D1543990

Football Outsiders Almanac 2017

THE ESSENTIAL GUIDE TO THE 2017 NFL AND COLLEGE FOOTBALL SEASONS

Edited by Aaron Schatz

With Greg A. Bedard, Ian Boyd, Bill Connelly, Cian Fahey,

Nathan Forster, Brian Fremeau, Tom Gower, Scott Kacsmar,

Bryan Knowles, Rivers McCown, Chad Peltier, Andrew Potter,

Mike Tanier, Vincent Verhei, Robert Weintraub, and Carl Yedor

Table of Contents

Introduction   v

Pregame Show   vii

Statistical Toolbox   xii

The Year In Quotes   xxxii

Full 2017 Projections   xxxvi

NFL TEAMS

Arizona Cardinals   1

Atlanta Falcons   9

Baltimore Ravens   18

Buffalo Bills   25

Carolina Panthers   32

Chicago Bears   40

Cincinnati Bengals   47

Cleveland Browns   54

Dallas Cowboys   61

Denver Broncos   67

Detroit Lions   76

Green Bay Packers   84

Houston Texans   92

Indianapolis Colts   99

Jacksonville Jaguars   106

Kansas City Chiefs   113

Los Angeles Chargers   122

Los Angeles Rams   130

Miami Dolphins   137

Minnesota Vikings   146

New England Patriots   153

New Orleans Saints   161

New York Giants   168

New York Jets   175

Oakland Raiders   182

Philadelphia Eagles   191

Pittsburgh Steelers   198

San Francisco 49ers   206

Seattle Seahawks   214

Tampa Bay Buccaneers   221

Tennessee Titans   229

Washington Redskins   236

NFL PLAYERS

Quarterbacks   243

Running Backs   273

Wide Receivers   310

Tight Ends   357

2017 Kicker Projections   376

2017 Fantasy Defense Projections   377

COLLEGE FOOTBALL

Introduction and Statistical Toolbox 378

NCAA Top 50 Teams   382

NCAA Win Projections   422

NCAA F/+ Projections   426

FURTHER RESEARCH

BackCAST 2017   429

FO Rookie Projections   434

Top 25 Prospects   436

Fantasy Projections   441

Statistical Appendix   446

Author Bios   464

About Sports Info Solutions   467

Introduction

Here is our 100 percent, no-doubt, absolutely-true-or-your-money-back guarantee for *Football Outsiders Almanac 2017*: some of the predictions in this book will be wrong.

It's a bit remarkable how much sanity has returned to the NFL over the last few years. After a series of improbable postseason runs, the last four Super Bowls have featured the best teams in the league.

Yet the unexpected still happens. In last year's book, we listed the Atlanta Falcons with only a 2.6 percent chance of making it to Super Bowl LI. That turned out to be a bit low.

In each individual game, the unexpected is possible. Remember when Atlanta had a 28-20 lead and a first down inside the Patriots 30 in the final five minutes of Super Bowl LI? Since 2000, teams in this situation are 221-4. That's a .982 winning percentage. Unfortunately for the Falcons, they are now one of the four teams that lost.

We have a lot of confidence that you'll learn more about the 2017 NFL and college football seasons by reading this book, and that we'll be right more often than we're wrong. Last year, New England was our favorite to represent the AFC in the Super Bowl, and we had Alabama and Clemson as our No. 1 and No. 3 teams in college football. But no matter what, some of the analysis in *Football Outsiders Almanac 2017* will be wrong. Players we say are likely to improve will not improve. Teams we say have strong odds to win will in fact lose.

That's one of the things that makes football so much fun. Some people may say that it takes away the fun of the game to analyze the odds of which teams are more likely to win or lose. But it doesn't take away the fun; it increases our appreciation when certain players and teams can overcome the odds. The NFL product has its flaws, but you can't say that it's boring.

Another reason that NFL football is fun right now: different teams can win with different approaches. This isn't like the mid-'70s, when every winning team was structured around a similar philosophy. Dallas built a winner around a great offensive line and a cheap defense. Seattle built a winner around a great defense and a cheap offensive line. The Titans built heavily around the running game. The Packers barely even had a running game. And the Patriots can do everything, depending on what they think their opponent can't stop.

Each of these approaches to building an NFL team has its strengths and weaknesses. The analytics you'll find in *Football Outsiders Almanac 2017* help us to highlight how these strengths and weaknesses—with a healthy dollop of luck stirred in—determine which teams succeed and which teams fail.

At its heart, the football analytics revolution is about learning more about the intricacies of the game instead of just accepting the boilerplate storylines produced by insipid pregame shows and crotchety old players from the past. It's about not accepting the idea that some guy "just wins." It's about understanding that the "skill players" aren't the only guys on the team with skills. It's about gaining insight into the complexity behind the modern offense, and that you don't just shove the ball into the line hoping to gain yardage. It's about understanding the dramatic way that strength of schedule affects the way we see a team's performance, especially at the college level. It's about figuring out which player skills translate from college to the pros, and which skills just produce meaningless scoutspeak. And it's about accepting that the pass dominates the run in the National Football League, and that it's been that way for 30 years.

There's more to this analysis than just numbers. Numbers are just one way to look at what happens on the football field. Words are the meat of our analysis; numbers are just the spice. There's a rumor that stat analysts don't watch game tape. In reality, stat analysts watch more tape than most beat writers or national Internet columnists, and *a lot* more tape than the average fan. We take everything we learn off the tape, synthesize it with the statistics, and deliver it to you.

Everybody who writes about football uses both statistics (whether they be basic yardage totals or more advanced stats like ours) and scouting (whether scouting reports by professionals or just their own eyes). The same goes for us, except that the statistics portion of our analysis is far more accurate than what you normally see from football coverage. Those numbers are based on two ideas:

1) **Conventional football statistics are heavily dependent on context.** If you want to see which teams are good and which are bad, which strategies work and which do not, you first need to filter out that context. Down and distance, field position, the current score, time left on the clock, the quality of the opponent—all of these elements influence the objective of the play and/or its outcome. Yet, the official NFL stats add together all yardage gained by a specific team or player without considering the impact of that particular yardage on wins and losses.

A close football game can turn on a single bounce of the ball. In a season of only 16 games, those effects can have a huge impact on a team's win-loss record, thus obscuring the team's true talent level. If we can filter out these bits of luck and random chance, we can figure out which teams are really more likely to play better for the rest of the season, or even in the following season.

2) **On any one play, the majority of the important action is not tracked by the conventional NFL play-by-play.** That's why we started the Football Outsiders game charting project in 2005. We now partner with both ESPN Stats & Info and Sports Info Solutions to collect data on every single NFL regular-season and postseason play. We know how many pass-rushers teams send on each pass, how often teams go three-wide or use two tight ends, how often teams use a play-fake or a zone blitz, and which defensive backs are in coverage, even when they don't get a tackle in the standard play-by-play.

There's also a third important precept that governs the work we do at Football Outsiders, although it's more about how to interpret numbers and not the numbers themselves. **A player's production in one year does not necessarily equal his production the next year.** This also applies to teams, of course. Even when stats are accurate, they're often extremely variable from year to year and subject to heavy forces of regression to the mean. Field goal percentage, red zone performance, third-down performance on defense, interceptions and fumble recoveries—these are but a few examples. In addition, the age curves for football players are much steeper than in other sports. Old players break down faster, and young players often improve faster. A number of football analysts concentrate on looking at what players did last year. We'll talk about that as well, but we're more interested in what players are going to do *this* year. Which performances from a year ago are flukes, and which ones represent long-term improvement or decline? What will one more year of experience do to this player's production? And how will a player's role change this year, and what does it mean for the team?

As with past books, *Football Outsiders Almanac 2017* starts off with "Pregame Show" (reviewing the most important research we've done in past books) and "Statistical Toolbox" (explaining all our stats). Once again, we preserve the ridiculousness of the football season for posterity with another version of "The Year in Quotes" and we introduce you to some of the more promising (and lesser-known) young bench players with our seventh annual list of Top 25 Prospects chosen in the third round or later.

Each NFL team gets a full chapter covering what happened in 2016 and our projections for the upcoming season. Are there reasons to believe that the team was inherently better or worse than its record last year? What did the team do in the offseason, and what does that mean for the team's chances to win in 2017? Each chapter also includes all kinds of advanced statistics covering 2016 performance and strategic tendencies, plus detailed commentary on each of the major units of the team: offensive line, defensive front seven, defensive secondary, special teams, and coaching staff.

"Skill players" (by which we mean "players who get counted in fantasy football") get their own section in the back of the book. We list the major players at each position alphabetically, along with commentary and a 2017 KUBIAK projection that will help you win your fantasy football league. We also have the most accurate projections anywhere for two fantasy football positions that people wrongly consider impossible to predict: kickers and team defense.

Next comes our preview of the college football season. We go in-depth with the top 50 projected teams in the nation. Just like with our NFL coverage, the goal of our college previews is to focus as much as possible on "why" and how," not just "which team is better." We're not just here to rank the Football Bowl Subdivision teams from 1 to 130. We break things down to look at offense and defense, pass and run, and clutch situations compared to all plays.

We hope our book helps you raise your level of football expertise, win arguments with your friends, and win your fantasy football league. Occasionally, there are also jokes. Just don't expect it all to be right. Being wrong sometimes is part of the fun.

Aaron Schatz
Framingham, MA
July 23, 2017

P.S. Don't forget to visit FootballOutsiders.com every day for fresh coverage of the NFL and college football, plus the most intelligent football discussion threads on the Internet.

Pregame Show

It has now been 14 years since we launched Football Outsiders. In that time, we've done a lot of primary research on the National Football League, and we reference that research in many of the articles and comments in *Football Outsiders Almanac 2017*. New readers may come across an offhand comment in a team chapter about, for example, the idea that fumble recovery is not a skill, and wonder what in the heck we are talking about. We can't repeat all our research in every new edition of *Football Outsiders Almanac*, so we start each year with a basic look at some of the most important precepts that have emerged from Football Outsiders research. You will see these issues come up again and again throughout the book.

You can also find this introduction online at http://www.footballoutsiders.com/info/FO-basics, along with links to the original research in the cases in which that research appeared online instead of (or as well as) in print.

Our various methods for projecting NFL success for college prospects are not listed below, but are referenced at times during the book. Those methods are detailed in an essay on page 434.

You run when you win, not win when you run.

If we could only share one piece of anti-conventional wisdom with you before you read the rest of our book, this would be it. The first article ever written for Football Outsiders was devoted to debunking the myth of "establishing the run." There is no correlation whatsoever between giving your running backs a lot of carries early in the game and winning the game. Just running the ball is not going to help a team score; it has to run successfully.

There are two reasons why nearly every beat writer and television analyst still repeats the tired old school mantra that "establishing the run" is the secret to winning football games. The first problem is confusing cause and effect. There are exceptions, but for the most part, winning teams have a lot of carries because their running backs are running out the clock at the end of wins, not because they are running wild early in games.

The second problem is history. Most of the current crop of NFL analysts came of age or actually played the game during the 1970s. They believe that the run-heavy game of that decade is how football is meant to be, and today's pass-first game is an aberration. Yet it was actually the game of the 1970s that was the aberration. The '70s were far more slanted towards the run than any era since the arrival of Paul Brown, Otto Graham, and the Cleveland Browns in 1946. Optimal strategies from 1974 are not optimal strategies for 2012.

A sister statement to "you have to establish the run" is "team X is 5-1 when running back John Doe runs for at least 100 yards." Unless John Doe is possessed by otherworldly spirits the way Adrian Peterson was a couple years ago, the team isn't winning because of his 100-yard games. He's putting up 100-yard games because his team is winning.

A great defense against the run is nothing without a good pass defense.

This is a corollary to the absurdity of "establish the run." With rare exceptions, teams win or lose with the passing game more than the running game—and by stopping the passing game more than the running game. Ron Jaworski puts it best: "The pass gives you the lead, and the run solidifies it." The reason why teams need a strong run defense in the playoffs is not to shut the run down early; it's to keep the other team from icing the clock if they get a lead. You can't mount a comeback if you can't stop the run.

Note that "good pass defense" may mean "good pass rush" rather than "good defensive backs."

Running on third-and-short is more likely to convert than passing on third-and-short.

On average, passing will always gain more yardage than running, with one very important exception: when a team is just one or two yards away from a new set of downs or the goal line. On third-and-1, a run will convert for a new set of downs 36 percent more often than a pass. Expand that to all third or fourth downs with 1-2 yards to go, and the run is successful 40 percent more often. With these percentages, the possibility of a long gain with a pass is not worth the tradeoff of an incomplete that kills a drive.

This is one reason why teams have to be able to both run and pass. The offense also has to keep some semblance of balance so they can use their play-action fakes, and so the defense doesn't just run their nickel and dime packages all game. Balance also means that teams do need to pass occasionally in short-yardage situations; they just need to do it less than they do now. Teams pass roughly 60 percent of the time on third-and-2 even though runs in that situation convert 20 percent more often than passes. They pass 68 percent of the time on fourth-and-2 even though runs in that situation convert twice as often as passes.

Standard team rankings based on total yardage are inherently flawed.

Check out the schedule page on NFL.com, and you will find that each game is listed with league rankings based on total yardage. That is still how the NFL "officially" ranks teams, but these rankings rarely match up with common sense. That is because total team yardage may be the most context-dependent number in football.

It starts with the basic concept that rate stats are generally more valuable than cumulative stats. Yards per carry says more about a running back's quality than total yardage, completion percentage says more than just a quarterback's total number of completions. The same thing is true for teams; in fact, it is even more important because of the way football strategy influences the number of runs and passes in the game plan. Poor teams will give up fewer passing yards and more rushing yards because opponents will stop passing once they have a late-game lead and will run out the clock instead. For winning teams, the opposite is true. For example, which team had a better pass defense last year: Detroit or the New York Giants? The answer is obviously the Giants, yet according to the official NFL rankings, Detroit (3,975 net yards allowed on 549 pass attempts, 6.9 net yards per pass) was a better pass defense than the Giants (4,018 net yards allowed on 630 pass attempts, 6.0 net yards per pass).

Total yardage rankings are also skewed because some teams play at a faster pace than other teams. For example, last year Arizona (5,868) had roughly the same number of yards as Green Bay (5,900). However, the Packers were the superior offense and much more efficient; they gained those yards on only 167 drives while the Cardinals needed 192 drives.

A team will score more when playing a bad defense, and will give up more points when playing a good offense.

This sounds absurdly basic, but when people consider team and player stats without looking at strength of schedule, they are ignoring this. In 2012, for example, rookie Russell Wilson had a higher DVOA rating than fellow rookie Robert Griffin III because he faced a more difficult schedule, even though Griffin had slightly better standard stats.

If their overall yards per carry are equal, a running back who consistently gains yardage on every play is more valuable than a boom-and-bust running back who is frequently stuffed at the line but occasionally breaks a long highlight-worthy run.

Our brethren at Baseball Prospectus believe that the most precious commodity in baseball is outs. Teams only get 27 of them per game, and you can't afford to give one up for very little return. So imagine if there was a new rule in baseball that gave a team a way to earn another three outs in the middle of the inning. That would be pretty useful, right?

That's the way football works. You may start a drive 80 yards away from scoring, but as long as you can earn 10 yards in four chances, you get another four chances. Long gains have plenty of value, but if those long gains are mixed with a lot of short gains, you are going to put the quarterback in a lot of difficult third-and-long situations. That means more punts and more giving the ball back to the other team rather than moving the chains and giving the offense four more plays to work with.

The running back who gains consistent yardage is also going to do a lot more for you late in the game, when the goal of running the ball is not just to gain yardage but to eat clock time. If you are a Chargers fan watching your team with a late lead, you don't want to see three straight Melvin Gordon stuffs at the line followed by a punt. You want to see a game-icing first down.

A common historical misconception is that our preference for consistent running backs means that "Football Outsiders believes that Barry Sanders was overrated." Sanders wasn't just any boom-and-bust running back, though; he was the greatest boom-and-bust runner of all time, with bigger booms and fewer busts. Sanders ranked in the top five in DYAR five times (third in 1989, first in 1990, and second in 1994, 1996, and 1997).

Rushing is more dependent on the offensive line than people realize, but pass protection is more dependent on the quarterback himself than people realize.

Some readers complain that this idea contradicts the previous one. Aren't those consistent running backs just the product of good offensive lines? The truth is somewhere in between. There are certainly good running backs who suffer because their offensive lines cannot create consistent holes, but most boom-and-bust running backs contribute to their own problems by hesitating behind the line whenever the hole is unclear, looking for the home run instead of charging forward for the four-yard gain that keeps the offense moving.

As for pass protection, some quarterbacks have better instincts for the rush than others, and are thus better at getting out of trouble by moving around in the pocket or throwing the ball away. Others will hesitate, hold onto the ball too long, and lose yardage over and over.

Note that "moving around in the pocket" does not necessarily mean "scrambling." In fact, a scrambling quarterback will often take more sacks than a pocket quarterback, because while he's running around trying to make something happen, a defensive lineman will catch up with him.

Shotgun formations are generally more efficient than formations with the quarterback under center.

Over the past five seasons, offenses have averaged roughly 5.9 yards per play from Shotgun (or Pistol), but just 5.1 yards per play with the quarterback under center. This wide split exists even if you analyze the data to try to weed out biases like teams using Shotgun more often on third-and-long, or against prevent defenses in the fourth quarter. Shotgun offense is more efficient if you only look at the first half, on every down, and even if you only look at running back carries rather than passes and scrambles.

It's hard to think of a Football Outsiders axiom that has been better assimilated by the people running NFL teams since we started doing this a decade ago. In 2001, NFL teams only used Shotgun on 14 percent of plays. Five years later, in 2006, that had increased slightly, to 20 percent of plays. By 2012, Shotgun was used on a 47.5 percent of plays (including the Pistol, but not counting the Wildcat or other direct snaps to non-quarterbacks). Last year, the league as a whole was up to an average of 64.4 percent of plays from Shotgun or Pistol. Remember, before 2007, no team had ever used Shotgun on more than half its offensive plays. Now, the league *averages* over 60 percent. At some point, defenses will adapt and the benefit of the formation will become less pronounced, but it doesn't look like it is happening yet.

A running back with 370 or more carries during the regular season will usually suffer either a major injury or a loss of effectiveness the following year, unless he is named Eric Dickerson.

Terrell Davis, Jamal Anderson, and Edgerrin James all blew out their knees. Larry Johnson broke his foot. Earl Campbell and Eddie George went from legendary powerhouses to plodding, replacement-level players. Shaun Alexander broke his foot *and* became a plodding, replacement-level player. This is what happens when a running back is overworked to the point of having at least 370 carries during the regular season. DeMarco Murray was the latest player to follow up a high workload with a disappointing season.

The "Curse of 370" was expanded in our book *Pro Football Prospectus 2005*, and now includes seasons with 390 or more carries in the regular season and postseason combined. Research also shows that receptions don't cause a problem, only workload on the ground.

Plenty of running backs get injured without hitting 370 carries in a season, but there is a clear difference. On average, running backs with 300 to 369 carries and no postseason appearance will see their total rushing yardage decline by 15 percent the following year and their yards per carry decline by two percent. The average running back with 370 or more regular-season carries, or 390 including the postseason, will see their rushing yardage decline by 35 percent, and their yards per carry decline by eight percent. However, the Curse of 370 is not a hard and fast line where running backs suddenly become injury risks. It is more of a concept where 370 carries roughly represent the point at which additional carries start to become more and more of a problem.

Wide receivers must be judged on both complete and incomplete passes.

Last year, for example, Kenny Britt had 1,033 receiving yards for Los Angeles while DeAndre Hopkins had 1,038 receiving yards for Houston. Neither played with a very good quarterback, and each ran his average route roughly 12 yards downfield. But there was a big difference between them: Britt caught 61 percent of intended passes, while Hopkins caught only 52 percent.

Some work has been done on splitting responsibility for incomplete passes between quarterbacks and receivers, but not enough that we can incorporate this into our advanced stats at this time. We know that wide receiver catch rates are almost as consistent from year to year as quarterback completion percentages, but it is also important to look at catch rate in the context of the types of routes each receiver runs. A few years ago, we expanded on this idea with a new plus-minus metric, which is explained in the introduction to the chapter on wide receivers and tight ends.

The total quality of an NFL team is four parts offense, three parts defense, and one part special teams.

There are three units on a football team, but they are not of equal importance. For a long time, the saying from Football Outsiders was that the total quality of an NFL team is three parts offense, three parts defense, and one part special teams. Further recent research suggests that offense is even more important than we originally believed. Recent recent work by Chase Stuart, Neil Paine, and Brian Burke suggests a split between offense and defense of roughly 58-42, without considering special teams. Our research suggests that special teams contributes about 13 percent to total performance; if you measure the remaining 87 percent with a 58-42 ratio, you get roughly 4:3:1. When we compare the range of offense, defense, and special teams DVOA ratings, we get the same results, with the best and worst offenses roughly 130 percent stronger than the best and worst defenses, and roughly four times stronger than the best and worst special teams.

Offense is more consistent from year to year than defense, and offensive performance is easier to project than defensive performance. Special teams is less consistent than either.

Nobody in the NFL understood this concept better than former Indianapolis Colts general manager Bill Polian. Both the Super Bowl champion Colts and the four-time AFC champion Buffalo Bills of the early 1990s were built around the idea that if you put together an offense that can dominate the league year after year, eventually you will luck into a year where good health and a few smart decisions will give you a defense good enough to win a championship. (As the Colts learned in 2006, you don't even need a year, just four weeks.) Even the New England Patriots, who are led by a defense-first head coach in Bill Belichick, have been more consistent on offense than on defense since they began their run of success in 2001.

Field goal percentage is almost entirely random from season to season, while kickoff distance is one of the most consistent statistics in football.

This theory, which originally appeared in the *New York Times* in October 2006, is one of our most controversial, but it is hard to argue against the evidence. Measuring every kicker from 1999 to 2006 who had at least ten field goal attempts in each of two consecutive years, the year-to-year correlation coefficient for field goal percentage was an insignificant .05. Mike Vanderjagt didn't miss a single field goal in 2003, but his percentage was a below-average 74 percent the year before and 80 percent the year after. Adam Vinatieri has long been considered the best kicker in the game. But even he had never enjoyed two straight seasons with accuracy better than the NFL average of 85 percent until 2010 and 2011.

On the other hand, the year-to-year correlation coefficient for kickoff distance, over the same period as our measurement of field goal percentage and with the same minimum of ten kicks per year, is .61. The same players consistently lead the league in kickoff distance. In recent years, that group includes Steven Hauschka, Graham Gano, Stephen Gostkowski, and Justin Tucker.

Teams with more offensive penalties generally lose more games, but there is no correlation between defensive penalties and losses.

Specific defensive penalties of course lose games; we've all sworn at the television when the cornerback on our favorite team gets flagged for a 50-yard pass interference penalty. Yet overall, there is no correlation between losses and the total of defensive penalties or even the total yardage on defensive penalties. One reason is that defensive penalties often represent *good* play, not bad. Cornerbacks who play tight coverage may be just on the edge of a penalty on most plays, only occasionally earning a flag. Defensive ends who get a good jump on rushing the passer will gladly trade an encroachment penalty or two for ten snaps where they get off the blocks a split-second before the linemen trying to block them.

In addition, offensive penalties have a higher correlation from year to year than defensive penalties. The penalty that correlates highest with losses is the false start, and the penalty that teams will have called most consistently from year to year is also the false start.

This is covered a bit more in this year's Oakland chapter.

Recovery of a fumble, despite being the product of hard work, is almost entirely random.

Stripping the ball is a skill. Holding onto the ball is a skill. Pouncing on the ball as it is bouncing all over the place is not a skill. There is no correlation whatsoever between the percentage of fumbles recovered by a team in one year and the percentage they recover in the next year. The odds of recovery are based solely on the type of play involved, not the teams or any of their players.

The Green Bay Packers are a good example. In 2015, they recovered 5 of 15 fumbles by opponents. Last year, there were fewer fumbles (11) but they recovered more of them (7).

Fumble recovery is equally erratic on offense. In 2014, the San Francisco 49ers fumbled 15 times and only recovered 4 of them. In 2015, the 49ers fumbled 15 times and instead recovered 12 of them.

Fumble recovery is a major reason why the general public overestimates or underestimates certain teams. Fumbles are huge, turning-point plays that dramatically impact wins and losses in the past, while fumble recovery percentage says absolutely nothing about a team's chances of winning games in the future. With this in mind, Football Outsiders stats treat all fumbles as equal, penalizing them based on the likelihood of each type of fumble (run, pass, sack, etc.) being recovered by the defense.

Other plays that qualify as "non-predictive events" include two-point conversions, blocked kicks, and touchdowns during turnover returns. These plays are not "lucky," per se, but they have no value whatsoever for predicting future performance.

Field position is fluid.

As discussed in the Statistical Toolbox, every yard line on the field has a value based on how likely a team is to score from that location on the field as opposed to from a yard further back. The change in value from one yard to the next is the same whether the team has the ball or not. The goal of a defense is not just to prevent scoring, but to hold the opposition so that the offense can get the ball back in the best possible field position. A bad offense will score as many points as a good offense if it starts each drive five yards closer to the goal line.

A corollary to this precept: The most underrated aspect of an NFL team's performance is the field position gained or lost on kickoffs and punts. This is part of why players such as Tyler Lockett and Cordarrelle Patterson can have such an impact on the game, even when they aren't taking a kickoff or punt all the way back for a touchdown.

The red zone is the most important place on the field to play well, but performance in the red zone from year to year is much less consistent than overall performance.

Although play in the red zone has a disproportionately high importance to the outcome of games relative to plays on the rest of the field, NFL teams do not exhibit a level of performance in the red zone that is consistently better or worse than their performance elsewhere, year after year. The simplest explanation why is a small(er) sample size and the inherent variance of football, with contributing factors like injuries and changes in personnel.

Defenses which are strong on first and second down, but weak on third down, will tend to improve the following year. Defenses which are weak on first and second down, but strong on third down, will tend to decline the following year.

Teams get fewer opportunities on third down, so third-down performance is more volatile—but it's also is a bigger part of a team's overall performance than first or second down, because the result is usually either very good (four more downs) or very bad (losing the ball to the other team with a punt). Over time, a team will play as well in those situations as it does in other situations, which will bring the overall defense in line with the = defense on first and second down.

This trend is even stronger between seasons. Struggles on third down are a pretty obvious problem, and teams will generally target their off-season moves at improving their third-down performance ... which often leads to an improvement in third-down performance.

However, we have discovered something surprising over the past few years. Originally, we discovered this effect on both offense and defense. But the third-down rebound effect seems to have disappeared on offense, as we explained in the Philadelphia chapter of *Football Outsiders Almanac 2010*. We still plan to do additional research on this to look at whether the third-down effect still exists, and how strong it is on offense and/or defense.

Injuries regress to the mean on the seasonal level, and teams that avoid injuries in a given season tend to win more games.

There are no doubt teams with streaks of good or bad health over multiple years. However, teams who were especially healthy or especially unhealthy, as measured by our adjusted games lost (AGL) metric, almost always head towards league average in the subsequent season. Furthermore, injury—or the absence thereof—has a huge correlation with wins, and a significant impact on a team's success. There's no doubt that a few high-profile teams have resisted this trend in recent years. The Patriots often deal with a high number of injuries, and a number of recent Super Bowl champions such as the 2010 Packers and 2011 Giants have overcome injuries to win the championship. Nonetheless, the overall rule still applies. Last year, Super Bowl opponents Atlanta and New England both ranked among the eight teams with the lowest AGL. Meanwhile, only two of the ten teams with the highest AGL made the playoffs, Kansas City and Miami.

In the past, we have written that teams with a high number of injuries are a good bet to improve the following season. However, work we did two years ago on a new team projection system suggests this may not actually be the case. AGL totals correlate strongly with how well a team plays in that year, but not necessarily with improvement or decline the following season.

By and large, a team built on depth is better than a team built on stars and scrubs.

Connected to the previous statement, because teams need to go into the season expecting that they will suffer an average number of injuries no matter how healthy they were the previous year. You cannot concentrate your salaries on a handful of star players because there is no such thing as avoiding injuries in the NFL. The game is too fast and the players too strong to build a team based around the idea that "if we can avoid all injuries this year, we'll win."

Running backs usually decline after age 28, tight ends after age 29, wide receivers after age 30, and quarterbacks after age 32.

This research was originally done by Doug Drinen (editor of pro-football-reference.com) in 2000. In recent years, a few players have had huge seasons above these general age limits, but the peak ages Drinen found a few years ago still apply to the majority of players.

As for "non-skill players," research we did in 2007 for *ESPN The Magazine* suggested that defensive ends and defensive backs generally begin to decline after age 29, linebackers and offensive linemen after age 30, and defensive tackles after age 31. However, because we still have so few statistics to use to study linemen and defensive players, this research should not be considered definitive.

The strongest indicator of how a college football team will perform in the upcoming season is their performance in recent seasons.

It may seem strange because graduation enforces constant player turnover, but college football teams are actually much more consistent from year to year than NFL teams. Thanks in large part to consistency in recruiting, teams can be expected to play within a reasonable range of their baseline program expectations each season. Our Program F/+ ratings, which represent a rolling five-year period of play-by-play and drive efficiency data, have an extremely strong (.76) correlation with the next year's F/+ rating.

Championship teams are generally defined by their ability to dominate inferior opponents, not their ability to win close games.

Football games are often decided by just one or two plays: a missed field goal, a bouncing fumble, the subjective spot of an official on fourth-and-1. One missed assignment by a cornerback or one slightly askew pass that bounces off a receiver's hands and into those of a defensive back five yards away and the game could be over. In a blowout, however, one lucky bounce isn't going to change things. Championship teams—in both professional and college football—typically beat their good opponents convincingly and destroy the cupcakes on the schedule.

Aaron Schatz

Statistical Toolbox

After 14 years of Football Outsiders, some of our readers are as comfortable with DVOA and ALY as they are with touchdowns and tackles. Yet to most fans, including our newer readers, it still looks like a lot of alphabet soup. That's what this chapter is for. The next few pages define and explain all of all the unique NFL statistics you'll find in this book: how we calculate them, what the numbers mean, and what they tell us about why teams win or lose football games. We'll go through the information in each of the tables that appear in each team chapter, pointing out whether those stats come from advanced mathematical manipulation of the standard play-by-play or simple counting of what we see on television with the Football Outsiders game charting project. This chapter covers NFL statistics only. College metrics such as Highlight Yards and F/+ are explained in the introduction to the college football section on page 378.

We've done our best to present these numbers in a way that makes them easy to understand. This explanation is long, so feel free to read some of it, flip around the rest of the book, and then come back. It will still be here.

Defense-Adjusted Value Over Average (DVOA)

One running back runs for three yards. Another running back runs for three yards. Which is the better run?

This sounds like a stupid question, but it isn't. In fact, this question is at the heart of nearly all of the analysis in this book.

Several factors can differentiate one three-yard run from another. What is the down and distance? Is it third-and-2, or second-and-15? Where on the field is the ball? Does the player get only three yards because he hits the goal line and scores? Is the player's team up by two touchdowns in the fourth quarter and thus running out the clock, or down by two touchdowns and thus facing a defense that is playing purely against the pass? Is the running back playing against the porous defense of the Saints, or the stalwart defense of the Seahawks?

Conventional NFL statistics value plays based solely on their net yardage. The NFL determines the best players by adding up all their yards no matter what situations they came in or how many plays it took to get them. Now, why would they do that? Football has one objective—to get to the end zone—and two ways to achieve that, by gaining yards and achieving first downs. These two goals need to be balanced to determine a player's value or a team's performance. All the yards in the world won't help a team win if they all come in six-yard chunks on third-and-10.

The popularity of fantasy football only exacerbates the problem. Fans have gotten used to judging players based on how much they help fantasy teams win and lose, not how much they help *real* teams win and lose. Typical fantasy scoring further skews things by counting the yard between the one and the goal line as 61 times more important than all the other yards on the field (each yard worth 0.1 points, a touchdown worth 6.0). Let's say Odell Beckham catches a pass on third-and-15 and goes 50 yards but gets tackled two yards from the goal line, and then Paul Perkins takes the ball on first-and-goal from the two-yard line and plunges in for the score. Has Perkins done something special? Not really. When an offense gets the ball on first-and-goal at the two-yard line, they are going to score a touchdown five out of six times. Perkins is getting credit for the work done by the passing game.

Doing a better job of distributing credit for scoring points and winning games is the goal of **DVOA**, or Defense-adjusted Value Over Average. DVOA breaks down every single play of the NFL season, assigning each play a value based on both total yards and yards towards a first down, based on work done by Pete Palmer, Bob Carroll, and John Thorn in their seminal book, *The Hidden Game of Football*. On first down, a play is considered a success if it gains 45 percent of needed yards; on second down, a play needs to gain 60 percent of needed yards; on third or fourth down, only gaining a new first down is considered success.

We then expand upon that basic idea with a more complicated system of "success points," improved over the past four years with a lot of mathematics and a bit of trial and error. A successful play is worth one point, an unsuccessful play zero points with fractional points in between (for example, eight yards on third-and-10 is worth 0.54 "success points"). Extra points are awarded for big plays, gradually increasing to three points for 10 yards (assuming those yards result in a first down), four points for 20 yards, and five points for 40 yards or more. Losing three or more yards is minus-1 point. Interceptions average minus-6 points, with an adjustment for the length of the pass and the location of the interception (since an interception tipped at the line is more likely to produce a long return than an interception on a 40-yard pass). A fumble is worth anywhere from minus-1.7 to minus-4.0 points depending on how often a fumble in that situation is lost to the defense—no matter who actually recovers the fumble. Red zone plays get a bonus: 20 percent for team offense, five percent for team defense, and 10 percent for individual players. There is a bonus given for a touchdown that acknowledges that the goal line is significantly more difficult to cross than the previous 99 yards (although this bonus is nowhere near as large as the one used in fantasy football).

(Our system is a bit more complex than the one in *Hidden Game* thanks to our subsequent research, which added larger penalty for turnovers, the fractional points, and a slightly higher baseline for success on first down. The reason why all fumbles are counted, no matter whether they are recovered by the offense or defense, is explained in the essay "Pregame

Show.")

Every single play run in the NFL gets a "success value" based on this system, and then that number gets compared to the average success values of plays in similar situations for all players, adjusted for a number of variables. These include down and distance, field location, time remaining in game, and the team's lead or deficit in the game score. Teams are always compared to the overall offensive average, as the team made its own choice whether to pass or rush. When it comes to individual players, however, rushing plays are compared to other rushing plays, passing plays to other passing plays, tight ends to tight ends, wideouts to wideouts, and so on.

Going back to our example of the three-yard rush, if Player A gains three yards under a set of circumstances in which the average NFL running back gains only one yard, then Player A has a certain amount of value above others at his position. Likewise, if Player B gains three yards on a play on which, under similar circumstances, an average NFL back gains four yards, that Player B has negative value relative to others at his position. Once we make all our adjustments, we can evaluate the difference between this player's rate of success and the expected success rate of an average running back in the same situation (or between the opposing defense and the average defense in the same situation, etc.). Add up every play by a certain team or player, divide by the total of the various baselines for success in all those situations, and you get VOA, or Value Over Average.

Of course, the biggest variable in football is the fact that each team plays a different schedule against teams of disparate quality. By adjusting each play based on the opposing defense's average success in stopping that type of play over the course of a season, we get DVOA, or Defense-adjusted Value Over Average. Rushing and passing plays are adjusted based on down and location on the field; passing plays are also adjusted based on how the defense performs against passes to running backs, tight ends, or wide receivers. Defenses are adjusted based on the average success of the *offenses* they are facing. (Yes, technically the defensive stats are "offense-adjusted." If it seems weird, think of the "D" in "DVOA" as standing for "opponent-Dependent" or something.)

The biggest advantage of DVOA is the ability to break teams and players down to find strengths and weaknesses in a variety of situations. In the aggregate, DVOA may not be quite as accurate as some of the other, similar "power ratings" formulas based on comparing drives rather than individual plays, but, unlike those other ratings, DVOA can be separated not only by player, but also by down, or by week, or by distance needed for a first down. This can give us a better idea of not just which team is better, but why, and what a team has to do in order to improve itself in the future. You will find DVOA used in this book in a lot of different ways—because it takes every single play into account, it can be used to measure a player or a team's performance in any situation. All Pittsburgh third downs can be compared to how an average team does on third down. Blaine Gabbert and Colin Kaepernick can each be compared to how an average quarterback performs in the red zone, or with a lead, or in the second half of the game.

Since it compares each play only to plays with similar circumstances, it gives a more accurate picture of how much better a team really is compared to the league as a whole. The list of top DVOA offenses on third down, for example, is more accurate than the conventional NFL conversion statistic because it takes into account that converting third-and-long is more difficult than converting third-and-short, and that a turnover is worse than an incomplete pass because it eliminates the opportunity to move the other team back with a punt on fourth down.

One of the hardest parts of understanding a new statistic is interpreting its scale, or what numbers represent good performance or bad performance. We've made that easy with DVOA. For each season, ratings are normalized so that 0% represents league average. A positive DVOA represents a situation that favors the offense, while a negative DVOA represents a situation that favors the defense. This is why the best offenses have positive DVOA ratings (last year, Atlanta led the NFL at 24.6%) and the best defenses have negative DVOA ratings (with Denver on top at -18.3%).

The scale of offensive ratings is wider than the scale of defensive ratings. In most years, the best and worst offenses tend to rate around +/- 30%, while the best and worst defenses tend to rate around +/- 20%. For starting players, the scale tends to reach roughly +/-40% for passing and receiving, and +/- 30% for rushing. As you might imagine, some players with fewer attempts will surpass both extremes.

Team DVOA totals combine offense and defense by subtracting the latter from the former because the better defenses will have negative DVOA ratings. (Special teams performance is also added, as described later in this essay.) Certain plays are counted in DVOA for offense and not for defense, leading to separate baselines on each side of the ball. In addition, although the league ratings for offense and defense are always 0%, the league averages for passing and rushing separately are *not* 0%. Because passing is more efficient than rushing, the average for team passing is almost always positive and the average for team rushing is almost always negative. However, ratings for individual players only compare passes to other passes and runs to other runs, so the league average for individual passing is 0%, as are the league averages for rushing and the three separate league averages for receiving by wide receivers, tight ends, and running backs.

Some other important notes about DVOA:

• Only four penalties are included in DVOA. Two penalties count as pass plays on both sides of the ball: intentional grounding and defensive pass interference. The other two penalties are included for offense only: false starts and delay of game. Because the inclusion of these penalties means a group of negative plays that don't count as either passes or runs, the league averages for pass offense and run offense are higher than the league averages for pass defense and run defense.

• Aborted snaps and incomplete backwards lateral passes are only penalized on offense, not rewarded on defense.

• Adjustments for playing from behind or with a lead in the fourth quarter are different for offense and defense, as are adjustments for the final two minutes of the first half when the offense is not near field goal range.

• Offense gets a slight penalty and defense gets a slight bonus for games indoors.

Does well does DVOA work? Using correlation coefficients, we can show that only actual points scored are better than DVOA at indicating how many games a team has won (Table 1) and DVOA is a does a better job of predicting wins in the coming season than either wins or points scored in the previous season (Table 2).

(Correlation coefficient is a statistical tool that measures how two variables are related by using a number between 1 and minus-1. The closer to minus-1 or 1, the stronger the relationship, but the closer to 0, the weaker the relationship.)

Table 1. Correlation of Various Stats to Wins, 2002-2014

Stat	Offense	Defense	Total
Points Scored/Allowed	.755	-.676	.920
DVOA	.708	-.490	.859
Yards Gained/Allowed	.546	-.371	.681
Yards Gained/Allowed per Play	.546	-.339	.725

Table 2. Correlation of Various Stats to Wins Following Year, 2002-2014

Stat	Correlation	Stat	Correlation
DVOA	.370	Yards per Play Differential	.316
Point Differential	.353	Wins	.307
Pythagorean Wins	.347	Yardage Differential	.298

Special Teams: The problem with a system based on measuring both yardage and yardage towards a first down is what to do with plays that don't have the possibility of a first down. Special teams are an important part of football and we needed a way to add that performance to the team DVOA rankings. Our special teams metric includes five separate measurements: field goals and extra points, net punting, punt returns, net kickoffs, and kick returns.

The foundation of most of these special teams ratings is the concept that each yard line has a different value based on the likelihood of scoring from that position on the field. In *Hidden Game*, the authors suggested that the each additional yard for the offense had equal value, with a team's own goal line being worth minus-2 points, the 50-yard line 2 points, and the opposing goal line 6 points. (-2 points is not only the value of a safety, but also reflects the fact that when a team is backed up in its own territory, it is likely that its drive will stall, forcing a punt that will give the ball to the other team in good field position. Thus, the negative point value reflects the fact that the defense is more likely to score next.) Our studies have updated this concept to reflect the actual likelihood that the offense or defense will have the next score from a given position on the field based on actual results from the past few seasons. The line that represents the value of field position is not straight, but curved, with the value of each yard increasing as teams approach either goal line.

Our special teams ratings compare each kick or punt to league average based on the point value of the position of the kick, catch, and return. We've determined a league average for how far a kick goes based on the line of scrimmage for each kick (almost always the 35-yard line for kickoffs, variable for punts) and a league average for how far a return goes based on both the yard line where the ball is caught and the distance that it traveled in the air.

The kicking or punting team is rated based on net points compared to average, taking into account both the kick and the return if there is one. Because the average return is always positive, punts that are not returnable (touchbacks, out of bounds, fair catches, and punts downed by the coverage unit) will rate higher than punts of the same distance which are returnable. (This is also true of touchbacks on kickoffs.) There are also separate individual ratings for kickers and punters that are based on distance and whether the kick is returnable, assuming an average return in order to judge the kicker separate from the coverage.

For the return team, the rating is based on how many points the return is worth compared to average, based on the location of the catch and the distance the ball traveled in the air. Return teams are not judged on the distance of kicks, nor are they judged on kicks that cannot be returned. As explained below, blocked kicks are so rare as to be statistically insignificant as predictors for future performance and are thus ignored. For the kicking team they simply count as missed field goals, for the defense they are gathered with their opponents' other missed field goals in Hidden value (also explained below).

Field goal kicking is measured differently. Measuring kickers by field goal percentage is a bit absurd, as it assumes that all field goals are of equal difficulty. In our metric, each field goal is compared to the average number of points scored on all field goal attempts from that distance over the past 15 years. The value of a field goal increases as distance from the goal line increases. Kickoffs, punts, and field goals are then adjusted based on weather and altitude. It will surprise no one to learn that it is easier to kick the ball in Denver or a dome than it is to kick the ball in Buffalo in December. Because we do not yet have enough data to tailor our adjustments specifically to each stadium, each one is assigned to one of four categories: Cold, Warm, Dome, and Denver. There is also an additional adjustment dropping the value of field goals in Florida (because the warm temperatures allow the ball to carry better).

The baselines for special teams are adjusted in each year for rule changes such as the introduction of the special teams-only "k-ball" in 1999, movement of the kickoff line, and the 2016 change in kickoff touchbacks. Baselines have also been adjusted each year to make up for the gradual improvement of kickers over the last two decades, and a new baseline was set last year for the longer distance on extra points.

Once we've totaled how many points above or below average can be attributed to special teams, we translate those points into DVOA so the ratings can be added to offense and defense to get total team DVOA.

There are three aspects of special teams that have an impact on wins and losses, but don't show up in the standard special teams rating because a team has little or no influence on them. The first is the length of kickoffs by the opposing team, with an asterisk. Obviously, there are no defenders standing on the 35-yard line, ready to block a kickoff after the whistle blows. However, over the past few years, some teams have deliberately kicked short in order to avoid certain top return men, such as Devin Hester and Cordarrelle Patterson. The special teams formula now includes adjustments to give teams extra credit for field position on kick returns if kickers are deliberately trying to avoid a return.

The other two items that special teams have little control over are field goals against your team, and punt distance against your team. Research shows no indication that teams can influence the accuracy or strength of field goal kickers and punters, except for blocks. As mentioned above, although blocked field goals and punts are definitely skillful plays, they are so rare that they have no correlation to how well teams have played in the past or will play in the future, thus they are included here as if they were any other missed field goal or botched punt, giving the defense no additional credit for their efforts. The value of these three elements is listed separately as "Hidden" value.

Special teams ratings also do not include two-point conversions or onside kick attempts, both of which, like blocks, are so infrequent as to be statistically insignificant in judging future performance.

Defense-Adjusted Yards Above Replacement (DYAR)

DVOA is a good stat, but of course it is not a perfect one. One problem is that DVOA, by virtue of being a percentage or rate statistic, doesn't take into account the cumulative value of having a player producing at a league-average level over the course of an above-average number of plays. By definition, an average level of performance is better than that provided by half of the league and the ability to maintain that level of performance while carrying a heavy work load is very valuable indeed. In addition, a player who is involved in a high number of plays can draw the defense's attention away from other parts of the offense, and, if that player is a running back, he can take time off the clock with repeated runs.

Let's say you have a running back who carries the ball 300 times in a season. What would happen if you were to remove this player from his team's offense? What would happen to those 300 plays? Those plays don't disappear with the player, though some might be lost to the defense because of the associated loss of first downs. Rather those plays would have to be distributed among the remaining players in the offense, with the bulk of them being given to a replacement running back. This is where we arrive at the concept of replacement level, borrowed from our friends at Baseball Prospectus. When a player is removed from an offense, he is usually not replaced by a player of similar ability. Nearly every starting player in the NFL is a starter because he is better than the alternative. Those 300 plays will typically be given to a significantly worse player, someone who is the backup because he doesn't have as much experience and/or talent. A player's true value can then be measured by the level of performance he provides above that replacement level baseline, totaled over all of his run or pass attempts.

Of course, the *real* replacement player is different for each team in the NFL. Last year, the player who originally was the backup running back in Seattle (Jordan Howard) ended up as the starter with a much higher DVOA than original starter Jeremy Langford. Sometimes a player such as Gary Barnidge or Danny Woodhead will be cut by one team and turn into a star for another. On other teams, the drop from the starter to the backup can be even greater than the general drop to replacement level. (The 2011 Indianapolis Colts will be the hallmark example of this until the end of time.) The choice to start an inferior player or to employ a sub-replacement level backup, however, falls to the team, not the starter being evaluated. Thus we generalize replacement level for the league as a whole as the ultimate goal is to evaluate players independent of the quality of their teammates.

Our estimates of replacement level are computed differently for each position. For quarterbacks, we analyzed situations where two or more quarterbacks had played meaningful snaps for a team in the same season, then compared the overall DVOA of the original starters to the overall DVOA of the replacements. We did not include situations where the backup was actually a top prospect waiting his turn on the bench, since a first-round pick is by no means a "replacement-level" player.

At other positions, there is no easy way to separate players into "starters" and "replacements," since unlike at quarterback, being the starter doesn't make you the only guy who gets in the game. Instead, we used a simpler method, ranking players at each position in each season by attempts. The players who made up the final 10 percent of passes or runs were split out as "replacement players" and then compared to the players making up the other 90 percent of plays at that position. This took care of the fact that not every non-starter is a freely available talent. (Think of Giovani Bernard or Duke Johnson, for example.)

As noted earlier, the challenge of any new stat is to present it on a scale that's meaningful to those attempting to use it. Saying that Andy Dalton's passes were worth 116 success value points over replacement in 2016 has very little value without a context to tell us if 116 is good total or a bad one. Therefore, we translate these success values into a number called "Defense-adjusted Yards Above Replacement, or DYAR. Thus, Dalton was fourth among quarterbacks with 1,135 passing DYAR. It is our estimate that a generic replacement-level quarterback, throwing in the same situations as Dalton, would have been worth 1,135 fewer yards. Note that this doesn't mean the replacement level quarterback would have gained exactly 1,135 fewer yards. First downs, touchdowns, and turnovers all have an estimated yardage value in this system, so what we are saying is that a generic replacement-level quarterback would have fewer yards and touchdowns (and more turnovers) that would total up to be equivalent to the value of 1,135 yards.

Problems with DVOA and DYAR

Football is a game in which nearly every action requires the work of two or more teammates—in fact, usually 11 teammates all working in unison. Unfortunately, when it comes to individual player ratings, we are still far from the point at which we can determine the value of a player independent from the performance of his teammates. That means that when we say, "In 2014, Le'Veon Bell had a DVOA of 8.6%," what we really are saying is, "In 2014, Le'Veon Bell, playing in Todd Haley's offensive system with the Pittsburgh offensive line blocking for him and Ben Roethlisberger selling the fake when necessary, had a DVOA of 8.6%."

DVOA is limited by what's included in the official NFL play-by-play or tracked by our game charting partners (explained below). Because we need to have the entire play-by-play of a season in order to compute DVOA and DYAR, these metrics are not yet ready to compare players of today to players throughout the league's history. As of this writing, we have processed 31 seasons, 1986 through 2016, and we add seasons at a rate of roughly two per year (the most recent season, plus one season back into history.)

In addition, because we need to turn around DVOA and DYAR quickly during the season before charting can be completed, we do not yet have charting data such as dropped passes incorporated into these advanced metrics. Eventually we will have two sets of metrics, one incorporating charting data and going back to 2005 or 2006, and another that does not incorporate charting and can be used to compare current players and teams to players and teams all the way back to 1986 or earlier.

Pythagorean Projection

The Pythagorean projection is an approximation of each team's wins based solely on their points scored and allowed. This basic concept was introduced by baseball analyst Bill James, who discovered that the record of a baseball team could be very closely approximated by taking the square of team runs scored and dividing it by the sum of the squares of team runs scored and allowed. Statistician Daryl Morey, now

general manager of the Houston Rockets, later extended this theorem to professional football, refining the exponent to 2.37 rather than 2.

The problem with that exponent is the same problem we've had with DVOA in recent years: the changing offensive levels in the NFL. 2.37 worked great based on the league 20 years ago, but in the current NFL it ends up slightly underprojecting teams that play high-scoring games. The most accurate method is actually to adjust the exponent based on the scoring environment of each individual team. Saints games have a lot of points. Jaguars games feature fewer points.

This became known as Pythagenport when Clay Davenport of Baseball Prospectus started doing it with baseball teams. In the middle of the 2011 season, we switched our measurement of Pythagorean wins to a Pythagenport-style equation, modified for the NFL.[1] The improvement is slight, but noticeable due to the high-scoring teams that have dominated the last few years.

For a long time, Pythagorean projections did a remarkable job of predicting Super Bowl champions. From 1984 through 2004, 10 of 21 Super Bowls were won by the team that led the NFL in Pythagorean wins. Seven other Super Bowls during that time were won by the team that finished second. Super Bowl champions that led the league in Pythagorean wins but not actual wins include the 2004 Patriots, 2000 Ravens, 1999 Rams, and 1997 Broncos.

Super Bowl champions have been much less predictable over the last few seasons. As of 2005, the 1980 Oakland Raiders held the mark for the fewest Pythagorean wins by a Super Bowl champion, 9.7. Then, between 2006 and 2012, four different teams won the Super Bowl with a lower Pythagorean win total: the 2006 Colts (9.6), the 2012 Ravens (9.4), the 2007 Giants (8.6), and the 2011 Giants (7.9), the first team in the 90-year history of the National Football League to ever be outscored during the regular season and still go on to win the championship. In the past four seasons, we've returned to more standard playoff results: six of the last eight Super Bowl teams ranked first or second in Pythagorean wins during the regular season, and Atlanta was third a year ago.

Pythagorean wins are also useful as a predictor of year-to-year improvement. Teams that win a minimum of one full game more than their Pythagorean projection tend to regress the following year; teams that win a minimum of one full game less than their Pythagorean projection tend to improve the following year, particularly if they were at or above .500 despite their underachieving. There is no team that qualifies from 2016; every team that underperformed its projection by at least one game had a losing record. On the other side, there are teams that seem set for a reversion of luck. Oakland went 12-4 despite just 8.7 projected wins, one of five different teams in 2016 with at least two more wins than projected wins. The others were Houston, Miami, New York Giants, and Dallas.

---

1 The equation, for those curious, is 1.5 x log ((PF+PA)/G).

Adjusted Line Yards

One of the most difficult goals of statistical analysis in football is isolating the degree to which each of the 22 men on the field is responsible for the result of a given play. Nowhere is this as significant as the running game, in which one player runs while up to nine other players—including not just linemen but also wideouts and tight ends—block in different directions. None of the statistics we use for measuring rushing—yards, touchdowns, yards per carry—differentiate between the contribution of the running back and the contribution of the offensive line. Neither do our advanced metrics DVOA and DYAR.

We do, however, have enough play-by-play data amassed that we can try to separate the effect that the running back has on a particular play from the effects of the offensive line (and other offensive blockers) and the opposing defense. A team might have two running backs in its stable: RB A, who averages 3.0 yards per carry, and RB B, who averages 3.5 yards per carry. Who is the better back? Imagine that RB A doesn't just average 3.0 yards per carry, but gets exactly 3 yards on every single carry, while RB B has a highly variable yardage output: sometimes 5 yards, sometimes minus-2 yards, sometimes 20 yards. The difference in variability between the runners can be exploited not only to determine the difference between the runners, but the effect the offensive line has on every running play.

At some point in every long running play, the running back passes all of his offensive line blocks as well as additional blocking backs or receivers. From there on, the rest of the play is dependent on the runner's own speed and elusiveness and the speed and tackling ability of the opposing defense. If David Johnson breaks through the line for 50 yards, avoiding tacklers all the way to the goal line, his offensive line has done a great job—but they aren't responsible for the majority of the yards gained. The trick is figuring out exactly how much they *are* responsible for.

For each running back carry, we calculated the probability that the back involved would run for the specific yardage on that play based on that back's average yardage per carry and the variability of their yardage from play to play. We also calculated the probability that the offense would get the yardage based on the team's rushing average and variability using all backs *other* than the one involved in the given play, and the probability that the defense would give up the specific amount of yardage based on its average rushing yards allowed per carry and variability.

A regression analysis breaks the value for rushing yardage into the following categories: losses, 0-4 yards, 5-10 yards, and 11+ yards. In general, the offensive line is 20 percent more responsible for lost yardage than it is for positive gains up to four yards, but 50 percent less responsible for additional yardage gained between five and ten yards, and not at all responsible for additional yardage past ten yards.

By applying those percentages to every running back carry, we were able to create **Adjusted Line Yards**, a statistic that measured offensive line performance. (We don't include carries by receivers, which are usually based on deception rather than straight blocking, or carries by quarterbacks, although we may need to reconsider that given the recent use of the read option in the NFL.) Those numbers are then adjusted based on down, distance, situation, opponent and whether or not a team is in the shotgun. (Because defenses are generally playing pass when the quarterback is in shotgun, the average running back carry from shotgun last year gained 4.52 yards, compared to just 3.94 yards on other carries.) The adjusted numbers are then normalized so that the league average for adjusted line yards per carry is the same as the league average for RB yards per carry. Starting with this book, adjusted line yards numbers are normalized differently in each season, so that normalization is based on that year's average for RB yards per carry rather than a historical average.

The NFL distinguishes between runs made to seven different locations on the line: left/right end, left/right tackle, left/right guard, and middle. Further research showed no statistically significant difference between how well a team performed on runs listed as having gone up the middle or past a guard, so we separated runs into just five different directions (left/right end, left/right tackle, and middle). Note that there may not be a statistically significant difference between right tackle and middle/guard either, but pending further research (and for the sake of symmetry) we still list runs behind the right tackle separately. These splits allow us to evaluate subsections of a team's offensive line, but not necessarily individual linemen, as we can't account for blocking assignments or guards who pull towards the opposite side of the line after the snap.

Success Rate

Success rate is a statistic for running backs that measures how consistently they achieve the yardage necessary for a play to be deemed successful. Some running backs will mix a few long runs with a lot of failed runs of one or two yards, while others with similar yards-per-carry averages will consistently gain five yards on first down, or as many yards as necessary on third down. This statistic helps us differentiate between the two.

Since Success Rate compares rush attempts to other rush attempts, without consideration of passing, the standard for success on first down is slightly lower than those described above for DVOA. In addition, the standard for success changes slightly in the fourth quarter when running backs are used to run out the clock. A team with the lead is satisfied with a shorter run as long as it stays in bounds. Conversely, for a team down by a couple of touchdowns in the fourth quarter, four yards on first down isn't going to be a big help.

The formula for Success Rate is as follows:

• A successful play must gain 40 percent of needed yards on first down, 60 percent of needed yards on second down, and

100 percent of needed yards on third or fourth down.

• If the offense is behind by more than a touchdown in the fourth quarter, the benchmarks switch to 50 percent, 65 percent, and 100 percent.

• If the offense is ahead by any amount in the fourth quarter, the benchmarks switch to 30 percent, 50 percent, and 100 percent.

The league-average Success Rate in 2016 was 45.2 percent. Success Rate is not adjusted based on defenses faced, and is not calculated for quarterbacks and wide receivers who occasionally carry the ball.

Approximate Value

Approximate Value is a system created by Doug Drinen of Pro Football Reference. The goal is to put a single number on every season of every NFL player since 1950, using a very broad set of guidelines. The goal is not to make judgments on individual seasons, but rather to have a format for studying groups of seasons that is more accurate than measuring players with a very broad brush such as "games started" or "number of Pro Bowls." Skill players are rated primarily using basic stats, while offensive linemen and defensive players are rated in large part based on team performance as well as individual accolades and games started. Advanced stats from Football Outsiders play-by-play breakdown are not part of this system. It is obviously imperfect—"approximate" is right there in the name—but it's valuable for studying groups of draft picks, groups of players by age, and so on. The system is introduced and explained at https://www.pro-football-reference.com/blog/index37a8.html

KUBIAK Projection System

Most "skill position" players whom we expect to play a role this season receive a projection of their standard 2017 NFL statistics using the KUBIAK projection system. KUBIAK takes into account a number of different factors including expected role, performance over the past two seasons, age, height, weight, historical comparables, and projected team performance on offense and defense. When we named our system KUBIAK, it was a play on the PECOTA system used by our partners at Baseball Prospectus—if they were going to name their system after a long-time eighties backup, we would name our system after a long-time eighties backup. Little did we know that Gary Kubiak would finally get a head coaching job the very next season. After some debate, we decided to keep the name, although discussing projections for Denver players was a bit awkward for a while.

To clear up a common misconception among our readers, KUBIAK projects individual player performances only, not teams.

2017 Win Projection System

In this book, each of the 32 NFL teams receives a **2017 Mean Projection** at the beginning of its chapter. These projections stem from three equations that forecast 2017 DVOA for offense, defense, and special teams based on a number of different factors. This offseason, we overhauled and improved the team projection system for the first time in a few years. The new system starts by considering the team's DVOA over the past three seasons and, on offense, a separate projection for the starting quarterback. The new system also does a much better job of measuring the value of offseason personnel changes by incorporating a measure that's based on the net personnel change in DYAR among non-quarterbacks (for offense) and the net change in Approximate Value above replacement level (for defense). Other factors include coaching experience, recent draft history, certain players returning from injury, and combined tenure on the offensive line.

These three equations produce precise numbers representing the most likely outcome, but also produce a range of possibilities, used to determine the probability of each possible offensive, defensive, and special teams DVOA for each team. This is particularly important when projecting football teams, because with only 16 games in a season, a team's performance may vary wildly from its actual talent level due to a couple of random bounces of the ball or badly timed injuries. In addition, the economic structure of the NFL allows teams to make sudden jumps or drops in overall ability more often than in other sports.

From 2003-2014, the mean DVOA forecast by the new projection system had a correlation coefficient of .539 with actual wins and a correlation coefficient of .642 with actual DVOA.

The next step in our forecast involves simulating the season one million times. We use the projected range of DVOA possibilities to produce 1,000 different simulated seasons with 32 sets of DVOA ratings. We then plug those season-long DVOA ratings into the same equation we use during the season to determine each team's likely remaining wins for our Playoff Odds Report. The simulation takes each season game-by-game, determining the home or road team's chance of winning each game based on the DVOA ratings of each team as well as home-field advantage. A random number between 0 and 100 determines whether the home or road team has won that game. We ran 1,000 simulations with each of the 1,000 sets of DVOA ratings, creating a million different simulations. The simulation was programmed by Mike Harris.

Two years ago, we began using a system we call a "dynamic simulation" to better approximate the true distribution of wins in the NFL. When simulating the season, each team had 2.0% DVOA added or subtracted after a win or loss, reflecting the fact that a win or loss tends to tell us whether a team is truly better or worse than whatever their mean projection had been before the season. Using this method, a team projected with 20.0% DVOA which goes 13-3 will have a 40.0% DVOA entering the playoffs, which is much more realistic. This change gave us more projected seasons at the margins, with fewer seasons at 8-8 and more seasons at 14-2 or 2-14. The dynamic simulation also meant a slight increase in projected wins for the best teams, and a slight decrease for the worst teams. However, the conservative nature of our projection system still means the distribution of mean projected wins has a much smaller spread than the actual win-loss records we will see by the end of December. We will continue to experiment with changes to the simulation in order to produce the most accurate possible forecast of the NFL season in future years.

Football Outsiders Game Charting Data

Each of the formulas listed above relies primarily on the play-by-play data published by the NFL. When we began to analyze the NFL, this was all that we had to work with. Just as a television broadcast has a color commentator who gives more detail to the facts related by the play-by-play announcer, so too do we need some color commentary to provide contextual information that breathes life into these plain lines of numbers and text. We added this color commentary with game charting.

Beginning in 2005, Football Outsiders began using a number of volunteers to chart every single play of every regular-season and postseason NFL game. To put it into perspective, there were over 54,000 lines of play-by-play information in each NFL season and our goal is to add several layers of detail to nearly all of them.

It gradually became clear that attempting to chart so much football with a crew of volunteers was simply not feasible, especially given our financial resources compared to those of our competitors. Over the past few years, we have partnered with larger companies to take on the responsibilities of game charting so that we can devote more time to analysis.

In 2015, Football Outsiders reached an agreement with Sports Info Solutions, formerly Baseball Info Solutions, to begin a large charting project that would replace our use of volunteers. We also have a partnership with ESPN Stats & Info, and use their data to check against the data collected by Sports Info Solutions. All charting data for the 2016 season is provided by one of these two companies.

Our partnership with Baseball Info Solutions has also resulted in the expansion of Football Outsiders Premium with a new Premium Charting Data subscription that updates some of our data such as cornerback charting and broken tackles every week during the season. We also produce the Off The Charts podcast, which explores data from game charting in a weekly discussion of the NFL season.[2]

Game charting is significantly easier now that the NFL makes coaches' film available through NFL Game Rewind. This tape, which was not publicly available when we began

charting with volunteers in 2005, includes sideline and end zone perspectives for each play, and shows all 22 players at all times, making it easier to see the cause-and-effect of certain actions taken on the field. Nonetheless, all game charting is still imperfect. You often cannot tell which players did their jobs particularly well or made mistakes without knowing the play call and each player's assignment, particularly when it comes to zone coverage or pass-rushers who reach the quarterback without being blocked. Therefore, the goal of game charting from both ESPN Stats & Info and Sports Info Solutions is *not* to "grade" players, but rather to attempt to mark specific events: a pass pressure, a blown block, a dropped interception, and so on.

We emphasize that all data from game charting is unofficial. Other sources for football statistics may keep their own measurements of yards after catch or how teams perform against the blitz. Our data will not necessarily match theirs. Even ESPN Stats & Info and Sports Info Solutions have a number of disagreements, marking different events on the same play because it can be difficult to determine the definition of a "pressure" or a "dropped pass." However, any other group that is publicly tracking this data is also working off the same footage, and thus will run into the same issues of difficulty and subjectivity.

There are lots of things we would like to do with all-22 film that we simply haven't been able to do yet, such as charting coverage by cornerbacks when they aren't the target of a given pass, or even when pass pressure prevents the pass from getting into the air. Unfortunately, we are limited by what our partners are able to chart given time constraints.

In the description of data below, we have tried to designate which data from 2016 comes from ESPN Stats & Info group (ESPN S&I), which data comes from Sports Info Solutions (SIS), and where we have combined data from both companies with our own analysis.

Formation/Personnel

For each play, we have the number of running backs, wide receivers, and tight ends on the field courtesy of ESPN S&I. Players were marked based on their designation on the roster, not based on where they lined up on the field. Obviously, this could be difficult with some hybrid players or players changing positions in 2016, but we did our best to keep things as consistent as possible.

SIS also tracked this data and added the names of players who were lined up in unexpected positions. This included marking tight ends or wide receivers in the backfield, and running backs or tight ends who were lined up either wide or in the slot (often referred to as "flexing" a tight end). SIS also marked when a fullback or tight end was actually a sixth (or sometimes even seventh) offensive lineman, and they marked the backfield formation as empty back, single back, I formation, offset I, split backs, full house, or "other." These notations of backfield formation were recorded directly before the snap and do not account for positions before pre-snap motion.

SIS then marked defensive formations by listing the number of linemen, linebackers, and defensive backs. There will be mistakes—a box safety may occasionally be confused for a linebacker, for example—but for the most part the data for defensive backs will be accurate. Figuring out how to mark whether a player is a defensive end or a linebacker is a different story. The rise of hybrid defenses has led to a lot of confusion. Edge rushers in a 4-3 defense may play standing up because they used to play for a 3-4 defense and that's what they are used to. A player who is usually considered an outside linebacker for a 3-4 defense may put his hand on the ground on third down (thus looking like a 4-3 defensive end), but the tackle next to him is still two-gapping (which is generally a 3-4 principle). SIS marked personnel in a simplified fashion by designating any front seven player in a standing position as a linebacker and designating any front seven player in a crouching position as a defensive lineman.

This year, for the first time, we also have data from SIS on where receivers lined up before each of their pass targets (wide, slot, tight, or backfield) and what routes they ran.

Rushers and Blockers: ESPN Stats & Info provided us with two data points regarding the pass rush: the number of pass-rushers on a given play, and the number defensive backs blitzing on a given play. SIS also tracked this data for comparison purposes and then added a count of blockers. Counting blockers is an art as much as a science. Offenses base their blocking schemes on how many rushers they expect. A running back or tight end's assignment may depend on how many pass-rushers cross the line at the snap. Therefore, an offensive player was deemed to be a blocker if he engaged in an actual block, or there was some hesitation before running a route. A running back that immediately heads out into the flat is not a blocker, but one that waits to verify that the blocking scheme is working and then goes out to the flat would, in fact, be considered a blocker.

Pass Play Details: Both companies recorded the following data for all pass plays:

• Did the play begin with a play-action fake, including read-option fakes that developed into pass plays instead of being handed to a running back?
• Was the quarterback in or out of the pocket?
• Was the quarterback under pressure in making his pass?
• Was this a screen pass?

SIS game charting also marks the name of the defender who caused the pass pressure. Charters were allowed to list two names if necessary, and could also attribute a hurry to "overall pressure." No defender was given a hurry and a sack on the same play, but defenders were given hurries if they helped force a quarterback into a sack that was finished by another

player. SIS also identified which defender(s) caused the pass pressure which forced a quarterback to scramble for yardage. If the quarterback wasn't under pressure but ran anyway, the play could be marked either as "coverage scramble" (if the quarterback ran because there were no open receivers) or "hole opens up" (if the quarterback ran because he knew he could gain significant yardage).

Football Outsiders (using our past game charting volunteers) reviewed a number of plays where there was disagreement between the two companies on pass pressure. All team pressure rate stats in this book are based on SIS data, adjusting for the plays where Football Outsiders felt that ESPN S&I charting was more accurate. All individual pressure counts for defenders are based on SIS data combined with Football Outsiders adjustments, even if ESPN S&I did not mark the play in question as a pass pressure.

Some places in this book, we divide pass yardage into two numbers: distance in the air and yards after catch. This information is tracked by the NFL, but it can be hard to find and the official scorers often make errors, so we corrected the original data based on input from both ESPN S&I and SIS. Distance in the air is based on the distance from the line of scrimmage to the place where the receiver either caught or was supposed to catch the pass. We do not count how far the quarterback was behind the line or horizontal yardage if the quarterback threw across the field. All touchdowns are counted to the goal line, so that distance in the air added to yards after catch always equals the official yardage total kept by the league.

Incomplete Passes: Quarterbacks are evaluated based on their ability to complete passes. However, not all incompletes should have the same weight. Throwing a ball away to avoid a sack is actually a valuable incomplete, and a receiver dropping an otherwise quality pass is hardly a reflection on the quarterback.

This year, our evaluation of incomplete passes began with ESPN Stats & Info, which marked passes as Overthrown, Underthrown, Thrown Away, Batted Down at the Line, Defensed, or Dropped. We then compared this data to similar data from SIS and made some changes. We also changed some plays to reflect a couple of additional categories we have kept in past years for Football Outsiders: Hit in Motion (indicating the quarterback was hit as his arm was coming forward to make a pass), Caught out of Bounds, and Hail Mary.

Our count of passes defensed will be different from the unofficial totals kept by the league for reasons explained below in the section on Defensive Secondary tables.

ESPN S&I and SIS also marked when a defender dropped an interception; Football Outsiders volunteers then analyzed plays where the two companies disagreed to come up with a final total. When a play is close, we tend to err on the side of not marking a dropped interception, as we don't want to blame a defender who, for example, jumps high for a ball and has it tip off his fingers. We also counted a few "defensed" interceptions, when a quarterback threw a pass that would have been picked off if not for the receiver playing defense on the ball. These passes counted as dropped interceptions for quarterbacks but not for the defensive players.

Defenders: The NFL play-by-play lists tackles and, occasionally, tipped balls, but it does not definitively list the defender on the play. SIS charters attempted to determine which defender was primarily responsible for covering either the receiver at the time of the throw or the location to which the pass was thrown, regardless of whether the pass was complete or not.

Every defense in the league plays zone coverage at times, some more than others, which leaves us with the question of how to handle plays without a clear man assigned to that receiver. Charters (SIS employees in 2015-2016, and FO volunteers in past seasons) had three alternatives:

• We asked charters to mark passes that found the holes in zone coverage as Hole in Zone, rather than straining to assign that pass to an individual defender. We asked the charter to also note the player who appeared to be responsible for that zone, and these defenders are assigned half credit for those passes. Some holes were so large that no defender could be listed along with the Hole in Zone designation.

• Charters were free to list two defenders instead of one. This could be used for actual double coverage, or for zone coverage in which the receiver was right between two close defenders rather than sitting in a gaping hole. When two defenders are listed, ratings assign each with half credit.

• Screen passes and dumpoffs are marked as Uncovered unless a defender (normally a linebacker) is obviously shadowing that specific receiver on the other side of the line of scrimmage.

Since we began the charting project in 2005, nothing has changed our analysis more than this information on pass coverage. However, even now with the ability to view all-22 film, it can be difficult to identify the responsible defender except when there is strict man-to-man coverage.

Additional Details: All draw plays were marked, whether by halfbacks or quarterbacks. Option runs and zone reads were also marked.

Both SIS and ESPN S&I when the formation was pistol as opposed to shotgun; the official play-by-play simply marks these plays all as shotgun.

Both SIS and ESPN S&I track yards after contact for each play.

SIS charters marked each quarterback sack with one of the following terms: Blown Block, Coverage Sack, QB Fault, Failed Scramble, or Blitz/Overall Pressure. Blown Blocks were listed with the name of a specific offensive player who allowed the defender to come through. (Some blown block sacks are listed with two blockers, who each get a half-sack..) Coverage Sack denotes when the quarterback has plenty of time to throw but cannot find an open receiver. QB Fault represents "self sacks" listed without a defender, such as when the quarterback drops back, only to find the ball slip out of his hands with no pass-rusher touching him. Failed Scramble rep-

resents plays where a quarterback began to run without major pass pressure because he thought he could get a positive gain, only to be tackled before he reached the line of scrimmage.

SIS tracked "broken tackles" on all runs or pass plays. We define a "broken tackle" as one of two events: Either the ballcarrier escapes from the grasp of the defender, or the defender is in good position for a tackle but the ballcarrier jukes him out of his shoes. If the ballcarrier sped by a slow defender who dived and missed, that did not count as a broken tackle. If the defender couldn't bring the ballcarrier down because he is being blocked out of the play by another offensive player, this did not count as a broken tackle. It was possible to mark multiple broken tackles on the same play. Broken tackles are not marked for special teams.

Please note that broken tackle numbers have gone up substantially over the past two years because of a change in methodology in 2014 and a looser definition of broken tackles used by Sports Info Solutions in 2015. Because of these changes, the league-wide total of broken tackles went up roughly 25 percent in 2015 and then another 10 percent in 2016. It is important to account for this when comparing a player's total in one year to his total in another year..

Acknowledgements

Thank you to all the past game charting volunteers who helped us collect data from 2005 through 2014, and who helped us clean data from our partners in 2015 and 2016.

Thanks as well to our two game charting partners that have helped free us up to do more analysis and less data collection, including ESPN Stats & Info (particularly John McTigue, Allison Loucks, and Henry Gargiulo) and Sports Info Solutions (particularly Greg Thomas, Dan Foehrenbach, and Matt Manocherian).

How to Read the Team Summary Box

Here is a rundown of all the tables and stats that appear in the 32 team chapters. Each team chapter begins with a box in the upper-right hand corner that gives a summary of our statistics for that team, as follows:

2016 Record gives each team's actual win-loss record. **Pythagorean Wins** gives the approximate number of wins expected last year based on this team's raw totals of points scored and allowed, along with their NFL rank. **Snap-Weighted Age** gives the average age of the team in 2016, weighted based on how many snaps each player was on the field and ranked from oldest (New Orleans, first at 27.5) to youngest (Los Angeles Rams, 32nd at 25.7). **Average Opponent** gives a ranking of last year's schedule strength based on the average DVOA of all 16 opponents faced during the regular season. Teams are ranked from the hardest schedule of 2016 (Cleveland) to the easiest (New England).

Total DVOA gives the team's total DVOA rating, with rank. **Offense**, **Defense**, and **Special Teams** list the team's DVOA rating in each category, along with NFL rank. Remember that good offenses and special teams have positive DVOA numbers, while a negative DVOA means better defense, so the lowest defensive DVOA is ranked No. 1 (last year, Denver).

2017 Mean Projection gives the average number of wins for this team based on the 2017 Win Projection System described earlier in this chapter. Please note that we do not expect any teams to win the exact number of games in their mean projection. First of all, no team can win 0.8 of a game. Second, because these projections represent a whole range of possible values, the averages naturally tend to drift towards 8-8. Obviously, we're not expecting a season where no team goes 4-12 or 12-4. For a better way to look at the projections, we offer **Postseason Odds**, which give each team's chance of making the postseason based on our simulation, and **Super Bowl Appearance** odds, which give each team's chance of representing its conference in Super Bowl XLIX. The average team will make the playoffs in 37.5 percent of simulations, and the Super Bowl in 6.3 percent of simulations.

Projected Average Opponent gives the team's strength of schedule for 2017; like the listing for last year's schedule strength in the first column of the box, this number is based not on last year's record but on the mean projected DVOA for each opponent. A positive schedule is harder, a negative schedule easier. Teams are ranked from the hardest projected schedule (Philadelphia, first) to the easiest (New England, 32nd). This strength of schedule projection does not take into account which games are home or away, or the timing of the bye week.

The final column of the box gives the team's chances of finishing in four different basic categories of success:

- On the Clock (0-4 wins; NFL average 12%)
- Mediocrity (5-7 wins; NFL average 32%)
- Playoff Contender (8-10 wins; NFL average 36%)
- Super Bowl Contender (11+ wins; NFL average 20%)

The percentage given for each category is dependent not only on how good we project the team to be in 2016, but the level of variation possible in that projection, and the expected performance of the teams on the schedule.

You'll also find a table with the team's 2017 schedule placed within each chapter, along with a graph showing each team's 2016 week-to-week performance by single-game DVOA. The second, dotted line on the graph represents a five-week moving average of each team's performance, in order to show a longer-term view of when they were improving and declining. After the essays come statistical tables and comments related to that team and its specific units.

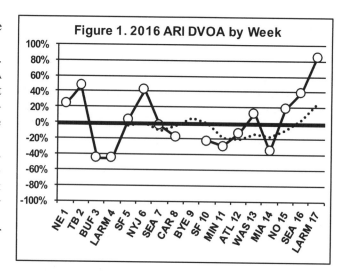

Figure 1. 2016 ARI DVOA by Week

Weekly Performance

The first table gives a quick look at the team's week-to-week performance in 2016. (Table X) This includes the playoffs for those teams that made the postseason, with the four weeks of playoffs numbered 18 (wild card) through 21 (Super Bowl). All other tables in the team chapters represent regular-season performance only unless otherwise noted.

Looking at the first week for the Arizona Cardinals in 2016, the first five columns are fairly obvious: Arizona opened the season with a 23-21 loss at home against New England. **YDF** and **YDA** are net yards on offense and net yards against the defense. These numbers do not include penalty yardage or special teams yardage. **TO** represents the turnover margin. Unlike other parts of the book in which we consider all fumbles as equal, this only represents actual turnovers: fumbles lost and interceptions. So, for example, the Cardinals forced two more turnovers than New England in Week 1, but then committed four more turnovers than Buffalo in Week 3.

Finally, you'll see DVOA ratings for this game: Total **DVOA** first, then offense (**Off**), defense (**Def**), and special teams (**ST**). Note that these are DVOA ratings, adjusted for opponent, so a loss to a good team will often be listed with a higher rating than a close win over a bad team. For example, the Cardinals have a positive DVOA for their Week 1 loss to New England, but a negative DVOA for their Week 10 win over San Francisco.

Trends and Splits

Next to the week-to-week performance is a table giving DVOA for different portions of a team's performance, on both offense and defense. Each split is listed with the team's rank among the 32 NFL teams. These numbers represent regular season performance only.

Total DVOA gives total offensive, and defensive DVOA in all situations. **Unadjusted VOA** represents the breakdown of play-by-play considering situation but not opponent. A team whose offensive DVOA is higher than its offensive VOA played a harder-than-average schedule of opposing defenses; a team with a lower defensive DVOA than defensive VOA player a harder-than-average schedule of opposing offenses.

Weighted Trend lowers the importance of earlier games to give a better idea of how the team was playing at the end of the regular season. The final four weeks of the season are full strength; moving backwards through the season, each week is given less and less weight until the first three weeks of the season, which are not included at all. **Variance** is the same as noted above, with a higher percentage representing less consistency. This is true for both offense and defense: Oakland, for example, was very consistent on defense (2.6%, fourth) but inconsistent on offense (9.5%, 28th). **Average Opponent** is that the same thing that appears in the box to open each chapter, except split in half: the average DVOA of all opposing defenses (for offense) or the average DVOA of all opposing offenses (for defense).

Passing and **Rushing** are fairly self-explanatory. Note that rushing DVOA includes all rushes, not just those by running backs, including quarterback scrambles that may have begun as pass plays.

The next three lines split out DVOA on **First Down, Second Down**, and **Third Down**. Third Down here includes fourth downs on which a team runs a regular offensive play instead of punting or attempting a field goal. **First Half** and **Second Half** represent the first two quarters and last two quarters (plus overtime), not the first eight and last eight games of the regular season. Next comes DVOA in the **Red Zone**, which is any offensive play starting from the defense's 20-yard line through the goal line. The final split is **Late and Close**, which includes any play in the second half or overtime when the teams are within eight points of each other in either direction. (Eight points, of course, is the biggest deficit that can be made up with a single score, a touchdown and two-point conversion.)

Five-Year Performance

This table gives each team's performance over the past five seasons. (Table X) It includes win-loss record, Pythagorean Wins, **Estimated Wins**, points scored and allowed, and turnover margin. Estimated wins are based on a formula that estimates how many games a team would have been expected to win based on 2016 performance in specific situations, normalized to eliminate luck (fumble recoveries, opponents' missed field goals, etc.) and assuming average schedule strength. The formula emphasizes consistency and overall DVOA as well as DVOA in a few specifically important situations. The next columns of this table give total DVOA along with DVOA for offense, defense, and special teams, and the rank for each among that season's 32 NFL teams.

The next four columns give the adjusted games lost (AGL) for starters on both offense and defense, along with rank. (Our total for starters here includes players who take over as starters due to another injury, such as Martellus Bennett or Brian Hoyer last year, as well as important situational players who may not necessarily start, such as pass-rush specialists and slot receivers.) Adjusted games lost was introduced in *Pro Football Prospectus 2008*; it gives a weighted estimate of the probability that players would miss games based on how they are listed on the injury report. Unlike a count of "starter games missed," this accounts for the fact that a player listed as questionable who does in fact play is not playing at 100 percent capability. Teams are ranked from the fewest injuries (2016: Los Angeles Rams on offense, New England on defense) to the most (2016: Minnesota on offense, Chicago on defense).

Individual Offensive Statistics

Each team chapter contains a table giving passing and receiving numbers for any player who either threw five passes or was thrown five passes, along with rushing numbers for any players who carried the ball at least five times. These numbers also appear in the player comments at the end of the book (except for runs by wide receivers). By putting them together in the team chapters we hope we make it easier to compare the performances of different players on the same team.

Players who are no longer on the team are marked with an asterisk. New players who were on a different team in 2016 are in italics. Changes should be accurate as of July 1. Rookies are not included.

All players are listed with DYAR and DVOA. Passing statistics then list total pass plays (**Plays**), net yardage (**NtYds**), and net yards per pass (**Avg**). These numbers include not just passes (and the positive yardage from them) but aborted snaps and sacks (and the negative yardage from them). Then comes average yards after catch (**YAC**), as determined by the game charting project. This

Chicago Bears Five-Year Performance

Year	W-L	Pyth W	Est W	PF	PA	TO	Total	Rk	Off	Rk	Def	Rk	ST	Rk	Off AGL	Rk	Def AGL	Rk	Off Age	Rk	Def Age	Rk	ST Age	Rk
2012	10-6	10.8	11.0	375	277	+20	20.5%	6	-10.9%	26	-26.7%	1	4.7%	6	17.6	8	13.6	4	27.2	12	27.9	4	26.9	6
2013	8-8	7.3	9.2	445	478	+5	6.6%	11	13.3%	6	8.7%	25	2.0%	11	6.9	1	55.6	30	27.5	8	27.3	10	27.5	1
2014	5-11	4.9	6.4	319	442	-5	-13.8%	26	-0.1%	14	10.6%	28	-3.1%	25	41.0	27	60.6	26	27.9	3	27.0	12	26.3	9
2015	6-10	6.3	6.8	335	397	-4	-5.7%	19	6.9%	10	11.3%	31	-1.2%	21	64.7	30	28.2	16	27.4	10	25.8	31	26.2	13
2016	3-13	4.7	6.2	279	399	-20	-8.3%	25	-2.6%	17	5.0%	23	-0.6%	18	84.0	31	71.1	32	26.7	16	26.0	24	26.2	11

average is based on charted receptions, not total pass attempts. The final three numbers are completion percentage (**C%**), passing touchdowns (**TD**), and interceptions (**Int**).

It is important to note that the tables in the team chapters contain Football Outsiders stats, while the tables in the player comments later in the book contain official NFL totals, at least when it comes to standard numbers like receptions and yardage. This results in a number of differences between the two:

• Team chapter tables list aborted snaps as passes, not runs, although aborted handoffs are still listed as runs. Net yardage for quarterbacks in the team chapter tables includes the lost yardage from aborted snaps, sacks, and intentional grounding penalties. For official NFL stats, all aborted snaps are listed as runs.

• Football Outsiders stats omit kneeldowns from run totals and clock-stopping spikes from pass totals.

• In the Football Outsiders stats, we have changed a number of lateral passes to count as passes rather than runs, under the theory that a pass play is still a pass play, even if the receiver is standing five inches behind the quarterback. This results in some small differences in totals.

• "Skill players" who played for multiple teams in 2016 are only listed in team chapters with stats from that specific team; combined stats are listed in the player comments section.

Sample Passing Table

Carolina Panthers Passing

Player	DYAR	DVOA	Plays	NtYds	Avg	YAC	C%	TD	Int
C.Newton	-64	-13.0%	543	3223	5.9	4.9	53.4%	19	14
D.Anderson	-27	-17.9%	53	453	8.5	4.5	67.9%	2	5

Rushing statistics start with DYAR and DVOA, then list rushing plays and net yards along with average yards per carry and rushing touchdowns. The final two columns are fumbles (**Fum**)—both those lost to the defense and those recovered by the offense—and Success Rate (**Suc**), explained earlier in this chapter. Fumbles listed in the rushing table include all quarterback fumbles on sacks and aborted snaps, as well as running back fumbles on receptions, but not wide receiver fumbles.

Sample Rushing Table

Dallas Cowboys Rushing

Player	DYAR	DVOA	Plays	Yds	Avg	TD	Fum	Suc
E.Elliott	303	16.0%	287	1394	4.9	15	0	57%
A.Morris	14	-3.4%	61	231	3.8	2	0	54%
D.Prescott	96	41.6%	36	235	6.5	6	0	-
L.Whitehead	38	43.9%	8	86	10.8	0	0	-
L.Dunbar*	5	8.9%	6	11	1.8	1	0	50%

Receiving statistics start with DYAR and DVOA and then list the number of passes thrown to this receiver (**Plays**), the number of passes caught (**Catch**) and the total receiving yards (**Yds**). Yards per catch (**Y/C**) includes total yardage per reception, based on standard play-by-play, while yards after catch (**YAC**) is based on information from our game charting project. Finally we list total receiving touchdowns, and catch percentage (**C%**), which is the percentage of passes intended for this receiver which were caught. Wide receivers, tight ends, and running backs are separated on the table by horizontal lines.

Sample Receiving Table

Denver Broncos Receiving

Player	DYAR	DVOA	Plays	Ctch	Yds	Y/C	YAC	TD	C%
D.Thomas	172	2.1%	144	90	1085	12.1	3.6	5	63%
E.Sanders	103	-3.3%	137	79	1032	13.1	3.0	5	58%
J.Norwood*	-61	-35.9%	34	20	215	10.8	3.4	1	59%
J.Taylor	32	2.7%	25	16	211	13.2	5.3	2	64%
B.Fowler	-16	-22.2%	24	11	145	13.2	5.8	2	46%
C.Latimer	2	-10.9%	15	8	76	9.5	3.0	0	53%
V.Green	-19	-14.8%	37	22	237	10.8	4.6	1	59%
A.J.Derby	1	-6.7%	20	16	161	10.1	3.2	0	80%
J.Heuerman	2	-5.6%	17	9	141	15.7	7.6	0	53%
J.Phillips*	4	-1.1%	8	5	40	8.0	3.4	1	63%
D.Booker	-41	-31.4%	45	31	270	8.7	8.3	1	69%
C.J.Anderson	-2	-15.4%	24	16	128	8.0	6.8	1	67%
J.Forsett*	-32	-64.7%	10	7	34	4.9	6.7	0	70%
A.Janovich	8	1.6%	7	5	44	8.8	6.0	0	71%

Performance Based on Personnel

These tables provide a look at performance in 2016 based on personnel packages, as defined above in the section on marking formation/personnel as part of Sports Info Solutions charting. There are four different tables, representing:

• Offense based on personnel
• Offense based on opponent's defensive personnel
• Defense based on personnel
• Defense based on opponent's offensive personnel

Most of these tables feature the top five personnel groupings for each team. Occasionally, we will list the personnel group which ranks sixth if the sixth group is either particularly interesting or nearly as common as the fifth group. Each personnel group is listed with its frequency among 2016 plays, yards per play, and DVOA. Offensive personnel are also listed with how often the team in question called a running play instead of a pass play from given personnel. (Quarterback scrambles are included as pass plays, not runs.)

Offensive personnel are given in the standard two-digit format where the first digit is running backs and the second digit is tight ends. You can figure out wide receivers by subtracting that total from five, with a couple of exceptions. Plays with six or seven offensive linemen will have a three-digit listing such as "611" or "622." Any play with a direct snap to a non-quarterback, or with a specific running quarterback taking the snap instead of the regular quarterback, was counted as "Wildcat." No team ends up with Wildcat listed among its top five offensive personnel groups.

When defensive players come in to play offense, defensive backs are counted as wide receivers and linebackers as tight ends. Defensive linemen who come in as offensive linemen are counted as offensive linemen; if they come in as blocking fullbacks, we count them as running backs.).

This year, we are not giving personnel data based on the number of defensive linemen and linebackers. This is because of the difficulty in separating between the two, especially with our simplified designation of players as defensive linemen or linebackers based simply on who has a hand on the ground. There are just too many hybrid defensive schemes in today's game: 4-3 schemes where one or both ends rush the passer from a standing position, or hybrid schemes that one-gap on one side of the nose tackle and two-gap on the other. Therefore, defensive personnel is listed in only five categories:

• Base (four defensive backs)
• Nickel (five defensive backs)
• Dime+ (six or more defensive backs)
• Big (either 4-4-3 or 3-5-3)
• Goal Line (all other personnel groups with fewer than four defensive backs)

11, or three-wide personnel, was by far the most common grouping in the NFL last year, used on 60 percent of plays, followed the standard two-tight end set 12 personnel (17 percent of plays) and the more traditional (and slowly dying) 21 personnel (7 percent). Defenses lined up in Base on 30 percent of plays, Nickel on 57 percent of plays, Dime+ on 11 percent of plays, and either Big or Goal Line on 1.9 percent of plays.

Strategic Tendencies

The Strategic Tendencies table presents a mix of information garnered from both the standard play by play and the Football Outsiders game charting project. It gives you an idea of what kind of plays teams run in what situations and with what personnel. Each category is given a league-wide **Rank** from most often (1) to least often (32) except as noted below. The sample table shown here lists the NFL average in each category for 2016.

The first column of strategic tendencies lists how often teams ran in different situations. These ratios are based on the type of play, not the actual result, so quarterback scrambles count as "passes" while quarterback sneaks, draws and option plays count as "runs."

Runs, first half and **Runs, first down** should be self-evident. **Runs, second-and-long** is the percentage of runs on second down with seven or more yards to go, giving you an idea of how teams follow up a failed first down. **Runs, power situations** is the percentage of runs on third or fourth down with 1-2 yards to go, or at the goal line with 1-2 yards to go. **Runs, behind 2H** tells you how often teams ran when they were behind in the second half, generally a passing situation. **Pass, ahead 2H** tells you how often teams passed when they had the lead in the second half, generally a running situation.

In each case, you can determine the percentage of plays that were passes by subtracting the run percentage from 100 (the reverse being true for "Pass, ahead 2H," of course).

The second column gives information about offensive formations and personnel, as tracked by ESPN Stats & Info.

The first two entries detail formation, i.e. where players were lined up on the field. **Form: Single Back** lists how often the team lined up with only one player in the backfield, and **Form: Empty Back** lists how often the team lined up with no players in the backfield.

The next three entries are based on personnel, no matter where players were lined up in the formation. **Pers: 3+ WR** marks how often the team plays with three or more wide receivers. **Pers: 2+ TE/6+ OL** marks how often the team plays with either more than one tight end or more than five offensive linemen. **Pers: 6+ OL** marks just plays with more than five offensive linemen. Finally, we give the percentage of plays where a team used **Shotgun or Pistol** in 2016. This does not count "Wildcat" or direct snap plays involving a non-quarterback.

The third column shows how the defensive **Pass Rush** worked in 2016.

Rush 3/Rush 4/Rush 5/Rush 6+: The percentage of pass plays (including quarterback scrambles) on which ESPN Stats & Info recorded this team rushing the passer with three or fewer defenders, four defenders, five defenders, and six or more defenders. These percentages do not include goal-line

NFL Average Strategic Tendencies, 2016

Run/Pass		Rk	Formation		Rk	Pass Rush		Rk	Secondary		Rk	Strategy		Rk
Runs, first half	38%	--	Form: Single Back	78%	--	Rush 3	8.3%	--	4 DB	30%	--	Play-action	18%	--
Runs, first down	47%	--	Form: Empty Back	8%	--	Rush 4	64.3%	--	5 DB	57%	--	Avg Box (Off)	6.20	--
Runs, second-long	30%	--	Pers: 3+ WR	66%	--	Rush 5	21.2%	--	6+ DB	11%	--	Avg Box (Def)	6.20	--
Runs, power sit.	56%	--	Pers: 2+ TE/6+ OL	28%	--	Rush 6+	6.2%	--	CB by Sides	76%	--	Offensive Pace	0.00	--
Runs, behind 2H	27%	--	Pers: 6+ OL	5%	--	Sacks by LB	37.6%	--	S/CB Cover Ratio	27%	--	Defensive Pace	30.55	--
Pass, ahead 2H	49%	--	Shotgun/Pistol	64%	--	Sacks by DB	8.6%	--	DB Blitz	9%	--	Go for it on 4th	1.00	--

plays on the one- or two-yard line.

Sacks by LB/Sacks by DB: The percentage of this team's sacks that came from linebackers and defensive backs. To figure out the percentage of sacks from defensive linemen, simply subtract the sum of these numbers from 100 percent.

The fourth column has more data on the use of defensive backs.

4 DB/5DB/6+ DB: The percentage of plays where this defense lined up with four, five, and six or more defensive backs, according to Sports Info Solutions.

CB by Sides: One of the most important lessons from game charting is that each team's best cornerback does not necessarily match up against the opponent's best receiver. Most cornerbacks play a particular side of the field and in fact cover a wider range of receivers than we assumed before we saw the charting data. This metric looks at which teams prefer to leave their starting cornerbacks on specific sides of the field.

To figure CB by Sides, we took the top two cornerbacks from each team and looked at the percentage of passes where that cornerback was in coverage on the left or right side of the field, ignoring passes marked as "middle." For each of the two cornerbacks, we took the higher number, right or left, and then we averaged the two cornerbacks to get the final CB by Sides rating. Teams which preferred to leave their cornerbacks in the same place last season, such as Cincinnati and Tampa Bay, will have high ratings. Teams that did more to move their best cornerback around to cover the opponent's top targets, such as Arizona and San Francisco, will have low ratings.

S/CB Cover Ratio: This is our attempt to track which teams like to use their safeties as hybrid safety/corners and put them in man coverage on wide receivers. This ratio takes all pass targets with a defensive back in coverage, and then gives what percentage of those targets belonged to a player who is rostered as a safety, ranging from Dallas, which used safety Byron Jones as a nickelback (35 percent) to the Los Angeles Rams, who sometimes used Lamarcus Joyner as a safety (20 percent).

DB Blitz: We have data on how often the defense used at least one defensive back in the pass rush courtesy of ESPN Stats & Info.

Finally, in the final column, we have some elements of game strategy.

Play action: The percentage of pass plays (including quarterback scrambles) which began with a play-action fake to the running back. This percentage does not include fake end-arounds unless there was also a fake handoff. It does include flea flickers.

Average Box: Another item added to our charting courtesy of ESPN Stats & Info Group is the number of defenders in the box before the snap. We list the average box faced by each team's offense and the average box used by this team's defense.

Offensive Pace: Situation-neutral pace represents the seconds of game clock per offensive play, with the following restrictions: no drives are included if they start in the fourth quarter or final five minutes of the first half, and drives are only included if the score is within six points or less. Teams are ranked from quickest pace (New York Giants, 28.7 seconds) to slowest pace (Tennessee, 33.1 seconds)

Defensive Pace: Situation-neutral pace based on seconds of game clock per defensive play. This is a representation of how a defense was approached by its opponents, not the strategy of the defense itself. Teams are ranked from quickest pace (New Orleans, 29.3seconds) to slowest pace (Detroit, 33.0 seconds).

Go for it on fourth: This is the aggressiveness index (AI) introduced by Jim Armstrong in *Pro Football Prospectus 2006*, which measures how often a team goes for a first down in various fourth down situations compared to the league average. A coach over 1.00 is more aggressive, and one below 1.00 is less aggressive. Coaches are ranked from most aggressive to least aggressive.

Following each strategic tendencies table, you'll find a series of comments highlighting interesting data from that team's charting numbers. This includes DVOA ratings split for things like different formations, draw plays, or play-action passing. Please note that all DVOA ratings given in these comments are standard DVOA with no adjustments for the specific situation being analyzed. The average DVOA for a specific situation will not necessarily be 0%, and it won't necessarily be the same for offense and defense. For example, the average offensive DVOA on play-action passes in 2016 was 28.3%, while the average defensive DVOA was 21.3%. The average offensive DVOA when the quarterback was hurried was minus-60.4%; even if we remove sacks, scrambles, and intentional grounding and only look at actual passes, the average offensive DVOA was minus-7.4%. On average last year, there was pressure marked on 27.1 percent of pass plays.

How to Read the Offensive Line Tables

SIS charters mark blown blocks not just on sacks but also on hurries, hits, and runs stuffed at the line. However, while we have blown blocks to mark bad plays, we still don't have a metric that consistently marks good plays, so blown blocks should not be taken as the end all and be all of judging individual linemen. It's simply one measurement that goes into the conversation.

All offensive linemen who had at least 160 snaps in 2016 (not including special teams) are listed in the offensive line tables along with the position they played most often and their **Age** as of the 2017 season, listed simply as the difference between birth year and 2017. Players born in January and December of the same year will have the same listed age.

Then we list games, games started, snaps, and offensive penalties (**Pen**) for each lineman. The penalty total includes declined and offsetting penalties. Finally, there are three numbers for blown blocks in 2016.

- Blown blocks leading directly to sacks
- All blown blocks on pass plays, not only including those

that lead to sacks but also those that lead to hurries, hits, or offensive holding penalties

• All blown blocks on run plays; generally, this means plays where the running back is tackled for a loss or no gain, but it also includes a handful of plays where the running back would have been tackled for a loss if not for a broken tackle, as well as offensive holding penalties on running plays

Players are given half a blown block when two offensive players are listed with blown blocks on the same play.

As with all player tables in the team chapters, players who are no longer on the team have an asterisk and those new to the team in 2017 are in italics.

The second offensive line table lists the last three years of our various line stats.

The first column gives standard yards per carry by each team's running backs (**Yds**). The next two columns give adjusted line yards (**ALY**) followed by rank among the 32 teams.

Power gives the percentage of runs in "power situations" that achieved a first down or touchdown. Those situations include any third or fourth down with one or two yards to go, and any runs in goal-to-go situations from the two-yard line or closer. Unlike the other rushing numbers on the Offensive Line table, Power includes quarterbacks.

Stuff gives the percentage of runs that are stuffed for zero or negative gain. Since being stuffed is bad, teams are ranked from stuffed least often (1) to most often (32).

Second-Level (**2nd Lev**) Yards and **Open-Field** Yards represent yardage where the running back has the most power over the amount of the gain. Second-level yards represent the number of yards per carry that come five to ten yards past the line of scrimmage. Open-field yards represent the number of yards per carry that come 11 or more yards past the line of scrimmage. A team with a low ranking in adjusted line yards but a high ranking in open-field yards is heavily dependent on its running back breaking long runs to make the running game work, and therefore tends to have a less consistent running attack. Second-level yards fall somewhere in between.

The next five columns give information about pass protection. That starts with total sacks, followed by adjusted sack rate (**ASR**) and its rank among the 32 teams. Some teams allow a lot of sacks because they throw a lot of passes; adjusted sack rate accounts for this by dividing sacks and intentional grounding by total pass plays. It is also adjusted for situation (sacks are much more common on third down, particularly third-and-long) and opponent, all of which makes it a better measurement than raw sacks totals. Remember that quarterbacks share responsibility for sacks, and two different quar-

terbacks behind the same line can have very different adjusted sack rates. This year, we've also listed pressure rate: this is the percentage of pass plays where we have marked pass pressure, based on Sports Info Solutions charting. Sacks or scrambles due to coverage are not counted as passes with pressure.

F-Start gives the number of false starts, which is the offensive penalty which best correlates to both wins and wins the following season. This total includes false starts by players other than offensive linemen, but it does not include false starts on special teams. Seattle and Philadelphia tied for the league lead with 26, Buffalo was last with 6, and the NFL average was 17.1. Finally, Continuity score (**Cont.**) tells you how much continuity each offensive line had from game-to-game in that season. It was introduced in the Cleveland chapter of *Pro Football Prospectus 2007*. Continuity score starts with 48 and then subtracts:

• The number of players over five who started at least one game on the offensive line;
• The number of times the team started at least one different lineman compared to the game before; and
• The difference between 16 and that team's longest streak where the same line started consecutive games.

The perfect continuity score is 48, which Atlanta received by starting the same five linemen in all 16 games. Last year's lowest score was 20 for the New York Jets.

Finally, underneath the table in italics we give 2016 adjusted line yards in each of the five directions with rank among the 32 teams. The league average was 4.31 on left end runs (**LE**), 4.32 on left tackle runs (**LT**), 4.19 on runs up the middle (**MID**), 4.18 on right tackle runs (**RT**), and 3.85 on right end runs (**RE**).

How to Read the Defensive Front Seven Tables

Defensive players make plays. Plays aren't just tackles—interceptions and pass deflections change the course of the game, and so does the act of forcing a fumble or beating the offensive players to a fumbled ball. While some plays stop a team on third down and force a punt, others merely stop a receiver after he's caught a 30-yard pass. We still cannot measure each player's opportunities to make a tackle. We can measure opportunities in pass coverage, however, thanks to

Baltimore Ravens Offensive Line

Player	Pos	Age	GS	Snaps	Pen	Sk	Pass	Run	Player	Pos	Age	GS	Snaps	Pen	Sk	Pass	Run
Jeremy Zuttah*	C	31	16/16	1109	6	4.0	10	4	Alex Lewis	LG/LT	25	10/8	538	4	1.0	4	2
Ricky Wagner*	RT	28	15/14	924	4	3.5	10	4	James Hurst	LT/RT	26	16/3	302	3	1.0	3	0
Marshal Yanda	RG	33	13/13	898	3	0.5	4	3	Ryan Jensen	C/G	26	7/3	272	2	0.0	3	0
Ronnie Stanley	LT	23	12/12	833	8	4.0	9	5	John Urschel	C/G	26	13/3	265	1	3.0	6	4
Vladimir Ducasse*	LG	30	10/8	554	6	1.5	6	5									

the Football Outsiders game charting project.

Defensive players are listed in these tables if they made at least 20 plays during the 2016 season, or if they played at least eight games and played 25 percent of defensive snaps in those games. We made a couple of exceptions to list a handful of players who just missed these minimums, including Jonson Bademosi, Ryan Davis, Barkevious Mingo, Rahim Moore, Cameron Wake, and Kyle Williams. Defensive players who were with two teams last year are only listed with the final team they played with.

Defensive Linemen/Edge Rushers: As we've noted earlier in this toolbox: as hybrid defenses become more popular, it becomes more and more difficult to tell the difference between a defensive end and an outside linebacker. What we do know is that there are certain players whose job is to rush the passer, even if they occasionally drop into coverage. We also know that the defensive ends in a two-gapping 3-4 system have a lot more in common with run-stuffing 4-3 tackles than with smaller 4-3 defensive ends.

Therefore, we have separated front seven players into three tables rather than two. All defensive tackles and defensive ends from 3-4 teams are listed as **Defensive Linemen**, and all ranked together. Defensive ends from 4-3 teams and outside linebackers from 3-4 teams are listed as **Edge Rushers**, and all ranked together. Most 4-3 linebackers are ranked along with 3-4 inside linebackers, and listed simply as **Linebackers**. For the most part this categorization puts players with similar roles together. Some players who have hybrid roles are ranked at the position more appropriate to their role, such as Joey Bosa and Jadeveon Clowney as edge rushers despite playing defensive end in 3-4 schemes.

The tables for defensive linemen and edge rushers are the same, although the players are ranked in two separate categories. Players are listed with the following numbers:

Age in 2017, determined by 2017 minus birth year, plus position (**Pos**) and the number of defensive **Snaps** played in 2016.

Plays (**Plays**): The total defensive plays including tackles,

pass deflections, interceptions, fumbles forced, and fumble recoveries. This number comes from the official NFL game-books and therefore does not include plays on which the player is listed by the Football Outsiders game charting project as in coverage, but does not appear in the standard play-by-play. Special teams tackles are also not included.

Percentage of team plays (**TmPct**): The percentage of total team plays involving this defender. The sum of the percentages of team plays for all defenders on a given team will exceed 100 percent, primarily due to shared tackles. This number is adjusted based on games played, so an injured player may be fifth on his team in plays but third in **TmPct**.

Stops (**Stop**): The total number of plays which prevent a "success" by the offense (45 percent of needed yards on first down, 60 percent on second down, 100 percent on third or fourth down).

Defeats (**Dfts**): The total number of plays which stop the offense from gaining first down yardage on third or fourth down, stop the offense behind the line of scrimmage, or result in a fumble (regardless of which team recovers) or interception.

Broken tackles (**BTkl**): The number of broken tackles recorded by SIS game charters.

The next five columns represent runs only, starting with the number of plays each player made on **Runs**. Stop rate (**St%**) gives the percentage of these run plays which were stops. Average yards (**AvYd**) gives the average number of yards gained by the runner when this player is credited with making the play.

Finally, we have pass rush numbers, starting with standard NFL **Sack** totals.

Hit: To qualify as a quarterback hit, the defender must knock the quarterback to the ground in the act of throwing or after the pass is thrown. We have listed hits on all plays, including those cancelled by penalties. (After all, many of the hardest hits come on plays cancelled because the hit itself draws a roughing the passer penalty.)

Hurries (**Hur**): The number of quarterback hurries recorded by Sports Info Solutions game charters. This includes both hurries on standard plays and hurries that force an offensive hold-

Buffalo Bills Defensive Line, Edge Rushers

Defensive Line	Age	Pos	G	Snaps	Plays	TmPct	Rk	Stop	Dfts	BTkl	Runs	St%	Rk	RuYd	Rk	Sack	Hit	Hur	Dsrpt
						Overall							vs. Run				Pass Rush		
Kyle Williams	34	DE	15	795	63	8.3%	8	45	17	11	55	71%	62	2.8	65	5.0	9	20	3
Leger Douzable*	31	DE	16	482	43	5.3%	32	30	10	5	37	68%	70	2.4	49	1.5	5	10	1
Marcell Dareus	28	DT	8	418	40	9.8%	2	30	9	1	33	73%	53	2.1	37	3.0	1	4	1
Adolphus Washington	23	DE	15	332	22	2.9%	--	19	5	2	18	83%	--	1.7	--	2.5	1	1	1
Corbin Bryant*	29	DT	8	234	11	2.7%	81	8	2	2	10	80%	38	2.4	52	0.0	0	2	0

Edge Rushers	Age	Pos	G	Snaps	Plays	TmPct	Rk	Stop	Dfts	BTkl	Runs	St%	Rk	RuYd	Rk	Sack	Hit	Hur	Dsrpt
						Overall							vs. Run				Pass Rush		
Jerry Hughes	29	OLB	16	860	50	6.1%	30	32	16	14	33	61%	90	3.5	84	6.0	8	33	3
Lorenzo Alexander	34	OLB	16	788	70	8.6%	6	54	28	7	41	76%	41	3.2	76	12.5	12	27	3
Shaq Lawson	23	OLB	10	237	14	2.8%	--	12	4	2	9	89%	--	0.8	--	2.0	3	10	1
Ryan Davis	28	DE	9	155	4	0.9%	--	2	2	0	4	50%	--	1.5	--	0.0	2	9	0

ing penalty that cancels the play and costs the offense yardage.

Disruptions (**Dsprt**): This stat combines two different but similar types of plays. First, plays where a pass-rusher forced an incomplete pass or interception by hitting the quarterback as he was throwing the ball. These plays are generally not counted as passes defensed, so we wanted a way to count them. Second, plays where the pass-rusher batted the ball down at the line of scrimmage or tipped it in the air. These plays are usually incomplete, but occasionally they lead to interceptions, and even more rarely they fall into the hands of offensive receivers. As with the "hit in motion" disruptions, some plays counted as tips by Football Outsiders were not counted as passes defensed by the NFL.

Defensive linemen and edge rushers are both ranked by percentage of team plays, run stop rate, and average yards per run tackle. The lowest number of average yards earns the top rank (negative numbers indicate the average play ending behind the line of scrimmage). Defensive linemen and edge rushers are ranked if they played at least 40 percent of defensive snaps in the games they were active. There are 86 defensive linemen ranked, and 100 edge rushers.

Linebackers: Most of the stats for linebackers are the same as those for defensive linemen. Linebackers are ranked in percentage of team plays, and also in stop rate and average yards for running plays specifically. Linebackers are ranked in these stats if they played at least five games and at least 35 percent of defensive snaps in the games they were active, with 87 linebackers ranked.

The final six columns in the linebacker stats come from Sports Info Solutions game charting.

Targets (**Tgts**): The number of pass players on which game charters listed this player in coverage.

Success rate (**Suc%**): The percentage plays of targeting this player on which the offense did not have a successful play. This means not only incomplete passes and interceptions, but also short completions which do not meet our baselines for success (45 percent of needed yards on first down, 60 percent on second down, 100 percent on third or fourth down). Success rate is adjusted for the quality of the receiver covered.

Adjusted yards per pass (**AdjYd**): The average number of yards gained on plays on which this defender was the listed target, adjusted for the quality of the receiver covered.

Passes defensed (**PD**): Football Outsiders' count of passes defensed. Unlike the official NFL count of passes defensed, this does not include passes batted down or tipped at the line.

These stats, including other differences between the NFL's count of passes defensed and our own, are explained in more detail in the section on secondary tables. Plays listed with two defenders or as "Hole in Zone" with this defender as the closest player count only for half credit in computing both success rate and average yards per pass. Eighty-two linebackers are ranked in the charting stats, based on hitting one of two minimums: 14 charted passes with fewer than eight games started, or 11 charted passes with eight or more games started. As a result of the different thresholds, some linebackers are ranked in standard stats but not charting stats.

Further Details: Just as in the offensive tables, players who are no longer on the team are marked with asterisks, and players who were on other teams last year are in italics. Other than the game charting statistics for linebackers, defensive front seven player statistics are not adjusted for opponent.

Numbers for defensive linemen and linebackers unfortunately do not reflect all of the opportunities a player had to make a play, but they do show us which players were most active on the field. A large number of plays could mean a strong defensive performance, or it could mean that the linebacker in question plays behind a poor part of the line. In general, defensive numbers should be taken as information that tells us what happened on the field in 2016, but not as a strict, unassailable judgment of which players are better than others—particularly when the difference between two players is small (for example, players ranked 20th and 30th) instead of large (players ranked 20th and 70th).

After the individual statistics for linemen and linebackers, the Defensive Front Seven section contains a table that looks exactly like the table in the Offensive Line section. The difference is that the numbers here are for all opposing running backs against this team's defensive front. As we're on the opposite side of the ball, teams are now ranked in the opposite order, so the No. 1 defensive front seven is the one that allows the fewest adjusted line yards, the lowest percentage in Power situations, and has the highest adjusted sack rate. Directions for adjusted line yards are given from the offense's perspective, so runs left end and left tackle are aimed at the right defensive end and (assuming the tight end is on the other side) weakside linebacker.

Houston Texans Linebackers

				Overall							vs. Run					Pass Rush			vs. Pass						
Linebackers	Age	Pos	G	Snaps	Plays	TmPct	Rk	Stop	Dfts	BTkl	Runs	St%	Rk	RuYd	Rk	Sack	Hit	Hur	Tgts	Suc%	Rk	AdjYd	Rk	PD	Int
Benardrick McKinney	25	ILB	16	915	130	17.3%	11	67	18	10	78	56%	72	3.9	63	5.0	6	8	36	48%	42	7.7	64	2	0
Brian Cushing	30	ILB	13	611	65	10.6%	50	38	8	4	45	73%	8	3.2	30	0.0	3	6	15	37%	74	7.8	65	0	0
Sio Moore	27	ILB	8	412	66	16.1%	15	40	9	8	40	70%	15	3.0	18	0.0	2	4	18	48%	41	6.4	37	1	0

How to Read the Secondary Tables

The first few columns in the secondary tables are based on standard play-by-play, not game charting, with the exception of broken tackles. Age, total plays, percentage of team plays, stops, and defeats are computed the same way they are for other defensive players, so that the secondary can be compared to the defensive line and linebackers. That means that total plays here includes passes defensed, sacks, tackles after receptions, tipped passes, and interceptions, but not pass plays on which this player was in coverage but was not given a tackle or passed defense by the NFL's official scorer.

The middle five columns address each defensive back's role in stopping the run. Average yardage and stop rate for running plays is computed in the same manner as for defensive linemen and linebackers.

The third section of statistics represents data from Sports Info Solutions game charting. In all game charting coverage stats, passes where two defenders are listed and those listed as "Hole in Zone" with this player as the closest zone defender count for half credit. We do not count pass plays on which this player was in coverage, but the incomplete was listed as Thrown Away, Batted Down, or Hit in Motion. Hail Mary passes are also not included.

Targets (**Tgts**): The number of pass plays on which our game charters listed this player in coverage.

Target percentage (**Tgt%**): The number of plays on which this player was targeted divided by the total number of charted passes against his defense, not including plays listed as Uncovered. Like percentage of team plays, this metric is adjusted based on number of games played.

Distance (**Dist**): The average distance in the air beyond the line of scrimmage of all passes targeted at this defender. It does not include yards after catch, and is useful for seeing which defenders were covering receivers deeper or shorter.

Adjusted Success rate (**Suc%**): The percentage plays of targeting this player on which the offense did not have a successful play. This means not only incomplete passes and interceptions, but also short completions which do not meet

our baselines for success (45 percent of needed yards on first down, 60 percent on second down, 100 percent on third or fourth down). Defensive pass interference is counted as a failure for the defensive player similar to a completion of equal yardage (and a new first down). This number is adjusted based on the quality of the receiver covered.

Adjusted Yards per Pass (**AdjYd**): The average number of yards gained on plays on which this defender was the listed target, adjusted for the quality of the receiver covered.

Passes Defensed (**PD**): This is our count of passes defensed, and will differ from the total found in NFL gamebooks. Our count includes:

- All passes listed by our charting as Defensed, based on Sports Info Solutions data.
- All interceptions, or tipped passes leading to interceptions.
- Any pass on which the defender is given a pass defensed by the official scorer, and our game charting is marked either Miscommunication or Catch Out of Bounds.

Our count of passes defensed does not include passes marked as defensed in the official gamebooks but listed by our charters as Overthrown, Underthrown, or Thrown Away. It also does not include passes tipped in the act of rushing the passer. In addition, we did a lot of work with both the NFL head office and the folks from ESPN Stats & Info and Sports Info Solutions to get the most accurate numbers possible for both drops and passes defensed. Official scorers and game charters will sometimes disagree on a drop vs. a pass defensed, or even an overthrown/underthrown ball vs. a pass defensed, and there are a number of passes where the league marked the official stats in one way and ESPN S&I or SIS marked their stats the other way.

Interceptions (**Int**) represent the standard NFL interception total.

With more and more wide receivers playing, that means more and more cornerbacks are playing, so we've had to increase our minimums so we aren't ranking a zillion cornerbacks. Cornerbacks need 50 charted passes or eight games started to be ranked in the defensive stats, with 87 cornerbacks ranked in total. Safeties require 20 charted passes or eight games started, with 74 safeties ranked in total. Strong and free

Cincinnati Bengals Defensive Secondary

Secondary	Age	Pos	G	Snaps	Plays	Overall TmPct	Rk	Stop	Dfts	BTkl	vs. Run Runs	St%	Rk	RuYd	Rk	vs. Pass Tgts	Tgt%	Rk	Dist	Suc%	Rk	AdjYd	Rk	PD	Int
Adam Jones	34	CB	16	1058	73	8.7%	39	23	9	12	17	41%	40	6.5	39	60	13.6%	1	9.7	41%	80	7.3	32	6	1
George Iloka	27	SS	16	1050	80	9.5%	42	27	7	9	33	36%	46	8.2	56	28	6.3%	12	15.6	42%	50	8.9	37	7	3
Dre Kirkpatrick	28	CB	15	974	56	7.1%	71	25	12	15	12	33%	55	9.2	71	69	17.0%	28	10.9	50%	40	5.5	6	10	3
Shawn Williams	26	FS	15	912	86	10.9%	26	25	7	13	40	35%	49	7.2	40	32	8.4%	37	13.5	34%	65	10.8	61	4	3
Josh Shaw	25	CB	16	618	50	6.0%	82	18	8	7	15	40%	41	7.1	50	37	14.2%	4	10.1	57%	8	7.4	37	2	1
Darqueze Dennard	26	CB	15	334	42	5.3%	--	13	4	2	11	18%	--	9.5	--	27	19.0%	--	8.6	34%	--	11.0	--	1	0

Year	Pass D Rank	vs. #1 WR	Rk	vs. #2 WR	Rk	vs. Other WR	Rk	vs. TE	Rk	vs. RB	Rk
2014	7	-28.9%	1	-32.8%	3	-24.4%	2	-20.4%	4	26.6%	29
2015	10	-4.5%	13	2.7%	17	-11.4%	8	-9.5%	12	10.0%	24
2016	14	-0.4%	13	8.1%	25	-2.2%	12	-1.8%	17	-7.7%	14

safeties are ranked together. Players listed with two positions, usually safeties who move to slot cornerback in nickel, are ranked at the first position listed.

Just like the front seven, the secondary has a table of team statistics following the individual numbers. This table gives DVOA figured against different types of receivers. Each offense's wide receivers have had one receiver designated as No. 1, and another as No. 2. (Occasionally this is difficult, due to injury or a situation with "co-No. 1 receivers," but it's usually pretty obvious.) The other receivers form a third category, with tight ends and running backs as fourth and fifth categories. The defense is then judged on the performance of each receiver based on the standard DVOA method, with each rating adjusted based on strength of schedule. (Obviously, it's a lot harder to cover the No. 1 receiver of the Pittsburgh Steelers than to cover the No.1 receiver of the Los Angeles Rams.) **Pass D Rank** is the total ranking of the pass defense, as seen before in the Trends and Splits table, and combines all five categories plus sacks and passes with no intended target.

The "defense vs. types of receivers" table should be used to analyze the defense as a whole rather than individual players. The ratings against types of receivers are generally based on defensive schemes, not specific cornerbacks, except for certain defenses that really do move one cornerback around to cover the opponent's top weapon (i.e., Arizona). The ratings against tight ends and running backs are in large part due to the performance of linebackers.

How to Read the Special Teams Tables

The special teams tables list the last three years of kick, punt, and return numbers for each team.

The first two columns list total special teams DVOA and rank among the 32 teams. The next two columns list the value in actual points of field goals and extra points (**FG/XP**) when compared to how a league average kicker would do from the same distances, adjusted for weather and altitude, and rank among the 32 teams. Next, we list the estimated value in actual points of field position over or under the league average based on net kickoffs (**Net Kick**), and rank that value among the 32 teams. That is followed by the estimated point values of field position for kick returns (**Kick Ret**), net punting (**Net Punt**), and punt returns (**Punt Ret**) and their respective ranks.

The final two columns represent the value of "**Hidden**" special teams, plays which throughout the past decade have usually been based on the performance of opponents without this team

being able to control the outcome. We combine the opposing team's value on field goals, kickoff distance, and punt distance, adjusted for weather and altitude, and then switch the sign to represent that good special teams by the opponent will cost the listed team points, and bad special teams will effectively hand them points. We have to give the qualifier of "usually" because, as explained above, certain returners such as Cordarrelle Patterson will affect opposing special teams strategy, and a handful of the missed field goals are blocked. Nonetheless, the "hidden" value is still "hidden" for most teams, and they are ranked from the most hidden value gained (Miami, 21.0 points) to the most value lost (Chicago, minus-12.9 points).

We also have methods for measuring the gross value of kickoffs and punts. These measures assume that all kickoffs or punts will have average returns unless they are touchbacks or kicked out of bounds, then judge the kicker or punter on the value with those assumed returns. These metrics may be listed in special teams comments as **KickPts+** and **PuntPts+**. We also count special teams tackles; these include both tackles and assists, but do not include tackles on two-point conversions, tackles after onside kicks, or tackles of the player who recovers a fumble after the punt or kick returner loses the ball. The best and worst individual values for kickers, punters, returners, and kick gunners (i.e. tackle totals) are listed in the statistical appendix at the end of the book.

Administrative Minutia

Receiving statistics include all passes intended for the receiver in question, including those that are incomplete or intercepted. The word passes refers to both complete and incomplete pass attempts. When rating receivers, interceptions are treated as incomplete passes with no penalty.

For the computation of DVOA and DYAR, passing statistics include sacks as well as fumbles on aborted snaps. We do not include kneeldown plays or spikes for the purpose of stopping the clock. Some interceptions which we have determined to be "Hail Mary" plays that end the first half or game are counted as regular incomplete passes, not turnovers.

All statistics generated by ESPN Stats & Info or Sports Info Solutions game charting, or our combination of the two sources, may be different from totals compiled by other sources.

Unless we say otherwise, when we refer to third-down performance in this book we are referring to a combination of third down and the handful of rushing and passing plays that take place on fourth down (primarily fourth-and-1).

Aaron Schatz

Detroit Lions Special Teams

Year	DVOA	Rank	FG/XP	Rank	Net Kick	Rank	Kick Ret	Rank	Net Punt	Rank	Punt Ret	Rank	Hidden	Rank
2014	-5.7%	31	-19.6	32	-4.0	24	-1.7	21	-0.6	17	-2.5	17	-6.6	26
2015	1.0%	13	6.0	5	-2.6	21	3.3	8	3.2	14	-4.7	24	-4.4	20
2016	3.5%	6	2.5	11	-2.9	24	-1.5	16	10.7	5	8.5	3	2.4	14

The Year In Quotes

TURNS OUT HE'S ABOUT AS GOOD AT KICKING AS WE ARE AT DRAFTING

"Not a lot of people will ever admit that a kicker is worth a first-round pick. I'm going to be jumping for joy when a few of the people in your business realize that some are... If we love a player we're going to go get him. Don't worry about it. Go get him. Don't worry about how other teams had him ranked, either. If you read that this guy is a sixth-round pick and you take him in the second, it doesn't matter. Get your guy."

—Tampa Bay Buccaneers general manager Jason Licht defends the selection of Roberto Aguayo. (Pewter Report)

"He's struggling... He's struggling a little bit right now. He's gotta work his way through it."

—Tampa Bay Buccaneers head coach Dirk Koetter, acknowledging the underperformance of second-round draft-pick kicker Roberto Aguayo, who was booed by fans after missing three of six attempts in an August practice. (ESPN.com)

#HUMBLEBRAGS

"I've been impressed with how Dak played. It kind of reminds me of a little bit back in the day in some capacity. He's playing great. To have depth at that position, it's a big bonus. Hopefully he can continue to do that. And he's a good kid, so you really root for him."

—Dallas Cowboys quarterback Tony Romo, giving mad props to rookie quarterback and preseason all-star Dak Prescott, as well as himself. (ESPN.com)

TRULY PISSED AT THE MOVE

"Join us every Sunday and hate watch the Rams with us all season long. Their losses are YOUR gains as we will offer Hotshots customers $1 off all domestic pitchers for every TD against the Rams, every week! The more they give up (which will be a lot), the more you can win while we root on literally ANYONE else. We have not forgotten what Stan and his cronies did to our city so we will have your shot to take a few jabs at them each week as well. Come root on the Rams to lose like only they can at Hotshots and get cheap beer! It's a win-win!"

—Website posting for St. Louis sports bar Hotshots, where folks were not happy with the Rams' move (back) to Los Angeles (Hotshots)

DRUGS ARE NOT GOOD, M'KAY

"Well, I think that in and of itself the reason we are talking about is in a way part of the learning process... But it's not good. It's just not good. It's just not good.... I would know how he is, and he needs to look at that. And the other thing is it's just not good."

—Dallas Cowboys owner Jerry Jones, criticizing Ezekiel Elliott after the rookie running back was spotted in a marijuana dispensary in Washington shortly before the Cowboys' preseason game against the Seattle Seahawks. (ESPN.com)

OFFENSIVE PHILOSOPHY 101

"No one is happy with the way the first offense operated... We need to improve, we need to make sure we are going forward... We need to execute better and we need to play forward. We can't be going backwards."

—New York Giants head coach Ben McAdoo, solving offensive strategy in just his first season in the job. (New York Post)

A CHIP ON CINCI'S SHOULDER

"I don't give no fucks about them... Zero. You can write that, too. I don't give no fucks about them. They're just another team. They don't scare me. Just another team."

—Cincinnati Bengals linebacker Vontaze Burfict, giving no f-cks about AFC North division rivals the Pittsburgh Steelers, who knocked the Bengals out of the playoffs in January of 2016. (MMQB)

NOT ALL AT THE SAME TIME, TO BE FAIR

"Teams have spent two first-round picks, a second and two fourths on Sam Bradford. What is that definition of insanity again?"

—NBC Sports writer Joe Posnanski, offering some perspective on the latest Sam Bradford trade. The Eagles had just traded Bradford to Minnesota in exchange for 2017 and 2018 draft picks, one year after acquiring Bradford in a trade with the Rams. (NBC Sports)

THIS I WOULD PAY TO SEE

"Good thing ESPN isn't coaching the Raiders."

—Oakland Raiders head coach Jack Del Rio, reacting to ESPN's criticism of his decision to go for two down 33-34 on the road to the New Orleans Saints with 47 seconds remaining in the game. The Raiders converted and won the game. (Jack Del Rio via Twitter)

I DON'T SEE HOW THAT WOULD HELP BUT OK

"For this city, for the coaching staff that worked their butts off and my teammates, I'll do anything to help us win, anything, cut my finger off, whatever I've got to do."

—Cleveland Browns wide receiver Terrelle Pryor, preparing to take one for the team ahead of their game against the Miami Dolphins on Sunday. (Cleveland Plain Dealer)

HE'S WELL KNOWN FOR BEING PRONE TO INJURY, AND BY ASSOCIATION DEATH

"There was a couple times he got hit—I thought he was dead. He wasn't moving, so I had to pick him up. I'm like, 'Sam, don't be dead.'"

—Minnesota Vikings guard Alex Boone, fearing for the life of quarterback Sam Bradford during the Vikings' 17-14 win over the Green Bay Packers in Week 2. (USA Today)

GIVE THIS MAN AN EXTENSION

"(Fisher) hands us the ball and he's like, 'Here.' Then he makes us stand in the end zone, and he's like, 'You see this? This is a football. This is the end zone. This is where you're supposed to be.'"

—Rams tight end Lance Kendricks, revealing Jeff Fisher's latest coaching techniques as the team looked for its first touchdown of the season. (TheRams.com)

JOKING ASIDE, HIS RECORD AGAINST THEM IS DREADFUL

"I don't think anybody has my phone number on the Vikings. Maybe Linval (Joseph), I'm not sure. I'm trying to think if I have anybody's number... I have (Sam) Bradford. I have his number. He's got my number. Can't think of anybody else's offhand, though. I'll look through my phone and get back to you."

—New York Giants quarterback Eli Manning, responding to a reporter's enquiry as to whether the Minnesota Vikings "have his number." (New York Daily News)

HOW ABOUT 'STRATEGICALLY UNDERPERFORMING?'

"I appreciate that folks have not seen a strategy quite like this before... but I would hardly call it tanking."

—Cleveland Browns' vice president of football operations Sashi Brown, answering critics who have accused the organization of deliberately trying to sabotage the team's 2016 season in order to improve their 2017 draft position. (ESPN)

SCARED FOR HIS HEALTH AND SINCE BLOCKING IS HARD, HE'S SWAPPING OUT LINE PLAY FOR LIFE AS A BARD

"I just want my time and mind intact, when you lose 'em both, you can't buy 'em back."

-- Former San Francisco 49ers offensive tackle Anthony Davis, poetically announcing his (second) retirement from the NFL due to health concerns. (Anthony Davis via Twitter)

TARGETING PENALTY

"After the play is over, unsportsmanlike conduct, No. 24. Shooting a bow and arrow."

—NFL referee Jeff Triplette, penalizing Washington cornerback Josh Norman for simulating a weapon during the team's 31-20 win over the Cleveland Browns in Week 4. In addition, Norman was fined $10,000 for the gesture. (MMQB)

IF YOU INSIST...

"Jack off to promising start."

—The Orlando Sentinel, headlining journalist Ryan O'Halloran's article on Jacksonville Jaguars rookie linebacker Myles Jack's debut in the Jags' 30-27 win over the Indianapolis Colts at London's Wembley Stadium in Week 4. (Orlando Sentinel)

COACH-SPEAK, OR GENUINELY CLUELESS?

"We don't have a plan."

—Chicago Bears head coach John Fox, discussing the Bears' direction (or lack thereof) at quarterback as they continued to start Brian Hoyer in Jay Cutler's injury-related absence in Week 5. (CSN Chicago)

A TROUBLED COUPLE

"Well, our relationship is growing. I thought we might as well make it serious. I proposed and she said yes. Me and the net are going to get married sometime soon. Hopefully it all works out. I'm 23, so I don't know much about marriage. She seems like a pretty nice gal."

—New York Giants wide receiver Odell Beckham, Jr., proposing to the kicking net that he had viciously attacked in the Giants' 27-29 loss to Washington back in Week 3, after scoring a touchdown to help the Giants defeat the Baltimore Ravens 27-23 in Week 6. (MMQB)

CHECK THE STANDINGS

"We run the damn East. Not Philly, not Dallas, not all of them. We run the damn East. Better remember we got that damn title."

—Washington defensive end Ricky Jean Francois, lording it up as his team defeated its NFC East rivals the Philadelphia Eagles 27-20 in Week 6. Washington finished third in the NFC East in 2016. (CSN Mid-Atlantic)

DON'T WORRY, NOBODY WAS WATCHING

"We blew it, this feeling is gross. It's like we pissed down our own leg."

—Indianapolis Colts linebacker Erik Walden, finding an apt comparison for the way his team blew a 14-point lead with three minutes to go before losing 26-23 in overtime to the Houston Texans in Week 6. (CBS Indianapolis)

NOT EVEN CLOSE

"We possibly have one of the best teams in the NFL, easily. Hands down."

—San Francisco 49ers linebacker Aaron Lynch, feeling good about the team's chances to improve on its 1-6 record, minus-75-point scoring differential, last-place ranking in yards per game, last-place rush defense... (CSN Bay Area)

WELL, THERE WERE SOME MISSED FIELD GOALS...

"I don't know how to react. I didn't know it was possible to tie. There was a tie last week, I was like, 'how the heck did they tie?'"

—Washington head coach Jay Gruden, expressing disbelief at tying 27-27 with the Cincinnati Bengals at London's Wembley Stadium in Week 8. (Washington Post)

NOTHIN' BUT A G THANG

"This is the G PODAWUND"

—Confused Cleveland Browns fans, showing support for their team in banner form during the Browns' 31-28 loss to the New York Jets in Week 8. (USA Today)

FOR THE LADIES

"We win a big game like that I'm going to the club wit full pads on."

—Oakland Raiders punter Marquette King, celebrating the Raiders' 30-20 Sunday Night Football win over the Denver Broncos in Week 9. (Marquette King via Twitter)

SALTY PEPPER

"Before we get started, there is no Pepper Johnson questions. I'm not answering any questions... There's no questions for me, then I'm not answering any questions... Er, D-line questions, no Pepper Johnson questions."

—New York Jets defensive line coach Pepper Johnson, refusing to answer questions about himself.

"No questions about you, but you'll answer questions about your guys?"

—Unknown reporter, asking Johnson for clarification.

"No, the other way round."

—Johnson, leaving everyone terribly confused. (NJ.com)

IF YOU'RE READING OUR BOOK, DOUG, THEN HELLO!

"I don't really like to look at stats, but DVOA is a stat that I look at seriously... and I think they were ranked No. 1, and we were ranked No. 2. That tells you just how efficient both teams are. So we knew coming in that it was going to be a battle, and we had to play at a high level."

—Seattle Seahawks wide receiver Doug Baldwin, bigging up Football Outsiders after a 26-15 win over the Philadelphia Eagles in Week 11. (ESPN)

IF YOU'RE READING OUR BOOK, BILL, THEN HELLO!

"The what now? What the hell is that? I mean, you can take those advanced websites and metric them in whatever you want. I don't know. I have no idea. I've never looked at one. I wouldn't even care to look at one. I don't care what they say."

—New England Patriots head coach Bill Belichick, dismissing the usefulness of advanced statistics. (NESN)

TIME FOR A RANDOM DRUG TEST

"It's top secret. For now, you guys call me Ronald... It's my new name. Ronald. For now, call me Ronald."

—Pittsburgh Steelers wide receiver Antonio Brown, insisting for some reason on being addressed as "Ronald" in a routine Week 13 presser. (ESPN)

ALERT RYAN FITZPATRICK AND BROCK OSWEILER

"Try to throw it to my team and not theirs."

—Jacksonville Jaguars quarterback Blake Bortles, outlining his plan to avoid so many interceptions for the rest of the season. (ESPN)

EVEN MIKE ZIMMER CAN SEE IT

"Everyone can see it. Stevie Wonder can see it."

—New York Giants wide receiver Odell Beckham Jr., complaining about the standard of officiating during the Giants' 24-14 loss to the Pittsburgh Steelers in Week 13. (New York Daily News)

TEDGINNITIS

"There's a virus going round in Chicago. Adams seems to have caught it... or not caught it."

—FOX color commentator John Lynch, using some choice words to describe the drop epidemic in the Green Bay Packers' Week 15 trip to Soldier Field, as wide receiver Davante Adams dropped his second sure touchdown of the day. (FOX)

...AND A MILLION CRYING JORDAN MEMES

"Looking back on it, it definitely wasn't worth it... I think the fact the photo made it... a picture is worth a thousand words."

—New York Giants wide receiver Victor Cruz, regretting the infamous Miami boat trip taken by the team's wide receivers the week before their wild-card playoff loss. (ESPN)

HE'S JUST JEALOUS

"As a team we kind of always pride ourselves on being well prepared, so when I saw some of those pictures, I was a little disappointed because obviously they didn't pack accordingly. They didn't have any shirts."

—New York Giants quarterback Eli Manning, expressing his disappointment about his receivers and their boat trip. (ESPN)

SURE

"I guarantee you we are going to win the Super Bowl next year."

—Then-Chicago wide receiver Alshon Jeffery, feeling confident about the Bears' chances to improve on their 3-13 record in 2016. Jeffery signed with the Philadelphia Eagles in March; maybe he was talking about them. (WGN Radio)

CONTINUING THE FINE TRADITION OF INSANE RAIDERS COACHES

"Can you smell it! Can you taste it!"

—Oakland Raiders head coach Jack Del Rio, getting fired up on the field before the Raiders' wild-card game against the Houston Texans, which they lost 14-27. (NFL Network)

SUPER BOWL LI IN QUOTES

"Have you ever been in a game where you start to think, 'it's not our day?'"

—BBC NFL pundit Mike Carlson, interviewing Miami Dolphins running back Jay Ajayi in studio during the BBC broadcast of Super Bowl LI.

(Silent nodding)

—Ajayi, in reply. (BBC)

"I think everybody is disappointed, for sure."

—Atlanta Falcons quarterback Matt Ryan, summing up the Falcons' improbable overtime Super Bowl loss. (ESPN)

"We are five weeks behind the rest of the NFL for the 2017 season."

—New England Patriots head coach Bill Belichick, already looking ahead to next year in the immediate aftermath of the Patriots' Super Bowl LI win. (ESPN)

DON'T FORGET SPECIAL TEAMS!

"Obviously, defense wins championships, but you have to score points."

—Newly-appointed Denver Broncos head coach Vance Joseph, clarifying an old adage in his introductory press conference. (Denver Post)

ME FOR THE NEXT FOUR YEARS

"Folks I am pumped. I can't tell you how excited I am to be the head coach of the San Diego, um, L.A. Chargers. Oops."

—Newly-appointed ~~San Diego~~ Los Angeles Chargers head coach Anthony Lynn, failing to come to terms with the team's move. (Fox Sports)

GOD FORGIVES, SAN DIEGO DOESN'T

"GOD WILL NEVER FORSAKE YOU—UNLIKE THE CHARGERS"

—Church sign in Fallbrook, San Diego, reacting to the Chargers' move to Los Angeles by condemning the franchise to hell. (Reddit)

EVERYBODY WINS

"As much as I'd like to see my buddy (Alex Mack) win a super bowl, I would sure love to see (Roger Goodell) have to hand a trophy to Brady!"

—Cleveland Browns offensive tackle Joe Thomas, rooting for Atlanta Falcons center and former teammate Alex Mack in Super Bowl LI, but happy to accept the consolation prize of an embarrassed league commissioner. (Joe Thomas via Twitter)

...AND FANS WHO DON'T CARE

"Rams have the only staff with defensive coordinator on Medicare and head coach in Daycare."

—Los Angeles Rams defensive coordinator Wade Phillips, joking about the respective ages of himself (69) (nice) and 31-year-old first-time head coach Sean McVay. (Wade Phillips via Twitter)

IN FIGHTING OR AT MADDEN?

"I honestly thing I can get a wolf 1-on-1 though... I'm 230lbs, wolves are what, 180-200 tops? He has no thumbs. If I control his neck he's dunzo... I've studied the wolf. He can't read. I know his weaknesses. Plus the thumb thing... Also hasn't been to four Pro Bowls, overcome those injuries and DOESN'T HAVE THUMBS."

—Recently retired NFL running back Arian Foster, backing himself to beat a wolf in heads-up combat. (Arian Foster via Twitter)

THE YEAR IN BENNETTS

"Marty, The Imagination Agency"

-- Patriots tight end Martellus Bennett, introducing himself on NBC's Sunday Night Football.

"There is no challenge. He threw for 100 yards."

-- Seahawks defensive end Michael Bennett, discussing the "challenge" of facing Blaine Gabbert as the Seahawks hammered the Niners, 37-18. (San Franciso Chronicle)

"They asked me if I needed a cart and I'm like, 'Shit, I'm going to look so weak.' I've been watching Luke Cage. He's the bulletproof brother from Marvel, and I'm like, 'What would Luke Cage do right now?' He'd get up and keep bouncing around, so I was like, 'I've got to get up and show them, get a moment, just run off the field and let them know I'm coming back in the game.'"

-- Martellus Bennett, on returning to the game after an early ankle injury as the Patriots beat the Cleveland Browns in Week 5, 33-13. Bennett caught three touchdown passes in the win. (CBS)

"That's how you know I am made of iron... He cheap-shotted me and he got a concussion. My wife was happy."

-- Michael Bennett, relishing in the injury suffered by New York Jets offensive guard Brian Winters after delivering a hit to Bennett during a Week 5 game. (Seattle Times)

"I'm never clear on the NFL rules... Two pumps get you a baby. Three pumps get you a fine."

-- Michael Bennett, after getting flagged for celebrating a sack against the Los Angeles Rams. (Seattle Post-Intelligencer)

"I prefer to play against a terrible team, because it makes the game a lot easier"

-- Michael Bennett, not relishing the prospect of playing against the Atlanta Falcons in the playoffs. (Tacoma News Tribune)

"It's cool. I'm kind of getting used to winning now, you know what I'm saying? At first it's like 'Yeah!' It's like the first time having sex. And then your second time and then your third time, it's like 'oh yeah, it's pretty cool. I'm getting better at it.' It's really fun."

-- Martellus Bennett, enjoying his move from Chicago to New England (Boston Herald)

QUOTE OF THE YEAR

"How many times have you heard me talk about the little things and what impact the little things have on the bigger things. How are you feeling, Tay? You good? Just cramped? What did you have for lunch? Two bananas... Little things are important, you follow me? I'm not fucking going 7-9 or 8-8 or 9-7, OK? Or 10-6 for that matter. This team's too talented. I'm not going to settle for that. I know what I'm doing. We had 7-9 bullshit this morning."

—Los Angeles Rams head coach Jeff Fisher, getting into wide receiver Tavon Austin after he left practice with a cramp during the Rams' training camp. Fisher was right—the Rams went 4-12. (HBO Hard Knocks)

compiled by Rob Eves

Full 2017 Projections

The following table lists the mean DVOA projections for all 32 NFL teams. We also list the average number of wins for each team in our one million simulations, along with how often each team made the playoffs, reached the Super Bowl, and won the NFL Championship.

Full 2017 Projections

Team	Avg Wins	Postseason Odds			Mean DVOA Projections								Schedule	
		Make Playoffs	Reach Super Bowl	Win Super Bowl	Total DVOA	Rk	Off DVOA	Rk	Def DVOA	Rk	ST DVOA	Rk	Average Opponent	Rk
NE	11.6	87.5%	35.2%	21.8%	27.3%	1	17.3%	2	-6.0%	3	4.1%	1	-3.5%	32
PIT	10.7	77.9%	25.0%	14.9%	23.2%	2	20.3%	1	-2.2%	13	0.7%	8	-1.6%	27
SEA	9.8	63.7%	17.3%	8.7%	16.8%	3	7.8%	5	-9.6%	1	-0.6%	17	-0.3%	21
GB	9.5	59.8%	14.5%	7.1%	13.0%	5	15.7%	3	1.8%	21	-0.8%	22	0.3%	12
DAL	9.3	54.7%	13.1%	6.5%	13.3%	4	10.6%	4	-2.9%	9	-0.2%	14	2.6%	2
OAK	8.8	50.4%	7.4%	3.7%	7.2%	6	5.0%	8	0.7%	18	2.9%	6	0.4%	11
CAR	8.6	46.4%	6.9%	2.9%	2.5%	9	-1.3%	18	-4.4%	8	-0.6%	19	-2.5%	30
ARI	8.3	39.4%	6.0%	2.8%	2.2%	11	-0.2%	16	-4.5%	5	-2.2%	31	0.1%	16
NYG	8.3	39.9%	6.5%	2.9%	5.1%	7	-1.3%	19	-4.4%	7	2.0%	7	2.2%	4
KC	8.3	42.5%	5.4%	2.6%	4.6%	8	0.9%	14	-0.6%	16	3.1%	5	1.6%	7
ATL	8.3	41.9%	6.1%	2.6%	2.5%	10	7.5%	6	3.0%	24	-2.0%	27	0.0%	17
TEN	8.1	43.0%	4.1%	1.9%	-1.6%	18	5.5%	7	5.4%	28	-1.7%	26	-2.1%	28
BAL	8.1	38.0%	3.9%	1.8%	0.3%	15	-5.3%	25	-1.8%	14	3.7%	2	-0.8%	25
LARM	8.0	34.4%	4.9%	2.1%	0.7%	13	-9.9%	28	-7.0%	2	3.7%	3	-0.1%	18
DET	8.0	35.0%	4.5%	1.8%	0.3%	14	1.3%	13	0.9%	19	-0.2%	13	0.5%	10
CIN	7.9	34.5%	3.1%	1.4%	-2.5%	19	-0.2%	17	0.2%	17	-2.1%	30	-1.3%	26
PHI	7.9	33.4%	4.8%	2.1%	2.1%	12	-3.7%	22	-2.4%	10	3.4%	4	2.9%	1
LACH	7.8	35.2%	3.3%	1.5%	-1.2%	17	2.0%	12	3.4%	26	0.3%	11	0.1%	14
WAS	7.8	31.3%	4.3%	1.8%	0.0%	16	2.5%	11	2.1%	23	-0.4%	16	2.5%	3
IND	7.6	35.1%	2.7%	1.1%	-5.4%	22	3.8%	9	7.2%	30	-2.1%	28	-2.4%	29
JAC	7.5	32.9%	2.3%	0.9%	-6.5%	23	-8.6%	27	-2.2%	12	-0.1%	12	-2.5%	31
CHI	7.5	27.6%	2.8%	1.1%	-5.3%	21	-2.8%	21	2.1%	22	-0.4%	15	0.1%	15
MIN	7.4	26.9%	2.7%	1.0%	-4.4%	20	-5.2%	24	-2.3%	11	-1.5%	23	0.6%	9
BUF	7.2	25.0%	1.7%	0.7%	-7.6%	26	-0.1%	15	6.9%	29	-0.6%	18	-0.7%	24
TB	7.2	25.8%	2.4%	0.9%	-7.5%	25	-1.7%	20	3.2%	25	-2.5%	32	-0.2%	19
NO	7.0	23.7%	1.9%	0.7%	-9.1%	28	2.8%	10	11.1%	32	-0.8%	21	-0.4%	22
DEN	7.0	24.6%	1.8%	0.7%	-6.9%	24	-12.8%	31	-5.6%	4	0.3%	10	1.8%	6
MIA	7.0	22.1%	1.5%	0.6%	-8.4%	27	-6.3%	26	1.5%	20	-0.6%	20	-0.2%	20
HOU	6.7	23.4%	1.4%	0.6%	-10.4%	29	-12.8%	30	-4.5%	6	-2.1%	29	1.1%	8
SF	6.5	16.2%	1.3%	0.4%	-11.6%	30	-4.8%	23	7.5%	31	0.7%	9	2.1%	5
NYJ	6.2	14.6%	0.7%	0.3%	-16.5%	32	-15.8%	32	-0.9%	15	-1.6%	24	-0.5%	23
CLE	6.0	13.5%	0.6%	0.2%	-16.1%	31	-10.2%	29	4.3%	27	-1.7%	25	0.2%	13

Arizona Cardinals

2016 Record: 7-8-1	Total DVOA: 1.3% (16th)	2017 Mean Projection: 8.3 wins	On the Clock (0-4): 8%
Pythagorean Wins: 9.4 (7th)	Offense: -6.0% (21st)	Postseason Odds: 39.4%	Mediocrity (5-7): 30%
Snap-Weighted Age: 26.8 (9th)	Defense: -13.6% (3rd)	Super Bowl Odds: 6.0%	Playoff Contender (8-10): 41%
Average Opponent: -4.3% (30th)	Special Teams: -6.3% (30th)	Proj. Avg. Opponent: 0.1% (16th)	Super Bowl Contender (11+): 21%

2016: *Great Expectations*—A dark, depressing tale of hopes dashed by cruel twists of fate.

2017: *The Old Curiosity Shop*—Can Palmer, Fitzgerald and the aging offense hold it together for one more year?

Putting together a championship-contending team in the salary-cap era is like playing a high-stakes game of Jenga. You have to balance the cap, players' primes and development, team chemistry, and efficiency in order to produce great teams, and it's difficult to keep it all in balance for very long. Fail to capitalize on your opportunities, and you get a prime spot in Camp Woulda-Coulda-Shoulda-Been alongside the '90s Bills and '70s Vikings. That's why the 2016 season hurt so much for Cardinals fans: it was a season that looked so promising on paper before the blocks came tumbling down.

The 2015 Arizona Cardinals were the best team the franchise put together since they moved to the desert. The most wins in franchise history. A powerful offense led by an MVP-caliber quarterback. An aggressive, risk-taking defense boasting three Pro Bowlers. Everything looked good for a dominant playoff run, until late injuries to Carson Palmer and Tyrann Mathieu derailed that train. But with all the key pieces still in place, and big additions like Chandler Jones and Evan Mathis, 2016 was going to be their year. They had the second-highest projected DVOA and, luck holding, were sure to be in the championship mix all year long.

Luck didn't hold. Some regression for the 37-year-old Palmer was expected, but no one predicted a drop from 34.4% to -7.4% DVOA. Some regression from Bruce Arians' 16-5 record in one-score games was expected, but a 2-5-1 record was a dramatic overcorrection. Add in injuries—to the offensive line in Mathis and Jared Veldheer and to the secondary in Mathieu, Tyvon Branch and Mike Jenkins—and you end up with a 7-8-1 season, no playoff berth, and a "thud" many fear is the sound of a Cardinal smacking headfirst into a shut window of opportunity.

In reality, of course, being competitive is a little more complicated than the window of opportunity metaphor implies. It's a great metaphor when your entire team is aging, or you have a roughly equal level of experience across the board, or contracts on both side of the ball are expiring at equal rate. That's not at all true for the Cardinals, where the offense and defense are on opposite sides of the development curve.

The Cardinals had the oldest snap-weighted offense in the league last season at 28.3, and it's only getting older. Carson Palmer will be 38 in December, which makes him the second-oldest starting quarterback in the league. Larry Fitzgerald turns 34 in August, and he has flirted with retirement in the past. Mike Iupati is 30. A.Q. Shipley is 31. Jared Veldheer is

30. We're not saying to pass out the canes and the Metamucil or anything, but age is definitely a concern here. Father Time eventually catches everyone, even greats like Fitzgerald.

On defense, however, the Cardinals were the fourth-*youngest* snap-weighted team last season at only 25.9. If anything, they have managed to get less experienced this offseason. Calais Campbell, Marcus Cooper, Kevin Minter, D.J. Swearinger, Tony Jefferson, Alex Okafor—all gone. If rookies Haason Reddick and Budda Baker play significant roles this season, the average age on defense might actually *drop* some. Youth is a great thing to have, but that's a lot of experience to replace in one season, and there may be growing pains as new players try to find their roles on defense.

So, really, what the Cardinals face is an offensive window sliding closed as players age, and a defensive window sliding open as young players get more experience. It's not a question if the windows are shut or not, but rather whether the Cardinals can thread the needle between them without getting crushed.

To thread that needle and be legitimate Super Bowl contenders, the Cardinals need three things to happen. On offense, they need their quarterback to play more like 2015 MVP-level Palmer and less like just-above-replacement-level 2016 Palmer. On defense, they need to replace nearly 5,000 defensive snaps without significantly hurting a unit that ranked third in DVOA last season. And on special teams, they need to not be quite so clown-shoes horrible in just about every way.

Let's start with Palmer. Palmer turns 38 at the end of December, and you just don't see starting quarterbacks last that long. Only 27 quarterbacks have thrown 200 or more passes at age 38 or older. It's miles off the wrong side of the quarterback aging curve. Aging quarterbacks usually fall off a cliff, too, with a final season well below their normal heights. 2015 looks like a massive outlier for Palmer in any rate stat you measure, but Palmer's 2016 falls below what he was able to do before that. The fear, of course, is that age has taken its toll and Palmer's time as a reliable starter is over.

On the other hand, that list of 27 quarterbacks is a *really* good list. Eleven are in the Hall of Fame. Two more are Tom Brady and Peyton Manning, who will be in Canton soon enough. With the exceptions of Steve DeBerg and Jon Kitna, the rest are Super Bowl champions and Pro Bowlers. These are players who push past the age curve and continue to show off strong skills as their contemporaries drop out. Palmer fits

2017 Cardinals Schedule

Week	Opp.	Week	Opp.	Week	Opp.
1	at DET	7	at LARM (U.K.)	13	LARM
2	at IND	8	BYE	14	TEN
3	DAL (Mon.)	9	at SF	15	at WAS
4	SF	10	SEA (Thu.)	16	NYG
5	at PHI	11	at HOU	17	at SEA
6	TB	12	JAC		

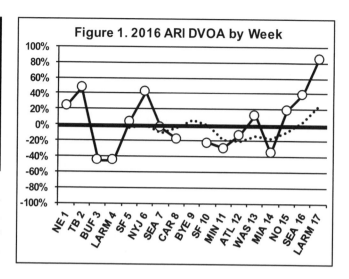

Figure 1. 2016 ARI DVOA by Week

right in—he has always been one of the most gifted quarterbacks in the league. He played better over the last five weeks, with a DVOA of 0.9%, so there are still signs of gas left in the tank. The Cardinals don't need MVP Palmer to win games on his own; they just need him to rebound to above-average.

So what will a 38-year-old Palmer look like in 2017? One way to estimate how much longer Palmer can go on is with similarity scores—looking at historical players with similar career arcs, and seeing how much longer they were able to play at a high level (Table 1). How many players similar to Palmer managed to chug along, and what can we learn from them?

Table 1. Most Similar Players to Carson Palmer, 2014-2016

Rank	Player	Year	Age	Starts Remaining	Sim Score
1	Dan Marino	1993-1995	34	56	581
2	Steve Beuerlein	1998-2000	35	5	543
3	John Elway	1992-1994	34	59	453
4	Steve Young	1996-1998	37	3	451
5	Kurt Warner	2006-2008	37	15	450
6	Tony Romo	2010-2012	32	34	446
7	Ken Anderson	1980-1982	33	24	430
8	Rich Gannon	1998-2000	35	42	427
9	Steve DeBerg	1989-1991	37	6	422
10	Jim Everett	1993-1995	32	16	400

It's a high-quality list of players, as you'd expect—if you're still lining up behind center after age 35, you've either had a fairly solid career, or you're Josh McCown. But we're not interested in the careers up to this point; we're interested in what came after. With that in mind, we can sort these players into three groups.

Three of them had great careers post-comparison, continuing to play at a high level even into their twilight. Elway had two Super Bowl championships still to come, and while he was helped by a strong running game, he also made the Pro Bowl in his final three seasons. Gannon was named MVP in 2002 at age 37. Romo had two more great seasons in him before injuries took their toll starting in 2015. If Palmer continues on like these three quarterbacks, then the Cardinals are going to be just fine.

Two more of them had solid careers post-comparison. Marino never again made the Pro Bowl in his last four seasons, but remained a regular starter and an above-average quarterback for a few more years before age and injuries caught up to him.

Warner had success in his final season in Arizona, with 14.5% DVOA. If Palmer can hit that good-but-not-great range, that would likely be enough for Arizona to at least contend.

The last five quarterbacks from Table 1 range from bad to nightmare scenarios. Young's career was ended by a concussion at Sun Devil Stadium the next season. Beuerlein and DeBerg lost their jobs to younger players as their skills deteriorated to below-average levels. Everett and Anderson sputtered on, less and less effective each season, and neither ever saw another winning campaign. Palmer has dealt with injuries, and Palmer already saw a sudden drop-off in his stats last season. This is the big fear—that Palmer has already started his downward spiral, either due to age or injury, and won't be an above-average quarterback again.

What separates the wheat from the chaff here? It might well be sack rate. The five successful quarterbacks all had a sack rate of 5.5 percent or lower over the remainder of their careers, while four of the five unsuccessful quarterbacks had a sack rate of 7.2 percent or higher. (Jim Everett is the outlier, playing behind an offensive line that included Willie Roaf and Jim Dombrowski.) It makes sense, because older players don't recover as quickly as their younger counterparts. Quarterbacks who are able to get rid of the ball and avoid taking big hits are going to have longer, more productive careers. There's less chance of damage, both in terms of major injuries and in terms of minor wear-and-tear over the course of a season.

Palmer's sack rate in 2015 was 4.4 percent, but it rose to 6.3 percent last season, placing him right between the successful and unsuccessful groups. Blame it on the offensive line, which dropped from fifth in adjusted sack rate in 2015 to 21st last season. Injuries were a huge part of that decline, as only A.Q. Shipley was able to start all 16 games and nine different players started at right tackle or right guard. Palmer is still good working in an unclean pocket, and still has some mobility to get around pressure. However, he ranked seventh among quarterbacks in pressure last season (30.8 percent of all dropbacks), and his DVOA under pressure dropped from second to 23rd in the league. He was hit 87 times and knocked down 127, both the most in the league. These conditions are not conducive to success for an aging passer.

For Palmer to have success, the offensive line has to remain healthier and provide more protection up front. If they do that, Palmer's numbers should rebound. Not to 2015 levels, of course, because those numbers are out of place when you consider Palmer's recent career, but to a level that should be more than adequate for playoff contention.

Of course, if the defense flatlines, then it doesn't matter if the offense rebounds, which brings us to Arizona's other big issue: finding replacements for 5,000 defensive snaps.

Arizona's defense has been its calling card for the last four seasons. It's a swarming, aggressive group which will bring pressure from anywhere and everywhere to disrupt opposing offenses. They blitzed five or more rushers on 39 percent of plays last season, third-most in the NFL. That's their basic philosophy—tons of pass-rushers from tons of positions so you don't have time to make a decision. They remained successful through a defensive coordinator switchover, going from Todd Bowles to James Bettcher without missing a beat. Now it's time to see if they can handle significant turnover on the field. Arizona finds itself facing the 2017 season having to replace five starters and two key members of their rotation (Table 2). This is not exactly ideal.

Table 2. Arizona's Defensive Snaps Lost

Pos	Player	Snaps	Def %
ILB	Kevin Minter	1,003	93.3%
S	Tony Jefferson	928	86.3%
S	D.J. Swearinger	837	77.9%
DE	Calais Campbell	828	77.0%
CB	Marcus Cooper	827	76.9%
ILB	Sio Moore	242	22.5%
OLB	Alex Okafor	231	21.5%
CB	Tharold Simon	76	7.1%
S	C.B. Bryant	2	0.2%
TOTAL		**4,974**	**42.1%**

The secondary is hardest hit. The Cardinals regularly use three safeties, sacrificing size to get more and more speed and athleticism on the field in both their coverage and blitz packages. Their defense was top-five in both blitzes from their defensive backs and S/CB cover ratio. Outside of maybe New Orleans, no team puts more weight on quality safety play than Arizona does. Jefferson and Swearinger weren't just bodies on the field; they were two of the top safeties in the game last season and key structural parts to how Arizona's defense works. Now they're out of town.

The Cardinals are going with the something old, something new approach to replacing them. Antoine Bethea comes over as a free agent from San Francisco. At 33, Bethea's best years are behind him, but a change of scenery and an actual competent defense around him could revitalize him. He's penciled in at strong safety. The third safety position could go to second-round pick Budda Baker, who's a perfect fit for this defense. He is most commonly compared to Tyrann Mathieu, and it only takes a few minutes of watching film to see why. Baker's a big-hitting thumper who terrorized the Pac-12 at the University of Washington, and he's going to be moved around everywhere

in the secondary. Tyvon Branch will probably start with more snaps, but in an ideal world, Baker takes over before too long.

The loss of Marcus Cooper is easier to swallow. While he did have four interceptions, Cooper ranked 67th in success rate last season. He was also picked on again and again, targeted on an estimated 24.1 percent of his snaps. While Cooper made big interceptions and deflected more than his fair share of passes, he was also largely responsible for Arizona's 27th-ranked pass defense against No. 2 wideouts. Cooper took the role from rookie Brandon Williams last season, as Williams was not ready for prime time. Williams was still a running back until his last year in college, so saying he's raw is an understatement. Arizona hopes that an extra year of experience will pay off, or else whoever plays opposite Patrick Peterson will once again be targeted early and often.

Eventually, Kevin Minter may be replaced by first-round pick Hasson Reddick, yet another player in the "athletic marvel with size questions" paradigm that has become the prototype for Arizona's defenders. However, Reddick's really a better fit for Deone Bucannon's moneybacker role. Instead, we'll likely see veteran Karlos Dansby get the initial nod to replace Minter, who got the starting job back in 2014 as a replacement for… Karlos Dansby. At least Dansby knows the system well, making the transition back to him less awkward. The other two linebackers are smaller losses; Okafor's rotational rusher role will be filled by Jarvis Jones, while Moore's role will be replaced by "maybe not having Deone Bucannon miss three weeks."

But the real challenge is the loss of Calais Campbell. The loss of production would be bad enough—the eight sacks, the team-leading 31 quarterback hurries, the 16 passes disrupted, the Pro Bowls, etc. The attention and extra blockers offenses were forced to spend accounting for Campbell allowed everyone else on the line to have an easier time. Add in his leadership both on and off the field, and you have a hole that's significantly larger than Campbell's 6-foot-8 frame.

Last year's first-round pick, Robert Nkemdiche, is penciled in as the starter, but suggesting that he'll *replace* Campbell is a bridge too far. He only had 83 snaps last season, spending time in Bruce Arians' doghouse thanks to a reported lack of work ethic. His production in college wasn't what you would expect out of a player with Nkemdiche's raw talent, either. He'll need to make the mother of all sophomore leaps to come close to filling Campbell's shoes.

Arizona knows better than to ask him to do it alone, though. Campbell's departure should also see increased snap counts for Josh Mauro, Frostee Rucker, and Rodney Gunter, as the Cardinals will go deeper into a rotation. You can't replace a player as integral as Campbell with just one guy; you take a bunch of different players, have them all tackle a piece of what Campbell did, and hope someone steps up.

It's not that the Cardinals don't have a plan in place for each of these losses, it's just that the sheer number of them presents a difficult challenge. Defensive chemistry and familiarity with a complex scheme doesn't happen overnight. There will be an adjustment period needed as all the new faces and new responsibilities try to mesh with the older crew. In an ideal world, this happens quickly, thanks to leadership from the veterans and potential from the rookies. In practice, there may be growing pains early on in the season. That could be trouble, because the schedule gives them few favors; a trifecta of Detroit, Indianapolis, and Dallas isn't exactly the offensive lineup you would choose to break in five new starters. If the defense clicks quickly, this shouldn't be an issue, but if there are growing pains, the Cardinals could find themselves behind the eight-ball very quickly.

Of course, all this talk about windows closing and opportunities squandered would be much quieter if the Cardinals had had even average special teams a year ago.

Arizona finished 30th in special teams DVOA and were below average in every individual aspect apart from kick returns. The big failures got the headlines—the missed field goals that cost them wins against New England and Seattle, the botched snaps which contributed to the loss in Buffalo, the poor tackling that lead to a loss against Los Angeles. Flip a few of those, and the Cardinals are in the playoffs last season.

But the special teams also misfired in smaller, more consistent ways that didn't always show up on the lowlight reel. Arizona's three-headed monster at punter—Drew Butler, replaced by Ryan Quigley, replaced by Butler again, replaced by Matt Wile—combined to average just 37 net yards per punt, worst in the league by nearly 2 yards. That's partly because they had trouble getting punts off—Arizona led the league in punts blocked, and had several snapping gaffes as well. Kicker Chandler Catanzaro not only had the second-worst field goal percentage in the league, he also was below-average on kickoffs, with a net of just 39.7 yards per kick. John Brown and Patrick Peterson averaged just 6.1 yards per punt return, third-worst in the league. They only had a positive special teams DVOA in three games, second-worst in the league behind Houston. They were regularly, and consistently, terrible.

The solution to that, of course, is to replace everyone. Butler and long-snapper Kameron Canaday were replaced last season. Catanzaro is gone, replaced by the more reliable Phil

Dawson. As for punt returns, the plan seems to still be "stick with Patrick Peterson, try to block him better lanes and hope he doesn't get injured." Frankly, Peterson hasn't been an above-average punt returner since 2011, when he was admittedly brilliant. The gap between Peterson and a less essential player—rookie T.J. Logan? Receivers J.J. Nelson or Brittan Golden?—isn't large enough to justify the added injury risk. No matter who they stick back there, Arizona is likely to see at least a little rebound on special teams, simply because of regression towards the mean. However, the Cardinals have not had a positive special teams DVOA since Bruce Arians and Steve Keim took over in 2013, and that's unlikely to change in 2017. It simply hasn't been a significant priority for the franchise in their personnel acquisition philosophy.

It's entirely possible that Palmer returns to something near his 2015 form, the defense doesn't miss a beat despite the personnel changes, and the special teams looks like an actual NFL unit. If that all happens, there's no reason Arizona can't compete with the likes of Seattle, Green Bay, and Dallas for a February trip to Minnesota.

It's also entirely possible that age hits Palmer like a ton of bricks, the defense doesn't gel until midway through the season, and the little errors continue to add up on special teams. If nothing works out, the Cardinals will be in perfect position to draft Palmer's successor in the 2018 draft.

All of this puts Arizona in an odd position for the 2017 season. They're not obvious contenders—there's too many moving parts, too many ways everything could go wrong and tumble to the ground. They're not obvious also-rans—every question has a potential answer in place, and most of 2015's near-miss team is still intact for another go. Few teams in the NFL have so much potential, both positive and negative.

At the very least, 2017's unlikely to be boring in the desert.

Bryan Knowles

2016 Cardinals Stats by Week

Wk	vs.	W-L	PF	PA	YDF	YDA	TO	Total	Off	Def	ST
1	NE	L	21	23	344	363	+2	24%	19%	-20%	-15%
2	TB	W	40	7	416	306	+5	47%	13%	-39%	-5%
3	at BUF	L	18	33	348	288	-4	-45%	-58%	-15%	-2%
4	LARM	L	13	17	420	288	-4	-46%	-24%	12%	-10%
5	at SF	W	33	21	288	286	+3	3%	-19%	-11%	10%
6	NYJ	W	28	3	396	257	0	42%	15%	-27%	-1%
7	SEA	T	6	6	443	257	0	-4%	-7%	-30%	-28%
8	at CAR	L	20	30	340	349	-1	-18%	-4%	12%	-2%
9	BYE										
10	SF	W	23	20	443	281	-3	-23%	-27%	-6%	-2%
11	at MIN	L	24	30	290	217	-1	-30%	-15%	-5%	-20%
12	at ATL	L	19	38	332	360	0	-13%	-16%	-3%	0%
13	WAS	W	31	23	369	333	+2	12%	0%	-22%	-10%
14	at MIA	L	23	26	300	314	-1	-35%	-40%	-17%	-12%
15	NO	L	41	48	425	488	-1	19%	38%	13%	-6%
16	at SEA	W	34	31	370	391	0	39%	38%	0%	1%
17	at LARM	W	44	6	344	123	+1	85%	5%	-81%	-1%

Trends and Splits

	Offense	Rank	Defense	Rank
Total DVOA	-6.0%	21	-13.6%	3
Unadjusted VOA	-3.2%	18	-13.3%	2
Weighted Trend	-3.3%	19	-12.2%	3
Variance	6.9%	22	5.5%	19
Average Opponent	1.5%	30	-3.1%	28
Passing	-4.7%	27	-9.8%	3
Rushing	0.2%	14	-18.3%	7
First Down	3.3%	16	-12.7%	6
Second Down	-15.6%	26	-19.1%	3
Third Down	-10.4%	23	-6.9%	10
First Half	-10.1%	25	-15.3%	2
Second Half	-4.5%	18	-6.7%	17
Red Zone	-0.2%	16	7.2%	24
Late and Close	-16.5%	26	-5.0%	15

Five-Year Performance

Year	W-L	Pyth W	Est W	PF	PA	TO	Total	Rk	Off	Rk	Def	Rk	ST	Rk	Off AGL	Rk	Def AGL	Rk	Off Age	Rk	Def Age	Rk	ST Age	Rk
2012	5-11	4.8	4.8	250	357	-1	-16.3%	26	-30.9%	32	-13.5%	6	1.1%	11	50.3	28	22.0	12	26.7	18	27.6	8	27.1	4
2013	10-6	9.5	10.4	379	324	-1	10.0%	10	-2.4%	20	-16.4%	2	-4.1%	27	26.8	11	36.1	22	27.9	4	28.0	2	27.0	3
2014	11-5	8.3	7.4	310	299	+8	-6.4%	22	-9.3%	23	-5.0%	7	-2.2%	21	24.0	8	48.8	24	27.3	10	27.1	9	26.4	5
2015	13-3	12.1	11.6	489	313	+9	27.4%	3	15.7%	4	-15.6%	3	-4.0%	29	21.2	4	41.3	25	28.2	3	26.0	26	25.8	21
2016	7-8-1	9.4	7.7	418	362	0	1.3%	16	-6.0%	21	-13.6%	3	-6.3%	30	35.4	17	42.4	21	28.3	1	25.9	29	25.5	27

2016 Performance Based on Most Common Personnel Groups

ARI Offense					ARI Offense vs. Opponents					ARI Defense				ARI Defense vs. Opponents			
Pers	Freq	Yds	DVOA	Run%	Pers	Freq	Yds	DVOA	Run%	Pers	Freq	Yds	DVOA	Pers	Freq	Yds	DVOA
11	56%	5.4	-0.7%	33%	Base	24%	5.2	-3.0%	55%	Base	19%	5.9	7.2%	11	73%	4.9	-19.8%
12	22%	5.4	-5.4%	49%	Nickel	62%	5.4	-2.0%	33%	Nickel	73%	4.8	-17.7%	12	11%	5.5	0.3%
10	12%	5.6	-24.5%	2%	Dime+	13%	6.5	-11.5%	4%	Dime+	6%	5.4	-56.1%	21	5%	6.4	16.8%
13	4%	6.4	14.3%	74%	Goal Line	1%	1.9	16.9%	80%	Goal Line	2%	0.6	4.5%	10	4%	4.5	-24.6%
20	2%	5.8	-71.8%	17%						Big	0%	7.4	23.3%	22	2%	3.5	-29.5%
21	2%	8.8	50.7%	43%													

Strategic Tendencies

Run/Pass		Rk	Formation		Rk	Pass Rush		Rk	Secondary		Rk	Strategy		Rk
Runs, first half	35%	27	Form: Single Back	79%	14	Rush 3	4.9%	20	4 DB	19%	28	Play-action	15%	31
Runs, first down	44%	25	Form: Empty Back	17%	1	Rush 4	56.8%	26	5 DB	73%	2	Avg Box (Off)	6.07	29
Runs, second-long	26%	24	Pers: 3+ WR	70%	10	Rush 5	29.0%	2	6+ DB	6%	19	Avg Box (Def)	6.23	15
Runs, power sit.	61%	9	Pers: 2+ TE/6+ OL	27%	16	Rush 6+	9.2%	6	CB by Sides	51%	32	Offensive Pace	30.56	17
Runs, behind 2H	19%	32	Pers: 6+ OL	1%	30	Sacks by LB	68.5%	6	S/CB Cover Ratio	33%	4	Defensive Pace	30.26	16
Pass, ahead 2H	50%	12	Shotgun/Pistol	49%	30	Sacks by DB	10.9%	7	DB Blitz	13%	5	Go for it on 4th	1.20	7

Arizona has ranked first or second in use of an empty backfield for four straight years. The Cardinals' offensive DVOA on these plays was roughly the same as their offensive DVOA overall. ☰ The Cardinals ran the ball only 8.4 percent of the time when the quarterback was in shotgun, the lowest rate in the league. ☰ The Cardinals had the worst offense in the league when they ran the ball on second-and-long: -68.7% DVOA and just 3.7 yards per carry. ☰ Despite the great season David Johnson had running the ball, the average men in the box against the Cardinals offense dropped from 6.31 (11th) in 2015 to 6.07 (29th) last year. ☰ Arizona was the beneficiary of a league-high 78 offensive penalties by opponents, and 152 total penalties, second behind Tennessee. This is the fourth straight year the Cardinals have ranked in the top five, which makes them the exception to the usually low year-to-year correlation of opponent penalties (correlation coefficient of roughly 0.15). ☰ Arizona opponents threw a league-high 26.1 percent of passes to No. 3 or "other" receivers. This is the second straight year the Cardinals led the league in this figure—although in 2016, it may have been somewhat related to the schedule since the Rams were right behind them at 25.6 percent. However, Arizona opponents only threw 14.3 percent of passes to tight ends, 31st in the NFL.

Passing

Player	DYAR	DVOA	Plays	NtYds	Avg	YAC	C%	TD	Int
C.Palmer	137	-7.8%	643	3908	6.1	4.6	61.7%	26	14
D.Stanton	-119	-50.9%	48	184	3.8	4.1	40.4%	2	2
B.Gabbert	-158	-25.4%	172	876	5.1	4.0	57.1%	5	6

Rushing

Player	DYAR	DVOA	Plays	Yds	Avg	TD	Fum	Suc
D.Johnson	113	1.8%	248	1085	4.4	16	0	49%
A.Ellington	-26	-32.2%	27	78	2.9	0	0	37%
C.Johnson*	7	-2.0%	25	95	3.8	1	0	48%
C.Palmer	19	59.0%	5	42	8.4	0	0	-
S.Taylor*	-5	-44.6%	4	12	3.0	0	0	50%
B.Gabbert	52	13.3%	38	175	4.6	2	0	-

Receiving

Player	DYAR	DVOA	Plays	Ctch	Yds	Y/C	YAC	TD	C%
L.Fitzgerald	71	-6.8%	152	109	1029	9.4	3.4	6	72%
J.Nelson	62	-2.3%	74	34	568	16.7	5.1	6	46%
Jo.Brown	61	-1.9%	73	39	517	13.3	2.7	2	53%
M.Floyd*	28	-7.6%	70	33	446	13.5	1.7	4	47%
Ja.Brown	7	-8.5%	22	11	187	17.0	5.3	1	50%
B.Golden	-18	-32.2%	14	8	83	10.4	1.6	1	57%
J.Gresham	-48	-18.7%	61	37	391	10.6	3.7	2	61%
D.Fells*	28	14.3%	18	14	154	11.0	6.4	1	78%
D.Johnson	274	27.7%	121	81	881	10.9	8.0	4	67%
A.Ellington	8	-4.3%	19	12	85	7.1	6.0	0	63%

Offensive Line

Player	Pos	Age	GS	Snaps	Pen	Sk	Pass	Run	Player	Pos	Age	GS	Snaps	Pen	Sk	Pass	Run
A.Q. Shipley	C	31	16/16	1148	5	0.5	5	4	John Wetzel	G/T	26	16/8	646	2	2.0	11	1
Mike Iupati	LG	30	15/15	1034	6	2.5	12	8	Jared Veldheer	LT	30	8/8	577	5	1.0	5	2
D.J. Humphries	RT	24	13/13	921	6	5.5	14	2	Ulrick John	RT	25	3/3	212	1	2.0	6	1
Earl Watford*	OL	27	15/11	787	5	4.0	8	2	Evan Mathis*	RG	36	4/3	199	0	0.0	2	0

Year	Yards	ALY	Rank	Power	Rank	Stuff	Rank	2nd Lev	Rank	Open Field	Rank	Sacks	ASR	Rank	Press	Rank	F-Start	Cont.
2014	3.47	3.93	24	59%	24	19%	14	0.92	32	0.42	30	28	4.8%	6	24.5%	17	22	42
2015	4.59	4.56	3	51%	29	20%	16	1.22	6	1.15	4	27	5.0%	5	28.1%	23	16	32
2016	4.28	4.54	7	72%	5	21%	20	1.23	12	0.82	11	41	6.3%	21	30.9%	29	13	22

2016 ALY by direction:	Left End 5.80 (3)	Left Tackle 4.23 (18)	Mid/Guard 4.43 (8)	Right Tackle 5.03 (5)	Right End 3.69 (18)

Mike Iupati struggled last season, finishing 87th out of 104 interior linemen with a blown block every 51.7 snaps. It's the third season in a row he has been outside the top 80; while still a road-grading run blocker, he whiffs more in pass protection than you'd like for the highest-paid lineman on the team. ☞ D.J. Humphries is moving to left tackle on a full-time basis. While Arizona's offensive DVOA was worse with Humphries on the left rather than the right last season, that's mostly just correlation and not causation; Humphries played solidly, if not spectacularly, after missing his entire rookie season. ☞ That moves Jared Veldheer to right tackle, a position he has never played. He is also coming off his second torn triceps in four seasons. ☞ Most of Arizona's issues last season were due to injuries. While the starters were generally solid at blocking, they had 28.1 adjusted games lost, and the added snaps for players like Ulrick John and Evan Boehm hurt. The starters averaged 71.8 snaps per blown block, the backups just 58.3. ☞ Dorian Johnson (Pitt) would have gone well before the fourth round if it wasn't for an overactive liver. He's a great pulling guard who rarely outright misses or botches blocks, though he can be pushed around somewhat. Don't be shocked if he starts ahead of Evan Boehm at right guard. ☞ Will Holden is a terrible name for an offensive lineman. The fifth-round pick played both left and right tackle at Vanderbilt, but his lack of quickness means that he's best fit for the right side in the NFL.

Defensive Front Seven

Defensive Line	Age	Pos	G	Snaps	Plays	TmPct	Rk	Stop	Dfts	BTkl	Runs	St%	Rk	RuYd	Rk	Sack	Hit	Hur	Dsrpt
Calais Campbell*	31	DE	16	828	58	7.1%	11	45	20	5	40	73%	55	1.9	33	8.0	13	31	7
Corey Peters	29	DE	15	497	21	2.7%	80	16	6	2	21	76%	48	1.3	11	0.0	2	8	0
Josh Mauro	26	DE	15	388	33	4.3%	--	28	10	3	28	82%	--	1.1	--	0.0	3	8	1
Frostee Rucker	34	DE	13	304	14	2.1%	--	11	4	2	11	73%	--	1.5	--	0.0	3	6	1

Edge Rushers	Age	Pos	G	Snaps	Plays	TmPct	Rk	Stop	Dfts	BTkl	Runs	St%	Rk	RuYd	Rk	Sack	Hit	Hur	Dsrpt
Chandler Jones	27	OLB	16	938	50	6.1%	31	41	24	5	28	75%	42	2.5	45	11.0	11	29	6
Markus Golden	26	OLB	16	761	51	6.2%	29	43	27	9	32	78%	32	2.3	40	12.5	17	29	1
Jarvis Jones	28	OLB	14	474	45	6.4%	24	31	8	1	29	66%	82	3.6	89	1.0	4	13	3

Linebackers	Age	Pos	G	Snaps	Plays	TmPct	Rk	Stop	Dfts	BTkl	Runs	St%	Rk	RuYd	Rk	Sack	Hit	Hur	Tgts	Suc%	Rk	AdjYd	Rk	PD	Int
Kevin Minter*	27	ILB	16	1003	81	9.9%	58	47	14	14	47	64%	38	3.2	29	3.5	5	9	23	50%	34	7.9	67	3	0
Deone Bucannon	25	ILB	13	818	94	14.1%	29	49	13	17	57	53%	78	4.4	77	0.0	1	9	31	55%	25	6.5	40	3	0
Sio Moore*	27	ILB	8	412	66	16.1%	15	40	9	8	40	70%	15	3.0	18	0.0	2	4	18	48%	41	6.4	37	1	0
Karlos Dansby	36	OLB	16	781	118	14.1%	31	66	19	10	65	68%	25	3.8	55	1.0	2	6	50	43%	56	7.8	66	6	0

Year	Yards	ALY	Rank	Power	Rank	Stuff	Rank	2nd Level	Rank	Open Field	Rank	Sacks	ASR	Rank	Press	Rank
2014	4.10	3.75	6	43%	1	26%	2	1.14	16	0.98	28	35	5.3%	28	29.1%	3
2015	3.71	3.32	2	62%	13	27%	2	1.05	8	0.87	21	36	5.7%	27	29.3%	3
2016	3.30	3.58	3	61%	13	23%	6	0.95	3	0.31	2	48	7.5%	3	32.1%	2
2016 ALY by direction:		Left End 4.00 (14)			Left Tackle 3.54 (7)			Mid/Guard 3.48 (3)			Right Tackle 3.85 (11)			Right End 3.45 (12)	

First-round pick Haason Reddick (Temple) had 22.5 tackles for a loss in 2016, third-most in the FBS. His lack of size is offset by his speed; his 4.52-second 40-yard dash was the fastest for any front seven player at the combine. ⚏ Jarvis Jones washed out in Pittsburgh thanks to a lack of any sort of pass-rush production; he had just 16 pass pressures in the last two years. Arizona may use him on rushing downs to give Chandler Jones or Markus Golden an occasional breather, though he was well below average in that department as well. ⚏ Karlos Dansby dropped from 98.5 percent to 71.8 percent of snaps last year in Cincinnati—at 35, age is beginning to catch up with him. He's still effective in moderate doses, and his 14 rush defeats are more than anyone in Arizona managed to put up last season. ⚏ Robert Nkemdiche was a healthy scratch in seven games last season, and missed three more due to injury, registering just three tackles on the year. That total nearly matches the number of times Bruce Arians publicly castigated him during a tumultuous rookie campaign. No pressure replacing Calais Campbell, then.

Defensive Secondary

Secondary	Age	Pos	G	Snaps	Plays	TmPct	Rk	Stop	Dfts	BTkl	Runs	St%	Rk	RuYd	Rk	Tgts	Tgt%	Rk	Dist	Suc%	Rk	AdjYd	Rk	PD	Int
Patrick Peterson	27	CB	16	1032	56	6.8%	75	24	10	5	14	64%	9	6.0	28	65	15.3%	9	12.7	55%	12	7.2	29	6	3
Tony Jefferson*	25	SS	15	928	97	12.6%	14	46	20	8	54	57%	11	4.1	4	36	9.3%	47	8.6	42%	49	7.1	15	4	0
D.J. Swearinger*	26	SS	16	837	72	8.8%	49	30	14	9	32	47%	22	4.9	11	22	6.2%	9	10.6	41%	52	9.0	39	8	3
Marcus Cooper*	27	CB	15	827	80	10.4%	11	23	12	8	15	7%	87	11.9	81	82	24.1%	77	11.0	45%	72	7.8	48	12	4
Tyrann Mathieu	25	FS/CB	10	560	38	7.4%	60	17	9	5	10	40%	36	6.4	33	28	11.9%	63	5.7	31%	71	10.0	54	4	1
Tyvon Branch	31	SS	7	270	31	8.7%	50	12	3	3	10	20%	71	10.2	67	26	22.9%	74	8.7	60%	3	8.7	35	4	0
Justin Bethel	27	CB	16	269	31	3.8%	--	15	5	2	7	43%	--	3.0	--	30	26.6%	--	11.8	56%	--	7.0	--	6	1
Brandon Williams	25	CB	13	240	26	3.9%	--	8	2	1	3	0%	--	4.0	--	35	34.9%	--	12.9	56%	--	7.7	--	3	0
Antoine Bethea	33	SS	16	1126	112	12.7%	13	38	11	15	60	40%	36	7.8	47	39	9.2%	46	13.3	37%	57	13.2	71	3	1

Year	Pass D Rank	vs. #1 WR	Rk	vs. #2 WR	Rk	vs. Other WR	Rk	vs. TE	Rk	vs. RB	Rk
2014	14	-4.0%	12	2.7%	19	-40.0%	1	16.9%	27	-26.2%	3
2015	4	-12.4%	6	-24.8%	3	-20.5%	5	-13.1%	7	9.7%	23
2016	3	-5.0%	10	17.2%	27	-1.2%	13	-19.7%	6	-43.5%	1

No defender in football played more than Antoine Bethea's 1,126 snaps in 2016 (and that even includes playoff totals). This is partially due to Bethea's health and longevity, and partially due to San Francisco being really bad. ⚏ Losing Tony Jefferson hurts in run defense; he led all defensive backs with 13 run defeats in 2016. ⚏ Patrick Peterson ranked 73rd in the league by allowing an average of 4.3 YAC. This is what happens when you shadow top receivers everywhere: occasionally you get burned. He was one of the ten least-targeted cornerbacks in 2016 despite constantly matching up with the best receivers in the league, which shows how respected he is. ⚏ Tyrann Mathieu had just a 31 percent success rate in coverage, the third-worst total of any defensive back with at least 20 targets or eight starts, and way down from 64 percent in 2015. He also dropped from 13 passes defensed to just four. A return to his elite 2015 form would really help offset the losses in the secondary. ⚏ If Budda

Baker were 2 inches taller, he would have been a first-round pick. What the Washington product lacks in size, he makes up for in speed—he was state champion in high school in both the 100 and 200 meters. ☞ Teams tested Brandon Williams early and often as a rookie—he was targeted on an estimated 34.9 percent of his coverage snaps, more than anyone else with at least 35 targets. Such is life across from Peterson; Justin Bethel and Marcus Cooper also had above-average target rates. With Cooper off to Chicago, Williams and Bethel will compete for the other perimeter cornerback spot. ☞ Arizona ranked last with 38.8 adjusted games lost for defensive backs, thanks to injuries to Tyvon Branch, Mike Jenkins, and Mathieu. It didn't hurt their pass defense, which still ranked third in the league.

Special Teams

Year	DVOA	Rank	FG/XP	Rank	Net Kick	Rank	Kick Ret	Rank	Net Punt	Rank	Punt Ret	Rank	Hidden	Rank
2014	-2.2%	21	0.0	16	2.0	13	-6.2	30	-9.6	30	3.0	11	-0.3	18
2015	-4.0%	29	-1.8	24	0.4	17	0.5	11	-12.7	30	-6.3	29	-11.4	31
2016	-6.3%	30	-8.9	30	-4.9	27	1.7	10	-14.7	31	-4.6	26	-2.8	20

Phil Dawson should be more accurate on field goals than Chandler Catanzaro, but don't allow him anywhere near kickoff duties. Dawson was one of the five worst kickers in the league on gross kickoff value in both 2014 and 2016 (and didn't kick off in 2015). Catanzaro wasn't much better last season. ☞ Punter Matt Wile was the best punter the Cardinals had in 2016 by default. He was worth minus-4.0 points in gross punt value, assuming average returns, compared to minus-6.3 for Drew Butler and minus-8.1 for Ryan Quigley. ☞ Andre Ellington was lousy on kick returns in 2016, so rookie T.J. Logan will get a chance this year alongside Brittan Golden. All three punt returners (Golden, John Brown, and Patrick Peterson) finished with negative value as well.

Atlanta Falcons

This past spring, a vagrant started a fire that wound up burning down a large elevated section of Interstate 85, which cuts through the heart of Atlanta. The collapse of a main thoroughfare is a major challenge for any American city. But the blow dealt to the collective Atlanta psyche was a distant second to the damage caused by the Falcons' collapse in Super Bowl LI. Everyone who bought this book knows that the Falcons blew a 28-3 third-quarter lead and lost in overtime to New England, denying the franchise and the title-starved city it represents on the gridiron a long-awaited championship.

Then again, considering where the Falcons stood just a few months earlier, perhaps the only thing more astonishing than the way the Super Bowl unfolded was that the team was in the game to begin with.

Atlanta went 8-8 in 2015, listing badly after a 5-0 start. Coming into 2016, owner Arthur Blank had put a "playoffs or else" mandate on the future of general manager Thomas Dimitroff and his staff. Head coach Dan Quinn was derided locally as "Coach Bro" for his insistence on peppering all interactions with fortune cookie bromides; he was derided nationally as being well out over his skis as a rookie shot caller. Offensive coordinator Kyle Shanahan was lucky to have a second season on the job, as the team struggled to produce points and rumors of a poor relationship with his players hit the media. Quarterback Matt Ryan was coming off a terrible 2015 season in which he made several crucial, inexplicable mistakes. On the wrong side of 30, questions arose over whether he would ever be a high-quality player again. Prized rookie Vic Beasley was invisible, and the pass rush nonexistent. Not even the awesomeness of wideout Julio Jones could lift the Falcon funk.

Defying virtually all prognostications, including ours, the Falcons responded to the disappointments of 2015 with an amazing 2016, one that shoulda/woulda/coulda ended with a Lombardi Trophy. Dimitroff infused the roster with gobs of young, athletic players. Quinn learned from his mistakes and implemented a swarming defense to go with an extremely potent offense. Said attack was designed by Shanahan, who had one of the greatest seasons in the annals of coordinatordom (until the final furlong, alas). Ryan rebounded to win the MVP, one year after his worst season as a pro. Beasley came from nowhere to lead the league in sacks.

As they say on the Internet, life comes at you fast.

As it happens, "fast" was a crucial element of the turnaround. The Falcons featured a lightning attack that led the NFL in points, touchdowns, and DVOA. The season-long efficiency was frightening to behold. Atlanta scored a jaw-dropping 540 points on just 175 drives. With a mere 11 turnovers and just 48 punts, the Falcons scored on 55.4 percent of their drives. That very nearly matches the record of 55.7 percent set by the 2007 Patriots, heretofore the team that leapt to mind when discussing unstoppable offensive juggernauts. With 3.06 points per drive, the Falcons became only the third offense since 1996 to average more than a field goal every time they took the field, though they fell short of the 2007 Pats and their insane 3.37 PPD.

The Falcons scored 58 touchdowns, meaning only one more drive ended with a punt or turnover than a touchdown. Last year's second-best team in this category, the Aaron Rodgers-led Packers, scored 51 touchdowns and had 73 drives end in punt or turnover.

Ryan was named MVP for directing this onslaught, a stunner given his 2015 struggles but not shocking when placed in the greater context of his strong, underrated career. He definitely struggled during Shanahan: Year 1, with rumors of discontent so pervasive it seemed certain the two would never fully mesh. But that undersold Ryan's adaptability and professionalism, and it stood to reason that simply erasing those terrible mistakes in key situations would turn his damp squib of 2015 into an outlier.

Still, rebounding to have a good season is one thing; playing at an MVP level is another. For that, Shanahan deserves plenty of credit. He had a season so overflowing with brilliant schematic design and timely play calls that the AP's new Assistant Coach of the Year Award, which he won, may have to be henceforth named for him—the "Shanny." Week after week, Shanahan embarrassed quality defensive coordinators across the league, while also ensuring Ryan was put into situations where he was not only comfortable but able to excel.

Shanahan surely ushered in the brilliance with an offseason move that dripped with good karma—inviting local media to watch game film with him! The underlying message of these sessions was that his offense should have worked in 2015, but for poor execution or bad luck. At the time, it seemed like a CYA maneuver disguised as PR, but in hindsight he was right.

One of the most important missing ingredients from the offense was the lack of an athletic center to trigger the

9

2017 Falcons Schedule

Week	Opp.	Week	Opp.	Week	Opp.
1	at CHI	7	at NE	13	MIN
2	GB	8	at NYJ	14	NO (Thu.)
3	at DET	9	at CAR	15	at TB (Mon.)
4	BUF	10	DAL	16	at NO
5	BYE	11	at SEA (Mon.)	17	CAR
6	MIA	12	TB		

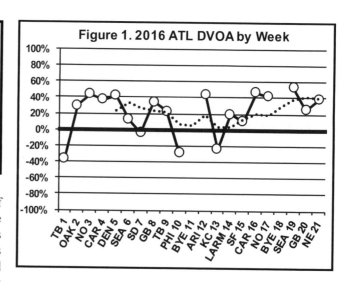

Figure 1. 2016 ATL DVOA by Week

zone-blocking attack. That was fixed by a single flourish of Blank's pen, when he signed the check that brought in free agent Alex Mack from Cleveland. Overnight, the offense was transformed. Ryan was no longer fielding ground-ball snaps and getting chased from the middle of the pocket, as he had throughout 2015. The outside zone run became not merely Shanahan's core concept (Atlanta used it on more than 40 percent of its handoffs), but an effective one. Most importantly, Mack's athleticism and caginess helped play-action off the outside zone to become almost scarily efficient. Atlanta's ability to consistently run well with Devonta Freeman and Tevin Coleman gave the play-action increased bite, and Shanahan took advantage, riffing on the scheme with all manner of boot actions and screens. No offense used play-action more than Atlanta, and few teams used it more effectively. Atlanta ranked fifth in DVOA (53.3%) and second in yards per pass (10.3), with Ryan throwing for 1,869 yards on play-action passes. Only two other passers (Russell Wilson and Kirk Cousins) topped 1,000, and both just barely.

Conversely, Atlanta used shotgun less often than any other team, operating from "old-fashioned" sets that employed fullbacks and multiple tight ends. Atlanta frequently employed three at once, at least until Jacob Tamme was injured in midseason. When passing from that "13" personnel grouping, Ryan went 24-for-29 with five touchdowns, and overall the team had a 54.9% DVOA. With the NFL massively shifting toward a three-receiver, shotgun-spread look, the Falcons and Shanahan caught defenses off guard by going retro.

What separated the Falcons attack from most mortal offenses was the ability to stretch the field to its full lateral width even when Ryan rolled out in one direction, a situation that theoretically should have cut his options in half. That was partially due to the brilliance of Jones, and his ability to get across the field with precision and explosiveness. It was partially due to wideout Taylor Gabriel's blinding speed that defenders had to honor, clearing space for the crossers to operate. And it was partially due to Freeman and Coleman's ability as receivers and to run various wheel route concepts. Defenders expecting them to be in one place coming off the play-action were often stunned to discover they were on the other side of the field. Or that while they had managed to locate the backs, one of the tight ends was now completely uncovered. Or that Jones had simply defeated their perfectly executed coverage. The dizzying array of playmakers enabled by Shanahan's scheme often led to defenses exploding in anger and confusion on their sideline, as the Seahawks did in a midseason game after the

Falcons scored 21 points in 11 minutes. It helped that Atlanta receivers hung on to the ball far more often. We charted the team with a league-high 32 drops two years ago; in 2016, the unit had just 16 drops, the fewest in the NFL.

One way to measure Shanahan's ability to get his playmakers into space is first downs created by yards after the catch—in other words, plays where the receiver caught the ball short of the sticks and converted on his own. Our Cian Fahey tracked the stat in his indispensable *Pre-Snap Reads QB Catalogue 2017*: Ryan easily led all passers with 118 YAC first downs. He also topped the league in gains on such plays of 11-plus and 21-plus yards, indicating that Shanahan was scheming receivers so wide open on third down that they could turn mere conversions into big plays. Opposing defenses might live with Jones taking a 5-yard pass and hurtling down the sideline for a big gain, but when the likes of Levine Toilolo or Aldrick Robinson did so, frustration mounted.

Of course, all of the hosannas to Shanahan come with a mighty "Yeah, but..." attached. When the situation called for slow-playing the clock and running the ball in the fourth quarter of the Super Bowl, Shanny went into "check this out" mode, and abetted the Patriots comeback by calling up deep-dropback passes that became disastrous sacks or clock-stopping incompletions. Shanahan reportedly moaned, "I blew it" after the game; certainly the Falcons' fan base blamed him for the unthinkable loss.

Under the circumstances, then, perhaps it is best that Shanahan left for a head coaching gig. There were few illusions that Shanahan would return to the Atlanta sideline in 2017 anyway, and when San Francisco fired Chip Kelly it was obvious Shanny would return to his father's old stomping grounds by the Bay. In his stead, the Falcons made a very surprising hire: Steve Sarkisian, best known for drinking his way out of the USC Trojans job, and fresh off his substitute teacher cameo with Alabama's offense in the national title game.

Sarkisian is respected throughout the sport for his offensive acumen, and no doubt the team put in the requisite vetting to feel comfortable bringing someone with Sark's troubled history on board. But he has precious little Sunday experience (he was quarterbacks coach in Oakland in 2004, and... that's it), and has never called a play in a pro game. Naturally, the line out of Falcon Land is "we aren't going to change anything" and "Matt Ryan is basically the coordinator, anyway," but every Atlanta fan has to feel a twinge of unease about the swap. Just in the last couple of seasons, Marc Trestman and Ken Zampese, both highly regarded offensive minds, struggled to replace Gary Kubiak and Hue Jackson in Baltimore and Cincinnati, respectively. That doesn't mean Sark can't have success, but expecting such robotic efficiency to continue seems foolish.

The good news for Atlanta is that teams that lose their offensive coordinators after awesome seasons don't often fall off much the next year. Since 1989, the top 20 teams in offensive DVOA to lose their coordinators have dropped from an average of 23.1% to 12.4%, and from second in the league to ninth (Table 1). These numbers are virtually indistinguishable from the usual regression towards the mean seen by top offenses that don't change coordinators.

A stronger regression trend relates to the offenses that improved the most over the previous season without changing quarterbacks. These teams tend to fall back the following season; on average, their rank in offensive DVOA rises from 19th in the league to fourth, and then drop backs to 14th (Table 2). Of course, none of these examples featured a season as excellent as the one Ryan had. Indeed, the 2016 Falcons are kind of *sui generis* in this department; no offense in the DVOA era has improved as much with the same quarterback/coordinator combo as the year before.

Table 1. Top 20 Offenses to Lose Offensive Coordinator, 1989-2015

Year	Team	OC	Off DVOA	Rk	OC Y+1	Off DVOA Y+1	Rk Y+1
2011	GB	J.Philbin	33.8%	1	T.Clements	19.5%	3
2011	NE	B.O'Brien	31.9%	3	J.McDaniels	30.8%	1
2005	DEN	G.Kubiak	26.9%	2	R.Dennison	-4.8%	18
2000	STL	M.Martz	26.7%	1	B.Jackson	20.5%	2
2006	SD	C.Cameron	25.7%	2	C.Shelmon	4.6%	14
1991	SF	M.Holmgren	24.0%	2	M.Shanahan	33.1%	1
2005	KC	A.Saunders	23.7%	4	M.Solari	6.3%	11
1998	MIN	B.Billick	23.6%	3	R.Sherman	11.7%	8
2004	NE	C.Weis	23.3%	3	J.McDaniels	17.5%	7
2013	SD	K.Whisenhunt	23.1%	2	F.Reich	7.0%	11
2012	DEN	M.McCoy	22.1%	2	A.Gase	33.5%	1
1993	DAL	N.Turner	21.8%	2	E.Zampese	18.4%	3
1991	BUF	T.Marchibroda	21.5%	3	T.Bresnahan	9.6%	6
2004	NYJ	P.Hackett	20.8%	4	M.Heimerdinger	-19.8%	31
2014	DEN	A.Gase	20.0%	3	R.Dennison	-8.7%	25
2008	DEN	R.Dennison	19.2%	1	M.McCoy	1.3%	18
1994	SF	M.Shanahan	18.9%	1	M.Trestman	18.6%	5
2000	SF	M.Mornhinweg	18.8%	4	G.Knapp	21.0%	1
2015	CIN	H.Jackson	18.6%	2	K.Zampese	7.5%	11
2001	OAK	B.Callahan	18.0%	3	M.Trestman	22.0%	2
	Average		23.1%	2.4		12.5%	9.0
	Average of all offenses over 18.0% DVOA		24.3%	2.3		12.4%	8.4

The takeaway from history is that good old-fashioned regression, rather than merely Shanahan's absence, is the more likely culprit should Atlanta fail to be as dominant in 2017. And regression is a virtual certainty, regardless of who calls the plays. Ryan and the offense just can't play any better; injuries are likely to hit harder than they did in 2016; the offensive line is already less cohesive, thanks to the retirement of guard Chris Chester; and on and on. And that's why our projection for the Falcons is more pessimistic than conventional wisdom, though we still expect Atlanta to be in the playoff mix.

It should be remembered that up until the final month of the 2016 season, the Falcons, for all their offensive wizardry, were hardly considered elite. Part of that was Atlanta's lack of success historically, to be sure, especially at winning time— Ryan doubled his career postseason win total last January. Then there was the good fortune that greased the skids towards the Super Bowl. After losing at home to Kansas City in bizarre fashion (an Eric Berry 2-point interception return), the Falcons were 7-5, mostly written off as the "same old Falcons" at that point by the pigskin commentariat. They were not considered a genuine title threat.

But the last month of the season was cushy, featuring dates with the hapless Rams, 49ers, and Panthers, plus a home game with hated rival (and defense-free) New Orleans. Atlanta swept the quartet, scoring 38.5 points per game in the process. Meanwhile, other NFC teams slipped and fell, handing the Falcons a playoff bye that seemed unlikely when December dawned. The tournament broke their way, too: opponents Seattle and Green Bay were far too broken physically to come to the Georgia Dome and win, and Atlanta avoided the one

Table 2. Top Offensive DVOA Improvements by Teams in Top 10, 1989-2016

Year	Team	Y-1 DVOA	Y-1 Rk	Off DVOA	Rk	Y+1 DVOA	Y+1 Rk	Change from Y-1	Change in Y+1
1991	DAL	-23.6%	28	17.6%	4	23.6%	2	41.3%	6.0%
2013	SD	-10.0%	24	23.1%	2	7.0%	11	33.1%	-16.1%
2014	BAL	-21.7%	30	9.4%	9	-5.2%	20	31.1%	-14.6%
1993	DEN	-15.7%	25	14.8%	3	1.0%	11	30.5%	-13.8%
1989	GB	-20.8%	27	8.9%	6	-13.6%	22	29.7%	-22.5%
2007	NE	14.1%	4	43.5%	1	12.5%	7	29.4%	-31.0%
2006	PHI	-7.5%	19	21.1%	3	12.4%	6	28.7%	-8.7%
1996	BAL	-5.0%	19	22.8%	1	1.8%	15	27.8%	-21.0%
2010	TB	-19.3%	26	8.0%	8	-11.5%	26	27.3%	-19.5%
2011	NO	6.4%	11	33.0%	2	11.9%	9	26.6%	-21.1%
2005	SEA	2.8%	12	28.5%	1	-11.2%	27	25.7%	-39.7%
2001	ARI	-19.6%	27	5.2%	9	-12.3%	27	24.8%	-17.5%
2002	KC	11.1%	5	35.4%	1	33.4%	1	24.3%	-2.0%
2013	CHI	-10.9%	26	13.3%	6	-0.1%	14	24.2%	-13.4%
1998	SF	5.5%	10	28.8%	2	-1.7%	16	23.3%	-30.6%
Average		**-7.6%**	**19.5**	**20.9%**	**3.9**	**3.2%**	**14.3**	**28.5%**	**-17.7%**
2016	ATL	-7.3%	23	24.6%	1	—	—	31.9%	—
2016	TEN	-15.7%	32	10.8%	9	—	—	26.5%	—

Note: Only includes teams with the same quarterback in the first two years.

contest that seemed problematic, visiting Dallas for the NFC Championship Game. Even the Patriots were a rather favorable matchup for the Falcons, which played out for 40 minutes of Super Bowl LI before it all went pear-shaped.

As it happens, a fresh example of the post-Super Bowl regression nightmare is right there in the division, just four hours to the north (when I-85 isn't broken). The Carolina Panthers' loss to Denver in Super Bowl 50 was merely incredibly disappointing, rather than unspeakable. Yet the team wasn't the same in 2016, for various reasons, few of which seemed plausible when the new season dawned and talk in Charlotte was of "unfinished business." That may be the worst-case scenario, but even a handful of the ills that shot down the Panthers could keep Atlanta out of the postseason entirely, especially with an improved division and a first-place schedule that makes them the only NFC South team to play Seattle or Dallas.

Instead of lurking in the shadows, the Falcons will be firmly in the spotlight this season. Increasing the notice will be the grand opening of Mercedes-Benz Stadium, a monstrously expensive edifice that will replace the perfectly fine Georgia Dome. Construction delays, mostly due to the new stadium's unique retractable roof—which doesn't, at present, fit on top of the stadium—have already pushed back the timeline, and forced Atlanta to start the preseason on the road. Few will remember come December, assuming games are happening as scheduled, but it's a dark omen coming off of that Super Bowl.

Nevertheless, optimism in the Peach City is as high as it has ever been. And there is a reason for optimism despite the expected regression of the high-flying Falcons offense. The franchise has the foundation of a viable defense for the first time in what feels like decades. A plodding group that scared no one has been replaced by high-velocity players who fly to the ball. Last year, rookies like safety Keanu Neal and linebackers Deion Jones and De'Vondre Campbell were all immediate impact defenders, if still raw in various facets. As noted earlier, Beasley led the NFL in sacks and helped transform a pass rush that was the league's worst in 2015. Young talent like Grady Jarrett, Robert Alford, and Brian Poole started to develop into quality playmakers.

It was hardly a finished product. In fact, the 2016 Falcons actually dropped five spots in defensive DVOA, to 26th (although their weighted DVOA was 22nd, indicating a glimmer of improvement over the season). To his credit, Quinn didn't stand pat in the coaching staff. Lost in all the hoopla over

Shanahan's departure is the fact that Atlanta changed out its defensive coordinator, too. Richard Smith is gone, replaced by Marquand Manuel. Manuel was the secondary coach in 2016, and has been rewarded for his role in maintaining the unit's cohesion despite losing star corner Desmond Trufant midway through the year. Defensive line coach Bryan Cox is also gone, booted for former 49ers standout Bryant Young. The Super Bowl collapse was a handy excuse for the departures, but word out of Flowery Branch is that the changes were likely regardless of the result in Houston.

Of course, this is fundamentally Quinn's defense, and he is still apparently searching for the right coaches to help him implement his vision (i.e., a southern replica of the Legion of Boom). As mentioned above, Quinn possesses a bumper sticker-ready slogan for every possible scenario, and he is ready for 2017 with the motto "Embrace the Suck." It is designed to meet the Super Bowl disaster head-on while encouraging the team to rededicate itself to the little things that breed success, all in one pithy shibboleth.

Of course, DQ is a product of the Pete Carroll coaching tree, a cadre bound by nature to espouse relentless enthusiasm in the face of professional horrors. The truth is, no t-shirt platitudes can counteract the aftermath of such a devastating defeat, and no mathematical equation can quantify it. For example, an *ESPN The Magazine* article in May[1] traced Seattle's surprising openness to trading Richard Sherman this offseason directly to the team's mind-blowing loss in Super Bowl XLIX, an unthinkable setback that has lingered even as the Seahawks returned to the playoffs twice since and remained one of the NFL's top teams. Sherman, it seems, just can't get over the game. Now New England has destroyed the dreams of another franchise, one that, unlike Seattle, doesn't have a recent title to fall back upon in the darkest hours.

It's an uncomfortable thing for an analytics-based publication to admit, but the Falcons season may rest less upon on-field efficiency and more upon off-field psychotherapy. Whatever happens, Super Bowl LI will hang over the team in Sword of Damoclesian fashion until they return to the big game—and win it this time. Fortunately, taking a roundhouse kick to the testicles and coming back to win it all is quite the rage of late, as proven in Clemson and Cleveland and Chapel Hill.

Hey, even I-85 was repaired in record time, so anything is possible.

Robert Weintraub

---

1 http://www.espn.com/nfl/story/_/id/19446657/seattle-seahawks-cornerback-richard-sherman-let-go-problem-nfl-2017

2016 Falcons Stats by Week

Wk	vs.	W-L	PF	PA	YDF	YDA	TO	Total	Off	Def	ST
1	TB	L	24	31	374	371	+1	-36%	-9%	31%	4%
2	at OAK	W	35	28	528	454	-1	29%	43%	30%	16%
3	at NO	W	45	32	442	474	+2	44%	40%	3%	7%
4	CAR	W	48	33	571	378	+1	36%	47%	13%	3%
5	at DEN	W	23	16	372	267	0	42%	18%	-19%	5%
6	at SEA	L	24	26	362	333	-2	12%	17%	3%	-2%
7	SD	L	30	33	386	426	+1	-5%	0%	8%	4%
8	GB	W	33	32	367	331	0	34%	42%	0%	-7%
9	at TB	W	43	28	461	396	+1	23%	41%	21%	3%
10	at PHI	L	15	24	303	429	0	-29%	-6%	14%	-9%
11	BYE										
12	ARI	W	38	19	360	332	0	45%	42%	-1%	2%
13	KC	L	28	29	418	389	0	-24%	18%	46%	5%
14	at LARM	W	42	14	286	312	+5	19%	15%	-3%	2%
15	SF	W	41	13	550	272	0	11%	19%	17%	8%
16	at CAR	W	33	16	408	302	+2	47%	26%	-25%	-4%
17	NO	W	38	32	465	473	+1	42%	28%	-10%	4%
18	BYE										
19	SEA	W	36	20	422	309	+2	54%	50%	-12%	-9%
20	GB	W	44	21	493	367	+2	25%	25%	1%	2%
21	vs. NE	L	28	34	344	546	+1	39%	40%	-10%	-12%

Trends and Splits

	Offense	Rank	Defense	Rank
Total DVOA	24.6%	1	7.3%	26
Unadjusted VOA	23.4%	1	6.7%	25
Weighted Trend	23.3%	2	4.1%	22
Variance	3.3%	5	3.5%	6
Average Opponent	-2.2%	4	-2.3%	26
Passing	50.8%	1	10.7%	18
Rushing	3.6%	6	1.7%	28
First Down	29.2%	1	-1.5%	17
Second Down	22.9%	4	13.2%	27
Third Down	16.2%	7	14.6%	26
First Half	23.5%	2	0.8%	18
Second Half	37.4%	1	1.9%	20
Red Zone	3.0%	14	23.3%	29
Late and Close	63.9%	1	14.2%	24

Five-Year Performance

Year	W-L	Pyth W	Est W	PF	PA	TO	Total	Rk	Off	Rk	Def	Rk	ST	Rk	Off AGL	Rk	Def AGL	Rk	Off Age	Rk	Def Age	Rk	ST Age	Rk
2012	13-3	11.2	9.1	419	299	+13	9.1%	10	6.1%	12	-2.9%	12	0.1%	16	17.3	7	35.6	21	28.6	1	28.0	3	26.5	9
2013	4-12	5.9	6.5	353	443	-7	-10.4%	25	3.2%	14	13.5%	29	-0.1%	17	53.9	27	36.1	23	27.6	7	26.7	15	25.9	21
2014	6-10	7.1	7.2	381	417	+5	-5.4%	20	7.2%	10	15.7%	32	3.0%	9	60.6	30	33.2	12	26.8	16	26.6	21	26.4	7
2015	8-8	7.8	5.8	339	345	-7	-16.3%	26	-7.3%	23	6.9%	22	-2.1%	22	10.9	2	17.8	5	27.5	8	26.9	14	26.7	5
2016	11-5	10.9	11.8	540	406	+11	19.8%	3	24.6%	1	7.3%	26	2.5%	7	19.3	2	32.9	16	27.8	5	26.0	25	27.3	2

2016 Performance Based on Most Common Personnel Groups

ATL Offense					ATL Offense vs. Opponents					ATL Defense				ATL Defense vs. Opponents			
Pers	Freq	Yds	DVOA	Run%	Pers	Freq	Yds	DVOA	Run%	Pers	Freq	Yds	DVOA	Pers	Freq	Yds	DVOA
11	45%	6.2	21.0%	24%	Base	46%	7.4	39.6%	51%	Base	19%	5.9	9.8%	11	68%	5.9	9.3%
21	26%	7.2	30.9%	56%	Nickel	46%	6.6	23.1%	32%	Nickel	63%	5.9	9.9%	12	11%	6.4	3.5%
12	17%	7.7	36.8%	50%	Dime+	7%	5.7	6.4%	6%	Dime+	18%	5.3	-12.7%	21	5%	5.2	-15.9%
13	7%	8.5	54.9%	42%	Goal Line	1%	2.8	34.8%	70%	Goal Line	1%	0.8	27.2%	10	4%	4.7	-30.3%
22	2%	6.2	12.6%	65%										00	2%	5.4	6.8%
														611	2%	8.2	42.8%
														13	2%	4.2	30.1%

Strategic Tendencies

Run/Pass		Rk	Formation		Rk	Pass Rush		Rk	Secondary		Rk	Strategy		Rk
Runs, first half	36%	25	Form: Single Back	63%	30	Rush 3	8.2%	14	4 DB	19%	29	Play-action	27%	1
Runs, first down	49%	12	Form: Empty Back	8%	12	Rush 4	74.7%	3	5 DB	63%	11	Avg Box (Off)	6.53	1
Runs, second-long	28%	21	Pers: 3+ WR	47%	31	Rush 5	15.3%	29	6+ DB	16%	9	Avg Box (Def)	5.65	32
Runs, power sit.	54%	21	Pers: 2+ TE/6+ OL	27%	18	Rush 6+	1.8%	31	CB by Sides	60%	30	Offensive Pace	29.10	4
Runs, behind 2H	31%	5	Pers: 6+ OL	1%	29	Sacks by LB	45.6%	16	S/CB Cover Ratio	32%	6	Defensive Pace	31.36	25
Pass, ahead 2H	51%	11	Shotgun/Pistol	40%	32	Sacks by DB	8.8%	12	DB Blitz	5%	28	Go for it on 4th	1.10	16

The biggest transformation of Atlanta's offense was on routes over the middle of the field. The Falcons were 31st in DVOA on passes up the middle in 2015, but improved to third in 2016. By comparison, DVOA on passes to the left improved from 19th to second, and on the right they improved from fifth to second. ☁ Atlanta's pace stats show what happens when a team goes 11-5 with a strong running game. The Falcons offense was fourth in situation-neutral pace but 23rd in total pace, as they slowed things down with a lead. The defense was the reverse: 25th in situation-neutral pace as opponents tried to keep it slow early on, but third in total pace because opponents tried to catch up late. ☁ While the running game was strong, the Falcons hardly ever used it when Matt Ryan was in the shotgun. The Falcons only ran the ball 13 percent of the time from shotgun, 27th in the NFL. And they were awful on these plays: a league-low 2.6 yards per carry with -34.2% DVOA. ☁ One strategy that worked against Matt Ryan: during the regular season, Ryan averaged only 4.9 yards per pass against a DB blitz. ☁ The Atlanta defense ranked fifth against the pass on first downs, but 31st against the run. ☁ Falcons opponents dropped 44 passes, third in the NFL. ☁ This year's reminder that time of possession doesn't really matter: three NFC South teams ranked in the top 10 of average time of possession in 2016. The team that didn't rank in the top 10 was Atlanta, which ranked 18th and won the division easily.

Passing

Player	DYAR	DVOA	Plays	NtYds	Avg	YAC	C%	TD	Int
M.Ryan	1885	39.1%	573	4690	8.2	6.1	70.0%	38	7

Receiving

Player	DYAR	DVOA	Plays	Ctch	Yds	Y/C	YAC	TD	C%
J.Jones	458	31.7%	129	83	1409	17.0	4.7	6	64%
M.Sanu	123	6.5%	81	59	653	11.1	4.9	4	73%
T.Gabriel	181	33.7%	51	36	579	16.1	7.7	6	71%
A.Robinson*	91	24.5%	32	20	323	16.2	3.8	2	63%
J.Hardy	70	14.8%	31	21	203	9.7	2.3	4	68%
N.Williams	25	28.8%	7	5	59	11.8	8.2	0	71%
A.Roberts	32	3.2%	25	14	188	13.4	4.5	1	56%
J.Tamme*	25	4.7%	31	22	210	9.5	4.4	3	71%
A.Hooper	106	46.8%	27	19	271	14.3	3.8	3	70%
L.Toilolo	85	57.5%	19	13	264	20.3	11.3	2	68%
D.Freeman	141	24.9%	65	54	462	8.6	7.7	2	83%
T.Coleman	136	48.8%	40	31	421	13.6	12.1	3	78%
P.DiMarco*	18	19.5%	10	7	52	7.4	4.1	1	70%

Rushing

Player	DYAR	DVOA	Plays	Yds	Avg	TD	Fum	Suc
D.Freeman	99	3.8%	182	791	4.3	11	0	48%
T.Coleman	93	17.1%	87	328	3.8	8	0	46%
T.Ward	7	-1.6%	25	99	4.0	0	0	56%
M.Ryan	29	14.4%	19	116	6.1	0	0	-

Offensive Line

Player	Pos	Age	GS	Snaps	Pen	Sk	Pass	Run	Player	Pos	Age	GS	Snaps	Pen	Sk	Pass	Run
Chris Chester*	RG	34	16/16	1039	5	6.0	14	9	Alex Mack	C	32	16/16	1018	4	1.0	7	4
Ryan Schraeder	RT	29	16/16	1038	10	5.0	18	7	Jake Matthews	LT	25	16/16	978	8	5.5	17	7
Andy Levitre	LG	31	16/16	1018	5	3.0	10	8									

Year	Yards	ALY	Rank	Power	Rank	Stuff	Rank	2nd Lev	Rank	Open Field	Rank	Sacks	ASR	Rank	Press	Rank	F-Start	Cont.
2014	3.93	4.23	14	67%	13	21%	20	1.02	24	0.68	17	31	5.1%	11	26.4%	22	16	27
2015	4.07	4.17	15	61%	21	22%	22	1.33	1	0.67	19	32	5.4%	9	24.3%	13	12	36
2016	4.66	4.40	10	61%	17	22%	23	1.30	7	1.20	3	37	6.5%	23	29.5%	25	19	48

2016 ALY by direction: Left End 4.04 (22)   Left Tackle 4.74 (10)   Mid/Guard 4.58 (4)   Right Tackle 5.14 (4)   Right End 3.39 (22)

The key number here is 80/80, as in 80 games started by the first stringers out of a possible 80. That stat, more than any individual mark, highlights how a good-but-not-great group buoyed such a high-powered attack. ≡ Alex Mack was, of course, the linchpin. His acquisition stemmed the broken dike that was the Falcons' interior in 2015. His athleticism and familiarity with Shanahan's scheme (they were together in Cleveland) allowed Atlanta's zone-blocking runs to work. Notably, whenever the Falcons backs ran anywhere near Mack, the results were near the top of the league. When they ran to the perimeter, the numbers plummeted. ≡ Surprisingly, Mack was in the bottom half of league centers in blown blocks, with 11, double his number with the Browns the season before. It was a trend that extended to the rest of the line, all of whom ranked 23rd or lower at their position. The caveat here is that our charting is not grading how often a block is good or average, just counting the ones that are obviously really screwed up. ≡ Left tackle Jake Matthews was the highly regarded early draft pick, while right tackle Ryan Schraeder wasn't drafted at all, but it's the mammoth (6-foot-7, 300-pound) Schraeder who has been the better pro, and who was rewarded with a $33-million extension last fall. Matthews had his fifth-year option picked up despite ostensibly regressing in his third season. Matthews ranked in the top five among left tackles in snaps per blown block two years ago, only to plummet to the bottom five in 2016. Thus far he has scarcely resembled his Hall of Fame father, Bruce. ≡ Andy Levitre has been passable as a Falcon, but is 31, and Chris Chester, who was mediocre last season, has retired, leaving guard an area of concern. Wes Schweitzer, a sixth-round pick out of San Jose State in 2016, enters training camp as the frontrunner to succeed Chester. A chemistry major, Schweitzer should understand the importance of working well together with his linemates. The Falcons picked Sean Harlow out of Oregon State in the fourth round this April to compete for the spot as well. Both Schweitzer and Harlow are strong, unathletic types who are transitioning from collegiate careers spent at tackle. Harlow at least has the bloodlines—his father Pat was a star tackle at USC and was a first-round choice of the Patriots back in 1991.

Defensive Front Seven

Defensive Line	Age	Pos	G	Snaps	Plays	TmPct	Rk	Stop	Dfts	BTkl	Runs	St%	Rk	RuYd	Rk	Sack	Hit	Hur	Dsrpt
						Overall							vs. Run				Pass Rush		
Grady Jarrett	24	DT	16	630	48	5.7%	25	32	10	7	41	66%	75	2.2	39	3.0	7	20	0
Jonathan Babineaux*	36	DT	16	426	23	2.8%	--	17	4	9	19	79%	--	2.4	--	0.0	2	12	1
Courtney Upshaw	28	DT	13	310	24	3.5%	--	21	6	4	18	89%	--	1.9	--	1.0	2	7	1
Dontari Poe	27	DT	16	821	30	3.5%	65	22	5	5	22	68%	66	3.0	72	1.5	9	18	6

Edge Rushers	Age	Pos	G	Snaps	Plays	TmPct	Rk	Stop	Dfts	BTkl	Runs	St%	Rk	RuYd	Rk	Sack	Hit	Hur	Dsrpt
						Overall							vs. Run				Pass Rush		
Vic Beasley	25	OLB	16	671	41	4.9%	48	32	24	7	18	67%	76	1.9	29	15.5	5	38	1
Adrian Clayborn	29	DE	13	583	21	3.1%	83	16	8	6	15	73%	53	2.9	66	4.5	12	22	0
Brooks Reed	30	DE	15	425	21	2.7%	93	17	5	3	16	75%	42	2.1	35	2.0	5	17	1
Dwight Freeney*	37	DE	15	415	8	1.0%	100	7	6	0	4	75%	42	3.0	67	3.0	7	29	2
Tyson Jackson*	31	DE	16	329	14	1.7%	--	9	1	3	12	58%	--	3.0	--	0.0	1	3	1
Ra'Shede Hageman	27	DE	12	265	18	2.9%	--	12	3	1	13	69%	--	2.1	--	2.0	3	7	0
Jack Crawford	29	DE	16	529	25	3.1%	84	16	7	4	19	58%	94	3.5	87	3.5	2	8	0

Linebackers	Age	Pos	G	Snaps	Plays	TmPct	Rk	Stop	Dfts	BTkl	Runs	St%	Rk	RuYd	Rk	Sack	Hit	Hur	Tgts	Suc%	Rk	AdjYd	Rk	PD	Int
						Overall							vs. Run				Pass Rush				vs. Pass				
Deion Jones	23	MLB	15	896	117	14.9%	22	54	22	12	48	58%	64	4.6	80	0.0	3	2	54	49%	38	4.8	8	10	3
De'Vondre Campbell	24	OLB	11	547	55	9.6%	60	26	11	5	27	59%	62	3.0	19	0.0	0	3	30	40%	64	6.3	34	7	1
Philip Wheeler*	33	OLB	16	339	27	3.2%	--	20	8	6	19	74%	--	3.1	--	0.0	2	4	9	40%	--	10.0	--	0	0
Sean Weatherspoon*	30	OLB	4	190	27	12.9%	--	9	3	4	11	18%	--	5.5	--	0.0	0	0	14	50%	--	9.2	--	0	0
Paul Worrilow*	27	MLB	12	162	20	3.2%	--	11	4	3	12	58%	--	3.2	--	0.0	1	2	7	62%	--	7.0	--	2	0
LaRoy Reynolds	27	MLB	16	138	23	2.8%	--	12	3	4	11	73%	--	2.6	--	0.0	1	1	6	34%	--	9.0	--	0	0

Year	Yards	ALY	Rank	Power	Rank	Stuff	Rank	2nd Level	Rank	Open Field	Rank	Sacks	ASR	Rank	Press	Rank
2014	4.09	4.45	24	80%	30	15%	30	1.11	12	0.54	6	22	4.5%	30	22.2%	26
2015	4.06	4.14	19	73%	27	18%	22	1.15	20	0.80	17	19	3.7%	32	21.5%	31
2016	4.28	4.47	25	63%	16	19%	18	1.29	26	0.64	13	34	5.4%	24	26.4%	20

2016 ALY by direction:	Left End 3.83 (12)	Left Tackle 3.94 (13)	Mid/Guard 4.56 (26)	Right Tackle 5.37 (32)	Right End 4.28 (24)

Vic Beasley had an unusually high success rate when it came to sacks. His 15.5 led the NFL, but he only knocked the quarterback down five other times, easily the fewest among players with double-digit sacks. We charted him with 38 hurries, giving him a sack/hit/hurry total of 58.5, good but hardly in the vicinity of Kahlil Mack (81) or Olivier Vernon (88). Even a relatively unheralded rusher like Philly's Brandon Graham amassed 77.5. Such a ratio naturally suggests a 2017 regression in his sack total. ☙ Beasley feasted on rookie quarterbacks—8.5 of his total came against Jared Goff, Paxton Lynch, and Carson Wentz—and benefitted from poor pocket awareness on many of his takedowns. His favorite ploy was to swat away the ball as he flew by. Beasley forced a league-leading six fumbles (tied with Bruce Irvin). ☙ The Falcons may list Beasley as a linebacker on their depth chart, but 13 of his sacks came from a three-point stance. ☙ Beasley disappeared completely in the postseason (no sacks and just two tackles in three games), part of why Atlanta traded up to draft what it hopes will be a bookend pass-rusher, Takkarist McKinley out of UCLA. McKinley was a relentless, high-energy player in college, to say nothing of the relentless high energy he showed on stage in Philadelphia after the Falcons selected him. He comes with injury concerns (he needed shoulder surgery in March, which could keep him out through training camp) and a lack of refinement to go with his all-out aggression. Beasley needed some coaching up too, so the hope is Dan Quinn and his staff will unlock similar production given the talent they have to work with. SackSEER penalizes him slightly for his poor testing numbers (his 3-cone time ranked in the 14th percentile among edge rushers), but his elite junior-year production leads to a promising overall outlook. If nothing else, McKinley can club enemy passers with the giant portrait of his late grandmother that he toted to the draft. ☙ Atlanta had major issues when teams ran to the right, finishing last in the NFL in that split. Neither Adrian Clayborn nor Dwight Freeney, last year's left defensive ends, are really employed for their run defense. ☙ Atlanta's poor numbers in second-level yards suggest a weakness at linebacker. Deion Jones had a quality rookie season but needs help, so the Falcons went back to Baton Rouge and picked up another LSU linebacker, Duke Riley, in the third round. Riley is a reliable tackler who lacks athleticism but should be an improvement over the likes of Paul Worrilow and Philip Wheeler. ☙ Grady Jarrett's breakout Super Bowl hinted at his immense gifts, mainly his quick first step. Jarrett doubled his defeat total from his rookie season and accrued 20 hurries after just two in 2015. He could form a dastardly tackle combo with free-agent pickup Dontari Poe. Poe fell out of favor in Kansas City due to weight, back, and character issues. But if focused and healthy, he can be a tremendous interior disruptor. He fits Atlanta's scheme better than the one in K.C. and is a bargain on a one-year, $8 million deal. Even in a down season he hit/hurried the passer as often as Jarrett, to go with six disruptions. So long as Poe sticks to ordering his Waffle House hash browns merely scattered, as opposed to smothered and covered, he should beat out Derrick Shelby as the starter. ☙ Tackle Jonathan Babineaux retired after seemingly 1,119 seasons with the Falcons, but Atlanta added free-agent end Jack Crawford from Dallas, giving the team enviable depth along its front.

Defensive Secondary

Secondary	Age	Pos	G	Snaps	Plays	Overall TmPct	Rk	Stop	Dfts	BTkl	vs. Run Runs	St%	Rk	RuYd	Rk	vs. Pass Tgts	Tgt%	Rk	Dist	Suc%	Rk	AdjYd	Rk	PD	Int
Ricardo Allen	26	FS	16	1101	93	11.1%	22	11	6	7	44	14%	73	12.5	73	27	5.0%	3	17.2	48%	32	9.0	41	3	2
Robert Alford	29	CB	16	1080	78	9.3%	30	35	12	6	15	27%	70	7.8	59	87	16.8%	23	12.0	50%	37	7.5	42	19	2
Keanu Neal	22	SS	14	920	111	15.2%	3	33	10	7	35	31%	54	5.0	12	71	16.1%	73	8.3	49%	26	6.3	7	9	0
Brian Poole	25	CB	16	835	68	8.1%	52	30	13	10	18	50%	19	6.9	47	55	13.7%	2	8.4	46%	61	7.2	30	10	1
Desmond Trufant	27	CB	9	591	34	7.2%	70	9	5	1	5	40%	41	5.6	21	44	15.3%	10	12.3	49%	43	6.1	11	4	1
Jalen Collins	24	CB	8	424	40	9.6%	26	16	11	6	5	20%	78	10.0	74	51	24.8%	82	11.9	51%	32	7.7	47	9	2
Kemal Ishmael	26	SS/LB	13	310	51	7.5%	--	16	8	7	19	42%	--	4.3	--	19	12.8%	--	4.9	37%	--	7.4	--	2	0

Year	Pass D Rank	vs. #1 WR	Rk	vs. #2 WR	Rk	vs. Other WR	Rk	vs. TE	Rk	vs. RB	Rk
2014	31	-12.9%	8	28.9%	28	15.7%	27	-8.9%	12	27.4%	30
2015	22	-11.1%	7	8.0%	20	-11.7%	7	-14.0%	6	31.9%	32
2016	18	-3.4%	11	-5.6%	8	14.5%	27	-5.6%	12	16.5%	25

The offense got all the credit for the Super Bowl run, but the secondary's performance in the second half of the season and the playoffs was a crucial element in the Falcons' success. Three of their best four pass defense performances by DVOA came in the final month—even more impressive since these games came after the unit's best player, Desmond Trufant, was lost for the season with a torn pectoral muscle. ☙ Trufant should be healthy to start 2017, meaning Robert Alford and Brian Poole can return to their more natural spots while Trufant takes the top role. The lack of depth turned up in the splits of DVOA against types of wide receivers, as the Falcons were significantly worse covering slot receivers. You can also see this in Poole's placement as one of the most targeted cornerbacks in the league. ☙ We charted only two cornerbacks with more passes defensed than Alford (one of whom, Brent Grimes, Alford was drafted to replace). Like Trufant, Alford was rewarded with a contract extension.

If both are healthy, it's a sturdy, unheralded corner combo. ≋ The Falcons moved cornerbacks around the field much more in 2016 than they did the year before, dropping from eighth to 30th in "CB by Sides," and the usage pattern did not change after Trufant's injury. ≋ Running backs also hurt Atlanta in the passing game, which is ironic given both Dan Quinn's emphasis on speedy personnel and Atlanta's own success throwing to its backs. Apparently practicing against the likes of Devonta Freeman and Tevin Coleman didn't help much. ≋ Strong safety Keanu Neal turned in a solid rookie season, particularly against the pass, where his willingness to thump dudes and generally play on the margins of the law clearly affected opposing receivers. He also missed just seven tackles, good for a 10 percent missed tackle rate which ranked in the top 25th percentile of all DBs with at least 25 tackles. Not bad considering his weakness coming out of Florida was bringing down ballcarriers. ≋ The Falcons had the biggest gap between average location of tackles by their two starting safeties, showing the preference for playing Ricardo Allen in centerfield with Neal close to stop the run. Seattle-influenced defenses ranked 1-2 in this stat, with Jacksonville second while the Seahawks themselves were seventh.

Special Teams

Year	DVOA	Rank	FG/XP	Rank	Net Kick	Rank	Kick Ret	Rank	Net Punt	Rank	Punt Ret	Rank	Hidden	Rank
2014	3.0%	9	8.8	2	-6.2	26	-0.3	16	5.2	8	7.7	6	-1.2	20
2015	-2.1%	22	-4.3	28	-3.9	26	0.2	13	-4.6	21	2.1	12	7.8	5
2016	2.5%	7	11.1	2	-3.0	25	-1.7	19	2.1	12	3.8	9	-4.3	22

The high overall unit DVOA was mostly driven by the continued excellence of kicker Matt Bryant. Only the otherworldly Justin Tucker had more value on field goals and extra points, though comparisons between the two aren't particularly relevant. Bryant was two points ahead of the third-place kicker, Chris Boswell of Pittsburgh, but 14.4 (!) points behind Tucker. ≋ Matt Bosher handled punts and kickoffs, though far more of the latter. His 44 punts were the fewest in the league, while his 105 kickoffs were the most in the NFL since Matt Prater in 2013. In this case, the higher the workload, the lesser the efficiency, as Bosher was a good punter (seventh in gross punt value) but below-average on kickoffs. ≋ Eric Weems pulled double duty as a return man, but has left for Tennessee. He will be most likely be replaced by free-agent signee Andre Roberts, who was even better than Weems on punt returns last year with Detroit, though not as good on kickoffs. Receiver Justin Hardy should get some opportunities as well.

Baltimore Ravens

2016 Record: 8-8	Total DVOA: 7.4% (12th)	2017 Mean Projection: 8.1 wins	On the Clock (0-4): 8%
Pythagorean Wins: 8.6 (13th)	Offense: -7.5% (24th)	Postseason Odds: 38.0%	Mediocrity (5-7): 32%
Snap-Weighted Age: 27.4 (2nd)	Defense: -9.9% (6th)	Super Bowl Odds: 3.9%	Playoff Contender (8-10): 41%
Average Opponent: 1.7% (7th)	Special Teams: 4.9% (4th)	Proj. Avg. Opponent: -0.8% (25th)	Super Bowl Contender (11+): 19%

2016: An offense so monotonous they made the kicker interesting.

2017: An offense so monotonous they will make the kicker interesting.

For the better part of the last 20 years, the Baltimore Ravens have been AFC royalty. Since stepping onto the scene in 2000 with a Super Bowl win and one of the best defenses in NFL history, the Ravens have finished with a losing record only four times. They've made the playoffs 10 times in 17 years and won two Super Bowls. Look past the Patriots dynasty, and their success is basically equivalent to any other team in that timespan, including the rival Steelers.

But times have been hard in Baltimore lately, even though their philosophy on defense and special teams is clearly working. Through Week 12, the Ravens were on pace to post the best run defense DVOA on record, shattering the record of minus-36.6% set by their own franchise in that 2000 season. But they then allowed 95, 169, 127, and 153 rushing yards during the last four weeks of the seasons as they fell from 7-5 to 8-8. None of their main front seven defenders missed much time in this stretch, except for Zach Orr sitting out Week 17. Instead, it seemed as if the unit just wore down. They finished fifth in run defense DVOA.

The Ravens were also boosted by the efforts of kicker Justin Tucker, who set a record in our measurement of placekicking value by adding 25.5 points over an average kicker. All Baltimore had to do was find the right side of the field, and Tucker would deliver for them. Baltimore finished fourth in special teams DVOA because of Tucker's leg, despite a lack of explosive returns. While this isn't something that we should count on happening again, it means a lot to the Ravens that they have a kicker who can reasonably be compared to peak Sebastian Janikowski (Table 1).

So Baltimore got two best-case scenarios from these two units, including a massive bounceback season from a defense that finished 20th in DVOA in 2015, and they still managed to go just 8-8. The Ravens were held back, yet again, by their offense.

In the heart of snarky writers, Baltimore's scrappy, through-the-trenches offense has become synonymous with the quest to win 13-9 and 10-7 games. But since Gary Kubiak left for Denver's head coaching job, you just need to drop the "s" in scrappy to realize what Baltimore has become on the offensive side of the ball.

It's easy to tell this tale through the eyes of noted elite quarterback Joe Flacco, Super Bowl champion. It's even easy to tell the tale of Flacco's enormous contract limiting the Ravens, who have had to be thrifty in free agency even as the cap has continually swelled. It's hard to maintain a power run game when you develop players such as guard Kelechi Osemele and tackle Rick Wagner and have to watch them walk because you can't afford them. It's hard to build a deep passing game when you can't afford to keep Torrey Smith. Flacco's cap figure this year is $24.5 million, the highest number for any active player in the NFL and nearly double the second-highest Raven (Jimmy Smith, $12.6 million). Flacco, unlike some quarterbacks, adds nothing as a runner to hold defenders in the box. There is no extra layer of hidden value that goes beyond the stats here. Flacco is a classic pocket passer who has thrown 34 touchdowns and 27 interceptions over the past two seasons, in a league that is increasingly becoming more about what your quarterback can do that is unique or different. The Ravens have become stale, and while they should have tempered expectations for Flacco as he returned from a 2015 torn ACL, his play is a big part of the reason that Baltimore is where it is.

Since Flacco plays an old-time style, it's no real surprise that looking for comparable quarterbacks means you encounter a stunning amount of old-time quarterbacks. The career comparables to Flacco on Pro Football Reference are led by names like Daryle Lamonica and Ken O'Brien. The only modern quarterbacks on the 10-player list are Alex Smith, Jay Cutler, David Garrard, and Jon Kitna. Flacco is headed into his age 32 season, and with the exception of the active Smith, Kitna is the only quarterback on the list who was a full-time starter past the age of 33. Medical technology being what it is, it's pretty hard to

Table 1. Best Kickers in FO's FG Pts+ Metric, 1986-2016

Year	Team	FG Pts +	FG Pts+, Y+1	Kicker
2016	BAL	+25.5	--	Justin Tucker
2005	ARI	+19.6	-2.8	Neil Rackers
1998	MIN	+19.1	-16.9	Gary Anderson
1997	KC	+17.4	+2.9	Pete Stoyanavich
1989	DET	+16.7	-8.6	Eddie Murray
2011	OAK	+16.6	+11.8	Sebastian Janikowski
1990	KC	+16.6	+4.3	Nick Lowery
2003	IND	+15.9	-4.6	Mike Vanderjagt
2002	NE	+15.6	-13.6	Adam Vinatieri
2009	OAK	+15.0	+3.6	Sebastian Janikowski
2003	STL	+14.7	+0.4	Jeff Wilkins

2017 Ravens Schedule

Week	Opp.	Week	Opp.	Week	Opp.
1	at CIN	7	at MIN	13	DET
2	CLE	8	MIA (Thu.)	14	at PIT
3	at JAC (U.K.)	9	at TEN	15	at CLE
4	PIT	10	BYE	16	IND (Sat.)
5	at OAK	11	at GB	17	CIN
6	CHI	12	HOU (Mon.)		

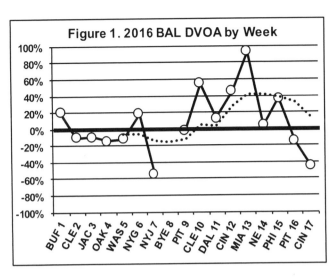

imagine injuries ending Flacco's career as easily as those suffered by quarterbacks in the '70s and '80s. But it's pretty startling to look at this list and think that a player similar to these guys is regarded as a true franchise quarterback.

Flacco, quite frankly, throws a lot of interceptable passes. Per Cian Fahey's charting in his *Pre-Snap Reads QB Catalogue 2017*, Flacco ranked sixth in the league last year. He had an even higher percentage of interceptable passes in 2014 when Kubiak schemed him into success. This is a quarterback who is prone to making dumb plays and not reading coverages correctly. When Flacco had success early in his career, it was because the passing game was complementary. When Flacco had success with Kubiak, it was because Kubiak fully understood how to use him. Kubiak understood that Flacco didn't really handle pressure well, so he drew up quick-hitters on pass-rush plays, and the Ravens managed 7.6 yards per attempt that season on the 38 percent of pass plays where defenses sent five or more rushers. All quarterbacks struggle under pressure, but in 2014, Flacco averaged 4.0 yards per attempt when it happened. In every other year from 2013 to 2016, he failed to crack 3.1 yards per attempt. And despite Flacco's big arm, the Ravens have been a terrible play-action team in each of the last three seasons. On a play where the average DVOA over the last three years is 11% to 15% higher than on a standard pass, Flacco's Ravens managed a minus-26.8% DVOA in 2016. They were one of only two teams to have a negative DVOA on play-action passes. They were at 5.0% in 2015, again second-worst in the league. But under Kubiak in 2014, the Ravens finished with a 30.3% play-action pass DVOA. That was the year where Torrey Smith drew 11 defensive pass interference penalties and the second-place finisher, Jordy Nelson, had six.

(Read that paragraph again, and replace the words "Flacco" and "Kubiak" with "Colin Kaepernick" and "Greg Roman." Ask yourself why one of these quarterbacks has the highest cap hit in the NFL and the other one is jobless. Rahim Moore? One goal-line stand and some kneels?)

It's not really fair to blame Flacco for making the money, of course. All he did was sign a contract that was offered to him. But by offering him the contract in the first place, one that valued him higher than all but a few quarterbacks in the NFL, the Ravens upped the difficulty level of their cap management. And where that has culminated this offseason is that Baltimore has nobody dangerous to catch the football.

Steve Smith, a Hall of Famer on his last tank of gas, officially retired. Dennis Pitta, a reliable underneath tight end who led Baltimore in targets in 2016, was released after re-dislocating his hip in OTAs. Kamar Aiken was allowed to join the Colts late in free

agency, and fullback Kyle Juszczyk signed a big deal with the 49ers. Say what you will about the quality of these players at this point, but that's four of the six most-targeted Ravens receivers in 2016. The Ravens employ zero players who caught more than 50 passes for them in each of the last two years, and just one who was targeted 100 times last year: the enigmatic Mike Wallace.

This has been Baltimore's M.O. for years. The Ravens love to take older, skilled receivers and make a passing offense with them. From Derrick Mason to Anquan Boldin to Smith, there hasn't been a season since 2006 that has elapsed without the Baltimore roster featuring an older Hall Of Very Good (or better) receiver let go by his original team. So it was no real surprise that the Ravens pounced all over Jeremy Maclin when the Chiefs released him. Per media reports in Baltimore, the Chiefs were concerned that Maclin had lost a step. That doesn't mean Maclin can't catch 100 balls here—someone has to—but if he doesn't add the deep threat, the Ravens still won't be able to keep defenses honest.

But let's share some words from John Harbaugh's final press availability at the end of the season, when we learned that Marty Mornhinweg would be back as offensive coordinator. "Marty was here, and Marty is a part of that system, but Marty has been coaching this offense since the late '80s. He started in the San Francisco system and through the [Mike] Holmgren system. That's a system I'm familiar with. It's the basic system they're running in Kansas City right now, and it's a good system for us. "

The word to focus on there is "familiar." Harbaugh fired Cam Cameron, replaced him with Jim Caldwell on an interim basis, then went to Kubiak and got instant results. Somehow what Harbaugh learned out of that exchange was not "changing up bad things with smart offensive minds leads to results" but instead "Joe Flacco must run the West Coast offense." Flacco has spent the last two seasons proving that without the Kubiak wrinkles, the West Coast offense doesn't help. The Chiefs finished 13th in offensive DVOA last year with sparkplugs like Tyreek Hill and Travis Kelce and the active quarterback with the career most similar to Flacco's. The closest thing the Ravens have to exciting on offense is Breshad Perriman, a burner who has started one game in two seasons. Trying to emulate Kansas City's offense without Kansas City's dynamic offensive personnel is like trying to run League of Legends on Windows 98.

The Ravens face a choice. After two years of Marc Trestman's Dumpoff Fiesta (if you buy the line that Mornhinweg was coaching with Trestman's playbook), it's clear that the Ravens need to run the ball a lot more to succeed. Baltimore's offense ranked seventh in their average lead per drive, yet only two teams had fewer rushing attempts (Table 2). The only other team with an average lead and rushing total anywhere near Baltimore's last year was Green Bay, and they A) have the best quarterback in the game and B) had to turn a wide receiver into their starting running back. The Ravens don't even have the excuse that the rushing game was unproductive, as Terrance West and Kenneth Dixon were each right around the league average in rushing DVOA. West was a spectacular reclamation project, and Dixon has true three-down ability if he ever stays on the field for a full season. (A PED suspension will cost him the first four games in 2017.) The offensive line could use some work, but so could the line for about 27 other teams, and those teams don't employ Marshal Yanda.

But just how much do they want to run the ball? Do they want to become like the Texans, a team that grinds clock at every opportunity and hopes to pile up wins while they hide their quarterback? Or do they just want to strive for a balance and hope that it somehow creates 2014 Flacco all over again? The Ravens can definitely compete no matter the offensive talent level, but it seems that a lot of the 50/50 games may come down to just how much faith they have in Flacco, and how much he rewards them for it.

The defense is still good, and after a meat and potatoes draft by general manager Ozzie Newsome, it's as stacked as a unit with questions about the individual pass-rushing talent can be. Our projection system tends to like teams that spend a lot of draft capital on defense, because the effect of defensive rookies is more predictable than the effect of offensive rookies. The projections say Baltimore has an easy schedule, despite predicting a strong season for Pittsburgh and some rebound from Cincin-

Table 2. Top 10 Teams in Average Lead per Offensive Possession, 2016

Team	Average Lead	Rush Attempts	Rank
NE	7.41	482	2
ATL	4.92	421	12
DAL	2.99	499	1
SEA	0.95	403	20
SD	0.85	398	22
GB	0.66	374	29
BAL	**0.60**	**367**	**30**
PIT	0.49	409	17
KC	0.29	412	14
CIN	0.13	446	9

nati. We also expect another valuable year for Baltimore special teams, which have ranked in the top four for five straight years. Even if Tucker is not as good as he was a year ago, it will probably be balanced out by better years from punter Sam Koch and the return game. This is why, despite some projected regression for the defense and a bland, gruel-esque offense, our mean projection puts the Ravens on the cusp of a playoff spot.

But the longer-term future of the franchise revolves around a way to bring the offense back to respectability, be it with Flacco as a supporting cog in a run-first offense, by finding more talented skill position players for him to do the work, or through an unlikely career renaissance at age 32. The results have not matched the reputation for a long time. Harbaugh tends to have a lot of patience with the people he trusts most, as you might have guessed from his quote about Mornhinweg and how long he employed Cameron.

But if Flacco makes it three straight duds, the spirit of the debate will shift from "is he elite?" to "is he still a starter?"

Rivers McCown

2016 Ravens Stats by Week

Wk	vs.	W-L	PF	PA	YDF	YDA	TO	Total	Off	Def	ST
1	BUF	W	13	7	308	160	-1	20%	-24%	-46%	-2%
2	at CLE	W	25	20	382	387	0	-11%	-18%	13%	21%
3	at JAC	W	19	17	283	216	0	-10%	-36%	-26%	0%
4	OAK	L	27	28	412	261	0	-14%	-8%	-5%	-12%
5	WAS	L	10	16	306	310	+1	-12%	-17%	-28%	-24%
6	at NYG	L	23	27	391	435	+3	18%	10%	1%	9%
7	at NYJ	L	16	24	245	344	-1	-54%	-64%	-3%	7%
8	BYE										
9	PIT	W	21	14	274	277	0	-2%	-52%	-37%	14%
10	CLE	W	28	7	396	144	+1	55%	0%	-50%	5%
11	at DAL	L	17	27	368	417	0	13%	34%	19%	-2%
12	CIN	W	19	14	311	325	+1	45%	-14%	-32%	27%
13	MIA	W	38	6	496	277	+1	93%	54%	-32%	8%
14	at NE	L	23	30	348	496	+2	4%	-13%	-1%	15%
15	PHI	W	27	26	340	328	-1	37%	19%	-16%	1%
16	at PIT	L	27	31	368	406	+1	-15%	15%	36%	6%
17	at CIN	L	10	27	335	371	-2	-44%	-15%	34%	5%

Trends and Splits

	Offense	Rank	Defense	Rank
Total DVOA	-7.5%	24	-9.9%	6
Unadjusted VOA	-3.7%	19	-6.3%	9
Weighted Trend	0.1%	15	-5.8%	12
Variance	9.1%	27	7.3%	29
Average Opponent	0.9%	24	3.1%	4
Passing	-0.8%	26	-0.9%	10
Rushing	-8.5%	21	-23.6%	4
First Down	-2.0%	17	-13.0%	5
Second Down	-19.3%	29	2.5%	18
Third Down	1.1%	15	-22.2%	2
First Half	-4.0%	20	-6.5%	11
Second Half	-16.6%	25	-19.6%	4
Red Zone	-13.8%	23	3.4%	22
Late and Close	-14.8%	23	-24.1%	5

Five-Year Performance

Year	W-L	Pyth W	Est W	PF	PA	TO	Total	Rk	Off	Rk	Def	Rk	ST	Rk	Off AGL	Rk	Def AGL	Rk	Off Age	Rk	Def Age	Rk	ST Age	Rk
2012	10-6	9.4	9.2	398	344	+9	9.8%	8	3.0%	13	2.2%	19	9.0%	1	8.1	2	46.4	25	27.3	10	27.7	7	26.9	7
2013	8-8	7.1	6.8	320	352	-5	-6.7%	23	-21.7%	30	-8.7%	7	6.3%	3	34.0	16	13.4	5	26.6	18	27.5	6	25.9	22
2014	10-6	10.9	11.5	409	302	+2	21.9%	5	9.4%	9	-4.6%	8	8.0%	2	25.0	10	27.6	8	27.4	8	26.8	15	25.4	31
2015	5-11	6.0	7.5	328	401	-14	-3.0%	17	-5.2%	20	5.1%	20	7.3%	1	70.1	32	26.0	12	26.5	18	27.1	10	25.6	27
2016	8-8	8.6	9.1	343	321	+5	7.4%	12	-7.5%	24	-9.9%	6	4.9%	4	29.4	12	30.9	14	28.0	3	27.2	5	26.1	18

2016 Performance Based on Most Common Personnel Groups

BAL Offense					BAL Offense vs. Opponents					BAL Defense					BAL Defense vs. Opponents			
Pers	Freq	Yds	DVOA	Run%	Pers	Freq	Yds	DVOA	Run%	Pers	Freq	Yds	DVOA	Pers	Freq	Yds	DVOA	
11	57%	5.6	3.2%	26%	Base	32%	5.7	2.0%	47%	Base	31%	5.0	-15.6%	11	64%	5.7	-5.3%	
12	19%	5.5	-0.2%	30%	Nickel	59%	5.1	-6.2%	27%	Nickel	62%	5.4	-8.9%	12	14%	5.2	-8.5%	
21	11%	5.0	-6.9%	50%	Dime+	7%	6.6	20.4%	3%	Dime+	5%	8.2	10.3%	21	6%	4.4	-23.9%	
13	4%	4.5	-37.3%	61%	Goal Line	1%	0.8	-101.9%	89%	Goal Line	1%	1.0	0.1%	621	2%	4.1	8.0%	
20	3%	6.5	22.0%	42%						Big	1%	2.2	-6.8%	13	2%	2.6	-45.4%	
22	2%	3.1	-68.6%	43%										611	2%	8.3	29.0%	

Strategic Tendencies

Run/Pass		Rk	Formation		Rk	Pass Rush		Rk	Secondary		Rk	Strategy		Rk
Runs, first half	30%	31	Form: Single Back	78%	18	Rush 3	5.7%	18	4 DB	31%	14	Play-action	18%	15
Runs, first down	43%	28	Form: Empty Back	8%	13	Rush 4	66.3%	14	5 DB	62%	13	Avg Box (Off)	6.17	17
Runs, second-long	26%	25	Pers: 3+ WR	62%	23	Rush 5	23.3%	11	6+ DB	5%	20	Avg Box (Def)	6.22	18
Runs, power sit.	53%	22	Pers: 2+ TE/6+ OL	27%	15	Rush 6+	4.6%	25	CB by Sides	83%	13	Offensive Pace	30.18	10
Runs, behind 2H	25%	21	Pers: 6+ OL	2%	25	Sacks by LB	54.8%	11	S/CB Cover Ratio	29%	10	Defensive Pace	30.50	20
Pass, ahead 2H	51%	9	Shotgun/Pistol	61%	21	Sacks by DB	9.7%	8	DB Blitz	8%	20	Go for it on 4th	1.17	10

Last season continued an odd trend for Joe Flacco: for three years, he's been better against a blitz, but not a big blitz. Last year, Flacco averaged 9.3 yards per pass against a five-man pass rush, but just 5.3 yards against three or four pass-rushers and just 5.1 yards against six or more. ☞ Reasons the Ravens may miss Kyle Juszczyk: Baltimore had 4.9 yards per carry and 7.4% DVOA with two backs compared to 3.7 yards per carry and minus-22.8% DVOA with just one back. ☞ Baltimore ranked second with 145 broken tackles after ranking near the bottom of the league with just 81 in 2015. Most of the change came from running backs, switching out Buck Allen (23 in 2015) and Justin Forsett (12) for Kenneth Dixon (34 in 2016) and Terrance West (49 on 227 touches in 2016 after eight on 66 touches in 2015). ☞ The Ravens had a league-high 37 percent of passes marked "middle" and a league-low 25 percent of passes marked "left." No other offense had fewer than 32 percent of passes marked left or more than 30 percent of passes marked middle. However, this may have been an issue with the official scorer preferences, because the Baltimore defense also faced the highest rate of passes marked "middle" (32 percent). Or perhaps this was just strategic, because the Ravens ranked ninth in offensive DVOA on middle passes but 29th on passes to the right and dead last on passes to the left. ☞ Baltimore opponents threw to their No. 3 or "other" wide receivers on a league-low 14 percent of passes. ☞ Baltimore had the league's largest gap between defense against single-back runs (3.5 yards per carry, minus-36.5% DVOA) and defense against multi-back runs (4.8, 2.4%). This seems to be a regular problem, as they also had a large gap in 2015. ☞ The Ravens had the No. 1 defensive DVOA in the league at home but ranked 23rd in defensive DVOA on the road.

Passing

Player	DYAR	DVOA	Plays	NtYds	Avg	YAC	C%	TD	Int
J.Flacco	-155	-14.6%	700	4055	5.8	4.8	65.7%	20	14
R.Mallett	-29	-84.9%	6	26	4.3	6.3	50.0%	0	1

Rushing

Player	DYAR	DVOA	Plays	Yds	Avg	TD	Fum	Suc
T.West	-3	-9.0%	165	661	4.0	5	0	44%
K.Dixon	29	2.9%	57	245	4.3	3	0	54%
J.Forsett*	-30	-34.0%	31	98	3.2	0	0	35%
J.Flacco	21	15.8%	12	64	5.3	2	0	-
B.Allen	-3	-18.0%	9	34	3.8	0	0	56%
M.Wallace	18	15.3%	5	31	6.2	0	0	-
D.Woodhead	30	33.7%	19	116	6.1	0	0	63%

Receiving

Player	DYAR	DVOA	Plays	Ctch	Yds	Y/C	YAC	TD	C%
M.Wallace	114	0.0%	116	72	1017	14.1	5.8	4	62%
S.Smith	158	7.2%	101	70	799	11.4	4.0	5	69%
B.Perriman	21	-8.7%	66	33	499	15.1	5.2	3	50%
K.Aiken*	-11	-15.5%	50	29	328	11.3	3.4	1	58%
C.Moore	-68	-66.1%	16	7	46	6.6	2.7	0	44%
J.Maclin	50	-4.3%	76	44	536	12.2	3.1	2	58%
D.Pitta*	-96	-19.7%	121	86	729	8.5	3.4	2	71%
D.Waller	-10	-15.1%	17	10	85	8.5	3.9	2	59%
C.Gillmore	-17	-26.3%	14	8	71	8.9	4.1	1	57%
N.Boyle	0	-7.7%	6	6	44	7.3	3.5	0	100%
K.Juszczyk*	6	-11.9%	49	37	266	7.2	5.9	0	76%
T.West	50	4.9%	45	34	236	6.9	7.0	1	76%
K.Dixon	-14	-20.6%	41	30	162	5.4	6.2	1	73%
J.Forsett*	-20	-38.6%	15	12	36	3.0	3.0	0	80%
D.Woodhead	18	26.0%	8	6	35	5.8	5.2	1	75%

Offensive Line

Player	Pos	Age	GS	Snaps	Pen	Sk	Pass	Run	Player	Pos	Age	GS	Snaps	Pen	Sk	Pass	Run
Jeremy Zuttah*	C	31	16/16	1109	6	4.0	10	4	Alex Lewis	LG/LT	25	10/8	538	4	1.0	4	2
Ricky Wagner*	RT	28	15/14	924	4	3.5	10	4	James Hurst	LT/RT	26	16/3	302	3	1.0	3	0
Marshal Yanda	RG	33	13/13	898	3	0.5	4	3	Ryan Jensen	C/G	26	7/3	272	2	0.0	3	0
Ronnie Stanley	LT	23	12/12	833	8	4.0	9	5	John Urschel	C/G	26	13/3	265	1	3.0	6	4
Vladimir Ducasse*	LG	30	10/8	554	6	1.5	6	5									

Year	Yards	ALY	Rank	Power	Rank	Stuff	Rank	2nd Lev	Rank	Open Field	Rank	Sacks	ASR	Rank	Press	Rank	F-Start	Cont.
2014	4.83	4.54	3	55%	28	21%	23	1.36	3	1.30	1	19	4.5%	4	23.0%	13	16	34
2015	3.97	4.22	14	54%	28	23%	25	1.21	11	0.62	21	24	3.8%	2	23.5%	12	18	25
2016	4.02	4.07	20	70%	9	20%	14	1.11	20	0.66	18	33	5.3%	8	26.9%	19	13	27

2016 ALY by direction:	Left End 4.32 (18)	Left Tackle 3.64 (25)	Mid/Guard 3.97 (24)	Right Tackle 3.92 (15)	Right End 6.02 (1)

Two Baltimore spots are well-assured. 2016 first-rounder Ronnie Stanley should stick at left tackle, looking to follow up a serviceable rookie season. And, of course, All-Pro guard Marshal Yanda will be mauling people inside. Yanda is getting long in the tooth, turning 33 in September, but his play has shown no sign of decline yet. In 2016, he made his sixth consecutive Pro Bowl (only cyborg/Twitter savant Joe Thomas has a longer streak among O-linemen) and finished fifth among right guards in snaps per blown block. He did, however, miss his first games since 2013 with a shoulder injury. ☞ The other spots are up for grabs after Rick Wagner's defection to Detroit and the trade of Jeremy Zuttah to San Francisco. Alex Lewis, who barely missed qualifying for our Top Prospects list on snaps, was playing left guard at OTAs. His play last year was spectacular, even when he had to fill in at left tackle briefly. Interior lineman John Urschel, the guy you know as the nerd in that J.J. Watt Bose commercial, should also start somewhere along the interior line. We could see either of them playing any position on the line (other than left tackle) based on who the fifth starter is. As far as blown blocks, both players played relatively clean last year. ☞ Ryan Jensen manned center at OTAs. Perhaps Baltimore's best alignment would be if fourth-round left guard Nico Siragusa—no, he's not related to *that* Siragusa—was able to start right away. That would force Lewis to right tackle and put Urschel at center. Siragusa's pass protection was questionable at San Diego State, but he should at least provide some beef up front for the Ravens this year. The top backup outside is the athletic James Hurst, who keeps getting chances to show why he went undrafted.

Defensive Front Seven

Defensive Line	Age	Pos	G	Snaps	Plays	Overall TmPct	Rk	Stop	Dfts	BTkl	Runs	vs. Run St%	Rk	RuYd	Rk	Sack	Pass Rush Hit	Hur	Dsrpt
Brandon Williams	28	DT	16	636	52	6.7%	17	43	8	2	50	82%	32	2.3	46	1.0	2	13	1
Timmy Jernigan*	25	DE	16	629	34	4.4%	46	31	14	1	24	92%	6	1.9	31	5.0	6	15	2
Lawrence Guy*	27	DE	16	484	26	3.4%	67	22	6	0	24	83%	26	1.8	29	1.0	9	16	1
Michael Pierce	25	DT	16	375	36	4.6%	--	34	10	1	33	94%	--	1.3	--	2.0	3	7	1

Edge Rushers	Age	Pos	G	Snaps	Plays	Overall TmPct	Rk	Stop	Dfts	BTkl	Runs	vs. Run St%	Rk	RuYd	Rk	Sack	Pass Rush Hit	Hur	Dsrpt
Terrell Suggs	35	OLB	15	695	38	5.2%	42	31	16	6	20	75%	42	1.0	9	8.0	9	24	6
Za'Darius Smith	25	OLB	13	494	19	3.0%	88	12	5	3	15	67%	76	3.2	77	1.0	4	16	1
Matt Judon	25	OLB	14	308	29	4.3%	--	15	7	2	19	47%	--	3.9	--	4.0	6	8	3
Elvis Dumervil*	33	OLB	8	272	11	2.8%	91	7	3	2	6	67%	76	3.7	91	3.0	6	24	0

Linebackers	Age	Pos	G	Snaps	Plays	Overall TmPct	Rk	Stop	Dfts	BTkl	Runs	vs. Run St%	Rk	RuYd	Rk	Pass Rush Sack	Hit	Hur	Tgts	vs. Pass Suc%	Rk	AdjYd	Rk	PD	Int
Zach Orr*	25	ILB	15	961	133	18.3%	7	77	26	14	75	71%	14	3.1	23	0.0	1	7	44	40%	63	8.8	75	5	3
C.J. Mosley	25	ILB	14	874	101	14.9%	23	41	14	11	48	52%	79	4.3	73	0.0	6	9	33	37%	73	8.9	77	7	4
Albert McClellan	31	ILB	16	603	52	6.7%	75	24	7	3	30	63%	44	3.4	35	1.0	1	4	18	40%	65	7.4	57	0	0

Year	Yards	ALY	Rank	Power	Rank	Stuff	Rank	2nd Level	Rank	Open Field	Rank	Sacks	ASR	Rank	Press	Rank
2014	3.53	3.80	7	55%	4	18%	19	0.86	2	0.46	2	49	8.0%	5	25.1%	15
2015	3.96	4.26	20	68%	21	18%	24	0.94	2	0.67	12	37	6.1%	19	23.9%	26
2016	3.82	3.95	10	50%	3	21%	12	1.05	8	0.59	11	31	5.7%	22	26.7%	19

2016 ALY by direction:	Left End 4.36 (18)	Left Tackle 5.12 (26)	Mid/Guard 3.82 (9)	Right Tackle 3.68 (8)	Right End 3.38 (11)

The Ravens didn't almost set an NFL record for run defense efficiency out of nowhere. Baltimore made it a big priority to re-sign nose tackle Brandon Williams, giving him $24.5 million fully guaranteed at signing and making him the second-highest paid defensive lineman in the league by average yearly value. Timmy Jernigan was the other player getting starter snaps at the position, but Jernigan was dealt to Philadelphia in the offseason in a salary-dump move. Jernigan actually had better run metrics than Williams, though that's likely a statement about who was facing the double-teams. ☞ The top candidates to get Jernigan's snaps are third-round rookie Chris Wormley and second-year UDFA Michael Pierce, who was incredible in a small sample size last season (94 percent run stop rate and 10 defeats). Wormley may also have been a bit of a steal. If you believe in the 10-yard split of the 40-yard dash is an important trait for defensive linemen, his 1.62-second split would be in the 80th percentile. Wormley, at 300 pounds, could grow into a physical mismatch between his speed and size, à la Sheldon Richardson. While none of the other linemen have been dominant or project to play much on passing downs, there's reason to think the Ravens can find solid depth snaps from Brent Urban, Willie Henry, Carl Davis, and Bronson Kaufusi. ☞ C.J. Mosley has become just what he seemed to be at Alabama: a stellar three-down linebacker. But next to him on the inside, the Ravens will have to fill the spot of Zach Orr, who surprisingly retired after just one year as a starter because of a congenital spinal condition. Kamalei Correa will get the first shot, though the 23-year-old is a fairly unknown quantity after moving over from outside linebacker. He's got the profile of the position athletically, but the instincts for pass coverage and run diagnosis are anyone's guess after a rookie year with just 48 defensive snaps. Long-time special teamer Albert McClellan is next in line. ☞ Should they falter, the best in-house candidate to replace Orr on passing downs is probably second-round pick Tyus Bowser. He played a hybrid role at the University of Houston, rushing the passer but also frequently asked to cover and be an overhang player. As shown in various Nintendo cartridges, Bowser has always been very versatile, even playing the reluctant hero in *Super Mario RPG*. Looking at the numbers, SackSEER loves Bowser, giving him a projection of 26.5 sacks in his first five seasons. His athletic profile screams upper-echelon pass-rusher, and the Ravens definitely need one of those as well. SackSEER may also be overrating Bowser because his hybrid role led to passes defensed that weren't necessarily passes batted down at the line of scrimmage. ☞ Terrell Suggs, the last of the legacy Ravens, continues to be a good edge player who still has the skill of his past even if the speed was left on the operating room table after his torn Achilles. Between Bowser and third-round pick Tim Williams, who had 19.5 sacks over the last two years at Alabama, the Ravens will hope they've found the right players to replace Suggs long-term. Elvis Dumervil's release opens up playing time on the outside, but the rookies will have to beat out Matt Judon on passing downs and Za'Darius Smith on running downs.

Defensive Secondary

| Secondary | Age | Pos | G | Snaps | Plays | Overall | | | | | vs. Run | | | | | vs. Pass | | | | | | | | | |
						TmPct	Rk	Stop	Dfts	BTkl	Runs	St%	Rk	RuYd	Rk	Tgts	Tgt%	Rk	Dist	Suc%	Rk	AdjYd	Rk	PD	Int
Eric Weddle	32	SS	16	1030	102	13.1%	9	50	15	6	53	58%	9	5.8	21	32	7.6%	28	11.0	53%	17	7.5	23	13	4
Lardarius Webb	32	FS	16	998	78	10.1%	37	19	8	11	20	25%	65	9.9	66	44	10.7%	57	11.0	35%	64	9.4	50	5	1
Tavon Young	23	CB	16	832	58	7.5%	68	32	17	11	8	38%	50	6.1	33	60	17.7%	35	8.3	50%	35	7.9	52	8	2
Shareece Wright*	30	CB	12	673	56	9.6%	24	23	7	8	14	43%	38	6.1	34	55	20.1%	56	12.4	53%	25	8.1	57	6	0
Jimmy Smith	29	CB	11	582	36	6.7%	77	15	4	2	3	67%	5	7.0	48	48	20.1%	55	12.3	54%	19	5.3	5	4	0
Jerraud Powers*	30	CB	13	508	38	6.0%	--	17	6	7	5	60%	--	3.6	--	31	15.0%	--	9.1	48%	--	4.8	--	5	2
Tony Jefferson	25	SS	15	928	97	12.6%	14	46	20	8	54	57%	11	4.1	4	36	9.3%	47	8.6	42%	49	7.1	15	4	0
Brandon Carr	31	CB	16	1015	70	8.6%	43	21	6	6	11	27%	67	5.1	17	88	18.0%	39	10.5	49%	51	7.9	51	9	1

Year	Pass D Rank	vs. #1 WR	Rk	vs. #2 WR	Rk	vs. Other WR	Rk	vs. TE	Rk	vs. RB	Rk
2014	15	3.4%	18	8.6%	23	11.7%	24	4.8%	21	-13.5%	9
2015	25	-5.4%	10	18.3%	26	21.5%	29	10.7%	23	-0.4%	16
2016	10	-5.9%	7	-6.3%	7	9.9%	22	-28.8%	3	12.7%	24

It seemed a bit odd when Baltimore rushed Marlon Humphrey to the podium with their first-round pick in April. While getting younger at cornerback was a must, Humphrey wasn't talked about much in the pre-draft process. Maybe he should have been. He started from Day 1 as a redshirt freshman at Alabama, and he's got the size (65th percentile among cornerbacks) and speed (80th percentile based on his combine 40) to be a true No. 1 cornerback. Humphrey was quite flammable in college though, giving up a lot of big plays on deep passes. Humphrey will immediately be on the spot after the promising Tavon Young tore his ACL in OTAs. ☜ Jimmy Smith has played like a low-end No. 1 cornerback for a couple years now, but he has missed almost a full season's worth of games over the past three years. Not coincidentally, Baltimore's three worst defensive DVOA weeks of the season came in games Smith missed. Over-maligned Brandon Carr was brought over from the Cowboys as a stop-gap, and in theory should be better than real cornerbacks who have started games for the Ravens over the past two years, with imaginary names like "Asa Jackson," "Shareece Wright," and "Anthony Levine." A bigger issue is that none of Baltimore's top three cornerbacks have much experience in the slot, the position Young occupied in 2016. ☜ For the second straight off-season, the Ravens bolstered their safety depth chart, this time bringing in Tony Jefferson from Arizona. Jefferson has been a monster near the line of scrimmage, as his 13 run defeats last season led all defensive backs, and may wind up playing more of a linebacker role. ☜ Eric Weddle is ending his Hall of Fame-caliber career with a very graceful decline, and will probably play up less than he did last year with the addition of Jefferson. Lardarius Webb will play deep safety, unless the Young injury forces him into the slot corner role. Webb was an excellent cornerback early in his career, but has never rediscovered his past level of play after a 2012 torn ACL, despite the position change.

Special Teams

Year	DVOA	Rank	FG/XP	Rank	Net Kick	Rank	Kick Ret	Rank	Net Punt	Rank	Punt Ret	Rank	Hidden	Rank
2014	8.0%	2	5.3	7	8.3	4	10.2	3	17.9	1	-1.9	14	-3.2	24
2015	7.3%	1	4.5	7	4.5	6	4.7	6	16.0	2	7.0	6	-0.6	17
2016	4.9%	4	25.5	1	7.0	3	-2.8	23	-1.0	16	-4.1	24	11.7	3

Holy Mark Moseley. Justin Tucker may not have won the MVP last year, but his 2016 season was arguably the greatest kicking campaign ever. Tucker added a whopping 25.5 points over average on field goals and extra points, the best mark in our database dating back to 1986 by nearly a full touchdown. To top things off, the Ravens gained 7.0 net points on kickoffs, which ranked third in the league. ☜ The biggest question for this unit in 2017 is what they'll do at returner. Devin Hester returned punts and kicks for most of last season, but was cut as Baltimore spiraled back to Earth towards the end of the year. His replacements were Walking Welker Comparison Michael Campanaro on punts and the speedy, raw Chris Moore on kicks. Moore barely returned kicks at all in college. It wouldn't be a surprise if camp competition produced a new answer at either spot. ☜ Sam Koch remains a strong punter who has finished first, sixth, and sixth the past three seasons in gross points added on punts. The problem in 2016 was the coverage rather than Koch, as the Ravens gave up an estimated 4.4 points worth of field position on punt returns. ☜ Undrafted rookie linebacker Patrick Onwuasor led the Ravens with 11 special teams tackles, five more than any of his teammates.

Buffalo Bills

2016 Record: 7-9	**Total DVOA:** 1.0% (17th)	**2017 Mean Projection:** 7.2 wins	**On the Clock (0-4):** 15%
Pythagorean Wins: 8.5 (15th)	**Offense:** 10.7% (10th)	**Postseason Odds:** 25.0%	**Mediocrity (5-7):** 41%
Snap-Weighted Age: 27.0 (6th)	**Defense:** 7.8% (27th)	**Super Bowl Odds:** 1.7%	**Playoff Contender (8-10):** 34%
Average Opponent: -3.5% (27th)	**Special Teams:** -1.9% (22nd)	**Proj. Avg. Opponent:** -0.7% (24th)	**Super Bowl Contender (11+):** 11%

2016: Rex Ryan's NFL coaching career ends not with a bang, but with a whimper.

2017: It looks like there are the first steps of a plan in place here—but just the first steps.

Ask Patriots owner Robert Kraft about being the steward of an NFL franchise, and he'll tell you there's a steep learning curve. He'll regale about many of the mistakes he made, mostly notably the messy personnel director/head coach situations involving Bobby Grier, Bill Parcells, and Pete Carroll. It took Kraft seven seasons to get it right when he hired Bill Belichick and let him direct all of the football operations.

Look at just about every new NFL owner, and you'll see how steep the learning curve is. Almost all of them have struggled to find consistent success: Jimmy Haslam (Browns), Shad Khan (Jaguars), Stan Kroenke (Rams), Stephen Ross (Dolphins), Woody Johnson (Jets), Dan Snyder (Redskins), and the Glazer family (Buccaneers).

The biggest mistake new owners make? Not getting the power structure correct. There's the inevitable holdover, whether it's the general manager or head coach, and the owner, wanting to assert his power, forces the holdover to work with whomever the owner selects. Then the holdover gets fired, and the cycle starts over again. Just look at the constant shake-ups of the Browns front office under Haslam before he finally hired the Moneyball front office of Paul DePodesta and Sashi Brown, then let them hire coach Hue Jackson. Haslam was the poster child of not having a clue.

He finally learned that, basically, you have one of two choices: either you hire a strong general manager, who hires and fires the coach, or you have a strong coach who plucks his own general manager. (There are exceptions that work out well, but they are rare.)

That brings us to the Bills, and owners Terry and Kim Pegula. After the Pegulas acquired the team in 2014, head coach Doug Marrone took advantage of a clause in his contract that allowed him to bolt if ownership changed. The Pegulas held onto general manager Doug Whaley, and forced Rex Ryan on him. That predictably ended in a disaster, with Ryan fired last season, and Whaley dismissed after the draft.

Now, three years after taking ownership of the team, the Pegulas deserve some credit by catching the curve and finally giving the Bills a chance at success.

The first step was to hire Panthers defensive coordinator Sean McDermott as head coach in January. The 43-year-old McDermott is, in many ways, the anti-Rex. While the former coach also possessed a great defensive mind, Ryan was boisterous and his teams reflected his undisciplined and impulsive personality. McDermott is quiet, measured, and disciplined, and his units with the Panthers reflected that.

Once Whaley was dispatched after the draft—and that delay is normal NFL practice because the general manager and his staff have done all the work on the prospects—the Bills hired Brandon Beane as general manager. Beane, not coincidentally, was the Panthers' assistant general manager and worked with McDermott for six years in Charlotte.

McDermott and Beane have had similar paths in the NFL, where both started as interns out of college and slowly worked their way (18 and 19 years, respectively) to get their first power positions in the league. The duo was close in Carolina, where they often went on runs together and McDermott gave Beane's son wrestling pointers—on the wrestling mat in McDermott's house.

Both served at the altar of another football lifer, Panthers general manager Dave Gettleman, and are following the same steps to sustained success that Gettleman has preached since taking over in Carolina.

"What you want is sustained success—that's what you're looking for," Gettleman said. "Any one team in any given year can go to the playoffs where everything just breaks right. But it's really about sustained success. If that's what you want, you must go through the process. You can't take shortcuts. You have to do the work and build it right."

Promoted by Gettleman, Beane was often by his bosses' side, whether it be in the film room, in the press box during games, or scouting on the sidelines. Those in the know have said that if you want to look at the future of the Bills, look to what the Panthers have done under Gettleman and coach Ron Rivera. Both Beane and McDermott were vital parts of the Panthers' 2015 NFC Championship team and believe the same approach will work to help the Bills end their league-leading 17-year playoff drought.

The path to sustained success is slow and steady, and it starts in player personnel. And Beane started almost completely from scratch, as he dismissed the scouting staff. Despite being handcuffed by the league calendar (most in personnel are locked into contracts by mid-May), Beane has assembled an impressive array of talent. Assistant general manager Joe Schoen worked for Beane in the Panthers' front office, and then branched out to become the Dolphins' director of player personnel. Brian Gaine, who worked for six years with Schoen

2017 Bills Schedule

Week	Opp.	Week	Opp.	Week	Opp.
1	NYJ	7	TB	13	NE
2	at CAR	8	OAK	14	IND
3	DEN	9	at NYJ (Thu.)	15	MIA
4	at ATL	10	NO	16	at NE
5	at CIN	11	at LACH	17	at MIA
6	BYE	12	at KC		

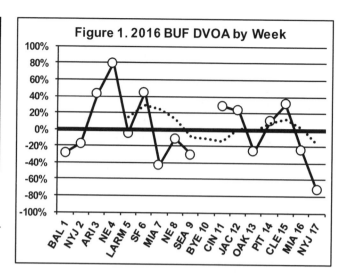

Figure 1. 2016 BUF DVOA by Week

in Miami, was named the Bills' vice president of player personnel after interviewing with the Pegulas for Beane's job. Gaine comes over from Houston, where he held the title of director of player personnel; he has been interviewed for a handful of general manager spots in recent years and will be running his own team in short order.

Additionally, Malik Boyd (director of pro personnel), Lake Dawson (assistant director of college scouting), Marvin Allen (national scout), Brian Adams (national scout), and former Dolphins general manager Dennis Hickey (senior college scout) each have more than 14 years of NFL experience and are well respected.

"Considering what time of year they had to hire, they have a very impressive staff," said one general manager. "To get both Schoen and Gaine is a real coup for Beane. They're both ego-less and real talents."

So we know that the new-look Bills, after years of skimping on a personnel staff, now have a talented, modern-day front office. We also know that McDermott and Beane want to build the Bills in the mold of the Panthers. What will that mean for the players on the field?

McDermott, who tabbed Tampa-2 disciple Leslie Frazier as his coordinator, uses a 4-3 scheme that relies on zone coverage. DVOA ranked his Carolina defense as the worst in the league when he started there in 2011, but his defenses have been above-average or better every year since (Table 1). While McDermott learned under Jim Johnson with the Eagles, he does not share his late mentor's love of the blitz. McDermott likes a beefy defensive line, athletes at linebacker, and ballhawks in the secondary.

On the defensive line, McDermott has plenty to work with.

Table 1. Sean McDermott as Defensive Coordinator, 2009-2016

Year	Team	Pass DVOA	Rk	Run DVOA	Rk	Def DVOA	Rk
2009	PHI	-17.1%	5	-10.4%	12	-14.3%	3
2010	PHI	-0.4%	8	-7.5%	12	-3.6%	11
2011	CAR	20.5%	29	10.7%	32	15.8%	32
2012	CAR	0.8%	12	-8.4%	11	-3.1%	11
2013	CAR	-15.6%	3	-16.0%	6	-15.7%	3
2014	CAR	0.0%	9	-4.0%	23	-1.7%	15
2015	CAR	-18.2%	2	-18.6%	6	-18.4%	2
2016	CAR	1.1%	11	-15.1%	9	-5.3%	10

Defensive tackles Kyle Williams and Marcell Dareus have anchored the Buffalo defense for years, and they're backed up by youngster Adolphus Washington. At end, 2016 first-round pick Shaq Lawson showed potential in limited playing time after missing training camp and the early part of the season with a shoulder injury. However, Jerry Hughes, who counts $10.45 million against the cap this year, is very light for a McDermott edge player. That being said, Hughes flourished in Jim Schwartz's pre-Rex 4-3 defense, combining for 19.5 sacks in 2013 and 2014.

Linebacker is going to be a problem. In Carolina, McDermott had three of the league's best athletes at the position with Luke Kuechly and converted safeties Thomas Davis and Shaq Thompson. They were terrific at dropping into coverage (often all the way down the seam for Kuechly) and blitzing when necessary. The Bills, on the other hand, have two players for one middle linebacker spot and one player, maybe, for two outside linebacker spots. They let run-and-hit linebacker Zach Brown, who had a career year last season, walk in free agency even though he was the best fit on the roster for McDermott's scheme. Both Preston Brown (who had success with Schwartz) and Reggie Ragland (a standard 3-4 ILB) are two-down middle linebackers who are better at stuffing the run than running with a tight end down the middle of the field. At strongside linebacker, Lorenzo Alexander was one of the few good fits for Ryan's scheme and had a remarkable late-career breakout in 2016, going from special teams ace to ranking third in the league with 12.5 sacks. But can he now be a standard 4-3 outside linebacker at the age of 34? Alexander won't do much pass-rushing on the first two downs, but he's a certain to be in the mix as a sub edge rusher. Veterans Gerald Hodges (formerly Vikings, 49ers) and Ramon Humber (formerly Saints, Colts) are in the mix at weakside linebacker, but neither is really an NFL-quality starter.

In the secondary, the Bills are virtually starting over from scratch. They released safeties Aaron Williams and Corey Graham as well as cornerback Nickell Robey-Coleman, and allowed the Patriots to scoop up free-agent cornerback Stephon Gilmore. The lone holdover from the starting lineup is cornerback Ronald Darby.

Beane showed he's not a complete Gettleman disciple when he decided to shell out questionable money for free-agent safeties Micah Hyde ($14 million guaranteed) and Jordan Poyer ($6 million). Hyde, who doesn't run well, cashed in after a career year for the Packers that included four interceptions in the last seven games. He does offer flexibility, however, as strong safety who frequently played slot cornerback for the Packers. Poyer was injured in a Week 6 game last season and missed the rest of the year with a lacerated kidney. The Bills are taking a risk that they've found a player who can flourish in a larger role, as Poyer was primarily a special teams standout until Cleveland made him a starter last season.

There are great expectations for first-round cornerback Tre'Davious White (LSU), who earned rave reviews during the offseason for his work with the first team. If Beane's right about Hyde and Poyer (and he had better be, considering their signings will hurt the Bills in the compensatory pick calculations, offsetting Gilmore's departure), Buffalo might have something cooking in the secondary.

The expectations for second-round wide receiver Zay Jones are as strong as those for White, and he'll certainly get plenty of opportunity after both Robert Woods and Marquise Goodwin signed elsewhere this offseason. But historical analysis suggests the odds are stacked against East Carolina product. Jones has a Playmaker Score of 37.6 percent, which makes him the most overrated wide receiver prospect in this class. Jones had only eight touchdowns as a senior, which isn't really a lot for a top-drafted wideout, and he had an extremely low average of 10.7 yards per reception. Possession receivers in college tend not to succeed in the NFL, even as possession receivers.

That's certainly not going to help the prospects of underrated quarterback Tyrod Taylor, who was wisely re-signed after some very public debate among team management. However, the arrival of Rick Dennison as offensive coordinator should be a major plus. Dennison directed the offense for the Texans (2010-13) and the Broncos (2015-16); in between, he was Taylor's quarterbacks coach with the Ravens in 2014. He's very much a Mike Shanahan and Gary Kubiak disciple, which means an offense with a high-percentage passing game and a reliance on the run through a zone-blocking scheme. Taylor can certainly execute the scheme, and his feet will be an asset on designed boot-action passes, but the talent around him has been unreliable. Sammy Watkins, the fourth overall pick in 2014, has only played 21 games the past two seasons as he has dealt with various injuries. Free agents Andre Holmes (56 percent catch rate) and Corey Brown (51 percent) add depth, but their hands have been unreliable. Tight end Charles Clay ranked 28th in both DYAR and DVOA last year, and continues to look like another big-money Whaley bust.

There is, however, great optimism for the Bills ground game, which ranked first in DVOA last year and should continue right where it left off as long as LeSean McCoy stays healthy. McCoy was terrific in 2016, as he ranked second in rushing DVOA and DYAR. It will be interesting to see if McCoy continues to flourish in Dennison's scheme. McCoy excels with his vision and improvisational style. Dennison prefers a more decisive one-cut runner, but McCoy certainly has the ability to do that. If McCoy deals with injuries again, which seem like an every-year occurrence now, the Bills could be in trouble. With backups Mike Gillislee now in New England, the Bills have little depth behind McCoy.

The Bills have hovered around the .500 mark for three seasons now, never quite able to break through. Scheme changes under a new coach usually take time, but everyone in the division is playing for second place behind the Patriots, so why should the Bills be any different? And with the Jets in expansion team mode, that leaves the Bills and Dolphins taking up the middle ground. Miami made the playoffs under a new coach last year. Could the Bills do the same in 2017? If McCoy, Watkins, and Taylor stay healthy, they have a chance. The bigger question will be whether McDermott can find the right pieces at linebacker and in the secondary to operate his scheme in the short term while keeping an eye on the future and sustained success. Given their history in Carolina, McDermott and Beane know doing both is possible. But it's not probable.

Greg A. Bedard

2016 Bills Stats by Week

Wk	vs.	W-L	PF	PA	YDF	YDA	TO	Total	Off	Def	ST
1	at BAL	L	7	13	160	308	+1	-29%	-26%	3%	0%
2	NYJ	L	31	37	393	493	0	-18%	22%	47%	8%
3	ARI	W	33	18	297	348	+4	43%	14%	-35%	-7%
4	at NE	W	16	0	378	277	+1	80%	28%	-43%	9%
5	at LARM	W	30	19	305	345	+3	-5%	6%	11%	1%
6	SF	W	45	16	492	300	-1	44%	26%	-7%	11%
7	at MIA	L	25	28	267	454	0	-43%	-12%	33%	2%
8	NE	L	25	41	376	357	0	-11%	9%	5%	-16%
9	at SEA	L	25	31	425	278	-1	-31%	34%	48%	-17%
10	BYE										
11	at CIN	W	16	12	342	300	+1	28%	-8%	-26%	11%
12	JAC	W	28	21	304	301	0	23%	30%	12%	5%
13	at OAK	L	24	38	382	399	-2	-27%	-3%	22%	-2%
14	PIT	L	20	27	275	460	+2	10%	13%	-8%	-10%
15	CLE	W	33	13	451	269	0	31%	42%	13%	1%
16	MIA	L	31	34	589	494	+1	-24%	30%	33%	-22%
17	at NYJ	L	10	30	230	329	-3	-73%	-54%	17%	-2%

Trends and Splits

	Offense	Rank	Defense	Rank
Total DVOA	10.7%	10	7.8%	27
Unadjusted VOA	12.2%	8	5.7%	23
Weighted Trend	10.7%	9	10.0%	28
Variance	6.3%	18	7.2%	28
Average Opponent	-0.3%	12	-3.2%	29
Passing	9.2%	18	12.3%	21
Rushing	17.0%	1	2.9%	30
First Down	11.4%	6	17.3%	31
Second Down	10.4%	9	-1.3%	15
Third Down	9.8%	9	2.5%	21
First Half	14.9%	8	12.6%	27
Second Half	16.0%	7	19.2%	29
Red Zone	27.0%	6	7.3%	25
Late and Close	5.1%	13	7.8%	21

Five-Year Performance

Year	W-L	Pyth W	Est W	PF	PA	TO	Total	Rk	Off	Rk	Def	Rk	ST	Rk	Off AGL	Rk	Def AGL	Rk	Off Age	Rk	Def Age	Rk	ST Age	Rk
2012	6-10	5.7	6.5	344	435	-13	-12.1%	23	-4.2%	20	10.6%	27	2.7%	9	51.5	29	28.2	16	26.2	25	26.7	18	26.5	10
2013	6-10	6.7	7.1	339	388	+3	-3.3%	18	-11.5%	25	-13.8%	4	-5.6%	30	17.9	6	26.4	12	26.4	24	26.0	26	26.1	12
2014	9-7	9.6	9.0	343	289	+7	10.5%	9	-11.2%	26	-15.5%	2	6.2%	4	27.2	14	31.9	11	26.6	21	26.1	26	26.1	15
2015	8-8	8.5	8.8	379	359	+6	2.7%	12	9.8%	9	8.6%	24	1.5%	12	37.2	19	43.3	28	26.2	21	26.4	21	26.5	9
2016	7-9	8.5	7.4	399	378	+6	1.0%	17	10.7%	10	7.8%	27	-1.9%	22	37.0	19	60.8	28	26.6	19	27.2	6	27.3	1

2016 Performance Based on Most Common Personnel Groups

BUF Offense

Pers	Freq	Yds	DVOA	Run%
11	46%	5.8	10.8%	23%
21	26%	5.7	11.3%	72%
12	16%	6.2	19.2%	34%
22	4%	5.1	15.2%	87%
611	2%	6.2	73.2%	41%

BUF Offense vs. Opponents

Pers	Freq	Yds	DVOA	Run%
Base	48%	5.9	18.5%	61%
Nickel	47%	5.7	8.9%	25%
Dime+	3%	6.0	47.0%	19%
Goal Line	1%	0.8	-28.9%	85%

BUF Defense

Pers	Freq	Yds	DVOA
Base	31%	5.5	5.6%
Nickel	51%	6.0	11.2%
Dime+	14%	6.5	15.1%
Goal Line	1%	1.6	-18.6%
Big	3%	2.9	-20.2%

BUF Defense vs. Opponents

Pers	Freq	Yds	DVOA
11	58%	6.4	18.1%
12	19%	5.4	-11.9%
10	6%	4.5	-22.4%
612	3%	6.2	-11.9%
21	3%	5.9	27.4%
611	3%	4.4	-2.0%

Strategic Tendencies

Run/Pass		Rk	Formation		Rk	Pass Rush		Rk	Secondary		Rk	Strategy		Rk
Runs, first half	42%	7	Form: Single Back	62%	32	Rush 3	16.8%	3	4 DB	31%	15	Play-action	21%	7
Runs, first down	55%	2	Form: Empty Back	5%	24	Rush 4	60.8%	22	5 DB	51%	27	Avg Box (Off)	6.46	2
Runs, second-long	31%	12	Pers: 3+ WR	47%	30	Rush 5	16.1%	27	6+ DB	11%	14	Avg Box (Def)	6.20	21
Runs, power sit.	66%	4	Pers: 2+ TE/6+ OL	26%	24	Rush 6+	6.4%	13	CB by Sides	94%	2	Offensive Pace	30.23	11
Runs, behind 2H	35%	2	Pers: 6+ OL	5%	13	Sacks by LB	61.5%	9	S/CB Cover Ratio	23%	26	Defensive Pace	30.79	22
Pass, ahead 2H	47%	20	Shotgun/Pistol	80%	3	Sacks by DB	2.6%	28	DB Blitz	7%	25	Go for it on 4th	1.04	19

The Bills offense threw just 14 percent of passes in the middle of the field; no other offense was below 19 percent. This was not an issue with the official scorers, as the Bills defense faced an above-average rate of passes marked as "middle." The Bills were eighth in offensive DVOA on passes in the middle, and No. 1 on passes in the deep middle, so perhaps they should run those routes more often.   The Bills were much better when they had a fullback or tight end in the backfield: 5.7 yards per carry and 24.4% DVOA from multi-back sets, compared to 4.6 yards and 7.4% DVOA from single-back sets. The Bills had 57 percent of their runs come out of multi-back sets last year, the highest rate in the league. Buffalo and New England were the only teams over 50 percent. Just five years ago, more than half the teams in the league were over 50 percent.   Through no fault of their own, the Bills were victimized by an excellent performance from opposing field goal kickers. Opponents only missed two field goals against Buffalo, both over 45 yards. (Arizona also had a field goal attempt against Buffalo blown by a fumbled snap.)   Buffalo's defense only recovered four of 15 opposition fumbles last season.   The Bills massively downshifted their use of defensive backs as pass-rushers in 2016, as the rate of both defensive back blitzes and big blitzes (six or more pass-rushers) dropped by half. The Bills went from getting 19 percent of sacks from defensive backs (first in 2015) to just 2.6 percent (28th). Overall, the Bills were not successful blitzing last season, allowing 6.4 yards per pass with three or four pass-rushers but 8.3 yards per pass with five or more and 9.8 yards per pass with at least one defensive back blitzing.   Buffalo's adjusted sack rate on defense went from 5.7 percent on first and second down (20th) to 10.3 percent on third down (second behind Carolina).   Only 15 percent of runs against the Bills came from two-back sets, 30th in the NFL. The other teams in the bottom six all had winning records.

Passing

Player	DYAR	DVOA	Plays	NtYds	Avg	YAC	C%	TD	Int
T.Taylor	275	-2.1%	477	2831	5.9	4.2	61.8%	17	6
EJ Manuel*	-58	-47.2%	29	112	3.9	2.5	42.3%	0	0
C.Jones	-62	-84.6%	12	94	7.8	4.2	54.5%	0	1

Rushing

Player	DYAR	DVOA	Plays	Yds	Avg	TD	Fum	Suc
L.McCoy	236	24.0%	186	978	5.3	14	0	47%
T.Taylor	76	8.5%	71	475	6.7	6	0	-
M.Gillislee*	199	55.3%	66	409	6.2	8	0	73%
J.Williams	-3	-12.3%	20	73	3.7	1	0	45%
R.Bush*	-22	-54.8%	11	5	0.5	1	0	45%
J.Felton*	-2	-12.8%	6	12	2.0	0	0	67%
M.Tolbert	-22	-27.2%	29	74	2.6	0	0	34%

Receiving

Player	DYAR	DVOA	Plays	Ctch	Yds	Y/C	YAC	TD	C%
R.Woods*	117	7.9%	75	50	613	12.3	2.5	1	67%
M.Goodwin	-56	-23.8%	68	29	413	14.2	2.8	3	43%
S.Watkins	48	-1.3%	52	28	430	15.4	1.9	2	54%
W.Powell	-18	-22.2%	25	14	142	10.1	2.6	0	56%
J.Hunter	46	10.3%	24	10	189	18.9	3.0	4	42%
B.Tate	38	30.9%	11	8	117	14.6	6.5	0	73%
G.Salas*	23	33.2%	6	4	89	22.3	8.3	1	67%
C.Brown	-55	-25.8%	53	27	271	10.0	4.2	1	51%
R.Streater	49	11.2%	27	18	191	10.6	3.7	2	67%
A.Holmes	6	-9.9%	25	14	126	9.0	1.9	3	56%
C.Clay	4	-6.5%	87	57	552	9.7	3.4	4	66%
N.O'Leary	5	-1.2%	14	9	114	12.7	4.8	0	64%
L.McCoy	117	21.2%	58	51	356	7.0	7.6	1	88%
M.Gillislee*	-18	-48.0%	11	9	50	5.6	5.1	1	82%
R.Bush*	40	50.9%	10	7	90	12.9	5.7	0	70%
J.Felton*	15	13.1%	9	6	57	9.5	5.7	0	67%
M.Tolbert	11	0.2%	15	10	72	7.2	8.7	1	67%
P.DiMarco	18	19.5%	10	7	52	7.4	4.1	1	70%

Offensive Line

Player	Pos	Age	GS	Snaps	Pen	Sk	Pass	Run	Player	Pos	Age	GS	Snaps	Pen	Sk	Pass	Run
Richie Incognito	LG	34	16/16	1059	7	0.5	5	9	Eric Wood	C	31	9/9	569	4	0.5	3	3
John Miller	RG	24	16/16	1047	4	2.0	5	2	Ryan Groy	C	27	16/7	541	0	0.0	1	1
Jordan Mills	RT	27	16/16	1033	7	5.5	12	6	Cyrus Kouandjio*	LT	24	12/5	407	2	0.5	3	8
Cordy Glenn	LT	28	11/11	656	7	2.0	5	0	Vladimir Ducasse	LG	30	10/8	554	6	1.5	6	5

Year	Yards	ALY	Rank	Power	Rank	Stuff	Rank	2nd Lev	Rank	Open Field	Rank	Sacks	ASR	Rank	Press	Rank	F-Start	Cont.
2014	3.83	3.87	26	63%	16	17%	7	0.94	30	0.64	20	39	6.9%	20	21.7%	8	19	37
2015	4.68	3.92	23	71%	10	21%	17	1.28	2	1.18	2	42	8.4%	27	26.8%	19	15	26
2016	5.12	4.16	16	60%	20	22%	22	1.41	1	1.32	2	46	9.3%	31	31.8%	30	6	32

2016 ALY by direction: Left End 4.59 (12)   Left Tackle 3.44 (30)   Mid/Guard 4.40 (9)   Right Tackle 3.74 (20)   Right End 4.01 (14)

Richie Incognito has been the unit's most reliable player since arriving in 2015. Incognito is one of 12 offensive linemen to play at least 1,000 regular season snaps each of the past two years. And last year, he was among the 11 offensive linemen to play over 1,000 snaps and allow less than one sack. ☞ Cordy Glenn and Eric Wood played every game from 2013 to 2015, but missed a combined 12 games in 2016. Glenn isn't going anywhere after inking a rich five-year extension last offseason, but the 31-year-old Wood is entering the final year of his deal. Ryan Groy was excellent in his stead, ranking first among centers in snaps per blown block. If Wood doesn't look like himself coming off a broken leg, the Bills at least don't have to wonder about his successor. ☞ Right tackle Jordan Mills was more passable last year after a rough 2015, but the plan is still for second-round rookie Dion Dawkins to take over sooner rather than later. Temple ran some of the outside zone blocking scheme Rick Dennison will import to Buffalo, so that experience might soften Dawkins' transition to the pros.

Defensive Front Seven

Defensive Line	Age	Pos	G	Snaps	Plays	TmPct	Rk	Stop	Dfts	BTkl	Runs	St%	Rk	RuYd	Rk	Sack	Hit	Hur	Dsrpt
						Overall						vs. Run				Pass Rush			
Kyle Williams	34	DE	15	795	63	8.3%	8	45	17	11	55	71%	62	2.8	65	5.0	9	20	3
Leger Douzable*	31	DE	16	482	43	5.3%	32	30	10	5	37	68%	70	2.4	49	1.5	5	10	1
Marcell Dareus	28	DT	8	418	40	9.8%	2	30	9	1	33	73%	53	2.1	37	3.0	1	4	1
Adolphus Washington	23	DE	15	332	22	2.9%	--	19	5	2	18	83%	--	1.7	--	2.5	1	1	1
Corbin Bryant*	29	DT	8	234	11	2.7%	81	8	2	2	10	80%	38	2.4	52	0.0	0	2	0

Edge Rushers	Age	Pos	G	Snaps	Plays	TmPct	Rk	Stop	Dfts	BTkl	Runs	St%	Rk	RuYd	Rk	Sack	Hit	Hur	Dsrpt
						Overall						vs. Run				Pass Rush			
Jerry Hughes	29	OLB	16	860	50	6.1%	30	32	16	14	33	61%	90	3.5	84	6.0	8	33	3
Lorenzo Alexander	34	OLB	16	788	70	8.6%	6	54	28	7	41	76%	41	3.2	76	12.5	12	27	3
Shaq Lawson	23	OLB	10	237	14	2.8%	--	12	4	2	9	89%	--	0.8	--	2.0	3	10	1
Ryan Davis	28	DE	9	155	4	0.9%	--	2	2	0	4	50%	--	1.5	--	0.0	2	9	0

Linebackers	Age	Pos	G	Snaps	Plays	TmPct	Rk	Stop	Dfts	BTkl	Runs	St%	Rk	RuYd	Rk	Sack	Hit	Hur	Tgts	Suc%	Rk	AdjYd	Rk	PD	Int
						Overall						vs. Run				Pass Rush					vs. Pass				
Preston Brown	25	ILB	16	1068	134	16.5%	14	71	31	11	97	60%	61	4.0	66	1.0	2	5	23	44%	52	6.1	30	1	0
Zach Brown*	28	ILB	16	980	152	18.7%	5	86	27	13	95	66%	29	3.7	49	3.5	6	6	45	46%	47	8.2	71	4	1
Gerald Hodges	25	ILB	15	583	82	9.9%	57	49	9	9	63	63%	43	4.1	68	3.0	2	6	16	55%	23	5.4	19	0	0

Year	Yards	ALY	Rank	Power	Rank	Stuff	Rank	2nd Level	Rank	Open Field	Rank	Sacks	ASR	Rank	Press	Rank
2014	3.99	3.58	4	64%	16	26%	1	1.14	17	0.83	23	54	8.8%	1	26.4%	7
2015	4.52	4.71	29	72%	25	16%	31	1.24	26	0.77	16	21	3.8%	31	21.8%	29
2016	4.50	4.41	22	57%	6	19%	16	1.30	28	0.88	25	39	7.1%	7	29.0%	9

2016 ALY by direction: Left End 4.11 (16)   Left Tackle 4.03 (15)   Mid/Guard 4.35 (20)   Right Tackle 4.02 (15)   Right End 7.18 (32)

An improvement in the Bills' 30th-ranked run defense starts with better play from Marcell Dareus and Kyle Williams. Both were extremely mediocre in this department under Rex Ryan; Williams in particular declined significantly after a strong 2014 in which he ranked seventh in run stop rate. Sean McDermott comes from a Carolina organization which valued its "hog mollies." Dareus and Williams rank first and seventh in cap hit, respectively, on Buffalo's 2017 cap sheet, so the duo needs to provide better return on investment. ☞ In his final draft, Ryan spent his top three picks on defensive players: Shaq Lawson, Reggie Ragland, and Adolphus Washington, who combined to play just over 550 snaps last year. As such, all three are essentially rookies learning a new scheme from a regime that didn't draft them. It's far too early to assume any of them will fail in Buffalo, but their ability to adapt will determine how much of a young foundation this unit really has. ☞ The Bills hope they have replaced Zach Brown with another bargain starter in Gerald Hodges. Buffalo inked the fifth-year vet to a one-year deal that barely pays him more than the minimum. As a part-time starter for the Niners last year, Hodges posted better coverage charting numbers than either Zach or Preston Brown—but the sample size was much smaller. ☞ The Bills drafted two smallish outside linebackers in Matt Milano (fifth round, Boston College) and Tanner Vallejo (sixth round, Boise State) that fit McDermott's preference for speed at linebacker better than the team's veterans, but it's likely special teams are in their immediate future.

Defensive Secondary

Secondary	Age	Pos	G	Snaps	Plays	Overall TmPct	Rk	Stop	Dfts	BTkl	Runs	vs. Run St%	Rk	RuYd	Rk	Tgts	vs. Pass Tgt%	Rk	Dist	Suc%	Rk	AdjYd	Rk	PD	Int
Corey Graham*	32	FS	16	1055	90	11.1%	23	36	12	15	49	43%	30	6.6	36	25	6.3%	13	14.8	48%	33	7.1	14	9	1
Stephon Gilmore*	27	CB	15	984	60	7.9%	63	24	8	5	13	46%	30	7.5	55	55	15.1%	8	14.8	49%	48	9.1	75	12	5
Ronald Darby	23	CB	14	824	82	11.5%	3	31	6	9	24	33%	55	10.6	76	66	21.8%	67	14.8	48%	57	9.5	82	12	0
Nickell Robey-Coleman*	25	CB	16	573	37	4.5%	--	15	7	5	7	43%	--	10.9	--	36	16.9%	--	9.6	51%	--	8.3	--	6	2
Corey White*	27	CB	15	413	32	4.2%	--	8	4	6	8	38%	--	5.8	--	25	16.2%	--	14.1	48%	--	7.8	--	4	2
Aaron Williams*	28	SS	7	339	25	7.0%	--	9	4	1	8	38%	--	5.8	--	15	11.7%	--	14.0	55%	--	6.9	--	5	0
Kevon Seymour	24	CB	15	285	17	2.2%	--	7	3	4	4	25%	--	7.8	--	18	16.7%	--	12.8	60%	--	6.9	--	3	0
Robert Blanton*	28	SS	10	270	26	5.1%	--	5	1	2	7	29%	--	7.9	--	10	10.1%	--	10.1	32%	--	9.4	--	0	0
Micah Hyde	27	CB/FS	16	821	65	8.1%	56	28	15	4	17	47%	28	6.1	30	51	13.9%	3	9.6	48%	53	8.5	65	9	3
Shareece Wright	30	CB	12	673	56	9.6%	24	23	7	8	14	43%	38	6.1	34	55	20.1%	56	12.4	53%	25	8.1	57	6	0
Jordan Poyer	26	FS	6	354	37	11.6%	--	9	1	2	13	38%	--	9.7	--	17	13.0%	--	10.3	25%	--	13.6	--	2	0
Leonard Johnson	27	CB	10	436	31	6.0%	--	12	7	9	5	40%	--	5.4	--	30	16.0%	--	6.7	50%	--	6.6	--	1	0

Year	Pass D Rank	vs. #1 WR	Rk	vs. #2 WR	Rk	vs. Other WR	Rk	vs. TE	Rk	vs. RB	Rk
2014	1	-22.6%	3	6.6%	22	-5.8%	12	-26.2%	2	-20.0%	5
2015	18	-13.3%	5	-12.9%	8	6.0%	18	-9.0%	13	16.5%	29
2016	21	3.1%	19	-0.4%	16	12.0%	25	-5.9%	11	7.9%	21

Ronald Darby is the last man standing from the 2016 starting secondary. If Darby plays more like he did in his rookie season of 2015, though, that's not necessarily a bad place to start. The Florida State product ranked sixth in adjusted yards per pass two seasons ago, but plummeted all the way to 82nd out of 87 qualifying cornerbacks in his sophomore campaign. Darby doesn't automatically shoulder all of that blame, as Ryan's notoriously aggressive scheme always placed lots of stress on his defensive backs. The charting numbers will most likely fall somewhere in between in 2017, but the bigger long-term question is whether or not Darby is a schematic fit in a predominantly zone defense after playing lots of man coverage under Ryan. ☞ Kevon Seymour will probably cede snaps at some point to Tre'Davious White, but the 2016 sixth-rounder could start opposite Darby to begin the year. As a rookie, Seymour actually posted a better adjusted success rate than either Darby or Stephon Gilmore. His lack of size (5-foot-11, 186 pounds) makes him a prototypical slot corner, though he did demonstrate sufficient quickness to indicate that he can succeed in that role. Additionally, Seymour thrived in a zone defense at USC, perhaps giving him a slight edge over the rest of the Bills' corners. ☞ Broken tackles may have been a clear sign that Corey Graham's career is over at age 32. We counted him with more than twice as many broken tackles in 2016 as we did in 2014 and 2015 combined. Tackling should improve with Micah Hyde and Jordan Poyer at safety, both of whom posted broken tackle rates under 10 percent. The bigger issue is the lack of safety depth. The top reserve right now is either career special-teamer Colt Anderson or street free agent Shamiel "Schilamzel, Hasenpfeffer Incorporated" Gary. Neither one played a single snap on defense last season. It's a dicey proposition if either Hyde or Poyer gets injured, and it could also prevent Hyde from bumping down to the slot in sub packages if either Seymour or White falters at cornerback.

Special Teams

Year	DVOA	Rank	FG/XP	Rank	Net Kick	Rank	Kick Ret	Rank	Net Punt	Rank	Punt Ret	Rank	Hidden	Rank
2014	6.2%	4	8.5	3	7.9	5	5.3	6	2.2	13	7.1	7	1.4	14
2015	1.5%	12	-1.7	23	18.2	1	-6.1	30	4.0	10	-6.9	31	-5.2	22
2016	-1.9%	22	-7.7	28	-2.6	21	-3.7	25	-2.9	21	7.6	5	-4.9	23

Dan Carpenter did not take well to the new extra point distance. A season after missing six PATs, Carpenter missed five last season, giving him a two-year average of just 87 percent on extra points. Among kickers who remained employed the last two seasons, only Jacksonville's Jason Myers was worse. Somehow, the Bills replaced Carpenter with one of the two kickers to miss *more* extra points last year. Steven (né Stephen) Hauschka missed three PATs in the final five minutes of one-score games last year. He also missed two field goals under 30 yards after missing just two such field goals over the first eight seasons of his career. Gambling that this is just typical kicker inconsistency and not a sign his career is over, the Bills forked over a three-year, $8.9 million deal this offseason. ☞ Brandon Tate had the best season of his career as a punt returner, ranking sixth in punt return value. He was much more average on kick returns, but his value in the third phase could help him stick around another season. ☞ Punters tend to be the most consistent part of special teams, but not Colton Schmidt. His gross value was minus-9.2 points last year (33rd of 34 punters), plus-4.8 points in 2015 (eighth), and minus-7.5 points in 2014 (28th).

Carolina Panthers

2016 Record: 6-10	**Total DVOA:** -5.5% (24th)	**2017 Mean Projection:** 8.6 wins	**On the Clock (0-4):** 6%
Pythagorean Wins: 7.1 (25th)	**Offense:** -8.4% (25th)	**Postseason Odds:** 46.4%	**Mediocrity (5-7):** 27%
Snap-Weighted Age: 26.6 (16th)	**Defense:** -5.3% (10th)	**Super Bowl Odds:** 6.9%	**Playoff Contender (8-10):** 43%
Average Opponent: 1.4% (8th)	**Special Teams:** -2.5% (25th)	**Proj. Avg. Opponent:** -2.5% (30th)	**Super Bowl Contender (11+):** 23%

2016: Dominance to decay, seemingly overnight.

2017: Not 2015 good, but good enough.

If the defining image of Carolina's magical 2015 season was Cam Newton's megawatt smile, then the 2016 disaster was best represented by Luke Kuechly's tears. Concussed during a Thursday night game against New Orleans in November, Kuechly lost control of his emotions as he was carted off the field. It's a common effect of brain bruising, but the sight of the NFL's foremost tough guy weeping openly on national television was disquieting for all football fans. Symbolically, it captured what all Carolina fans felt about a season that defined Super Bowl hangover.

How bad was it? The Panthers plummeted from 15-1 to 6-10. They dropped by more than 30 percentage points in DVOA, from fourth to 24th overall (Table 1). After leading the NFL with 500 points scored in 2015, they dropped to 369, good for 15th. And Newton went from Most Valuable Player to Crash Test Dummy, a battered and beaten figure with nary a dab in sight.

The Panthers basically flipped seasons with their hated division rivals in Atlanta. In retrospect, perhaps the Falcons' win in the penultimate game of 2015, which ended Carolina's unbeaten season, set up the *Freaky Friday* nature of 2016. Both teams had awesome runs to the Super Bowl one season and very disappointing years that saw the star quarterback massively underperform the other, one right after the next—though in reverse order. For each of these NFC South fanbases, the question for 2017 is clear: which extreme will their team approach more closely in the coming season?

If you are reading this *Almanac* in sequential order, you know we think the Falcons will come back to the pack a bit in 2017. The Panthers' projection, meanwhile, anticipates a strong rebound season—mainly driven by the defense—that puts them slightly ahead of the Falcons. (The Saints and Bucs are closely bunched as well; every game will count in the NFC South this season.) The last-place schedule will help. We project Atlanta to have an average schedule, which includes the Cowboys and Seahawks, while Carolina plays one of the league's five easiest schedules, by contrast featuring the Eagles and 49ers. It's not completely a cakewalk: in October, the Panthers play four of five games on the road. At the same time, the first half is quite manageable on paper, with only a trip to New England seemingly beyond their grasp. December brings three straight home games before the finale at Atlanta, which just might be for the division title.

To make our forecast into a reality, the Panthers need to resuscitate Newton, which in large part means protecting him better and improving the offense around him. Since drafting

Table 1. Largest Year-to-Year DVOA Drop, Teams with Same Starting QB, 1987-2016

Years	Team	Year 1			Year 2				Year 3			
		W-L	DVOA	Rk	W-L	DVOA	Rk	Change	W-L	DVOA	Rk	Change
89-91	CLE1	9-6-1	24.4%	2	3-13	-30.3%	26	-54.6%	6-10	1.0%	15	+31.2%
05-07	SEA	13-3	28.4%	3	9-7	-13.0%	24	-41.4%	10-6	14.7%	9	+27.7%
91-93	WAS	14-2	56.9%	1	9-7	17.0%	5	-39.8%	4-12	-21.4%	24	-38.4%
88-90	NYJ	8-7-1	13.3%	7	4-12	-25.5%	26	-38.8%	6-10	-7.1%	15	+18.5%
98-00	ATL	14-2	18.8%	7	5-11	-19.2%	26	-38.0%	4-12	-32.5%	28	-13.3%
00-02	TEN	13-3	33.3%	1	7-9	-2.8%	18	-36.1%	11-5	9.2%	11	+12.0%
12-13	WAS	10-6	9.3%	9	3-13	-26.2%	29	-35.5%	4-12	-27.0%	28	-0.9%
13-15	CAR	12-4	24.6%	3	7-8-1	-8.5%	24	-33.1%	15-1	26.0%	4	+34.5%
87-89	DEN	8-3-1	17.9%	4	8-8	-14.8%	23	-32.7%	11-5	19.0%	4	+33.8%
12-14	GB	11-5	26.3%	5	8-7-1	-6.0%	20	-32.4%	12-4	23.3%	3	+29.4%
15-17	CAR	15-1	26.0%	4	6-10	-5.5%	24	-31.6%	—	—	—	—
89-91	LARM	11-5	19.9%	3	5-11	-11.3%	20	-31.3%	3-13	-10.7%	22	+0.6%
00-02	IND	10-6	19.9%	7	6-10	-11.3%	23	-31.2%	10-6	-1.2%	20	+10.1%
15-17	SEA	10-6	38.1%	1	10-5-1	8.0%	11	-30.1%	—	—	—	—

Note: Only includes teams which kept the same starting quarterback in Year 3 as well.

2017 Panthers Schedule

Week	Opp.	Week	Opp.	Week	Opp.
1	at SF	7	at CHI	13	at NO
2	BUF	8	at TB	14	MIN
3	NO	9	ATL	15	GB
4	at NE	10	MIA (Mon.)	16	TB
5	at DET	11	BYE	17	at ATL
6	PHI (Thu.)	12	at NYJ		

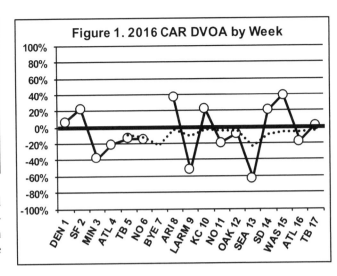

Figure 1. 2016 CAR DVOA by Week

the Battering Cam in 2011, the Panthers have concentrated their attack around Newton's physical gifts to an unusual degree. Unsurprisingly, he has also taken more punishment than any franchise quarterback should expect to take, even one who sports Superman's physique.

The 2016 season opener set the tone for the bashing to come. Sent to Denver for a Super Bowl rematch (a rather unfair bit of scheduling that head coach Ron Rivera is still complaining about), Carolina watched in horror as Denver turned back the clock to the "YOU GOT JACKED UP!!" era. Broncos defenders took turns launching themselves at Newton's *cabeza*, with little to no protection from the refs or the sideline *medicos*. The ugly strategy left Newton groggy, though officially un-concussed (no one on the Panthers sideline bothered to put him in the protocol).

There were more beatings down the line. In an October game against Atlanta, Newton styled like it was 2015 as he approached the goal line on a keeper, only to get leveled by Deion Jones, and was most definitely concussed. The shot may have convinced Newton to curb his running instincts, as he set career lows in carries and yards, not to mention by far his worst mark in rushing DVOA (it was Newton's first trip into negativity in that regard). Meanwhile, he was sacked or hit 99 times, ninth in the NFL in knockdowns as a percentage of dropbacks. That doesn't fully excuse his poor play—Matt Ryan, for example, was knocked down more often and was Newton's successor as MVP—but it certainly didn't help.

The latest entry on Newton's HIPAA form is a torn rotator cuff, which he suffered in December. He proceeded to play through it, attempted to rehab it without surgery, watched it worsen, then finally had it operated upon in March. The shoulder surgery gets tacked on to three years of medical trauma that also includes the concussion(s), ankle surgery, cracked ribs, a back fracture after a terrifying car crash, and a wisdom tooth extraction. (Remember this list when excoriating Cam for having fun on the sidelines during the good times.) Newton was benched for a series for not wearing a tie to a game, but never missed a snap due to the rotator cuff injury.

In retrospect, the decision to keep throwing Newton out on the field to finish up a lost season seems imprudent at best. Clearly, the team didn't think the injury was as bad as it turned out to be—otherwise Newton would have had surgery far earlier. But they also told the world Cam's issue was "pain management," NFL code for "don't be a pussy and take the damn Toradol already," and that there was no tear, a claim that the Panthers later admitted was false. The Panthers also waited

until June to reveal defensive tackle Star Lotulelei had shoulder surgery months earlier, so the team seems to be comfortable with duplicity when it comes to medical manners. But the dissonance between sending the clearly limited franchise quarterback out for more whacking while babying the concussed franchise linebacker was glaring.

By the time you read this, Newton may have actually thrown his first offseason pass—after teasing he would be ready for OTAs in June, the Panthers pushed his ready date back to training camp. He is way behind when it comes to getting in tune with his new weaponry: namely, Carolina's first two picks in the draft, Christian McCaffrey and Curtis Samuel. Their selections scream that the Panthers want to de-emphasize the deep-passing, big-receiver approach they have prized since Newton came to Charlotte, or at least mix it up some with a Patriots-style short game based on slippery, versatile players.

McCaffrey and Samuel certainly fit that mold, especially the former. The Stanford running back is such a receiving weapon he could make the roster as a slot wideout. His combine numbers made Draft Twitter spontaneously combust with ecstasy, highlighting his exceptional quickness. As a runner, McCaffrey has superb vision and great footwork, which overcome his lack of top-end size and speed. McCaffrey put up almost 7,000 total yards in college, including returns, highlighting how he will be deployed from various angles in Carolina (though draft night exclamations of 30 touches a game seem extreme, not to mention malpractice). Combining McCaffrey with Newton in shotgun looks almost automatically puts defenses in a mismatch situation. Plays that became Newton runs in the past can now be schemed into wheel routes, slants, and screens to a player who can handle all of them, or can simply take a handoff and get tough yards when needed, relieving the quarterback of added burden.

Samuel is a less exceptional version of McCaffrey. He played running back and wideout at Ohio State, though he will mostly be the latter in Charlotte. His 4.31 40-yard dash at the combine was overlooked after John Ross blistered a 4.22, but Samuel adds another element of pure speed to the plodding Panthers attack. (Samuel actually sports a higher Playmaker

Rating than Ross, though much of that is based on his rushing attempts.) He needs plenty of work to become a polished NFL receiver, but the Panthers envision him taking short passes and weaving through the enemy, à la Taylor Gabriel in Atlanta.

The problem with all of this, beyond the learning curve the rookies will require, is that Newton isn't a quarterback well-suited to the short, surgical passing game. Newton only completed 44 passes to his running backs last year, a number the Panthers hope McCaffrey can exceed all by his lonesome in 2017. But Newton's strength is deep and intermediate ball accuracy. Small ball is just not in his wheelhouse. It's like asking Aaron Judge to bunt.

Our own Cian Fahey broke down Newton's accuracy in his *Pre-Snap Reads Quarterback Catalogue 2017*. Newton led the NFL in average depth of target, with his average pass travelling more than 10 yards past the line of scrimmage. He had more attempts deeper than 20 yards than he had dump-off passes behind the line of scrimmage. Meanwhile, Fahey's accuracy table lists Newton as the 32nd-ranked quarterback in throws up to 5 yards from the line of scrimmage, and 30th in throws up to 10 yards past the line. But only Touchdown Tommy is better when it comes to passes 11 to 20 yards downfield, and Cam ranks in the top ten on those 20-plus-yarders as well.

We've all seen Newton gun his typical fastball to a receiver too close to handle that kind of velocity, or spray a seemingly simple dump pass one play after lasering a dime 40 yards downfield. Newton is a rare beast: precise, but only within the framework of the intermediate/downfield passing offense. So Mike Shula, Carolina's offensive coordinator, has built his attack around Newton's downfield capability. Given the lack of consistent deep threats and quality offensive line play, the fact that Newton excels operating these game plans is testimony to his incredible talents.

The question now becomes whether Shula intends to truly change his scheme, or just make smaller modifications. Working quick-strike players like McCaffrey and Samuel into the existing framework will lessen their impact, and risks blunting the best of both approaches. Yet building entirely around the rookies' skill sets not only works against the best attributes of the quarterback but negates the previous drafting of big-framed, slow-twitch wideouts Kelvin Benjamin and Devin Funchess. Whatever the blend, it will be up to Newton to make it all work. He is most certainly capable of doing so, if healthy, but missing all of the offseason won't help get that important timing down (and McCaffrey wasn't available until the final day of June minicamp, thanks to Stanford being on the quarters system).

However long it takes the offensive plans to slip into gear, the hope is the defense remains the bulwark and identity of the team. As mentioned above, we foresee the unit to be better, though it was hardly poor in 2016 (10th in DVOA, down from second in 2015).

A return to greatness for the Panthers defense will have to come under new leadership. Defensive coordinator Sean McDermott has shuffled off to Buffalo to coach the Bills. McDermott was less guru than grinder, a conventional schemer who was successful through ultra-preparedness and intelligent use of his personnel. Secondary (and assistant head) coach Steve Wilks takes over—unsurprisingly, as he and Rivera are joined at the hip. Wilks has coached under Riverboat Ron at three separate NFL stops. He's a hometown hero of sorts, who grew up in Charlotte, played college ball at nearby Appalachian State, and even went both ways for the Charlotte Rage of the Arena League—not exactly in the Steph Curry pantheon of athletes from the Queen City, but not bad. Changes from McDermott's 4-3 scheme—the front four rushes the passer, plenty of Cover-3 zone behind it, let the athletes win out—will be few. One player to watch under Wilks figures to be linebacker Shaq Thompson. The speedster has been excellent in coverage, but seldom gets unleashed to attack the quarterback (one sack and a dozen hits or hurries in two seasons). If anything looks new on the Carolina defense, it will be Thompson coming off the edge more often to augment the rush.

If Wilks is to lead a top-five defense, having Kuechly healthy for the entire season obviously is condition No. 1. The dominant linebacker insists he is healthy and could have played at the end of last season had the games merited his presence. But the team and its fans will be on eggshells as Kuechly hurls himself into the ruck and maul of NFL Sundays. Meanwhile, fellow linebacker Thomas Davis remains among the best in the game, but he is 35 with a notable history of injury himself. If the Dynamic Duo, along with Thompson (does that make him Commissioner Gordon in this metaphor?), can stay together and up to standards in 2017, the defense can't help but be strong.

What can make it special again will be the further development of the young cornerbacks. After Josh Norman was surprisingly dumped last offseason, rookies Daryl Worley and James Bradberry were thrust into the fray long before they were ready. The two performed quite well, all things considered, but the Norman Effect was felt. In 2015, Carolina was third in the NFL in DVOA against the opposing No. 1 wide receivers. In 2016, they fell to 24th. At least the yo-yo didn't swing all the way back to 2014 levels, when the Panthers were 27th in that split. It is reasonable to expect that with seasoning, and the addition of veterans Captain Munnerlyn and Mike Adams, the Panthers secondary should head back toward 2015 levels, if not actually reach those heights.

Another standout year from the pass rush will also help. Carolina took the quarterback down 47 times last year, second in the league, while they were tied for fourth in adjusted sack rate. General manager Dave Gettleman has shown he prizes the front four, while willing to be cheap in the secondary, and this offseason only underscored that trait. With the exception of end Kony Ealy, who was traded to New England, Gettleman managed to get the band back together despite a host of free agents. Dominant defensive tackle Kawann Short was re-signed to a monster deal, as was expected, and ends Mario Addison (9.5 sacks), Wes Horton, and Charles Johnson were also brought back, despite expectations at least one would leave. Gettleman even added old friend Julius Peppers, who is back in Carolina for one last rodeo. Having at long last been freed from salary-cap prison, Gettleman showed that he is a savvy operator when there are no handcuffs.

Gettleman also loves to trade up for draft picks, having

moved up in the past to snag Worley, Funchess, and tackle Darryl Williams, in addition to slot corner Bene Benwikere, who was very good in 2015 only to sink along with his team a year later and get released (he's now in Cincinnati). Trader Dave got aggressive in the draft once again this April, dealing away a fourth-round pick to move up in the third and select defensive end Daeshon Hall from Texas A&M to further augment the pass rush and pack the D-line meeting room with quality athletes.

If there was one move that didn't fit Gettleman's usual m.o., it was the free-agent signing of oft-injured, mostly bad left tackle Matt Kalil to a sizable deal. Gettleman has been reticent to throw big money at the offensive line in the past, and it has been four years since Kalil was either healthy or productive. The signing shows how desperate the team is to protect Newton, and just how much the season hinges on getting the quarterback back to his 2015 form.

It seems ridiculous to say Gettleman and Rivera are feeling the heat so soon after an 18-2 season and a Super Bowl trip. Yet a repeat of 2016 could see a fresh start on South Mint Street. There is a long list of veterans who could be cut after this year without dire cap consequences, including Davis, Peppers, Johnson, running back Jonathan Stewart, tight end Greg Olsen, and center/older brother Ryan Kalil. A slingshot back into the playoffs ensures everyone keeps getting paid.

The stakes are right there in the center of the table for all to see, unmissable even to those whose eyes are filled with tears.

Robert Weintraub

Right as we were finishing up *FOA 2017*, Carolina threw a massive spanner into the works with the stunning firing of Dave Gettleman. There was no immediate reasoning given. Reports from beat writers and insiders indicate owner Jerry Richardson may have wearied of Gettleman's unusual approach to team-building, i.e., not paying the going rate to offensive linemen and cornerbacks, two crucial pillars of any modern team. It might also have something to do with a Tweet sent out by former Panthers running back DeAngelo Williams, who wrote "I want to publicly say the Panthers is off my list of teams I won't play for due to the firing of that snake Dave gettleman (sic)." Seems the locker room wasn't always behind the general manager. The Panthers hired Marty Hurney, the man Gettleman replaced in 2012, to serve as interim general manager until a new full-time hire is made after the season. Regardless of why it happened, the fall from 17-2 and the Super Bowl to the unemployment line in 17 months is shocking. It turns out Gettleman's job *didn't* depend on a turnaround in 2017.

2016 Panthers Stats by Week

Wk	vs.	W-L	PF	PA	YDF	YDA	TO	Total	Off	Def	ST
1	at DEN	L	20	21	333	307	+2	6%	15%	-6%	-14%
2	SF	W	46	27	529	302	-1	22%	3%	-11%	9%
3	MIN	L	10	22	306	211	-3	-38%	-25%	-6%	-18%
4	at ATL	L	33	48	378	571	-1	-21%	-10%	15%	4%
5	TB	L	14	17	414	315	-4	-14%	-2%	-4%	-16%
6	at NO	L	38	41	406	523	-1	-15%	10%	19%	-6%
7	BYE										
8	ARI	W	30	20	349	340	+1	36%	18%	-9%	9%
9	at LARM	W	13	10	244	339	+1	-53%	-15%	25%	-13%
10	KC	L	17	20	341	256	-1	22%	-1%	-25%	-2%
11	NO	W	23	20	223	371	+2	-20%	-33%	-15%	-2%
12	at OAK	L	32	35	358	366	0	-8%	-8%	-11%	-11%
13	at SEA	L	7	40	271	534	-1	-63%	-33%	29%	-1%
14	SD	W	28	16	272	278	+4	20%	-29%	-34%	16%
15	at WAS	W	26	15	438	335	+3	39%	4%	-30%	5%
16	ATL	L	16	33	302	408	-2	-18%	-34%	-4%	12%
17	at TB	L	16	17	335	300	-1	1%	-11%	-24%	-11%

Trends and Splits

	Offense	Rank	Defense	Rank
Total DVOA	-8.4%	25	-5.3%	10
Unadjusted VOA	-9.3%	24	-2.1%	15
Weighted Trend	-12.2%	26	-7.9%	5
Variance	3.1%	3	3.6%	7
Average Opponent	0.0%	13	1.5%	8
Passing	2.5%	24	1.1%	11
Rushing	-11.8%	23	-15.1%	9
First Down	-6.5%	23	1.3%	20
Second Down	-17.3%	27	-6.0%	11
Third Down	1.5%	14	-18.3%	4
First Half	-6.0%	22	-15.5%	1
Second Half	-5.6%	19	-2.5%	18
Red Zone	-15.8%	25	-19.3%	5
Late and Close	-11.9%	22	-8.7%	9

Five-Year Performance

Year	W-L	Pyth W	Est W	PF	PA	TO	Total	Rk	Off	Rk	Def	Rk	ST	Rk	Off AGL	Rk	Def AGL	Rk	Off Age	Rk	Def Age	Rk	ST Age	Rk
2012	7-9	7.8	8.8	357	363	+1	5.5%	13	7.2%	10	-3.1%	11	-4.8%	29	23.1	10	53.0	27	27.1	15	25.7	28	26.0	19
2013	12-4	11.7	11.0	366	241	+11	24.6%	3	7.9%	10	-15.7%	3	1.0%	13	42.4	21	28.4	17	28.2	2	26.6	16	26.6	7
2014	7-8-1	7.0	7.4	339	374	+3	-8.5%	24	-4.7%	20	-1.7%	15	-5.5%	30	39.7	25	11.7	1	26.4	26	27.2	8	26.4	6
2015	15-1	12.4	11.1	500	308	+20	26.0%	4	10.1%	8	-18.4%	2	-2.4%	23	28.2	14	22.7	8	27.0	14	28.1	3	26.8	3
2016	6-10	7.1	6.7	369	402	-2	-5.5%	24	-8.4%	25	-5.3%	10	-2.5%	25	36.9	18	19.6	7	27.0	12	26.2	23	26.6	6

2016 Performance Based on Most Common Personnel Groups

CAR Offense					CAR Offense vs. Opponents					CAR Defense				CAR Defense vs. Opponents			
Pers	Freq	Yds	DVOA	Run%	Pers	Freq	Yds	DVOA	Run%	Pers	Freq	Yds	DVOA	Pers	Freq	Yds	DVOA
11	53%	6.0	6.0%	34%	Base	31%	4.9	-13.6%	58%	Base	40%	6.2	-0.9%	11	56%	5.4	-11.6%
12	27%	5.0	-15.6%	34%	Nickel	56%	5.8	-1.0%	35%	Nickel	59%	5.3	-8.7%	12	17%	6.4	10.1%
21	9%	5.1	-24.4%	63%	Dime+	9%	5.5	-3.4%	9%	Goal Line	0%	0.8	3.4%	21	8%	6.8	-0.7%
22	4%	2.6	-55.0%	74%	Goal Line	3%	0.5	18.6%	81%					13	4%	9.0	32.8%
612	3%	5.1	-2.9%	91%	Big	1%	6.9	16.6%	80%					611	3%	3.6	-34.7%
622	2%	1.7	43.7%	83%										612	3%	3.9	-14.0%

Strategic Tendencies

Run/Pass		Rk	Formation		Rk	Pass Rush		Rk	Secondary		Rk	Strategy		Rk
Runs, first half	42%	6	Form: Single Back	66%	29	Rush 3	3.2%	28	4 DB	40%	5	Play-action	18%	16
Runs, first down	51%	8	Form: Empty Back	8%	11	Rush 4	73.0%	5	5 DB	59%	16	Avg Box (Off)	6.35	6
Runs, second-long	37%	4	Pers: 3+ WR	54%	28	Rush 5	17.9%	25	6+ DB	0%	32	Avg Box (Def)	6.27	10
Runs, power sit.	63%	7	Pers: 2+ TE/6+ OL	37%	4	Rush 6+	5.9%	16	CB by Sides	86%	10	Offensive Pace	30.24	12
Runs, behind 2H	32%	3	Pers: 6+ OL	6%	11	Sacks by LB	11.5%	23	S/CB Cover Ratio	23%	25	Defensive Pace	29.46	3
Pass, ahead 2H	52%	8	Shotgun/Pistol	78%	4	Sacks by DB	11.5%	6	DB Blitz	10%	13	Go for it on 4th	1.01	20

Clearly the strategy against the Panthers is to send blitzes at Cam Newton. Newton was blitzed a league-high 38 percent of pass plays. Thirteen percent of pass plays were big blitzes with six or more pass-rushers, while no other quarterback was big-blitzed on more than 7.9 percent of passes. The strategy was very successful, as Carolina went from 7.1 yards per play with three or four pass-rushers to 6.1 yards with five pass-rushers and 4.3 yards with six or more pass-rushers. ☙ Department of *A Change Is Gonna Come*: Carolina was dead last with only 12 percent of passes going to running backs in 2016. The Panthers were also last in 2015 and 31st in 2014. ☙ Carolina only went three-and-out on 17.0 percent of drives (fourth in the NFL) despite ranking 25th in offensive DVOA. ☙ The Panthers used play-action on 24 percent of first-down passes, which ranked only 27th in the NFL. But they were average using play-action on 20 percent of second-down passes, and then led the league by using play-action on 8.7 percent of third-down passes. This seems to be a specific tendency of the Panthers offense, not a fluke, as they've been first or second in using play-action on third down for three straight seasons. ☙ Then again, maybe this tendency needs to change, as the Panthers averaged 6.0 yards with play-action but 6.6 yards on other passes. They were one of just three teams with negative DVOA on play-action. ☙ Carolina recovered just two of 10 offensive fumbles last season. ☙ Carolina had the league's second-largest gap between defense against single-back runs (3.5 yards per carry, -25.3% DVOA) and defense against multi-back runs (4.7, -2.2%). This may be a one-year fluke, as their gap went in the other direction in 2015. ☙ Carolina was the only team in the NFL we didn't mark using six defensive backs on a single play last season. ☙ Although the Panthers didn't blitz a defensive back any more often than they had in 2015, they had 2.5 times as many sacks from defensive backs. ☙ The Panthers (and 49ers) had the league's most interchangeable safeties, as the average gain on a tackle by Kurt Coleman was within 0.1 yards of the average gain on a tackle by Tre Boston. ☙ Carolina's adjusted sack rate on defense went from 6.0 percent on first and second down (17th) to a league-leading 10.5 percent on third down. ☙ Carolina defenders were only called for defensive pass interference three times for a league-low 26 yards. ☙ The Panthers benefited from 47 opponent drops, second in the league behind Tennessee.

Passing

Player	DYAR	DVOA	Plays	NtYds	Avg	YAC	C%	TD	Int
C.Newton	-64	-13.0%	543	3223	5.9	4.9	53.4%	19	14
D.Anderson	-27	-17.9%	53	453	8.5	4.5	67.9%	2	5

Rushing

Player	DYAR	DVOA	Plays	Yds	Avg	TD	Fum	Suc
J.Stewart	11	-7.0%	162	579	3.6	9	0	43%
C.Newton	20	-7.1%	73	320	4.4	5	0	-
F.Whittaker	-18	-18.8%	47	223	4.7	0	0	38%
C.Artis-Payne	6	-4.5%	36	144	4.0	2	0	50%
M.Tolbert*	-22	-27.2%	29	74	2.6	0	0	34%
T.Ginn*	33	9.1%	12	74	6.2	0	0	-

Receiving

Player	DYAR	DVOA	Plays	Ctch	Yds	Y/C	YAC	TD	C%
K.Benjamin	145	3.0%	118	63	941	14.9	3.7	7	53%
T.Ginn*	13	-10.8%	95	54	752	13.9	3.4	4	57%
D.Funchess	26	-7.4%	58	23	371	16.1	4.5	4	40%
C.Brown*	-55	-25.8%	53	27	271	10.0	4.2	1	51%
B.Bersin	-6	-21.7%	6	2	17	8.5	1.0	0	33%
R.Shepard	89	15.7%	40	23	341	14.8	3.3	2	58%
C.Johnson	-13	-17.0%	37	20	232	11.6	3.5	0	54%
G.Olsen	134	8.3%	129	80	1073	13.4	4.4	3	62%
E.Dickson	6	-2.6%	19	10	134	13.4	6.9	1	53%
F.Whittaker	37	6.2%	33	25	226	9.0	9.5	0	76%
J.Stewart	-67	-70.1%	21	8	60	7.5	9.3	0	38%
M.Tolbert*	11	0.2%	15	10	72	7.2	8.7	1	67%

Offensive Line

Player	Pos	Age	GS	Snaps	Pen	Sk	Pass	Run	Player	Pos	Age	GS	Snaps	Pen	Sk	Pass	Run
Andrew Norwell	LG	26	16/16	1109	5	4.0	13	5	Tyler Larsen	C	26	9/5	356	0	0.0	3	6
Mike Remmers*	LT/RT	28	16/16	1107	15	8.5	20	7	Chris Scott	G/T	30	12/4	294	1	1.0	3	3
Trai Turner	RG/RT	24	16/16	1099	10	2.5	14	5	Gino Gradkowski	C	29	10/3	235	1	0.5	2	1
Daryl Williams	RT	25	13/10	647	1	1.5	11	3	Michael Oher	LT	31	3/3	233	1	3.0	5	2
Ryan Kalil	C	32	8/8	506	4	1.0	2	1									

Year	Yards	ALY	Rank	Power	Rank	Stuff	Rank	2nd Lev	Rank	Open Field	Rank	Sacks	ASR	Rank	Press	Rank	F-Start	Cont.
2014	3.93	3.85	27	68%	10	20%	17	1.14	18	0.59	25	42	7.9%	22	21.5%	7	17	26
2015	4.10	4.24	12	76%	2	18%	8	1.23	5	0.61	22	33	6.9%	21	25.7%	17	12	34
2016	3.90	3.83	25	73%	3	22%	24	1.10	23	0.63	19	36	6.2%	19	26.8%	17	14	27

2016 ALY by direction:	Left End 4.81 (10)	Left Tackle 3.45 (28)	Mid/Guard 3.73 (29)	Right Tackle 3.65 (22)	Right End 4.56 (8)

Despite the pounding Cam Newton took, the line's adjusted sack rate was actually slightly better in 2016 than in 2015. Not so with adjusted line yards, however, and the run numbers across the board were mostly bottom third. Only in power situations was the ranking up to snuff, which of course is mostly about Newton anyway. ⬥ Carolina essentially swapped tackles with Minnesota, signing Matt Kalil from the Vikings and letting Mike Remmers—famously undressed by Von Miller in Super Bowl 50 and not much better in 2016—head north in a subsequent free agency move. Kalil got $31 million guaranteed (sixth among offensive tackles) after playing just two games in 2016 due to a hip injury. He wasn't exactly dynamite before that, finishing fourth in the league in blown blocks during an awful 2015 campaign. He has generally played (poorly) with one injury or another for most of his career. Hopefully fraternal bonds lead to more cohesive line play, as Matt joins brother Ryan, the Panthers center, in Charlotte. ⬥ Michael Oher's well-documented pigskin journey appears to be at an end, thanks to a nasty Week 3 concussion that lingered well into the summer. Darryl Williams remains the right tackle for now, though he struggled enough that guard Trai Turner was kicked outside late in the season, with predictable results. Turner regressed some at his natural position too, falling from third to 24th among right guards in snaps per blown block. ⬥ Taylor Moton, picked in the second round from Western Michigan, will prove a critical figure. A massive dude (6-foot-5, 319 pounds) with footwork issues, Moton is a more natural guard at the pro level, though he played tackle well enough in college. (He did play guard as a junior, and excelled.) The sooner he can become a contributor on this line, the better, be it inside or out.

Defensive Front Seven

Defensive Line	Age	Pos	Overall								vs. Run					Pass Rush			
			G	Snaps	Plays	TmPct	Rk	Stop	Dfts	BTkl	Runs	St%	Rk	RuYd	Rk	Sack	Hit	Hur	Dsrpt
Kawann Short	28	DT	16	779	58	7.0%	13	53	19	6	45	91%	7	0.9	8	6.0	13	23	4
Star Lotulelei	28	DT	16	702	26	3.1%	71	18	9	1	16	69%	64	1.5	18	4.0	4	12	1
Vernon Butler	23	DT	10	225	14	2.7%	--	10	4	0	9	78%	--	3.4	--	1.5	1	3	1
Kyle Love	31	DT	10	224	16	3.1%	--	11	6	2	13	62%	--	2.5	--	1.5	1	5	0

Edge Rushers	Age	Pos	G	Snaps	Plays	TmPct	Rk	Stop	Dfts	BTkl	Runs	St%	Rk	RuYd	Rk	Sack	Hit	Hur	Dsrpt
					Overall						vs. Run					Pass Rush			
Kony Ealy*	26	DE	16	623	34	4.1%	65	26	10	7	21	81%	21	2.4	42	5.0	2	19	2
Charles Johnson	31	DE	13	541	28	4.1%	64	22	10	4	14	86%	8	2.4	43	4.0	9	25	3
Mario Addison	30	DE	14	433	25	3.4%	79	19	15	3	9	78%	33	0.2	2	9.5	5	20	1
Wes Horton	27	DE	11	332	11	1.9%	99	10	4	1	8	88%	5	1.4	18	2.5	2	13	0
Lavar Edwards	27	DE	10	195	13	2.3%	--	10	4	0	8	88%	--	1.6	--	2.0	1	3	1
Julius Peppers	37	OLB	16	587	26	3.2%	80	22	12	4	13	77%	36	1.8	26	7.5	5	18	6

Linebackers	Age	Pos	G	Snaps	Plays	TmPct	Rk	Stop	Dfts	BTkl	Runs	St%	Rk	RuYd	Rk	Sack	Hit	Hur	Tgts	Suc%	Rk	AdjYd	Rk	PD	Int
					Overall						vs. Run					Pass Rush			vs. Pass						
Thomas Davis	34	OLB	16	1008	110	13.2%	38	51	15	7	49	57%	67	3.7	53	2.5	2	9	46	58%	13	4.2	2	5	3
Luke Kuechly	26	MLB	10	655	108	20.7%	1	62	23	3	54	69%	20	2.9	16	2.0	2	10	30	56%	21	8.1	70	5	1
Shaq Thompson	23	OLB	14	535	60	8.2%	68	37	9	9	28	79%	3	2.4	6	0.0	3	5	22	58%	12	4.6	5	3	1
A.J. Klein*	26	OLB	15	351	30	3.8%	86	16	7	4	13	85%	2	1.2	1	1.0	0	1	18	35%	76	10.4	80	1	0

Year	Yards	ALY	Rank	Power	Rank	Stuff	Rank	2nd Level	Rank	Open Field	Rank	Sacks	ASR	Rank	Press	Rank
2014	4.51	3.90	10	79%	29	21%	8	1.07	10	1.27	32	40	7.5%	7	25.0%	17
2015	3.78	3.50	4	87%	32	24%	6	1.02	6	0.76	15	44	7.1%	11	26.3%	12
2016	3.83	3.61	4	78%	32	24%	5	1.10	10	0.73	17	47	7.3%	5	30.2%	7

2016 ALY by direction:	Left End 4.44 (19)	Left Tackle 3.13 (4)	Mid/Guard 3.56 (4)	Right Tackle 4.22 (16)	Right End 3.55 (13)

The Panthers stepped up and signed tackle Kawann Short to a monster new deal, one he has clearly earned with stellar play. Short saw his sack total decline from 2015, but accrued 8.5 more hurries and turned into an elite run-stuffer. His fellow "Hog Molly" (Dave Gettleman's fond term for continent-sized linemen) Star Lotulelei becomes the next decision point after Carolina picked up his rookie option for 2017. Lotulelei isn't the run-stuffer Damon Harrison is, but will command similar money in the marketplace, meaning 2016 second-rounder Vernon Butler (Louisiana Tech) may be groomed as an interstellar replacement if the Panthers get outbid for Star. ☜ Somehow, despite all that tackle talent and Short's run defense improvement, the Panthers were dead last in the NFL at stopping power runs for the second straight season. Considering they don't even have to play against Cam Newton, that's poor. ☜ Kony Ealy was dealt to the Patriots for a song in one of those "Belichick must know something" deals. His long-term replacement could be third-rounder Daeshon Hall, who was the "other" defensive end at Texas A&M. While not as explosive an athlete as top overall pick Myles Garrett, Hall has pretty good bend and flexibility considering he was primarily a linebacker until last season. SackSEER likes him considerably more than ends selected ahead of him such as Taco Charlton, Charles Harris, and Derek Rivers. Pass-rush aside, developing his edge-setting abilities will be key to Hall's playing time. ☜ Meanwhile, Julius Peppers returns home to rush the passer. If his 2016 season with the Packers is any indication, the second-greatest Julius in sports history still has quality snaps left in his tank. ☜ He gets lost behind Luke and T.D., but Shaq Thompson broke out in an excellent second season. Thompson's speed allows the Panthers to play their base 4-3 even when the opponents play three wide receivers. Carolina's -40.5% DVOA in base defense was easily tops in the league last season. Even if Davis' age and Kuechly's concussions become issues, the second-greatest Shaq in sports history (edging out New England's Shaq Mason) should pick up the slack.

Defensive Secondary

Secondary	Age	Pos	G	Snaps	Plays	TmPct	Rk	Stop	Dfts	BTkl	Runs	St%	Rk	RuYd	Rk	Tgts	Tgt%	Rk	Dist	Suc%	Rk	AdjYd	Rk	PD	Int
					Overall						vs. Run					vs. Pass									
Kurt Coleman	29	FS	15	995	100	12.8%	11	35	9	8	50	46%	25	6.1	27	34	8.0%	31	13.1	35%	63	9.9	53	7	4
Daryl Worley	22	CB	16	866	95	11.4%	4	33	10	8	25	44%	36	5.8	24	68	18.6%	46	14.8	54%	14	7.1	28	9	1
Tre Boston*	25	FS	15	840	59	7.6%	57	22	13	8	22	45%	26	6.0	24	24	6.6%	17	16.7	62%	1	6.0	5	6	2
James Bradberry	24	CB	13	798	69	10.2%	15	23	9	4	14	29%	66	4.6	12	72	21.2%	62	12.4	50%	39	6.0	9	10	2
Leonard Johnson*	27	CB	10	436	31	6.0%	--	12	7	9	5	40%	--	5.4	--	30	16.0%	--	6.7	50%	--	6.6	--	1	0
Robert McClain	29	CB	14	326	35	4.8%	--	13	7	8	14	50%	--	3.2	--	19	14.4%	--	9.7	18%	--	10.6	--	1	0
Michael Griffin*	32	FS	13	285	35	5.2%	--	14	2	4	23	61%	--	5.6	--	7	5.8%	--	12.0	34%	--	12.6	--	0	0
Captain Munnerlyn	29	CB	15	637	56	7.6%	65	21	9	1	11	45%	31	8.7	67	42	15.9%	14	7.6	50%	42	6.9	23	3	0
Mike Adams	36	SS	15	998	81	10.6%	30	18	7	7	37	24%	68	9.8	65	29	6.7%	21	8.4	34%	66	10.1	57	0	0

Year	Pass D Rank	vs. #1 WR	Rk	vs. #2 WR	Rk	vs. Other WR	Rk	vs. TE	Rk	vs. RB	Rk
2014	9	15.1%	27	-0.6%	16	7.9%	23	-11.6%	7	-29.5%	2
2015	2	-24.7%	3	-9.5%	12	-30.4%	3	-40.4%	1	-10.5%	8
2016	11	6.1%	24	-1.1%	15	10.1%	23	-7.9%	9	-8.4%	12

All the talk in 2016 was about the rookie corners expected to replace Josh Norman. This year the chatter is about experience, as in veteran additions Captain Munnerlyn, back in Carolina after a three-year stretch in Minnesota; and Mike Adams, the 36-year-old safety signed from Indy to replace Tre Boston alongside Kurt Coleman. Munnerlyn is no shrinking violet, so the idea that he will mentor the young corners while quietly holding down the nickel role is a little kumbaya for reality, but he should be an upgrade over the likes of Robert McClain and Leonard Johnson. As for the kids, James Bradberry had the better rep, Daryl Worley the slightly better success rate. By adjusted yards per target, however, Bradberry was the best of any qualifying rookie cornerback. Both are quite promising, and should only be better after the gauntlet of their rookie seasons. Ready for a strange sentence? Boston is now in L.A. Yes, Tre signed with the Chargers after the Panthers dumped him, reportedly because he angered the coaches with his inconsistency and inability to communicate with his teammates. However, he was our top graded safety in success rate, albeit in a small sample. Adams, his replacement, was targeted about as frequently, and was successful about half as often as Boston. On the other hand, the Panthers ranked 30th in defensive DVOA on passes we charted as "deep middle" (over 15 yards downfield), so something was rotten in the defensive backfield.

Special Teams

Year	DVOA	Rank	FG/XP	Rank	Net Kick	Rank	Kick Ret	Rank	Net Punt	Rank	Punt Ret	Rank	Hidden	Rank
2014	-5.5%	30	-0.2	18	-2.2	20	2.3	9	-23.1	32	-4.1	22	0.0	17
2015	-2.4%	23	-1.5	21	-5.1	28	-1.8	19	-6.3	24	2.8	11	5.5	10
2016	-2.5%	25	-3.8	21	5.2	7	1.0	12	-10.4	29	-4.3	25	4.2	12

Before last season, the Panthers traded a 2018 fourth-round pick to Cleveland for Andy Lee, but he didn't show much gratitude for being sprung from the Browns—he was mediocre before getting hurt midseason (though he did set a franchise record with a 76-yard punt in Denver's thin air). Michael Palardy took over the job and wasn't much better, but got far better coverage from his gunners (minus-2.0 points worth of estimated field position, compared to 7.6 points for Lee), likely due to the improvement of Carolina's young players as the season progressed. Or maybe they just liked Palardy better. Ted Ginn Jr. added little as a punt returner and was worse on kickoffs, part of the reason he is now in New Orleans. Candidates for returns in 2017 include Fozzy Whittaker, Brenton Bersin, and Joe Webb, the NFL's only kick-returning third-string quarterback. Graham Gano wasn't very good at kickoffs, and his placekicking numbers weren't great either. Most of the damage was due to three missed field goals in the season finale, a 1-point loss at Tampa Bay. He only missed five other field goals all year, though one was in the final seconds in the opener at Denver, ensuring a loss that set the tone for Carolina's *annus horribilis*. The team drafted Harrison Butker from Georgia Tech in the seventh round to give Gano some competition.

Chicago Bears

2016 Record: 3-13	Total DVOA: -8.3% (25th)	2017 Mean Projection: 7.5 wins	On the Clock (0-4): 13%
Pythagorean Wins: 4.7 (28th)	Offense: -2.6% (17th)	Postseason Odds: 27.6%	Mediocrity (5-7): 39%
Snap-Weighted Age: 26.3 (23rd)	Defense: 5.0% (23rd)	Super Bowl Odds: 2.8%	Playoff Contender (8-10): 36%
Average Opponent: -0.8% (21st)	Special Teams: -0.6% (18th)	Proj. Avg. Opponent: 0.1% (15th)	Super Bowl Contender (11+): 12%

2016: This is what happens when a team with no depth leads the league in injuries.

2017: If you have two quarterbacks, you have no quarterback, but what if only one of those quarterbacks actually matters?

"Mike Glennon is our starting quarterback." That's what Ryan Pace said, and he might have even believed it. The Bears' general manager was standing in front of assembled media after the draft, with his team having just acquired Mitchell Trubisky after a trade for the second overall pick. Pace went as far as to say that there would be no quarterback competition before repeating, "Glennon is our starting quarterback."

Was Pace trying to convince the crowd or was he trying to convince himself? Recent history suggests the latter.

Pace is trying to follow the Eagles' blueprint from 12 months ago. There's only one problem: even the Eagles didn't follow that blueprint. The Eagles traded up in the first round of the 2016 draft to select Carson Wentz, despite having re-signed Sam Bradford to an extension to keep him off the free-agent market. Bradford was repeatedly labelled the starter, and Wentz was going to sit and learn before taking over for Bradford in the future. It turned out that the future was August. Bradford was sent to Minnesota before Week 1, and Wentz started all 16 games of his rookie season.

Glennon isn't likely to attract a trade partner. Even if another team loses its starter during training camp or the preseason, Glennon's lack of pedigree doesn't make him as attractive as Bradford was.

Since it's likely that Glennon will still be on the roster by the time the season comes around, Trubisky will be in a position where he has to take the job from the *incumbent* starter. Instead of looking like what the Eagles did last year, this is more likely to follow the route of the Los Angeles Rams and Jared Goff, or the Jacksonville Jaguars and Blake Bortles. Jaguars GM Dave Caldwell vehemently stated and repeated that Bortles was going to sit for at least his first season. They were happy to start Chad Henne, even if that meant losing games. Bortles would indeed sit—for two weeks. He played in 14 games, starting 13, and threw 475 passes during his rookie season.

In reality, Trubisky gains nothing from sitting. A quarterback whose primary knock coming out of college was that he only played in 13 games isn't going to benefit from not playing. Should Trubisky sit for the entirety of his rookie season and then start the next year, he will have started 13 games (all in college) between leaving high school in 2013 and his first NFL start in 2018. That's not the way to develop a quarter-back. It's especially not the way to develop a quarterback with Trubisky's skill set.

The Bears drafted Trubisky because they saw his poise, his accuracy, his footwork, and his willingness to deliver the ball against impending hits. Sure, he had issues at North Carolina. Most notably, he threw two awful interceptions against Stanford when the defense baited him into bad throws with the same action. On both plays, Trubisky failed to recognize that a safety rotated down just before the ball was snapped, changing the coverage. He threw the ball directly to a defender twice, with the second interception being run back for an easy touchdown.

Those plays were exceptions in that game, and exceptions for his college career. Trubisky can learn to read coverages better, and he can do so while throwing interceptions on the field. Sitting on the sideline being told how coverages work isn't the same as adjusting to the speed of the NFL and figuring things out through game action. Furthermore, the Bears are set up to protect him.

Regardless of who the starting quarterback is, Jordan Howard should be the focal point of the Bears offense in 2017. Howard had an excellent rookie season. He ran the ball 252 times for 1,313 rushing yards, 5.2 yards per carry, and six touchdowns, while only fumbling twice. He finished fifth in DYAR and 10th in DVOA. Howard is a physically imposing back who shows patience and vision running between the tackles. He can break off big plays—he had 10 plays that gained 20 or more yards last year, and two that gained 40 or more—while showing off subtle feet to evade defenders in space. Howard offers the Bears someone who can combine efficiency and explosiveness while carrying the ball 20 times per game.

Using the run to set up the pass will allow the Bears to simplify Trubisky's responsibilities. Instead of putting him in shotgun and expecting him to diagnose coverages, they can rely on play-action that distorts the defense's assignments while also creating clearly defined reads by using specific route combinations and half-field reads. Trubisky may not be advanced mentally, but he has a natural ability to react to pressure and the balance to set and reset in the pocket. His athleticism allows him to push the ball downfield accurately or throw on the run outside of the pocket. The offense would look something like Mark Sanchez's early years with the Jets,

2017 Bears Schedule

Week	Opp.	Week	Opp.	Week	Opp.
1	ATL	7	CAR	13	SF
2	at TB	8	at NO	14	at CIN
3	PIT	9	BYE	15	at DET (Sat.)
4	at GB (Thu.)	10	GB	16	CLE
5	MIN (Mon.)	11	DET	17	at MIN
6	at BAL	12	at PHI		

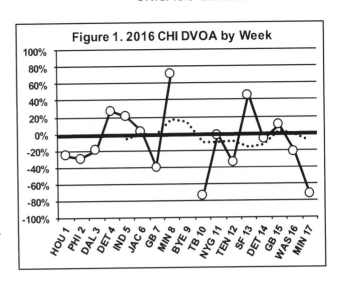

Figure 1. 2016 CHI DVOA by Week

except the Bears would be hoping to gradually shift more responsibility onto their quarterback as he develops.

While the Bears have limited receiving options, especially if Kevin White isn't healthy again, they do have an exceptional offensive line. The Bears had an adjusted sack rate of 4.9 percent last year, seventh in the league. It's not just that the Bears have a good offensive line, it's that their offensive interior excels in pass protection. Interior pressure is the worst kind for a quarterback, because it's tougher to adjust to. You can mitigate edge pressure with your movement or with a quicker release if you have space in front of you. It's much harder to do the same when that space is taken away and you have to move sideways. For a young quarterback who is going to be a touch slow reading defenses, that interior protection is huge. Josh Sitton has been one of the best pass-blocking guards in the NFL for a decade. He didn't fall off after being released by the Green Bay Packers last year. Cody Whitehair enjoyed his first NFL season last year and was an outstanding center. Kyle Long moved back inside after struggling more at right tackle to give the Bears three above-average starters inside.

The quality of the Bears' pass protection was the primary reason for Brian Hoyer and Matt Barkley's prolonged periods of competence last year. Barkley inevitably imploded and Hoyer likely would have too if he had stayed on the field long enough.

Putting Trubisky into the Bears offense won't be throwing him to the wolves (or the Vikings or Lions, in this scenario). He will be set up for success and should be able to learn his position without being overwhelmed or torpedoing the offense's output. Sitting him for the more experienced Glennon would likely make the offense better in 2017, but not dramatically. Glennon has legitimate starter potential and could be an above-average producer in the right setup but his long-term value to the franchise now is as a backup. The repetitions in training camp and practice, and scarce opportunities to play in the regular season, should all be focused on Trubisky. Whether the Bears want to publicly admit it now or not, he is the future of the franchise and he will be the biggest determining factor in the success or failure of this regime.

Another important factor will be Chicago's ability to hang on to Vic Fangio. Fangio was the target of his former employers, the San Francisco 49ers, who wanted to bring him back as defensive coordinator this offseason. The Bears blocked the approach and expanded Fangio's role, making him both the team's defensive coordinator and its linebackers coach. That's not new for Fangio—he did it with great success with

the 49ers—but it's notable because of who the Bears' outside linebackers are. Willie Young led the team with 7.5 sacks last year, yet he's not the primary reason the position is so intriguing. He's not even the secondary reason.

When Fangio was the defensive coordinator in San Francisco, he watched over the development of Aldon Smith. Smith spent his rookie season as a situational pass-rusher, but still managed 14 sacks. Leonard Floyd, whom the Bears selected high in the first round of the 2016 draft, started all 12 of the games he played in last year and managed seven sacks. Floyd came out of college as an athletic freak. Football Outsiders' SackSEER projection model loved him, giving him an 81 percent rating and projecting him for 26.9 sacks through five years. For comparison, Aldon Smith was projected for 20.0 sacks through five years. Floyd's workout numbers were phenomenal, but he was considered a raw prospect coming out of college. His rookie season was encouraging because his play speed and intensity were consistent, while he showed an ability to beat offensive linemen across their faces. Floyd was more of a high-energy player than a refined pass-rusher and he doesn't know how to bend the edge consistently at this point, but the potential for growth is there. His insane testing numbers combined with that comfort on the field suggest that Fangio could develop him into something special.

Floyd could very quickly be the Bears' best defender and even their best player. He has that kind of upside. First, though, he needs to surpass Pernell McPhee as the team's best outside linebacker. McPhee endured a frustrating 2016 season, missing the first six weeks because of knee issues. He finished the season with four sacks in nine games, but ultimately played only 274 snaps while not starting a game. McPhee didn't have the same explosiveness and physicality that had allowed him to constantly disrupt plays the previous year. McPhee is one of the more versatile defenders in the league; if he is healthy, he and Floyd would create one of the NFL's best outside linebacker combinations. Despite an offseason shoulder surgery, McPhee is optimistic about his ability to rebound in 2017 thanks to his weight loss. He claims to have lost 25 pounds since before the 2016 season. That should help his explosiveness, but could limit his physicality.

Relying on Floyd, McPhee, Young, the impressive Akiem Hicks, and maybe a breakout season from Jonathan Bullard, the Bears will be hoping that the pressure their front seven creates can mask some of the holes that still exist in the secondary.

Some onlookers pegged defensive backs such as Marshon Lattimore or Malik Hooker for the Bears' first-round selection, but the Trubisky trade cost Chicago a chance at either player even as they both slipped out of the top ten. Prince Amukamara was once one of the best young cornerbacks in the NFL, but was let go by the New York Giants two years ago before failing to land a second contract with the Jaguars after last season. Amukamara should start across from Kyle Fuller. Fuller was a highly respected cornerback coming out of college, but injuries and struggles with the athleticism of NFL receivers have resulted in an underwhelming career. The Bears didn't pick up Fuller's option for the end of his rookie deal, so he is entering a make-or-break season with the franchise. The Bears' depth at cornerback is impressive and diverse but none of the backups are suited to push for starting roles. That's a major problem when you share a division with three passing games that ranked in the top 20 of DVOA.

Improving a bad pass defense is always a priority in today's NFL. The Bears run defense was actually worse than its pass defense last year, though it has to be acknowledged that the two are largely intertwined. Defenses that stop the run on early downs put themselves in better position to stop the pass in obvious passing situations. Fangio will need to create an understanding between the players in his patchwork secondary, because he doesn't have individuals who can simply win their matchups. He can indirectly help the secondary by fixing the run defense, 29th in DVOA last year. A huge reason for that was the absence of nose tackle Eddie Goldman. The 320-pound nose tackle has shown promise when he has played and is only 23 years old, but he spent most of last season on the sideline after a high ankle sprain in Week 2. His presence alongside Akiem Hicks would not only improve the first-level run defense, but also create cleaner routes to the running back for the inside linebackers behind them. Assuming Goldman's development hasn't been derailed by missing most of last season, he should prove to be a valuable piece for what looks like an improving defensive front in Chicago.

Goldman was part of a historically bad season of injuries for the Bears last season. Chicago's 155.1 AGL was the highest in Football Outsiders' database since 2000, eclipsing the 141.3 AGL of the 2013 Giants. For the defense to really take a step forward, it can't afford to be without its key pieces. Health is always a defining element of any team's season. Seven of the ten teams since 2002 with the most injuries in comparison to that year's average won more games in the following season (Table 1). It's rare that an injury-crippled team wins the Super Bowl; the 2010 Green Bay Packers are the only obvious example from recent years. Health is even more relevant for a team such as Chicago, which not only lacks depth but also major stars it can rely on to offset weaknesses on the field.

Table 1. Worst AGL in a Season by Z-Score, 2002-2016

Rk	Team	Year	AGL	Rk	W-L	Z-Score	AGL Y+1	Rk	W-L Y+1
1	CLE	2006	98.0	32	4-12	-3.42	42.4	14	10-6
2	OAK	2003	91.5	32	4-12	-3.12	70.4	30	5-11
3	NYG	2015	138.7	32	6-10	-3.07	52.4	7	11-5
4	NYG	2013	141.3	32	7-9	-3.07	137.1	32	6-10
5	BUF	2009	122.5	32	6-10	-2.94	41.6	11	4-12
6	**CHI**	**2016**	**155.1**	**32**	**3-13**	**-2.70**	—	—	—
7	CHI	2002	67.7	32	4-12	-2.65	23.2	9	7-9
8	NYG	2014	137.1	32	6-10	-2.59	138.7	32	6-10
9	NYJ	2005	74.1	32	4-12	-2.49	16.5	2	10-6
10	NE	2005	72.4	31	10-6	-2.38	38.9	20	12-4
11	CIN	2008	107.8	32	4-11-1	-2.37	70.6	24	10-6
12	TEN	2004	88.4	32	5-11	-2.33	28.9	12	4-12

Z-Score represents how many standard deviations away from the mean that team's AGL score was for the season listed.

The Bears lack big-name stars on both sides of the ball. That doesn't mean they are destined to be a bad team. They do have enough pieces to at least be an average team. If they fall to the depths of the league standings, it will be because they are relying on inexperienced players or players who again couldn't stay healthy. It's not a great spot to be in, but it's better than having an old, expensive roster that is going nowhere.

Cian Fahey

2016 Bears Stats by Week

Wk	vs.	W-L	PF	PA	YDF	YDA	TO	Total	Off	Def	ST
1	at HOU	L	14	23	258	344	0	-26%	-19%	7%	-1%
2	PHI	L	14	29	284	280	-3	-29%	-23%	14%	8%
3	at DAL	L	17	31	390	447	-1	-19%	4%	25%	2%
4	DET	W	17	14	408	263	+2	27%	18%	-43%	-33%
5	at IND	L	23	29	522	396	-1	20%	27%	1%	-5%
6	JAC	L	16	17	389	317	+2	3%	-5%	-1%	7%
7	at GB	L	10	26	189	406	-1	-40%	-50%	4%	14%
8	MIN	W	20	10	403	258	0	72%	42%	-21%	9%
9	BYE										
10	at TB	L	10	36	283	360	-3	-74%	-70%	5%	1%
11	at NYG	L	16	22	315	329	-1	-2%	14%	18%	2%
12	TEN	L	21	27	411	375	-2	-35%	-13%	25%	3%
13	SF	W	26	6	326	147	-1	46%	13%	-44%	-11%
14	at DET	L	17	20	296	323	+2	-7%	-16%	-7%	2%
15	GB	L	27	30	449	451	-4	10%	26%	20%	4%
16	WAS	L	21	41	458	478	-5	-22%	15%	30%	-6%
17	at MIN	L	10	38	323	374	-4	-72%	-30%	36%	-6%

Trends and Splits

	Offense	Rank	Defense	Rank
Total DVOA	-2.6%	17	5.0%	23
Unadjusted VOA	-1.6%	17	7.2%	26
Weighted Trend	-3.9%	20	6.5%	25
Variance	9.0%	26	5.6%	20
Average Opponent	1.8%	32	0.5%	12
Passing	8.1%	20	6.9%	17
Rushing	-4.8%	18	2.7%	29
First Down	12.5%	5	7.1%	24
Second Down	-9.3%	21	3.1%	19
Third Down	-27.6%	29	4.3%	23
First Half	10.3%	9	6.7%	22
Second Half	-23.2%	27	2.6%	21
Red Zone	-11.9%	21	-4.7%	13
Late and Close	0.8%	17	17.2%	27

Five-Year Performance

Year	W-L	Pyth W	Est W	PF	PA	TO	Total	Rk	Off	Rk	Def	Rk	ST	Rk	Off AGL	Rk	Def AGL	Rk	Off Age	Rk	Def Age	Rk	ST Age	Rk
2012	10-6	10.8	11.0	375	277	+20	20.5%	6	-10.9%	26	-26.7%	1	4.7%	6	17.6	8	13.6	4	27.2	12	27.9	4	26.9	6
2013	8-8	7.3	9.2	445	478	+5	6.6%	11	13.3%	6	8.7%	25	2.0%	11	6.9	1	55.6	30	27.5	8	27.3	10	27.5	1
2014	5-11	4.9	6.4	319	442	-5	-13.8%	26	-0.1%	14	10.6%	28	-3.1%	25	41.0	27	60.6	26	27.9	3	27.0	12	26.3	9
2015	6-10	6.3	6.8	335	397	-4	-5.7%	19	6.9%	10	11.3%	31	-1.2%	21	64.7	30	28.2	16	27.4	10	25.8	31	26.2	13
2016	3-13	4.7	6.2	279	399	-20	-8.3%	25	-2.6%	17	5.0%	23	-0.6%	18	84.0	31	71.1	32	26.7	16	26.0	24	26.2	11

2016 Performance Based on Most Common Personnel Groups

CHI Offense				CHI Offense vs. Opponents					CHI Defense				CHI Defense vs. Opponents			
Pers	Freq	Yds	DVOA	Run%	Pers	Freq	Yds	DVOA	Run%	Pers	Freq	Yds	DVOA	Pers	Freq	Yds	DVOA
11	65%	6.4	7.5%	25%	Base	31%	5.8	-6.2%	60%	Base	22%	5.0	-2.4%	11	66%	6.0	6.1%
12	23%	6.5	6.9%	55%	Nickel	57%	6.3	6.0%	32%	Nickel	69%	5.8	8.8%	12	12%	5.3	8.2%
21	7%	4.2	-45.5%	71%	Dime+	11%	6.3	-6.7%	3%	Dime+	6%	8.7	4.7%	01	5%	6.9	7.8%
13	3%	2.3	-44.9%	73%	Goal Line	1%	1.0	110.7%	100%	Goal Line	2%	0.3	-9.3%	21	3%	4.2	-13.1%
23	1%	1.1	124.5%	100%						Big	1%	5.9	-23.2%	612	2%	7.5	40.8%

Strategic Tendencies

Run/Pass		Rk	Formation		Rk	Pass Rush		Rk	Secondary		Rk	Strategy		Rk
Runs, first half	43%	4	Form: Single Back	83%	8	Rush 3	11.1%	8	4 DB	22%	24	Play-action	20%	9
Runs, first down	47%	16	Form: Empty Back	4%	31	Rush 4	73.1%	4	5 DB	69%	6	Avg Box (Off)	6.21	12
Runs, second-long	27%	22	Pers: 3+ WR	65%	17	Rush 5	12.1%	32	6+ DB	6%	18	Avg Box (Def)	6.02	29
Runs, power sit.	61%	8	Pers: 2+ TE/6+ OL	28%	14	Rush 6+	3.7%	26	CB by Sides	65%	24	Offensive Pace	31.08	23
Runs, behind 2H	27%	16	Pers: 6+ OL	0%	31	Sacks by LB	58.1%	10	S/CB Cover Ratio	26%	19	Defensive Pace	31.57	27
Pass, ahead 2H	47%	18	Shotgun/Pistol	63%	19	Sacks by DB	2.7%	27	DB Blitz	7%	26	Go for it on 4th	0.80	24

The Bears threw in the middle of the field twice as often as they had in 2015, going from last in the league to above-average. ☞ Here's a very fluky stat: Chicago was the No. 2 offense in the league in the second quarter, but ranked 20th or lower in each of the other three quarters. ☞ The Bears used play-action on 25 percent of passes with Jay Cutler at quarterback, but only 18 percent of passes with Brian Hoyer or Matt Barkley. ☞ Chicago's defense was sixth in forcing three-and-outs (25.8 percent of drives) despite ranking just 23rd in defensive DVOA. ☞ Another thing Chicago's defense did well was prevent yards after the catch: they allowed an average of just 4.2, second in the league behind the Patriots.

Passing

Player	DYAR	DVOA	Plays	NtYds	Avg	YAC	C%	TD	Int
M.Barkley*	4	-10.9%	222	1568	7.1	4.2	59.7%	8	13
B.Hoyer*	404	19.4%	204	1435	7.0	5.2	67.8%	6	0
J.Cutler*	-69	-18.5%	154	955	6.2	5.1	59.1%	4	5
D.Fales*	-9	-34.3%	6	17	2.8	7.5	40.0%	0	0
M.Sanchez	-119	-96.5%	21	68	3.2	5.4	55.6%	0	2
M.Glennon	65	65.8%	11	75	6.8	3.7	90.9%	1	0

Rushing

Player	DYAR	DVOA	Plays	Yds	Avg	TD	Fum	Suc
J.Howard	103	4.2%	194	969	5.0	6	0	46%
J.Langford	16	-0.4%	44	152	3.5	4	0	57%
K.Carey	7	-3.0%	31	125	4.0	0	0	39%
J.Cutler*	3	-0.1%	5	24	4.8	0	0	-
B.Cunningham	-2	-11.4%	21	101	4.8	0	0	48%

Receiving

Player	DYAR	DVOA	Plays	Ctch	Yds	Y/C	YAC	TD	C%
C.Meredith	128	4.1%	98	67	898	13.4	4.5	4	68%
A.Jeffery*	132	5.0%	94	52	821	15.8	3.7	2	55%
E.Royal*	41	0.6%	43	33	372	11.3	5.9	2	77%
J.Bellamy	4	-11.2%	38	19	282	14.8	2.7	1	50%
D.Thompson	65	10.0%	36	22	249	11.3	2.0	2	61%
K.White	-64	-35.6%	36	19	187	9.8	2.8	0	53%
M.Wilson*	63	37.4%	16	9	160	17.8	5.6	1	56%
V.Cruz	6	-11.7%	72	39	586	15.0	4.8	1	54%
K.Wright	119	21.9%	43	29	416	14.3	4.3	3	67%
M.Wheaton	-9	-25.8%	9	4	51	12.8	2.0	1	44%
Z.Miller	85	12.5%	64	47	486	10.3	4.6	4	73%
D.Brown	15	4.1%	20	16	124	7.8	2.8	1	80%
L.Paulsen*	-57	-84.0%	10	3	15	5.0	1.3	0	30%
B.Braunecker	0	-8.1%	6	4	41	10.3	1.8	0	67%
D.Sims	34	6.3%	35	26	256	9.8	5.0	4	74%
J.Howard	17	-7.5%	50	29	298	10.3	10.3	1	58%
J.Langford	9	-7.1%	27	19	142	7.5	6.8	0	70%
K.Carey	24	41.5%	7	5	55	11.0	12.0	0	71%
B.Cunningham	-12	-24.0%	21	16	91	5.7	5.0	0	76%

Offensive Line

Player	Pos	Age	GS	Snaps	Pen	Sk	Pass	Run	Player	Pos	Age	GS	Snaps	Pen	Sk	Pass	Run
Charles Leno	LT	26	16/16	1011	6	4.5	13	7	Ted Larsen*	RG	30	16/8	582	7	0.5	3	6
Cody Whitehair	C	25	16/16	1009	5	1.0	2	12	Kyle Long	RG	29	8/8	430	2	0.0	0	7
Bobby Massie	RT	28	15/15	914	3	3.0	12	4	Eric Kush	G	28	8/4	279	1	0.0	2	2
Josh Sitton	LG	31	13/12	734	6	2.0	4	2									

Year	Yards	ALY	Rank	Power	Rank	Stuff	Rank	2nd Lev	Rank	Open Field	Rank	Sacks	ASR	Rank	Press	Rank	F-Start	Cont.
2014	3.97	4.21	15	68%	10	18%	10	1.21	12	0.38	32	41	6.3%	18	22.1%	11	24	23
2015	3.89	4.46	7	74%	4	16%	2	1.05	23	0.30	32	34	5.6%	12	30.1%	27	19	26
2016	4.69	4.48	8	75%	1	18%	11	1.27	10	1.06	5	28	4.9%	7	23.4%	9	18	29

2016 ALY by direction: Left End 5.01 (8)   Left Tackle 4.79 (7)   Mid/Guard 4.22 (16)   Right Tackle 4.54 (9)   Right End 4.35 (9)

Despite the poor quality of offensive line play across the NFL right now, a few teams have concentrated enough talent to create truly great units. Soon, the Bears may be part of this conversation alongside Dallas, Oakland, and Pittsburgh. ☞ The arrival of Josh Sitton and Cody Whitehair in 2016 elevated the Bears' interior to one of the best groups in the league. Only the Raiders can compete with Sitton, Whitehair, and Kyle Long when it comes to pass protection. Long particularly took well to a move back to guard after playing out of position at right tackle in 2015, going from a team-high 6.5 sacks allowed two years ago to none over eight games last season. ☞ For the Bears to become a celebrated unit, they need to get better play from their tackles. The franchise's pursuit of Rick Wagner during the offseason suggests they know it too. The player Wagner would have replaced, Bobby Massie, was signed to be the starter only 12 months ago but was too inconsistent during his first year in Chicago. He played better over the second half of the year, ultimately keeping his job, and no real competition arrived over the offseason. ☞ Left tackle Charles Leno hasn't particularly excelled, but shows enough that the Bears hope to re-sign him before the start of his contract year. GM Ryan Pace called Leno "one of the brightest spots (on the roster)," before adding, "I like Leno a lot. I like his makeup. I like his intelligence. I am so hopeful we will get back on this track because last year was a little bumpy." At 25, Leno still has the potential to improve his consistency; that would solidify the position and provide some of the continuity that the Bears line has been lacking over recent years.

Defensive Front Seven

Defensive Line	Age	Pos	G	Snaps	Plays	TmPct	Rk	Stop	Dfts	BTkl	Runs	St%	Rk	RuYd	Rk	Sack	Hit	Hur	Dsrpt
					Overall							vs. Run					Pass Rush		
Akiem Hicks	28	DE	16	930	55	6.7%	16	42	17	3	45	71%	61	2.4	48	7.0	11	30	3
Mitch Unrein	30	DE	13	436	26	3.9%	53	22	3	1	22	86%	20	3.0	72	1.0	3	9	0
Cornelius Washington*	28	DE	15	364	21	2.7%	--	12	5	1	16	56%	--	3.9	--	2.0	3	12	2
Jonathan Bullard	24	DE	14	297	17	2.4%	--	12	4	1	16	69%	--	2.8	--	1.0	1	4	0
Will Sutton*	26	DT	8	173	16	3.9%	--	11	2	2	14	71%	--	1.8	--	0.0	0	1	1
Jaye Howard	29	DE	8	359	24	5.6%	28	18	4	4	21	71%	58	2.7	60	1.0	6	7	1

Edge Rushers	Age	Pos	G	Snaps	Plays	TmPct	Rk	Stop	Dfts	BTkl	Runs	St%	Rk	RuYd	Rk	Sack	Hit	Hur	Dsrpt
					Overall							vs. Run					Pass Rush		
Willie Young	32	OLB	16	713	40	4.9%	50	30	13	5	27	74%	50	2.1	31	7.5	2	22	2
Leonard Floyd	25	OLB	12	537	35	5.7%	37	26	11	5	21	67%	76	4.0	95	1.0	5	13	1
Sam Acho	29	OLB	16	499	25	3.1%	85	18	6	4	17	71%	65	2.4	41	1.0	5	13	1
Pernell McPhee	28	OLB	9	274	16	3.5%	75	13	7	2	12	75%	42	2.8	59	4.0	6	13	1

Linebackers	Age	Pos	G	Snaps	Plays	TmPct	Rk	Stop	Dfts	BTkl	Runs	St%	Rk	RuYd	Rk	Sack	Hit	Hur	Tgts	Suc%	Rk	AdjYd	Rk	PD	Int
					Overall							vs. Run					Pass Rush				vs. Pass				
Jerrell Freeman	31	ILB	12	806	114	18.6%	6	70	18	6	67	63%	47	3.9	59	0.0	4	5	42	68%	4	4.6	7	7	0
Danny Trevathan	27	ILB	9	565	69	15.0%	21	41	12	6	44	66%	32	3.4	37	1.0	0	6	25	46%	46	7.3	56	2	0
Nick Kwiatkoski	24	ILB	14	457	44	6.1%	78	25	4	7	29	69%	18	3.0	20	1.0	0	6	14	33%	79	7.5	61	1	0
John Timu	25	ILB	11	185	18	3.2%	--	13	8	5	12	83%	--	2.4	--	0.0	0	1	7	59%	--	5.3	--	1	0
Dan Skuta	31	OLB	13	267	19	2.9%	--	11	4	0	17	59%	--	2.9	--	0.0	2	4	2	0%	--	9.8	--	0	0

Year	Yards	ALY	Rank	Power	Rank	Stuff	Rank	2nd Level	Rank	Open Field	Rank	Sacks	ASR	Rank	Press	Rank
2014	4.45	4.68	30	53%	2	15%	31	1.12	13	0.84	24	39	6.4%	22	24.4%	18
2015	4.33	5.01	32	68%	21	15%	32	1.27	27	0.44	5	35	6.2%	18	24.7%	20
2016	4.41	4.33	20	60%	10	17%	24	1.13	14	0.84	24	37	7.3%	4	28.1%	13

2016 ALY by direction:	Left End 4.97 (26)	Left Tackle 4.51 (19)	Mid/Guard 4.40 (23)	Right Tackle 3.88 (13)	Right End 3.98 (19)

Leonard Floyd is the Chicago defender most likely to become a league-wide star in 2017. Seven sacks is a significant number for a first-year player, topped by only 20 rookies over the past decade. There are a couple of oddities on that list—such as Stylez G. White and Mark Anderson—but the list is primarily made up of pass-rushers who proved to be effective every-down players over the course of their careers. More importantly, the majority of rookies who were more productive than Floyd came out of college as more polished prospects. Floyd was very clearly a project coming out of college: an athlete rather than a refined pass-rusher. Yet Floyd not only had seven sacks but also 21 hurries; that prorates to 28 hurries over 16 games, which would have been the most by any Bears pass-rusher over the past three seasons. He still needs to expand his pass-rushing tool kit, as he primarily relied on effort and inside counter moves in 2016, but his overall play was much better than expected. The comfort Floyd showed off in his assignments allowed him to play with intensity while making good decisions. The Bears don't need Floyd to have a Vic Beasley-type of sophomore explosion for the defense to be good, but it would go a long way if he could draw extra attention coming off the edge. ⇒ Inside linebackers Jerrell Freeman and Danny Trevathan combined to miss 12 games last year, with Trevathan suffering a debilitating ruptured patellar tendon injury in November. What makes the duo such an integral part of the Bears defense is their versatility. They are both disciplined and violent enough to play the run between the tackles. Both players diagnose well to track down runs that break outside without over- or under-pursuing. It's hard to find two linebackers who can comfortably drop into zones and read-and-react to different route combinations, but Trevathan and Freeman can both do it. That diversifies Chicago's blitz packages and makes it easier to stay in base packages on early downs. ⇒ Vic Fangio's defensive line is a work in progress, though Akiem Hicks was a nice free-agent addition. He turned into a three-down interior disruptor who played nearly as many defensive snaps last year as he had the prior two seasons combined. Ideally, the Bears are looking for a healthy season from nose tackle Eddie Goldman and a second-year leap from 2016 third-rounder Jonathan Bullard to pair next to Hicks in base packages. The Bears no longer have a single defensive lineman left from the season before Fangio arrived; in theory, the unit's rebuilt core should be in place after a multi-year overhaul.

Defensive Secondary

Secondary	Age	Pos	G	Snaps	Plays	Overall TmPct	Rk	Stop	Dfts	BTkl	vs. Run Runs	St%	Rk	RuYd	Rk	vs. Pass Tgts	Tgt%	Rk	Dist	Suc%	Rk	AdjYd	Rk	PD	Int
Tracy Porter*	31	CB	16	944	57	7.0%	72	17	5	14	12	17%	81	14.0	83	73	18.6%	47	12.3	45%	65	9.5	79	11	2
Adrian Amos	24	FS	15	939	66	8.6%	51	25	10	11	30	43%	28	7.8	48	35	9.0%	44	8.9	37%	59	8.1	27	5	0
Harold Jones-Quartey	24	SS	16	731	79	9.7%	41	21	7	10	30	33%	51	6.0	24	33	11.0%	59	10.5	34%	67	10.4	59	4	1
Cre'Von LeBlanc	23	CB	13	695	53	8.0%	61	22	8	5	15	33%	55	7.1	49	44	15.4%	11	13.3	51%	30	8.6	68	10	2
Bryce Callahan	26	CB	11	488	36	6.4%	79	15	4	5	4	25%	73	11.3	79	47	23.4%	73	14.9	60%	4	5.8	8	6	0
Deon Bush	24	SS	11	333	22	3.9%	--	4	1	3	12	25%	--	9.3	--	5	3.3%	--	11.0	60%	--	6.3	--	1	0
Jacoby Glenn	24	CB	7	244	32	8.9%	--	15	6	3	9	44%	--	5.2	--	26	25.9%	--	15.2	47%	--	11.3	--	6	1
Demontre Hurst*	26	CB	10	223	14	2.7%	--	7	4	1	4	50%	--	13.0	--	13	14.1%	--	8.4	44%	--	8.8	--	0	0
Marcus Cooper	27	CB	15	827	80	10.4%	11	23	12	8	15	7%	87	11.9	81	82	24.1%	77	11.0	45%	72	7.8	48	12	4
Quintin Demps	32	SS	13	693	63	10.3%	34	30	14	4	32	47%	22	6.2	30	25	8.4%	36	12.8	48%	28	8.5	33	10	6
Prince Amukamara	28	CB	14	871	54	7.7%	64	21	7	2	11	36%	52	7.2	52	69	20.3%	58	12.1	45%	73	7.6	45	6	0
B.W. Webb	27	CB	14	589	38	5.4%	87	13	3	2	4	25%	73	10.0	74	50	19.1%	48	13.2	41%	82	8.8	72	11	1

Year	Pass D Rank	vs. #1 WR	Rk	vs. #2 WR	Rk	vs. Other WR	Rk	vs. TE	Rk	vs. RB	Rk
2014	15	3.4%	18	8.6%	23	11.7%	24	4.8%	21	-13.5%	9
2015	25	-5.4%	10	18.3%	26	21.5%	29	10.7%	23	-0.4%	16
2016	10	-5.9%	7	-6.3%	7	9.9%	22	-28.8%	3	12.7%	24

When Kyle Fuller came out of college, he showed off phenomenal footwork to shift his weight in space. He isn't big, but he's big enough that his quickness and balance should have allowed him to thrive. That hasn't been the story of his NFL career. Fuller has never been an imposing figure on the outside, nor has he shown an ability to thrive in the slot. A year away from the NFL because of a knee injury is unlikely to make Fuller a more aggressive or athletic presence outside the numbers. Yet the Bears still need him to make an impact in the secondary because of the unit's limitations. ☞ Prince Amukamara is in a similar situation as a talented but underwhelming performer to this point in his career, while the remaining options on the depth chart are all limited role players. Bryce Callahan was a decent find as an undrafted rookie, as he assumed the slot role and ranked fourth in adjusted success rate. But the Bears' decision to take fliers on several veterans speaks to their opinion of the current personnel. In a division with Aaron Rodgers, Matthew Stafford, and Sam Bradford, it's going to be difficult for the Bears to hide poor cornerback play. ☞ Brad Biggs of the *Chicago Tribune* made a shocking revelation during the offseason. Biggs said that Quintin Demps was guaranteed his starting spot (the not-shocking part of his statement) before suggesting that rookie Eddie Jackson has a real chance to unseat Adrian Amos as the other starting safety. Jackson was a priority pick for the Bears, who traded up for him in the fourth round. Jackson likely wouldn't have fallen that far if he hadn't suffered a broken leg during his final season in college. The Alabama prospect will need to perform well during training camp to unseat Amos, but the fact that he's competing with Amos and not Demps is shocking considering Demps is a journeyman while Amos is theoretically still young enough to develop into a quality starter.

Special Teams

Year	DVOA	Rank	FG/XP	Rank	Net Kick	Rank	Kick Ret	Rank	Net Punt	Rank	Punt Ret	Rank	Hidden	Rank
2014	-3.1%	25	-5.9	29	0.2	16	1.6	10	-6.9	25	-4.3	23	-1.4	21
2015	-1.2%	21	3.5	9	-15.0	32	3.3	9	3.0	15	-0.9	18	-8.2	27
2016	-0.6%	18	-4.8	24	2.9	10	-1.5	17	-1.4	17	1.5	11	-12.9	32

The departure of Robbie Gould saw Chicago regress significantly in placekicking value. Well-traveled vet Connor Barth was a shaky 4-for-7 from 40 yards or longer, and was almost exactly average on kickoffs. Undrafted rookie Andy Phillips (Utah) provides camp competition. ☞ Eddie Royal was useful on punt returns last year, but was released because he wasn't very good at his primary job. Chicago may use some combination of Deonte Thompson and Cre'von LeBlanc on returns. The halcyon days of Devin Hester, these are not. ☞ The Bears ranked last in hidden points added, which measures opposing special teams performance. No specific area stood out; Bears opponents were above-average in field goal accuracy, punt distance, and kickoff distance. After two years with high Hidden values, Chicago would surely appreciate some better luck in the third phase in 2017.

Cincinnati Bengals

2016 Record: 6-9-1	Total DVOA: 4.0% (13th)	2017 Mean Projection: 7.9 wins	On the Clock (0-4): 10%
Pythagorean Wins: 8.3 (19th)	Offense: 7.5% (11th)	Postseason Odds: 34.5%	Mediocrity (5-7): 34%
Snap-Weighted Age: 27.3 (3rd)	Defense: 0.8% (17th)	Super Bowl Odds: 3.1%	Playoff Contender (8-10): 40%
Average Opponent: 1.2% (12th)	Special Teams: -2.7% (28th)	Proj. Avg. Opponent: -1.3% (26th)	Super Bowl Contender (11+): 16%

2016: All great wild-card Saturday dynasties come to an end someday.

2017: Is Anthony Munoz available?

Football is family, as you may have heard and/or absorbed through the NFL's relentless ad campaign. And if football is family, no team is more football than the Cincinnati Bengals, who have plucked the ethos of the hardworking, unambitious Midwestern family that all stays in the same county for life and created a football team around it.

Head coach Marvin Lewis appears to be the unimpeachable head of the household. Lewis has led Cincinnati to its best days since Sam Wyche was inventing no-huddle offenses, of course, but he has done so while winning zero playoff games and leaving a bevy of odd challenges and assorted other weird play calls in his wake. It's not just him. The Bengals, per an independent study from SB Nation's Jeff Hunter, have retained the largest percentage of their draft picks from 2011-2013 (Table 1). And over the last three years. And, naturally, in total over the course of the six-year study. The only free agents that ever leave Cincinnati are the ones who get paid like a top-of-the-line starter by the market: Johnathan Joseph, Marvin Jones, and now, Kevin Zeitler and Andrew Whitworth.

Table 1. Percentage of Draft Picks Retained, 2011-2016

2011-2013 Drafts			2014-2016 Drafts		
Team	% of Picks	Rank	Team	% of Picks	Rank
CIN	35.7%	1	CIN	87.5%	1
ATL	30.0%	2	JAC	87.5%	1
DAL	27.3%	3	DEN	87.0%	3
CAR	25.0%	4	SD	84.2%	5
NO/PHI	25.0%	4	NYG	84.2%	5

It would be easy to paint a rosy picture for Cincinnati if not for those two defections. Andy Dalton and the passing offense struggled last year with Jones gone and Tyler Eifert and A.J. Green limited, but the Bengals immediately went to work at top of their draft board. By reeling in Washington receiver John Ross and Oklahoma running back Joe Mixon, the Bengals revitalized their skill positions. Ross comes with injury concerns, while Mixon punched a woman and fell to the second round as a result. On the field, it's hard to question either selection; our player projection systems adore both Ross and Mixon. And to concentrate on reloading at the skill positions is necessary when your quarterback is Andy Dalton. Cincinnati could be the ultimate litmus test for building a team around the quarterback, rather than trusting the quarterback to carry the team. Dalton is a capable performer, but one who needs to be elevated to greatness by the players who surround him.

But seemingly unconditional loyalty comes at a cost, and the cost is that sometimes you will commit to players who don't deserve it, because they are family. Rey Maualuga was family, starting 104 games despite performance issues that were evident by the end of his rookie contract. Domata Peko was family, starting 156 games as nose tackle even though the Bengals finished in the bottom 12 in run defense DVOA three of the last five years. And, now, Cedric Ogbuehi and Jake Fisher are family, because they are going to be protecting Dalton from edge rushers despite absolutely nothing in their pro resumes that says they have earned the chance.

It has been pre-ordained that the Bengals would replace Whitworth and Andre Smith with Ogbuehi and Fisher since the latter were selections in the 2015 draft. There was some talk early in the draft process that year that Ogbuehi would be a top-10 pick, but he fell to the Bengals at 21 after tearing an ACL in Texas A&M's bowl game. While NFL types raved about Ogbuehi's athleticism, he did not do any pre-draft testing because of the injury and scouts were concerned about his lack of functional power. Through his first two seasons, including what Ogbuehi himself termed a "shit" 2016 season, he has been a complete waste of a pick on the field.

Ogbuehi is saying the right things and acting the right way. He has spent the offseason training with Jay Glazer at Unbreakable. He's finally going to have a full year of OTAs after two injury-plagued years. But you can sum up the first two years of his career through this exchange related to the *Cincinnati Enquirer*:

"Not playing right tackle is going to be a big thing for me. That's not my position. It's not comfortable. I know against the Texans I gave up two sacks but besides the two sacks, out of 41 pass plays, my guy was nowhere near the quarterback. But those two plays were sacks so I've got to fix that."

In Ogbuehi's mind, that game (his first at left tackle) was a turning point for him. So much so that he sought out Marvin Lewis when the team returned to Cincinnati.

"Even though maybe we would have graded it a little dif-

47

2017 Bengals Schedule

Week	Opp.	Week	Opp.	Week	Opp.
1	BAL	7	at PIT	13	PIT (Mon.)
2	HOU (Thu.)	8	IND	14	CHI
3	at GB	9	at JAC	15	at MIN
4	at CLE	10	at TEN	16	DET
5	BUF	11	at DEN	17	at BAL
6	BYE	12	CLE		

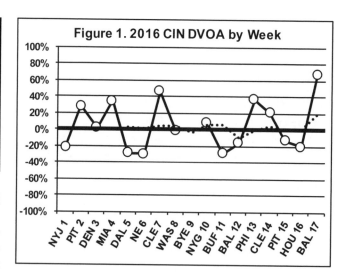

Figure 1. 2016 CIN DVOA by Week

ferently, his grade for himself on the curve he felt pretty good about and that's good," Lewis said.

You can sum up so much about the Bengals in that paragraph. Lewis considers himself a father figure for many of the players the Bengals draft, and works hard to get the most out of them. Ogbuehi is happy that he only allowed two sacks, and Lewis wants to spin that as a positive. There's an inherent level of belief in Ogbuehi in those words, even with the fact that his performance wasn't good in that game. That extends up the front office to director of player personnel Duke Tobin, who gushed about Ogbuehi at the combine: "I think Cedric is a marvelously talented young man. I think he's made of the right stuff to work at it, and I'm bullish on him and his ability to play."

As for Fisher, you can look at him one of two ways. You could say that he wasn't anywhere near as bad as Ogbuehi in his short trial at the end of last season. You could also say that he has had fewer snaps on the offensive line than NFLPA president Eric Winston in each of the last two seasons. Neither statement is particularly flattering, and he had the same ding on him coming out that Ogbuehi did: a lack of functional strength on the field. If that's enough to make you wonder who the backups are at tackle, I've got good news: Andre Smith is back! In guard form!

Three of Lewis' former assistants have graduated to head coaching positions: Mike Zimmer, Jay Gruden, and Hue Jackson. The Bengals have promoted from within after each departure. Offensive coordinator Ken Zampese has been with the Bengals since 2003, mostly as a quarterbacks coach. Paul Guenther had been a Bengals linebackers coach and special teams coach since 2005 before taking the defensive coordinator job. Nepotism is fairly common in the NFL, but even Donald Trump thinks the Bengals might want to look for some outside ideas.

Last year's Bengals defense finished in the bottom half of the league in defensive DVOA for the first time since 2011. It was stocked with—you're not going to believe this—veterans who continued to get chances or returning Bengals. Michael Johnson was a free-agent washout in Tampa Bay after a big year with the Bengals, and played last year with three forks sticking out of his back. Pat Sims came over from the Raiders after—you guessed it—originally arriving in the NFL as a Bengals UDFA back in 2010. He got an enormous amount of playing time. Margus Hunt came to Cincinnati with the body of a Greek god; after four years, we've learned that body is mostly good for blocking kicks, but Hunt continued to get

pass-rushing snaps in 2016.

While the Bengals finally shed Maualuga and Peko this offseason, replacing Maualuga with two-down run-stuffer Kevin Minter, they didn't put much of an effort into finding passable solutions beyond that. If their young edge rushers fail, the answer is still Michael Johnson. Pat Sims is still here. Wallace Gilberry is still here. Reinard Wilson is still here. OK, OK, we made that last one up. But you get our gist: there's very little upside here unless the Bengals have hit on their draft picks. The stopgap solutions are just the same guys you saw in 2011, but older and slower.

Now, let's remember some good things about the Bengals. Over the past seven or eight years, they have been excellent drafters on the whole. In addition to Green and Dalton, they have landed players such as Geno Atkins and George Iloka on Day 3 of the draft. They broke in Shawn Williams successfully at safety last season. Their decision to take a flier on the undrafted Vontaze Burfict paid off magnificently. This is exactly what makes Cincinnati's hesitancy on the mistakes so annoying. This team absolutely has the upper-echelon talent up and down the roster to make a deep playoff run, if not a Super Bowl. Dalton isn't Aaron Rodgers, but the only chance he had to play on a truly great offense failed to result in a playoff win only because he got hurt before the playoffs and the Bengals skidded their way to a 2-3 finish without him. The roster was almost talented enough to get A.J. McCarron a playoff win.

The Bengals had a chance to look at what was happening with their offensive line, pony up for Zeitler and Whitworth, and come into this year as a solid favorite for a wild-card spot, if not an AFC North title. Given how Ben Roethlisberger has tended to miss games by the bushel over the last few years and almost retired this offseason, you can argue that the Steelers aren't exactly the sturdiest contender to be chasing after, either. Cincinnati had plenty of chaff to cut through to free up cap room, and came into OTAs with about $20 million in unused cap space. According to the team's own website, they never even offered Zeitler a contract.

So instead, the family presses on. The Bengals are well-positioned, in our reckoning, for a rebound this year. We think they have one of the weaker schedules in the NFL, though it's mostly because of an absence of top teams rather than a true slate of bottom feeders. They went 1-6-1 in one-score games in 2016. The kicker is that we're not actually projecting great things for Cincinnati in 2017. We have them as a middle-of-the-pack offense and a middle-of-the-pack defense, and project them to essentially be a league-average team.

There are reasons to believe that they can outperform that projection significantly. If Mixon can come in and re-invigorate what was a dead rushing attack based on 2-yard runs up the middle with Jeremy Hill, the Bengals can re-establish an offensive identity that will make Dalton more effective. In college, John Ross was a touchdown reception waiting to happen every time he stepped on the field, and the 4.22 speedster was also extremely effective in the red zone. Eifert and Green could come back healthy and stay that way. The Bengals have a significant amount of highly touted youth on hand that could be ready to step in and play right away, both from this draft

and last year's class. Andrew Billings was as rare a size-speed specimen in college as Atkins was, and could take over at nose tackle and run with it (or, more specifically, stop other teams from running with it). And, hey, maybe those tackles do pan out after all and we're not subjected to a year of Dalton under pressure, which is one of the worst forms of Andy Dalton there is.

There are also reasons to believe that they shouldn't even be aiming for a wild-card spot. That it's incredibly sad that we're even here thinking about a team that won 10 or more games in each of the four years prior to 2016 rebounding to "just" eight wins.

But in the end, the Bengals are family. You don't always understand what they're doing. You just have to be content with the knowledge that it seems to be working out how they expect it to.

Rivers McCown

2016 Bengals Stats by Week

Wk	vs.	W-L	PF	PA	YDF	YDA	TO	Total	Off	Def	ST
1	at NYJ	W	23	22	381	340	0	-22%	8%	16%	-14%
2	at PIT	L	16	24	412	374	0	28%	9%	-19%	0%
3	DEN	L	17	29	332	355	-1	1%	31%	24%	-5%
4	MIA	W	22	7	362	222	+2	35%	-26%	-52%	9%
5	at DAL	L	14	28	345	402	+1	-29%	14%	32%	-11%
6	at NE	L	17	35	357	437	0	-30%	10%	31%	-9%
7	CLE	W	31	17	559	352	+1	47%	72%	5%	-21%
8	WAS	T	27	27	415	546	-1	-1%	10%	8%	-3%
9	BYE										
10	at NYG	L	20	21	264	351	+1	8%	-6%	3%	17%
11	BUF	L	12	16	300	342	-1	-29%	-34%	-13%	-8%
12	at BAL	L	14	19	325	311	-1	-16%	-26%	-9%	1%
13	PHI	W	32	14	412	359	+1	36%	31%	-9%	-4%
14	at CLE	W	23	10	360	254	+1	21%	9%	-6%	6%
15	PIT	L	20	24	222	382	-1	-13%	-10%	17%	14%
16	at HOU	L	10	12	294	250	-1	-20%	-12%	-4%	-12%
17	BAL	W	27	10	371	335	+2	67%	58%	-12%	-4%

Trends and Splits

	Offense	Rank	Defense	Rank
Total DVOA	7.5%	11	0.8%	17
Unadjusted VOA	6.5%	11	0.0%	17
Weighted Trend	5.9%	14	-0.9%	16
Variance	8.5%	25	4.6%	14
Average Opponent	-2.0%	6	-0.9%	22
Passing	20.8%	11	4.3%	14
Rushing	0.3%	13	-4.0%	20
First Down	-5.9%	22	-2.1%	15
Second Down	22.9%	5	3.8%	20
Third Down	8.8%	10	1.4%	20
First Half	17.2%	6	-2.1%	16
Second Half	5.6%	11	6.3%	23
Red Zone	0.5%	15	-2.0%	17
Late and Close	12.9%	8	8.3%	22

Five-Year Performance

Year	W-L	Pyth W	Est W	PF	PA	TO	Total	Rk	Off	Rk	Def	Rk	ST	Rk	Off AGL	Rk	Def AGL	Rk	Off Age	Rk	Def Age	Rk	ST Age	Rk
2012	10-6	9.9	8.7	391	320	+4	6.10%	12	-1.8%	17	-3.78%	10	4.1%	7	37.0	21	22.2	13	25.1	32	27.3	11	26.0	17
2013	11-5	11.1	10.1	430	305	+1	14.2%	9	0.4%	17	-12.6%	5	1.2%	12	11.2	2	30.5	19	26.0	29	27.4	8	26.3	9
2014	10-5-1	8.6	9.0	365	344	0	5.0%	12	-1.4%	18	-2.3%	14	4.2%	6	48.5	28	23.2	5	25.9	29	28.1	2	26.1	14
2015	12-4	11.7	12.3	419	279	+11	27.9%	2	18.6%	2	-7.1%	10	2.2%	8	10.0	1	18.2	6	26.2	23	28.1	2	26.5	10
2016	6-9-1	8.3	8.0	325	315	+3	4.0%	13	7.5%	11	0.8%	17	-2.7%	28	24.7	7	10.4	2	26.7	17	28.2	1	26.4	7

2016 Performance Based on Most Common Personnel Groups

CIN Offense					CIN Offense vs. Opponents					CIN Defense				CIN Defense vs. Opponents			
Pers	Freq	Yds	DVOA	Run%	Pers	Freq	Yds	DVOA	Run%	Pers	Freq	Yds	DVOA	Pers	Freq	Yds	DVOA
11	70%	6.0	21.6%	31%	Base	29%	4.6	-8.6%	58%	Base	27%	5.6	2.1%	11	58%	5.7	-0.6%
12	17%	5.3	-10.8%	51%	Nickel	58%	6.0	19.2%	35%	Nickel	68%	5.5	1.8%	12	21%	5.3	5.1%
611	3%	6.1	14.3%	55%	Dime+	11%	6.5	41.2%	8%	Dime+	3%	7.8	-17.6%	21	8%	4.8	-12.0%
21	3%	3.3	-17.6%	73%	Goal Line	2%	0.5	-17.5%	88%	Goal Line	2%	1.6	-22.0%	10	3%	5.7	28.8%
13	2%	3.9	-12.0%	65%	Big	1%	3.1	-25.1%	57%					13	2%	6.1	-28.0%
22	2%	4.1	21.0%	84%													

Strategic Tendencies

Run/Pass		Rk	Formation		Rk	Pass Rush		Rk	Secondary		Rk	Strategy		Rk
Runs, first half	39%	12	Form: Single Back	79%	13	Rush 3	3.8%	27	4 DB	27%	20	Play-action	24%	2
Runs, first down	50%	10	Form: Empty Back	5%	28	Rush 4	79.0%	2	5 DB	68%	7	Avg Box (Off)	6.20	15
Runs, second-long	32%	9	Pers: 3+ WR	70%	9	Rush 5	12.4%	30	6+ DB	3%	24	Avg Box (Def)	6.10	25
Runs, power sit.	65%	6	Pers: 2+ TE/6+ OL	27%	19	Rush 6+	4.8%	24	CB by Sides	96%	1	Offensive Pace	29.65	7
Runs, behind 2H	27%	14	Pers: 6+ OL	6%	9	Sacks by LB	9.1%	25	S/CB Cover Ratio	24%	23	Defensive Pace	29.73	8
Pass, ahead 2H	42%	30	Shotgun/Pistol	64%	17	Sacks by DB	3.0%	26	DB Blitz	7%	24	Go for it on 4th	0.79	25

Three years ago, Andy Dalton destroyed big blitzes, averaging an amazing 12.0 yards per pass against six or more pass-rushers. The last two seasons, this has totally reversed. In 2015, Dalton went from 7.7 yards per play with three or four pass-rushers to 7.1 with five and 5.9 with six or more. Last season, these numbers were 7.1, 6.4, and 4.6, respectively. ☜ The Bengals moved significantly away from two-TE sets last year, using more three-WR sets instead. In 2015, they ranked sixth in the former and 26th in the latter. ☜ Only Kansas City ran more wide receiver or tight end screens than the Bengals. Cincinnati averaged 5.9 yards on these plays with 33.4% DVOA. ☜ Cincinnati used play-action on a league-high 30 percent of passes on second down. ☜ Cincinnati opponents threw a league-low 17 percent of passes to their No. 1 receivers, but were at the top of the league in passes to running backs (23 percent) and second in passes to tight ends (27 percent). ☜ This was the third straight year the Bengals really struggled against draw plays. Since 2014, opposing running backs have gained 7.1 yards per carry with 39.4% DVOA on 71 draws. ☜ Cincinnati had real trouble tackling. By our count, the Bengals led the NFL in both broken tackles (142) and the percentage of defensive plays that had broken tackles (12.7 percent). ☜ Pace of play increased for both the Bengals and their opponents; situation-neutral pace on both sides of the ball went from below-average in 2015 to top-ten in 2016. ☜ The Bengals finished last in the NFL with only 104 penalties and 726 penalty yards.

Passing

Player	DYAR	DVOA	Plays	NtYds	Avg	YAC	C%	TD	Int
A.Dalton	738	7.6%	605	3915	6.5	5.1	65.0%	18	8

Rushing

Player	DYAR	DVOA	Plays	Yds	Avg	TD	Fum	Suc
J.Hill	66	-0.6%	195	788	4.0	9	0	45%
G.Bernard	24	-2.1%	91	337	3.7	2	0	49%
A.Dalton	56	21.7%	31	185	6.0	4	0	-
R.Burkhead*	58	39.2%	28	151	5.4	2	0	71%

Receiving

Player	DYAR	DVOA	Plays	Ctch	Yds	Y/C	YAC	TD	C%
B.LaFell	202	10.8%	107	64	862	13.5	5.5	6	60%
A.J.Green	250	19.1%	100	66	964	14.6	3.9	4	66%
T.Boyd	96	2.4%	81	54	603	11.2	3.7	1	67%
C.Core	4	-10.8%	27	17	200	11.8	6.9	0	63%
J.Wright	-5	-16.3%	19	13	106	8.2	2.4	0	68%
A.Erickson	15	12.5%	8	6	71	11.8	5.2	0	75%
T.Eifert	57	9.6%	47	29	394	13.6	5.0	5	62%
C.J.Uzomah	18	-0.2%	38	25	234	9.4	4.0	1	66%
T.Kroft	5	0.0%	12	10	92	9.2	3.1	0	83%
G.Bernard	101	22.4%	51	39	337	8.6	6.4	1	76%
J.Hill	27	3.1%	27	21	174	8.3	7.8	0	78%
R.Burkhead*	22	7.3%	20	17	145	8.5	8.4	0	85%

Offensive Line

Player	Pos	Age	GS	Snaps	Pen	Sk	Pass	Run	Player	Pos	Age	GS	Snaps	Pen	Sk	Pass	Run
Kevin Zeitler*	RG	27	16/16	1086	5	1.0	5	8	Cedric Ogbuehi	RT	24	14/12	677	3	4.5	14	7
Andrew Whitworth*	LT	36	16/16	1065	7	2.5	6	4	Jake Fisher	OT	24	15/3	295	4	3.0	7	2
Russell Bodine	C	25	16/16	1060	2	3.0	3	7	Eric Winston	OT	34	16/2	282	1	2.0	2	2
Clint Boling	LG	28	14/14	942	2	4.5	8	13	Andre Smith	RT	30	4/4	181	3	1.5	3	1

Year	Yards	ALY	Rank	Power	Rank	Stuff	Rank	2nd Lev	Rank	Open Field	Rank	Sacks	ASR	Rank	Press	Rank	F-Start	Cont.
2014	4.53	4.31	11	68%	9	15%	3	1.16	16	1.04	3	23	4.6%	5	19.1%	3	18	24
2015	4.00	4.59	1	68%	13	17%	3	1.20	14	0.42	31	32	5.9%	15	21.2%	6	18	36
2016	3.91	4.20	14	60%	19	20%	15	1.04	26	0.55	23	41	7.3%	26	22.5%	8	15	38

2016 ALY by direction: Left End 2.52 (30)   Left Tackle 4.60 (11)   Mid/Guard 4.44 (6)   Right Tackle 4.44 (11)   Right End 3.01 (28)

We talked a lot about some of these guys already. Let's focus on the others. Andre Smith was part of the famed Minnesota offensive line "Meet You at Sam Bradford Jambaroo" last year, or at least he was for the first four games before he tore his triceps. The Bengals want Smith to play guard, which might be the best fit for his skill set right now. That makes the nominal swing tackle Eric Winston, a 33-year-old who hasn't been a starter since 2013. These are the players Cincinnati would turn to if Jake Fisher and Cedric Ogbuehi go bust. This is fine. ☙ Inside, the Bengals have the pieces to be average if Smith can make the transition. Russell Bodine has driven a lot of derision over the past couple of years, but had his best season in 2016, finishing 15th among centers in snaps per blown block, up from 23rd and 26th the prior two seasons. Bodine will never be a good pass-blocking center, but can contribute as long as he plays like he did in the run game last year. ☙ Clint Boling is probably the best lineman the Bengals have at this point, though even he had some strength issues last year as a result of playing through an injured shoulder. ☙ 2016 fifth-round pick Christian Westerman (Arizona State) was regarded as a bit of a steal by the draft cognoscenti, and it would be really nice for the Bengals if he proved them right. Like, immediately. ☙ 2017 fifth-round pick J.J. Dielman (Utah) played a lot of tackle before moving to center and breaking his foot in the middle of last season. On this team, his versatility might help him see the field sooner rather than later, but he'll have to get more physical at the point of attack.

Defensive Front Seven

Defensive Line	Age	Pos	G	Snaps	Plays	Overall TmPct	Rk	Stop	Dfts	BTkl	Runs	vs. Run St%	Rk	RuYd	Rk	Pass Rush Sack	Hit	Hur	Dsrpt
Geno Atkins	29	DT	16	779	31	3.7%	60	29	17	7	20	90%	11	1.4	16	9.0	17	37	0
Domata Peko*	33	DT	16	593	40	4.8%	40	35	6	4	34	85%	24	1.7	28	0.5	2	4	3
Pat Sims	32	DT	16	408	37	4.4%	--	27	10	1	34	74%	--	1.6	--	1.5	3	8	0

Edge Rushers	Age	Pos	G	Snaps	Plays	Overall TmPct	Rk	Stop	Dfts	BTkl	Runs	vs. Run St%	Rk	RuYd	Rk	Pass Rush Sack	Hit	Hur	Dsrpt
Carlos Dunlap	28	DE	16	838	62	7.4%	16	40	17	8	29	52%	97	4.0	95	7.0	17	48	16
Michael Johnson	30	DE	16	831	48	5.7%	36	38	16	8	34	76%	37	3.1	72	4.0	7	26	1
Will Clarke	26	DE	16	373	16	1.9%	--	12	5	3	9	67%	--	2.8	--	4.0	1	9	3
Margus Hunt*	30	DE	15	322	16	2.0%	--	13	5	5	11	82%	--	1.1	--	0.0	5	8	2
Wallace Gilberry	33	DE	9	265	15	3.2%	81	11	5	0	10	70%	69	4.1	98	2.5	7	11	0

Linebackers	Age	Pos	G	Snaps	Plays	Overall TmPct	Rk	Stop	Dfts	BTkl	Runs	vs. Run St%	Rk	RuYd	Rk	Pass Rush Sack	Hit	Hur	vs. Pass Tgts	Suc%	Rk	AdjYd	Rk	PD	Int
Karlos Dansby*	36	OLB	16	781	118	14.1%	31	66	19	10	65	68%	25	3.8	55	1.0	2	6	50	43%	56	7.8	66	6	0
Vontaze Burfict	27	OLB	11	674	109	18.9%	4	54	14	18	55	60%	58	3.7	54	2.0	2	5	37	44%	55	6.9	48	8	2
Vincent Rey	30	OLB	16	592	86	10.3%	53	54	13	7	47	66%	31	3.3	33	0.0	0	3	30	64%	6	5.1	14	6	1
Rey Maualuga*	30	MLB	14	325	29	4.0%	--	17	4	6	18	61%	--	2.8	--	0.0	0	2	12	59%	--	6.6	--	2	1
Kevin Minter	27	MLB	16	1003	81	9.9%	58	47	14	14	47	64%	38	3.2	29	3.5	5	9	23	50%	34	7.9	67	3	0

Year	Yards	ALY	Rank	Power	Rank	Stuff	Rank	2nd Level	Rank	Open Field	Rank	Sacks	ASR	Rank	Press	Rank
2014	4.31	4.53	27	69%	23	17%	24	1.27	27	0.60	12	20	4.5%	31	19.3%	32
2015	4.20	3.97	14	60%	10	22%	11	1.11	16	0.94	26	42	7.0%	12	26.6%	9
2016	4.44	4.33	19	66%	23	17%	22	1.28	24	0.80	20	33	5.9%	16	30.8%	6

2016 ALY by direction:	Left End 4.14 (17)	Left Tackle 3.96 (14)	Mid/Guard 4.50 (25)	Right Tackle 4.61 (22)	Right End 4.02 (21)

This was a star-studded unit last year, but the stars could only drag the weak areas up to around average. Geno Atkins has been one of the best interior linemen in the league for the better part of a decade now, and is still a tough matchup for guards and centers who can't keep up with his speed and power. His comeback from a torn ACL was a success, as only Aaron Donald had more hurries among defensive tackles. Carlos Dunlap is a strong edge rusher, solidly a No. 1 pass-rusher in the league even if he's not really regarded as a star. Vontaze Burfict carries a lot of baggage, but also carries the kind of emotion that is looked at as a good thing for other, more successful teams. And a whuppin' stick. ☞ On the edge, a lot depends on how good Jordan Willis (Kansas State) and Carl Lawson (Auburn) can be, and how quickly they can get there. Willis blew up the combine, posting a 4.53 40-yard dash and a 39-inch vertical leap. He had the second-highest SackSEER score in the draft, behind only Myles Garrett, and was productive at Kansas State, with a program-record 25.5 career sacks. The only issue with him, and the reason he fell to the third round, is that he weighed only 255 pounds at the combine and isn't much to look at. Lawson was bandied about as a potential first-round pick a year ago before he returned to Auburn, but he had missed a year-and-a-half of games between ACL and hip injuries in 2014 and 2015, and that scared some teams off him. The Bengals have been using him at linebacker some at OTAs. ☞ Nick Vigil came on late in 2016 and helped spur the Bengals defense to some impressive results down the stretch. Five of their seven games with a negative DVOA came after Vigil started getting defensive snaps in Week 11. He should start at the SAM position in base packages. ☞ Andrew Billings missed the entire season, but was highly regarded in the same way that Atkins was coming out: men that big shouldn't be able to move that fast. If these four can even be average, the Bengals will have a frightening front seven. If not, you know the story on the type of guy the Bengals will have waiting to replace them with: he's been here, and he's not great.

Defensive Secondary

Secondary	Age	Pos	G	Snaps	Plays	Overall TmPct	Rk	Stop	Dfts	BTkl	vs. Run Runs	St%	Rk	RuYd	Rk	vs. Pass Tgts	Tgt%	Rk	Dist	Suc%	Rk	AdjYd	Rk	PD	Int
Adam Jones	34	CB	16	1058	73	8.7%	39	23	9	12	17	41%	40	6.5	39	60	13.6%	1	9.7	41%	80	7.3	32	6	1
George Iloka	27	SS	16	1050	80	9.5%	42	27	7	9	33	36%	46	8.2	56	28	6.3%	12	15.6	42%	50	8.9	37	7	3
Dre Kirkpatrick	28	CB	15	974	56	7.1%	71	25	12	15	12	33%	55	9.2	71	69	17.0%	28	10.9	50%	40	5.5	6	10	3
Shawn Williams	26	FS	15	912	86	10.9%	26	25	7	13	40	35%	49	7.2	40	32	8.4%	37	13.5	34%	65	10.8	61	4	3
Josh Shaw	25	CB	16	618	50	6.0%	82	18	8	7	15	40%	41	7.1	50	37	14.2%	4	10.1	57%	8	7.4	37	2	1
Darqueze Dennard	26	CB	15	334	42	5.3%	--	13	4	2	11	18%	--	9.5	--	27	19.0%	--	8.6	34%	--	11.0	--	1	0

Year	Pass D Rank	vs. #1 WR	Rk	vs. #2 WR	Rk	vs. Other WR	Rk	vs. TE	Rk	vs. RB	Rk
2014	7	-28.9%	1	-32.8%	3	-24.4%	2	-20.4%	4	26.6%	29
2015	10	-4.5%	13	2.7%	17	-11.4%	8	-9.5%	12	10.0%	24
2016	14	-0.4%	13	8.1%	25	-2.2%	12	-1.8%	17	-7.7%	14

This is perhaps the deepest unit on the Bengals roster. Shawn Williams was able to take over for the departed Reggie Nelson without much of a hiccup, and he and George Iloka combine to create one of the better safety combinations in the NFL. They aren't disruptors who change how offenses approach the game or create a lot of turnovers, but rather steady performers without an obvious weakness in coverage or run defense. ☞ Perhaps you've heard of the movie being made about Cincinnati's cornerbacks: *Three First-Round Babies and a Pac-Man*. OK, Dre Kirkpatrick clearly doesn't qualify as a youngster anymore after getting a five-year, $52 million contract in the offseason. Kirkpatrick has prototypical outside size, though he isn't much of a tackler and hasn't had the kind of year yet that would make you think of him as a No. 1 cornerback. Jones fell from fifth in adjusted success rate to 80th in a year. Normally we would write that off to the typical inconsistency of cornerback charting metrics, but it's reasonable to think age also played a part. For the second straight year, no defense was more likely to leave its cornerbacks on specific sides of the field: Dre Kirkpatrick on the defensive left and Adam Jones on the defensive right. ☞ Darqueze Dennard has been the weakest of the first-round trio, with a success rate that tells you all you need to know about how tight his coverage was. He has the physical attributes to play corner and none of the success in his limited samples thus far. William Jackson III, who missed his entire rookie season with a torn pec, could be in line for a sizeable role if Dennard and Kirkpatrick struggle. ☞ Former fourth-rounder and first-rate injury storyteller Josh Shaw played a swing role between safety and slot corner, and he could also see more time this year. At any rate, he's definitely the first man off the bench at both positions.

Special Teams

Year	DVOA	Rank	FG/XP	Rank	Net Kick	Rank	Kick Ret	Rank	Net Punt	Rank	Punt Ret	Rank	Hidden	Rank
2014	4.2%	6	-2.6	23	0.3	15	4.2	7	12.1	3	6.8	8	5.5	7
2015	2.2%	8	1.5	13	7.2	3	-2.0	20	3.4	13	1.1	15	0.9	15
2016	-2.7%	28	-12.1	31	0.9	14	9.0	3	-2.7	20	-8.7	30	-11.4	29

Mike Nugent has spent his entire career shining the light of truth on the notion that you need to value kickers. A second-round pick who made more than 80.6 percent of his field goals once in four seasons with the Jets, he was released and washed up in Cincinnati. He somehow managed to con a franchise tag out of this team in 2012. Nugent is the main reason Bengals special teams were awful last year, as the team finished second-to-last in FG/XP value mostly due to his six missed extra points. Those are the ones that are supposed to be easy. Randy Bullock replaced him in December and missed a game-winning field goal against the Texans. Fifth-round rookie Jake Elliott (Memphis) will be given every chance to win the job. Roberto Aguayo will have to carry on Nugent's cause, if he even manages to last as long as Nugent has. ⚏ Kevin Huber was once one of the better punters in the NFL, but he has been very average the last two seasons. ⚏ UDFA rookie Alex Erickson was excellent on kickoff returns and poor on punt returns. These are different skills, and some players can't excel at both, but this also could be just random variation. Adam Jones isn't really at an age where he should be an alternative on punt returns anymore. Perhaps John Ross could take a crack at it. We hear he's pretty fast.

Cleveland Browns

2016 Record: 1-15	**Total DVOA:** -30.4% (31st)	**2017 Mean Projection:** 6.0 wins	**On the Clock (0-4):** 29%
Pythagorean Wins: 3.3 (31st)	**Offense:** -13.4% (29th)	**Postseason Odds:** 13.5%	**Mediocrity (5-7):** 45%
Snap-Weighted Age: 25.7 (31st)	**Defense:** 14.5% (30th)	**Super Bowl Odds:** 0.6%	**Playoff Contender (8-10):** 22%
Average Opponent: 6.7% (1st)	**Special Teams:** -2.5% (26th)	**Proj. Avg. Opponent:** 0.2% (13th)	**Super Bowl Contender (11+):** 5%

2016: Dumps like a truck, truck, truck.

2017: Draft picks like what, what, what.

We are now two offseasons into the "Moneyball era" of the Cleveland Browns, and one thing is clear: the men running this franchise are very smart. They made a smart coaching hire. They have made smart cuts to the roster. They have made smart decisions to let players leave in free agency, and made smart moves with the players they have brought in. They have made smart trades. They have made smart draft picks.

Despite all these smart moves, however, the Browns are likely to still be a terrible football team this fall. Because before the smart men took over, the folks running the show in Cleveland had been acting very, very dumb.

That dumbness goes back a long way. We do not have the time, space, or emotional stability necessary to chronicle all the dumb things the Browns have done since returning to the NFL in 1999, and most of those dumb decisions are ancient history at this point anyway. So here we will focus on the more recent eras of Browns futility—specifically, the reigns of general manager Tom Heckert and team president Mike Holmgren, who ran the team from 2010 to 2012; general manager Mike Lombardi, who was in charge in 2013; and Ray Farmer, general manager from 2014 to 2015. Off the bat, you can see that some of the dumb decisions in Cleveland the past decade come from ownership, with a repeated refusal to stick with any kind of long-term plan in the front office. We must also acknowledge that at different times it has been hard to tell whether the coach, the GM, or somebody else was really calling the shots. But these are the official job titles for the seasons in question, and so these are the men we are going to blame today.

These are not dumb football men. Holmgren was a key cog in the building of Super Bowl teams in Green Bay and Seattle. Heckert was part of the Philadelphia front office that put the Eagles in the playoffs every year, and also helped build a Super Bowl winner in Denver. Lombardi has been an NFL personnel man since the early '90s and was working for the Patriots when they won Super Bowl XLIX. There's still time for Farmer to find success should he get another opportunity—the former linebacker, currently an analyst for ESPN, is only 43.

These men have spent decades in and around the NFL, and on the whole they have been a part of winning teams more often than not. Yet somehow, when they got to Cleveland, they all acted… well, dumb. That's especially evident when it comes to the draft.

You can't fault this crew for effort. They tried everything. From 2010 to 2015, they traded up 11 times, and they traded down five times. They traded picks to acquire veterans five times, and traded veterans for picks seven times. They traded present picks for future picks, and future picks for immediate selections. In six years, they wound up with nine picks in the first round, seven in the second, and eight in the third. According to Chase Stuart's research at Football Perspective on expected value within a player's first five years, the Browns were second only to the Rams in total capital spent in the draft, and 30 percent higher than the average team.

And they spread those picks all over the field—linemen, linebackers, corners, running backs. They drafted an immature quarterback in 21-year-old Johnny Manziel, then an overly mature quarterback in 28-year-old Brandon Weeden. Fifty players in all, each now theoretically between their third and eighth NFL seasons, who should have formed the backbone of the Browns roster in 2017.

Instead, the Browns are left with a black hole of talent. Only ten of those 50 players remained on Cleveland's roster in mid-May. That was tied with Tennessee, Indianapolis, and Buffalo for the fewest number of home-grown players at the time. (Cleveland's cross-state rivals, the Bengals, had the most with 26.) Seven of those 10 players came from Farmer's last draft in 2015, and in many cases the jury is still out on them. Taking that year away leaves three current players in total drafted between 2010 and 2014: Joe Haden, Joel Bitonio, and Christian Kirksey. That's the lowest total from that time period on any roster.

Jimmy Haslam replaced Farmer by promoting from within the organization, changing Sashi Brown's title from "Executive Vice President/General Counsel" to "Executive Vice President of Football Operations" and giving him full control of the coaching staff and team roster. Brown then looked outside the organization—outside the sport, for that matter—for his next hire. Paul DePodesta made his name in baseball, most notably working with Billy Beane in Oakland, in an era that was chronicled in Michael Lewis' book *Moneyball*. DePodesta has been one of the key figures in pushing advanced statistical analysis into mainstream sports management.

The last piece of the Browns brain trust came a few weeks later when they added head coach Hue Jackson, who went 8-8 with Oakland in 2011 before being fired so the Raiders could start a long string of losing seasons. (The Raiders were going through their own stretch of dumb decisions at the time.)

2017 Browns Schedule

Week	Opp.	Week	Opp.	Week	Opp.
1	PIT	7	TEN	13	at LACH
2	at BAL	8	MIN (U.K.)	14	GB
3	at IND	9	BYE	15	BAL
4	CIN	10	at DET	16	at CHI
5	NYJ	11	JAC	17	at PIT
6	at HOU	12	at CIN		

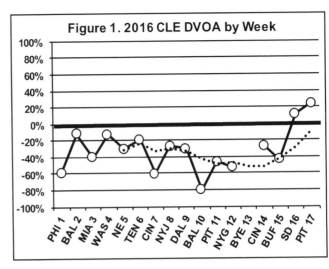

Figure 1. 2016 CLE DVOA by Week

Jackson then spent four years on the Bengals' staff before the Browns offered him their job.

And ever since, things in Cleveland have gotten a lot smarter. The first sign was obvious on the surface, but must have been a hard pill to swallow: Brown, DePodesta, and Jackson were smart enough to know that they were now in charge of a very bad football team, and there was nothing they could do to make it good right away. Once they came to grips with their situation, the Browns' next smart move was to get a lot younger. That meant immediately releasing two starters in their thirties, Karlos Dansby and Donte Whitner. It also meant letting a lot of good talent walk out the door—safety Tashaun Gipson and wide receiver Travis Benjamin in 2015, and Alex Mack and Mitchell Schwartz in 2016. These are good players, but they didn't fit into Cleveland's budget anymore. All told, those four players signed contracts with their new teams that included $74.2 million in guaranteed money.

The Browns, however, needed bodies everywhere, and by letting their own players go, they were able to add talent on the cheap. In two offseasons, Cleveland has guaranteed money to ten players in free agency, for a total of $73.6 million. Effectively, the Browns have traded four players to get ten—none older than 30 and up to six of whom could be starting in 2017.

The next smart decision for Cleveland: don't get married to one quarterback. We have seen too many teams reach for questionable passers in the draft. They hope for a messiah and instead get a Bortles. Worse, many teams have been so smitten with specific quarterbacks that they mortgage the present and future in massive trade deals to move up in the draft. In hindsight, you think Washington regrets giving up three firsts and a second to get Robert Griffin?

Rather than go all-in on one passer, the Browns did another smart thing by stocking up on as many draft picks as possible. They found a trading partner in the Philadelphia Eagles, giving up the second pick in the 2016 draft (used by the Eagles to take Carson Wentz) and a 2017 fourth-rounder in exchange for first-, third- and fourth-round picks in 2016, plus a first-round pick in 2017 and a second-rounder in 2018. The Browns took two of those picks and traded down twice more, winding up with 14 players in a seven-round draft. The star of the group was Emmanuel Ogbah, who started all 16 games and led the Browns in sacks. Other highlights include Corey Coleman, Cleveland's second-leading wide receiver despite missing six games; Spencer Drango, entrenched as a starter on the offensive line by the end of the year; and Cody Kessler, the team's best quarterback in 2016 and perhaps beyond.

After all those smart decisions, the Browns still went 1-15 in 2016. But you'd be hard-pressed to find a one-win season that gave a team more cause for optimism. Five of those losses came by one score, two in overtime. And the Browns weren't especially healthy either, finishing 23rd in adjusted games lost on both offense and defense. That includes a league-worst finish in adjusted games lost at quarterback. With just a little more health and a little more luck, this could easily have been a run-of-the-mill five- or six-win team, not the worst team in football.

Still, there was plenty of room for improvement. So the Browns made what might have been their smartest move yet. Technically, it was a trade to acquire Houston quarterback Brock Osweiler. For all intents and purposes, though, the Browns simply bought a 2018 second-round pick by taking on the burden of Osweiler's $16 million guaranteed salary this season. It's a no-lose situation for the Browns—they can cut Osweiler at any point with no long-term repercussions, but that second-round pick could become an important part of the roster for a half-decade or more.

This was not the last time the Browns made shrewd use of their $100 million-plus in cap space. While many teams with money to burn would have splurged on big-name free agents right away, Cleveland was still thrifty. Twenty free agents signed for at least $12 million guaranteed this offseason, and only one (Kevin Zeitler) joined the Browns. Instead, the Browns were patient. Months into free agency and even weeks after the draft, they were still acquiring veterans, signing defensive back Jason McCourty and trading for safety Calvin Pryor. All these bargain-bin acquisitions will make the Browns a better football team in 2017, while still giving them long-term roster flexibility. The Browns already have more than $9 million in 2018 salary-cap space, which ranks 20th in the league, and they can vault into the top ten just by cutting Osweiler and his non-guaranteed $18 million base salary.

Then the Browns picked up even more picks by making another deal with Houston on draft day. (Table 1.) All these moves have left Cleveland with a massive pile of draft capital in 2018: each of their own picks, plus Houston's first-rounder; second-rounders from Houston and Philadelphia; Carolina's fourth-rounder; and Pittsburgh's sixth-rounder. That's 12 picks waiting to be made or dealt for more players.

The biggest deal, though, may have been one Cleveland didn't make. Most pre-draft speculation had the Browns taking Texas A&M defensive end Myles Garrett with the No. 1 overall pick. Then, just days before the draft, rumors began to float that Cleveland might take North Carolina quarterback Mitchell Trubisky. Even stranger, the rumors said that the analytics department was pushing Trubisky over Garrett, even though no team with a strong analytical background would gamble on a risky one-year starter. In the end, the Browns took Garrett, then sat back and watched as Chicago traded up to grab Trubisky. The rest of this paragraph is purely speculation, but it seems likely the Browns knew Chicago was looking to make a deal and were leaking the Trubisky rumors to try to bait the Bears into a mega-package. In the end, they could not get an offer they liked more than Garrett, and stood pat. This is why Browns management was shown on the draft broadcast congratulating each other after the pick was made—they had done their due diligence in exploring all options with that first pick and chosen the option that best fit their needs. And it was another sign of the new intelligence in Cleveland—while the old Browns might have been happy to make a deal, the new Browns are only interested in the *right* deal.

In addition to Garrett, the Browns had two other first-round picks this year, and both should end up starting on Day 1. Jabrill Peppers provides an instant upgrade for a secondary that saw some of the NFL's worst safety play in 2016, while the Browns guaranteed David Njoku the starting tight end job when they released Gary Barnidge shortly after the draft.

All three first-rounders are 21 or younger, which will help make a team that was very young in 2016 even younger. By snap-weighted age, the Browns were the league's youngest team on defense and special teams last year, while ranking 15th on offense. Exact starting lineups are still fluid, of course, but the average age of Cleveland's projected first-string offense is 25.6, while the average age of the starting defense is 25.2. Each of those would have been the second-youngest unit in 2016. Only one starter on offense (tackle Joe Thomas) and one potential starter on defense (McCourty) is age 30 or older.

So where does that leave the Browns for 2017? The front seven is suddenly loaded with potential studs such as Garrett, Ogbah, Danny Shelton, Jamie Collins, and Christian Kirksey. The secondary has received a much-needed talent infusion from Peppers and McCourty. The offensive line has been rebuilt with free-agent additions Zeitler and J.C. Tretter. There is plenty of youth and upside at running back, receiver, and tight end, plus veteran Kenny Britt, who should be at least a reasonable replacement for the departed Terrelle Pryor.

That leaves quarterback, where the Browns are sticking with the crap-against-the-wall methodology that, frankly, didn't work out too well in 2016. None of Cleveland's half-dozen quarterbacks last year was satisfactory, but the best was Kessler, who had a higher passing DVOA than "franchise" quarterbacks such as Ryan Tannehill, Cam Newton, Joe Flacco, and, yes, Carson Wentz. He will have to win the job in a battle against Osweiler and DeShone Kizer, the Notre Dame project who arrived in the second round. Odds are against any one of

Table 1: Two Browns-Texans Trades in One

Trade Date	Browns Get	Texans Get
March 9	• Brock Osweiler • 2017 sixth (traded for a fifth, used on Roderick Johnson) • 2018 second	• 2017 fourth (Carlos Watkins)
April 27	• 2017 first (Jabrill Peppers) • 2018 first	• 2017 first (Deshaun Watson)

them turning into a superstar, but that's why the Browns are hedging their bets—they only need one of these lottery tickets to be a winner. And if none of them pans out? Cleveland will just find their franchise quarterback in the 2018 draft—and they will have the picks to trade up if necessary, with enough talent around that pick to ensure he has some chance of success.

If there's a concern about Cleveland's young talent, it's that they might repeat the sins of Browns busts past. It's amazing how many of Cleveland's disappointments showed an obvious lack of motivation, sometimes before arriving in the league. Brandon Weeden only turned to football after failing at baseball. Trent Richardson admitted after his career that he had gotten lazy in the NFL. Josh Gordon was such a screw-up that he was kicked off the Baylor football team by Art Briles. (That one's really astonishing.) Justin Gilbert's effort was publicly questioned by ex-teammate Joe Thomas after he was traded away. He is currently unsigned, and he and Gordon are both suspended for drug abuse. Johnny Manziel's partying was legendary in his college days, and he was often seen drinking in public even after his NFL career was derailed by a stint in rehab. Terrance West ran for 673 yards as a rookie, but was traded one year later because he showed up for training camp overweight.

That's why whispers about the attitudes of Cleveland's current youngsters are more distressing than they might be for another team. Hall of Fame defensive lineman Warren Sapp said that Garrett was a "lazy kid" who "ain't even close" to being the top player in the draft. Peppers had a diluted urine sample at the combine and was accused of illegal drug use after the draft. Osweiler may not be in Cleveland's long-term plans, but he didn't help himself when he blamed his struggles in Houston on Texans coaches, while simultaneously saying his film proved he deserved to start. However, while you can't blame Cleveland fans for being paranoid, it would be a mistake to hold the new players accountable for the sins of their predecessors, just as it would be a mistake to doubt the current front office based on the failures of past regimes.

The Browns would be thrilled to get into the playoffs in 2017, but that is not the goal. Nor is the goal simply to tank—there is an inherent value in building a winning culture, overcoming adversity, and all those other cheesy sportswriter clichés that hold more than a nugget of truth. Cleveland's real goal is simply to give its young talent a chance to develop and grow, and to sort out which of its young stars have the most potential. The goal in 2017 is to prepare for a playoff game in 2019.

Smart money says they can pull it off.

Vincent Verhei

2016 Browns Stats by Week

Wk	vs.	W-L	PF	PA	YDF	YDA	TO	Total	Off	Def	ST
1	at PHI	L	10	29	288	403	-1	-59%	-33%	21%	-5%
2	BAL	L	20	25	387	382	0	-12%	13%	2%	-23%
3	at MIA	L	24	30	430	426	+2	-40%	-18%	3%	-20%
4	at WAS	L	20	31	380	301	-2	-13%	0%	19%	6%
5	NE	L	13	33	262	501	-1	-31%	-23%	7%	0%
6	at TEN	L	26	28	341	407	+1	-19%	-2%	17%	0%
7	at CIN	L	17	31	352	559	-1	-61%	-2%	63%	5%
8	NYJ	L	28	31	407	393	-2	-27%	-7%	27%	7%
9	DAL	L	10	35	222	423	0	-30%	6%	26%	-10%
10	at BAL	L	7	28	144	396	-1	-80%	-54%	22%	-4%
11	PIT	L	9	24	209	313	-2	-46%	-50%	-4%	0%
12	NYG	L	13	27	343	296	-2	-53%	-19%	27%	-8%
13	BYE										
14	CIN	L	10	23	254	360	-1	-27%	-11%	11%	-4%
15	at BUF	L	13	33	269	451	0	-44%	-6%	36%	-1%
16	SD	W	20	17	251	356	+1	11%	-11%	-13%	9%
17	at PIT	L	24	27	437	312	-3	24%	-6%	-21%	8%

Trends and Splits

	Offense	Rank	Defense	Rank
Total DVOA	-13.4%	29	14.5%	30
Unadjusted VOA	-15.1%	29	19.2%	32
Weighted Trend	-15.1%	28	14.3%	31
Variance	3.4%	6	4.1%	10
Average Opponent	-2.2%	3	4.3%	2
Passing	-12.1%	29	26.7%	29
Rushing	0.4%	12	1.6%	27
First Down	-22.8%	31	0.6%	19
Second Down	-12.9%	25	33.2%	32
Third Down	6.8%	12	12.3%	24
First Half	2.1%	18	8.7%	25
Second Half	-31.0%	30	25.2%	31
Red Zone	-6.6%	18	25.1%	31
Late and Close	-56.6%	31	31.2%	31

Five-Year Performance

Year	W-L	Pyth W	Est W	PF	PA	TO	Total	Rk	Off	Rk	Def	Rk	ST	Rk	Off AGL	Rk	Def AGL	Rk	Off Age	Rk	Def Age	Rk	ST Age	Rk
2012	5-11	6.1	6.2	302	368	+3	-13.5%	24	-15.2%	27	4.5%	22	6.1%	2	26.4	13	57.0	29	25.7	30	26.1	26	25.2	30
2013	4-12	5.5	4.4	308	406	-8	-21.8%	28	-14.4%	26	8.2%	24	0.9%	14	24.8	9	16.3	8	26.6	21	25.4	30	24.9	31
2014	7-9	6.9	7.2	299	337	+6	-6.7%	23	-10.2%	24	-3.0%	11	0.4%	14	30.5	16	36.6	14	26.6	18	26.4	22	25.8	23
2015	3-13	4.0	4.5	278	432	-9	-23.0%	30	-13.2%	27	10.5%	29	0.7%	15	37.1	18	33.7	21	27.4	9	27.1	8	25.6	25
2016	1-15	3.3	1.5	264	452	-12	-30.4%	31	-13.4%	29	14.5%	30	-2.5%	26	46.2	23	50.2	23	26.7	15	25.1	32	24.5	32

2016 Performance Based on Most Common Personnel Groups

CLE Offense					CLE Offense vs. Opponents						CLE Defense					CLE Defense vs. Opponents			
Pers	Freq	Yds	DVOA	Run%	Pers	Freq	Yds	DVOA	Run%		Pers	Freq	Yds	DVOA		Pers	Freq	Yds	DVOA
11	64%	5.2	-6.0%	25%	Base	33%	5.2	-13.1%	44%		Base	38%	5.7	7.4%		11	56%	6.3	16.6%
12	16%	4.7	-5.4%	35%	Nickel	59%	5.2	-2.4%	27%		Nickel	57%	6.2	16.1%		12	18%	6.7	21.9%
21	10%	5.9	-8.6%	42%	Dime+	6%	5.0	-22.5%	5%		Dime+	3%	7.6	72.2%		21	9%	5.0	-0.9%
13	3%	5.1	-6.7%	62%	Goal Line	1%	3.1	13.0%	60%		Goal Line	2%	1.2	27.4%		22	3%	3.9	-20.0%
22	3%	8.9	34.5%	70%	Big	1%	3.4	-14.1%	40%							13	3%	6.3	-11.9%
																10	3%	8.3	104.9%

Strategic Tendencies

Run/Pass		Rk	Formation		Rk	Pass Rush		Rk	Secondary		Rk	Strategy		Rk
Runs, first half	36%	23	Form: Single Back	77%	21	Rush 3	7.3%	17	4 DB	38%	6	Play-action	17%	19
Runs, first down	40%	31	Form: Empty Back	5%	25	Rush 4	65.8%	17	5 DB	57%	19	Avg Box (Off)	6.22	11
Runs, second-long	31%	15	Pers: 3+ WR	64%	19	Rush 5	21.2%	17	6+ DB	3%	23	Avg Box (Def)	6.26	11
Runs, power sit.	57%	13	Pers: 2+ TE/6+ OL	26%	23	Rush 6+	5.8%	18	CB by Sides	70%	20	Offensive Pace	30.26	13
Runs, behind 2H	23%	28	Pers: 6+ OL	3%	19	Sacks by LB	48.1%	15	S/CB Cover Ratio	22%	29	Defensive Pace	31.59	28
Pass, ahead 2H	58%	3	Shotgun/Pistol	72%	8	Sacks by DB	7.4%	15	DB Blitz	8%	21	Go for it on 4th	1.52	4

There's no way the Browns had any luck last year, right? Think again. Opposing field goal kickers were terrible against Cleveland, connecting on just 19 of 27 attempts (70 percent). Only one of those was actually blocked by the Browns. ☞ On the other hand, some awful luck: It's bad enough that Cleveland only forced eight fumbles on defense, but it's worse that the Browns only recovered one of those. ☜ The Browns led the league with 25 percent of passes going to running backs, but they were 31st with only 13 percent of passes going to No. 3 and "other" wide receivers. ☜ Cleveland used the draw play more frequently than any offense except Philadelphia, ranking second in both yards per carry (7.9) and DVOA (57.4%). Perhaps nobody expects the draw when the offense is down by three touchdowns.

Passing

Player	DYAR	DVOA	Plays	NtYds	Avg	YAC	C%	TD	Int
C.Kessler	50	-7.6%	218	1225	5.6	5.0	66.0%	6	2
J.McCown*	-269	-34.4%	184	966	5.3	5.2	54.9%	6	6
R.Griffin*	-270	-36.0%	170	743	4.4	5.0	59.2%	2	3
K.Hogan	-131	-86.2%	28	94	3.4	3.8	53.8%	0	2
C.Whitehurst*	-5	-14.1%	26	168	6.5	3.0	58.3%	1	1
T.Pryor*	-27	-48.7%	10	40	4.0	6.0	55.6%	0	0
B.Osweiler	-558	-26.8%	535	2739	5.1	3.9	59.5%	15	15

Rushing

Player	DYAR	DVOA	Plays	Yds	Avg	TD	Fum	Suc
I.Crowell	136	14.0%	155	718	4.6	7	0	41%
D.Johnson	46	12.1%	60	295	4.9	1	0	45%
R.Griffin*	8	1.0%	11	68	6.2	2	0	-
T.Pryor*	-22	-71.6%	8	21	2.6	1	0	-
K.Hogan	45	108.2%	8	105	13.1	1	0	-
C.Kessler	-9	-37.1%	7	19	2.7	0	0	-
J.McCown*	-6	-37.8%	5	21	4.2	0	0	-

Receiving

Player	DYAR	DVOA	Plays	Ctch	Yds	Y/C	YAC	TD	C%
T.Pryor*	112	-2.5%	140	77	1007	13.1	2.8	4	55%
C.Coleman	-57	-22.9%	73	33	413	12.5	2.9	3	45%
A.Hawkins*	1	-12.5%	54	33	324	9.8	3.9	3	61%
R.Louis	-82	-42.6%	36	18	205	11.4	5.1	0	50%
R.Higgins	-14	-26.4%	12	6	77	12.8	5.2	0	50%
K.Britt	166	6.4%	111	68	1002	14.7	4.4	5	61%
G.Barnidge*	89	10.0%	81	55	612	11.1	3.7	2	68%
S.DeValve	52	57.5%	12	10	127	12.7	4.4	2	83%
R.Telfer	-45	-107.6%	7	2	4	2.0	4.5	0	29%
D.Johnson	134	19.2%	74	53	514	9.7	8.0	0	72%
I.Crowell	33	-2.4%	53	40	319	8.0	8.4	0	75%
M.Johnson	6	2.5%	7	5	44	8.8	10.6	0	71%

Offensive Line

Player	Pos	Age	GS	Snaps	Pen	Sk	Pass	Run	Player	Pos	Age	GS	Snaps	Pen	Sk	Pass	Run
Joe Thomas	LT	33	16/16	1030	4	3.0	9	3	Alvin Bailey	LG/RG	26	14/5	373	2	4.0	6	2
Austin Pasztor*	RT	27	16/16	1020	9	8.0	16	6	Joel Bitonio	LG	26	5/5	331	0	1.0	1	1
John Greco	RG	32	12/12	746	5	2.5	8	3	Jonathan Cooper*	RG	27	5/3	183	1	1.0	1	1
Cameron Erving	C	25	13/13	700	8	3.0	6	2	Kevin Zeitler	RG	27	16/16	1086	5	1.0	5	8
Spencer Drango	LG	25	16/9	599	0	4.5	7	2	J.C. Tretter	C	26	7/7	488	2	2.3	5	4

Year	Yards	ALY	Rank	Power	Rank	Stuff	Rank	2nd Lev	Rank	Open Field	Rank	Sacks	ASR	Rank	Press	Rank	F-Start	Cont.
2014	3.79	3.88	25	61%	19	22%	31	1.13	19	0.60	22	31	6.0%	15	27.0%	25	19	31
2015	3.75	3.61	29	65%	17	26%	31	0.98	30	0.78	14	53	8.1%	26	33.7%	31	23	35
2016	4.82	3.73	28	71%	7	22%	27	1.40	2	1.36	1	66	10.6%	32	30.5%	28	20	23

2016 ALY by direction: Left End 1.52 (32)   Left Tackle 4.94 (4)   Mid/Guard 3.85 (27)   Right Tackle 3.89 (16)   Right End 3.37 (23)

You'd be hard pressed to find an NFL team that suffered a bigger talent drop-off at any one position from 2015 to 2016 than the Browns did at center. While Alex Mack was voted to another Pro Bowl in Atlanta (a game Mack missed because he was preparing to play in the Super Bowl instead), Cam Erving and the Browns were struggling just to function in Cleveland. The Browns surrendered 19 sacks to defensive tackles and 10 more to inside linebackers. No other team gave up more than 11 or five, respectively. The Browns were 27th in adjusted line yards on runs up the middle and tied for first in fumbled snaps, and Erving was one of five centers with at least seven penalties. ☜ J.C. Tretter was signed from Green Bay to take Erving's spot at center, though that's not a guaranteed upgrade. Tretter only started 11 games in four seasons in Green Bay (including the playoffs), and ranked 33rd out of 39 centers last season in snaps per blown block. With Tretter at center, Erving will battle 2016 third-rounder Shon Coleman at right tackle to replace Austin Pasztor, who was unsigned as of press time. ☜ The other new starter, right guard Kevin Zeitler, comes up I-71 after five strong seasons in Cincinnati. Now the highest-paid guard in football, Zeitler was 11th at his position in blown block rate in 2016, tenth in 2015, and fourth in 2014. ☜ The Browns make for a good reminder that judging individual linemen by directional rushing stats can be a mistake. They ranked 23rd in adjusted line yards to right end, but 32nd to left end. However, many of those good runs to the right side came with Joe Thomas and Joel Bitonio pulling across the formation from left to right, Joe Gibbs-counter trey style. Thomas is perpetually excellent, and though Bitonio has missed 17 games the last two years, the Browns like him enough to have signed him to a six-year deal with $23.7 million guaranteed in March. ≡ At the moment, Cleveland has a hair under $48.5 million in salary-cap hits committed to the unit this season, or over 30 percent of their adjusted cap. Both those figures lead the league.

Defensive Front Seven

Defensive Line	Age	Pos	G	Snaps	Plays	TmPct	Rk	Stop	Dfts	BTkl	Runs	St%	Rk	RuYd	Rk	Sack	Hit	Hur	Dsrpt
						Overall						vs. Run					Pass Rush		
Danny Shelton	24	DT	16	746	59	7.0%	12	51	6	3	55	87%	19	2.5	54	1.5	4	9	0
Jamie Meder	26	DE	16	721	48	5.7%	27	31	7	1	43	65%	77	3.4	82	1.0	5	14	1
Carl Nassib	24	DE	14	540	24	3.2%	70	18	4	3	13	77%	44	2.8	64	2.5	4	13	4
Xavier Cooper	26	DE	13	451	20	2.9%	75	13	4	1	17	65%	78	3.2	76	0.0	4	5	0
Stephen Paea*	29	DE	13	321	12	1.7%	--	10	2	3	11	82%	--	2.4	--	0.5	2	6	0

Edge Rushers	Age	Pos	G	Snaps	Plays	TmPct	Rk	Stop	Dfts	BTkl	Runs	St%	Rk	RuYd	Rk	Sack	Hit	Hur	Dsrpt
						Overall						vs. Run					Pass Rush		
Emmanuel Ogbah	24	DE	16	850	55	6.5%	23	39	16	3	40	68%	75	3.3	78	5.5	11	22	3
Cam Johnson	27	OLB	12	351	29	4.6%	57	24	6	4	25	80%	26	2.7	55	3.0	3	6	0

Linebackers	Age	Pos	G	Snaps	Plays	TmPct	Rk	Stop	Dfts	BTkl	Runs	St%	Rk	RuYd	Rk	Sack	Hit	Hur	Tgts	Suc%	Rk	AdjYd	Rk	PD	Int
						Overall						vs. Run					Pass Rush				vs. Pass			
Christian Kirksey	25	ILB	16	1112	146	17.2%	12	89	24	10	98	68%	21	3.2	28	2.5	4	13	40	41%	62	7.4	58	3	0
Jamie Collins	27	OLB	15	980	112	14.1%	30	56	19	17	56	64%	36	3.8	57	3.0	5	8	26	44%	54	6.3	36	0	0
Demario Davis*	28	ILB	16	788	100	11.8%	44	56	14	13	75	57%	66	4.0	67	2.0	3	7	20	45%	48	7.7	63	2	0

Year	Yards	ALY	Rank	Power	Rank	Stuff	Rank	2nd Level	Rank	Open Field	Rank	Sacks	ASR	Rank	Press	Rank
2014	4.45	4.66	29	58%	8	15%	29	1.32	28	0.67	14	31	6.1%	25	20.5%	30
2015	4.57	4.73	30	70%	24	17%	28	1.27	28	0.86	20	29	5.8%	25	23.6%	27
2016	4.50	4.85	32	61%	12	15%	30	1.25	22	0.69	14	26	5.7%	21	23.7%	28

2016 ALY by direction:	Left End 4.94 (25)	Left Tackle 5.94 (31)	Mid/Guard 4.32 (19)	Right Tackle 5.10 (30)	Right End 5.52 (29)

The Browns played an odd defense last year, both in the odd/even sense and in the odd/normal sense. Scrambling to field a defense with the spare parts left over from terrible regimes of the past and injuries of the present, their most frequent formation was a mutant kind of 3-3-5 nickel set that featured Emmanuel Ogbah at "end-backer." He was tied with New England's Rob Ninkovich for most pass targets by a defensive end, with seven. That's far from his bread-and-butter, but he should play in a three-point stance far more frequently in 2017. ≡ The Browns fired Ray Horton after the season and replaced him with Gregg Williams. In two decades with seven NFL franchises as a head coach or defensive coordinator, Williams' defenses have been built around a 4-3 base package. That means this year's pass rush will be keyed by Ogbah (third in 2016 SackSEER projections) and Myles Garrett (first by far in SackSEER projections this year). After 31.0 sacks in three seasons at Texas A&M, Garrett is the most promising defensive prospect to hit Cleveland since Courtney Brown in 2000, with one of the top 10 SackSEER projections of the past 20 years. Here's hoping Garrett enjoys more success than Brown did. ≡ At the second level, both Christian Kirksey and Jamie Collins were among the NFL's top 30 defenders in percentage of team plays last season. Very quietly, Kirksey was first in the league in both total successful plays and successful run tackles. Collins, acquired midseason for a 2017 compensatory third-round pick, is more of a do-it-all space player. He was one of six defenders (and four linebackers) with at least 3.0 sacks and 50 pass tackles last season. Both players signed four-year deals worth a combined total of $46 million in guarantees after the season.

Defensive Secondary

Secondary	Age	Pos	G	Snaps	Plays	Overall					vs. Run					vs. Pass									
						TmPct	Rk	Stop	Dfts	BTkl	Runs	St%	Rk	RuYd	Rk	Tgts	Tgt%	Rk	Dist	Suc%	Rk	AdjYd	Rk	PD	Int
Jamar Taylor	27	CB	15	920	69	8.7%	40	32	11	3	16	50%	19	7.9	60	56	16.8%	26	11.2	49%	47	6.4	14	13	3
Joe Haden	28	CB	13	855	59	8.6%	45	27	5	8	15	53%	17	6.7	43	62	20.1%	54	15.7	50%	41	9.2	76	11	3
Tramon Williams*	34	CB	12	624	41	6.5%	--	20	10	9	10	70%	--	4.9	--	36	16.1%	--	9.3	49%	--	7.0	--	5	1
Briean Boddy-Calhoun	24	CB	14	571	51	6.9%	74	26	15	9	15	60%	12	7.6	57	51	24.9%	84	15.4	45%	66	9.5	78	11	3
Derrick Kindred	24	FS	12	537	49	7.7%	--	17	5	8	26	35%	--	5.9	--	17	8.8%	--	14.9	33%	--	12.4	--	5	0
Ed Reynolds	26	FS	10	505	41	7.7%	--	14	3	7	25	40%	--	7.2	--	6	3.3%	--	13.3	49%	--	9.2	--	1	0
Ibraheim Campbell	25	SS	14	419	43	5.8%	70	12	3	6	20	40%	36	6.6	35	10	6.7%	19	15.5	43%	47	12.3	68	0	0
Jordan Poyer*	26	FS	6	354	37	11.6%	--	9	1	2	13	38%	--	9.7	--	17	13.0%	--	10.3	25%	--	13.6	--	2	0
Tracy Howard	23	FS	15	281	17	2.1%	--	6	0	5	10	20%	--	7.2	--	9	8.4%	--	9.2	76%	--	4.8	--	1	0
Jason McCourty*	30	CB	14	813	79	11.3%	5	27	9	2	9	33%	55	13.3	82	94	23.4%	74	11.6	52%	28	8.0	54	12	2
Calvin Pryor	25	FS	15	813	66	9.3%	44	31	15	13	31	58%	10	4.7	10	36	10.4%	54	7.8	47%	38	9.5	52	4	0

Year	Pass D Rank	vs. #1 WR	Rk	vs. #2 WR	Rk	vs. Other WR	Rk	vs. TE	Rk	vs. RB	Rk
2014	2	-17.6%	6	-5.9%	13	-17.6%	5	-5.7%	15	-41.1%	1
2015	27	4.2%	19	8.7%	21	28.9%	31	-1.7%	17	16.1%	28
2016	29	14.9%	30	6.0%	23	-4.5%	10	39.7%	32	3.5%	20

Cleveland's safeties were so terrible last year it often felt as if the defense only had nine or ten men on the field. As a group, the Browns safeties finished last in the league in pass defeats (five) and total defeats (12), and they didn't intercept a single pass all season. There were 21 individual safeties with at least 12 defeats last year. Landon Collins by himself doubled the Browns' group with 24. Cleveland safeties were also in the bottom five in successful pass plays, total successes, percentage of team's run plays, and percentage of team's total plays. This is partly due to a scheme that kept the safeties deep to prevent big pass plays, but they weren't good at that either—the Browns gave up 19 completions and DPIs more than 25 yards downfield, among the five worst defenses in the NFL. About the only thing Cleveland safeties did with any regularity was miss tackles, where they were in the top 10. ☞ The Browns exhausted every possible option to try and upgrade the position. First they turned to the draft, taking Michigan's Jabrill Peppers 25th overall. The 2016 winner of the Paul Hornung Award as college football's most versatile player, Peppers shined on defense, offense (five rushing touchdowns), and special teams (leading the Big Ten in punt return average last season) at Michigan. With just one interception on defense and ten receptions on offense, he may not have the best hands in the world, but that'll be OK as long as he's roaming sideline to sideline putting ballcarriers on the ground. ☞ After the draft, Cleveland signed long-time Tennessee cornerback Jason McCourty; they might move him to safety. Then the Browns traded for 2014 first-rounder Calvin Pryor, a bust in New York who still would have been Cleveland's best safety in 2016. Derrick Kindred or Ed Reynolds might still get plenty of playing time as centerfielders. ☞ At corner, Jamar Taylor, Joe Haden, and Briean Boddy-Calhoun all return. Haden's reputation as a shutdown corner has eroded spectacularly. After a horrendous injury-plagued 2015, Haden ranked 76th out of 87 qualifying cornerbacks in adjusted yards per pass in 2016. Quarterbacks certainly aren't afraid anymore, as Haden's estimated target percentage has been over 20 percent each of the past three seasons. McCourty should be an upgrade over the departed Tramon Williams. The Browns also drafted Howard Wilson (University of Houston) in the fourth round and added four more undrafted free agents at the position, so they'll certainly have depth there this year.

Special Teams

Year	DVOA	Rank	FG/XP	Rank	Net Kick	Rank	Kick Ret	Rank	Net Punt	Rank	Punt Ret	Rank	Hidden	Rank
2014	0.4%	14	-6.2	30	10.4	1	-5.5	28	9.9	7	-6.6	30	-10.9	29
2015	0.7%	15	-0.3	16	1.4	11	-4.0	25	-2.4	20	8.7	3	-2.6	18
2016	-2.5%	26	-4.5	23	3.3	9	-6.6	28	-1.4	18	-3.6	23	4.5	9

Two draftees could end up being critical players in the kicking game for Cleveland. Duke Johnson handled punt returns last year while four players split time as kickoff returners, but Jabrill Peppers could take both duties on Day 1. Meanwhile, seventh-round pick Zane Gonzalez figures to take over placekicking duties from Cody Parkey. Gonzalez set an FBS record with 96 field goals at Arizona State. He went 23-of-25 as a senior, including 7-of-9 from 50 yards or more. In the past four seasons, Browns kickers have gone just 4-of-11 from 50-plus yards. Gonzalez is also good on kickoffs, with a 75 percent touchback rate in the last two years. ☞ Britton Colquitt returns as punter, though that may not last long—2016 was his third straight year with negative gross value on punts. ☞ Joe Schobert, a fourth-round rookie out of Wisconsin, led the Browns with 12 special teams tackles.

Dallas Cowboys

2016 Record: 13-3	Total DVOA: 20.3% (2nd)	2017 Mean Projection: 9.3 wins	On the Clock (0-4): 4%
Pythagorean Wins: 11.0 (2nd)	Offense: 19.9% (3rd)	Postseason Odds: 54.7%	Mediocrity (5-7): 20%
Snap-Weighted Age: 26.4 (21st)	Defense: 1.1% (18th)	Super Bowl Odds: 13.1%	Playoff Contender (8-10): 43%
Average Opponent: 1.8% (6th)	Special Teams: 1.6% (9th)	Proj. Avg. Opponent: 2.6% (2nd)	Super Bowl Contender (11+): 33%

2016: Forget sunlight. In the NFL, a cost-controlled young quarterback is the best disinfectant.

2017: Not as many breaks will go their way, but they're still the big dog in the NFC East dogfight.

The Dallas Cowboys Ministry of Truth and Creative Retcons wants you to know that it always planned for things to work out this way.

The franchise's plan was always to build the dominant offensive line of its generation, then replace Tony Romo with Dak Prescott (whom the team began scouting in elementary school) just when a younger, healthier, more cost-effective quarterback solution became necessary. Add Ezekiel Elliott to the mix and the master plan came to fruition: a young, talented, affordable and balanced offense, capable of cramming its running game down your throat or beating you over the top.

Forget for a moment that the offensive line plan grew from the team's decision to go rogue on its own draft board in 2013 ("reaching" for Travis Frederick in the first round despite an internal second-round grade) and a family drama that culminated with a Johnny Manziel draft card getting pried from Jerry Jones' hand and replaced with one for Zack Martin. Also forget that the Cowboys openly preferred both Connor Cook and Paxton Lynch to Prescott and planned to bury Prescott behind Kellen Moore on the depth chart before Moore got hurt in training camp.

Forget it all, because the Cowboys are The Contender That Happy Accidents Built. It doesn't matter what might have happened if they had drafted Manziel or spent last season goofing around with Moore. What matters is that the Cowboys built a sustainable, high-quality offense at exactly the point in their history when all of their bad past decisions should be coming back to roost.

We should be in Year One of the Romocalypse, the period of forced austerity caused by Romo's $24 million cap hit, which itself was caused by the Cowboys using Romo's salary like a line of revolving debt for many years. Jones kept converting Romo's salary into signing bonuses year after year, playing a game of voodoo caponomics which provided immediate cap space but prorated the team's lofty (often foolish) spending under the rug, to be dealt with in some far-flung future.

That future was supposed to be 2017. Romo's $24 million gut-buster, even spread across two seasons, should be crippling the team competitively right now. The only solution to the Romo cap dilemma, besides going 5-11 for two seasons of credit repair, was a real longshot: find a quality starting quarterback who essentially plays for free.

Sure enough, the Cowboys landed Prescott, who will earn $540,000 this year and $630,000 next year in base salary. He doesn't even have a contractual right to complain about it until after 2018, by which time the collection agencies will have ceased calling about Romo's old signing bonuses.

To be fair, the Cowboys made their own luck when it came to Prescott. Their All-Pro-studded offensive line provided a heck of a cockpit for a rookie quarterback. So did Elliott, Jason Witten, Dez Bryant (when healthy), and a commitment by Jason Garrett to lean into the strengths of his offensive personnel.

The Cowboys were the best first-down rushing offense in the NFL, with a DVOA of 20.4%. They ran the ball on 59.4 percent of first downs, averaging 5.1 yards per rush and keeping them unpredictable on second downs, where they ranked first in both passing DVOA (61.6%) and overall DVOA (30.8%). With the running game sucking linebackers and safeties into the box, the Cowboys executed play-action on 24 percent of all plays, the third-highest rate in the NFL. They averaged 8.9 yards per play on play-action, which ranked ninth.

The Cowboys weren't a great third-down offense (17th in DVOA), but all of those productive first and second downs led them to face just 11.8 third downs per game, the third lowest total in the NFL. The Cowboys also had the best red zone rushing offense in the NFL (65.5% DVOA) and the No. 2 goal-to-go offense (65.0%), making it easy to convert drives into touchdowns, usually with minimal need for quarterback heroics.

We can keep dumping percentages and splits on you, but in summary, Prescott got plenty of opportunities to throw passes when life is generally easy for a quarterback (second-and-medium, off play-action, with a lead) and had a lower-than-average number of attempts when things are hard (third-and-long when trailing in the second half). There were lots of nature-nurture arguments about where the Cowboys offense ended and Prescott's talents began last year, most of them tedious and irrelevant. Prescott proved capable of capitalizing on the ideal situation he was placed in last season. The circumstances will be very similar this season. There is no good reason to suspect a "sophomore slump" any more excessive than some understandable regression to the mean.

There is more reason to be concerned about the Cowboys defense, which finished 17th in the NFL last season and, like Prescott, benefitted from an offense which forgave multiple sins. The Cowboys defense had multiple chinks in its 2016 ar-

2017 Cowboys Schedule

Week	Opp.	Week	Opp.	Week	Opp.
1	NYG	7	at SF	13	WAS (Thu.)
2	at DEN	8	at WAS	14	at NYG
3	at ARI (Mon.)	9	KC	15	at OAK
4	LARM	10	at ATL	16	SEA
5	GB	11	PHI	17	at PHI
6	BYE	12	LACH (Thu.)		

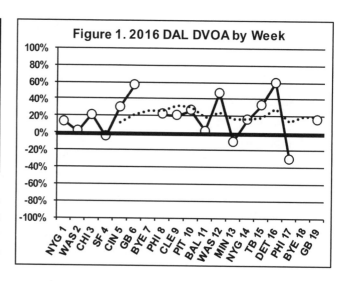

Figure 1. 2016 DAL DVOA by Week

mor, including an ineffective pass-rush and coverage vulnerable to short passes (29th in DVOA), passes over the middle (28th), and to tight ends (30th). Luckily, when a team is getting steamrolled by the opponent's offensive line, dinks and dunks to the tight ends aren't a very effective counterattack, and fourth-quarter desperation for opponents can help a bad pass rush produce a healthy adjusted sack rate (6.5 percent, 12th in the NFL) despite a lack of overall pass pressure (29th).

The Cowboys felt some of the brunt of the Romo cap situation on defense, losing Brandon Carr (another mild dead-money headache), J.J. Wilcox, Morris Claiborne, Barry Church, Terrell McClain, Jack Crawford, and Ryan Davis all in one offseason. Furthermore, neither Randy Gregory nor Rolando McClain has been able to outrun his demons and become a real contributor.

None of the players listed above are superstars, and many were disappointments. But they represent thousands of meaningful snaps, particularly along the secondary and the defensive line, not to mention major recent cap expenditures (Carr) or draft investments (Claiborne, Gregory). Under normal circumstances, the Cowboys would be projected to become the Saints: a great offensive team that is incapable of competing defensively and likely to go .500 over the course of a fun-but-frustrating season of 38-35 final scores.

Then good luck played another hand for the Cowboys. Their major defensive cap crunch just happened to coincide with one of the deepest defensive drafts in NFL history.

First-round selection Taco Charlton (Michigan) received much more love from the scouting community than from SackSEER. Scouts loved his breakout senior season, size, and agility. SackSEER hates "breakout senior seasons" because most NFL pass-rushers demonstrate their sack potential long before they become college seniors. Skepticism about his long-range potential notwithstanding, Charlton was a need pick for a team whose sack leader in 2016 was Benson Mayowa, a 20- to 30-snap wave player.

After Taco Thursday, the Cowboys spent most of the remainder of the draft rebuilding their secondary. Cornerback Chidobe Awuzie (Colorado) dropped to 60th overall but had a first-round grade on many draft boards. Third-rounder Jourdan Lewis (Michigan) was less highly regarded, but sixth-round safety Xavier Woods (Louisiana Tech) was a draftnik darling, and both Woods and sixth-round cornerback Marquez White (Florida State) would have gone much higher in typical drafts that lacked the depth of the 2016 class. The later-round players are also strong Rod Marinelli system fits. Lewis and

Woods, in particular, have the diagnostic chops to shine while playing a lot of Cover-2.

The rookies, plus budget-friendly free agents like Nolan Carroll and Robert Blanton, won't make the Cowboys defense great. But they will keep it competitive while making it far cheaper, and also younger and capable of improving. Instead of becoming the 2014-16 Saints, the Cowboys are poised to become the 2016 Falcons: an offensive powerhouse with a defense that generates just enough turnovers to compensate for the chunks of yardage it allows—and gets better as the season wears on. That last part is what makes these Cowboys different from a year ago; this version is younger with a higher ceiling.

Most remarkably, the Cowboys have built something sustainable. Jason Witten and Sean Lee will be the only regulars over 30 years old when the season starts. Zack Martin and Tyron Smith will turn 27 late in the season; the rest of the offensive line is younger. Recent free-agent contracts, like defensive tackle Cedric Thornton's four-year deal last year, are more thoughtfully structured than the whoppers of years past. There are still some cap-proration shenanigans going on—Frederick converted his base salary to a bonus in February, freeing up $10 million in operational cap space in exchange for another round of future dead money hassles—but the new Cowboys core can remain intact for several years without any financial tomfoolery.

What the Cowboys accomplish in 2017 will come down to how their still-developing youngsters adjust to a schedule more difficult than the one they faced in 2016. The Cowboys will visit the Falcons and host the Packers this season, and they face a tough slate of AFC and NFC West defenses. There are no cupcakes in the NFC East, and the Giants' overloaded receiving corps presents a particularly difficult matchup for the Cowboys' peach-fuzz secondary. The Cowboys also play five prime-time games, which can create brutal scheduling blocks. For example, they end the season traveling to Oakland on Sunday night, then hosting the Seahawks, then traveling to Philly for an early game.

The Cowboys went 7-2 in games decided by less than a touchdown last year. A little regression on that front will keep the Cowboys from 13 wins, but it won't keep them from the playoffs, and this year their opponents won't face a rookie quarterback in January. The Cowboys should be strong Super Bowl contenders in 2017 and for several years afterward.

That means more Jerry Jones stories about how he rated Prescott as the next Tom Brady, invented the concept of build-ing a good offensive line, personally scouted every 2017 rookie cornerback, and so on. You don't have to believe the tall tales. It doesn't matter how these Cowboys were assembled. What matters is that they are built to last.

Mike Tanier

2016 Cowboys Stats by Week

Wk	vs.	W-L	PF	PA	YDF	YDA	TO	Total	Off	Def	ST
1	NYG	L	19	20	328	316	+1	13%	16%	11%	8%
2	at WAS	W	27	23	380	432	0	1%	-1%	-3%	-1%
3	CHI	W	31	17	447	390	+1	21%	39%	12%	-6%
4	at SF	W	24	17	428	295	+1	-5%	12%	10%	-7%
5	CIN	W	28	14	402	345	-1	30%	51%	20%	-1%
6	at GB	W	30	16	424	372	+2	56%	16%	-42%	-3%
7	BYE										
8	PHI	W	29	23	460	291	0	22%	14%	-8%	0%
9	at CLE	W	35	10	423	222	0	20%	25%	10%	5%
10	at PIT	W	35	30	422	448	-1	26%	37%	26%	15%
11	BAL	W	27	17	417	368	0	3%	46%	48%	5%
12	WAS	W	31	26	353	505	0	47%	57%	16%	6%
13	at MIN	W	17	15	264	318	-1	-11%	-13%	9%	11%
14	at NYG	L	7	10	260	260	0	15%	-24%	-44%	-4%
15	TB	W	26	20	449	276	+3	33%	18%	-22%	-7%
16	DET	W	42	21	375	319	+2	60%	47%	-15%	-2%
17	at PHI	L	13	27	195	346	-2	-30%	-30%	8%	7%
18	BYE										
19	GB	L	31	34	429	413	0	16%	18%	17%	15%

Trends and Splits

	Offense	Rank	Defense	Rank
Total DVOA	19.9%	3	1.1%	18
Unadjusted VOA	18.9%	3	1.8%	19
Weighted Trend	19.1%	5	-1.0%	15
Variance	7.0%	23	5.8%	22
Average Opponent	-0.7%	10	0.0%	17
Passing	38.2%	3	11.0%	19
Rushing	11.5%	2	-15.8%	8
First Down	20.1%	3	-7.4%	8
Second Down	30.0%	1	11.8%	26
Third Down	0.6%	16	0.7%	17
First Half	22.4%	4	6.2%	21
Second Half	18.7%	5	-11.7%	9
Red Zone	47.0%	3	2.8%	21
Late and Close	29.4%	4	0.0%	19

Five-Year Performance

Year	W-L	Pyth W	Est W	PF	PA	TO	Total	Rk	Off	Rk	Def	Rk	ST	Rk	Off AGL	Rk	Def AGL	Rk	Off Age	Rk	Def Age	Rk	ST Age	Rk
2012	8-8	7.4	7.9	376	400	-13	-0.4%	17	6.1%	11	6.7%	23	0.2%	15	29.0	17	57.5	30	27.2	11	26.7	19	25.6	26
2013	8-8	8.2	8.2	439	432	+8	-2.8%	17	7.5%	11	13.8%	30	3.4%	8	16.4	5	50.2	29	26.5	22	26.1	24	25.3	28
2014	12-4	10.8	10.3	467	352	+6	13.7%	6	16.8%	4	4.0%	22	0.9%	13	9.3	2	66.8	28	26.4	25	26.1	25	25.6	29
2015	4-12	5.2	4.4	275	374	-22	-18.0%	27	-15.6%	31	4.1%	19	1.8%	11	24.1	11	27.6	15	26.9	15	25.9	29	25.7	23
2016	13-3	11	11.8	421	306	+5	20.3%	2	19.9%	3	1.1%	18	1.6%	9	37.5	20	33.1	17	26.6	20	26.3	20	26.1	16

2016 Performance Based on Most Common Personnel Groups

DAL Offense					DAL Offense vs. Opponents					DAL Defense				DAL Defense vs. Opponents			
Pers	Freq	Yds	DVOA	Run%	Pers	Freq	Yds	DVOA	Run%	Pers	Freq	Yds	DVOA	Pers	Freq	Yds	DVOA
11	60%	6.3	31.3%	33%	Base	34%	5.7	10.1%	66%	Base	19%	4.8	-8.1%	11	70%	5.8	5.8%
12	15%	5.8	2.7%	69%	Nickel	57%	6.6	34.7%	35%	Nickel	56%	5.7	1.9%	12	14%	5.5	9.1%
21	8%	6.2	1.2%	56%	Dime+	6%	6.2	4.4%	8%	Dime+	25%	5.7	5.0%	21	3%	6.2	-7.3%
612	5%	4.0	-10.9%	93%	Goal Line	1%	4.4	70.6%	71%					13	3%	3.0	-46.5%
22	3%	4.6	-21.6%	85%	Big	3%	3.0	-9.5%	92%					01	2%	7.5	5.0%
01	3%	11.6	121.1%	0%										20	2%	3.9	-31.9%

Strategic Tendencies

Run/Pass		Rk	Formation		Rk	Pass Rush		Rk	Secondary		Rk	Strategy		Rk
Runs, first half	42%	5	Form: Single Back	79%	15	Rush 3	17.8%	2	4 DB	19%	26	Play-action	24%	3
Runs, first down	58%	1	Form: Empty Back	10%	6	Rush 4	61.3%	21	5 DB	56%	23	Avg Box (Off)	6.38	4
Runs, second-long	30%	17	Pers: 3+ WR	63%	21	Rush 5	19.8%	19	6+ DB	25%	5	Avg Box (Def)	5.85	31
Runs, power sit.	70%	3	Pers: 2+ TE/6+ OL	29%	12	Rush 6+	1.2%	32	CB by Sides	92%	4	Offensive Pace	32.19	30
Runs, behind 2H	38%	1	Pers: 6+ OL	9%	5	Sacks by LB	8.8%	28	S/CB Cover Ratio	35%	1	Defensive Pace	29.45	2
Pass, ahead 2H	42%	27	Shotgun/Pistol	51%	28	Sacks by DB	5.9%	22	DB Blitz	10%	11	Go for it on 4th	0.90	22

Dallas led the league with 8.2 yards per pass, 58.1% DVOA, and 11.2 average yards after the catch on passes thrown at or behind the line of scrimmage. Only two other teams, Denver and Tampa Bay, averaged more than 6.5 yards on such passes. Even without Ezekiel Elliott's 83-yard touchdown against Pittsburgh from Week 10, the Cowboys still would have ranked third. The Cowboys' rank in "S/CB Cover Ratio" depends entirely on whether we count Byron Jones as a safety first or a cornerback first. In 2015, we counted him as a cornerback, and the Cowboys ranked 31st. In 2016, we counted him as a safety, and the Cowboys ranked No. 1. The Dallas defense had a 7.0 percent adjusted sack rate on first and second down (fourth) but dropped to 4.7 percent on third down (24th). We only charted Cowboys opponents with 25 dropped passes (tied for 26th), which equaled 4.2 percent of opportunities (30th).

Passing

Player	DYAR	DVOA	Plays	NtYds	Avg	YAC	C%	TD	Int
D.Prescott	1302	31.6%	483	3527	7.3	5.0	68.1%	23	4
M.Sanchez*	-119	-96.5%	21	68	3.2	5.4	55.6%	0	2

Rushing

Player	DYAR	DVOA	Plays	Yds	Avg	TD	Fum	Suc
E.Elliott	303	16.0%	287	1394	4.9	15	0	57%
A.Morris	14	-3.4%	61	231	3.8	2	0	54%
D.Prescott	96	41.6%	36	235	6.5	6	0	-
L.Whitehead	38	43.9%	8	86	10.8	0	0	-
L.Dunbar*	5	8.9%	6	11	1.8	1	0	50%

Receiving

Player	DYAR	DVOA	Plays	Ctch	Yds	Y/C	YAC	TD	C%
C.Beasley	341	31.0%	99	76	840	11.1	5.3	5	77%
D.Bryant	153	7.5%	96	50	796	15.9	2.9	8	52%
T.Williams	214	31.1%	61	44	594	13.5	3.8	4	72%
B.Butler	6	-10.4%	32	16	219	13.7	1.2	3	50%
J.Witten	0	-7.2%	95	69	673	9.8	3.7	3	73%
G.Swaim	3	-2.3%	8	6	69	11.5	8.3	0	75%
G.Escobar*	5	4.4%	7	4	30	7.5	2.3	1	57%
E.Elliott	82	26.9%	40	32	363	11.3	12.2	1	80%
L.Dunbar*	-5	-17.5%	24	16	122	7.6	5.2	0	67%
A.Morris	-13	-53.4%	6	3	11	3.7	3.7	0	50%

Offensive Line

Player	Pos	Age	GS	Snaps	Pen	Sk	Pass	Run	Player	Pos	Age	GS	Snaps	Pen	Sk	Pass	Run
Travis Frederick	C	26	16/16	1060	5	0.0	1	5	Ronald Leary*	LG	28	13/12	805	4	0.0	5	3
Zack Martin	RG	25	16/16	1060	2	1.5	2	0	La'el Collins	LG	24	3/3	186	2	0.0	1	1
Doug Free*	RT	33	16/16	1055	7	5.5	14	11	Jonathan Cooper	RG	27	5/3	183	1	1.0	1	1
Tyron Smith	LT	27	13/13	837	7	4.5	8	4									

Year	Yards	ALY	Rank	Power	Rank	Stuff	Rank	2nd Lev	Rank	Open Field	Rank	Sacks	ASR	Rank	Press	Rank	F-Start	Cont.
2014	4.86	4.71	1	76%	4	18%	11	1.38	2	1.10	2	30	6.1%	16	22.0%	10	13	32
2015	4.53	4.48	6	66%	15	17%	4	1.21	12	1.01	8	33	6.6%	19	20.9%	5	26	34
2016	4.68	4.63	4	73%	3	15%	5	1.36	5	0.98	8	28	5.6%	13	28.8%	24	14	37

2016 ALY by direction:	Left End 5.29 (6)	Left Tackle 4.12 (21)	Mid/Guard 4.78 (2)	Right Tackle 5.01 (6)	Right End 4.22 (10)

The Cowboys' unspectacular adjusted sack rate and pressure metrics can be traced back to two linemen. Guard La'el Collins got pushed around by the Giants interior line in the season opener, then settled down for two games before hitting injured reserve with a toe injury. Right tackle Doug Free was a weak link all season long. Collins is penciled in as Free's replacement at right tackle. If he cannot handle the move, Chaz Green may get an opportunity. Green, a 2015 third-round pick from Florida, played two games at left tackle in relief of Tyron Smith last year without being credited with a sack allowed. It helped a little that those games were against the Bears and 49ers. Freefalling former first-rounder Jonathan Cooper, a key component of last year's Chandler Jones trade who could not stick with the Patriots, is the favorite to take over for Ronald Leary at left guard.

Cooper looked like the best guard prospect in a decade when coming out of North Carolina in 2015. Take a moment to imagine what the Cowboys offensive line will be like if both Collins and Cooper achieve the potential they once displayed. ⚊ Mere competence from those two positions should allow the Cowboys to retain their unofficial "Best O-Line in the NFL" title belt. By snaps per blown block, Travis Frederick and Zack Martin were the league's two best interior linemen in 2016. Tyron Smith never ranks as well in blown blocks as his reputation would suggest, but having the uber-athletic left tackle under contract through the rapture isn't a bad thing.

Defensive Front Seven

Defensive Line	Age	Pos	G	Snaps	Plays	Overall TmPct	Rk	Stop	Dfts	BTkl	Runs	vs. Run St%	Rk	RuYd	Rk	Pass Rush Sack	Hit	Hur	Dsrpt
Maliek Collins	22	DT	16	656	23	2.8%	78	18	8	2	15	67%	71	3.0	71	5.0	6	11	0
David Irving	24	DT	15	489	22	2.9%	77	21	13	4	11	100%	1	0.0	1	4.0	13	26	6
Terrell McClain*	29	DT	15	471	40	5.3%	33	30	6	3	34	76%	47	2.9	68	2.5	5	5	0
Cedric Thornton	29	DT	13	278	22	3.3%	--	18	7	0	16	88%	--	1.1	--	1.5	3	4	1
Stephen Paea	29	DE	13	321	12	1.7%	--	10	2	3	11	82%	--	2.4	--	0.5	2	6	0

Edge Rushers	Age	Pos	G	Snaps	Plays	Overall TmPct	Rk	Stop	Dfts	BTkl	Runs	vs. Run St%	Rk	RuYd	Rk	Pass Rush Sack	Hit	Hur	Dsrpt
Tyrone Crawford	28	DE	14	627	28	3.9%	68	23	12	2	22	77%	35	1.2	13	4.5	5	22	0
Jack Crawford*	29	DE	16	529	25	3.1%	84	16	7	4	19	58%	94	3.5	87	3.5	2	8	0
Benson Mayowa	26	DE	13	383	25	3.8%	70	20	13	0	16	81%	20	1.1	12	6.0	1	6	0
Demarcus Lawrence	25	DE	9	329	11	2.4%	97	9	5	1	8	88%	5	-0.6	1	1.0	5	17	3
Ryan Davis*	28	DE	9	155	4	0.9%	--	2	2	0	4	50%	--	1.5	--	0.0	2	9	0

Linebackers	Age	Pos	G	Snaps	Plays	Overall TmPct	Rk	Stop	Dfts	BTkl	Runs	vs. Run St%	Rk	RuYd	Rk	Pass Rush Sack	Hit	Hur	Tgts	vs. Pass Suc%	Rk	AdjYd	Rk	PD	Int
Sean Lee	31	OLB	15	977	144	18.9%	3	77	28	10	79	65%	34	3.1	26	0.0	2	7	43	38%	69	7.2	55	1	0
Anthony Hitchens	25	MLB	16	581	78	9.6%	59	36	7	5	47	64%	38	4.1	70	1.5	4	4	15	34%	78	11.0	81	1	0
Damien Wilson	24	MLB	16	284	30	3.7%	--	13	6	3	16	44%	--	4.9	--	0.5	1	2	12	55%	--	4.7	--	1	0
Justin Durant	32	OLB	13	282	40	6.1%	--	20	10	3	13	46%	--	4.8	--	1.0	1	4	10	42%	--	10.3	--	2	0

Year	Yards	ALY	Rank	Power	Rank	Stuff	Rank	2nd Level	Rank	Open Field	Rank	Sacks	ASR	Rank	Press	Rank
2014	4.46	4.12	17	67%	20	18%	20	1.16	19	1.02	30	28	4.6%	29	22.1%	27
2015	4.31	4.26	21	76%	30	21%	17	1.35	29	0.74	14	31	6.5%	16	24.6%	22
2016	4.02	4.01	13	69%	25	22%	8	1.28	25	0.58	10	36	6.5%	12	23.1%	29

2016 ALY by direction:	Left End 3.12 (3)	Left Tackle 3.47 (6)	Mid/Guard 4.37 (21)	Right Tackle 3.74 (10)	Right End 4.74 (27)

Twelve of the Cowboys' 38 sacks last year came when opponents trailed by 14 points or more. Tyrone Crawford and David Irving (suspended for the first four games of the season, because he is a Cowboys pass-rusher) were the only remotely consistent pass-rushers, with package player Benson Mayowa sprinkling in some flash plays. Really, the team's best pass-rusher was the offense, which applied constant pressure on opponents to play catch-up. ⚊ The SackSEER system has multiple reasons to be skeptical of Taco Charlton. In addition to unimpressive college stats over his first three seasons, Charlton ran a dismal 40 (4.92 seconds) and tested average or worse at other agility and explosiveness drills at the Combine. Tape study shows a big, toolsy pass-rusher who may be quicker than his 40 time suggests. It also shows a player in a college defense full of playmakers who generated most of his pressure by sliding around the formation, coming unblocked, or exploiting mismatches against right tackles. Doom and gloom aside, Charlton can help the Cowboys just by being a 5-6 sack role player early on, because the team really needs talented edge players who can stay on the field. ⚊ Weakside linebacker remains an important position in Rod Marinelli's descendant of the Tampa-2 defense, and Sean Lee remains the cornerstone of the Cowboys front seven: an exceptional run defender, coverage linebacker, and decision-maker in space. ⚊ There's reason for cautious optimism surrounding Jaylon Smith, as the 2016 second-rounder participated in OTAs after missing his entire rookie year with an ACL/LCL injury. Counting on a full season from Smith might be too great a leap of faith, but it's also possible the linebacking corps isn't simply Lee or bust for yet another season.

Defensive Secondary

Secondary	Age	Pos	G	Snaps	Plays	TmPct	Rk	Stop	Dfts	BTkl	Runs	St%	Rk	RuYd	Rk	Tgts	Tgt%	Rk	Dist	Suc%	Rk	AdjYd	Rk	PD	Int
						Overall						**vs. Run**					**vs. Pass**								
Brandon Carr*	31	CB	16	1015	70	8.6%	43	21	6	6	11	27%	67	5.1	17	88	18.0%	39	10.5	49%	51	7.9	51	9	1
Byron Jones	25	FS/CB	16	985	89	11.0%	25	36	12	11	30	37%	44	6.1	27	67	14.1%	72	10.5	55%	9	6.4	10	11	1
Anthony Brown	24	CB	16	717	59	7.3%	69	20	7	2	9	33%	55	5.8	25	58	16.8%	24	13.1	47%	58	7.5	43	8	1
Barry Church*	29	SS	12	675	89	14.6%	4	27	11	9	40	38%	43	6.0	23	27	8.3%	34	6.3	43%	46	7.5	22	5	2
Orlando Scandrick	30	CB	12	645	52	8.5%	46	20	10	5	4	75%	2	3.5	4	50	15.9%	15	9.8	43%	75	7.3	36	7	1
J.J. Wilcox*	26	FS	13	557	51	7.7%	55	22	11	6	20	25%	65	10.7	70	23	8.6%	39	8.8	59%	4	5.2	1	5	1
Morris Claiborne*	27	CB	7	406	31	8.7%	--	15	9	4	5	40%	--	9.2	--	42	21.4%	--	12.2	62%	--	4.4	--	5	1
Nolan Carroll	30	CB	16	910	64	8.5%	47	29	7	9	11	36%	52	10.8	77	73	18.0%	40	12.4	52%	26	8.1	55	8	1
Robert Blanton	28	SS	10	270	26	5.1%	--	5	1	2	7	29%	--	7.9	--	10	10.1%	--	10.1	32%	--	9.4	--	0	0

Year	Pass D Rank	vs. #1 WR	Rk	vs. #2 WR	Rk	vs. Other WR	Rk	vs. TE	Rk	vs. RB	Rk
2014	22	-2.2%	14	29.5%	29	-24.3%	3	-9.0%	11	-6.3%	12
2015	17	19.6%	30	-11.5%	10	9.0%	21	-25.0%	3	8.2%	20
2016	19	-5.0%	9	3.1%	18	-11.9%	8	31.2%	30	-2.2%	18

Byron Jones has grown into one of the Cowboys' best defenders. Jones slides around from deep safety to slot cornerback, like many versatile defensive backs do these days. His athleticism has always been outstanding, his instincts have developed, and he gets the job done in run support. ☜ While Jeff Heath is still on the roster, look for fifth-round pick Xavier Woods (Louisiana Tech) to make a push to start beside Jones. Woods is a tough little guided missile with great play recognition chops. ☜ Neither Morris Claiborne nor Brandon Carr became the players the Cowboys expected them to be when the team invested the sixth overall pick in the former and $26.4 million guaranteed in the latter. But Claiborne (now with the Jets) was playing well before suffering a midseason groin injury, while Carr (Ravens) was durable and baseline reliable. Between the departures of those two plus erstwhile starting safeties Barry Church and J.J. Wilcox, the Cowboys have more than 2,500 defensive snaps to replace from last year in the secondary alone. ☜ Nolan Carroll is expected to start beside incumbent cornerback Orlando Scandrick until Day 2 picks Chidobe Awuzie (Colorado) or Jourdan Lewis (Michigan) develop. Carroll looked good at the start of the season last year for the Eagles, though appearances may have been deceiving; Carroll's good game against the Steelers consisted mainly of showing up at the last second to defend deep passes that hung in the air. The Cowboys will really want Awuzie (physical but mistake-prone on deep routes) and Lewis (technically proficient Cover-2 type with so-so measureables) to come around quickly. Both would have been late first- or early second-round selections in a cornerback draft that wasn't populated by metahumans.

Special Teams

Year	DVOA	Rank	FG/XP	Rank	Net Kick	Rank	Kick Ret	Rank	Net Punt	Rank	Punt Ret	Rank	Hidden	Rank
2014	0.9%	13	5.3	6	5.0	8	-3.0	23	-0.6	19	-2.5	16	3.1	11
2015	1.8%	11	8.6	3	-6.2	29	-0.1	14	13.3	4	-6.7	30	5.8	8
2016	1.6%	9	4.5	7	1.0	13	-2.0	20	6.1	7	-1.8	19	10.2	5

Rookie Ryan Switzer should jump-start return units which have had little juice since Dwayne Harris left two years ago. Switzer returned seven punts for touchdowns at North Carolina, five of them as a freshman in 2013. While Switzer fits the stereotypical, problematic "little white slot receiver" scouting report, he's powerfully built, incredibly agile, and able to take a licking in the open field: three skills that translate well to an NFL return role.

Denver Broncos

2016 Record: 9-7	Total DVOA: 3.7% (14th)	2017 Mean Projection: 7.0 wins	On the Clock (0-4): 17%
Pythagorean Wins: 9.1 (9th)	Offense: -12.3% (28th)	Postseason Odds: 24.6%	Mediocrity (5-7): 42%
Snap-Weighted Age: 26.4 (22nd)	Defense: -18.3% (1st)	Super Bowl Odds: 1.8%	Playoff Contender (8-10): 31%
Average Opponent: 2.9% (4th)	Special Teams: -2.3% (24th)	Proj. Avg. Opponent: 1.8% (6th)	Super Bowl Contender (11+): 9%

2016: A late-season scoring drought eliminates the defending champs.

2017: New coaches, same old dilemma.

Ever since John Elway came to Denver in 1983, the Broncos' fortunes have generally revolved around the quarterback position. First, there was Elway's 16-year Hall of Fame career, followed by the monumental task of replacing him. The replacement plans only kept getting shorter and shorter. Brian Griese lasted five seasons (1998-2002) in Denver. Jake Plummer spent four years (2003-2006) there before giving way to Jay Cutler, who was traded after his third season (2008). During his third season in 2011, Kyle Orton was lost in the rapture known as Tim Tebow mania, which led to a surprise playoff appearance.

By then, Elway was heading into his second year as Denver's general manager, and he had the clout to replace the popular Tebow with the only other quarterback he could sell fans on: Peyton Manning. The Broncos instantly became Super Bowl contenders, reached the big game twice, and won a championship in Super Bowl 50. However, that team was led by a historically-strong defense rather than its quarterback play. Manning rode off into the sunset, and Elway correctly decided that Brock Osweiler was not worth the $18-million-per-season gamble. Rather than trade for someone with Super Bowl experience, such as Colin Kaepernick, Elway traded for Mark Sanchez and selected Paxton Lynch in the first round of the 2016 draft. Trevor Siemian, a 2015 seventh-round pick, ended up winning the job for the regular season, sparing us the sight of Sanchez in a meaningful game. While the conventional passing stats looked better in 2016, the offense actually dropped from 25th in DVOA to 28th behind the young quarterbacks.

The defense was still championship caliber, coming away with two touchdown returns in the fourth quarter to put away the Colts in Week 2—a game so reminiscent of Denver's 2015 wins. Fortune was kind to Denver in the kicking game as well. Graham Gano missed a 50-yard field goal on opening night that would have won the Super Bowl rematch for Carolina. In New Orleans, Drew Brees appeared to have thrown a go-ahead touchdown pass late, but a blocked extra point was returned by Will Parks for two points and the win in a wild 25-23 finish. Denver lost to the heavyweights on its schedule (Atlanta, Oakland, and Kansas City), but the team still was in control of its playoff destiny at 8-4.

Then the offensive woes became too much to overcome. In a three-game losing streak that ultimately sunk Denver's title defense, the offense mustered a total of 23 points against the Titans, Patriots, and Chiefs. Tennessee (13-10) and New England (16-3) didn't even crack 17 points in victories over the Broncos. In his career, Manning was 89-0 in games he finished when his team allowed fewer than 17 points. The Broncos weren't missing Manning's body as much as they were his mind. When the defense also put on one of its worst efforts in years on Christmas in Kansas City (33-10 loss), you knew the 2016 Broncos were finished. The only gift that week was a Derek Carr injury that helped Denver beat Oakland's overmatched backup quarterbacks in Week 17 to finish 9-7.

Denver's defense is primed for championship runs right now, but may have to settle for just the one because they don't have a proper quarterback. This is usually what happens to defensively-driven contenders.

This happened to Mike Ditka's Bears in the 1980s. The 1986 team was ready to dominate again, but ended up starting four different quarterbacks, including little Doug Flutie in a one-and-done postseason after managing to go 14-2. Chicago won one playoff game ("The Fog Bowl") the rest of the decade. The 2000s Ravens also experienced this problem after letting Trent Dilfer leave the team following its lone Super Bowl win. Sure, Elvis Grbac was actually an upgrade in 2001, but the offense was still lacking, and then the Ravens made a huge mistake drafting Kyle Boller as their quarterback of the future in 2003. The Buccaneers were closer to their end than their beginning after they won in 2002. Quarterback Brad Johnson struggled the following season, and by 2004, veterans such as Warren Sapp and John Lynch already moved on to other teams. Every Super Bowl winner since the 2002 Buccaneers has featured a legitimate franchise quarterback, though with the way Joe Flacco has played since his title run got him paid (thanks, Rahim Moore), he might not even be able to lead this Denver team to another championship. Siemian (-7.3%) finished eight spots higher in passing DVOA than Flacco (-13.9%) in 2016.

A typical Tony Romo season would have certainly been good enough to make Denver a real contender, and that type of power move certainly fits with Elway's modus operandi. Alas, any hopes of Romo going to Denver ended when the veteran announced his retirement in April. On the bright side for Broncos fans, you'll hear Romo instead of Phil Simms during your CBS games from now on. (For those unfamiliar

2017 Broncos Schedule

Week	Opp.	Week	Opp.	Week	Opp.
1	LACH (Mon.)	7	at LACH	13	at MIA
2	DAL	8	at KC (Mon.)	14	NYJ
3	at BUF	9	at PHI	15	at IND (Thu.)
4	OAK	10	NE	16	at WAS
5	BYE	11	CIN	17	KC
6	NYG	12	at OAK		

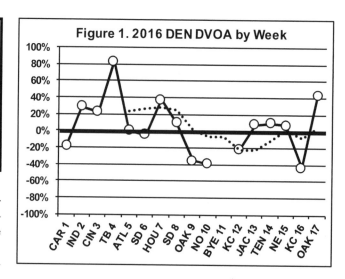

Figure 1. 2016 DEN DVOA by Week

with the story, more than 40,000 Broncos fans signed a petition in 2014 that proposed a ban of Simms from calling Denver games. So at least Romo's retirement has brought some good fortune to the team.)

This means that Denver is locked into a quarterback competition between Siemian and Lynch. We'll get to them later, but if we assume that quarterback is a weakness for the 2017 Broncos, then we can focus on the significant changes that happened this offseason.

It is not often that a team of Denver's caliber makes wholesale changes along the coaching staff, but here we are. Head coach Gary Kubiak quickly announced his retirement after the team's final game of the season. Kubiak has had a few scary health incidents in the last few years, including a hospitalization that caused him to miss Denver's Week 6 loss in San Diego. Offensive coordinator Rick Dennison has long been joined at the hip with Kubiak, and upon the news of Kubiak's retirement, Dennison went to Buffalo for the same position. Sorry LeBron, but famed defensive coordinator Wade Phillips has taken his talents to the Golden State Warriors. No, check that... Phillips went off to La La Land to see if he can bring out the best in an underachieving Rams defense.

Elway played for Phillips and was a teammate to Kubiak and Dennison in the '80s, so this is really saying goodbye to three old friends. With three big spots to fill, the Broncos made one promotion, brought back one familiar name, and took one big roll of the dice on the most important hiring.

Vance Joseph, who got his start in the league coaching defensive backs for the Mike Nolan-era 49ers, will turn 45 in September and is a first-time NFL head coach. In fact, he was just a first-time defensive coordinator in 2016 for the Dolphins, an average defense (19th in DVOA) that was shredded by New England and Pittsburgh in the final two games of the season. Not exactly the most recent fact you want on your resume when you are trying to land a job with an AFC contender.

One might wonder why Denver did not hire Kyle Shanahan instead, as he was one of the three candidates Elway and team president Joe Ellis interviewed. After all, he is the son of Mike Shanahan, who Elway won his two Super Bowls with, and he also worked under Kubiak's guidance in Houston. This wouldn't even be nepotism or favoritism. Shanahan just coached an incredibly productive Atlanta offense to a near Super Bowl win, led by MVP quarterback Matt Ryan. Surely he could help develop Lynch in Denver, right?

The fact is Denver was high on Joseph before this year, and he has more Denver ties than you might think. After the Broncos let John Fox go following the 2014 season, the first interview to be Fox's replacement went to offensive coordinator Adam Gase. However, their second interview was Joseph, a little-known defensive backs coach who had just completed his first season under Marvin Lewis in Cincinnati. Lewis and the Bengals were protective of Joseph, who they expected to have a future as a coordinator or head coach. Of course, the job ultimately went to Kubiak, who Joseph coached under in Houston (2011-13). And when Gase eventually earned the top gig in Miami last year, he made Joseph his coordinator.

Joseph's lack of experience in making big decisions makes him very difficult to project around. We don't know if he'll make Andy Reid look like a clock-managing genius, or if he has the tact to ever out-coach Bill Belichick. Joseph's preference is to not be a play caller, and he stressed at his introductory press conference that he wants to fit the scheme to the players instead of the other way around. Joseph is here to be the leader, and to maintain a culture that does not tolerate pettiness, such as when Aqib Talib pushed teammate Jordan Norwood after a muffed punt last season. When Joseph was coaching defensive backs in Houston during a 14-game losing streak in 2013, he was commended for his unwavering effort to make sure his unit was the most prepared each week, even though the team was a huge disappointment that season.

Not every report on Joseph was squeaky clean. In 2003, two female trainers alleged that Joseph sexually assaulted them while he was an assistant at the University of Colorado. Joseph has denied the allegations, and was never charged or arrested. Sexual harassment was investigated at the school, and Joseph left Colorado during that time. The Broncos looked into the reports and it obviously did not change their hiring decision.

Something that could affect a team's decision to hire a coach is when that coach has earned a reputation for creating a dysfunctional work environment. That was the case with the younger Shanahan in Washington in 2013, where he worked under his father. In talking to Jason La Canfora at CBS Sports[1],

---

a former member of the organization summed it up: "Kyle bitches about everything, and then his father has to fix it. He bitches about the food in the cafeteria, he bitches about the field, he bitches about the equipment. He complains and then Mike takes care of it. Kyle is a big problem there. He is not well liked." Shanahan also allegedly had no real relationship with young quarterback Robert Griffin III, who he treated like "a JV quarterback," according to one staff member.

Again, these are the stories that are out there about these men, and Denver made the call on which one to pick. The success of Shanahan in San Francisco compared to Joseph in Denver is something the fan base will likely keep an eye on, but like with any coach, that success is still largely determined by the other people around them.

That includes a person like Mike McCoy, who is getting a second shot as Denver's offensive coordinator, a position he held in 2009-2012. It is strange how Adam Gase has earned the reputation as a "quarterback whisperer" for his work with Tim Tebow and Peyton Manning in Denver. Maybe it helps to build that perception when Gase was the offensive coordinator for Denver's record-breaking 2013 offense, but Gase was just the quarterbacks coach in 2011-12. McCoy was the playcaller, and he had no problem shifting midseason to a run-heavy, zone-read option scheme to accommodate Tebow's unusual skill set. When Manning came to town, McCoy of course changed the Denver offense to fit the style that had produced incredible results for Manning in the past.

That led to McCoy taking the head coaching job in San Diego in 2013. He made the playoffs that year, and helped Philip Rivers to an excellent bounce-back season. But the rest of McCoy's tenure there was marred by a gross amount of injuries, timid game management, and way too many blown leads. Fortunately, the Broncos will just ask McCoy to get back to playcalling duties, leaving a lot of the other decisions to Joseph. McCoy's history suggests he'll do a good job of scheming around the players Denver has instead of forcing them into a specific system.

McCoy and the winner of the quarterback competition will both have to work around other offensive deficiencies that have hurt Denver in the previous two seasons. First, there is still a lack of a third receiving weapon behind Demaryius Thomas and Emmanuel Sanders. The Broncos never really replaced Wes Welker or Julius Thomas after 2014, meaning the likes of Bennie Fowler, Cody Latimer, Virgil Green, A.J. Derby, and Jeff Heuerman will have to step up. They did not last year when rookie back Devontae Booker was third on the team in targets (45) and catches (31). Denver drafted Carlos Henderson (third round) and tight end Jake Butt (fifth round) this year, but Henderson is a long-term project who may play primarily on special teams as a rookie, while Butt still has to recover from the torn ACL he suffered in the Orange Bowl. A serious injury to Sanders or Thomas would be absolutely devastating to this offense.

The other major issue is the offensive line, where Elway has struggled at constructing a competent unit. Russell Okung lasted one subpar year at left tackle before leaving without his option picked up. Five years into his career, Donald Stephenson doesn't instill much confidence as a starting tackle, and 2015 second-round pick Ty Sambrailo has only started seven games in two seasons. The signing of ex-Dallas left guard Ronald Leary should help this season. He actually has the sixth-highest cap hit ($8.4 million) on the team this year, and last season in Dallas he ranked sixth among left guards in snaps per blown block. He won't have the benefit of lining up between two All-Pros in Denver, but the Broncos had to add a quality lineman somewhere to get the running game (30th in DVOA) back on track.

The defense is still loaded with talent, which is great news for first-time coordinator Joe Woods. He has huge shoes to fill in replacing Wade Phillips, but Woods' background is a lot like that of Joseph's. He worked alongside Mike Tomlin in Tampa Bay (2004-05) and Minnesota (2006) where defensive backs were his specialty. In the last two years, Woods has coached Denver's "No Fly Zone" secondary with great results. Denver has finished No. 1 in pass defense DVOA in both seasons. The great pass rush also had the highest pressure rate in both seasons, but that is hardly the only reason for the success. Woods' secondary can cover with the best of them. In 2016, Denver's defense had -8.8% DVOA without pressure, the best mark for any defense in the last seven years. The league average is usually around 30-35% DVOA when there's no pressure on the quarterback, so it is really impressive for the Broncos to post a negative number.

In January, Elway stated that Denver's No. 1 priority this offseason was to "stay great" on defense. On paper, so far things look just dandy. The most notable loss was the retirement of DeMarcus Ware, a future Hall of Famer, but the Broncos knew this was coming eventually. That's why Shane Ray was drafted in the first round in 2015, and he already had to fill an injured Ware's shoes last season when he racked up 8.0 sacks. Denver's combination of having arguably the best pass-rusher (Von Miller) and best secondary in the game gives this unit an edge over any other defense. All five key members of the No Fly Zone return: Chris Harris Jr., Aqib Talib, Bradley Roby, Darian Stewart, and T.J. Ward. None of these players will be older than 31 this season. Denver's run defense slipped to 21st in DVOA last year, including games in Oakland and Kansas City where the Broncos allowed over 200 rushing yards, but the ability to defend the pass is still far more important.

Denver is poised to have another strong defensive season, but there's a difference between strong defense and spectacular defense. Even defenses that consistently excel have a hard time staying at the peak of the 2015-2016 Broncos for very long. In fact, the 2015-2016 Broncos are just the third defense since 1986 to lead the NFL in DVOA in consecutive seasons. The 1993-1994 Steelers and 2013-2014 Seahawks also ranked No. 1 in back-to-back seasons, but no defense has ever had three years in a row on top.

In May, Roby set his eyes on leading the league in pass defense for a third-straight season. "That is our biggest goal—to be the No. 1 pass defense three years straight, just to really show that in history, they can go back and show that the Broncos secondary was one of the best—if not the best—secondary to ever play. And the numbers don't lie," Roby said. Well, the numbers do lie a bit if you're using yards allowed to rank defenses, but it is true that no defense since the merger has allowed the fewest passing yards three years in a row. The 1964-1968 Packers had a streak of five seasons, winning three championships in the process under Vince Lombardi.

Using DVOA instead of total yardage allowed also shows how difficult it is to play historically great pass defense for an extended length of time. The Broncos are only the third team in the past 30 years to put up pass defense DVOA below -25.0% for two straight seasons, along with the 1991-1992 New Orleans Saints and the 1988-1989 Minnesota Vikings. No team has ever reached that benchmark for three straight seasons. Only one team in DVOA history has even reached a pass defense DVOA of -20.0% for more than two straight seasons: Tampa Bay, in five straight seasons from 1999 to 2003.

The trends are similar with total defensive DVOA, where the Broncos have ranked fourth or better for three consecutive seasons. Only seven other defenses have since 1986 have matched or exceeded that streak. They are all featured in Table 1, which shows where they ranked in DVOA over a five-year period.

Table 1. Five-Year Outlook for Top-Four Defenses in DVOA, 1986-2016

Team	Seasons	T4 Streak	Y1	Y2	Y3	Y4	Y5
PHI	1988-1992	5	2	1	3	1	2
PIT	1993-1997	5	1	1	4	4	2
SEA	2012-2015	4	2	1	1	4	5
SF	1995-1997	3	1	2	1	16	30
BAL	1999-2001	3	1	2	4	6	1
TB	2001-2003	3	2	1	3	8	8
CHI	2010-2012	3	4	4	1	25	28
DEN	2014-2016	3	4	1	1	-	-

While defense is not as consistent as offense, there have been a few teams who were capable of extending a long run of high-caliber play. The Eagles actually managed a top-five ranking in DVOA for nine years (1987-1995) and then finished No. 8 in 1996; somehow, they still only went 2-6 in the playoffs for that decade. Seattle's defense began to drop-off last season, though the injury to Earl Thomas was a major reason. The mid-'90s 49ers got old and lost veterans, which led to a sharp decline; the same thing happened to the Bears after Lovie Smith left in 2013. The Broncos are not facing this problem as of yet, so they can hope to match some of the long-term success the Ravens had. From 1999 through 2011, the meat of the Ray Lewis era, Baltimore ranked in the top eight in defensive DVOA for 13 straight seasons.

Defense is what Denver hangs its hat on, but as the teams on Table 1 show, quarterback play is still the difference-maker in this league. Neither Lynch nor Siemian threw a regular-season pass before 2016, so both are operating at similar experience levels. Siemian just had the 14 starts last year to two for Lynch, and did reasonably well for an unheralded seventh-round pick in his second year. Since Lynch only threw 83

passes, we don't want to make a huge deal out of the 2016 statistics. However, we did put together a comparison between the two quarterbacks for last season in a variety of statistics that showcase both efficiency and playing style (Table 2).

Table 2. Denver's Young Quarterback Competition

2016 Statistic	Trevor Siemian	Paxton Lynch
Pass attempts	486	83
Yards per attempt	7.0	6.0
Air yards per attempt	8.8	11.0
Off-target pass% (ESPN)	20.7%	24.7%
Passing DVOA	-7.3%	-19.0%
Total QBR (ESPN)	55.8	28.8
ALEX (3rd down only)	1.5	3.0
Passing plus-minus	+0.4	-2.4
Out of pocket%	14.1%	19.2%
Out of pocket DVOA	-20.4%	-35.3%
Knockdown%	16.1%	18.4%
Pressure rate	25.7%	29.3%
DVOA with pressure	-71.7%	-166.8%
DVOA no pressure	29.6%	57.2%
Red zone DVOA	-48.0%	7.4%
Red zone QBR (ESPN)	19.2	39.0
Shotgun/Pistol DVOA	-18.6%	-12.3%
QB Under Center DVOA	8.3%	-25.8%

While Siemian boasted better overall numbers, this looks like the classic low ceiling (Siemian) vs. high potential (Lynch) argument. Siemian exhibited a lot of traits shared by division rival Alex Smith in his careful way of protecting the ball; at least he costs only a small fraction of what Smith makes in Kansas City. Meanwhile, Lynch was more of the deep-throwing, get-on-the-move wild child with questionable accuracy. We're not calling him Tebow 2.0, but Lynch's 24.7 percent rate of off-target throws (over or underthrown passes according to ESPN Stats & Info) was the second highest in 2016 for all passers with at least 50 attempts.

Again, the sample sizes are small, but there are some areas that suggest Lynch's potential for growth is worth exploring over the consistent mediocrity of Siemian. For example, while Lynch was abysmal under pressure, his DVOA was nearly twice as high as Siemian's from a clean pocket, one of the best indicators of good quarterback play. Siemian also really struggled in the red zone, and he did not fare well in the shotgun. Lynch was a shotgun-only quarterback in college, and did not adjust well to Kubiak's system that favored non-shotgun plays. This is where McCoy's flexibility to adapt to his players should help quicken Lynch's development.

While this coaching staff is not tied to either quarterback, make no mistake: Elway, like any GM, wants to see his first-round pick deliver. Since 1978, only 22 of 84 first-round quarterbacks (26.2 percent) did not start the season opener in their second season. The last three quarterbacks to fit that description were Johnny Manziel, Tim Tebow, and Brady Quinn.

That's not the company that Lynch wants to join. Of those 22 quarterbacks, only four turned out to be long-time quality starters, and two of them (Philip Rivers and Aaron Rodgers) sat behind future Hall of Famers (Drew Brees and Brett Favre). Lynch just has to beat out Siemian. Training camp and preseason performance will still determine Denver's Week 1 starter, but unless Lynch is the second coming of Heath Shuler, which would make Siemian the new Gus Frerotte, then the first-round pick should get a good shot this year.

The Broncos still have the tamest offense in the AFC West, arguably the league's best division. They also have to play four games against the NFC East, the league's other contender for best division, as part of a challenging schedule that projects as one of the league's toughest. Still, our mean projection of 7.0 wins does feel low, especially for a franchise that has just six losing seasons in the last 40 years. This year marks the 40th anniversary of Denver's "Orange Crush" defense, the moniker given to Denver's first Super Bowl team back in 1977. Today's defense is even better, but we have likely seen the peak of its power. Without the steadiness of a veteran quarterback or a reliable running game, combined with some expected growing pains from the new coaching staff, this Denver team is too defense-reliant in an offense-driven league. Miller and the No Fly Zone should keep the Broncos relevant into December, but until there is equilibrium found at quarterback, we'll best remember Denver for 2015's triumph, just as we remember the 1985 Bears, 2000 Ravens, and 2002 Buccaneers.

Scott Kacsmar

2016 Broncos Stats by Week

Wk	vs.	W-L	PF	PA	YDF	YDA	TO	Total	Off	Def	ST
1	CAR	W	21	20	307	333	-2	-19%	-11%	6%	-1%
2	IND	W	34	20	400	253	+1	28%	8%	-28%	-8%
3	at CIN	W	29	17	355	332	+1	22%	19%	2%	5%
4	at TB	W	27	7	307	215	+3	83%	17%	-67%	0%
5	ATL	L	16	23	267	372	0	0%	-32%	-25%	7%
6	at SD	L	13	21	304	265	0	-5%	-10%	-7%	-2%
7	HOU	W	27	9	347	271	+2	37%	25%	-8%	3%
8	SD	W	27	19	324	369	0	9%	-25%	-38%	-5%
9	at OAK	L	20	30	299	397	-2	-36%	-19%	17%	0%
10	at NO	W	25	23	337	373	+2	-39%	-46%	-9%	-3%
11	BYE										
12	KC	L	27	30	464	273	-1	-21%	0%	-14%	-35%
13	at JAC	W	20	10	206	333	+3	7%	-23%	-25%	5%
14	at TEN	L	10	13	348	253	-2	9%	-14%	-20%	4%
15	NE	L	3	16	309	313	-3	7%	-33%	-41%	-1%
16	at KC	L	10	33	246	484	-2	-44%	-39%	8%	3%
17	OAK	W	24	6	349	221	+2	43%	-14%	-66%	-9%

Trends and Splits

	Offense	Rank	Defense	Rank
Total DVOA	-12.3%	28	-18.3%	1
Unadjusted VOA	-11.5%	28	-16.3%	1
Weighted Trend	-18.9%	30	-19.1%	1
Variance	4.5%	9	6.0%	23
Average Opponent	0.7%	22	3.9%	3
Passing	3.6%	22	-31.1%	1
Rushing	-22.7%	29	-3.8%	21
First Down	-15.6%	28	-10.3%	7
Second Down	-9.8%	23	-15.7%	5
Third Down	-10.2%	22	-35.9%	1
First Half	-10.1%	26	-14.7%	3
Second Half	-27.1%	29	-14.7%	7
Red Zone	-37.9%	30	-2.6%	16
Late and Close	-15.0%	24	-6.5%	13

Five-Year Performance

Year	W-L	Pyth W	Est W	PF	PA	TO	Total	Rk	Off	Rk	Def	Rk	ST	Rk	Off AGL	Rk	Def AGL	Rk	Off Age	Rk	Def Age	Rk	ST Age	Rk
2012	13-3	12.5	14.7	481	289	-1	36.5%	2	22.1%	2	-13.8%	5	0.6%	13	27.8	15	21.4	11	28.3	5	27.0	15	25.9	21
2013	13-3	11.7	14.1	606	399	0	32.7%	2	33.5%	1	-0.2%	15	-1.0%	21	37.8	19	45.8	26	27.9	3	26.3	18	26.8	5
2014	12-4	11.0	13.3	482	354	+5	29.5%	2	20.0%	3	-13.2%	4	-3.7%	27	11.7	4	25.2	6	28.6	2	25.7	31	25.6	27
2015	12-4	9.7	10.7	355	296	-4	17.7%	8	-8.7%	25	-25.8%	1	0.7%	14	42.9	22	13.8	2	28.3	2	26.5	19	25.6	26
2016	9-7	9.1	8.5	333	297	+2	3.7%	14	-12.3%	28	-18.3%	1	-2.3%	24	26.0	8	34.2	18	26.6	18	26.7	12	25.1	30

2016 Performance Based on Most Common Personnel Groups

DEN Offense					DEN Offense vs. Opponents					DEN Defense				DEN Defense vs. Opponents			
Pers	Freq	Yds	DVOA	Run%	Pers	Freq	Yds	DVOA	Run%	Pers	Freq	Yds	DVOA	Pers	Freq	Yds	DVOA
11	52%	5.8	-1.3%	28%	Base	33%	4.7	-15.5%	56%	Base	57%	5.1	-14.5%	11	41%	4.5	-26.5%
21	20%	4.7	-8.7%	65%	Nickel	51%	5.7	-5.3%	30%	Nickel	7%	4.5	-25.0%	12	27%	4.9	-19.5%
12	11%	4.8	-26.5%	39%	Dime+	14%	4.9	-3.8%	12%	Dime+	33%	4.6	-30.5%	21	9%	5.3	-11.7%
10	10%	4.2	-29.6%	20%	Goal Line	1%	0.5	24.1%	69%	Goal Line	1%	0.8	57.9%	13	5%	4.8	-18.3%
01	2%	6.0	1.8%	0%						Big	2%	4.1	-16.7%	611	4%	6.0	-14.3%
20	1%	6.5	18.4%	67%										22	3%	6.1	12.5%
00	1%	4.7	-4.6%	10%										612	3%	3.4	-17.8%

Strategic Tendencies

Run/Pass		Rk	Formation		Rk	Pass Rush		Rk	Secondary		Rk	Strategy		Rk
Runs, first half	36%	22	Form: Single Back	72%	26	Rush 3	4.6%	24	4 DB	57%	1	Play-action	18%	17
Runs, first down	43%	27	Form: Empty Back	6%	19	Rush 4	57.6%	25	5 DB	7%	32	Avg Box (Off)	6.17	18
Runs, second-long	31%	11	Pers: 3+ WR	66%	15	Rush 5	26.7%	5	6+ DB	33%	1	Avg Box (Def)	6.42	2
Runs, power sit.	58%	11	Pers: 2+ TE/6+ OL	14%	30	Rush 6+	11.0%	3	CB by Sides	73%	18	Offensive Pace	29.19	5
Runs, behind 2H	21%	31	Pers: 6+ OL	2%	26	Sacks by LB	68.3%	7	S/CB Cover Ratio	33%	3	Defensive Pace	30.00	11
Pass, ahead 2H	41%	31	Shotgun/Pistol	43%	31	Sacks by DB	7.3%	17	DB Blitz	8%	22	Go for it on 4th	0.99	21

Without Peyton Manning around, Gary Kubiak reverted to his usual form. The Broncos fell from 14th to 31st in usage of the shotgun, and from third to 26th in usage of single-back sets. ☞ Trevor Siemian did a strong job of diagnosing the blitz last season, going from 5.5 yards per pass against a standard pass rush to 7.9 yards against five pass-rushers and 8.9 yards against six or more. Paxton Lynch also did well against the blitz in his limited playing time, going from 4.5 average yards with a regular pass rush to 7.0 yards with a blitz. ☞ Nickel defense is now the base for most NFL teams, but not in Denver. The Broncos were the only NFL team to use only four defensive backs on more than half of all plays, then also led the league by using six or more defensive backs on 33 percent of plays. ☞ Isn't one of the goals of the play-action pass to slow down an opposing pass rush? If so, why did Denver opponents only use play-action on 12.5 percent of pass plays? That's the lowest figure in the NFL for the second straight year, particularly odd since only the Giants and Packers had a larger gap between DVOA allowed with play-action and DVOA allowed on other passes. ☞ The Broncos were No. 2 in the league in defensive penalties for the second straight season, another example of how a high number of penalties often signifies a good defense rather than a bad one. ☞ The Broncos not only cover well, but also tackle well, with a league-low broken-tackle rate of 7.4 percent. ☞ Denver's defense ranked 21st in DVOA through the first quarter, then was the best in the league the rest of the way.

Passing

Player	DYAR	DVOA	Plays	NtYds	Avg	YAC	C%	TD	Int
T.Siemian	137	-7.1%	516	3182	6.2	4.9	59.6%	18	9
P.Lynch	-46	-18.8%	91	455	5.0	3.2	59.8%	2	1

Rushing

Player	DYAR	DVOA	Plays	Yds	Avg	TD	Fum	Suc
D.Booker	-92	-23.0%	146	510	3.5	4	0	42%
C.J.Anderson	-23	-13.5%	110	437	4.0	4	0	39%
J.Forsett*	-58	-39.7%	43	155	3.6	1	2	33%
K.Bibbs*	14	2.7%	29	129	4.4	0	0	52%
T.Siemian	-5	-17.7%	16	60	3.8	0	0	-
P.Lynch	-12	-43.0%	8	29	3.6	0	0	-
A.Janovich	21	60.4%	4	33	8.3	1	0	100%
J.Charles	6	2.6%	12	40	3.3	1	0	42%

Receiving

Player	DYAR	DVOA	Plays	Ctch	Yds	Y/C	YAC	TD	C%
D.Thomas	172	2.1%	144	90	1085	12.1	3.6	5	63%
E.Sanders	103	-3.3%	137	79	1032	13.1	3.0	5	58%
J.Norwood*	-61	-35.9%	34	20	215	10.8	3.4	1	59%
J.Taylor	32	2.7%	25	16	211	13.2	5.3	2	64%
B.Fowler	-16	-22.2%	24	11	145	13.2	5.8	2	46%
C.Latimer	2	-10.9%	15	8	76	9.5	3.0	0	53%
V.Green	-19	-14.8%	37	22	237	10.8	4.6	1	59%
A.J.Derby	1	-6.7%	20	16	161	10.1	3.2	0	80%
J.Heuerman	2	-5.6%	17	9	141	15.7	7.6	0	53%
J.Phillips*	4	-1.1%	8	5	40	8.0	3.4	1	63%
D.Booker	-41	-31.4%	45	31	270	8.7	8.3	1	69%
C.J.Anderson	-2	-15.4%	24	16	128	8.0	6.8	1	67%
J.Forsett*	-32	-64.7%	10	7	34	4.9	6.7	0	70%
A.Janovich	8	1.6%	7	5	44	8.8	6.0	0	71%

Offensive Line

Player	Pos	Age	GS	Snaps	Pen	Sk	Pass	Run	Player	Pos	Age	GS	Snaps	Pen	Sk	Pass	Run
Max Garcia	LG	26	16/16	1080	5	4.0	9	9	Donald Stephenson	RT	29	13/12	747	9	3.0	20	8
Matt Paradis	C	28	16/16	1080	3	1.0	2	6	Ty Sambrailo	RT	25	10/4	246	3	6.5	14	2
Russell Okung*	LT	30	16/16	1067	11	7.0	18	2	Ronald Leary	LG	28	13/12	805	4	0.0	5	3
Michael Schofield	RG	27	16/16	1048	7	1.5	9	5	Menelik Watson	RT	29	10/5	255	4	1.0	2	2

Year	Yards	ALY	Rank	Power	Rank	Stuff	Rank	2nd Lev	Rank	Open Field	Rank	Sacks	ASR	Rank	Press	Rank	F-Start	Cont.
2014	4.39	4.26	12	75%	5	18%	9	1.24	10	0.83	7	17	3.7%	1	13.4%	1	18	36
2015	4.33	4.07	17	61%	23	23%	23	1.24	3	0.93	9	39	5.8%	13	27.5%	22	11	32
2016	3.78	4.09	18	51%	29	21%	21	1.19	13	0.50	26	40	7.4%	27	24.6%	12	20	32

2016 ALY by direction:	Left End 5.80 (2)	Left Tackle 4.17 (20)	Mid/Guard 4.34 (11)	Right Tackle 3.59 (23)	Right End 2.12 (32)

Serving as his own agent, Russell Okung bet on himself when he signed a deal worth just over $5 million to become Denver's left tackle in 2016. After staying healthy enough to start every game, the bet sort of worked, but Okung will collect his next fat check from the Chargers this season. Denver declined to pick up his option, but that leaves the Broncos with a big hole at left tackle this season. ≡ The replacement for Okung is probably Donald Stephenson, the former Chiefs lineman who is best known for being the player drafted one spot before Russell Wilson in 2012. Stephenson was at right tackle last year, but ranked 34th at the position in blown block rate. That job may now go to Ty Sambrailo, who so far has moved from left to right, and from tackle to guard, but has yet to prove he is an asset to the Broncos. ≡ Given the hole at the position, it was no surprise when John Elway used Denver's first-round pick on a left tackle, Garett Bolles of Utah. Bolles has been noted for his athletic ability and mean streak, but he lacks experience (only one year of FBS ball) and will be a 25-year-old rookie. That's not exactly a plug-and-play pick for Week 1, but Bolles will have his opportunity on a line that needs better performance. Eventually, the left tackle position should be his. ≡ Left guard Ronald Leary is the most accomplished lineman on the team without even playing a snap yet for Denver. He should help the running game, even if he doesn't get to play between Tyron Smith and Travis Frederick anymore. ≡ Center Matt Paradis (ninth) and right guard Max Garcia (20th) had much higher rankings in snaps per blown block in 2016 than they did the previous year. Both are still young enough to improve, although Paradis will be limited in the preseason after two hip surgeries this offseason.

Defensive Front Seven

Defensive Line	Age	Pos	G	Snaps	Plays	TmPct	Rk	Stop	Dfts	BTkl	Runs	St%	Rk	RuYd	Rk	Sack	Hit	Hur	Dsrpt
Jared Crick	28	DE	16	942	59	7.0%	14	49	11	2	45	80%	38	2.5	53	3.0	10	19	7
Derek Wolfe	27	DE	14	666	55	7.4%	9	43	11	1	42	71%	58	2.9	67	6.0	12	21	4
Sylvester Williams*	29	DT	16	649	30	3.5%	64	18	4	3	25	60%	84	3.1	74	1.0	5	15	1
Billy Winn	28	DE	16	344	18	2.1%	--	15	2	1	18	83%	--	2.2	--	0.0	1	3	1
Domata Peko	33	DT	16	593	40	4.8%	40	35	6	4	34	85%	24	1.7	28	0.5	2	4	3
Zach Kerr	27	DT	12	318	19	3.1%	--	18	8	3	15	100%	--	0.5	--	2.5	6	6	0

Edge Rushers	Age	Pos	G	Snaps	Plays	TmPct	Rk	Stop	Dfts	BTkl	Runs	St%	Rk	RuYd	Rk	Sack	Hit	Hur	Dsrpt
Von Miller	28	OLB	16	933	80	9.4%	3	62	29	4	50	76%	40	3.1	74	13.0	11	38	4
Shane Ray	24	OLB	16	667	48	5.7%	39	30	14	4	34	56%	96	3.4	83	8.0	13	26	0
Shaquil Barrett	25	OLB	16	422	32	3.8%	--	26	6	2	23	83%	--	2.0	--	1.5	3	9	3
DeMarcus Ware*	35	OLB	10	318	16	3.0%	86	11	6	2	10	50%	98	3.7	93	4.0	5	14	1

Linebackers	Age	Pos	G	Snaps	Plays	TmPct	Rk	Stop	Dfts	BTkl	Runs	St%	Rk	RuYd	Rk	Sack	Hit	Hur	Tgts	Suc%	Rk	AdjYd	Rk	PD	Int
Todd Davis	25	ILB	16	699	99	11.7%	46	53	9	3	75	56%	74	4.3	72	0.5	4	5	24	51%	33	8.7	73	3	0
Brandon Marshall	28	ILB	11	601	55	9.4%	61	30	7	3	36	61%	55	3.9	60	0.0	0	5	17	77%	1	5.3	18	2	0
Corey Nelson	26	ILB	16	545	66	7.8%	69	31	9	5	37	46%	84	4.4	74	0.0	2	5	25	51%	32	4.9	10	5	0

Year	Yards	ALY	Rank	Power	Rank	Stuff	Rank	2nd Level	Rank	Open Field	Rank	Sacks	ASR	Rank	Press	Rank
2014	3.55	3.43	2	55%	7	22%	7	0.97	5	0.60	11	41	6.3%	23	26.8%	5
2015	3.07	3.35	3	83%	31	24%	5	0.73	1	0.37	2	52	8.1%	1	32.7%	1
2016	4.03	4.60	28	65%	20	11%	32	0.91	1	0.52	7	42	7.6%	2	32.2%	1

2016 ALY by direction:	Left End 4.56 (20)	Left Tackle 5.02 (25)	Mid/Guard 4.60 (28)	Right Tackle 4.76 (24)	Right End 2.84 (6)

DeMarcus Ware only played his final three seasons with Von Miller in Denver, but they will go down as one of the top pass-rushing duos from this decade. During their three-year run, no team had more sacks than the Broncos (135), and Denver never finished worse than fifth in pressure rate. You can expect Ware to be part of the Hall of Fame Class of 2022 now that he is retired. ☞ Next, the Broncos hope Shane Ray can combine with Miller for an even longer run of success. So far, the results are looking good, but Miller's sidekick needs to get better against the run. Stunningly, Ray (96th) and Ware (98th) were both near the bottom of all edge rushers in run stop rate. Should something happen to Miller or Ray this season, Shaquil Barrett is a capable backup, though he could miss the beginning of the season after suffering a hip injury in May. ☞ Todd Davis and the reliable Brandon Marshall return at middle linebacker, though the latter saw his run defense metrics decline significantly from a stellar 2015. Marshall's stop rate went from 71 percent to 61 percent, and the average depth of his run tackles ballooned from 2.7 yards (11th among 2015 linebackers) to 3.9 yards (60th). ☞ John Elway also swapped out some personnel on the defensive line in an effort to help the run defense rebound. 2013 first-round pick Sylvester Williams moved on after an underwhelming four seasons in Denver. He'll be replaced by ex-Cincinnati veteran Domata Peko, who is used to playing alongside Geno Atkins in a 4-3 defense, but also big enough at 318 pounds to handle the nose tackle position in a 3-4. Peko's not one for getting after the quarterback, but neither was Williams. Peko's backup will be his own cousin, Kyle Peko, who Denver signed out of Oregon State as an undrafted free agent a year ago. ☞ Defensive end Derek Wolfe is another one of the young building blocks returning to this defense, but the Broncos added some needed insurance for their defensive line with the second-round selection of DeMarcus Walker. He had big numbers at Florida State, posting 25 sacks in the last two years alone, but lacked the physical traits to be a first-round pick. With Jared Crick set to hit free agency in 2018, Walker is a scheme fit who could be Wolfe's bookend in the future.

Defensive Secondary

Secondary	Age	Pos	G	Snaps	Plays	Overall TmPct	Rk	Stop	Dfts	BTkl	Runs	vs. Run St%	Rk	RuYd	Rk	Tgts	vs. Pass Tgt%	Rk	Dist	Suc%	Rk	AdjYd	Rk	PD	Int
Chris Harris	28	CB	16	1099	74	8.7%	38	40	16	4	19	26%	72	9.6	73	71	17.5%	32	10.7	67%	3	4.7	2	11	2
Darian Stewart	29	FS	16	1087	74	8.8%	48	24	9	13	36	39%	40	8.7	59	25	6.3%	11	10.8	47%	35	7.4	20	7	3
T.J. Ward	31	SS	14	989	95	12.8%	12	43	16	13	43	51%	15	6.2	29	50	13.7%	69	10.5	57%	7	6.5	11	9	1
Aqib Talib	31	CB	13	872	55	8.0%	59	25	14	5	12	50%	19	5.8	23	56	17.4%	29	11.3	55%	13	4.7	3	11	3
Bradley Roby	25	CB	16	691	48	5.7%	86	22	11	11	8	63%	11	6.5	40	62	24.5%	79	11.4	48%	55	8.3	61	8	2
Justin Simmons	24	FS	13	296	27	3.9%	--	11	6	2	9	56%	--	5.3	--	11	10.2%	--	9.1	47%	--	8.7	--	4	2
Will Parks	23	SS	16	270	20	2.4%	--	6	4	2	6	33%	--	6.7	--	15	14.7%	--	9.3	43%	--	7.6	--	3	1

Year	Pass D Rank	vs. #1 WR	Rk	vs. #2 WR	Rk	vs. Other WR	Rk	vs. TE	Rk	vs. RB	Rk
2014	5	-18.6%	5	-36.0%	2	5.3%	22	-7.0%	13	-1.4%	17
2015	1	-20.7%	4	-22.1%	4	-28.0%	4	-12.0%	8	-33.4%	2
2016	1	-29.6%	2	-58.5%	1	-24.0%	4	-20.7%	5	-7.1%	15

The 2016 Broncos are the first team in NFL history to have a pair of cornerbacks (Aqib Talib and Chris Harris) as first-team All-Pro selections in the same season. This is a bit misleading in that 2016 was the first time that voters had an extra spot for another defensive back, which went to Harris. Still, it's a fantastic secondary with four players that ranked in the top 20 in adjusted yards per pass. ☞ The only key member of the No Fly Zone who did not chart well was Bradley Roby, who had much stronger numbers in 2015. However, if Harris was to get injured or Talib was suspended after acting the fool again, the Broncos should feel very confident about sliding in Roby to start. ☞ Justin Simmons had solid metrics for a third-round rookie and could continue to push Darian Stewart for playing time at safety. Simmons is one of the twitchier safety prospects in recent seasons, as he ranked in the 85th percentile or better in the vertical jump, broad jump and 3-cone drill. ☞ Third-round rookie Brendan Langley was added for depth, but the former wide receiver for FCS-level Lamar University will mostly see snaps on special teams at first. Langley would be a liability in coverage this season, but has plenty of time to develop under Vance Joseph and Joe Woods, two experts on coaching defensive backs. ☞ The preferred strategy against Denver seems pretty clear: use your tight ends, but avoid Denver's depth at cornerback. Last year, the Broncos defense was last in the league in the percentage of passes targeting opposing No. 2 receivers (14.6 percent) and 31st in the percentage targeting No. 3 receivers (14.8 percent). However, they led the league with 26.8 percent of opposing passes thrown to tight ends. Denver had similar splits in 2015, and to a lesser extent in 2013 and 2014.

Special Teams

Year	DVOA	Rank	FG/XP	Rank	Net Kick	Rank	Kick Ret	Rank	Net Punt	Rank	Punt Ret	Rank	Hidden	Rank
2014	-3.7%	27	-4.4	27	-6.3	27	6.3	4	-7.7	26	-6.3	29	7.8	4
2015	0.7%	14	-0.6	17	0.1	18	-2.2	22	4.9	7	1.3	14	-2.8	19
2016	-2.3%	24	1.6	12	-8.6	29	-0.9	14	3.3	11	-6.8	28	4.3	11

Brandon McManus is more than serviceable on field goals and extra points, but his kickoffs have gotten worse each season. In 2016, he was next to last in gross kickoff value after our adjustments for the altitude at Mile High. ⚏ Rookie punter Riley Dixon was not a strength for the team last year, but he did save the Broncos a few million dollars over what would have been a more expensive choice in Britton Colquitt. Dixon finished 25th in gross punt value a year after Colquitt finished 26th in 2015. Strong punt coverage, led by Cody Latimer and Zaire Anderson, helped mitigate the damage. ⚏ On kick returns, the Broncos took a gym-class approach where every kid gets a turn regardless of skill. Seriously, the Broncos had four players with at least three kick returns. Latimer did the best with his eight opportunities, and the need to extract more special teams value out of the former second-round pick might help him get more chances in 2017. ⚏ Jordan Norwood handled most of the punt return duties, but only three individual returners had less value by our metrics. Emmanuel Sanders held this job in 2015, but did not return a punt in 2016. Denver may be best served to turn these return jobs over to some rookies, including third-rounder Carlos Henderson, who had three touchdowns on returns at Louisiana Tech. Fifth-round pick Isaiah McKenzie returned five punts for touchdowns at Georgia.

Detroit Lions

2016 Record: 9-7	Total DVOA: -15.6% (27th)	2017 Mean Projection: 8.0 wins	On the Clock (0-4): 9%
Pythagorean Wins: 7.7 (22nd)	Offense: -0.6% (15th)	Postseason Odds: 35.0%	Mediocrity (5-7): 33%
Snap-Weighted Age: 26.2 (24th)	Defense: 18.5% (32nd)	Super Bowl Odds: 4.5%	Playoff Contender (8-10): 41%
Average Opponent: -0.3% (18th)	Special Teams: 3.5% (6th)	Proj. Avg. Opponent: 0.5% (10th)	Super Bowl Contender (11+): 17%

2016: A record number of fourth-quarter comebacks…

2017: …and an active four-game losing streak.

While the 2016 Lions reached the playoffs for the third time since 2011, the quick exit was all too familiar to fans. It was the eighth consecutive playoff appearance where the Lions lost in the wild-card round, and their ninth playoff loss in a row dating back to the 1991 NFC Championship Game. Both of those are new NFL records, breaking the ties Detroit previously had with the Cincinnati Bengals.

The season-ending 26-6 loss to Seattle was about as dramatic as Jim Caldwell's facial expressions, but the path Detroit followed just to get to the playoffs was certainly striking. Detroit set an NFL record with eight fourth-quarter comeback wins in the regular season. Even if we included the playoffs, no team in the NFL's 97-year history had won eight games after trailing in the fourth quarter until the Lions, who had the record sewn up by Week 14. Of course, the Lions did not win another game after that eighth comeback.

One might think such a historic run of close wins doesn't bode well for Detroit in 2017. Historically, teams that load up on late comebacks regress the following season. Prior to this past season, there were 52 teams in NFL history that won at least six games (including playoffs) with the game-winning points scored in the fourth quarter or overtime. Those teams won 67.2 percent of their games in that "clutch" season, but dropped to 57.3 percent the following season, with half of the teams missing the playoffs. This may just sound like normal regression, but it's a bit stronger. Historically, 60 percent of 9-7 teams fail to improve their record in the following season. Of the 52 clutch teams, 75 percent had a worse record the next year, and only four teams improved their record by at least 20 percentage points: the 1990-91 Cowboys, the 1997-98 Bills, the 2001-02 Buccaneers, and the 2011-12 Broncos.

None of those four teams are particularly comparable to the 2017 Detroit Lions. Dallas began to reap the benefits of the Herschel Walker trade, and had three young, future Hall of Famers on offense start to peak. The Bills got an unexpected lift when Doug Flutie ended his long wanderings in the CFL wilderness. The Buccaneers brought in a new head coach, Jon Gruden, specifically to improve a weak offense. The Broncos replaced Tim Tebow with Peyton Manning, who got right back into All-Pro form. Needless to say, the Lions are keeping the status quo at head coach and quarterback, and have not owned the last few drafts with an abundance of extra picks.

It is very difficult to continue pulling out close wins over multiple seasons. That's where the "clutch" teams really regress the next year. We have specific game-winning drive data going back to 1980, and the results are striking. The 44 "clutch" teams since 1980 were 286-142 (.668) at game-winning drive opportunities in that clutch season, but 121-181-1 (.401) in the following season. Only two of the 44 teams actually improved their record in close games: the aforementioned 1990-91 Cowboys and the 2008-09 Colts.

Yes, Jim Caldwell was a rookie head coach for the 2009 Colts when they started 14-0 and eventually reached the Super Bowl. Yes, that team set the previous record for fourth-quarter comebacks in a season with seven, so Caldwell has the top two seasons now. However, any team with prime Peyton Manning at quarterback should have an asterisk, and Caldwell could have been mistaken for a *Weekend at Bernie's* character as far as his impact on that team.

Those two Manning-Caldwell Indianapolis teams are also a good cautionary tale about how comeback regression is real. The 2010 Colts went 0-5 in comeback opportunities, with Manning throwing three notable game-ending interceptions. The team ultimately lost at home to the Jets in the wild-card round on the final play of the game. A year after setting the record with seven comebacks, 2010 was the only season of Manning's career where he did not lead a fourth-quarter comeback win.

Unlike seven years ago, Caldwell is not returning with a Super Bowl team. A 9-7 record hides the fact that the 2016 Lions were outscored by 12 points on the season, finished 27th in DVOA, and had the second-fewest "estimated wins" (4.9) for any team with a winning record since 1988. Essentially, the Lions were like a 5-11 team that pulled off four extra miracles, often in the final minute of the game.

It's not like late game-winning drives are new to Matthew Stafford, who garnered MVP consideration for the first time in his career. He led four of them in 2011 and five more in 2014, which happen to be Detroit's previous two playoff appearances. Stafford's 25 fourth-quarter comeback wins are tied for the most in NFL history through a player's first 10 seasons. The crazy part about that stat is that Stafford just finished his *eighth* season, and he missed 19 games in his first two years. He's far from perfect, but Stafford is the main reason that Detroit might have a better than usual chance to resist regression on close wins in 2017. He was the most consistent factor in the

2017 Lions Schedule

Week	Opp.	Week	Opp.	Week	Opp.
1	ARI	7	BYE	13	at BAL
2	at NYG (Mon.)	8	PIT	14	at TB
3	ATL	9	at GB (Mon.)	15	CHI (Sat.)
4	at MIN	10	CLE	16	at CIN
5	CAR	11	at CHI	17	GB
6	at NO	12	MIN (Thu.)		

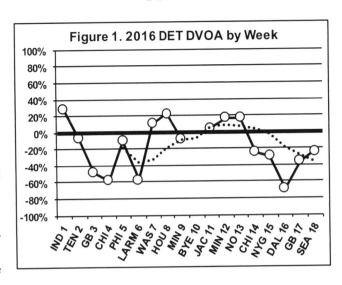

Figure 1. 2016 DET DVOA by Week

team's success last season. On the 14 drives in the fourth quarter and overtime that led to Detroit's eight comeback wins, Stafford completed 41-of-56 passes for 563 yards with four touchdowns and no turnovers.

For as good as those numbers look, they are only one piece of the puzzle that was Detroit's season. Odd as it may sound, despite a record number of comeback wins, the 2016 Lions were *not* a good fourth-quarter team. No, really. The defense was dead last in "late and close" situations, defined as all plays within eight points after halftime. The offense as a whole, and Stafford in particular, had their worst DVOA ranking in the fourth quarter and overtime (Table 1). Stafford threw a game-ending interception against the Titans after the defense blew a 12-point lead, or else we might be talking about nine comeback wins.

Table 1. Table 1. 2016 Lions: DVOA By Quarter

Quarter	Offensive DVOA	Rk	M.Stafford DVOA	Rk*	Defensive DVOA	Rk
1	4.9%	13	21.8%	9	19.8%	29
2	8.3%	11	14.5%	11	11.1%	24
3	-11.3%	21	3.7%	13	43.8%	32
4/OT	-9.0%	23	-9.1%	19	9.7%	22
Late & Close	-11.6%	23	-0.1%	15	27.0%	32

Minimum 50 passes for quarterback to qualify for quarter DVOA ranking.

This season really was a case of "great when he absolutely had to be" for Stafford. Take the record-setting eighth comeback against Chicago in Week 14, for example. With Detroit leading, Stafford threw two interceptions in the fourth quarter: the first came in the red zone, and the second was returned for a touchdown to give Chicago a 17-13 lead. So Detroit set the comeback record with a self-imposed opportunity after Stafford's mistake. He made up for it by driving the offense 76 yards with a game-winning touchdown scramble, but that earlier sloppy play set up the opportunity.

Detroit only trailed to start the fourth quarter in one of its eight comeback wins. Five times, the Lions took a lead into the final quarter, lost it, and regained it at the end. None of Detroit's comebacks were from a deficit of more than seven points, and six of them were from deficits of four points or less. When the 2009 Colts and 2011 Giants had seven fourth-quarter comebacks, the average deficit they overcame was 5.7

points, compared to 3.4 points for Detroit. We looked at win probability data from EDJ Analytics on the four 2016 teams with at least six game-winning scores in the fourth quarter or overtime (Table 2). Detroit's lowest win probability in the fourth quarter of its "clutch wins" averaged out to 22.9 percent, which was actually a little higher than the average triumphs engineered by the Dolphins (19.5 percent) and Raiders (22.4 percent). So maybe this team didn't quite have as much luck as one might expect from a team with a record number of late comebacks.

Table 2. Lowest Win Probability in Fourth-Quarter Wins for 2016's "Clutch" Teams

Rk	Miami		Oakland		Detroit		N.Y. Giants	
1	at LARM	1.5%	at NO	4.4%	at MIN	1.6%	BAL	19.6%
2	at BUF	10.9%	at TB	12.9%	PHI	6.8%	at DAL	19.7%
3	CLE	12.8%	HOU	15.1%	LARM	20.2%	CIN	36.2%
4	BUF	12.9%	CAR	20.4%	at IND	22.8%	at WAS	36.4%
5	at SD	18.7%	at BAL	26.4%	MIN	22.9%	LARM	43.8%
6	NYJ	31.4%	at SD	32.9%	WAS	25.2%	NO	50.3%
7	ARI	48.1%	BUF	44.8%	CHI	40.9%	--	--
8	--	--	--	--	JAC	43.1%	--	--
AVG		19.5%		22.4%		22.9%		34.3%

Source: EDJAnalytics.com

There were three games where Detroit did not trail for the entire game until the final 65 seconds. Stafford saved his best for last with throws to pull those games out against the Colts, Redskins, and Vikings. Caldwell does get credit for managing his timeouts well in these games, saving Stafford just enough time to pull out those low-probability wins. Matt Prater's 58-yard field goal to send the first Minnesota game to overtime was the thinnest line the Lions navigated between a win and loss last season as the win probability dipped as low as 1.6 percent.

One way to ease Stafford's workload is to finally give him a running game. It seems like ever since Barry Sanders brought the blues to Motown with his early retirement in 1999, the

Lions have been cursed in trying to find a franchise running back. Last season was just the latest example, as the Lions led the NFL in adjusted games lost at the running back position. Second-year back Ameer Abdullah was lost to foot surgery after just two games, and receiving back Theo Riddick missed six games plus the playoff loss in Seattle. By season's end, Detroit was relying on second-year UDFA Zach Zenner. The Lions did not add any backs in free agency or the draft, so they are clearly depending on a better bill of health to improve at the position in 2017. If injury luck regresses towards the mean, this group has the talent to be productive as runners and receivers.

Even though Stafford was getting rid of the ball faster than ever, his pressure rate was a career-high 28.5 percent in 2016. Fortunately, his -34.1% DVOA while pressured was also a career best, but he could always use better protection. The Lions were very aggressive in free agency, rebuilding the right side of the offensive line with guard T.J. Lang from rival Green Bay and making Baltimore's Ricky Wagner the highest-paid right tackle in NFL history at $9.5 million per season. Both players are better known for their pass protection rather than run-blocking, but Detroit should expect to see better offensive production behind the right side of this line. Unfortunately, the left side could be a letdown; 2016 first-round left tackle Taylor Decker will miss a large part of the season after undergoing surgery for a torn labrum in June.

On the surface, Detroit's offense would seem to have more ground to make up than its defense. After all, the Lions ranked 20th in points scored and 13th in points allowed. However, those general scoring stats fail to account for pace and opportunity. Detroit's small-ball offense averaged the most plays per drive (6.66), and Lions games had the fewest possessions in 2016. In fact, Detroit's 152 offensive possessions are the third fewest in a season since 1996, while the defense's 155 drives are tied with the 2006 Colts for the second fewest.

Yes, Caldwell was on Tony Dungy's coaching staff for those Manning-led Indianapolis teams that we keep drawing comparisons to. A trademark of those teams was to have few possessions because of so many successful runs and pass completions that kept the clock running. Well, the 2016 Lions

set an NFL record by allowing quarterbacks to complete 72.7 percent of their throws. The previous record was 71.2 percent by the 2011 Colts, a 2-14 Manning-less team that got Caldwell fired in Indianapolis. Furthermore, four of the 12 highest completion percentages in NFL history have been allowed by the Detroit defense since 2007. In addition to Caldwell, the top 12 is littered with coaches with links to Dungy and his Tampa-2 defense, including Lovie Smith, Leslie Frazier, and Rod "0-16" Marinelli (Table 3).

That Cover-2 style of defense can be exploited for a lot of easy completions, and Detroit did not benefit from many dropped passes from opponents, as only five defenses had a lower drop rate. However, defensive coordinator Teryl Austin is not a Tampa-2 disciple, and has a reputation for favoring more of a standard 4-3 defense. A big problem for Austin last year was a slow start caused by injuries to some of the defense's best players, including Ezekiel Ansah, Darius Slay, Haloti Ngata, and DeAndre Levy. The defense was continuously exploited for easy completions against soft zones because pressure did not get home. The Lions ranked 29th in pressure rate and 31st in yards per pass against play-action passes. Against short passes, thrown to receivers within 15 yards of the line of scrimmage, the Lions were 32nd in DVOA.

By allowing so many successful plays on a consistent basis, particularly with the league's worst defense on first down, the Lions finished 32nd in defensive DVOA. Detroit's rank of 26th in points per drive allowed matches this unit's caliber of play much better than the No. 13 ranking in total points allowed.

Still, the Lions lost three games in which the defense only allowed 16 or 17 points, and the brunt of blame would fall more heavily on the offense for those losses. While the defense was shredded at times by lesser quarterbacks, including Case Keenum and Brian Hoyer, it did come away with critical takeaways to help seal wins. Despite only ranking 28th in takeaways per drive, the Lions led the league with four interceptions in the final two minutes of the fourth quarter in one-score games. Those interceptions shut the door on the Eagles, Rams, and Jaguars, and even set up an easy game-winning field goal on Thanksgiving against the Vikings. Again, this was part of Detroit's "timely play" in 2016, even though the

Table 3. Highest Completion Percentage Allowed in NFL History

Rk	Team	Year	Comp.	Att.	Pct.	Yds	TD	INT	Pass Def DVOA	Rk	Head Coach/ Defensive Coordinator
1	DET	2016	399	549	72.68%	3975	33	10	38.1%	32	Jim Caldwell/Teryl Austin
2	IND	2011	351	493	71.20%	3632	25	8	18.2%	27	Jim Caldwell/Larry Coyer
3	DET	2007	422	602	70.10%	4131	32	17	22.8%	31	Rod Marinelli/Joe Barry
4	TB	2015	378	540	70.00%	3852	31	11	20.6%	26	Lovie Smith/Leslie Frazier
5	TB	2014	387	563	68.74%	4084	28	14	14.9%	23	Lovie Smith/Leslie Frazier
6	DET	2008	304	444	68.47%	3712	25	4	32.8%	32	Rod Marinelli/Joe Barry
7	IND	2008	330	482	68.46%	3013	6	15	-1.3%	12	Tony Dungy/Ron Meeks
8	NO	2015	372	544	68.38%	4544	45	9	48.1%	32	Sean Payton/Rob Ryan
9	SF	2015	375	549	68.31%	4179	21	9	25.0%	30	Jim Tomsula/Eric Mangini
10	MIN	2011	367	538	68.22%	4019	34	8	22.9%	32	Leslie Frazier/Fred Pagac
11	DET	2015	360	528	68.18%	3789	27	9	13.4%	19	Jim Caldwell/Teryl Austin
12	STL	2014	368	540	68.15%	3861	18	13	8.9%	20	Jeff Fisher/Gregg Williams

defense was still 32nd in DVOA in "late and close" situations due to how often it surrendered the lead in the first place.

Austin earned high praise for his work with the 2014 defense, which ranked third in DVOA. But recent results have not been as favorable, and he has yet to land that first head coaching gig despite numerous opportunities that were available. This year he'll try to manage a defense with an interesting mix of core veterans (Ansah, Ngata, Slay, and safety Glover Quin), young draft picks (second-year tackle A'Shawn Robinson and first-round rookie middle linebacker Jarrad Davis), and free-agent castoffs (D.J. Hayden and Paul Worrilow). More pressure should generate more takeaways, but much of that has to come from Ansah getting back to form. He had just two sacks in 2016, although he did manage 20 hurries in 13 games. He'll just need to finish more plays.

Even if the Lions develop a newfound running game or impressive defense, this once again will be one of the league's more quarterback-dependent teams in 2017. Stafford, still just 29 years old, is second in NFL history in passing yards per game (278.0). He ended 2016 by surpassing 30,000 passing yards in his 109th game, the fewest games to that milestone in NFL history, so he is still on pace to one day be the league's all-time leading passer. Peyton Manning will get a good test for that record from Drew Brees, while fellow contemporary Matt Ryan is also producing yardage at a historic rate in today's pass-happy climate. Stafford has never really matched the efficiency of that trio, and his yardage is more of the result of averaging the most pass attempts per game (39.3) in NFL history.

However, 2017 will be Stafford's ninth season. Manning (2006), Brees (2009), and Ryan (2016) each reached their first Super Bowl and played arguably the finest football of their careers in their ninth season. If Stafford is to get more respect for his late-game heroics and volume passing, then the narrative in Detroit has to change. Right now, there is an impending sense of doom any time the Lions have to play a winning team.

Home-field advantage was still very much in play when the Lions sat at 9-4 last year. It would have been well-earned, too, with wins over playoff teams in Weeks 15-17. Instead, the Lions lost each game. Stafford's MVP case closed after the offense was unable to score more than six points against the Giants. Then the defense failed to slow down the high-scoring Cowboys and Packers—the latter in a home game that would have clinched the NFC North for Detroit. It was more of the same in the playoffs, with Stafford unable to generate any big plays on the road even though Seattle's pass defense had struggled without Earl Thomas.

This has become a hallmark of the Lions in the Stafford era. Since 2009, Detroit's 7-55 (.113) mark in games against teams with winning records for the season is the second-worst record in the NFL. Meanwhile, in that same time Detroit has gone 49-20 (.710) against non-winning teams, the eighth-best winning percentage in the league. That difference of almost 60 percentage points is more than double the league average. No team falters as much from its usual performance against winning teams like the Lions. Stafford's record as a starter in games against winning teams is 5-46 (.098). That includes a 3-19 record under Caldwell and a 1-25 record in road games.

Naturally, the struggles are not always the quarterback's fault, but this is something that has persisted through each of Stafford's first eight seasons. Hell, this has persisted in Detroit for each of the last six decades, but Stafford is by far the most promising quarterback that this franchise has had since Bobby Layne, who infamously cursed the team after he was traded to Pittsburgh in 1958. Stafford was drafted one year after Layne's curse that the Lions would "not win for 50 years," but the Lions have still not won a playoff game in this era.

Detroit's 2017 schedule is front-loaded with many challenges in the first eight games, including contests with the Giants, Falcons, Steelers, and Packers, as well as Arizona and Carolina teams that we expect to rebound. If this failure to beat the good teams continues, then Detroit's playoff goose could be cooked long before the team gets another Week 17 crack at a home win against the Packers, or even before the Thanksgiving rematch with the Vikings. After all, it's not like Sam Bradford can gift a team an interception with 30 seconds left in a tied game two years in a row, right?

While Stafford's passing will keep the Lions a competitive team, chances are he won't pull off one or two of the last-minute drives that he saved the team with in 2016. A margin that tiny is how a team can go from 9-7 and the playoffs to 7-9 and vacationing in January.

Scott Kacsmar

2016 Lions Stats by Week

Wk	vs.	W-L	PF	PA	YDF	YDA	TO	Total	Off	Def	ST
1	at IND	W	39	35	448	450	0	27%	54%	32%	5%
2	TEN	L	15	16	375	363	0	-7%	-17%	2%	13%
3	at GB	L	27	34	418	324	-1	-49%	4%	47%	-6%
4	at CHI	L	14	17	263	408	-2	-58%	-51%	33%	26%
5	PHI	W	24	23	244	346	+1	-10%	1%	12%	1%
6	LARM	W	31	28	348	387	+1	-57%	6%	65%	2%
7	WAS	W	20	17	344	413	+2	10%	9%	-7%	-6%
8	at HOU	L	13	20	289	269	+1	22%	31%	2%	-7%
9	at MIN	W	22	16	311	337	-1	-8%	-1%	14%	6%
10	BYE										
11	JAC	W	26	19	277	285	+1	5%	-27%	-13%	18%
12	MIN	W	16	13	308	306	+1	17%	13%	0%	4%
13	at NO	W	28	13	422	369	+3	17%	0%	-14%	2%
14	CHI	W	20	17	323	296	-2	-25%	-15%	16%	5%
15	at NYG	L	6	17	324	300	-2	-30%	-8%	20%	-1%
16	at DAL	L	21	42	319	375	-2	-69%	-17%	51%	0%
17	GB	L	24	31	408	448	-1	-35%	11%	39%	-7%
18	at SEA	L	6	26	231	387	0	-24%	-19%	17%	12%

Trends and Splits

	Offense	Rank	Defense	Rank
Total DVOA	-0.6%	15	18.5%	32
Unadjusted VOA	-1.3%	16	18.0%	31
Weighted Trend	-2.7%	17	16.2%	32
Variance	5.7%	14	5.7%	21
Average Opponent	0.3%	17	-0.5%	20
Passing	16.0%	13	36.2%	32
Rushing	-16.8%	25	-4.1%	19
First Down	-5.0%	20	22.0%	32
Second Down	9.3%	10	14.5%	29
Third Down	-8.7%	20	17.6%	28
First Half	7.5%	13	13.2%	28
Second Half	-10.9%	21	39.3%	32
Red Zone	-22.6%	27	49.6%	32
Late and Close	-16.8%	27	39.5%	32

Five-Year Performance

Year	W-L	Pyth W	Est W	PF	PA	TO	Total	Rk	Off	Rk	Def	Rk	ST	Rk	Off AGL	Rk	Def AGL	Rk	Off Age	Rk	Def Age	Rk	ST Age	Rk
2012	4-12	6.4	7.6	372	437	-16	0.1%	16	12.3%	8	7.1%	24	-5.1%	30	23.2	11	58.3	31	28.3	4	26.7	17	27.8	1
2013	7-9	8.5	7.7	395	376	-12	-1.5%	16	-1.9%	19	-0.8%	14	-0.4%	20	31.9	14	30.7	20	27.0	14	27.0	13	26.8	6
2014	11-5	9.2	8.7	321	282	+7	4.4%	14	-3.8%	19	-13.9%	3	-5.7%	31	26.4	13	41.1	21	27.0	15	27.5	6	25.9	20
2015	7-9	6.9	7.4	358	400	-6	1.2%	13	1.8%	13	1.6%	16	1.0%	13	21.7	5	55.0	30	26.2	24	27.3	6	26.2	15
2016	9-7	7.7	5.3	346	358	-1	-15.6%	27	-0.6%	15	18.5%	32	3.5%	6	40.0	22	29.4	13	26.2	25	26.4	18	25.9	21

2016 Performance Based on Most Common Personnel Groups

DET Offense					DET Offense vs. Opponents					DET Defense					DET Defense vs. Opponents			
Pers	Freq	Yds	DVOA	Run%	Pers	Freq	Yds	DVOA	Run%	Pers	Freq	Yds	DVOA		Pers	Freq	Yds	DVOA
11	75%	6.1	11.2%	24%	Base	20%	4.8	-19.4%	58%	Base	22%	7.2	29.6%		11	59%	6.3	20.4%
12	9%	3.9	-31.9%	60%	Nickel	64%	5.5	8.2%	28%	Nickel	57%	5.7	16.8%		12	23%	5.5	10.5%
21	4%	4.7	-22.6%	73%	Dime+	15%	8.2	26.0%	10%	Dime+	18%	7.2	22.5%		21	6%	8.3	34.3%
10	3%	6.1	8.5%	6%	Goal Line	1%	0.7	-13.8%	80%	Goal Line	1%	0.8	64.0%		612	2%	3.3	-39.4%
620	1%	4.8	-6.9%	75%						Big	3%	1.6	-66.2%		22	2%	1.8	-48.3%
611	1%	10.0	37.8%	73%											13	2%	7.6	-6.8%

Strategic Tendencies

Run/Pass		Rk	Formation		Rk	Pass Rush		Rk	Secondary		Rk	Strategy		Rk
Runs, first half	33%	29	Form: Single Back	87%	7	Rush 3	3.2%	29	4 DB	22%	25	Play-action	16%	24
Runs, first down	45%	22	Form: Empty Back	6%	23	Rush 4	64.2%	18	5 DB	57%	20	Avg Box (Off)	6.08	28
Runs, second-long	24%	26	Pers: 3+ WR	81%	3	Rush 5	26.5%	7	6+ DB	17%	7	Avg Box (Def)	6.08	28
Runs, power sit.	44%	29	Pers: 2+ TE/6+ OL	16%	29	Rush 6+	6.1%	14	CB by Sides	64%	25	Offensive Pace	31.27	25
Runs, behind 2H	24%	22	Pers: 6+ OL	6%	12	Sacks by LB	0.0%	32	S/CB Cover Ratio	33%	5	Defensive Pace	32.98	32
Pass, ahead 2H	61%	1	Shotgun/Pistol	84%	2	Sacks by DB	11.5%	4	DB Blitz	10%	16	Go for it on 4th	1.14	12

The slowdown in Lions games came mostly from opponents, not the Lions themselves. In 2015, they ranked even lower in situation-neutral pace on offense (30th). But they went from third to dead last in situation-neutral pace on defense. ☞ The Lions either ran long extended drives or they closed up shop early: they were first in plays per drive (6.66) but 25th in three-and-out drives (22.4 percent). ☞ The Lions mostly retired fullback Michael Burton from the offense, going from 71 percent (23rd) to 87 percent (seventh) in frequency of single-back sets. ☞ Detroit used a max-protect blocking scheme on just 4.5 percent of passes, last in the NFL. (This is defined as seven or more blockers with at least two more blockers than pass-rushers.)

Passing

Player	DYAR	DVOA	Plays	NtYds	Avg	YAC	C%	TD	Int
M.Stafford	761	7.2%	628	4094	6.5	5.8	65.8%	24	10

Rushing

Player	DYAR	DVOA	Plays	Yds	Avg	TD	Fum	Suc
T.Riddick	-5	-9.8%	92	357	3.9	1	0	42%
D.Washington	-32	-20.1%	69	212	3.1	1	0	38%
Z.Zenner	-24	-18.9%	53	186	3.5	4	0	43%
M.Stafford	54	27.7%	26	202	7.8	2	0	-
A.Abdullah	18	16.5%	18	101	5.6	0	0	61%
J.Forsett*	-15	-35.7%	13	38	2.9	1	0	38%
G.Tate	-38	-119.7%	9	4	0.4	0	0	-
M.Asiata	-15	-11.3%	107	354	3.3	6	0	49%
M.James	-2	-24.4%	4	19	4.8	0	0	50%

Receiving

Player	DYAR	DVOA	Plays	Ctch	Yds	Y/C	YAC	TD	C%
G.Tate	114	-1.8%	135	91	1077	11.8	6.8	4	67%
M.Jones	202	10.9%	103	55	930	16.9	4.3	4	53%
A.Boldin*	140	5.2%	95	67	584	8.7	3.4	8	71%
A.Roberts*	32	3.2%	25	14	188	13.4	4.5	1	56%
T.J.Jones	-20	-33.6%	14	5	93	18.6	6.0	0	36%
E.Ebron	149	20.1%	85	61	711	11.7	4.6	1	72%
D.Fells	28	14.3%	18	14	154	11.0	6.4	1	78%
T.Riddick	67	3.9%	67	53	371	7.0	7.3	5	79%
Z.Zenner	80	51.4%	23	18	196	10.9	11.4	0	78%
D.Washington	-5	-20.1%	15	10	62	6.2	7.6	0	67%
M.Asiata	54	11.5%	38	32	263	8.2	8.2	0	84%

Offensive Line

Player	Pos	Age	GS	Snaps	Pen	Sk	Pass	Run	Player	Pos	Age	GS	Snaps	Pen	Sk	Pass	Run
Taylor Decker	LT	23	16/16	1037	8	7.5	14	8	Corey Robinson	OT	25	14/3	164	1	1.0	4	1
Larry Warford*	RG	26	15/15	970	2	4.5	9	5	Ricky Wagner	RT	28	15/14	924	4	3.5	10	4
Riley Reiff*	RT	29	14/14	889	5	3.5	11	5	T.J. Lang	RG	30	13/13	791	5	3.0	7	4
Travis Swanson	C	26	12/12	766	3	0.0	2	4	Greg Robinson	LT	25	14/14	893	15	6.5	14	4
Graham Glasgow	C/LG	25	15/11	706	6	2.0	14	7	Cyrus Kouandjio	LT	24	12/5	407	2	0.5	3	8
Laken Tomlinson	LG	25	16/10	649	3	2.0	6	4									

Year	Yards	ALY	Rank	Power	Rank	Stuff	Rank	2nd Lev	Rank	Open Field	Rank	Sacks	ASR	Rank	Press	Rank	F-Start	Cont.
2014	3.75	4.05	21	65%	15	22%	30	0.99	26	0.59	26	45	6.9%	21	20.8%	5	12	23
2015	3.76	3.93	22	69%	12	24%	29	1.11	20	0.59	24	44	6.9%	22	21.6%	9	12	26
2016	3.64	3.49	31	56%	26	23%	29	1.10	21	0.47	27	37	6.1%	18	27.1%	20	16	30

2016 ALY by direction:	Left End 2.74 (28)	Left Tackle 3.05 (32)	Mid/Guard 4.07 (20)	Right Tackle 3.13 (29)	Right End 3.15 (26)

You cannot deny Detroit's efforts to build a good offensive line in front of Stafford. Since 2012, the Lions have spent six picks within the first three rounds (including three first-rounders) on offensive linemen, most of any team over that span. While right tackle Riley Reiff and right guard Larry Warford did not receive a second contract from the Lions, the team immediately used free agency to refill those positions. ☞ Rookie left tackle Taylor Decker had a few growing pains, surrendering just as many sacks in one season as the now-departed Reiff allowed in the last two seasons. Decker underwent surgery in June for a torn labrum suffered in practice, and is likely out for at least half the year. Detroit took a pair of fliers on 2014 draft busts, inking Cyrus Kouandjio and trading for Greg Robinson shortly after Decker's injury. There will be an open competition between these two players and 2016 fifth-rounder Joe Dahl to fill the left tackle void to start the season. ☞ T.J. Lang was a big signing from Green Bay, but a hip injury is expected to keep him out until training camp. Lang should be an upgrade over Warford, especially in pass protection, where he has allowed just six sacks combined over the last three seasons. ☞ Ricky Wagner will get a lot of attention at right tackle because of his hefty contract, but he has ranked sixth in snaps per blown block in each of the last two seasons. He'll have the fortune of playing next to Lang after lining up beside Marshal Yanda the first four seasons of his career. ☞ Travis Swanson is reliable at center, but left guard is the big question mark. Laken Tomlinson was a first-round pick in 2015, but he has been benched multiple times already. We had Tomlinson as middle-of-the-road in snaps per blown block, but potential starter Graham Glasgow was dead last in that metric among 2016 centers. He filled in for an injured Swanson down the stretch, but also played left guard. Detroit will have to get much better play out of this position no matter which player ultimately wins the job.

Defensive Front Seven

Defensive Line	Age	Pos	G	Snaps	Plays	TmPct	Rk	Stop	Dfts	BTkl	Runs	St%	Rk	RuYd	Rk	Sack	Hit	Hur	Dsrpt
						Overall						vs. Run				Pass Rush			
Haloti Ngata	33	DT	13	527	25	3.8%	57	21	9	2	16	81%	33	2.6	57	1.5	2	12	3
A'Shawn Robinson	22	DT	16	408	37	4.5%	--	29	7	2	27	70%	--	2.3	--	2.0	0	1	7
Tyrunn Walker*	27	DT	15	350	25	3.3%	--	14	5	1	20	60%	--	3.2	--	0.0	2	7	0
Khyri Thornton	28	DT	13	307	19	2.9%	--	11	3	2	18	56%	--	2.6	--	1.0	1	4	0
Stefan Charles*	29	DT	12	236	12	2.0%	--	10	2	3	11	82%	--	2.1	--	0.0	2	2	1
Akeem Spence	26	DT	16	362	18	2.2%	--	16	5	3	17	88%	--	2.1	--	0.5	2	4	0
Cornelius Washington	28	DE	15	364	21	2.7%	--	12	5	1	16	56%	--	3.9	--	2.0	3	12	2

Edge Rushers	Age	Pos	G	Snaps	Plays	TmPct	Rk	Stop	Dfts	BTkl	Runs	St%	Rk	RuYd	Rk	Sack	Hit	Hur	Dsrpt
						Overall						vs. Run				Pass Rush			
Devin Taylor*	28	DE	16	665	29	3.6%	74	15	8	6	18	33%	100	4.4	99	4.5	5	21	1
Kerry Hyder	26	DE	16	655	37	4.5%	58	27	16	3	22	64%	85	2.9	61	8.0	12	25	1
Ezekiel Ansah	28	DE	13	495	34	5.1%	44	26	10	7	27	74%	50	2.0	30	2.0	14	22	1
Anthony Zettel	25	DE	13	214	13	2.0%	--	8	1	0	12	58%	--	3.3	--	1.0	0	3	0

Linebackers	Age	Pos	G	Snaps	Plays	TmPct	Rk	Stop	Dfts	BTkl	Runs	St%	Rk	RuYd	Rk	Sack	Hit	Hur	Tgts	Suc%	Rk	AdjYd	Rk	PD	Int
						Overall						vs. Run				Pass Rush				vs. Pass					
Tahir Whitehead	27	MLB	15	933	137	17.9%	9	59	16	13	68	49%	83	5.0	82	0.0	1	3	50	47%	43	7.4	59	5	0
Josh Bynes*	28	OLB	9	373	42	9.2%	63	23	10	5	19	63%	45	2.1	4	0.0	0	2	20	56%	18	5.4	20	3	0
Antwione Williams	24	OLB	14	203	20	2.8%	--	9	3	6	12	58%	--	3.3	--	0.0	1	0	7	19%	--	9.7	--	0	0
DeAndre Levy*	30	OLB	5	199	22	8.6%	67	12	3	1	14	57%	67	3.1	27	0.0	1	2	5	51%	--	7.1	--	0	0
Nick Bellore	28	MLB	14	691	82	10.6%	51	57	15	12	55	75%	5	2.6	9	1.0	2	5	20	44%	51	5.3	17	5	1
Paul Worrilow	27	MLB	12	162	20	3.2%	--	11	4	3	12	58%	--	3.2	--	0.0	1	2	7	62%	--	7.0	--	2	0

Year	Yards	ALY	Rank	Power	Rank	Stuff	Rank	2nd Level	Rank	Open Field	Rank	Sacks	ASR	Rank	Press	Rank
2014	3.17	3.01	1	63%	15	25%	3	0.86	1	0.50	5	42	6.6%	18	25.9%	10
2015	4.08	3.60	5	56%	7	24%	4	1.06	11	1.02	28	43	7.3%	8	24.9%	18
2016	4.35	4.40	21	73%	31	15%	29	1.20	20	0.73	15	26	5.4%	25	23.1%	30

2016 ALY by direction:	Left End 6.89 (32)	Left Tackle 5.20 (28)	Mid/Guard 4.11 (14)	Right Tackle 4.43 (19)	Right End 2.76 (5)

DeAndre Levy was once one of the building blocks to this defense, but the Lions released the veteran in March. Injuries had limited him to six games since 2015, so Detroit has essentially been playing without the leader of its linebacker corps for two years. The Lions may have found their long-term replacement with first-round pick Jarrad Davis (Florida), the "safe pick" in comparison with the red-flagged Reuben Foster. Some fans will keep an eye on Foster's career to see if their team made the right choice, but Davis should be a Week 1 starter at MIKE. ☙ Tahir Whitehead will move to the weak side; he had some trouble in pass coverage and lots of problems against the run last season. Whitehead's 49 percent run stop rate was second-worst among linebackers with at least 600 snaps. Veteran Paul Worrilow should compete with fourth-round rookie Jalen Reeves-Maybin for the other starting spot. Reeves-Maybin is a smaller linebacker with durability concerns, but he did have back-to-back 100-tackle seasons at Tennessee. Worrilow slipped to JAG status in Atlanta after four seasons, but his one-year deal is only for $3 million. ☙ Ezekiel Ansah and Haloti Ngata are the stars up front, but both would like to be a bit healthier in 2017 after suffering through ankle and calf injuries, respectively. The Lions have fallen from 10th to 18th to 30th in pressure rate over the past three seasons, and Ndamukong Suh isn't walking back through that door anytime soon. ☙ Second-round rookie A'Shawn Robinson led Detroit's defensive line in stops. He might not rush the passer much, but he was able to bat down seven passes and was not a liability against the run. ☙ The other defensive end job will come down to Kerry Hyder and Cornelius Washington. Hyder was a pleasant surprise for the Lions last year, leading the team in both sacks and hurries after seeing almost no regular-season snaps in his first two NFL seasons. Washington had an uneventful four seasons in Chicago, so it certainly would make sense for the Lions to stick with a player they developed themselves.

Defensive Secondary

Secondary	Age	Pos	G	Snaps	Plays	TmPct	Rk	Stop	Dfts	BTkl	Runs	St%	Rk	RuYd	Rk	Tgts	Tgt%	Rk	Dist	Suc%	Rk	AdjYd	Rk	PD	Int
Glover Quin	31	SS	16	1026	73	9.0%	47	23	12	12	30	30%	57	7.6	44	26	6.2%	8	14.7	53%	19	8.4	30	5	2
Nevin Lawson	26	CB	16	923	65	8.0%	60	22	5	5	13	15%	83	9.5	72	58	15.5%	13	11.8	42%	78	8.7	70	9	0
Darius Slay	26	CB	13	730	57	8.6%	44	24	11	6	9	33%	55	14.4	86	52	17.5%	33	12.0	48%	54	6.6	16	13	2
Tavon Wilson	27	FS	15	707	89	11.6%	18	41	7	9	42	57%	12	4.5	8	30	10.5%	56	10.5	48%	30	9.5	51	0	0
Rafael Bush*	30	FS	16	500	51	6.3%	68	20	10	7	18	33%	51	8.8	60	21	10.4%	53	11.1	53%	15	7.4	19	3	2
Quandre Diggs	24	CB	12	420	43	7.0%	--	18	10	4	6	83%	--	3.2	--	35	20.4%	--	8.8	30%	--	10.2	--	1	0
Johnson Bademosi	27	CB	16	283	23	2.8%	--	9	3	6	5	0%	--	7.2	--	23	20.2%	--	15.4	39%	--	12.2	--	5	1
Miles Killebrew	24	SS	16	149	21	2.6%	--	11	11	1	4	50%	--	4.8	--	11	17.5%	--	7.0	41%	--	9.3	--	0	0
D.J. Hayden	27	CB	11	477	43	8.1%	54	19	10	0	8	25%	73	14.3	85	50	24.5%	80	12.3	50%	38	8.4	63	6	0

Year	Pass D Rank	vs. #1 WR	Rk	vs. #2 WR	Rk	vs. Other WR	Rk	vs. TE	Rk	vs. RB	Rk
2014	8	-26.4%	2	-11.9%	9	2.4%	20	-10.0%	8	14.8%	23
2015	19	9.5%	24	5.5%	18	-5.0%	14	26.0%	29	-10.7%	7
2016	32	11.5%	26	5.0%	21	27.4%	32	21.7%	29	34.4%	29

Darius Slay is a known quantity as the No. 1 cornerback; now the task is to found other cornerbacks who can help him. Nevin Lawson struggled last season and Quandre Diggs was a slot corner limited by injury. D.J. Hayden, a bust in four years with Oakland, is likely not the answer either. Hayden and Lawson were two of the league's 13 corners with zero interceptions on at least 50 targets last year. ⚜ Detroit drafted Jalen "Teez" Tabor in the second round out of Florida. One AFC South scout said Tabor is "a good football player and can cover in our league, but he's also going to be a pain in the ass for whoever takes him." Some of Tabor's warning flags include a molasses-slow 4.62 40 time that four defensive linemen managed to beat at the combine, a lack of physicality, too many missed tackles, and past suspensions for drug tests. If he's a poor man's Slay, then the Lions will probably still be OK with that, but expectations should be very low in 2017. ⚜ Tavon Wilson was the secondary's only solid run-stopper, but a mixed bag in pass coverage. Wilson was the only defender in 2016 to face at least 30 targets and have zero passes defensed. Wilson had an uneventful four seasons in New England after the Patriots drafted him 48th overall in 2012, but perhaps we should cut him some slack in his first real year as a starter. In 2016, he played just 47 fewer defensive snaps than he did his first four seasons combined. ⚜ The Lions climbed from 23rd to seventh in use of dime defense, frequently a three-safety set that added veteran Rafael Bush or rookie Miles Killebrew. In 2017, that should mostly be Killebrew, whom the Lions see as their version of Deone Bucannon or Su'a Cravens.

Special Teams

Year	DVOA	Rank	FG/XP	Rank	Net Kick	Rank	Kick Ret	Rank	Net Punt	Rank	Punt Ret	Rank	Hidden	Rank
2014	-5.7%	31	-19.6	32	-4.0	24	-1.7	21	-0.6	17	-2.5	17	-6.6	26
2015	1.0%	13	6.0	5	-2.6	21	3.3	8	3.2	14	-4.7	24	-4.4	20
2016	3.5%	6	2.5	11	-2.9	24	-1.5	16	10.7	5	8.5	3	2.4	14

Detroit's No. 6 ranking in special teams DVOA was its highest since 2004, when the Lions were fifth. ⚜ Matt Prater has been a fairly clutch kicker in his career. He helped legitimize some of those Tim Tebow-branded miracles for the 2011 Broncos, and delivered four game-winning (and two game-tying) field goals for Detroit last season. ⚜ Sam Martin ranked third in gross punt value, but was lacking in his other duty on kickoffs. We estimate shorter kicks cost the Lions 2.6 points of estimated field position, ranking Martin 28th out of 35 kickers in gross kickoff value. ⚜ Andre Roberts was the return specialist in Detroit last season, and he did really well on punts, returning two for touchdowns. However, he went to Atlanta this offseason, opening up jobs that could be filled by Golden Tate (mediocre on punt returns for Detroit in 2015), running back Dwayne Washington (had a 96-yard kick return touchdown against Pittsburgh last preseason), or fifth-round rookie cornerback Jamal Agnew (returned punts at the University of San Diego).

Green Bay Packers

2016 Record: 10-6	**Total DVOA:** 12.3% (7th)	**2017 Mean Projection:** 9.5 wins	**On the Clock (0-4):** 3%
Pythagorean Wins: 9.1 (8th)	**Offense:** 16.6% (4th)	**Postseason Odds:** 59.8%	**Mediocrity (5-7):** 18%
Snap-Weighted Age: 26.2 (25th)	**Defense:** 2.5% (20th)	**Super Bowl Odds:** 14.5%	**Playoff Contender (8-10):** 43%
Average Opponent: -0.2% (17th)	**Special Teams:** -1.9% (21st)	**Proj. Avg. Opponent:** 0.3% (12th)	**Super Bowl Contender (11+):** 36%

2016: What's wrong with Aaron Rodgers? It turns out: nothing.

2017: R-E-L-A-X is supposed to be an admonition for the Green Bay fans, not the Green Bay front office.

The Patriots just won the Super Bowl thanks in large part to a series of veteran talent acquisitions. LeGarrette Blount was signed as a free agent after he was cut by Pittsburgh, and went on to score 19 touchdowns. Chris Hogan and Danny Amendola were signed in free agency; they added 11 touchdowns. Martellus Bennett scored seven touchdowns and significantly softened the loss of Rob Gronkowski to injury; he was acquired in a trade. Chris Long, Alan Branch, Patrick Chung, and Eric Rowe played roles on defense as free agent/trade acquisitions. It was the second time in three years that New England won the Super Bowl with a roster that had maxed out its talent by spending in free agency, making trades, and drafting well.

It's not just a Patriots thing; it's what Super Bowl teams do. T.J. Ward, Aqib Talib, Louis Vasquez, Darian Stewart, Peyton Manning, Emmanuel Sanders, and DeMarcus Ware won a Super Bowl with the Denver Broncos between New England's two championships. The Seattle Seahawks team that won in 2013 featured Marshawn Lynch, Percy Harvin, Cliff Avril, Michael Bennett, and Chris Clemons. Super Bowl teams max out their talent by exploring every avenue with which they can improve their roster. Competing with them requires doing the same.

Ted Thompson has made a career of not maxing out his rosters. Thompson's philosophy is to build through the draft, and while it is admirable how he consistently trades down in that process, his level of trust in such an inexact science is troubling. Sometimes, there's a hole on the roster that can be better filled with established production rather than another gamble on young talent. Think of what Reggie White and Charles Woodson brought to the Packers in years past, key additions to Super Bowl championship defenses. (Thompson himself brought in Woodson, but that was over a decade ago.) While other teams go shopping for established talent in free agency, Thompson saves his energy almost exclusively for the draft. This would not be a complaint if Thompson was crushing draft after draft, but no one in this business is good enough to consistently have that type of success.

Back in 2015, PackersNews.com wrote an article tracking how well Thompson has drafted in Green Bay.[1] It measured success by how many starts his drafted players had accumu-

lated. Thompson had "drafted 104 players since 2005, more than any team. The Packers lead the NFL with 1,860 starts and 3,267 games played from drafted players. They have 119 more starts and 106 more games played by drafted players than any NFL team."

Well, of course. When you're not signing free agents or acquiring established players in trades, you're going to get a lot of starts from the players you draft. This kind of analysis celebrates Thompson's approach because of his approach, not because it is the right approach or because he has been particularly good at building great teams.

Right now, the Packers are enjoying the prime of one of the greatest quarterbacks in NFL history. Aaron Rodgers enjoyed another phenomenal season last year. He carried an offense that was riddled with limited, inconsistent players and led it to a top-five finish in offensive DVOA. Thompson should have entered this offseason looking to be aggressive in setting Rodgers up for greater success while also trying to add to a below-average defense. Instead, he let another key piece of the offense walk away to save money.

Less than 12 months ago, the Packers made the shocking move to release Josh Sitton. Sitton had been the team's starting left guard for eight seasons. He had made three All-Pro teams and started all 16 games in 2015. Sitton was released just before the start of the 2016 season, so the Packers didn't have an opportunity to bring in another high-priced player to improve the team elsewhere. Sitton proceeded to join the Chicago Bears, and he again played at an All-Pro level even though he didn't officially get the nod. Sitton's loss hurt the Packers, but Lane Taylor proved to be a capable replacement. Taylor played the most snaps of any Packers lineman last year. It was the first time the 27-year-old, former undrafted player out of Oklahoma State was a full-time starter. He wasn't as good as Sitton, but he played well enough that Thompson wasn't going to be criticized for letting Sitton leave.

T.J. Lang was Sitton's counterpart at guard. Lang and Sitton had been considered the best guard pairing in the league for a long time. Their ability to shut down interior penetration was huge, allowing Rodgers to mitigate edge pressure with his movement within the confines of the pocket. Therefore, it

---

1 http://pck.rs/2rGOezB

2017 Packers Schedule

Week	Opp.	Week	Opp.	Week	Opp.
1	SEA	7	NO	13	TB
2	at ATL	8	BYE	14	at CLE
3	CIN	9	DET (Mon.)	15	at CAR
4	CHI (Thu.)	10	at CHI	16	MIN (Sat.)
5	at DAL	11	BAL	17	at DET
6	at MIN	12	at PIT		

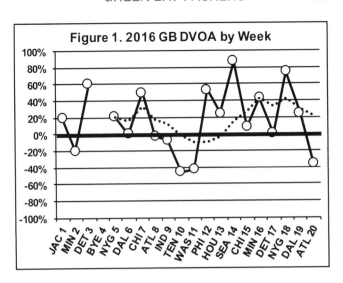

Figure 1. 2016 GB DVOA by Week

was just as startling to watch Lang depart for the Detroit Lions this year as it was less than 12 months ago when Sitton was unceremoniously kicked to the curb.

Taylor wasn't a premium replacement for Sitton, but he's a more inspiring option than what the Packers plan to move forward with at right guard now. Letting Lang leave might have made some sense if they had kept Sitton, or if Jason Spriggs was going to start. Spriggs is a former second-round pick on whom the Packers coaching staff is very high. He is presumably one of their five best offensive linemen, but has no chance of starting at left tackle over David Bakhtiari or at right tackle over Brian Bulaga. The natural conclusion would be to move Spriggs inside to start at right guard.

Head coach Mike McCarthy has already dismissed that notion. "Spriggs is a tackle," he told reporters at the NFL meetings in Phoenix in March. "The first thing you have to say about Jason is he can play left tackle in this league—and that's huge. ... I think we're very fortunate we have David, Bryan Bulaga, and Jason, so we have three high-quality tackles."

McCarthy didn't just dismiss the idea of Spriggs playing guard, he also dismissed the idea of moving Bulaga inside to accommodate Spriggs. "Bulaga had his best year at right tackle last year," he said. "I'm not really looking to move him because ... Bryan and David gave us an outstanding combination of right and left tackle play."

Instead of having a replacement who had been groomed to assume Lang's role, the Packers are left with Don Barclay and Jahri Evans. Barclay has repeatedly proven throughout a long career that he's not an NFL-caliber player. He has played both inside and outside without any success. Evans should be the Week 1 starter. Despite not making the Seahawks roster out of training camp last year, Evans started 16 games for the New Orleans Saints. The Saints were familiar with Evans' skill set because he had started 153 games there previously. Despite enjoying an All-Pro career, Evans has never been a strong pass-blocker, and now he's 34 years old. He's extremely unlikely to replicate what Lang did for the Packers in pass protection. He won't be comfortable with one-on-one assignments in space. With Taylor rather than Sitton at left guard, the Packers now have two guards who can't be expected to execute difficult pass-blocking assignments.

Evans being the expected starter confirms that Lang and Sitton were only let go to save money. It's not like either player was in decline. Sitton will be 31 at the start of this season, while Lang will turn 30 in September. The Packers downgraded on both players and got significantly older at one spot.

That's not maximizing your talent.

By neglecting the interior of their line, the Packers are putting more pressure on Rodgers to carry the offense. Even though the Packers offense ranked fourth in DVOA—seventh in passing and fifth in rushing—this unit's success hinged on the quarterback more than most. Rodgers constantly found himself holding the ball longer than the play called for because his receivers couldn't create separation against aggressive coverage or find soft spots in zones within the timing of the play. Rodgers' patience and footwork allows him to extend plays within the pocket and create leverage for his linemen while slowing the pass rush from the beginning of the play. But he still needs that offensive line to be effective when he has to wait for his receivers to get open. Jordy Nelson put up big numbers after returning from 2015's torn ACL, but Nelson wasn't the same player he had been previously. He could no longer separate with ease, and it took him longer to get downfield on vertical routes. Nelson's athleticism improved as the season wore on, but his inability to get open was a big part of what forced Rodgers to execute more difficult plays on a more regular basis.

It's easier to be a wide receiver in Green Bay than it is anywhere else. To be productive, Nelson only needed to consistently catch the ball rather than create his own separation within the design of the route each play. Davante Adams couldn't even do that, and he was still productive. Adams finished the season with 12 touchdowns and should have had more, but failed to catch six accurate throws into the end zone. Randall Cobb's career has fallen off over recent years through a combination of health and inconsistency. Cobb needs more help getting open with route combinations that McCarthy simply refuses to run. The inconsistency that had previously marred Jared Cook's career was ignored last season so he could be celebrated as an integral piece of the offense. Cook offered vertical speed that the offense didn't have otherwise, but his lack of consistency is why he wasn't retained in the offseason.

Martellus Bennett became the exception to the rule when he was signed to replace Cook. Bennett is a legitimate star player. He is a far superior player to Cook. Cook is faster in a straight line, but Bennett runs better routes, makes better adjustments at the catch point, performs better against tight coverage, and catches the ball more consistently. He is also a true tight end because he offers legitimate value as a run-blocker. Bennett can manhandle defensive ends in the running game without help from a teammate. He is one of the best tight ends in the league and should diversify the Packers' skill position group while creating more consistency.

Outside of the draft, Bennett represents the only real effort the Packers made to get better this offseason. Along with not adequately replacing Lang on the interior of the line, they let Eddie Lacy leave without a clear replacement. The Packers took three running backs in the draft, but none before the fourth round. Ty Montgomery was a wide receiver less than a year ago—now he's the veteran and lead back on the depth chart. If the wide receiver group is to improve, it will do so with the same faces from last season. It's hard to rationally expect the receiving corps to be better than it has been over recent seasons. (The biggest variable is whether Nelson's athleticism continues to return in the second year after ACL surgery, or if he starts an age-related decline at the age of 32.) Without an offensive line that can consistently give him time, it will be dramatically tougher for Rodgers to elevate that group. If anything, the Packers offense is more likely to regress.

Should that happen, it will be the responsibility of the defense to create a more balanced team in Wisconsin. The Green Bay defense ranked 20th by DVOA last year. Former Packers cornerback Davon House was Thompson's most notable free-agent signing from the offseason. House played well when he was last in Green Bay but struggled as a full-time starter for the Jacksonville Jaguars. His one-year deal suggests he will be forced to earn his playing time. House will re-join a secondary that boasts two former first-round picks, three former second-round picks, and one former third-round pick. Noting where Quinten Rollins and Damarious Randall were drafted is the highest compliment you can pay to those guys at this point. Rollins has missed games in both of his seasons so far but even when healthy his athleticism hasn't allowed him to become an above-average starting cornerback. Randall is another impressive athlete who made the peculiar move of becoming a cornerback in the NFL after playing safety in college. He also hasn't played a full 16 games since being drafted and has only shown sporadic flashes of quality.

Two more second-round picks arrive this year, and both are expected to make an immediate impact. Kevin King was widely touted as a first-round pick but slipped far enough that the Packers could pick him early in the second round after trading down. The Washington product is an extremely long defender. He officially measured at 6-foot-3 and 200 pounds. Consider that Richard Sherman officially measured at 6-foot-3 and 195 pounds. King is going to need to rely on his size to be an effective NFL starter. He tested well at the combine in cone and shuttle drills, but his foot speed reacting to shorter receivers suggests that he won't be able to play in the slot. A 4.43-second 40 makes him fast enough, but not a fast NFL defender. King will rely on his length and ball skills while looking to leverage the sideline with receivers from press coverage. So long as the Packers keep him outside, he will have a chance to contribute early and develop into a quality long-term starter.

Josh Jones of North Carolina State was the team's other second-round pick this year. With Ha Ha Clinton-Dix and Morgan Burnett entrenched as the team's first-string safeties, Jones can't expect to start straight away. Still, there is a clear route to playing time thanks to Micah Hyde's departure. Dom Capers used Hyde in different ways. He was primarily a safety, but moved around the field and could be used in coverage like a cornerback against specific matchups. In theory Hyde was "only" a nickel player, but he played an impactful role in the defense. At 6-foot-1 and 220 pounds, Jones has the size to line up in the box, but he also has the range to be used as a weapon of deception. He has the physical profile that will allow him to execute strenuous coverage assignments, whether that be dropping into a deeper zone after threatening to blitz or being used as a single-high defender. What Jones lacks is discipline and consistency. Being the third safety in Green Bay is a perfect role for him because he won't be expected to play every snap or be part of every package. He will be able to focus on his specific roles in specific packages. His mistakes should be less egregious, but his big hits and aggressive mindset can still be shown off.

Green Bay can tie an NFL record with a ninth-consecutive playoff appearance in 2017. Given that Rodgers was able to lead last year's roster to an NFC Championship Game, that record should be in the bag. The question is: will the Packers produce more than one Super Bowl appearance out of this streak? How do you overtake teams when you're not trying to speed up? The teams that beat Green Bay in the playoffs consistently go out to add even more talent in the offseason. The 2015 Seahawks traded for Jimmy Graham, the 2016 Cardinals traded for Chandler Jones, and this year's Falcons added Dontari Poe to their defense.

In the last three offseasons, Thompson's biggest outside moves were signing Jared Cook and signing Martellus Bennett to replace Cook this year. That's it. At some point, the Packers became complacent in just making the playoffs, and hoping Rodgers has a great run that month. This has made Green Bay one of the league's most predictable teams each year, and to be honest, one of the disappointments. Playoff appearances are not a great measure of success for a team with a generational talent at quarterback; Super Bowls are. The Packers continue to not do enough to maximize every chance Rodgers has at a Super Bowl while he is still in his prime.

Cian Fahey

2016 Packers Stats by Week

Wk	vs.	W-L	PF	PA	YDF	YDA	TO	Total	Off	Def	ST
1	at JAC	W	27	23	294	348	+1	19%	16%	-5%	-2%
2	at MIN	L	14	17	263	284	-2	-20%	-28%	-9%	-1%
3	DET	W	34	27	324	418	+1	60%	60%	4%	3%
4	BYE										
5	NYG	W	23	16	406	221	-1	20%	16%	-10%	-6%
6	DAL	L	16	30	372	424	-2	0%	-24%	-11%	13%
7	CHI	W	26	10	406	189	+1	50%	11%	-51%	-12%
8	at ATL	L	32	33	331	367	0	-3%	9%	16%	4%
9	IND	L	26	31	405	355	+1	-7%	16%	-1%	-25%
10	at TEN	L	25	47	402	446	-3	-46%	-4%	32%	-9%
11	at WAS	L	24	42	424	515	-2	-43%	5%	39%	-9%
12	at PHI	W	27	13	387	292	+1	53%	52%	4%	5%
13	HOU	W	21	13	309	307	0	25%	24%	8%	9%
14	SEA	W	38	10	330	354	+6	86%	42%	-47%	-3%
15	at CHI	W	30	27	451	449	+4	8%	32%	22%	-2%
16	MIN	W	38	25	348	446	+2	42%	55%	19%	6%
17	at DET	W	31	24	448	408	+1	0%	20%	18%	-2%
18	NYG	W	38	13	406	365	+2	74%	58%	3%	19%
19	at DAL	W	34	31	413	429	0	24%	27%	6%	4%
20	at ATL	L	21	44	367	493	-2	-35%	-1%	28%	-7%

Trends and Splits

	Offense	Rank	Defense	Rank
Total DVOA	16.6%	4	2.5%	20
Unadjusted VOA	16.9%	4	3.4%	21
Weighted Trend	20.2%	4	5.6%	23
Variance	6.5%	19	6.1%	24
Average Opponent	1.3%	27	0.1%	15
Passing	31.3%	7	13.2%	23
Rushing	4.4%	5	-13.2%	14
First Down	6.9%	9	10.6%	28
Second Down	21.3%	6	-16.8%	4
Third Down	28.4%	3	16.4%	27
First Half	23.9%	1	6.1%	20
Second Half	0.0%	16	-21.2%	3
Red Zone	29.6%	5	16.1%	27
Late and Close	11.2%	9	-8.2%	10

Five-Year Performance

Year	W-L	Pyth W	Est W	PF	PA	TO	Total	Rk	Off	Rk	Def	Rk	ST	Rk	Off AGL	Rk	Def AGL	Rk	Off Age	Rk	Def Age	Rk	ST Age	Rk
2012	11-5	10.5	11.8	433	336	+7	26.3%	5	19.5%	3	-7.0%	8	-0.2%	18	38.7	23	62.8	32	26.9	16	25.8	27	24.9	32
2013	8-7-1	7.8	7.3	417	428	-3	-6.0%	20	8.6%	9	14.4%	31	-0.3%	19	59.1	29	43.9	24	26.0	30	26.3	19	25.2	29
2014	12-4	11.2	10.8	486	348	+14	23.3%	3	24.7%	1	-1.0%	16	-2.3%	22	11.0	3	31.0	9	25.7	30	26.7	18	25.9	19
2015	10-6	9.3	9.9	368	323	+5	9.9%	10	2.2%	11	-7.3%	9	0.4%	17	29.7	15	26.5	14	26.7	16	26.3	23	25.5	28
2016	10-6	9.1	9.8	432	388	+8	12.3%	7	16.6%	4	2.5%	20	-1.9%	21	35.2	16	35.3	19	26.8	14	25.8	30	25.4	28

2016 Performance Based on Most Common Personnel Groups

GB Offense					GB Offense vs. Opponents					GB Defense					GB Defense vs. Opponents			
Pers	Freq	Yds	DVOA	Run%	Pers	Freq	Yds	DVOA	Run%	Pers	Freq	Yds	DVOA		Pers	Freq	Yds	DVOA
11	57%	6.5	31.9%	23%	Base	16%	6.0	13.9%	58%	Base	10%	6.5	8.7%		11	66%	6.3	6.4%
01	10%	5.7	21.8%	14%	Nickel	63%	6.0	22.8%	29%	Nickel	59%	5.6	-0.3%		12	16%	5.7	-1.9%
20	8%	4.5	2.4%	60%	Dime+	20%	6.4	25.8%	12%	Dime+	30%	6.9	5.9%		13	6%	6.6	23.4%
12	7%	6.7	28.0%	46%	Goal Line	0%	-0.3	-80.4%	100%	Goal Line	0%	0.0	-55.9%		21	5%	5.2	-28.9%
21	5%	6.0	-15.6%	44%						Big	0%	3.5	83.8%		22	3%	4.5	-24.5%
00	4%	4.7	-1.7%	4%														
10	3%	7.0	29.7%	35%														

Strategic Tendencies

Run/Pass		Rk	Formation		Rk	Pass Rush		Rk	Secondary		Rk	Strategy		Rk
Runs, first half	29%	32	Form: Single Back	67%	28	Rush 3	3.1%	30	4 DB	10%	32	Play-action	15%	28
Runs, first down	41%	30	Form: Empty Back	10%	8	Rush 4	68.0%	11	5 DB	59%	17	Avg Box (Off)	5.96	32
Runs, second-long	22%	29	Pers: 3+ WR	83%	2	Rush 5	22.7%	13	6+ DB	29%	2	Avg Box (Def)	6.08	27
Runs, power sit.	49%	26	Pers: 2+ TE/6+ OL	12%	31	Rush 6+	6.1%	15	CB by Sides	87%	9	Offensive Pace	30.81	20
Runs, behind 2H	22%	29	Pers: 6+ OL	3%	23	Sacks by LB	73.1%	2	S/CB Cover Ratio	25%	20	Defensive Pace	30.23	15
Pass, ahead 2H	57%	4	Shotgun/Pistol	76%	5	Sacks by DB	11.5%	4	DB Blitz	15%	2	Go for it on 4th	1.87	1

Numbers certainly back up the idea that there's something special about Aaron Rodgers' ability to draw opposing penalties. Packers opponents had 72 defensive penalties in 2016 after 81 defensive penalties in 2015. No other offense drew more than 63 opposition flags in either season. And it's not an issue of the specific officials, as the Packers were below-average in defensive penalties both years. ☞ This was the second straight year where Rodgers has struggled against the blitz, with fewer yards per pass as more pass-rushers come. Last year, he averaged 7.3 yards with three or four pass-rushers, 6.6 yards with five, and only 5.0 yards with six or more. This would be a bigger problem except that opponents only blitzed Rodgers 24 percent of the time, the fifth-lowest rate in the league. ☞ The Packers went without a tight end on 15.5 percent of plays, the second straight season they ranked second in the league behind the Jets. ☞ Forty-five percent of Packers runs came from multi-back sets, third in the NFL. Yet they were much better running from single-back sets: 4.8 yards per carry and 2.6% DVOA with one back, 3.7 yards per carry and minus-17.9% DVOA otherwise. ☞ The Packers were just 25th with 11.8% DVOA on play-action passes, but they were third with 41.2% DVOA on other passes. It was the second year in a row where the Packers had one of the league's three largest reverse splits on play-action. (Most teams will be better with play-action than without.) ☞ Also for the second year in a row, the Packers defense got killed by play-action, allowing 58.0% DVOA (31st in the NFL) compared to 4.3% DVOA on other passes (16th). In 2015, these ranks were 23rd and fifth, respectively. ☞ Green Bay opponents have been watching the film: The Packers faced 30 percent of passes in the middle of the field, the second-highest rate in the NFL, and ranked 29th in DVOA on these passes. (In an interesting example of Simpson's paradox, the Packers were 21st against deep middle passes and 25th against short middle passes.) ☞ Despite their other defensive problems in 2016, the Packers dramatically improved their tackling from past seasons. The Packers tied Jacksonville with a league-low 79 broken tackles and ranked third with broken tackles on just 7.6 percent of plays, after ranking 30th and 31st in broken-tackle rate the previous two years. Blake Martinez led the Packers with just eight broken tackles; every other defense in the league had at least three players with eight or more broken tackles.

Passing

Player	DYAR	DVOA	Plays	NtYds	Avg	YAC	C%	TD	Int
A.Rodgers	1279	18.7%	644	4175	6.5	5.1	66.0%	40	6
B.Hundley	-80	-109.2%	11	16	1.5	6.5	20.0%	0	1

Rushing

Player	DYAR	DVOA	Plays	Yds	Avg	TD	Fum	Suc
E.Lacy*	84	20.4%	71	360	5.1	0	0	49%
J.Starks*	-54	-29.6%	62	151	2.4	0	0	32%
T.Montgomery	28	6.2%	44	228	5.2	3	0	55%
A.Rodgers	66	20.5%	39	305	7.8	4	0	-
A.Ripkowski	6	-4.3%	25	89	3.6	2	0	48%
C.Michael*	7	0.1%	20	59	3.0	1	0	50%
D.Jackson*	-12	-40.9%	10	32	3.2	0	0	50%
R.Cobb	11	-22.8%	10	33	3.3	0	0	-
K.Davis*	-22	-114.6%	5	5	1.0	0	0	0%

Receiving

Player	DYAR	DVOA	Plays	Ctch	Yds	Y/C	YAC	TD	C%
J.Nelson	382	19.2%	152	97	1257	13.0	3.7	14	64%
D.Adams	230	11.3%	121	75	1017	13.6	5.2	12	62%
R.Cobb	133	6.6%	84	60	610	10.2	6.0	4	71%
G.Allison	47	15.2%	22	12	202	16.8	4.2	2	55%
J.Janis	-25	-27.8%	19	11	93	8.5	2.7	1	58%
T.Davis	21	22.2%	7	3	24	8.0	2.7	1	43%
J.Cook*	-15	-11.5%	51	30	377	12.6	4.9	1	59%
R.Rodgers	-6	-9.1%	47	30	271	9.0	3.5	2	64%
L.Kendricks	-70	-19.7%	87	50	499	10.0	5.5	2	57%
M.Bennett	197	33.4%	73	55	701	12.7	7.6	7	75%
T.Montgomery	33	-4.2%	56	44	348	7.9	7.3	0	79%
J.Starks*	-20	-28.1%	26	20	128	6.4	8.3	2	77%
A.Ripkowski	10	2.7%	10	9	46	5.1	3.2	1	90%
E.Lacy*	-12	-45.4%	7	4	28	7.0	10.0	0	57%

Offensive Line

Player	Pos	Age	GS	Snaps	Pen	Sk	Pass	Run	Player	Pos	Age	GS	Snaps	Pen	Sk	Pass	Run
Lane Taylor	LG	28	16/16	1086	5	2.0	10	5	Corey Linsley	C	26	9/9	599	2	0.5	7	8
Bryan Bulaga	RT	28	16/16	1058	5	1.5	16	10	J.C. Tretter*	C	26	7/7	488	2	2.3	5	4
David Bakhtiari	LT	26	16/16	1057	7	4.8	9	4	Jason Spriggs	OT	23	16/2	239	3	0.8	3	3
T.J. Lang*	RG	30	13/13	791	5	3.0	7	4	Jahri Evans	RG	34	16/16	1137	6	2.5	4	4

Year	Yards	ALY	Rank	Power	Rank	Stuff	Rank	2nd Lev	Rank	Open Field	Rank	Sacks	ASR	Rank	Press	Rank	F-Start	Cont.
2014	4.39	4.36	8	59%	25	21%	24	1.29	5	0.83	8	30	5.5%	13	20.6%	4	11	43
2015	4.00	3.88	25	61%	21	23%	27	1.11	19	0.73	16	47	7.4%	23	30.2%	29	10	28
2016	4.36	4.08	19	49%	30	20%	17	1.15	15	0.94	9	35	5.5%	11	26.3%	16	13	33

2016 ALY by direction:	Left End 4.17 (20)	Left Tackle 5.25 (2)	Mid/Guard 4.08 (19)	Right Tackle 3.77 (19)	Right End 3.35 (24)

It's tough to find quality offensive linemen in the NFL right now. Part of the reason for that is linemen are being asked to pass-block in space more than ever before, which is inherently tougher than run-blocking considering the size of the people who play these positions. The Packers are fortunate in this regard to have two bookend offensive tackles in Bryan Bulaga and David Bakhtiari who are squarely in their prime and under contract through at least 2019. Bulaga is the elder of the pair and he turned 28 after last season. Bakhtiari enjoyed the more successful 2016, finishing in the top 10 in snaps per blown block, but Bulaga himself has conceded only 3.5 sacks combined the past two seasons. Assuming both can stay healthy moving forward—a tougher assumption with Bulaga than Bakhtiari because of multiple ACL tears earlier in his career—Rodgers will have a pair of established, talented tackles to escort him through the final stages of his career. Unfortunately, the same can't be said for the interior of the line. ☞ Lane Taylor played well enough in 2016 to justify his starting spot heading into the 2017 season but he was by no means a star. Still, with T.J. Lang's departure, Taylor will mostly likely be penciled in at left guard, leaving the opposite guard spot as the most uncertain area on the line. ☞ The goal for the Packers should be to keep Don Barclay off the field. Barclay has stuck around for years because of his ability to line up at different spots on the field, but the key words there are "line up at." Barclay has always been able to play guard or tackle in theory, but he has never proven capable of being effective in either spot. When asked to play meaningful snaps in 2015, he ranked 37th out of 38 qualifying right tackles in snaps per blown block. Barclay has torpedoed his quarterback's protection and disrupted the whole offense whenever he has been on the field. ☞ Jahri Evans may have limitations at this point of his career, as his athleticism continues to decline, but he should still be the favorite to start ahead of Barclay simply due to his value in the running game. 2016 tackle draftees Jason Spriggs and Kyle Murphy have also been cross-training at guard, which really represents their only immediate avenue to playing time.

Defensive Front Seven

Defensive Line	Age	Pos		Overall								vs. Run					Pass Rush			
			G	Snaps	Plays	TmPct	Rk	Stop	Dfts	BTkl	Runs	St%	Rk	RuYd	Rk	Sack	Hit	Hur	Dsrpt
Mike Daniels	28	DE	16	664	34	4.2%	49	30	9	4	26	92%	3	1.4	17	4.0	8	23	1
Letroy Guion	30	DT	15	449	31	4.1%	50	25	8	3	28	79%	42	1.6	24	0.0	1	3	1
Kenny Clark	22	DT	16	335	23	2.9%	--	17	4	0	20	75%	--	2.0	--	0.0	2	8	2
Ricky Jean-Francois	31	DE	16	442	33	3.8%	56	28	6	2	27	89%	13	2.0	35	1.5	0	4	1

Edge Rushers	Age	Pos		Overall								vs. Run					Pass Rush			
			G	Snaps	Plays	TmPct	Rk	Stop	Dfts	BTkl	Runs	St%	Rk	RuYd	Rk	Sack	Hit	Hur	Dsrpt
Nick Perry	27	OLB	14	606	56	7.9%	10	49	25	3	35	86%	8	2.5	44	11.0	5	21	3
Julius Peppers*	37	OLB	16	587	26	3.2%	80	22	12	4	13	77%	36	1.8	26	7.5	5	18	6
Datone Jones*	27	OLB	15	548	24	3.2%	82	21	6	4	20	90%	2	1.4	20	1.0	12	21	4
Clay Matthews	31	OLB	12	479	27	4.5%	60	19	11	4	16	69%	73	1.8	27	5.0	4	17	3

Linebackers	Age	Pos		Overall								vs. Run				Pass Rush			vs. Pass				
			G	Snaps	Plays	TmPct	Rk	Stop	Dfts	BTkl	Runs	St%	Rk	RuYd	Rk	Sack	Hit	Hur	Tgts	Suc%	Rk	AdjYd	Rk	PD	Int
Joe Thomas	26	ILB	16	634	73	9.1%	64	36	13	7	28	57%	67	3.7	52	0.0	2	4	38	50%	37	8.8	74	6	1
Jake Ryan	25	ILB	14	558	84	11.9%	42	49	10	4	59	71%	13	3.0	21	0.0	4	5	14	48%	40	5.7	23	3	0
Blake Martinez	23	ILB	13	438	69	10.5%	52	38	7	8	50	58%	65	3.9	62	1.0	0	1	22	56%	19	5.0	12	4	1

Year	Yards	ALY	Rank	Power	Rank	Stuff	Rank	2nd Level	Rank	Open Field	Rank	Sacks	ASR	Rank	Press	Rank
2014	4.09	4.51	26	63%	14	17%	25	1.19	21	0.42	1	41	6.9%	14	25.2%	14
2015	4.15	3.87	11	67%	17	25%	3	1.21	24	0.92	25	43	6.7%	15	26.5%	10
2016	4.12	3.84	9	72%	30	20%	13	1.16	17	0.82	22	40	7.0%	8	27.0%	16

2016 ALY by direction:	Left End 3.52 (11)	Left Tackle 2.93 (3)	Mid/Guard 3.84 (10)	Right Tackle 5.15 (31)	Right End 3.59 (16)

Even during games when opponents eviscerated the Packers defense last year, defensive lineman Mike Daniels consistently stood out. It was true during the regular season and especially true during the playoff loss against the Falcons. Daniels has developed into a consistent, well-rounded player who doesn't get big sack numbers but consistently wins his matchups. Last year, he even turned into a disruptive force against the run, posting the best run defense charting numbers of his career. ☞ The Packers hope second-year lineman Kenny Clark develops into a similarly disruptive presence alongside Daniels, but his relative youth means it may not happen in the near future. Clark occasionally flashed potential during an underwhelming rookie season but didn't fill a big role and finished the season without a sack despite playing all 16 games. It's not unusual for young defensive linemen to take time to adjust after being drafted, and this should be especially true for one as young as Clark. He could play three or four more seasons and still be considered young. ☞ Although Clay Matthews was an effective inside linebacker, he struggled to impact the game as much from that position, and the Packers played him more outside again last year. It's unclear if Matthews has lost a step over the course of his career, but it was not that long ago that he was a truly dominant pass-rusher off the edge. After averaging more than 10 sacks per season during his first six years in the league, Matthews has had just 11.5 sacks the past two seasons combined. With Julius Peppers' departure, it behooves the Packers to keep Matthews outside across from Nick Perry. ☞ Fourth-round rookie Vince Biegel is a local hero, a high school All-American out of Wisconsin Rapids who went on to play for the Badgers. But unless he's immediately capable of being an impactful, three-down edge defender, the Packers should rely more on Joe Thomas as the nickel linebacker alongside Jake Ryan, rather than letting Biegel kick Matthews back inside. Ryan and Blake Martinez will likely start in base packages, which for the Packers essentially means a 2-4-5 alignment.

Defensive Secondary

Secondary	Age	Pos	G	Snaps	Plays	Overall TmPct	Rk	Stop	Dfts	BTkl	vs. Run Runs	St%	Rk	RuYd	Rk	vs. Pass Tgts	Tgt%	Rk	Dist	Suc%	Rk	AdjYd	Rk	PD	Int
Ha Ha Clinton-Dix	25	FS	16	1031	85	10.5%	32	22	11	4	40	28%	62	8.1	55	36	7.8%	29	12.8	42%	51	9.1	42	7	5
Morgan Burnett	28	SS	15	948	100	13.2%	8	41	15	6	36	50%	16	5.5	18	41	9.7%	51	9.9	48%	29	6.3	6	11	2
Ladarius Gunter	25	CB	16	861	65	8.1%	56	22	10	7	7	14%	84	18.4	87	63	16.6%	21	12.9	51%	33	8.3	60	12	0
Micah Hyde*	27	CB/FS	16	821	65	8.1%	56	28	15	4	17	47%	28	6.1	30	51	13.9%	3	9.6	48%	53	8.5	65	9	3
Quinten Rollins	25	CB	13	704	49	7.5%	67	14	5	3	5	40%	41	6.6	42	60	19.1%	49	10.5	33%	87	9.8	85	7	1
Damarious Randall	25	CB	10	497	46	9.1%	33	16	10	6	6	17%	81	7.7	58	54	24.6%	81	14.7	45%	68	9.5	80	9	3
Kentrell Brice	23	SS	16	261	21	2.6%	--	5	2	2	7	43%	--	4.7	--	7	5.6%	--	14.2	35%	--	15.7	--	1	0
Davon House	28	CB	16	272	16	2.0%	--	5	2	2	6	50%	--	4.3	--	22	20.8%	--	13.0	26%	--	10.9	--	0	0

Year	Pass D Rank	vs. #1 WR	Rk	vs. #2 WR	Rk	vs. Other WR	Rk	vs. TE	Rk	vs. RB	Rk
2014	11	-1.5%	15	-14.2%	7	-11.4%	9	-5.8%	14	1.0%	19
2015	6	7.5%	21	-31.7%	2	6.4%	19	-20.8%	4	-24.7%	4
2016	23	12.3%	28	18.0%	28	13.7%	26	-17.4%	7	-7.9%	13

You never want to rely on rookies too much, especially in your secondary. Cornerbacks need to be young because of the athleticism of NFL receivers, but they also need to be comfortable in their coverage assignments. Kevin King's development and capacity to contribute immediately will be big for the overall success of the unit. Sam Shields' departure means the Packers don't have a veteran who can athletically match up with opposing team's top receivers. Davon House is better than anyone they had last year but House didn't impress during his time in Jacksonville. ☞ Rebound seasons from Damarious Randall and Quinten Rollins would give the Packers a suddenly deep cornerback depth chart, but both have lots of ground to make up. Rollins finished with the worst adjusted success rate among 87 qualifying cornerbacks, while Randall had persistent issues with the deep ball, finishing 80th in adjusted yards per target. ☞ Ha Ha Clinton-Dix is developing into a very good safety. His improved recognition and ball skills resulted in five interceptions during his third season. Clinton-Dix and Morgan Burnett have skill sets that complement each other perfectly. The only concern for Clinton-Dix is his decision-making consistency. The Packers ask him to cover vast amounts of space at times but he doesn't have the most stressful free safety role in the league. With Clinton-Dix and Burnett as the starters and rookie Josh Jones filling the old Micah Hyde role, safety play should once again be an area of strength for the Packers in 2017.

Special Teams

Year	DVOA	Rank	FG/XP	Rank	Net Kick	Rank	Kick Ret	Rank	Net Punt	Rank	Punt Ret	Rank	Hidden	Rank
2014	-2.3%	22	-2.9	24	-7.0	28	-2.9	22	-9.4	29	10.5	4	0.1	16
2015	0.4%	17	5.0	6	-7.8	31	5.4	5	4.7	9	-5.6	25	-4.9	21
2016	-1.9%	21	0.7	13	-8.7	30	-2.5	22	0.1	14	1.1	13	-8.4	26

Mason Crosby continues to deliver yearly competency in one of the league's harshest kicking environments. Crosby's 2016 season will be remembered for his divisional round heroics in Dallas, but he also had positive gross value on kickoffs. The problem was in Green Bay's kickoff coverage units, which conceded an estimated 11.6 points of field position to opposing returners. The Packers ranked 31st and 27th in that category the previous two seasons, so this is a problem that has needed fixing for a while. ≋ Jacob Schum was a below-average punter last season, while his predecessor Tim Masthay was one of the five worst punters by net points added the two seasons prior to that. Rookie free agent Justin Vogel (Miami) hopes to end the revolving door at the position, and the Packers don't currently have competition for him on the roster. ≋ The Ty Montgomery-Jeff Janis kickoff return duo regressed in 2016. Each was among the 12 best returners by net points added in 2015, and then each was below average last season. Second-year receiver Trevor Davis, who was an above-average punt returner as a rookie, could theoretically take on more of these duties depending on how the roster shakes out at receiver. ≋ Green Bay was one of eight teams not to have a player with double-digit tackles on special teams. Kyler Fackrell led the team with nine, eight of which came for that beleaguered kickoff coverage unit. ≋ The poor "Hidden" rating came from opposing field goal kickers going 27-for-29 against Green Bay. Both misses came from Matt Prater of Detroit.

Houston Texans

2016 Record: 9-7	Total DVOA: -21.9% (29th)	2017 Mean Projection: 6.7 wins	On the Clock (0-4): 19%
Pythagorean Wins: 6.5 (26th)	Offense: -21.2% (30th)	Postseason Odds: 23.4%	Mediocrity (5-7): 44%
Snap-Weighted Age: 26.1 (27th)	Defense: -5.8% (9th)	Super Bowl Odds: 1.4%	Playoff Contender (8-10): 29%
Average Opponent: 1.0% (13th)	Special Teams: -6.5% (31st)	Proj. Avg. Opponent: 1.1% (8th)	Super Bowl Contender (11+): 8%

2016: Of all the teams to ever make the playoffs, this was truly one of them.

2017: Deshaun really beat Bama, and a quarterback from UNC named Mitsubishi is gonna go before him?

"I'm comin' straight out of the South with my nuts in my hand," rapped esteemed Houstonian Paul Wall in a verse that couldn't be any more about this year's Texans if it tried. After back-to-back offseasons of bold moves aimed to fix the quarterback position, the Texans now have to ask if Deshaun Watson will reward their faith, or leave them stuck firmly in quarterback purgatory until 2019.

Houston came hard after quarterback Brock Osweiler last offseason. The weirdest thing about the move was that, outside of the clear and aching need for a quarterback the Texans have had since 2012, there didn't seem to be any empirical reason behind it. Our QBASE system gave Osweiler the worst projection of any quarterback of the past 20 years (Table 1). Former FO writer and Rookie Scouting Portfolio author Matt Waldman ranked Osweiler as the 10th-best quarterback in his class, behind quarterbacks we're sure you remember such as Jacory Harris and B.J. Coleman. Waldman wrote of Osweiler: "On a physical level, his mechanics need work and this could sidetrack his career before it ever has a chance to get started." Osweiler's 2015 starts with the Broncos were underwhelming statistically (-3.2% DVOA, 153 DYAR) and look worse when you consider that Denver's skill position talent and Gary Kubiak's offensive scheme both minimized Osweiler's need to excel at the difficult parts of playing quarterback. The Texans had a hole at quarterback and reacted by selecting someone with a large track record of not being able to play quarterback, one that dated back to his college days at Arizona State.

On the other hand, Osweiler was certainly tall and looked the part of an NFL starting quarterback. And, after all, it only cost the Texans money to try. The fact that Mike Glennon essentially got a lower-key version of this deal one year later tells you that NFL teams are willing to gamble on tools like Osweiler has. Why this schism exists and why teams seem to only target tall, big-armed quarterbacks for their gambles is beyond the scope of this essay.

Osweiler flopped. After two weeks of NFL teams getting a feel for the kind of throws he makes, they bottled up the big-armed thrower and asked him to make precise strikes over the middle or on post routes. The Texans had three weeks of positive pass offense DVOA over the course of the season: Week 1 against the Bears (3.6% DVOA), Week 6's furious comeback against the inept Colts defense (3.5% DVOA), and Week 15 when Osweiler was benched for Tom Savage (3.8% DVOA). Osweiler finished with 16 interceptions and 15 touchdowns despite playing in a super conservative offense. Then, if media reports are to be believed, he wore out his welcome with head coach Bill O'Brien and the two had a physical altercation at halftime of the Week 17 game in Tennessee. It was supposedly the reason that the Texans got rid of Osweiler this offseason, sending him to Cleveland with a 2018 second-round pick for a seventh-round pick and a fourth-round pick in this year's draft.

The odd thing about that trade, though, was that the Texans never actually used the cap space they freed up from the deal. From the outside, it could be perceived that the Texans simply thought Tony Romo was in the bag before they made the deal—something that would have made the cap space much more valuable. But it certainly looked odd in hindsight to trade Osweiler and not even make the final day of deliberations with cornerback A.J. Bouye, who signed with the division rival Jaguars. Was a second-round pick spent solely on keeping the clubhouse calm? That seems like a stretch. Occam would suggest that the Texans thought they'd outlast the competition for Romo, only to find out that he'd rather play for CBS.

The quarterbacks that O'Brien has collected seem to come in two molds: those with New England experience and those who look like focus-grouped interpretations of what a quarterback looks like. While O'Brien has disavowed ever wanting Osweiler—through his camp leaking it to any corner of the

Table 1. 10 Lowest-Projected Quarterbacks by QBASE, 1996-2017

Name	Team	Pick	Year	Projection	Actual DYAR (Yr 3-5)
Josh McCown	ARI	81	2002	-339	-102
Connor Cook	OAK	100	2016	-380	N/A
Jacoby Brissett	NE	91	2016	-381	N/A
Kevin O'Connell	NE	94	2008	-381	0
Marques Tuiasosopo	OAK	59	2001	-427	-49
Christian Hackenberg	NYJ	51	2016	-436	N/A
Mark Sanchez	NYJ	5	2009	-469	-649
Trent Edwards	BUF	92	2007	-520	-564
Charlie Batch	DET	60	1998	-597	59
Brock Osweiler	DEN	57	2012	-847	-421

2017 Texans Schedule

Week	Opp.	Week	Opp.	Week	Opp.
1	JAC	7	BYE	13	at TEN
2	at CIN (Thu.)	8	at SEA	14	SF
3	at NE	9	IND	15	at JAC
4	TEN	10	at LARM	16	PIT (Mon./Xmas)
5	KC	11	ARI	17	at IND
6	CLE	12	at BAL (Mon.)		

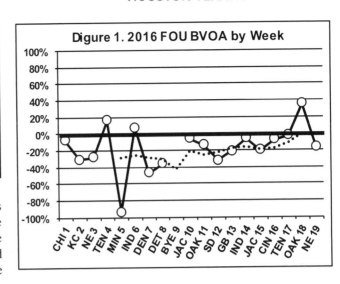

Digure 1. 2016 FOU BVOA by Week

media that will hear him—it's hard to ignore that the Texans have a type. Between Osweiler, Savage, and Ryan Mallet, the Texans clearly idealized physical traits over on-field play. We don't say that as a jab. It's common to pick NFL players based on traits and try to teach them to play. Just look at what Seattle tries to do with its offensive line. Or, to use a more successful interpretation, look at what our SackSEER system tries to measure in terms of raw athletic ability. Those pass-rushers don't all come into the league knowing all the moves. They get taught.

But the Seattle offensive line and Houston quarterback situation are shared examples of this same approach: willful focus on one set of skills at the expense of all others. Seattle has Russell Wilson to help bail them out of their mistakes. The Texans have… uh, a bad division and some emergency plans for a Jonathan Grimes wildcat formation.

That's why Houston's trade up for Clemson's national championship-winning quarterback was so stunning. Not only was it a complete abandonment of the "we don't need to make a real investment in a quarterback when we can just teach these male models" philosophy, it was a complete abandonment of their whole idea of a quarterback. The quarterback for those principles was Patrick Mahomes III. Watson has a slim build that worries outside scouts who know that there's a transition between college football punishment and NFL punishment. Even though he fits the technical definition of most size-focused scouts at 6-foot-3 with 9 3/4-inch hands, he does so just barely. Watson doesn't have a body to "dream on," he simply makes the most of what is there.

While Watson was presumed to be the most pro-ready of this year's prospects, he does come with some flaws. He was quite turnover-prone last year, putting up 17 interceptions in 15 starts. Those are numbers that point to poor decisions after the snap, especially in crowded zones. And while he has a quick release, there was some concern over Watson's fastball velocity after he was clocked throwing 49 miles per hour at the combine, the lowest of any quarterback invited. Then, of course, there were the typical "spread quarterback" criticisms, as if Dak Prescott never happened.

Our system is bearish on Watson's future, giving him a projection of just 261 DYAR in his third through fifth seasons. In a lot of ways, that says a lot about what our new system thinks of Watson's teammates. QBASE has an adjustment for quarterbacks that play with top-level talent. It sees Mike Williams' draft status and wonders if this isn't another situation such as Johnny Manziel and Mike Evans, where the quarterback

was made to look good by his supporting cast. Jordan Leggett, Watson's tight end, was drafted in the fifth round. Artavis Scott, another Clemson wideout, signed with the Chargers as an undrafted free agent. Because there is a historical precedent for quarterbacks being lifted by top-class receivers, QBASE approaches Watson with some skepticism.

While there has been some discussion of Watson's athleticism as a mitigating factor, he is, in Waldman's words, "not the next Michael Vick." Watson can do some damage on the ground and can make some run-pass options viable, but he's probably not going to draw quarterback spies or change the game in the box to a significant extent.

The local camp talk has mostly revolved around a quarterback competition, but it's a competition that has no real point. Tom Savage might get some starts if he can stay healthy long enough to do it. (That in itself would be a deviation from the norm, as he has ended two seasons on IR and made it almost two games before bowing out last year.) But the future of the entire Houston organization is riding on the Watson pick.

With both their first- and second-round picks gone next year, the Texans have fired every bullet from the chamber in their quest to win this year. They looked at this team as being one quarterback away from being good, prepared to get one, and perhaps backed into this play after Romo went to CBS. The die has been cast.

Here's what the Texans believe will happen: they believe that Watson is their Prescott, and despite being surrounded by a less illustrious supporting cast, hope that he can be the kind of quarterback to get them past the divisional round. They saw what happened last season without J.J. Watt, and know that their defense may have an even higher ceiling if they can let a rejuvenated Watt, Whitney Mercilus, and Jadeveon Clowney feast together.

The problem with that vision is that it's a very flowery re-telling of the last few years of the Texans. The Texans believe that they are a near-contender with back-to-back division titles, coming off a tough playoff loss on the road in Foxboro. When asked about analytics, O'Brien told local CBS Houston radio that: "Yeah, we look at it. There's no doubt we look at stats and analytics and all those things, but what I've learned over the years is it's gotta be what you see on the field and what you see on tape."

The reality is that, to make that game, the Texans had to hold off an Oakland team with a third-string rookie quarterback making his first NFL start. The reality is that the Texans were a bad team last year. They finished 29th in DVOA despite the league's seventh-best defense, and won nine games by going 8-2 in games decided by seven points or less. They were outscored by 49 points. When they won the AFC South in 2015, they did so with a point differential of plus-26 and another negative DVOA.

The Texans haven't finished higher than 24th in offensive DVOA under O'Brien. O'Brien's offense doesn't manufacture any easy yardage and spends a lot of time looking too cute for its own good, especially in the red zone. (Hello, Vince Wilfork and J.J. Watt in the goal-line set.) The demand for change led to the firing of offensive coordinator George Godsey, but Houston didn't replace him with anybody and now will watch O'Brien call the plays.

The Texans haven't finished higher than 28th in special teams DVOA since 2011. In each of their last two playoff losses, they gave up return touchdowns. There's been plenty of talk from O'Brien about getting this corrected. They even hired former Patriot Larry Izzo as the new coordinator last year. But be it through poor coaching, poor personnel, a lack of focus, or all of the above, this unit is a black hole just waiting to suck close games away from Houston.

So while we project the Texans to miss the playoffs and do poorly, our projection system isn't actually calling for much to change. It expects the defense to be good, it expects the offense and special teams units to continue to be bad, and it expects the Texans to have a record more commensurate with those underlying factors. It doesn't see Watson as a savior, and without that boost, it can't figure out where this team is going to get better.

Through January, smoke was billowing about O'Brien potentially being fired or leaving for a different job. O'Brien never exactly quashed those rumors, saying after the Oakland win: "Yeah, no, I have a five-year contract here. I have two years left on my contract. I'm looking forward to coaching here, and I'm looking forward to getting ready for this next game." Longtime general manager Rick Smith has been rumored to either be getting kicked up the front office or fired multiple times over the last five years.

Right now, the Texans look very much like a team that has gambled their future on Watson reinvigorating a dead passing offense. It could work, but it's more likely to work in the longer term. Rookie quarterbacks being good right away is a hard thing for projection systems to catch on to, and we have no empirical data that points to Watson excelling immediately. We also have a lot of evidence proving that the other teams in this division have gotten better. The Colts finally got rid of their dead-end general manager and stopped fielding an AARP defense. The Jaguars are building a great defense and are only tied to Blake Bortles for one more year. The Titans are relying a lot on green defenders, but have become a much scarier team on the other side of the ball. These are some of the things that O'Brien may begin to see show up on tape this year, rather than abstract analytical terms.

And given just how much draft capital is tied up in this year being a success, it would not at all be shocking if this team found itself with an entirely new leadership base at this time next year. From a statistical standpoint, they're sittin' sideways, and the boys are in a daze.

Rivers McCown

2016 Texans Stats by Week

Wk	vs.	W-L	PF	PA	YDF	YDA	TO	Total	Off	Def	ST
1	CHI	W	23	14	344	258	0	-8%	-22%	-16%	-3%
2	KC	W	19	12	351	291	+1	-31%	-39%	-28%	-20%
3	at NE	L	0	27	284	282	-3	-28%	-29%	-12%	-11%
4	TEN	W	27	20	359	320	-1	16%	-15%	-18%	13%
5	at MIN	L	13	31	214	351	-1	-94%	-45%	23%	-26%
6	IND	W	26	23	414	392	0	7%	7%	-3%	-4%
7	at DEN	L	9	27	271	347	-2	-48%	-11%	29%	-7%
8	DET	W	20	13	269	289	-1	-36%	-25%	8%	-2%
9	BYE										
10	at JAC	W	24	21	273	327	+2	-6%	7%	8%	-5%
11	at OAK	L	20	27	354	325	-1	-14%	-17%	-9%	-6%
12	SD	L	13	21	353	302	-3	-32%	-16%	15%	-1%
13	at GB	L	13	21	307	309	0	-22%	-9%	5%	-8%
14	at IND	W	22	17	316	348	+2	-6%	-31%	-18%	7%
15	JAC	W	21	20	387	150	-1	-21%	-30%	-25%	-16%
16	CIN	W	12	10	250	294	+1	-8%	-31%	-27%	-4%
17	at TEN	L	17	24	289	236	0	-3%	-28%	-36%	-11%
18	OAK	W	27	14	291	203	+3	34%	-20%	-64%	-10%
19	at NE	L	16	34	302	377	0	-18%	-42%	-26%	-2%

Trends and Splits

	Offense	Rank	Defense	Rank
Total DVOA	-21.2%	30	-5.8%	9
Unadjusted VOA	-18.2%	30	-3.4%	13
Weighted Trend	-18.7%	29	-6.0%	11
Variance	2.1%	1	3.7%	8
Average Opponent	1.6%	31	2.4%	6
Passing	-19.5%	30	-4.7%	5
Rushing	-19.1%	27	-7.2%	18
First Down	-22.1%	30	-3.2%	14
Second Down	-19.1%	28	-3.7%	12
Third Down	-22.7%	28	-13.4%	8
First Half	-34.3%	32	-7.1%	9
Second Half	-19.8%	26	-21.8%	2
Red Zone	-42.1%	31	-1.6%	18
Late and Close	-20.6%	29	-30.7%	3

Five-Year Performance

Year	W-L	Pyth W	Est W	PF	PA	TO	Total	Rk	Off	Rk	Def	Rk	ST	Rk	Off AGL	Rk	Def AGL	Rk	Off Age	Rk	Def Age	Rk	ST Age	Rk
2012	12-4	10.2	8.3	416	331	+12	6.7%	11	0.1%	16	-14.2%	4	-7.7%	32	6.7	1	30.6	19	28.1	6	26.5	22	26.4	11
2013	2-14	4.2	3.9	276	428	-20	-26.5%	30	-18.9%	29	2.5%	18	-5.1%	29	35.1	18	28.6	18	27.5	9	26.2	22	25.7	26
2014	9-7	9.8	6.7	372	307	+12	-4.5%	19	-6.8%	21	-6.2%	6	-3.9%	28	18.8	6	41.1	20	27.2	12	26.0	28	26.1	17
2015	9-7	8.8	7.8	339	313	+5	-4.8%	18	-8.5%	24	-9.3%	8	-5.7%	32	49.8	26	15.0	3	26.5	17	26.2	24	25.8	20
2016	9-7	6.5	4.6	279	328	-7	-21.9%	29	-21.2%	30	-5.8%	9	-6.5%	31	51.8	27	40.0	20	25.7	30	26.5	17	26.2	12

2016 Performance Based on Most Common Personnel Groups

HOU Offense					HOU Offense vs. Opponents					HOU Defense				HOU Defense vs. Opponents			
Pers	Freq	Yds	DVOA	Run%	Pers	Freq	Yds	DVOA	Run%	Pers	Freq	Yds	DVOA	Pers	Freq	Yds	DVOA
11	61%	5.4	-12.2%	29%	Base	29%	4.0	-32.7%	56%	Base	34%	5.4	-7.0%	11	58%	5.9	0.1%
12	15%	4.2	-22.0%	44%	Nickel	51%	5.4	-15.2%	36%	Nickel	38%	5.3	-9.0%	12	17%	4.1	-28.2%
21	7%	4.3	-25.7%	59%	Dime+	17%	5.4	-4.4%	15%	Dime+	24%	6.0	-4.8%	21	10%	5.7	-3.7%
611	4%	3.2	-69.2%	73%	Goal Line	2%	0.3	18.5%	88%	Goal Line	2%	0.4	13.4%	611	3%	4.7	-34.9%
20	3%	5.8	-43.2%	59%	Big	1%	2.5	-65.9%	92%	Big	3%	4.6	16.6%	22	3%	8.6	64.0%
22	3%	4.4	-22.9%	86%										621	2%	3.4	-7.9%

Strategic Tendencies

Run/Pass		Rk	Formation		Rk	Pass Rush		Rk	Secondary		Rk	Strategy		Rk
Runs, first half	42%	8	Form: Single Back	78%	19	Rush 3	11.8%	7	4 DB	34%	11	Play-action	17%	21
Runs, first down	45%	20	Form: Empty Back	6%	21	Rush 4	56.4%	27	5 DB	38%	31	Avg Box (Off)	6.23	8
Runs, second-long	43%	3	Pers: 3+ WR	67%	13	Rush 5	26.6%	6	6+ DB	24%	6	Avg Box (Def)	6.29	9
Runs, power sit.	56%	16	Pers: 2+ TE/6+ OL	27%	17	Rush 6+	5.3%	20	CB by Sides	74%	17	Offensive Pace	30.50	16
Runs, behind 2H	26%	17	Pers: 6+ OL	8%	7	Sacks by LB	51.6%	14	S/CB Cover Ratio	22%	27	Defensive Pace	32.02	29
Pass, ahead 2H	42%	29	Shotgun/Pistol	67%	14	Sacks by DB	6.5%	19	DB Blitz	5%	27	Go for it on 4th	1.26	6

The Texans threw 31 percent of passes to tight ends, the highest rate in the league, after throwing just 13 percent of passes to tight ends in 2015. They also threw a league-low 12 percent of passes to No. 3 and "other" wide receivers. Theoretically, that number should go up if Braxton Miller is healthier. ▪ The Texans ran on second-and-long more than any other team except San Francisco, even though they were horrible at it: 3.8 yards per carry and minus-58.9% DVOA. ▪ Houston receivers ranked 31st with just 3.9 average yards after the catch, after ranking dead last with 3.8 in 2015. ▪ Another problem was a lack of broken tackles. For the second straight year, the Texans ranked dead last in broken-tackle rate, although they did improve from breaking tackles on just 5.8 percent of plays to breaking tackles on 7.5 percent of plays. ▪ The Texans were horrendous on play-action passes, with a league-low minus-40.2% DVOA. In his limited sample, Savage (-43.5%) was actually worse than Osweiler (-39.7%). ▪ The Texans were also dismal when they used an extra offensive lineman. They did this on 8.2 percent of plays, seventh in the league, but averaged just 2.1 yards per play with minus-51.5% DVOA. ▪ However, the Texans defense was as good on play-action as the offense was bad. The Texans allowed just 5.7 yards per pass with minus-31.5% DVOA on play-action passes, leading the league in both figures. Jacksonville was the only other defense to allow less than 6.9 yards per pass on play-action. These stats are even more remarkable considering that the Texans had the exact opposite gap in 2015, when they allowed 9.0 yards per pass on play-action but only 5.0 average yards on other passes. ▪ The Texans defense was fantastic when it sent extra pressure. The Texans allowed 7.0 yards per pass with the standard four pass-rushers, but that dropped to 5.9 yards with five pass-rushers and just 3.3 yards with six or more. ▪ Houston's adjusted sack rate on third down (9.2 percent, sixth) was more than double what it was on first or second down (4.3 percent, 31st). ▪ Houston opponents threw a league-high 28 percent of passes to their No. 1 receivers. ▪ Houston gave up 330 yards on penalties for defensive pass interference; no other team was above 255 yards.

Passing

Player	DYAR	DVOA	Plays	NtYds	Avg	YAC	C%	TD	Int
B.Osweiler*	-558	-26.8%	535	2739	5.1	3.9	59.5%	15	15
T.Savage	31	-5.4%	78	432	5.5	3.7	63.0%	0	0

Rushing

Player	DYAR	DVOA	Plays	Yds	Avg	TD	Fum	Suc
L.Miller	-28	-11.5%	246	1014	4.1	5	0	46%
A.Blue	30	2.0%	67	318	4.7	1	0	54%
B.Osweiler*	44	30.5%	17	144	8.5	2	0	-
A.Hunt	12	12.5%	16	88	5.5	0	0	44%
J.Grimes*	5	6.7%	14	86	6.1	0	0	29%

Receiving

Player	DYAR	DVOA	Plays	Ctch	Yds	Y/C	YAC	TD	C%
D.Hopkins	43	-9.3%	151	78	951	12.2	3.3	4	52%
W.Fuller	-15	-14.8%	92	47	630	13.4	4.7	2	51%
B.Miller	-79	-48.3%	28	15	99	6.6	3.5	1	54%
J.Strong	-32	-29.5%	24	14	131	9.4	2.3	0	58%
K.Mumphery*	-11	-24.2%	12	10	69	6.9	2.0	0	83%
W.Williams	7	0.2%	7	4	75	18.8	3.3	0	57%
C.Fiedorowicz	-67	-18.8%	89	54	559	10.4	3.9	4	61%
R.Griffin	-77	-22.9%	74	50	442	8.8	3.4	2	68%
S.Anderson	17	8.0%	16	11	93	8.5	3.5	1	69%
L.Miller	-1	-14.4%	39	31	199	6.4	6.0	1	79%
J.Grimes*	-5	-18.2%	18	13	94	7.2	6.4	0	72%
A.Blue	-42	-59.7%	16	12	40	3.3	2.3	0	75%

Offensive Line

Player	Pos	Age	GS	Snaps	Pen	Sk	Pass	Run	Player	Pos	Age	GS	Snaps	Pen	Sk	Pass	Run
Greg Mancz	C	25	16/16	1121	3	0.5	5	6	Derek Newton	RT	30	6/6	358	1	2.5	6	1
Chris Clark	RT	32	16/14	1079	14	5.5	22	5	Oday Aboushi*	LG	26	4/3	269	1	0.0	3	2
Xavier Su'a-Filo	LG	26	16/15	1056	2	5.0	11	4	Kendall Lamm	OT	25	15/3	166	0	3.0	4	1
Jeff Allen	RG	27	14/14	889	5	4.0	10	8	Breno Giacomini*	RT	32	5/5	267	5	1.0	5	1
Duane Brown	LT	32	12/12	778	1	0.0	6	6									

Year	Yards	ALY	Rank	Power	Rank	Stuff	Rank	2nd Lev	Rank	Open Field	Rank	Sacks	ASR	Rank	Press	Rank	F-Start	Cont.
2014	4.07	3.97	23	67%	13	21%	25	1.07	22	0.80	12	26	4.9%	8	24.8%	19	15	39
2015	3.79	4.06	18	65%	16	19%	9	1.02	25	0.47	29	36	6.3%	17	21.3%	8	18	24
2016	4.14	4.16	15	61%	18	16%	6	1.14	16	0.61	20	32	5.6%	12	30.2%	27	7	29

2016 ALY by direction:	Left End 4.47 (14)	Left Tackle 4.85 (5)	Mid/Guard 4.13 (17)	Right Tackle 3.53 (24)	Right End 3.95 (16)

The big news on the offensive line is that the Texans will be without the services of right tackle Derek Newton, who had the incredible misfortune of tearing both patellar tendons on the same play in Denver. He has already been placed on injured reserve. There are a couple of candidates to man his spot. Incumbent Chris Clark, who replaced Newton last year after the injury, had a rough season, ranking 28th among 34 right tackles in snaps per blown block. Late free-agent addition Breno Giacomini has been average at best with the Seahawks and Jets, but might provide more in the running game. ☞ The long-term hope is that fourth-round pick Juli'en Davenport (Bucknell) develops into something. Davenport proved he's got the athleticism to be a left tackle in the NFL after putting up a 20-yard shuttle time of 4.69 seconds and a 3-cone drill of 7.57 seconds at the Senior Bowl. But Davenport made it to the fourth round because, in the words of college football fans everywhere, he ain't played nobody. Davenport could slide in at right tackle in the near term while the Texans wait out the end of stellar left tackle Duane Brown's career. Brown skipped out on OTAs in a contract dispute, as he has no more guaranteed money remaining over the final two years of his deal. ☞ Inside there will likely be a shake-up as 2016 second-rounder Nick Martin returns from an ankle injury that put him out for his rookie year. Martin was drafted as a center, which puts 2015 UDFA Greg Mancz on the spot after he started all of last year. Mancz has the speed, if not the size, to be a solid center. However, if the Texans divvy things out on pure merit, they might consider having Martin start at guard. Former Chiefs guard Jeff Allen was brutal in the first year of his four-year, $28 million deal and has lost 20 pounds this offseason. Xavier Su'a-Filo, the guy the Texans picked instead of Derek Carr or Teddy Bridgewater, has become a decent run blocker but still struggles with pass protection.

Defensive Front Seven

Defensive Line	Age	Pos	G	Snaps	Plays	Overall TmPct	Rk	Stop	Dfts	BTkl	Runs	St%	vs. Run Rk	RuYd	Rk	Sack	Pass Rush Hit	Hur	Dsrpt
Vince Wilfork*	36	DT	15	507	22	3.1%	72	18	6	6	21	81%	34	1.7	27	0.0	3	6	0
Christian Covington	24	DE	16	415	27	3.6%	62	19	6	7	24	71%	63	2.9	66	1.0	2	7	1
D.J. Reader	23	DT	16	404	23	3.1%	73	21	9	1	20	90%	11	1.4	13	1.0	1	10	1
Antonio Smith*	36	DE	13	246	4	0.7%	--	3	1	0	3	67%	--	3.0	--	0.5	5	7	1
Joel Heath	24	DE	12	234	8	1.4%	--	7	2	0	5	80%	--	2.6	--	2.0	2	4	0

Edge Rushers	Age	Pos	G	Snaps	Plays	Overall TmPct	Rk	Stop	Dfts	BTkl	Runs	St%	vs. Run Rk	RuYd	Rk	Sack	Pass Rush Hit	Hur	Dsrpt
Whitney Mercilus	27	OLB	15	869	54	7.7%	13	34	21	3	40	60%	91	2.9	62	7.5	14	31	3
Jadeveon Clowney	24	DE	14	736	53	8.1%	8	42	22	5	41	80%	24	1.1	11	6.0	12	33	4
John Simon*	27	OLB	11	518	52	10.1%	1	35	12	6	31	74%	48	3.1	71	3.5	6	13	2

Linebackers	Age	Pos	G	Snaps	Plays	Overall TmPct	Rk	Stop	Dfts	BTkl	Runs	St%	vs. Run Rk	RuYd	Rk	Sack	Pass Rush Hit	Hur	Tgts	vs. Pass Suc%	Rk	AdjYd	Rk	PD	Int
Benardrick McKinney	25	ILB	16	915	130	17.3%	11	67	18	10	78	56%	72	3.9	63	5.0	6	8	36	48%	42	7.7	64	2	0
Brian Cushing	30	ILB	13	611	65	10.6%	50	38	8	4	45	73%	8	3.2	30	0.0	3	6	15	37%	74	7.8	65	0	0
Sio Moore	27	ILB	8	412	66	16.1%	15	40	9	8	40	70%	15	3.0	18	0.0	2	4	18	48%	41	6.4	37	1	0

Year	Yards	ALY	Rank	Power	Rank	Stuff	Rank	2nd Level	Rank	Open Field	Rank	Sacks	ASR	Rank	Press	Rank
2014	4.10	3.75	6	43%	1	26%	2	1.14	16	0.98	28	35	5.3%	28	29.1%	3
2015	3.71	3.32	2	62%	13	27%	2	1.05	8	0.87	21	36	5.7%	27	29.3%	3
2016	3.30	3.58	3	61%	13	23%	6	0.95	3	0.31	2	48	7.5%	3	32.1%	2

2016 ALY by direction:	Left End 4.00 (14)	Left Tackle 3.54 (7)	Mid/Guard 3.48 (3)	Right Tackle 3.85 (11)	Right End 3.45 (12)

J.J. Watt practiced with no restrictions at OTAs. If Watt comes back to the Texans as prime J.J. Watt, this unit is terrifying. They were just fine without him in 2016 as Jadeveon Clowney blossomed and Whitney Mercilus continued to show improvement as a pass-rusher. Even with a hampered Watt, the Texans project as an above-average pass-rushing group, given that they maintained almost the exact same pressure rate from 2015. ≡ Houston got a two-sack game from Joel Heath inside in Week 17, and he projects as someone to watch athletically. ≡ Vince Wilfork retired, but the Texans got a nice first season out of Clemson's D.J. Reader, and he should be beefy enough to plug the middle of the defense. ≡ Christian Covington played a lot in Watt's absence last year, and is solid depth if nothing you can dream on at this point. ≡ One question about this unit is who will replace the departed John Simon at outside linebacker on run downs. Clowney has stood up outside before and done okay, but it might limit his pass-rushing ability. Brennan Scarlett is the incumbent backup at the position, though he's not really getting talked up much after playing just 113 snaps in his rookie season. Another option could be to use second-rounder Zach Cunningham (Vanderbilt) inside early. Cunningham is the first Texans linebacker you can credibly say has the coverage skills to handle the middle of the field, a big problem for the team that was exposed by the Patriots in their playoff loss. The reason Cunningham slipped to the second round is he weighed in at just 234 pounds at the combine, and will face a transition as a tackler in the NFL. Bernardrick McKinney was a second-team All-Pro in his second season, but is better getting after the quarterback than covering, which is an odd combination of traits for a middle linebacker and might be an interesting fit outside on run downs. Brian Cushing is still a punishing hitter, even at 30 years old, but has lost a step after a multitude of injuries. If Cunningham can learn to tackle like Cushing, he'll replace him sooner rather than later.

Defensive Secondary

Secondary	Age	Pos	G	Snaps	Plays	TmPct	Rk	Stop	Dfts	BTkl	Runs	St%	Rk	RuYd	Rk	Tgts	Tgt%	Rk	Dist	Suc%	Rk	AdjYd	Rk	PD	Int
Andre Hal	25	FS	15	813	53	7.5%	58	19	9	12	26	35%	50	8.2	57	21	5.9%	6	13.7	32%	69	10.0	55	7	2
A.J. Bouye*	26	CB	15	722	78	11.1%	6	37	19	4	15	20%	78	8.5	65	73	23.4%	72	11.5	59%	6	6.4	13	16	1
Kareem Jackson	29	CB	14	720	66	10.0%	16	30	12	5	15	27%	70	6.1	31	67	21.5%	63	11.6	51%	34	8.3	62	4	1
Quintin Demps*	32	SS	13	693	63	10.3%	34	30	14	4	32	47%	22	6.2	30	25	8.4%	36	12.8	48%	28	8.5	33	10	6
Johnathan Joseph	33	CB	13	619	53	8.7%	41	20	7	7	10	30%	65	5.9	27	59	22.0%	68	11.7	46%	60	7.4	38	8	0
Corey Moore	24	FS	16	392	26	3.5%	74	10	1	5	13	46%	24	5.2	14	11	6.5%	16	9.1	38%	56	11.2	63	3	0
Kevin Johnson	25	CB	6	288	24	8.5%	--	8	2	1	4	50%	--	4.5	--	23	18.6%	--	9.3	56%	--	6.0	--	4	0
Eddie Pleasant	29	SS	14	249	22	3.3%	--	11	10	3	7	29%	--	7.7	--	18	16.8%	--	7.2	67%	--	4.0	--	4	0

Year	Pass D Rank	vs. #1 WR	Rk	vs. #2 WR	Rk	vs. Other WR	Rk	vs. TE	Rk	vs. RB	Rk
2014	6	1.0%	16	-39.4%	1	4.5%	21	-24.1%	3	-8.6%	11
2015	7	-7.6%	8	10.7%	23	-39.3%	1	-11.6%	9	2.2%	18
2016	5	1.8%	17	-38.1%	2	1.8%	17	-40.6%	2	23.3%	28

Here's where things start to get a bit sketchy. Johnathan Joseph has had a terrific career and is a rare example of a free-agent signing that completely paid off. He's also 33 with 50-year-old legs, and seems to get hurt every other week, despite playing at least 13 games each of his six seasons in Houston. After losing A.J. Bouye to the Jaguars, the Texans will likely turn to Kareem Jackson as the second corner. In his prime, Jackson was a pretty good player, but he had a down 2016 and spent the whole off-season trying to dodge rumors that he was moving to safety. Kevin Johnson, Houston's first-round pick in 2015, missed most of last season with a foot issue and could be asked to play outside rather than inside if Jackson is found wanting. The upside is that Johnson has been pretty stellar when he has been on the field. Next man up is probably fifth-round rookie Treston DeCoud (Oregon State), a cousin of former NFL safety Thomas DeCoud. This DeCoud has all the physical attributes of a good press-man corner, but didn't show the play skill for it last year. ☜ More than one outside observer has remarked that the Texans have the worst safety group in the league. Free safety Andre Hal is a horrendous open-field tackler whose 27.9 percent missed tackle rate was third-worst among defenders with at least 30 tackles last season. The strong safety battle between K.J. Dillon, Eddie Pleasant, and Corey Moore also doesn't inspire much in the way of hope. This could be a spot where the Texans look to sign a veteran free agent as training camps open. ☜ Houston lost Quintin Demps to the Bears in free agency. Did you know that Quintin Demps got an All-Pro vote at safety? It's amazing what a few right-spot, right-time interceptions will do for you.

Special Teams

Year	DVOA	Rank	FG/XP	Rank	Net Kick	Rank	Kick Ret	Rank	Net Punt	Rank	Punt Ret	Rank	Hidden	Rank
2014	-3.9%	28	0.5	15	-2.0	19	-5.2	27	-6.5	24	-6.1	27	2.3	13
2015	-5.7%	32	-3.7	27	1.0	12	-2.6	24	-15.1	31	-8.1	32	5.6	9
2016	-6.5%	31	-5.9	26	-12.9	32	-7.5	30	-13.0	30	6.7	6	1.4	15

Let's approach this section with the same amount of effort the Texans have approached fixing their special teams.

Wait, we have to write something? Well, let's say this for the Texans special teams: they do have some good pieces to work with. Jonathan Weeks has been a good long snapper. When they let Will Fuller return punts, he immediately took a 67-yarder to the house. Tyler Ervin has the skills to be a good punt returner as well. Shane Lechler still has a big leg even after qualifying for AARP. The Texans just make a lot of mental errors and aren't able to field a full squad of good special teamers. There's a reason Houston's special teams unit has finished in the bottom five of DVOA each of the past five seasons, including three last-place finishes. ☜ Kicker Nick Novak will be pushed in training camp by Ka'imi Fairbairn, who is surprisingly not an NPC in any MMO sidequests that we know of. The UCLA grad's full name is John Christian Ka'iminoeauloameka'ikeokekumupa'a Fairbairn. ☜ Akeem Hunt is the favorite to return kicks if he makes the roster, though the Texans might be better off seeing what else the bottom of the roster can produce for them in this area.

Indianapolis Colts

2016 Record: 8-8	Total DVOA: -4.6% (23rd)	2017 Mean Projection: 7.6 wins	On the Clock (0-4): 12%
Pythagorean Wins: 8.5 (16th)	Offense: 3.7% (12th)	Postseason Odds: 35.1%	Mediocrity (5-7): 38%
Snap-Weighted Age: 26.7 (12th)	Defense: 12.5% (29th)	Super Bowl Odds: 2.7%	Playoff Contender (8-10): 37%
Average Opponent: -3.9% (28th)	Special Teams: 4.1% (5th)	Proj. Avg. Opponent: -2.4% (29th)	Super Bowl Contender (11+): 14%

2016: The judge calls *The State of This Franchise v. Andrew Luck*, all sides come to order.

2017: They can't help but improve somewhere, but they might have more baggage to shed before the AFC South is afraid again.

There's a lot of revisionist history in the air about Andrew Luck these days, which is no surprise. Special quarterbacks are supposed to transcend their situations forever and not have excuses made for them. They're not supposed to get hurt or stay hurt. And, most importantly, they are supposed to win no matter what. The no-win vultures have been circling the Colts after two lost campaigns, squawking about how Luck isn't what they thought he was. That maybe the media was too hasty in declaring him the next great quarterback.

Let's put Luck aside for a minute, and put him in bubble wrap for the sake of Colts fans, then look at the franchise assets that aren't Luck.

If you were looking to declare one NFL owner the most Donald Trump, Jim Irsay would be that owner. He's got a history of erratic behavior even beyond the well-known incident where he was pulled over with a briefcase full of drugs and cash. A 2014 *Outside the Lines* piece about "The Shadow Life" of Irsay detailed his long affair with a woman who overdosed, his troubles with painkiller addiction, and the way his Twitter trivia contests helped create a new affair with a married woman. As a football publication, we're not here to trash a man who clearly has needed and received a lot of help dealing with himself over the years. Irsay had more money than he knew what to do with after his father passed away when Jim was 37. He hasn't had many people hold him accountable, because this stage of American capitalism is an exercise in captive listening to rich people who don't really know what they're doing. These are, if not excuses for his behavior, at least contributing factors that were beyond his control.

As a young owner, Irsay was gifted Bill Polian and Tony Dungy. He learned a lot about stability. And he has desperately tried to hang on to that idea even as the Colts, talent-depleted from years of bad Polian drafting in the 2010s, found themselves flying high with Luck and making the AFC Championship Game in 2014. It was a place they didn't belong, and it was a place where the Patriots easily dispatched them even though all anyone remembers from that game is talking about the ideal gas law for months afterward.

NFL sources are always talking, and were questioning the job security of head coach Chuck Pagano and general manager Ryan Grigson for the last two seasons. The only problem with this is that Irsay is the guy they need the actual scoop from, and it's pretty hard to read Irsay. So even though a plu-

rality of well-sourced people thought Grigson and Pagano would and should both be gone after 2015, they had to preface that analysis with ¯_(ツ)_/¯. Irsay took to Twitter after a six-game suspension to these words: "What can I say? I could say something, but nothing IS something; nothing isn't nothing, if I say it; it's something. No things are nothing things." And that's just who he is. That is the kind of public persona he embraces. There is nothing Irsay could say or do that would surprise anybody who follows the league.

Irsay tried to have Grigson and Pagano stay together for the kids last year. It didn't work. Grigson's roster continued to lack both depth and stars, and Pagano's coaching is straight out of the 1980s in a way that is particularly distasteful to Colts fans who watched Peyton Manning conduct one of the best offenses in modern NFL history. Because of Irsay's stubbornness in insisting that Pagano can get it right, he has handicapped a bad roster with a coach that Bill Belichick can play like a fiddle.

Into this situation came new general manager Chris Ballard, who has been a well-regarded front office prospect for some time. He came up as a scout with the Bears, then ran Kansas City's personnel and football ops departments for four years before getting the call from Irsay. Ballard immediately went to work tearing up the Colts defense, one of the saddest things in the NFL last year. On paper, it sure looks like the Colts won't be starting a single defensive player in 2017 who started their 2016 opener (Table 1).

How sad was that Colts front seven last year? Out of their top five linebackers (the four listed plus Trent Cole), only Sio Moore even has an NFL job as of training camp. Cole, Robert Mathis, Erik Walden, and D'Qwell Jackson were a unique combination of old, bad, and overpaid. Zach Kerr was miscast as a starter because Arthur Jones, another huge free-agent bust, was too hurt and/or suspended to even make the opening day roster. Henry Anderson's torn ACL in the middle of 2016 left the team with veteran stopgap Kendall Langford at end, and David Parry was just the latest in a long line of Colts draft picks at nose tackle who proved inadequate.

And while the defense definitely looks better when perennial Pro Bowl corner Vontae Davis isn't hurt, the opening secondary was just as bad. Mike Adams was coming off two years as a Pro Bowl alternate, but it's risky to trust a 35-year-old safety. He's in Carolina now. Patrick Robinson is a last-gasp

2017 Colts Schedule

Week	Opp.	Week	Opp.	Week	Opp.
1	at LARM	7	JAC	13	at JAC
2	ARI	8	at CIN	14	at BUF
3	CLE	9	at HOU	15	DEN (Thu.)
4	at SEA	10	PIT	16	at BAL (Sat.)
5	SF	11	BYE	17	HOU
6	at TEN (Mon.)	12	TEN		

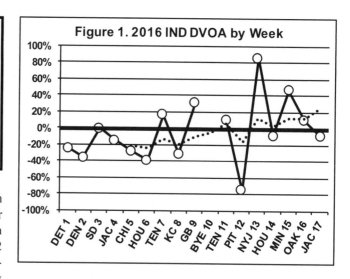

Figure 1. 2016 IND DVOA by Week

veteran in Philadelphia. Antonio Cromartie is another addition to the tally of Colts defenders who haven't found a job for 2017. T.J. Green was quickly dispatched in favor of Clayton Geathers, and Darryl Morris is a depth cornerback. Of the 12 starters—given the proliferation of three-wide sets, the "starting lineup" really includes both base and nickel sets—only four have a legitimate shot at starting a game for the Colts this year: Parry, Langford, Green, and Morris.

It may not surprise you to learn that the Colts lost their opener, 39-35, to a team that finished 15th in offensive DVOA. It may actually surprise you that three teams finished with a worse defensive DVOA than Indianapolis, although to be fair, most of the upward pull was replacing clearly out-of-their-depth veterans with youngsters and seeing what happened.

The offense around Luck has some legitimate talent, but, again, is muted by Pagano's direction. Pagano, from the moment he arrived in Indianapolis, has wanted the Colts to be a run-first offense that sustains drives. It's the reason that they traded a first-round pick for Trent Richardson, and it's the reason that they brought in Hall of Fame candidate Frank Gore after Richardson reached his absolute floor as an NFL player.

The problem, though, is that Gore was 33 years old last season. He's 34 as you're reading this. Gore is a beast of a player, and it's amazing that he's still able to handle the workload he does at his age, given that other star backs of his era (such as Edgerrin James and Steven Jackson) were effectively done in their early thirties. But it is an inconvenient truth for Pagano that Gore has little burst left at this point. He's a low-upside

Table 1. Colts Opening Day Defense, 2016 vs. 2017

2016		Projected 2017	
DE	Zach Kerr	DE	Henry Anderson
DT	David Parry	DT	Johnathan Hankins
DE	Kendall Langford	DE	Hassan Ridgeway
OLB	Robert Mathis	OLB	Jabaal Sheard
OLB	Erik Walden	OLB	John Simon
ILB	Sio Moore	ILB	Antonio Morrison
ILB	D'Qwell Jackson	ILB	Sean Spence
CB	Patrick Robinson	CB	Vontae Davis
CB	Antonio Cromartie	CB	Quincy Wilson
NB	Darryl Morris	NB	Rashaan Melvin
SS	T.J. Green	SS	Clayton Geathers
FS	Mike Adams	FS	Malik Hooker

player with little going for him beyond his top-notch mental approach to running.

The Colts saw how slow they were in the backfield and still decided to let Gore and street free agent Robert Turbin combine for 392 offensive touches out of 982 rushes and targets the Colts had last year. That's nearly 40 percent of the total offensive workload being distributed to two players who, to be blunt, had no reason to be a focal point of the offense at this point in their careers.

Then there was the receiving depth, a perennial problem for the Luck-era Colts dating back to the days of Griff Whalen and Darrius Heyward-Bey. Dwayne Allen, traded to the Patriots this offseason, somehow never seemed to be appreciated by the coaching staff for his gifts as a receiver. Coby Fleener was allowed to leave in free agency after a few lackluster years. Donte Moncrief, a solid receiver the Colts should still have some long-term hope for, was hurt and missed half the season. Phillip Dorsett, a deep "threat" in that he threatens to sometimes catch a deep pass, has been an absolute waste of a first-round pick. The Colts have invested a ton of premium picks on this area and are right back where they started from: asking low-round and undrafted afterthoughts like Jack Doyle and Chester Rogers to assume real roles in the offense. Sometimes your general manager finds enough hidden gems that this works, and sometimes you employ Grigson and wind up throwing 47 passes at Frank Gore.

Ballard has a wildly complicated task in front of him over these next few years. He has an owner who could change the plan at any moment. He has a coach who has shown little aptitude for the modern NFL. And he has a roster that, despite the presence of Luck and T.Y. Hilton, is a rebuilding project.

Then there's the question of Luck's actual health. Luck had offseason surgery on labrum damage in his throwing shoulder, which was rumored to have been dogging Luck for much of last season. When Luck will actually be able to return to the field is an open question. And it should be noted that there is a lot of risk in Luck's optimal game. He buys a lot of time in the pocket, and isn't afraid to run outside the pocket and take shots. (It is funny, though, to watch the people who complained about RG3 not sliding stay mum or redirect the blame for Luck's injuries to the offensive line.) All reports say that Luck will be ready at the beginning of the season. Luck has said that he feels great, but hasn't thrown a football yet as we go to press. Irsay said in June that Luck was "healing tremendously," which is only one step removed from healing bigly.

Ballard has been able to turn over an impressive amount of the roster so far, even if we assume he won't hit on every pick and signing. Most of his moves have been smart plays, not desperate grabs to validate scouting missteps, like Grigson's dreadful Walden signing. The Colts are a strong bounce-back candidate this season. They have one of the weakest schedules in the NFL, and they have the quarterback who can erase a lot of problems if he is right and healthy. They also play in a division where anything is possible, which is always a big help.

But for the Colts to make an immediate beeline to the play-offs would take some things going right even beyond Luck's health. It would take an immediate reconsolidation by a defense that, in many ways, is pieced together on the fly without any continuity. It would take a healthy supporting cast around Luck. It would probably require fourth-round rookie Marlon

Mack to show some juice and make hay out of Pagano's preferred offensive style. That's a lot of change necessary for a team that hasn't changed much at all over the four years since it drafted Luck.

At the very least, this year can be a step in the right direction for the Colts. Even if all they get out of this season are some good Ballard finds, some good fortune on Luck's shoulder, and an easy path to firing Pagano, they can still be well positioned to take advantage of Luck's talent in the long term. That's a damned sight better than where they were ten months ago, when they were in Year 4 of Grigson's tour of veteran presents.

Luck showed off plenty of his early-career witchcraft last season. As long as he's healthy, all he needs from this organization are for Irsay, Ballard, and Pagano to give him the tools and resources to take the Colts to a better place.

The jury is still out on Ballard, but so far, the other two have proven that they can't be trusted to do anything. No things are nothing things, as a famous philosopher once said.

Rivers McCown

2016 Colts Stats by Week

Wk	vs.	W-L	PF	PA	YDF	YDA	TO	Total	Off	Def	ST
1	DET	L	35	39	450	448	0	-25%	26%	55%	5%
2	at DEN	L	20	34	253	400	-1	-36%	-5%	29%	-2%
3	SD	W	26	22	410	352	+1	-1%	-8%	-5%	2%
4	at JAC	L	27	30	284	331	-1	-16%	-9%	14%	7%
5	CHI	W	29	23	396	522	+1	-28%	-17%	37%	26%
6	at HOU	L	23	26	392	414	0	-40%	1%	42%	2%
7	at TEN	W	34	26	422	331	+1	16%	31%	14%	-1%
8	KC	L	14	30	277	422	-2	-31%	-21%	0%	-10%
9	at GB	W	31	26	355	405	-1	31%	10%	6%	27%
10	BYE										
11	TEN	W	24	17	327	351	-1	11%	-1%	-13%	-1%
12	PIT	L	7	28	310	369	-2	-75%	-37%	39%	0%
13	at NYJ	W	41	10	421	250	+2	86%	46%	-19%	22%
14	HOU	L	17	22	348	316	-2	-9%	-4%	-6%	-11%
15	at MIN	W	34	6	411	282	+3	46%	18%	-22%	7%
16	at OAK	L	25	33	390	463	-3	10%	28%	23%	4%
17	JAC	W	24	20	384	470	0	-9%	10%	9%	-10%

Trends and Splits

	Offense	Rank	Defense	Rank
Total DVOA	3.7%	12	12.5%	29
Unadjusted VOA	1.4%	13	9.8%	28
Weighted Trend	6.3%	12	6.2%	24
Variance	4.6%	10	5.4%	18
Average Opponent	-0.6%	11	-3.1%	27
Passing	13.6%	17	17.9%	26
Rushing	1.2%	10	4.5%	32
First Down	-7.5%	25	11.7%	29
Second Down	27.3%	3	20.9%	31
Third Down	-12.2%	24	-1.2%	15
First Half	-4.8%	21	10.1%	26
Second Half	11.5%	9	7.9%	26
Red Zone	4.5%	13	-14.2%	6
Late and Close	0.5%	18	11.6%	23

Five-Year Performance

Year	W-L	Pyth W	Est W	PF	PA	TO	Total	Rk	Off	Rk	Def	Rk	ST	Rk	Off AGL	Rk	Def AGL	Rk	Off Age	Rk	Def Age	Rk	ST Age	Rk
2012	11-5	7.2	6.2	357	387	-12	-16.0%	25	-2.9%	18	14.0%	31	0.9%	12	44.4	24	43.1	24	25.9	28	26.6	20	25.2	31
2013	11-5	9.4	9.5	391	336	+13	3.2%	13	4.3%	13	0.9%	16	-0.1%	18	75.5	30	25.2	11	25.8	31	27.7	4	26.0	20
2014	11-5	10.2	8.8	458	369	-5	4.5%	13	-1.1%	17	-2.3%	13	3.3%	8	56.6	29	48.2	23	26.2	28	28.3	1	26.1	12
2015	8-8	6.0	5.5	333	408	-5	-12.9%	23	-15.6%	30	-2.2%	13	0.5%	16	22.0	6	43.1	26	27.1	13	28.6	1	26.3	11
2016	8-8	8.5	7.0	411	392	-5	-4.6%	23	3.7%	12	12.5%	29	4.1%	5	27.3	9	51.1	24	25.8	27	28.0	2	25.9	20

2016 Performance Based on Most Common Personnel Groups

IND Offense					IND Offense vs. Opponents					IND Defense				IND Defense vs. Opponents			
Pers	Freq	Yds	DVOA	Run%	Pers	Freq	Yds	DVOA	Run%	Pers	Freq	Yds	DVOA	Pers	Freq	Yds	DVOA
11	61%	6.2	9.6%	23%	Base	37%	5.6	5.3%	49%	Base	30%	5.6	0.4%	11	62%	6.6	22.8%
12	31%	5.8	11.3%	46%	Nickel	53%	6.4	14.9%	26%	Nickel	51%	6.5	18.1%	12	12%	6.9	8.8%
13	5%	3.8	-25.1%	69%	Dime+	8%	5.0	-10.6%	5%	Dime+	16%	6.6	25.9%	21	8%	4.4	-22.7%
02	1%	9.5	72.5%	0%	Goal Line	1%	0.4	-13.7%	79%	Goal Line	1%	0.6	38.2%	611	3%	5.5	13.7%
622	1%	0.5	9.3%	100%						Big	2%	4.5	-40.8%	10	3%	5.2	-20.4%

Strategic Tendencies

Run/Pass		Rk	Formation		Rk	Pass Rush		Rk	Secondary		Rk	Strategy		Rk
Runs, first half	35%	28	Form: Single Back	73%	25	Rush 3	13.4%	5	4 DB	30%	16	Play-action	20%	10
Runs, first down	40%	32	Form: Empty Back	10%	7	Rush 4	58.5%	23	5 DB	51%	26	Avg Box (Off)	6.21	13
Runs, second-long	23%	27	Pers: 3+ WR	62%	24	Rush 5	20.9%	18	6+ DB	16%	8	Avg Box (Def)	6.09	26
Runs, power sit.	42%	30	Pers: 2+ TE/6+ OL	39%	3	Rush 6+	7.2%	9	CB by Sides	79%	16	Offensive Pace	30.36	15
Runs, behind 2H	24%	24	Pers: 6+ OL	1%	28	Sacks by LB	71.9%	4	S/CB Cover Ratio	28%	12	Defensive Pace	29.48	4
Pass, ahead 2H	50%	15	Shotgun/Pistol	60%	22	Sacks by DB	0.0%	30	DB Blitz	10%	14	Go for it on 4th	1.11	14

Respect for the Colts running game dropped, as opponents went from an average of 6.37 men in the box in 2015 (fifth) to 6.09 in 2016 (26th). ⬤ The Colts ranked dead last with just 84 broken tackles, the second straight year they were 30th or worse. ⬤ The Colts had just six plays we marked as wide receiver or tight end screens, the lowest figure in the league. ⬤ The Colts' adjusted sack rate on offense increased from 6.6 percent on first and second down (tenth) to 10.6 percent on third down (third). ⬤ Indianapolis had a strange reverse home-field advantage on offense, ranking third in offensive DVOA on the road but 23rd at home. (We write this just because it's interesting; it doesn't really have any predictive value for the upcoming season.) ⬤ Indianapolis had the league's biggest yardage gap between defense against multi-back runs (3.6 yards per carry, -11.9% DVOA) and defense against single-back runs (5.3, 8.3%). The Colts had a similarly large gap in both 2014 and 2015. ⬤ The Indianapolis defense couldn't bring pressure no matter how many pass-rushers it sent. Even with a blitz, the Colts had a pressure rate of just 24 percent, two-thirds of the NFL average.

Passing

Player	DYAR	DVOA	Plays	NtYds	Avg	YAC	C%	TD	Int
A.Luck	719	7.3%	586	3958	6.8	4.9	64.0%	31	13
S.Tolzien	-59	-33.6%	40	196	4.9	3.5	62.2%	1	2

Rushing

Player	DYAR	DVOA	Plays	Yds	Avg	TD	Fum	Suc
F.Gore	114	4.2%	208	797	3.8	5	0	48%
A.Luck	97	33.8%	40	318	8.0	2	0	-
R.Turbin	50	23.0%	30	98	3.3	6	0	53%
J.Ferguson	-31	-71.6%	13	19	1.5	0	0	15%
J.Todman*	21	101.5%	5	40	8.0	0	0	60%
C.Michael	52	-0.6%	148	583	3.9	7	1	49%

Receiving

Player	DYAR	DVOA	Plays	Ctch	Yds	Y/C	YAC	TD	C%
T.Y.Hilton	360	17.3%	155	91	1448	15.9	3.8	6	59%
P.Dorsett	107	10.2%	59	33	528	16.0	4.5	2	56%
D.Moncrief	50	-1.9%	56	30	307	10.2	2.6	7	54%
C.Rogers	51	5.4%	34	19	276	14.5	2.8	0	56%
D.Street*	-20	-61.1%	6	1	20	20.0	2.0	0	17%
K.Aiken	-11	-15.5%	50	29	328	11.3	3.4	1	58%
J.Doyle	131	18.7%	75	59	584	9.9	4.2	5	79%
D.Allen*	108	21.8%	52	35	406	11.6	3.4	6	67%
E.Swoope	85	46.7%	22	15	297	19.8	8.9	1	68%
F.Gore	40	0.7%	48	39	274	7.0	7.6	4	81%
R.Turbin	-1	-14.2%	35	26	179	6.9	8.4	1	74%
J.Ferguson	14	-3.7%	25	20	136	6.8	8.1	0	80%
C.Michael	-44	-40.1%	29	22	109	5.0	5.6	1	76%

Offensive Line

Player	Pos	Age	GS	Snaps	Pen	Sk	Pass	Run	Player	Pos	Age	GS	Snaps	Pen	Sk	Pass	Run
Anthony Castonzo	LT	29	16/16	1076	4	5.0	16	2	Denzelle Good	RG	26	12/10	606	4	5.5	12	3
Ryan Kelly	C	24	16/16	1020	3	1.5	7	1	Jonotthan Harrison*	C	26	13/4	451	2	2.0	9	1
Joe Haeg	G/T	24	15/14	953	4	4.5	14	1	Joe Reitz	RT	32	13/6	423	5	3.0	7	0
Jack Mewhort	LG	26	10/10	669	3	0.0	4	2	Le'Raven Clark	OT	24	8/3	200	1	0.0	3	0

Year	Yards	ALY	Rank	Power	Rank	Stuff	Rank	2nd Lev	Rank	Open Field	Rank	Sacks	ASR	Rank	Press	Rank	F-Start	Cont.
2014	3.91	4.21	16	52%	31	19%	15	1.20	13	0.46	29	29	4.8%	7	22.6%	12	20	19
2015	3.52	3.78	27	60%	24	23%	24	0.99	29	0.48	28	37	6.1%	16	25.8%	18	12	26
2016	3.83	4.69	2	63%	15	13%	1	1.01	28	0.26	32	44	7.6%	28	33.3%	31	18	24
2016 ALY by direction:			Left End 3.81 (24)			Left Tackle 4.19 (19)			Mid/Guard 5.32 (1)			Right Tackle 3.72 (21)			Right End 3.41 (21)			

The butt of many jokes over the last few years, the Colts offensive line actually turned the corner in 2016—at least when it came to run-blocking. First-round center Ryan Kelly helped spearhead a unit that had the lowest stuff rate in the NFL. Imagine if they had someone to block for. ❧ As bad as Grigson had been at assembling a defense, it's true that he nailed a lot of his offensive line picks. Jack Mewhort, mercifully moved off right tackle, has been a very good left guard while healthy. Anthony Castonzo had one of his better years and is a capable left tackle. ❧ To the extent that the Colts were bad on the line, it mostly came because of replacement players subbing in for the injured, and what happened on the right side of the line. So, naturally, that right side is a bit more in-flux for 2017. 2015 seventh-round pick Denzelle Good started most of last year and struggled, but 2016 fifth-round find Joe Haeg showed quite a bit in his limited action, particularly as a run blocker. Behind both of them is last year's third-round pick, Le'Raven Clark, who has the athleticism to be a great tackle. Ultimately, Indianapolis' best combination might be to put Clark at right tackle and Haeg inside at guard. But Good may get some more rope to play his way out of the comfy space that Pagano often affords his guys. ❧ Another youngster to monitor here is fourth-round wide-load Zach Banner (USC), who has weighed as much as 385 pounds and could be a nice fit as a drive-blocking guard. He'll have to adjust after playing tackle in college, but most scouts didn't believe he had the athleticism to stay on the edge.

Defensive Front Seven

Defensive Line	Age	Pos	G	Snaps	Plays	TmPct	Rk	Stop	Dfts	BTkl	Runs	St%	Rk	RuYd	Rk	Sack	Hit	Hur	Dsrpt
						Overall							vs. Run				Pass Rush		
David Parry	25	DT	16	645	47	5.8%	24	30	6	3	42	62%	82	3.3	77	3.0	5	6	0
Hassan Ridgeway	23	DE	16	445	22	2.7%	81	19	5	1	17	88%	16	1.6	22	1.5	4	9	2
Arthur Jones*	31	DE	8	323	30	7.4%	10	16	1	0	30	53%	86	3.4	83	0.0	0	2	0
Zach Kerr*	27	DT	12	318	19	3.1%	--	18	8	3	15	100%	--	0.5	--	2.5	6	6	0
Henry Anderson	26	DE	11	309	14	2.5%	84	12	1	3	12	83%	26	3.8	86	0.0	7	8	2
T.Y. McGill	25	DT	13	298	7	1.1%	--	7	6	2	3	100%	--	0.3	--	2.0	6	12	1
Johnathan Hankins	25	DT	16	764	43	5.1%	35	35	12	5	38	79%	41	2.3	44	3.0	6	15	0
Al Woods	30	DT	12	248	18	3.0%	--	13	5	2	16	81%	--	2.2	--	0.0	0	3	0

Edge Rushers	Age	Pos	G	Snaps	Plays	TmPct	Rk	Stop	Dfts	BTkl	Runs	St%	Rk	RuYd	Rk	Sack	Hit	Hur	Dsrpt
						Overall							vs. Run				Pass Rush		
Erik Walden*	32	OLB	16	761	42	5.2%	43	29	16	5	24	63%	86	5.1	100	11.0	8	13	1
Robert Mathis*	36	OLB	14	534	19	2.7%	94	13	7	0	11	73%	56	3.1	73	5.0	2	10	1
Akeem Ayers	28	OLB	16	365	20	2.5%	--	13	3	3	12	75%	--	2.7	--	2.0	3	7	0
Jabaal Sheard	28	DE	15	580	36	4.9%	49	28	12	7	17	76%	37	2.5	48	5.0	4	26	1
John Simon	27	OLB	11	518	52	10.1%	1	35	12	6	31	74%	48	3.1	71	3.5	6	13	2
Margus Hunt	30	DE	15	322	16	2.0%	--	13	5	5	11	82%	--	1.1	--	0.0	5	8	2

Linebackers	Age	Pos	G	Snaps	Plays	TmPct	Rk	Stop	Dfts	BTkl	Runs	St%	Rk	RuYd	Rk	Sack	Hit	Hur	Tgts	Suc%	Rk	AdjYd	Rk	PD	Int
						Overall							vs. Run				Pass Rush				vs. Pass				
D'Qwell Jackson*	34	ILB	12	708	80	13.1%	40	42	6	14	58	62%	51	3.9	58	1.0	1	3	21	38%	70	8.8	76	3	0
Edwin Jackson	26	ILB	16	497	60	7.4%	71	28	3	6	31	52%	80	5.5	86	2.0	0	2	17	44%	53	6.6	41	0	0
Antonio Morrison	23	ILB	16	333	45	5.5%	--	19	3	4	31	55%	--	3.6	--	0.0	1	2	10	21%	--	13.8	--	0	0
Sean Spence	27	ILB	15	505	53	7.1%	73	27	7	3	22	64%	41	3.2	31	3.0	2	2	24	55%	24	6.0	28	4	0

Year	Yards	ALY	Rank	Power	Rank	Stuff	Rank	2nd Level	Rank	Open Field	Rank	Sacks	ASR	Rank	Press	Rank
2014	4.20	4.34	22	67%	20	20%	15	1.23	23	0.68	15	41	7.3%	9	22.7%	24
2015	4.16	4.08	17	59%	9	20%	18	1.05	9	1.00	27	35	5.7%	28	26.5%	11
2016	4.81	4.83	31	48%	2	16%	28	1.42	31	0.82	21	33	6.3%	13	19.0%	32

2016 ALY by direction:	Left End 3.49 (10)	Left Tackle 5.98 (32)	Mid/Guard 4.67 (29)	Right Tackle 4.81 (26)	Right End 6.14 (31)

Earlier in the chapter we discussed the old guys; now let's meet the replacements. ☙ Up front the Colts got a kick start on rebuilding their run defense when the Giants and Johnathan Hankins found themselves in a contract stalemate. Hankins, like Dontari Poe, seemed to misread the market on nose tackles and rooted down for a bigger deal. In the end, the Colts snagged him for just $16.9 million in guarantees on a three-year, $30 million deal. Hankins should be a centerpiece in the middle of Pagano's 3-4 after posting career-bests in hurries and defeats in 2016. ☙ The Colts also reeled in Cincinnati kick-blocker Margus Hunt, nominally a defensive lineman, and former Titans nose tackle Al Woods. However, the player the Colts would most like to see manning a spot next to Hankins is a healthy Henry Anderson, who kicked people around as a rookie before tearing his ACL late in the season. ☙ There's a lot of highly drafted youth on this roster, but perhaps no one as intriguing as fourth-rounder Grover Stewart. Stewart put up some very interesting workout numbers, including a 7.71 3-cone drill time at 347 pounds. That's a faster time at a higher weight than Dontari Poe, B.J. Raji, and Haloti Ngata had coming out of college. Stewart, though, was a fourth-round pick, because he went to Albany State. ☙ On the edges, the Colts are relying on three free-agent pickups. Jabaal Sheard had a bizarre year in New England, starting eight games as the Patriots' top pass-rusher but also getting benched for entire games by Bill Belichick. Sheard is more of a 1B pass-rusher than a true No. 1, but that's closer to average than what the Colts had in 2016. John Simon, signed away from the rival Texans, sets a good edge and cleans up with hustle sacks. Barkevious Mingo looked like a future star in his first year in Cleveland and we've all spent the three years since wondering what the hell happened. The Colts will get a chance to find out! ☙ Third-round pick Tarrell Basham (Ohio) was an interesting selection. He was highly productive in college, but has no real experience winning by bending the edge and plays very stiff at times. His combine performances show someone who should at least have a chance at being an average pass-rusher, but he might take some development time. ☙ At inside linebacker, Sean Spence has always had the athleticism to be a good coverage linebacker, but his body simply refuses to stay healthy. The Colts could desperately use a full season from Spence, as only the Saints were worse at covering running backs last season. ☙ Antonio Morrison is a two-down, downhill stuffer, and went underdrafted because a severe knee injury hampered his play at Florida. ☙ Northwestern's Anthony Walker, a fifth-round pick in this year's draft, is a guy most NFL teams want to see lose a little weight. Either he follows in Morrison's footsteps, or becomes more of a special teams maven for his first few seasons.

Defensive Secondary

Secondary	Age	Pos	G	Snaps	Plays	TmPct	Rk	Stop	Dfts	BTkl	Runs	St%	Rk	RuYd	Rk	Tgts	Tgt%	Rk	Dist	Suc%	Rk	AdjYd	Rk	PD	Int
						Overall						vs. Run					vs. Pass								
Mike Adams*	36	SS	15	998	81	10.6%	30	18	7	7	37	24%	68	9.8	65	29	6.7%	21	8.4	34%	66	10.1	57	0	0
Vontae Davis	29	CB	14	823	47	6.6%	78	21	6	4	4	75%	2	2.0	1	69	19.2%	50	14.6	54%	17	6.9	22	10	1
Rashaan Melvin	28	CB	15	655	67	8.8%	37	23	5	6	20	35%	54	6.3	36	67	23.6%	75	10.1	46%	62	7.3	33	9	0
Clayton Geathers	25	SS	9	561	63	13.8%	6	28	10	5	28	50%	16	5.2	15	34	14.0%	71	8.9	49%	27	8.4	31	4	0
T.J. Green	22	FS	15	479	45	5.9%	69	14	8	5	14	43%	30	8.4	58	29	14.0%	70	13.9	39%	55	10.2	58	2	0
Darius Butler	31	CB	12	472	40	6.6%	--	17	8	9	5	20%	--	10.6	--	31	15.1%	--	12.3	58%	--	8.6	--	7	3
Patrick Robinson*	30	CB	7	401	30	8.4%	--	7	2	5	7	14%	--	7.1	--	36	20.4%	--	13.8	43%	--	7.8	--	5	0
Darryl Morris	27	CB	12	360	40	6.6%	--	13	5	1	10	30%	--	7.4	--	25	15.7%	--	11.6	43%	--	9.6	--	6	1

Year	Pass D Rank	vs. #1 WR	Rk	vs. #2 WR	Rk	vs. Other WR	Rk	vs. TE	Rk	vs. RB	Rk
2014	10	-11.8%	9	-7.4%	11	-2.6%	14	16.1%	26	29.0%	31
2015	12	-4.8%	11	-10.5%	11	23.4%	30	6.5%	20	-7.9%	11
2016	26	13.7%	29	-3.3%	12	-1.1%	14	33.1%	31	38.5%	31

The Colts started off their draft with back-to-back secondary selections, and even Ballard seemed surprised to see Ohio State's Malik Hooker still on the board at 15. Hooker got this sum up from the man who drafted him: "I thought Hooker was the best athlete in the draft. And he's got a unique skill set. He's got size. He's got speed. He's got great instincts and ball skills. And guys that can take away the football are hard to find, and we think he can do that at this level." ☙ Second-rounder Quincy Wilson from Florida is a press corner at 6-foot-1, 211 pounds. Wilson has a few bad habits to break: he's a gambler, and his overly contact-prone style may lead to some early bumps. ☙ It was bound to happen sooner or later—Vontae Davis had a down year. After ranking in the top 10 in adjusted success rate the last three years, Davis fell all the way to 20th! Dealing with ankle issues, hip issues, and a concussion probably helped contribute in some small way. Regardless, Davis is the one defensive player the Colts have who can play with anybody, no questions asked. ≈ Clayton Geathers had a very nice rookie season, but was not practicing at all at OTAs after undergoing neck surgery in March. Should he be unable to go, the primary backups will be slot corner/safety hybrid Darius Butler, who has been a rare example of a solid role player in Indianapolis, and T.J. Green—if they can get the burn marks off his uniform after last year's performance. Rashaan Melvin was decent outside when pressed into service and should be the third corner at the start of the season.

Special Teams

Year	DVOA	Rank	FG/XP	Rank	Net Kick	Rank	Kick Ret	Rank	Net Punt	Rank	Punt Ret	Rank	Hidden	Rank
2014	3.3%	8	8.4	4	4.9	9	0.4	14	11.2	6	-8.5	31	2.4	12
2015	0.5%	16	4.5	8	4.8	5	-1.2	18	-0.1	19	-5.6	26	6.9	6
2016	4.1%	5	8.9	4	1.6	12	9.0	4	3.5	10	-2.3	21	4.4	10

With long-time punter Pat McAfee retired, the Colts have only clutch kicker Adam Vinatieri to call their own. Vinatieri broke the NFL record for consecutive field goals made, and though that's less impressive in a domed stadium, it's still quite a feat for the oldest man in the NFL. However, without McAfee, the Colts will no longer have a booming leg who can hide Vinatieri from kickoffs. Jeff Locke (Ex-Vikings) and Rigoberto Sanchez (UDFA from Hawaii) will have a camp battle for the punter role, with the winner a potential kickoff specialist as well. ≈ The Colts rotated through a bevy of returners last year, with nobody getting more than 16 returns on either kicks or punts. Quan Bray was slated to be the main returner, but broke his ankle in October. Coming off an injury and with a new sheriff in the front office, it's no guarantee he'll get the job back. Chester Rogers returned punts after Bray went down, and Jordan Todman returned most of the kicks. Todman was not retained, however, so it's possible the role will fall to someone like Josh Ferguson.

Jacksonville Jaguars

2016 Record: 3-13	Total DVOA: -10.4% (26th)	2017 Mean Projection: 7.5 wins	On the Clock (0-4): 13%
Pythagorean Wins: 5.8 (27th)	Offense: -11.3% (27th)	Postseason Odds: 32.9%	Mediocrity (5-7): 39%
Snap-Weighted Age: 25.7 (30th)	Defense: -3.1% (12th)	Super Bowl Odds: 2.3%	Playoff Contender (8-10): 36%
Average Opponent: -1.7% (25th)	Special Teams: -2.3% (23rd)	Proj. Avg. Opponent: -2.5% (31st)	Super Bowl Contender (11+): 13%

2016: One more chance for Gus yields yet another high pick

2017: One more chance for Blake yields…

Something changed in Jacksonville last season. For the first time in five years, and just the second time in the past decade, the Jaguars fielded a quality defense. Some of the young talent from all those high picks shined, as Jalen Ramsey confounded those positional questions and our perennial doubt about the rookie impact of corners with a fine season. Third-rounder Yannick Ngakoue led the team in sacks, providing some of the pass-rush that previous first-round pick Dante Fowler did not. Yet there they were again in late April, with their fifth consecutive top-five pick in the draft.

With yet another failed season, there were unsurprising consequences. The defensive improvement was not enough to save Gus Bradley, whose indefatigable enthusiasm came to ring hollow, and he was sent packing with the nine-game losing streak that dropped the Jaguars to 2-12. Enter Doug Marrone, initially on an interim basis and then after season's end with the full-time tag. Enter as well, again, Tom Coughlin. No, general manager Dave Caldwell, you get to stick around, at least for now. Coughlin is, officially, Executive Vice President of Football Operations. Unofficially, well, the fact that Coughlin's introductory press conference started five minutes before its official start in non-Coughlin time said all that was needed. Anybody who missed the news got a reminder when the new offensive line coach was Tom Flaherty, Coughlin's assistant with the Giants, rather than Marrone compadre Kevin Mawae.

The much-improved defense meant it was easy to pinpoint the team's failings on a particular source: the offense. Most of the NFL commentariat expected further offensive improvement after Blake Bortles threw for 35 touchdowns and the Jaguars ranked 14th in the league in points scored in 2015. But that improvement never happened. The offense sputtered. Bortles' nominally impressive 2015 campaign was revealed to be just garbage-time production.

Last season's offensive disappointment was most apparent in close games, where Jacksonville went 2-8 in games decided by no more than 7 points. From a failed fourth-and-1 against Green Bay in the season opener to opportunities squandered in the season finale against Indianapolis, the Jaguars repeatedly failed to either burn clock to protect a late lead or take advantage of late-game comeback opportunities. But these games suggest that the Jaguars are in the same position as most other losing teams, with a long list of "if onlys" that suggest where and how the results could greatly improve.

That recap should not be so surprising. These are the Jaguars that perennially appear on May lists of "most improved teams," not the near-expansion squads left in the wake of Gene Smith. Only the truly dreadful or the truly great manage to escape their share of close games, and most of those come down to a play, a series, a drive managed well or mismanaged by one team or the other. Really, Jacksonville's struggles on offense were not so hard to fathom. Our team projections in *Football Outsiders Almanac 2016* forecast the Bortles-led squad with a minus-10.9% DVOA, 29th in the league. Their actual minus-11.4% DVOA was 27th. We foresaw the defensive surge as well: they were projected at minus-1.4% (12th) and ended up at minus-3.1% (13th). What did we see that everybody missed? Well, perhaps everything.

Our numbers struck a note of caution on Bortles two years ago. Despite the 35 touchdowns and more than 4,400 passing yards, Bortles' minus-9.9% DVOA put him 25th in the league among qualifying passers. Our metrics marked him as still a below-average quarterback, no matter how many points he accumulated for your fantasy team. 2016 saw no progression in his game, as Bortles posted an identical minus-9.9% passing DVOA.

There are four key questions about Bortles we need to answer. First, why are our numbers telling us that he was equally good in 2015 and 2016 when conventional wisdom says otherwise? Second, what are we to make of this apparent stagnation? Third, what about the public perception that Bortles is a garbage-time player? Does he really play better with the game out of reach? Fourth, can the Jaguars help mitigate Bortles' weaknesses by building their offense around a power running game led by first-round pick Leonard Fournette?

The first question has a number of easy answers, starting with opponent adjustments. The Jaguars faced an easier than average schedule of pass defenses in 2015 and a tougher than average one in 2016. Bortles also improved in 2016 when it came to turnovers and sacks. He threw fewer interceptions on more pass attempts (though Cian Fahey in his *Pre-Snap Reads Quarterback Catalogue* charted him with the fourth-highest total of interceptable passes in the league). And Bortles and the Jaguars offense ranked ninth in adjusted sack rate in 2016 at 5.3 percent after ranking 25th at 7.9 percent in 2015 and last-place 11.3 percent in Bortles' rookie season. This seems to be an area where there has been genuine growth in his game over his first three seasons.

2017 Jaguars Schedule

Week	Opp.	Week	Opp.	Week	Opp.
1	at HOU	7	at IND	13	IND
2	TEN	8	BYE	14	SEA
3	BAL (U.K.)	9	CIN	15	HOU
4	at NYJ	10	LACH	16	at SF
5	at PIT	11	at CLE	17	at TEN
6	LARM	12	at ARI		

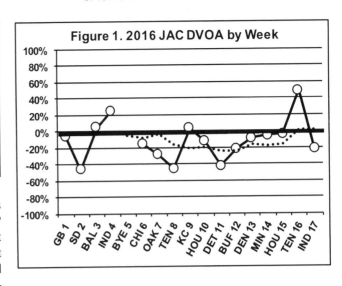

Figure 1. 2016 JAC DVOA by Week

Second, who are some other pedigreed young quarterbacks who stagnated at a below average (by DVOA) level early on? Table 1 collects some of the names that seemed most relevant from the history of DVOA (1986-present). The most recent name on that list is fairly interesting. While Ryan Tannehill was not a disaster as a rookie like Bortles was, he posted back-to-back seasons of basically identical DVOA before improving some the next season, only to revert back to his prior performance level the next two seasons. Like Bortles, Tannehill was a high pick but was widely considered to be in need of seasoning and development when he was drafted.

Table 1. Bortles Passing DVOA v. Comparable Quarterbacks, Years 1-5

Player	B.Bortles	R.Tannehill	Da.Carr	J.Losman	D.McNabb	C.Miller
Year 1	-40.7%	-9.9%	-47.4%	N/A	-51.6%	-50.8%
Year 2	-9.9%	-9.8%	-7.0%	-41.5%	-1.4%	-10.0%
Year 3	-9.9%	4.1%	-3.2%	-9.0%	-3.7%	-8.2%
Year 4	--	-10.6%	-29.2%	-12.7%	-0.8%	-0.1%
Year 5	--	-11.6%	-8.2%	-62.3%	5.4%	13.5%

The other quarterbacks on Table 1 were more like Bortles, though, miserable in their first action before improving greatly. Their fates are much more of a mixed bag. J.P. Losman only had one full season as a starter, his third; his fifth season was his last as a significant player. If pressure can ruin a passer, David Carr's failure to develop can be blamed on the disaster that was the expansion Texans' offensive line. Donovan McNabb (a controversial choice as the second overall pick, and the second quarterback in a QB-heavy draft) and Chris Miller (the 13th overall pick by the Falcons) are the encouraging examples. After plateauing in his first two seasons as a primary starter, Miller came with the sort of steady progression you find in handbooks, while McNabb bounced around average until breaking through in his sixth season with Terrell Owens when the Eagles made it to the Super Bowl. By itself, this sort of agglomeration of names suggests that Bortles' fate is far from written—he could improve, stay the same, or get worse. That answer is, of course, thoroughly unsatisfying, but it at least does suggest he is not doomed.

Third, is Bortles a garbage-time player? Some of the stats make this easy to answer. Much of his statistical production—58 of his 69 career touchdown passes—have come with the Jaguars trailing, many of those by multiple scores. He was

also a better passer while trailing by more than a touchdown the past two seasons. Yet the unexpected lesson of Table 2 is that, by DVOA, quarterbacks are not normally better when their teams are trailing. Bortles is. What should we make of this?

Table 2. Passing DVOA by Score Margin

	Down 8-plus	Leading or Score within 7
Bortles 2015	-5.1%	-12.8%
NFL Average 2015	-0.6%	0.2%
Bortles 2016	23.0%	-27.3%
NFL Average 2016	-6.6%	2.4%

The details of what may be going on seem to be interesting. The split seems to run across personnel packages and situations, so it is not as simple as "a power running game with the quarterback under center will make Bortles better" or "just play more three-wide receiver sets." Rather, a couple counterintuitive points come up. First, Bortles' sack rate goes down when trailing, when the league's sack rate goes up. The difference here is not too large—from 5.8 percent adjusted sack rate to 4.5 percent, when the league went from 5.9 percent to 6.5 percent in 2016—but it does suggest Bortles' play style is affected. Second, his overall success rate goes up. NFL quarterbacks, as a group, posted identical 46 percent success rates in both score situations in 2016, but Bortles' was 51 percent when down multiple scores and just 39 percent otherwise. This greater success when trailing remains when looking at all kinds of statistical splits: at different depth of passes, from at or behind the line of scrimmage to bombs, to the left, right, or middle, and to backs, tight ends, and receivers.

That brings us to the fourth question: How much might Bortles be helped by Jacksonville's decision to draft Fournette with the fourth overall selection and attempt to refashion the offense more around a sustaining ground game than around Bortles' arm? Part of the problem is that this was already supposed to be last offseason's plan, with T.J. Yeldon and Chris Ivory leading the lightning-and-thunder attack. It proved to be a comprehensive failure. The offensive line struggled and both backs were hamstrung by the bad situation rather than transcending it in any way. So enter Fournette with the fourth overall pick as take two, and a statement of who Coughlin and Marrone want to be.

Fournette at LSU was a certain kind of runner, a downhill between-the-tackles physical runner who has drawn comparisons to Adrian Peterson since he was a high school phenom. The LSU Fournette played almost exclusively from under center, and did much better there than he did in shotgun. He often played with a traditional fullback, and indeed the 2017 offseason saw one of those rare creatures again spotted in Duval.

Let us accept what the numbers suggest as true, that Bortles is a better performer down multiple scores. The numbers do not suggest a why, so we enter the realm of speculation. One possible answer is that what Fahey and others write is accurate, that Bortles' biggest problem is an inability to read defenses. His garbage-time performance then might be the result of defenses playing more conservatively and giving him easier-to-read looks. Once a deficit closes, they make his job harder, and he falters. If this is truly the case, the Jaguars have a serious dilemma by midseason, facing a decision to either give up on Bortles to avoid guaranteeing his fifth-year option by injury or to admit the season is over by turning to Chad Henne or Brandon Allen.

But if Bortles' improved garbage-time performance is the result of greater mental comfort on his part, then what the Fournette selection may do is put him in a more comfortable position to succeed before the game reaches garbage time. Some of the time, at least. Every offense, no matter how good, ends up in two-minute drills and other obvious passing situations like third-and-long, and Bortles has no choice but to be better there. And in competitive situations, a Fournette-based offense does not suggest greater success given the makeup of the rest of the Jacksonville roster.

Downhill running plays typically come with a fullback and a tight end (sometimes two) on the field. Yet the brightest spots for the Jaguars offense have been their trio of young receivers.

Allen Robinson and Allen Hurns ranked among the top twenty wideouts in both DYAR and DVOA in 2015, and Marqise Lee did in 2016. All three players are entering their fourth seasons and could be the core of a truly improved offense. Except the selection of Fournette, unless he is a much more prolific and advanced shotgun and passing-downs player than he demonstrated with a Bayou Bengals, ensures they will not be.

If Jacksonville's offensive plan is to use more regular personnel (21 or 12) on early downs, well, they were the second-worst passing offense in the league in those situations last year. With second-round pick Cam Robinson and trade acquisition Brandon Albert added to the offensive line, Fournette may help improve Jacksonville's rushing offense, which also ranked 31st on first and second downs. But at a certain point, it's going to come down to the quarterback. Blake Bortles just has to play better for this team to win more games.

The good news for Jacksonville is that we once again project every team in the AFC South to be below average. The defense could improve even more, and we only have to go back to 2016 to find a team that won this division with a really good defense and an offense every bit as bad as Jacksonville's could be again. Alternatively, any significant defensive regression not coupled with great offensive improvement would give the Jaguars another very high pick. Our most likely scenario, though, is between the two extremes: a 7-9 or 8-8 season, and a draft pick in the low teens. The defense should be solid again, but will probably not be great. The offense will be a little bit better, but not good. Some better luck in close games will help improve the overall record. Next offseason brings a big decision on Bortles. More likely than not, the Jacksonville chapter of *Football Outsiders Almanac 2018* will discuss a Jaguars playoff drought that has reached a decade and the brand-new quarterback who seeks to end it.

Tom Gower

2016 Jaguars Stats by Week

Wk	vs.	W-L	PF	PA	YDF	YDA	TO	Total	Off	Def	ST
1	GB	L	23	27	348	294	-1	-6%	-19%	1%	14%
2	at SD	L	14	38	388	357	-2	-47%	-12%	27%	-8%
3	BAL	L	17	19	216	283	0	4%	-22%	-28%	-2%
4	IND	W	30	27	331	284	+1	25%	-1%	-21%	4%
5	BYE										
6	at CHI	W	17	16	317	389	-2	-16%	-19%	2%	5%
7	OAK	L	16	33	344	344	-3	-29%	-30%	-12%	-11%
8	at TEN	L	22	36	370	494	-1	-46%	3%	47%	-2%
9	at KC	L	14	19	449	231	-4	3%	-6%	-25%	-16%
10	HOU	L	21	24	327	273	-2	-13%	7%	13%	-6%
11	at DET	L	19	26	285	277	-1	-42%	-48%	-20%	-15%
12	at BUF	L	21	28	301	304	0	-21%	-7%	7%	-7%
13	DEN	L	10	20	333	206	-3	-9%	-22%	-15%	-2%
14	MIN	L	16	25	315	377	+1	-6%	9%	5%	-10%
15	at HOU	L	20	21	150	387	+1	-4%	-39%	-10%	24%
16	TEN	W	38	17	415	263	0	49%	19%	-21%	9%
17	at IND	L	20	24	470	384	0	-22%	-7%	3%	-13%

Trends and Splits

	Offense	Rank	Defense	Rank
Total DVOA	-11.3%	27	-3.1%	12
Unadjusted VOA	-11.2%	27	-3.8%	11
Weighted Trend	-10.2%	25	-3.1%	13
Variance	3.2%	4	4.1%	11
Average Opponent	1.2%	26	-0.4%	19
Passing	3.5%	23	5.6%	15
Rushing	-22.7%	28	-13.5%	12
First Down	-5.2%	21	-4.2%	11
Second Down	-3.8%	18	-6.5%	10
Third Down	-34.2%	31	4.1%	22
First Half	-15.2%	30	-6.7%	10
Second Half	-2.8%	17	10.8%	28
Red Zone	14.5%	9	-3.5%	14
Late and Close	3.2%	15	17.7%	28

Five-Year Performance

Year	W-L	Pyth W	Est W	PF	PA	TO	Total	Rk	Off	Rk	Def	Rk	ST	Rk	Off AGL	Rk	Def AGL	Rk	Off Age	Rk	Def Age	Rk	ST Age	Rk
2012	2-14	3.3	2.7	255	444	-3	-33.0%	31	-18.4%	28	11.7%	28	-3.0%	25	63.7	30	36.2	22	26.5	20	27.0	14	25.8	23
2013	4-12	3.1	3.2	247	449	-6	-38.2%	32	-29.8%	32	10.9%	28	2.5%	9	47.3	24	26.8	14	26.6	20	26.2	23	24.7	32
2014	3-13	3.6	3.3	249	412	-6	-29.5%	32	-24.3%	31	1.5%	20	-3.6%	26	33.5	19	44.3	22	24.7	32	26.1	27	25.5	30
2015	5-11	6.2	5.8	376	448	-10	-16.0%	25	-5.4%	21	9.7%	26	-0.9%	20	25.7	12	43.2	27	25.6	30	26.4	22	25.4	29
2016	3-13	5.8	5.4	318	400	-16	-10.4%	26	-11.3%	27	-3.1%	12	-2.3%	23	47.6	26	25.0	10	25.6	31	25.9	28	25.5	26

2016 Performance Based on Most Common Personnel Groups

JAC Offense					JAC Offense vs. Opponents					JAC Defense					JAC Defense vs. Opponents			
Pers	Freq	Yds	DVOA	Run%	Pers	Freq	Yds	DVOA	Run%	Pers	Freq	Yds	DVOA		Pers	Freq	Yds	DVOA
11	75%	5.8	0.8%	26%	Base	23%	4.3	-20.6%	50%	Base	36%	4.9	-0.9%		11	55%	5.6	-4.2%
12	20%	4.0	-27.6%	53%	Nickel	56%	5.5	-0.9%	32%	Nickel	61%	5.6	-2.7%		12	17%	5.2	-1.8%
10	1%	3.4	-7.1%	27%	Dime+	19%	6.1	-6.2%	9%	Dime+	0%	-0.8	-199.9%		21	9%	6.0	11.9%
13	1%	5.4	-16.7%	73%	Goal Line	1%	1.0	15.1%	50%	Goal Line	2%	0.5	-7.9%		13	4%	4.4	9.5%
01	1%	2.7	-166.0%	0%											22	4%	4.8	4.2%
612	1%	2.3	-21.0%	75%														

Strategic Tendencies

Run/Pass		Rk	Formation		Rk	Pass Rush		Rk	Secondary		Rk	Strategy		Rk
Runs, first half	37%	18	Form: Single Back	91%	3	Rush 3	4.1%	25	4 DB	36%	8	Play-action	15%	30
Runs, first down	44%	24	Form: Empty Back	6%	18	Rush 4	71.8%	6	5 DB	61%	14	Avg Box (Off)	6.11	26
Runs, second-long	29%	20	Pers: 3+ WR	77%	7	Rush 5	19.1%	22	6+ DB	0%	30	Avg Box (Def)	6.39	5
Runs, power sit.	31%	32	Pers: 2+ TE/6+ OL	23%	25	Rush 6+	5.0%	22	CB by Sides	62%	27	Offensive Pace	30.08	9
Runs, behind 2H	24%	26	Pers: 6+ OL	2%	27	Sacks by LB	9.1%	25	S/CB Cover Ratio	27%	16	Defensive Pace	30.30	17
Pass, ahead 2H	58%	2	Shotgun/Pistol	75%	6	Sacks by DB	7.6%	14	DB Blitz	9%	19	Go for it on 4th	1.45	5

Jacksonville's use of two-TE sets dropped in half, from 45 percent (fourth) in 2015 to 23 percent (25th) last season. ≡ The Jaguars faced play-action on 23 percent of passes; only San Francisco faced it more often. But the Jaguars defense was excellent on these plays, second in the league with just 6.1 yards allowed per pass and seventh with minus-1.6% DVOA. ≡ Jacksonville's young defense has improved its tackling significantly. In 2015, the Jaguars had 122 broken tackles and ranked 26th in broken-tackle rate. In 2016, they tied the Packers with a league-low 79 broken tackles, and ranked second in broken-tackle rate behind Denver. ≡ Two years ago, the Jaguars allowed a league-low 3.1 yards per pass when they blitzed a defensive back. Last year, even though the Jaguars defense improved overall, they allowed a league-high 10.5 yards per pass when blitzing a defensive back. ≡ Jacksonville led the NFL with 37 penalties and 294 penalty yards on special teams.

Passing

Player	DYAR	DVOA	Plays	NtYds	Avg	YAC	C%	TD	Int
B.Bortles	52	-10.0%	662	3704	5.6	5.1	59.0%	23	16

Rushing

Player	DYAR	DVOA	Plays	Yds	Avg	TD	Fum	Suc
T.J.Yeldon	-78	-25.5%	120	432	3.6	1	0	38%
C.Ivory	-132	-43.0%	93	350	3.8	3	0	41%
B.Bortles	91	30.3%	44	340	7.7	3	0	-
D.Robinson*	-18	-20.7%	37	127	3.4	0	0	41%
M.Lee	16	13.4%	6	35	5.8	0	0	-
C.Grant	-3	-22.0%	5	15	3.0	1	0	40%

Receiving

Player	DYAR	DVOA	Plays	Ctch	Yds	Y/C	YAC	TD	C%
A.Robinson	8	-12.0%	151	73	883	12.1	2.8	6	48%
M.Lee	211	12.2%	105	63	851	13.5	5.5	3	60%
A.Hurns	-71	-24.0%	76	35	477	13.6	6.0	3	46%
B.Walters	70	12.5%	35	25	235	9.4	4.3	2	71%
A.Benn	18	10.6%	10	5	116	23.2	10.6	1	50%
R.Greene	-21	-48.6%	8	5	32	6.4	3.4	0	63%
J.Thomas*	-23	-13.8%	51	30	281	9.4	3.4	4	59%
M.Lewis	-16	-14.8%	30	20	169	8.5	5.3	1	67%
B.Koyack	38	16.6%	24	19	161	8.5	2.4	1	79%
N.Sterling	3	-4.5%	16	12	110	9.2	4.0	0	75%
M.Rivera	23	6.4%	25	18	192	10.7	3.4	1	72%
T.J.Yeldon	-52	-27.9%	68	50	312	6.2	7.1	1	74%
C.Ivory	3	-12.0%	28	20	186	9.3	9.5	0	71%
C.Grant	8	9.3%	7	4	35	8.8	8.0	1	57%

Offensive Line

Player	Pos	Age	GS	Snaps	Pen	Sk	Pass	Run	Player	Pos	Age	GS	Snaps	Pen	Sk	Pass	Run
A.J. Cann	RG	26	16/16	1112	5	2.0	7	7	Chris Reed	LG	25	10/4	334	1	0.0	3	2
Jermey Parnell	RT	31	16/16	1112	12	5.5	14	6	Tyler Shatley	C/G	26	16/4	316	1	2.0	2	5
Kelvin Beachum*	LT	28	15/15	1023	10	6.0	14	7	Luke Joeckel*	LG	26	4/4	221	3	1.0	3	1
Brandon Linder	C	25	14/14	908	2	2.0	5	5	Earl Watford	OL	27	15/11	787	5	4.0	8	2
Patrick Omameh	LG	28	10/7	453	3	0.0	5	1	Branden Albert	LT	33	12/12	721	3	1.5	9	3

Year	Yards	ALY	Rank	Power	Rank	Stuff	Rank	2nd Lev	Rank	Open Field	Rank	Sacks	ASR	Rank	Press	Rank	F-Start	Cont.
2014	3.98	3.76	30	58%	26	21%	22	0.96	27	0.81	10	71	11.3%	32	26.6%	23	8	29
2015	3.80	4.11	16	39%	31	22%	21	1.01	28	0.63	20	51	7.9%	25	27.4%	21	8	41
2016	3.80	3.73	27	58%	24	20%	18	1.06	24	0.55	24	34	5.3%	9	22.2%	7	18	28
2016 ALY by direction:			Left End 4.10 (21)			Left Tackle 3.62 (26)			Mid/Guard 3.96 (25)			Right Tackle 3.08 (30)			Right End 3.09 (27)			

The Fournette-based offense the Jaguars want to run requires the offensive line to be more of a sustaining force than it was in 2016. Post-draft flux everywhere on the line makes that harder to achieve. ☜ Branden Albert, acquired from Miami for Julius Thomas in a swap of players who were deemed surplusage, will replace Kelvin Beachum at left tackle. Albert huffed and puffed about getting a new contract, but eventually reported to minicamp. The 32-year-old has no guaranteed money left on the final two years of his deal, with cap hits of $8.9 million and $9.6 million, making his roster standing potentially vulnerable. ☜ Second-round pick Cam Robinson (Alabama) would likely play left tackle if Albert retires or gets released, and maybe left guard otherwise. Considering many draftniks saw him as more of a right tackle, he will likely need to be protected if he starts on the blind side. Playing him inside would let him uncork his power and make for a softer transition. ☜ Marrone mentioned this offseason that the Jaguars now view right tackle as the second most important offensive line spot, rather than center. He's likely hoping for a cleaner season from Jermey Parnell, who had 12 penalties in the second season of his five-year deal. Like Albert, Parnell has no more fully guaranteed money remaining and can be released at any point without dead money on the cap. ☜ Brandon Linder is Jacksonville's best interior lineman, and worked in OTAs at his old right guard position after playing center in 2016. ☜ A.J. Cann was underwhelming last year, while Patrick Omameh emerged as the best option on the rotating wheel of left guards. Neither is a lineup lock this year. ☜ Luke Bowanko, who missed most of 2016 after labrum surgery, may start at center if Linder plays guard.

Defensive Front Seven

Defensive Line	Age	Pos	G	Snaps	Plays	TmPct	Overall Rk	Stop	Dfts	BTkl	Runs	vs. Run St%	Rk	RuYd	Rk	Sack	Pass Rush Hit	Hur	Dsrpt
Malik Jackson	27	DT	16	717	36	4.5%	42	33	16	5	21	90%	9	0.8	7	6.5	12	29	4
Sen'Derrick Marks*	30	DT	16	537	22	2.8%	79	20	12	0	13	92%	3	0.5	3	3.5	5	12	1
Abry Jones	26	DT	15	465	33	4.4%	45	30	5	0	27	93%	2	1.4	15	0.0	0	8	1
Calais Campbell	31	DE	16	828	58	7.1%	11	45	20	5	40	73%	55	1.9	33	8.0	13	31	7
Stefan Charles	29	DT	12	236	12	2.0%	--	10	2	3	11	82%	--	2.1	--	0.0	2	2	1

Edge Rushers	Age	Pos	G	Snaps	Plays	TmPct	Overall Rk	Stop	Dfts	BTkl	Runs	vs. Run St%	Rk	RuYd	Rk	Sack	Pass Rush Hit	Hur	Dsrpt
Yannick Ngakoue	22	DE	16	706	24	3.0%	89	19	11	2	9	89%	3	2.7	54	8.0	8	21	1
Dante Fowler	23	DE	16	570	37	4.6%	56	33	16	2	22	82%	17	1.4	17	4.0	6	31	5
Tyson Alualu*	30	DE	14	509	35	5.0%	46	28	6	2	31	81%	23	2.8	60	2.5	4	3	0

Linebackers	Age	Pos	G	Snaps	Plays	TmPct	Overall Rk	Stop	Dfts	BTkl	Runs	vs. Run St%	Rk	RuYd	Rk	Sack	Pass Rush Hit	Hur	Tgts	vs. Pass Suc%	Rk	AdjYd	Rk	PD	Int
Paul Posluszny	33	MLB	16	1057	136	17.0%	13	77	26	14	72	65%	33	3.7	48	1.5	2	10	29	63%	7	7.2	54	3	1
Telvin Smith	26	OLB	16	1048	125	15.6%	19	74	27	18	73	62%	54	3.9	65	1.0	1	11	53	66%	5	5.2	15	8	2
Dan Skuta*	31	OLB	13	267	19	2.9%	--	11	4	0	17	59%	--	2.9	--	0.0	2	4	2	0%	--	9.8	--	0	0
Myles Jack	22	OLB	16	239	24	3.0%	--	14	2	1	18	56%	--	6.3	--	0.5	1	1	5	81%	--	1.3	--	2	0

Year	Yards	ALY	Rank	Power	Rank	Stuff	Rank	2nd Level	Rank	Open Field	Rank	Sacks	ASR	Rank	Press	Rank
2014	4.06	3.86	9	70%	24	21%	9	1.05	9	0.88	27	45	8.5%	2	20.1%	31
2015	3.68	3.82	8	68%	19	23%	9	1.11	15	0.58	9	36	5.8%	24	21.7%	30
2016	3.76	3.73	7	64%	18	21%	11	0.96	4	0.74	18	33	5.9%	17	27.2%	15

2016 ALY by direction:	Left End 3.23 (4)	Left Tackle 3.61 (9)	Mid/Guard 4.38 (22)	Right Tackle 2.73 (3)	Right End 2.23 (2)

With a better pass-rush off the edge, the Jaguars front seven would have an argument as one of league's best. As is, it is still an integral part of the much improved defense. ≋ Malik Jackson's 29 hurries ranked fifth among interior linemen, a testament to the consistent pressure he provided. He also upped his run stop rate from his Denver days. ≋ Calais Campbell was this offseason's big addition in the front seven, and he was one of the four linemen with more hurries than Jackson. He may play end in the base four-man sets before kicking inside on third downs. ≋ Abry Jones has become a good rotational run-stuffer. Between Jones, Jackson, Yannick Ngakoue, and Sen'Derrick Marks, the Jaguars had four defensive linemen finish in the top 10 at their position in run stop rate, the most of any team. ≋ Dante Fowler's first real season (after missing 2015 due to injury) is a Rorschach test. If you liked him coming out, his 31 hurries are a sign of greater things to come in 2017. If you were skeptical, the fact that rookie third-rounder Ngakoue surpassed him as the team's primary pass-rusher is telling, and his high hurries-to-sacks ratio is a sign of the limited athleticism that made him only SackSEER's No. 6 edge-rushing prospect in 2015. ≋ Myles Jack was eased into the lineup as a rookie. He will have a bigger role in 2017, replacing Paul Posluszny as the middle linebacker with Poz shifting to the strong side and more of a rotational role. Jack's athleticism was evident as a rookie, but harnessing it properly should be a priority this offseason. The defensive line keeping him clean so he is not forced to beat or run around blockers will also improve his game. ≋ Missed tackles may end up being a fact of life for Telvin Smith, listed at just 215 pounds. As long as his strong work in coverage and improvement in using his athleticism effectively continues, the Jaguars will willingly make that tradeoff. Plus, his broken tackle rate was just 17th among the 42 linebackers with at least 50 solo tackles, part of the overall improvement of tackling in Jacksonville last season.

Defensive Secondary

Secondary	Age	Pos	G	Snaps	Plays	TmPct	Rk	Stop	Dfts	BTkl	Runs	St%	Rk	RuYd	Rk	Tgts	Tgt%	Rk	Dist	Suc%	Rk	AdjYd	Rk	PD	Int
Johnathan Cyprien*	27	SS	16	1070	130	16.3%	2	58	15	9	72	60%	7	4.3	6	52	12.4%	66	9.8	46%	39	8.5	34	6	0
Jalen Ramsey	23	CB	16	1059	79	9.9%	18	38	19	10	16	50%	19	6.9	45	94	22.7%	71	12.0	57%	10	6.4	15	14	2
Tashaun Gipson	27	FS	16	1040	43	5.4%	71	7	5	4	19	21%	70	11.5	71	19	4.6%	1	14.7	28%	73	13.5	73	2	1
Prince Amukamara*	28	CB	14	871	54	7.7%	64	21	7	2	11	36%	52	7.2	52	69	20.3%	58	12.1	45%	73	7.6	45	6	0
Aaron Colvin	26	CB	10	292	22	4.4%	--	10	7	3	2	50%	--	6.0	--	20	17.6%	--	8.3	54%	--	5.7	--	0	0
Davon House*	28	CB	16	272	16	2.0%	--	5	2	2	6	50%	--	4.3	--	22	20.8%	--	13.0	26%	--	10.9	--	0	0
Josh Johnson	28	CB	8	134	10	2.5%	--	5	2	1	3	67%	--	7.0	--	6	10.5%	--	10.1	85%	--	1.8	--	1	0
A.J. Bouye	26	CB	15	722	78	11.1%	6	37	19	4	15	20%	78	8.5	65	73	23.4%	72	11.5	59%	6	6.4	13	16	1
Barry Church	29	SS	12	675	89	14.6%	4	27	11	9	40	38%	43	6.0	23	27	8.3%	34	6.3	43%	46	7.5	22	5	2

Year	Pass D Rank	vs. #1 WR	Rk	vs. #2 WR	Rk	vs. Other WR	Rk	vs. TE	Rk	vs. RB	Rk
2014	17	37.0%	32	-9.8%	10	22.3%	28	5.9%	22	-5.8%	13
2015	31	9.9%	25	13.4%	24	17.7%	26	23.8%	28	14.2%	27
2016	15	0.9%	15	4.4%	19	16.1%	29	-1.9%	16	-28.5%	2

Our standard expectation is that rookie corners, even those with heaps of potential, often struggle as rookies. Jalen Ramsey was an exception. Teams were willing to test him enough to make Ramsey the league's most targeted cornerback, and he used his size and length to make receivers work for the catches they managed to get against him. Ramsey led all rookies in adjusted success rate and passes defensed. ☞ Prince Amukamara was solid opposite him, eschewing the paid vacation mentality former Giants corner Aaron Ross once brought to Duval. The oft-injured cornerback managed to play 14 games and 838 snaps, his highest totals since 2013, but took his talents to Chicago over the offseason. ☞ Ramsey's fine play meant a limited role for 2015 big-money free agent Davon House. Jacksonville cut him and he returned to Green Bay this offseason. ☞ Safety for the Jaguars in 2016 was pretty easy: Tashaun Gipson up top and Johnathan Cyprien down low, thus their charting stats. The difference in average depth of tackle between the two was 7.3 yards, the second-highest total of any safety tandem in the league. Replacing Cyprien with Barry Church should give defensive coordinator Todd Wash more flexibility in how he deploys his safeties in 2017, not that he should necessarily use it. ☞ Aaron Colvin is a solid option as the nickel corner. His 5.2 adjusted yards per pass would have ranked fourth among qualified corners, though he only faced 20 targets in 10 games.

Special Teams

Year	DVOA	Rank	FG/XP	Rank	Net Kick	Rank	Kick Ret	Rank	Net Punt	Rank	Punt Ret	Rank	Hidden	Rank
2014	-3.6%	26	-1.8	21	2.6	12	0.5	12	-13.2	31	-6.2	28	-3.0	23
2015	-0.9%	20	-4.6	29	2.4	10	-0.9	17	-9.3	27	7.8	5	6.0	7
2016	-2.3%	23	0.5	14	0.0	16	8.9	5	-8.9	28	-11.8	32	-3.7	21

Now that he's no longer missing extra points on a biweekly basis (29-of-32, 91 percent after hitting 32-of-39, 81 percent as a rookie), Jason Myers is at least a league-average kicker. His overall field goal rate was ugly at 79 percent, but more than one-third of his attempts (12 of 34) were from 50 yards and beyond. He was above average on kickoffs once again. ☞ Like Bryan Anger the year before, Brad Nortman was fine on gross punt distance but undone by coverage. Jacksonville allowed an estimated 9.4 points above average on punt returns, the worst figure in the league. ☞ Rashad Greene went from second-best punt returner in 2015 to second-worst in 2016, in just eight games. Ball security was a big part of his issue, with four fumbles in the eight games he played, but he was third-worst even with all fumbles removed. His replacement, Bryan Walters, was last in that category. Fourth-round pick Dede Westbrook may have a role to play here, and on kickoff returns, where Marqise Lee (second in return value, but perhaps needed more on offense) and Corey Grant (average) split duties in 2016.

Kansas City Chiefs

2016 Record: 12-4

Pythagorean Wins: 10.1 (4th)

Snap-Weighted Age: 26.0 (28th)

Average Opponent: -1.1% (22nd)

Total DVOA: 13.5% (6th)

Offense: 2.9% (13th)

Defense: -2.8% (14th)

Special Teams: 7.8% (1st)

2017 Mean Projection: 8.3 wins

Postseason Odds: 42.5%

Super Bowl Odds: 5.4%

Proj. Avg. Opponent: 1.6% (7th)

On the Clock (0-4): 8%

Mediocrity (5-7): 30%

Playoff Contender (8-10): 42%

Super Bowl Contender (11+): 20%

2016: A dream season that left fans wanting again.

2017: More likely to play second fiddle in the AFC West this time.

After clinching the AFC West and a first-round bye, they looked prepared as ever for a deep playoff run. Once again, the head coach was getting the most out of his skill players, and thanks to improved play in the secondary, this was the year the team could finally outscore a Tom Brady or Ben Roethlisberger in the playoffs. While skepticism still surrounded the veteran quarterback, there was also optimism— with strong play from the rest of the squad, his risk-averse style could lead them deep into the playoffs. The team was coming off two recent January disappointments, but perhaps the third time would be the charm.

It was not to be. The Steelers came to town and ended another postseason for the team in disappointing fashion. The defense struggled to get stops, and the offense sputtered. Where can this team go from here? The draft brought a surprising trade to move up in the first round and select a gunslinger quarterback. Do his raw skills make up for the fact that he couldn't even lead his college team to a winning record? He may not be the answer this season, but clearly his predecessor's days are numbered.

With a roster that is still very talented, this team should be in the thick of things again, but the question remains: why should we expect this team to outscore New England, Pittsburgh, or even Indianapolis in the AFC playoffs?

While we have been talking about the Kansas City Chiefs all of this time, every word of the last three paragraphs also applies to the Denver Broncos in advance of the 2006 season. In 2005, Mike Shanahan's team finished 13-3, second in the AFC, and quarterback Jake Plummer was playing mistake-free football for a change. Denver was making its third straight playoff appearance, but in the AFC Championship Game the defense was picked apart by Ben Roethlisberger and the Steelers, and Plummer turned into his old self with four giveaways. The Broncos then traded up to the No. 11 pick to select Vanderbilt's Jay Cutler. A 32-year-old Plummer retained his job to start the 2006 season, and the team even started 7-2 thanks to a strong defense. But the offense had fallen off in a major way, and Plummer, who would retire after the season, looked finished. Cutler started the final five games of the season. Denver missed the playoffs at 9-7, and failed to return to the postseason until 2011.

Essentially, the Broncos plateaued in an AFC that had basically the same Super Bowl contenders as it does today: New England and Pittsburgh, plus a young up-and-coming California team, and, to a much lesser extent, Indianapolis. Now Andy Reid's Chiefs have to worry that they are in the same position with a 33-year-old Alex Smith at quarterback: good, but never good enough to take the next step.

2016 sure looked like a golden opportunity for the Chiefs. They began the year with a franchise-record 21-point comeback win over San Diego, and also had a 17-point comeback win in Carolina. They swept an Oakland team that otherwise went 12-1 when Derek Carr started, holding them to 23 points in two games combined. They held Andrew Luck to his season-low scoring output in Indianapolis, winning 30-14. They outscored the No. 1 offense in Atlanta, winning the game 29-28 with a "pick-two" by Eric Berry. They even cracked Denver's No. 1 defense on the road, coming back with a late 75-yard touchdown drive and two-point conversion before winning 30-27 in overtime. On Christmas, the Chiefs completed their sweep of the defending champions by rolling up 484 yards of offense, the most that Denver has allowed in the last three seasons.

With the Patriots missing Rob Gronkowski, there was hope that the Chiefs would be a tougher match for New England than they had been in 2015's divisional-round loss when some of their own best players were injured. However, they never made it to that rematch after falling at home to six field goals by the Steelers. There was another time-consuming touchdown drive late in a playoff game, and this time it would have been welcomed... had Eric Fisher not been called for a hold against James Harrison, negating a tying two-point conversion. The Chiefs were unable to get the ball back, and Pittsburgh held on for an 18-16 win.

Was that Kansas City's best shot at a championship? Smith is heading into his 13th season, and Reid will be in his 19th year as a head coach. Only one quarterback (John Elway, 15th season) and one head coach (Bill Cowher, 14th season) won their first championship more than a dozen years into their careers.

In fact, all 31 Super Bowl-winning duos of a head coach and quarterback won their first championship within seven years of being together. The longest waits are listed in Table 1. While Steve Young was with George Seifert for six years, he backed up Joe Montana in 1989-1990, so Young was actually a fourth-year starter in 1994. Likewise, Ken Stabler backed

2017 Chiefs Schedule

Week	Opp.	Week	Opp.	Week	Opp.
1	at NE (Thu.)	7	at OAK (Thu.)	13	at NYJ
2	PHI	8	DEN (Mon.)	14	OAK
3	at LACH	9	at DAL	15	LACH (Sat.)
4	WAS (Mon.)	10	BYE	16	MIA
5	at HOU	11	at NYG	17	at DEN
6	PIT	12	BUF		

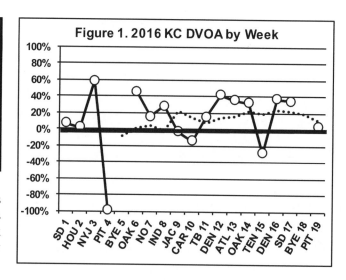

Figure 1. 2016 KC DVOA by Week

up Daryle Lamonica in Oakland, and he was John Madden's full-time starter for a fourth year in 1976. Jeff Hostetler was Bill Parcells' long-time backup for Phil Simms in New York for seven years, but Hostetler finally had his moment of glory in the 1990 playoffs in placed of an injured Simms.

Table 1. Longest Waits for Super Bowl-Winning QB/HC Duos

Quarterback	Head Coach	1st Title Win	Team	Years	QB Note
Terry Bradshaw	Chuck Noll	1974	PIT	5	
Mark Rypien	Joe Gibbs	1991	WAS	5	4th-year starter
Brett Favre	Mike Holmgren	1996	GB	5	
Peyton Manning	Tony Dungy	2006	IND	5	
Aaron Rodgers	Mike McCarthy	2010	GB	5	3rd-year starter
Joe Flacco	John Harbaugh	2012	BAL	5	
Steve Young	George Seifert	1994	SF	6	4th-year starter
Ken Stabler	John Madden	1976	OAK	7	4th-year starter
Jeff Hostetler	Bill Parcells	1990	NYG	7	P.Simms' backup

Call it The Five-Year Rule: no team has ever started the same quarterback under the same head coach for more than five years and seen that duo win its first championship. Reid already experienced this in Philadelphia when he was with Donovan McNabb. The duo reached their only Super Bowl in 2004, their sixth year together, and the fifth that McNabb was a full-time starter. Believe it or not, but several of the most noteworthy ringless duos had their greatest shot in Year 5:

• John Elway and Dan Reeves: they reached three Super Bowls together, but the only one that looked optimistic was Super Bowl XXII, when Denver opened up a 10-0 lead before an avalanche of points by Washington buried the 1987 Broncos 42-10.

• Boomer Esiason and Sam Wyche: the high-powered offense was shut down by San Francisco in Super Bowl XXIII, but one more defensive stop would have clinched a title for the 1988 Bengals.

• Jim Kelly and Marv Levy: the Bills lost Super Bowl XXV after Scott Norwood missed a potential game-winning field goal. Buffalo lost the next three Super Bowls as well, but never came closer to winning than in the 1990 season.

• Steve McNair and Jeff Fisher: McNair was a third-year starter in 1999, but it was his fifth season with Fisher, and the only time the two got to the Super Bowl (with a major assist from the Music City Miracle). The Titans came up 1 yard short (of overtime) against the Rams in Super Bowl XXXIV.

• Matt Hasselbeck and Mike Holmgren: it took five seasons in Green Bay for Holmgren and Brett Favre to break through the NFC to win a championship. In their fifth season in Seattle (2005), Holmgren and Hasselbeck shook off two tough playoff defeats to reach the franchise's first Super Bowl, but lost an ugly game to the Steelers in Super Bowl XL.

• Matt Ryan and Mike Smith: the Falcons never had back-to-back winning seasons before Ryan was drafted and Smith was hired in 2008. Then they had five winning seasons in a row, but the peak was 2012 when the Falcons blew a 17-point lead at home to the 49ers in the NFC Championship Game.

• Cam Newton and Ron Rivera: the 2015 Panthers finished 15-1 and beat Seattle and Arizona in dominant fashion in the playoffs. However, the Denver defense was too much for Carolina in Super Bowl 50.

Either ultimate success comes early, or the situation deteriorates and someone has to go. With the Chiefs entering Year 5 of Reid/Smith, it is really on Smith to deliver this season. We know Reid isn't going anywhere after the team signed him to a four-year extension in June. Clearly, there have been limitations within this offense that start at the quarterback position. The Chiefs jumped on the opportunity to trade up with Buffalo for Texas Tech quarterback Patrick Mahomes, moving from 27th to 10th by giving up a third-round pick (91st overall) and a first-round pick in 2018. Going from Smith to an Air Raid quarterback sounds like a huge change, but it's likely not one we will see until 2018 at the earliest. The Chiefs have not won a regular-season game with a quarterback they drafted since September 13, 1987 (Todd Blackledge), and that streak is all but guaranteed to extend beyond 30 years.

The 2017 Chiefs are the first team coming off a playoff season since those 2006 Broncos to draft a first-round quarterback while also returning the same starting quarterback. In fact, there have only been nine first-round quarterbacks drafted by playoff teams since 1990, including three in the last two drafts. Mahomes would have been the first one since Cutler, which would have made our 2006 Broncos comparison even better, but Brock Osweiler literally spoils everything. Osweiler could have replaced a retired Peyton Manning in Denver, but left for more money in Houston, which led to the Broncos drafting Paxton Lynch. Houston then dumped Osweiler after one season, opting for Deshaun Watson two spots after Mahomes went off the board. These picks are rare occurrences, and the new quarterback rarely works out well. Table 2 looks at the nine quarterbacks, the incumbent quarterback they each had to replace, how many regular-season games it took for that draft pick to make his first start, and how many starts he made overall for his draft team.

Table 2. Teams That Used First-Round Pick on Quarterback After Playoff Season (Since 1990)

Year	Team	Incumbent QB	Age	Rookie QB	Pick	Games to First Start	Career GS for Draft Team
1991	LARD	J.Schroeder	30	T.Marinovich	24	16	8
1992	DEN	J.Elway	32	T.Maddox	25	11	4
1997	SF	S.Young	36	J.Druckenmiller	26	2	1
1999	MIN	R.Cunningham	36	D.Culpepper	11	17	80
2005	GB	B.Favre	36	A.Rodgers	24	49	135
2006	DEN	J.Plummer	32	J.Cutler	11	12	37
2016	DEN	T.Siemian*	25	P.Lynch	26	5	2**
2017	KC	A.Smith	33	P.Mahomes	10	-	-**
2017	HOU	T.Savage*	27	D.Watson	12	-	-**

Brock Osweiler would have been the incumbent quarterback for the 2016 Broncos and 2017 Texans if he didn't suck.
** *Still with team.*

The two successes, Daunte Culpepper and Aaron Rodgers, each sat for at least a season before taking over. That will probably happen with the raw Mahomes, who had a few nicknames in college, ranging from "Fat Pat" to "Mahomie" to "2 P.M." His NFL nickname might just be "Not Alex Smith," because he is a much different type of quarterback when it comes to aggressive play and getting into shootouts. Mahomes had 20 games in college with 350 passing yards. Smith has three such games in his NFL career (147 games). According to ESPN Stats & Info, Mahomes had 2016's highest QBR and second-highest air yards on third down among Power 5 quarterbacks. That is a big departure from Smith's reputation on third down, where he usually turns into Negative ALEX. Last season was the first time Smith had positive ALEX (plus-0.4) since 2007, though he still ranked 24th in the league and 18th in conversion rate.

Smith showed a little effort to be more aggressive last season, with varying results. His eight interceptions were the most he has thrown in a season since 2010, and a few were crucial plays in the red zone in low-scoring games Kansas City went on to lose against the Titans and Buccaneers. Including the playoffs, the Chiefs lost three games at home last season in which the team allowed fewer than 20 points. Oddly

enough, the Chiefs were 4-1 when allowing 27-plus points in 2016. Smith's teams were 3-29 from 2005-2015 when allowing that many points, so last year looks like an outlier in that regard. Still, unless the defense is going to step up in a huge way in the playoffs, Smith will likely have to post a high point total against the offense-driven contenders in his conference.

In May, Smith addressed the new quarterback situation, telling ESPN that he thinks the Chiefs are committed to him through this year. "Whether or not we drafted Patrick, it doesn't change that, right? If you're not good enough and didn't get it done, you're not going to be around long. That's just our culture. I know it. That's the nature of the position." Smith knows what it is like to lose a job to a promising young player. After a concussion sidelined him halfway through the 2012 season, Smith watched Colin Kaepernick lead the 49ers to a Super Bowl. Smith was traded to Kansas City the next offseason.

The rookie who is unlikely to help the Chiefs in 2017 is a big part of the story of the 2017 Chiefs. This team has been close in the AFC the last few years, but this trade is unlikely to help them get any closer this fall. To play devil's advocate, maybe there wasn't any rookie who could really help them get over the hump this year. Were the Chiefs going to draft a first-round tight end when they already have one of the best in the game in Travis Kelce? Unlikely. No wide receiver went off the board in picks 10 through 36, so that value was really unavailable to Kansas City. If the Chiefs hadvstayed put at 27, they could have replaced Jamaal Charles with Dalvin Cook (41st to Minnesota) or Joe Mixon (48th to Cincinnati), but those would have felt like reaches.

The truth is that rookies at any positon are rarely big factors on Super Bowl winners. Since 2000, only 13 rookies started at least 10 games for Super Bowl-winning teams, and eight of those players were offensive linemen. All but one of those linemen (Kelechi Osemele) had the luxury of playing with Tom Brady, Peyton Manning, or Aaron Rodgers, so it is debatable how much value they really added. No one's going to say left guard Joe Thuney really put the Patriots over the top last season. The last prominent rookie starter who didn't play offensive line was Colts safety Antoine Bethea way back in 2006. However, think of the impact cornerback Marcus Peters had on the Chiefs defense as a rookie in 2015: that caliber of player could have elevated the Chiefs in 2017.

The other problem with this trade is that, barring any future moves, the Chiefs won't have a first-round pick in 2018 either. For a team in a Super Bowl window, mortgaging two first-round picks on a quarterback of the future doesn't make a whole lot of sense. Next year we can probably write about all of the great things Reid may get out of Mahomes, but it's just not expected to be the story for the 2017 Chiefs.

Of course, stories change quickly in the NFL. We thought we had the Chiefs pegged pretty well, but two big moves in June give a reason for pause. First, the Chiefs released presumed No. 1 wideout Jeremy Maclin without a clear replacement on the roster. Maclin had a career-low 536 receiving yards in 2016, but a groin injury was partly to blame. The fact that Maclin, who Reid originally drafted in Philadelphia, was released on a Friday via a voice mail from general manager John Dorsey may have led to the Chiefs' other big move.

While Reid received his contract extension, the Chiefs parted ways with Dorsey after four seasons. Sources have told *The Kansas City Star* that Dorsey's communication skills and management style were factors in the decision. For instance, Dorsey removed two front-office executives without much explanation, to which a source said "John does stuff and doesn't tell people why." While Reid is more calculated in his decisions, Dorsey tends to go with the flow. It is especially troubling that the Chiefs already lost Chris Ballard to the Colts. Just before we went to press, the Chiefs filled the GM role by promoting co-director of player personnel Brett Veach, a former college scout whose connections to Reid go back to Philadelphia. Regardless, Reid is thought to be pulling most of the strings in Kansas City these days. This is why Dorsey's removal should not have much impact on the 2017 season, but the timing certainly is odd from a franchise that seemed to be promoting stability.

If the draft does not boost the Chiefs this year, then free agency is always the other option, and arguably the more attractive one for a team with instant championship aspirations. Unfortunately, free agents cost money, and Dorsey's cap management was a bit shoddy. Veach will take over a situation that sees the Chiefs with the lowest cap space ($1.3 million in the red) in 2018 according to overthecap.com. The Chiefs made Eric Berry the highest-paid safety in the game after his stellar 2016 season, signing him to a six-year deal worth $78 million with $40 million guaranteed. His cap number will shoot up to $13 million in 2018.

Keeping Berry was definitely the right move, but it came at a cost. Kansas City's one major move in free agency came at nose tackle, but even that move was because of cap issues, not despite them. Dontari Poe could have been given the franchise tag, but he would have earned over $13 million for just one season of play. Poe was a two-time Pro Bowler for the defense, but typically a team should not break the bank on a defensive tackle who is not a premier pass rusher à la Aaron Donald or Ndamukong Suh. Poe had 6.0 sacks in 2014, but just 2.5 sacks in his last two seasons combined. Sure, the cute jump-pass touchdown at the end of the game against Denver was well done, but Poe's impact was diminishing with a lack

of pass-rush productivity and the Chiefs' slumping run defense. The Chiefs were 30th in adjusted line yards on defense, and only 19th at forcing stuffed runs for no gain or a loss. Worse, the Chiefs were 32nd against runs right up the middle, and offenses knew this weakness with a league-high 74 percent of runs coming in that direction (2016 league average: 56 percent).

Poe likely wanted a long-term deal with the Chiefs, so Dorsey made the decision to let him walk. Poe eventually signed a one-year deal for $8 million to play with Atlanta. Some incentives could boost him a little higher, but it's a deal that is hardly any more lucrative than the one-year deal the Chiefs ultimately gave to Bennie Logan. While he is a good 30 pounds lighter than Poe, Logan has experience at playing nose tackle in a 3-4 defense from his time in Philadelphia. He is also versatile enough to play in a 4-3, and his run defense metrics have been superior to Poe's for years now. We looked at the two players' production since 2014 when Logan became a full-time starter (Table 3). Logan actually has 32 more stops on 834 fewer snaps, though snaps are a big area of difference between the two. Poe was very durable and rarely left the field in Kansas City. Logan has not taken on such a workload in his career, and the Chiefs may need to rely more on depth to help him out. Poe's pass-rushing production is also clearly superior, but Logan will be asked to stop the run more, and is seemingly better suited to do that than his predecessor.

The Chiefs already lost cornerback Sean Smith in free agency a year ago; now Poe is another cornerstone of the defense to leave the team. However, this shouldn't be a significant loss. In the end, Poe was not worth more than $13 million this season, and Logan should be a more than adequate replacement.

The middle of the field is an area to keep an eye on with Derrick Johnson returning from a ruptured Achilles tendon. He will be 35 in November, and the Chiefs did not find his successor yet. But the middle of the field may not be such a focal point if the edges return to past glory. Star pass-rusher Justin Houston has been limited to 16 games over the past two seasons. His 32 hurries in those games are barely more than the 29 hurries Dee Ford produced last season in his first crack at a starting job. If Houston's health permits him to return to past form, the Chiefs can pair him with an emerging Ford and have veteran Tamba Hali available to spell them That should

Table 3. Defensive Production for Dontari Poe and Bennie Logan, 2014-16

2014	Snaps	Stop	Dfts	BTkl	Runs	St%	Rk	RuYd	Rk	Sack	Hit	Hur	Dsrpt
Dontari Poe	944	34	10	3	38	68%	84	2.8	72	6.0	1	8.8	1
Bennie Logan	639	47	14	1	55	78%	45	1.3	18	0.0	1	6.0	1
2015	Snaps	Stop	Dfts	BTkl	Runs	St%	Rk	RuYd	Rk	Sack	Hit	Hur	Dsrpt
Dontari Poe	759	27	4	1	35	74%	48	3.0	66	1.0	2	12.0	0
Bennie Logan	584	48	12	6	51	88%	10	2.0	35	1.0	1	3.5	0
2016	Snaps	Stop	Dfts	BTkl	Runs	St%	Rk	RuYd	Rk	Sack	Hit	Hur	Dsrpt
Dontari Poe	821	22	5	5	22	68%	66	3.0	72	1.5	9	18	6
Bennie Logan	467	20	10	5	18	89%	13	0.6	4	2.5	3	9	0
2014-16 Totals	Snaps	Stop	Dfts	BTkl	Runs	St%	Rk	RuYd	Rk	Sack	Hit	Hur	Dsrpt
Dontari Poe	2,524	83	19	9	95	70%	-	2.9	-	8.5	12	38.8	7
Bennie Logan	1,690	115	36	12	124	85%	-	1.3	-	3.5	5	18.5	1

give the Chiefs a much stronger pass rush than the one that ranked 27th in pressure rate (24.4 percent) and only produced 28 sacks.

One thing is for sure: we will get plenty of exposure to the Chiefs this season. Kansas City has a league-high six games scheduled for prime time, including the season opener at New England. That should instantly be a good barometer for where the Chiefs are compared to the AFC's best team. In fact, the Chiefs have to play both No. 1 seeds from last season on the road, while the rival Raiders get New England and Dallas at home. The Raiders also get to avoid Pittsburgh, which will make another trip to Kansas City in Week 6. Oakland even gets the Giants at home, while the Chiefs go to the Meadowlands and get the NFC East's two non-playoff teams (Philadelphia and Washington) as home games instead. The schedule certainly works in Oakland's favor. Head-to-head matchups will be as important as ever, and the Chiefs could have to clinch their playoff berth in Week 17 at Mile High, which is always a tough place to play.

There are some big changes going on in the AFC West, yet the Chiefs have kept the status quo at head coach, defensive coordinator, and quarterback since 2013. That formula has been good enough for four winning seasons, but when your main tweaks are a swap of nose tackles and the addition of a quarterback-in-waiting, things might start to turn stale. When your brand of football is designed to be less quarterback-dependent than your competitors, but you lack the funds to build up the roster, then sustaining that success is going to be a lot more difficult. This is still one of the AFC's six best teams, but it looks like we're on the other side of the peak now. The Reid/Smith era may be remembered best for the time the Chiefs let six field goals end a dream season.

Scott Kacsmar

2016 Chiefs Stats by Week

Wk	vs.	W-L	PF	PA	YDF	YDA	TO	Total	Off	Def	ST
1	SD	W	33	27	413	388	-1	7%	29%	27%	4%
2	at HOU	L	12	19	291	351	-1	1%	-31%	-19%	14%
3	NYJ	W	24	3	293	305	+7	58%	-6%	-58%	6%
4	at PIT	L	14	43	357	436	-2	-99%	-31%	59%	-9%
5	BYE										
6	at OAK	W	26	10	406	285	+2	46%	33%	-19%	-7%
7	NO	W	27	21	326	463	+2	15%	22%	10%	3%
8	at IND	W	30	14	422	277	+2	28%	-5%	-27%	6%
9	JAC	W	19	14	231	449	+4	-4%	-25%	-6%	15%
10	at CAR	W	20	17	256	341	+1	-14%	-25%	-4%	6%
11	TB	L	17	19	343	442	-1	15%	23%	11%	3%
12	at DEN	W	30	27	273	464	+1	41%	20%	14%	36%
13	at ATL	W	29	28	389	418	0	36%	39%	-1%	-5%
14	OAK	W	21	13	323	244	-3	32%	-17%	-28%	21%
15	TEN	L	17	19	316	389	+2	-29%	-26%	1%	-2%
16	DEN	W	33	10	484	246	+2	37%	26%	-16%	-4%
17	at SD	W	37	27	365	398	+1	34%	15%	16%	36%
18	BYE										
19	PIT	L	16	18	227	389	-1	3%	-13%	-6%	10%

Trends and Splits

	Offense	Rank	Defense	Rank
Total DVOA	2.9%	13	-2.8%	14
Unadjusted VOA	0.5%	15	-4.6%	10
Weighted Trend	6.0%	13	-2.0%	14
Variance	6.6%	20	7.2%	27
Average Opponent	-1.2%	8	-0.4%	18
Passing	21.2%	10	-4.2%	7
Rushing	-7.9%	19	-1.1%	25
First Down	3.9%	15	0.5%	18
Second Down	-0.5%	15	-8.7%	9
Third Down	5.8%	13	-0.5%	16
First Half	8.9%	10	-3.6%	15
Second Half	-13.5%	23	-8.1%	16
Red Zone	-25.8%	28	-35.0%	2
Late and Close	5.4%	12	-7.2%	12

Five-Year Performance

Year	W-L	Pyth W	Est W	PF	PA	TO	Total	Rk	Off	Rk	Def	Rk	ST	Rk	Off AGL	Rk	Def AGL	Rk	Off Age	Rk	Def Age	Rk	ST Age	Rk
2012	2-14	2.5	2.4	211	425	-24	-40.1%	32	-25.1%	31	13.0%	30	-2.0%	22	50.0	27	29.3	17	26.3	24	26.1	25	26.0	14
2013	11-5	11.1	10.0	430	305	+18	17.5%	6	3.0%	15	-6.7%	9	7.8%	1	29.4	13	10.6	3	26.1	27	26.4	17	25.8	23
2014	9-7	10.1	9.4	353	281	-3	10.4%	10	5.0%	12	1.3%	19	6.7%	3	36.0	20	62.8	27	26.6	19	26.6	20	25.7	26
2015	11-5	11.2	11.4	405	287	+14	25.2%	5	11.7%	6	-11.6%	6	2.0%	9	26.3	13	28.6	18	25.8	28	27.4	5	25.8	19
2016	12-4	10.1	9.7	389	311	+16	13.5%	6	2.9%	13	-2.8%	14	7.8%	1	33.2	14	66.1	30	25.9	26	26.5	16	25.1	31

2016 Performance Based on Most Common Personnel Groups

KC Offense					KC Offense vs. Opponents					KC Defense				KC Defense vs. Opponents			
Pers	Freq	Yds	DVOA	Run%	Pers	Freq	Yds	DVOA	Run%	Pers	Freq	Yds	DVOA	Pers	Freq	Yds	DVOA
11	51%	5.6	11.0%	28%	Base	39%	5.5	-1.6%	52%	Base	29%	5.8	5.5%	11	60%	5.9	-0.2%
12	18%	5.9	4.7%	39%	Nickel	47%	6.1	12.5%	31%	Nickel	40%	5.4	-14.4%	12	15%	6.8	14.5%
13	9%	5.8	0.5%	57%	Dime+	12%	4.9	31.9%	13%	Dime+	29%	6.1	2.6%	21	9%	5.0	-3.6%
21	9%	4.7	-15.6%	51%	Goal Line	1%	0.0	-30.1%	71%	Goal Line	1%	1.5	43.5%	10	6%	3.6	-85.8%
22	2%	4.9	-4.9%	95%	Big	1%	2.6	-17.9%	80%	Big	1%	4.9	-42.2%	22	2%	3.7	14.3%
01	2%	6.6	41.1%	32%													
621	2%	3.1	-23.9%	100%													

Strategic Tendencies

Run/Pass		Rk	Formation		Rk	Pass Rush		Rk	Secondary		Rk	Strategy		Rk
Runs, first half	37%	17	Form: Single Back	80%	10	Rush 3	13.1%	6	4 DB	29%	18	Play-action	17%	20
Runs, first down	46%	18	Form: Empty Back	6%	20	Rush 4	68.1%	10	5 DB	40%	30	Avg Box (Off)	6.24	7
Runs, second-long	32%	10	Pers: 3+ WR	56%	27	Rush 5	15.5%	28	6+ DB	27%	3	Avg Box (Def)	6.24	14
Runs, power sit.	60%	10	Pers: 2+ TE/6+ OL	36%	6	Rush 6+	3.3%	29	CB by Sides	90%	7	Offensive Pace	31.76	28
Runs, behind 2H	23%	27	Pers: 6+ OL	4%	18	Sacks by LB	74.1%	1	S/CB Cover Ratio	28%	11	Defensive Pace	29.80	9
Pass, ahead 2H	51%	10	Shotgun/Pistol	68%	11	Sacks by DB	3.7%	25	DB Blitz	4%	31	Go for it on 4th	1.05	17

The strange saga of the Kansas City Chiefs in the red zone continues. After three straight years where the Chiefs offense was much better in the red zone than it was overall, they collapsed in the red zone in 2016: a dismal 28th in DVOA and 30th in goal-to-go situations. But the defense rebounded, ranking second in red zone DVOA. So on both sides of the ball, Kansas City has now been better in the red zone in three out of four years. 2016 was the exception on offense, and 2015 on defense. ☞ Once again, the Chiefs led the league by throwing 25 percent of passes at or behind the line of scrimmage. The NFL average was 16 percent, and no other team was above 22 percent. ☞ In a connected stat, Kansas City also ran more wide receiver and tight end screens than any other offense. We had them charted with 68 such plays, while no other team had more than 50. The Chiefs had 7.8 yards per pass with 34.6% DVOA on these plays. ☞ Kansas City sent only three pass-rushers more than three times as often as in 2015. They also sent a defensive back on a blitz half as often as the year before. ☞ The Chiefs defense was relatively much stronger against passes thrown beyond the line of scrimmage (second in DVOA) than against passes thrown behind the line of scrimmage (24th). ☞ The Chiefs benefited from opposing kickers only hitting touchbacks on 43 percent of kickoffs, the second-lowest figure in the league.

Passing

Player	DYAR	DVOA	Plays	NtYds	Avg	YAC	C%	TD	Int
A.Smith	688	9.4%	518	3372	6.5	5.5	67.3%	16	8
N.Foles*	5	-9.9%	59	376	6.4	5.5	65.5%	3	0

Rushing

Player	DYAR	DVOA	Plays	Yds	Avg	TD	Fum	Suc
S.Ware	35	-4.1%	183	790	4.3	3	0	50%
C.West	-29	-22.1%	54	195	3.6	1	0	33%
A.Smith	5	-6.4%	18	71	3.9	5	0	-
T.Hill	47	13.1%	14	89	6.4	3	0	-
J.Charles*	6	2.6%	12	40	3.3	1	0	42%
K.Davis*	-10	-54.6%	7	14	2.0	0	0	29%

Receiving

Player	DYAR	DVOA	Plays	Ctch	Yds	Y/C	YAC	TD	C%
T.Hill	87	0.8%	83	61	599	9.8	4.5	6	73%
J.Maclin*	50	-4.3%	76	44	536	12.2	3.1	2	58%
C.Conley	74	1.1%	69	44	530	12.0	3.4	0	64%
A.Wilson	-37	-22.1%	51	31	279	9.0	4.8	2	61%
D.Thomas	-23	-44.2%	9	7	35	5.0	3.9	0	78%
T.Kelce	261	26.0%	117	85	1125	13.2	7.4	4	73%
D.Harris	-63	-36.9%	31	17	123	7.2	2.4	1	55%
R.Travis	-21	-58.2%	6	3	15	5.0	5.0	0	50%
G.Escobar	5	4.4%	7	4	30	7.5	2.3	1	57%
S.Ware	115	32.7%	42	33	447	13.5	11.4	2	79%
C.West	21	-3.0%	34	28	188	6.7	6.5	2	82%
A.Sherman	-29	-97.4%	6	4	11	2.8	1.8	0	67%
C.J.Spiller	-17	-52.9%	9	5	43	8.6	4.4	1	56%

Offensive Line

Player	Pos	Age	GS	Snaps	Pen	Sk	Pass	Run	Player	Pos	Age	GS	Snaps	Pen	Sk	Pass	Run
Eric Fisher	LT	26	16/16	1024	10	5.0	15	4	Laurent Duvernay-Tardif	RG	26	14/14	892	5	0.0	3	4
Mitchell Schwartz	RT	28	16/16	1024	8	8.0	23	7	Zach Fulton	LG	26	16/12	803	2	0.5	4	6
Mitch Morse	C	25	16/16	1021	2	0.5	5	6	Parker Ehinger	LG	25	5/4	229	0	0.5	4	1

Year	Yards	ALY	Rank	Power	Rank	Stuff	Rank	2nd Lev	Rank	Open Field	Rank	Sacks	ASR	Rank	Press	Rank	F-Start	Cont.
2014	4.47	4.36	7	60%	21	17%	5	1.15	17	0.97	4	49	9.4%	28	27.0%	26	16	40
2015	4.43	4.53	5	70%	11	18%	6	1.22	8	0.84	11	46	8.7%	28	25.0%	15	15	22
2016	3.91	4.10	17	59%	21	18%	10	1.04	27	0.57	22	32	5.7%	14	21.0%	5	23	32

2016 ALY by direction:	Left End 4.95 (9)	Left Tackle 4.39 (16)	Mid/Guard 4.01 (22)	Right Tackle 3.15 (28)	Right End 4.06 (11)

Eric Fisher's 2016 season should not be defined by a holding penalty on a crucial two-point conversion in the playoffs. It is better to just acknowledge that the Chiefs got another mediocre effort out of the left tackle, who at this point may best be known for going No. 1 overall in a very weak draft (2013). Last season was arguably his best and he still finished 16th in snaps per blown block among left tackles. Fisher should be the left tackle for at least the next two seasons, but the team has an out in 2019 from the deal he signed last summer. ⬧ Like Fisher, right tackle Mitchell Schwartz could cite "being there every snap" as one of the highlights of his season. The former Cleveland lineman fell from ninth with the Browns to 31st with the Chiefs in snaps per blown block at his positon. The Chiefs were at their worst (28th in adjusted line yards) when running off right tackle. ⬧ Center Mitch Morse is the best of an average group. He didn't make any huge improvements over his rookie season, though he did not allow a full sack like he did three times in 2015. ⬧ Guard has been in flux around Morse the last two seasons. Third-year veteran Zach Fulton had to take over for injured rookie left guard Parker Ehinger, though he fared better in pass protection. Right guard Laurent Duvernay-Tardif was the unit's best pass protector, finishing sixth in blown block rate at his position. Ehinger will likely get his starting job back, so the Chiefs will return the same starting unit in 2017.

Defensive Front Seven

Defensive Line	Age	Pos	G	Snaps	Plays	TmPct	Rk	Stop	Dfts	BTkl	Runs	St%	Rk	RuYd	Rk	Sack	Hit	Hur	Dsrpt
						Overall						vs. Run				Pass Rush			
Dontari Poe*	27	DT	16	821	30	3.5%	65	22	5	5	22	68%	66	3.0	72	1.5	9	18	6
Chris Jones	23	DE	16	574	32	3.8%	58	26	9	3	26	77%	44	2.3	45	2.0	7	21	4
Jaye Howard*	29	DE	8	359	24	5.6%	28	18	4	4	21	71%	58	2.7	60	1.0	6	7	1
Rakeem Nunez-Roches	24	DE	11	286	23	3.9%	--	14	6	3	20	60%	--	3.0	--	0.5	3	4	0
Kendall Reyes*	28	DE	12	236	21	3.3%	--	10	4	0	18	44%	--	4.0	--	1.0	3	5	1
Bennie Logan	28	DT	13	467	24	3.9%	52	20	10	5	18	89%	13	0.6	4	2.5	3	9	0

Edge Rushers	Age	Pos	G	Snaps	Plays	TmPct	Rk	Stop	Dfts	BTkl	Runs	St%	Rk	RuYd	Rk	Sack	Hit	Hur	Dsrpt
						Overall						vs. Run				Pass Rush			
Dee Ford	26	OLB	15	798	39	4.9%	52	32	21	3	22	82%	17	2.5	45	10.0	7	29	1
Tamba Hali	34	OLB	16	596	34	4.0%	67	20	8	5	26	62%	88	4.1	97	3.5	5	19	0
Frank Zombo	30	OLB	16	490	41	4.8%	54	21	7	4	25	60%	91	3.0	67	1.0	3	7	1
Justin Houston	28	OLB	5	295	22	8.3%	7	18	9	2	15	80%	26	1.3	14	4.5	2	9	2

Linebackers	Age	Pos	G	Snaps	Plays	TmPct	Rk	Stop	Dfts	BTkl	Runs	St%	Rk	RuYd	Rk	Sack	Hit	Hur	Tgts	Suc%	Rk	AdjYd	Rk	PD	Int
						Overall						vs. Run				Pass Rush				vs. Pass					
Derrick Johnson	35	ILB	13	844	93	13.4%	35	53	16	16	62	65%	35	3.6	45	1.0	1	3	24	60%	10	5.0	11	3	1
Ramik Wilson	25	ILB	11	524	78	13.3%	36	36	10	5	61	44%	85	5.0	83	0.0	0	3	17	61%	9	3.4	1	2	1
Justin March-Lillard	24	ILB	5	162	24	9.0%	66	13	2	2	16	63%	49	3.7	50	0.0	0	1	5	34%	--	10.2	--	1	0

Year	Yards	ALY	Rank	Power	Rank	Stuff	Rank	2nd Level	Rank	Open Field	Rank	Sacks	ASR	Rank	Press	Rank
2014	4.96	4.89	32	55%	4	18%	23	1.57	32	0.84	25	46	8.3%	3	23.3%	22
2015	3.83	3.82	7	50%	2	22%	10	1.06	10	0.58	8	47	7.7%	4	28.1%	5
2016	4.43	4.72	30	65%	22	18%	19	1.39	30	0.47	5	28	5.1%	26	24.4%	27

2016 ALY by direction:	Left End 3.45 (8)	Left Tackle 5.17 (27)	Mid/Guard 4.99 (32)	Right Tackle 3.65 (7)	Right End 2.91 (8)

No front seven suffered more injuries than the Chiefs in 2016. Kansas City's defensive line and linebackers both had the most adjusted games lost in the league. Derrick Johnson, Allen Bailey, Jaye Howard, Josh Mauga, and Justin March-Lillard all finished 2016 on injured reserve. ☞ Dee Ford helped pick up the slack for Justin Houston's absence and Tamba Hali's aging in appropriate fashion for a former first-round pick. Ford blew away his previous career-bests in every pass-rushing category and even increased his run stop rate from 2015. ☞ Ramik Wilson was not as successful at leading the inside linebackers once Johnson ruptured his Achilles, particularly against the run, where he had the third-worst run stop rate among linebackers. ☞ The defensive line is where this defense should look the most different in 2017. Beyond the switch from Dontari Poe to Bennie Logan in the middle, the Chiefs could soon be relying on second-round picks from the last two drafts. Chris Jones, who also works inside, may not have impressed many with his 2.0 sacks as a rookie, but that can be a misleading stat. He was second on the team with 21 hurries. Kansas City would love that type of production from this year's second-round selection, Tanoh Kpassagnon, but the Villanova prospect figures to fit the "raw, athletic freak needing development time" mold. There's some question among draftniks about whether Kpassagnon fits in Kansas City's two-gap scheme rather than playing a more traditional one-gap defensive end position where he can utilize his burst to rush the passer. Nonetheless, Kpassagnon is clearly in the team's future, though Rakeem Nunez-Roches is more likely to be the Week 1 starter.

Defensive Secondary

Secondary	Age	Pos	G	Snaps	Plays	Overall TmPct	Rk	Stop	Dfts	BTkl	vs. Run Runs	St%	Rk	RuYd	Rk	vs. Pass Tgts	Tgt%	Rk	Dist	Suc%	Rk	AdjYd	Rk	PD	Int
Ron Parker	30	SS/CB	16	1106	73	8.6%	52	27	9	10	26	38%	41	7.4	42	40	8.4%	35	11.1	47%	36	6.9	13	12	1
Eric Berry	29	FS	16	1085	85	10.0%	38	31	14	11	37	41%	34	5.8	20	41	8.6%	40	11.5	53%	20	8.4	32	9	4
Steven Nelson	24	CB	15	1012	80	10.0%	17	28	13	12	16	13%	85	8.4	63	78	17.8%	37	11.3	49%	45	7.8	50	14	0
Marcus Peters	24	CB	15	1010	65	8.1%	53	34	18	9	12	42%	39	5.4	19	78	17.7%	34	13.0	54%	15	7.4	39	18	6
Daniel Sorensen	27	SS	16	541	59	6.9%	63	26	15	3	24	33%	51	8.1	53	31	13.0%	68	8.6	57%	6	7.3	17	5	3
Phillip Gaines	26	CB	11	450	49	8.4%	49	15	4	4	9	33%	55	6.9	46	55	28.3%	86	13.6	43%	77	11.3	87	7	1
Terrance Mitchell	25	CB	7	239	25	6.7%	--	10	4	1	2	0%	--	9.0	--	32	30.5%	--	10.8	57%	--	4.9	--	8	0

Year	Pass D Rank	vs. #1 WR	Rk	vs. #2 WR	Rk	vs. Other WR	Rk	vs. TE	Rk	vs. RB	Rk
2014	13	5.9%	22	-3.9%	14	1.6%	19	7.3%	23	-2.4%	15
2015	5	7.6%	22	-15.7%	7	9.0%	20	-36.4%	2	-28.9%	3
2016	7	0.2%	14	-10.0%	6	-24.9%	3	3.4%	20	-20.5%	4

While the Chiefs were decimated by injuries in the front seven, the secondary had the third-lowest AGL in 2016. Including the postseason, Kansas City was the only team to have four defensive backs play more than 1,000 snaps last season. ☞ The Chiefs pulled off a rare feat of having two defensive backs (Eric Berry and Marcus Peters) named to the first-string All-Pro team by the Associated Press. ☞ While Berry's coverage metrics slipped a little from 2015, his overall impact (and his highlight reel) may have never been greater. Berry made some incredible takeaways, including a pick-six off of Cam Newton to help spark a fourth-quarter comeback in Carolina. Berry also famously returned a Matt Ryan pass for a touchdown in Atlanta, then won the game with the first-ever return of a two-point conversion pass for a defensive score in Kansas City's 29-28 win. Berry's whopping $13 million annual salary may be a little high for a player going into his age-29 season, but the Chiefs had no choice but to lock up a player who is so productive. ☞ Peters was the most-targeted cornerback in the NFL as a rookie, but offenses eased up a bit on testing him in 2016. He still proved to be a ball magnet with six more picks to give him 14 career interceptions, most in a player's first two seasons since Orlando Thomas also had 14 from 1995-96. ☞ The problem is the cornerback depth after Peters. Steven Nelson did a respectable job in his first year as a starter, but Phillip Gaines ranked dead last in adjusted yards per target by more than a full yard over all other qualified cornerbacks. Terrance Mitchell had far better coverage metrics than Gaines, and one more pass defensed on 23 fewer targets. The Chiefs ranked a respectable 12th in pass DVOA over the first 12 weeks, but jumped up to fourth from Weeks 13-17, when Mitchell replaced Gaines in the nickel package. ☞ Safety Ron Parker is very active on the field, often moving inside to cover slot receivers man-to-man. The Chiefs also got a surprising boost from Daniel Sorensen, including on special teams, where all nine of his tackles stopped returners short of an average gain. Kansas City locked him up with a four-year extension in March.

Special Teams

Year	DVOA	Rank	FG/XP	Rank	Net Kick	Rank	Kick Ret	Rank	Net Punt	Rank	Punt Ret	Rank	Hidden	Rank
2014	6.7%	3	-1.5	20	-2.7	23	12.4	1	11.6	4	13.7	2	0.1	15
2015	2.0%	9	-2.9	25	0.6	16	-0.8	16	16.2	1	-3.1	20	2.8	12
2016	7.8%	1	0.5	15	0.5	15	5.7	7	11.3	4	20.8	1	3.2	13

The Chiefs never ranked higher than 13th in special teams DVOA in the nine seasons (2004-2012) prior to Andy Reid taking over as head coach in 2013. They have been seventh or better in these last four seasons, including a second No. 1 finish in 2016. Special teams are not often consistent from year to year, but Chiefs special teams coordinator Dave Toub is a notable exception to that rule. Before he came to Kansas City, Toub had a remarkable run in Chicago where the Bears finished with top-six special teams for seven straight seasons (2006-2012). ▪ Talent still matters too, and just as Toub had Devin Hester in Chicago, he has a new All-Pro returner in Tyreek Hill, who led the league in punt return yards (592) and average (15.2). He also scored two punt return touchdowns in addition to a kickoff return score. Hill's punt return success was the strongest part of Kansas City's special teams, and the only question is if an increased role as the No. 1 wide receiver will take away from his return effectiveness this season. ▪ Punter Dustin Colquitt and kicker Cairo Santos return, but both had mediocre seasons in 2016. That's out of the norm for Colquitt, as he relied significantly on his coverage team last season. Though the Chiefs were fourth in net punting value, Colquitt himself was only 21st in gross punting value.

Los Angeles Chargers

2016 Record: 5-11	Total DVOA: -1.1% (19th)	2017 Mean Projection: 7.8 wins	On the Clock (0-4): 10%
Pythagorean Wins: 7.7 (21st)	Offense: -3.2% (18th)	Postseason Odds: 35.2%	Mediocrity (5-7): 36%
Snap-Weighted Age: 26.6 (13th)	Defense: -6.8% (7th)	Super Bowl Odds: 3.3%	Playoff Contender (8-10): 38%
Average Opponent: -0.2% (16th)	Special Teams: -4.8% (29th)	Proj. Avg. Opponent: 0.1% (14th)	Super Bowl Contender (11+): 15%

2016: An 8-8 team if games were three quarters long.

2017: Clean slate means a clean BINGO card too.

One repetitive task faced by modern sportswriters is the need to change things up between writing a team's nickname or its city name, all for the sake of variety. As the author of the Chargers' chapter in *Football Outsiders Almanac 2015*, I used "San Diego" 26 times and "Chargers" 24 times. For all the data we use at Football Outsiders, this is something we aren't actually tracking, but the near 50-50 split makes me feel good.

However, this year won't even come close to 50-50, because it just does not feel natural to think of the Chargers as "Los Angeles." Not many of us can remember the 1960 Los Angeles Chargers, the team's inaugural (and only) season in Los Angeles with the AFL. At least with the Rams and Raiders, most of us were alive when those teams actually played in L.A., and long-time Football Outsiders readers know about our "LARM" and "LARD" abbreviations. What is a "LACH" supposed to represent? It is surely not a nod to former Pro Bowl tackle Jim Lachey, the Chargers' first-round pick in 1985.

As you might imagine, this group of spreadsheet-loving football nerds does not take too kindly to owner Dean Spanos moving the team, and not just because it makes "SD" obsolete in our databases.

The San Diego fans deserve better after decades of support for a team that has a rich history, which includes some of the NFL's all-time great players, but unfortunately no Super Bowl wins to show for it. Pro Football Reference has an Approximate Value (AV) metric that's weighted for a player's career[1], and among the top 32 players in career AV, only three never played in a Super Bowl. Incredibly, they are all San Diego greats: LaDainian Tomlinson, Philip Rivers, and Dan Fouts. It is ludicrous to think that 1994, the year "Deno" took over the team from his father, remains the only season a San Diego team reached the Super Bowl. That team only had Stan Humphries and Natrone Means in the backfield, for crying out loud. Instead of a legendary tight end such as Kellen Winslow or Antonio Gates, the 1994 Chargers started Alfred Pupunu. It sure would have been nice to see if future San Diego teams could have brought that long-awaited championship home to the fans. Now should that happen, it will largely be enjoyed by people who used to root for the Raiders, or have grown tired of watching the current Rams.

At the same time, if any franchise could use a fresh start, or a hit of the reset button, it is the Chargers. This team has managed just one playoff appearance in the last seven seasons, a wild card in 2013. Once we wipe the slate clean on injuries, blown leads, contract squabbles, and general disappointment, then 2017 can actually start with optimism for the Chargers. No, we are not likely looking at a Super Bowl team here, but that 5-11 record in 2016 does not do this team justice either. There is enough talent here to make the playoffs. The question is, can they get enough things to go their way this time?

The 2016 Chargers were a dangerous team, including as a threat to themselves. The Chargers ranked second in injuries according to adjusted games lost, and tied for the most blown fourth-quarter leads (six). These are areas where we would typically expect to see regression in 2017, moving the Chargers closer to average health and fewer late-game disappointments. For example, teams since 2001 with at least four blown fourth-quarter leads won an average of 2.2 more games the following season (Table 1).

Table 1. Win Changes by Blown 4th-Quarter Leads

Blown Q4 Leads	Teams	Wins in Y	Wins in Y+1	Dif
0	74	10.3	8.1	-2.2
1	111	9.1	8.5	-0.6
2	143	7.7	8.0	+0.3
3	89	6.9	7.4	+0.5
4	43	5.7	7.9	+2.2
5+	19	5.9	8.1	+2.2

Note: 2016 Chargers had six blown leads.

Of course, we could have written the same thing about regression and the Chargers for the past few seasons, but they still kept dropping like flies and finding new ways to lose games. The 2015 Chargers tied for the league lead with five blown fourth-quarter leads, making San Diego the first team

---

1 http://www.pro-football-reference.com/leaders/career_av_career.htm

2017 Chargers Schedule

Week	Opp.	Week	Opp.	Week	Opp.
1	at DEN (Mon.)	7	DEN	13	CLE
2	MIA	8	at NE	14	WAS
3	KC	9	BYE	15	at KC (Sat.)
4	PHI	10	at JAC	16	at NYJ
5	at NYG	11	BUF	17	OAK
6	at OAK	12	at DAL (Thu.)		

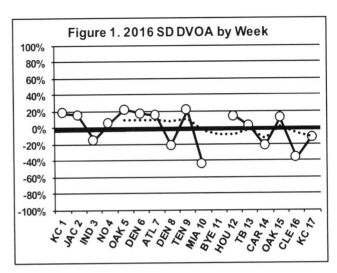

Figure 1. 2016 SD DVOA by Week

since the 2001-02 Carolina Panthers to blow at least five fourth-quarter leads in consecutive regular seasons. And the Chargers ranked 26th or worse in AGL in each of the last four seasons. Something had to change here.

One way to promote change is new leadership. The Chargers fired head coach Mike McCoy after four seasons, and hired Buffalo offensive coordinator Anthony Lynn for his first head coaching job in the NFL. Time will tell if Lynn was the best hire, but it was certainly time for McCoy to go. After he snuck into the playoffs at 9-7 in 2013, the Chargers consistently declined over the rest of his tenure, only winning nine games in the last two seasons combined. That's just one more win than the number of children for quarterback Philip Rivers. Rivers never dipped below 4,286 passing yards or 29 touchdown passes in a season under McCoy, but the Chargers have essentially been wasting a highly-paid quarterback in his mid-thirties.

The very first game of McCoy's tenure back in 2013 was really a harbinger of things to come. The Chargers were hosting Houston in the *Monday Night Football* double-header, and managed to blow a 28-7 lead in the second half en route to a

Figure 2. Crazy Philip Rivers Losses

B	I	N	G	O
2013 HOU: Blew 28-7 lead at home	2008 DEN: Ed Hochuli botched Cutler fumble call	Missed a game-tying FG against the Patriots (2x)	2012 BAL: Ray Rice converted a 4th-and-29 checkdown	2016 MIA: Rivers 4Q pick parade (game-losing pick-6)
2006 NE: Fumbled Tom Brady's INT on 4th down	2015 PIT: Le'Veon Bell GW TD run w/0:00 left	2011 DEN: Tebow'd in OT	2012 NO: Rivers game-ending strip-sack	2010 OAK: Down 1 point, Rivers fumble-6
2016 CLE: Missed game-tying FG vs. 0-14 team	2016 IND: Henry fumble w/1:02 left, down 4		2016 KC: Blew a 17-pt 4Q lead to Alex Smith	2016 NO: Blew a 34-21 lead in last 5:00
2011 KC: Rivers fumbled snap at KC 15 w/0:48 left	2016 OAK: botched hold on game-tying FG	2013 TEN: Allowed 34-yd TD pass w/0:15 left	2009 NYJ: N.Kaeding missed 3 FGs	2010 SEA: Allowed 99-yd GW kick return TD
2008 CAR: Allowed GW TD pass on final play	2008 PIT: Only 11-10 loss in NFL history	2012 DEN: Rivers pick-6 after blowing 24-0 lead	2015 OAK: Turnover on downs in OT, down 3	2013 WAS: Allowed TD drive to start OT

31-28 loss. Fast forward to 2016, and not much had changed. The Chargers led 27-10 in the fourth quarter of Week 1 at Kansas City, but blew that lead and lost in overtime, setting the tone for a season of missed opportunities.

During McCoy's tenure (2013-16), the Chargers lost an NFL-high 16 games in which they had a fourth-quarter lead. That is a fourth of McCoy's San Diego tenure that the Chargers spent losing games they looked like they were going to win. The Chargers sure found some excruciating ways to lose these games, and while the defense takes the brunt of the blame, there were also some doozies for the offense, the special teams, and even the officials. In fact, in the Week 10 edition of *Clutch Encounters* on our website, we put together a BINGO card for the "Crazy Chargers Losses" of the Rivers era (Figure 2). There were classics such as the time Marlon McCree fumbled a Tom Brady interception on fourth down in the playoffs (2006), Ray Rice's conversion on fourth-and-29 (2012), and when referee Ed Hochuli blew a call on an obvious Jay Cutler fumble in the red zone (2008). But there was also a lot of 2016 featured, including the 13-point blown lead in the final five minutes against the Saints, the game-losing pick-six Rivers threw to Miami's Kiko Alonso, a late fumble in Indianapolis, and a botched hold by punter Drew Kaser on a game-tying field goal attempt against Oakland. The Chargers even kept adding to the list after that, missing a game-tying field goal try in Cleveland on Christmas Eve to give the 1-15 Browns their only win of the season.

In the Week 15 rematch with Oakland, McCoy quit on the game when he did not use his final timeout with 17 seconds left and the Raiders holding a 19-16 lead. While the Chargers likely would have lost 22-16 after an Oakland field goal on fourth down, there was still time to try something crazy: first an all-out field goal block, then a Hail Mary or a crazy play full of laterals. But apparently crazy things only happen to the Chargers, not for them. Still, that surrender is symbolic of McCoy's time as San Diego's coach. In our Aggressiveness Index metric, which looks at fourth-down decisions, McCoy ranks just 131st out of 149 coaches since 1989.

To play devil's advocate, McCoy was never dealt a healthy roster. In his four seasons, the Chargers ranked 28th, 31st,

26th, and 31st in adjusted games lost (AGL). While AGL and winning percentage do not necessarily have a strong correlation, it is certainly better to have a healthier team than one of the league's most injured rosters. Out of the 70 coaches with three years of experience that we studied since 2002, McCoy's teams averaged the most AGL (104.8), the worst average AGL rank (29.0), and the worst average z-score (minus-1.3) in AGL.[2]

So if McCoy ever wanted to break coaching protocol and actually give a candid take on his time in San Diego, he would have a legitimate gripe about never having a healthy enough roster. This is something that usually regresses to the mean, but certain teams—the Giants in recent years, or the Bill Polian-era Colts—have had extended runs of bad injury numbers. We did not find any proof that a coach's work habits influence his team's AGL. Under Lynn, the Chargers have made John Lott their new strength and conditioning coach. Lott is famous for his energetic behavior at the bench press for the scouting combine. For what it's worth, Lott left his strength and conditioning job with the Browns after a 2006 season where Cleveland had the highest AGL in the league. When he started in Arizona in 2007, the Cardinals fell from fourth to 26th in AGL. Again, injuries are tough to predict.

If the Chargers can finally stay healthy this year, then Lynn is inheriting a very talented starting roster on both sides of the ball. Depth is of course an issue, but let's consider the range of talent that this team has put together. As always, we have to start at the quarterback. The fact that Rivers has started every game since 2006—185 and counting when we include the playoffs—has been remarkable, especially when so many of his offensive teammates have been hurt. This is the weakness in blaming injuries for McCoy's ineffective tenure. Yes, there have been a lot of injuries, but a top player at the most important position remained healthy enough to suit up every single week, and the Chargers still went 27-37 over that stretch.

Lynn is now tasked with keeping Rivers healthy as he reaches his age-36 season. Given Lynn's background, he has a good shot to do this. Lynn was a backup to Terrell Davis in Denver when the Broncos helped an old John Elway to two Super Bowls by giving Davis an astronomical number of touches over those seasons. He learned the "ground and pound" philosophy while coaching running backs under Rex Ryan with the Jets (2009-2014) and Bills (2015-16). Lynn was promoted to offensive coordinator in Week 3 last year after Ryan fired Greg Roman, and then served as interim head coach in Week 17 when Ryan was fired. However, he has not completely turned over the Chargers staff. Lynn has retained offensive coordinator Ken Whisenhunt, who has worked with Rivers in 2013 and 2016.

Offenses like to promote a balanced attack, but the NFL's best rushing teams often operate with a run-first mentality. While Lynn was in Buffalo, the Bills had the No. 1 rushing offense by DVOA, gaining 2,630 yards and scoring 29 times on the ground. Tyrod Taylor's mobility is not something that Rivers will replicate, but the rushing numbers were still great without Taylor's added effectiveness, and it's not like the Bills had a Dallas-like offensive line. Lynn can certainly work with Melvin Gordon, who dismissed criticism of his failure to score a touchdown as a rookie by scoring at least one in each of his first five games of 2016 (12 touchdowns overall). Gordon still only averaged 3.93 yards per carry, but his offensive line did him few favors. According to ESPN Stats & Info, Gordon ranked 34th in 2016 with 1.95 yards before first contact per rush. Buffalo's two leading backs under Lynn, LeSean McCoy (3.93) and Mike Gillislee (3.89), led the league. Gordon did finish eighth in yards after contact per rush (1.98), so a new scheme and revamped line could do him wonders, especially if the Chargers are going to start putting more responsibility on the third-year back.

Rivers could use the balance, which means he won't have to keep throwing 600-plus passes per season as he gets closer to the end of his career. Rivers has led the league in interceptions in two of the last three seasons, including 21 picks last season. However, that number again speaks to some of the bad luck for the Chargers in 2016. Defenders caught almost everything Rivers offered them, as he only had one dropped interception. Compare that to 2004 draft classmates Ben Roethlisberger (12) and Eli Manning (11), who both had dropped interception totals in the double digits.

The Chargers have also added depth at the "skill positions" around Rivers so as to avoid a situation like last year when the offense added 45 AGL from Stevie Johnson (16), Keenan Allen (15), and Danny Woodhead (14) alone. Allen has especially had a rough two seasons, losing time to a kidney injury and a torn ACL in Week 1 last year. He is a No. 1 wide receiver, but the Chargers added some insurance with Clemson rookie Mike Williams with the No. 7 overall pick. Williams' size makes him a dangerous red zone target, but Playmaker Score barely puts him above 70.0 percent, which pales in comparison to the two wideouts he was drafted in between: Corey Davis (90.6 percent) and John Ross (96.9 percent). The Chargers still have Tyrell Williams, who had a breakout year in Allen's absence, and Travis Benjamin can fill the Malcom Floyd role of taking the top off the defense. Future Hall of Fame tight end Antonio Gates will return for his 15th season, but Hunter Henry looked like the real deal with a team-high eight touchdowns as a rookie. If Gordon, Henry, and Williams continue to develop, then the Chargers will have a strong collection of young skill players for Rivers' twilight years.

On defense, long-time assistant and defensive coordinator John Pagano moved on to Oakland. He will be replaced by Gus Bradley, who also tied the Chargers with six blown fourth-quarter leads as Jacksonville's head coach last year. But Bradley can get back to focusing on just the defense here, and the Chargers will change from their long-time 3-4 scheme to the 4-3 defense Bradley used in Jacksonville and as Seattle's defensive coordinator under Pete Carroll before that.

Bradley was interested in drafting Joey Bosa a year ago, but

---

2 http://www.footballoutsiders.com/stat-analysis/2017/nfl-head-coaches-adjusted-games-lost

the Chargers snatched the reigning Defensive Rookie of the Year first. Bosa played in a 4-3 in college, so he is very excited about the opportunity to play for the energetic Bradley, who he met during the draft process. "When I heard [Bradley] was going to be our defensive coordinator I couldn't have been happier with the decision. I feel what we are running this year fits me better," Bosa said in April. Bosa was already very impressive as a rookie with 10.5 sacks, despite missing four games after a long contract dispute and a hamstring injury. The Chargers also locked up edge rusher Melvin Ingram this offseason with a four-year deal worth $66 million, with $42 million guaranteed. This gives the Chargers a pair of edge rushers that can rival their division foes in Oakland (Khalil Mack and Bruce Irvin), Kansas City (Justin Houston and Dee Ford), and Denver (Von Miller and Shane Ray). The Chargers should also provide Bradley with a standout pair of cornerbacks in Casey Hayward and Jason Verrett. Last season, Verrett missed 12 games with a partially torn ACL while Hayward stepped up to lead the NFL with seven interceptions. Any coordinator would love to run a defense with two strong pass-rushers and two cover corners, so Bradley is in an ideal positon.

If you are starting to get jazzed up over this roster, then let's acknowledge the clear weakness that could hold this team back: the offensive line. It has been a mess for years despite past efforts to fix it. Free-agent signing Orlando Franklin was a bust at guard, and the Chargers released him just two years into his five-year deal. Left tackle King Dunlap was released and retired this offseason. Whether he was at tackle or guard, D.J. Fluker never lived up to his first-round potential and was released in March.

In the latest attempt to repair the line, the Chargers signed left tackle Russell Okung (88 career starts) to a four-year deal worth $53 million. The draft was used to beef up the team's disappointing guard situation with second-round pick Forrest Lamp (Western Kentucky) and third-round pick Dan Feeney (Indiana), both four-year starters in college. The two became fast friends after meeting at the Senior Bowl, and could be lining up next to each other this season. "We think [Feeney] can play center for us. We've got two guards and a center position where we're kind of looking at different combinations, and he's definitely in the mix," Lynn said in May.

The offensive line must protect Rivers better and open up more holes for Gordon. If Lynn cannot get the line to improve, then this dream of the Chargers reshaping into a playoff team will not be a reality. However, do not underestimate the im-

Table 2. First-Year Results After Relocation Since 1980

Team	Years	Old City	W-L	New City	W-L
Chargers	2016-17	San Diego	5-11	Los Angeles	TBD
Rams	2015-16	St. Louis	7-9	Los Angeles	4-12
Oilers	1996-97	Houston	8-8	Tennessee	8-8
Browns/Ravens	1995-96	Cleveland	5-11	Baltimore	4-12
Raiders	1994-95	Los Angeles	9-7	Oakland	8-8
Rams	1994-95	Los Angeles	4-12	St. Louis	7-9
Cardinals	1987-88	St. Louis	7-8	Phoenix	7-9
Colts	1983-84	Baltimore	7-9	Indianapolis	4-12
Raiders	1981-82	Oakland	7-9	Los Angeles	8-1

Note: Expansion teams not included.

pact of a new coach and the potential of new, high draft picks.

In summary, if Angelenos did not enjoy the city's return to the NFL with the Rams last year, then consider the differences with the Chargers. You get a young, talented roster with a franchise quarterback instead of Case Keenum and Jared Goff, and the rookie coach is a wild card instead of Jeff Fisher, the master of 7-9 bullshit. In fact, Fisher was an overseer of the NFL's last two relocations. Past relocations have not gone so well in the first year. None of the last nine teams in new cities won more than eight games, though the Raiders finished 8-1 in a strike-shortened 1982 season (Table 2).

The Chargers will make their Los Angeles return official in Week 2 against Miami. This is the first of three seasons where the team will play its home games at StubHub Center in Carson, California, until the new stadium is ready for 2020. So the Chargers are actually closer to Compton than Hollywood. It will be odd to see an NFL team play in front of a capacity crowd of 30,000 fans, but perhaps that could help create a more raucous, intimate setting. Of course, the Chargers have to give fans something to cheer for first, but this team is good enough to split games in a tough AFC West division. The post-bye schedule also features the Jets, Browns, Bills, and Jaguars, so there are good opportunities for the Chargers to get back to a winning record, and perhaps a wild-card berth.

You can take the Chargers out of San Diego, but does that leave the crazy losses behind as well? We'll keep a fresh marker for our BINGO card, just in case.

Scott Kacsmar

2016 Chargers Stats by Week

Wk	vs.	W-L	PF	PA	YDF	YDA	TO	Total	Off	Def	ST
1	at KC	L	27	33	388	413	+1	18%	39%	8%	-14%
2	JAC	W	38	14	357	388	+2	15%	20%	6%	1%
3	at IND	L	22	26	352	410	-1	-15%	-21%	-13%	-8%
4	NO	L	34	35	346	275	-1	5%	-22%	-23%	4%
5	at OAK	L	31	34	423	389	-3	22%	21%	-14%	-13%
6	DEN	W	21	13	265	304	0	17%	10%	-5%	1%
7	at ATL	W	33	30	426	386	-1	14%	-3%	-19%	-1%
8	at DEN	L	19	27	369	324	0	-22%	-24%	-12%	-10%
9	TEN	W	43	35	476	393	+3	20%	26%	4%	-1%
10	MIA	L	24	31	379	337	-3	-45%	-50%	14%	19%
11	BYE										
12	at HOU	W	21	13	302	353	+3	14%	16%	0%	-2%
13	TB	L	21	28	330	349	-1	1%	14%	8%	-4%
14	at CAR	L	16	28	278	272	-4	-22%	-33%	-20%	-9%
15	OAK	L	16	19	263	345	0	11%	-21%	-34%	-1%
16	at CLE	L	17	20	356	251	-1	-37%	-35%	-9%	-11%
17	KC	L	27	37	398	365	-1	-12%	21%	8%	-26%

Trends and Splits

	Offense	Rank	Defense	Rank
Total DVOA	-3.2%	18	-6.8%	7
Unadjusted VOA	-4.3%	20	-8.0%	6
Weighted Trend	-9.2%	24	-6.9%	8
Variance	7.1%	24	1.9%	2
Average Opponent	0.4%	19	0.2%	14
Passing	14.1%	15	-2.5%	9
Rushing	-14.7%	24	-12.6%	15
First Down	-4.4%	18	-4.2%	10
Second Down	-1.3%	16	-11.5%	7
Third Down	-3.6%	18	-4.9%	11
First Half	8.1%	12	-11.6%	4
Second Half	9.6%	10	7.0%	25
Red Zone	-6.7%	19	-12.1%	7
Late and Close	-6.7%	19	20.8%	29

Five-Year Performance

Year	W-L	Pyth W	Est W	PF	PA	TO	Total	Rk	Off	Rk	Def	Rk	ST	Rk	Off AGL	Rk	Def AGL	Rk	Off Age	Rk	Def Age	Rk	ST Age	Rk
2012	7-9	8.0	6.6	350	350	+2	-9.05%	22	-10.0%	24	2.0%	18	3.0%	8	30.2	18	19.3	10	28.4	2	27.8	6	27.1	2
2013	9-7	9.2	8.8	396	348	-4	6.4%	12	23.1%	2	17.5%	32	0.8%	15	46.3	23	44.8	25	27.5	10	25.8	28	26.0	17
2014	9-7	8.0	8.0	348	348	-5	-0.6%	16	7.0%	11	4.9%	25	-2.7%	23	82.1	32	37.0	15	27.9	4	26.7	17	26.6	4
2015	4-12	5.9	6.0	320	398	-4	-14.8%	24	0.9%	15	10.4%	28	-5.3%	31	55.7	27	25.7	10	27.6	7	25.9	30	26.5	7
2016	5-11	7.7	6.9	410	423	-7	-1.1%	19	-3.2%	18	-6.8%	7	-4.8%	29	61.7	29	66.0	29	27.9	4	25.7	31	25.7	24

2016 Performance Based on Most Common Personnel Groups

LACH Offense					LACH Offense vs. Opponents					LACH Defense					LACH Defense vs. Opponents			
Pers	Freq	Yds	DVOA	Run%	Pers	Freq	Yds	DVOA	Run%	Pers	Freq	Yds	DVOA	Pers	Freq	Yds	DVOA
11	61%	6.0	3.9%	25%	Base	33%	5.3	-6.5%	60%	Base	35%	5.3	-13.3%	11	55%	5.9	-8.4%
12	19%	5.7	4.3%	52%	Nickel	56%	6.3	9.1%	28%	Nickel	47%	5.7	-7.4%	12	18%	5.9	1.1%
21	6%	4.3	-35.8%	54%	Dime+	8%	3.8	-28.2%	7%	Dime+	15%	6.5	7.2%	21	8%	4.9	0.0%
22	5%	5.8	28.3%	81%	Goal Line	1%	0.7	28.7%	67%	Goal Line	2%	0.6	31.2%	13	4%	4.2	-30.8%
13	4%	4.9	1.1%	58%	Big	0%	2.6	-7.3%	60%	Big	1%	2.1	-57.3%	611	3%	3.7	-39.6%

Strategic Tendencies

Run/Pass		Rk	Formation		Rk	Pass Rush		Rk	Secondary		Rk	Strategy		Rk
Runs, first half	38%	15	Form: Single Back	81%	9	Rush 3	9.6%	13	4 DB	35%	10	Play-action	17%	23
Runs, first down	52%	7	Form: Empty Back	7%	14	Rush 4	65.8%	16	5 DB	47%	28	Avg Box (Off)	6.22	10
Runs, second-long	21%	32	Pers: 3+ WR	63%	22	Rush 5	21.2%	16	6+ DB	15%	11	Avg Box (Def)	6.26	12
Runs, power sit.	51%	24	Pers: 2+ TE/6+ OL	33%	8	Rush 6+	3.4%	27	CB by Sides	68%	21	Offensive Pace	30.87	21
Runs, behind 2H	29%	11	Pers: 6+ OL	3%	20	Sacks by LB	52.9%	13	S/CB Cover Ratio	25%	21	Defensive Pace	30.37	18
Pass, ahead 2H	52%	7	Shotgun/Pistol	64%	18	Sacks by DB	1.4%	29	DB Blitz	8%	23	Go for it on 4th	0.73	26

The Chargers recovered only six of 18 fumbles on offense, but they also recovered nine of 13 fumbles on defense. ⬛ This was the first time since 2012 that the Chargers did not rank dead last in use of play-action. Perhaps they finally figured out that Philip Rivers is really good on the play-action deep pass. The Chargers led the NFL with 83.9% DVOA on play-action passes but were 26th with -1.5% DVOA on other passes, matching a trend we've seen for the last few years. ☞ With Melvin Gordon proving much more dangerous in his second season, the average number of men in the box against the Chargers offense went from 31st to 10th. Philip Rivers faced a blitzing defensive back on only 5.9 percent of pass plays—only Alex Smith faced a pass-rushing defensive back less often—but he crushed these plays for an average gain of 10.4 yards. ☞ As for the Chargers themselves, they dropped from seventh to 23rd in use of defensive backs in the pass rush, and dropped from third to 29th in the percentage of sacks that came from defensive backs.

Passing

Player	DYAR	DVOA	Plays	NtYds	Avg	YAC	C%	TD	Int
P.Rivers	498	1.4%	615	4120	6.7	5.8	60.7%	33	21

Rushing

Player	DYAR	DVOA	Plays	Yds	Avg	TD	Fum	Suc
M.Gordon	2	-8.4%	254	997	3.9	10	0	45%
K.Farrow	11	-1.5%	36	125	3.5	0	0	53%
D.Woodhead*	30	33.7%	19	116	6.1	0	0	63%
P.Rivers	5	4.2%	6	40	6.7	0	0	-
K.Barner	46	38.1%	24	123	5.1	2	0	58%

Receiving

Player	DYAR	DVOA	Plays	Ctch	Yds	Y/C	YAC	TD	C%
T.Williams	201	9.0%	118	68	1032	15.2	6.0	7	58%
D.Inman	140	5.5%	97	58	810	14.0	3.7	4	60%
T.Benjamin	144	12.1%	75	47	677	14.4	5.2	4	63%
K.Allen	33	36.8%	7	6	63	10.5	3.0	0	86%
A.Gates	4	-6.6%	93	53	548	10.3	3.5	7	57%
H.Henry	148	33.4%	53	36	478	13.3	5.4	8	68%
M.Gordon	105	21.0%	57	41	419	10.2	10.1	2	72%
K.Farrow	-35	-54.5%	16	13	70	5.4	6.8	0	81%
D.McCluster*	-23	-52.0%	11	7	36	5.1	6.3	0	64%
R.Hillman*	-3	-19.3%	9	4	49	12.3	15.8	0	44%
D.Woodhead*	18	26.0%	8	6	35	5.8	5.2	1	75%
K.Barner	-15	-40.7%	11	5	42	8.4	9.4	0	45%

Offensive Line

Player	Pos	Age	GS	Snaps	Pen	Sk	Pass	Run	Player	Pos	Age	GS	Snaps	Pen	Sk	Pass	Run
Matt Slauson	C	31	16/16	1019	1	1.0	8	6	King Dunlap*	LT	32	12/12	775	7	4.5	17	3
D.J. Fluker*	RG	26	16/16	992	7	2.5	8	6	Chris Hairston	LT	28	15/5	325	1	2.0	5	1
Joseph Barksdale	RT	28	15/15	971	9	7.0	14	7	Spencer Pulley	C	24	16/0	222	2	1.5	6	1
Orlando Franklin*	LG	30	16/16	920	3	2.5	13	5	Russell Okung	LT	30	16/16	1067	11	7.0	18	2

Year	Yards	ALY	Rank	Power	Rank	Stuff	Rank	2nd Lev	Rank	Open Field	Rank	Sacks	ASR	Rank	Press	Rank	F-Start	Cont.
2014	3.51	3.51	31	78%	3	21%	28	0.95	28	0.52	27	37	6.1%	17	21.8%	9	14	27
2015	3.53	3.47	31	73%	6	20%	15	0.85	32	0.53	27	40	5.4%	11	24.3%	14	20	22
2016	3.92	3.97	23	66%	13	21%	19	1.01	30	0.76	12	36	6.6%	24	28.7%	23	19	37

2016 ALY by direction: Left End 2.82 (27) Left Tackle 3.44 (29) Mid/Guard 4.10 (18) Right Tackle 4.48 (10) Right End 3.80 (17)

There will be a lot of competition for starting jobs along this line, but the tackles appear to be set in stone. On the right side, Joe Barskdale is unlikely to wow anyone, and he has ranked 20th in snaps per blown block in each of the last two seasons (out of 38 right tackles in 2015, then 34 last year). Left tackle is a bit more interesting. King Dunlap dealt with injury issues throughout his career, but the same can be said about Russell Okung, whom the Chargers made the highest-paid left tackle in the league. Last year was the first time in his seven-year career that Okung played 16 games, but he should be an upgrade over Dunlap. Okung ranked 18th in snaps per blown block compared to 31st for Dunlap. And this is really the first time since his rookie year with Matt Hasselbeck in 2010 that Okung will play with a veteran pocket passer who gets rid of the ball quickly. ☞ The Chargers have numerous options along the interior of the line. Matt Slauson struggled at center last year (28th in snaps per blown block), but could move to left guard where he played for the Jets under Lynn in New York. ☞ The Chargers drafted Max Tuerk in the third round of the 2016 draft, but the USC product did not see the field last year. He could battle for the starting center job with Spencer Pulley, a second-year UDFA from Vanderbilt who got some first-team reps at OTAs. ☞ Second-round rookie Forrest Lamp is a favorite for the right guard job, but he is versatile enough to play center or tackle as well. Lamp was a draft favorite for many analysts, so it was a little surprising to see him slip to the second round. He should be a strong pass protector for Rivers. Fellow rookie Dan Feeney is more of a natural at right guard, but he should also be considered for the center position that the Chargers have struggled to fill since Nick Hardwick's career ended in 2014.

Defensive Front Seven

Defensive Line	Age	Pos	G	Snaps	Plays	Overall TmPct	Rk	Stop	Dfts	BTkl	Runs	vs. Run St%	Rk	RuYd	Rk	Pass Rush Sack	Hit	Hur	Dsrpt
Corey Liuget	27	DE	16	811	37	4.5%	43	33	13	3	31	90%	10	1.6	26	0.0	7	26	3
Tenny Palepoi	27	DE	13	378	13	1.9%	86	10	4	0	12	83%	26	2.2	38	0.0	6	15	0
Damion Square	28	DT	11	362	13	2.3%	85	12	5	3	9	89%	13	0.3	2	2.5	1	1	0
Brandon Mebane	32	DT	10	340	22	4.3%	48	14	5	1	19	63%	81	1.9	32	1.0	2	4	0
Darius Philon	23	DE	14	265	11	1.5%	--	10	1	1	10	90%	--	2.3	--	1.0	1	3	0

Edge Rushers	Age	Pos	G	Snaps	Plays	Overall TmPct	Rk	Stop	Dfts	BTkl	Runs	vs. Run St%	Rk	RuYd	Rk	Pass Rush Sack	Hit	Hur	Dsrpt
Melvin Ingram	28	OLB	16	959	65	7.9%	11	45	21	10	38	71%	62	2.6	52	8.0	12	42	5
Joey Bosa	22	DE	12	563	41	6.6%	22	35	21	2	28	79%	30	1.1	10	10.5	11	26	2
Kyle Emanuel	26	OLB	16	545	56	6.8%	21	34	12	2	40	73%	57	3.1	70	0.5	3	6	0
Jeremiah Attaochu	24	OLB	8	176	7	1.7%	--	4	3	1	3	33%	--	4.3	--	2.0	3	13	0

Linebackers	Age	Pos	G	Snaps	Plays	Overall TmPct	Rk	Stop	Dfts	BTkl	Runs	vs. Run St%	Rk	RuYd	Rk	Pass Rush Sack	Hit	Hur	Tgts	vs. Pass Suc%	Rk	AdjYd	Rk	PD	Int
Jatavis Brown	23	ILB	12	600	82	13.3%	37	41	21	7	32	50%	81	4.4	76	3.0	0	4	33	54%	28	6.3	33	6	0
Korey Toomer	29	ILB	13	543	73	10.9%	48	49	20	8	48	73%	9	2.8	15	1.0	2	3	19	68%	3	6.7	44	2	0
Denzel Perryman	24	ILB	12	485	72	11.6%	47	35	11	11	40	60%	58	3.6	41	2.0	2	3	22	35%	75	7.6	62	2	1

Year	Yards	ALY	Rank	Power	Rank	Stuff	Rank	2nd Level	Rank	Open Field	Rank	Sacks	ASR	Rank	Press	Rank
2014	4.03	4.30	20	58%	9	20%	14	1.20	22	0.56	7	26	5.5%	27	25.8%	11
2015	4.95	4.60	28	73%	27	18%	25	1.38	31	1.21	32	32	5.8%	26	25.2%	16
2016	3.85	3.65	6	71%	28	24%	4	1.18	18	0.73	16	35	5.9%	15	26.8%	18

2016 ALY by direction: Left End 3.40 (7)   Left Tackle 5.21 (29)   Mid/Guard 3.46 (2)   Right Tackle 3.16 (5)   Right End 4.14 (22)

Melvin Ingram may not have a lot of fame with national fans, but the 2012 first-round pick is finally living up to his potential and has a shiny new $66 million contract to show for it. Ingram started off as a situational pass-rusher, and missed 19 games in 2013-14. He had 10.5 sacks in 2015, his first full year as a starter, and racked up 8.0 sacks and 42 hurries last season. He did get credit for a league-high 13 split hurries where more than one defender helped create the pressure, but if Ingram is only a team's second-best edge rusher, then that's a very good thing. ⬧ All eyes will be on Joey Bosa this year, showing what he can do with a full training camp and in a 4-3 system that better suits his skill set. ⬧ Nose tackle Brandon Mebane played for Gus Bradley in Seattle, so he should feel more comfortable after some struggles against the run in his Chargers debut last year. ⬧ Corey Liuget was the team's franchise player a few years ago, but failed to produce a sack for the first time in his career in 2016. Out of 91 players charted with at least 20 hurries in 2016, Liuget was the only one without a sack, so he'll hope to finish more plays this year. ⬧ At inside linebacker, 2015 second-round pick Denzel Perryman is the big name, but he experienced a bit of a sophomore slump. As a rookie in 2015, Perryman had six more stops on 99 fewer snaps compared to what he did in 2016. ⬧ Jatavis Brown and Korey Toomer had better production and coverage stats than Perryman, as well as fewer missed tackles. Brown's performance as a rookie made Manti Te'o expendable after four injury-riddled seasons. Te'o went to New Orleans, which we imagine offers plenty of catfish options.

Defensive Secondary

Secondary	Age	Pos	G	Snaps	Plays	TmPct	Rk	Stop	Dfts	BTkl	Runs	St%	Rk	RuYd	Rk	Tgts	Tgt%	Rk	Dist	Suc%	Rk	AdjYd	Rk	PD	Int
Dwight Lowery	31	FS	16	1003	69	8.4%	53	26	11	5	24	50%	16	9.4	62	39	8.7%	42	11.2	47%	37	8.8	36	8	1
Casey Hayward	28	CB	16	986	77	9.3%	31	37	14	3	12	67%	5	5.1	16	80	18.4%	43	12.5	52%	27	6.8	20	19	7
Adrian Phillips	25	SS	14	543	38	5.3%	--	12	3	5	19	32%	--	10.3	--	11	4.4%	--	16.6	49%	--	8.3	--	3	1
Jahleel Addae	27	SS	8	510	52	12.6%	15	25	10	7	27	59%	8	5.3	16	19	8.3%	33	11.5	40%	53	8.1	28	4	1
Craig Mager	25	CB	11	408	34	6.0%	81	12	6	4	9	44%	33	4.8	13	30	16.5%	19	9.8	38%	85	8.7	69	4	1
Trevor Williams	24	CB	12	388	35	5.7%	--	17	10	2	10	80%	--	2.6	--	41	23.8%	--	14.2	44%	--	7.5	--	5	0
Brandon Flowers*	31	CB	6	351	33	10.7%	--	16	10	2	8	50%	--	3.5	--	32	20.4%	--	7.6	50%	--	9.3	--	5	1
Dexter McCoil	26	SS	16	249	27	3.3%	--	9	4	4	6	17%	--	11.5	--	13	11.9%	--	7.8	42%	--	9.8	--	3	1
Steve Williams	26	CB	6	219	20	6.5%	--	3	0	0	3	0%	--	7.3	--	22	23.0%	--	10.9	34%	--	6.7	--	2	0
Tre Boston	25	FS	15	840	59	7.6%	57	22	13	8	22	45%	26	6.0	24	24	6.6%	17	16.7	62%	1	6.0	5	6	2

Year	Pass D Rank	vs. #1 WR	Rk	vs. #2 WR	Rk	vs. Other WR	Rk	vs. TE	Rk	vs. RB	Rk
2014	25	-3.6%	13	11.2%	26	12.9%	26	-4.0%	16	17.3%	27
2015	21	4.9%	20	7.6%	19	-10.5%	9	34.8%	31	14.1%	26
2016	9	-10.4%	6	5.7%	22	-25.0%	2	-2.1%	15	-3.5%	17

Jason Verrett was a first-round selection in 2014, but has missed as many games (24) as he has played through three seasons. Durability has always been a concern, but when healthy, Verrett provides the Chargers with strong coverage on the outside and in the slot. ☞ If defenses choose to target Casey Hayward instead, he can make quarterbacks pay. Hayward's league-best seven interceptions were reminiscent of his 2012 rookie season, when he picked off six passes for the Packers. Injuries caused him to fall out of favor in Green Bay, but he still charted well in 2015, making him a smart signing by the Chargers. Hayward has ranked in the top 20 in adjusted yards per pass in consecutive seasons. Now the Chargers just hope he and Verrett can stay healthy together for 16 games. Third corner Craig Mager was a liability last season and has not proven much through two seasons. ☞ The safety duo of Dwight Lowery and Jahleel Addae was passable, not making the team miss Eric Weddle too much. Still, after the offensive line, safety may be the position group where the Chargers are least impressive. One move the team made to solve that problem: signing Tre Boston two weeks after Carolina released him in May. Boston had his most productive season in 2016, finishing No. 1 among safeties in adjusted success rate, albeit against just 24 targets. He ended 2016 on injured reserve, so he's an ideal fit for the Chargers. ☞ The team also added safety depth by using a fourth-round pick on Rayshawn Jenkins (Florida) and a fifth-round pick on Desmond King (Iowa). Bradley will look to use Jenkins as his Kam Chancellor "enforcer" type. That might sound unlikely, but you'll have to remember that even Chancellor was just a fifth-round pick in 2010 before becoming a Pro Bowl starter in his second season. King has good ball skills, but a lack of athleticism has moved him from college corner to NFL safety.

Special Teams

Year	DVOA	Rank	FG/XP	Rank	Net Kick	Rank	Kick Ret	Rank	Net Punt	Rank	Punt Ret	Rank	Hidden	Rank
2014	-2.7%	23	0.6	13	-8.3	29	-1.4	20	-3.0	20	-1.6	13	-0.4	19
2015	-5.3%	31	-1.2	19	-2.7	22	-4.3	26	-12.3	29	-6.1	28	-7.8	25
2016	-4.8%	29	-8.7	29	-2.6	20	-4.7	26	-5.8	25	-2.2	20	-12.3	31

The Chargers continued to field one of the league's worst special teams units. Kicker Josh Lambo missed four extra points for the second year in a row, but more importantly were the failed game-tying field goals in losses to the Raiders and Browns. The first was not his fault as punter/holder Drew Kaser botched the hold, but Lambo has not done well in crunch time in his two years. In the fourth quarter and overtime during his career, he's 15-of-19 (78.9 percent) on field goals. He's also just 4-of-8 on field goals from 50-plus yards. ☞ Kaser was below average on his punts, and the coverage units were also not sharp. ☞ As you might imagine, the returns were also not good. The Chargers averaged 18.1 yards per kick return, ranked 30th in the league, and did not have a return specialist rank in the top 24 of our value metric on kickoffs or punts. Isaiah Burse mostly handled those duties, but none of his 24 combined returns gained more than 30 yards. Travis Benjamin is still an option on punt returns, and he returned three for touchdowns as a member of the Browns. He averaged 6.6 yards per punt return for the Chargers last year.

Los Angeles Rams

2016 Record: 4-12	Total DVOA: -28.6% (30th)	2017 Mean Projection: 8.0 wins	On the Clock (0-4): 10%
Pythagorean Wins: 3.3 (32nd)	Offense: -37.8% (32nd)	Postseason Odds: 34.4%	Mediocrity (5-7): 33%
Snap-Weighted Age: 25.7 (32nd)	Defense: -2% (15th)	Super Bowl Odds: 4.9%	Playoff Contender (8-10): 40%
Average Opponent: -1.4% (24th)	Special Teams: 7.1% (3rd)	Proj. Avg. Opponent: -0.1% (18th)	Super Bowl Contender (11+): 18%

2016: A bad case of whuppin' Goff.

2017: Rams may approach platonic ideal of a no-offense, great-defense team.

As they prepared for their first season in Los Angeles since 1994, the Rams sought to make a splash to spark interest in their new (old) fan base. They traded up in the 2016 draft, moving from No. 15 to the first overall pick, and took a huge gamble on Jared Goff to be the franchise quarterback that would push the team over the top and into the playoffs. The cost was steep, much like the 2012 trade between the Rams and the Washington Redskins that sent the No. 2 pick (Robert Griffin III) to Washington. But if Goff could eventually lead the Rams to the promised land, it was a cost the Rams wanted to pay.

Head coach Jeff Fisher and general manager Les Snead were likely under pressure to win immediately upon the team's arrival in Los Angeles, as evidenced by Fisher's famous *Hard Knocks* speech proclaiming that he wasn't going to go 7-9 again. And Fisher didn't go 7-9, but not for the reason he would have liked. Instead of contending for a playoff spot, the Rams limped to a 4-12 record in 2016. Goff lost the quarterback competition to Case Keenum to start the year, and when he finally did get on the field, it wasn't pretty. No matter who was at quarterback in Los Angeles, the offense was a mess, ranking dead last in DVOA and derailing the Rams' playoff hopes.

With three games remaining in the season, Fisher got the ax, leaving behind an absolute disaster of an offense in need of major upgrades across the board. Los Angeles hired Redskins offensive coordinator Sean McVay as head coach just two weeks shy of his 31st birthday, and his goal is to fix Goff and, by extension, the rest of the offense. On one hand, it would be nearly impossible for the offense to be worse in 2017 than it was in 2016, due in large part to how terrible Los Angeles's quarterback and offensive line play was. But when you sell the farm to trade up for a quarterback, moving from "abysmal" to "mediocre" isn't the type of year-to-year improvement you have in mind.

Keenum began the year as the starter in order to help ease Goff into the league. Many questioned the logic of starting Keenum after using so much draft capital to trade for Goff, and the voices calling for Goff to start only got louder as Keenum posted -19.5% DVOA through nine games, good for 31st among 34 quarterbacks with a minimum of 200 pass attempts. After a 9-6 road win over the Jets pushed the Rams' record to 4-5, Fisher made the change at quarterback and inserted Goff into the starting lineup ahead of their Week 11 tilt against the Dolphins. What soon followed had fans that had initially been clamoring for Goff furiously deleting social media posts.

To put it bluntly, Goff was terrible. Among the 34 quarterbacks who met the minimum threshold for inclusion of 200 pass attempts, Goff finished dead last in both DYAR (-881) and DVOA (-74.8%). Granted, this was only across a seven-game sample without much help from his offensive line or wide receivers, but Goff's performance was historically bad.

All quarterbacks struggle when under pressure, and given that Goff led the league in pressure rate at 40.4 percent, it might be tempting to try and explain away his performance by saying he didn't get any help from his offensive line. However, Keenum faced a pressure rate of 21.2 percent with largely the same personnel in front of him, which suggests that Goff created some of that pass pressure with his own style of play. And when he did have time to throw, he didn't suddenly see a massive improvement in relative performance à la Andy Dalton. No, Goff turned in the worst performance without pressure of any quarterback in our database: -45.2%. The next-worst season for any quarterback with at least 200 passes since 2010? Brady Quinn had -6.7% DVOA without pressure for the 2012 Kansas City Chiefs; he hasn't taken a regular-season snap since. In 2016, Goff played worse *without* pressure than ten other quarterbacks did *with* pressure. The 2017 season will be critical for Goff's development, but based on historical precedent, it will be difficult for Goff to turn into an above-average starter after his mess of a half season.

It will certainly help Goff's development if the players around him provide a better support system than they did in 2016. The offensive line, led by 2014 No. 2 overall pick Greg Robinson at left tackle, finished 29th in both adjusted sack rate and adjusted line yards. Robinson's play was so disappointing that he ended up getting benched late in the year, but he was hardly the only player along the line underperforming for the Rams.

At OTAs, there was a lot of discussion of Robinson competing for the starting job at right tackle, but that plan changed when Los Angeles declined his fifth-year option and subsequently shipped him to Detroit in exchange for a 2018 sixth-round pick. Surely this is not what the Rams were hoping for with their final pick of the RG3 bounty. The Rams have clearly identified this weakness and made a big move to fix it,

2017 Rams Schedule

Week	Opp.	Week	Opp.	Week	Opp.
1	IND	7	ARI (U.K.)	13	at ARI
2	WAS	8	BYE	14	PHI
3	at SF (Thu.)	9	at NYG	15	at SEA
4	at DAL	10	HOU	16	at TEN
5	SEA	11	at MIN	17	SF
6	at JAC	12	NO		

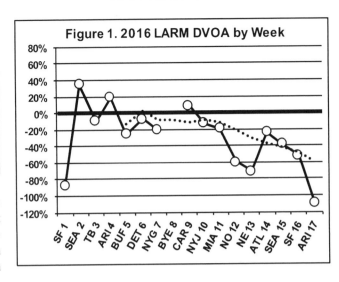

Figure 1. 2016 LARM DVOA by Week

signing former Bengals left tackle Andrew Whitworth in free agency. Whitworth finished third in snaps per blown block at left tackle in 2016 and was named first-team All-Pro at the position in 2015. He's also going to be 36 in December, so even if Goff does develop into a quality NFL starter, Whitworth probably won't be protecting him by the time he gets there.

As if the offensive line play in Los Angeles wasn't enough of a problem in 2016, the receiving corps didn't help matters either. Fresh off signing a four-year contract worth up to $42 million, Tavon Austin managed to finish 93rd in both DYAR and DVOA for wide receivers. Only 93 receivers met the 50-pass threshold to qualify for the rankings. As usual, Austin somewhat offset his lack of contribution in the passing game with some gadget runs and appearances in the backfield, but the negative receiving DYAR (-220) significantly outweighs the positive rushing DYAR (46). Brian Quick did not set the world on fire either, ranking 79th in both categories.

Quick is now in Washington, while the Rams' best receiver, Kenny Britt, departed in free agency for the greener pastures of Northeast Ohio. Britt's contract with the Browns has a lower average salary per year and fewer guarantees than Austin's despite the fact that Austin has only posted a positive receiving DYAR once in his four seasons in the NFL. A large part of Austin's value comes from his contributions running the ball and on special teams, but when you pay a player No. 1 receiver money, you expect an impact in the passing game as well.

Of those three, the only one still on Los Angeles' roster is Austin, but between 2016-17 wide receiver draftees Pharoh Cooper, Mike Thomas, Cooper Kupp, and Josh Reynolds, the Rams have reason to hope that their new wave of young players will develop alongside their second-year starting quarterback. With their second-round pick in 2017 the Rams added tight end Gerald Everett from South Alabama; Everett will be in line to compete for targets with incumbent tight end Tyler Higbee.

After winning offensive rookie of the year in 2015, running back Todd Gurley followed up his impressive debut season with a major disappointment, falling from fourth to 37th in rushing DYAR. As with Goff, some of Gurley's struggles from 2016 can be ascribed to the offensive line, but that was hardly the only issue. At Rams minicamp, some of Gurley's linemen suggested to the media that the line was not always on the same page with their young running back in 2016.[1] Regardless of whose fault it was, a stronger running game would take pressure off Goff to perform right away. In 2016, the Rams ranked dead last in rushing DVOA, which forced the Rams to rely on their quarterbacks to move the ball downfield despite the fact that they weren't any good. On first downs, the Rams ran the ball 52 percent of the time, sixth in the league. However, because the rushing offense was so bad, this set up longer second-down plays for the worst offense in second-and-medium and second-and-long situations, when teams are much more likely to pass.

With the addition of Whitworth fortifying the offensive line, Gurley should see more success in his third season. Combine that with a new wave of receiving talent, and Goff will hopefully be able to make the leap from "historically terrible" to "just plain bad" or even "mediocre." Normally, that wouldn't be anything to write home about, but with the talent on the Rams' defense and special teams, that would be enough for them to hit our projection as a borderline wild-card team.

At first glance, that seems awfully unlikely. The Rams defense scuffled a bit during the first season back in Los Angeles, falling from seventh to 15th in overall defensive DVOA. Their run defense, led by world-destroying defensive tackle Aaron Donald, finished sixth in DVOA, but their pass defense only managed a disappointing 20th.

However, the Rams made a very important addition for 2017. It's not a star player in free agency, or a draft pick to fill a specific hole. Instead, they added sage defensive coordinator Wade Phillips to make the jump from a talented defense to an elite one. In addition to being more than twice the age of head coach Sean McVay, Phillips brings with him years of experience turning bad defenses into good ones and good defenses into great ones. Since 1988, Phillips has taken over seven different defenses. Every single one of those teams improved by at least five places in the defensive DVOA rankings, except for the Broncos who moved from fourth to first in 2015 (Table 1). With a talented front seven stocked with former first-round picks such as edge rusher Robert Quinn, defensive tackle Michael Brockers, linebacker Alec Ogletree, and Donald, Phillips has all the pieces he needs up front to generate a major improvement in Year 1 as the Rams transition from a 4-3 to a 3-4.

Quinn will nominally be shifting from defensive end to outside linebacker in the 3-4, but his role as a pass-rusher will not be changing significantly. Injuries have shortened both the 2015 and 2016 seasons for Quinn, but Phillips is just the right person to help Quinn come close to his earlier peak performance. In Quinn's age-22 through age-24 seasons, he totaled 40 sacks, including 19 in 2013. Between Quinn, Donald, and free-agent addition Connor Barwin, opposing quarterbacks will be quaking in their cleats.

Table 1. Defenses Before and After Wade Phillips

Team	Years	Pre-Wade	Rk	Wade Y1	Rk
DEN	1988-89	13.9%	27	-16.6%	4
BUF	1994-95	3.8%	19	-6.5%	10
ATL	2001-02	11.8%	26	-4.1%	12
SD	2003-04	12.0%	30	-4.2%	13
DAL (HC)	2006-07	-1.5%	14	-6.8%	9
HOU	2010-11	17.5%	31	-9.5%	6
DEN	2014-15	-13.2%	4	-36.0%	1
AVG		**6.3%**	**21.6**	**-12.0%**	**7.9**

Hiring Phillips has been an immediate ticket to massive improvement on defense for the past 30 years, but if there's any reason to question whether he can perform his usual defensive wizardry with the Rams, it's because of the secondary. Losing cornerback Janoris Jenkins to the Giants in 2016 free agency hurt the Rams' depth in the defensive backfield, which played a role in them finishing 30th in DVOA against "other" wide receivers.

Los Angeles had to make the tough decision to let Jenkins go because fellow cornerback Trumaine Johnson was also up for contract after the 2015 season. The Rams elected to use the franchise tag on Johnson for the 2016 season, and with that large cap number devoted to one of their corners, they could not afford to keep Jenkins around long-term as well. Jenkins went on to finish second in the league in adjusted success rate with 18 passes defensed and three interceptions, while Johnson did not match that level of production playing on the tag.

Of course, Johnson was still their No. 1 corner, so the Rams decided to keep him around for 2017. However, that required Los Angeles to franchise Johnson for a second year in a row because the team finds itself in the unenviable position of having been lousy in 2016 and having very little cap space for 2017. As of the end of June, according to Spotrac.com, the Rams have approximately $4 million in cap space for 2017 coming off a season in which they finished 30th overall in DVOA. Meanwhile, the Texans, who finished 29th overall, have over $31 million in space available, even with $9 million of dead money for quarterback Brock Osweiler on Houston's cap sheet. If the Rams want to give Aaron Donald an extension in 2017, it will take some creative cap maneuvering to fit him in without restructuring any existing contracts, but it will obviously be worth it in the long run, given the talent level of the fourth-year pro out of Pittsburgh.

The Rams will need to be clever to get their stars on defense locked up long-term, but they already have their standout performer from one of the best special teams units in the league under team control for the foreseeable future. Los Angeles finished third in the league in special teams DVOA, led by a record-setting punting unit (Table 2). In breaking his own record, Johnny Hekker was worth an estimated 29.5 points of field position above average, which was more than double what Tampa Bay managed in second place (13.6). Punters are the most consistent part of special teams from year to year, so it should not be surprising if Hekker is again at the top in 2017. He has been worth at least 10 points of field position each of the past four seasons. Hekker's current contract runs through the 2020 season, so Los Angeles will not have to worry about him leaving for greener pastures any time soon.

Table 2. Highest Net Punting Value, 1989-2016

Year	Team	Punt Pts+	Punter	Punt Pts Y+1
2016	**LARM**	**+29.5**	**Johnny Hekker**	--
2013	STL	+22.4	Johnny Hekker	+11.3
2002	HOU	+20.9	Chad Stanley	+6.0
2008	BAL	+19.7	Sam Koch	-3.3
2012	ARI	+19.7	Dave Zastudil	+3.9
2011	CHI	+19.7	Adam Podlesh	+18.8
1992	PHX	+19.1	Rich Camarillo	+6.0
1990	PHX	+19.1	Rich Camarillo	+16.1
1989	PHX	+19.0	Rich Camarillo	+19.1
2012	CHI	+18.8	Adam Podlesh	5.3
2002	DET	+18.7	John Jett	-1.9*
2007	SF	+18.1	Andy Lee	+4.4

*Jett only played in four games in 2003.

The Rams' skill on special teams, particularly with punting, plays an important role in their projection as well. Given how impressive their special teams units have been in recent years and the likely improvement on the defensive side of the ball thanks to Phillips, if Goff can just be a normal level of bad (as opposed to his horrific level from 2016), that should be enough for the Rams to hit their projection. However, when Los Angeles gave up all those picks to move up to take Goff, they were expecting more out of the top pick in the draft. For the Rams to truly be a Super Bowl contender in the next few years, they will need him to be above average—and given what 2016 looked like, above average may be too much to ask.

Carl Yedor

2016 Rams Stats by Week

Wk	vs.	W-L	PF	PA	YDF	YDA	TO	Total	Off	Def	ST
1	at SF	L	0	28	185	320	-1	-88%	-97%	-4%	5%
2	SEA	W	9	3	283	306	+1	35%	3%	-23%	9%
3	at TB	W	37	32	320	472	0	-10%	-2%	10%	2%
4	at ARI	W	17	13	288	420	+4	19%	-5%	-15%	9%
5	BUF	L	19	30	345	305	-3	-26%	-35%	-5%	4%
6	at DET	L	28	31	387	348	-1	-7%	12%	19%	0%
7	NYG	L	10	17	345	232	-3	-21%	-33%	-10%	2%
8	BYE										
9	CAR	L	10	13	339	244	-1	9%	-3%	-9%	3%
10	at NYJ	W	9	6	280	296	+1	-13%	-27%	1%	15%
11	MIA	L	10	14	227	240	0	-20%	-40%	-13%	8%
12	at NO	L	21	49	247	555	-1	-60%	-48%	34%	22%
13	at NE	L	10	26	162	402	-2	-71%	-89%	-4%	13%
14	ATL	L	14	42	312	286	-5	-24%	-55%	-20%	10%
15	at SEA	L	3	24	183	299	+1	-38%	-53%	-12%	3%
16	SF	L	21	22	177	323	0	-52%	-60%	0%	9%
17	ARI	L	6	44	123	344	-1	-109%	-106%	2%	-1%

Trends and Splits

	Offense	Rank	Defense	Rank
Total DVOA	-37.8%	32	-2.0%	15
Unadjusted VOA	-35.2%	32	-2.2%	14
Weighted Trend	-45.7%	32	-0.5%	17
Variance	13.2%	32	2.1%	3
Average Opponent	0.3%	16	0.0%	16
Passing	-38.2%	32	11.6%	20
Rushing	-26.6%	32	-20.3%	6
First Down	-40.9%	32	-14.2%	4
Second Down	-34.9%	32	-0.1%	16
Third Down	-36.1%	32	18.2%	29
First Half	-30.4%	31	-4.4%	13
Second Half	-51.8%	32	-11.3%	11
Red Zone	-34.0%	29	18.1%	28
Late and Close	-26.7%	30	-16.2%	7

Five-Year Performance

Year	W-L	Pyth W	Est W	PF	PA	TO	Total	Rk	Off	Rk	Def	Rk	ST	Rk	Off AGL	Rk	Def AGL	Rk	Off Age	Rk	Def Age	Rk	ST Age	Rk
2012	7-8-1	6.6	8.2	299	348	-1	1.5%	15	-4.2%	21	-9.1%	7	-3.4%	26	28.0	16	8.3	3	26.3	23	26.3	24	25.5	29
2013	7-9	7.6	7.8	348	364	+8	2.4%	14	-9.5%	22	-5.7%	11	6.3%	4	26.1	10	21.4	10	26.1	28	25.0	31	25.0	30
2014	6-10	7.1	6.1	324	354	-2	-3.8%	18	-11.1%	25	-3.8%	9	3.5%	7	37.6	21	26.5	7	26.5	23	25.0	32	25.2	32
2015	7-9	6.5	7.9	280	330	+5	-2.2%	16	-15.0%	29	-10.5%	7	2.4%	7	32.3	16	48.0	29	25.2	32	26.1	25	24.9	32
2016	4-12	3.3	4.6	224	394	-11	-28.6%	30	-37.8%	32	-2.0%	15	7.1%	3	7.7	1	21.3	8	25.5	32	26.0	26	25.4	29

2016 Performance Based on Most Common Personnel Groups

LARM Offense					LARM Offense vs. Opponents					LARM Defense					LARM Defense vs. Opponents			
Pers	Freq	Yds	DVOA	Run%	Pers	Freq	Yds	DVOA	Run%	Pers	Freq	Yds	DVOA		Pers	Freq	Yds	DVOA
11	65%	4.3	-46.2%	27%	Base	30%	4.7	-7.8%	58%	Base	19%	5.8	3.1%		11	57%	5.6	-1.1%
12	24%	5.1	-10.2%	52%	Nickel	60%	4.5	-40.4%	30%	Nickel	72%	5.3	-2.5%		12	17%	5.0	-5.3%
13	3%	3.5	-14.4%	79%	Dime+	8%	5.3	-90.0%	5%	Dime+	7%	6.0	0.2%		21	7%	5.1	-26.3%
21	2%	4.8	15.5%	90%	Goal Line	1%	-0.7	-59.1%	67%	Goal Line	1%	0.6	-28.1%		10	7%	5.9	24.3%
01	2%	3.3	-46.5%	40%											13	3%	5.7	12.2%
611	1%	7.7	-24.7%	54%											20	3%	4.5	13.8%

Strategic Tendencies

Run/Pass		Rk	Formation		Rk	Pass Rush		Rk	Secondary		Rk	Strategy		Rk
Runs, first half	39%	13	Form: Single Back	80%	11	Rush 3	9.9%	12	4 DB	19%	27	Play-action	16%	26
Runs, first down	52%	6	Form: Empty Back	5%	26	Rush 4	54.6%	29	5 DB	72%	3	Avg Box (Off)	6.15	23
Runs, second-long	26%	23	Pers: 3+ WR	68%	12	Rush 5	26.0%	8	6+ DB	7%	17	Avg Box (Def)	6.23	16
Runs, power sit.	47%	28	Pers: 2+ TE/6+ OL	31%	10	Rush 6+	9.6%	4	CB by Sides	86%	11	Offensive Pace	31.79	29
Runs, behind 2H	29%	12	Pers: 6+ OL	3%	21	Sacks by LB	3.2%	30	S/CB Cover Ratio	20%	31	Defensive Pace	31.01	23
Pass, ahead 2H	48%	17	Shotgun/Pistol	59%	23	Sacks by DB	12.9%	3	DB Blitz	17%	1	Go for it on 4th	0.55	30

Two years ago, the Rams led the league by running 73 percent of the time in short-yardage/power situations. Last year, that dropped below half, even though success on short-yardage runs barely dropped. Perhaps the massive drop in success on all the other runs bled over into strategy in short-yardage situations. ☞ We also saw a lot less Cory Harkey, as the Rams went from dead last to above-average in use of single-back formations. ☞ Opponents blitzed a defensive back on 12.5 percent of Rams pass plays, including 16.3 percent of passes with Jared Goff at quarterback. Goff had a hideous 2.8 yards per play on these blitzes. ☞ It took a lot of work, but we found something the Rams offense did well last year: play-action passing! The Rams gained 8.3 yards per pass with play-action (12th in the NFL) with 15.6% DVOA (21st). They were, of course, dead last in both stats on other passes. ☞ The Rams were first or second in the percentage of DB blitzes for the third straight year. That's about to change; Wade Phillips defenses are usually near the bottom of the league in rushing defensive backs. ☞ However, Phillips is likely to continue the Rams' presence near the top of the league in blitzes. Denver and Los Angeles tied last year, bringing five pass-rushers on 27 percent of passes and six pass-rushers on 10 percent. And the Rams were much better on those big blitzes, allowing just 4.3 yards per pass with six or more pass-rushers. ☞ Rams opponents threw to their No. 3 or "other" wide receivers on 25.6 percent of passes. The Rams and Cardinals were the only defenses above 23 percent. ☞ The Rams led the league with 497 penalty yards on defense, although three defenses had more flags thrown. ☞ We charted Rams opponents with a league-low 19 dropped passes. ☞ Rams opponents only threw deep (16-plus yards) on a league-low 13 percent of pass attempts. ☞ Opposing kickers only hit touchbacks on 41 percent of kickoffs against the Rams, the lowest figure in the league.

Passing

Player	DYAR	DVOA	Plays	NtYds	Avg	YAC	C%	TD	Int
C.Keenum*	-183	-19.5%	345	2054	6.0	5.3	60.9%	9	11
J.Goff	-881	-74.8%	230	876	3.8	5.1	54.9%	5	7
S.Mannion	-45	-108.8%	6	19	3.2	4.7	50.0%	0	1

Rushing

Player	DYAR	DVOA	Plays	Yds	Avg	TD	Fum	Suc
T.Gurley	-54	-14.3%	227	740	3.3	6	0	42%
B.Cunningham*	-2	-11.4%	21	101	4.8	0	0	48%
T.Austin	33	-10.5%	21	118	5.6	1	0	-
C.Keenum*	25	22.2%	13	58	4.5	1	0	-
M.Brown	-37	-88.4%	11	30	2.7	0	0	27%
L.Dunbar	5	8.9%	6	11	1.8	1	0	50%

Receiving

Player	DYAR	DVOA	Plays	Ctch	Yds	Y/C	YAC	TD	C%
K.Britt*	166	6.4%	111	68	1002	14.7	4.4	5	61%
T.Austin	-219	-39.1%	106	58	509	8.8	4.7	3	55%
B.Quick*	-28	-17.1%	77	41	564	13.8	4.3	3	53%
P.Cooper	-30	-36.0%	20	14	106	7.6	5.1	0	70%
M.Thomas	-20	-43.3%	9	3	37	12.3	4.3	0	33%
B.Marquez	-4	-20.1%	7	3	37	12.3	7.3	0	43%
R.Woods	117	7.9%	75	50	613	12.3	2.5	1	67%
L.Kendricks*	-70	-19.7%	87	50	499	10.0	5.5	2	57%
T.Higbee	-109	-68.5%	29	11	85	7.7	2.4	1	38%
T.Gurley	13	-9.9%	58	43	327	7.6	8.2	0	74%
B.Cunningham*	-12	-24.0%	21	16	91	5.7	5.0	0	76%
L.Dunbar	-5	-17.5%	24	16	122	7.6	5.2	0	67%

Offensive Line

Player	Pos	Age	GS	Snaps	Pen	Sk	Pass	Run	Player	Pos	Age	GS	Snaps	Pen	Sk	Pass	Run
Tim Barnes*	C	29	16/16	1005	2	5.3	11	8	Cody Wichmann	RG	25	12/11	594	2	3.0	9	2
Rob Havenstein	RT	25	15/15	935	4	5.8	20	4	Jamon Brown	G/T	24	11/5	397	2	3.5	8	2
Rodger Saffold	LG	29	15/15	916	3	2.5	14	10	Andrew Donnal	G/T	25	16/4	297	3	0.0	4	4
Greg Robinson*	LT	25	14/14	893	15	6.5	14	4	Andrew Whitworth	LT	36	16/16	1065	7	2.5	6	4

Year	Yards	ALY	Rank	Power	Rank	Stuff	Rank	2nd Lev	Rank	Open Field	Rank	Sacks	ASR	Rank	Press	Rank	F-Start	Cont.
2014	4.08	4.17	18	53%	30	21%	29	1.18	14	0.71	16	47	8.6%	23	31.5%	30	20	38
2015	4.24	3.88	24	64%	20	23%	28	1.03	24	1.17	3	18	3.5%	1	27.0%	20	16	25
2016	3.23	3.66	29	61%	16	22%	28	0.89	31	0.30	30	49	8.1%	29	28.0%	21	20	29

| 2016 ALY by direction: | Left End 1.61 (31) | Left Tackle 4.42 (15) | Mid/Guard 3.93 (26) | Right Tackle 2.34 (31) | Right End 4.66 (6) |

The Rams finished 29th in both adjusted line yards and adjusted sack rate in 2016, providing just about the worst environment possible for rookie quarterback Jared Goff and second-year running back Todd Gurley to develop. As a response to left tackle Greg Robinson allowing 6.5 sacks and blowing a block every 49.6 snaps (21st among left tackles), Los Angeles signed former Bengals standout Andrew Whitworth to provide some stability on Goff's blind side. At 35 years old, Whitworth is unlikely to be around for the long haul, but he will play a key role for the 2017 Rams in trying to right the good ship Goff. Then the Rams finally gave up on Robinson, dumping him on the Lions in June for a 2018 sixth-round pick. ☞ The Rams will also be replacing Tim Barnes at center with former Vikings starter John Sullivan, who spent 2016 as a backup in Washington after missing all of 2015 with a back injury. ☙ Left guard Rodger Saffold finished dead last in snaps per blown block at his position, yet he's probably the second-best player on this unit after Whitworth. ☙ Right tackle Rob Havenstein had unimpressive blown-block numbers, but the Rams were at their best when running off the right end. Initial depth charts from Rams OTAs have Havenstein moving inside to right guard while Jamon Brown takes over at right tackle.

Defensive Front Seven

Defensive Line	Age	Pos	G	Snaps	Plays	TmPct	Rk	Stop	Dfts	BTkl	Runs	St%	Rk	RuYd	Rk	Sack	Hit	Hur	Dsrpt
						Overall						vs. Run				Pass Rush			
Aaron Donald	26	DT	16	828	52	6.3%	20	45	24	4	36	81%	36	0.7	6	8.0	24	44	10
Dominique Easley	25	DT	16	470	36	4.3%	47	29	12	2	26	81%	35	2.7	59	3.5	3	7	1
Michael Brockers	27	DT	14	418	21	2.9%	76	17	4	1	14	86%	23	1.6	21	0.0	5	3	3
Cam Thomas*	31	DT	16	392	15	1.8%	--	13	1	4	13	92%	--	1.9	--	1.0	1	6	0
Tyrunn Walker	27	DT	15	350	25	3.3%	--	14	5	1	20	60%	--	3.2	--	0.0	2	7	0

Edge Rushers	Age	Pos	G	Snaps	Plays	TmPct	Rk	Stop	Dfts	BTkl	Runs	St%	Rk	RuYd	Rk	Sack	Hit	Hur	Dsrpt
						Overall						vs. Run				Pass Rush			
Eugene Sims*	31	DE	16	536	24	2.9%	90	21	8	3	20	85%	12	1.6	22	2.5	3	14	2
Ethan Westbrooks	27	DE	16	533	25	3.0%	87	21	9	4	21	86%	8	1.0	8	2.0	8	22	1
William Hayes*	32	DE	14	513	43	5.9%	34	33	15	2	34	76%	37	1.4	16	5.0	13	28	1
Robert Quinn	27	DE	9	370	12	2.6%	95	9	5	1	6	50%	98	3.7	91	4.0	3	8	1
Connor Barwin	31	DE	16	713	36	4.8%	55	25	12	5	21	71%	61	3.0	69	5.0	6	21	2

Linebackers	Age	Pos	G	Snaps	Plays	TmPct	Rk	Stop	Dfts	BTkl	Runs	St%	Rk	RuYd	Rk	Sack	Hit	Hur	Tgts	Suc%	Rk	AdjYd	Rk	PD	Int
						Overall						vs. Run				Pass Rush				vs. Pass					
Alec Ogletree	26	MLB	16	1089	146	17.6%	10	81	24	16	91	63%	48	4.4	78	0.0	3	11	24	42%	60	6.6	42	5	2
Mark Barron	28	OLB	16	1086	125	15.1%	20	70	16	15	64	67%	26	3.8	56	1.0	2	2	48	56%	17	5.5	22	7	2

Year	Yards	ALY	Rank	Power	Rank	Stuff	Rank	2nd Level	Rank	Open Field	Rank	Sacks	ASR	Rank	Press	Rank
2014	3.88	3.54	3	55%	4	24%	5	1.12	14	0.82	22	40	6.7%	15	26.2%	8
2015	3.97	3.70	6	63%	14	24%	7	1.13	17	0.90	24	41	6.3%	17	28.3%	4
2016	3.99	3.43	1	64%	19	29%	1	1.10	11	1.04	30	31	5.0%	29	28.4%	11

2016 ALY by direction:	Left End 3.29 (6)	Left Tackle 2.58 (1)	Mid/Guard 3.79 (8)	Right Tackle 2.81 (4)	Right End 3.57 (14)

Under the leadership of new defensive coordinator Wade Phillips, the Rams will be transitioning from a 4-3 defense to a 3-4. Sometimes, such a transition comes with growing pains, but with defensive tackle Aaron Donald around, the only pains likely to be felt will be by opposing quarterbacks. Donald managed 44 hurries from the interior for the Rams last season, which is even more impressive if we consider the fact that the Rams spent so much time trailing. The third-year man out of Pittsburgh paired that pass-rushing ability with 45 stops and 24 defeats (tied with Ndamukong Suh for most among interior defensive linemen), making his case as the league's best all-around defensive lineman not named J.J. Watt even stronger. ☙ Former Philadelphia edge rusher Connor Barwin joins the incumbent Robert Quinn to form what could be a potent duo on the outside to complement Donald. Quinn hasn't made it through a full season since 2014, but a return to health and form would go a long way towards the Rams making good on their projection of having one of the league's top defenses. ☙ Michael Brockers and Ethan Westbrooks will fill the other two starting spots along the defensive line. Westbrooks is transitioning inside to a 5-technique role and may get competition from former Patriots first-round pick Dominique Easley. It's a less important role because Phillips defenses tend to play only two linemen in passing situations. ☙ Mark Barron and Alec Ogletree are a strong pair of starting inside linebackers, but the depth players do not have much experience. The Rams were so rarely in "base" defense last season that Cory Littleton (2016 UDFA), Josh Forrest (2016 sixth-round pick), and Bryce Hager (2015 seventh-round pick) combined to play only 19.5 percent of defensive snaps.

Defensive Secondary

Secondary	Age	Pos	G	Snaps	Plays	TmPct	Rk	Stop	Dfts	BTkl	Runs	St%	Rk	RuYd	Rk	Tgts	Tgt%	Rk	Dist	Suc%	Rk	AdjYd	Rk	PD	Int
T.J. McDonald*	26	SS	16	1069	68	8.2%	54	35	16	8	31	55%	13	6.8	38	28	6.4%	15	8.6	53%	14	6.3	8	6	2
Trumaine Johnson	27	CB	14	953	68	9.4%	29	27	10	10	13	23%	77	9.2	70	66	16.9%	27	9.2	52%	29	6.1	10	12	1
Maurice Alexander	26	SS	14	918	54	7.4%	59	18	7	12	16	44%	27	9.4	63	24	6.4%	14	15.1	36%	60	13.4	72	3	2
Lamarcus Joyner	27	CB	14	699	71	9.8%	19	39	16	12	25	64%	10	5.1	18	46	16.0%	16	8.8	60%	5	6.8	21	5	0
E.J. Gaines	25	CB	11	613	63	11.1%	7	24	11	5	12	50%	19	11.3	79	55	21.8%	66	9.9	36%	86	7.9	53	7	0
Troy Hill	26	CB	12	335	40	6.4%	--	15	6	8	9	33%	--	5.8	--	29	21.3%	--	13.4	34%	--	11.4	--	2	0
Cody Davis	28	FS	16	273	13	1.6%	--	4	2	5	2	0%	--	10.0	--	8	6.7%	--	18.4	51%	--	11.6	--	3	1
Mike Jordan	25	CB	5	177	22	8.5%	--	9	3	5	5	60%	--	3.6	--	22	30.5%	--	8.8	33%	--	9.3	--	2	0
Nickell Robey-Coleman	25	CB	16	573	37	4.5%	--	15	7	5	7	43%	--	10.9	--	36	16.9%	--	9.6	51%	--	8.3	--	6	2

Year	Pass D Rank	vs. #1 WR	Rk	vs. #2 WR	Rk	vs. Other WR	Rk	vs. TE	Rk	vs. RB	Rk
2014	20	3.5%	19	33.8%	31	-1.0%	15	-12.2%	6	-9.9%	10
2015	8	-26.4%	2	-19.1%	6	4.1%	16	-4.0%	16	-3.0%	13
2016	20	3.7%	21	-3.8%	11	17.8%	30	-6.0%	10	-20.1%	6

As the only NFL cornerback on the franchise tag for 2017, Johnson will be the highest-paid defensive back in the league for what is very likely his final season with the Rams. The Rams lost cornerback Janoris Jenkins to the Giants in free agency in 2016 with only a 2017 compensatory third-round pick to show for it, and chances are good they receive a similar return for Johnson in the near future. Incumbent starter E.J. Gaines will compete with free-agent signings Nickell Robey-Coleman (ex-Bills) and Kayvon Webster (ex-Broncos, and a personal Phillips favorite) to fill out the starting lineup alongside Johnson. Gaines struggled mightily in his return from the Lisfranc injury that cost him the 2015 season, in the proper tradition of cornerback inconsistency. He had been in the top 20 in both our charting stats as a rookie in 2014. ☞ Strong safety T.J. McDonald led the Rams' defensive backs in snaps in 2016, but the hard hitter from USC left for Miami in free agency and will be looking to leave a mark on unsuspecting receivers there once he returns from an eight-game suspension. Los Angeles will look to replace McDonald internally with fourth-year safety Maurice Alexander, though McDonald outperformed Alexander in our charting numbers across the board. ☞ Lamarcus Joyner will be moving from cornerback to free safety to form the starting duo over the top, though he may still drop back down to the slot in sub packages. Playing primarily in the slot last season, he posted the best charting numbers of his career.

Special Teams

Year	DVOA	Rank	FG/XP	Rank	Net Kick	Rank	Kick Ret	Rank	Net Punt	Rank	Punt Ret	Rank	Hidden	Rank
2014	3.5%	7	-4.7	28	0.1	17	-1.2	19	11.3	5	12.1	3	4.4	10
2015	2.4%	7	-6.7	30	2.5	9	4.0	7	10.4	5	1.6	13	1.0	14
2016	7.1%	3	3.8	9	4.0	8	1.3	11	29.2	1	-2.6	22	0.7	16

On the back of another strong season from punter Johnny Hekker, the Rams special teams unit was again one of the best in the league. Hekker continued a three-year run finishing first or second in gross punt value, leading the pack in 2016 at 18.8 points above average. Oakland's Marquette King finished second at 8.2 points above average, but he was closer to Jeff Locke of the Vikings (who ranked 26th) than he was to Hekker. The Rams also finished with 29.5 net points of estimated field position from punts, dwarfing Kansas City's league-leading mark of 16.2 from 2015. ☞ After posting two of the worst marks in the league on placekicking in the Rams' last two seasons in St. Louis, kicker Greg Zuerlein adapted well to the warm Los Angeles weather in 2016. ☞ With Benny Cunningham departed for Chicago, kick returns likely belong to some combination of receivers Mike Thomas and Pharoh Cooper. Tavon Austin will again be involved on punt returns, though the Rams will surely be hoping for more of an impact on offense from the former first-round pick. Again.

Miami Dolphins

2016 Record: 10-6	Total DVOA: 1.0% (18th)	2017 Mean Projection: 7.0 wins	On the Clock (0-4): 17%
Pythagorean Wins: 7.5 (24th)	Offense: 1.8% (14th)	Postseason Odds: 22.1%	Mediocrity (5-7): 43%
Snap-Weighted Age: 26.4 (20th)	Defense: 1.6% (19th)	Super Bowl Odds: 1.5%	Playoff Contender (8-10): 31%
Average Opponent: -3.2% (26th)	Special Teams: 0.8% (12th)	Proj. Avg. Opponent: -0.2% (20th)	Super Bowl Contender (11+): 9%

2016: Unlike the Jets and Bills, the Dolphins can still make the playoffs.

2017: Hello 8-8, my old friend.

Every NFL team, including the Super Bowl contenders, has flaws. The salary cap just does not allow for a true "super team" to exist in today's game. Teams combat this by playing to their strengths, something they can hang their hat on that will keep them competitive. For example, the Broncos still have great trust in their talented defense, and the Colts like to feature the one-man show known as Andrew Luck. Even the lowly Jets, dead last in DVOA for 2016, still had the No. 1 run defense thanks to a stout line.

Championship teams don't do everything well, but they usually are great at *something*. The 2016 Miami Dolphins were great at balls to the wall mediocrity. The No. 17 ranking in DVOA does not even begin to do this feat justice. Once you start looking through the rankings of relevant stats, the 2016 Dolphins show you more teens and twentysomethings than the crowd at a Justin Bieber concert.

By DVOA, Miami's No. 14 offense ranked 17th in passing and 16th in rushing. Quarterback Ryan Tannehill finished 25th with minus-12 passing DYAR, the first time he had negative DYAR in a season. Running back Jay Ajayi fared better in our stats, ranked seventh in DYAR and 13th in DVOA, but he was 32nd in success rate, so it was really a boom-or-bust season for the young back. Only Tampa Bay had a higher rate of stuffed runs than Miami. In pass protection, Miami finished a sub-par 21st in pressure rate and 22nd in adjusted sack rate. The Dolphins were 16th in turnovers per drive, so it wasn't like a great job of protecting the ball made up for the lackluster production. Only one offense (Rams) had fewer first downs, and only four offenses went three-and-out more often than Miami, which ranked 25th in third-down conversion rate. Also, it's not like the Dolphins capitalized often in the red zone, where they finished 18th in points per red zone appearance.

The No. 19 defense was game to match this effort. Miami finished 14th against the pass and 22nd against the run. While Miami's pass rush had the league's fourth-highest pressure rate, the pressure was not very effective. The Dolphins finished 27th in DVOA with pressure, picked up 33 sacks, and ranked next to last in adjusted sack rate. The big-name defensive line saw backs get past them often, as Miami finished 32nd in second-level yards. The defense finished 11th in take-aways per drive, meaning the Dolphins were only plus-2 in turnover differential, tied for 13th in the league.

Even Miami's special teams, which easily had the biggest advantage in hidden points from factors generally out of the team's control, finished a ho-hum 12th in DVOA. No team made (16) or attempted (21) fewer field goals than Miami.

It's not just our metrics and charting data that paint a picture of mediocrity. Check the scoreboard. The 2016 Dolphins are only the sixth playoff team to ever win at least 10 games with a negative scoring differential. Yes, the Dolphins allowed 17 more points than they scored last season. Meanwhile, regular old defensive passer rating ranked Miami (88.5) at No. 17, and ESPN's Total QBR (62.6) ranked Miami 21st against opposing quarterbacks. Tannehill's 54.6 QBR ranked 24th in the league, right behind two quarterbacks unlikely to have a Week 1 starting job this year: Colin Kaepernick (55.2) and Brock Osweiler (55.3).

One stat that is inarguably *above* average: 10 wins in 16 games. But given all of this, you might be wondering how the heck Miami finished 10-6 after such a mediocre season.

Well, you can always start with the schedule, which ranked 26th in average DVOA. Including the playoffs, Miami played a league-low six games against teams with a winning record, but went 1-5 in those games, only beating the Steelers in Week 6 when Ben Roethlisberger tore his meniscus. When the QB1 injuries were reversed for the playoff rematch, the Dolphins were quickly dispatched 30-12 in Pittsburgh. Miami beefed up the win count by sweeping the Bills and Jets, and squeaked out close wins over the 49ers and Browns, two teams that combined for one win going into Christmas Eve. Talk about gifts.

Speaking of close wins, the Dolphins had a surplus of them. As we analyzed in the Detroit chapter (page 77), the Dolphins won seven games with a decisive score in the fourth quarter or overtime, including four games where Miami's win probability dipped below 13.0 percent in the final frame. Overall, Miami has not fared well in such games in the Tannehill era. The career record in game-winning drive opportunities with Tannehill at quarterback is 14-24 (.368), but it was 4-3 last season, and later 2-0 with backup Matt Moore. That does not include the win over the Jets where the Dolphins got a 96-yard game-winning kick return touchdown from Kenyan Drake. Oh yes, Miami pulled a few rabbits out of the hat in 2016. The Dolphins looked dead for 55 minutes in Los Angeles before erasing a 10-0 deficit against the Rams, the franchise's first double-digit road comeback since 2005. Kiko Alonso intercepted a Philip Rivers pass for a 60-yard touchdown with just

2017 Dolphins Schedule

Week	Opp.	Week	Opp.	Week	Opp.
1	TB	7	NYJ	13	DEN
2	at LACH	8	at BAL (Thu.)	14	NE (Mon.)
3	at NYJ	9	OAK	15	at BUF
4	NO (U.K.)	10	at CAR (Mon.)	16	at KC
5	TEN	11	BYE	17	BUF
6	at ATL	12	at NE		

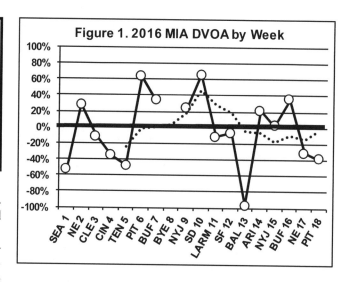

Figure 1. 2016 MIA DVOA by Week

over a minute left to give Miami a 31-24 win in San Diego. And the Bills and Browns both missed game-winning field goals in games the Dolphins went on to win in overtime.

While Miami made some great plays in crunch time, reversing just those two missed field goals would have put the Dolphins in the same territory as every other Miami team since 2009: no better than 8-8. If we think of Miami as a mediocre ball club rather than a 10-6 playoff team with a healthy quarterback returning, then it is a lot easier to project where this team can go in 2017.

What can the Dolphins hope to hang their hats on this year? If head coach Adam Gase has his way in his second season, then it looks like Ajayi is the answer. It is hard to believe that the Dolphins toyed with signing Chris Johnson, actually signed Arian Foster to delay his inevitable retirement, and left Ajayi as a healthy scratch in Week 1 last season. Ajayi's emergence and surprising 204-yard rushing day against the Steelers in Week 6 really turned Miami's season around. The team won nine out of 11 games after a 1-4 start where the offense was struggling in a pass-centric, no-huddle attack. Miami shifted towards the run, and actually had the slowest pace of play in the league, which helps to explain why the Dolphins averaged the fewest plays per drive (5.03). Miami had the eighth-fastest pace in 2015, so this was a big change, but Gase is used to being able to switch things up on the fly from his time in Denver and Chicago.

However, to say that growing pains concluded and Miami consistently ran the ball well would be misleading. We mentioned earlier that Ajayi ranked 32nd in rushing success rate, but his game-to-game production was also very up and down. In addition to gashing Pittsburgh, Ajayi rushed for more than 200 yards in both games against the Bills (No. 30 rush defense), which made him the fourth player to rush for at least 200 yards in three games in a season. That's awesome, but that also means that 49 percent of his rushing yards last season came in three games. Ajayi failed to exceed 61 rushing yards in six of his last seven games, including the playoff loss where he rushed for 33 yards on 16 carries in Pittsburgh.

Of course, with the way the Steelers jumped out to such a huge early lead, a running back is difficult to build an offense around. This is especially true when Ajayi is limited as a receiver. Ajayi ranked 47th (out of 53 backs) in receiving DVOA, and the Dolphins relied on Damien Williams in that role, which takes Ajayi off the field on third downs. According to ESPN Stats & Info, 36 running backs played more third-down snaps than Ajayi's 70 last season, which were only

one more than Williams had for Miami. Ajayi still has a lot of room for improvement to become a consistent, all-around threat in this offense.

Furthermore, the success of the Dolphins remains largely tied to whether or not Tannehill finally breaks that label of Next Year's Breakout Quarterback. Gase has garnered a bit of a reputation as a quarterback whisperer, and he did get a few career-best marks out of Tannehill, such as in completion percentage (67.1 percent), yards per attempt (7.70), and passer rating (93.5). That's all good, but makes it only more peculiar that advanced stats (DVOA and QBR) were so down on Tannehill's season.

So what gives? For starters, Gase likes an offense to utilize screens and short passes, so Tannehill only ranked 25th in average air yards per pass (7.9). That helps explain the career-high completion percentage, but Tannehill still took some deep shots too. Five of his interceptions were thrown at least 25 yards beyond the line of scrimmage, which helped lead to a career-high 3.1 interception rate. He fumbled nine times, which he does every year, but his fumble rate was higher because he had fewer plays. He was also strip-sacked five times, including a late sack that set up Cleveland for a missed, would-be game-winning 46-yard field goal.

As has been the case in his career, Tannehill struggled under pressure in 2016. His DVOA under pressure (-108.8%) was the third lowest in the NFL, sandwiched between Brock Osweiler and Los Angeles' unsightly duo of Jared Goff and Case Keenum. When Tannehill wasn't under pressure, his DVOA was 54.8%, good for eighth in the league. That difference of -163.7% in DVOA when getting pressured was the season's largest, so that is still an area he has to handle better.

Another explanation for Tannehill's low rankings in advanced metrics is a simple one: Tannehill had a poor start to 2016 before playing better. Through five games, Tannehill ranked dead last in passing DYAR (-311) and his QBR (37.4) was only higher than Keenum's. Starting with the Pittsburgh game in Week 6 through his injury in Week 14, Tannehill ranked 13th in DYAR (321) and 12th in QBR (65.0). That's still not the stuff of legends, but Miami can work with that. Furthermore, Moore had 259 DYAR, 34.8% passing DVOA, and an 81.7 QBR in the short period of time that he played for Tannehill. Those are MVP-caliber numbers if done over a full season. Now Moore is one of the league's best backups, and he got to throw four touchdowns against a disinterested Jets team, but these numbers give hope to Miami fans who want to believe that Gase has the offense moving in the right direction after those first five games.

It was very unfortunate that Tannehill suffered a major knee sprain when he did last season, the first significant injury of his career. At the very least, his ACL was spared and Miami expects no issues with the knee this fall. The injury robbed us of a chance to see Tannehill in important late-season games with Buffalo and New England, and of course what would have been his first playoff start in Pittsburgh.

After five seasons and 77 starts, the jury is still out on Tannehill. Some see future stardom held back by a dysfunctional organization, while others see a deluxe Sam Bradford with a lesser bank account. When you watch Tannehill, flat-footed and under pressure, deliver two deep-bucket throws to perfect spots for huge gains in San Diego last season, then you can understand why there's still a lot of excitement about his future. The talent is there, but the consistency has not been.

The truth is, if Tannehill was going to be a Hall of Fame-caliber quarterback, we would have seen it already in these five seasons, as we did from the likes of Peyton Manning, Kurt Warner, Tom Brady, Drew Brees, Ben Roethlisberger, and even 2012 draft mates Andrew Luck and Russell Wilson. Through five seasons, Tannehill has 731 passing DYAR. We looked at how that stacks up to the 27 other quarterbacks who debuted since 1987 and threw at least 100 passes in each of their first five seasons (Table 1). As you might imagine, Tannehill's results are average.

Barring major drop-offs for Cam Newton and Andy Dalton, the top 13 quarterbacks from Table 1 all exceeded 1,600 DYAR and will be decade-long starters in this league. Tannehill is bunched closely with Donovan McNabb, who had a miserable rookie season but also had a lot more rushing value than Tannehill, as well as four playoff appearances starting in 2000. The 13 quarterbacks below Tannehill are generally not good company, including a few notable busts such as Tim Couch, Rick Mirer, and David Carr. Michael Vick rebounded for one big year with Andy Reid on the 2010 Eagles, but he's a unique case.

If there is a silver lining for Tannehill, it would be that some of those quarterbacks below him still went on to some success. In fact, we looked at DYAR through five seasons for

Table 1. Passing DYAR Through Five Seasons, 1987-2016

Rk	Player	From	To	1stTm	Y1	Y2	Y3	Y4	Y5	Total
1	Peyton Manning	1998	2002	IND	697	1,581	1,882	965	1,075	6,200
2	Matt Ryan	2008	2012	ATL	1,012	702	1,122	1,120	1,196	5,153
3	Jeff Garcia	1999	2003	SF	333	1,642	1,057	936	450	4,418
4	Russell Wilson	2012	2016	SEA	872	770	503	1,190	562	3,897
5	Ben Roethlisberger	2004	2008	PIT	908	885	616	668	97	3,173
6	Troy Aikman	1989	1993	DAL	-299	-251	866	1,237	1,234	2,787
7	Andy Dalton	2011	2015	CIN	573	194	541	237	1,135	2,680
8	Andrew Luck	2012	2016	IND	257	650	879	-126	744	2,404
9	Joe Flacco	2008	2012	BAL	232	667	697	413	358	2,366
10	Drew Bledsoe	1993	1997	NE	72	584	7	799	809	2,272
11	Cam Newton	2011	2015	CAR	407	422	421	-105	630	1,775
12	Jay Cutler	2006	2010	DEN	-17	865	1,141	-390	80	1,678
13	Eli Manning	2004	2008	NYG	-191	632	529	-190	840	1,619
Rk	Player	From	To	1stTm	Y1	Y2	Y3	Y4	Y5	Total
14	Donovan McNabb	1999	2003	PHI	-629	389	251	267	557	835
15	**Ryan Tannehill**	**2012**	**2016**	**MIA**	**39**	**54**	**630**	**20**	**-12**	**731**
16	Josh Freeman	2009	2013	TB	-392	816	-96	118	-176	271
17	Don Majkowski	1987	1991	GB	-68	42	618	78	-422	248
18	Jake Plummer	1997	2001	ARI	-137	108	-405	-34	705	237
19	Rodney Peete	1989	1993	DET	-60	107	75	182	-385	-81
20	Kerry Collins	1995	1999	CAR	-369	699	-393	-253	220	-96
21	Michael Vick	2001	2005	ATL	-171	514	-44	-510	36	-175
22	Jeff George	1990	1994	IND	-211	-590	-374	497	341	-337
23	Tony Banks	1996	2000	STL	-519	292	-56	-158	-83	-524
24	Vinny Testaverde	1987	1991	TB	-153	-202	153	-16	-356	-574
25	Joey Harrington	2002	2006	DET	-279	-250	41	-93	-97	-679
26	Tim Couch	1999	2003	CLE	-478	-54	-421	98	-43	-898
27	Rick Mirer	1993	1997	SEA	-190	-34	-279	-244	-387	-1,133
28	David Carr	2002	2006	HOU	-1,130	83	258	-565	92	-1,263

Minimum 100 passes each season.

every quarterback with at least 1,000 pass attempts since 1987 to find comparisons for Tannehill. Those 12 examples, sorted by descending passing DYAR through five years, are listed in Table 2, but you'll notice that almost all of these players had to find success with a franchise other than their initial team (1stTm), such as Jake Plummer's move to Denver or Vinny Testaverde escaping Tampa Bay to be coached by Bill Belichick (Browns), Ted Marchibroda (Ravens), and Bill Parcells (Jets). Alex Smith, who needed Jim Harbaugh to come coach the 49ers in 2011, is the one exception to the rule, a quarterback who stayed with the same team through years of poor production and then eventually (in his seventh season) improved.

Table 2. Late Bloomers and Limited Successes

Player	Debut	1stTm	DYAR Yrs 1-5	Later Success
Steve Beuerlein	1988	LARD	711	1999 CAR: 5th in DYAR, 36 TD passes
Jim Harbaugh	1987	CHI	681	1995 IND: 8th in DVOA, AFC-CG loss
Jon Kitna	1997	SEA	612	2003 CIN: 7th in DYAR, 26 TD passes
Brad Johnson	1992	MIN	506	2002 TB: Won SB XXXVIII
Jake Plummer	1997	ARI	237	2003-05 DEN: three playoff seasons
Chris Chandler	1988	IND	193	1998 ATL: 5th in DVOA, lost SB XXXIII
Erik Kramer	1987	ATL	42	1995 CHI: 1st in DYAR, 3rd in DVOA
Kerry Collins	1995	CAR	-96	2000 NYG: 8th in DYAR, lost SB XXXV
Matt Cassel	2005	NE	-267	2010 KC: 27 TD passes, lost AFC-WC
Jeff George	1990	IND	-337	Made playoffs with ATL and MIN
Vinny Testaverde	1987	TB	-574	1996 BAL: 1st in passing DYAR
Alex Smith	2005	SF	-1,776	Made playoffs with SF (1) and KC (3)

Several of these quarterbacks reached conference championship games and Super Bowls, so that should be encouraging for Tannehill believers. Even better is the fact that Kerry Collins (2000 Giants), Chris Chandler (1998 Falcons), and Jim Harbaugh (1995 Colts) each had a big season in his second year with a new team. While Tannehill is stuck in Miami for the time being, maybe his second year in Gase's system brings out the best in him.

Miami has never really found a solid tight end for Tannehill, but made a trade to take another shot: Julius Thomas, who left Peyton Manning in Denver to become a JAG for the Jaguars. It's hard to expect much at this point, so the offense will also look for improved contributions from DeVante Parker and Kenny Stills. The latter is a solid deep threat, while Parker showed good hands and some playmaking ability last year. Still, he's not yet at the level of Demaryius Thomas or Alshon Jeffery, who were the No. 1 options in Gase's last two offenses.

The No. 1 option in this offense still seems to be Jarvis Landry, who is an unusual No. 1 wide receiver since he led all receivers in yards gained from the slot last year. Sure, Julian Edelman serves a similar role for the Patriots, but that offense still features a dominant threat in Rob Gronkowski, and also traded for Brandin Cooks. Landry has been far and away the targets leader in Miami, but that has not necessarily been a good thing for his offense.

For many fans, Landry is even more divisive than his quarterback. While 2016 was his best season yet, Landry's ranking as the No. 7 wide receiver in the NFL Network's Top 100 Players of 2017 is a bit absurd. Landry still did not crack the top 40 wide receivers in DVOA, and finished in the top three in failed receptions for the third year in a row. Landry has only averaged a paltry 10.6 yards per reception for his career, though he raised that average to 12.1 yards in 2016. He only catches about a handful of touchdowns per season too, so he doesn't have specific talent for breaking big plays or producing in the red zone.

The number most associated with praise for Landry is 288, the record number of receptions for a player in his first three seasons. Of course, fellow 2014 rookie Odell Beckham Jr. also has 288 catches, but he has 35 touchdown catches compared to 13 for Landry. The fact is that Landry's catches are just not as valuable as those made by his peers. We looked at the correlation between receiving stats and an offense's passing DVOA for each game from 2014 to 2016. We looked at Landry compared to the five wide receivers (minus Tyreek Hill) voted ahead of him on the Top 100 list (Table 3), and then compared to the five most productive slot receivers (in receptions) of the last three years (Table 4).

Though it is not a strong correlation, Landry is the only player on either table with a negative correlation between his receptions and his offense's passing DVOA. As Landry's targets and catches go up, Miami's passing DVOA goes down. The same cannot be said of the other players for the most part. Landry also pales greatly in comparison with his peers on the top table when it comes to receiving DYAR. We're not saying Miami should let Landry walk in free agency after the season, but paying him like a top-flight receiver would be a mistake. For the Dolphins to take the next step offensively, Parker is the receiver who needs to make the biggest strides. As long as Landry is far and away the leading receiver in Miami's offense, it is unlikely that this passing game will rise above mediocrity.

The Dolphins have done a suspect job of making the team around Tannehill better after an underwhelming offseason. Beyond the receiving corps, Tannehill's pass protection has always been an area of scrutiny. Miami has three first-round picks on the offensive line, but the guards leave a lot to be desired.

General manager Chris Grier's offseason moves were largely focused on defense for new coordinator Matt Burke, who is replacing Vance Joseph (Broncos' new head coach). Burke coached linebackers in Detroit (2009-2013), Cincinnati (2014-15), and Miami last year. He'll have some new options to work with this year after Grier added Lawrence Timmons from Pittsburgh, as well as safeties Nate Allen and T.J. McDonald. But veterans at this stage of their careers are really just lateral, low-impact moves. Second-round linebacker Raekwon McMillian (Ohio State) may have the best shot to start out of Miami's top three draft picks, which also included first-round defensive end Charles Harris (Missouri) and third-round cornerback Cordera Tankersley (Clemson).

The pick of Harris really needs to work out after the loss

Table 3. Landry vs. Top 5 WR: Correlation with Pass Offense DVOA by Game, 2014-16

Player	Team	Correlation with Pass DVOA			StDev of Passes	DYAR
		Pass	Rec	Yards		
Jarvis Landry	MIA	-0.26	-0.14	0.13	3.64	344
A.J. Green	CIN	-0.13	0.11	0.20	3.98	820
Julio Jones	ATL	-0.19	0.11	0.28	3.79	1,157
Odell Beckham	NYG	-0.06	0.17	0.30	3.74	862
Antonio Brown	PIT	0.04	0.23	0.31	3.60	1,347
Mike Evans	TB	0.08	0.31	0.43	3.79	716

Table 4. Landry vs. Top Slot WR: Correlation with Pass Offense DVOA by Game, 2014-16

Player	Team	Correlation with Pass DVOA			StDev of Passes	DYAR
		Pass	Rec	Yards		
Jarvis Landry	MIA	-0.26	-0.14	0.13	3.64	344
Larry Fitzgerald	ARI	-0.13	0.03	0.13	3.17	494
Randall Cobb	GB	-0.01	0.03	0.28	3.39	679
Doug Baldwin	SEA	0.06	0.12	0.37	3.02	823
Jordan Matthews	PHI	0.12	0.12	0.16	3.16	305
Julian Edelman	NE	0.08	0.13	-0.05	3.30	329

Miami took on the decision to let Olivier Vernon walk and replace him with Mario Williams. Vernon led the NFL with 66 hurries for the Giants, while Williams was unproductive, benched, and ultimately cut after one failure of a season. However, not all of Miami's moves from last offseason backfired. Kiko Alonso managed to stay healthy, even if he was not much help against the run, so that's at least a positive. Cornerback Byron Maxwell also showed that he was not as dreadful away from Seattle as his 2015 season in Philadelphia suggested. He even shut down Antonio Brown in the first matchup with Pittsburgh, but again, Miami would like to forget what happened the second time around when the defense couldn't tackle Brown.

This defense will still go as Ndamukong Suh and Cameron Wake do, but the additions are not very inspiring for 2017. Will a first-time coordinator, a few retreads, and no obvious Week 1 rookie starters close the gap between Miami and the AFC's top teams? At this point, believing in Miami is about believing in Gase.

Miami fans will take a shot in the tournament over yet another 8-8 season, but the current makeup of the AFC makes it very difficult to trust the Dolphins to do anything relevant into January. The offense is unlikely to outscore New England, Pittsburgh, or Oakland in a shootout, and the defense is unlikely to stifle those potent offenses enough to make a low-scoring win a possibility. Even if the Dolphins improved to 10th on both sides of the ball, teams like that just haven't had postseason success in this era. Updating our 2016 study[1] on building a Super Bowl winner, 27 of the last 30 champions ranked in the top seven on at least one side of the ball. Only the 2001 Patriots, 2007 Giants, and 2012 Ravens didn't have a dominant side, but they had the Tuck Rule/Adam Vinatieri, David Tyree's helmet catch, and Jacoby Jones. They had miracles, and that's what it would take for the Dolphins to win a Super Bowl this season unless Gase finally has the recipe for getting Tannehill to take the next step.

Some Dolphins fans can still recall the consistent winning under the head coach-quarterback duo of Dan Marino and Don Shula. But younger Dolphins fans only know a world where the consistent winners are Tom Brady and Bill Belichick, and Miami is left chasing a wild-card spot every year. It seems very unlikely for Miami to return to the playoffs without another four wins over the Bills and Jets, which are certainly possible given the depressed state of those division rivals. The rest of the schedule will not be as easy on the Dolphins, especially if the team continues to lack an identity. Miami has early home games with Tennessee and Tampa Bay, two teams that appear to be on the right track behind their young quarterbacks, and will see Denver's stingy defense in December. The Dolphins lose a true home game by having to go to London to take on the Saints and Drew Brees. The road slate has tough trips to Atlanta, Baltimore, Carolina, Kansas City, and the first regular-season game for the Chargers in Los Angeles since 1960. Miami should be a frequent underdog in 2017.

Then again, Miami has often been an underdog ever since Marino retired over 17 years ago. Without that type of quarterback play or an all-world defense to carry the team, mediocrity is the most likely outcome. On the bright side, Brady is another year closer to retirement, and the Dolphins won't see the 40-year-old quarterback until after Thanksgiving, unless Father Time gets to him first. On the other hand, the Patriots were up 24-0 on Miami last year with Jimmy Garoppolo at quarterback, so the status quo may not be changing any time soon in the AFC East until Miami finds something to be great at.

Scott Kacsmar

1 http://www.footballoutsiders.com/stat-analysis/2016/building-super-bowl-winner-part-i

2016 Dolphins Stats by Week

Wk	vs.	W-L	PF	PA	YDF	YDA	TO	Total	Off	Def	ST
1	at SEA	L	10	12	214	352	+2	-52%	-48%	-6%	-10%
2	at NE	L	24	31	457	463	-3	28%	34%	1%	-5%
3	CLE	W	30	24	426	430	-2	-11%	-14%	7%	10%
4	at CIN	L	7	22	222	362	-2	-36%	-50%	-15%	0%
5	TEN	L	17	30	200	398	-2	-48%	-47%	22%	22%
6	PIT	W	30	15	474	297	+2	64%	45%	-25%	-7%
7	BUF	W	28	25	454	267	0	33%	29%	-18%	-13%
8	BYE										
9	NYJ	W	27	23	274	331	+2	24%	-5%	-8%	21%
10	at SD	W	31	24	337	379	+3	66%	33%	-40%	-7%
11	at LARM	W	14	10	240	227	0	-12%	-2%	2%	-7%
12	SF	W	31	24	358	475	+2	-6%	20%	29%	2%
13	at BAL	L	6	38	277	496	-1	-97%	-30%	61%	-7%
14	ARI	W	26	23	314	300	+1	21%	-15%	-33%	3%
15	at NYJ	W	34	13	303	360	+3	2%	-2%	-7%	-3%
16	at BUF	W	34	31	494	589	-1	35%	31%	14%	18%
17	NE	L	14	35	280	396	-2	-31%	0%	28%	-3%
18	at PIT	L	12	30	305	367	-1	-39%	-38%	10%	9%

Trends and Splits

	Offense	Rank	Defense	Rank
Total DVOA	1.8%	14	1.6%	19
Unadjusted VOA	4.2%	12	1.1%	18
Weighted Trend	7.5%	10	2.8%	21
Variance	9.9%	31	6.8%	26
Average Opponent	0.3%	18	-1.7%	23
Passing	14.1%	16	5.8%	16
Rushing	-3.9%	17	-3.4%	22
First Down	5.2%	13	-5.2%	9
Second Down	-5.4%	20	16.3%	30
Third Down	7.5%	11	-9.4%	9
First Half	-10.9%	27	6.8%	23
Second Half	20.4%	4	-10.5%	13
Red Zone	38.9%	4	1.1%	20
Late and Close	14.5%	6	-21.4%	6

Five-Year Performance

Year	W-L	Pyth W	Est W	PF	PA	TO	Total	Rk	Off	Rk	Def	Rk	ST	Rk	Off AGL	Rk	Def AGL	Rk	Off Age	Rk	Def Age	Rk	ST Age	Rk
2012	7-9	7.1	7.6	288	317	-10	-7.2%	21	-8.4%	22	-0.8%	14	0.4%	14	19.7	9	18.0	7	25.7	29	26.8	16	25.7	25
2013	8-8	7.5	6.8	317	335	-2	-6.5%	22	-1.8%	18	2.4%	17	-2.4%	23	41.3	20	18.6	9	26.5	23	27.3	11	26.0	18
2014	8-8	8.4	8.8	388	373	+2	3.5%	15	10.1%	8	0.5%	17	-6.1%	32	40.3	26	39.1	18	26.2	27	27.3	7	25.7	25
2015	6-10	5.8	5.8	310	389	-3	-19.0%	29	-7.3%	22	9.0%	25	-2.7%	24	23.0	7	40.5	24	25.5	31	26.6	16	25.3	30
2016	10-6	7.5	8.9	363	380	+2	1.0%	18	1.8%	14	1.6%	19	0.8%	12	46.3	24	52.8	25	26.3	23	26.9	10	25.6	25

2016 Performance Based on Most Common Personnel Groups

MIA Offense					MIA Offense vs. Opponents					MIA Defense					MIA Defense vs. Opponents			
Pers	Freq	Yds	DVOA	Run%	Pers	Freq	Yds	DVOA	Run%	Pers	Freq	Yds	DVOA	Pers	Freq	Yds	DVOA	
11	75%	6.0	1.2%	36%	Base	21%	6.9	27.6%	58%	Base	35%	5.9	7.7%	11	56%	5.8	2.9%	
12	14%	6.8	24.2%	58%	Nickel	69%	5.8	0.8%	39%	Nickel	60%	5.8	0.6%	12	18%	6.5	18.6%	
13	3%	3.0	-15.4%	65%	Dime+	7%	5.2	-8.3%	8%	Dime+	2%	5.7	16.5%	21	10%	5.6	2.1%	
612	2%	3.4	2.2%	82%	Goal Line	1%	0.8	4.3%	80%	Goal Line	2%	1.2	-59.9%	10	5%	5.5	19.6%	
611	2%	3.7	-32.5%	82%	Big	2%	3.6	-43.6%	79%	Big	0%	5.2	-0.4%	22	4%	5.0	-3.9%	

Strategic Tendencies

Run/Pass		Rk	Formation		Rk	Pass Rush		Rk	Secondary		Rk	Strategy		Rk
Runs, first half	43%	3	Form: Single Back	88%	6	Rush 3	4.8%	22	4 DB	35%	9	Play-action	22%	5
Runs, first down	54%	3	Form: Empty Back	7%	15	Rush 4	68.9%	8	5 DB	60%	15	Avg Box (Off)	6.20	14
Runs, second-long	36%	5	Pers: 3+ WR	78%	5	Rush 5	19.5%	21	6+ DB	2%	25	Avg Box (Def)	6.20	20
Runs, power sit.	55%	20	Pers: 2+ TE/6+ OL	22%	26	Rush 6+	6.8%	10	CB by Sides	82%	14	Offensive Pace	32.44	31
Runs, behind 2H	31%	7	Pers: 6+ OL	5%	15	Sacks by LB	3.0%	31	S/CB Cover Ratio	24%	24	Defensive Pace	32.51	31
Pass, ahead 2H	47%	22	Shotgun/Pistol	63%	20	Sacks by DB	13.6%	2	DB Blitz	10%	10	Go for it on 4th	0.28	32

Adam Gase's offense meant a big change in run/pass ratios, even before considering Miami's 10-6 record. Two years ago, the Dolphins ranked 22nd in run/pass ratio in the first half, and 29th in run/pass ratio on first down. Shotgun usage dropped by 14 percentage points, and situation-neutral pace dropped from average to the bottom of the league. ☞ Ironically for a team that moved so strongly towards the run, the Dolphins were fabulous from empty-backfield sets: 8.9 yards per play and a league-leading 95.0% DVOA. ☞ However, the Dolphins were awful on wide receiver screens, gaining just 3.8 yards per play with -26.7% DVOA. ☞ Ryan Tannehill had struggled against big blitzes for his entire career, but that turned around massively in 2016. Tannehill averaged 6.1 yards per pass against a standard pass rush but 10.5 against five pass-rushers and 10.1 against six or more. Matt Moore showed similar splits in his limited time, but there's no indication that this is a specific strength of the Adam Gase scheme, as his previous offenses did not show similar splits. ☞ Miami was the league's most-penalized team on defense, with 66 penalties for 495 yards. This was the second straight year the Dolphins ranked in the top three. ☞ Miami had the league's biggest DVOA gap between defense against multi-back runs (3.7 yards per carry, -34.8% DVOA) and defense against single-back runs (4.9, -0.6%).

Passing

Player	DYAR	DVOA	Plays	NtYds	Avg	YAC	C%	TD	Int
R.Tannehill	10	-10.8%	419	2743	6.5	5.5	67.6%	19	12
M.Moore	259	34.7%	87	718	8.3	6.6	64.7%	8	3
D.Fales	-9	-34.3%	6	17	2.8	7.5	40.0%	0	0

Rushing

Player	DYAR	DVOA	Plays	Yds	Avg	TD	Fum	Suc
J.Ajayi	167	13.2%	193	957	5.0	8	0	43%
R.Tannehill	8	-7.0%	32	168	5.3	1	0	-
D.Williams	30	15.7%	30	110	3.7	3	0	40%
A.Foster*	-24	-33.6%	22	55	2.5	0	0	27%
K.Drake	35	39.3%	20	97	4.9	2	0	50%
I.Pead*	-16	-60.3%	8	22	2.8	0	0	38%

Receiving

Player	DYAR	DVOA	Plays	Ctch	Yds	Y/C	YAC	TD	C%
J.Landry	174	4.8%	131	94	1136	12.1	6.6	4	72%
D.Parker	141	7.8%	88	56	744	13.3	4.2	4	64%
K.Stills	121	6.8%	81	42	726	17.3	4.6	9	52%
L.Carroo	2	-7.5%	6	3	29	9.7	4.3	1	50%
D.Sims*	34	6.3%	35	26	256	9.8	5.0	4	74%
M.Gray	37	22.2%	17	14	174	12.4	4.9	0	82%
J.Cameron*	6	0.6%	11	8	60	7.5	3.5	1	73%
D.Jones*	3	-2.9%	10	7	61	8.7	6.3	1	70%
J.Thomas	-23	-13.8%	51	30	281	9.4	3.4	4	59%
A.Fasano	13	5.2%	14	8	83	10.4	4.8	2	57%
J.Ajayi	-14	-20.7%	35	27	151	5.6	4.9	0	77%
D.Williams	45	12.5%	31	23	256	11.1	9.0	3	74%
K.Drake	8	0.6%	10	9	46	5.1	7.1	0	90%
A.Foster*	-1	-15.1%	10	6	78	13.0	11.3	0	60%

Offensive Line

Player	Pos	Age	GS	Snaps	Pen	Sk	Pass	Run	Player	Pos	Age	GS	Snaps	Pen	Sk	Pass	Run
Jermon Bushrod	RG	33	16/16	946	7	3.3	9	8	Anthony Steen	C	27	15/7	408	2	0.0	1	3
Ja'Wuan James	RT	25	16/16	935	11	5.3	18	8	Kraig Urbik	C	32	16/6	388	0	0.0	2	4
Laremy Tunsil	LG	23	14/14	802	5	0.5	3	2	Mike Pouncey	C	28	5/5	301	1	0.0	2	1
Branden Albert*	LT	33	12/12	721	3	1.5	9	3	Ted Larsen	RG	30	16/8	582	7	0.5	3	6

Year	Yards	ALY	Rank	Power	Rank	Stuff	Rank	2nd Lev	Rank	Open Field	Rank	Sacks	ASR	Rank	Press	Rank	F-Start	Cont.
2014	4.63	4.34	9	63%	17	18%	12	1.42	1	0.82	9	46	6.9%	19	26.1%	21	20	26
2015	4.28	3.76	28	58%	27	24%	30	1.22	7	1.01	7	45	7.6%	24	28.2%	25	19	33
2016	4.59	3.97	22	52%	28	24%	31	1.40	3	1.13	4	30	6.3%	21	26.8%	18	14	25

2016 ALY by direction: Left End 5.43 (5)   Left Tackle 3.93 (22)   Mid/Guard 3.97 (23)   Right Tackle 3.46 (26)   Right End 3.51 (20)

Laremy Tunsil did not quite live up to the "draft him in the first round and start him at left tackle for a decade" pipe dream that gets thrown around for every highly touted prospect since the early 2000s. Then again, no one since Joe Thomas (2007) has really pulled that off without some growing pains. Tunsil started his career at left guard, and he was more than adequate, actually finishing No. 1 in snaps per blown block at his position. He'll now take over for Branden Albert at left tackle, which is good news for Ryan Tannehill's blindside, but not so good for the now-open spot at left guard. ☞ Anthony Steen filled in at center for Mike Pouncey last year. "I was scared to death, honestly," is what Steen, also a guard, said about that surprise fill-in job last year. He eventually lost his spot to veteran Kraig Urbik, but a nagging ankle injury was part of the issue. This spring he has split his time between guard and center, but is still an option at left guard since the main competition is middling free-agent backup Ted Larsen. ☞ Mike is usually the more durable Pouncey brother, but his hip has been an issue. He had a stem cell procedure this offseason, and the Dolphins cannot afford to lose him for 11 games again like last year. Miami had a -5.1% rushing DVOA without Pouncey in the lineup, but a sensational 22.1% DVOA in the five games he did play. For reference, the Bills led the league in rushing DVOA last year at 16.1%. ☞ Jermon Bushrod struggled in his move to right guard last season, ranked 26th in snaps per blown block. Urbik is still there for depth, versatility, and experience. Long-term, the job may belong to fifth-round pick Isaac Asiata (Utah), a powerful prospect who needs to harness his aggression with better technique. ☞ Ja'Wuan James is the third first-round pick along Miami's line, but he ranked 30th at right tackle in snaps per blown block, as pass protection is still his weakness.

Defensive Front Seven

Defensive Line	Age	Pos	G	Snaps	Plays	TmPct	Rk	Stop	Dfts	BTkl	Runs	St%	Rk	RuYd	Rk	Sack	Hit	Hur	Dsrpt
					Overall							**vs. Run**					**Pass Rush**		
Ndamukong Suh	30	DT	16	973	75	8.7%	6	64	24	2	56	80%	37	2.3	47	5.5	11	35	7
Jordan Phillips	25	DT	16	622	26	3.0%	74	22	10	2	19	84%	25	1.5	19	0.5	4	15	2
Earl Mitchell*	30	DT	9	308	18	3.7%	59	16	8	3	16	88%	18	0.7	5	0.0	1	8	0

Edge Rushers	Age	Pos	G	Snaps	Plays	TmPct	Rk	Stop	Dfts	BTkl	Runs	St%	Rk	RuYd	Rk	Sack	Hit	Hur	Dsrpt
					Overall							**vs. Run**					**Pass Rush**		
Andre Branch	28	DE	16	774	49	5.7%	38	38	20	7	31	74%	48	1.8	28	5.5	9	20	3
Cameron Wake	35	DE	16	589	31	3.6%	73	27	18	8	15	73%	53	3.4	82	11.0	14	36	0
Jason Jones*	31	DE	14	516	38	5.1%	45	29	9	1	23	78%	31	3.3	81	3.5	8	13	1
Mario Williams*	32	DE	13	449	14	2.0%	98	13	5	7	11	91%	1	0.3	3	1.5	3	19	2
Terrence Fede	26	DE	8	173	13	3.0%	--	5	0	2	11	45%	--	4.5	--	0.0	0	8	0
William Hayes	*32*	*DE*	*14*	*513*	*43*	*5.9%*	*34*	*33*	*15*	*2*	*34*	*76%*	*37*	*1.4*	*16*	*5.0*	*13*	*28*	*1*

Linebackers	Age	Pos	G	Snaps	Plays	TmPct	Rk	Stop	Dfts	BTkl	Runs	St%	Rk	RuYd	Rk	Sack	Hit	Hur	Tgts	Suc%	Rk	AdjYd	Rk	PD	Int
					Overall							**vs. Run**					**Pass Rush**				**vs. Pass**				
Kiko Alonso	27	MLB	15	1050	119	14.8%	25	54	19	14	74	42%	87	5.2	84	0.0	6	7	35	54%	27	7.2	52	4	2
Jelani Jenkins*	25	OLB	9	372	29	6.0%	79	16	4	5	18	72%	11	3.9	64	0.0	1	2	13	30%	--	7.5	--	1	0
Donald Butler*	29	OLB	14	356	28	3.7%	87	16	6	2	22	73%	10	1.7	2	0.0	0	0	6	12%	--	7.9	--	0	0
Neville Hewitt	24	OLB	16	353	57	6.6%	--	26	12	6	38	63%	--	4.0	--	1.0	0	2	13	38%	--	5.0	--	0	0
Spencer Paysinger*	29	OLB	15	333	54	6.7%	--	27	10	6	22	50%	--	6.5	--	0.0	2	3	18	54%	26	4.4	3	3	0
Koa Misi	30	OLB	3	128	22	13.7%	--	10	1	1	17	53%	--	3.5	--	0.0	0	1	5	48%	--	6.5	--	0	0
Lawrence Timmons	*31*	*ILB*	*16*	*950*	*119*	*14.8%*	*24*	*65*	*18*	*12*	*59*	*68%*	*24*	*3.1*	*25*	*2.5*	*10*	*17*	*42*	*39%*	*68*	*6.9*	*49*	*5*	*2*

Year	Yards	ALY	Rank	Power	Rank	Stuff	Rank	2nd Level	Rank	Open Field	Rank	Sacks	ASR	Rank	Press	Rank
2014	4.12	4.11	15	65%	19	21%	10	1.08	11	0.80	20	39	7.5%	8	24.1%	20
2015	4.08	3.85	10	66%	16	24%	8	1.21	23	0.84	19	31	5.9%	22	25.3%	15
2016	4.54	4.32	18	57%	6	22%	10	1.45	32	0.82	23	33	4.7%	31	31.4%	4
2016 ALY by direction:	Left End 6.12 (31)			Left Tackle 4.23 (16)			Mid/Guard 3.98 (12)			Right Tackle 4.97 (28)			Right End 2.76 (4)		

Ndamukong Suh and Cameron Wake are well-known commodities, but the Dolphins can really field a talented line if recent high draft picks Jordan Phillips and Charles Harris develop. Phillips showed improvement in his second season, but still isn't anywhere near the level of an elite run-stuffer to complement Suh's pressure. He'll have to improve in that facet to stay on the field, as the 335-pounder only had a handful of hurries and doesn't profile as much of a pass-rusher. ☞ Second-round linebacker Raekwon McMillan (Ohio State) doesn't have much competition, so he could be Miami's best rookie starter this season. Scouts see his future as an average starter, but that's basically what the Dolphins have gotten out of Koa Misi on the other side. They'll just hope that McMillan has better durability than Misi, who has missed 28 games since 2011. ☞ Miami signed Lawrence Timmons for $12 million over the next two seasons. He is now 31, but only missed two games in a decade in Pittsburgh. Timmons showed some life last year after a miserable 2015 season, particularly against the run. He's not the same force he used to be, but he is easily the most accomplished linebacker on the team. The Dolphins aren't paying him just to ride the bench, but he is good insurance for the unreliable starter ahead of him on the depth chart. ☞ Kiko Alonso signed a four-year deal for $28.9 million in March even though he was subpar against the pass and the run last year. Alonso's career is a masterwork of getting people to believe he is a very good player, contrary to the evidence. The first step is to make a strong first impression, like when Alonso intercepted four passes in September of 2013—an unusual stretch of play for a linebacker, let alone a rookie. He also did it in Buffalo, where assisted tackle stats are artificially inflated by the official scorer, before suffering a torn ACL ahead of his second season. In his first game with the Eagles in 2015, he made an athletic interception off Matt Ryan in the end zone on Monday Night Football, the type of big play in front of a national audience that will get people remembering what you did as a rookie. Alonso has charted outside the top 50 in pass coverage for each of the last two seasons, but since he had a game-winning pick-six in San Diego last year, his reputation continues to exceed his performance.

Defensive Secondary

Secondary	Age	Pos	G	Snaps	Plays	Overall TmPct	Rk	Stop	Dfts	BTkl	vs. Run Runs	St%	Rk	RuYd	Rk	vs. Pass Tgts	Tgt%	Rk	Dist	Suc%	Rk	AdjYd	Rk	PD	Int
Isa Abdul-Quddus*	28	FS	15	951	81	10.1%	36	29	9	6	42	40%	35	7.9	51	27	7.4%	27	12.7	44%	43	10.7	60	5	2
Tony Lippett	25	CB	16	863	77	9.0%	35	28	12	7	24	33%	55	8.2	62	64	19.6%	53	10.3	49%	49	7.5	40	11	4
Byron Maxwell	29	CB	13	846	67	9.6%	25	31	14	7	14	50%	19	7.4	54	64	20.2%	57	13.6	50%	36	6.7	19	15	2
Bobby McCain	24	CB	16	620	49	5.7%	85	22	13	4	11	27%	67	4.6	11	39	16.8%	25	9.0	45%	67	7.1	27	6	1
Michael Thomas	28	FS	16	572	40	4.7%	73	14	6	6	23	30%	56	9.3	61	13	6.1%	7	10.0	46%	40	9.3	49	1	0
Xavien Howard	24	CB	7	528	46	12.2%	--	13	3	8	7	14%	--	7.4	--	43	21.5%	--	13.5	44%	--	10.1	--	6	0
Bacarri Rambo*	27	SS	9	469	42	8.7%	--	14	5	6	20	40%	--	6.5	--	14	8.0%	--	12.4	42%	--	12.6	--	3	1
Reshad Jones	29	SS	6	431	55	17.1%	--	24	9	4	29	45%	--	6.8	--	12	7.4%	--	8.6	50%	--	6.2	--	2	1
Nate Allen	30	FS	14	231	29	4.3%	--	13	5	2	17	59%	--	4.3	--	8	8.1%	--	14.6	27%	--	14.2	--	3	2
T.J. McDonald	26	SS	16	1069	68	8.2%	54	35	16	8	31	55%	13	6.8	38	28	6.4%	15	8.6	53%	14	6.3	8	6	2

Year	Pass D Rank	vs. #1 WR	Rk	vs. #2 WR	Rk	vs. Other WR	Rk	vs. TE	Rk	vs. RB	Rk
2014	16	5.9%	21	-13.4%	8	29.1%	30	-16.5%	5	15.5%	25
2015	29	29.4%	32	21.5%	27	9.2%	22	-10.5%	11	6.3%	19
2016	16	-15.1%	5	-15.6%	4	22.9%	31	4.7%	21	-11.1%	10

While the secondary lacks any star players, three of the top 12 Dolphins by 2017 cap hit belong to this unit, led by Byron Maxwell (fourth on the team at $8.5 million). It was only two years ago when Maxwell served up burnt toast regularly with the Eagles, ranking 64th in adjusted success rate and 71st in adjusted yards per pass. He ranked 36th and 19th, respectively, in those categories with Miami, proving once again that cornerback coverage stats are prone to large variation from year to year. ☞ The Dolphins better hope to see improvement from Xavien Howard in his second season. As a result of Miami's shoddy secondary depth, Howard was an immediate starter despite missing the entire preseason with a knee injury. Defenses targeted the rookie frequently with success before another knee injury cost him nine games. Howard has a good chance to start again this year, but Bobby McCain and Tony Lippett showed more last season. The good news is that many top-drafted cornerbacks take two, three, or even four years to fully develop. ☞ Clemson cornerback Cordrea Tankersley was added for depth in the third round. Scouting reports peg him as a speedy corner who doesn't want to get involved against the run. In two years as a starter, he intercepted eight passes but also had eight pass interference penalties. ☞ Safety Reshad Jones is one of the four likely starters on Miami's defense who was drafted by the Dolphins. He missed 10 games last year, and Bacarri Rambo allowed more than twice as many yards per pass as Jones did. Miami signed four-year veteran T.J. McDonald from the Rams to help avoid that type of situation again, but McDonald will miss the first eight games of 2017 due to a suspension for violating the league's substance abuse policy. ☞ Miami's other starting safety, Nate Allen, brings a second-round pedigree from the Eagles and Raiders, but has mostly been a JAG for his career. He could be replaced at midseason by McDonald, or sooner by Walt Aikens, the special-teamer who has flopped around from corner to safety in his time with Miami.

Special Teams

Year	DVOA	Rank	FG/XP	Rank	Net Kick	Rank	Kick Ret	Rank	Net Punt	Rank	Punt Ret	Rank	Hidden	Rank
2014	-6.1%	32	-8.8	31	-12.6	32	0.1	15	-4.3	22	-4.8	26	15.3	2
2015	-2.7%	24	-1.7	22	0.8	14	-9.1	31	-11.2	28	7.9	4	18.8	1
2016	0.8%	12	-6.2	27	6.0	5	6.6	6	-3.5	22	1.2	12	21.0	1

We mentioned earlier in the chapter that Miami had a league-low 21 field goal attempts in 2016, but that was actually up from the 16 attempts the team had in 2015. Yes, 37 field goal attempts in two years when the rest of the league has averaged 63.2 attempts is an odd-looking stat. Kicker Andrew Franks also hasn't been very successful in his first two seasons, connecting on 7-of-13 field goals from 40-plus yards. However, he was sixth in gross kickoff value in 2016. ☞ Punter Matt Darr didn't help Miami's special teams improve to 12th in DVOA, but the return game did. Kenyan Drake's game-winning kick return touchdown against the Jets helped him to the fifth-most kick return value of the season. Jarvis Landry and Jakeem Grant split time returning punts; Landry had more value even though Grant was the one with a touchdown return. ☞ Miami blocked a league-high three extra points. They also benefited from a league-high nine missed field goals (opponents were 26-for-35, 74 percent). ☞ Safety Michael Thomas and linebacker Mike Hull each made 18 special teams plays for the Dolphins, tied for second in the league. Nate Ebner of the Patriots, with 19, was the only other player in the league with more than 15 combined tackles and assists on kick or punt returns.

Minnesota Vikings

2016 Record: 8-8	Total DVOA: -1.7% (20th)	2017 Mean Projection: 7.4 wins	On the Clock (0-4): 13%
Pythagorean Wins: 8.6 (14th)	Offense: -9.8% (26th)	Postseason Odds: 26.9%	Mediocrity (5-7): 40%
Snap-Weighted Age: 27.2 (4th)	Defense: -6.6% (8th)	Super Bowl Odds: 2.7%	Playoff Contender (8-10): 35%
Average Opponent: -0.4% (19th)	Special Teams: 1.5% (10th)	Proj. Avg. Opponent: 0.6% (9th)	Super Bowl Contender (11+): 12%

2016: The quarterback injury set off the alarms, but the offensive line injuries burned down the house.

2017: The defense should make the Vikings wild-card contenders, but our projection system is cynical.

Fifteen times last season, the Minnesota Vikings threw the ball when they needed to gain 1 yard for a first down. They converted 11 times. On 39 other occasions, the Vikings needed a yard but decided to run the ball. They converted 25 times. Only five teams in the league were more efficient gaining first downs when they threw the ball in those situations; 24 teams were more efficient when they ran. Yet the Vikings were committed to running the ball in short-yardage situations. Not only that, but they were committed to running the ball with a fullback and multiple tight ends on the field. Mike Zimmer would bring every defender as close as possible to the ball so that his offense could prove its toughness and impose itself on the defense.

Send a message.

Zimmer is talking about being tougher this offseason. "We're going to get back to being the Vikings and be blue collar," he told Chris Tomasson of the *St. Paul Pioneer Press*. "I don't care how long practice goes. If the schedule says two hours and I'm not happy, we're going to 2:30."

Those words came later in the offseason, after Zimmer had told the team's official website that the running game was the biggest issue facing their offense: "We've got to run the football better than we did. I think that was part of the problem, we had way too many negative-yardage runs." Of course, he's right. The Vikings were 30th in adjusted line yards and 26th in stuff rate last season. Awful offensive line play was a big issue. The Vikings cycled through different linemen all season long. Matt Kalil entered the season as the starter at left tackle, but he only played two games before landing on IR. Kalil was soon followed by starting right tackle Andre Smith. Smith earned his job by default during the offseason because Phil Loadholt decided to retire instead of coming back from injury. The Vikings were forced to start T.J. Clemmings for most of the season, more often than not at left tackle. Clemmings was essentially the third-string left tackle, while Jeremiah Siles was the third-string right tackle. Clemmings played 933 snaps, the most of any lineman on the team; Sirles played 817, which ranked fifth.

The interior wasn't much better. Only Alex Boone remained in place from Week 1 through season's end, and even he missed two games. Adding Mike Remmers and Riley Reiff won't dramatically improve the Vikings' line. Remmers and Reiff are subpar starters who, if healthy, will be upgrades over the players they are replacing, but not dramatically so.

Zimmer's commitment to an archaic running philosophy is only serving to stress the weaknesses of his offense. When you put extra tight ends and a fullback onto the field, you are theoretically bringing in players who are better blockers than the wide receivers who are being replaced. That gives you a better chance of executing blocks, and it allows you to use more creative blocking designs to create space. It also puts more pressure on those blockers to execute. It brings more defenders into positions where they can stop the run and forces you to create space that would already be there if the defense were stretched horizontally with three or four receivers. In his attempt to directly help his linemen and be a tougher team, Zimmer was outsmarting himself. He was doing a perfect Rex Ryan impression—the prototype defensive genius who prioritized trying to be physical over trying to be effective. That stubbornness was a catalyst in anchoring the Minnesota offense to the lower third of the league. The Vikings passing game ranked 18th in DVOA, but the offense as a whole ranked 26th because the running game was the second-worst in the league. Only Todd Gurley's Los Angeles Rams managed to be worse, and everyone saw how ugly that was.

Notably, running back is a position where the Vikings made significant investments in this offseason. Adrian Peterson's departure was inevitable and Latavius Murray's arrival suggested that the Vikings were looking at a like-for-like replacement. Murray is a bigger back with more receiving skills than Peterson, but he is not generally regarded for having a diverse skill set. Murray and Jerick McKinnon would have made a fine combination atop the depth chart, but then the Vikings traded up to in the second round to make Dalvin Cook their first 2017 draft selection. (They had lost their first-round pick in the Sam Bradford trade a year prior.)

Our new BackCAST projection system certainly approves of the decision to select Cook. Our introduction to BackCAST elsewhere in the book (page 429) explains why Cook has one of the system's best running back projections of the last 20 years. Cook sported an unusual combination of usage and efficiency during his time at Florida State. There have been plenty of running backs who have been used as heavily as Cook *or* have been as efficient as Cook, but only one running back (Ricky Williams) ever has been used as heavily *and* been as efficient as Cook. Cook's BackCAST score of plus-136.0 percent was second behind Leonard Fournette this year, but

2017 Vikings Schedule

Week	Opp.	Week	Opp.	Week	Opp.
1	NO (Mon.)	7	BAL	13	at ATL
2	at PIT	8	at CLE (U.K.)	14	at CAR
3	TB	9	BYE	15	CIN
4	DET	10	at WAS	16	at GB (Sat.)
5	at CHI (Mon.)	11	LARM	17	CHI
6	GB	12	at DET (Thu.)		

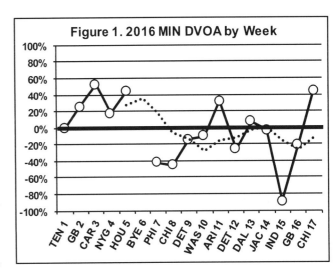

Figure 1. 2016 MIN DVOA by Week

ranks fifth overall since 1998, behind Fournette and just ahead of LaDainian Tomlinson.

On the other hand, Cook's combine performance is a significant concern. BackCAST incorporates combine numbers, but does not solely rely on them. And Cook's combine numbers were the reason why he was available in the second round. Josh Norris of Rotoworld noted that no running back with Cook's athletic profile had been drafted in the first round for 18 years prior to the 2017 draft. Cook tested in the ninth percentile of SPARQ's athleticism rankings because of bad performances in essentially all of the combine drills. His tape at Florida State was undeniably great, but his transition to the NFL, especially playing behind the Vikings offensive line in the Vikings scheme, is a real concern.

Further concerning evidence that Zimmer is becoming the next Rex Ryan is the perilous position of Laquon Treadwell. Ryan repeatedly proved that he could develop defensive prospects, but no skill position players on offense ever made significant strides under his guidance. Treadwell, whom Zimmer called "the best blocking receiver that I have ever seen" 12 months ago, seemingly developed backwards in his rookie season. Treadwell is in position to be Minnesota's third receiver in 2017, but he couldn't take Cordarrelle Patterson's job last year despite being given every opportunity to do so—and Patterson isn't exactly a high bar to clear. With Patterson now in Oakland, Treadwell will battle with Jarius Wright and Michael Floyd for the third receiver spot. Floyd is the best receiver of the three, but he is facing a suspension to start the year and is coming off his worst season in the NFL. In Arizona last season, he continually failed to take advantage of accurate Carson Palmer passes. Floyd is a good blocker, and has also proven that he can beat press coverage off the line of scrimmage and use his athleticism to get open vertically. Treadwell showed off no route-running ability, athleticism, or ball skills during his one-catch, 80-snap season.

The only young offensive player in Minnesota who has shown any real development since Zimmer arrived is Adam Thielen. 2016 was Thielen's breakout season. He and Sam Bradford developed an instant understanding that allowed the quarterback to consistently find the receiver downfield with precision and timing. Thielen led team in yards and had two more touchdowns than fellow starter Stefon Diggs despite catching 15 fewer passes. Diggs is likely still the Vikings' best receiver, but the gap between the two isn't notable. Improving the running game and offensive line will give the Vikings more opportunities to push the ball downfield. Bradford

is an exceptionally accurate deep passer, one of the best in the league, but most fans don't consider that one of his skills because he has never been in an offense where he had opportunities to consistently be aggressive. Thielen will be his primary target if the Vikings can create that situation in 2017. Sixteen of Thielen's 69 receptions last year gained at least 20 yards. All 10 of the receivers who caught more big plays than him were also targeted more times than him. His combination of athleticism and subtlety in his vertical routes allows him to beat any kind of coverage from any kind of defensive back.

With Thielen and Diggs outside, the Vikings have the potential to create a passing game that is both efficient and explosive. Everything hinges on better play calling and better offensive line play.

NFL teams often rely on great strengths to overcome great weaknesses. The best example from recent times was the Carolina Panthers team that reached the Super Bowl in 2015. That offense had phenomenal quarterback play, a good interior offensive line, and a running game that could consistently create hesitation in every level of the defense on each snap. Even on the defensive side, the Panthers relied on their front seven to execute tougher assignments so the secondary could be filled with disciplined but unathletic older players. Unfortunately for the Vikings, it's harder to rely on receivers as your strength to cover weaknesses on the offensive line than it is to do the inverse. A bad offensive line requires expert play calling from the coaching staff to set the quarterback up to negate the inevitable pressure.

For all the issues the Vikings have on offense, the defense is coming off a top-10 finish in DVOA and should get better this season. Save for Brian Robison and Terence Newman, the Vikings don't have any players in line to make significant contributions who are past their prime. Danielle Hunter has two years of experience and won't turn 23 until midseason; this should be the year when he finally replaces Robison in the starting lineup. Hunter is the superior athlete with greater pass-rushing ability. Forcing Newman out is tougher. Newman was released by the Dallas Cowboys because of he seemed to be declining… six years ago. He rebounded under Zimmer's coaching in Cincinnati, followed him to Minnesota, and is still playing strong at the age of 39. Newman offers the Vikings a buffer against any failure in the development of Trae Waynes and Mackensie Alexander. If one of the high-potential youngsters struggles or fails to fill the requirements of his role, the Vikings can turn to Newman.

That blend of youth and experience extends into the Vikings' foundation. Hunter is a part of it. So is fellow defensive end Everson Griffen (29 years old). Linebackers Anthony Barr (25) and Eric Kendricks (25) offer Zimmer versatility in his play calling. Few linebackers in the league can play the run as well as those two while showing off controlled aggression and range in coverage. Harrison Smith (28) is widely acknowledged as one of the best safeties in the league due to his versatility and consistency. Cornerback Xavier Rhodes (26) is coming off his best season. Zimmer has built this defense by developing versatile players in key positions. From that group, Zimmer will look to Griffen, Barr, and Smith to lead on each level of his defense. Barr in particular needs to have a greater impact than he had last year. The linebacker only had two sacks, one forced fumble, and four pass deflections. He didn't have a single interception and had 37 solo tackles in 16 games, after having more than 50 in each of his first two seasons while playing no more than 14 games either year. Barr's explosiveness and rounded athleticism wasn't evident last year like it had been previously. His head coach said in December that he "has a tendency to coast a little bit."

Sharrif Floyd's uncertain status is the only major concern the Vikings defense has. Floyd tore his meniscus last September. He played 25 total snaps in 2016. It was supposed to be a routine procedure, but complications led to nerve damage that never healed. Tom Pellisero of *USA Today* (now NFL.com) reported that Floyd's career is under threat. He is under contract for 2017, but nobody knows if he will ever play again. Even if Floyd doesn't return, Shamar Stephen and Tom Johnson played well in his absence last year, while Jaleel Johnson of Iowa was a widely praised pick in the fourth round of the 2017 draft. A fully healthy Floyd would give the Vikings an excellent pass-rushing complement to the impressive Linval Joseph on the interior of the Vikings defensive line. Without him, the defense is more reliant on disguising its pass rushes to create confusion. Zimmer's double A-Gap blitzes weren't as successful last year as they have been in the past.

Our statistical forecast ended up surprisingly pessimistic about the Vikings season, for a somewhat odd reason: essentially, the defense projects to rank lower because it stands still while other teams added talent this offseason. But the Minnesota defense won't stand still if the young talent keeps improving. Even after an uninspired offseason that didn't see the franchise make any dramatic upgrades except at running back, the Vikings roster is talented enough to be a contender in the NFC. Minnesota's odds of making the playoffs are likely higher than our forecast indicates, but they would also need a huge step forward to be a serious Super Bowl contender.

The Vikings are trying to be the team that started last season 5-0 rather than the one that finished 3-8. Since health was such a big issue in 2016, it's rational for the franchise to be optimistic about the outlook in 2017. Coaching will be the biggest determining factor in Minnesota.

Cian Fahey

2016 Vikings Stats by Week

Wk	vs.	W-L	PF	PA	YDF	YDA	TO	Total	Off	Def	ST
1	at TEN	W	25	16	301	316	+3	-1%	-2%	-14%	-13%
2	GB	W	17	14	284	263	+2	26%	-32%	-50%	7%
3	at CAR	W	22	10	211	306	+3	53%	5%	-29%	19%
4	NYG	W	24	10	366	339	+2	17%	26%	8%	-1%
5	HOU	W	31	13	351	214	+1	44%	14%	-17%	13%
6	BYE										
7	at PHI	L	10	21	282	239	0	-42%	-50%	-25%	-17%
8	at CHI	L	10	20	258	403	0	-46%	-24%	25%	3%
9	DET	L	16	22	337	311	+1	-14%	-16%	-8%	-7%
10	at WAS	L	20	26	331	388	0	-10%	2%	11%	-1%
11	ARI	W	30	24	217	290	+1	32%	-5%	-18%	19%
12	at DET	L	13	16	306	308	-1	-26%	-28%	1%	2%
13	DAL	L	15	17	318	264	+1	7%	-10%	-33%	-17%
14	at JAC	W	25	16	377	315	-1	-3%	1%	13%	9%
15	IND	L	6	34	282	411	-3	-89%	-67%	26%	4%
16	at GB	L	25	38	446	348	-2	-21%	-3%	16%	-2%
17	CHI	W	38	10	374	323	+4	44%	18%	-21%	5%

Trends and Splits

	Offense	Rank	Defense	Rank
Total DVOA	-9.8%	26	-6.6%	8
Unadjusted VOA	-9.9%	26	-7.7%	7
Weighted Trend	-12.8%	27	0.2%	18
Variance	6.1%	17	4.9%	17
Average Opponent	1.5%	29	1.2%	10
Passing	8.6%	19	-2.8%	8
Rushing	-23.3%	31	-11.7%	16
First Down	-10.2%	26	2.8%	21
Second Down	2.7%	14	-12.1%	6
Third Down	-28.4%	30	-16.6%	5
First Half	-15.0%	29	4.5%	19
Second Half	2.5%	14	-33.0%	1
Red Zone	-21.1%	26	-7.2%	10
Late and Close	14.3%	7	-34.2%	2

Five-Year Performance

Year	W-L	Pyth W	Est W	PF	PA	TO	Total	Rk	Off	Rk	Def	Rk	ST	Rk	Off AGL	Rk	Def AGL	Rk	Off Age	Rk	Def Age	Rk	ST Age	Rk
2012	10-6	8.8	8.8	379	348	-1	2.0%	14	0.3%	15	3.1%	21	4.7%	5	10.4	3	18.5	8	25.5	31	27.2	12	25.5	28
2013	5-10-1	6.1	6.5	391	480	-12	-11.4%	26	-4.7%	21	10.5%	27	3.8%	6	21.4	8	32.5	21	26.6	19	27.1	12	25.8	24
2014	7-9	7.5	7.2	325	343	-1	-8.7%	25	-7.4%	22	4.3%	23	3.0%	10	39.0	23	17.1	3	26.7	17	25.9	29	25.6	28
2015	11-5	9.8	9.5	365	302	+5	5.7%	11	0.0%	16	-1.8%	14	3.9%	4	36.5	17	22.5	7	26.4	19	27.5	4	25.7	22
2016	8-8	8.6	8.6	327	307	+11	-1.7%	20	-9.8%	26	-6.6%	8	1.5%	10	92.1	32	28.6	12	27.1	10	27.8	3	26.3	10

2016 Performance Based on Most Common Personnel Groups

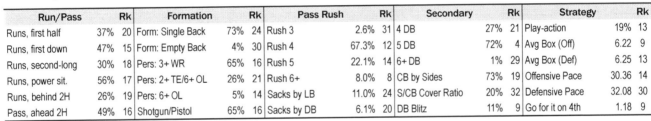

MIN Offense					MIN Offense vs. Opponents					MIN Defense				MIN Defense vs. Opponents			
Pers	Freq	Yds	DVOA	Run%	Pers	Freq	Yds	DVOA	Run%	Pers	Freq	Yds	DVOA	Pers	Freq	Yds	DVOA
11	63%	5.3	-4.9%	24%	Base	29%	5.1	2.0%	56%	Base	27%	5.0	-9.8%	11	65%	5.3	-5.4%
12	13%	6.0	8.0%	30%	Nickel	57%	5.3	-3.2%	29%	Nickel	72%	5.4	-6.0%	12	18%	5.4	-6.1%
21	9%	4.6	-18.2%	63%	Dime+	10%	5.4	-19.8%	3%	Dime+	1%	4.9	-18.2%	21	4%	5.0	-27.3%
22	6%	5.1	11.3%	80%	Goal Line	2%	0.6	-24.8%	71%	Goal Line	1%	0.8	32.7%	13	3%	5.3	0.1%
13	2%	3.8	-5.2%	73%	Big	2%	5.0	-15.1%	88%					01	2%	9.3	12.1%
20	2%	5.6	52.1%	69%										10	2%	2.4	-36.9%
622	2%	0.5	-63.1%	73%													

Strategic Tendencies

Run/Pass		Rk	Formation		Rk	Pass Rush		Rk	Secondary		Rk	Strategy		Rk
Runs, first half	37%	20	Form: Single Back	73%	24	Rush 3	2.6%	31	4 DB	27%	21	Play-action	19%	13
Runs, first down	47%	15	Form: Empty Back	4%	30	Rush 4	67.3%	12	5 DB	72%	4	Avg Box (Off)	6.22	9
Runs, second-long	30%	18	Pers: 3+ WR	65%	16	Rush 5	22.1%	14	6+ DB	1%	29	Avg Box (Def)	6.25	13
Runs, power sit.	56%	17	Pers: 2+ TE/6+ OL	26%	21	Rush 6+	8.0%	8	CB by Sides	73%	19	Offensive Pace	30.36	14
Runs, behind 2H	26%	19	Pers: 6+ OL	5%	14	Sacks by LB	11.0%	24	S/CB Cover Ratio	20%	32	Defensive Pace	32.08	30
Pass, ahead 2H	49%	16	Shotgun/Pistol	65%	16	Sacks by DB	6.1%	20	DB Blitz	11%	9	Go for it on 4th	1.18	9

In past years, we have frequently showed evidence that there's no correlation between the quality of a run game and the quality of the play-action passing attack. The Vikings were a great example in 2016. They gained 9.2 yards per play with play-action compared to just 6.0 yards per play otherwise, the largest gap in the league. (The second-largest gap belonged to the Rams, another team that could barely run the ball last season.) ☞ The Vikings were the only defense in the NFL with a better DVOA against deep passes (27.1%, second) than against short passes (28.6%, 16th). They had the worst defense in the NFL against short middle passes but the best defense in the NFL against deep middle passes. (These may differ from numbers on our website because passes batted down or thrown away on purpose are removed.) ☞ Part of Minnesota's issue with short passes: they got absolutely killed by running back screens. No defense faced more of them, and the Vikings gave up 8.4 yards per play with 58.7% DVOA. ☞ Once again, the Vikings were fantastic when they brought a blitz. They allowed 6.3 yards per pass with three or four pass-rushers, but that dropped to 5.7 with five and 3.2 with six or more. ☞ Minnesota's defense ranked 19th in the NFL before halftime, but was No. 1 in the league after halftime. ☞ The Vikings also ranked last in defensive DVOA on third-and-short, but 10th on third down with 3 or more yards to go.

Passing

Player	DYAR	DVOA	Plays	NtYds	Avg	YAC	C%	TD	Int
S.Bradford	510	2.2%	589	3576	6.1	5.0	71.7%	20	5
S.Hill*	15	-4.4%	36	235	6.5	3.5	54.3%	0	0
C.Keenum	-183	-19.5%	345	2054	6.0	5.3	60.9%	9	11

Rushing

Player	DYAR	DVOA	Plays	Yds	Avg	TD	Fum	Suc
J.McKinnon	-31	-14.7%	129	388	3.0	2	0	40%
M.Asiata*	-15	-11.3%	107	354	3.3	6	0	49%
A.Peterson*	-30	-33.6%	31	50	1.6	0	0	39%
R.Hillman*	-15	-29.6%	18	50	2.8	0	0	50%
Z.Line*	2	-3.0%	7	15	2.1	0	0	57%
C.Patterson	28	51.4%	7	43	6.1	0	0	-
S.Bradford	12	33.3%	5	37	7.4	0	0	-
L.Murray	139	10.3%	162	656	4.0	12	0	51%
C.Keenum	25	22.2%	13	58	4.5	1	0	-

Receiving

Player	DYAR	DVOA	Plays	Ctch	Yds	Y/C	YAC	TD	C%
S.Diggs	186	8.2%	111	84	903	10.8	3.8	3	76%
A.Thielen	270	26.2%	92	69	967	14.0	4.3	5	75%
C.Patterson*	17	-9.5%	70	52	453	8.7	6.4	2	74%
C.Johnson*	-13	-17.0%	37	20	232	11.6	3.5	0	54%
J.Wright	12	-1.8%	14	11	67	6.1	3.8	1	79%
M.Floyd	43	-5.6%	76	37	488	13.2	1.9	5	49%
K.Rudolph	-17	-9.1%	132	83	840	10.1	4.3	7	63%
R.Ellison*	-41	-51.9%	14	9	57	6.3	3.8	0	64%
J.McKinnon	10	-10.7%	53	43	255	5.9	6.3	2	81%
M.Asiata*	54	11.5%	38	32	263	8.2	8.2	0	84%
R.Hillman*	-1	-15.6%	7	4	43	10.8	9.3	0	57%
A.Peterson*	-30	-109.4%	6	3	8	2.7	3.7	0	50%
L.Murray	10	-9.4%	43	33	264	8.0	8.5	0	77%

Offensive Line

Player	Pos	Age	GS	Snaps	Pen	Sk	Pass	Run	Player	Pos	Age	GS	Snaps	Pen	Sk	Pass	Run
T.J. Clemmings	LT	26	15/14	882	10	9.5	20	12	Nick Easton	C	25	11/5	414	1	1.5	5	3
Alex Boone	LG	30	14/14	873	5	1.0	5	10	Jake Long*	LT	32	4/3	210	0	3.5	7	0
Joe Berger	C	35	14/14	852	1	2.5	3	5	Andre Smith*	RT	30	4/4	181	3	1.5	3	1
Brandon Fusco*	RG	28	14/14	834	2	3.5	13	10	Mike Remmers	LT/RT	28	16/16	1107	15	8.5	20	7
Jeremiah Sirles	RT	26	14/10	772	8	6.0	13	5	Riley Reiff	RT	29	14/14	889	5	3.5	11	5

Year	Yards	ALY	Rank	Power	Rank	Stuff	Rank	2nd Lev	Rank	Open Field	Rank	Sacks	ASR	Rank	Press	Rank	F-Start	Cont.
2014	4.11	4.25	13	68%	10	15%	2	1.07	21	0.61	21	51	9.1%	27	29.8%	27	16	28
2015	4.55	4.31	10	76%	2	20%	12	1.24	4	1.12	5	45	8.8%	29	36.0%	32	13	48
2016	3.15	3.64	30	47%	31	22%	26	0.81	32	0.28	31	38	6.0%	17	23.6%	10	18	23

2016 ALY by direction: Left End 4.24 (19)   Left Tackle 3.12 (31)   Mid/Guard 3.72 (30)   Right Tackle 3.86 (17)   Right End 3.18 (25)

Desperation was the theme for the Vikings this offseason. After watching a litany of awful offensive linemen repeatedly destroy the design of plays and the overall functionality of the offense in Minnesota, Vikings brass were overly aggressive in free agency. Riley Reiff arrives from the Lions after an underwhelming five-year tenure. Reiff might benefit somewhat from playing left tackle rather than right tackle. He's a pass-blocking specialist who offers no real value in the running game. He is an assignment run-blocker, someone who gets to the right spot and might execute his block but won't ever make any impact at the point of contact. Moreover, he was never good enough as a pass-blocker to offset his limitations as a run-blocker in Detroit. Reiff's charting in Detroit ranked him as an average right tackle. It will be difficult for him to replicate that relative success in Minnesota because he is moving into a scheme that stresses the tackles more with deeper drops where the quarterback is expected to hold the ball. ☞ Mike Remmers is used to playing in an offense that stresses the tackles. Remmers is best known for his Super Bowl undressing at the hands of Von Miller two seasons ago. Yes, Miller has made a career of doing that to offensive tackles, but Remmers can't use that excuse: he has been repeatedly exposed by average NFL defenders throughout his career. When injuries forced him to play left tackle last year, it further exacerbated his slow feet and tendency to lose his balance by leaning too far forward. By blown blocks, Remmers ranked 29th out of 35 qualifying left tackles. He was also tied with Greg Robinson for the league lead with 15 offensive penalties. Now Remmers will return to the right side in Minnesota, where the Vikings hope he provides value in the running game and plays well enough to be effective with help in pass protection. Sam Bradford has shown that he can get the ball out quickly and deliver the ball against arriving pressure. He doesn't need great tackles, but he can't sidestep the work of matadors either. ☞ Third-round pick Pat Elflein was the only addition of significance made to the interior of the line. The Ohio State product has a chance to start from Day 1 but will have to beat out veteran Nick Easton. With Elflein and Easton vying for the center spot, Joe Berger can concentrate on exclusively playing right guard. Berger is old and was inconsistent last year while playing multiple positions and missing time because of a concussion. If he and starting left guard Alex Boone can remain in the same positions for 16 games, it would go a long way towards solidifying the Vikings offensive line. ☙ The Vikings have few young players who could step up to compete with Berger for playing time. Clemmings doesn't have the body to transition to guard, Willie Beavers offers limited ability/upside, and Sirles is better suited to playing outside. That leaves rookie fifth-round pick Danny Isidora, a three-year starter at Miami who could be a viable starter in the NFL if he corrects some footwork issues that cause imbalance in pass protection.

Defensive Front Seven

Defensive Line	Age	Pos	G	Snaps	Plays	Overall TmPct	Rk	Stop	Dfts	BTkl	Runs	vs. Run St%	Rk	RuYd	Rk	Sack	Pass Rush Hit	Hur	Dsrpt
Linval Joseph	29	DT	16	721	75	9.6%	3	51	11	6	68	66%	73	3.6	84	4.0	12	20	0
Shamar Stephen	26	DT	16	550	39	5.0%	37	25	1	3	35	69%	65	3.1	75	0.0	4	6	0
Tom Johnson	33	DT	14	475	18	2.6%	83	14	6	1	14	71%	58	3.3	77	2.0	24	21	1

Edge Rushers	Age	Pos	G	Snaps	Plays	Overall TmPct	Rk	Stop	Dfts	BTkl	Runs	vs. Run St%	Rk	RuYd	Rk	Sack	Pass Rush Hit	Hur	Dsrpt
Everson Griffen	30	DE	16	888	49	6.3%	28	38	16	5	34	71%	65	3.5	85	8.0	18	42	3
Brian Robison	34	DE	16	837	29	3.7%	72	23	13	5	18	72%	58	2.2	36	7.5	8	28	1
Danielle Hunter	23	DE	16	598	55	7.0%	17	43	18	9	36	72%	58	3.5	86	12.5	8	19	1
Datone Jones	27	OLB	15	548	24	3.2%	82	21	6	4	20	90%	2	1.4	20	1.0	12	21	4

Linebackers	Age	Pos	G	Snaps	Plays	Overall TmPct	Rk	Stop	Dfts	BTkl	Runs	vs. Run St%	Rk	RuYd	Rk	Sack	Pass Rush Hit	Hur	Tgts	vs. Pass Suc%	Rk	AdjYd	Rk	PD	Int
Anthony Barr	25	OLB	16	1025	72	9.2%	62	38	9	10	47	64%	38	4.4	75	2.0	7	14	27	35%	77	7.1	51	1	0
Eric Kendricks	25	MLB	15	869	116	15.8%	17	67	25	11	63	62%	52	3.9	61	2.5	1	5	52	57%	14	4.9	9	9	1
Chad Greenway*	34	OLB	16	403	40	5.1%	83	29	4	6	28	75%	4	2.7	13	0.0	0	1	15	52%	30	11.9	82	0	0

Year	Yards	ALY	Rank	Power	Rank	Stuff	Rank	2nd Level	Rank	Open Field	Rank	Sacks	ASR	Rank	Press	Rank
2014	4.49	4.88	31	73%	26	14%	32	1.25	25	0.64	13	41	7.0%	12	22.9%	23
2015	4.23	4.37	25	53%	3	18%	23	1.22	25	0.63	10	43	7.1%	10	28.0%	7
2016	4.17	4.46	24	59%	9	15%	31	1.08	9	0.56	8	41	7.8%	1	31.2%	5

2016 ALY by direction:	Left End 4.09 (15)	Left Tackle 4.58 (20)	Mid/Guard 4.56 (27)	Right Tackle 4.79 (25)	Right End 4.22 (23)

Danielle Hunter has been the definition of a rotation player for the Vikings to this point of his career. Hunter played 58 percent of snaps last year while Brian Robison and Everson Griffen both eclipsed 80 percent. As a rookie in 2015, he played only 37 percent of snaps. Yet despite playing sparingly over his first two seasons in the league, only 32 players in league history had more sacks over their first two seasons than Hunter. Only three players—Shawne Merriman (27), Terrell Suggs (22.5), and Jason Pierre-Paul (21)—had more sacks than Hunter's 18.5 at age 22. Hunter has started one game in his career; Merriman had started 22, Suggs 17, and Pierre-Paul 12. ☙ Mike Zimmer teams have always prioritized a deep defensive line rotation and quality cornerback play. Now that Zimmer has been involved in shaping the roster for a few years, the defensive line depth is an obvious strength. Robison's demotion to the second string offers the Vikings a proven every-down player if either Hunter or Griffen gets injured. He also offers a baseline for the younger players to eclipse before they can see the field, so nobody will be rushed into a role that they aren't ready to fill. ☙ The Vikings will have a number of rookie defensive linemen in training camp, but it's a second-year player who sparks the most intrigue. Stephen Weatherly was a seventh-round pick in the 2016 draft who didn't make the initial 53-man roster out of training camp. He became a favorite of Vikings defensive line coach Andre Patterson, which allowed him to hold onto a practice squad spot, and Mike Zimmer and Rick Spielman both praised him when he was brought onto the active roster later in the season. The 23-year-old Weatherly is transitioning from playing as an outside linebacker in college to putting his hand on the ground as a defensive end for the Vikings, but he offers intriguing length and athleticism. Like a poor man's Hunter, Weatherly could develop into an underrated gem if he takes to the Vikings' coaching. ☙ The linebacker spots are settled, and Anthony Barr and Eric Kendricks will likely remain the core of the Minnesota defense for most of the next decade. However, the development of these players has not been a straight line upward. Barr played well in 2016 but didn't offer the kind of impact his talent suggests he could. For the Vikings defense to be at its very best, Barr should be contributing more in coverage, but last year his charting numbers regressed significantly from his first two seasons. With a plethora of pass-rushers on the defensive line, Barr doesn't need to blitz or be used off the edge. He can instead be used as a movable chess piece, picking his spots in nickel packages as a change-up.

Defensive Secondary

Secondary	Age	Pos	G	Snaps	Plays	Overall TmPct	Rk	Stop	Dfts	BTkl	vs. Run Runs	St%	Rk	RuYd	Rk	vs. Pass Tgts	Tgt%	Rk	Dist	Suc%	Rk	AdjYd	Rk	PD	Int
Harrison Smith	28	FS	14	893	93	13.6%	7	33	6	7	50	48%	21	5.1	13	27	7.4%	26	11.6	37%	58	11.0	62	2	0
Andrew Sendejo	30	SS	14	855	69	10.1%	35	23	10	7	30	43%	28	5.9	22	22	6.3%	10	12.2	33%	68	11.9	66	3	2
Xavier Rhodes	27	CB	14	786	63	9.2%	32	26	15	2	14	50%	19	9.1	69	72	22.3%	69	13.7	51%	31	6.6	17	9	5
Terence Newman	39	CB	15	752	46	6.3%	80	22	8	5	9	67%	5	3.9	6	45	14.6%	6	15.3	58%	7	5.2	4	7	1
Captain Munnerlyn*	29	CB	15	637	56	7.6%	65	21	9	1	11	45%	31	8.7	67	42	15.9%	14	7.6	50%	42	6.9	23	3	0
Trae Waynes	25	CB	15	579	58	7.9%	62	21	7	2	10	40%	41	5.7	22	66	27.8%	85	13.5	46%	63	7.5	41	12	3
Anthony Harris	25	SS	16	234	36	4.6%	--	7	2	2	23	22%	--	6.9	--	7	7.3%	--	13.9	48%	--	15.4	--	1	0

Year	Pass D Rank	vs. #1 WR	Rk	vs. #2 WR	Rk	vs. Other WR	Rk	vs. TE	Rk	vs. RB	Rk
2014	19	11.7%	26	-22.3%	5	-15.2%	6	-2.0%	17	15.8%	26
2015	11	-6.1%	9	17.0%	25	-30.4%	2	16.1%	25	8.7%	22
2016	8	-1.9%	12	-4.2%	10	-23.9%	5	12.3%	24	-12.1%	8

Andrew Sendejo is the forgotten man in the Vikings secondary, but his absence was felt when he missed two games in 2016. Sendejo fits a role that is similar to the one Ryan Clark filled behind Troy Polamalu for years in Pittsburgh. While he doesn't always sit deep behind Harrison Smith, Sendejo's role is to be reliable and consistent. He's not a big-play threat like Smith, but he's a consistent tackler who is always in the right position even if his less impressive athleticism can hold him back. Sendejo isn't a spectacular player, but if he's the fourth (or arguably the fifth) best player in your secondary, then you've got a spectacular secondary. So long as Sendejo and Smith are healthy, the Vikings will have no concerns about their coverage over the deep middle. ☞ Much like with Brian Robison on the defensive line, Terence Newman sets a standard of consistency and execution that the younger players at his position have to eclipse if they are going to see the field. He was reportedly at the center of a bizarre Week 16 player coup which resulted in Jordy Nelson torching the Minnesota secondary, but the ancient corner seemed to patch things up with Zimmer this offseason. Newman is capable of playing inside or outside, offering the Vikings versatility in how they use him but also in who they play alongside him. ☞ Xavier Rhodes is assured of his starting spot. Trae Waynes is close to establishing himself as an unquestioned starter but has been an inconsistent performer throughout his career, putting up ugly charting numbers as offenses targeted him more than any other Minnesota defensive back. It would not be shocking if Waynes struggled enough to lose his starting spot. ☞ 2016 second-rounder Mackensie Alexander is in position to play a big role if Waynes has problems, and many Vikings observers project him to eventually take over the slot role Captain Munnerlyn vacated this offseason. ☞ Alexander was widely discussed as a top-20 pick last year, and his size likely contributed to his drop into the second round. On another team it might be an issue that Alexander isn't 6 feet tall, but with Rhodes' ability to line up in different spots on the field and follow specific matchups, Alexander's size can become a positive rather than a negative. He can take the Randall Cobbs of the world while Rhodes focuses on the Jordy Nelsons.

Special Teams

Year	DVOA	Rank	FG/XP	Rank	Net Kick	Rank	Kick Ret	Rank	Net Punt	Rank	Punt Ret	Rank	Hidden	Rank
2014	3.0%	10	-3.6	25	6.0	7	5.5	5	3.4	9	3.7	10	7.2	5
2015	3.9%	4	2.0	11	-3.7	25	16.1	1	1.1	16	4.0	7	-8.7	28
2016	1.5%	10	-5.5	25	-10.7	31	9.4	2	5.9	8	8.3	4	-6.4	25

Blair Walsh's wild-card PTSD dragged down the overall performance of this unit. Walsh had declined precipitously after an excellent rookie season, but eight total misses last season between field goals and extra points were enough to bring his Vikings tenure to an unceremonious end. Replacement Kai Forbath managed to tread water enough that he'll probably retain his job in 2017. ☞ Minnesota's kick return game ranked in the top five for the fourth straight season thanks to Cordarrelle Patterson, but the former first-rounder left for Oakland this spring. Rookie Rodney Adams, who averaged over 25 yards per kick return at South Florida, is the leading candidate to replace him. ☞ The good news is that the Vikings still retain the other half of the league's best return duo from last year. Marcus Sherels ranked second in estimated points added on punt returns last season, and has taken three punts to the house the past two seasons.

New England Patriots

2016 Record: 14-2	Total DVOA: 24.9% (1st)	2017 Mean Projection: 11.6 wins	On the Clock (0-4): 0%
Pythagorean Wins: 12.8 (1st))	Offense: 20.8% (2nd)	Postseason Odds: 87.5%	Mediocrity (5-7): 4%
Snap-Weighted Age: 26.8 (10th)	Defense: -1.8% (16th)	Super Bowl Odds: 35.2%	Playoff Contender (8-10): 24%
Average Opponent: -7.5% (32nd)	Special Teams: 2.3% (8th)	Proj. Avg. Opponent: -3.5% (32nd)	Super Bowl Contender (11+): 71%

2016: The Tom Brady Revenge Tour ends with the greatest playoff comeback win in NFL history.

2017: The strongest team with the weakest schedule. It's almost unfair.

Bill Belichick has never been one to rest on his laurels. So it was expected that New England would do some tweaking to the 2016 team that went 14-2 and then shocked the world—and spawned a thousand online dissertations on clock management—by overcoming a 28-3 late third-quarter deficit to win Super Bowl LI, 34-28 in overtime.

But the Patriots didn't need a whole lot entering the offseason. Their 25.3% team DVOA was easily the best in the league, and second-highest for any of their championship teams (2004 at 34.2% still holds the crown). Sure, they'd have some key departures for various reasons, like cost (tight end Martellus Bennett, cornerback Logan Ryan), ineffectiveness (defensive end Jabaal Sheard, linebacker Barkevious Mingo, wide receiver Michael Floyd) and age (defensive end Chris Long, running back LeGarrette Blount). There's turnover in every offseason, so the Patriots figured to make a few additions. But not many figured the Patriots would be adding entire floors to their foundation that would help them look down even further at their competition.

Instead, that's exactly what they did. A flurry of offseason moves left them in our projected top five for all three units: offense, defense and special teams. They also have the easiest projected schedule in the league, not only because of the

Table 1. Top Team Projections in Football Outsiders Almanac, 2012-2017

Team	Year	Mean Wins	Final W-L	Playoffs
NE	2012	12.0	12-4	Lost AFC-CG
NE	**2017**	**11.6**	--	--
GB	2012	11.1	11-5	Lost NFC-Div
PIT	**2017**	**10.7**	--	--
SEA	2015	10.7	10-6	Lost NFC-Div
DEN	2014	10.7	12-4	Lost AFC-Div
NE	2013	10.6	12-4	Lost AFC-CG
SEA	2016	10.5	10-5-1	Lost NFC-Div
NE	2015	10.5	12-4	Won Super Bowl
GB	2013	10.4	8-7-1	Lost NFC-WC
ARI	2016	10.4	7-8-1	Missed playoffs
DEN	2013	10.3	13-3	Lost Super Bowl
WAS	2013	10.3	3-13	Missed playoffs
SEA	2013	10.3	13-3	Won Super Bowl

weakness of the AFC East but also because our forecast is lower than conventional wisdom on a number of this year's opponents (Atlanta, Denver, Tampa Bay). Put it together, and the Patriots are prohibitive favorites to become the first back-to-back Super Bowl champions since they did it themselves back in 2004.

New England's listed mean projection of 11.6 wins may not look impressive, but it's quite extraordinary for a team to come out of our preseason simulations with a number that high. Since Football Outsiders introduced a more conservative simulation system in 2012, only one team has come out with a better forecast: the Patriots themselves five years ago, when they were coming off a loss in Super Bowl XLVI. The 2017 Patriots are the only team in the past five years to emerge from the simulation with an average forecast above 11 wins. There's no question that the Patriots start the season in pole position, and everyone else is at least three or four car-lengths back.

How did the Patriots open up such a huge gap in expectations between themselves and the rest of the league? It starts with a big move of the kind New England has rarely made over the last few years. Instead of basically starting over at cornerback by dealing Malcolm Butler so somebody else could pay him, the Patriots held onto Butler and then signed Bills standout Stephon Gilmore to a whopping four-year, $65 million contract.

Why Gilmore? Both Butler and Eric Rowe struggled at times covering bigger No. 1 receivers, and the Patriots ranked 20th in DVOA covering No. 1s. At 6-foot-1, Gilmore can be more effective in that role and allow the 5-foot-11 Butler to play more size-appropriate receivers, and possibly play in the slot with Ryan now in Tennessee.

You can certainly make the case that the Patriots vastly overpaid for Gilmore, who has yet to play up to his No. 1 cornerback reputation. With the Bills, Gilmore's statistics weren't all that different than those of teammate Ronald Darby, and Gilmore was certainly well off Butler's pace in terms of FO charting stats such as success rate and adjusted yards per pass.

But the Patriots don't make moves like this without something in mind to increase the player's future productivity. On film, it's evident that Gilmore was caught up in the overall malaise of the Bills' two-year transition in Rex Ryan's defense. For whatever reason (and it was likely personnel short-

2017 Patriots Schedule

Week	Opp.	Week	Opp.	Week	Opp.
1	KC (Thu.)	7	ATL	13	at BUF
2	at NO	8	LACH	14	at MIA (Mon.)
3	HOU	9	BYE	15	at PIT
4	CAR	10	at DEN	16	BUF
5	at TB (Thu.)	11	at OAK (Mex.)	17	NYJ
6	at NYJ	12	MIA		

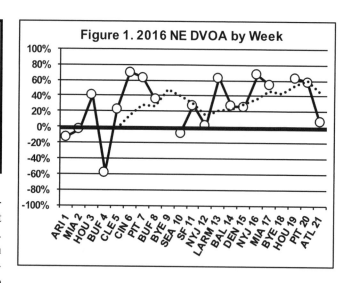

Figure 1. 2016 NE DVOA by Week

comings left by now-departed general manager Doug Whaley), Ryan was never able to fully implement the predominant man-to-man scheme that was a staple of his Revis Island Jets. Gilmore was basically caught in no-man's land playing both man and zone, and he never looked fully comfortable, especially in space. You don't need Belichick's football resume to see that Gilmore has vast potential as just a press corner, and the Patriots will likely give him every opportunity to do just that. No team is going to pay $65 million for a (to this point) average cornerback and expect the same average results. No, Belichick and defensive coordinator Matt Patricia are likely going to give Gilmore every chance to use his underrated physicality and catch-up speed at the line to smother the opponent's top receiver.

Having Gilmore and Butler together should also help the pass rush to improve on its adjusted sack rate, which ranked 26th. (The Patriots had ranked second in 2015, though a lot of those were coverage sacks). So should edge rusher Kony Ealy, who was acquired in one of two trades the Patriots made after signing Gilmore.

Ealy was a star in the Panthers' Super Bowl 50 loss to the Broncos, but he has yet to deliver on that promise with consistency. After teasing his potential with 21 hurries in 2015, Ealy's development stagnated with 19 last season. But the Panthers' struggles in the secondary post-Josh Norman may have had as much to do with that as anything. The adjustments the Panthers had to make in the back end would mask any improvement Ealy might have shown.

Ealy and third-round draft pick Derek Rivers will be looking to replace some of the production (nine sacks, 12 hits, and 56 hurries) that departed with Long and Sheard. What will be interesting to see is how effective Ealy can be playing with his hand off the ground, which most of the Patriots' edge players to do at least on early downs. Ealy is a one-directional rusher and has played stiff in his hips to this point. Rivers is more versatile, with athletic skills that give him the proverbial "huge upside" label, but he's a raw prospect who will need to adjust to the big gap between FCS Youngstown State and the NFL.

Lawrence Guy was added from the Ravens to give the Patriots a little more athletic ability on the interior of the line, especially against the run. He ranked in the top 30 for stops and average gain per tackle, which is better than anyone on the Patriots, including Alan Branch. The late addition of Jets veteran inside linebacker David Harris doesn't look like much of a move considering the 33-year-old is well past his prime,

but he won't have to play 900 snaps in New England like he did for the Jets. The durable Harris allows the Patriots to deploy re-signed defensive heartbeat Dont'a Hightower wherever they see fit depending on the opponent.

With the additions of Gilmore, Early, Guy, and Harris—and, especially, the trickle-down effect their presence will have on players like Butler, Rowe, Hightower, and rising star pass-rusher Trey Flowers—the Patriots undoubtedly feel that they have improved a unit that dropped from 12th to 16th in defensive DVOA last season. Ignore the Patriots' No. 1 finish in points allowed, which was more a product of a) the easiest defensive schedule in the league and b) the field-position advantage they got from strong special teams and an offense that never turned the ball over. The Patriots defense was especially subpar against the pass (23rd in DVOA), and looked slow and outclassed by the Falcons through nearly three quarters of the Super Bowl.

Of course, one way to keep the defense from looking slow is to get them a lot of rest, and the Patriots offense is going to spend a lot of time on the field this season. That unit has loaded up as well, in the form of a 5-foot-10 speedster receiver, and not one but two quality running backs. This is, of course, a case of the rich getting richer, because the Patriots finished second to the Falcons in offensive DVOA, and likely would have been in the top spot had they had full seasons from Brady and Rob Gronkowski.

It certainly wouldn't appear that the Patriots need former Saints first-round pick Brandin Cooks, not with Julian Edelman signed to an extension; Chris Hogan delivering after his escape from Buffalo; Danny Amendola showing his clutch gene; and Malcolm Mitchell becoming the rarest of New England birds: a rookie receiver who doesn't go into the witness protection program after earning the inevitable disdain from the demanding Brady. But Cooks isn't just some receiver: he led the legendary class of 2014 in Playmaker Score, higher than Odell Beckham or Mike Evans, and he's produced in the NFL with two straight seasons over 1,100 yards. Cooks will give the Patriots a little bit more oomph where they were a little lacking (again, it's relative). He's a deep threat who runs a 4.33 40, and his agility gives offensive coordinator Josh

McDaniels more opportunity to diversify near the goal line, where the Patriots surprisingly ranked 22nd in DVOA in goal-to-go situations.

With so many parts to tinker with, McDaniels could use Cooks in a utility-knife role, similar to how Aaron Hernandez was deployed once Gronkowski asserted himself as the traditional tight end. Cooks can line up anywhere from wideout to slot receiver to running back, and will cause defensive coordinators to lose sleep thinking up ways to match up against him, especially if the Patriots bring back their hurry-up offense. It's hard to believe that Cooks only totaled 21 rushes in 42 games for Saints coach Sean Payton, who is known for his creative passing game but lacks conviction on the ground. In New England, Julian Edelman had 12 rushes last season alone.

Still, Cooks wasn't acquired for a first-round pick to carry the ball—he's going to make his future money through the air. Despite being short (but strongly built), Cooks is actually better on the outside. In fact, Cooks' DVOA (32.1%) when lined up wide was the highest in the league for any receiver with at least 35 targets there. His DVOA from the slot (-0.7%) was in the bottom half for receivers with at least 35 targets there, but it was better than Edelman's last season. (In an off-year, Edelman had -4.8% DVOA from the slot and -24.0% DVOA when lined up wide.) And it doesn't matter where he lines up, Cooks catches the ball at the same rate: a very good 68 percent. Edelman's catch rate was 66 percent in the slot and dropped to 43 percent on the outside. Cooks ranked fourth in the league last year with 24 targets thrown 25 yards or more downfield, and should get the first shot at being Brady's top vertical threat. How that meshes with Brady's age (40 in August) and talents, which have never stood out in the deep part of the field, should be interesting. But both the Texans and the Falcons in the postseason showed that the way to slow Brady and the Patriots (without Gronkowski, at least) is to clamp down on his targets within 5 yards of the line of scrimmage, and force Brady to beat you with intermediate and deep passes. The Patriots obviously felt the need to back defenses off with Cooks' speed.

Brady's future figures to be a huge story this season in more ways than one, and the Patriots seem dead set on easing his load as much as possible. LeGarrette Blount's spectacular fantasy football numbers (including 18 touchdowns) masked the fact that the Patriots' run offense slumped to 15th in DVOA, the team's lowest rank since 2005. Blount was a bit of a plodding two-down back, 28th in success rate last year, and the Patriots didn't make much of an effort to re-sign him. Instead, they replaced him by poaching two AFC rivals for Rex Burkhead (Bengals) and Mike Gillislee (Bills).

To get Gillislee, the Patriots went discount shopping at their favorite neighborhood bodega (thanks, Doug Whaley) for the second year in a row and didn't even have to break the bank that much in a restricted free-agent offer sheet. Now Gillislee goes from a secondary role in Buffalo to being the main two-down threat behind Brady. Gillislee has too much experience to make our Top Prospects list, but he's certainly the starting tailback on the Football Outsiders Ready to Bust Out team. Gillislee had only 101 carries, just barely enough for our run-

ning back rankings, and ended up fourth in DYAR, first in DVOA, and first in success rate. He possesses great vision, a good feel in the hole, and enough pop to get into the secondary.

Backing up Gillislee on the FO Ready to Bust Out team would be his new running mate, Burkhead, who was clearly the Bengals' best back last season but was only given one start behind Jeremy Hill and Giovani Bernard. Burkhead might not be a 25-touch back in every game, but there isn't anything he doesn't do well, from picking holes to picking up the blitz. Only two running backs with at least 20 carries finished with rushing DVOA over 40%, and the Patriots went out and bought both of them in Gillislee (44.9%) and Burkhead (41.9%, though he didn't qualify to be ranked with just 74 carries). Third-down scat backs Dion Lewis and James "Should Have Been Super Bowl MVP" White are here as well. Now it's up to McDaniels and running backs coach Ivan Fears to figure out how to get everyone enough touches to keep them engaged. With White agreeing to a new contract extension, don't be surprised if Lewis is dangled in a trade at some point. A healthy Lewis certainly helps, but his durability issues could make him expendable should everyone emerge from the preseason at full strength.

With a young and improving offensive line under the continued tutelage of coach Dante Scarnecchia and the subtle addition of Colts tight end Dwayne Allen (another trade), the Patriots seem primed on offense. The plight of Allen should be interesting. He looked to be a looming (distant) rival to Gronkowski as one the league's most complete tight ends after an outstanding rookie campaign, but hasn't been the same since missing most of 2013 with a hip injury. The Patriots are betting that he's on the way back. When healthy, Allen, while not a freak talent, can line up anywhere on the field and be a devastating blocker at the point of attack.

Perhaps the most curious player on the Patriots roster is not one of the new arrivals but instead a player everyone expected to make a departure. Tom Brady—coming off one of his best seasons ever at age 39, still noshing on TB12 Snacks (available now for just $50 per 12-pack!), and armed with potentially the deepest and most diverse array of weapons in his career—looks capable of going on forever. So what the heck is backup Jimmy Garoppolo still doing in New England, entering a contract year after which he could leave without compensation should the Patriots elect not to grant him a $20 million-plus franchise tag?

At the least, the Patriots are buying themselves one more year of insurance for Brady, who may appear to be Gumby, but in fact is a human with bones and joints that can break. At the other end of the spectrum, the Patriots are letting Brady, with potentially his best team ever, have one more season before he either calls it a career, or the Patriots enter the Jimmy G Era and jettison Brady in the nicest, most polite way possible.

"Dude, bro. There's no way Belichick is letting is letting the GOAT go to another team, dude. You're a wicked idiot."

It's certainly possible, especially if Brady exhibits a little more of the slippage that he displayed late last season. Cian

Fahey, in his *Pre-Snap Reads Quarterback Catalogue 2017*, makes an interesting and subtle case that while most were celebrating the Patriots' historic comeback and heralding Brady's greatness, what they really should have been doing was talking about how average he looked in two postseason games against the Texans and Falcons. This isn't about Brady specifically; it's part and parcel of a general trend Fahey has found that shows older quarterbacks lose accuracy late in the season.

"Playing four fewer regular-season games probably bought Brady enough time before his arm completely died for the Patriots to win the Super Bowl," writes Fahey, who pointed out that after throwing seven interceptable passes in 12 regular-season games, Brady threw nine in two against the Texans and Falcons (four were in the fourth quarter and overtime, when most thought Brady was playing his best). "His arm strength gradually got worse as the regular season wore on."

"In two of his three playoff games Brady looked old… If he falls off in 2017 there will have been warning signs, but it can't reasonably be expected given the totality of his season."

If Belichick saw the same thing approaching this offseason, doesn't it stand to reason that he may be alarmed entering 2018 with a 41-year-old Brady when Garoppolo—who posted a better DVOA, QBR and completion percentage than his mentor in two starts—will only be 26? If you look at it in those terms, the Patriots' sudden offseason gusto seems to make a little more sense: give Brady the sendoff he deserves, while setting up the heir apparent pretty well to take over and give Belichick his crowning achievement, a title without Brady.

In the meantime, this isn't Boston sports talk radio. Let's talk about what we do know. Brady played great last season, and the Patriots won another Super Bowl in dramatic fashion. They figure to be even better this season after adding even more talent. The Patriots are coming for another stab at back-to-back titles, and the scary thing is it might be getting to the point where it doesn't even matter which quarterback they play. Yes, that's how good the Patriots are.

Greg A. Bedard

2016 Patriots Stats by Week

Wk	vs.	W-L	PF	PA	YDF	YDA	TO	Total	Off	Def	ST
1	at ARI	W	23	21	363	344	-2	-13%	2%	25%	10%
2	MIA	W	31	24	463	457	+3	-4%	29%	27%	-6%
3	HOU	W	27	0	282	284	+3	40%	10%	-5%	25%
4	BUF	L	0	16	277	378	-1	-58%	-38%	3%	-16%
5	at CLE	W	33	13	501	262	+1	22%	17%	-14%	-9%
6	CIN	W	35	17	437	357	0	70%	56%	-4%	10%
7	at PIT	W	27	16	362	375	-1	63%	57%	-18%	-12%
8	at BUF	W	41	25	357	376	0	36%	21%	2%	16%
9	BYE										
10	SEA	L	24	31	385	420	-2	-8%	14%	19%	-3%
11	at SF	W	30	17	444	299	0	28%	23%	-5%	1%
12	at NYJ	W	22	17	377	333	+2	1%	23%	23%	1%
13	LARM	W	26	10	402	162	+2	63%	20%	-39%	4%
14	BAL	W	30	23	496	348	-2	27%	33%	2%	-4%
15	at DEN	W	16	3	313	309	+3	26%	-8%	-25%	9%
16	NYJ	W	41	3	325	239	+4	67%	19%	-38%	10%
17	at MIA	W	35	14	396	280	+2	55%	50%	-5%	0%
18	BYE										
19	HOU	W	34	16	377	302	0	63%	12%	-31%	20%
20	PIT	W	36	17	431	368	+2	58%	43%	-10%	5%
21	vs. ATL	W	34	28	546	344	-1	6%	7%	5%	4%

Trends and Splits

	Offense	Rank	Defense	Rank
Total DVOA	20.8%	2	-1.8%	16
Unadjusted VOA	22.4%	2	-6.5%	8
Weighted Trend	24.3%	1	-6.4%	10
Variance	5.6%	13	4.2%	12
Average Opponent	-0.7%	9	-6.7%	32
Passing	49.6%	2	13.1%	22
Rushing	-2.2%	15	-23.3%	5
First Down	20.9%	2	-3.6%	12
Second Down	-2.7%	17	0.8%	17
Third Down	57.8%	1	-3.0%	12
First Half	22.4%	3	-8.3%	7
Second Half	30.8%	3	-2.1%	19
Red Zone	24.6%	7	-6.5%	12
Late and Close	55.0%	2	-4.3%	16

Five-Year Performance

Year	W-L	Pyth W	Est W	PF	PA	TO	Total	Rk	Off	Rk	Def	Rk	ST	Rk	Off AGL	Rk	Def AGL	Rk	Off Age	Rk	Def Age	Rk	ST Age	Rk
2012	12-4	12.7	13.4	557	331	+25	34.9%	3	30.8%	1	1.4%	15	5.5%	4	46.7	25	28.0	15	27.9	7	25.6	29	26.2	12
2013	12-4	10.5	11.0	444	338	+9	18.9%	5	16.4%	4	4.2%	20	6.7%	2	47.8	25	49.8	28	27.6	6	25.8	29	25.6	27
2014	12-4	11.8	10.8	468	313	+12	22.1%	4	13.5%	6	-3.0%	12	5.7%	5	24.4	9	37.6	16	27.7	5	26.6	19	26.1	16
2015	12-4	11.7	10.9	465	315	+7	22.6%	6	15.4%	5	-3.3%	12	3.9%	5	60.6	29	32.7	19	27.2	12	25.9	27	25.9	18
2016	14-2	12.8	11.9	441	250	+12	24.9%	1	20.8%	2	-1.8%	16	2.3%	8	47.2	25	7.3	1	27.3	7	26.6	14	26.3	9

2016 Performance Based on Most Common Personnel Groups

NE Offense					NE Offense vs. Opponents					NE Defense				NE Defense vs. Opponents			
Pers	Freq	Yds	DVOA	Run%	Pers	Freq	Yds	DVOA	Run%	Pers	Freq	Yds	DVOA	Pers	Freq	Yds	DVOA
11	47%	6.9	43.3%	28%	Base	36%	5.5	11.0%	60%	Base	11%	5.0	-8.0%	11	64%	5.2	-5.6%
12	18%	5.8	19.9%	37%	Nickel	51%	6.2	28.9%	31%	Nickel	62%	5.5	1.1%	12	17%	6.3	14.4%
21	16%	4.8	3.5%	62%	Dime+	9%	9.0	85.1%	16%	Dime+	26%	5.1	-2.9%	21	6%	5.8	11.4%
22	5%	3.3	-48.6%	91%	Goal Line	3%	1.9	6.5%	92%	Goal Line	1%	-0.3	-65.6%	10	4%	4.1	-17.5%
20	4%	7.3	49.4%	42%										20	3%	5.7	7.8%
621	3%	5.3	9.0%	93%										13	2%	2.7	-39.9%
611	3%	8.2	35.3%	25%													

Strategic Tendencies

Run/Pass		Rk	Formation		Rk	Pass Rush		Rk	Secondary		Rk	Strategy		Rk
Runs, first half	40%	10	Form: Single Back	63%	31	Rush 3	23.9%	1	4 DB	11%	31	Play-action	20%	11
Runs, first down	53%	4	Form: Empty Back	9%	10	Rush 4	54.8%	28	5 DB	62%	12	Avg Box (Off)	6.42	3
Runs, second-long	34%	7	Pers: 3+ WR	52%	29	Rush 5	18.0%	24	6+ DB	25%	4	Avg Box (Def)	5.97	30
Runs, power sit.	70%	2	Pers: 2+ TE/6+ OL	33%	9	Rush 6+	3.3%	28	CB by Sides	66%	23	Offensive Pace	29.23	6
Runs, behind 2H	25%	20	Pers: 6+ OL	9%	6	Sacks by LB	13.6%	22	S/CB Cover Ratio	27%	17	Defensive Pace	29.62	6
Pass, ahead 2H	50%	13	Shotgun/Pistol	53%	27	Sacks by DB	9.1%	11	DB Blitz	9%	17	Go for it on 4th	1.11	15

Between special teams and a lack of turnovers, the Patriots constantly played in strong field position. They started drives with an average of just 69.3 yards to go (second in NFL) and opponents started drives with an average of 75.1 yards to go (first in NFL). ≡ Remarkably, the Patriots were 27th in percentage of drives ending three-and-out (24.9 percent). Both the Patriots and the Detroit Lions ranked in the top 10 of yards per drive but the bottom 10 of three-and-outs. The only other two offenses to accomplish this in the past 10 seasons were the 2010 Packers and the 2009 Vikings. This isn't specifically related to life without Tom Brady, as the Patriots still went three-and-out on 23.8 percent of drives (25th) after Brady's return. ≡ The Patriots were one of two teams (along with the Bills) to have over half their runs come from multi-back sets. They essentially had the same DVOA either way, with a slightly lower yards per carry average from one-back sets because those were more frequently short-yardage situations. ≡ In 2015, Tom Brady reversed a long-time weakness against defensive back blitzes and that continued in 2016, as he averaged 8.5 yards on these plays. ≡ Possibly connected: New England used a max-protect blocking scheme on a league-leading 19 percent of passes. (This is defined as seven or more blockers with at least two more blockers than pass-rushers.) ≡ The Patriots themselves blitzed a defensive back twice as often as they had the year before; they were just average on these plays (6.8 yards per pass) with a pressure rate (30 percent) much lower than the NFL average (43 percent). ≡ One significant problem for the Patriots defense in 2016 was tackling. After three years ranking first or second in fewest broken tackles, the Patriots dropped to 21st with 99 broken tackles last season. ≡ Nobody wanted to run screens against the Patriots. They faced only eight wide receiver screens all year, and just seven running back screens. This was the second straight year the Patriots were last in the league in both figures. ≡ The Patriots led the NFL by allowing just 4.0 average yards after the catch on defense. That may seem like it's been a staple of the Patriots defense for a long time, but actually, it hasn't; the Patriots were fifth in 2015 but average or worse from 2012-2014.

Passing

Player	DYAR	DVOA	Plays	NtYds	Avg	YAC	C%	TD	Int
T.Brady	1286	33.4%	446	3447	7.7	6.0	67.8%	28	2
J.Garoppolo	225	44.4%	68	489	7.2	5.8	68.8%	4	0
J.Brissett	4	-10.0%	61	360	5.9	9.7	61.8%	0	0

Rushing

Player	DYAR	DVOA	Plays	Yds	Avg	TD	Fum	Suc
L.Blount*	130	3.7%	248	1029	4.1	18	0	45%
J.White	22	8.4%	33	132	4.0	0	0	55%
D.Lewis	37	42.2%	19	88	4.6	0	0	68%
T.Brady	-11	-21.1%	18	67	3.7	0	0	-
J.Brissett	-8	-24.4%	13	86	6.6	1	0	-
J.Edelman	22	0.5%	11	51	4.6	0	0	-
D.J.Foster	-11	-58.3%	6	17	2.8	0	0	50%
M.Gillislee	199	55.3%	66	409	6.2	8	0	73%
R.Burkhead	58	39.2%	28	151	5.4	2	0	71%
B.Cooks	14	13.7%	5	28	5.6	0	0	-

Receiving

Player	DYAR	DVOA	Plays	Ctch	Yds	Y/C	YAC	TD	C%
J.Edelman	43	-9.2%	159	98	1106	11.3	5.0	3	62%
C.Hogan	145	18.0%	58	38	680	17.9	6.3	4	66%
M.Mitchell	132	19.6%	48	32	401	12.5	5.2	4	67%
D.Amendola	85	27.0%	29	23	243	10.6	3.2	4	79%
M.Floyd*	14	18.6%	6	4	42	10.5	3.5	1	67%
B.Cooks	226	11.6%	118	79	1175	14.9	4.9	8	67%
A.Hawkins	1	-12.5%	54	33	324	9.8	3.9	3	61%
M.Bennett*	197	33.4%	73	55	701	12.7	7.6	7	75%
R.Gronkowski	136	44.5%	38	25	540	21.6	9.1	3	66%
D.Allen	108	21.8%	52	35	406	11.6	3.4	6	67%
J.White	163	20.1%	86	60	551	9.2	8.8	5	70%
D.Lewis	-25	-31.9%	24	17	94	5.5	4.9	0	71%
L.Blount*	-7	-31.0%	8	7	38	5.4	6.1	0	88%
J.Develin	-16	-51.9%	6	3	18	6.0	3.3	0	50%
R.Burkhead	22	7.3%	20	17	145	8.5	8.4	0	85%
M.Gillislee	-18	-48.0%	11	9	50	5.6	5.1	1	82%

Offensive Line

Player	Pos	Age	GS	Snaps	Pen	Sk	Pass	Run	Player	Pos	Age	GS	Snaps	Pen	Sk	Pass	Run
David Andrews	C	25	16/16	1115	6	0.0	8	5	Nate Solder	LT	29	15/15	1030	6	4.0	13	6
Joe Thuney	LG	25	16/16	1115	10	3.0	15	8	Shaq Mason	RG	24	16/15	1018	4	4.5	15	6
Marcus Cannon	RT	29	15/15	1032	6	2.5	14	7	Cameron Fleming	OT	25	16/5	282	1	0.0	0	3

Year	Yards	ALY	Rank	Power	Rank	Stuff	Rank	2nd Lev	Rank	Open Field	Rank	Sacks	ASR	Rank	Press	Rank	F-Start	Cont.
2014	4.11	4.51	5	59%	23	21%	27	1.22	11	0.59	23	26	4.4%	2	23.3%	14	19	28
2015	3.88	4.56	2	64%	19	16%	1	1.17	16	0.42	30	38	6.5%	18	25.5%	16	13	15
2016	3.99	4.46	9	59%	22	20%	16	1.10	22	0.60	21	24	4.6%	6	25.6%	14	14	38

2016 ALY by direction: Left End 5.19 (7)   Left Tackle 3.79 (23)   Mid/Guard 4.43 (7)   Right Tackle 4.31 (12)   Right End 5.90 (3)

A year after finishing with the worst offensive line continuity score we've ever measured, the Patriots finished tied for the second-best score in 2016. Offensive line coach Dante Scarnecchia ended his brief retirement and eschewed the bizarre series-by-series rotation New England employed at times during Dave DeGuglielmo's final season. Thus, a season after no lineman played over 900 regular-season snaps, the Patriots had all five starters exceed that threshold in 2016. ☞ Stability at tackle also served as a critical element in this unit's improvement. Marcus Cannon went from being the LVP of the 2015 AFC Championship Game to earning a deserved five-year extension last November. Nate Solder also stayed healthy after missing all but four games with a torn biceps the previous season. Together, they conceded just 6.5 sacks in 2016, compared to 12 sacks allowed by Patriots tackles in 2015. ☞ The interior trio of David Andrews, Joe Thuney and Shaq Mason had some inconsistencies, but the Pats basically got them at a bulk rate from Costco. The three have combined cap hit of $2.8 million in 2017, which would rank 97th among *individual* offensive linemen this year. All three are under contract for at least the next two seasons, and the unit could get even cheaper next spring if third-round pick Antonio Garcia (Troy) replaces Solder, who is entering the final year of his contract. Garcia is an agile, athletic blocker with a mean streak, but needs to bulk up and add strength, particularly in his legs, if he's going to be a starting left tackle in the NFL.

Defensive Front Seven

Defensive Line	Age	Pos	G	Snaps	Plays	TmPct	Rk	Stop	Dfts	BTkl	Runs	St%	Rk	RuYd	Rk	Sack	Hit	Hur	Dsrpt
						Overall						**vs. Run**					**Pass Rush**		
Alan Branch	33	DT	16	625	52	6.6%	18	40	10	7	46	76%	49	1.9	34	1.5	0	7	3
Malcom Brown	23	DT	16	596	49	6.3%	21	36	5	9	46	72%	57	2.5	55	3.0	2	13	0
Vincent Valentine	23	DT	13	289	19	3.0%	--	15	3	2	17	82%	--	1.4	--	1.0	1	4	0
Lawrence Guy	27	DE	16	484	26	3.4%	67	22	6	0	24	83%	26	1.8	29	1.0	9	16	1

Edge Rushers	Age	Pos	G	Snaps	Plays	TmPct	Rk	Stop	Dfts	BTkl	Runs	St%	Rk	RuYd	Rk	Sack	Hit	Hur	Dsrpt
						Overall						**vs. Run**					**Pass Rush**		
Chris Long*	32	DE	16	677	35	4.5%	59	23	6	6	23	61%	89	2.9	64	4.0	8	30	2
Jabaal Sheard*	28	DE	15	580	36	4.9%	49	28	12	7	17	76%	37	2.5	48	5.0	4	26	1
Trey Flowers	24	DE	16	563	46	5.9%	35	34	14	5	34	71%	65	2.1	34	7.0	8	19	2
Rob Ninkovich	33	DE/LB	12	461	32	5.4%	40	20	5	9	17	59%	93	3.3	80	4.0	1	11	2
Kony Ealy	26	DE	16	623	34	4.1%	65	26	10	7	21	81%	21	2.4	42	5.0	2	19	2

Linebackers	Age	Pos	G	Snaps	Plays	TmPct	Rk	Stop	Dfts	BTkl	Runs	St%	Rk	RuYd	Rk	Sack	Hit	Hur	Tgts	Suc%	Rk	AdjYd	Rk	PD	Int
						Overall						**vs. Run**				**Pass Rush**				**vs. Pass**					
Dont'a Hightower	27	MLB	13	708	65	10.2%	54	36	9	11	35	57%	67	2.9	17	2.5	6	11	23	43%	57	5.8	24	1	0
Kyle Van Noy	26	OLB	14	524	53	7.7%	70	31	8	12	34	62%	53	3.0	22	1.0	1	9	24	53%	29	6.0	27	3	1
Shea McClellin	28	OLB	14	382	40	5.8%	80	19	4	6	22	59%	63	3.5	39	1.0	2	7	8	41%	--	6.5	--	0	0
Elandon Roberts	23	OLB	13	270	43	6.8%	--	20	3	2	28	54%	--	2.7	--	0.0	3	1	10	35%	--	8.8	--	0	0
David Harris	33	MLB	15	900	96	13.5%	34	48	10	7	58	55%	76	3.7	47	0.5	1	11	27	44%	50	6.4	38	2	0

Year	Yards	ALY	Rank	Power	Rank	Stuff	Rank	2nd Level	Rank	Open Field	Rank	Sacks	ASR	Rank	Press	Rank
2014	4.78	4.27	19	74%	28	18%	22	1.32	29	1.17	31	34	6.0%	26	25.1%	16
2015	5.06	4.74	31	68%	20	16%	30	1.46	32	1.20	31	31	6.0%	20	21.3%	32
2016	4.21	4.09	15	65%	20	20%	14	1.13	13	0.94	27	30	5.0%	28	27.3%	14
2016 ALY by direction:		Left End 4.76 (23)			Left Tackle 4.80 (23)			Mid/Guard 3.75 (7)			Right Tackle 3.86 (12)			Right End 4.71 (26)		

Trey Flowers is the player the Patriots are counting on to become the next foundational piece on their defense. Flowers had 7.0 sacks in his sophomore season, the second-highest total by any second-year Patriots defender under Bill Belichick. With 34 1/4-inch arms, Flowers is the type of strong lengthy disruptor Belichick loves to move around, as he'll play anything from the 3-technique to the 7-technique depending on the front. Given the inexperience behind the top three edge rushers, expect Flowers to see a big spike in workload this season. ≡ On the other hand, fellow second-year defender Malcom Brown didn't quite take the leap everyone expected. Brown wasn't bad, but he saw declines in total stops, defeats and run stop rate, while also contributing little as a pass-rusher. The former first-rounder should remain a part of the rotation, but his expected role remains a quandary: Flowers and Lawrence Guy are likely better interior rushers on passing downs, but Alan Branch and Vincent Valentine are sturdier run stuffers. ≡ David Harris may have the inside edge to playing next to Dont'a Hightower on rushing downs. The Jets defector is certainly cerebral enough to play in the middle, but it's unclear how much he has left physically. The 33-year-old saw a decline in his run defense charting numbers from 2015, and probably isn't a candidate to play much in sub packages. Elandon Roberts, who was supposed to be The Next Man Up after the Jamie Collins trade, may get more of an opportunity to play on passing downs in his second season. ≡ Roberts may be on our Top Prospects list, but Kyle Van Noy was probably the Patriots' best coverage option last season. Still, Van Noy's natural fit coming out of BYU was as a 3-4 outside linebacker, a role he never got to play in Detroit either. If Roberts can develop steadier habits in coverage, perhaps that allows the Pats to re-assign Van Noy to edge-rushing duties.

Defensive Secondary

Secondary	Age	Pos	G	Snaps	Plays	Overall TmPct	Rk	Stop	Dfts	BTkl	vs. Run Runs	St%	Rk	RuYd	Rk	vs. Pass Tgts	Tgt%	Rk	Dist	Suc%	Rk	AdjYd	Rk	PD	Int
Devin McCourty	30	FS	16	1021	85	10.9%	27	25	10	6	38	26%	63	7.5	43	34	7.1%	23	12.6	48%	31	7.4	18	7	1
Malcolm Butler	27	CB	16	1007	80	10.2%	14	40	16	8	12	67%	5	4.1	7	83	17.8%	36	12.6	54%	20	7.8	49	17	4
Patrick Chung	30	SS	16	1005	90	11.5%	19	32	9	9	42	36%	47	6.0	26	41	8.7%	43	11.9	52%	22	7.8	25	3	1
Logan Ryan*	26	CB	16	897	103	13.2%	1	41	17	5	24	58%	13	4.4	10	81	19.5%	52	11.1	45%	70	7.6	44	11	2
Duron Harmon	26	FS	16	507	28	3.6%	--	5	3	6	5	0%	--	12.0	--	11	4.7%	--	16.9	44%	--	15.5	--	0	0
Eric Rowe	25	CB	9	452	34	7.7%	--	17	9	2	9	56%	--	6.4	--	43	20.4%	--	15.3	63%	--	5.7	--	8	1
Justin Coleman	24	CB	10	226	11	2.2%	--	5	3	5	0	0%	--	0.0	--	21	19.7%	--	14.4	65%	--	5.1	--	3	0
Stephon Gilmore	27	CB	15	984	60	7.9%	63	24	8	5	13	46%	30	7.5	55	55	15.1%	8	14.8	49%	48	9.1	75	12	5

Year	Pass D Rank	vs. #1 WR	Rk	vs. #2 WR	Rk	vs. Other WR	Rk	vs. TE	Rk	vs. RB	Rk
2014	12	-14.4%	7	1.8%	17	-13.8%	7	22.0%	30	-4.6%	14
2015	15	-1.2%	17	1.1%	15	21.4%	28	-8.3%	15	1.7%	17
2016	22	3.6%	20	-5.6%	9	4.0%	19	-3.4%	14	9.2%	22

We dissected the Gilmore-Butler tandem earlier in the chapter, but one more underrated area to watch is how they tackle. Belichick has typically placed an emphasis on secure tackling on the back end, but he lost his best player in that facet when Logan Ryan and his 6.7 percent broken tackle rate left for Tennessee. Stephon Gilmore was nearly double that at 12.5 percent last year, while Malcolm Butler saw his own rate rise from 7.8 percent to an unsightly 14.5 percent in 2016. ☜ In that regard, one player the Patriots don't have to worry about is Devin McCourty. The free safety posted a stellar 8.7 percent missed tackle rate last year, sixth among defensive backs with least 50 tackles. Indeed, McCourty's greatest asset is his reliability. Since moving to safety in 2012, McCourty has missed just three games and played at least 850 snaps every season. Only three other safeties (Malcolm Jenkins, Glover Quin and Reggie Nelson) have reached that snap threshold the past five years. ☜ McCourty's partner in crime Patrick Chung should remain the starting strong safety in 2017and the Patriots often use him in the hybrid strong safety/nickel role so popular these days. New England gave Chung a goodwill incentive boost to his current contract, bumping his cap hit up to $6.2 million for 2017.

Special Teams

Year	DVOA	Rank	FG/XP	Rank	Net Kick	Rank	Kick Ret	Rank	Net Punt	Rank	Punt Ret	Rank	Hidden	Rank
2014	5.7%	5	10.8	1	8.4	3	0.5	13	0.2	16	8.4	5	8.9	3
2015	3.9%	5	14.1	1	8.2	2	0.7	10	-6.7	25	3.1	10	0.1	16
2016	2.3%	8	0.2	17	10.4	2	-3.6	24	12.1	3	-7.7	29	11.6	4

Patriots kickers have been among the most bankable aspects of the league's most bankable franchise, but not in 2016. Stephen Gostkowski posted his lowest field goal percentage since 2012 and missed three extra points after going 52-for-52 during the first regular season with the 33-yard distance. Still, New England brought in no challengers for the 33-year-old, so the leash remains long with Gostkowski. ☜ The same can't be said for Cyrus Jones, who was truly appalling as a punt returner during his rookie season. Jones was worth an estimated minus-6.5 points on punt returns, the worst mark by any returner over the last three seasons. Jones held on to only seven of 11 punt returns, with three muffs and one fumble; he also fumbled once on a kick return. Ironically, Belichick highlighted Jones' special teams prowess at Alabama as the tiebreaker for selecting him with the 60th overall pick in 2016 over several similarly graded prospects. Jones admitted that his issues as a returner wrecked his confidence, but the Pats will try to rebuild him in Year 2. ☜ Matthew Slater may be the six-time Pro Bowl selection, but Nate Ebner was the real star of the unit last season. Fresh off an Olympics appearance in rugby, Ebner led the league with 19 special teams tackles and was one of only two players with double-digit tackles in punt coverage.

New Orleans Saints

2016 Record: 7-9	**Total DVOA:** -1.9% (21st)	**2017 Mean Projection:** 7.0 wins	**On the Clock (0-4):** 17%
Pythagorean Wins: 8.3 (17th)	**Offense:** 15.4% (6th)	**Postseason Odds:** 23.7%	**Mediocrity (5-7):** 42%
Snap-Weighted Age: 27.5 (1st)	**Defense:** 14.6% (31st)	**Super Bowl Odds:** 1.9%	**Playoff Contender (8-10):** 31%
Average Opponent: 0.1% (15th)	**Special Teams:** -2.6% (27th)	**Proj. Avg. Opponent:** -0.4% (22nd)	**Super Bowl Contender (11+):** 9%

2016: Good offense, bad defense, rinse, repeat.

2017: Good offense, bad defense, rinse, but an end to the repeats is nigh.

They are who we thought they were.

Dennis Green's most iconic quote, from one of the most memorable postgame press conferences of the past 15 years, has now turned into a sports-talk cliché. Usually deployed to describe people or teams messing up in easily predictable ways, the criticism is not always merited, is often an oversimplification, and commonly omits important details in favor of a trite soundbite.

The 2016 New Orleans Saints, though, were exactly who we thought they were.

DVOA has ranked the Saints offense in the top third of the league every year since Drew Brees joined the team, and in the top ten every year since 2011. Although the Saints offense has now ranked sixth or seventh in each of the past three individual seasons, that year-to-year consistency means they have had the fourth-best offense by mean DVOA over that span (Table 1).

Brees has been the core of that success. For six consecutive years, he has passed for at least 4,800 yards and ranked in the top eight in both DYAR and DVOA. Last year, at age 37, he ranked second in DYAR and fourth in DVOA.

The success of Brees in the Saints offense is, of course, reflected in the numbers of the supporting cast. Second-round receiver Michael Thomas had an all-time great rookie year in 2016, his DYAR total of 429 rivaled only by Randy Moss in 1998 (428 DYAR) and Odell Beckham in 2013 (393 DYAR in 12 games). Brandin Cooks also performed like a legitimate top receiver, ranking 15th by DYAR, while tight end Coby Fleener ranked 24th.

Halfbacks Mark Ingram and Tim Hightower each ranked in the top 16 for both rushing DYAR and receiving DYAR. As a team, the Saints ranked third in rushing DVOA, their most ef-

ficient season in five years. This balanced, versatile offense led the league in both yards and first downs per game. They ranked third in yards per play, second in scoring, and sixth in DVOA.

The Saints finished 7-9. Again.

Despite the success of Brees and the consistently excellent Saints offense, the team has now finished 7-9 in four of the past five seasons, and each of the past three. No other team in our table of the top five offenses since 2014 has even missed the playoffs once; the Saints have missed the playoffs every year. No other team in that top five has had a losing record since 2012; the Saints have had a losing record both for the five-year period and in four of the past five individual seasons. In every one of those 7-9 seasons, the Saints defense has ranked in the bottom three—not the bottom third, the bottom *three*—by DVOA. The lone exception, 2013, is also the lone playoff season. Taking the past three years as a whole, the Saints have had far and away the worst defense in the entire NFL.

Those numbers are having a very direct impact on the team's results: New Orleans has lost while scoring 28-plus points more often than any other team in the NFL since 2014. That's not a cherry-picked cut-off, either. They either lead the league or are tied for the lead in losses at every number of points from 21 through 34 inclusive. (Only the Giants have lost more than once while scoring at least 35 points.)

Black and gold. The Louisiana Superdome. Good offense, terrible defense. We know exactly who the Saints are, because they're like this *every single year*.

It's not that they haven't tried to fix it. Jairus Byrd arrived as a hot free agent in 2014 on a six-year, $56 million contract. He was released this offseason, exactly halfway through that deal. Brandon Browner arrived off two straight Super Bowl championship years with the Seahawks and Patriots. He left

Table 1. Best Offenses and Worst Defenses by Mean DVOA, 2014-2016

Top 5 Offenses						Bottom 5 Defenses					
Rk	Team	Mean	2014	2015	2016	Rk	Team	Mean	2014	2015	2016
1	PIT	17.0%	2	3	7	28	WAS	7.5%	27	21	25
2	NE	16.7%	6	5	2	29	TEN	7.9%	29	23	24
3	GB	14.4%	1	11	4	30	CHI	8.9%	28	31	23
4	**NO**	**12.3%**	7	7	6	31	ATL	10.2%	32	22	26
5	SEA	10.9%	5	1	16	32	**NO**	**17.7%**	**31**	**32**	**31**

161

2017 Saints Schedule

Week	Opp.	Week	Opp.	Week	Opp.
1	at MIN (Mon.)	7	at GB	13	CAR
2	NE	8	CHI	14	at ATL (Thu.)
3	at CAR	9	TB	15	NYJ
4	at MIA (U.K.)	10	at BUF	16	ATL
5	BYE	11	WAS	17	at TB
6	DET	12	at LARM		

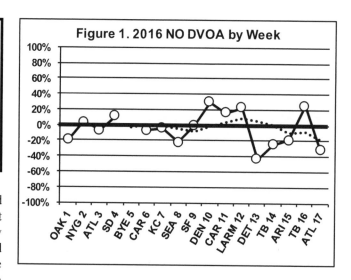

Figure 1. 2016 NO DVOA by Week

with an unwanted NFL record as the all-time most penalized player in a single season. Veteran James Laurinaitis didn't make it past November before being released with an injury settlement. Curtis Lofton, Champ Bailey, Keenan Lewis, and Kyle Wilson have all come and gone. Whatever the root cause of the Saints' issues on defense, simply switching out veteran pieces isn't the cure.

Those issues also go deeper than simply an awful overall ranking. The Saints haven't ranked higher than 22nd against opposing No. 1 receivers since 2013, nor higher than 26th against opposing No. 2 receivers. They haven't ranked higher than 31st against opposing running backs, with a ridiculously bad average DVOA of 38.1%. They had the best DVOA in the league against tight ends in 2014, but have since ranked 32nd (2015, 46.0%) and 22nd (2016, 4.6%). They've struggled rushing the passer (averaging 25th by adjusted sack rate) and stopping the run (average DVOA rank: 26th). In the areas where they aren't below average, they're terrible. In the areas where they aren't terrible, they're below average. There's no quick and easy fix for that breadth of underperformance.

All of which makes our 2017 projection a depressingly familiar read for Saints fans. Seven wins. A top-ten offense. The worst defense in the league. Third place in the division. And the world spins on.

The good news is that there appears to be hope for the future. Gone are high-priced busts like Byrd and Browner, replaced with young draftees Vonn Bell and P.J. Williams. Marshon Lattimore, widely considered the draft's top cornerback, fell to the Saints in April, and should start opposite Delvin Breaux. Kenny Vaccaro had some success last year as a big nickel safety and occasional blitzer, often featuring alongside Byrd and Bell in that hybrid safety-linebacker role which is becoming so popular in modern defenses. Marcus Williams also arrived in April's draft as a versatile, athletic third safety who should feature prominently in those same big nickel sets. Assuming all of the core players can stay healthy, this could give the Saints their most talented defensive backfield since the Super Bowl squad.

In the front seven, linebacker A.J. Klein arrives from Carolina with plenty to prove away from the shadows of Luke Kuechly and Thomas Davis. Former Browns veteran Craig Robertson performed well in multiple spots throughout last year. Cameron Jordan is still here, and Hau'oli Kikaha should be back after missing all of last year with a torn ACL. The interior defensive line is both talented and deep, though both the front-line talent and the depth have taken a hit now that

Nick Fairley's heart condition has forced him to take the year off (and may yet force him to retire).

The bad news is that this is still just switching out pieces, with little confidence that the coaches know how best to use them. The Saints haven't had a defensive coordinator with a strong pedigree since Gregg Williams, and his name conjures all manner of specters for the team's fans and coaches. Dennis Allen was the secondary coach when the Saints won the Super Bowl, but has never been the coordinator or head coach of a defense in the top half of the league. (New linebackers coach Mike Nolan has achieved that much at least once in every one of his seven previous coordinator jobs, which may or may not bode well for Allen's future.)

Also, Drew Brees isn't getting any younger. The last time the Saints had a defense in the top half of the league, Brees was 34 and the team made the divisional round of the playoffs. In fact, every time in the Brees era that the Saints have had a defensive DVOA outside the bottom eight—that is, higher than 25th—the team has made the postseason. Brees is now 38, however, and there are genuine questions around how much longer he has left. Every negative DVOA game the Saints offense had in 2016 came in the last five weeks of the season, and almost half (seven) of the quarterback's 15 interceptions came in that span. Brees can't be expected to shoulder another near-700-attempt season.

The addition of Adrian Peterson suggests that the coaches agree, but it's extremely rare for 32-year-old running backs to be difference-making players. That's particularly true if they were injured and ineffective the previous year; Peterson only managed three games last season, with a -50.9% DVOA.

The closest comparisons in our similarity scores—30-year-old backs or older who had a 1,000-plus-yard season, then missed more than half of the following year due to injury—averaged barely 10 carries per game for under 700 total yards on returning from their major injury. Peterson has proven a special case in the past, in particular with his ACL recovery, but he's five years older now than he was then. He'll definitely get opportunities—even his lack of utility as a pass blocker and receiver won't keep him off the field outside pure passing downs—but he'll have to run an awful lot better than he did last year to make his signing worthwhile.

Then there's the departure of Brandin Cooks. Young, fast, productive No. 1 receivers are very valuable commodities in the current NFL, in part because there are so few players who fit all of those criteria. The Saints had two, but traded Cooks—admittedly a vocal malcontent at times last season—to replace him with Ted Ginn and a young right tackle. That is likely to hurt the offense, even with Willie Snead and Michael Thomas still around. Brees has made productive receivers out of worse players than Ted Ginn—Joe Morgan had 135 DYAR with a sub-50 percent catch rate in 2012—but even if Ginn doubled his previous career-best DYAR (he had 77 in 2015) he would still provide less value than Cooks did in either of the past two years. At least Ginn can both take and fake an end-around as effectively as Cooks, and he is a willing downfield block-

er—all very useful functions in the Saints offense. Ultimately though, his success or failure as Cooks' replacement will be determined by how his own inconsistency synchs up with the strength of his 38-year-old quarterback's arm.

Which brings us right back to the issue of Drew Brees' age. Unlike the Sisyphus of Greek mythology, Brees has been to the top of the mountain. Since 2011, though, the career of the Saints quarterback has been positively Sisyphean: perennially tasked with dragging a rock-bottom defense uphill to the play-offs, always to have it roll away from him in the end. Also unlike the mythical Sisyphus, Brees cannot go on like this forever, so it's yet again up to the Saints coaching staff to find a defense before time runs out for their legendary quarterback.

Andrew Potter

2016 Saints Stats by Week

Wk	vs.	W-L	PF	PA	YDF	YDA	TO	Total	Off	Def	ST
1	OAK	L	34	35	507	486	-1	-20%	23%	30%	-13%
2	at NYG	L	13	16	288	417	+3	4%	12%	7%	-2%
3	ATL	L	32	45	474	442	-2	-7%	19%	24%	-1%
4	at SD	W	35	34	275	346	+1	11%	7%	-1%	3%
5	BYE										
6	CAR	W	41	38	523	406	+1	-7%	26%	33%	-1%
7	at KC	L	21	27	463	326	-2	-4%	23%	28%	1%
8	SEA	W	25	20	375	359	0	-22%	0%	19%	-3%
9	at SF	W	41	23	571	486	+4	0%	41%	25%	-15%
10	DEN	L	23	25	373	337	-2	30%	16%	-19%	-6%
11	at CAR	L	20	23	371	223	-2	16%	4%	-17%	-5%
12	LARM	W	49	21	555	247	+1	23%	46%	10%	-14%
13	DET	L	13	28	369	422	-3	-43%	-23%	23%	2%
14	at TB	L	11	16	294	270	-3	-25%	-33%	-1%	7%
15	at ARI	W	48	41	488	425	+1	-19%	39%	56%	-1%
16	TB	W	31	24	417	349	+2	26%	30%	9%	6%
17	at ATL	L	32	38	473	465	-1	-31%	-5%	26%	-1%

Trends and Splits

	Offense	Rank	Defense	Rank
Total DVOA	15.4%	6	14.6%	31
Unadjusted VOA	13.4%	7	10.5%	29
Weighted Trend	14.5%	6	13.2%	29
Variance	4.8%	11	3.7%	9
Average Opponent	-2.2%	2	-2.3%	24
Passing	31.9%	6	27.4%	30
Rushing	5.4%	3	-3.2%	23
First Down	18.6%	4	16.5%	30
Second Down	5.0%	12	8.2%	24
Third Down	25.0%	6	21.9%	30
First Half	2.4%	17	26.5%	32
Second Half	31.2%	2	2.6%	22
Red Zone	11.6%	10	3.7%	23
Late and Close	51.4%	3	-4.2%	17

Five-Year Performance

Year	W-L	Pyth W	Est W	PF	PA	TO	Total	Rk	Off	Rk	Def	Rk	ST	Rk	Off AGL	Rk	Def AGL	Rk	Off Age	Rk	Def Age	Rk	ST Age	Rk
2012	7-9	8.2	6.4	461	454	+2	-5.2%	19	11.9%	9	14.8%	32	-2.3%	24	11.5	4	23.6	14	28.3	3	26.6	21	25.9	22
2013	11-5	10.8	10.0	414	304	0	19.3%	4	16.0%	5	-5.8%	10	-2.5%	24	12.3	3	59.0	31	28.4	1	26.0	25	26.2	10
2014	7-9	7.4	7.6	401	424	-13	-0.9%	17	10.6%	7	13.1%	31	1.6%	11	26.4	12	31.6	10	29.0	1	26.2	24	25.9	22
2015	7-9	6.4	5.2	408	476	+2	-18.7%	28	10.5%	7	26.1%	32	-3.2%	26	19.7	3	36.3	23	28.2	4	26.5	20	26.7	4
2016	7-9	8.3	8.6	469	454	-3	-1.9%	21	15.4%	6	14.6%	31	-2.6%	27	22.4	5	58.9	27	28.3	2	26.8	11	27.0	4

2016 Performance Based on Most Common Personnel Groups

\ NO Offense					NO Offense vs. Opponents					NO Defense				NO Defense vs. Opponents			
Pers	Freq	Yds	DVOA	Run%	Pers	Freq	Yds	DVOA	Run%	Pers	Freq	Yds	DVOA	Pers	Freq	Yds	DVOA
11	57%	6.4	22.3%	26%	Base	37%	6.7	24.7%	49%	Base	18%	6.0	10.6%	11	62%	6.5	14.6%
12	10%	6.8	10.1%	44%	Nickel	47%	5.9	12.5%	32%	Nickel	66%	6.5	14.0%	12	19%	5.6	10.5%
21	10%	6.9	33.5%	37%	Dime+	15%	7.4	50.3%	9%	Dime+	14%	5.8	24.6%	21	7%	8.3	22.0%
611	6%	7.1	14.3%	72%	Goal Line	1%	0.7	29.4%	87%	Goal Line	2%	0.4	17.0%	13	2%	5.9	20.7%
612	2%	6.2	9.7%	63%	Big	1%	-2.7	-56.0%	33%					10	2%	6.6	28.0%
10	2%	7.4	64.2%	15%										22	2%	5.2	4.3%
610	2%	3.7	-24.2%	56%													
620	2%	4.7	16.7%	81%													

Strategic Tendencies

Run/Pass		Rk	Formation		Rk	Pass Rush		Rk	Secondary		Rk	Strategy		Rk
Runs, first half	38%	14	Form: Single Back	74%	23	Rush 3	7.3%	16	4 DB	18%	30	Play-action	17%	22
Runs, first down	44%	26	Form: Empty Back	12%	2	Rush 4	51.1%	31	5 DB	66%	9	Avg Box (Off)	6.13	24
Runs, second-long	22%	30	Pers: 3+ WR	65%	18	Rush 5	29.0%	3	6+ DB	13%	13	Avg Box (Def)	6.32	6
Runs, power sit.	57%	15	Pers: 2+ TE/6+ OL	28%	13	Rush 6+	12.6%	2	CB by Sides	84%	12	Offensive Pace	28.95	2
Runs, behind 2H	27%	13	Pers: 6+ OL	16%	2	Sacks by LB	25.0%	19	S/CB Cover Ratio	35%	2	Defensive Pace	29.35	1
Pass, ahead 2H	55%	6	Shotgun/Pistol	55%	25	Sacks by DB	6.7%	18	DB Blitz	14%	3	Go for it on 4th	0.86	23

The Saints had a league-leading 23.9% DVOA on runs from the shotgun, although they only ran on 12 percent of their shotgun snaps (29th in NFL). ☞ Over the last three seasons, New Orleans' usage of six offensive linemen has gone from 0.3 percent of plays to 4.5 percent to 15.7 percent, second in the NFL last year. ☞ The Saints offense ranked 16th in DVOA for both the first and second quarters, then ranked second in DVOA for both the third and fourth quarters (behind Atlanta and Pittsburgh, respectively). ☞ The Saints were both lucky and unlucky on defense. They recovered 12 of 15 opposition fumbles, but only benefited from 22 dropped passes by opponents, tied for 30th in the NFL. ☞ New Orleans dramatically increased its use of the blitz in 2016, with use of five or more pass-rushers going from 26.8 percent to 41.6 percent. The Saints were slightly better with more pass-rushers, going from 7.9 yards per pass with three or four pass-rushers (32nd in the NFL) to 7.3 yards per pass with five or six (23rd). ☞ Sean Payton is one of the most aggressive head coaches in NFL history, and this is the first time he has ever finished a season with an Aggressive Index under 1.0.

Passing

Player	DYAR	DVOA	Plays	NtYds	Avg	YAC	C%	TD	Int
D.Brees	1599	23.3%	694	4987	7.2	5.1	71.1%	37	14

Rushing

Player	DYAR	DVOA	Plays	Yds	Avg	TD	Fum	Suc
M.Ingram	105	9.4%	143	758	5.3	6	0	52%
T.Hightower*	63	4.8%	105	422	4.0	4	0	47%
J.Kuhn	50	41.9%	15	33	2.2	4	0	73%
D.Lasco	4	-0.8%	11	32	2.9	0	0	45%
D.Brees	22	22.7%	9	26	2.9	2	0	-
B.Cooks*	14	13.7%	5	28	5.6	0	0	-
A.Peterson	-30	-33.6%	31	50	1.6	0	0	39%
T.Ginn	33	9.1%	12	74	6.2	0	0	-

Receiving

Player	DYAR	DVOA	Plays	Ctch	Yds	Y/C	YAC	TD	C%
M.Thomas	431	31.6%	121	92	1137	12.4	5.1	9	76%
B.Cooks*	226	11.6%	118	79	1175	14.9	4.9	8	67%
W.Snead	206	12.5%	104	72	895	12.4	5.4	4	69%
B.Coleman	77	12.2%	38	26	281	10.8	2.8	3	68%
T.Lewis	0	-12.7%	11	7	76	10.9	2.9	0	64%
T.Ginn	13	-10.8%	95	54	752	13.9	3.4	4	57%
C.Fleener	16	-4.5%	82	50	633	12.7	4.2	3	61%
J.Hill	-20	-20.4%	22	15	149	9.9	5.1	1	68%
J.Phillips	-5	-19.1%	6	5	32	6.4	1.4	0	83%
M.Ingram	81	10.6%	58	46	319	6.9	7.1	4	79%
T.Cadet	44	-1.2%	54	40	281	7.0	5.2	4	74%
T.Hightower*	73	32.1%	26	22	200	9.1	9.5	1	85%
J.Kuhn	-8	-20.2%	20	16	70	4.4	3.1	1	80%
A.Peterson	-30	-109.4%	6	3	8	2.7	3.7	0	50%

Offensive Line

Player	Pos	Age	GS	Snaps	Pen	Sk	Pass	Run	Player	Pos	Age	GS	Snaps	Pen	Sk	Pass	Run
Jahri Evans*	RG	34	16/16	1137	6	2.5	4	4	Senio Kelemete	RG	27	15/9	662	4	1.5	6	2
Zach Strief	RT	34	16/16	1124	5	2.5	8	0	Tim Lelito*	LG	28	16/7	406	2	1.0	5	4
Max Unger	C	31	15/15	1090	1	1.0	5	3	Terron Armstead	LT	26	7/7	398	1	0.0	1	1
Andrus Peat	LG/LT	24	15/15	1040	4	4.5	11	3	Larry Warford	RG	26	15/15	970	2	4.5	9	5

Year	Yards	ALY	Rank	Power	Rank	Stuff	Rank	2nd Lev	Rank	Open Field	Rank	Sacks	ASR	Rank	Press	Rank	F-Start	Cont.
2014	4.36	4.69	2	59%	22	18%	13	1.25	8	0.73	15	30	5.3%	12	21.0%	6	10	33
2015	4.00	4.23	13	74%	5	20%	14	1.17	17	0.68	18	32	5.1%	7	21.3%	7	19	25
2016	4.53	4.93	1	70%	9	14%	2	1.11	19	0.85	10	27	4.5%	5	18.9%	3	19	21

2016 ALY by direction:	Left End 5.53 (4)	Left Tackle 4.77 (9)	Mid/Guard 4.71 (3)	Right Tackle 5.87 (1)	Right End 3.60 (19)

It's probably time to officially slap the "injury-prone" label on left tackle Terron Armstead. After missing 12 games the past two seasons, Armstead suffered a torn labrum this offseason that will keep him sidelined until midseason at best. Andrus Peat filled the left tackle spot during last season's absences, but the Saints would be much happier to keep Peat at left guard if possible. That could mean a temporary switch of sides for first-round pick Ryan Ramczyk (Wisconsin), who is expected to ultimately supplant the soon-to-be 34-year-old Strief at right tackle. Strief isn't ready for the pasture quite yet; even at age 33, he was second at his position in snaps per blown block. ▰ Center Max Unger has been sidelined during the summer due to foot surgery, but is expected to return in time for preseason. Senio Kelemete is his deputy, just in case. ▰ Only Jahri Evans does not return from last year's starting five. Evans had a nice Saints homecoming after a brief training camp foray with Seattle, but free-agent signing Larry Warford should provide a more stable long-term solution at right guard. ▰ The Saints have now ranked in the top third of the league by adjusted sack rate every year since Drew Brees joined the team, and have only been outside the top seven once. That's a good indicator of how sacks are in large part a quarterback stat, but this line is still a good one.

Defensive Front Seven

Defensive Line	Age	Pos	G	Snaps	Plays	TmPct	Rk	Stop	Dfts	BTkl	Runs	St%	Rk	RuYd	Rk	Sack	Hit	Hur	Dsrpt
						Overall						vs. Run				Pass Rush			
Nick Fairley	29	DT	16	723	43	5.4%	31	30	12	2	34	65%	78	3.3	79	6.5	16	25	1
Tyeler Davison	25	DT	15	438	25	3.3%	68	22	3	3	22	91%	8	1.6	23	0.0	1	4	2
David Onyemata	25	DT	16	393	18	2.2%	--	11	0	4	15	60%	--	4.2	--	0.0	4	6	0
Sheldon Rankins	23	DT	9	336	20	4.4%	44	13	5	0	12	75%	50	2.9	69	3.5	2	6	0
John Jenkins	28	DT	9	208	13	2.9%	--	6	0	2	12	50%	--	3.7	--	0.0	0	2	0

Edge Rushers	Age	Pos	G	Snaps	Plays	TmPct	Rk	Stop	Dfts	BTkl	Runs	St%	Rk	RuYd	Rk	Sack	Hit	Hur	Dsrpt
						Overall						vs. Run				Pass Rush			
Cameron Jordan	28	DE	16	965	63	7.9%	12	54	25	4	46	83%	15	0.8	5	7.0	19	50	6
Paul Kruger*	31	DE	15	571	26	3.5%	78	20	10	5	19	79%	29	1.7	25	1.5	9	17	1
Darryl Tapp	33	DE	16	292	17	2.1%	--	15	2	1	14	93%	--	2.2	--	0.5	8	12	1

Linebackers	Age	Pos	G	Snaps	Plays	TmPct	Rk	Stop	Dfts	BTkl	Runs	St%	Rk	RuYd	Rk	Sack	Hit	Hur	Tgts	Suc%	Rk	AdjYd	Rk	PD	Int
						Overall						vs. Run				Pass Rush				vs. Pass					
Craig Robertson	29	MLB	15	972	118	15.7%	18	60	15	11	76	61%	57	3.1	24	1.0	5	7	29	50%	35	6.0	26	4	1
Dannell Ellerbe	32	OLB	9	444	46	10.2%	55	24	9	2	25	56%	74	3.4	38	4.5	4	6	13	33%	80	7.9	68	2	0
Nate Stupar	29	MLB	16	376	50	6.2%	77	29	4	10	29	69%	18	4.4	79	1.0	1	0	16	41%	61	6.0	29	2	1
A.J. Klein	26	OLB	15	351	30	3.8%	86	16	7	4	13	85%	2	1.2	1	1.0	0	1	18	35%	76	10.4	80	1	0

Year	Yards	ALY	Rank	Power	Rank	Stuff	Rank	2nd Level	Rank	Open Field	Rank	Sacks	ASR	Rank	Press	Rank
2014	4.78	4.27	19	74%	28	18%	22	1.32	29	1.17	31	34	6.0%	26	25.1%	16
2015	5.06	4.74	31	68%	20	16%	30	1.46	32	1.20	31	31	6.0%	20	21.3%	32
2016	4.21	4.09	15	65%	20	20%	14	1.13	13	0.94	27	30	5.0%	28	27.3%	14

2016 ALY by direction:	Left End 4.76 (23)	Left Tackle 4.80 (23)	Mid/Guard 3.75 (7)	Right Tackle 3.86 (12)	Right End 4.71 (26)

A three-way battle beckons between Hau'oli Kikaha, Alex Okafor, and third-round rookie Trey Hendrickson at defensive end opposite Cameron Jordan. Okafor's 13.5 sacks in the past three seasons for Arizona would have ranked second on the Saints over that period, but 8.0 of those came in 2014. Kikaha, who lost his sophomore season to a torn ACL, had more sacks as a rookie in 2015 (4.0) than Okafor has managed in either of the past two seasons. Hendrickson is a SackSEER sleeper, with strong speed and explosion testing numbers and a productive career at Florida Atlantic. ☜ Defensive tackle Nick Fairley will miss the entire 2017 season with a heart condition, and at least one of the three heart specialists he has consulted has advised him to retire from football. He was diagnosed with an enlarged heart in 2011 following a pre-draft physical, and his recent symptoms are believed to be related to that. Fairley finally earned a long-term deal last year after playing on a series of one-year prove-it contracts, but may now have played his final down. The Saints have since added veteran Tony McDaniel, and have confidence in David Onyemata and Tyeler Davison, but they may still need more veteran depth next to Sheldon Rankins if Fairley's career is over. ☜ Competition is the buzzword for the linebacker corps after previous linebackers coach Joe Vitt was replaced with Mike Nolan. Seven players will battle for three starting roles, with free-agent arrival A.J. Klein the closest thing to a projected starter. Among the returnees, Craig Robertson was unspectacular as the team's lone three-down linebacker last season, while former first-rounder Stephone Anthony may have finally reached the end of the team's rope after playing just 133 defensive snaps. ☜ Third-round rookie Alex Anzalone is one linebacker to watch, as long as he can stay out of the treatment room. The athletic Florida product will battle Dannell Ellerbe for the weakside linebacker spot, assuming the oft-injured pair aren't battling for the trainer's attention instead.

Defensive Secondary

Secondary	Age	Pos	G	Snaps	Plays	Overall TmPct	Rk	Stop	Dfts	BTkl	vs. Run Runs	St%	Rk	RuYd	Rk	vs. Pass Tgts	Tgt%	Rk	Dist	Suc%	Rk	AdjYd	Rk	PD	Int
Jairus Byrd*	31	FS	16	893	85	10.6%	31	23	10	9	26	38%	41	6.3	32	31	7.9%	30	9.7	39%	54	9.3	47	4	2
Vonn Bell	23	FS	16	891	87	10.8%	28	26	11	2	35	43%	30	6.8	37	45	11.5%	61	9.3	35%	62	9.2	46	4	0
Sterling Moore	27	CB	13	806	69	10.6%	10	19	11	6	11	9%	86	14.2	84	62	17.5%	30	11.8	38%	84	8.2	58	11	2
Kenny Vaccaro	26	SS	11	724	71	12.9%	10	38	16	7	28	68%	2	3.6	1	30	9.4%	49	6.3	44%	44	7.5	21	4	2
B.W. Webb*	27	CB	14	589	38	5.4%	87	13	3	2	4	25%	73	10.0	74	50	19.1%	48	13.2	41%	82	8.8	72	11	1
Ken Crawley	24	CB	15	503	51	6.8%	76	19	9	10	5	20%	78	5.8	26	54	24.4%	78	12.9	47%	59	8.5	66	9	0
Roman Harper*	35	SS	16	303	25	3.1%	--	6	1	4	15	33%	--	5.6	--	9	6.4%	--	15.4	28%	--	13.4	--	0	0
Delvin Breaux	28	CB	6	296	22	7.3%	--	8	4	5	5	100%	--	0.6	--	33	25.0%	--	11.3	42%	--	7.6	--	1	0
Rafael Bush	30	FS	16	500	51	6.3%	68	20	10	7	18	33%	51	8.8	60	21	10.4%	53	11.1	53%	15	7.4	19	3	2

Year	Pass D Rank	vs. #1 WR	Rk	vs. #2 WR	Rk	vs. Other WR	Rk	vs. TE	Rk	vs. RB	Rk
2014	27	25.1%	30	8.6%	24	-5.2%	13	-26.7%	1	40.7%	32
2015	32	14.9%	29	23.0%	29	18.9%	27	46.0%	32	28.7%	31
2016	30	5.5%	23	11.3%	26	15.3%	28	4.8%	22	43.4%	32

After the release of Jairus Byrd, Delvin Breaux is now the only presumed starter in the Saints secondary who was not drafted by the team. Even Breaux has never played for another NFL team; he played in the GDFL, Arena League, and CFL between leaving LSU in 2012 and joining the Saints in early 2015. Kenny Vaccaro (first round, 2013), Vonn Bell (second, 2016), P.J. Williams (third, 2016), Marshon Lattimore (first, 2017), and Marcus Williams (second, 2017) all arrived in the first three rounds of their respective draft classes. ☜ That group of the team's top six defensive backs has an average age of 23, which would make the Saints secondary one of the youngest individual units in the league. A healthy season from Breaux, who ranked 15th in adjusted success rate in 2015 before missing 10 games with leg and shoulder injuries in 2016, would go a long way towards stabilizing this callow unit. ☜ Not one of the top three Saints cornerbacks from last year projects to be any higher than the fourth cornerback on this year's depth chart. B.W. Webb is now in Chicago, while Sterling Moore and Ken Crawley saw far more playing time than expected in 2016 because of early-season injuries to Breaux and P.J. Williams. Nothing came of the offseason flirtation with Malcolm Butler, which gives Lattimore a clear path to an immediate full-time gig. ☜ Vaccaro was often deployed as a big nickelback/small linebacker in three-safety sets, which is reflected in his charting numbers. He allowed an average of only 6.0 yards per play made (pass deflection, interception, sack, or tackle), tied with Kam Chancellor for the lowest average among starting safeties. His run stop rate of 68 percent was second among safeties by a rounding error, and he also contributed 16 defeats, tied for fourth among safeties. ☜ Second-round draft pick Marcus Williams (Utah) gives the Saints a younger option to replace Byrd as the presumptive third safety in the aforementioned three-safety packages. Vonn Bell, Jairus Byrd, and Kenny Vaccaro each played at least 68 percent of the team's defensive snaps in 2016, with veteran Roman Harper also given substantial playing time. This year, Harper's role of veteran reserve passes to Rafael Bush, who rejoins the Saints after a year in Detroit.

Special Teams

Year	DVOA	Rank	FG/XP	Rank	Net Kick	Rank	Kick Ret	Rank	Net Punt	Rank	Punt Ret	Rank	Hidden	Rank
2014	1.6%	11	-4.1	26	-2.5	21	4.0	8	13.4	2	-2.6	18	-23.1	32
2015	-3.2%	26	-15.4	31	-2.4	20	-2.1	21	3.8	11	0.2	16	14.0	3
2016	-2.6%	27	0.0	18	-5.1	28	-8.0	31	0.8	13	-1.0	15	-6.3	24

The winner of last year's Barth-Forbath bloodbath was ultimately rookie Wil Lutz, who went on to provide precisely zero (as in 0.0) value over average on field goals and extra points. The Saints lost two games on crucial field goal and extra point returns, against the Giants in Week 2 and the Broncos in Week 10, but you can't blame Lutz for that. Lutz finished the year better than he started it, with no missed field goals or extra points in the final six weeks of the season. However, he was still well below average on kickoff distance. ≞ Instead of a kicker battle, this year Saints fans (for)get to witness a long-snapper battle between futures contract signee Jesse Schmitt and undrafted rookie Chase Dominguez. Previous incumbent Justin Drescher remains unsigned. ≞ Newly-signed receiver Ted Ginn is determined to return punts, a role recently filled to good effect by Tommylee Lewis. Ginn may be of more use on kick returns, where the Saints ranked 30th by estimated points added and 31st by average return yardage last year. Rookie running back Alvin Kamara also has experience as a returner, and may be expected to contribute on special teams. ≞ Thomas Morstead still punts well, when asked to do so. The Saints punted less than 27 other teams in 2016, outpunting the league-leading Falcons offense by around one punt every two games.

New York Giants

2016 Record: 11-5	Total DVOA: 9.6% (8th)	2017 Mean Projection: 8.3 wins	On the Clock (0-4): 8%
Pythagorean Wins: 8.8 (11th)	Offense: -6% (22nd)	Postseason Odds: 39.9%	Mediocrity (5-7): 30%
Snap-Weighted Age: 26.1 (26th)	Defense: -14.5% (2nd)	Super Bowl Odds: 6.5%	Playoff Contender (8-10): 42%
Average Opponent: 2.7% (5th)	Special Teams: 1.2% (11th)	Proj. Avg. Opponent: 2.2% (4th)	Super Bowl Contender (11+): 21%

2016: Radical defensive reconstruction powers the Giants back into the postseason.

2017: Loading up to give Eli Manning one last shot at the Super Bowl.

It was August of 2011, the summer when the NFL lockout ended at the last possible moment and players hustled back to training camp just hours after learning of the settlement.

Teams tried to cram four months of personnel moves into a few days. The Eagles grabbed every available free agent in pursuit of what Vince Young tragically labeled a Dream Team. Other teams dropped big money on players who would not benefit from OTAs or minicamps with the teams that signed them.

But the Giants hardly did anything. They shed a few expensive veterans, extended the contracts of some low-level roster fodder, and started camp with rookies and street free agents slotted for significant roles. Giants fans—spurred on by the Big Apple media, more overstimulated than usual in those hectic days—howled so loudly for the team to keep up with the big spenders that general manager Jerry Reese called an unscheduled press conference at the end of a steamy afternoon practice in East Rutherford.

"We are not looking to make every sexy splash that can be made," Reese said. Then he started repeating the word "sexy" so often it sounded like he was trying to revolutionize dubstep.

"How many big, sexy moves did the Green Bay Packers make last year?" Reese asked of the then-defending champions. "I don't remember a lot. Who won before? Pittsburgh? How many big, sexy moves did they have? You develop players. The making a splash, the big, sexy moves: I don't know if that always works. I don't know if all the big, sexy moves are the right way to go."

The Giants won the Super Bowl that year, of course, playing the unsexy tortoise while hares like the Eagles flamed out. But 2011 feels like a lifetime ago now that the Giants are the sexiest, splashiest team in the NFL. And no, "sexy splash" doesn't just represent the sound of a wide receiver's Timberlands on the deck of a pre-playoffs party boat.

For the second straight offseason, Reese and the Giants leapt head-first into the free agency hot tub. Last year, they invited Olivier Vernon, Snacks Harrison and Janoris Jenkins to what had previously been a very private party. This year, they climbed out with Brandon Marshall and D.J. Fluker.

The Giants also extended Jason Pierre-Paul's contract this offseason—who would have expected that two summers ago? —and added an extra dose of sizzle in the draft by selecting both a big-play tight end of the present (Evan Engram) and a possible quarterback of the future (Davis Webb).

The change of tactics has been remarkable, considering the relative lack of change elsewhere in the organization. Reese is still Reese. The transfer of coaching power from Tom Coughlin to Ben McAdoo was orderly. The cultural upheaval in East Rutherford is not the result of a regime change. It's simply a recognition that the Eli Manning era will soon end. The Giants are in Win Now mode.

There is nothing wrong with a franchise led by a 36-year-old quarterback adjusting its priorities after two Super Bowl wins in a decade. Last year's splash, compounded with the switch from Coughlin to McAdoo, jumpstarted the organization after a pair of 6-10 seasons. The question is whether the Giants have constructed a true contender or the type of "Dream Team" Reese dissed six years ago.

The Giants have assembled one of the league's best receiving corps. Marshall's low DVOA last year was largely the result of the confusion and incompetence of the Jets quarterbacks. From Week 7 (when Ryan Fitzpatrick was briefly benched for Geno Smith) through the end of the season (when Bryce Petty began making cameos), the Jets were just 4-of-21 for 77 yards throwing deep passes to Marshall, with two interceptions. Marshall caught just one of 11 targets from Petty against the Dolphins in Week 16, albeit with a pair of drops. Given even replacement-level quarterbacking, Marshall can still win 1-on-1 matchups against most cornerbacks, which is all he will need to do for the Giants, because Odell Beckham, Engram and Sterling Shepard will keep opposing safeties more than occupied.

The talent upgrade at receiver will make the Giants offense more consistent. Beckham and Shepard were the only reliable weapons last year, with Beckham often reduced to catching shallow drag routes because opponents could safely roll all deep coverage in his direction. Victor Cruz aged quickly, an injury to Shane Vereen (and Rashad Jennings' age/injuries) minimized the receiving threat out of the backfield, and the tight ends were comic relief. The Giants ranked 31st in the NFL with three-and-outs on 31 percent of their drives. They lived and died by the big play.

Manning now has all the multi-purpose weaponry he needs to sustain drives. But there are still several questions. One is whether the offensive line is good enough to give Manning time to get Beckham, Marshall and the others the ball.

The Giants ranked second in the NFL in adjusted sack rate and sixth in pressure rate allowed. Both are surprising

2017 Giants Schedule

Week	Opp.	Week	Opp.	Week	Opp.
1	at DAL	7	SEA	13	at OAK
2	DET (Mon.)	8	BYE	14	DAL
3	at PHI	9	LARM	15	PHI
4	at TB	10	at SF	16	at ARI
5	LACH	11	KC	17	WAS
6	at DEN	12	at WAS (Thu.)		

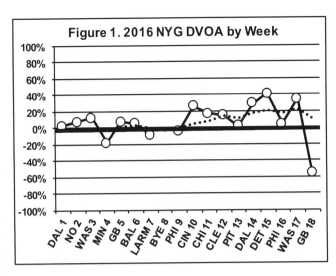

Figure 1. 2016 NYG DVOA by Week

statistics, because it often looked like the Giants could improve their blocking by replacing tackles Ereck Flowers and Bobby Hart with rain barrels. Manning can audible and hot-read his way out of much danger, and the Giants interior line was stouter than the tackles. But the Giants' run blocking was weak across the line, ranking 24th in adjusted line yards and making the Giants one-dimensional offensively. Bad blocking led to third-and-long situations, which led to pressured throws, punts and interceptions, even when Manning avoided taking a sack. Fluker is a one-dimensional piledriver of a blocker whom the Chargers moved to guard two seasons ago to hide his lateral stiffness and general immobility. He might be able to play right tackle in a pinch, but the Giants kept him inside during OTAs. The only other newcomer on the offensive line is sixth-round pick Adam Bisnowaty, so Flowers will probably get another year on scholarship to try to master the subtleties of NFL pass-blocking footwork.

The Giants also let Jennings go at running back. They plan to split carries among three scatbacks this season: Paul Perkins, Vereen and fourth-round pick Wayne Gallman. It's a puzzling backfield configuration, both for a team that averaged just 2.98 yards per rush on first downs last year and for one that will sometimes want to grind down the clock at the ends of victories. Also, there is no backfield pass-protector in that bunch, though the team presumably grabbed former Vikings fullback/H-back Rhett Ellison for that role.

Defensively, everything starts with a defensive line which eats up about $35 million in cap space this year and flows through a secondary which absorbs another $20 million. The Vernon-Snacks-JPP line recoded an underwhelming 35 sacks last season but produced the sixth-highest pressure rate in the NFL and allowed Steve Spagnuolo to revive some of the mix-and-match creativity his displayed when he coordinated the 2007 Giants defense.

The pressure also helped Dominique Rodgers-Cromartie and Janoris Jenkins rank first and second in adjusted success rate among cornerbacks. Meanwhile, strong safety Landon Collins emerged as an all-purpose weapon, helping to hide the fact that the Giants once again had a whole lot of nothing at linebacker. Youngsters Eli Apple and Darrian Thompson, plus newcomer Valentino Blake, give the Giants enviable depth in the secondary.

The Giants' overall strategy for 2017 is easy to understand. They plan to launch a full-throttle aerial assault on offense, then punish opponents for trying to catch up with sacks and turnovers. It's a formula McAdoo imported from Green Bay,

right down to the very ordinary running backs.

It's also a plan which meshes well with some of the other innovations McAdoo pushed once Coughlin stopped showing up at team headquarters every day like a creepy father-in-law after a wedding. McAdoo hired a new conditioning staff, rearranged the weight rooms, changed practice schedules, and enacted some sports science initiatives. It probably wasn't a coincidence that the Giants finished seventh in adjusted games lost last season after finishing either 31st or dead last for several consecutive years. The McAdoo Giants should be a healthy, well-conditioned team, ready to play up-tempo on both sides of the ball for 60 minutes.

But great receivers, great defensive playmakers and modernized practice routines probably won't be enough to win the NFC East, let alone the conference or the league.

The Giants face a potential sustainability problem on defense. Last year, they leapt from 30th to second in the league in defensive DVOA. That's the largest year-to-year leap ever in rank, and one of the largest in terms of actual DVOA percentage points. The reasons for the improvement have already been covered: Vernon, Snacks, Collins, drastically improved injury luck. But history shows that teams that take sudden leaps forward in defensive DVOA in one year tend to settle back toward the pack in their second year (Table 1). A minor, central-tendency fueled backslide on defense will partially offset the gains on offense. In an unforgiving division, the Giants can't afford to take one step forward and even a half-step back.

Inexperienced big spenders that they are, the Giants also did not purchase everything they needed. Both their offense and defense are designed to go boom-or-bust, and the only kicker on the roster by the end of OTAs was an undrafted free agent from the NAIA. There will be long touchdowns, big sacks and costly turnovers on both sides of the ball, plus probably an important missed field goal or two.

There may also be some drama. This is not the space to discuss receivers cruisin' it up before playoff games or Beckham punching holes in stadium walls after losses. But the Giants have assembled a combustible mix of personalities. Marshall's efforts to raise awareness of mental illness and work for the socially-conscious RISE Foundation are laudable, but he got used to a role as receiver/team spokesman/de facto general manager with the Jets. That will not go over well in East Rutherford. Jenkins, Snacks, JPP and DRC can be outspoken dudes when things aren't going well. Beckham is on his own emotional plateau. This is a team with the potential to soar, spiral, or do both several times over the course of the season.

It's hard to tell whether this sexy splash was too sexy (from a team chemistry standpoint) or not sexy enough (from the standpoint of getting everything the Giants need to win a Super Bowl). It just doesn't feel like they found the Goldilocks Zone. And while the selection of Webb points to a plan for life after Eli Manning, the rest of the roster is built for the short

term. Few of the expensive veterans currently on the roster will still be here two seasons from now.

The 2017 Giants will be fun to watch. They will cause some mayhem. They could well return to the playoffs. But in those moments when everything is going wrong for them, Reese may harken back to those days when the Giants won Super Bowls with unimpressive rosters but a slow-and-steady pace. Big, sexy, splashy moves really aren't the way to go most of the time. But with the Manning window of opportunity closing fast, the Giants had no choice but to give them a try.

Mike Tanier

Table 1. Top Defensive DVOA Improvements after Season in Bottom 10, 1986-2016

Year	Team	DVOA Y-1	Rk	DVOA	Rk	DVOA Y+1	Rk	Change from Y-1	Change in Y+1
1998	MIA	11.7%	28	-22.4%	1	-9.4%	5	-34.1%	+13.0%
1989	DEN	13.9%	27	-16.6%	4	8.4%	19	-30.5%	+25.0%
2009	DEN	20.7%	31	-9.8%	7	16.6%	30	-30.5%	+26.4%
1998	OAK	14.4%	29	-15.2%	3	-5.6%	11	-29.6%	+9.6%
2011	JAC	17.7%	32	-11.3%	5	11.7%	28	-29.0%	+23.0%
2011	HOU	17.5%	31	-9.5%	6	-14.2%	4	-27.0%	-4.7%
2001	STL	14.9%	27	-11.7%	5	-4.5%	11	-26.7%	+7.3%
1996	DEN	10.5%	27	-15.3%	3	-5.9%	8	-25.8%	+9.4%
1990	MIA	18.3%	28	-7.2%	8	14.5%	28	-25.5%	+21.6%
2016	**NYG**	**10.7%**	**30**	**-14.5%**	**2**	--	--	**-25.2%**	--
2013	BUF	10.6%	27	-13.8%	4	-15.5%	2	-24.4%	-1.7%
2004	WAS	8.6%	24	-15.4%	4	-11.6%	4	-24.0%	+3.8%
AVERAGE (except NYG)		14.4%	28.3	-13.5%	4.5	-1.4%	13.6	-27.9%	+12.1%

2016 Giants Stats by Week

Wk	vs.	W-L	PF	PA	YDF	YDA	TO	Total	Off	Def	ST
1	at DAL	W	20	19	316	328	-1	3%	1%	-10%	-8%
2	NO	W	16	13	417	288	-3	7%	-10%	-23%	-6%
3	WAS	L	27	29	457	403	-2	12%	3%	-19%	-10%
4	at MIN	L	10	24	339	366	-2	-19%	5%	24%	0%
5	at GB	L	16	23	221	406	+1	7%	-25%	-21%	10%
6	BAL	W	27	23	435	391	-3	5%	5%	7%	7%
7	at LARM	W	17	10	232	345	+3	-9%	-17%	-1%	7%
8	BYE										
9	PHI	W	28	23	302	443	0	-4%	-9%	-16%	-11%
10	CIN	W	21	20	351	264	-1	26%	2%	-32%	-8%
11	CHI	W	22	16	329	315	+1	17%	11%	-13%	-6%
12	at CLE	W	27	13	296	343	+2	14%	-3%	-10%	7%
13	at PIT	L	14	24	234	389	0	1%	-9%	-5%	5%
14	DAL	W	10	7	260	260	0	29%	-52%	-70%	11%
15	DET	W	17	6	300	324	+2	41%	6%	-23%	12%
16	at PHI	L	19	24	470	286	-2	4%	3%	4%	5%
17	at WAS	W	19	10	332	284	+3	34%	-15%	-46%	4%
18	at GB	L	13	38	365	406	-2	-55%	-26%	18%	-11%

Trends and Splits

	Offense	Rank	Defense	Rank
Total DVOA	-6.0%	22	-14.5%	2
Unadjusted VOA	-5.6%	23	-11.1%	4
Weighted Trend	-6.9%	22	-18.0%	2
Variance	2.4%	2	4.8%	15
Average Opponent	1.5%	28	2.6%	5
Passing	5.3%	21	-6.7%	4
Rushing	-16.9%	26	-25.3%	2
First Down	-6.7%	24	-3.4%	13
Second Down	-4.3%	19	-27.4%	1
Third Down	-7.2%	19	-15.3%	6
First Half	-2.3%	19	-7.8%	8
Second Half	-12.9%	22	-17.9%	5
Red Zone	10.6%	11	-28.5%	3
Late and Close	-8.3%	21	-14.4%	8

Five-Year Performance

Year	W-L	Pyth W	Est W	PF	PA	TO	Total	Rk	Off	Rk	Def	Rk	ST	Rk	Off AGL	Rk	Def AGL	Rk	Off Age	Rk	Def Age	Rk	ST Age	Rk
2012	9-7	10.2	9.5	429	344	+14	13.4%	7	12.8%	7	1.5%	16	2.0%	10	26.1	12	56.6	28	27.8	8	27.2	13	26.2	13
2013	7-9	5.6	5.5	294	383	-15	-15.7%	27	-22.0%	31	-11.4%	6	-5.1%	28	80.9	32	60.3	32	27.4	12	27.4	7	26.1	15
2014	6-10	7.5	7.0	380	400	-2	-5.8%	21	-0.3%	15	4.9%	24	-0.6%	15	65.9	31	71.3	30	26.6	20	27.6	5	26.7	3
2015	6-10	7.5	7.4	420	442	+7	-7.1%	20	-1.8%	19	10.7%	30	5.4%	2	66.9	31	71.8	31	26.2	22	27.0	13	26.5	8
2016	11-5	8.8	9.8	310	284	-2	9.6%	8	-6.0%	22	-14.5%	2	1.2%	11	27.7	11	24.7	9	26.3	22	25.9	27	26.2	13

2016 Performance Based on Most Common Personnel Groups

NYG Offense					NYG Offense vs. Opponents					NYG Defense					NYG Defense vs. Opponents			
Pers	Freq	Yds	DVOA	Run%	Pers	Freq	Yds	DVOA	Run%	Pers	Freq	Yds	DVOA		Pers	Freq	Yds	DVOA
11	92%	5.4	-3.2%	35%	Base	5%	4.0	-17.3%	65%	Base	31%	5.8	-6.6%		11	62%	5.0	-23.7%
12	5%	4.4	-2.7%	55%	Nickel	87%	5.4	-3.2%	38%	Nickel	52%	4.8	-23.8%		12	16%	6.5	7.8%
610	2%	4.0	-6.8%	76%	Dime+	9%	5.7	-0.9%	15%	Dime+	16%	6.1	2.9%		21	7%	5.6	-11.9%
										Goal Line	1%	0.1	-28.1%		13	5%	5.4	1.0%
															612	3%	4.8	-34.0%

Strategic Tendencies

Run/Pass		Rk	Formation		Rk	Pass Rush		Rk	Secondary		Rk	Strategy		Rk
Runs, first half	36%	24	Form: Single Back	93%	1	Rush 3	7.8%	15	4 DB	31%	12	Play-action	15%	29
Runs, first down	50%	9	Form: Empty Back	2%	32	Rush 4	66.2%	15	5 DB	52%	25	Avg Box (Off)	6.01	30
Runs, second-long	29%	19	Pers: 3+ WR	94%	1	Rush 5	16.5%	26	6+ DB	15%	10	Avg Box (Def)	6.31	7
Runs, power sit.	52%	23	Pers: 2+ TE/6+ OL	8%	32	Rush 6+	9.4%	5	CB by Sides	60%	29	Offensive Pace	28.72	1
Runs, behind 2H	24%	23	Pers: 6+ OL	3%	22	Sacks by LB	8.6%	29	S/CB Cover Ratio	26%	18	Defensive Pace	31.23	24
Pass, ahead 2H	42%	28	Shotgun/Pistol	73%	7	Sacks by DB	20.0%	1	DB Blitz	14%	4	Go for it on 4th	1.66	2

The movement of the NFL towards a three-wide base offense continues unabated—all 32 teams had 11 personnel as their most common package in 2016—but nobody is as dedicated as the Giants. Big Blue had 11 personnel on 92 percent of plays last season; the next-highest team was at 76 percent. ⚌ Despite going three-wide on nearly every play, the Giants didn't use many wide receiver screens (just 11 plays). However, they were second in the NFL with 36 running back screens and had a phenomenal 7.9 yards per play and 43.6% DVOA on these plays. ⚌ Opposing defenses blitzed Eli Manning a bit more than the year before, but he still ranked dead last in the percentage of passes where he faced extra pass-rushers, just 21 percent. Manning was pressured on only 26 percent of blitzes, putting the Giants third in the league behind New Orleans and Oakland. Yards per pass were basically the same no matter the number of pass-rushers. ⚌ It's probably not a surprise with that pass rush that Giants opponents used a lot of screen passes. The Giants defense ranked second in wide receiver screens and third in running back screens. They were average against the former, a little better than average against the latter. ⚌ Though use of defensive backs in the pass rush only went up slightly from 2015, the Giants went from 26th to first in the percentage of sacks that came from defensive backs. ⚌ The Giants allowed just 5.1 yards per pass with a blitz, second in the NFL behind Minnesota, compared to 6.8 yards per pass with three or four pass-rushers. ⚌ Giants opponents threw deep (16+ yards) on a league-high 24.5 percent of pass attempts, even though the Giants had a voracious pass rush and ranked third in DVOA against deep passes. ⚌ One of the most remarkable facts about the 2016 New York Giants is that they are the most consistent team ever tracked by Football Outsiders in terms of week-to-week total DVOA. Twelve of their 16 regular-season performances fell in a thin band between -20% and 20% DVOA. This is a fun, quirky stat, but it also has no bearing whatsoever on the Giants' performance in 2017. The correlation coefficient of DVOA variance this year and next year is only 0.12, and the correlation of variance to both next year's DVOA and next year's change in DVOA is less than half that.

Lowest Week-to-Week Variance in Regular Season, 1986-2016

Year	Team	Total DVOA	Total Rk	W-L	VAR
2016	NYG	9.6%	8	11-5	2.5%
1988	IND	1.1%	13	9-7	3.2%
1990	LARD	26.0%	3	12-4	3.3%
2015	BAL	-3.0%	17	5-11	3.6%
2015	DAL	-18.0%	27	4-12	4.5%
2013	NE	18.9%	5	12-4	4.5%
2016	SD	-1.1%	19	5-11	4.7%
2016	NO	-1.9%	21	7-9	4.7%
2003	CAR	0.6%	16	11-5	4.7%
2006	SD	29.5%	1	14-2	4.9%
1991	SD	1.6%	14	4-12	4.9%
1987	MIN	1.3%	12	8-4	4.9%

Passing

Player	DYAR	DVOA	Plays	NtYds	Avg	YAC	C%	TD	Int
E.Manning	188	-6.5%	620	3882	6.3	5.3	63.2%	26	15
G.Smith	-68	-70.8%	17	105	6.2	10.4	57.1%	1	1

Receiving

Player	DYAR	DVOA	Plays	Ctch	Yds	Y/C	YAC	TD	C%
O.Beckham	161	-1.1%	169	101	1367	13.5	5.2	10	60%
S.Shepard	91	-1.8%	105	65	683	10.5	4.0	8	62%
V.Cruz*	6	-11.7%	72	39	586	15.0	4.8	1	54%
R.Lewis	-29	-31.5%	19	7	97	13.9	0.6	2	37%
B.Marshall	-35	-16.1%	127	58	788	13.6	3.0	3	46%
W.Tye	-68	-22.2%	70	48	395	8.2	3.8	1	69%
L.Donnell*	-61	-48.1%	22	15	92	6.1	2.7	1	68%
J.Adams	-17	-19.4%	21	16	123	7.7	4.4	1	76%
R.Ellison	-41	-51.9%	14	9	57	6.3	3.8	0	64%
R.Jennings*	-28	-25.6%	43	36	207	5.8	7.7	1	84%
B.Rainey*	10	-7.0%	25	20	153	7.7	9.0	0	80%
P.Perkins	-1	-14.4%	24	15	162	10.8	11.3	0	63%
S.Vereen	-19	-33.6%	19	11	94	8.5	8.0	0	58%
S.Draughn	60	14.2%	39	29	263	9.1	6.4	2	74%

Rushing

Player	DYAR	DVOA	Plays	Yds	Avg	TD	Fum	Suc
R.Jennings*	-38	-15.5%	135	453	3.4	3	0	41%
P.Perkins	-18	-15.6%	65	230	3.5	0	0	38%
S.Vereen	-2	-9.9%	31	147	4.7	1	0	45%
O.Darkwa	18	6.9%	30	111	3.7	2	0	40%
B.Rainey*	8	1.8%	17	63	3.7	0	0	53%
S.Draughn	17	2.9%	37	120	3.2	4	0	35%

Offensive Line

Player	Pos	Age	GS	Snaps	Pen	Sk	Pass	Run	Player	Pos	Age	GS	Snaps	Pen	Sk	Pass	Run
Ereck Flowers	LT	23	16/16	1061	13	4.0	19	4	Justin Pugh	LG	27	11/11	686	3	2.0	8	4
John Jerry	RG	31	16/16	1059	4	1.5	6	5	Marshall Newhouse*	RT	29	10/6	461	4	2.0	3	2
Weston Richburg	C	26	16/16	1046	3	1.0	4	9	D.J. Fluker	RG	26	16/16	992	7	2.5	8	6
Bobby Hart	RT	23	14/13	865	5	1.5	14	3									

Year	Yards	ALY	Rank	Power	Rank	Stuff	Rank	2nd Lev	Rank	Open Field	Rank	Sacks	ASR	Rank	Press	Rank	F-Start	Cont.
2014	3.62	4.02	22	61%	20	20%	18	0.94	29	0.47	28	30	5.0%	10	23.5%	15	18	37
2015	4.02	4.31	11	47%	30	19%	11	1.10	21	0.59	23	27	5.1%	6	23.3%	11	13	28
2016	3.70	3.89	24	63%	14	17%	9	1.01	29	0.40	29	22	3.9%	2	21.6%	6	11	30

2016 ALY by direction: Left End 4.46 (15)   Left Tackle 4.59 (12)   Mid/Guard 3.83 (28)   Right Tackle 2.27 (32)   Right End 4.72 (5)

Ereck Flowers isn't your typical former first-round left tackle who turns out to be bad. He's on a special plateau of disappointment all his own. Blown block and sacks allowed totals don't do Flowers justice, because they miss all the plays in between where he looks subpar. He's awkward in his backpedal, takes all kinds of strange little hop-steps to get into position, and can't adjust or mirror when pass-rushers work inside or otherwise surprise him. Even by the playoffs, he still looked like a big dude from New Zealand or someplace who is taking his first real reps in American football. ☞ Flowers was working hard to rebuild his game from the ground up during OTAs. Meanwhile, sixth-round pick Adam Bisnowaty was getting all the love from the press. Bisnowaty is athletically limited and technically unspectacular, but he's a gamer-brawler-finisher type who proved very effective when protecting Nathan Peterman and opening holes for James Connor at Pitt. ☞ The rest of the line is really in decent shape. Groot-like D.J. Fluker is likely to replace replacement-level starter John Jerry and upgrade the run blocking at right guard. Center Weston Richburg has allowed just one sack the last two seasons combined, while left guard Justin Pugh should be better in 2017 after missing time with an MCL injury last year. ☞ Still, it's down to Last Chance Prospect versus Extra-Thirsty Try Hard at the position that will determine whether Eli Manning will have time to play with all of his new toys. It's quite a gamble, considering the outpouring of investments everywhere else.

Defensive Front Seven

Defensive Line	Age	Pos	G	Snaps	Plays	TmPct	Rk	Stop	Dfts	BTkl	Runs	St%	Rk	RuYd	Rk	Sack	Hit	Hur	Dsrpt
						Overall						vs. Run					Pass Rush		
Johnathan Hankins*	25	DT	16	764	43	5.1%	35	35	12	5	38	79%	41	2.3	44	3.0	6	15	0
Damon Harrison	29	DT	16	674	87	10.3%	1	70	16	11	78	83%	26	2.3	43	2.5	1	9	1

Edge Rushers	Age	Pos	G	Snaps	Plays	Overall TmPct	Rk	Stop	Dfts	BTkl	Runs	vs. Run St%	Rk	RuYd	Rk	Sack	Pass Rush Hit	Hur	Dsrpt
Olivier Vernon	27	DE	16	1040	63	7.4%	15	52	20	11	47	81%	22	2.3	38	9.0	19	66	1
Jason Pierre-Paul	28	DE	12	792	59	9.3%	4	45	15	2	38	68%	74	2.9	65	7.0	10	28	9
Romeo Okwara	22	DE	16	368	22	2.6%	--	20	7	1	14	93%	--	2.4	--	1.0	4	10	2
Devin Taylor	28	DE	16	665	29	3.6%	74	15	8	6	18	33%	100	4.4	99	4.5	5	21	1

Linebackers	Age	Pos	G	Snaps	Plays	Overall TmPct	Rk	Stop	Dfts	BTkl	Runs	vs. Run St%	Rk	RuYd	Rk	Sack	Pass Rush Hit	Hur	Tgts	vs. Pass Suc%	Rk	AdjYd	Rk	PD	Int
Jonathan Casillas	30	OLB	16	796	100	11.8%	44	61	18	13	43	72%	12	3.2	32	1.5	1	8	34	57%	15	6.6	43	6	0
Keenan Robinson	28	OLB	16	780	86	10.2%	56	45	14	9	37	62%	50	3.7	51	0.0	1	4	31	56%	20	6.4	39	6	0
Devon Kennard	26	OLB	16	533	58	6.8%	74	35	11	3	42	67%	27	2.6	11	1.5	4	13	11	39%	67	7.2	53	0	0
Kelvin Sheppard*	29	MLB	16	453	49	5.8%	81	20	3	6	35	43%	86	4.3	71	0.0	0	3	13	56%	22	5.4	21	2	0

Year	Yards	ALY	Rank	Power	Rank	Stuff	Rank	2nd Level	Rank	Open Field	Rank	Sacks	ASR	Rank	Press	Rank
2014	4.81	4.61	28	62%	13	16%	27	1.37	31	1.00	29	47	7.8%	6	29.4%	2
2015	4.35	4.33	22	67%	17	20%	19	1.18	21	0.88	22	23	4.1%	30	25.9%	13
2016	3.64	4.12	16	63%	14	17%	20	0.91	2	0.45	4	35	5.5%	23	29.2%	8

2016 ALY by direction:	Left End 3.48 (9)	Left Tackle 4.44 (18)	Mid/Guard 4.27 (18)	Right Tackle 4.23 (17)	Right End 3.88 (18)

Last season, Jason Pierre-Paul was the flashy front man, Olivier Vernon the mysterious brooder, Damon "Big Snacks" Harrison the fun-loving quipster, and Johnathan Hankins the quiet big brother type. Depending on whether that's your formula for a boy band or a superhero team, the linebackers were either roadies or extras. ⚏ This year, second-round pick Dalvin Tomlinson (Alabama) is expected to replace Hankins (now in Indianapolis), so replace the quiet-guy archetype with more of a nerdy intellectual. Tomlinson, like many 320-pound behemoths from the Deep South, is a big-time anime fan with a pair of finance-related bachelor degrees. His primary job will be to keep blockers away from the others, particularly Snacks, who emerged as the both the best playmaker and the most vocal leader of the bunch last year. ⚏ JPP underwent groin surgery in December and was still not a full participant by the start of OTAs. This could be problematic for one of the most top-heavy pass rushes in the league. Vernon led all defenders last year with 66 total hurries, while JPP had a respectable 28, giving the two 94 hurries together. The rest of the team combined for 95 hurries. There is no quality depth behind JPP and Vernon, nor is there any big-play capability at linebacker (where the Giants are still trying to make Devon Kennard happen), so JPP's return to health is key to the team's defensive plans.

Defensive Secondary

Secondary	Age	Pos	G	Snaps	Plays	Overall TmPct	Rk	Stop	Dfts	BTkl	Runs	vs. Run St%	Rk	RuYd	Rk	Tgts	vs. Pass Tgt%	Rk	Dist	Suc%	Rk	AdjYd	Rk	PD	Int
Landon Collins	23	SS	16	1105	138	16.3%	1	70	24	11	59	61%	6	4.3	5	59	12.4%	67	10.6	53%	16	7.6	24	13	5
Janoris Jenkins	29	CB	15	956	67	8.4%	48	39	24	7	11	45%	31	6.5	41	68	16.5%	20	14.6	69%	2	5.6	7	18	3
Andrew Adams	25	FS	14	746	50	6.7%	65	18	9	8	21	29%	60	7.7	45	16	5.0%	4	15.4	54%	11	12.3	69	6	1
Dominique Rodgers-Cromartie	31	CB	15	733	70	8.8%	36	42	19	6	12	75%	2	3.3	3	61	19.5%	51	15.0	71%	1	4.5	1	21	6
Eli Apple	22	CB	14	701	56	7.6%	66	21	9	9	15	40%	41	6.3	38	53	17.5%	31	13.2	41%	81	10.0	86	6	1
Leon Hall*	33	CB	12	383	32	5.0%	--	14	5	4	7	57%	--	8.7	--	23	14.0%	--	8.0	44%	--	7.5	--	2	1
Trevin Wade*	28	CB	16	355	26	3.1%	--	15	9	1	3	100%	--	1.7	--	33	21.7%	--	12.6	64%	--	8.0	--	4	0
Coty Sensabaugh*	29	CB	13	217	24	3.5%	--	9	5	1	10	80%	--	3.2	--	13	29.7%	--	7.8	9%	--	12.7	--	0	0
Duke Ihenacho	28	SS	15	636	61	7.6%	56	21	7	13	38	39%	39	6.5	34	12	4.6%	2	8.8	28%	74	11.3	64	2	0
Valentino Blake	27	CB	16	364	42	5.3%	--	13	4	1	5	60%	--	3.0	--	49	27.4%	--	12.8	42%	--	8.1	--	6	0

Year	Pass D Rank	vs. #1 WR	Rk	vs. #2 WR	Rk	vs. Other WR	Rk	vs. TE	Rk	vs. RB	Rk
2014	21	7.8%	23	-3.1%	15	1.1%	18	13.9%	25	2.1%	20
2015	28	-1.7%	15	1.1%	16	-6.0%	12	20.5%	27	8.5%	21
2016	4	-29.7%	1	-12.8%	5	-14.2%	7	15.7%	26	-25.8%	3

Continuity was a huge factor in this unit's success last season. Though the Giants secondary only finished 22nd in adjusted games lost, a large chunk of that was due to a season-ending injury to rookie starting free safety Darian Thompson after just two games. Undrafted rookie Andrew Adams stepped in ably and ranked third among Giants defensive backs in snaps. Including the postseason, New York had five defensive backs play at least 700 snaps, tied with Pittsburgh for the most in the league. ☜ Landon Collins went from a liability in coverage as a rookie to one of the league's best all-around defenders with a year under his belt. Now the Giants coaches hope Thompson can make a similar leap in his second season. Thompson played well early in the season before suffering a Lisfranc injury. A slick, smart centerfielder-type at Boise State, Thompson impressed coaches with his ability to absorb the defense last season. He was running at close to full speed at the start of OTAs. ☜ If Thompson emerges, he will join Collins, Dominique Rodgers-Cromartie, Janoris Jenkins, and the still-developing Eli Apple in a secondary that has the potential to be the best in the league east of Colorado.

Special Teams

Year	DVOA	Rank	FG/XP	Rank	Net Kick	Rank	Kick Ret	Rank	Net Punt	Rank	Punt Ret	Rank	Hidden	Rank
2014	-0.6%	15	3.7	8	7.0	6	-5.9	29	-5.2	23	-2.8	19	-13.3	30
2015	5.4%	2	9.5	2	-3.1	24	9.1	2	7.4	6	4.0	8	-6.4	24
2016	1.2%	11	4.6	6	-3.0	26	2.5	9	10.6	6	-8.7	31	-11.3	27

Undrafted rookie Aldrick Rosas was the only kicker on the roster by the end of minicamp. Rosas kicked for a pair of NAIA National Champions while at Southern Oregon, but he tore his ACL in 2015, limiting all the pre-draft clamor and hype NAIA kickers usually receive. Rosas went to camp with the Titans last year but was released and became your basic tryout kicker, finally signing a futures deal with the Giants in January. Jerry Reese said that he plans to sign a veteran kicker before training camp, but we're finalizing this book three weeks into July and Rosas is still lonesome. After last year's Josh Brown's fiasco, let's hope Reese is doing the proverbial "due diligence" in addition to watching them kick field goals. ☜ Trading anything for a punter is an invitation for others to mock you, but Brad Wing has stabilized the position since arriving in 2015. The Giants ranked sixth in net points gained from punts for the second straight season; when isolating the punter's kicks alone, Wing ranked fourth in 2016. ☜ Dwayne Harris is entrenched as the return man at this point, but he was disastrous on punt returns last season. Only Rashad Greene and Cyrus Jones provided less value in that department in 2016; Odell Beckham and Bobby Rainey were also net negatives when given the opportunity. Harris was a top-10 punt returner in 2015, though, so some positive regression might be in store there. Harris also led the Giants with nine special teams tackles, followed by Zak DeOssie, whose eight tackles (all on punts) were the most for any long snapper.

New York Jets

2016 Record: 5-11	**Total DVOA:** -32.4% (32nd)	**2017 Mean Projection:** 6.2 wins	**On the Clock (0-4):** 26%
Pythagorean Wins: 4.4 (29th)	**Offense:** -21.9% (31st)	**Postseason Odds:** 14.6%	**Mediocrity (5-7):** 45%
Snap-Weighted Age: 26.8 (11th)	**Defense:** 3.7% (21st)	**Super Bowl Odds:** 0.7%	**Playoff Contender (8-10):** 24%
Average Opponent: 1.4% (10th)	**Special Teams:** -6.8% (32nd)	**Proj. Avg. Opponent:** -0.5% (23rd)	**Super Bowl Contender (11+):** 5%

2016: Everything collapses except the run defense.

2017: You're doing it wrong.

This is it, ladies and gentlemen. We have reached peak New York Jets. Over the last half-decade, this franchise has suffered embarrassment from head (brain-dead interceptions) to toe (foot fetish gossip) and everywhere in between (butt-fumble!), but we have never seen anything like this. It's hard to deny that the Jets are going into 2017 looking to deliberately lose as many games as possible. That's not the embarrassing part, though. The embarrassing thing is that despite those best efforts, our projections don't give them the best chance to land the first overall pick in 2018. Only the Jets would find themselves in this situation: they can't even tank correctly.

The problem for the Jets is that they waited too long to tank, long after the perfect opportunity had presented itself. You know what would have been an ideal time to begin the process? January of 2015. The Jets were coming off a 4-12 season, their worst record since 2007. They had finished 27th in total DVOA, 27th on offense and 21st on defense. And the roster was old: ninth in snap-weighted age on offense, and 11th on defense. With Mike Maccagnan replacing John Idzik as general manager and Todd Bowles taking over for Rex Ryan as head coach, the Jets were in a perfect position to start rebuilding—chop salary, get younger, and start stockpiling draft picks.

Instead, the Jets went out and got older. They traded draft picks to acquire Ryan Fitzpatrick and Brandon Marshall, and signed eight other free agents age 30 or older, including Darrelle Revis and Antonio Cromartie. The worst-case scenario then unfolded for the Jets: they were moderately successful, finishing 10-6 and contending for the playoffs until the fourth quarter of Week 17. The Jets were a legitimately good team that season, finishing ninth in total DVOA. But they were also a very old team, the oldest team in the league on offense and ninth-oldest on defense. The roster desperately needed an overhaul, but those 10 wins convinced the Jets they were on the right track, and the rebuild that was already a year too late got delayed another season.

So the Jets added more aging players, signing five more 30-year-olds. That included Fitzpatrick, who was re-signed after a long and awkward courtship. Like a couple who should have split up after their best days had come and gone, Fitzpatrick and the Jets stayed together out of comfort. In the draft, rather than trade down and accumulate extra pics, the Jets made just one deal, giving up a 2017 fourth-rounder to take tackle Brandon Shell in the fifth round—a minor transaction, but one that cost New York future capital in exchange for an immediate payoff.

It should have come as no surprise the Jets fell apart in 2016. They won five games thanks largely to a soft schedule (the teams they beat averaged five wins apiece), but DVOA said they were the worst team in football. They did one thing exceptionally well, leading the league in run defense DVOA, and were also in the middle of the pack running the ball on offense. But they were next to last in passing offense. And passing defense. And dead last in special teams. Some of those old players severely declined in quality (Fitzpatrick found himself benched at times for Geno Smith and Bryce Petty). Others got hurt. Matt Forte, Steve McLendon, Ryan Clady, Kellen Davis, Nick Mangold, Breno Giacomini, and Erin Henderson each missed at least three starts. Thirteen of the 75 different players to hit the field in a Jets uniform in 2016 were 30 or older, but only two of them played in all 16 games: kicker Nick Folk and long snapper Tanner Purdum. The Jets finished 22nd in adjusted games lost on defense and 30th on offense.

The Maccagnan/Bowles regime was now entering Year 3, and it was clearly time for a rebuild that should have begun in Year 1. Still, the Jets dragged their feet in the process, and often showed signs of internal confusion or a failure to work together.

Let's start with the things they did right. First, there was a salary purge of aging veterans. Most of the team's 30-year-olds were released or allowed to sign elsewhere in free agency. To replace them the Jets signed free agents still in their twenties, including Kelvin Beachum, Morris Claiborne, and Chandler Catanzaro. Then they entered the draft ready to deal. New York made five trades during the draft—four moves down for more picks, and one pick traded from this year's draft for an extra pick in 2018. These were all minor trades, none involving anything more than a third-round pick, but on paper each made sense for a rebuilding team.

At quarterback, though, the Jets made the puzzling decision to replace an aging, mediocre Ryan Fitzpatrick with Josh McCown, who at 38 is significantly older and significantly worse. Since turning 35—the same age Fitzpatrick will be this year—McCown has ranked 35th and 23rd in DVOA, and he would have ranked 34th last year if he had thrown enough passes to qualify for our leaderboards. In the same three seasons, Fitzpatrick has ranked 12th, 14th, and 23rd. As a rule, old players tend to get worse, not better, so it's quite likely that McCown's play

2017 Jets Schedule

Week	Opp.	Week	Opp.	Week	Opp.
1	at BUF	7	at MIA	13	KC
2	at OAK	8	ATL	14	at DEN
3	MIA	9	BUF (Thu.)	15	at NO
4	JAC	10	at TB	16	LACH
5	at CLE	11	BYE	17	at NE
6	NE	12	CAR		

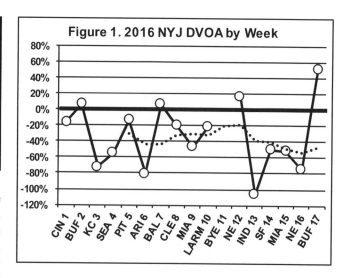

Figure 1. 2016 NYJ DVOA by Week

will decline. Further, signing McCown takes away some of the opportunity for young quarterbacks Bryce Petty and Christian Hackenberg to show what they can or can't do, and gives the Jets less of a chance to evaluate either player's future prospects. The only benefit to acquiring McCown is that he will likely bring good draft mojo along with him—McCown's last three teams have finished with the first, second, and first overall selections in the following seasons' drafts.

Speaking of the draft, it was also puzzling that the Jets didn't trade down in the first round this year. In hindsight, we know for a fact that the Chiefs and Texans were both willing to give up first-round draft picks in 2017 *and* 2018 to move up in search of quarterbacks. In theory, the Jets could have gotten an even bigger bounty for the sixth overall pick. Even if that's not the case, though, the Jets would have been better off taking either of those deals and getting an extra first-round pick next year. Forget what the trade value charts say, because in this case they are irrelevant. The Jets need a lot of good players, and they need a lot of young players, and by standing pat at six they cost themselves a shot at filling a need (or getting ammunition to trade up the board) in 2018. This can only turn out one of two ways: either Jamal Adams is the second coming of Kam Chancellor, or the Jets will regret being asleep at the wheel here.

Actually, there is a third possibility, which is that the Jets still had not fully decided whether they were rebuilding or not. Some of their post-draft moves showed conflicting motivations. The drafting of Adams in the first round and Marcus Maye in the second made Calvin Pryor expendable, but the time to trade Pryor would have been during the draft, when they could have gotten a rookie or two in return. Instead the Jets waited until June, trading him to Cleveland for Demario Davis, a linebacker they had allowed to leave in free agency just one year earlier who is three years older than Pryor. And then things got really weird later that month when linebacker David Harris and wide receiver Eric Decker were also let go. Again, these were not strange moves in a vacuum—Harris will be 33 this season, Decker 30—but the timing was bizarre. Why not try to trade one or both players before or during the draft? Even a 2018 seventh-round pick would have been something added in exchange for the loss of a player. Instead, the best wide receiver and best linebacker on the roster were both unceremoniously kicked out the door. The Jets had achieved a remarkable feat: the roster was worse going into training camp than it was going into the draft, and that almost never happens outside of major injuries.

Maccagnan was described as "somber" when speaking to the press after Harris was released. He was asked point-blank if the Jets were tanking for a better draft pick in 2018. "That's not something we're focused on," he replied. He was also asked whether they had the worst roster in the NFL. "I'm not going to speculate on our roster compared to anybody else's roster," he said. For the record, neither of those answers was a denial.

Bowles didn't have much useful to add. The Jets could easily have afforded Harris' $6.5 million salary, so why not keep him on the roster? "That's a good question," Bowles said. Why wasn't the situation with Harris resolved months earlier? "That's a good question," Bowles said again. In short, nobody in charge of things on the Jets actually seemed to know what was going on.

If Maccagnan and Bowles were in the dark, that means the cuts were decided by owner Woody Johnson. Johnson even admitted that "the timing is not ideal" in a press release announcing Harris' release, which is stunning since *he was the one who picked the time.* And it really was horrible timing for Harris and Decker as players, for the Jets as a team, and for the Jets' fans. Primary payments for Jets season-ticket packages this year were due in May, about a month before the Pryor trade and Harris and Decker releases.

But then things got even weirder, as NFL Network analyst Steve Smith revealed to his colleagues that the Jets had reached out to him and tried to talk him out of retirement. This is mind-boggling. Why on earth would a tanking team amidst a serious youth movement try to sign a wide receiver who had recently retired at the age of 37? What purpose would he have served on the roster? How would that have helped them get a better draft pick in 2018?

This kind of one-foot-in, one-foot-out approach to tanking has left the Jets in an impossible spot. While their offense could well turn out to be the worst in the league, there are several reasons to believe that the defense will improve significantly this fall. For the second year in a row, the Jets' run defense was one of the best we have ever measured. (Table 1). However, their pass defense was terrible. No team on record has ever had a bigger gap between run defense DVOA and pass defense DVOA. This is critical, because run defense is more consistent from year-to-year than pass defense. Over the past decade, the year-to-year correlation coefficient for run defense is .43, as opposed to .29 for pass defense. Most of the other teams with big gaps between run and pass defense have improved their overall defense the following season (Table 2.)

Table 1. Best Run Defenses 1986-2016

Year	Team	DVOA	Yds/Carry
2000	BAL	-36.6%	3.72
1991	PHI	-34.9%	2.97
2015	NYJ	-33.3%	3.58
1998	SD	-32.9%	2.70
2014	DET	-31.4%	3.17
2006	MIN	-30.5%	2.83
1995	KC	-30.5%	3.28
2010	PIT	-29.0%	3.02
2008	BAL	-28.6%	3.56
2016	NYJ	-28.1%	3.69
2000	TEN	-27.4%	3.97
2007	BAL	-27.3%	2.84

So we would expect the Jets defense to improve anyway, based on how great they have been against the run, and the fact that they were very good in 2015. That's not even considering the new talent in the draft, and the projection system upgrades the Jets for taking two safeties in the first 39 picks this year. In theory, there's a lot to like about this defense. That should help balance out an offense that looks dreadful.

For the sake of argument, let's say the Jets go 5-11 again this year. What then? They'll miss out on a top-three draft pick, and with no extra first-round selection, they would have to move heaven and earth to get to the top of the draft to find a quarterback. They should have a ton of cap space, but what youngsters will be available to come in and save the franchise? Teddy Bridgewater? Rex Burkhead? Tyler Eifert? Dontari Poe?

This all assumes that when September comes and the real games kick off, the Jets will do their best to win games with their limited roster. Given the disconnect among those at the top of the organization, it's entirely possible that players will be ordered to go out and drop passes or miss tackles in hopes of getting the top pick in 2018. This leaves Maccagnan and Bowles in a no-win situation. They could be fired for losing too many games, but they could also be fired for winning too often and failing to tank. In all likelihood, their fates are sealed either way, and the 2018 Jets will have new names running the show. At this point, though, it's hard to see why anyone would want these jobs.

Vincent Verhei

Table 2. Biggest Gap Between Run Defense and Pass Defense, 1986-2016

Year	Team	Pass D	Rk	Run D	Rk	Gap	All D	Rk	All D Y+1	Change
2016	NYJ	28.9%	31	-28.1%	1	-57.0%	3.7%	21	--	--
2015	NO	48.1%	32	-2.4%	27	-50.5%	26.1%	32	14.6%	-11.5%
2009	JAC	35.8%	31	-13.6%	9	-49.4%	11.3%	28	17.7%	+6.4%
1996	BAL	42.0%	30	-6.4%	14	-48.4%	17.5%	29	-2.4%	-19.9%
1990	ATL	24.7%	27	-23.4%	1	-48.1%	3.0%	17	1.2%	-1.8%
1991	NE	27.7%	26	-19.8%	2	-47.6%	5.9%	20	10.8%	+4.9%
1999	SF	41.7%	31	-4.5%	18	-46.2%	20.4%	30	16.0%	-4.4%
2014	WAS	29.5%	32	-14.2%	9	-43.7%	9.9%	27	5.4%	-4.5%
2009	SEA	30.9%	30	-11.7%	10	-42.6%	12.0%	29	12.0%	0.0%
1989	DAL	36.4%	28	-5.6%	11	-42.0%	13.6%	25	-5.9%	-19.5%
2000	CIN	32.4%	30	-9.0%	8	-41.4%	11.7%	26	0.5%	-11.2%
2001	TEN	28.4%	30	-12.8%	6	-41.2%	10.3%	25	-0.2%	-10.5%
AVERAGE EXCEPT JETS		34.3%		-11.2%			12.9%		6.3%	-6.5%

2016 Jets Stats by Week

Wk	vs.	W-L	PF	PA	YDF	YDA	TO	Total	Off	Def	ST
1	CIN	L	22	23	340	381	0	-16%	-2%	11%	-3%
2	at BUF	W	37	31	493	393	0	7%	25%	10%	-8%
3	at KC	L	3	24	305	293	-7	-73%	-79%	-11%	-4%
4	SEA	L	17	27	305	354	-3	-55%	-26%	30%	2%
5	at PIT	L	13	31	316	436	+1	-14%	10%	15%	-9%
6	at ARI	L	3	28	230	396	-2	-80%	-45%	39%	4%
7	BAL	W	24	16	344	245	+1	7%	-6%	-37%	-24%
8	at CLE	W	31	28	393	407	+2	-20%	-5%	14%	-1%
9	at MIA	L	23	27	331	274	-2	-47%	-32%	-15%	-30%
10	LARM	L	6	9	296	280	-1	-21%	-7%	2%	-13%
11	BYE										
12	NE	L	17	22	333	377	-2	16%	21%	1%	-4%
13	IND	L	10	41	250	421	-2	-106%	-62%	36%	-7%
14	at SF	W	23	17	404	364	-1	-50%	-29%	25%	4%
15	MIA	L	13	34	360	303	-3	-51%	-43%	-6%	-13%
16	at NE	L	3	41	239	325	-4	-75%	-66%	-3%	-12%
17	BUF	W	30	10	329	230	+3	51%	-13%	-56%	9%

Trends and Splits

	Offense	Rank	Defense	Rank
Total DVOA	-21.9%	31	3.7%	21
Unadjusted VOA	-19.4%	31	6.3%	24
Weighted Trend	-25.8%	31	0.9%	19
Variance	9.5%	28	6.4%	25
Average Opponent	0.7%	21	1.2%	9
Passing	-25.7%	31	28.9%	31
Rushing	-8.3%	20	-28.1%	1
First Down	-17.3%	29	-2.0%	16
Second Down	-29.0%	31	13.2%	28
Third Down	-19.3%	26	0.8%	18
First Half	-8.6%	24	15.8%	29
Second Half	-26.2%	28	-15.9%	6
Red Zone	-55.3%	32	-7.2%	11
Late and Close	-15.8%	25	-36.3%	1

Five-Year Performance

Year	W-L	Pyth W	Est W	PF	PA	TO	Total	Rk	Off	Rk	Def	Rk	ST	Rk	Off AGL	Rk	Def AGL	Rk	Off Age	Rk	Def Age	Rk	ST Age	Rk
2012	6-10	5.3	5.6	281	375	-14	-18.0%	27	-20.7%	30	-4.2%	9	-1.5%	21	37.7	22	41.0	23	26.6	19	28.1	2	26.0	16
2013	8-8	5.4	7.5	290	387	-14	-7.7%	24	-15.3%	27	-5.6%	12	2.1%	10	33.9	15	9.1	1	26.2	26	26.7	14	26.1	13
2014	4-12	4.8	5.9	283	401	-11	-15.5%	27	-11.2%	27	3.5%	21	-0.8%	16	18.7	5	22.8	4	27.3	9	27.0	11	26.1	13
2015	10-6	10.0	9.7	387	314	+6	12.4%	9	1.6%	14	-13.8%	5	-2.9%	25	48.7	25	13.2	1	28.5	1	27.1	9	26.6	6
2016	5-11	4.4	4.6	275	409	-20	-32.4%	32	-21.9%	31	3.7%	21	-6.8%	32	67.6	30	42.9	22	27.5	6	26.4	19	26.0	19

2016 Performance Based on Most Common Personnel Groups

NYJ Offense					NYJ Offense vs. Opponents					NYJ Defense					NYJ Defense vs. Opponents			
Pers	Freq	Yds	DVOA	Run%	Pers	Freq	Yds	DVOA	Run%	Pers	Freq	Yds	DVOA	Pers	Freq	Yds	DVOA
11	40%	5.4	-20.0%	46%	Base	23%	5.4	-13.5%	60%	Base	37%	5.2	-7.7%	11	58%	6.2	15.1%
10	33%	5.3	-27.6%	15%	Nickel	60%	5.2	-23.3%	36%	Nickel	56%	6.3	18.2%	12	19%	5.7	-0.2%
12	16%	5.7	4.7%	62%	Dime+	16%	6.0	-4.0%	14%	Dime+	4%	6.2	-20.9%	21	9%	3.6	-26.1%
20	4%	5.6	-31.8%	27%	Goal Line	1%	0.7	8.0%	83%	Goal Line	2%	3.2	-34.9%	13	4%	7.1	13.2%
611	2%	5.3	8.4%	68%						Big	1%	4.0	-12.4%	10	2%	10.4	42.8%

Strategic Tendencies

Run/Pass		Rk	Formation		Rk	Pass Rush		Rk	Secondary		Rk	Strategy		Rk
Runs, first half	40%	11	Form: Single Back	77%	20	Rush 3	10.7%	11	4 DB	37%	7	Play-action	16%	25
Runs, first down	49%	13	Form: Empty Back	11%	4	Rush 4	49.2%	32	5 DB	56%	22	Avg Box (Off)	6.00	31
Runs, second-long	31%	16	Pers: 3+ WR	78%	6	Rush 5	27.3%	4	6+ DB	4%	21	Avg Box (Def)	6.42	3
Runs, power sit.	55%	18	Pers: 2+ TE/6+ OL	21%	27	Rush 6+	12.9%	1	CB by Sides	63%	26	Offensive Pace	31.43	26
Runs, behind 2H	30%	10	Pers: 6+ OL	4%	17	Sacks by LB	31.5%	18	S/CB Cover Ratio	27%	14	Defensive Pace	29.58	5
Pass, ahead 2H	43%	26	Shotgun/Pistol	68%	12	Sacks by DB	7.4%	15	DB Blitz	12%	6	Go for it on 4th	0.56	29

The Jets once again minimized the tight end position like no other team in the NFL. The Jets had no tight end on the field on 37.5 percent of plays; the NFL average was 4.1 percent and no other team was above 16 percent. They threw just 5.4 percent of passes to tight ends; every other team was at 14 percent or higher. ☞ It took a lot of time and effort, but we were finally able to find something the Jets offense did well last year: running back screens. They ran more of these than any other team in the NFL and averaged 7.0 yards with 31.6% DVOA. ⚘ Meanwhile, the Jets defense only faced nine running back screens all season, fewer than anyone except New England. They allowed 2.9 yards per play, with a DVOA of minus-88.2%. ⚘ Jets games generally featured officials who kept their whistles in their pockets; the Jets were 28th in the NFL with just 111 penalties while Jets opponents were dead last with just 91 penalties. ⚘ The Jets ranked fifth in defensive DVOA against passes thrown behind the line of scrimmage, but 31st against passes beyond the line of scrimmage. ⚘ Jets opponents sent only two or three pass-rushers on 16 percent of pass plays, the highest figure in the league by more than three percentage points.

Passing

Player	DYAR	DVOA	Plays	NtYds	Avg	YAC	C%	TD	Int
R.Fitzpatrick*	-319	-22.6%	423	2601	6.1	4.9	56.7%	12	16
B.Petty	-414	-57.5%	146	732	5.0	5.1	56.4%	3	7
G.Smith*	-68	-70.8%	17	105	6.2	10.4	57.1%	1	1
J.McCown	-269	-34.4%	184	966	5.3	5.2	54.9%	6	6

Rushing

Player	DYAR	DVOA	Plays	Yds	Avg	TD	Fum	Suc
M.Forte	-11	-9.9%	214	792	3.7	7	0	41%
B.Powell	129	32.4%	71	395	5.6	3	0	55%
R.Fitzpatrick*	10	-3.6%	22	119	5.4	0	0	-
J.Todman	21	101.5%	5	40	8.0	0	0	60%
J.McCown	-6	-37.8%	5	21	4.2	0	0	-

Receiving

Player	DYAR	DVOA	Plays	Ctch	Yds	Y/C	YAC	TD	C%
B.Marshall*	-35	-16.1%	127	58	788	13.6	3.0	3	46%
Q.Enunwa	69	-4.5%	105	58	857	14.8	6.1	4	55%
R.Anderson	-31	-17.9%	78	42	587	14.0	2.8	2	54%
C.Peake	-51	-32.6%	35	19	186	9.8	3.7	0	54%
J.Marshall	20	-2.2%	23	14	162	11.6	3.3	2	61%
E.Decker*	48	17.3%	21	9	194	21.6	3.3	2	43%
Q.Patton	-84	-29.5%	63	37	408	11.0	5.4	0	59%
A.Seferian-Jenkins	-6	-12.7%	17	10	110	11.0	2.8	0	59%
B.Bostick*	-13	-25.2%	11	8	63	7.9	4.9	0	73%
B.Powell	49	-1.9%	75	59	388	6.6	7.2	2	79%
M.Forte	21	-5.6%	43	30	263	8.8	9.2	1	70%

Offensive Line

Player	Pos	Age	GS	Snaps	Pen	Sk	Pass	Run	Player	Pos	Age	GS	Snaps	Pen	Sk	Pass	Run
James Carpenter	LG	28	16/16	994	3	1.0	6	3	Brent Qvale	RT	26	12/5	347	3	1.0	4	2
Benjamin Ijalana	LT/RT	28	16/13	868	4	5.5	13	5	Breno Giacomini*	RT	32	5/5	267	5	1.0	5	1
Brian Winters	RG	26	13/13	807	6	2.0	9	5	Brandon Shell	RT	25	8/3	204	0	1.0	4	3
Wesley Johnson	C	26	16/8	659	2	0.5	8	2	Kelvin Beachum	LT	28	15/15	1023	10	6.0	14	7
Ryan Clady*	LT	31	9/8	538	6	1.5	11	2	Jonotthan Harrison	C	26	13/4	451	2	2.0	9	1
Nick Mangold*	C	33	8/8	433	0	0.0	1	2									

Year	Yards	ALY	Rank	Power	Rank	Stuff	Rank	2nd Lev	Rank	Open Field	Rank	Sacks	ASR	Rank	Press	Rank	F-Start	Cont.
2014	4.20	4.11	20	75%	5	18%	8	1.12	20	0.65	19	47	8.8%	25	30.2%	28	17	37
2015	4.06	3.87	26	59%	26	23%	26	1.14	18	0.90	10	22	4.1%	3	22.4%	10	21	35
2016	4.25	4.30	12	74%	2	16%	7	1.24	11	0.66	17	35	6.3%	20	24.9%	13	16	20

2016 ALY by direction:	Left End 4.42 (16)	Left Tackle 4.52 (14)	Mid/Guard 4.38 (10)	Right Tackle 4.22 (13)	Right End 2.81 (29)

With Ryan Clady and Breno Giacomini both released after the season, the Jets will turn to two younger linemen to play tackle. The first is Ben Ijalana, who was re-signed after his first season as a starter in the NFL. The other is Kelvin Beachum, who arrives after four years in Pittsburgh and one in Jacksonville. Though Ijalana played at left and right tackle last season, most expect him to start on the right side with Beachum on the left. Beachum got three years and $12 million guaranteed; Ijalana, two years and $3 million. Beachum missed 2015 with a torn ACL while Ijalana had arthroscopic surgery in June, but both were expected to be ready for training camp. The two were essentially identical by charting last season; they finished with almost the exact same snaps per blown block rate and both struggled more in pass protection than run blocking. Brandon Shell, a fifth-round rookie last season (and the great-nephew of Raiders Hall of Famer Art Shell), started three games at right tackle last year, and could also make a push for playing time this year. ⚘ There is also a new face at center, where the release of Nick Mangold means Wesley Johnson will be the full-time starter going forward. A fifth-round draft pick by the Steelers in 2014, Johnson has only nine starts in his career and is largely untested. But with no other options at the position, the Jets had little choice but to re-sign him to a one-year deal for $2.7 million. ⚘ Things are much more stable at guard. Brian Winters returns for his fifth season as a starter, fresh off a four-year extension with $15 million guaranteed. James Carpenter could never stay healthy in Seattle, but has started every game in his two years with the Jets. He was likely New York's best offensive player in 2016. Well, somebody had to be.

Defensive Front Seven

Defensive Line	Age	Pos	G	Snaps	Plays	TmPct	Overall Rk	Stop	Dfts	BTkl	vs. Run Runs	St%	Rk	RuYd	Rk	Pass Rush Sack	Hit	Hur	Dsrpt
Leonard Williams	23	DE	16	896	67	8.9%	5	60	23	6	57	88%	17	1.4	14	7.0	14	29	0
Muhammad Wilkerson	28	DE	15	845	59	8.3%	7	50	15	5	44	86%	20	2.0	36	4.5	7	19	3
Steve McLendon	31	DT	11	381	27	5.2%	34	23	10	0	23	83%	31	2.2	41	3.5	2	4	1
Deon Simon	27	DT	16	205	23	3.0%	--	19	5	3	21	81%	--	1.8	--	1.5	0	3	0

Edge Rushers	Age	Pos	G	Snaps	Plays	TmPct	Overall Rk	Stop	Dfts	BTkl	vs. Run Runs	St%	Rk	RuYd	Rk	Pass Rush Sack	Hit	Hur	Dsrpt
Sheldon Richardson	27	OLB	15	762	63	8.9%	5	47	21	6	52	73%	55	2.3	37	1.5	7	20	1
Jordan Jenkins	23	OLB	14	513	42	6.3%	26	29	13	1	26	69%	72	3.3	79	2.5	1	15	1
Lorenzo Mauldin	25	OLB	11	353	18	3.5%	77	16	6	3	12	83%	14	2.3	39	2.5	12	12	0
Julian Stanford	27	OLB	9	244	19	4.5%	61	11	2	1	9	67%	76	3.6	88	0.0	1	2	0
Mike Catapano*	27	OLB	11	209	4	0.8%	--	2	2	0	2	50%	--	2.0	--	0.0	2	6	0

Linebackers	Age	Pos	G	Snaps	Plays	TmPct	Overall Rk	Stop	Dfts	BTkl	vs. Run Runs	St%	Rk	RuYd	Rk	Pass Rush Sack	Hit	Hur	vs. Pass Tgts	Suc%	Rk	AdjYd	Rk	PD	Int
David Harris*	33	ILB	15	900	96	13.5%	34	48	10	7	58	55%	76	3.7	47	0.5	1	11	27	44%	50	6.4	38	2	0
Darron Lee	23	ILB	13	641	73	11.9%	43	39	11	8	33	70%	16	2.3	5	1.0	1	1	40	42%	59	8.0	69	3	0
Demario Davis	28	ILB	16	788	100	11.8%	44	56	14	13	75	57%	66	4.0	67	2.0	3	7	20	45%	48	7.7	63	2	0
Spencer Paysinger	29	OLB	15	333	54	6.7%	--	27	10	6	22	50%	--	6.5	--	0.0	2	3	18	54%	26	4.4	3	3	0

Year	Yards	ALY	Rank	Power	Rank	Stuff	Rank	2nd Level	Rank	Open Field	Rank	Sacks	ASR	Rank	Press	Rank
2014	3.81	4.06	13	64%	18	19%	16	0.89	3	0.69	17	45	8.2%	4	26.7%	6
2015	3.35	3.19	1	62%	12	28%	1	0.96	4	0.55	6	39	6.0%	21	28.0%	6
2016	3.99	3.62	5	51%	4	27%	2	1.16	16	0.91	26	27	4.3%	32	26.3%	21

2016 ALY by direction:	Left End 2.93 (1)	Left Tackle 3.59 (8)	Mid/Guard 3.71 (5)	Right Tackle 3.93 (14)	Right End 3.57 (15)

Officially, Sheldon Richardson was labeled as an outside linebacker last year. In reality, he did a little bit of everything—outside and inside linebacker, defensive end, even some 3-technique defensive tackle. We only tracked two plays where he was listed as the primary defender in pass coverage, so he was really a lineman more than anything. What he was not was an effective pass rusher—his sack, hit, and hurry numbers were all down from 2015. The Jets have said Richardson will play a more standard defensive end role in 2017. What happens after that, though, is anybody's guess. His contract is up after the season, and if the Jets want to retain him, they will likely need to franchise him at either $13.5 million (if he's counted as a defensive tackle) or $17 million (if he's a defensive end). The alternative would be to let him leave and get nothing in return. This makes it all the more curious why the Jets didn't trade him over the offseason for younger players or picks, and shows again that the right hand in New York often doesn't know what the left hand is doing. ☞ With Richardson struggling as an edge rusher, the Jets' pass rush quite literally turned inside-out. Leonard Williams led the team with 7.0 sacks, and every one of them came as an interior lineman, with an end or linebacker lined up to the outside. ☞ On that note, it would be great for the Jets if just one of their young pass-rusher prospects would actually develop. Lorenzo Mauldin and Jordan Jenkins were back-to-back third-rounders in 2015 and 2016, and so far they have produced a total of nine sacks in 40 games. (Joey Bosa, the reigning defensive rookie of the year, has 10.5 sacks in only 12 games.) This is how you end up dead last in adjusted sack rate despite fielding a trio of Pro Bowl-caliber defensive linemen. ☞ Longtime stalwart David Harris was in the post-draft wave of cap casualties, leaving Darron Lee as the returning starting inside linebacker. Lee was billed as a speedy modern prototype for the position, but the undersized rookie actually fared best against the run in his first season. Pass coverage presents a steep learning curve for any rookie defender, but if Lee can sustain his success against the run while also improving in the area he was actually drafted for, the Jets might have their Harris successor. Old friend Demario Davis will reassume a starting spot next to Lee after a year in Cleveland, completing an extremely depressing NFL round trip.

Defensive Secondary

Secondary	Age	Pos	G	Snaps	Plays	TmPct	Rk	Stop	Dfts	BTkl	Runs	St%	Rk	RuYd	Rk	Tgts	Tgt%	Rk	Dist	Suc%	Rk	AdjYd	Rk	PD	Int
Darrelle Revis*	32	CB	15	922	58	8.2%	50	17	6	11	9	44%	33	8.8	68	63	16.1%	17	12.0	44%	74	9.0	74	5	1
Marcus Gilchrist*	29	SS	13	819	57	9.3%	45	13	7	5	28	25%	65	13.7	74	23	6.6%	18	13.1	36%	61	8.9	38	4	2
Buster Skrine	28	CB	14	815	53	8.0%	58	21	8	9	9	44%	33	6.1	32	63	18.1%	42	10.6	39%	83	7.3	34	5	1
Calvin Pryor*	25	FS	15	813	66	9.3%	44	31	15	13	31	58%	10	4.7	10	36	10.4%	54	7.8	47%	38	9.5	52	4	0
Marcus Williams	26	CB	13	457	38	6.2%	--	10	5	2	4	25%	--	5.5	--	36	18.6%	--	12.7	36%	--	11.8	--	6	2
Rontez Miles	29	FS	16	394	49	6.5%	--	24	6	3	32	50%	--	6.3	--	14	8.4%	--	9.8	75%	--	10.3	--	1	0
Darryl Roberts	27	CB	12	285	27	4.8%	--	10	2	1	6	17%	--	8.7	--	34	27.7%	--	13.2	55%	--	5.6	--	7	0
Morris Claiborne	27	CB	7	406	31	8.7%	--	15	9	4	5	40%	--	9.2	--	42	21.4%	--	12.2	62%	--	4.4	--	5	1

Year	Pass D Rank	vs. #1 WR	Rk	vs. #2 WR	Rk	vs. Other WR	Rk	vs. TE	Rk	vs. RB	Rk
2014	24	2.7%	17	19.0%	27	34.0%	31	30.5%	31	-23.0%	4
2015	9	-2.1%	14	-51.8%	1	10.6%	24	-8.8%	14	-3.0%	12
2016	31	11.5%	25	25.1%	32	7.7%	21	0.9%	19	-5.9%	16

The end for Darrelle Revis came fast and hard, but at age 31 some decline should have been expected. Revis' demise was hardly New York's only problem, as the Jets fell from first to last in defense against No. 2 wide receivers. This is why the entire secondary was due for an overhaul, with Calvin Pryor traded and Revis and Marcus Gilchrist released. (Gilchrist tore his patellar tendon in December, and might miss the entire 2017 season.) ⚡ Buster Skrine is nobody's idea of a top cornerback, so the Jets brought in Morris Claiborne from Dallas. Claiborne had outstanding coverage numbers last year, but in a small sample of plays. This is part of the problem for Claiborne: he can't stay healthy, missing exactly half of the Cowboys' regular-season games in the past four years. ⚡ It should be noted that Claiborne's charting numbers for most of his career have been quite poor. In fact, in 11 combined NFL seasons, only once has either Skrine or Claiborne ever finished among the top 30 corners in either yards per target allowed or adjusted success rate. (Skrine was third in yards allowed per target with the Browns in 2013.) ⚡ Wondering why the Jets doubled down at safety in the first two rounds of the draft? They were last in DVOA against passes over the middle, and 29th against deep passes over the middle. Besides releasing Gilchrist, the Jets also jettisoned former first-rounder Calvin Pryor. They almost can't help but be better here in 2017. ⚡ Each of the two rookies can play either strong safety or free, but first-rounder Jamal Adams fits more as a box defender. He was noted more at LSU for his leadership and hitting than his coverage ability. Mike Mayock called him the safest prospect in the draft. Meanwhile, second-rounder Marcus Maye showed sideline-to-sideline coverage ability at Florida, with a knack for getting his hands on the ball in the air.

Special Teams

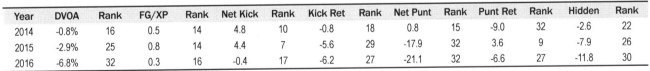

Year	DVOA	Rank	FG/XP	Rank	Net Kick	Rank	Kick Ret	Rank	Net Punt	Rank	Punt Ret	Rank	Hidden	Rank
2014	-0.8%	16	0.5	14	4.8	10	-0.8	18	0.8	15	-9.0	32	-2.6	22
2015	-2.9%	25	0.8	14	4.4	7	-5.6	29	-17.9	32	3.6	9	-7.9	26
2016	-6.8%	32	0.3	16	-0.4	17	-6.2	27	-21.1	32	-6.6	27	-11.8	30

There was so much terrible football in Jets games last year that their poor performance on special teams went overlooked. In particular, they had the NFL's worst punting unit. There was nothing wrong with the coverage teams, but seventh-round rookie Lac Edwards was last in net punting value and third-worst in gross punting average. That's just looking at what happened when he got a punt off—it doesn't even account for his fumbled snap against Baltimore that was recovered for a Ravens touchdown. Remember, kids: never draft a punter. The good news for Edwards is that the Jets were so busy dealing with problems elsewhere that they didn't bother bringing anyone in to challenge him, so he will get a chance to improve on his dreadful performance. ⚡ It was the second year in a row the Jets had the NFL's worst punt units, but in 2015 the issue was less Ryan Quiqley's punts and more the league's worst coverage teams. ⚡ Nick Folk was close to average last year in both placekicking and kickoffs, so of course the Jets replaced him with Chandler Catanzaro, who was in the bottom six in both categories with Arizona. In fact, in three years in the desert, Catanzaro never finished in the top half of the league in placekicking value. He also had a pair of high-profile failures last season, missing potential game-winning kicks against the Patriots and Seahawks. Good luck in the Meadowlands, kid! ⚡ If you can return kicks, please send your resume to 1 Jets Drive in Florham Park, N.J. Jalin Marshall was New York's primary returner on both punts and kickoffs in 2016, and finished in the bottom 10 at both jobs. After the draft, the Jets signed undrafted free agent Brisly Estime, who twice led the ACC in punt return average while playing for Syracuse. Unfortunately, Estime tore his Achilles in OTAs and was placed on injured reserve. So Marshall, like Edwards, will likely retain his job by default.

Oakland Raiders

2016 Record: 12-4	Total DVOA: 8.2% (10th)	2017 Mean Projection: 8.8 wins	On the Clock (0-4): 5%
Pythagorean Wins: 8.8 (12th)	Offense: 12.2% (8th)	Postseason Odds: 50.4%	Mediocrity (5-7): 25%
Snap-Weighted Age: 26.6 (14th)	Defense: 4.3% (22nd)	Super Bowl Odds: 7.4%	Playoff Contender (8-10): 43%
Average Opponent: 1.0% (14th)	Special Teams: 0.3% (14th)	Proj. Avg. Opponent: 0.4% (11th)	Super Bowl Contender (11+): 26%

2016: Sweet emotion, but the Raiders' return to the playoffs is short-lived.

2017: Sweet regression, but Connor Cook probably isn't getting a playoff start again.

For the first time since 2003, the Raiders enter a season with actual winning expectations. Back then, Oakland was a veteran club trying to regroup from a crushing Super Bowl loss. This is a younger team with an emerging quarterback, who finished third in MVP voting, and the reigning Defensive Player of the Year. Oakland finally ended its long playoff drought with a surprising 12-4 season, but the playoffs were almost an afterthought once Derek Carr broke his leg in Week 16. To make matters worse, the Raiders lost backup Matt McGloin a week later, forcing rookie fourth-round pick Connor Cook to make his first start in the playoffs. Naturally, Cook was overwhelmed in Houston, the offense finished 2-of-16 on third down, and the Raiders fell 27-14.

Carr was already back to full health for OTAs. He'll return behind one of the league's top offensive lines, playing alongside unretired local hero Marshawn Lynch. The defense spawns optimism of the "it can't get worse" variety; despite the presence of Khalil Mack, the Raiders ranked 32nd in net yards allowed per pass last season. Conventional wisdom says that Oakland is as likely as any team, including Pittsburgh, to challenge the Patriots in a parity-lacking AFC. If the Steelers are just going to keep losing to New England in the same fashion that they always do, then why can't this be Oakland's year to rage against the machine?

The main problem with this thinking is that Oakland's track record of success is limited to one season, and it was atypical for a 12-4 season. In fact, Oakland's plus-31 scoring differential is the smallest in NFL history for a 12-win team (Table 1).

Table 1. 12-4 Teams with Lowest Scoring Differential, 1978-2016

Team	Year	W-L	Pt Dif	Result	W-L Y+1	Pt Dif	Result
OAK	2016	12-4	+31	Lost AFC-WC	TBD	-	-
DET	1991	12-4	+44	Lost NFC-CG	5-11	-59	No Playoffs
LARD	1985	12-4	+46	Lost AFC-DIV	8-8	-23	No Playoffs
DEN	2015	12-4	+59	Won SB	9-7	+36	No Playoffs
IND	2006	12-4	+67	Won SB	13-3	+188	Lost AFC-DIV
LARD	1990	12-4	+69	Lost AFC-CG	9-7	+1	Lost AFC-WC
DEN	1991	12-4	+69	Lost AFC-CG	8-8	-67	No Playoffs
GB	2002	12-4	+70	Lost NFC-WC	10-6	+135	Lost AFC-DIV

The next three teams on that list all failed to make the playoffs the following season, including the Raiders in 1986.

Oakland's 8.2% DVOA is the seventh lowest for a 12-win team since 1986. Each of the six teams lower than the Raiders won fewer games the next year, and only teams with Peyton Manning (2000 Colts) and Brett Favre (2003 Packers) at quarterback still finished 10-6 to make the playoffs again. However, wouldn't the Raiders probably sign up for a guaranteed 10-6 playoff season with Carr healthy this time? After 13 straight losing seasons, this should sound like a sweet deal.

It is not an insult to believe that the Raiders will regress and win fewer games this season. Stacking 12-win seasons is a very difficult thing to do in this league. Joe Montana, Steve Young, Roger Staubach, Drew Brees, Aaron Rodgers, Ben Roethlisberger, and Matt Ryan have never stacked together consecutive 12-win seasons, to give a few notable examples. A team basically has to have Peyton Manning or Tom Brady at quarterback to consistently win 12 games a year, and Carr is not at that level yet. Last year's team was rough around the edges despite the record, and the inability to beat Kansas City limited them to a wild-card berth. Lesser competition also tended to give the Raiders all they could handle.

If not for Detroit's record-breaking eight late-game triumphs last season, there might have been more attention paid to what Oakland did in the fourth quarter. The Raiders had seven fourth-quarter comeback wins in the regular season, a mark only the 2009 Colts had reached prior to 2016. The Raiders lived on the edge all season, and managed an incredible 7-2 record on fourth-quarter comeback opportunities. As we covered further in the Detroit chapter (page 77), teams like this almost always regress the following season, winning fewer games overall and especially producing a worse record in close games. In the first two seasons with Carr at quarterback (2014-15), the Raiders were 5-13 in such games, so 7-2 is a huge difference. Carr's play was impressive at times in these moments, but he also got away with what could have been a game-ending interception, dropped by Eric Weddle when the Raiders trailed Baltimore 27-21 with 2:12 left. On the very next play, Carr threw a game-winning touchdown pass to Michael Crabtree. It was that kind of season for Oakland.

The much-maligned Oakland defense also did a very good job at closing games out, protecting the leads the offense provided. The Raiders were 2016's only team to not lose a game

2017 Raiders Schedule

Week	Opp.	Week	Opp.	Week	Opp.
1	at TEN	7	KC (Thu.)	13	NYG
2	NYJ	8	at BUF	14	at KC
3	at WAS	9	at MIA	15	DAL
4	at DEN	10	BYE	16	at PHI (Mon./Xmas)
5	BAL	11	NE (Mex.)	17	at LACH
6	LACH	12	DEN		

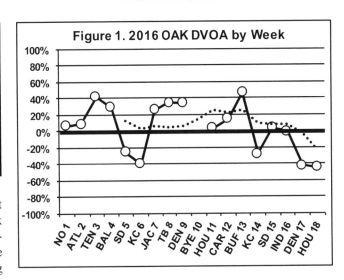

Figure 1. 2016 OAK DVOA by Week

with a fourth-quarter lead. That includes holding up one-point leads against the Saints and Ravens, and getting a strip-sack from Khalil Mack against Cam Newton to finish off the Panthers in a 35-32 game. The defense also received help from the bumbling Chargers, who botched the snap on a game-tying 36-yard field goal in Week 5 and then fumbled in their own end to help Oakland's comeback in Week 15.

Head coach Jack Del Rio is no stranger to rolling the dice. He entered 2016 ranked eighth in Aggressiveness Index (AI) on fourth down among head coaches with at least 50 attempts since 1989. While the Raiders were only 11th in AI this season, their gambles often paid off. There were eight fourth-down plays in which Del Rio let Carr and the offense go for it in the late stages of the game, and the offense converted five times, including three touchdown passes. Against San Diego, the Raiders could have kicked a field goal late in the third quarter, but Del Rio went for it on fourth-and-3, and Carr's 21-yard touchdown pass to Michael Crabtree put the Raiders ahead for the rest of the game. Carr's game-winning touchdown pass in overtime to Seth Roberts in Tampa Bay was also a fourth-down call. This does not even include the Week 1 decision when Del Rio went for a two-point conversion in New Orleans to give his team a 35-34 lead with 47 seconds left. A failure to convert likely would have led to a failed onside kick and a 34-33 loss. Instead, the last-minute win set the tone for the wild season Oakland had up until the Carr injury.

Oakland also had the league's best starting field position differential at plus-6.26. That is the eighth-best mark for any team since 2002. While some teams have been able to consistently dominate field position over multiple seasons—namely,

Table 2. Most Accepted Penalties in a Season, NFL History

Rk	Team	Year	W-L	Penalties	Yards
1	OAK	2011	8-8	163	1,358
2	KC	1998	7-9	158	1,304
3	LARD	1994	9-7	156	1,186
3	OAK	1996	7-9	156	1,266
5	HOIL	1989	9-7	149	1,153
6	LARD	1993	10-6	148	1,181
6	OAK	2010	8-8	148	1,279
8	OAK	2005	4-12	147	1,132
8	**OAK**	**2016**	**12-4**	**147**	**1,247**
10	ARI	2005	5-11	145	1,184

Jim Harbaugh's 49ers (2011-2013) and the Patriots—most don't. Just two seasons before in 2014, Oakland was minus-8.30 in field position differential, the worst of the 480 teams since 2002.

Penalties were also favorable to the Raiders in 2016. This sounds odd because Oakland led the NFL with 147 accepted penalties, tied for eighth in NFL history. Seven of the top nine seasons in penalties belong to the Raiders, keeping alive their reputation as the NFL's bad boys (Table 2). Since 2002, 20 teams have been called for more than 30 penalties than their opponents, and Oakland has eight of those 20 slots.

The young Oakland offense led the league with 73 accepted penalties last year. Is that more harmful than a defense that leads the league in penalties? There is basically zero correlation between win percentage and total penalties or penalty yards, including as a beneficiary too. However, there is a difference when things are broken down by offense and defense. Since 2002, offensive penalties and winning percentage have a correlation of minus-0.22, compared to minus-0.03 correlation between defensive penalties and winning percentage. Penalties can be a nuisance, but aggressive play on defense is often a good thing in the NFL, and some really good teams, dating back to Paul Brown's Cleveland teams in the 1950s, have been among the most penalized in the league. It's not like officials are brave enough to call everything, so test the waters, and do your best to avoid the significant penalties in crucial moments.

In those crucial moments, the penalties mostly swung in Oakland's favor. Leaguewide last season, there were seven offensive plays in the fourth quarter on fourth down that earned a first down via penalty. Carr and the Raiders were the beneficiaries of three of those seven calls. For example, Oakland set an NFL record with 23 penalties in its overtime win in Tampa Bay in Week 8. However, the biggest call of the game went in Oakland's favor. Down 24-17 with 1:49 left, Carr faced a fourth-and-3 at the Tampa Bay 5. He badly missed Crabtree in the end zone, but the Buccaneers were flagged for a soft defensive holding penalty that was inconsequential to the play. One play later, Carr threw the game-tying touchdown and Oakland eventually won in overtime.

Similarly, the Raiders started the season getting a break on a fourth-and-5 in New Orleans with 1:37 left. Carr missed a throw out of bounds, but the Saints were still penalized for defensive pass interference even though the pass looked uncatchable. (Carr actually had 19 flags drawn for defensive pass interference in 2016, the most by any quarterback in a season in our database.) Two plays later, Carr threw the go-ahead touchdown and game-winning two-point conversion pass.

There is a pattern here. The Raiders avoid a near calamity, and Carr throws a significant touchdown pass. That is how thin the margin was between this team going 12-4 versus 8-8 at best. While that usually works both ways, Oakland was fairly outclassed in its losses last season.

Carr will be the focal point again in Oakland this season, and that should be the case for years to come. In June, Oakland signed Carr to a record-breaking five-year extension worth $125 million, making Carr the first $25 million-per-season player in NFL history. While that sounds outrageous given Carr's meager list of career achievements, this is the current status of the quarterback market. Next year we will surely write about how Kirk Cousins or Matthew Stafford has topped Carr's contract.

Carr showed his biggest improvement from his rookie season to his second year, but his third season was his best yet. Should we expect to see him continue to rise in Year 4? The gut may say yes, but NFL history is filled with examples of promising young quarterbacks, especially those on teams that were still developing, who did not deliver in their fourth seasons. To research this, we looked for quarterbacks who met two requirements: they had a third season better than their first two, and they had a third-season passer rating index higher than 105 (Carr's was 110) as listed at Pro Football Reference. This way we did not consider early breakouts such as Dan Marino, Daunte Culpepper, Ben Roethlisberger, or Russell Wilson.

Ultimately, we found 24 quarterbacks that qualified, including Carr. Fifteen of the other 23 declined in their fourth seasons. In some cases, a preseason injury was the culprit, robbing Roger Staubach (1972) and Chad Pennington (2003) of a proper fourth season. Even Joe Montana (for the last time as a starter) missed the playoffs in his fourth season, as San Francisco had a 3-6 record in a strike-shortened 1982.

Some of Carr's contemporaries, including players to whom he has drawn direct comparisons, offer the best cautionary tales. Peyton Manning had another stellar season for the Colts in 2000, but his defense declined to the worst in the league in 2001, and he missed the playoffs for the last time in his career with a 6-10 record. Matthew Stafford and Andrew Luck each had 40-touchdown seasons in their third year, but regressed the following year. Luck's play in 2015 was poor even before a lacerated kidney ended his season. Cam Newton really struggled in 2014, finishing 5-8-1 as a starter and 33rd in passing DVOA, and he was fortunate that the NFC South was so historically bad that he still made the playoffs that year. Carson Palmer might be the best comparison for Carr, since he too once led a struggling franchise (Cincinnati) back to the

playoffs in his third year with an offense that featured two very good wide receivers. Palmer's season ended in the wild-card round after he tore his ACL on his first pass, dooming the Bengals the way Carr's injury doomed the Raiders' playoff chances last season. Palmer was able to return with a good, but less-efficient season in 2006, and the Bengals missed the playoffs at 8-8.

On the flip side, we only found eight notable quarterbacks since 1950 who really blossomed in their fourth seasons. Johnny Unitas (1959), Joe Namath (1968), and Troy Aikman (1992) each won a championship in arguably the most iconic season of their Hall of Fame careers. The other five examples are really just guys who operated at peak efficiency in their fourth season, and are best known to NFL statheads: Milt Plum (1960), Ken Anderson (1974), Bert Jones (1976), Neil Lomax (1984), and Jim "Chris" Everett (1989). Jones in particular had a really strong MVP season for the Baltimore Colts in 1974, and Carr would definitely be living up to a new contract and the hype if he played anything like *that* in 2017. Despite the six MVP votes he received in 2016, Carr's season was not up to par with his peers who were also on ballots (Table 3).

Table 3. Quarterbacks Receiving MVP Votes in 2016

Quarterback	MVP Votes	Pass DYAR	Rk	Pass DVOA	Rk	QBR	Rk	Pass YPA	Rk
Matt Ryan	25	1,918	1	40.2%	1	83.3	1	9.26	1
Tom Brady	10	1,295	5	33.8%	2	83.0	2	8.23	2
Derek Carr	**6**	**1,169**	**7**	**19.9%**	**6**	**62.1**	**16**	**7.03**	**18**
Aaron Rodgers	2	1,251	6	18.2%	8	76.9	4	7.26	14
Dak Prescott	1	1,301	4	31.5%	3	81.5	3	7.99	4

One of the key statistical areas where Carr has always underperformed in the NFL is in yards per pass attempt (YPA). We'll just forget his abysmal rookie season for a second, but even in 2015 Carr only ranked 26th at 6.96 YPA. This past season he ranked 18th at 7.03, below league average, barely beating out Sam Bradford (7.02) and Trevor Siemian (7.00).

A big part of this is Carr's odd playing style. He would win an award for Most Cautious Gunslinger, if such a thing existed. If any quarterback embodies the "touchdown or checkdown" mentality, it is Carr. His great arm gives him the confidence to try fitting any throw into a small window or against tight coverage, and that plays a big factor in the number of pass interference flags he is able to draw. However, he also loves to get rid of the ball quickly despite usually strong pass protection. Carr's knockdown rate of 6.3 percent was the lowest in 2016, and he now has the sixth-lowest sack rate (3.94 percent) in NFL history. Carr also loves checkdowns almost as much as AFC West rival Alex Smith. In fact, Carr set a single-game record (since 1989) for failed completions[1] with 16 against Tampa Bay last year. In 2016, Carr finished 29th in

---

1 i.e. completions that don't meet Football Outsiders' baselines for a successful play given the down and distance.

failed completion rate, 27th in ALEX (all downs), and 23rd in passing plus-minus. He has shown neither the accuracy nor the aggressiveness that typifies a quarterback pulling in a salary of roughly $25 million per season.

Carr and this offense are still growing together. You could see moments of brilliance last season, as well as plays that were just a tad off. For instance, Carr had seven incompletions that were caught out of bounds, the most of any 2016 quarterback. Five of those plays were in the end zone, and Amari Cooper was the target on four of them. Sometimes the throw was just off, and sometimes the receiver needed to show better awareness with his feet and the boundary line. Carr also had the fourth-highest dropped pass rate in 2016. The Raiders can't continue to miss opportunities like this given how heavily they rely on the offense to deliver.

For the Raiders to win the AFC West this season, they will likely have to beat the Chiefs at least once. Kansas City has won five straight in the rivalry, and Carr has yet to have a good game against Bob Sutton's defense. Oakland's offense has not cracked 20 points in any of the five losses. Carr's YPA is a miniscule 4.92 against Kansas City, compared to 6.72 against the rest of the NFL. In his last shot at the Chiefs in December, Carr threw for 117 yards on 41 attempts (2.85 YPA), his MVP chances fading with the night in a 21-13 loss. That was only the second time in NFL history that a quarterback passed for fewer than 120 yards on at least 40 attempts. Jesse "The Bachelor" Palmer did it in 2003, and while he also looks dreamy, that is not the company any quarterback wants to keep.

Kansas City has done a wonderful job against this offense. The pass rush has gotten to Carr, and the secondary has held up well against the receivers. Carr has 14 games in his 47-game career with at least a 25.0 percent pressure rate, and four of those games were against the Chiefs. According to ESPN's data, three of Carr's four worst games in terms of off-target pass percentage have come against the Chiefs. Last season, the Chiefs decided not to blitz Carr. He has four games in his career where he has faced a blitz rate under 15.0 percent, and two of them were against Kansas City last year. The defense still pressured him well and forced him into bad throws. The Chiefs were the only 2016 defense to hold the Carr-led Raiders under 17 points, and they did it twice.

To help Carr out this year, the Raiders added Cordarrelle Patterson (kick returner and bubble-screen catcher) and tight end Jared Cook (occasional spectacular catch maven), but perhaps the most interesting addition is Marshawn Lynch coming out of retirement to play for his hometown Raiders. "Beast Mode" was one of the best in the game just a few years ago with Seattle, but his 2015 season did not go well, partly due to health. After an early retirement a year ago, Lynch is back at age 31, because what other profession allows you to run through a motherfucker's face for money?

Lynch's toughness after contact is certainly a departure from speed back Latavius Murray, who left in free agency for Minnesota. Murray only ranked 23rd in rushing DVOA in 2016, but young backs Jalen Richard and DeAndre Washington both flashed big-play potential with more than 5.4 yards per carry each. Even fullback Jamize Olawale had a 75-yard

reception, so the backs weren't a weakness on the team a year ago. The Raiders could just use a little more balance and consistency from a lead back, which is something Lynch used to provide well for Seattle. He still won't be much of a receiver in Oakland, but he could take double-digit carries each week. The offensive line is built more for pass protection, which is not something Lynch is used to from his time in Seattle, but the Raiders can run-block with some of the best lines in the league too.

For a running back in his thirties returning from a year out of action, there are not many historical comparisons for Lynch. Only two running backs have ever returned from a true "gap year" to rush for at least 600 yards in a season in their thirties. Washington's John Riggins sat out the 1980 season over a contract dispute before returning to rush for 714 yards at age 32 in 1981. Garrison Hearst is a modern medical miracle after he returned from a broken ankle and avascular necrosis to rush for 1,206 yards at age 30 for the 49ers in 2001. He actually missed both the 1999 and 2000 seasons for rehab. Finally, it is worth noting that Denver's Mike Anderson missed the 2004 season due to torn groin muscles, but he suffered those in the preseason, so he technically did try to play that year. Anderson returned at age 32 in 2005 to rush for 1,014 yards and 12 touchdowns.

We don't know if Lynch's healthy year off will neutralize the effects of general aging, but he's a back with a lot of wear and tear on his body. There have been 24 1,000-yard rushing seasons by running backs age 31 or older, but Frank Gore (twice) is the only player to do so in the last seven seasons. The NFL has moved away from hanging onto older backs, but Oakland is taking a small risk—Lynch's 2017 cap hit is $2.9 million—to see if someone with a borderline Hall of Fame case can put the team over the top.

General manager Reggie McKenzie's moves on offense have generally been working, but the defense is a different story. Del Rio hasn't had much impact as a defensive-minded coach, and it was very strange to see the Defensive Player of the Year (Khalil Mack) come from a defense that ranked 23rd in DVOA, including 25th against the pass. Mack was quite good, of course, tied for third in the NFL with 50 total quarterback hurries. His sacks dipped down to 11.0, but that was because of a slow start where he had one sack in five games. Still, the pressure was there from him, and the sacks eventually came. Bruce Irvin came over from Seattle and formed a pretty solid pass-rushing duo with Mack, producing 38 of his own pressures.

The problem was a lack of support from the rest of the defense, including a revolving door at defensive line that produced little in the form of pass rush. The other linebackers, including Malcolm Smith and Cory James, also struggled against the run and in pass coverage.

Perhaps the most disappointing piece of the defense was cornerback Sean Smith, a prized free-agent addition from Kansas City who struggled in his first year with the Raiders. Smith finished 84th in adjusted yards per pass out of 87 ranked cornerbacks. Cornerback metrics tend to have a lot of variation from year to year, but the eye test certainly agreed with the numbers that Smith was far from a lockdown corner. The team made a controversial draft selection to strengthen the position, taking Ohio State cornerback Gareon Conley 24th overall. Conley reportedly passed a polygraph test issued by the Raiders following accusations that he raped a woman in a Cleveland hotel earlier in April. Conley has not been charged and has strongly denied the accusation. This is just one early career hurdle he will face, but for on-field purposes, the Raiders should have a starter-caliber player here. It is just unfair to assume that a rookie corner will be a difference-maker, especially against the likes of Brandin Cooks (Patriots) and Antonio Brown (Steelers).

There is the sentiment that Oakland just needed a healthy Carr to win in the playoffs, and that may have been true against the Texans, but it is unlikely that the defense would have gotten the job done in New England the following week. If the Raiders could make Brock Osweiler look competent, then imagine what Tom Brady could have done to a Del Rio-schemed defense that he has terrorized throughout his career. Seriously, Osweiler had two games with a QBR above 80.0 in 2016, and both were against Oakland, including his season-high 85.4 QBR in the wild-card win.

Oakland still has a long way to go on defense before we can expect playoff success against the AFC's offensively-potent contenders such as New England and Pittsburgh. Shootouts will likely be needed, and that has just never been a formula for deep playoff runs.

Finally, we have to consider the potential impact of the schedule. Last season's 12-4 record was built against a schedule that had very few lightweights and ranked 10th in terms of difficulty. It was loaded with teams that hovered around .500, but Oakland finished 0-3 against double-digit-win teams. This season's schedule features a very tough slate following Oakland's Week 10 bye. After getting the Patriots in Mexico City, the Raiders host the Broncos and Giants, travel for a huge matchup at Arrowhead Stadium, and then wrap up a grueling five-game stretch against Dallas, last year's top seed in the NFC. Oakland ends the season with road games against the Eagles and Chargers, who are hardly pushovers either.

The saving grace is that Oakland definitely has the better draw of the schedule than rival Kansas City, which has to play the Patriots, Cowboys, and Giants on the road. The Raiders will get all three of those opponents at "home," even if the Mexico City game with the Patriots is really a neutral site. Oakland also doesn't have to play AFC runner-up Pittsburgh like the Chiefs will in Week 6. Still, those head-to-head games are most likely to determine the AFC West again, but the Raiders even get a little schedule advantage there when they host the Chiefs on a Thursday night (short week) in Week 7.

Oakland is one of the trendy Super Bowl picks this year, although some of that is just New England fatigue. However, the Patriots remain the safest bet to win it all, while the Raiders are a great bet to be a team that plays better than it did a year ago, but does not see it reflected in the win-loss record. Oakland is still too rough around the edges to reliably make that deep playoff run, but even the slightest improvement on both sides of the ball still makes this team the favorite in the AFC West. It's just that come playoff time, the Raiders are most likely to take their lumps in Gillette Stadium or Heinz Field rather than host the AFC Championship Game. It is best to save those Raiders Super Bowl tokens for the future when the team is in the best place to spend tokens: Las Vegas.

Scott Kacsmar

2016 Raiders Stats by Week

Wk	vs.	W-L	PF	PA	YDF	YDA	TO	Total	Off	Def	ST
1	at NO	W	35	34	486	507	+1	7%	21%	19%	4%
2	ATL	L	28	35	454	528	+1	9%	46%	21%	-17%
3	at TEN	W	17	10	368	393	+2	42%	9%	-25%	8%
4	at BAL	W	28	27	261	412	0	29%	18%	8%	20%
5	SD	W	34	31	389	423	+3	-26%	-1%	24%	0%
6	KC	L	10	26	285	406	-2	-40%	-4%	30%	-6%
7	at JAC	W	33	16	344	344	+3	26%	5%	-11%	9%
8	at TB	W	30	24	626	270	-1	35%	37%	-10%	-12%
9	DEN	W	30	20	397	299	+2	34%	41%	5%	-2%
10	BYE										
11	HOU	W	27	20	325	354	+1	3%	10%	8%	1%
12	CAR	W	35	32	366	358	0	14%	7%	3%	11%
13	BUF	W	38	24	399	382	+2	47%	35%	-2%	10%
14	at KC	L	13	21	244	323	+3	-28%	-16%	-14%	-26%
15	at SD	W	19	16	345	263	0	3%	-23%	-14%	12%
16	IND	W	33	25	463	390	+3	-1%	25%	20%	-5%
17	at DEN	L	6	24	221	349	-2	-43%	-44%	-2%	-1%
18	at HOU	L	14	27	203	291	-3	-45%	-42%	10%	6%

Trends and Splits

	Offense	Rank	Defense	Rank
Total DVOA	12.2%	8	4.3%	22
Unadjusted VOA	9.9%	10	4.4%	22
Weighted Trend	6.9%	11	2.0%	20
Variance	6.0%	15	2.6%	4
Average Opponent	-2.2%	5	-0.8%	21
Passing	35.8%	4	15.1%	25
Rushing	-2.3%	16	-8.4%	17
First Down	10.3%	7	7.2%	25
Second Down	6.3%	11	5.1%	22
Third Down	26.2%	4	-2.7%	13
First Half	8.8%	11	-3.7%	14
Second Half	5.1%	12	19.2%	30
Red Zone	8.1%	12	8.7%	26
Late and Close	3.8%	14	29.8%	30

Five-Year Performance

Year	W-L	Pyth W	Est W	PF	PA	TO	Total	Rk	Off	Rk	Def	Rk	ST	Rk	Off AGL	Rk	Def AGL	Rk	Off Age	Rk	Def Age	Rk	ST Age	Rk
2012	4-12	4.1	3.7	290	443	-7	-27.8%	29	-9.5%	23	12.5%	29	-5.8%	31	31.8	19	35.0	20	27.1	13	27.5	9	26.6	8
2013	4-12	4.9	2.1	322	453	-9	-34.1%	31	-16.7%	28	10.3%	26	-7.1%	31	49.7	26	27.2	15	26.7	17	27.6	5	26.1	16
2014	3-13	3.1	4.8	253	452	-15	-27.4%	29	-19.4%	30	6.3%	26	-1.7%	18	26.1	11	77.5	32	26.5	22	27.7	4	26.2	11
2015	7-9	6.9	7.4	359	399	+1	0.1%	14	-1.3%	18	-1.5%	15	-0.1%	19	23.7	8	33.9	22	26.2	20	26.6	17	27.2	1
2016	12-4	8.8	8.9	416	385	+16	8.2%	10	12.2%	8	4.3%	22	0.3%	14	32.5	13	32.4	15	26.5	21	26.6	13	26.9	5

2016 Performance Based on Most Common Personnel Groups

OAK Offense					OAK Offense vs. Opponents					OAK Defense					OAK Defense vs. Opponents			
Pers	Freq	Yds	DVOA	Run%	Pers	Freq	Yds	DVOA	Run%	Pers	Freq	Yds	DVOA		Pers	Freq	Yds	DVOA
11	55%	6.3	25.3%	27%	Base	30%	5.5	3.0%	55%	Base	44%	6.3	6.4%		11	52%	6.9	10.8%
611	11%	4.9	-5.8%	69%	Nickel	49%	6.4	28.4%	31%	Nickel	53%	6.3	0.6%		12	18%	5.0	-28.7%
12	7%	5.6	16.8%	35%	Dime+	18%	6.1	24.4%	22%	Dime+	1%	10.0	75.8%		21	12%	5.4	6.9%
610	5%	5.3	-6.9%	45%	Goal Line	2%	0.6	35.8%	82%	Goal Line	1%	2.2	26.4%		13	5%	8.5	54.4%
21	4%	7.8	22.3%	34%	Big	1%	4.4	-24.5%	69%	Big	1%	1.6	-20.4%		22	4%	6.6	14.9%
612	4%	2.8	-35.1%	87%											10	2%	5.1	-54.2%
20	3%	5.9	40.0%	26%														
22	3%	8.3	45.8%	52%														

Strategic Tendencies

Run/Pass		Rk	Formation		Rk	Pass Rush		Rk	Secondary		Rk	Strategy		Rk
Runs, first half	37%	16	Form: Single Back	78%	17	Rush 3	4.9%	21	4 DB	44%	3	Play-action	15%	27
Runs, first down	45%	23	Form: Empty Back	11%	3	Rush 4	67.1%	13	5 DB	53%	24	Avg Box (Off)	6.15	22
Runs, second-long	36%	6	Pers: 3+ WR	67%	14	Rush 5	22.9%	12	6+ DB	1%	27	Avg Box (Def)	6.40	4
Runs, power sit.	55%	19	Pers: 2+ TE/6+ OL	34%	7	Rush 6+	5.2%	21	CB by Sides	89%	8	Offensive Pace	30.78	19
Runs, behind 2H	30%	9	Pers: 6+ OL	24%	1	Sacks by LB	32.0%	17	S/CB Cover Ratio	25%	22	Defensive Pace	29.82	10
Pass, ahead 2H	47%	19	Shotgun/Pistol	69%	10	Sacks by DB	0.0%	30	DB Blitz	5%	30	Go for it on 4th	1.16	11

The Raiders led the league in usage of six-lineman sets, with an extra lineman on 24 percent of plays. No other team was above 16 percent. The Raiders gained 4.7 yards per play with six linemen, higher than the NFL average of 3.9, but they had just -4.1% DVOA. One-third of these plays were passes. ≋ When the Raiders didn't go heavy, they went light. They ranked third in usage of empty backfields, and they were awesome on those plays: 7.1 yards per play and 46.7% DVOA. ≋ Raiders receivers dropped fewer passes than in years past, but still ranked 23rd in drop rate. They've ranked 23rd or worse in drop rate for five straight seasons. ≋ Derek Carr was better against the blitz than he was against a regular pass rush. Carr had 6.8 yards per play against four pass-rushers or fewer, but 7.9 yards per play against a blitz. That included 8.2 yards per play against DB blitzes with 91.2% DVOA, highest in the NFL. Carr was also better against the blitz in 2015, though he was worse as a rookie in 2014. ≋ The Raiders allowed a league-high 5.7 average yards after the catch. They had issues both on passes behind the line of scrimmage (9.7 YAC, 28th) and passes beyond the line of scrimmage (4.8 YAC, 32nd). ≋ And yet for some reason, opponents didn't try to slow down Khalil Mack with screen passes—a strategy which would make even more sense given Oakland's propensity for giving up yards after the catch. The Raiders faced only 24 wide receiver screens, below the NFL average, and only 12 running back screens, which was tied for 29th in the league. ≋ Related: Oakland opponents threw a league-low 14 percent of passes to running backs. ≋ Oakland gave up 9.67 yards per pass on play-action passes. That was the worst figure in the league by 0.33 yards per pass, although four teams had a worse defensive DVOA than Oakland's 48.7%.

Passing

Player	DYAR	DVOA	Plays	NtYds	Avg	YAC	C%	TD	Int
D.Carr	1164	19.8%	575	3833	6.7	5.1	64.2%	28	6
C.Cook	-21	-23.9%	23	141	6.1	6.1	66.7%	1	1
M.McGloin*	6	-4.0%	15	50	3.3	1.1	53.3%	0	0
EJ Manuel	-58	-47.2%	29	112	3.9	2.5	42.3%	0	0

Rushing

Player	DYAR	DVOA	Plays	Yds	Avg	TD	Fum	Suc
L.Murray*	139	10.3%	162	656	4.0	12	0	51%
J.Richard	53	13.1%	68	386	5.7	1	0	47%
D.Washington	11	-4.4%	63	302	4.8	2	0	49%
D.Carr	-47	-64.9%	19	72	3.8	0	0	-
J.Olawale	-1	-9.4%	17	47	2.8	2	0	35%
J.Holton	16	25.0%	5	43	8.6	0	0	-

Receiving

Player	DYAR	DVOA	Plays	Ctch	Yds	Y/C	YAC	TD	C%
M.Crabtree	212	5.3%	145	89	1003	11.3	2.8	8	61%
A.Cooper	231	8.8%	132	83	1153	13.9	5.3	5	63%
S.Roberts	-37	-18.6%	77	38	397	10.4	5.3	5	49%
A.Holmes*	6	-9.9%	25	14	126	9.0	1.9	3	56%
C.Patterson	17	-9.5%	70	52	453	8.7	6.4	2	74%
C.Walford	9	-4.7%	52	33	359	10.9	3.7	3	63%
M.Rivera*	23	6.4%	25	18	192	10.7	3.4	1	72%
L.Smith	-12	-40.6%	6	6	29	4.8	5.3	0	100%
J.Cook	-15	-11.5%	51	30	377	12.6	4.9	1	59%
L.Murray*	10	-9.4%	43	33	264	8.0	8.5	0	77%
J.Richard	9	-8.8%	39	29	194	6.7	4.9	2	74%
D.Washington	1	-12.9%	23	17	115	6.8	6.8	0	74%
J.Olawale	71	84.8%	14	12	227	18.9	14.4	1	86%

Offensive Line

Player	Pos	Age	GS	Snaps	Pen	Sk	Pass	Run	Player	Pos	Age	GS	Snaps	Pen	Sk	Pass	Run
Rodney Hudson	C	28	16/16	1119	8	0.0	3	5	Austin Howard	RT	30	11/10	721	3	5.5	18	5
Gabe Jackson	RG	26	16/16	1118	6	0.5	5	3	Vadal Alexander	G/T	23	9/5	305	10	0.0	1	3
Donald Penn	LT	34	16/16	1111	10	2.5	7	8	Menelik Watson*	RT	29	10/5	255	4	1.0	2	2
Kelechi Osemele	LG	28	15/15	1041	7	0.0	5	6	Marshall Newhouse	RT	29	10/6	461	4	2.0	3	2

Year	Yards	ALY	Rank	Power	Rank	Stuff	Rank	2nd Lev	Rank	Open Field	Rank	Sacks	ASR	Rank	Press	Rank	F-Start	Cont.
2014	3.80	3.81	28	55%	29	21%	21	0.94	31	0.65	18	28	4.4%	3	24.6%	18	17	32
2015	3.98	4.02	19	72%	7	18%	6	1.02	26	0.74	15	33	4.6%	4	20.7%	3	28	33
2016	4.66	4.39	11	59%	23	17%	8	1.28	8	1.00	7	18	3.4%	1	17.7%	1	24	31

2016 ALY by direction:	Left End 3.72 (25)	Left Tackle 5.15 (3)	Mid/Guard 4.51 (5)	Right Tackle 3.50 (25)	Right End 2.55 (31)

Non-breaking news: the Oakland offensive line is excellent, featuring three Pro Bowl selections last year. It was the first year since 2002 that any Oakland offensive lineman made the Pro Bowl, and the first time the offensive line had three Pro Bowlers since 1977. The team has come a long way from the Robert Gallery days. ☞ Left tackle Donald Penn (eighth), left guard Kelechi Osemele (seventh), center Rodney Hudson (seventh), and right guard Gabe Jackson (fourth) all ranked in the top eight at their positions in snaps per blown block. All return to the starting lineup this season. ☞ The weak spot was right tackle, where Austin Howard (33rd in snaps per blown block) and Menelik Watson (an athletic prospect who never panned out) struggled. Howard had surgery in January for a torn labrum and rotator cuff, and he should remain the starter. Watson departed for Denver in free agency. Newly signed backup Marshall Newhouse has spent most of his career as a turnstile, so it's not like there's an improvement ready on the roster. ☞ Howard did at least one thing well: avoiding penalties. He had only three. The other four Oakland linemen had at least six penalties each. Even Vadal Alexander, the team's sixth offensive lineman, picked up 10 penalties on only 305 offensive snaps.

Defensive Front Seven

Defensive Line	Age	Pos	G	Snaps	Plays	Overall TmPct	Rk	Stop	Dfts	BTkl	Runs	vs. Run St%	Rk	RuYd	Rk	Pass Rush Sack	Hit	Hur	Dsrpt
Dan Williams*	30	DT	16	366	17	2.2%	--	12	2	0	14	71%	--	2.4	--	0.5	4	8	1
Justin Ellis	27	DT	16	336	21	2.7%	--	17	2	0	21	81%	--	1.8	--	0.0	0	0	0
Darius Latham	23	DT	14	308	18	2.7%	--	13	4	3	14	79%	--	2.0	--	0.0	2	2	1
Stacy McGee*	27	DT	9	220	17	3.9%	--	13	7	0	14	71%	--	2.3	--	2.5	1	3	0

Edge Rushers	Age	Pos	G	Snaps	Plays	Overall TmPct	Rk	Stop	Dfts	BTkl	Runs	vs. Run St%	Rk	RuYd	Rk	Pass Rush Sack	Hit	Hur	Dsrpt
Khalil Mack	26	DE	16	949	75	9.7%	2	57	29	7	54	74%	50	2.6	51	11.0	20	50	3
Bruce Irvin	30	OLB	16	927	58	7.5%	14	40	17	5	39	74%	47	2.1	33	7.0	22	38	2
Denico Autry	27	DE	16	690	31	4.0%	66	28	11	5	24	88%	5	1.4	18	3.0	1	14	2
Jihad Ward	23	DE	16	636	29	3.8%	71	19	4	3	23	70%	71	2.7	56	0.0	8	18	0
Shilique Calhoun	25	OLB	10	170	6	1.2%	--	3	1	1	4	50%	--	3.0	--	0.0	2	3	0

Linebackers	Age	Pos	G	Snaps	Plays	Overall TmPct	Rk	Stop	Dfts	BTkl	Runs	vs. Run St%	Rk	RuYd	Rk	Pass Rush Sack	Hit	Hur	Tgts	vs. Pass Suc%	Rk	AdjYd	Rk	PD	Int
Malcolm Smith*	28	OLB	15	934	106	14.6%	26	53	14	16	56	64%	36	5.2	85	0.0	2	7	49	47%	44	6.3	35	3	1
Perry Riley*	29	MLB	11	628	48	9.0%	65	27	6	3	33	64%	41	3.4	34	0.0	0	3	15	59%	11	4.5	4	1	0
Cory James	24	MLB	16	375	38	4.9%	84	21	6	4	19	74%	7	3.6	46	0.0	0	1	14	28%	82	10.0	79	0	0
Jelani Jenkins	25	OLB	9	372	29	6.0%	79	16	4	5	18	72%	11	3.9	64	0.0	1	2	13	30%	--	7.5	--	1	0

Year	Yards	ALY	Rank	Power	Rank	Stuff	Rank	2nd Level	Rank	Open Field	Rank	Sacks	ASR	Rank	Press	Rank
2014	4.08	4.11	16	62%	12	20%	12	1.13	15	0.72	18	22	4.1%	32	24.4%	19
2015	3.93	4.09	18	53%	4	22%	12	1.07	12	0.72	13	38	5.9%	23	24.1%	25
2016	4.52	4.43	23	63%	17	16%	26	1.13	15	0.98	28	25	4.9%	30	26.9%	17

2016 ALY by direction:	Left End 4.88 (24)	Left Tackle 3.85 (12)	Mid/Guard 4.25 (17)	Right Tackle 5.00 (29)	Right End 5.31 (28)

While Bruce Irvin was a fine addition to the defense last year, this front seven really thrives on Khalil Mack's ability to produce pressure. He had an odd season with zero sacks in the first three games and zero sacks in the last four games (including playoffs), but 11 sacks in between. He went from averaging 2.4 hurries per game through Week 5 to an average of 3.5 hurries in the final 11 games, a stretch that led to him winning the Defensive Player of the Year award. Mack can absolutely get better in his fourth season, but if he doesn't, it is hard to see this unit making a big leap in performance. ≡ Right up the middle is where Oakland generated little push. Justin Ellis and Darius Latham return as probable defensive tackle starters, but combined for just two hurries last season. ≡ All of the Raiders' defensive tackles are part-timers, meaning that the interior rushing burden should fall on either Jihad Ward or Mario Edwards Jr. Ward didn't have a spectacular rookie season, but he still outpaced Edwards' 2015 rookie year in terms of sacks, defeats, and hurries. The latter lost all but two games to a hip injury in 2016, so both former second-rounders should be at similar stages of their development. ≡ Oakland's highest draft pick in the front seven was third-round tackle Eddie Vanderdoes (UCLA). Draft experts raved about his 2014 tape, but he tore his ACL in the first game of 2015, put on a bit too much weight, and never looked the same last season. ≡ At linebacker, Cory James and Malcolm Smith were picked on in coverage. Smith has moved on, and James was only a sixth-round rookie, but he'll have to take on a bigger role this year. ≡ The biggest addition was Jelani Jenkins, who started the last three seasons for Miami. He was reliable against the run, but nothing special in coverage or rushing the passer (six hurries in his last 37 games). Perry Riley, who was clearly Oakland's best three-down linebacker last season, remains a free agent as of now.

Defensive Secondary

Secondary	Age	Pos	G	Snaps	Plays	Overall TmPct	Rk	Stop	Dfts	BTkl	Runs	vs. Run St%	Rk	RuYd	Rk	Tgts	vs. Pass Tgt%	Rk	Dist	Suc%	Rk	AdjYd	Rk	PD	Int
Reggie Nelson	34	FS	16	1049	77	10.0%	39	24	12	8	31	26%	64	9.7	64	30	6.7%	20	15.7	61%	2	9.0	40	13	5
David Amerson	26	CB	15	960	80	11.1%	8	32	16	10	15	33%	55	8.7	66	85	20.6%	60	12.6	48%	56	8.1	56	17	2
Sean Smith	30	CB	15	885	50	6.9%	73	26	11	5	13	54%	16	5.5	20	62	16.4%	18	12.4	49%	44	9.7	84	11	2
Karl Joseph	23	SS	12	593	66	11.4%	21	20	5	0	35	29%	60	7.1	39	24	9.5%	50	15.9	55%	10	6.7	12	5	1
D.J. Hayden*	27	CB	11	477	43	8.1%	54	19	10	0	8	25%	73	14.3	85	50	24.5%	80	12.3	50%	38	8.4	63	6	0
T.J. Carrie	27	CB	16	325	25	3.2%	--	10	4	3	6	50%	--	11.5	--	30	21.2%	--	13.7	51%	--	11.4	--	5	1
Nate Allen*	30	FS	14	231	29	4.3%	--	13	5	2	17	59%	--	4.3	--	8	8.1%	--	14.6	27%	--	14.2	--	3	2

Year	Pass D Rank	vs. #1 WR	Rk	vs. #2 WR	Rk	vs. Other WR	Rk	vs. TE	Rk	vs. RB	Rk
2014	28	16.7%	28	2.5%	18	12.1%	25	-9.1%	10	15.4%	24
2015	16	-4.6%	12	-1.1%	14	4.8%	17	-11.0%	10	17.0%	30
2016	25	-17.0%	4	5.0%	20	6.0%	20	7.7%	23	9.8%	23

In the latest tale of "Cornerback Stats Often Fluctuate," Sean Smith and David Amerson did not deliver for the Raiders in 2016 after both played well in the previous season. Both players had ranked in the top 20 for adjusted yards per pass in 2015, before falling to 84th and 56th, respectively. Smith's performance, which led to multiple benchings during the season, was especially disappointing after he signed on for nearly $10 million per year. D.J Hayden also continued to play poorly, and Oakland did not bring him back for 2017. T.J. Carrie was not targeted often, but had problems allowing big plays after some flashes of potential in the past. Defensive backs coach Marcus Robertson fell on his sword in the offseason, but Del Rio was also not afraid to criticize Smith, and the secondary as a whole, for allowing too many big plays. ✒ Oakland's other secondary additions worked out a lot better than Smith. Safety Reggie Nelson, who was a draft pick by Del Rio's Jaguars in 2007, moved over from Cincinnati to Oakland and continued his strong late-career production. He has made back-to-back Pro Bowls, intercepted 19 passes since turning 30 in 2013 (most in the league over that span), and played in the postseason for six straight years. Unfortunately, his team lost in the wild-card round for the sixth year in a row too, and his Pro Bowl seasons have been for teams that had to start A.J. McCarron and Connor Cook in January. Perhaps this is the year Nelson can finally put his ball-hawking skills to use deep into the playoffs. ✒ Oakland drafted Connecticut safety Obi Melifonwu in the second round, but expect him to replace the 34-year-old Nelson down the road rather than in 2017. Melifonwu needs to refine his mental processing, but the physical tools are beyond drool-worthy: among defensive backs, he ranks in the 95th percentile or better in height, weight, 40 time, vertical jump, and broad jump. ✒ Oakland's future in the secondary could be bright if Melifonwu and rookie first-round cornerback Gareon Conley pan out. Conley allowed a 37 percent completion rate at Ohio State, according to NFL.com. They would form a solid young trio with strong safety Karl Joseph, who missed a quarter of his rookie season due to injury but showed plenty of promise with both coverage and excellent tackling. Joseph was the only defender in the league to make more than 40 solo tackles without getting charted with a broken tackle by Sports Info Solutions.

Special Teams

Year	DVOA	Rank	FG/XP	Rank	Net Kick	Rank	Kick Ret	Rank	Net Punt	Rank	Punt Ret	Rank	Hidden	Rank
2014	-1.7%	18	8.2	5	-5.4	25	-9.3	32	2.7	12	-4.7	24	6.3	6
2015	-0.1%	19	-1.4	20	-6.2	30	-2.3	23	14.0	3	-4.6	23	16.4	2
2016	0.3%	14	-1.6	19	5.3	6	-1.4	15	-5.5	24	4.9	7	13.2	2

"If I'm going to be the punter, I'm going to rock this visor, I'm going to put armbands on, I'm going to wear this swag rag on my side. I'm good." That was what Oakland punter Marquette King told ESPN this offseason about his transition from wide receiver to punter in college. He's not just having fun out there, because King was one of the NFL's most effective punters in 2016, ranking second to only Johnny Hekker in gross punt value by out metrics. The Raiders coverage was poor, leading to negative net punt value. However, in Oakland's defense, this may somewhat be an indicator of our need to figure out some sort of opponent adjustments for our special teams stats. Oakland gave up three returns of 50 or more yards, but two of those (including a 78-yard touchdown) were by Tyreek Hill. The other was a 73-yard return from Atlanta's Eric Weems. ✒ Kicker Sebastian Janikowski returns for his 18th season, but the veteran's placekicking value was below average for the second season in a row. ✒ The big change comes at kick returner, where the Raiders added Cordarrelle Patterson, who led all players in kick return value in 2015 and 2016. He is no stranger to returning the ball from deep in the end zone, has five career touchdowns on kick returns, and his 30.4 yards per kick return ranks second in NFL history to only Gale Sayers (30.6). However, keep in mind he only averages 33.5 kick returns per season, or a little more than two per game. The NFL has made sure kick returns are a less significant part of the game in the name of safety, but Patterson is as good as anyone in this department. The Raiders have produced negative value on kick returns every year since 2011, a streak which should end this season. ✒ Jalen Richard should remain as the team's punt returner, and he had some moderate success last season, ranking ninth in individual punt return value.

Philadelphia Eagles

2016 Record: 7-9	**Total DVOA:** 14.4% (5th)	**2017 Mean Projection:** 7.9 wins	**On the Clock (0-4):** 10%
Pythagorean Wins: 9.0 (10th)	**Offense:** -5.5% (20th)	**Postseason Odds:** 33.4%	**Mediocrity (5-7):** 34%
Snap-Weighted Age: 27.0 (7th)	**Defense:** -12.4% (4th)	**Super Bowl Odds:** 4.8%	**Playoff Contender (8-10):** 39%
Average Opponent: 5.7% (2nd)	**Special Teams:** 7.5% (2nd)	**Proj. Avg. Opponent:** 2.9% (1st)	**Super Bowl Contender (11+):** 17%

2016: The Gang Tries to Clean Up Chip Kelly's Mess.

2017: The Gang Gets Carson Some Weapons.

Carson Wentz's rookie season was a rookie season like any other, only more so.

The highs were dizzying. The lows reached the planet's core. The hype and backlash were contentious and deafening. Dak Prescott and Jared Goff provided a wide set of uprights for great and miserable rookie quarterbacking in 2016, and Wentz doinked his debut season off both uprights and landed on the crossbar on New Year's Day.

Wentz's rookie offseason was a harbinger of the whirlwind of a season to come. The Eagles traded a value pack of draft picks to select him, then plopped him third on the depth chart. Sam Bradford left South Philly in a huff when Wentz arrived, then returned for OTAs when he remembered how much money his brand of sturdy mediocrity is worth, then got shipped off to Minnesota when Teddy Bridgewater got injured. Wentz, whose deep passes had a Tebow wobble during minicamp (when coaches fiddled with his throwing mechanics), leapfrogged Chase Daniel and claimed the Opening Day starting job with hours to spare in early September.

Wentz's first few weeks were magical: five touchdowns and zero interceptions in three straight wins over the Browns, Bears, and Steelers by a combined 92-27 score. Philadelphia, Pennsylvania, became Carson City, Wentzylvania. Prescott vs. Wentz was prematurely christened the NFL's next great quarterback rivalry.

But trouble was brewing, and it could be seen with a careful scan of the statistics. Football Outsiders' Scott Kacsmar noted after Week 3 that Wentz ranked second from the bottom of the league in Air Yards, the measure of how far passes travel in the air. Anyone who watched those early Eagles blowouts had to notice that Wentz was completing lots of itsy-bitsy passes (20 completions netted less than 5 yards in those three games) and getting a lot of mileage out of screen passes to Darren Sproles and others (Wentz completed 15 screens for 124 yards in the games in question). It was not a sustainable recipe for success, so Kacsmar wrote and tweeted that the good times would not roll on forever.

Well, you don't want to rile up any local media base in the middle of Coronate the Rookie Quarterback hysteria, especially not the pugnacious Philly legions. For several weeks, Philly bloggers relentlessly attacked Football Outsiders analysts, and golly, it sure was fun to be stuck in the middle.

But while the guys at the NovaCare Complex press annex thumped their chests about the ridiculousness of "Air Yards," a funny thing happened: Wentz's game began to collapse. First, he began getting off to slow starts. The slow starts deteriorated into full-bore early-game turnover jags: three first-quarter turnovers against the Vikings, two first-quarter interceptions against the Giants.

Wentz proved adept at powering through early-game disasters, but something was totally missing from his game: the big passing play. Wentz's longest pass plays against the Lions and Vikings were each 27 yards. In the midseason loss to the Cowboys, his longest pass play gained 20 yards. From Week 7 through Week 12, Wentz's only pass play longer than 27 yards was a screen pass to Zach Ertz that turned into a 54-yard rumble against the Seahawks.

The Eagles remained competitive at the start of Wentz's decline, thanks to good defense, outstanding special teams, and the ability of opponents like the Vikings to trade turnover for turnover. Their first four losses all came by a touchdown or less. In early November, despite a 5-4 record, Philadelphia was somehow sitting at No. 1 in our DVOA ratings: 20th on offense, but first for both defense and special teams. But as soon as the defense faltered even slightly, the Eagles bottomed out in a series of blowout losses. Doug Pederson stuck with Wentz through the lows and some minor injuries, and it paid off with a pair of dignity-restoring late wins, one against a Cowboys team with nothing to play for. But for the season, Wentz was 4-of-32 on passes that traveled 25-plus yards in the air, for 187 yards, two touchdowns and six interceptions. The Eagles utterly lacked deep-pass capability, and it kept them from riding their early-season success into the playoffs.

This being a chapter in a Football Outsiders publication that illustrates how a Football Outsiders statistical principle proved accurate in the face of condemnation and scorn, you probably expect a little back-patting right now. And yes, if a neutral national stat analyst contradicts the local hero-worship narrative after a three-game hot streak, it might be wise to listen to the messengers instead of shooting them. But the Wentz story is not a simple matter of "bad rookie has three fluky starts." There were significant extenuating circumstances last year.

Take the Eagles receivers last year (plz). Jordan Matthews, Nelson Agholor, and Dorial Green-Beckham combined to drop 21 passes, but there was so much more to their misery than dropped passes. Agholor never developed in Chip Kelly's

2017 Eagles Schedule

Week	Opp.	Week	Opp.	Week	Opp.
1	at WAS	7	WAS (Mon.)	13	at SEA
2	at KC	8	SF	14	at LARM
3	NYG	9	DEN	15	at NYG
4	at LACH	10	BYE	16	OAK (Mon./Xmas)
5	ARI	11	at DAL	17	DAL
6	at CAR (Thu.)	12	CHI		

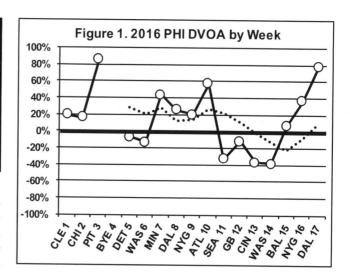

Figure 1. 2016 PHI DVOA by Week

program, which wasn't keen on coaching NFL fundamentals, and suffered an early-season confidence crisis that turned him into one of the NFL's worst regular players. Green-Beckham arrived late in camp and knew about three pass routes by the time he was given a regular role. Matthews was an adequate-at-best No. 2 receiver pretending to be a No. 1 receiver. Behind the three disappointing, fast-fading prospects was nothing but bean dip. Eagles receivers were masters of giving up on contested balls, getting one foot inbounds, and misjudging passes in flight. In addition to the drops, they cost Wentz at least two or three passes per game that a league-average receiving corps would have converted into productive gains. So Wentz checked down (and scrambled, improvised, and took sacks) because downfield reads were rarely open and unlikely to get the job done when they were.

The running game, while effective on a per-play basis, also abandoned the Eagles at the worst possible moments. Ryan Mathews fumbled while running out the clock late in the fourth quarter against the Lions, costing the Eagles a win. Wendell Smallwood impersonated Mathews by coughing one up when the Eagles led 23-16 in the fourth quarter against the Cowboys. That sort of thing never happened to Prescott.

The Eagles loaded up at the skill positions this year to provide Wentz with more support in his second season. Alshon Jeffery replaces Matthews as the No. 1 receiver. Torrey Smith and fifth-round pick Shelton Gibson will compete for the role of designated deep threat. Fourth-round pick Mack Hollins has Green-Beckham's body, but the mind of a student council president. LeGarrette Blount arrives from New England to grind out tough yards without putting the ball on the ground. Fourth-round pick Donnell Pumphrey is Darren Sproles: The Next Generation.

Even with all the changes, Wentz doesn't have a skill-position corps that ranks anywhere near the top five in the league. But last year's units were bottom five. This group is deep, multi-dimensional, and capable. At the start of OTAs, Smith and Jeffrey looked as good as advertised, while Matthews and Agholor were sharper than last year, a sign that the increased competition has everyone on notice. It was a pronounced, encouraging change from 2016 OTAs, when Rueben Randle was the closest thing the incumbents had to "veteran challengers." When Wentz throws downfield this year, there is a chance someone will catch it. That should encourage him (and Pederson) to take a few more chances.

The Eagles could not invest quite as many resources on defense, but they still made an impressive set of upgrades. Last

year's defense, still being rebuilt from the ravages of the Kelly era (a 3-4 scheme that never gelled, dubious personnel decisions, getting stuck on the field for close to 40 minutes per game), was strong early but buckled late. Edge rusher Connor Barwin was out of position as a 4-3 end, Fletcher Cox had a penalty-plagued early season after signing a fat contract, and the excellent safeties found it harder and harder to compensate for the awful cornerbacks as the season progressed.

With Barwin now reunited with Wade Phillips in Los Angeles, first-round pick Derek Barnett and veteran Chris Long will share the right end position, with rock-solid Brandon Graham on the other side. Barnett broke Reggie White's all-time Tennessee sack record and looked like the real deal at OTAs. Long proved in New England that he can still bring the heat as a rotation player. Cox played well despite some bonehead plays last year, Vinny Curry is a valuable rotation player, and Timmy Jernigan arrives from Baltimore to provide some extra interior quickness. This defensive line is going to be formidable. It had better be, because the cornerback situation will remain a problem until second-round pick Sidney Jones gets healthy and third-round pick Rasul Douglas develops.

The Eagles should be more stable on both sides of the ball this season than last. That increased stability will extend to the coaching staff. While coordinators Jim Schwartz and Frank Reich reintroduced NFL concepts on defense and offfense last offseason after three years of Kelly experiments, Pederson felt his way along as a first-year head coach. Basic questions like the amount of contact during training camp took him by surprise last year: he was an advocate of an extra-physical camp until the first injury, then everyone spent a week playing two-hand touch. Pederson was randomly aggressive on fourth downs, suddenly becoming a risk-taker midway through the season. Pederson and the organization did not make the transition easier by juggling quarterbacks and mixing messages right up until the week before the season started. The rookie head coach, like his quarterback, showed promise mixed with long stretches of futility.

The pace at Eagles practices during OTAs was faster this year; last season, even drill schedules felt poorly planned. Instead of firing flutterballs on a far field while refining his mechanics, Wentz barked hard-counts, pointed out blitzers, and commanded the first-team offense this spring. Everyone looked like they knew what they were doing in June of 2017, which is more than could be said of the Eagles in June of 2016.

But there's a big difference between stability and excellence. The 2017 Eagles roster reflects three different sets of goals: winning in the future (when Wentz has developed into a superstar), winning now (and helping Wentz become that superstar), and repairing the leftover damage from Hurricane Chip. General manager Howie Roseman, along with new Vice President of Player Personnel Joe Douglas, are trying to address all three goals simultaneously. Jeffrey's one-year contract, for example, is a win-now move which is also designed to correct for Kelly's eclectic taste in wide receivers. Keeping Jason Peters and his massive contract is also a win-now move, albeit one necessitated by the fact that Lane Johnson's suspensions have slowed his transition from right to left tackle. Drafting Jones, who is still on the mend from a pre-draft foot injury and unlikely to be a major factor this season, was an obvious move for the future. Slow decisions on other pricey Kelly holdovers who don't really fit the new regime, such as Mychal Kendricks and Ryan Mathews, show that the Eagles still have not finished their roster and salary-cap cleanup operations.

The result of the three-tiered management plan is an expensive roster that should hover among the wild-card contenders this season, but is too weak at cornerback to do much else, unless Wentz suddenly becomes 1984 Dan Marino. The "win now" leg of the tripod may be cut down by the ultracompetitive NFC East, where all four teams ranked in DVOA's top ten last season. Add in games against the powerful defenses of the AFC and NFC West, and we have the Eagles projected with the toughest schedule in the league.

But if all goes according to plan, when Wentz graduates into the upper echelon of quarterbacks in 2018 or 2019, this year's rookies may be anchoring a great cornerback corps, and the wide receiver situation will finally be straightened out. The Eagles will then be contenders … if Johnson replaces Peters, someone replaces Johnson, veterans like Malcolm Jennings don't fade, Brandon Graham's contract gets extended, and lots of other problems are solved. All of those problems are manageable if Wentz truly does become a franchise quarterback.

It's trite to say that everything depends on Wentz's continued development, but it's true, which is why so many short-term resources are devoted to giving him the best possible opportunity for short-term success. Wentz now has receivers who can get open and catch passes downfield. He has no excuse for not connecting with them. If he can start doing it with some consistency, the Eagles can take the training wheels off and spend their money and energy building a real contender.

Mike Tanier

2016 Eagles Stats by Week

Wk	vs.	W-L	PF	PA	YDF	YDA	TO	Total	Off	Def	ST
1	CLE	W	29	10	403	288	+1	19%	-8%	-25%	1%
2	at CHI	W	29	14	280	284	+3	16%	7%	-20%	-11%
3	PIT	W	34	3	426	251	+2	86%	36%	-45%	5%
4	BYE										
5	at DET	L	23	24	346	244	-1	-7%	-17%	-7%	4%
6	at WAS	L	20	27	239	493	+1	-14%	-36%	6%	28%
7	MIN	W	21	10	239	282	0	43%	-34%	-50%	27%
8	at DAL	L	23	29	291	460	0	25%	-3%	-19%	9%
9	at NYG	L	23	28	443	302	0	19%	-4%	-8%	16%
10	ATL	W	24	15	429	303	0	57%	2%	-53%	2%
11	at SEA	L	15	26	308	439	-2	-33%	-6%	28%	1%
12	GB	L	13	27	292	387	-1	-12%	-1%	21%	11%
13	at CIN	L	14	32	359	412	-1	-38%	-28%	11%	1%
14	WAS	L	22	27	383	334	-1	-39%	-22%	12%	-5%
15	at BAL	L	26	27	328	340	+1	6%	-8%	7%	21%
16	NYG	W	24	19	286	470	+2	36%	19%	-3%	15%
17	DAL	W	27	13	346	195	+2	77%	12%	-68%	-3%

Trends and Splits

	Offense	Rank	Defense	Rank
Total DVOA	-5.5%	20	-12.4%	4
Unadjusted VOA	-4.4%	21	-9.2%	5
Weighted Trend	-7.6%	23	-7.9%	6
Variance	3.7%	7	8.1%	32
Average Opponent	0.2%	15	5.3%	1
Passing	0.8%	25	-11.8%	2
Rushing	0.7%	11	-13.3%	13
First Down	6.7%	10	-14.6%	3
Second Down	-9.4%	22	-26.3%	2
Third Down	-22.3%	27	13.0%	25
First Half	-8.5%	23	-1.0%	17
Second Half	15.5%	8	-9.0%	14
Red Zone	-2.2%	17	-36.4%	1
Late and Close	7.8%	11	-3.9%	18

Five-Year Performance

Year	W-L	Pyth W	Est W	PF	PA	TO	Total	Rk	Off	Rk	Def	Rk	ST	Rk	Off AGL	Rk	Def AGL	Rk	Off Age	Rk	Def Age	Rk	ST Age	Rk
2012	4-12	3.9	4.5	280	444	-24	-22.4%	28	-10.8%	25	9.4%	26	-2.2%	23	65.2	32	8.1	2	26.8	17	26.5	23	25.6	27
2013	10-6	9.4	10.2	442	382	+12	15.2%	8	22.9%	3	4.9%	23	-2.8%	25	21.2	7	11.0	4	27.5	11	26.2	21	26.0	19
2014	10-6	9.7	9.7	474	400	-8	12.8%	7	1.1%	13	-3.3%	10	8.3%	1	32.2	18	16.4	2	27.2	11	26.9	13	26.9	1
2015	7-9	6.7	6.8	377	430	-5	-11.2%	22	-10.1%	26	3.0%	17	1.9%	10	23.7	10	28.3	17	27.2	11	26.7	15	26.9	2
2016	7-9	9.0	9.9	367	331	+6	14.4%	5	-5.5%	20	-12.4%	4	7.5%	2	20.6	3	17.8	5	27.0	11	26.9	9	27.0	3

2016 Performance Based on Most Common Personnel Groups

PHI Offense					PHI Offense vs. Opponents					PHI Defense					PHI Defense vs. Opponents			
Pers	Freq	Yds	DVOA	Run%	Pers	Freq	Yds	DVOA	Run%	Pers	Freq	Yds	DVOA	Pers	Freq	Yds	DVOA
11	58%	5.4	7.9%	34%	Base	27%	5.3	5.7%	54%	Base	23%	5.2	-23.5%	11	68%	6.2	-3.5%
12	27%	4.8	-15.9%	31%	Nickel	64%	5.1	0.5%	33%	Nickel	73%	5.9	-10.3%	12	14%	5.6	-25.4%
13	6%	6.1	34.5%	47%	Dime+	8%	5.9	-11.7%	11%	Dime+	2%	6.7	-5.7%	21	7%	4.9	-59.5%
612	4%	4.2	-13.2%	81%	Goal Line	1%	0.7	10.4%	70%	Goal Line	1%	8.6	65.8%	20	3%	3.6	-30.4%
611	2%	2.7	-59.5%	89%	Big	1%	1.7	-81.3%	86%	Big	1%	4.9	-19.4%	610	2%	3.2	-31.6%

Strategic Tendencies

Run/Pass		Rk	Formation		Rk	Pass Rush		Rk	Secondary		Rk	Strategy		Rk
Runs, first half	36%	21	Form: Single Back	90%	4	Rush 3	1.8%	32	4 DB	23%	22	Play-action	19%	12
Runs, first down	45%	21	Form: Empty Back	7%	16	Rush 4	79.3%	1	5 DB	73%	1	Avg Box (Off)	6.15	21
Runs, second-long	31%	14	Pers: 3+ WR	60%	26	Rush 5	12.3%	31	6+ DB	2%	26	Avg Box (Def)	6.30	8
Runs, power sit.	57%	14	Pers: 2+ TE/6+ OL	40%	2	Rush 6+	6.6%	12	CB by Sides	92%	5	Offensive Pace	31.45	27
Runs, behind 2H	27%	15	Pers: 6+ OL	7%	8	Sacks by LB	9.1%	25	S/CB Cover Ratio	28%	13	Defensive Pace	30.11	12
Pass, ahead 2H	46%	25	Shotgun/Pistol	67%	13	Sacks by DB	6.1%	21	DB Blitz	10%	12	Go for it on 4th	1.52	3

You already know about the huge schematic changes that came from replacing Chip Kelly with Doug Pederson, but Jim Schwartz also brought a number of schematic changes on defense. The Eagles went from 13th to first in how often they brought the standard four pass-rushers, and dropped from 14th to dead last in rushing three. They also went from 48 percent (24th) to 73 percent (first) in how often they used five defensive backs, and from 4.9 percent (31st) to 10.2 percent (12th) in how often they blitzed a defensive back. ☜ One thing that didn't change: for the second straight year, Philadelphia was dead last in the frequency of opposing passes targeting tight ends (13.8 percent). ☜ A year after Kelly's Eagles didn't run a single draw play, Pederson's Eagles led the league by running draws on 11 percent of running back carries. However, the Eagles were below average on draws, with just 4.3 yards per carry and -12.7% DVOA. ☜ Philadelphia fumbled 22 times on offense last year, but recovered 16 of them. ☜ One big problem for the Philadelphia defense was tackling. By our count, the Eagles ranked third in broken tackles (131) and second in the percentage of defensive plays that had broken tackles (12.6 percent). ☜ Philadelphia had a league-low 11 penalties on special teams.

Passing

Player	DYAR	DVOA	Plays	NtYds	Avg	YAC	C%	TD	Int
C.Wentz	-36	-12.0%	641	3580	5.6	4.7	62.7%	16	14
N.Foles	5	-9.9%	59	376	6.4	5.5	65.5%	3	0
M.McGloin	6	-4.0%	15	50	3.3	1.1	53.3%	0	0

Rushing

Player	DYAR	DVOA	Plays	Yds	Avg	TD	Fum	Suc
R.Mathews	-3	-9.2%	117	483	4.1	8	0	53%
D.Sproles	74	15.4%	78	366	4.7	2	0	53%
W.Smallwood	17	-3.4%	77	314	4.1	1	0	49%
C.Wentz	-22	-26.1%	27	104	3.9	2	0	-
K.Barner*	46	38.1%	24	123	5.1	2	0	58%
L.Blount	130	3.7%	248	1029	4.1	18	0	45%

Receiving

Player	DYAR	DVOA	Plays	Ctch	Yds	Y/C	YAC	TD	C%
J.Matthews	-4	-13.2%	117	73	804	11.0	3.2	3	62%
D.Green-Beckham	-34	-18.6%	74	36	392	10.9	4.2	2	49%
N.Agholor	-60	-23.3%	70	37	373	10.1	3.3	2	53%
J.Huff	-14	-23.4%	17	13	72	5.5	7.2	1	76%
P.Turner	20	5.9%	14	9	126	14.0	5.8	0	64%
B.Treggs	-23	-38.2%	12	3	80	26.7	5.3	0	25%
A.Jeffery	132	5.0%	94	52	821	15.8	3.7	2	55%
T.Smith	-78	-33.0%	49	20	267	13.4	3.1	3	41%
Z.Ertz	75	3.4%	106	78	816	10.5	3.4	4	74%
T.Burton	-83	-27.9%	60	37	327	8.8	3.6	1	62%
B.Celek	-12	-16.7%	19	14	152	10.9	6.0	0	74%
D.Sproles	65	3.0%	71	52	427	8.2	7.9	2	73%
R.Mathews	33	19.6%	14	13	115	8.8	8.7	1	93%
W.Smallwood	-9	-27.6%	13	6	55	9.2	8.3	0	46%
K.Barner*	-15	-40.7%	11	5	42	8.4	9.4	0	45%
L.Blount	-7	-31.0%	8	7	38	5.4	6.1	0	88%

Offensive Line

Player	Pos	Age	GS	Snaps	Pen	Sk	Pass	Run	Player	Pos	Age	GS	Snaps	Pen	Sk	Pass	Run
Jason Kelce	C	30	16/16	1133	9	0.0	6	12	Halapoulivaati Vaitai	RT	24	7/6	423	1	2.0	7	1
Jason Peters	LT	35	16/16	1100	13	4.0	15	7	Lane Johnson	RT	27	6/6	407	2	0.5	3	1
Brandon Brooks	RG	28	14/14	991	2	1.0	6	2	Isaac Seumalo	G/T	24	9/4	335	2	1.0	4	3
Allen Barbre	LG	33	12/12	672	6	2.0	11	2	Brian Schwenke	C	26	16/3	247	0	0.5	1	1
Stefen Wisniewski	C/G	28	16/6	607	1	0.0	2	2									

Year	Yards	ALY	Rank	Power	Rank	Stuff	Rank	2nd Lev	Rank	Open Field	Rank	Sacks	ASR	Rank	Press	Rank	F-Start	Cont.
2014	4.36	3.77	29	81%	1	21%	26	1.24	9	0.93	6	32	4.9%	9	26.7%	24	17	27
2015	4.09	3.54	30	84%	1	21%	18	1.21	10	0.81	13	37	6.6%	20	20.8%	4	20	34
2016	4.28	4.28	13	57%	25	18%	12	1.36	6	0.67	16	33	5.4%	10	25.7%	15	26	26

2016 ALY by direction:	Left End 4.36 (17)	Left Tackle 4.56 (13)	Mid/Guard 4.26 (14)	Right Tackle 4.81 (8)	Right End 4.01 (15)

Carson Wentz's period of maximum futility coincided neatly with Lane Johnson's midseason suspension. Halapoulivaati Vaitai, Isaac Seumalo, and Matt Tobin all started in Johnson's place, with various degrees of ineffectiveness. By comparison, Johnson finished fourth among right tackles in snaps per blown block. Bad pass protection didn't directly cause Wentz to go on his early-game turnover sprees, but it didn't help. ▬ Johnson is back this season, as is left tackle Jason Peters. Apart from a league-high 10 false start penalties, the 35-year-old is still playing at a high level despite mounting aches and pains. No one appears ready to step up at tackle, so the long-range plan to move Johnson to left tackle to replace Peters remains a long-range plan. ▬ Jason Kelce had a rough season in 2016: six holding penalties, some big whiffs on open-field blocks, too many low snaps and botched exchanges with Wentz. Wentz took the blame for some of the mishandled snaps, saying he took his eyes off the ball to read the defense. Fair enough; many of the snaps were still heading straight for his lower shin. Kelce may be traded to a team in need of a veteran center or even released at the end of camp. The team has veteran Stefan Wisniewski in the wings to replace Kelce, plus several prospects they like, including Seumalo (who started at guard for much of OTAs, with Vaitai subbing for the absent Peters) and undrafted rookie Tyler Orlosky out of West Virginia.

Defensive Front Seven

Defensive Line	Age	Pos	G	Snaps	Plays	Overall TmPct	Rk	Stop	Dfts	BTkl	Runs	vs. Run St%	Rk	RuYd	Rk	Sack	Pass Rush Hit	Hur	Dsrpt
Fletcher Cox	27	DT	16	773	45	6.0%	22	33	13	4	33	73%	53	1.5	20	6.5	12	29	2
Bennie Logan*	28	DT	13	467	24	3.9%	52	20	10	5	18	89%	13	0.6	4	2.5	3	9	0
Beau Allen	26	DT	16	412	29	3.9%	55	25	11	3	25	92%	5	1.0	9	0.5	5	7	0
Destiny Vaeao	24	DT	16	268	15	2.0%	--	12	3	1	11	73%	--	2.2	--	2.0	1	5	0
Timmy Jernigan	25	DE	16	629	34	4.4%	46	31	14	1	24	92%	6	1.9	31	5.0	6	15	2

Edge Rushers	Age	Pos	G	Snaps	Plays	Overall TmPct	Rk	Stop	Dfts	BTkl	Runs	vs. Run St%	Rk	RuYd	Rk	Sack	Pass Rush Hit	Hur	Dsrpt
Brandon Graham	29	DE	16	765	60	8.0%	9	46	22	6	49	78%	34	0.8	6	5.5	20	52	4
Connor Barwin*	31	DE	16	713	36	4.8%	55	25	12	5	21	71%	61	3.0	69	5.0	6	21	2
Vinny Curry	29	DE	16	435	26	3.5%	76	17	10	5	21	62%	87	1.7	24	2.5	9	26	0
Chris Long	32	DE	16	677	35	4.5%	59	23	6	6	23	61%	89	2.9	64	4.0	8	30	2

Linebackers	Age	Pos	G	Snaps	Plays	Overall TmPct	Rk	Stop	Dfts	BTkl	Runs	vs. Run St%	Rk	RuYd	Rk	Sack	Pass Rush Hit	Hur	Tgts	vs. Pass Suc%	Rk	AdjYd	Rk	PD	Int
Nigel Bradham	28	OLB	16	990	102	13.6%	32	65	25	11	52	69%	17	2.6	10	2.0	1	6	36	57%	16	6.1	31	6	1
Jordan Hicks	25	MLB	16	971	95	12.6%	41	62	20	10	48	67%	27	3.6	43	1.0	4	5	28	70%	2	5.0	13	8	5
Mychal Kendricks	27	OLB	15	273	29	4.1%	--	18	3	7	19	63%	--	3.4	--	0.0	2	4	10	60%	--	4.4	--	1	0

Year	Yards	ALY	Rank	Power	Rank	Stuff	Rank	2nd Level	Rank	Open Field	Rank	Sacks	ASR	Rank	Press	Rank
2014	3.64	3.98	11	80%	30	21%	11	1.02	7	0.48	4	49	7.1%	10	29.6%	1
2015	4.57	4.36	23	74%	29	17%	27	1.18	22	1.04	29	37	6.8%	13	24.9%	19
2016	4.20	3.44	2	70%	27	24%	3	1.20	19	1.13	31	34	6.6%	11	31.6%	3

2016 ALY by direction: Left End 3.10 (2)   Left Tackle 3.76 (10)   Mid/Guard 3.72 (6)   Right Tackle 2.21 (1)   Right End 3.36 (10)

Like most other Eagles units, the pass rush started off hot, with 14 sacks in four weeks, before bottoming out midseason and rebounding a little bit at the end. Defensive coordinator Jim Schwartz, who knows a little bit about analytics, talked about the issues during OTAs. "We did a lot of studies in the offseason. We did studies of different teams and things like that. Sacks go hand-in-hand with so many other things. A lot of it has to do with our corner position. If you can cover for a long time, you can buy time to get the sackers there. If they're rushing well, it helps the corners out. But I think that both of those can go hand-in-hand. [Sacks] also go hand-in-hand with score. I don't think there is any surprise that a lot of games we were sacking the quarterback—Pittsburgh and Minnesota and things like that—we were playing with the lead." In other words, if your offense turns the ball over twice in the first quarter and your cornerbacks cannot cover, your front four had better be the Steel Curtain if you want high sack totals. ☞ The Eagles defensive line is hardly the Steel Curtain, but Brandon Graham has slowly developed into an excellent all-around defender, and more than tripled his hurry total from 2015 (17 to 52, which ranked second in the league). ☞ Vinny Curry is also more disruptive than raw sack totals suggest. Schwartz pointed out that Curry often got initial penetration but failed to finish plays, and the coaching staff focused on ways to clean up the ends of his snaps in the spring. ☞ Newcomers Derek Barnett and Chris Long impressed in the early stages of camp and should add the edge-rushing depth that first-round bust Marcus Smith never did. The Eagles have the personnel to be among the NFL's sack leaders … assuming everyone else holds up their ends of the bargain. ☞ Fletcher Cox frustrated fans with some sloppy roughness penalties but played close enough to expectations after signing a massive contract that it didn't become a story. Cox's measure-of-impact numbers (sacks, hits, hurries, stops, defeats) declined across the board from 2015, but he remains an ideal three-down fit for Schwartz's system. ☞ The Eagles swapped out Bennie Logan for Timmy Jernigan as Cox's partner in crime on the interior. Jernigan will get paid after 2017, but in the short-term the Eagles will benefit from a younger, more athletic 1-technique who developed into a premier run-stuffer last season.

Defensive Secondary

Secondary	Age	Pos	G	Snaps	Plays	TmPct	Rk	Stop	Dfts	BTkl	Runs	St%	Rk	RuYd	Rk	Tgts	Tgt%	Rk	Dist	Suc%	Rk	AdjYd	Rk	PD	Int
Malcolm Jenkins	30	SS	16	1019	78	10.4%	33	42	19	14	31	65%	4	4.7	9	54	12.0%	64	9.3	53%	13	7.1	16	9	3
Rodney McLeod	27	FS	16	1014	86	11.5%	20	25	9	18	41	29%	59	11.7	72	23	5.1%	5	17.4	45%	41	12.1	67	7	3
Nolan Carroll*	30	CB	16	910	64	8.5%	47	29	7	9	11	36%	52	10.8	77	73	18.0%	40	12.4	52%	26	8.1	55	8	1
Jalen Mills	23	CB	16	661	68	9.1%	34	28	10	9	13	38%	47	6.2	35	73	24.8%	83	13.1	56%	11	7.3	35	7	0
Leodis McKelvin*	32	CB	13	587	59	9.7%	23	25	11	6	11	27%	67	6.8	44	79	30.2%	87	13.7	54%	16	9.7	83	16	2
Jaylen Watkins	26	SS	16	388	33	4.4%	--	12	5	5	15	47%	--	4.1	--	14	8.2%	--	12.6	58%	--	6.2	--	3	0
Patrick Robinson	30	CB	7	401	30	8.4%	--	7	2	5	7	14%	--	7.1	--	36	20.4%	--	13.8	43%	--	7.8	--	5	0

Year	Pass D Rank	vs. #1 WR	Rk	vs. #2 WR	Rk	vs. Other WR	Rk	vs. TE	Rk	vs. RB	Rk
2014	18	10.2%	24	4.4%	20	-6.1%	11	0.2%	19	19.7%	28
2015	14	7.8%	23	-5.1%	13	-12.4%	6	4.7%	19	-0.8%	15
2016	2	-18.5%	3	1.6%	17	2.3%	18	-52.8%	1	-11.9%	9

Safeties good. Cornerbacks bad.

Because you expect deeper analysis than that from *Football Outsiders Almanac*, here is Jim Schwartz from OTAs talking about Jalen Mills: "I'll sum his rookie season up: it was a rookie season." Mills, a camp phenom who turned into a burnt cinder last season, is expected to start opposite oft-injured newcomer Patrick Robinson. Second-round pick Sidney Jones (Washington) spent the summer rehabbing the Achilles injury he suffered at his pro day. Long-armed, athletic third-round pick Rasul Douglas (West Virginia) looked phenomenal at the start of OTAs, but so did Mills last year. Jones and Douglas may be the future of the Eagles secondary, but September will probably be rough. ☙ Malcolm Jenkins does double duty as a safety and matchup slot corner. He's excellent at what he does, but some of the slot matchups he draws are a little too ambitious. Still, Jenkins has ranked in the top 20 in adjusted success rate and the top five in run stop rate each of the past two seasons. Mills is being cross-trained in the slot and may move there if Douglas emerges or Jones can return to play a role this year. ☙ Rodney McLeod was a valuable addition last year and returns as the free safety. The Eagles had clearly delineated roles for Jenkins and McLeod; only Atlanta and Jacksonville had a larger gap on the average gain on tackles by the two starting safeties.

Special Teams

Year	DVOA	Rank	FG/XP	Rank	Net Kick	Rank	Kick Ret	Rank	Net Punt	Rank	Punt Ret	Rank	Hidden	Rank
2014	8.3%	1	3.5	9	9.8	2	12.3	2	1.7	14	14.2	1	23.5	1
2015	1.9%	10	-2.9	26	0.7	15	-0.2	15	1.0	18	11.1	2	-13.8	32
2016	7.5%	2	3.5	10	14.3	1	15.1	1	0.1	15	4.8	8	-11.3	28

The Eagles' return and coverage units covered up for the inconsistency of the offense and defense again last year, just as they did for the 2015 squad and many past Eagles teams. Darren Sproles averaged 13.2 yards per punt return. Wendell Smallwood and Josh Huff each returned kickoffs for touchdowns. Bennie Logan blocked a pair of kicks. Terrance Brooks forced a pair of special teams fumbles. Chris Maragos was everywhere. Big special teams plays kept Eagles in games that looked like blowouts after the first quarter. ☙ With Sproles aging, the Eagles signed pocket-sized Donnel Pumphrey to learn the art of surviving in the NFL despite being too short to ride the really fun rollercoasters. Pumphrey didn't return punts at San Diego State, but he has a returner's toolkit. Nonetheless, Sproles should still start the season as the primary punt returner. ☙ Maragos and Brooks remain the anchors of the coverage units. Fourth-round pick Mack Hollins captained the North Carolina special teams for several seasons and should make the team as a third-string receiver and first-team gunner. ☙ Kicker Caleb Sturgis has been reliable on kickoffs, and every kickoff travels precisely 65 yards, with good-to-excellent hang time.

Pittsburgh Steelers

2016 Record: 11-5	**Total DVOA:** 17.1% (4th)	**2017 Mean Projection:** 10.7 wins	**On the Clock (0-4):** 1%
Pythagorean Wins: 9.9 (5th)	**Offense:** 12.5% (7th)	**Postseason Odds:** 77.9%	**Mediocrity (5-7):** 9%
Snap-Weighted Age: 26.6 (15th)	**Defense:** -4.7% (11th)	**Super Bowl Odds:** 25.0%	**Playoff Contender (8-10):** 32%
Average Opponent: 1.2% (11th)	**Special Teams:** -0.1% (16th)	**Proj. Avg. Opponent:** -1.6% (27th)	**Super Bowl Contender (11+):** 58%

2016: The offense was mostly healthy and the defense was fine, putting the Steelers in position to lose the AFC Championship Game to New England.

2017: If the offense can stay mostly healthy and the defense is a little better, the Steelers will be in position to lose the AFC Championship Game to New England.

They say the definition of insanity is doing the same thing over and over and expecting different results. In Pittsburgh, that means hoping every year that finally, the Steelers' stars will be available for a full season, and especially in the playoffs. In theory, this should be the league's most talented offense. Suspensions and injuries, however, have cost Pittsburgh multiple games at quarterback, running back, and wide receiver—and all too often, those absences have come in the postseason.

They say the definition of insanity is doing the same thing over and over and expecting different results. In Pittsburgh, that means hoping every year that finally, all those draft picks invested in the defense will start to pay off. The Steelers' defense hasn't finished in the top 10 in DVOA since James Farrior retired. Pittsburgh has really, really tried to find good young players and develop them into a unit on par with the team's own offense, but thus far those efforts have resulted in a defense that has maxed out at "slightly above average."

They say the definition of insanity is doing the same thing over and over and expecting different results. In Pittsburgh, that means hoping every year that finally, the Steelers will establish that they, and not the New England Patriots, are the best team in the AFC. Six years ago, the Steelers were coming off their second Super Bowl appearance in three years and looked to have taken the crown as the AFC's team to beat. Since then, the Patriots have rebounded to play in three Super Bowls, winning two. Meanwhile, the Steelers have only made it as far as one conference championship game—last year, when they fell to the Patriots.

The Pittsburgh Steelers have been stuck in a Groundhog Day-style bugaboo for years now, where every season feels like a missed chance at greatness, and usually for those same three reasons: an offense that always seems to be missing important pieces, a defense that never seems to be more than a complementary part of the team, and a mismatch against the Patriots that never seems to go their way. Let's break these down one-by-one to see how they have hurt the team in the past, and whether the Steelers can get those fortunes turned around in 2017.

THE OFFENSE

It sounds strange to say that an offense that has finished in the top ten in DVOA three years in a row has underachieved, but it definitely feels that way in Pittsburgh. You would expect more from a team with Ben Roethlisberger, Le'Veon Bell, and Antonio Brown, arguably the NFL's best "Big Three" in recent years. As if that weren't enough, the Steelers have one of the league's most dangerous No. 2 receivers in Martavis Bryant, a deep threat with few peers in today's NFL.

But that fearsome foursome has very rarely appeared on the same field at the same time. Roethlisberger, of course, has been taking dozens of beatings every season since entering the league in 2004. In the last five years alone, he has been listed on the injury report with maladies to his head, shoulder, hand, knee (twice, with two different injuries), ankle, and foot. More often than not, he has played through the injuries, but he has still played 16 regular-season games only three times in 13 NFL seasons.

Martavis Bryant has had his own injury problems, most notably an AC sprain that knocked him out for three games in 2014. The bigger issue, though, has been an inability to stay away from drugs—suspensions wiped out his first four games of 2015, and his entire 2016 season. He has been conditionally cleared to play this year, but it's hard to rely on a guy who has been suspended for nearly as many games (20) as he has played (21) in a three-year NFL career.

For Le'Veon Bell, the problems have been related to both health and behavior. He missed three games in 2013 with a foot injury and eight in 2015 with torn knee ligaments. He is also coming off groin surgery, and there is no timetable for his return other than the team saying that he won't suit up until he is 100 percent healthy. On top of all that, Bell missed the first two games of 2015 and the first three of 2016 for assorted violations of the league's drug policy.

Compared to his teammates, Brown has been an iron man. He has played 110 regular-season and playoff games in a Steelers uniform since he was drafted in 2010, and only missed two games (Week 17 last year when Pittsburgh rested its starters against Cleveland, and a 2015 playoff game) in the past four years. Still, he is perhaps the team's best player, and

2017 Steelers Schedule

Week	Opp.	Week	Opp.	Week	Opp.
1	at CLE	7	CIN	13	at CIN (Mon.)
2	MIN	8	at DET	14	BAL
3	at CHI	9	BYE	15	NE
4	at BAL	10	at IND	16	at HOU (Mon./Xmas)
5	JAC	11	TEN (Thu.)	17	CLE
6	at KC	12	GB		

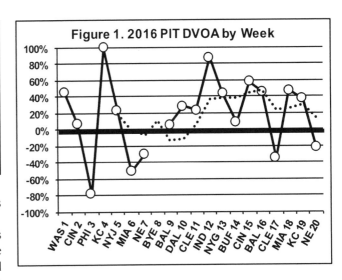

Figure 1. 2016 PIT DVOA by Week

it's important to at least try to analyze the kind of impact his absence has had on the team.

With all of that in mind, let's take a look at how the Steelers have performed in recent years with and without each of the big four. We'll go back to 2013, the year when Le'Veon Bell was drafted, and the first time that Antonio Brown finished in the top 10 in receptions or yards. (Table 1)

Table 1. Steelers Offense With And Without Big Stars, 2013-2016

Status	Games	Win%	Off. DVOA	Pts/ Gm	Yds/ Gm	TO/ Gm
Overall	70	0.614	12.6%	25.0	379.2	1.5
Regular Season	64	0.625	13.4%	25.6	379.2	1.4
Playoffs	6	0.500	4.2%	19.3	379.3	1.8
Healthy Roethlisberger	55	0.636	14.7%	25.8	382.5	1.5
Injured Roethlisberger*	9	0.556	10.2%	23.3	394.9	1.4
No Roethlisberger	6	0.500	-3.4%	20.8	324.7	1.0
Bell	50	0.640	14.3%	25.0	372.7	1.2
No Bell	20	0.550	8.4%	25.2	395.4	2.1
Brown	68	0.618	12.8%	25.1	379.9	1.5
No Brown	2	0.500	7.0%	21.5	354.0	1.0
Bryant	24	0.667	18.7%	27.8	412.0	1.9
No Bryant**	46	0.587	9.4%	23.6	362.0	1.2
All Four Played	11	0.727	24.8%	29.3	414.0	1.5
One Player Missing	46	0.652	12.4%	25.2	377.9	1.4
Two or More Missing	13	0.385	3.0%	21.1	354.2	1.5

Includes regular season and playoff games.

* Includes all games in which Roethlisberger was listed on the injury report but did play.

** Includes 16 games in 2013, when Bryant was still in college.

The Steelers have performed worse when Roethlisberger played hurt and even worse when he was out, but this of course is true of any team missing a good quarterback. Brown's two missed games is far too small a sample size from which to draw any meaningful conclusions.

More enlightening is the decline when either Bell or Bryant has been out. The Steelers' win percentage drops when either Bell or Bryant is absent, but for different reasons. Turnovers have risen sharply when Bell hasn't played. We focus so often on Bell's big plays that we overlook his ball security. He has fumbled only five times in 1,135 career NFL touches. In the same time frame, Pittsburgh's other running backs have eight fumbles in just 505 touches.

Meanwhile, Bryant's presence in the lineup has led to more wins, points, and yards, but also more turnovers. That's more bad luck than anything to do with Bryant though. He has been the target on just three interceptions, two of which were thrown by Landry Jones, and has fumbled just once in 24 games. In those same games, Antonio Brown has fumbled four times. And despite the rise in turnovers, Pittsburgh's DVOA is significantly higher with Bryant than without, which shows just what kind of explosive player he is.

The bottom section of the table is most important. When all four stars have been on the field, the Steelers have gone 8-3, a rate that works out to 11.6 wins in a 16-game season. When any one of the four has been absent—as has usually been the case—the Steelers have gone 30-16, or 10.4 wins per 16 games. And with two or more of these players absent, the Steelers have gone 4-8, more like a team drafting in the top ten than a playoff hopeful.

This is why it is so vital that Pittsburgh keeps its four stars on the field, especially in the playoffs. The Steelers have never had all four participate in the same playoff game.

THE DEFENSE

By snap-weighted age, Pittsburgh fielded the NFL's oldest defense every year from 2007 to 2013. Only five defenses since 2006 had a snap-weighted age of 29.0 or higher, and four of those were the Steelers from 2009 to 2012.

Obviously, that couldn't last forever. And to be fair, general manager Kevin Colbert has done his best to replace greybeards such as Brett Keisel, Ike Taylor, Troy Polamalu, and Ryan Clark. Pittsburgh has drafted 25 defenders in the past five years. That includes all five first-round picks, three second-rounders, two thirds, and two fourths. The defense has certainly gotten younger, finishing third in SWA in 2014, 11th in 2015, and 15th last year. Seven defenders from those drafts are likely to be starters this season, and incoming first-round draft pick T.J. Watt could make it eight if he can supplant James Harrison, who is his senior by *16 years*.

For all that youth, though, the Steelers remain a good defense, not a great one. They have found reliable defenders in the draft, but no stars. Not a single Pittsburgh defender drafted in the past five years has been elected to the Pro Bowl. Will that change in 2017?

The most likely candidate is linebacker Ryan Shazier, who played in last year's Pro Bowl as an injury replacement. When healthy, Shazier is a true triple-threat, capable of stuffing running backs, rushing the passer, or making plays in coverage. Despite missing three games last season, he was one of 37 defenders with at least nine defeats on both running and passing plays, and he and the Giants' Landon Collins were the only players in the league with at least three interceptions and three sacks. He should play an even bigger role this year given the departure of Lawrence Timmons to Miami in free agency. Trouble is, Shazier has often been injured, playing in 40 of 54 possible games (including playoffs) in his three-year career. He also misses too many tackles—a league-high 20 last year—to warrant Pro Bowl consideration.

Shazier's fellow 2014 draftee, defensive end Stephon Tuitt, is another good breakout candidate. He brings an unusually high amount of pass pressure for a 3-4 end. Tuitt led the team in combined sacks, hits, and hurries last year, and was third the year before. If he can just find that extra half-step of quickness that will turn more hits and hurries into sacks, he could be the Steelers' next breakout star.

Pass-rusher Bud Dupree, Pittsburgh's 2015 first-round pick, went on a tear at the end of last year. Limited to situational pass-rush duty as a rookie, Dupree missed the first ten weeks of 2016 with a groin injury, but then played 455 out of 460 defensive snaps from Week 14 through the Steelers' loss in the playoffs. In those seven games, he produced five run stuffs, five sacks, two passes defensed and one forced fumble.

The last veteran linebacker to consider is Vince Williams, who started 11 games as a rookie in 2013, but then was banished to the bench, with only six starts since. He'll take Timmons' spot in the lineup this fall by default.

A trio of 2016 draftees started at least eight games for Pittsburgh's defense. First-rounder Artie Burns played in all 16 games, starting every game after the Week 8 bye. His charting numbers were quite poor, but many highly-drafted cornerbacks struggle as rookies and take two, three, or even four seasons to fully develop. Second-round safety Sean Davis started the last seven games of the regular season and all three playoff games. He showed promising potential as an in-the-box type, though he must improve his tackling. Third-round nose tackle Javon Hargrave outplayed the two men picked before him, starting 16 games including the playoffs. As a nose tackle, it's doubtful he'll ever put up big individual numbers of any kind, but his continued development would solve a lot of problems for a defense that hasn't finished in the top 10 in adjusted line yards since leading the league in 2010.

The secondary offers two potential breakout stars, neither of whom offered much cause for optimism just a year ago. Ross Cockrell played only 11 defensive snaps as a rookie with the Bills in 2014 and failed to make the team in 2015. The Steelers grabbed him just before the season, and he spent that year bouncing in and out of the starting lineup. Then he started all 16 games last season, often matching up with top receivers like Odell Beckham, Brandon Marshall, or DeSean Jackson. The longshot in the defensive backfield is Senquez Golson, who has more arrests (one) than games played (zero) in his first two NFL seasons. Injuries to his shoulder and foot robbed him of his first two seasons, and he was caught with a gun and ammunition going through a Florida airport in April. Still, he was a second-round pick for a reason, he is reportedly 100 percent healthy now, and is still only 23—two years younger than Cockrell.

That leaves Watt, the 30th overall pick in the draft this year. Watt was only a starter for one year at Wisconsin, but it was a very productive season, with 11.5 sacks, an interception, and four passes defensed in 14 games. He had the second-best SackSEER projection in the 2017 draft behind Myles Garrett. On most teams, he would be a lock to start in Week 1. In Pittsburgh, he must beat out the ageless Harrison, whose first career sack came against Jeff Garcia and the Browns in 2004 when Watt was 10 years old.

The key here is that Pittsburgh's defense has not been great in recent years, but it has been good. A breakout year by just one or two of these youngsters could be enough to push things over the top. But given the unreliable nature of the offense, the defense must improve this fall. They can't be "sort of good" again and expect to return to the Super Bowl.

Now, speaking of the Super Bowl…

THE PATRIOTS

Since drafting Ben Roethlisberger in 2004, the Steelers are third in the league with 137 regular-season wins, and tied for second with 13 playoff wins. They need just two more regular-season wins than the Colts and one more playoff win than the Seahawks this year to move into sole possession of second place in both categories.

Problem is, they would still be a distant second, because the Patriots have 162 wins in the regular season and 19 more in the playoffs. (This is starting in 2004, which means Tom Brady's first two Super Bowl wins are not even included.) If the Patriots didn't exist, we might be talking about Roethlisberger's Steelers as one of sports' greatest dynasties. Of course, the Patriots do exist, which means the Steelers will probably need to beat them to win another Lombardi Trophy.

Since drafting Roethlisberger, the Steelers have gone 3-8 against the Patriots, including the playoffs. That includes a 2008 win when Matt Cassel was under center for New England, and a 2016 loss when Landry Jones was taking snaps for Pittsburgh. A winning percentage of .273 certainly isn't very good—but it ranks tenth against New England in that time frame, and five of the nine teams with better records against the Patriots are NFC teams that have played New England five times or less. The Steelers have averaged 23.9 points per game against New England (fifth-best) and allowed 30.0 (17th), with a differential of minus-6.1 (tenth). That's not as good as Pittsburgh usually ranks, but it's close, and again, we're only talking about a handful of games here. It's not so much that the Patriots are a bad matchup for Pittsburgh—they're a bad matchup for everybody.

Recent games paint a slightly grimmer picture. The Steelers have won just one of their last seven games against Tom Brady, and that one win came six years ago. They have lost four in a row since, by scores of 55-31, 28-21 (which wasn't really that close—Pittsburgh scored a touchdown with two seconds left in the game), 27-16 (the Landry Jones game), and then 36-17 in the AFC Championship Game last year. But now we are talking about miniscule sample sizes, and games that took place several generations ago. In the Steelers' last win against New England, their leading rushers were Rashard Mendenhall and Mewelde Moore, and their top receivers were Emmanuel Sanders and Mike Wallace. New England's offensive leaders that day included Kevin Faulk, BenJarvus Green-Ellis, and Aaron Hernandez. This game is ancient history, and it's foolish to think there's much we can learn from it now.

What we do know is that Pittsburgh hosts New England in Week 15, right after back-to-back games against the Bengals and Ravens. This is likely the stretch that will decide the Steelers' season. Wins over Cincinnati and Baltimore would go a long way toward clinching the division, and a third win over New England might be necessary to clinch home-field advantage in the playoffs. Then, no matter what happens in the regular season, Pittsburgh will probably need to beat the Patriots to get back to the Super Bowl.

They say the definition of insanity is doing the same thing over and over and expecting different results. In Pittsburgh, that means hoping for offensive health, defensive growth, and a big win over football's best team.

They could get all three. But expecting it to happen is kind of insane.

Vincent Verhei

2016 Steelers Stats by Week

Wk	vs.	W-L	PF	PA	YDF	YDA	TO	Total	Off	Def	ST
1	at WAS	W	38	16	437	384	+1	46%	27%	-16%	3%
2	CIN	W	24	16	374	412	0	7%	-3%	-6%	4%
3	at PHI	L	3	34	251	426	-2	-79%	-24%	46%	-9%
4	KC	W	43	14	436	357	+2	99%	63%	-32%	4%
5	NYJ	W	31	13	436	316	-1	22%	24%	16%	15%
6	at MIA	L	15	30	297	474	-2	-51%	-11%	34%	-7%
7	NE	L	16	27	375	362	+1	-30%	-2%	26%	-1%
8	BYE										
9	at BAL	L	14	21	277	274	0	5%	-27%	-50%	-18%
10	DAL	L	30	35	448	422	+1	28%	46%	12%	-6%
11	at CLE	W	24	9	313	209	+2	23%	-11%	-34%	0%
12	at IND	W	28	7	369	310	+2	87%	45%	-42%	0%
13	NYG	W	24	14	389	234	0	43%	31%	-6%	6%
14	at BUF	W	27	20	460	275	-2	8%	-10%	-9%	10%
15	at CIN	W	24	20	382	222	+1	58%	26%	-22%	10%
16	BAL	W	31	27	406	368	-1	45%	61%	10%	-5%
17	CLE	W	27	24	312	437	+3	-35%	-26%	2%	-6%
18	MIA	W	30	12	367	305	+1	48%	19%	-36%	-7%
19	at KC	W	18	16	389	227	+1	37%	3%	-23%	11%
20	at NE	L	17	36	368	431	-2	-21%	-3%	17%	-1%

Trends and Splits

	Offense	Rank	Defense	Rank
Total DVOA	12.5%	7	-4.7%	11
Unadjusted VOA	16.3%	5	-3.8%	12
Weighted Trend	13.4%	8	-7.7%	7
Variance	9.7%	29	7.7%	30
Average Opponent	0.8%	23	1.0%	11
Passing	29.3%	8	1.7%	12
Rushing	2.3%	7	-14.0%	11
First Down	5.2%	14	-15.6%	1
Second Down	13.9%	7	5.1%	23
Third Down	25.9%	5	1.1%	19
First Half	5.6%	14	-9.3%	5
Second Half	-6.3%	20	-11.2%	12
Red Zone	24.0%	8	-26.3%	4
Late and Close	2.2%	16	-7.8%	11

Five-Year Performance

Year	W-L	Pyth W	Est W	PF	PA	TO	Total	Rk	Off	Rk	Def	Rk	ST	Rk	Off AGL	Rk	Def AGL	Rk	Off Age	Rk	Def Age	Rk	ST Age	Rk
2012	8-8	8.7	7.4	336	314	-10	-1.2%	18	-4.0%	19	-2.9%	13	-0.1%	17	64.3	31	19.1	9	26.5	21	29.2	1	25.9	20
2013	8-8	8.2	8.3	379	370	-4	0.9%	15	4.4%	12	4.0%	19	0.5%	16	55.3	28	27.5	16	26.4	25	28.4	1	25.7	25
2014	11-5	9.7	9.4	436	368	0	12.1%	8	22.5%	2	11.3%	30	0.9%	12	4.1	1	38.7	17	26.5	24	27.8	3	26.2	10
2015	10-6	10.7	10.8	423	319	+2	21.3%	7	17.3%	3	-3.8%	11	0.1%	18	43.2	23	23.9	9	28.2	5	27.0	11	26.2	14
2016	11-5	9.9	10.2	399	327	+5	17.1%	4	12.5%	7	-4.7%	11	-0.1%	16	35.2	15	26.7	11	27.1	9	26.5	15	25.7	23

2016 Performance Based on Most Common Personnel Groups

PIT Offense					PIT Offense vs. Opponents					PIT Defense				PIT Defense vs. Opponents			
Pers	Freq	Yds	DVOA	Run%	Pers	Freq	Yds	DVOA	Run%	Pers	Freq	Yds	DVOA	Pers	Freq	Yds	DVOA
1.1	63%	6.5	29.8%	26%	Base	32%	5.6	-0.6%	60%	Base	28%	4.7	-18.1%	1.1	67%	6.2	1.5%
1.2	13%	5.8	-5.9%	39%	Nickel	59%	6.0	22.8%	30%	Nickel	64%	6.0	2.0%	1.2	15%	5.7	7.8%
62.1	6%	3.9	2.0%	93%	Dime+	8%	8.6	86.6%	6%	Dime+	7%	6.2	14.2%	2.1	4%	3.0	-102.6%
2.1	6%	4.8	-23.8%	59%	Goal Line	1%	3.4	-44.3%	43%	Goal Line	1%	-0.8	-86.7%	1.3	3%	4.8	-14.5%
1.3	5%	6.2	40.8%	60%	Big	1%	3.3	25.7%	92%	Big	1%	6.4	-7.2%	61.2	2%	4.5	-8.6%
61.2	4%	6.0	-7.6%	79%										1.0	2%	3.7	0.7%

Strategic Tendencies

Run/Pass		Rk	Formation		Rk	Pass Rush		Rk	Secondary		Rk	Strategy		Rk
Runs, first half	37%	19	Form: Single Back	76%	22	Rush 3	13.7%	4	4 DB	28%	19	Play-action	14%	32
Runs, first down	47%	14	Form: Empty Back	11%	5	Rush 4	57.8%	24	5 DB	64%	10	Avg Box (Off)	6.16	20
Runs, second-long	34%	8	Pers: 3+ WR	64%	20	Rush 5	26.0%	9	6+ DB	7%	16	Avg Box (Def)	6.20	19
Runs, power sit.	39%	31	Pers: 2+ TE/6+ OL	31%	11	Rush 6+	2.6%	30	CB by Sides	81%	15	Offensive Pace	31.06	22
Runs, behind 2H	24%	25	Pers: 6+ OL	11%	3	Sacks by LB	63.2%	8	S/CB Cover Ratio	27%	15	Defensive Pace	30.54	21
Pass, ahead 2H	46%	24	Shotgun/Pistol	66%	15	Sacks by DB	9.2%	9	DB Blitz	9%	18	Go for it on 4th	1.12	13

Pittsburgh used six offensive linemen on 11.4 percent of plays last season, one of three teams to use an extra lineman more than 10 percent of the time. ☞ The Steelers also used a max-protect blocking scheme on a 17.4 percent of passes, second in the NFL. (This is defined as seven or more blockers with at least two more blockers than pass-rushers.) ☞ Pittsburgh recovered 11 of 14 offensive fumbles last season. ☞ The Steelers were the only offense last season to use play-action more often on second down (18 percent) than on first down (16 percent, the lowest rate in the league). ☞ Pittsburgh was third in the league in use of wide receiver screens, but had just 4.5 yards per play with minus-1.2% DVOA on these plays. ☞ The Steelers cut their use of DB blitzes in half after ranking second by sending a defensive back on 19 percent of passes in 2015. But the DB blitzes they called did work well, as they allowed 5.7 yards per pass compared to 6.4 average yards on other passes. ☞ Pittsburgh opponents dropped 41 passes, which was 7.5 percent of opportunities, third in the NFL.

Passing

Player	DYAR	DVOA	Plays	NtYds	Avg	YAC	C%	TD	Int
B.Roethlisberger	807	12.1%	524	3678	7.0	5.2	64.8%	29	13
L.Jones	-14	-13.7%	89	524	5.9	4.6	62.4%	4	2

Rushing

Player	DYAR	DVOA	Plays	Yds	Avg	TD	Fum	Suc
L.Bell	188	12.9%	218	1054	4.8	7	0	53%
D.Williams*	-3	-9.5%	75	276	3.7	4	0	49%
F.Toussaint	-9	-31.3%	11	44	4.0	0	0	55%
B.Roethlisberger	7	14.8%	5	26	5.2	1	0	-
K.Davis	-42	-75.3%	18	28	1.6	0	1	17%

Receiving

Player	DYAR	DVOA	Plays	Ctch	Yds	Y/C	YAC	TD	C%
A.Brown	295	11.1%	154	106	1284	12.1	3.8	12	69%
E.Rogers	150	18.3%	66	48	594	12.4	4.3	3	73%
S.Coates	0	-12.7%	49	21	435	20.7	5.4	2	43%
C.Hamilton	64	14.9%	28	17	234	13.8	1.3	2	61%
D.Heyward-Bey	-12	-21.0%	19	6	114	19.0	3.0	2	32%
D.Ayers	7	-7.0%	13	6	53	8.8	4.7	1	46%
M.Wheaton*	-9	-25.8%	9	4	51	12.8	2.0	1	44%
J.James	-26	-13.7%	60	39	338	8.7	3.2	3	65%
L.Green*	14	-0.4%	34	18	304	16.9	5.4	1	53%
X.Grimble	-2	-8.5%	21	11	118	10.7	3.5	2	52%
D.Johnson	0	-6.7%	11	7	80	11.4	7.7	0	64%
L.Bell	165	16.2%	94	75	616	8.2	8.9	2	80%
D.Williams*	-3	-15.7%	27	18	118	6.6	7.1	2	67%

Offensive Line

Player	Pos	Age	GS	Snaps	Pen	Sk	Pass	Run	Player	Pos	Age	GS	Snaps	Pen	Sk	Pass	Run
Alejandro Villanueva	LT	29	16/16	1083	7	4.0	10	3	Marcus Gilbert	RT	29	13/13	847	7	3.0	3	5
David DeCastro	RG	27	16/16	1081	13	0.0	7	5	Chris Hubbard	G/T	26	15/4	325	3	0.0	3	1
Maurkice Pouncey	C	28	15/15	959	2	0.0	4	6	B.J. Finney	C	26	13/3	300	2	0.5	2	2
Ramon Foster	LG	31	14/14	906	1	0.5	6	5									

Year	Yards	ALY	Rank	Power	Rank	Stuff	Rank	2nd Lev	Rank	Open Field	Rank	Sacks	ASR	Rank	Press	Rank	F-Start	Cont.
2014	4.50	4.38	6	69%	8	15%	1	1.18	15	0.96	5	33	5.8%	14	17.5%	2	15	27
2015	4.53	4.45	8	60%	24	19%	10	1.22	9	1.01	6	33	5.4%	8	19.2%	1	17	39
2016	4.47	4.68	3	71%	7	15%	4	1.40	4	0.52	25	21	4.1%	4	18.6%	2	21	31

2016 ALY by direction:	Left End 6.65 (1)	Left Tackle 4.78 (8)	Mid/Guard 4.25 (15)	Right Tackle 5.51 (3)	Right End 4.61 (7)

In an era when entire rosters seem to turn over in the span of a few seasons, the continuity along Pittsburgh's offensive line warrants full notice and appreciation. (It's also part of the reason Pittsburgh has the league's best mean projection for offensive DVOA.) ⬤ Ramon Foster and Maurkice Pouncey are each about to enter their seventh seasons as full-time starters in yellow and black; David DeCastro and Marcus Gilbert, their sixth seasons; and even the youngster of the group, Alejandro Villanueva, will be in his third season as the starter and his fourth season on the Pittsburgh roster. There have been some injuries and long absences along the way—last season was the first time the older quartet each played at least 800 snaps together—but this has essentially been the starting quintet in Pittsburgh for years and is unlikely to change in the near future. ⬤ That continuity could be key to the Steelers' rock-solid pass protection—note those stellar ranks in adjusted sack rate and pressure rate. (Ben Roethlisberger also deserves some credit for that—see his player page on page 264 for more info.) Pittsburgh has also fared very well in adjusted line yards year in and year out, ranking in the top 10 each of the past three years, even as Le'Veon Bell has missed 14 games in that span. Dallas gets all the attention, but numerically speaking, the NFL's best line plays at Heinz Field. ⬤ Teamwork and coordination play a big part in that success, but there's also a lot of individual talent on hand here. Villanueva, Foster, DeCastro, and Gilbert each ranked in the top ten at their positions snaps per blown block. Pouncey was just average in his first year back from a broken fibula, but ranked third among centers prior to that in 2014.

Defensive Front Seven

Defensive Line	Age	Pos		G	Snaps	Plays	TmPct	Rk	Stop	Dfts	BTkl		Runs	St%	Rk	RuYd	Rk		Sack	Hit	Hur	Dsrpt
			Overall									vs. Run					Pass Rush					
Stephon Tuitt	24	DE		14	764	40	5.7%	26	33	15	9		29	86%	22	1.3	12		3.5	11	21	3
Javon Hargrave	24	DT		15	492	27	3.6%	63	19	8	2		22	68%	66	2.6	56		2.0	1	15	0
Cameron Heyward	28	DE		7	364	24	6.8%	15	19	9	2		13	77%	44	1.3	10		3.0	3	5	5
Ricardo Mathews*	30	DE		16	311	13	1.6%	--	11	2	0		12	83%	--	1.8	--		1.0	2	6	0
Leterrius Walton	25	DE		10	254	9	1.8%	--	8	2	1		6	83%	--	1.3	--		0.0	2	1	1

Edge Rushers	Age	Pos		G	Snaps	Plays	TmPct	Rk	Stop	Dfts	BTkl		Runs	St%	Rk	RuYd	Rk		Sack	Hit	Hur	Dsrpt
			Overall									vs. Run					Pass Rush					
James Harrison	39	OLB		15	587	53	7.0%	18	33	12	2		32	66%	81	2.5	45		5.0	5	20	0
Jarvis Jones	28	OLB		14	474	45	6.4%	24	31	8	1		29	66%	82	3.6	89		1.0	4	13	3
Arthur Moats	29	OLB		16	396	22	2.7%	--	17	6	0		9	89%	--	2.7	--		3.5	3	6	1
Bud Dupree	24	OLB		7	318	24	6.8%	20	17	8	2		10	70%	69	2.9	62		4.0	2	8	0
Anthony Chickillo	25	OLB		15	316	22	2.9%	--	18	9	2		12	75%	--	3.3	--		2.5	4	5	0
Tyson Alualu	30	DE		14	509	35	5.0%	46	28	6	2		31	81%	23	2.8	60		2.5	4	3	0

Linebackers	Age	Pos		G	Snaps	Plays	TmPct	Rk	Stop	Dfts	BTkl	Runs	St%	Rk	RuYd	Rk	Sack	Hit	Hur	Tgts	Suc%	Rk	AdjYd	Rk	PD	Int
			Overall									vs. Run					Pass Rush			vs. Pass						
Lawrence Timmons*	31	ILB		16	950	119	14.8%	24	65	18	12	59	68%	24	3.1	25	2.5	10	17	42	39%	68	6.9	49	5	2
Ryan Shazier	25	ILB		13	771	95	14.5%	27	58	21	20	42	74%	6	2.7	13	3.5	3	16	40	42%	58	9.4	78	8	3
Vince Williams	28	ILB		16	269	40	5.0%	--	22	9	2	20	70%	--	4.8	--	2.0	2	2	11	12%	--	8.2	--	0	0

Year	Yards	ALY	Rank	Power	Rank	Stuff	Rank	2nd Level	Rank	Open Field	Rank	Sacks	ASR	Rank	Press	Rank
2014	4.36	4.32	21	53%	3	18%	21	1.32	30	0.75	19	33	6.4%	21	24.0%	21
2015	3.80	4.06	16	55%	5	21%	14	1.13	18	0.56	7	48	7.4%	7	24.2%	24
2016	4.39	4.07	14	67%	24	22%	9	1.24	21	0.99	29	38	5.8%	19	24.7%	24

2016 ALY by direction:	Left End 5.37 (29)	Left Tackle 2.65 (2)	Mid/Guard 4.18 (16)	Right Tackle 4.64 (23)	Right End 2.34 (3)

We discussed Pittsburgh's young defenders in our main essay, so we'll focus on their older players here. And when you're talking about old defenders, there's no better place to start than James Harrison. Since sacks became an official statistic in 1982, Harrison is just the 20th player to pick up a sack at age 38 or older. (That total includes Clay Matthews Sr. twice, and Bruce Smith three times.) Only five players had a sack at age 39, and only Matthews and Smith got one at age 40. In other words, we're approaching uncharted territory for older pass-rushers here. The Steelers still believe in Harrison, as evidenced by the two-year, $3.5 million contract he signed in May. But Father Time, as they say, is undefeated. ☛ Cameron Heyward had not missed a game since he was a first-round draft pick in 2011, and had not missed a start since 2013, but then missed most of 2016 with hamstring and pectoral injuries. He still collected 3.0 sacks last year and now has 22.5 over the last four seasons. In Heyward's place, Stephon Tuitt led the team with a career-high 21 hurries. Heyward and Tuitt usually stay on the field in nickel sets, and their success has done a lot to mask the failures of Pittsburgh's young linebackers over the years. ☛ Speaking of young linebackers, it's worth mentioning that Bud Dupree actually led this unit with 45.4 snaps per game. In each of the past two seasons, though Harrison's hits and hurries have dwarfed Dupree's, Dupree's sack totals have nearly matched Harrison's. So while Dupree has not matched Harrison's consistency as a pass-rusher, he does have that extra gear to finish plays and put quarterbacks on the ground.

Defensive Secondary

Secondary	Age	Pos	G	Snaps	Plays	TmPct	Rk	Stop	Dfts	BTkl	Runs	St%	Rk	RuYd	Rk	Tgts	Tgt%	Rk	Dist	Suc%	Rk	AdjYd	Rk	PD	Int
Ross Cockrell	26	CB	16	1025	76	9.4%	27	31	12	9	13	38%	47	4.8	14	79	18.4%	44	12.8	49%	46	7.2	31	14	0
Mike Mitchell	30	SS	16	1004	86	10.7%	29	19	8	9	36	17%	72	10.4	68	31	7.4%	25	13.0	51%	24	9.1	43	10	1
William Gay	32	CB	16	844	65	8.1%	55	31	13	9	16	56%	15	4.3	9	53	14.8%	7	9.2	54%	21	6.2	12	5	1
Artie Burns	22	CB	16	810	76	9.4%	27	32	11	9	17	24%	76	11.0	78	71	20.7%	61	10.6	49%	52	9.3	77	13	3
Sean Davis	24	SS	16	740	74	9.2%	46	30	11	15	33	42%	33	7.9	50	27	8.5%	38	8.9	52%	21	5.9	4	6	1
Robert Golden	27	FS	13	377	33	5.0%	72	13	6	4	13	54%	14	5.7	19	13	8.2%	32	13.5	45%	42	12.6	70	1	0
Coty Sensabaugh	29	CB	13	217	24	3.5%	--	9	5	1	10	80%	--	3.2	--	13	29.7%	--	7.8	9%	--	12.7	--	0	0

Year	Pass D Rank	vs. #1 WR	Rk	vs. #2 WR	Rk	vs. Other WR	Rk	vs. TE	Rk	vs. RB	Rk
2014	30	4.4%	20	-6.8%	12	39.3%	32	17.4%	28	13.3%	22
2015	13	12.2%	26	10.2%	22	-9.2%	11	-16.1%	5	-8.6%	9
2016	12	19.8%	32	-18.9%	3	-30.4%	1	-4.4%	13	3.3%	19

Remember when Al Davis and the Raiders took Mike Mitchell and his seventh-round projection in the second round in 2009 and everyone laughed? And then he started only nine games in four years in Oakland before leaving as a major bust? Well, he has started 62 games since: 14 for Carolina, then 48 for Pittsburgh. Only two players drafted after him (Andy Levitre and Glover Quin) have started more games in the past four seasons. So in the long run, Mitchell proved Davis was right to have faith in him—not that it actually did the Raiders any good. ☛ Ross Cockrell was Pittsburgh's top corner last season. He may not be the best corner in the league—in two years as a starter he has yet to finish in the top 30 in either success rate or yards allowed per target—but he is one of the best values at the position, signing a $1.8 million one-year deal as a restricted free agent to return to Pittsburgh in 2017. If he plays well again, he'll be a lot more expensive to re-sign in 2018. ☛ It says a lot that neither Mitchell nor Cockrell, the two best players in Pittsburgh's secondary, was actually drafted by the Steelers. Since Troy Polamalu in 2003, Steelers defensive draftees have combined for just three Pro Bowl selections, with none making more than one. ☛ Sean Davis started his rookie season at slot corner, but soon moved to strong safety and stuck there. His top priority will be to improve as a tackler, as his 15 missed tackles were tied for second-most among defensive backs. Davis' 25 percent missed tackle rate was also second-worst among all defenders with at least 40 tackles (distressingly, only teammate Ryan Shazier was worse). ☛ William Gay was moved to nickel corner after five years as a starter for the Steelers and Cardinals and played very well, but his job may be in jeopardy. If Senquez Golson or third-round rookie Cameron Sutton can pass him on the depth chart, the Steelers may decide it's not worth keeping a 32-year-old corner on the bench at the expense of younger players with more upside.

Special Teams

Year	DVOA	Rank	FG/XP	Rank	Net Kick	Rank	Kick Ret	Rank	Net Punt	Rank	Punt Ret	Rank	Hidden	Rank
2014	0.9%	12	2.5	10	-2.6	22	-4.6	26	3.2	10	5.8	9	-13.5	31
2015	0.1%	18	-1.0	18	3.7	8	-4.8	27	3.4	12	-0.6	17	-11.1	30
2016	-0.1%	16	9.1	3	-2.2	19	-1.6	18	-4.4	23	-1.3	17	-0.2	17

Chris Boswell has been excellent for two years now. (Pittsburgh's mediocre placekicking value in 2015 includes Josh Scobee's 6-of-10 performance.) His 88 percent field goal percentage ranks 10th since 2015, including a 28-of-29 mark inside of 40 yards. When you account for kicking in Heinz Field, where field goals go to die, he has been in the top four in placekicking value in each of the last two seasons. ⇒ Like Boswell, Jordan Berry joined the Steelers in 2015. Unlike Boswell, he has been decidedly mediocre at his job, ranking within one point of an average punter each season. ⇒ In the past three years, Antonio Brown has ranked seventh, 15th, and 13th in punt return value. That's certainly not bad, but is it good enough to justify the risk of using one of the best wide receivers in the league to return punts? ⇒ Sammie Coates and Fitzgerald Toussaint split kickoff return duties and were both essentially average. The Steelers didn't bring in anyone to compete with them. ⇒ One of the weirder events of draft weekend was the Steelers selecting Louisville long snapper Colin Holba in the sixth round. On the one hand, it makes sense, because incumbent Greg Warren turns 36 in October and has suffered two torn ACLs in his career. On the other hand, it makes no sense, because who drafts a long snapper? The answer to that would be Bill Belichick, who drafted Joe Cardona in the fifth round in 2015. Since the draft, Kevin Colbert has said bizarre things about a training camp competition between Holba and Warren, and even suggested the loser might end up on the practice squad. When asked whether any long snapper warranted a sixth-round pick, Colbert replied that in the past, sixth- and seventh-rounders have failed to make the team. A better question for Colbert might be, has anyone ever found a superstar player in the sixth round? And the answer to that would also be Bill Belichick.

San Francisco 49ers

2016 Record: 2-14	Total DVOA: -19.6% (28th)	2017 Mean Projection: 6.5 wins	On the Clock (0-4): 23%
Pythagorean Wins: 3.9 (30th)	Offense: -7.2% (23rd)	Postseason Odds: 16.2%	Mediocrity (5-7): 45%
Snap-Weighted Age: 26.5 (18th)	Defense: 12.1% (28th)	Super Bowl Odds: 1.3%	Playoff Contender (8-10): 26%
Average Opponent: -1.4% (23rd)	Special Teams: -0.3% (17th)	Proj. Avg. Opponent: 2.1% (5th)	Super Bowl Contender (11+): 7%

2016: Ship of fools on a cruel sea. Ship of fools, sail away from me.

2017: Come hear Uncle John's band, playing to the Crimson Tide linebacker.

In hindsight, maybe firing Jim Harbaugh wasn't such a good idea after all.

The robust 7-25 record the 49ers have had over the last two seasons backs up that claim. So does the fact that they're on their fourth head coach in four years. This isn't just a case of hindsight being 20/20, because it was easy to mock the move at the time. *FOA 2015* claimed that the 49ers were "about to learn some much-needed lessons in humility." Consider those lessons learned.

The firing was the end result of a power struggle between Harbaugh, notoriously prickly to work with even at the best of times, and general manager Trent Baalke. The relationship crumbled to a point where the two men simply couldn't work together anymore, and owner Jed York sided with Baalke. In retrospect, perhaps they should have stuck with the coach with the fifth-highest winning percentage in NFL history.

Even if they had kept Harbaugh, however, it's unlikely that the 49ers would have entirely avoided the slide that has plunged them from the Super Bowl to the dregs of the league in five seasons. Under Baalke's management, the 49ers suffered an enormous talent drain, and failed miserably at replenishing talent though the draft.

Baalke was quite adept at moving around in the draft, gathering more picks and targeting the players he wanted. From 2012 to 2016, the 49ers ended up making 51 selections, three more than any other team. The problem is that almost none of the players the 49ers selected actually worked out.

The 49ers have only managed to squeeze 402 games started and 202 points of Approximate Value out of those draft picks, an absolutely abysmal hit rate. (Table 1) To put that in perspective, the only team with less AV from their draft picks (196 points) is the New Orleans Saints, and they have had 20 fewer players to draw from. Cleveland pips San Francisco to the line for most expected value lost over the past five seasons, but the two teams are in a league of their own when it comes to whiffing on the draft.

So when the 49ers tried to replace stars such as Patrick Willis, Frank Gore, or Justin Smith, they found the cupboard bare. Some players just couldn't play at the NFL level, such as first-round bust A.J. Jenkins. Other players couldn't stay healthy, including the seven players with preexisting ACL injuries the 49ers drafted from 2013-16, who have combined for just one start. Undrafted free-agent signings were more likely to feature former rugby players or discus throwers than experienced college prospects who could contribute. The lack of any real talent coming in to replenish the roster has driven the 49ers down to the bottom of the league.

As a result, the 2016 San Francisco 49ers were one of the most talent-starved and directionless franchises in the NFL. The first step in fixing a problem of that scale is to acknowledge that the problem exists; the second step is to make the front-office changes that will start to fix the problem. This message finally hit home for York, and Baalke was summarily dismissed, making way for new blood and a new strategy.

The new blood are new head coach Kyle Shanahan and new general manager John Lynch, each with six-year contracts and a directive to shape the franchise to their vision. The length of the contracts are what's important here. Six years is an *extraordinarily* long commitment to a first-time coach and general manager. In fact, Shanahan has a longer contract than any other active head coach, as opposed to the more conventional four-year deals given to Jim Tomsula and Chip Kelly.

It's a sign that the 49ers are aware that rebuilding a team that finished in the bottom five in DVOA in each of the last two seasons isn't something that's going to happen overnight. The long deals should give Shanahan and Lynch a couple of seasons to revamp and turn over the roster before results can reasonably be expected.

The new administration certainly didn't wait to start that turnover process. As of June 3, 51 players on the 90-man roster were new Shanahan-Lynch signees. They let 27 of their 31 free agents walk, including all four quarterbacks. They are

Table 1. Worst Drafting Teams, 2012-2016

Team	No. of Picks	Starts	AV	AV/Pick	Exp. AV	Difference
CLE	48	506	260	5.42	343.2	-83.2
SF	51	402	202	3.96	281.2	-79.2
NYJ	40	438	215	5.38	263.2	-48.2
JAX	38	595	307	8.08	336.2	-29.2
CIN	44	495	287	6.52	307.5	-20.5
TEN	40	491	268	6.70	288.5	-20.5
SD	32	441	231	7.22	246.0	-15.0
BUF	37	572	283	7.65	292.0	-9.0
BAL	47	490	274	5.83	282.5	-8.5
DEN	37	388	236	6.38	242.5	-6.5

2017 49ers Schedule

Week	Opp.	Week	Opp.	Week	Opp.
1	CAR	7	DAL	13	at CHI
2	at SEA	8	at PHI	14	at HOU
3	LARM (Thu.)	9	ARI	15	TEN
4	at ARI	10	NYG	16	JAC
5	at IND	11	BYE	17	at LARM
6	at WAS	12	SEA		

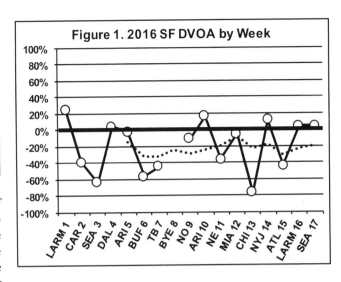

Figure 1. 2016 SF DVOA by Week

projected to have a dozen new starters compared to Week 1 of 2016. They're switching offensive philosophies from the Chip Kelly spread to a West Coast attack, and switching defensive schemes from a 3-4 front to a Seattle-inspired 4-3. About the only thing that will remain the same from 2016 to 2017 are the jerseys on the field—and even those are undergoing a minor overhaul.

It's not surprising that San Francisco chose Kyle Shanahan to guide the team through these changes. Shanahan has been a hot head coaching candidate since the 2014 season, and the 49ers flirted with bringing him in with his father Mike as a package deal before they promoted Tomsula in 2015. His offense in Atlanta last season put up a 25.3% DVOA, the best performance of the last three years. His schemes don't only work when you have someone like Matt Ryan calling the shots; he has also helped Robert Griffin, Rex Grossman, and Matt Schaub have career seasons. His average offensive DVOA as a coordinator has only been 1.2%, but he has managed that with some pretty sorry quarterback situations. The 49ers would love to have an offense hit 1.2%, a baseline the franchise has only reached twice since 2004. Shanahan is a logical, conventional choice to shape a franchise going forward.

John Lynch, on the other hand, is anything but a conventional choice. Picking a general manager from the broadcasting booth with no prior front-office experience was met with equal parts skepticism and incredulity, especially as it came out of the blue. All reports had the 49ers interviewing front office veterans such as George Paton and Terry McDonough before the surprise pick of the ex-FOX analyst. Lynch's complete lack of credentials quickly drew comparisons to famous TV talking head-turned-front office exec Matt Millen, who led the Detroit Lions to a 31-97 record including the only 0-16 season in NFL history. The hiring of Lynch, with no evidence of any front-office skills, was just another boneheaded move by a franchise floundering in the wilderness, right?

Well, the absence of evidence is not necessarily evidence of absence. While we obviously won't be able to judge Lynch and Shanahan's success before anything happens on the field, their offseason has quickly made believers out of the fan base. Part of that is Lynch's more open style. Coming from a media background, it's clear that Lynch is more comfortable with reporters and cameras than Baalke ever was. It's a far cry from the old regime, where leaks to national media were about the only information a fan could get on just what the plan was at 49ers HQ.

The good vibes continued among the fans when the new administration was surprisingly active in free agency. As part of that aforementioned massive roster turnover, the 49ers spent nearly $150 million in new deals for free agents, bringing in Brian Hoyer, Kyle Juszczyk, Pierre Garcon, Earl Mitchell, and Malcom Smith. The 49ers handed out more money in new contracts this offseason than they had in the past four offseasons combined. This isn't just a factor of cap space opening up suddenly this offseason; the 49ers have rolled over huge chunks of their cap from the previous two seasons, opting simply to move nearly $40 million in cap room to 2017 rather than signing players to help improve either Tomsula or Kelly's squads. This inaction is part of what drove the fan base crazy. Not only was the team floundering on the field, but it felt like nothing was being done about it. It remains to be seen if the 49ers' spending spree will pay off, but it at least feels like an attempt is being made to improve the on-field product.

Of course, all the draft kudos, free-agent acquisitions, and media savvy in the world won't matter if the actual on-field plan is scattershot. Free agency isn't a panacea that can turn a struggling team into a playoff contender. Glowing articles written after the draft don't mean the class will perform on the field. Confidence and charisma in interviews do not necessarily lead to competence in player acquisition. Positive first steps need to be followed up by a coherent and functioning plan to undo years of poor player acquisition and on-field results.

So, what *is* the grand Lynch-Shanahan plan to bring the 49ers back to relevance? With so many holes on the roster, the 49ers couldn't possibly fix everything in one go, so what was their strategy to begin the rebuild?

An old Bill Walsh axiom stated that scheme and coaching can boost an offense, but you need talent and better athletes to make a defense work. That philosophy seemed to guide the 49ers' plans this offseason. They spent time and money in free agency adding players who could help install Shanahan's offensive scheme and organizational culture, and then spent the majority of their draft capital on adding athletes to the defense.

The offense still has a great many question marks up and down the depth chart, and there's every chance that their performance will only be marginally improved from 2016. What's important is that the new additions are building a framework for Shanahan to install his system and culture—and then replace the subpar talent and square pegs in the future as the rebuild continues.

Shanahan's offensive philosophy is a dramatic change from Chip Kelly's spread attack, but one that should feel very familiar for longtime 49ers fans. In the passing game, it's a modern take on the classic West Coast system. It's focused on getting the ball out of the quarterback's hands quickly and producing yards after the catch, using short routes to the running back and fullback as extensions of the running game. (Atlanta was second in the league with an average of 6.1 yards after the catch last season.) However, it also incorporates a more vertical aspect, stretching the field with go routes and fades. Andre Johnson in Houston, Pierre Garcon in Washington, Julio Jones in Atlanta—Shanahan likes to design his passing concepts around one key receiver. This top receiver will stretch and stress the defense on one side of the field, simplifying both the reads and precision needed from the quarterback.

In the running game, Shanahan's offense resembles the offenses his father ran in Denver, with a zone-blocking scheme that features heavy use of stretch plays to get backs to the outside. By moving the defense laterally and pinning them inside, it gives running backs plenty of open room to run. It's the system that helped make Terrell Davis a Hall of Famer, dragged 1,000-yard seasons out of marginal players like Mike Anderson and Tatum Bell, and produced the two-headed monster of Devonta Freeman and Tevin Coleman down in Atlanta.

It's a system that's proven to work, even with subpar talent. With exceptional talent, it explodes. Shanahan set franchise records in offensive DVOA in his time in Houston and Atlanta, improved Washington's offense to a level it hadn't seen since the glory days of the '90s, and produced the best offense Cleveland has had in the last six seasons.

To install that system, though, Shanahan needed some players who had run it before. Enter Brian Hoyer, who worked with Shanahan in Cleveland in 2014. Welcome Pierre Garcon, who was with Shanahan in Washington in 2012 and 2013. Even the additions who don't have direct Shanahands-on experience are bringing with them skills that fit the team's new direction. Center Jeremy Zuttah operated out of a zone-blocking scheme in Baltimore. Fullback Kyle Juszczyk is, well, a fullback—a position which had no role in Kelly's offense but sees significant work in Shanahan's system. He'll play fullback, running back, slot receiver, wideout, and tight end, filling some of the role in the passing game that Freeman and Coleman played in Atlanta.

With the possible exception of Juszczyk, these are not players who are going to be key parts in the next great 49ers team. They're role players—solid veterans who will help install the system, teach young colleagues what to do, and then eventually be replaced as the rebuild continues. When we get talk about the dangers of attempting to build a team through free agency, we're talking about overpaying for aging veterans in an attempt to build a competitive team out of whole cloth rather than building it organically through the draft. That's not what the 49ers did this offseason, though. The bulk of their

free agent spending was on short-term deals that will put a more entertaining product on the field in 2017 and help them build a culture without locking them into anything long-term.

Take Hoyer, for example. The 49ers could have used their second pick in the draft on Mitchell Trubisky or Patrick Mahomes, or put together a package of picks and pried Kirk Cousins from Washington. That would have tied the franchise to that particular quarterback, however—with that much draft capital invested in one player, the fate of Shanahan and Lynch would be directly tied to his development.

By offering an inexpensive two-year deal to Hoyer, the 49ers have left all their options open. Maybe Hoyer somehow duplicates his lucky 2016 season. Maybe third-round pick C.J. Beathard shows promise and surprising tools in his rookie season. If not, they can attempt to sign Kirk Cousins next offseason, or take Sam Darnold or Josh Allen in a much deeper 2018 quarterback class. It's a multi-year rebuild; the 49ers can afford to wait until they get players they love rather than settling for who's available. Garcon doesn't prevent them from drafting a true No. 1 receiver; Zuttah doesn't mean they can't pick up new additions to the offensive line in the future.

Improvement on offense will be measured in fits and starts. It will be spurred by a better scheme and players who can operate it, rather than a dramatic talent infusion. Improvement on defense, on the other hand, will be measured in talent added *this* year, and will likely see a quicker and more dramatic boost thanks to a stellar draft.

John Lynch and company made headlines by trading down in the first round. They swapped with Chicago to drop down from 2 to 3, picking up three mid-round picks in the process. According to media reports, they expected to get the third player on their draft board—Alabama linebacker Reuben Foster. Instead, the Bears went quarterback. That meant the 49ers ended up taking who they would have picked at No. 2 anyway—Stanford lineman Solomon Thomas—and still managed to trade back up and take Foster at the end of the first round. Not bad for your first draft day.

The 49ers have now spent three consecutive first-round picks on big Pac-12 interior defensive linemen. Thomas projects as an elite run defender with exceptional athletic talent and the ability to play anywhere along the line. He had an athletic SPARQ score of 140.7, putting him in the 94th percentile among NFL edge rushers, thanks to his lateral agility and recovery speed. Combine him with DeForest Buckner, who had a very strong rookie season, and Arik Armstead, whose sophomore season was cut short due to injury, and you have three young, promising players to build around.

Unfortunately, there are only two natural slots for these three players in new defensive coordinator Robert Saleh's scheme. Each player projects well as a 5-technique defensive end or as a 3-technique defensive tackle. But they would each be an awkward fit in the pivotal LEO role, the hybrid defensive end/linebacker asked to be the best pass-rusher on the team *and* play C-gap run support. That's a tough task to handle, and none of the 49ers' big three is really the ideal player for it.

That won't matter in sub packages, when all three can be exploited to rush the quarterback. In the base formation, though, expect Buckner to stay locked in as the 3-technique tackle with Thomas opposite him as the 5-technique end. Armstead will try to convert from a 4-technique end to the LEO role, battling with Aaron Lynch to fill that spot. Add in free-agent acquisition Earl Mitchell at nose tackle, and you have the makings of a promising line. At the very least, they should improve their poor performance against the run a year ago, 29th in adjusted line yards.

The 49ers followed up the first-round selections of Thomas and Foster by grabbing cornerback Ahkello Witherspoon of Colorado at the top of the third round. That's three straight picks to bolster the defense, all three of whom could realistically start in 2017, though it will depend somewhat on Foster's recovery from a torn rotator cuff. He may start as a nickel player and ease into free agent Malcom Smith's role as the Will linebacker. Either way, the 49ers took the opportunity presented by a deep defensive draft and added a trio of players who should have an immediate impact.

Not every defensive problem could be addressed in one year, of course. The 49ers cut last year's top cornerback, Tramaine Brock, after an April domestic violence arrest; they'll use some combination of Witherspoon, Rashard Robinson, Dontae Johnson and Keith Reaser to cover that role. They could really use a top shutdown corner—or a great safety, allowing Jimmie Ward to fill an extra corner role—but with so many needs, it wasn't possible to fill *everything* in one year. The rebuild seems to be further along on defense, but remains a work in progress.

That's the underlying phrase to remember this season for the 49ers: work in progress. With the luxury of six-year deals, Shanahan and Lynch do not feel the pressure to win right away—and faced with a brutal schedule and massive roster turnover, they probably won't. There's a strong chance they'll end up with the first pick in the draft next season.

But wins and losses aren't how you should judge the 2017 49ers. Even if they turn in a third straight double-digit loss season, it's quite possible they will see notable improvement on the field, as their young defensive talent begins to gel and the offense becomes more comfortable in Shanahan's system. Only time will tell if any of these moves will work, or if it was just shuffling deck chairs around. However, for the first time since Harbaugh was fired, 49ers fans can dare to believe that their team might be pointed in the right direction, even if it might take a year or two to actually see that result in a better record.

Bryan Knowles

2016 49ers Stats by Week

Wk	vs.	W-L	PF	PA	YDF	YDA	TO	Total	Off	Def	ST
1	LARM	W	28	0	320	185	+1	25%	-2%	-31%	-4%
2	at CAR	L	27	46	302	529	+1	-40%	-10%	25%	-4%
3	at SEA	L	18	37	254	418	+1	-64%	-37%	13%	-14%
4	DAL	L	17	24	295	428	-1	4%	14%	8%	-1%
5	ARI	L	21	33	286	288	-3	-3%	4%	0%	-7%
6	at BUF	L	16	45	300	492	+1	-57%	-27%	26%	-3%
7	TB	L	17	34	273	513	-2	-45%	-17%	35%	7%
8	BYE										
9	NO	L	23	41	486	571	-4	-11%	-1%	27%	17%
10	at ARI	L	20	23	281	443	+3	16%	0%	-6%	10%
11	NE	L	17	30	299	444	0	-36%	-11%	13%	-11%
12	at MIA	L	24	31	475	358	-2	-5%	26%	26%	-6%
13	at CHI	L	6	26	147	326	+1	-77%	-61%	32%	17%
14	NYJ	L	17	23	364	404	+1	11%	26%	3%	-11%
15	at ATL	L	13	41	272	550	0	-44%	-15%	25%	-4%
16	at LARM	W	22	21	323	177	0	4%	-9%	-16%	-2%
17	SEA	L	23	25	253	376	-2	4%	-6%	5%	14%

Trends and Splits

	Offense	Rank	Defense	Rank
Total DVOA	-7.2%	23	12.1%	28
Unadjusted VOA	-9.7%	25	12.3%	30
Weighted Trend	-6.6%	21	13.6%	30
Variance	4.9%	12	3.4%	5
Average Opponent	-1.3%	7	-2.3%	25
Passing	-8.7%	28	21.7%	28
Rushing	1.2%	9	3.3%	31
First Down	9.5%	8	9.4%	27
Second Down	-21.6%	30	5.0%	21
Third Down	-16.8%	25	29.8%	31
First Half	5.1%	15	17.8%	31
Second Half	-42.7%	31	-8.4%	15
Red Zone	55.1%	2	24.3%	30
Late and Close	-62.5%	32	-6.1%	14

Five-Year Performance

Year	W-L	Pyth W	Est W	PF	PA	TO	Total	Rk	Off	Rk	Def	Rk	ST	Rk	Off AGL	Rk	Def AGL	Rk	Off Age	Rk	Def Age	Rk	ST Age	Rk
2012	11-4-1	11.4	12.5	397	273	+9	29.5%	4	16.5%	5	-14.4%	3	-1.5%	20	11.7	5	4.5	1	27.1	14	27.3	10	26.9	5
2013	12-4	11.5	10.6	406	272	+12	17.4%	7	9.1%	8	-4.6%	13	3.7%	7	34.7	17	46.8	27	27.8	5	27.4	9	26.9	4
2014	8-8	7.0	9.0	306	340	+7	6.6%	11	-0.4%	16	-10.1%	5	-3.0%	24	30.0	15	71.8	31	27.6	6	26.8	16	26.4	8
2015	5-11	3.8	4.1	238	387	-5	-27.5%	32	-14.0%	28	9.9%	27	-3.6%	27	58.2	28	25.8	11	27.7	6	25.4	32	25.1	31
2016	2-14	3.9	4.6	309	247	-5	-19.6%	28	-7.2%	23	12.1%	28	-0.3%	17	39.0	21	58.5	26	27.0	13	26.2	22	26.1	17

2016 Performance Based on Most Common Personnel Groups

SF Offense					SF Offense vs. Opponents					SF Defense				SF Defense vs. Opponents			
Pers	Freq	Yds	DVOA	Run%	Pers	Freq	Yds	DVOA	Run%	Pers	Freq	Yds	DVOA	Pers	Freq	Yds	DVOA
12	19%	4.5	0.1%	61%	Nickel	79%	5.2	0.4%	38%	Nickel	41%	6.3	17.1%	12	27%	5.5	1.2%
11	76%	5.3	-3.1%	35%	Base	14%	4.2	-11.0%	66%	Base	48%	5.6	4.3%	11	48%	6.5	21.7%
12	19%	4.5	0.1%	61%	Nickel	79%	5.2	0.4%	38%	Nickel	41%	6.3	17.1%	12	27%	5.5	1.2%
10	2%	3.4	-37.3%	31%	Dime+	7%	4.4	-32.0%	14%	Dime+	10%	8.1	36.9%	21	9%	7.4	23.4%
20	1%	3.5	-45.7%	42%	Goal Line	0%	-4.0	-198.2%	100%	Goal Line	1%	0.2	16.2%	10	5%	5.6	-21.1%
13	1%	5.7	-28.7%	86%										611	3%	6.1	-5.4%

Strategic Tendencies

Run/Pass		Rk	Formation		Rk	Pass Rush		Rk	Secondary		Rk	Strategy		Rk
Runs, first half	46%	1	Form: Single Back	92%	2	Rush 3	10.9%	9	4 DB	48%	2	Play-action	23%	4
Runs, first down	46%	19	Form: Empty Back	5%	29	Rush 4	62.7%	20	5 DB	41%	29	Avg Box (Off)	6.12	25
Runs, second-long	48%	1	Pers: 3+ WR	80%	4	Rush 5	21.6%	15	6+ DB	8%	15	Avg Box (Def)	6.44	1
Runs, power sit.	74%	1	Pers: 2+ TE/6+ OL	21%	28	Rush 6+	4.8%	23	CB by Sides	55%	31	Offensive Pace	28.97	3
Runs, behind 2H	31%	6	Pers: 6+ OL	0%	32	Sacks by LB	53.2%	12	S/CB Cover Ratio	31%	7	Defensive Pace	30.14	13
Pass, ahead 2H	47%	23	Shotgun/Pistol	99%	1	Sacks by DB	8.1%	13	DB Blitz	12%	8	Go for it on 4th	1.19	8

Use of the shotgun in the NFL keeps going up year after year, particularly if we count pistol formations and shotgun formations together, but it's hard to imagine it going further than last year's San Francisco 49ers. San Francisco had a quarterback under center on only 10 plays all year. Even stranger, these were not specifically short-yardage plays; most were first-and-10 or second-and-10. In the final five weeks of the season, San Francisco didn't run a single play with the quarterback under center. ⬤ Under Kyle Shanahan, the 49ers offense will change dramatically. Atlanta ranked dead last, using shotgun or pistol on only 40 percent of plays last year. And while the 49ers only used multi-back sets on 11 carries by running backs last season, or 3 percent, Atlanta used multi-back sets on 43 percent of running plays. And Baltimore, previous home of Kyle Juszczyk, had 4.9 yards per carry and 7.4% DVOA with two backs, compared to 3.7 yards per carry and minus-22.8% DVOA with just one back. ⬤ This was the first time Chip Kelly's offense did not lead the league in situation-neutral pace. His Philadelphia offenses were five or six seconds ahead of the rest of the league; the 49ers finished third, slightly behind the Giants and Saints. ⬤ 49ers opponents used play-action on a league-high 25 percent of passes, though the 49ers had roughly the same defensive DVOA with or without play-action. ⬤ San Francisco was one of only two defenses (along with Denver) to use four defensive backs as the most common personnel package. ⬤ San Francisco opponents threw a league-low 17 percent of passes in the middle of the field even though the 49ers were 25th in DVOA against these passes. ⬤ San Francisco benefited from a league-low 25 defensive penalties by opponents, for just 221 yards.

Passing

Player	DYAR	DVOA	Plays	NtYds	Avg	YAC	C%	TD	Int
C.Kaepernick*	-145	-17.5%	366	2044	5.6	5.7	59.4%	16	4
B.Gabbert*	-158	-25.4%	172	876	5.1	4.0	57.1%	5	6
B.Hoyer	404	19.4%	204	1435	7.0	5.2	67.8%	6	0
M.Barkley	4	-10.9%	222	1568	7.1	4.2	59.7%	8	13

Rushing

Player	DYAR	DVOA	Plays	Yds	Avg	TD	Fum	Suc
C.Hyde	201	18.5%	188	857	4.6	6	0	48%
C.Kaepernick*	136	40.1%	53	418	7.9	2	0	-
B.Gabbert*	52	13.3%	38	175	4.6	2	0	-
S.Draughn*	17	2.9%	37	120	3.2	4	0	35%
D.Harris*	-9	-15.4%	34	139	4.1	0	0	38%
M.Davis*	-28	-38.1%	19	50	2.6	1	0	47%
T.Hightower	63	4.8%	105	422	4.0	4	0	47%
K.Bibbs	14	2.7%	29	129	4.4	0	0	52%

Receiving

Player	DYAR	DVOA	Plays	Ctch	Yds	Y/C	YAC	TD	C%
J.Kerley	-124	-26.4%	115	64	667	10.4	3.3	3	56%
Q.Patton*	-84	-29.5%	63	37	408	11.0	5.4	0	59%
T.Smith*	-78	-33.0%	49	20	267	13.4	3.1	3	41%
R.Streater*	49	11.2%	27	18	191	10.6	3.7	2	67%
C.Harper*	-2	-13.9%	21	13	133	10.2	3.7	0	62%
A.Burbridge	-12	-22.6%	16	7	88	12.6	6.1	0	44%
P.Garcon	262	16.3%	114	79	1041	13.2	4.3	3	69%
A.Robinson	91	24.5%	32	20	323	16.2	3.8	2	63%
G.Celek	-6	-9.0%	50	29	357	12.3	4.2	3	58%
V.McDonald	41	6.7%	45	24	391	16.3	8.6	4	53%
B.Bell	5	2.7%	9	4	85	21.3	7.8	0	44%
L.Paulsen	-57	-84.0%	10	3	15	5.0	1.3	0	30%
S.Draughn*	60	14.2%	39	29	263	9.1	6.4	2	74%
C.Hyde	38	6.2%	34	28	162	5.8	5.4	3	82%
D.Harris*	36	59.6%	9	8	115	14.4	15.1	1	89%
K.Juszczyk	6	-11.9%	49	37	266	7.2	5.9	0	76%
T.Hightower	73	32.1%	26	22	200	9.1	9.5	1	85%

Offensive Line

Player	Pos	Age	GS	Snaps	Pen	Sk	Pass	Run	Player	Pos	Age	GS	Snaps	Pen	Sk	Pass	Run
Zane Beadles	LG/LT/C	31	16/16	1034	3	1.5	14	7	Joshua Garnett	RG	23	15/11	715	6	5.0	15	7
Trenton Brown	RT	24	16/16	1034	11	4.5	12	12	Andrew Tiller*	LG/RG	28	15/7	485	4	2.0	3	3
Joe Staley	LT	33	13/13	844	3	4.0	12	6	Jeremy Zuttah	C	31	16/16	1109	6	4.0	10	4
Daniel Kilgore	C	30	13/13	793	3	2.0	6	3	Garry Gilliam	RT	27	14/13	811	5	2.5	11	8

Year	Yards	ALY	Rank	Power	Rank	Stuff	Rank	2nd Lev	Rank	Open Field	Rank	Sacks	ASR	Rank	Press	Rank	F-Start	Cont.
2014	4.15	4.33	10	48%	32	21%	19	1.26	6	0.59	24	52	9.8%	30	30.5%	29	14	22
2015	3.51	3.44	32	67%	14	26%	31	1.05	22	0.57	26	53	9.1%	31	30.2%	28	16	35
2016	3.99	3.46	32	69%	11	22%	25	1.12	17	0.72	14	47	8.4%	30	28.6%	22	15	32

2016 ALY by direction:	Left End 3.89 (23)	Left Tackle 3.57 (27)	Mid/Guard 3.42 (32)	Right Tackle 3.84 (18)	Right End 2.56 (30)

Every offensive lineman who played at least 100 snaps for the Niners last season is back. There isn't anyone in the pipeline to threaten the incumbents right now, as the front office chose not to spend a draft pick on the position for the first time since 2009. ⚡ At age 32, Joe Staley may be beginning to slowly decline. He missed the Pro Bowl for the first time since 2010, and struggled a little more against the elite pass-rushers of the league when compared to his All-Pro heyday. But he's still a very good lineman and the only guaranteed starter on the line. ⚡ Joshua Garnett had major rookie struggles, with a blown block once every 32.5 plays, the worst rate for any qualifying interior offensive lineman in the league. He may move to left guard, his college position, where he would benefit from working next to Staley. ⚡ Only Jason Peters had more false starts than Trent Brown did last season (six). Brown's 12 blown run blocks were the worst among right tackles as well, though he was better at pass protection. ⚡ Zane Beadles' best seasons came in a Denver zone-blocking scheme, where he was a highly effective run blocker. ⚡ Jeremy Zuttah gets first crack at center, displacing Daniel Kilgore. Kilgore was a strong run blocker but struggled in pass protection; he may replace Beadles at a guard position. ⚡ Garry Gilliam comes over from Seattle to compete for the right tackle position. He ranked 24th and 32nd in snaps per blown block at right tackle over the last two seasons. He should fit right in.

Defensive Front Seven

Defensive Line	Age	Pos	G	Snaps	Plays	TmPct	Rk	Stop	Dfts	BTkl	Runs	St%	Rk	RuYd	Rk	Sack	Hit	Hur	Dsrpt
					Overall							vs. Run					Pass Rush		
DeForest Buckner	23	DE	15	1005	74	9.0%	4	49	12	8	59	66%	74	3.4	81	6.0	14	23	2
Quinton Dial	27	DE	14	477	38	4.9%	38	25	4	5	35	66%	76	2.3	42	0.0	1	5	2
Glenn Dorsey*	32	DT	12	400	24	3.6%	61	14	3	4	23	57%	85	3.7	85	1.0	2	5	0
Arik Armstead	24	DE	8	335	15	3.4%	66	11	4	4	12	67%	71	3.3	80	2.5	0	7	0
Ronald Blair	24	DE	15	311	16	1.9%	--	11	5	2	9	67%	--	4.0	--	2.5	5	8	1
Chris Jones	27	DE	13	301	21	2.9%	--	17	4	2	21	81%	--	1.7	--	0.0	2	4	0
Mike Purcell	26	DT	16	279	26	3.0%	--	19	3	3	26	73%	--	3.2	--	0.0	0	0	0
Earl Mitchell	30	DT	9	308	18	3.7%	59	16	8	3	16	88%	18	0.7	5	0.0	1	8	0

Edge Rushers	Age	Pos	G	Snaps	Plays	TmPct	Rk	Stop	Dfts	BTkl	Runs	St%	Rk	RuYd	Rk	Sack	Hit	Hur	Dsrpt
					Overall							vs. Run					Pass Rush		
Ahmad Brooks	33	OLB	16	918	56	6.4%	25	46	19	6	41	80%	24	2.1	32	6.0	2	16	2
Eli Harold	23	OLB	16	688	37	4.2%	63	30	9	8	28	82%	16	2.5	49	3.5	3	10	0
Elvis Dumervil	33	OLB	8	272	11	2.8%	91	7	3	2	6	67%	76	3.7	91	3.0	6	24	0

Linebackers	Age	Pos	G	Snaps	Plays	TmPct	Rk	Stop	Dfts	BTkl	Runs	St%	Rk	RuYd	Rk	Sack	Hit	Hur	Tgts	Suc%	Rk	AdjYd	Rk	PD	Int
					Overall							vs. Run					Pass Rush				vs. Pass				
Nick Bellore*	28	ILB	14	691	82	10.6%	51	57	15	12	55	75%	5	2.6	9	1.0	2	5	20	44%	51	5.3	17	5	1
Gerald Hodges*	25	ILB	15	583	82	9.9%	57	49	9	9	63	63%	43	4.1	68	3.0	2	6	16	55%	23	5.4	19	0	0
Michael Wilhoite*	31	ILB	16	511	47	5.3%	82	23	6	5	28	54%	77	4.1	69	0.5	0	2	17	49%	39	5.2	16	2	0
NaVorro Bowman	29	ILB	4	252	37	16.8%	--	25	11	3	26	69%	--	2.4	--	1.0	1	3	10	65%	--	4.6	--	2	1
Malcolm Smith	28	OLB	15	934	106	14.6%	26	53	14	16	56	64%	36	5.2	85	0.0	2	7	49	47%	44	6.3	35	3	1

Year	Yards	ALY	Rank	Power	Rank	Stuff	Rank	2nd Level	Rank	Open Field	Rank	Sacks	ASR	Rank	Press	Rank
2014	4.04	4.45	25	71%	25	16%	26	1.00	6	0.59	9	36	6.6%	16	26.0%	9
2015	4.19	4.53	27	64%	15	17%	29	1.01	5	0.81	18	28	5.4%	29	25.7%	14
2016	4.97	4.68	29	71%	28	16%	27	1.27	23	1.29	32	33	5.8%	20	22.6%	31
2016 ALY by direction:		Left End 4.73 (22)			Left Tackle 5.41 (30)			Mid/Guard 4.75 (30)			Right Tackle 4.41 (18)			Right End 2.89 (7)		

When John Lynch went back to Stanford in 2014 to finish his degree, he took a Management Science and Engineering class. There, he worked on a group project with a freshman named Solomon Thomas. That's next-level scouting for you; expect the scouting reports of the future to be filled with information about penmanship and tardiness. Despite missing a game with a foot injury, DeForest Buckner's 1,005 snaps were most in the league amongst defensive linemen—partially due to a lack of talent in the rotation behind him. Buckner was more promising as a pass-rusher than run-stuffer as a rookie, leading the team with 23 hurries but ranking 74th among D-linemen in run stop rate. He did improve in the latter facet as the season went along, however, as issues with pad level and playing too high gradually went away. Arik Armstead is an odd fit for the LEO position; he had only seven hurries last season and has just 4.5 career sacks. He dealt with shoulder issues all last season, ending with surgery on a torn labrum, but the 49ers hope a healthier, lighter Armstead can become a pass-rushing specialist. If Earl Mitchell could match last year's 88 percent run stop rate, it would be the highest for a 49ers lineman since Aubrayo Franklin in 2010. Aaron Lynch's much-anticipated breakout season in 2016 turned out to be more of a breakdown season. He had 34.5 hurries in 2015, but that number plummeted to nine last year, as he dealt with suspensions and ankle injuries. He also reported to training camp 20 pounds overweight, which rarely bodes well. When Reuben Foster is healthy, he should take over at weakside linebacker. The "when" is the key point here; Foster's rotator cuff tear and subsequent surgery were reportedly enough for some teams to medically reject him.

Defensive Secondary

Secondary	Age	Pos	G	Snaps	Plays	TmPct	Rk	Stop	Dfts	BTkl	Runs	St%	Rk	RuYd	Rk	Tgts	Tgt%	Rk	Dist	Suc%	Rk	AdjYd	Rk	PD	Int
Antoine Bethea*	33	SS	16	1126	112	12.7%	13	38	11	15	60	40%	36	7.8	47	39	9.2%	46	13.3	37%	57	13.2	71	3	1
Tramaine Brock*	29	CB	16	1101	72	8.2%	51	25	17	9	22	32%	64	8.1	61	75	18.1%	41	15.7	53%	24	7.7	46	14	1
Eric Reid	26	FS	10	743	67	12.2%	16	21	3	5	32	31%	55	7.2	41	34	12.2%	65	10.3	52%	23	8.1	26	6	1
Jimmie Ward	26	CB	11	668	63	10.4%	12	28	9	5	16	44%	37	8.4	63	57	22.6%	70	10.7	43%	76	8.6	67	12	1
Jaquiski Tartt	25	SS	15	615	52	6.3%	67	20	12	9	26	50%	16	7.7	46	21	9.1%	45	10.5	42%	48	8.3	29	3	0
Rashard Robinson	22	CB	14	544	36	4.7%	--	13	6	7	10	20%	--	10.9	--	37	18.2%	--	12.3	53%	--	7.1	--	7	1
Keith Reaser	26	CB	15	353	28	3.4%	--	14	5	4	7	71%	--	4.0	--	29	21.5%	--	12.5	42%	--	10.4	--	5	0

Year	Pass D Rank	vs. #1 WR	Rk	vs. #2 WR	Rk	vs. Other WR	Rk	vs. TE	Rk	vs. RB	Rk
2014	4	-6.0%	11	-22.4%	4	-11.8%	8	-9.7%	9	-16.5%	8
2015	30	2.9%	18	22.0%	28	10.2%	23	9.1%	22	11.7%	25
2016	28	19.1%	31	7.6%	24	-7.0%	9	17.5%	27	17.1%	27

Last season, third-round pick Ahkello Witherspoon allowed just a 26.5 percent completion rate at Nevada with 20 passes defensed. He's also a tremendous athlete, running a 4.45 40 and playing that fast on the field. When it comes to tackling, however, he's hesitant at best, and will need to stop playing matador in order to earn a starting role over Dontae Johnson or Keith Reaser. ⬚ Jimmie Ward's charting metrics dropped in 2016; his adjusted yards ballooned from 7.2 to 8.6 and his adjusted success rate dropped from 50 percent to 43 percent. Some of this was due to offenses running him nearly 3 yards further downfield; Ward allowed about the same completion percentage in each year. A move to free safety will use his talents better. ⬚ Rashard Robinson flashed promise as a rookie; he would have been second in YAC allowed and in the top 20 in success rate had he qualified for the leaderboards. He'll be thrust into the top corner role with Tramaine Brock gone. ⬚ Will Redmond is the ghost of Trent Baalke injury picks past. Redmond missed his entire rookie season with a torn ACL, a yearly occurrence in the Baalke era. He only played 19 games at Mississippi State, but flashed athleticism and cover skills when healthy. He'll battle for the nickel role with K'Waun Williams, who started 10 games for Cleveland in 2014-2015 but failed a physical in Chicago and sat out last season. ⬚ Eric Reid was a Pro Bowler as a rookie, but it's been downhill from there. He'll be battling with Jaquiski Tartt for the strong safety role, and Tartt's run stop rate and tackling ability are much more suited to the role than Reid's have ever been. Entering the final year of his rookie deal, Reid might not be much longer for San Francisco.

Special Teams

Year	DVOA	Rank	FG/XP	Rank	Net Kick	Rank	Kick Ret	Rank	Net Punt	Rank	Punt Ret	Rank	Hidden	Rank
2014	-3.0%	24	-2.0	22	0.7	14	-0.8	17	-8.3	28	-4.8	25	-6.4	25
2015	-3.6%	27	0.7	15	-4.3	27	-5.3	28	-4.6	22	-4.4	22	11.3	4
2016	-0.3%	17	3.9	8	-2.7	23	-6.7	29	5.1	9	-0.9	14	-1.2	19

Ted Ginn returned a kickoff and a punt for a touchdown against Seattle in Week 1 of 2011. Since then, the 49ers have returned 477 kickoffs and punts and have failed to hit paydirt. Only Tampa Bay has a longer dry spell. Fifth-round rookie receiver Trent Taylor (Louisiana Tech) or veterans Bruce Ellington and Jeremy Kerley may get cracks at finally sniffing the end zone. ⬚ Bradley Pinion and Phil Dawson split kickoff duties in 2016, with Pinion being the touchback guy and Dawson trying to pin teams inside the 20. On gross kick value, Pinion was about league-average with minus-0.3 points added, but Dawson ranked fourth-worst at minus-4.1. Expect punter Pinion to return to the full-time kickoff duties he had in 2015. ⬚ Robbie Gould replaces Dawson as the 49ers' balding veteran placekicker. He saves the 49ers $1 million per year at the cost of about a percentage point of field goal accuracy. Gould made seven field goals of 50-plus yards two years ago in Chicago, but didn't have a single attempt at that distance last year with the Giants.

Seattle Seahawks

2016 Record: 10-5-1

Pythagorean Wins: 9.8 (6th)

Snap-Weighted Age: 26.4 (19th)

Average Opponent: -3.9% (29th)

Total DVOA: 8.0% (11th)

Offense: -2.6% (16th)

Defense: -10.6% (5th)

Special Teams: -0.1% (15th)

2017 Mean Projection: 9.8 wins

Postseason Odds: 63.7%

Super Bowl Odds: 17.3%

Proj. Avg. Opponent: -0.3% (21st)

On the Clock (0-4): 2%

Mediocrity (5-7): 15%

Playoff Contender (8-10): 41%

Super Bowl Contender (11+): 41%

2016: A broken leg also snaps the Seattle DVOA dynasty.

2017: The Legion of Boom wants to go out with a bang.

The Seahawks entered 2016 with high expectations for postseason success. Our preseason projections gave them a 23.1 percent chance to win the Super Bowl and a mean forecast of 10.5 wins, the highest of any team in both categories. Seattle also held the distinction of finishing first in DVOA in each of Russell Wilson's first four seasons in the league. At the start of the season, the team's only glaring weakness was the offensive line. But the offensive line was just as much of a weakness in 2015, and Seattle still finished first in offensive DVOA. Was it really going to be a bigger problem in 2016?

It took only one game to find out. Early in the third quarter of their opener against the Dolphins, Ndamukong Suh accidentally stepped on Russell Wilson's foot and significantly injured Wilson's ankle in the process. This injury, in addition to an MCL sprain sustained against the 49ers in Week 3, sapped Wilson of his mobility for much of the season and threw off his throwing mechanics in his lower body. Wilson's inability to make as many plays with his legs through both running the ball and extending pass plays outside the pocket substantially limited the Seahawks' offensive options and brought the deficiencies on the offensive line into even clearer focus than before. In Weeks 1-9, Wilson was outside the pocket on 20.9 percent of plays, averaging 4.4 yards on those plays; in Weeks 10-17 (as he progressively got healthier), he was outside the pocket on 26.5 percent of plays, gaining 6.3 yards per play.

Without having to account for Wilson's ability as a runner, opposing teams were free to devote more of their resources towards overwhelming the Seahawks' offensive line in the running game. And Wilson wasn't the only Seattle runner to deal with injuries: running backs Thomas Rawls and C.J. Prosise both spent a substantial portion of the season on the sidelines. Christine Michael fell out of favor with the coaching staff and ended up getting released midseason before catching on with Green Bay, even though he would finish the 2016 season as the leading rusher for the Seahawks. When your leading rusher finishes the year on another team, that generally does not bode well for your offensive outlook, as illustrated by Seattle finishing 23rd in rushing DVOA and 17th in overall offensive DVOA.

Despite this combination of injuries and ineffectiveness, the defense remained one of the most fearsome in the league and kept the team in a great position to make a deep postseason run once key playmakers on offense like Rawls and Prosise

returned to health. In November, it still looked like the team would be one to be reckoned with come playoff time. They went into Foxborough against New England on a Sunday night and emerged as the only team to beat the Tom Brady-led Patriots all year long. The following week, they faced off against the Eagles in the 2016 version of the "DVOA Bowl," featuring the (at the time) top-ranked Eagles and the second-ranked Seahawks. Seattle won the game and regained the DVOA crown in Week 11.

But their stay at the top would prove short-lived. Third-year offensive lineman Justin Britt, a bright spot on the offensive line in his first year as the starting center, missed Seattle's game in Tampa Bay the following week. In his absence, the Seahawks managed only five points (two via a safety) after going down 14-0 early on. It snapped the team's NFL-record streak of leading or being within one score in the fourth quarter at 98 games. But while failing to extend the streak hurt, it pales in comparison to the loss the Seahawks would suffer the following week against Carolina.

On a jump ball thrown deep down the middle of the field, star safeties Earl Thomas and Kam Chancellor collided, which resulted in a broken leg for Thomas and represented the death knell for the team's viability as a Super Bowl contender in 2016. Seattle had defensive DVOA above zero (i.e., worse than average) in four of the seven games Thomas missed in 2016, including the playoffs (Table 1). The pass defense finished outside the DVOA top ten for the first time since Thomas' rookie season of 2010, when the Seahawks infamously won the NFC West at 7-9. Seattle allowed 38 points on the road to Green Bay in Week 14 and then 34 to Arizona at home on Christmas Eve; the latter cost the Seahawks a chance at a first-round bye in the playoffs. That certainly would have helped against Atlanta, whom the Seahawks had to play in the Georgia Dome instead of the friendly confines of CenturyLink Field.

Table 1. Seattle Defense with and without Earl Thomas, 2016

Weeks	PA/G	Yd/Play	TO/G	DVOA	vs. Pass	vs. Run
Weeks 1-11, 13	16.4	4.98	1.3	-15.9%	-7.0%	-26.4%
Weeks 12, 14-19	22.0	5.39	0.7	0.0%	25.9%	-25.6%

2017 Seahawks Schedule

Week	Opp.	Week	Opp.	Week	Opp.
1	at GB	7	at NYG	13	PHI
2	SF	8	HOU	14	at JAC
3	at TEN	9	WAS	15	LARM
4	IND	10	at ARI (Thu.)	16	at DAL
5	at LARM	11	ATL (Mon.)	17	ARI
6	BYE	12	at SF		

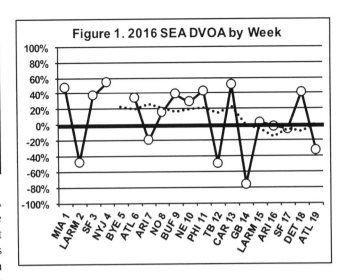

Figure 1. 2016 SEA DVOA by Week

Seattle managed to finish fifth overall in defensive DVOA even without Thomas, though that was aided by one of the strongest seasons against the run we have ever measured. At -26.8%, the Seahawks finished one of the 12 best run defenses in DVOA history. Compare that to their pass defense, which finished in 13th place last season. Not terrible, but certainly not what we have come to expect from the Legion of Boom.

When healthy, the defensive stars for the Seahawks produced at a high level, but it is fair to wonder how much gas is left in the tank for some of them. Defensive end Cliff Avril set a career high with 11.5 sacks and was named to the Pro Bowl for the first time in his career, joining fellow defensive end Michael Bennett, cornerback Richard Sherman, and linebackers Bobby Wagner and K.J. Wright in Orlando as representatives for the Seahawks defense. However, Avril and Bennett are over 30 years old, and Sherman and Kam Chancellor are both 29, meaning that the next generation of Seahawks defenders will likely need to take on a larger role in 2017 and beyond.

The Seahawks defense was at its most fearsome in 2013 when it had the depth to send wave after wave of defensive linemen at opposing quarterbacks. Between Bennett, Avril, Bruce Irvin, Chris Clemons, and Clinton McDonald, the Seahawks were able to keep their pass-rushers fresh and quarterbacks under duress. McDonald in particular was quite valuable, contributing 5.5 sacks as a pass-rushing defensive tackle. The following season, the Seahawks got another 5.5 sacks from a different pass-rushing defensive tackle, 2013 third-rounder Jordan Hill. In the two years since, the Seahawks haven't gotten more than two sacks from an interior defensive lineman (this does not count cases when defensive ends like Bennett and Frank Clark lined up at defensive tackle to rush the passer).

Young defensive linemen Clark and Jarran Reed appear to be the heirs to the throne, with special teams standout Cassius Marsh also capable of filling in as an extra pass-rusher in obvious passing situations. Clark logged ten sacks and two forced fumbles over the course of the 2016 season, making five starts when Bennett was out with a knee injury. Reed served as a run-stuffer on early downs in his rookie year, taking the place of Brandon Mebane after the veteran tackle moved on to the Chargers as a free agent in the 2016 offseason.

Adding to the youth movement on the defensive line will be 2017 second-round pick Malik McDowell from Michigan

State. Projected by some as an early first-round pick entering the 2016 college season, McDowell slipped to 35th overall after an underwhelming junior season in East Lansing where he dealt with an ankle injury. Anonymous scouts questioned McDowell's work ethic, and teams were thoroughly unimpressed with his interviews at the scouting combine. With that said, McDowell, who will barely be 21 years old at the start of training camp, is probably falling into one of the better situations for him in the Seahawks defensive line room with the veteran leadership of Avril, Bennett, and Ahtyba Rubin.

Defensive line was not the only position group where the Seattle front office looked to get younger in the 2017 draft. From 2011 to 2016, the Seahawks did not draft a defensive back before the fifth round; in 2014 and 2016, they didn't draft a single one. Not the case in 2017, when the Seahawks used two of their four third-round picks on defensive backs Shaquill Griffin (Central Florida) and Delano Hill (Michigan) and then followed that up in the fourth and sixth rounds with safeties Tedric Thompson (Colorado) and Mike Tyson (Cincinnati). Tyson, unrelated to the boxer, will be transitioning to cornerback instead of his college position of safety, which makes sense given the injury situation of the Seattle secondary.

After 2016 starter DeShawn Shead tore his ACL in the divisional round against Atlanta, the second cornerback spot is up for grabs this offseason while Shead works his way back from the injury. Griffin, Tyson, and incumbent nickel corner Jeremy Lane will be competing to land the starting job across from four-time Pro Bowler Richard Sherman. While Sherman will be the starter for Seattle in 2017, that may not be the case in 2018 and beyond. Trade "rumors" surrounding Sherman were proven to be more than just that, with both Sherman and GM John Schneider confirming that the Stanford alum was the subject of trade discussions. In an interview with the Seattle Post-Intelligencer, Schneider (in a surprisingly transparent display) explained the logic behind the move[1]: "It's OK, and we feel like it would clear cap room and we would be able to get younger, but that's the only reason we'd do it. The guy's

1 http://bit.ly/2sQEZuw

one of the top cornerbacks in the league. You don't just like give him away, you know?"

That makes perfect sense, but it does seem to indicate that the window may be closing on the Legion of Boom-era Seattle defense. In addition to the advancing age of some of the stars, Sherman, Thomas, Chancellor, Avril, Rubin, and K.J. Wright will all be free agents in 2018 or 2019. Seattle has done an excellent job keeping as many of the young stars from the 2012 and 2013 teams together as possible given the constraints of the salary cap, but the team is approaching an inflection point for how it wants to move forward on the defensive side of the ball.

While the combination of age and impending free agency brings new questions for the defense, the questions around the offense entering 2016 remain largely the same a year later. The offensive line is again in flux, with only one starter from 2016 entering the 2017 offseason program at the same position (center Justin Britt). In 2015 and 2016, new holes were largely a product of Russell Okung and J.R. Sweezy signing expensive free-agent contracts with Denver and Tampa Bay, respectively. Restricted free-agent right tackle Garry Gilliam headed south for San Francisco this offseason, but the larger changes will come as a result of competition at all four non-center line spots heading into 2017.

Rookie second-round pick Ethan Pocic (Louisiana State) will compete with 2016 right guard Germain Ifedi at right tackle while free-agent signing Oday Aboushi (ex-Jets, Texans) will duke it out with 2016 left guard Mark Glowinski at right guard. On the left side, free-agent signing Luke Joeckel (ex-Jaguars) will compete with incumbent 2016 left tackle George Fant and backup Rees Odhiambo for the two spots on Russell Wilson's blind side. Seattle made an aggressive push to sign former Packers guard T.J Lang in free agency to shore up a major position of need, but Lang, one of the best offensive guards on the market, instead signed with his hometown team in Detroit.

No matter who ends up starting at guard and tackle, they will have to help keep Russell Wilson healthier for this team to make a serious run. The Seahawks' decision to not devote many cap dollars to their offensive line can work when Wilson is healthy, as evidenced by his performance down the stretch in 2015. And while we may criticize the constant turnover on the Seattle line, the players they let walk have not exactly been stars for their new teams.

The 2013 offensive line, from left to right, featured Russell Okung, James Carpenter, Max Unger, J.R. Sweezy, and Breno Giacomini. Carpenter and Giacomini both signed with the Jets as free agents in consecutive seasons. Giacomini was cut this offseason to save salary cap space, although Carpenter has been a reasonable starter for New York over the past two

years. Sweezy signed a five-year contract with Tampa Bay before last season but didn't play a single down because of a back injury, so the jury is still out there. Okung started all 16 games for the first time in his career in his lone season in Denver, parlaying that into a four-year deal with the Chargers. And while Unger, who has dealt with injury issues of his own, was the best of the bunch, Seattle didn't just let him go for free, and Seattle's strongest position on the offensive line entering 2017 is at center with Justin Britt. The Seahawks didn't let five Pro Bowlers walk out the door, but it wasn't like they were all terrible either.

Taken individually, the decision to move on from each of those linemen makes sense given the substantial raises the free agents received on their second contract and the acquisition of Jimmy Graham in the Unger trade with New Orleans. But letting all five leave resulted in a major lack of experience along the line that seriously hindered Seattle's championship aspirations in 2016. Veteran free-agent signings Bradley Sowell and J'Marcus Webb both lost starting spots as the season progressed, leaving Britt (in his third new position in three years) and Gilliam (originally a college tight end) as the elder statesmen along the offensive line.

In addition to the offensive line questions, the Seahawks also find themselves waiting on the return from late-season injuries of key starters entering 2017. In 2015, Rawls and Graham both suffered leg injuries late in the season, and their 2016 performance was a mixed bag, with Graham setting franchise records for receptions and receiving yards by a tight end while Rawls had an ineffective season while struggling through more injuries. Entering 2017, Seattle is hoping for a full return to health from wide receiver Tyler Lockett (recovering from a broken leg suffered in Week 16 against Arizona) along with the aforementioned Shead and Thomas. Of those three, Thomas is clearly the most important, but getting all three back and performing at a high level would add a major boost to their chances of bringing home another Lombardi trophy.

Seattle is stocked with talent at the offensive skill positions between Baldwin, Graham, Lockett, Rawls, Prosise, and free-agent signee Eddie Lacy. It will just be a question of whether the offensive line gives Wilson and company enough of a chance to shine, taking the pressure off the defense to stand on its head week in and week out. If Seattle can keep Wilson firing on all cylinders and the defense returns to form with Thomas back healthy, the Seahawks will again be a threat to win it all. If that doesn't happen, not only will Seattle's season end earlier than it would like, it could also mean that the Legion of Boom's championship window is closing.

Carl Yedor

2016 Seahawks Stats by Week

Wk	vs.	W-L	PF	PA	YDF	YDA	TO	Total	Off	Def	ST
1	MIA	W	12	10	352	214	-2	48%	-10%	-62%	-4%
2	at LARM	L	3	9	306	283	-1	-48%	-27%	20%	-1%
3	SF	W	37	18	418	254	-1	37%	-5%	-32%	9%
4	at NYJ	W	27	17	354	305	+3	54%	23%	-18%	12%
5	BYE										
6	ATL	W	26	24	333	362	+2	35%	10%	-30%	-6%
7	at ARI	T	6	6	257	443	0	-20%	-17%	-11%	-14%
8	at NO	L	20	25	359	375	0	15%	-7%	-18%	3%
9	BUF	W	31	25	278	425	+1	38%	49%	8%	-2%
10	at NE	W	31	24	420	385	+2	28%	23%	-5%	0%
11	PHI	W	26	15	439	308	+2	43%	37%	-13%	-6%
12	at TB	L	5	14	245	338	-1	-49%	-42%	10%	3%
13	CAR	W	40	7	534	271	+1	51%	22%	-20%	9%
14	at GB	L	10	38	354	330	-6	-76%	-72%	8%	4%
15	LARM	W	24	3	299	183	-1	3%	-28%	-23%	8%
16	ARI	L	31	34	391	370	0	-2%	20%	18%	-4%
17	at SF	W	25	23	376	253	+2	-6%	-7%	-13%	-12%
18	DET	W	26	6	387	231	0	42%	8%	-24%	9%
19	at ATL	L	20	36	309	422	-2	-33%	-30%	10%	7%

Trends and Splits

	Offense	Rank	Defense	Rank
Total DVOA	-2.6%	16	-10.6%	5
Unadjusted VOA	0.5%	14	-11.1%	3
Weighted Trend	-2.3%	16	-6.7%	9
Variance	9.8%	30	4.5%	13
Average Opponent	0.5%	20	-3.2%	30
Passing	14.8%	14	2.5%	13
Rushing	-11.3%	22	-24.9%	3
First Down	6.7%	11	-14.7%	2
Second Down	-10.4%	24	-3.6%	13
Third Down	-9.1%	21	-13.5%	7
First Half	2.9%	16	-8.4%	6
Second Half	-15.8%	24	-11.7%	10
Red Zone	-15.4%	24	-11.3%	8
Late and Close	-20.2%	28	1.4%	20

Five-Year Performance

Year	W-L	Pyth W	Est W	PF	PA	TO	Total	Rk	Off	Rk	Def	Rk	ST	Rk	Off AGL	Rk	Def AGL	Rk	Off Age	Rk	Def Age	Rk	ST Age	Rk
2012	11-5	12.5	13.0	412	245	+13	38.7%	1	18.5%	4	-14.5%	2	5.7%	3	14.8	6	15.0	6	25.9	27	25.6	31	26.0	18
2013	13-3	12.8	13.0	417	231	+20	40.0%	1	9.4%	7	-25.9%	1	4.7%	5	43.8	22	16.2	7	25.7	32	26.0	27	26.1	14
2014	12-4	11.9	12.7	394	254	+10	31.9%	1	16.8%	5	-16.8%	1	-1.7%	19	39.5	24	35.3	13	25.3	31	26.3	23	25.8	24
2015	10-6	11.8	12.5	423	277	+7	38.1%	1	18.7%	1	-15.2%	4	4.2%	3	23.7	9	16.4	4	25.9	25	27.0	12	26.3	12
2016	10-5-1	9.8	9.1	354	525	+1	8.0%	11	-2.6%	16	-10.6%	5	-0.1%	15	23.8	6	17.3	4	25.7	29	27.2	7	26.4	8

2016 Performance Based on Most Common Personnel Groups

SEA Offense				SEA Offense vs. Opponents					SEA Defense				SEA Defense vs. Opponents			
Pers	Freq	Yds	DVOA	Run%	Pers	Freq	Yds	DVOA	Run%	Pers	Freq	Yds	DVOA	Pers	Freq	Yds	DVOA
11	63%	5.9	2.3%	26%	Base	25%	5.8	10.5%	54%	Base	31%	4.9	-11.3%	11	60%	5.0	-13.7%
12	18%	6.8	19.5%	48%	Nickel	59%	5.8	4.2%	30%	Nickel	66%	5.3	-10.2%	12	15%	5.3	-4.2%
21	6%	4.7	-17.0%	61%	Dime+	15%	6.8	-3.1%	14%	Dime+	1%	6.1	-3.4%	21	6%	5.2	-7.6%
13	4%	6.3	29.6%	51%	Goal Line	1%	-0.4	-55.7%	78%	Goal Line	1%	0.3	-11.4%	10	6%	7.1	10.0%
01	3%	6.1	-10.8%	0%										13	3%	9.2	58.2%

Strategic Tendencies

Run/Pass		Rk	Formation		Rk	Pass Rush		Rk	Secondary		Rk	Strategy		Rk
Runs, first half	33%	30	Form: Single Back	79%	12	Rush 3	5.7%	19	4 DB	31%	13	Play-action	20%	8
Runs, first down	42%	29	Form: Empty Back	10%	9	Rush 4	68.8%	9	5 DB	66%	8	Avg Box (Off)	6.16	19
Runs, second-long	31%	12	Pers: 3+ WR	69%	11	Rush 5	19.6%	20	6+ DB	1%	28	Avg Box (Def)	6.12	24
Runs, power sit.	50%	25	Pers: 2+ TE/6+ OL	26%	20	Rush 6+	5.9%	17	CB by Sides	67%	22	Offensive Pace	30.75	18
Runs, behind 2H	26%	18	Pers: 6+ OL	2%	24	Sacks by LB	22.6%	20	S/CB Cover Ratio	29%	9	Defensive Pace	31.44	26
Pass, ahead 2H	56%	5	Shotgun/Pistol	70%	9	Sacks by DB	0.0%	30	DB Blitz	3%	32	Go for it on 4th	0.71	27

Without Beast Mode or a healthy Thomas Rawls, the Seahawks dropped from running in 67 percent of short-yardage/power situations (fifth) to 50 percent (25th). They ran less often in pretty much every situation, although use of play-action fakes on passes only dropped from sixth to eighth. ⚌ Seattle's offense also plummeted from second to 29th in broken tackles, and from third to 24th in broken-tackle rate. ⚌ The Seahawks ran 36 percent of the time with three or more wide receivers in the game, more than any other team, but were near the bottom of the league with just -18.4% DVOA and 3.88 yards per carry on these plays. ⚌ Seattle only blitzed a defensive back on 15 plays all year; every other defense did this at least 25 times. ⚌ The Seahawks ranked 18th in defensive DVOA in the first quarter, then fifth for the rest of the game.

Passing

Player	DYAR	DVOA	Plays	NtYds	Avg	YAC	C%	TD	Int
R.Wilson	569	4.0%	592	3941	6.7	5.0	65.4%	21	11
T.Boykin	0	-11.2%	19	140	7.4	5.5	72.2%	1	1

Rushing

Player	DYAR	DVOA	Plays	Yds	Avg	TD	Fum	Suc
C.Michael*	40	-1.0%	117	469	4.0	6	0	49%
T.Rawls	41	4.7%	71	293	4.1	3	0	46%
R.Wilson	27	1.4%	41	219	5.3	1	0	-
C.J.Prosise	38	19.6%	31	172	5.5	1	0	52%
A.Collins	-28	-46.1%	17	42	2.5	1	0	29%
T.Pope	1	-7.2%	11	43	3.9	0	0	36%
E.Lacy	84	20.4%	71	360	5.1	0	0	49%
M.Davis	-28	-38.1%	19	50	2.6	1	0	47%

Receiving

Player	DYAR	DVOA	Plays	Ctch	Yds	Y/C	YAC	TD	C%
D.Baldwin	263	13.0%	128	97	1131	11.7	4.9	7	76%
J.Kearse	-114	-28.7%	89	41	510	12.4	3.4	1	46%
T.Lockett	99	5.5%	68	43	612	14.2	5.7	1	63%
P.Richardson	56	7.9%	36	21	288	13.7	4.6	1	58%
T.McEvoy	67	67.8%	11	9	140	15.6	3.3	2	82%
J.Graham	204	25.1%	96	66	923	14.0	5.0	6	69%
L.Willson	13	2.5%	21	15	129	8.6	5.0	2	71%
C.Michael*	-32	-37.6%	26	20	98	4.9	5.7	1	77%
C.J.Prosise	62	55.2%	19	17	208	12.2	6.9	0	89%
T.Rawls	22	10.9%	17	13	96	7.4	6.3	0	76%
A.Collins	37	35.7%	11	11	84	7.6	7.4	0	100%
C.J.Spiller*	-17	-52.9%	9	5	43	8.6	4.4	1	56%
E.Lacy	-12	-45.4%	7	4	28	7.0	10.0	0	57%

Offensive Line

Player	Pos	Age	GS	Snaps	Pen	Sk	Pass	Run	Player	Pos	Age	GS	Snaps	Pen	Sk	Pass	Run
Mark Glowinski	LG	25	16/16	1059	5	2.0	12	10	Bradley Sowell*	LT/RT	28	10/9	630	8	3.0	13	6
Justin Britt	C	26	15/15	994	4	0.0	3	6	J'Marcus Webb	RG	29	9/3	224	1	1.0	3	2
Germain Ifedi	RG	23	13/13	840	7	4.5	18	5	Oday Aboushi	LG	26	4/3	269	1	0.0	3	2
Garry Gilliam*	RT	27	14/13	811	5	2.5	11	8	Luke Joeckel	LG	26	4/4	221	3	1.0	3	1
George Fant	LT	25	14/10	664	7	6.0	19	7									

Year	Yards	ALY	Rank	Power	Rank	Stuff	Rank	2nd Lev	Rank	Open Field	Rank	Sacks	ASR	Rank	Press	Rank	F-Start	Cont.
2014	4.62	4.52	4	78%	2	17%	6	1.34	4	0.80	11	42	8.7%	24	39.3%	32	29	25
2015	4.44	4.56	4	71%	8	18%	5	1.20	15	0.81	12	46	9.0%	30	31.8%	30	21	30
2016	3.82	3.77	26	53%	27	23%	30	1.12	18	0.70	15	42	6.9%	25	33.7%	32	26	28

2016 ALY by direction: Left End 2.69 (29)   Left Tackle 4.36 (17)   Mid/Guard 3.60 (31)   Right Tackle 4.17 (14)   Right End 4.04 (12)

The Seahawks ranked in the top 10 in adjusted line yards to all five directions in 2015 despite four of the team's starters ranking 25th or worse in snaps per blown block. No such luck in 2016. Center Justin Britt ranked 13th at his position with 110.4 snaps per blown block and zero sacks allowed, but no other offensive linemen did better than left guard Mark Glowinski's 48.1. In spite of Britt's play, Seattle still ranked 31st in the league in adjusted line yards up the middle. ⚌ Having both Glowinski and right guard Germain Ifedi rank in the bottom five in blown blocks at their respective positions certainly did not help. Bringing up the rear was left tackle George Fant (did you hear that he played basketball in college?) at 25.5 snaps per blown block, which led to 6.0 sacks allowed. Fant finished last among 35 ranked left tackles in 2016, but the man he replaced in the starting lineup, Bradley Sowell, was only slightly better at 33rd. Fant at least has time to develop as he enters his second season. ⚌ Seattle signed left tackle/left guard Luke Joeckel and guard Oday Aboushi in the offseason, then added versatile LSU center Ethan Pocic in the second round of the draft. Many fans were surprised when the Seahawks listed Pocic as a tackle when they announced his selection, but that's in fact how they see him. He will be competing for playing time at right tackle with Ifedi, who is moving back to his collegiate position. ⚌ Entering OTAs, the only player with an entrenched starting position is Britt, which is probably a good thing given the overall poor play of the rest of the offensive line in 2016. In 2015, a healthy Russell

Wilson and Thomas Rawls papered over some of the weaknesses in the running game. The combination of those two plus newly acquired running back Eddie Lacy could do the same in 2017, though as last season showed, their health is no guarantee.

Defensive Front Seven

Defensive Line	Age	Pos	G	Snaps	Plays	TmPct	Rk	Stop	Dfts	BTkl	Runs	St%	Rk	RuYd	Rk	Sack	Hit	Hur	Dsrpt
						Overall						vs. Run				Pass Rush			
Ahtyba Rubin	31	DT	16	602	39	4.7%	41	28	9	1	34	68%	69	2.4	51	1.0	1	5	2
Tony McDaniel*	32	DT	16	486	46	5.6%	29	35	4	4	40	75%	50	1.8	30	0.0	1	6	3
Jarran Reed	25	DT	15	477	37	4.8%	39	26	3	0	31	68%	68	2.7	61	1.5	3	5	3

Edge Rushers	Age	Pos	G	Snaps	Plays	TmPct	Rk	Stop	Dfts	BTkl	Runs	St%	Rk	RuYd	Rk	Sack	Hit	Hur	Dsrpt
						Overall						vs. Run				Pass Rush			
Cliff Avril	31	DE	16	830	41	5.0%	47	35	20	9	22	82%	17	1.7	23	11.5	14	39	5
Frank Clark	24	DE	15	682	47	6.1%	32	36	20	6	31	71%	63	2.6	50	10.0	7	22	0
Michael Bennett	32	DE	11	563	34	6.0%	33	30	17	5	28	86%	8	0.5	4	5.0	14	27	0
Cassius Marsh	25	DE	16	387	15	1.8%	--	11	7	5	10	70%	--	1.9	--	3.0	4	14	1
David Bass	27	OLB	13	226	12	1.9%	--	8	1	0	8	88%	--	1.8	--	0.0	1	2	0

Linebackers	Age	Pos	G	Snaps	Plays	TmPct	Rk	Stop	Dfts	BTkl	Runs	St%	Rk	RuYd	Rk	Sack	Hit	Hur	Tgts	Suc%	Rk	AdjYd	Rk	PD	Int
						Overall						vs. Run				Pass Rush				vs. Pass					
Bobby Wagner	27	MLB	16	1072	170	20.7%	2	86	24	12	109	57%	71	3.6	42	4.5	14	14	44	45%	49	7.4	60	2	1
K.J. Wright	28	OLB	16	1051	131	15.9%	16	72	27	10	71	56%	73	3.4	36	4.0	4	10	40	62%	8	5.9	25	6	0
Mike Morgan*	29	OLB	9	138	11	2.4%	--	8	3	2	7	86%	--	0.1	--	0.0	0	2	5	62%	--	11.4	--	0	0
Michael Wilhoite	31	MLB	16	511	47	5.3%	82	23	6	5	28	54%	77	4.1	69	0.5	0	2	17	49%	39	5.2	16	2	0

Year	Yards	ALY	Rank	Power	Rank	Stuff	Rank	2nd Level	Rank	Open Field	Rank	Sacks	ASR	Rank	Press	Rank
2014	3.54	3.64	5	59%	10	23%	6	0.92	4	0.59	8	37	7.0%	13	25.4%	13
2015	3.54	3.93	12	72%	26	21%	15	0.94	3	0.42	3	37	6.7%	14	29.3%	2
2016	3.42	3.81	8	58%	8	23%	7	0.97	6	0.40	3	42	6.7%	10	28.6%	10

2016 ALY by direction:	Left End 4.63 (21)	Left Tackle 4.83 (24)	Mid/Guard 3.43 (1)	Right Tackle 3.68 (9)	Right End 3.63 (17)

Michael Bennett and Cliff Avril put up stellar seasons again, combining for 66 hurries in 2016 despite Bennett missing five games due to injury. Second-year player Frank Clark added 22 hurries of his own, and if Seattle can get some interior pressure from talented rookie defensive tackle Malik McDowell, this could be an even scarier unit in 2017. The key with McDowell will be his work ethic, as attitude and effort were the major reasons that he fell to the early part of the second round. ☜ Tony McDaniel and Jarran Reed combined to fill the void left by Brandon Mebane's move to the Chargers, though with McDaniel now in New Orleans, Seattle will likely turn to McDowell, Quinton Jefferson, and third-round rookie Nazair Jones (North Carolina) to replace McDaniel's 486 snaps at defensive tackle. ☜ Mike Morgan nominally replaced Bruce Irvin as the team's starting strongside linebacker, but due to the combination of a sports hernia and the league-wide shift towards nickel defenses, Morgan only ended up playing 25.5 percent of the team's snaps. At training camp, former 49er Michael Wilhoite will be competing with Arthur Brown and 2014 fourth-rounder Kevin Pierre-Louis, among others, to replace Morgan as the third linebacker. ☜ Conversely, Bobby Wagner and K.J. Wright both played more than 97 percent of the team's snaps and combined for more than 300 plays made. Wagner made 109 plays against the run by himself and was the only player in the league involved in more than 20 percent of his team's defensive plays.

Defensive Secondary

Secondary	Age	Pos	G	Snaps	Plays	Overall TmPct	Rk	Stop	Dfts	BTkl	Runs	St%	vs. Run Rk	RuYd	Rk	Tgts	Tgt%	Rk	Dist	vs. Pass Suc%	Rk	AdjYd	Rk	PD	Int
Richard Sherman	29	CB	16	1053	71	8.6%	42	31	18	9	18	50%	19	3.8	5	71	16.7%	22	14.8	54%	22	9.5	81	15	4
DeShawn Shead	28	CB	15	918	93	12.1%	2	38	11	6	29	52%	18	7.1	51	76	20.5%	59	13.4	42%	79	8.9	73	14	1
Jeremy Lane	27	CB	16	769	49	6.0%	83	17	9	11	12	58%	13	4.1	7	48	15.4%	12	10.6	46%	64	8.5	64	2	0
Kam Chancellor	29	SS	12	731	88	14.3%	5	53	16	8	48	65%	3	3.7	2	34	11.4%	60	12.6	58%	5	5.5	3	6	2
Earl Thomas	28	FS	11	693	56	9.9%	40	16	8	12	15	13%	74	8.0	52	24	8.6%	41	15.0	47%	34	9.3	48	10	2
Steven Terrell*	27	FS	16	383	24	2.9%	--	4	1	2	11	9%	--	14.6	--	8	5.2%	--	24.9	55%	--	9.0	--	1	0
Kelcie McCray*	29	FS	16	338	36	4.4%	--	16	4	3	19	63%	--	5.4	--	16	11.8%	--	8.8	57%	--	3.9	--	1	0
Bradley McDougald	27	FS	16	1012	100	12.1%	17	32	11	13	52	37%	45	6.3	31	41	9.3%	48	13.6	53%	18	6.4	9	8	2

Year	Pass D Rank	vs. #1 WR	Rk	vs. #2 WR	Rk	vs. Other WR	Rk	vs. TE	Rk	vs. RB	Rk
2014	3	-22.0%	4	-18.3%	6	-19.2%	4	-0.8%	18	-2.0%	16
2015	3	-33.3%	1	-21.5%	5	-9.5%	10	20.0%	26	-17.8%	5
2016	13	1.3%	16	22.3%	31	-3.2%	11	-1.3%	18	-20.3%	5

Kam Chancellor may have missed four games during the regular season, but when he was on the field, he was a force to be reckoned with, posting excellent numbers across the board. ≋ The magnificent Earl Thomas is occasionally forgotten because so much of what makes him special happens out of the camera shot on a standard broadcast; once he got injured, Steven Terrell's play in his stead only amplified just how important Thomas is to the underlying structure of the Seattle pass defense. After seeing how the defense fell apart without Thomas in the lineup, the Seattle front office went out and signed safety Bradley McDougald in free agency, and the coaching staff will find ways to get all three on the field together. ≋ Richard Sherman again saw about one-sixth of the targets Seattle faced, though his continued success on the field was somewhat overshadowed by the drama off the field related to his mysterious MCL injury and the trade rumors he was involved in leading up to the draft. ≋ Sherman's cornerback counterpart DeShawn Shead stepped in as the fourth member of the Legion of Boom in 2016; the former undrafted free agent tore his ACL in the divisional round against Atlanta, leaving the Week 1 outside corner spot up for grabs. Shead had the worst success rate of any Seattle defensive back in the past three seasons, so whoever wins the right cornerback job could hold it for the forseeable future. Third-round rookie Shaquill Griffin (Central Florida) has the athletic profile to replace Shead initially. ≋ Perhaps Seattle needs to use Sherman to follow opposing No. 1 receivers more. With the Seahawks having problems at the other outside cornerback spot, Seattle opponents threw 27 percent of passes to No. 1 receivers, near the top of the league. The Seahawks had ranked 30th or 31st in this figure the three previous seasons. ≋ Nickel cornerback Jeremy Lane had a forgettable season in the first year of his new contract, which makes this upcoming season all the more critical for him given that Seattle used four draft picks on defensive backs in 2017. The 2017 season marks an important transition season for the Seattle secondary as the stars continue to age, and the new wave of rookie talent will play a major role in 2018 and beyond in determining how bright the future is post-Legion of Boom.

Special Teams

Year	DVOA	Rank	FG/XP	Rank	Net Kick	Rank	Kick Ret	Rank	Net Punt	Rank	Punt Ret	Rank	Hidden	Rank
2014	-1.7%	19	0.8	12	4.5	11	-7.5	31	-4.0	21	-2.4	15	5.3	8
2015	4.2%	3	6.6	4	0.8	13	7.6	4	-5.4	23	11.3	1	-8.9	29
2016	-0.1%	15	-4.0	22	6.2	4	3.1	8	-7.4	27	1.6	10	8.7	7

Seattle's special teams unit dropped from being one of the best in 2015 to the middle of the pack. Steven Hauschka's six missed extra points (three in the final five minutes of the fourth quarter) and four missed field goals (two from less than 30 yards out) played a factor in the team's decision to let him walk in free agency. The Seahawks brought in Blair Walsh as Hauschka's replacement at a much lower price than what Hauschka received from Buffalo, but it's going to be a problem if Walsh can't recover from his post-2016 wild-card yips. ≋ Seattle's punting game looks consistently bad in our metrics, but in reality 2016 was a surprise off-year for Jon Ryan. In previous seasons, the problem was poor punt coverage, while last year the problem was Ryan's gross punt distance. ≋ After a standout season returning punts and kicks as a rookie, Tyler Lockett struggled through several different injuries that limited his effectiveness in 2016. Lockett suffered a broken leg in Week 16 against Arizona, leading to Seattle signing Devin Hester for the playoff push. Hester is now retired, but the Seahawks could potentially get rookie free agent Cyril Grayson and his 4.33 40 time involved in the 2017 return game. Grayson ran track at LSU before working out at the Tigers' pro day in April.

Tampa Bay Buccaneers

2016 Record: 9-7	**Total DVOA:** -3.0% (22nd)	**2017 Mean Projection:** 7.2 wins	**On the Clock (0-4):** 15%
Pythagorean Wins: 7.6 (23rd)	**Offense:** -4.1% (19th)	**Postseason Odds:** 25.8%	**Mediocrity (5-7):** 41%
Snap-Weighted Age: 25.9 (29th)	**Defense:** -2.9% (13th)	**Super Bowl Odds:** 2.4%	**Playoff Contender (8-10):** 33%
Average Opponent: 1.4% (9th)	**Special Teams:** -1.8% (20th)	**Proj. Avg. Opponent:** -0.2% (19th)	**Super Bowl Contender (11+):** 10%

2016: Offseason focus on the defense pays immediate dividends.

2017: Offseason focus on the offense needs to pay immediate dividends.

It's all about Jameis Winston.

That statement has been true to a greater or lesser extent ever since Tampa Bay drafted the Florida State redshirt sophomore with the first overall pick in 2015, but this offseason has brought it into the sharpest possible focus. Off the field, the offseason started with Winston's maturity and leadership being questioned again by the media over some innocuous but ill-chosen public comments. On the field, an offseason filled with splash moves gives Winston his deepest and most talented receiving corps yet, and heaps pressure on the shoulders of the young quarterback to play up to the level of his supporting cast.

It's easy to see why Jason Licht and Dirk Koetter have taken this approach. Last offseason's quiet focus on plugging defensive holes bore fruit in the second half of the year. Robert Ayers, Noah Spence, Brent Grimes, and Vernon Hargreaves all played key roles in what DVOA considered the best Buccaneers pass defense since 2008. Even with a secondary comprised mostly of spare parts—four former undrafted free agents, a former sixth-round career backup (Keith Tandy), a free-agency bust from 2014 (Alterraun Verner), and the adjective-defying Chris Conte—the Buccaneers ranked sixth in DVOA against the pass and held half of their opponents to 21 or fewer points. As the defense performed, so did the team. The Buccaneers won every game in which the defense allowed under 24 points, lost every game in which it allowed more than 24, and was 1-1 when allowing exactly 24 in regulation (a 30-24 overtime loss to Oakland versus a 31-24 opening-day win in Atlanta).

The run defense numbers make less pleasant reading. With basically the same personnel, Tampa Bay's run defense DVOA ranked in the top ten in both 2014 and 2015 before dropping to 26th in 2016. The Bucs responded by signing Chris Baker away from Washington, adding to a formidable-looking defensive front, while J.J. Wilcox arrived from Dallas as the direct replacement for Seattle-bound strong safety Bradley McDougald. Texas A&M product Justin Evans was drafted in the second round as a rangy if undisciplined free safety, and pass-rusher Jacquies Smith returns after losing nearly all of last season to an opening-day ACL tear. Any other changes on the defense would come from the existing depth chart, as the Buccaneers will mostly put last season's defensive personnel back on the field.

Instead, as mentioned earlier, the front office made its biggest moves on offense. DeSean Jackson arrives from Washington with a deserved reputation as one of the best receivers of the past decade: an explosive deep threat who has also proven an ability to translate his punt returner skills to the short passing game. Jackson has never had fewer than 900 yards in any season with at least 13 starts. He has a career average of 17.7 yards per reception and at least one reception of 60 yards or longer in every single season of his professional career. In theory, he is a perfect fit for Dirk Koetter's offense of deep routes, clear-out concepts, and play-action.

Jackson has, however, already proven an example of the general league-wide trend that losing a top receiver hurts his old team more than gaining a top receiver helps his new one. When Jackson moved to Washington from Philadelphia in 2014, his old team's pass DVOA dropped 18.4% from 30.0% (fifth) to 11.6% (15th); but his new team's DVOA increased by less than half that margin, from -13.9% (26th) to -5.3% (25th). Even though Jackson had career-bests in DVOA (27.0%, sixth) and second-bests in yards per reception (20.5) and DYAR (306, 10th), the needle barely moved on either team's end-of-season record.

Even that season's result outperformed the general trend. Since 1981, receivers who moved teams after a year in which they had at least 800 yards with at least 16 yards per reception have averaged 42 receptions for 645 yards and 3.6 touchdowns the following year. Only three of those 16 players—Santana Moss for the 2005 Redskins, Vincent Jackson for the 2012 Bucs, and Jackson himself in 2014—had more than 800 yards and 16 yards per reception again the following year. Jackson is a very exciting signing for a fan base unaccustomed to exciting signings, but he is unlikely to be the primary difference between playoff contention and a warm couch in January.

That tempering of expectations is doubly true for top draftee O.J. Howard. Already, Howard is being touted as a potential star: the next great in-line tight end in the mold of Jason Witten or Martellus Bennett. A talented and willing blocker as well as a proficient receiver, Howard has been praised for his route-running and his outstanding athleticism. By all accounts, the only reason for his relatively low receiving numbers at Alabama was his role in the Crimson Tide offense. He is already a popular pick in fantasy circles as a potential stud rookie, ready and able to take advantage

2017 Buccaneers Schedule

Week	Opp.	Week	Opp.	Week	Opp.
1	at MIA	7	at BUF	13	at GB
2	CHI	8	CAR	14	DET
3	at MIN	9	at NO	15	ATL (Mon.)
4	NYG	10	NYJ	16	at CAR
5	NE (Thu.)	11	BYE	17	NO
6	at ARI	12	at ATL		

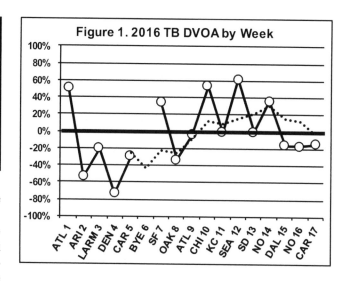

Figure 1. 2016 TB DVOA by Week

when Jackson and Mike Evans open up the middle of the field with their deep routes.

History is not on Howard's side—at least not for his rookie year. No rookie tight end has topped the 1,000-yard mark since Mika Ditka all the way back in 1961. Only four rookie tight ends have ever topped 800 yards, and only ten have even topped 600. All but two of those came before the turn of the millennium, and the only 600-yard rookie season in the past ten years belongs to a name few people would guess: John Carlson had 627 yards on 55 receptions for the 2008 Seahawks. The only other rookie tight end to top 600 receiving yards in the 21st century was Jeremy Shockey, who had 894 yards on 74 receptions in 2002. Shockey still finished a mere 17th in DYAR that year, with a DVOA of -1.5%, while Carlson ranked eighth in DYAR in what was by far the best season of his career.

A more realistic total for Howard, if the past is any indication, is between 500 and 600 yards on around 50 catches—roughly in the same neighborhood as Tim Wright in 2013, Dwayne Allen in 2012, or Rob Gronkowski, Aaron Hernandez, and Tony Moeaki in 2010. Even that would be one of the most productive seasons for a rookie tight end this century,[1] and it assumes Howard is able to displace incumbent Cameron Brate from the starting lineup. Howard may well be a better player in both the short and long term than Brate, Wright, Allen, and Moeaki, and he will certainly hope for a longer career than Hernandez. His presence doesn't factor into this year's team projection at all though, because historically most guys in his situation simply don't break out until their second year.

While we're bursting bubbles, there are two other question marks still attached to the Buccaneers offense heading into training camp. The first of those is running back, where Doug Martin faces a three-game suspension to open the season and has a $7 million contract with no cap hit for releasing him. Martin has drawn praise for his work during the offseason, but *everybody* draws praise during the offseason. The real test will come when his suspension ends in September, especially if the ground game is effective in Martin's absence and/or fifth-round pick Jeremy McNichols proves the steal that many observers suspect he will.

Even if Martin does return, there are valid concerns about his effectiveness: he has performed above replacement level precisely once in the past four years, missing 23 games over that span, and ranked 38th of 42 qualifying rushers in DYAR

last year. Charles Sims fared little better; the most efficient rusher for the Buccaneers was Jacquizz Rodgers, who was forced into action only when Martin and Sims were both injured. Both Martin and Sims were more effective than Rodgers as receiving backs, but nobody is queuing up to give Darren Sproles or James White a $7 million-a-year contract.

The other area of uncertainty is the offensive line, where significant changes are expected despite basically the same personnel. Ali Marpet has been moved to center in place of Joe Hawley, with Hawley and third center Evan Smith retained as depth at both center and guard. Kevin Pamphile has also practiced snapping the ball during the offseason, but Pamphile and J.R. Sweezy are expected to be the starting guards when the real action begins. Donovan Smith remains at left tackle, where he alternates between excellent and execrable with alarming frequency, while right tackle Demar Dotson is yet to return to his previous level after missing most of the 2015 season through injury. Unless this reshuffling can substantially elevate the play of the unit as a whole, the line is still likely to be mediocre at best, with the potential to be devastating on any given play—but devastating to either team's benefit.

Put that all together, and it's easy to understand why our projection is wary of the hype. DeSean Jackson is one player, and one player only. Jameis Winston threw six more touchdowns as a sophomore than he did as a rookie, but also had seven more turnovers (three more interceptions, four more fumbles). His raw passing yardage numbers will probably increase—Winston ranked 16th in yards per game last year, and the team didn't sign all of these receivers to use them as run blockers—but that does not necessarily correlate to more touchdowns, or an improvement in overall efficiency. Jackson will get his numbers as long as he's healthy, but will probably siphon much of his value from other players rather than adding raw value of his own. The rest of the offense hasn't changed a bit: O.J. Howard and Cameron Brate will be competing for many of the same snaps, with Brate more likely to provide immediate receiving value. Chris Godwin is considered an outside receiver, not a slot guy, so Adam Humphries will still

---

play in the slot. Last year's 28th-ranked running game is still a huge question mark, particularly with so much uncertainty on the offensive line. The team's high 2016 DVOA on screens and play-action is probably unsustainable, and very likely to regress toward the mean. Winston still throws too many interceptions, and far too many interceptable passes. The Buccaneers offense ranked 18th in DVOA last year and has a mean projection of 20th for this year. It's not that we expect the Buccaneers to be appreciably *worse*; we just aren't convinced they're going to be that much *better*.

While our projection for the offense is underwhelming, it's the defensive projection that really hoists the red flags. Last year's Buccaneers posted the team's best pass defense DVOA since 2008, but the underlying components of that rating suggest a number of concerns for the future.

The most obvious of those was visible throughout last year: unless Justin Evans immediately lives up to all the best bits of his Earl Thomas comparisons, the Buccaneers do not have a reliable deep safety. Last year, the Bucs ranked 25th in DVOA against deep passes (thrown 16 or more yards downfield). Sixty of those 107 deep throws (56.1 percent) resulted in a first down or a touchdown, the fourth-worst rate behind Green Bay, New Orleans, and San Francisco. No team allowed more completions of 40 yards or longer. J.J. Wilcox is a solid player, but he does not quite fit that deeper-than-the-deepest role. Neither do Keith Tandy and Chris Conte, as last season again demonstrated. Evans is the only player on the roster who might, and he has a reputation for poor coverage discipline, being suckered by play-fakes, and misjudging pursuit angles. That is not a recipe for successful deep coverage in a division that features two of the league's best pass offenses.

Brent Grimes' age is also a concern. A Mike Smith favorite from their time in Atlanta, Grimes arrived from Miami last offseason to join Smith and performed better in Central Florida than he ever did in the south. He turns 34 before the new season though, and may be the oldest starting cornerback in the league (depending on the status of Minnesota's 39-year-old Terence Newman). 2016 fourth-rounder Ryan Smith is currently the closest thing to a direct backup for Grimes, but Smith spent last season trying unsuccessfully to transition to safety—hardly a ringing endorsement of his cornerback credentials. If Grimes does begin to show his age, the Buccaneers will probably have to suffer through it until next offseason.

A mention of age and depth leads us to peek behind another possible facade: Tampa Bay's defense had exceptionally good health last year, ranking sixth-healthiest with only 17.9 adjusted games lost. No NFL team can rely on starting the same 11 players in all 16 games, but the Buccaneers were far healthier than most. Every major starter on defense played at least 12 games, and only Ayers played fewer than 14. While the idea that health is a skill is true to a certain extent, there is also a lot of luck involved—luck from which the Buccaneers almost certainly benefited last year. Any regression on that front will mean a lot more playing time for what appears to be a very shallow pool of backups.

Similarly, we expect the rate of turnovers to regress toward the mean. Last year's Buccaneers defense ranked third in total takeaways, snagging 17 interceptions and recovering 12 opposing fumbles. They intercepted 3.1 percent of opponents' passes, the second-highest rate behind only San Diego, and claimed a turnover on 1.7 percent of their plays (fourth). That's good, of course, but in 2015 they intercepted only 2.0 percent of passes (24th) and their total turnover rate was 1.1 percent (24th). Turnover frequency simply is not consistent from year to year, and has more to do with opponent and game situation than the pure ability of the defense. Last year's high turnover rate tells us very little about this season.

Finally, our system is not impressed with the team's pass rush despite the Bucs ranking seventh in adjusted sack rate last year. The Buccaneers ranked in the bottom quarter of the league by pressure rate, meaning that 25 percent of the team's pressures resulted in sacks, well above the league average of 20.5 percent. The only teams with a higher rate of converting pressures to sacks were the Colts and 49ers. Pressure rate is more consistent from year to year than sack rate, a reason for pessimism in 2017.

While it's true that the team has four solid defensive ends rostered, one of those (Smith) is recovering from a torn ACL and another (Ayers) will be 32 on opening day. William Gholston is a solid run defender rather than an impactful pass-rusher, while Noah Spence is nothing but a pass-rusher and will have a limited role outside of obvious passing situations. Everybody in the Buccaneers front seven will contribute a few sacks here and there, but not even Gerald McCoy was that one difference-making pocket crusher last season.

Though all of these are admittedly potential issues rather than certainties, taken together they paint a picture of a defense that is unlikely to repeat its success from a year ago. The NFC South is likely to be very unforgiving of defensive weaknesses, meaning that even if the offense does live up to its hype, any defensive regression could still be enough to keep the Buccaneers out of the postseason. Special teams are unlikely to tilt anything in Tampa Bay's favor—that's an essay in itself—so the best hope for Buccaneers fans is another year of near-perfect health, Brent Grimes defying Father Time, and Justin Evans playing like a professional-caliber free safety from the start.

More likely, as was mentioned at the start, a lot of pressure will land on Jameis Winston's shoulders. We haven't spent a lot of time analyzing Winston himself, because we don't expect to see a huge difference from what he's already shown us. We certainly expect to see *some* progress as he heads into his third season, but we have also seen the same strengths and weaknesses consistently over the past two years. He's in the same scheme, with the same coaches and most of the same teammates. It's reasonable to say that Winston needs to diagnose coverages better, cut out the silly throws, and seriously improve his accuracy. It's less reasonable to expect him to improve drastically in all three areas during a single offseason. Nor is he going to suddenly lose his positive qualities: presence and maneuverability in the pocket, variety of throws, and velocity.

Any time a team makes such a huge investment in "weapons," fans want to see an immediate return or questions begin to be asked of the quarterback. Subjectively, Tampa Bay may have the widest projection swing of any team in the NFL this season. If Winston clicks with his new weapons and the defense plays at a high level again, the Bucs could be Super Bowl contenders. If the offensive additions fizzle while the defense regresses to its 2015 form, even a moderately healthy Bucs team could end up picking in the top five of the draft. It would be unfair to pin such an outcome on Winston, who has proven that he belongs as a starter at this level. We don't expect that to change, even if we do expect his playoff debut to be postponed for at least another year.

Andrew Potter

2016 Buccaneers Stats by Week

Wk	vs.	W-L	PF	PA	YDF	YDA	TO	Total	Off	Def	ST
1	at ATL	W	31	24	371	374	-1	50%	19%	-29%	2%
2	at ARI	L	7	40	306	416	-5	-54%	-27%	23%	-4%
3	LARM	L	32	37	472	320	0	-20%	9%	20%	-9%
4	DEN	L	7	27	215	307	-3	-74%	-56%	21%	2%
5	at CAR	W	17	14	315	414	+4	-29%	-11%	11%	-8%
6	BYE										
7	at SF	W	34	17	513	273	+2	34%	25%	-24%	-15%
8	OAK	L	24	30	270	626	+1	-33%	-11%	18%	-5%
9	ATL	L	28	43	396	461	-1	-4%	10%	15%	1%
10	CHI	W	36	10	360	283	+3	53%	-11%	-57%	7%
11	at KC	W	19	17	442	343	+1	-1%	7%	10%	2%
12	SEA	W	14	5	338	245	+1	62%	16%	-48%	-3%
13	at SD	W	28	21	349	330	+1	-1%	11%	10%	-1%
14	NO	W	16	11	270	294	+3	36%	-14%	-50%	0%
15	at DAL	L	20	26	276	449	-3	-16%	-19%	1%	4%
16	at NO	L	24	31	349	417	-2	-17%	-7%	16%	6%
17	CAR	W	17	16	300	335	+1	-15%	-18%	-12%	-9%

Trends and Splits

	Offense	Rank	Defense	Rank
Total DVOA	-4.1%	19	-2.9%	13
Unadjusted VOA	-5.0%	22	-0.1%	16
Weighted Trend	-2.8%	18	-9.0%	4
Variance	4.2%	8	7.9%	31
Average Opponent	0.1%	14	1.7%	7
Passing	20.3%	12	-4.7%	6
Rushing	-22.8%	30	-0.7%	26
First Down	-12.4%	27	5.8%	23
Second Down	4.4%	13	-3.2%	14
Third Down	-1.2%	17	-21.5%	3
First Half	-12.1%	28	-4.9%	12
Second Half	16.1%	6	6.4%	24
Red Zone	-7.5%	20	-8.9%	9
Late and Close	15.4%	5	15.8%	26

Five-Year Performance

Year	W-L	Pyth W	Est W	PF	PA	TO	Total	Rk	Off	Rk	Def	Rk	ST	Rk	Off AGL	Rk	Def AGL	Rk	Off Age	Rk	Def Age	Rk	ST Age	Rk
2012	7-9	7.9	7.8	389	394	+3	-6.6%	20	0.6%	14	2.9%	20	-4.3%	27	26.7	14	30.1	18	26.4	22	25.6	30	25.7	24
2013	4-12	5.3	6.3	288	389	+10	-5.1%	19	-10.4%	24	-6.8%	8	-1.5%	22	75.6	31	9.6	2	27.0	16	25.0	32	26.2	11
2014	2-14	4.4	4.1	277	410	-8	-28.3%	30	-26.3%	32	1.1%	18	-0.8%	17	31.1	17	56.1	25	27.5	7	25.7	30	26.0	18
2015	6-10	6.0	6.7	342	417	-5	-9.1%	21	-1.1%	17	3.3%	18	-4.7%	30	42.2	21	32.8	20	25.9	27	25.9	28	26.2	16
2016	9-7	7.6	7.2	354	369	+2	-3.0%	22	-4.1%	19	-2.9%	13	-1.8%	20	59.6	28	17.9	6	25.7	28	26.2	21	25.8	22

2016 Performance Based on Most Common Personnel Groups

TB Offense					TB Offense vs. Opponents					TB Defense					TB Defense vs. Opponents			
Pers	Freq	Yds	DVOA	Run%	Pers	Freq	Yds	DVOA	Run%	Pers	Freq	Yds	DVOA		Pers	Freq	Yds	DVOA
11	60%	5.8	3.0%	26%	Base	38%	5.0	-1.6%	57%	Base	41%	5.3	-14.0%		11	55%	6.3	4.6%
12	23%	5.4	-2.7%	53%	Nickel	51%	5.6	-3.1%	29%	Nickel	58%	6.4	4.7%		12	17%	5.0	-9.8%
612	5%	4.1	-23.3%	78%	Dime+	9%	6.4	26.9%	6%	Dime+	0%	27.0	496.2%		21	13%	6.0	-16.3%
13	4%	4.5	27.7%	58%	Goal Line	2%	1.4	26.0%	79%	Goal Line	1%	0.4	12.8%		611	3%	4.7	-12.4%
611	2%	4.6	-22.3%	92%											13	3%	4.6	-50.8%
21	2%	4.7	-10.8%	35%											10	2%	9.1	81.1%

Strategic Tendencies

Run/Pass		Rk	Formation		Rk	Pass Rush		Rk	Secondary		Rk	Strategy		Rk
Runs, first half	41%	9	Form: Single Back	78%	16	Rush 3	3.9%	26	4 DB	41%	4	Play-action	22%	6
Runs, first down	53%	5	Form: Empty Back	7%	17	Rush 4	70.4%	7	5 DB	58%	18	Avg Box (Off)	6.19	16
Runs, second-long	22%	31	Pers: 3+ WR	62%	25	Rush 5	18.9%	23	6+ DB	0%	31	Avg Box (Def)	6.23	17
Runs, power sit.	58%	12	Pers: 2+ TE/6+ OL	37%	5	Rush 6+	6.8%	11	CB by Sides	93%	3	Offensive Pace	29.79	8
Runs, behind 2H	22%	30	Pers: 6+ OL	9%	4	Sacks by LB	21.1%	21	S/CB Cover Ratio	29%	8	Defensive Pace	29.67	7
Pass, ahead 2H	47%	21	Shotgun/Pistol	50%	29	Sacks by DB	5.3%	23	DB Blitz	5%	29	Go for it on 4th	0.67	28

In last year's book, we wrote about the Bucs' absurd jump from the worst team in the league on play-action passes in 2014 to one of the best in 2015. That improvement did carry over to 2016; the Bucs were close to average with 8.1 yards per pass when using play-action, but they ranked second in the NFL with 67.0% DVOA. ☞ The Bucs were dead last in the league with just 3.9 average yards after the catch, even though they were fifth with 9.7 average YAC on passes behind the line of scrimmage. That's because they had just 2.6 average YAC on passes past the line of scrimmage; every other offense averaged 3.3 YAC or more on such passes. ☞ Tampa Bay ran the ball only 9.4 percent of the time when the quarterback was in shotgun, the second-lowest rate in the league—and they were terrible on these 50 plays, 3.7 yards per carry with a league-worst minus-39.9% DVOA. ☞ Tampa Bay's offense ranked 28th in the first half of games, then sixth in the second half of games, including fifth in "late and close" situations. ☞ Mike Smith blitzed defensive backs on only 4.6 percent of opposing pass plays, the fourth-lowest rate in 2016. Nickelback Jude Adjei-Barimah was the only defensive back to register a sack. Those few secondary blitzes worked well overall, however, producing a league-best minus-58.8% DVOA. The Buccaneers were excellent in general on big blitzes, allowing just 3.9 yards per pass when sending six or more pass-rushers. ☞ Tampa Bay's defense ranked 29th in DVOA against red zone runs, but ranked third in DVOA against red zone passes. ☞ Tampa Bay had both good and bad luck on special teams. On one hand, the Bucs benefited from a league-high nine field goals missed by opponents (tied with Miami), although six of those were from 50 or more yards. On the other hand, opposing kickers hit touchbacks on a league-high 74 percent of kickoffs.

Passing

Player	DYAR	DVOA	Plays	NtYds	Avg	YAC	C%	TD	Int
J.Winston	556	3.6%	603	3824	6.3	3.9	61.0%	28	16
M.Glennon*	65	65.8%	11	75	6.8	3.7	90.9%	1	0
R.Fitzpatrick	-319	-22.6%	423	2601	6.1	4.9	56.7%	12	16

Rushing

Player	DYAR	DVOA	Plays	Yds	Avg	TD	Fum	Suc
D.Martin	-81	-26.9%	105	313	3.0	4	0	38%
J.Rodgers	45	3.1%	95	422	4.4	2	0	52%
P.Barber	-24	-20.2%	50	204	4.1	1	0	46%
C.Sims	-45	-34.7%	41	116	2.8	1	0	37%
J.Winston	-27	-34.9%	25	126	5.0	1	0	-
A.Smith*	-23	-73.3%	10	46	4.6	0	0	60%
A.Humphries	5	-20.4%	5	18	3.6	0	0	-
M.James*	-2	-24.4%	4	19	4.8	0	0	50%
R.Fitzpatrick	10	-3.6%	22	119	5.4	0	0	-

Receiving

Player	DYAR	DVOA	Plays	Ctch	Yds	Y/C	YAC	TD	C%
M.Evans	309	10.0%	173	96	1321	13.8	1.8	12	55%
A.Humphries	68	-1.9%	83	55	622	11.3	6.9	2	66%
R.Shepard*	89	15.7%	40	23	341	14.8	3.3	2	58%
V.Jackson*	-18	-20.0%	32	15	173	11.5	1.1	0	47%
C.Shorts*	-28	-27.0%	27	11	152	13.8	2.4	0	41%
F.Martino	41	40.3%	11	8	142	17.8	3.8	1	73%
J.Huff	-2	-16.4%	6	3	41	13.7	8.3	0	50%
D.Jackson	241	16.4%	100	56	1005	17.9	5.1	4	56%
C.Brate	149	20.4%	81	57	660	11.6	2.4	8	70%
B.Myers*	-22	-27.9%	14	7	59	8.4	2.0	1	50%
L.Stocker	-30	-64.1%	8	5	23	4.6	4.0	0	63%
C.Sims	32	3.5%	32	24	190	7.9	7.3	1	75%
D.Martin	30	24.7%	16	14	134	9.6	7.6	0	88%
J.Rodgers	19	9.3%	16	13	98	7.5	6.9	0	81%
A.Cross	9	-1.4%	10	6	38	6.3	1.8	1	60%
A.Smith*	12	10.0%	9	6	77	12.8	13.2	0	67%
P.Barber	1	-10.2%	6	5	28	5.6	2.8	0	83%

Offensive Line

Player	Pos	Age	GS	Snaps	Pen	Sk	Pass	Run	Player	Pos	Age	GS	Snaps	Pen	Sk	Pass	Run
Ali Marpet	RG	24	16/16	1138	10	2.0	10	11	Demar Dotson	RT	32	13/13	944	12	5.5	17	3
Donovan Smith	LT	24	16/16	1138	12	3.0	15	11	Gosder Cherilus	RT	33	15/3	222	3	2.0	5	3
Joe Hawley	C	29	15/15	983	5	2.5	9	9	Evan Dietrich-Smith	C	31	12/2	174	0	0.0	1	0
Kevin Pamphile	LG	27	14/14	960	3	4.0	15	8									

Year	Yards	ALY	Rank	Power	Rank	Stuff	Rank	2nd Lev	Rank	Open Field	Rank	Sacks	ASR	Rank	Press	Rank	F-Start	Cont.
2014	3.73	3.44	32	69%	7	23%	32	0.99	25	0.79	13	52	9.4%	29	32.3%	31	17	33
2015	4.86	4.36	9	71%	8	20%	13	1.20	13	1.40	1	27	5.8%	14	29.3%	26	19	25
2016	3.61	4.01	21	47%	32	24%	32	1.06	25	0.45	28	35	5.9%	16	29.9%	26	16	32

2016 ALY by direction:	Left End 3.40 (26)	Left Tackle 3.72 (24)	Mid/Guard 4.26 (13)	Right Tackle 3.36 (27)	Right End 4.03 (13)

Former Seahawks left guard J.R. Sweezy should finally make his debut for Tampa Bay this year after missing all of last season with a back injury. The resultant reshuffle will probably see Ali Marpet move to center and incumbent left guard Kevin Pamphile move to right guard. No new offensive linemen of note have been signed. ≡ Including all players, not just linemen, the Buccaneers had 157 blown blocks in 2016, more than any other team. Counting only offensive linemen, they had 126, second-most behind only Seattle (127). Donovan Smith's 26 blown blocks tied for third-most among left tackles, Kevin Pamphile's 23 tied for second-most among left guards, and Joe Hawley's 18 tied for third-most among centers. Smith also gave up exactly 100 yards in penalties, one of only two offensive linemen to reach triple figures. Only right tackle Demar Dotson did not have at least the sixth-most blown blocks at his position, and Dotson missed three games. ≡ Though the Buccaneers were league-average by ASR, Jameis Winston tied with Carson Palmer for the most hits taken of any quarterback (87). Winston was knocked down 120 times in total, third-most behind Palmer and Andrew Luck. He was pressured on 203 plays, third-most behind Luck and Russell Wilson, though he only faced the seventh-highest *rate* of pressure (31.7 percent). What this Winston wouldn't give for a jump pack and a barrier projector.

Defensive Front Seven

Defensive Line	Age	Pos	G	Snaps	Plays	TmPct	Rk	Stop	Dfts	BTkl	Runs	St%	Rk	RuYd	Rk	Sack	Hit	Hur	Dsrpt
							Overall					vs. Run				Pass Rush		
Gerald McCoy	29	DT	15	794	39	5.0%	36	34	17	5	24	83%	26	1.6	25	6.0	5	28	4
Clinton McDonald	30	DT	12	484	36	5.8%	23	25	9	5	30	63%	80	2.6	58	3.5	2	10	0
Akeem Spence*	26	DT	16	362	18	2.2%	--	16	5	3	17	88%	--	2.1	--	0.5	2	4	0
Chris Baker	30	DE	16	783	48	5.6%	30	34	12	4	37	73%	52	2.2	40	4.0	7	21	2

Edge Rushers	Age	Pos	G	Snaps	Plays	TmPct	Rk	Stop	Dfts	BTkl	Runs	St%	Rk	RuYd	Rk	Sack	Hit	Hur	Dsrpt
							Overall					vs. Run				Pass Rush		
William Gholston	26	DE	14	585	50	6.9%	19	37	13	3	41	71%	64	2.7	53	3.5	4	7	0
Robert Ayers	32	DE	12	575	30	4.8%	53	26	11	2	20	80%	26	1.0	7	7.0	13	25	2
Noah Spence	23	DE	16	572	23	2.8%	92	17	9	6	14	57%	95	3.1	75	5.5	6	24	3
DaVonte Lambert	23	DE	11	374	14	2.5%	96	9	1	1	14	64%	83	3.6	90	0.0	0	5	0
Ryan Russell	25	DE	8	174	4	1.0%	--	3	3	1	3	67%	--	5.3	--	1.0	3	9	0

Linebackers	Age	Pos	G	Snaps	Plays	TmPct	Rk	Stop	Dfts	BTkl	Runs	St%	Rk	RuYd	Rk	Sack	Hit	Hur	Tgts	Suc%	Rk	AdjYd	Rk	PD	Int
							Overall					vs. Run				Pass Rush				vs. Pass					
Lavonte David	27	OLB	16	1041	89	10.7%	49	52	29	14	41	68%	22	2.5	7	5.0	3	8	38	38%	71	7.0	50	3	1
Kwon Alexander	23	MLB	16	1022	150	18.1%	8	79	28	19	77	61%	56	3.6	44	3.0	4	8	46	51%	31	6.8	46	7	1
Daryl Smith*	35	OLB	16	475	35	4.2%	85	19	4	4	25	68%	23	2.6	8	0.0	0	5	9	30%	--	13.5	--	0	0

Year	Yards	ALY	Rank	Power	Rank	Stuff	Rank	2nd Level	Rank	Open Field	Rank	Sacks	ASR	Rank	Press	Rank
2014	3.94	3.81	8	67%	20	25%	4	1.14	18	0.81	21	36	6.5%	19	21.9%	28
2015	3.55	4.06	15	69%	23	21%	16	1.07	13	0.29	1	38	7.6%	5	24.4%	23
2016	4.20	4.53	26	57%	5	19%	17	1.29	27	0.57	9	38	7.1%	6	24.7%	25

2016 ALY by direction:	Left End 5.25 (28)	Left Tackle 4.73 (21)	Mid/Guard 4.78 (31)	Right Tackle 4.46 (20)	Right End 2.14 (1)

Gerald McCoy had fewer sacks and quarterback hits last year than in any of the previous three seasons. Nonetheless, he still tied for the sixth among interior defensive linemen in total defeats. He'll play next to free-agent arrival Chris Baker, who profiles as an interior rusher on passing downs. Baker supplied unheralded work on an otherwise shaky Washington defensive line for years, but he did see declines in sacks, hits and defeats last season. ≡ Always the bridesmaid, never the bride. Lavonte David yet again ranked second in total defeats, this time tied with three other players behind Preston Brown rather than J.J. Watt. Kwon Alexander was tied for fifth, with one fewer defeat than David. The Buccaneers and Bills were the only two teams with more than one player in the top ten. ≡ When healthy, third-round rookie Kendell Beckwith should immediately become the team's third linebacker alongside David and Alexander. A powerful two-down run-stuffer, Beckwith led LSU in tackles last year until he tore his ACL in November. In the meantime, 2016 sixth-rounder Devante Bond is the favorite to man the strong side in base personnel sets. ☞ The last Buccaneers player to have double-digit sacks in a season remains Simeon Rice, who managed 14 in 2005. Every other team has had at least one player reach double-digits since. Michael Bennett (9 in 2012) and Gerald McCoy (9.5 in 2013) have each come within one sack of that target. ☞ Seventh-round pick Stevie Tu'ikolovatu (USC) has a chance to stick on the roster as a true 1-technique nose tackle who has earned favorable comparisons to Baltimore's Brandon Williams. With Akeem Spence now in Detroit, all of the team's established defensive tackles are generally considered 3-techniques.

Defensive Secondary

Secondary	Age	Pos	G	Snaps	Plays	TmPct	Rk	Stop	Dfts	BTkl	Runs	St%	Rk	RuYd	Rk	Tgts	Tgt%	Rk	Dist	Suc%	Rk	AdjYd	Rk	PD	Int
						Overall							vs. Run					vs. Pass							
Vernon Hargreaves	22	CB	16	1036	85	10.3%	13	32	13	16	23	39%	46	6.3	37	96	21.6%	64	9.9	45%	69	8.8	71	10	1
Bradley McDougald*	27	FS	16	1012	100	12.1%	17	32	11	13	52	37%	45	6.3	31	41	9.3%	48	13.6	53%	18	6.4	9	8	2
Brent Grimes	34	CB	16	997	81	9.8%	20	37	17	2	16	38%	50	7.6	56	77	17.9%	38	13.6	53%	23	6.7	18	24	4
Chris Conte	28	SS	14	713	68	9.4%	43	15	6	13	27	22%	69	10.5	69	32	10.3%	52	12.4	30%	72	16.1	74	5	2
Keith Tandy	28	SS	16	403	61	7.4%	61	23	10	5	31	35%	48	7.8	49	20	11.6%	62	12.8	56%	8	9.1	45	9	4
Jude Adjei-Barimah	25	CB	10	290	24	4.6%	--	10	4	4	6	33%	--	7.7	--	14	11.3%	--	9.1	48%	--	7.3	--	2	0
J.J. Wilcox	26	FS	13	557	51	7.7%	55	22	11	6	20	25%	65	10.7	70	23	8.6%	39	8.8	59%	4	5.2	1	5	1

Year	Pass D Rank	vs. #1 WR	Rk	vs. #2 WR	Rk	vs. Other WR	Rk	vs. TE	Rk	vs. RB	Rk
2014	23	27.1%	31	5.6%	21	-0.9%	16	4.0%	20	-17.9%	7
2015	26	-1.4%	16	41.6%	32	34.0%	32	2.9%	18	-8.0%	10
2016	6	-5.5%	8	-2.1%	13	-18.5%	6	-22.4%	4	16.6%	26

Chris Conte was one of only three safeties to allow more than 14 yards per pass play on more than 32 plays charted in coverage. Ricardo Allen (Atlanta) and Rodney McLeod (Philadelphia) were the other two. All three also made their average run tackle after a gain of over 10 yards. ☞ The disparity between the adjusted yards per pass figures recorded by Brent Grimes and Vernon Hargreaves was the fourth-widest of any starting cornerback tandem last year. Hargreaves also missed 16 tackles, third-most of any defensive back last season. Last year's 11th overall pick is still entrenched in the spot opposite Grimes, though, especially after Alterraun Verner's release this offseason. ☞ 2016 fourth-round pick Ryan Smith has been moved back to cornerback this offseason after failing to make the conversion to safety. Though Smith is expected to retain a roster spot, he will be strictly a backup at outside corner. Adjei-Barimah, Javien Elliott, and veteran Robert McClain are competing to play in the slot. ☞ J.J. Wilcox comes over from Dallas to play one safety position, but we have absolutely no idea who will be the other starting safety. The Bucs hope second-round pick Justin Evans (Texas A&M) is a long-term solution. Evans profiles as a physical hitter with the athleticism to also play deep, important in a defense that utilizes a two-high safety coverage foundation. In the short term, though, it's anybody's guess.

Special Teams

Year	DVOA	Rank	FG/XP	Rank	Net Kick	Rank	Kick Ret	Rank	Net Punt	Rank	Punt Ret	Rank	Hidden	Rank
2014	-0.8%	17	1.7	11	-1.4	18	-3.5	24	-0.6	18	-0.3	12	4.6	9
2015	-4.7%	30	-17.5	32	-3.1	23	0.2	12	1.1	17	-4.3	21	2.8	11
2016	-1.8%	20	-15.0	32	2.6	11	-8.9	32	13.6	2	-1.2	16	9.6	6

Remember that Seahawks-Cardinals overtime tie with what seemed like a dozen implausibly missed field goals? Buccaneers fans have witnessed kicking that bad throughout most of the past two years. Last year's second-round pick Roberto Aguayo was the worst kicker in the league at converting field goals and extra points, but his value was somehow still more than two points "higher" than 2015's Connor Barth-Kyle Brindza catastrophe. Aguayo was slightly above average on kickoffs, but that barely makes a dent in the deficit from his missed field goals. Veteran Nick Folk was signed as competition over the summer; whether that's more worrying for Folk's prospects or Aguayo's remains to be seen. ☞ The kick return game was also a hot mess throughout last season, setting a league record for the lowest average return since the merger. The previous official record low belonged to the 1993 Giants with 14.7 yards per return; last year's Buccaneers averaged 14.6. The team's longest return was 26 yards, also the lowest in the league. All three main Buccaneers kick returners finished below 17 yards per return; 80 different players exceeded that mark for other teams (min. 2 attempts). ☞ Punt returners fared much better; the team ranked 12th with

9.2 yards per punt return. That still cost the team an estimated 1.2 points of field position compared to an average team, though; over a quarter of those returns were muffed, fumbled, or resulted in penalties against the Buccaneers. ☙ On November 7th, 2010, Micheal Spurlock returned a kickoff for a touchdown against Atlanta. No Buccaneers player has scored a punt or kick return touchdown since, the longest ongoing drought in the league. Special teams coordinator Nate Kaczor has overseen exactly one kick or punt return touchdown in eight seasons with the Buccaneers, Titans, and Jaguars: a Mike Thomas punt return for Jacksonville against Indianapolis in December, 2010. 2010 is also the only time a special teams unit coached by Kaczor, either as an assistant or coordinator, has ranked above 20th in our ratings. ☙ Despite a net punting average that wasn't even in the top ten, Bryan Anger led the second-best punting unit in the league, adding 13.6 points of value over the season. The coverage allowed only 5.3 yards per return on 24 returns, the fourth-lowest and sixth-lowest figures in the league respectively. That added value was enough to lift the Buccaneers' overall special teams ranking to 21st; without it, they would have ranked 30th.

Tennessee Titans

2016 Record: 9-7	Total DVOA: 3.5% (15th)	2017 Mean Projection: 8.1 wins	On the Clock (0-4): 9%
Pythagorean Wins: 8.1 (20th)	Offense: 10.8% (9th)	Postseason Odds: 43.0%	Mediocrity (5-7): 32%
Snap-Weighted Age: 26.5 (17th)	Defense: 6.4% (24th)	Super Bowl Odds: 4.1%	Playoff Contender (8-10): 41%
Average Opponent: -5.8% (31st)	Special Teams: -1.0% (19th)	Proj. Avg. Opponent: -2.1% (28th)	Super Bowl Contender (11+): 19%

2016: Great shot, kid.

2017: Now don't get cocky.

The 2016 season represented a big improvement for the Tennessee Titans. A 9-7 season nearly doubled their five wins from the previous two seasons combined. Our numbers give virtually all of the credit for that improvement to the offense, which went from dead last in 2015 to ninth in DVOA in 2016. The improvement was split between the passing game (which jumped from 29th to ninth) and the running game (29th to eighth). Of course, since the range of passing performance is generally wider than the range of rushing performance, the passing game improvement made the biggest difference to the team's fate. Why, then, would the Titans use three of their first four picks to find new targets for quarterback Marcus Mariota?

Part of the answer is simple: the much-improved overall numbers concealed that the Titans essentially fielded two different offenses in 2016. One offense appeared on passing third downs (basically, 2 or more yards to go), in the two-minute drill, and in comeback situations. It featured Mariota in the shotgun, three receivers, and just the five offensive linemen blocking. The other offense is the one the Titans want to feature, with Mariota under center, frequent use of heavy protection (seven or more blockers on 43 percent of pass plays, the third-highest rate in the league), one or two receivers, often two tight ends, and sometimes two backs in the backfield. Those two offenses had very different results when they tried to throw the ball: the former was fantastic, the latter not.

With the quarterback operating from shotgun, the Titans had a pass offense DVOA of 34.4%, ranked fourth in the league. With the quarterback under center, their pass offense DVOA of 7.3% was just 23rd, or not far behind where the Jets and Bears ranked. Only Houston and Pittsburgh showed a greater improvement in their pass offense going from under center to shotgun. The Titans want to play as much of the under center "base" offense as possible. Given that, it makes perfect sense that improving the passing game in that preferred look was a high priority. Mariota, the backs, and the line are in place, so better pass game targets are the easiest way to do that. With feature receivers in short supply in free agency, the draft became the place to meet that need. And the Titans complied, adding Western Michigan's Corey Davis with the fifth overall pick, then Western Kentucky's Taywan Taylor and tight end Jonnu Smith out of Florida International in the third round.

Davis, Taylor, and Smith have a couple things in common,

beyond just their selection by the Titans. Each had only a single scholarship offer coming out of high school. Each attended an FBS school from what is now known as the Group of 5 (a.k.a. "the mid-majors") rather than a school in one of the power conferences. Most NFL draft picks, especially in the early rounds, are highly pedigreed players who had multiple offers out of high school and played in power conferences such as the SEC or Big Ten. Choosing Davis over, for example, Clemson's Mike Williams required a leap of faith on the part of general manager Jon Robinson, trusting in his evaluation abilities. Williams starred in showcase games, including the 2017 National Championship Game, against other highly pedigreed players like first-round corner Marlon Humphrey, while not a single corner Davis faced in 2016 was drafted this past April. Does drafting smaller-school players such as Davis, Taylor, and Smith present a larger risk?

There are a couple different ways to attack this question. First, just how many of the NFL's players come from major conference schools versus smaller schools? Second, just how many of the NFL's *better* players come from major conference schools versus smaller schools? Third, are players from major conference schools more likely to turn into better players? Fourth, looking specifically at Davis, how have first-round receivers from outside the major conferences fared, both overall and as rookies?

To answer these questions, we have to start by defining some terms. Our base measure of value, so we can look at more than just fantasy players, is Pro Football Reference's Approximate Value (AV). Any Tennessee fan who has looked at PFR's 2015 Titans page and seen Jeremiah Poutasi with 4 AV to Derrick Morgan's 3 is aware of the deep limitations of AV as a method of player evaluation. Much like some form of majoritarian rule with minority rights as a form of government, though, its primary value is that the other systems are all worse. Limitations aside, AV is a comprehensive number that includes an adjustment for team unit quality, acknowledges player participation data, and uses league-wide honors to reward players whose superior performance is acknowledged. Its limitations are more pronounced when comparing specific players, but to analyze players in the aggregate, it's a very useful tool.

Defining the power conferences is pretty easy. Schools that had a privileged path to a BCS game are power conference

2017 Titans Schedule

Week	Opp.	Week	Opp.	Week	Opp.
1	OAK	7	at CLE	13	HOU
2	at JAC	8	BYE	14	at ARI
3	SEA	9	BAL	15	at SF
4	at HOU	10	CIN	16	LARM
5	at MIA	11	at PIT (Thu.)	17	JAC
6	IND (Mon.)	12	at IND		

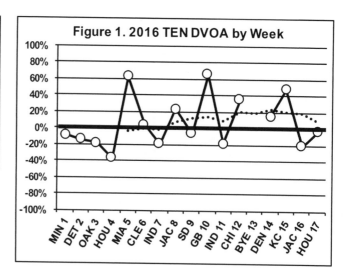

Figure 1. 2016 TEN DVOA by Week

schools. This includes the ACC, Big 12, Big Ten, Pac-12, SEC, the old Big East[1], and Notre Dame. The schools that did not are "mid-majors," those FBS schools now commonly known as the Group of 5; schools in FCS (f/k/a Division I-AA); and small schools, those that do not play Division I football.

We started our study with every offensive player since 2007. First, we specifically split out all player-seasons with at least 3 AV, a rough estimate of "replacement-level" value on offense. This sample includes almost every player who played a significant rotational role over the past ten years. Then we split out a second sample that included seasons with at least 8 AV, essentially the star players who truly mattered. The 2016 Titans had nine players with at least 8 AV, five of them on offense (Mariota, Jack Conklin, DeMarco Murray, Taylor Lewan, and Rishard Matthews).

Table 1 shows the first cut, players with at least 3 AV. A couple things stand out in the table, aside from just how unsurprising the death of Big East football was. One is that, as a collective group, the mid-majors produce plenty of talented players. Yes, there are many more mid-majors than there are schools in any particular power conference, but mid-majors produced more player-seasons than any power conference for linemen, quarterbacks, and wide receivers, and nearly as many running back seasons as the SEC. Only in tight ends did they lag behind. The dominance of the SEC is clear in this table, as is the quality of offensive line play in the Big Ten and just how few Pac-12 receivers have made an impact in the NFL.

Table 2 looks at the next cut, players with at least 8 AV. Once again, mid-majors fare extremely well outside of tight ends. They once again rank first at three of the five position groups and are just behind the leader in a fourth. The dominance of Big Ten offensive linemen becomes even more evident in this table, as does just how good receivers from the ACC have been.

Tables 1 and 2 make it clear that going to a mid-major is no bar to earning a regular role in the NFL, or even becoming a very good player in the NFL. The next question is, are players from smaller schools more likely to be just average players instead of good ones?

Table 3 makes it clear that the answer to that question is, by and large, absolutely not. Outside of tight ends—where 8 AV may not be a particularly meaningful bar just because there are so many fewer seasons to meet the threshold relative to other positions—mid-majors are just as good or even slightly

better at producing star NFL players. Individual positions may stand out for specific conferences, such as Big Ten offensive linemen and ACC wide receivers, plus just how many Big 12 quarterbacks have gotten NFL snaps but failed to emerge into regular starters. So far, this study suggests that no pessimism or skepticism about Davis or Taylor is warranted by their mid-major pedigrees. Perhaps slight skepticism about Smith is valid, but his projection to an early role is less certain than that of the other two players.

What about our last question: are things different for first-round picks specifically? The data shows just how rare it is for a receiver outside the power conference schools to be drafted that high. Going back to 1990, the highest draft position for a wide receiver from outside a power conference came in 1999, when Pittsburgh selected Louisiana Tech's Troy Edwards with the 13th pick. When Tennessee chose Davis No. 5 overall, they made him the highest-drafted receiver from a non-power conference school in the 51 years of the common draft era. Davis is just the fourth receiver from a smaller school chosen in the top ten at all, following in the footsteps of Haven Moses (San Diego State, No. 9 to Buffalo in 1968), Ken Burrough (Texas Southern, No. 10 to New Orleans in 1970), and Frank Lewis (Grambling, if you consider it a non-power school in 1971, No. 8 to Pittsburgh). To some extent, the Titans with Davis are dealing with uncharted territory. As with the selection of Conklin in the first round last year, the Titans and their supporters have no choice but to trust in Robinson's scouting acumen.

Davis' college production was truly impressive, and he became the unicorn, a senior receiver that Playmaker Score actually liked. He has an easy path to playing time, supplanting Tajae Sharpe. Sharpe was a surprise Week 1 starter as a fifth-round rookie but lost playing time as the season went on and posted the worst receiving DVOA of any Titans receiver other than The Player Formerly Known as Andre Johnson (Before He Retired Midseason). Taylor projects more as a slot receiver, while Smith seems likely to be eased into Delanie Walker's role as a move receiving tight end. The Titans added

---

1 Players drafted since 2014 from the leftover Big East football schools, now the American Athletic Conference, were counted as players from mid-major schools.

Eric Decker in late June, so he will factor into the receiving group somehow. However, by June minicamp Davis was fully recovered from the ankle injury that kept him out of pre-draft workouts, and he should still see significant work on offense as a rookie. Check back in *Football Outsiders Almanac 2018* for early returns on how he fared.

Last year's Jared Goff trade gave the Titans the additional first-round pick they used on Davis, while their own went for the other side of the ball. USC cornerback Adoree' Jackson snapped a couple of this team's trends. Unlike Davis and Conklin, he was a highly touted recruit and had many scholarship offers out of high school. The Titans had used their past seven first-round picks (including Davis) on offensive players. Jackson was also the first pure corner selected in the first round by a team with Dick LeBeau as their head coach or defensive coordinator in his more than 25 years in such jobs. On the other hand, Jackson's specific talents clearly fit the way the Titans execute their philosophy in the draft. The Titans preach versatility, and Jackson offers not just outside corner potential but the athleticism to match up to the two-way go from the slot, plus explosive return ability on punts and kicks. USC even featured him on offense some, and the Titans might do the same, fitting with the "exotic" part of Mike Mularkey's "exotic smashmouth" scheme.

Jackson's ability to match up with slot receivers fits with the implied plan of the Titans' big free-agent acquisitions on defense: corner Logan Ryan from New England, safety Johnathan Cyprien from Jacksonville, and nose tackle Sylvester Williams from Denver. Each of the four addresses the middle of the field, with Ryan featuring as the Patriots' slot corner for their Super Bowl run, Cyprien at his best in coverage and run support as a box player, and Williams, well, being a nose tackle.

But are the Titans really weak over the middle of the field? The Titans did not have a good DVOA against passes thrown in the middle of the field, but they weren't terrible: 20th against deep middle passes, 21st against short middle passes. Teams also did not attack the middle of the field at an above-average rate. By direction, their weakest area was against short throws on the right side. By position, they ranked 30th in the league against both No. 2 receivers and running backs in the passing game. Ryan or Jackson should help cover those No. 2 receivers, but linebacker, either inside or outside, was only addressed starting in the fifth round of the draft.

Another, potentially more fruitful point of attention might have been the pass rush. The Titans turned into a rush-5 team; this was a useful and necessary move, because they ranked just 29th with a 21 percent pressure rate when rushing only four players but 21st with a 35 percent pressure rate when blitzing. Both Derrick Morgan and Brian Orakpo had at least 9.0 sacks with commensurate hurry totals, but the two of them and Jurrell Casey needed more help from the rest of the front seven, and Williams is not likely to be the answer there.

Nevertheless, even if the defensive additions fail to improve things, it may not hold the Titans back in 2017. This year's forecast, like the progress the Titans made a year ago, is driven by the offense. It's driven by the rest of the AFC South, where

Table 1. Player-Seasons with at Least 3 AV by College Conference, 2007-2016

Conference	OL	QB	RB	WR	TE
ACC/Notre Dame	232	43	82	137	68
Big 12	209	37	78	104	28
Big East	100	18	51	65	14
Big Ten	290	50	58	107	39
Pac-10/12	177	58	102	84	57
SEC	333	56	113	160	44
All BCS/Power 5	1,341	262	484	657	250
Mid-Major	339	64	111	195	48
FCS	109	39	39	43	12
Division II/III	90	4	42	75	16
ALL non-BCS/Power 5	538	107	192	313	76
TOTAL	1,899	369	676	970	326

Table 2. Player-Seasons with at Least 8 AV by College Conference, 2007-2016

Conference	OL	QB	RB	WR	TE
ACC/Notre Dame	85	31	23	49	13
Big 12	85	17	24	30	1
Big East	36	9	16	26	3
Big Ten	123	34	17	27	4
Pac-10/12	63	31	28	24	11
SEC	120	42	28	46	10
All BCS/Power 5	512	164	136	202	42
Mid-Major	121	42	38	66	7
FCS	35	27	7	15	1
Division II/III	33	3	11	19	1
ALL non-BCS/Power 5	189	72	56	100	9
TOTAL	701	236	192	302	51

Table 3. Percentage of 3-Plus AV Player Seasons with at Least 8 AV by College Conference, 2007-2016

Conference	OL	QB	RB	WR	TE
ACC/Notre Dame	36.6%	72.1%	28.0%	35.8%	19.1%
Big 12	40.7%	45.9%	30.8%	28.8%	3.6%
Big East	36.0%	50.0%	31.4%	40.0%	21.4%
Big Ten	42.4%	68.0%	29.3%	25.2%	10.3%
Pac-10/12	35.6%	53.4%	27.5%	28.6%	19.3%
SEC	36.0%	75.0%	24.8%	28.8%	22.7%
All BCS/Power 5	38.2%	62.6%	28.1%	30.7%	16.8%
Mid-Major	35.7%	65.6%	34.2%	33.8%	14.6%
FCS	32.1%	69.2%	17.9%	34.9%	8.3%
Division II/III	36.7%	75.0%	26.2%	25.3%	6.3%
ALL non-BCS/Power 5	35.1%	67.3%	29.2%	31.9%	11.8%
TOTAL	36.9%	64.0%	28.4%	31.1%	15.6%

once again all four teams have a mean DVOA projection below average. And it's driven by one of the league's easiest schedules, enough to project the Titans as slight favorites in the division over Indianapolis. The Titans were the best team in the division by DVOA last year and ended up missing the postseason by virtue of a tiebreaker loss. If they can again avoid major long-term injuries, end the 11-game losing streak against Indianapolis, and maybe even go .500 or better in the division for the first time since 2011, that's probably enough to return Tennessee to the postseason for the first time since 2008. Like Houston last year, they might even be fortunate enough to face a playoff foe missing their starting quarterback and make it to the divisional round before one of the AFC's really good teams ends their season with a resounding defeat.

Tom Gower

2016 Titans Stats by Week

Wk	vs.	W-L	PF	PA	YDF	YDA	TO	Total	Off	Def	ST
1	MIN	L	16	25	316	301	-3	-9%	1%	2%	-8%
2	at DET	W	16	15	363	375	0	-15%	-9%	-9%	-15%
3	OAK	L	10	17	393	368	-2	-18%	-24%	-4%	2%
4	at HOU	L	20	27	320	359	+1	-37%	-9%	10%	-18%
5	at MIA	W	30	17	398	200	+2	62%	41%	-50%	-29%
6	CLE	W	28	26	407	341	-1	4%	24%	23%	3%
7	IND	L	26	34	331	422	-1	-19%	8%	32%	5%
8	JAC	W	36	22	494	370	+1	24%	53%	32%	3%
9	at SD	L	35	43	393	476	-3	-7%	24%	36%	4%
10	GB	W	47	25	446	402	+3	65%	51%	-6%	8%
11	at IND	L	17	24	351	327	+1	-18%	-15%	-1%	-4%
12	at CHI	W	27	21	375	411	+2	35%	36%	6%	5%
13	BYE										
14	DEN	W	13	10	253	348	+2	15%	9%	1%	8%
15	at KC	W	19	17	389	316	-2	48%	20%	-19%	9%
16	at JAC	L	17	38	263	415	0	-21%	-2%	26%	7%
17	HOU	W	24	17	236	289	0	-3%	-16%	-7%	6%

Trends and Splits

	Offense	Rank	Defense	Rank
Total DVOA	10.8%	9	6.4%	24
Unadjusted VOA	12.2%	9	2.3%	20
Weighted Trend	14.4%	7	8.3%	27
Variance	6.0%	16	4.9%	16
Average Opponent	1.2%	25	-4.1%	31
Passing	28.3%	9	18.8%	27
Rushing	1.7%	8	-14.4%	10
First Down	-4.6%	19	9.4%	26
Second Down	10.8%	8	8.4%	25
Third Down	39.7%	2	-2.4%	14
First Half	18.7%	5	16.1%	30
Second Half	0.4%	15	-13.7%	8
Red Zone	57.1%	1	-1.4%	19
Late and Close	-7.7%	20	-30.3%	4

Five-Year Performance

Year	W-L	Pyth W	Est W	PF	PA	TO	Total	Rk	Off	Rk	Def	Rk	ST	Rk	Off AGL	Rk	Def AGL	Rk	Off Age	Rk	Def Age	Rk	ST Age	Rk
2012	6-10	4.6	3.3	330	471	-4	-29.4%	30	-20.5%	29	7.5%	25	-1.4%	19	49.9	26	14.6	5	27.7	9	25.3	32	26.0	15
2013	7-9	7.5	6.6	362	381	0	-6.1%	21	1.4%	16	4.2%	22	-3.2%	26	28.3	12	15.6	6	27.3	13	26.2	20	26.4	8
2014	2-14	3.3	4.0	254	438	-10	-29.3%	31	-16.4%	29	11.2%	29	-1.8%	20	38.8	22	40.9	19	27.0	14	27.0	10	26.7	2
2015	3-13	4.8	4.4	299	423	-14	-26.6%	31	-15.7%	32	7.1%	23	-3.8%	28	38.7	20	26.5	13	25.6	29	26.5	18	25.7	24
2016	9-7	8.1	8.7	381	378	0	3.5%	15	10.8%	9	6.4%	24	-1.0%	19	21.0	4	11.0	3	26.2	24	27.0	8	26.2	14

2016 Performance Based on Most Common Personnel Groups

TEN Offense					TEN Offense vs. Opponents					TEN Defense					TEN Defense vs. Opponents			
Pers	Freq	Yds	DVOA	Run%	Pers	Freq	Yds	DVOA	Run%	Pers	Freq	Yds	DVOA	Pers	Freq	Yds	DVOA
11	40%	6.3	26.7%	20%	Base	43%	5.5	4.1%	65%	Base	29%	5.0	-14.5%	11	69%	6.0	15.8%
12	19%	5.5	-1.7%	53%	Nickel	41%	6.2	17.7%	28%	Nickel	56%	6.0	14.7%	12	14%	5.4	-15.4%
21	13%	6.4	14.0%	51%	Dime+	11%	6.8	46.1%	5%	Dime+	14%	6.5	26.6%	21	4%	6.4	1.9%
13	9%	6.6	17.0%	70%	Goal Line	2%	1.1	24.2%	88%	Goal Line	1%	0.4	-26.0%	13	2%	3.2	-32.2%
22	7%	4.5	-4.4%	81%	Big	2%	5.6	28.3%	76%					22	2%	7.3	42.7%
612	2%	3.3	-21.1%	75%										01	2%	4.4	-7.1%

Strategic Tendencies

Run/Pass		Rk	Formation		Rk	Pass Rush		Rk	Secondary		Rk	Strategy		Rk
Runs, first half	44%	2	Form: Single Back	70%	27	Rush 3	10.8%	10	4 DB	29%	17	Play-action	18%	14
Runs, first down	49%	11	Form: Empty Back	5%	27	Rush 4	53.6%	30	5 DB	56%	21	Avg Box (Off)	6.36	5
Runs, second-long	46%	2	Pers: 3+ WR	44%	32	Rush 5	30.1%	1	6+ DB	14%	12	Avg Box (Def)	6.14	23
Runs, power sit.	66%	5	Pers: 2+ TE/6+ OL	43%	1	Rush 6+	5.5%	19	CB by Sides	91%	6	Offensive Pace	33.08	32
Runs, behind 2H	32%	4	Pers: 6+ OL	6%	10	Sacks by LB	73.1%	2	S/CB Cover Ratio	22%	28	Defensive Pace	30.14	14
Pass, ahead 2H	40%	32	Shotgun/Pistol	56%	24	Sacks by DB	5.1%	24	DB Blitz	10%	15	Go for it on 4th	0.43	31

Tennessee was the only team to run more often than it passed on second downs, with a 53/47 ratio. ☞ Despite their run-heavy attack, the Titans ran less often than any other offense when they had three or more wide receivers on the field: just 21 percent of plays. However, the Titans were second in the NFL in both DVOA (14.9%) and yards per carry (5.53) on runs from three-wide or four-wide sets. ☞ The Titans ranked fifth in defensive DVOA on third- or fourth-and-short but 23rd on all other third and fourth downs. ☞ Tennessee benefited from 156 opposition penalties for 1,191 yards. Both numbers led the NFL. ☞ The Titans also benefited from a league-high 54 dropped passes from opponents, seven more than any other defense. It was a huge change from 2015, when the Titans were near the bottom with just 11 opponent drops.

Passing

Player	DYAR	DVOA	Plays	NtYds	Avg	YAC	C%	TD	Int
M.Mariota	681	11.1%	473	3252	6.9	4.6	61.7%	26	9
M.Cassel	-38	-23.1%	54	261	4.8	2.4	61.2%	2	2

Rushing

Player	DYAR	DVOA	Plays	Yds	Avg	TD	Fum	Suc
D.Murray	17	-6.9%	230	1043	4.5	10	0	49%
D.Henry	68	14.6%	70	312	4.5	5	0	54%
M.Mariota	38	5.9%	41	316	7.7	2	0	-

Receiving

Player	DYAR	DVOA	Plays	Ctch	Yds	Y/C	YAC	TD	C%
R.Matthews	229	14.4%	108	65	945	14.5	3.1	9	60%
T.Sharpe	23	-9.2%	83	41	522	12.7	2.1	2	49%
K.Wright*	119	21.9%	43	29	416	14.3	4.3	3	67%
A.Johnson	-23	-25.1%	23	9	85	9.4	1.7	2	39%
H.Douglas	63	22.4%	22	15	210	14.0	3.9	0	68%
D.Walker	102	8.4%	103	66	808	12.2	4.3	7	64%
A.Fasano*	13	5.2%	14	8	83	10.4	4.8	2	57%
D.Murray	40	-3.2%	67	53	377	7.1	6.5	3	79%
D.Henry	45	46.9%	15	13	137	10.5	9.5	0	87%

Offensive Line

Player	Pos	Age	GS	Snaps	Pen	Sk	Pass	Run	Player	Pos	Age	GS	Snaps	Pen	Sk	Pass	Run
Jack Conklin	RT	23	16/16	1060	3	1.0	3	4	Quinton Spain	LG	26	14/13	819	8	0.3	1	6
Ben Jones	C	28	16/16	1060	3	1.8	5	2	Brian Schwenke*	C	26	16/3	247	0	0.5	1	1
Taylor Lewan	LT	26	16/16	989	14	2.3	7	7	Tim Lelito	LG	28	16/7	406	2	1.0	5	4
Josh Kline	RG	28	14/14	928	4	2.0	5	5									

Year	Yards	ALY	Rank	Power	Rank	Stuff	Rank	2nd Lev	Rank	Open Field	Rank	Sacks	ASR	Rank	Press	Rank	F-Start	Cont.
2014	3.82	4.18	17	63%	17	17%	4	1.06	23	0.39	31	50	8.9%	26	26.0%	20	16	29
2015	3.66	3.98	20	37%	32	22%	20	0.95	31	0.58	25	54	9.6%	32	28.1%	24	10	24
2016	4.39	4.63	5	68%	12	19%	13	1.27	9	0.72	13	28	5.7%	15	20.8%	4	15	33
2016 ALY by direction:		Left End 4.71 (11)		Left Tackle 5.54 (1)		Mid/Guard 4.04 (21)		Right Tackle 5.52 (2)		Right End 5.98 (2)								

Mike Mularkey, offensive coordinator Terry Robiskie, and line coach Russ Grimm deserve a lot of credit for Jack Conklin's numbers. The trio made sure he was only asked to do what he could do well, and the rookie responded marvelously. He ranked atop our snaps per blown block rankings for all tackles. ☞ Taylor Lewan's Pro Bowl selection was more deserving than Conklin's All-Pro nod. He responded to the new coaches with his best season, while most of the help was directed to the right side of the line. ☞ Ben Jones gave the Titans what they needed after he was signed away from the Texans last offseason. The veteran starter finished fifth among centers in snaps per blown block; the year before, the brutal Andy Gallik/Joe Looney tag team both finished in the bottom seven at the position. ☞ Josh Kline was a waiver wire claim forced into the lineup by Chance Warmack's season-ending injury, but he played surprisingly well given his past struggles for the Patriots. ☞ Backups Dennis Kelly (tackle) and Tim Lelito (center, new, ex-Saints) both have experience as a sixth lineman and may play there often this season with the departure of blocking tight end Anthony Fasano. ⬦ Challenge for the Titans: are they content with what they have, or do they look to upgrade at guard? Josue Matias, a Florida State product who went undrafted in 2015, might have challenged Quinton Spain's starting spot but for injury, and 2016 sixth-round pick Sebastian Tretola may be in the mix as well.

Defensive Front Seven

Defensive Line	Age	Pos	G	Snaps	Plays	TmPct	Overall Rk	Stop	Dfts	BTkl	Runs	vs. Run St%	Rk	RuYd	Rk	Pass Rush Sack	Hit	Hur	Dsrpt
Jurrell Casey	28	DE	15	724	49	6.6%	19	37	16	5	32	72%	56	2.8	63	5.0	16	23	6
DaQuan Jones	26	DE	16	674	26	3.3%	69	19	4	4	22	77%	43	2.7	62	1.5	4	12	0
Karl Klug	29	DE	14	397	27	3.9%	54	17	6	2	21	62%	82	3.0	70	1.5	4	10	1
Angelo Blackson	25	DE	13	251	10	1.5%	--	8	4	0	8	75%	--	3.0	--	0.0	2	4	1
Al Woods*	30	DT	12	248	18	3.0%	--	13	5	2	16	81%	--	2.2	--	0.0	0	3	0
Austin Johnson	23	DT	10	190	15	3.0%	--	12	3	0	13	77%	--	2.2	--	0.5	0	0	1
Sylvester Williams	*29*	*DT*	*16*	*649*	*30*	*3.5%*	*64*	*18*	*4*	*3*	*25*	*60%*	*84*	*3.1*	*74*	*1.0*	*5*	*15*	*1*

Edge Rushers	Age	Pos	G	Snaps	Plays	TmPct	Overall Rk	Stop	Dfts	BTkl	Runs	vs. Run St%	Rk	RuYd	Rk	Pass Rush Sack	Hit	Hur	Dsrpt
Brian Orakpo	31	OLB	16	864	50	6.3%	27	35	19	4	25	64%	84	3.8	94	10.5	8	29	3
Derrick Morgan	28	OLB	15	765	33	4.4%	62	26	15	6	17	88%	4	1.5	21	9.0	12	33	0
David Bass*	27	OLB	13	226	12	1.9%	--	8	1	0	8	88%	--	1.8	--	0.0	1	2	0
Kevin Dodd	25	OLB	9	179	5	1.1%	--	3	1	1	2	100%	--	2.0	--	1.0	1	5	0

Linebackers	Age	Pos	G	Snaps	Plays	TmPct	Overall Rk	Stop	Dfts	BTkl	Runs	vs. Run St%	Rk	RuYd	Rk	Pass Rush Sack	Hit	Hur	vs. Pass Tgts	Suc%	Rk	AdjYd	Rk	PD	Int
Avery Williamson	25	ILB	16	908	105	13.2%	39	54	13	3	65	66%	30	4.8	81	2.0	3	8	28	32%	81	8.5	72	0	0
Wesley Woodyard	31	ILB	16	612	57	7.2%	72	32	14	12	35	63%	46	2.7	12	2.0	3	7	18	37%	72	6.7	45	6	1
Sean Spence*	27	ILB	15	505	53	7.1%	73	27	7	3	22	64%	41	3.2	31	3.0	2	2	24	55%	24	6.0	28	4	0

Year	Yards	ALY	Rank	Power	Rank	Stuff	Rank	2nd Level	Rank	Open Field	Rank	Sacks	ASR	Rank	Press	Rank
2014	4.41	4.36	23	73%	27	19%	17	1.25	26	0.84	26	39	7.0%	11	20.8%	29
2015	3.91	4.47	26	56%	6	18%	26	1.10	14	0.44	4	39	7.8%	3	25.2%	16
2016	3.80	3.97	12	45%	1	20%	15	0.96	5	0.60	12	40	6.2%	14	24.9%	23
2016 ALY by direction:		*Left End 5.73 (30)*			*Left Tackle 3.82 (11)*			*Mid/Guard 4.13 (15)*			*Right Tackle 2.64 (2)*			*Right End 3.10 (9)*		

The Titans return most of their defensive front seven, swapping rotational nose tackle Al Woods for the Broncos' Sylvester Williams and drafting fifth-rounder Jayon Brown (UCLA) to eventually step into Sean Spence's sub package linebacker job. The moves not made are more interesting than those that were, because while the run defense was good, there was not a diversified or strong-enough pass rush to help the coverage units. ⬦ Rotational pass-rushing tackle Karl Klug was re-signed after tearing his Achilles in Week 15. He missed the offseason but is expected back during training camp. ⬦ The key player might be Kevin Dodd. The 33rd overall pick of the 2016 draft suffered a foot injury in his first rookie minicamp and made little impact before going to injured reserve with some pointed comments from Mularkey. A second surgery followed after the season, and he was not running until June. The next two backups at outside linebacker are a pair of seventh-round picks (Aaron Wallace, UCLA, 2016; and Josh Carraway, TCU, 2017), so the Titans are clearly counting on him. We remain skeptical of overage and unathletic prospects (25 in July, SackSEER rating of 9.0%). ⬦ The Titans stabilized as a five-man pass rush, with one of the inside linebackers most commonly joining the front four. ⬦ Casey, Morgan, and Orakpo are the clear top three, but DaQuan Jones might have been the fourth-best player in the unit. He has become a very good player against the run and also increased his hurry total in 2016. ⬦ An impact three-down inside linebacker will probably make the priority list for next offseason.

Defensive Secondary

Secondary	Age	Pos	G	Snaps	Plays	Overall TmPct	Rk	Stop	Dfts	BTkl	vs. Run Runs	St%	Rk	RuYd	Rk	vs. Pass Tgts	Tgt%	Rk	Dist	Suc%	Rk	AdjYd	Rk	PD	Int
Brice McCain	31	CB	16	842	47	5.9%	84	21	8	8	6	50%	19	5.0	15	59	14.2%	5	10.4	57%	9	7.0	26	10	2
Jason McCourty*	30	CB	14	813	79	11.3%	5	27	9	2	9	33%	55	13.3	82	94	23.4%	74	11.6	52%	28	8.0	54	12	2
Kevin Byard	24	SS	16	655	55	6.9%	64	26	9	7	25	68%	1	4.4	7	24	7.3%	24	10.1	50%	25	5.4	2	3	0
Perrish Cox*	30	CB	11	623	53	9.7%	22	23	12	6	4	100%	1	2.8	2	73	23.7%	76	12.3	45%	71	8.3	59	11	3
Daimion Stafford*	26	SS	15	613	53	7.1%	62	23	7	12	19	63%	5	4.1	3	32	10.4%	55	7.2	44%	45	9.1	44	2	1
Da'Norris Searcy	29	SS	14	555	45	6.5%	66	17	8	5	16	50%	16	5.4	17	19	6.8%	22	11.3	54%	12	10.1	56	6	1
Rashad Johnson*	31	FS	14	550	39	5.6%	--	12	6	8	19	32%	--	6.6	--	15	5.4%	--	11.1	59%	--	7.1	--	1	0
Valentino Blake*	27	CB	16	364	42	5.3%	--	13	4	1	5	60%	--	3.0	--	49	27.4%	--	12.8	42%	--	8.1	--	6	0
LeShaun Sims	24	CB	13	235	20	3.1%	--	4	4	2	1	0%	--	5.0	--	39	33.7%	--	12.8	47%	--	8.1	--	3	1
Logan Ryan	26	CB	16	897	103	13.2%	1	41	17	5	24	58%	13	4.4	10	81	19.5%	52	11.1	45%	70	7.6	44	11	2
Johnathan Cyprien	27	SS	16	1070	130	16.3%	2	58	15	9	72	60%	7	4.3	6	52	12.4%	66	9.8	46%	39	8.5	34	6	0
Demontre Hurst	26	CB	10	223	14	2.7%	--	7	4	1	4	50%	--	13.0	--	13	14.1%	--	8.4	44%	--	8.8	--	0	0

Year	Pass D Rank	vs. #1 WR	Rk	vs. #2 WR	Rk	vs. Other WR	Rk	vs. TE	Rk	vs. RB	Rk
2014	26	-6.3%	10	53.9%	32	-8.1%	10	9.0%	24	0.5%	18
2015	24	12.2%	27	33.3%	31	14.3%	25	15.8%	24	-39.0%	1
2016	27	2.5%	18	21.7%	30	0.2%	16	-14.8%	8	36.3%	30

Key question going into 2016: how would the Titans use Kevin Byard? He played free safety in college but was used primarily as a modern versatile strong safety as a rookie. The decision paid off with his excellent charting numbers against the run, an area where Johnathan Cyprien also excelled in Jacksonville. He would be the right complement to Cyprien if he went back to playing single high but right now seems likely to continue to play the more versatile role. That leaves Da'Norris Searcy, still nominally a strong safety, as the single high player in Cover-1 looks behind that five-man pass rush. 🏈 Brice McCain was probably the most successful corner in his role last year, but showed in the past he is just a slot corner. Will he play there, and is there a fit for him with the Titans talking up the slot ability of Jackson and Ryan? 🏈 LeShaun Sims' first significant action was disastrous, but he ended the season playing well after the bye. Unlike McCain, Ryan, and Adoree' Jackson, he is just an outside corner. But you need two of those, which might earn him significant playing time. 🏈 Jason McCourty tailed off badly, which probably contributed to his offseason release. He had an outstanding 69 percent success rate in coverage through Week 7, but just 40 percent thereafter. 🏈 Perrish Cox posted the worst success rate in coverage in the league from Week 8 onward, which definitely contributed to his release after Week 12.

Special Teams

Year	DVOA	Rank	FG/XP	Rank	Net Kick	Rank	Kick Ret	Rank	Net Punt	Rank	Punt Ret	Rank	Hidden	Rank
2014	-1.8%	20	-0.1	17	-9.4	30	1.1	11	2.7	11	-3.3	20	-9.5	28
2015	-3.8%	28	1.5	12	-1.2	19	-10.0	32	-6.7	26	-2.4	19	-5.9	23
2016	-1.0%	19	8.1	5	-2.7	22	-2.5	21	-6.4	26	-1.4	18	5.1	8

Bobby April coordinated great special teams for Mularkey's Bills in 2004 and 2005 but was canned four weeks into the season with the Titans 31st in special teams DVOA. Poor coverage units stood out as the reason for the firing, as Tennessee ranked last on kickoffs and 31st on punts, including Braxton Miller's score that provided the eventual margin of victory in Houston's Week 4 win. Both coverage units got somewhat better after April's firing. From Week 5 on, the Titans were 27th in punt coverage and 19th in kick return coverage. 🏈 Improving special teams personnel was a big priority this offseason, as the Titans targeted Oakland gunners Brynden Trawick and Daren Bates early in free agency before adding veteran return man Eric Weems. Trawick led the NFL with 10 stops on kickoffs (plays that stopped a kickoff return short of our average baseline). 🏈 Marc Mariani was below average but reliable on both punts and kickoffs. Weems was good for the Falcons on punts and average on kickoffs. He also finished tied for second behind Trawick with nine stops on kickoffs. Rookies Adoree' Jackson and Khalfani Muhammad both have return experience and could provide more explosiveness.

Washington Redskins

2016 Record: 8-7-1	Total DVOA: 9.5% (9th)	2017 Mean Projection: 7.8 wins	On the Clock (0-4): 11%
Pythagorean Wins: 8.3 (18th)	Offense: 15.8% (5th)	Postseason Odds: 31.3%	Mediocrity (5-7): 36%
Snap-Weighted Age: 27.1 (5th)	Defense: 6.8% (25th)	Super Bowl Odds: 4.3%	Playoff Contender (8-10): 37%
Average Opponent: 4.3% (3rd)	Special Teams: 0.4% (13th)	Proj. Avg. Opponent: 2.5% (3rd)	Super Bowl Contender (11+): 15%

2016: You can choose a ready guide in some celestial voice.

2017: If you choose not to decide, you still have made a choice.

As offseason strategies go, firing your personnel guru amid a noxious cloud of innuendo during the crucial combine/free agency period is certainly unique, even by Washington's lofty standards.

The Redskins fired Scot McCloughan, the F. Scott Fitzgerald of football scouting, just hours before the start of free agency in March, having left their general manager of two years—one of the most respected personnel evaluators in the NFL—home from both the combine and the Senior Bowl.

Depending on which set of rumors you believed in the weeks before and after McCloughan's firing, the executive who helped build the Jim Harbaugh 49ers and Legion of Boom Seahawks either:

• Suffered a relapse of his documented alcoholism issues;
• Lost a power struggle with Dan Snyder and team president George Allen, who then surreptitiously spread alcohol rumors to cover their tracks after firing the popular personnel guru; or
• Some combination of the two, like a relapse that was used as justification for dismissal by those who wanted him out anyway.

It is waaaaay beyond the parameters of *Football Outsiders Almanac* to sort through a scandal like this. Those of us who were on the road in the offseason heard variations on all of the McCloughan rumors in Mobile and Indianapolis; ironically, they were hot topics of conversation at midnight watering holes. Whatever the truth may have been, something was happening in Washington, and those with vested interests on multiple sides of the conflict were loudly whispering their version of events down the lane.

By the time the draft arrived, McCloughan sounded chipper and lucid during radio interviews. He claimed he had no hard feelings against the organization that canned him and revealed that he was now consulting with multiple organizations. Allen, not surprisingly, decided that the perfect replacement for McCloughan was Allen himself. Director of College Scouting Scott Campbell, elevated to a higher-profile role under Allen, revealed before the draft that the team was still using modified, updated versions of McCloughan's original draft board. Yes, that would be the draft board he completed while being kept away from all-star games and the combine. Allen and Campbell consolidated power while simultaneously cribbing notes from the man they ousted to gain that power. Doug Williams also earned a promotion, though he cannily avoided a nominal "general manager" title, choosing Senior Vice President of Player Personnel over the catchier but more descriptive Well-Respected Figurehead.

The McCloughan-Allen skullduggery underscores a fundamental problem with Washington's offseason. The team made several very good acquisitions. Most of their moves, studied in isolation, would earn a B or B-plus, with an A or two sprinkled in. But the franchise took several steps backward at the macro level.

First, losing McCloughan will have a negative impact for a team coming off two straight productive drafts. Even if McCloughan was staggering around the facility in full *Days of Wine and Roses* mode—and that almost certainly was not the case—there are modern methods for helping a valued employee treat his illness. But forces within the organization chose to orchestrate a coup instead, despite the fact that they were happy to photocopy McCloughan's notes and drive to Philly with them for the draft. That speaks volumes about the acumen and priorities of the folks now making the Redskins' decisions.

Losing offensive coordinator Sean McVay was the second step backward. McVay, now the Rams head coach, has a stellar reputation as one of the league's up-and-coming offensive minds. Matt Cavanaugh, formerly the team's quarterback coach and a West Coast offense lifer, replaces McVay. He is likely to bring more competence than innovation.

Washington also replaced ineffective defensive coordinator Joe Berry with Greg Manusky, another excitingly ordinary coach who spent much of his coordinator career behind mediocre defensive-minded head coaches (Chuck Pagano, Mike Singletary). There are new faces all over the coaching staff, but there is no evidence that any will offer much more than professionalism, tempered with the kind of change-for-change's sake that can cause an organization to list sideways.

The final step backward was also the highest-profile potential blunder. The franchise's effort to permanently friend-zone Kirk Cousins moved far past the point of counterproductivity over the last two years. By applying the franchise tag to Cousins for two consecutive seasons, Washington has simultaneously paid top dollar for his services and alienated the most important player on the roster.

Cousins is the latest inkblot-test franchise quarterback; how

2017 Redskins Schedule

Week	Opp.	Week	Opp.	Week	Opp.
1	PHI	7	at PHI (Mon.)	13	at DAL (Thu.)
2	at LARM	8	DAL	14	at LACH
3	OAK	9	at SEA	15	ARI
4	at KC (Mon.)	10	MIN	16	DEN
5	BYE	11	at NO	17	at NYG
6	SF	12	NYG (Thu.)		

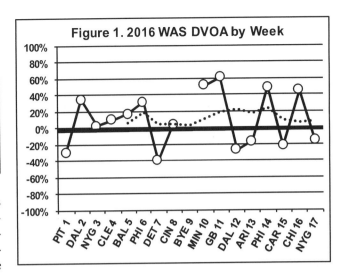

Figure 1. 2016 WAS DVOA by Week

you think and talk about him reveals your underlying attitudes toward the nature of modern football and the meaning you apply to terms like "franchise quarterback." But forget your personal opinions about Cousins' actual value as an NFL quarterback for a moment, whatever they may be, and consider the supply-and-demand aspect of his situation.

Cousins is about to either have a successful or an unsuccessful season. If he is successful, he will be within range for a contract in excess of $100 million, because that's what quarterbacks with three years as a productive starter earn. Washington will almost certainly be outbid for Cousins' services on the open market because: a) their cap situation isn't great and b) two years under the franchise tag have soured the relationship between Cousins and the team, making a "hometown discount" unlikely if Kyle Shanahan shows up with a wad of Jed York's money.

If Cousins has an unsuccessful season, well, so do the Redskins, who have no replacement at all on the roster. Cousins would still likely garner attention on the open market, and he probably won't be amenable to low-ball offers from the team that refused to lock him down when his stock was high. So it's very likely that the Redskins will be starting from scratch at quarterback in 2018, whether it's because Cousins proved to be too good or not good enough.

McCloughan, according to most sources, wanted to lock Cousins into a long-term deal after the 2015 season. That follows logically; McCloughan came from San Francisco and Seattle, two franchises that reached the Super Bowl by surrounding unheralded quarterback prospects with outstanding talent. Allen, Campbell, Dan Snyder, Jay Gruden and whoever else is currently involved in the Cousins decision all lack the long-range vision to recognize the corner they have painted themselves into. The Redskins are essentially in Super Bowl-or-Bust mode with Cousins in 2017; they need over-the-top success to justify the cost of keeping him beyond this season. But none of the team's other offseason moves suggests that whoever was making the decisions felt any urgency.

Pierre Garcon and DeSean Jackson, two of Cousins' primary weapons, were lost to free agency. Terrelle Pryor (on a one-year contract), Brian Quick, and redshirted 2016 first-round pick Josh Doctson are the replacements. Pryor is an impressive athlete who put up fine numbers last year, but he is also an enigma. Were all of those five-catch, 48-yard games in 2016 signs of a budding superstar coping with terrible quarterbacking, or just the numbers any competent receiver racks up when his team is blown out 33-13? Quick

has been similarly trapped in dreadful offenses for his entire career. Both players (plus Doctson) may blossom under Gruden with Cousins pulling the trigger. But it's hard to see them as an upgrade over Jackson and Garcon, either (or both) of whom could have been retained if Washington freed some cap space by constructing a long-term deal for Cousins. Meanwhile, Doctson hadn't even separated himself from fourth-year backup Ryan Grant as of OTAs.

Washington's defensive changes are more obviously upgrades. Each level of the defense received both a free-agent and high draft-pick overhaul. Top draft pick Jonathan Allen joins Terrell McClain and Phil Taylor on a rebuilt defensive line. Zach Brown and second-round pick Ryan Anderson add an interior defender and an edge rusher to the linebacking corps. D.J. Swearinger gives Washington a traditional free safety. Fabian Moreau is such a Richard Sherman-like prospect at cornerback that his draft card should have been dusted for McCloughan's fingerprints.

Assuming Manusky and his staff can get everyone on the same page swiftly, Washington's defense will improve upon last year's No. 25 overall ranking in DVOA. The defense ranked 30th in stopping deep passes last season; Swearinger can help put the fire out there. The new linemen will shore up a run defense that ranked 26th in short-yardage situations and 25th in stuffing runners at the line. Brown, tied for eighth in the NFL with 27 defeats last year, will be an across-the-board upgrade over Will Compton. Swearinger and Moreau will make it harder for teams to get their top receivers open by just hiding them from Josh Norman. An improved overall defense will take pressure off Cousins and the offense to win games.

Washington is a better team this year than last. So are all three division opponents. There's a strong chance that Washington moved just forward enough to stand still, placing them in the playoff hunt for the third consecutive year. But whereas the Cowboys and Eagles are building for the long haul and the Giants went all-in for this season, Washington faces a future beyond 2017 without its best draft strategist, without the young coach who was more Jon Gruden-like than any sibling could ever be, and—in all likelihood—led by a quarterback who is not on the current roster.

Ironically, the team that didn't want to make a major commitment to the sturdy-but-limited Cousins has done just that. The Redskins have a very good offensive line, but they are not the Cowboys. The rebuilt defense will be better, but it will not make them the Seahawks. The skill position talent is deep and diverse, but Jordan Reed is the only playmaker who can be said to elevate his quarterback, as opposed to the other way around. This is a balanced team with capable coaches. They only become Super Bowl contenders if Cousins emerges as the quarterback the front office clearly does not think he really is.

The Redskins have been doing this sort of thing since Snyder purchased the team, of course. Organizational politics, rumor-mongering, and sending mixed messages to the would-be franchise quarterback are what makes this team one of the NFL's greatest soap operas and most frustrated, frustrating franchises.

But it felt like everything was going to be different with McCloughan calling the shots. McCloughan arrived like a savior, as did Mike Shanahan, Donovan McNabb, Robert Griffin, the second iteration of Joe Gibbs, and a dozen overpaid free agents before him. The seeds of McCloughan's downfall may have been present at his arrival, and not just because alcoholism hung over his story like Chekov's Gun (whether to destroy him or be used against him). Ride into Ashburn, Virginia among palm branches and hosannas, and you can guarantee that someone whose power is being threatened will soon be itching to take you down.

This is Scot McCloughan's last Redskins team. It will be fine. The problem is that no one in the organization has any plan for the team that comes after it.

Mike Tanier

2016 Redskins Stats by Week

Wk	vs.	W-L	PF	PA	YDF	YDA	TO	Total	Off	Def	ST
1	PIT	L	16	38	384	437	-1	-30%	-20%	15%	4%
2	DAL	L	23	27	432	380	0	34%	16%	-14%	5%
3	at NYG	W	29	27	403	457	+2	2%	5%	12%	9%
4	CLE	W	31	20	301	380	+2	9%	27%	22%	4%
5	at BAL	W	16	10	310	306	-1	17%	-7%	-2%	22%
6	PHI	W	27	20	493	239	-1	31%	39%	-14%	-22%
7	at DET	L	17	20	413	344	-2	-40%	-17%	17%	-7%
8	at CIN	T	27	27	546	415	+1	4%	24%	4%	-15%
9	BYE										
10	MIN	W	26	20	388	331	0	51%	41%	1%	12%
11	GB	W	42	24	515	424	+2	61%	59%	3%	5%
12	at DAL	L	26	31	505	353	0	-27%	25%	38%	-14%
13	at ARI	L	23	31	333	369	-2	-17%	-8%	13%	4%
14	at PHI	W	27	22	334	383	+1	49%	44%	-6%	-1%
15	CAR	L	15	26	335	438	-3	-23%	-2%	16%	-4%
16	at CHI	W	41	21	478	458	+5	45%	49%	8%	3%
17	NYG	L	10	19	284	332	-3	-16%	-17%	2%	3%

Trends and Splits

	Offense	Rank	Defense	Rank
Total DVOA	15.8%	5	6.8%	25
Unadjusted VOA	14.3%	6	7.9%	27
Weighted Trend	21.2%	3	7.3%	26
Variance	6.8%	21	1.8%	1
Average Opponent	-3.2%	1	0.3%	13
Passing	34.4%	5	13.4%	24
Rushing	4.5%	4	-1.7%	24
First Down	5.7%	12	5.3%	22
Second Down	29.4%	2	-9.6%	8
Third Down	14.7%	8	37.5%	32
First Half	17.0%	7	8.1%	24
Second Half	2.9%	13	8.2%	27
Red Zone	-12.9%	22	-3.0%	15
Late and Close	8.0%	10	15.3%	25

Five-Year Performance

Year	W-L	Pyth W	Est W	PF	PA	TO	Total	Rk	Off	Rk	Def	Rk	ST	Rk	Off AGL	Rk	Def AGL	Rk	Off Age	Rk	Def Age	Rk	ST Age	Rk
2012	10-6	9.2	9.8	436	388	+17	9.3%	9	15.3%	6	1.7%	17	-4.3%	28	34.8	20	48.8	26	26.1	26	27.8	5	27.1	3
2013	3-13	4.8	4.2	334	478	-8	-26.2%	29	-10.0%	23	4.2%	21	-12.0%	32	14.6	4	26.8	13	27.0	15	28.0	3	27.1	2
2014	4-12	4.5	4.4	301	438	-12	-27.0%	28	-11.8%	28	9.9%	27	-5.4%	29	21.9	7	67.6	29	27.1	13	26.9	14	25.9	21
2015	9-7	8.2	7.8	388	379	+5	-0.3%	15	1.9%	12	5.4%	21	3.2%	6	44.0	24	75.1	32	25.9	26	27.1	7	26.0	17
2016	8-7-1	8.3	9.7	396	383	0	9.5%	9	15.8%	5	6.8%	25	0.4%	13	27.6	10	68.9	31	27.1	8	27.4	4	26.1	15

2016 Performance Based on Most Common Personnel Groups

WAS Offense					WAS Offense vs. Opponents					WAS Defense				WAS Defense vs. Opponents			
Pers	Freq	Yds	DVOA	Run%	Pers	Freq	Yds	DVOA	Run%	Pers	Freq	Yds	DVOA	Pers	Freq	Yds	DVOA
11	73%	6.5	19.8%	28%	Base	21%	7.5	22.9%	49%	Base	23%	5.7	6.0%	11	68%	6.3	13.2%
12	15%	7.7	37.7%	46%	Nickel	63%	6.4	21.7%	35%	Nickel	72%	5.9	5.0%	12	14%	4.4	-30.0%
13	6%	6.2	11.7%	68%	Dime+	13%	6.7	21.0%	8%	Dime+	4%	8.5	39.0%	13	4%	5.2	16.6%
612	3%	7.7	-28.3%	85%	Goal Line	1%	5.9	56.4%	92%	Goal Line	1%	2.7	32.2%	21	4%	4.6	-29.1%
622	1%	1.1	20.5%	75%	Big	1%	8.3	-12.5%	89%					22	1%	7.3	53.4%
611	1%	10.8	15.7%	67%										612	1%	6.8	47.1%

Strategic Tendencies

Run/Pass		Rk	Formation		Rk	Pass Rush		Rk	Secondary		Rk	Strategy		Rk
Runs, first half	35%	26	Form: Single Back	88%	5	Rush 3	4.7%	23	4 DB	23%	23	Play-action	18%	18
Runs, first down	47%	17	Form: Empty Back	6%	22	Rush 4	63.1%	19	5 DB	72%	5	Avg Box (Off)	6.10	27
Runs, second-long	23%	28	Pers: 3+ WR	74%	8	Rush 5	24.0%	10	6+ DB	3%	22	Avg Box (Def)	6.15	22
Runs, power sit.	47%	27	Pers: 2+ TE/6+ OL	26%	22	Rush 6+	8.2%	7	CB by Sides	62%	28	Offensive Pace	31.08	24
Runs, behind 2H	30%	8	Pers: 6+ OL	5%	16	Sacks by LB	71.1%	5	S/CB Cover Ratio	21%	30	Defensive Pace	30.38	19
Pass, ahead 2H	50%	14	Shotgun/Pistol	55%	26	Sacks by DB	9.2%	9	DB Blitz	12%	7	Go for it on 4th	1.04	18

Washington was dead last in run offense DVOA in 2015 and improved to fourth last year. Yet run/pass ratios in nearly every situation went *down* in 2016: from sixth to 26th running in the first half, for example, and from eighth to 17th running on first down. Did running less often make the run game more effective? That's a tough question to answer. ☞ One example of the effectiveness of the run: Washington was by far the best offense running the ball on second-and-long, leading the league with 20.5% DVOA and 6.4 yards per carry. (No other team was above 5.6.) ☞ One of the biggest changes for the Washington offense, particularly in the running game, was a massive improvement in broken tackles. In 2015, the Redskins were dead last with 81 broken tackles. In 2016, they ranked first with 149 broken tackles. Matt Jones had 19 broken tackles in each season, and Jordan Reed had only 12 last year compared to 19 the year before. However, Rob Kelley had 43 broken tackles in 2016 compared to just 12 for Alfred Morris in 2015, while Chris Thompson went from eight broken tackles on 70 touches to 30 broken tackles on 117 touches. ☞ Washington used play-action on 35.7 percent of first-down passes, fourth in the NFL. But they were dead last on second down, using play-action on just 9.5 percent of passes compared to the NFL average of 20 percent. ☞ Washington had used six linemen on a league-leading 15.2 percent of plays in 2015, but that dropped to just 4.6 percent of plays last year. ☞ Washington dramatically increased use of the blitz, from 21.7 percent of passes in 2015 to 32.2 percent in 2016. The Redskins defense improved sending five pass-rushers, going from 6.9 yards per pass to just 5.9 yards per pass, but then got torn apart for 8.7 yards per pass when sending a big blitz of six or more. They also doubled their use of defensive back blitzes from 2015, but allowed 8.2 yards per pass on these plays. ☞ Washington had the worst defense in the league against red zone runs, but ranked sixth in DVOA against red zone passes.

Passing

Player	DYAR	DVOA	Plays	NtYds	Avg	YAC	C%	TD	Int
K.Cousins	1317	20.9%	626	4738	7.6	4.8	67.3%	25	12
T.Pryor	-27	-48.7%	10	40	4.0	6.0	55.6%	0	0

Rushing

Player	DYAR	DVOA	Plays	Yds	Avg	TD	Fum	Suc
R.Kelley	112	12.0%	128	587	4.6	6	0	51%
M.Jones	83	10.2%	99	461	4.7	1	0	54%
C.Thompson	93	31.5%	60	321	5.4	3	0	52%
K.Cousins	-14	-26.5%	15	69	4.6	4	0	-
T.Pryor	-22	-71.6%	8	21	2.6	1	0	-

Receiving

Player	DYAR	DVOA	Plays	Ctch	Yds	Y/C	YAC	TD	C%
P.Garcon*	262	16.3%	114	79	1041	13.2	4.3	3	69%
D.Jackson*	241	16.4%	100	56	1005	17.9	5.1	4	56%
J.Crowder	129	4.6%	99	67	847	12.6	5.6	7	68%
R.Grant	-35	-34.9%	19	9	76	8.4	2.8	0	47%
M.Harris	-7	-19.7%	12	8	66	8.3	1.3	0	67%
J.Doctson	2	-9.3%	6	2	66	33.0	7.5	0	33%
T.Pryor	112	-2.5%	140	77	1007	13.1	2.8	4	55%
B.Quick	-28	-17.1%	77	41	564	13.8	4.3	3	53%
J.Reed	102	9.9%	89	66	690	10.5	4.0	6	74%
V.Davis	96	16.8%	59	44	581	13.2	5.4	2	75%
C.Thompson	77	10.6%	62	49	349	7.1	5.1	2	79%
R.Kelley	10	-4.8%	18	12	82	6.8	6.5	1	67%
M.Jones	45	76.6%	8	8	73	9.1	7.1	0	100%

Offensive Line

Player	Pos	Age	GS	Snaps	Pen	Sk	Pass	Run	Player	Pos	Age	GS	Snaps	Pen	Sk	Pass	Run
Brandon Scherff	RG	26	16/16	1047	8	1.5	11	4	Spencer Long	C	27	15/12	807	2	0.0	8	8
Morgan Moses	RT	26	16/16	1020	8	4.5	14	2	Trent Williams	LT	29	12/12	796	3	1.0	2	5
Shawn Lauvao	LG	29	14/14	916	5	4.5	9	6	Ty Nsekhe	LT	32	16/4	389	3	0.0	8	2

Year	Yards	ALY	Rank	Power	Rank	Stuff	Rank	2nd Lev	Rank	Open Field	Rank	Sacks	ASR	Rank	Press	Rank	F-Start	Cont.
2014	4.22	4.14	19	58%	27	20%	16	1.26	7	0.75	14	58	9.8%	31	23.9%	16	20	29
2015	3.82	3.96	21	65%	18	22%	19	1.02	27	0.68	17	27	5.4%	10	20.4%	2	13	34
2016	4.67	4.57	6	72%	5	15%	3	1.15	14	1.06	6	23	3.9%	3	24.2%	11	25	28
2016 ALY by direction:			Left End 4.53 (13)			Left Tackle 4.81 (6)			Mid/Guard 4.30 (12)			Right Tackle 4.89 (7)			Right End 4.90 (4)			

The entire unit returns in 2017, including Bill Callahan, the most important position coach to be retained through the team's staff shakeup. Under Callahan, Washington finished sixth in adjusted line yards, its highest rank since 2008. ☞ Callahan's influence can be seen in both the development of young players like Brandon Scherff and Spencer Long and the team's overall offensive philosophy. Like the Cowboys when Callahan coached there, the Redskins get a lot of mileage out of two and three-tight end sets both in the running game (5.15 yards per carry on 151 carries) and passing game (8.73 yards per attempt and just two sacks on 123 dropbacks). ☞ Washington also runs outside more than most teams, with 33 percent of their runs marked as going around left or right end. The NFL average last year was 19 percent; only the Eagles and Packers ran outside more often. Callahan likes to get fast linemen like Trent Williams on the perimeter while tight ends or rugged-blocking receivers seal the edge and/or crack back. ☞ Left guard Shaun Lauvao was the relative weak link of this strong unit. There was camp chatter about Arie Kouandjio or undrafted rookie Tyler Catalina (Georgia) pushing Lauvao. Otherwise, all positions are set, right down to backup left tackle, where Ty Nsekhe aced his midseason relief appearance last year when Williams was suspended. Callahan's best bet for improving this unit's performance lies with maintaining continuity, bringing along rookie blocking tight end Jeremy Sprinkle, and hoping for more consistency at running back.

Defensive Front Seven

Defensive Line	Age	Pos	G	Snaps	Plays	Overall TmPct	Rk	Stop	Dfts	BTkl	Runs	vs. Run St%	Rk	RuYd	Rk	Pass Rush Sack	Hit	Hur	Dsrpt
Chris Baker*	30	DE	16	783	48	5.6%	30	34	12	4	37	73%	52	2.2	40	4.0	7	21	2
Ziggy Hood	30	DT	16	661	35	4.1%	51	28	7	1	29	79%	40	2.4	50	1.0	4	10	2
Ricky Jean-Francois*	31	DE	16	442	33	3.8%	56	28	6	2	27	89%	13	2.0	35	1.5	0	4	1
Cullen Jenkins*	36	DE	15	308	15	1.9%	--	11	5	1	13	77%	--	1.5	--	1.0	2	4	0
Stacy McGee	27	DT	9	220	17	3.9%	--	13	7	0	14	71%	--	2.3	--	2.5	1	3	0
Terrell McClain	29	DT	15	471	40	5.3%	33	30	6	3	34	76%	47	2.9	68	2.5	5	5	0

Edge Rushers	Age	Pos	G	Snaps	Plays	Overall TmPct	Rk	Stop	Dfts	BTkl	Runs	vs. Run St%	Rk	RuYd	Rk	Pass Rush Sack	Hit	Hur	Dsrpt
Ryan Kerrigan	29	OLB	16	788	33	3.8%	69	30	19	3	19	84%	13	1.3	15	11.0	9	40	4
Preston Smith	25	OLB	16	768	42	4.9%	51	31	16	6	27	70%	68	2.8	58	5.0	8	26	2
Trent Murphy	27	OLB	16	675	46	5.4%	41	35	20	4	32	72%	60	2.7	57	8.5	17	23	0

Linebackers	Age	Pos	G	Snaps	Plays	Overall TmPct	Rk	Stop	Dfts	BTkl	Runs	vs. Run St%	Rk	RuYd	Rk	Pass Rush Sack	Hit	Hur	vs. Pass Tgts	Suc%	Rk	AdjYd	Rk	PD	Int
Will Compton	28	ILB	15	938	109	13.5%	33	51	14	15	55	60%	58	3.6	40	0.0	3	8	28	39%	66	6.8	47	4	1
Mason Foster	28	ILB	16	770	124	14.4%	28	57	16	5	72	49%	82	5.8	87	1.0	4	5	35	47%	45	6.2	32	2	0
Su'a Cravens	22	ILB	11	297	37	6.3%	76	25	12	3	12	92%	1	2.0	3	1.0	2	7	17	50%	36	4.6	6	3	1
Zach Brown	28	ILB	16	980	152	18.7%	5	86	27	13	95	66%	29	3.7	49	3.5	6	6	45	46%	47	8.2	71	4	1

Year	Yards	ALY	Rank	Power	Rank	Stuff	Rank	2nd Level	Rank	Open Field	Rank	Sacks	ASR	Rank	Press	Rank
2014	3.97	4.03	12	60%	11	20%	13	1.04	8	0.69	16	36	6.6%	17	25.8%	12
2015	4.68	4.37	24	49%	1	19%	20	1.35	30	1.07	30	38	7.3%	9	22.6%	28
2016	4.52	4.54	27	69%	26	17%	25	1.37	29	0.76	19	38	6.9%	9	28.4%	12
2016 ALY by direction:			Left End 5.13 (27)			Left Tackle 4.76 (22)			Mid/Guard 4.4 (24)			Right Tackle 4.49 (21)			Right End 4.32 (25)

Zach Brown announced during OTAs that his personal goal for 2017 is to win the league's Defensive MVP award. The first step will be earning a starting job—Brown was still playing behind Mason Foster and Will Compton in May—but once Brown unseats Compton, he can start aiming to unlock other achievements. Brown came to Washington to stay in a 3-4 defense after the Bills changed schemes this offseason. An MVP award may be unlikely, but Brown will provide a noticeable upgrade over Compton as a run defender and in coverage. Jonathan Allen fell to Washington in the draft mostly because of fears about a degenerative condition in his shoulder, though there were some scheme-fit issues as well. Regardless, Washington was one of three teams to finish in the bottom 10 of adjusted line yards each of the past two years, making Allen's fall a happy solution to its biggest positional need. Allen is talented enough to play a variety of defensive line roles, but he fits best as a two-gap end in a traditional 3-4, making him ideal for Washington's scheme. The shoulder ailment appears to be the type of thing to worry about two contracts down the road. Allen will grow into an upgrade over Chris Baker; Baker was a very solid all-around player and system fit, but Allen can provide more disruption and pass rush from a position which doesn't necessarily have to just be about eating up blockers. Fellow Crimson Tide draftee Ryan Anderson may also help out immediately on the edge. Washington's edge-rushing depth opposite stalwart Ryan Kerrigan has been mostly theoretical between the inconsistencies of Preston Smith and Trent Murphy and Achilles injuries of Junior Galette. The track record of Alabama edge rushers in the NFL under Nick Saban is stunningly barren; the best they've had to offer is either Courtney Upshaw (who is now a defensive tackle) or Brandon Deaderick. Anderson is the first Alabama edge rusher since Upshaw to be drafted as high as the second round, though, and he should at least receive the opportunity to break the mold.

Defensive Secondary

Secondary	Age	Pos	G	Snaps	Plays	TmPct	Rk	Stop	Dfts	BTkl	Runs	St%	Rk	RuYd	Rk	Tgts	Tgt%	Rk	Dist	Suc%	Rk	AdjYd	Rk	PD	Int
						Overall					vs. Run					vs. Pass									
Josh Norman	30	CB	16	1059	84	9.8%	21	36	19	9	15	47%	29	6.0	28	81	18.5%	45	12.2	54%	18	6.9	25	19	3
Bashaud Breeland	25	CB	14	764	81	10.8%	9	31	11	7	21	38%	49	7.4	53	69	21.8%	65	9.5	49%	50	6.9	24	13	3
Duke Ihenacho*	28	SS	15	636	61	7.6%	56	21	7	13	38	39%	39	6.5	34	12	4.6%	2	8.8	28%	74	11.3	64	2	0
Will Blackmon	33	FS	15	573	42	5.2%	--	11	8	8	15	13%	--	11.1	--	18	7.6%	--	12.4	57%	--	7.6	--	3	1
Donte Whitner*	32	SS	11	566	65	11.0%	24	15	3	4	34	29%	58	8.1	54	25	10.7%	58	8.6	32%	70	11.6	65	0	0
Kendall Fuller	22	CB	13	478	42	6.0%	--	13	5	3	5	40%	--	5.8	--	38	19.1%	--	11.8	41%	--	10.8	--	2	0
Quinton Dunbar	25	CB	14	300	30	4.0%	--	11	4	1	4	25%	--	10.8	--	27	21.5%	--	11.3	43%	--	8.8	--	5	1
David Bruton*	30	SS	4	235	29	13.5%	--	11	3	5	17	35%	--	7.1	--	6	5.7%	--	8.3	45%	--	6.7	--	2	0
D.J. Swearinger	26	SS	16	837	72	8.8%	49	30	14	9	32	47%	22	4.9	11	22	6.2%	9	10.6	41%	52	9.0	39	8	3

Year	Pass D Rank	vs. #1 WR	Rk	vs. #2 WR	Rk	vs. Other WR	Rk	vs. TE	Rk	vs. RB	Rk
2014	32	19.9%	29	32.5%	30	22.8%	29	21.7%	29	-18.0%	6
2015	20	13.2%	28	23.7%	30	-5.3%	13	8.0%	21	-17.8%	6
2016	24	4.4%	22	18.1%	29	10.5%	24	13.0%	25	-16.4%	7

Historically, when the Redskins sign a major free agent like Josh Norman, they assemble a think tank of the most creative minds not employed by Pixar to discover a new way to foul everything up (see: moving Albert Haynesworth to a 3-4 defense, everything involved with Donovan McNabb). Last year, the imagineers decided not just to keep Norman on one side of the formation for the first half of the year but to publicly and belligerently commit to the tactic, as if the rest of us were crazy to expect Joe Barry to slightly adjust his scheme just because Dan Snyder plunked down $75 million on an All-Pro cornerback. Poor Bashaud Breeland got broiled by Antonio Brown in the season opener and Dez Bryant in Week 2 before cooler heads prevailed and Norman started shadowing top receivers much more frequently. Breeland fared much better when not constantly in the crosshairs against a Murderer's Row of great receivers. But Washington also lacked depth at safety and the nickel-dime slots, with opponents targeting DeShaun Phillips early in the year, Greg Toler late, and safety Donte Whitner any time they could isolate him against anyone faster than a fullback. The Redskins announced in the offseason that Norman will shadow opponents' top receivers. One of these days they will figure out that they don't have to reveal their strategies to the nation in advance. Norman will have to cut down on the clutching and grabbing: he led the NFL with 15 penalties last season. Four of those came when the officials got a bit weird about Illegal Use of Hands against Cincinnati in Week 8, but even without those flags, Norman would have been tied for second in the league. Norman is not quite in Brandon Browner territory, however: he does an excellent job of actually covering receivers when not fondling them. Breeland finished last season with a career-best 6.9 adjusted yards per pass and should remain a capable No. 2. Third-round rookie Fabian Moreau (UCLA) has the talent to quickly solve the nickel problem, provided he's fully recovered from the torn pectoral he suffered at his pro day workout. Hybrid player Su'a Cravens is slated to replace Whitner at strong safety, which leaves free-agent arrival D.J. Swearinger with the task of switching to free safety. Washington plays a fair amount of two-high coverage, so Swearinger won't suddenly have to turn into an Earl Thomas-type centerfield patroller. However, Washington had a big deep-ball problem in 2016, ranking 30th in DVOA against deep passes. Inconveniently, the problem was at its worst in the deep middle, where Washington's 117.3% DVOA ranked 31st. So, no pressure with the new position or anything. ⬆ Also still in the picture: DeAngelo Hall, who spent OTAs on the PUP list while rehabbing an ACL. Hall has been such a *Football Outsiders Almanac* redheaded stepchild for so long that it feels weird to type this, but … as a situational dime defensive back (as opposed to an overpriced human slot machine of a would-be shutdown cornerback), one of the cagiest ballhawks in NFL history could be a useful role player.

Special Teams

Year	DVOA	Rank	FG/XP	Rank	Net Kick	Rank	Kick Ret	Rank	Net Punt	Rank	Punt Ret	Rank	Hidden	Rank
2014	-5.4%	29	-0.5	19	-10.1	31	-4.0	25	-8.0	27	-4.1	21	-8.4	27
2015	3.2%	6	3.0	10	5.1	4	8.9	3	4.8	8	-5.8	27	2.5	13
2016	0.4%	13	-3.7	20	-1.5	18	0.6	13	-2.4	19	9.3	2	-0.2	18

Kicker Dustin Hopkins was the NFL's Special Teams Player of the Month in September, making all 11 of his September field goal attempts. Then, as if to prove every principle about central tendency, streaks, and small sample sizes that Football Outsiders harps upon when discussing placekickers, Hopkins slumped badly. He missed several important field goals, including a 34-yarder in overtime that would have beaten the Bengals, and was never really on track for the rest of the season. Hopkins hit an upright on four different attempts, which sounds like it should be a record. The Redskins didn't even bring in a camp leg, so Hopkins has job security for better or worse. At least he is solid on kickoffs (70.7 percent touchbacks last year, fourth in the NFL), which longtime readers know are less likely to bloom in September but also less likely to wilt in overtime in October. ⬆ Jamison Crowder was one of the league's top punt returners last year, but he was one of the worst the year before. Special teams sure are inconsistent.

Quarterbacks

On the following pages, we provide the last three years of statistics for the top two quarterbacks on each team's depth chart, as well as a number of other quarterbacks who played significant time in 2016.

Each quarterback gets a projection from our KUBIAK fantasy football projection system, based on a complicated regression analysis that takes into account numerous variables including projected role, performance over the past two years, performance on third down vs. all downs, experience of the projected offensive line, historical comparables, collegiate stats, height, age, and strength of schedule.

It is difficult to accurately project statistics for a 162-game baseball season, but it is exponentially more difficult to accurately project statistics for a 16-game football season because of the small size of the data samples involved. With that in mind, we ask that you consider the listed projections not as a prediction of exact numbers, but the mean of a range of possible performances. What's important is not so much the exact number of yards and touchdowns we project, but whether or not we're projecting a given player to improve or decline. Along those same lines, rookie projections will not be as accurate as veteran projections due to lack of data.

Our quarterback projections look a bit different than our projections for the other skill positions. At running back and wide receiver, second-stringers see plenty of action, but, at quarterback, either a player starts or he does not start. We recognize that, when a starting quarterback gets injured in Week 8, you don't want to grab your *Football Outsiders Almanac* to find out if his backup is any good only to find that we've projected that the guy will throw 12 passes this year. Therefore, each year we project all quarterbacks to start all 16 games. If Aaron Rodgers goes down in November, you can look up Brett Hundley, divide the stats by 16, and get an idea of what we think he will do in an average week (and then, if you are a Green Bay fan, pass out). There are full-season projections for the top two quarterbacks on all 32 depth charts.

The first line of each quarterback table contains biographical data—the player's name, height, weight, college, draft position, birth date, and age. Height and weight are the best data we could find; weight, of course, can fluctuate during the offseason. **Age** is very simple: the number of years between the player's birth year and 2017, but birthdate is provided if you want to figure out exact age.

Draft position gives draft year and round, with the overall pick number with which the player was taken in parentheses. In the sample table, it says that Cam Newton was chosen in the first round of the 2011 NFL draft, with the first overall pick. Undrafted free agents are listed as "FA" with the year they came into the league, even if they were only in training camp or on a practice squad.

To the far right of the first line is the player's Risk variable for fantasy football in 2017, which measures the likelihood of the player hitting his projection. The default rating for each player is Green. As the risk of a player failing to hit his projection rises, he's given a rating of Yellow or, in the worst cases, Red. The Risk variable is not only based on age and injury probability, but how a player's projection compares to his recent performance as well as our confidence (or lack thereof) in his offensive teammates. A few players with the strongest chances of surpassing their projections are given a Blue rating. Most players marked Blue will be backups with low projections, but a handful are starters or situational players who can be considered slightly better breakout candidates.

Next, we give the last three years of player stats. The majority of these statistics are passing numbers, although the final five columns on the right are the quarterback's rushing statistics.

The first few columns after the year and team the player played for are standard numbers: games and games started (**G/GS**), offensive **Snaps**, pass attempts (**Att**), pass completions (**Cmp**), completion percentage (**C%**), passing yards (**Yds**), passing touchdowns (**TD**). These numbers are official NFL totals and therefore include plays we leave out of our own metrics, such as clock-stopping spikes, and omit plays we include in our metrics, such as sacks and aborted snaps. (Other differences between official stats and Football Outsiders stats are described in the "Statistical Toolbox" introduction at the front of the book.)

The column for interceptions contains two numbers, representing the official NFL total for interceptions (**Int**) as well as our own metric for adjusted interceptions (**Adj**). For example, if you look at our sample table, Cam Newton had 14 interceptions and 22 adjusted interceptions in 2016. Adjusted interceptions use game charting data to add dropped interceptions, plays where a defender most likely would have had an interception but couldn't hold onto the ball. Then we remove Hail Mary passes and interceptions thrown on fourth down when losing in the final two minutes of the game. We also re-

Cam Newton				Height: 6-5		Weight: 248		College: Auburn			Draft: 2011/1 (1)		Born: 11-May-1989			Age: 28			Risk: Yellow	
Year	Team	G/GS	Snaps	Att	Comp	C%	Yds	TD	INT/Adj	FUM	ASR	NY/P	Rk	DVOA	Rk	DYAR	Rk	YAR	Runs	Yds	TD	DVOA	DYAR	QBR
2014	CAR	14/14	927	448	262	58.5%	3127	18	12/14	9	8.4%	5.9	30	-14.5%	32	-105	32	-46	103	539	5	16.3%	146	56.9
2015	CAR	16/16	1077	495	296	59.8%	3837	35	10/14	5	6.9%	6.8	11	7.6%	12	630	11	855	132	636	10	8.1%	142	66.0
2016	CAR	15/14	1023	510	270	52.9%	3509	19	14/22	3	6.8%	6.0	25	-13.0%	28	-64	28	-64	90	359	5	-12.5%	-2	53.1
2017	CAR			513	310	60.4%	3680	25	12	5		6.5		2.4%					81	410	4	25.9%		
2015:	34% Short		42% Mid		12% Deep		11% Bomb		YAC: 5.0 (27)		ALEX: 3.0		2016:	31% Short		47% Mid		12% Deep		10% Bomb		YAC: 4.9 (24)	ALEX: 3.5

move "tipped interceptions," when a perfectly catchable ball deflected off the receiver's hands or chest and into the arms of a defender.

Overall, adjusted interception rate is higher than standard interception rate, so most quarterbacks will have more adjusted interceptions than standard interceptions. On average, a quarterback will have one additional adjusted interception for every 120 pass attempts. Once this difference is accounted for, adjusted interceptions are a better predictor of next year's interception total than standard interceptions.

The next column is fumbles (**FUM**), which adds together all fumbles by this player, whether turned over to the defense or recovered by the offense (explained in the essay "Pregame Show"). Even though this fumble total is listed among the passing numbers, it includes all fumbles, including those on sacks, aborted snaps, and rushing attempts. By listing fumbles and interceptions next to one another, we're giving readers a general idea of how many total turnovers the player was responsible for.

Next comes Adjusted Sack Rate (**ASR**). This is the same statistic you'll find in the team chapters, only here it is specific to the individual quarterback. It represents sacks per pass play (total pass plays = pass attempts + sacks) adjusted based on down, distance, and strength of schedule. For reference, the NFL average was 6.6 percent in 2014, 6.4 percent in 2015, and 6.1 percent in 2016.

The next two columns are Net Yards per Pass (**NY/P**), a standard stat but a particularly good one, and the player's rank (**Rk**) in Net Yards per Pass for that season. Net Yards per Pass consists of passing yards minus yards lost on sacks, divided by total pass plays.

The five columns remaining in passing stats give our advanced metrics: **DVOA** (Defense-Adjusted Value Over Average), **DYAR** (Defense-Adjusted Yards Above Replacement), and **YAR** (Yards Above Replacement), along with the player's rank in both DVOA and DYAR. These metrics compare each quarterback's passing performance to league-average or replacement-level baselines based on the game situations that quarterback faced. DVOA and DYAR are also adjusted based on the opposing defense. The methods used to compute these numbers are described in detail in the "Statistical Toolbox" introduction at the front of the book. The important distinctions between them are:

• DVOA is a rate statistic, while DYAR is a cumulative statistic. Thus, a higher DVOA means more value per pass play, while a higher DYAR means more aggregate value over the entire season.

• Because DYAR is defense-adjusted and YAR is not, a player whose DYAR is higher than his YAR faced a harder-than-average schedule. A player whose DYAR is lower than his YAR faced an easier-than-average schedule.

To qualify for a ranking in Net Yards per Pass, passing DVOA, and passing DYAR in a given season, a quarterback must have had 200 pass plays in that season. 37 quarterbacks ranked for 2014, 37 quarterbacks ranked for 2015, and 34 for 2016.

The final five columns contain rushing statistics, starting with **Runs**, rushing yards (**Yds**), and rushing touchdowns (**TD**). Once again, these are official NFL totals and include kneeldowns, which means you get to enjoy statistics such as Eli Manning rushing 21 times for minus-9 yards. The final two columns give **DYAR** and **DVOA** for quarterback rushing, which are calculated separately from passing. Rankings for these statistics, as well as numbers that are not adjusted for defense (YAR and VOA) can be found on our website, FootballOutsiders.com.

The last number listed is the Total QBR metric from ESPN Stats & Information. Total QBR is based on the expected points added by the quarterback on each play, then adjusts the numbers to a scale of 0-100. There are five main differences between Total QBR and DVOA:

• Total QBR incorporates information from game charting, such as passes dropped or thrown away on purpose.

• Total QBR splits responsibility on plays between the quarterback, his receivers, and his blockers. Drops, for example, are more on the receiver, as are yards after the catch, and some sacks are more on the offensive line than others.

• Total QBR has a clutch factor which adds (or subtracts) value for quarterbacks who perform best (or worst) in high-leverage situations.

• Total QBR combines passing and rushing value into one number and differentiates between scrambles and planned runs.

• Total QBR is now adjusted for strength of opponent, unlike in past seasons.

The italicized row of statistics for the 2017 season is our 2017 KUBIAK projection, as detailed above. Again, in the interest of producing meaningful statistics, all quarterbacks are projected to start a full 16-game season, regardless of the likelihood of them actually doing so.

The final line below the KUBIAK projection represents data from the Football Outsiders game charting project. First, we break down charted passes based on distance: **Short** (5 yards or less), **Mid** (6-15 yards), **Deep** (16-25 yards), and **Bomb** (26 or more yards). These numbers are based on distance in the air only and include both complete and incomplete passes. Passes thrown away or tipped at the line are not included, nor are passes on which the quarterback's arm was hit by a defender while in motion. We also give average yards after catch (**YAC**) with the Rank in parentheses for the 45 quarterbacks who qualify.

Some of the comments that follow also reference two metrics charted by Football Outsiders writer Cian Fahey for his own book *Pre-Snap Reads QB Catalogue 2017*:

• **Interceptable Passes** is a somewhat different concept from adjusted interceptions. Fahey includes all plays where he has determined that a defender had an opportunity to make an interception based on a quarterback mistake, even if that pass is not obviously dropped by the defender. He removes passes tipped at the line of scrimmage as well as plays similar to those removed by adjusted interceptions: passes tipped by receivers, Hail Mary and desperation situations, etc. This is a more subjective measurement than adjusted interceptions, but each quarterback is analyzed with the same standard since one person (Fahey) is doing all the charting.

• **Accuracy Percentage** measures how often a quarterback but the ball in a place where the receiver could easily catch it. Essentially, it looks for plays where the ball is not over-

thrown or underthrown, even if the ball is dropped. Passes defensed are judged based on the placement of the ball. Accuracy percentages were ranked for a number of categories for pass distance, and those stats are mentioned a few times in our quarterback comments.

A number of third- and fourth-string quarterbacks are briefly discussed at the end of the chapter in a section we call "Going Deep."

Top 20 QB by Passing DYAR (Total Value), 2016

Rank	Player	Team	DYAR
1	Matt Ryan	ATL	1,885
2	Drew Brees	NO	1,599
3	Kirk Cousins	WAS	1,317
4	Dak Prescott	DAL	1,302
5	Tom Brady	NE	1,286
6	Aaron Rodgers	GB	1,279
7	Derek Carr	OAK	1,164
8	Ben Roethlisberger	PIT	807
9	Matthew Stafford	DET	761
10	Andy Dalton	CIN	738
11	Andrew Luck	IND	719
12	Alex Smith	KC	688
13	Marcus Mariota	TEN	681
14	Russell Wilson	SEA	569
15	Jameis Winston	TB	556
16	Sam Bradford	MIN	510
17	Philip Rivers	SD	498
18	Brian Hoyer	CHI	404
19	Tyrod Taylor	BUF	275
20	Matt Moore	MIA	259

Minimum 200 passes.

Top 20 QB by Passing DVOA (Value per Pass), 2016

Rank	Player	Team	DVOA
1	Matt Ryan	ATL	39.1%
2	Tom Brady	NE	33.4%
3	Dak Prescott	DAL	31.6%
4	Drew Brees	NO	23.3%
5	Kirk Cousins	WAS	20.9%
6	Derek Carr	OAK	19.8%
7	Brian Hoyer	CHI	19.4%
8	Aaron Rodgers	GB	18.7%
9	Ben Roethlisberger	PIT	12.1%
10	Marcus Mariota	TEN	11.1%
11	Alex Smith	KC	9.6%
12	Andy Dalton	CIN	7.6%
13	Andrew Luck	IND	7.3%
14	Matthew Stafford	DET	7.2%
15	Russell Wilson	SEA	4.0%
16	Jameis Winston	TB	3.6%
17	Sam Bradford	MIN	2.2%
18	Philip Rivers	SD	1.4%
19	Tyrod Taylor	BUF	-2.1%
20	Eli Manning	NYG	-6.5%

Minimum 200 passes.

Derek Anderson

Height: 6-6 Weight: 229 College: Oregon State Draft: 2005/6 (213) Born: 15-Jun-1983 Age: 34 Risk: Red

Year	Team	G/GS	Snaps	Att	Comp	C%	Yds	TD	INT/Adj	FUM	ASR	NY/P	Rk	DVOA	Rk	DYAR	Rk	YAR	Runs	Yds	TD	DVOA	DYAR	QBR
2014	CAR	6/2	177	97	65	67.0%	701	5	0/2	2	5.2%	6.7	--	27.8%	--	254	--	282	8	24	0	34.3%	14	82.8
2015	CAR	3/0	25	6	4	66.7%	36	0	0/0	1	1.8%	6.0	--	-11.9%	--	0	--	1	7	-2	0	-137.8%	-19	9.7
2016	CAR	5/2	86	53	36	67.9%	453	2	5/4	1	0.8%	8.5	--	-17.9%	--	-27	--	-41	1	4	0	-200.4%	-13	18.2
2017	CAR			534	335	62.7%	3757	22	19	7		6.4		-8.3%					26	4	1	-25.0%		

2015:	50% Short	0% Mid	33% Deep	17% Bomb	YAC: 5.3 (--)	ALEX: 0.7	2016:	35% Short	43% Mid	20% Deep	2% Bomb	YAC: 4.5 (--)	ALEX: 3.8

In Week 13, Anderson got his big chance to shine. Starter Cam Newton was benched for the opening series for failing to wear a tie to the game. That gave Anderson, who has only thrown 160 passes across the last six seasons as Newton's safety net, a rare start. Coach Ron Rivera was looking to send a message, so a touchdown drive led by Anderson might well have led to more action. Instead, the backup's pass on the very first play bounced off of Mike Tolbert's hands for an interception, thus ending Newton's slap on the wrist, and sending Anderson back to his baseball cap. Given Anderson's age and rust, and the laundry list of injuries Newton has suffered of late, the Panthers might want to invest in a new backup soon.

Matt Barkley Height: 6-2   Weight: 230   College: USC   Draft: 2013/4 (98)   Born: 8-Sep-1990   Age: 27   Risk: Red

Year	Team	G/GS	Snaps	Att	Comp	C%	Yds	TD	INT/Adj	FUM	ASR	NY/P	Rk	DVOA	Rk	DYAR	Rk	YAR	Runs	Yds	TD	DVOA	DYAR	QBR
2014	PHI	1/0	6	1	0	0.0%	0	0	0/0	0	0.0%	0.0	--	-116.9%	--	-7	--	-8	3	0	0	--	--	0.1
2016	CHI	7/6	412	216	129	59.7%	1611	8	14/14	4	2.7%	7.1	7	-10.9%	26	4	26	127	7	2	0	-321.8%	-34	39.2
2017	SF			545	322	59.2%	3882	22	21	9		6.0		-20.0%					24	25	0	-22.1%		

		2016:	33% Short	43% Mid	14% Deep	9% Bomb	YAC: 4.2 (32) ALEX: 4.3

Barkley received the first starts of his career last year after both Jay Cutler and Brian Hoyer went down with injuries. He produced about what you would expect from a practice-squad player forced into unexpected action: the second-worst QBR among qualified quarterbacks and severe ball security problems. Things bottomed out at the end of the year, with 11 turnovers in Chicago's last three games. Barkley threw an interception on 6.5 percent of his passes, the worst rate since Heath Shuler in 1997. Between Barkley and Brian Hoyer, the Bears had quarterbacks with historically high and historically low turnover rates last season. Football is weird sometimes. Barkley will sit behind Hoyer to start the season in San Francisco, but don't be shocked if he starts a game or two if and when the team flounders.

Blake Bortles Height: 6-4   Weight: 232   College: Central Florida   Draft: 2014/1 (3)   Born: 16-Dec-1991   Age: 26   Risk: Red

Year	Team	G/GS	Snaps	Att	Comp	C%	Yds	TD	INT/Adj	FUM	ASR	NY/P	Rk	DVOA	Rk	DYAR	Rk	YAR	Runs	Yds	TD	DVOA	DYAR	QBR
2014	JAC	14/13	896	475	280	58.9%	2908	11	17/20	7	10.5%	4.8	37	-40.7%	36	-955	37	-935	56	419	0	24.7%	100	21.9
2015	JAC	16/16	1058	606	355	58.6%	4428	35	18/26	14	8.0%	6.3	18	-9.9%	25	54	25	100	52	310	2	24.5%	86	46.4
2016	JAC	16/16	1111	625	368	58.9%	3905	23	16/17	8	5.3%	5.6	30	-10.0%	24	52	23	3	58	359	3	23.3%	90	49.2
2017	JAC			577	342	59.2%	3892	25	16	9		5.9		-7.0%					56	297	3	22.3%		

2015:	45% Short	29% Mid	19% Deep	7% Bomb	YAC: 5.2 (21) ALEX: 2.6	2016:	47% Short	34% Mid	14% Deep	6% Bomb	YAC: 5.1 (15) ALEX: 1.7

The best part of Bortles' game is his mobility, as he has always been effective on the move. The offensive line is part of that, of course, but quarterbacks do a lot to influence how often they are sacked. Improvement in 2017 will require him to do as good a job against cover players as he does against pass-rushers. That is a much different task, and one with which he has struggled throughout his career. His offseason work on improving his throwing motion and mechanics, returning to Tom House and company for an extended period after only a brief pilgrimage last offseason, drew most of the headlines. As long as he continues to struggle against even relatively basic defenses, neither perfect technique, nor even perfect health after playing through nagging injuries, will make much of a difference. 2017 is a pivotal season for Bortles after the offseason surprisingly brought no real competition at his position. Play well, and the Jaguars will be happy they picked up the fifth-year option after passing on a passer in the draft. Play poorly, and a backup job elsewhere likely awaits.

Trevone Boykin Height: 6-0   Weight: 213   College: TCU   Draft: 2016/FA   Born: 22-Aug-1993   Age: 24   Risk: Yellow

Year	Team	G/GS	Snaps	Att	Comp	C%	Yds	TD	INT/Adj	FUM	ASR	NY/P	Rk	DVOA	Rk	DYAR	Rk	YAR	Runs	Yds	TD	DVOA	DYAR	QBR
2016	SEA	5/0	53	18	13	72.2%	145	1	1/1	1	4.5%	7.4	--	-11.2%	--	0	--	14	8	1	0	-89.0%	-18	71.0
2017	SEA			499	300	60.1%	3416	22	18	11		5.8		-16.0%					104	574	4	17.9%		

		2016:	65% Short	24% Mid	6% Deep	6% Bomb	YAC: 5.5 (--) ALEX: -0.9

Most of Boykin's action last year came in blowouts, but he did play 15 snaps in the regular-season finale against the 49ers, a game that the Seahawks needed to win to secure the third seed in the NFC—and a game that remained close all the way to the end. Fortunately, Boykin was able to ice the game away on the final drive, eating up the final five minutes of the game to finish off a 25-23 win in San Francisco. Boykin showed flashes of potential in both the preseason and his limited action during the regular season, but for the second time in two offseasons, his play on the field was overshadowed by an incident off of it when he was arrested on charges of marijuana possession and public intoxication. As a result of the uncertainty surrounding Boykin's legal situation, Seattle signed another backup quarterback, Austin Davis, to serve as insurance in case Russell Wilson gets hurt again.

Sam Bradford

Height: 6-4　Weight: 236　College: Oklahoma　Draft: 2010/1 (1)　Born: 8-Nov-1987　Age: 30　Risk: Yellow

Year	Team	G/GS	Snaps	Att	Comp	C%	Yds	TD	INT/Adj	FUM	ASR	NY/P	Rk	DVOA	Rk	DYAR	Rk	YAR	Runs	Yds	TD	DVOA	DYAR	QBR
2015	PHI	14/14	987	532	346	65.0%	3725	19	14/15	9	6.2%	6.3	16	-8.2%	24	107	24	221	26	39	0	-76.7%	-43	41.8
2016	MIN	15/15	978	552	395	71.6%	3877	20	5/9	10	6.3%	6.1	24	2.2%	17	510	16	571	20	53	0	54.3%	23	49.2
2017	MIN			581	394	67.8%	4109	23	12	8		6.0		2.6%					26	30	1	-18.0%		

2015: 56% Short　28% Mid　12% Deep　4% Bomb　YAC: 5.6 (12)　ALEX: -0.5　2016: 62% Short　24% Mid　10% Deep　5% Bomb　YAC: 5.0 (18)　ALEX: -1.2

For the first time since 2012, Sam Bradford will enter training camp 100 percent healthy and with a chance to spend all of his preparation time with the same team. Bradford never looked lost with the Vikings last year. Norv Turner's staff did a good job of playing to his strengths early in the season. Once Bradford got comfortable they reverted back to their regular offense, an offense that put more pressure on the quarterback. Bradford had an excellent season last year, reflected by his completion percentage record, the highest single-season mark in NFL history. Sure, Bradford's propensity to check down has a lot to do with that record, but he also completed 49 percent of deep/bomb attempts (16 or more yards through the air), which ranked fourth among qualified quarterbacks. (Matt Ryan, Andrew Luck, and Drew Brees were ahead of him, Tom Brady and Dak Prescott right behind him.)

If that quality of play is going to resonate in a more meaningful way, Bradford will need to get better protection from his offensive line. He has never been mobile enough to buy time inside or outside of the pocket. At 30 years old with multiple knee surgeries in his history, he's not suddenly going to turn into Russell Wilson or Aaron Rodgers. That doesn't mean he can't pick apart a defense and deliver the ball against pressure. It does mean he needs a more competent line to push the ball downfield consistently.

Tom Brady

Height: 6-4　Weight: 225　College: Michigan　Draft: 2000/6 (199)　Born: 3-Aug-1977　Age: 40　Risk: Yellow

Year	Team	G/GS	Snaps	Att	Comp	C%	Yds	TD	INT/Adj	FUM	ASR	NY/P	Rk	DVOA	Rk	DYAR	Rk	YAR	Runs	Yds	TD	DVOA	DYAR	QBR
2014	NE	16/16	1062	582	373	64.1%	4109	33	9/11	6	3.9%	6.6	16	18.1%	5	1176	6	1096	36	57	0	-25.1%	-19	74.3
2015	NE	16/16	1105	624	402	64.4%	4770	36	7/9	6	6.5%	6.9	7	19.5%	5	1312	2	1269	34	53	3	6.5%	25	64.4
2016	NE	12/12	819	432	291	67.4%	3554	28	2/3	5	4.2%	7.8	2	33.4%	2	1286	5	1361	28	64	0	-18.9%	-9	83.0
2017	NE			587	393	66.9%	4813	36	8	7		7.6		27.1%					39	65	1	5.5%		

2015: 50% Short　33% Mid　11% Deep　7% Bomb　YAC: 6.0 (6)　ALEX: 1.1　2016: 54% Short　27% Mid　11% Deep　7% Bomb　YAC: 6.0 (2)　ALEX: 2.1

Do you think Brady knows how to spot a big blitz? According to ESPN Stats & Information, Brady has thrown 70 touchdowns with zero interceptions when defenses rush at least six pass-rushers since 2006 (including the playoffs).

Brady's 2017 offensive cast may be the best he has had since that 2007 season when he threw 50 touchdowns and the Patriots broke the single-season scoring record (since broken by the 2013 Broncos). This year's offense should be great, but record-setting levels are hard to project. As talented as the receivers are, the only Randy Moss-level talent is Rob Gronkowski, who doesn't have the greatest history of durability. Should Gronk go down, Dwayne Allen would be an underwhelming replacement starter. Brady also has to bank on Julian Edelman continuing to stay healthy, and a more vertically inclined Brandin Cooks fitting in immediately.

Another big difference between the 2007 Patriots and the 2017 Patriots: the offensive line is not nearly as impenetrable as it appeared a decade ago (during the regular season, at least). Regardless of how many avocados you put in your diet, the hits on an older quarterback are harder to shake off. Brady has never really suffered a serious injury outside of that one time Patriot-killer Bernard Pollard got to his ACL in 2008, but Father Time remains undefeated. While Brady has only thrown 40 touchdowns in a season once, 40 is really the operative number in his career right now. We are getting into territory that few have entered in NFL history. Joe Montana, John Elway, Steve Young, and Dan Marino were all done at 38. Concussions did in Young, but even a great athlete like Elway was missing games in his final season after injuring himself while lifting weights or pulling a muscle in pre-game warmups. Peyton Manning stopped at 39, and Johnny Unitas should have, but instead played a forgettable 40-year-old season with the Chargers in 1973. Brett Favre was still brilliant at 40 for the Vikings, but his body (and ironman streak) finally failed him in 2010 at age 41. Besides Favre, Warren Moon and Vinny Testaverde are the only other quarterbacks who were able to start 10-plus games in a season in their forties.

Our projection would give Brady the best season ever by a quarterback in his forties, so there is certainly a lot of risk here in terms of fantasy football. As for real life, Brady might be able to get through this season unscathed. When the decline does happen, however, it will likely be swift and dramatic, much like his rise to fame 16 years ago.

Drew Brees

Height: 6-0 Weight: 209 College: Purdue Draft: 2001/2 (32) Born: 15-Jan-1979 Age: 38 Risk: Yellow

Year	Team	G/GS	Snaps	Att	Comp	C%	Yds	TD	INT/Adj	FUM	ASR	NY/P	Rk	DVOA	Rk	DYAR	Rk	YAR	Runs	Yds	TD	DVOA	DYAR	QBR
2014	NO	16/16	1140	659	456	69.2%	4952	33	17/19	7	5.2%	7.0	8	15.7%	6	1225	4	1224	27	68	1	17.7%	27	71.6
2015	NO	15/15	1089	627	428	68.3%	4870	32	11/13	5	5.3%	7.0	5	15.8%	7	1111	6	1184	24	14	1	32.1%	21	75.5
2016	NO	16/16	1151	673	471	70.0%	5208	37	15/14	5	4.5%	7.3	5	23.3%	4	1599	2	1473	23	20	2	17.2%	21	72.0
2017	NO			626	418	66.8%	4833	35	12	5		6.9		17.2%					25	25	1	1.2%		

2015:	54% Short	26% Mid	13% Deep	7% Bomb	YAC: 5.6 (15)	ALEX: 1.1	2016:	54% Short	28% Mid	11% Deep	6% Bomb	YAC: 5.1 (12)	ALEX: 1.5

Drew Brees had three bad games last year. Unfortunately, two came in successive weeks in early December to finally knock the Saints out of the wild-card picture. Six of Brees' 15 interceptions came in those two games against Detroit and Tampa Bay. It might be significant that all three of those bad games came in December, while his best spell came after a bye week—or it might be overfitting the narrative to the data. On the other hand, the stretch prior to that was incredible: following the team's Week 5 bye, Brees had five straight games (and six out of seven) with at least 140 DYAR. The Saints have invested heavily in defense and rushing this offseason to theoretically take some pressure off their aging quarterback. That's a story we have read before though, and the conclusion is usually written somewhere around the 700th attempt.

Teddy Bridgewater

Height: 6-2 Weight: 214 College: Louisville Draft: 2014/1 (32) Born: 10-Nov-1992 Age: 25 Risk: Red

Year	Team	G/GS	Snaps	Att	Comp	C%	Yds	TD	INT/Adj	FUM	ASR	NY/P	Rk	DVOA	Rk	DYAR	Rk	YAR	Runs	Yds	TD	DVOA	DYAR	QBR
2014	MIN	13/12	794	402	259	64.4%	2919	14	12/11	3	9.1%	6.1	23	-16.9%	34	-159	34	-82	47	209	1	-8.5%	8	50.2
2015	MIN	16/16	994	447	292	65.3%	3231	14	9/11	8	8.8%	6.0	29	-5.1%	22	187	21	93	44	192	3	5.3%	32	62.7
2017	MIN			573	389	67.9%	4156	26	14	7		6.2		2.4%					44	185	2	15.2%		

2015:	56% Short	25% Mid	14% Deep	6% Bomb	YAC: 6.2 (2)	ALEX: -0.7

After tearing his ACL and dislocating his knee last August, just wearing a jersey again will be a victory for Teddy Bridgewater. He's back working out and throwing the ball, but that doesn't guarantee he will be back on the field at any point in the future. The Vikings have the luxury of waiting on Bridgewater, and offseason reports indicated the final year of his rookie contract may toll to 2018 if he begins the year on the PUP list. Even if he's healthy, he probably won't play ahead of Sam Bradford in 2017.

Jacoby Brissett

Height: 6-4 Weight: 231 College: North Carolina State Draft: 2016/3 (91) Born: 11-Dec-1992 Age: 25 Risk: Yellow

Year	Team	G/GS	Snaps	Att	Comp	C%	Yds	TD	INT/Adj	FUM	ASR	NY/P	Rk	DVOA	Rk	DYAR	Rk	YAR	Runs	Yds	TD	DVOA	DYAR	QBR
2016	NE	3/2	156	55	34	61.8%	400	0	0/0	3	9.4%	5.9	--	-10.0%	--	4	--	-4	16	83	1	-24.4%	-8	44.8
2017	NE			525	330	62.9%	3834	24	14	11		6.4		-3.2%					87	435	3	16.7%		

													016:	63% Short	14% Mid	13% Deep	11% Bomb	YAC: 9.7 (--)	ALEX: 0.4

Brissett was never supposed to sniff the active game-day roster in his rookie campaign, but as they say, you're just one hit and one Second Circuit court decision away. The North Carolina State rookie managed to tiptoe around trouble enough for the Patriots to win two out of the three games he played, though he was also one of two players last season to attempt at least 50 passes without throwing a touchdown. There have been rumblings about the Patriots supposedly holding Brissett in very high regard due to a variety of circumstantial evidence—his mentor-mentee relationship with Bill Parcells, his toughness in playing through a torn thumb ligament in Week 4, and New England's decision to use their lone short-term IR spot on Brissett despite his lack of game-day value. Of course, all that was supposedly part of the lead-up to a Jimmy Garoppolo trade which never materialized. Realistically, Brissett is a long-term project who shouldn't see the field again anytime soon, though you can rest assured he'll enjoy the same buzz and reputation bump every Patriots backup quarterback seems to receive.

Derek Carr

Height: 6-3 Weight: 220 College: Fresno St. Draft: 2014/2 (36) Born: 3/28/1991 Age: 26 Risk: Green

Year	Team	G/GS	Snaps	Att	Comp	C%	Yds	TD	INT/Adj	FUM	ASR	NY/P	Rk	DVOA	Rk	DYAR	Rk	YAR	Runs	Yds	TD	DVOA	DYAR	QBR
2014	OAK	16/16	986	599	348	58.1%	3270	21	12/16	10	4.0%	5.0	36	-14.9%	33	-150	33	-355	29	92	0	28.4%	40	38.4
2015	OAK	16/16	1014	573	350	61.1%	3987	32	13/15	10	4.6%	6.2	22	4.1%	13	582	12	428	33	138	0	-25.3%	-13	49.2
2016	OAK	15/15	1048	560	357	63.8%	3937	28	6/12	5	3.3%	6.7	12	19.8%	6	1164	7	1038	39	70	0	-50.3%	-39	62.1
2017	OAK			578	370	64.0%	4171	29	11	7		6.7		11.3%					38	93	1	0.1%		

2015:	48% Short	32% Mid	12% Deep	7% Bomb	YAC: 5.1 (23)	ALEX: 0.7	2016:	51% Short	33% Mid	9% Deep	7% Bomb	YAC: 5.1 (13)	ALEX: 1.0

After becoming the latest highest-paid player in NFL history, Derek Carr may have taken a little jab at the Seattle Seahawks. "There's no pressure, there's no, you know... we'll be on the 1-yard line and I won't give it to Marshawn [Lynch]—I'll throw it," Carr told reporters in June. "There's none of that stuff. I don't care about the stats. That's not my No. 1 objective. I don't care if I throw 10 touchdowns next year. If we win every game, that's all I care about."

We'll see if Carr keeps his promise on that goal-line strategy. Handing the ball off to the bruising Lynch behind a stout line may actually be the smart thing to do. Carr's red zone stats declined once again last year. His red zone performance as a rookie—when he had 57.1% DVOA and threw a touchdown on 40.9 percent of his attempts, the second-highest rate (minimum 30 attempts) since 2006—was never sustainable. However, Carr's numbers have fallen off the last two years, and he was down to -0.9% DVOA and a 21.1 percent touchdown rate in the red zone in 2016. This despite the lowest pressure rate (10.9 percent) of any quarterback in the red zone. As we mentioned in the Oakland chapter, Carr had way too many near-misses in the end zone, mostly to Amari Cooper. If they can clean that up, then Carr might be able to set a new career high in touchdown passes, but he'll probably still be handing off to Lynch for plenty of scores as well. Either way, the weight of the new contract and Super Bowl expectations should put more pressure on Carr to perform at a higher level than what we have seen in his first three seasons.

Matt Cassel

| | | Height: 6-5 | | Weight: 230 | | College: USC | | | | Draft: 2005/7 (230) | | Born: 17-May-1982 | | Age: 35 | | | Risk: Yellow |

Year	Team	G/GS	Snaps	Att	Comp	C%	Yds	TD	INT/Adj	FUM	ASR	NY/P	Rk	DVOA	Rk	DYAR	Rk	YAR	Runs	Yds	TD	DVOA	DYAR	QBR
2014	MIN	3/3	140	71	41	57.7%	425	3	4/3	3	7.7%	4.9	--	-40.4%	--	-147	--	-150	9	18	0	-10.5%	0	28.9
2015	2TM	9/8	415	204	119	58.3%	1276	5	7/7	4	6.6%	5.5	35	-23.7%	35	-172	34	-210	15	78	0	-29.3%	-10	33.7
2016	TEN	4/1	98	51	30	58.8%	284	2	2/2	1	9.4%	4.8	--	-23.1%	--	-38	--	-68	4	3	0	-107.8%	-7	71.7
2017	TEN			485	277	57.2%	3152	22	15	8		5.5		-17.7%					35	111	1	3.3%		
2015:	48% Short		31% Mid		13% Deep		8% Bomb		YAC: 4.8 (30)		ALEX: 0.2		2016:	45% Short		41% Mid		9% Deep		5% Bomb		YAC: 2.4 (--)	ALEX: 0.8

Cassel's player comment in *Football Outsiders Almanac 2016* ended with the prediction that in Tennessee, Cassel likely wouldn't "have the burden of trying to keep a team in playoff contention if pressed into action." Yet, there he was in Week 16, forced into the lineup after Marcus Mariota suffered a broken leg, asked to rally the Titans from a 15-point deficit late in the third quarter to keep playoff hopes alive. A win in the finale was enough for Tennessee to keep him around, but a hand injury of his own knocked him out of offseason workouts. If asked to play a lot, expect many short passes and too many sacks.

Kellen Clemens

| | | Height: 6-2 | | Weight: 224 | | College: Oregon | | | | Draft: 2006/2 (49) | | Born: 6-Jun-1983 | | Age: 34 | | | Risk: Green |

Year	Team	G/GS	Snaps	Att	Comp	C%	Yds	TD	INT/Adj	FUM	ASR	NY/P	Rk	DVOA	Rk	DYAR	Rk	YAR	Runs	Yds	TD	DVOA	DYAR	QBR
2014	SD	2/0	15	3	1	33.3%	10	0	0/0	0	23.6%	0.3	--	-92.7%	--	-20	--	-20	0	0	0	--	--	1.3
2015	SD	2/0	15	6	5	83.3%	63	1	0/0	0	-0.9%	10.5	--	157.4%	--	67	--	62	1	-1	0	--	--	99.9
2016	SD	12/0	5	1	0	0.0%	0	0	0/0	0	0.0%	0.0	--	-116.1%	--	-6	--	-6	2	-1	0	--	--	0.1
2017	LACH			557	335	60.1%	3559	17	17	12		5.5		-19.8%					40	99	1	-7.8%		
2015:	17% Short		50% Mid		33% Deep		0% Bomb		YAC: 0.8 (--)		ALEX: 4.0		2016:	0% Short		0% Mid		0% Deep		100% Bomb		YAC: 0.0 (--)	ALEX: 28.0

When former NFL quarterback Vince Young recently sounded off on all the "garbage" quarterbacks who still have jobs, he could have been talking about Clemens, who was drafted 46 spots after Young in 2006. Clemens is going into his 12th season but has just 21 career starts, none since 2013. The Chargers haven't found a successor for Philip Rivers yet, so they'll hope he continues his ironman streak, because Clemens has never proven to be a competent starter in this league. However, he probably stands for every national anthem with great pride.

Connor Cook

| | | Height: 6-4 | | Weight: 217 | | College: Michigan State | | | | Draft: 2016/4 (100) | | Born: 29-Jan-1993 | | Age: 24 | | | Risk: Yellow |

Year	Team	G/GS	Snaps	Att	Comp	C%	Yds	TD	INT/Adj	FUM	ASR	NY/P	Rk	DVOA	Rk	DYAR	Rk	YAR	Runs	Yds	TD	DVOA	DYAR	QBR
2016	OAK	1/0	32	21	14	66.7%	150	1	1/1	2	8.2%	6.1	--	-23.9%	--	-21	--	-66	0	0	0	--	--	18.1
2017	OAK			520	293	56.3%	3304	18	17	8		5.4		-16.3%					23	47	1	1.6%		
													2016:	57% Short		29% Mid		14% Deep		0% Bomb		YAC: 6.1 (--)	ALEX: -1.3

A successful 2017 for Cook would involve beating out EJ Manuel for the No. 2 quarterback spot. As much as an Oakland fan may want to see whether Cook can improve on his brutal playoff outing in Houston last year, it is for the best if Derek Carr remains healthy.

Kirk Cousins

Height: 6-3 Weight: 214 College: Michigan State Draft: 2012/4 (102) Born: 19-Aug-1988 Age: 29 Risk: Green

Year	Team	G/GS	Snaps	Att	Comp	C%	Yds	TD	INT/Adj	FUM	ASR	NY/P	Rk	DVOA	Rk	DYAR	Rk	YAR	Runs	Yds	TD	DVOA	DYAR	QBR
2014	WAS	6/5	357	204	126	61.8%	1710	10	9/9	2	3.8%	7.7	1	4.6%	14	223	22	213	7	20	0	9.0%	7	46.9
2015	WAS	16/16	1026	543	379	69.8%	4166	29	11/13	8	5.4%	7.0	6	16.9%	6	1023	7	1125	26	48	5	-3.1%	8	70.1
2016	WAS	16/16	1063	606	406	67.0%	4917	25	12/16	9	3.9%	7.6	3	20.9%	5	1317	3	1197	34	96	4	1.9%	18	71.7
2017	WAS			577	372	64.5%	4316	26	15	11		6.6		5.4%					25	84	2	12.0%		

| 2015: | 58% Short | 23% Mid | 13% Deep | 6% Bomb | YAC: 5.0 (28) | ALEX: 0.9 | 2016: | 51% Short | 29% Mid | 12% Deep | 8% Bomb | YAC: 4.8 (26) | ALEX: 2.3 |

Cousins is not a great passer near the goal line: he was 15-of-40 from inside the 10-yard line last season, with eight touchdowns and two interceptions. Part of the problem is that Washington's offense is not built for red zone dominance. There's no powerhouse running back or jump-ball wide receiver, and the top tight end is always dinged up. But the goal line also reveals Cousins' limitations as a player: he can't fire fastballs through windows like Matt Ryan, outthink the defense like Tom Brady, or do as much with his legs as Aaron Rodgers or Cam Newton.

It's easy to overthink a quarterback like Cousins—which may be precisely what his employers are doing. Given a stout line and well-constructed offense, a solid veteran starting quarterback nowadays is going to have a 4,000-plus-yard, 25-touchdown season. Under the same circumstances, a solid veteran can post impressive DVOA results, because DVOA can only do so much to separate quarterback from supporting cast and scheme. Solid veteran quarterbacks are not the same as Rodgers-Brady types, but there is still a finite supply of them, and possessing one is among the bare minimum requirements of competing for a Super Bowl.

Every year, teams trade up in the draft and rearrange their organizational priorities because they lack a quarterback as good as Cousins. It's OK for Washington to want something better. But there's an old saying about a bird in the hand being worth two in the bush, and this franchise spent an awful lot of its recent history getting lost in the shrubbery.

Jay Cutler

Height: 6-3 Weight: 220 College: Vanderbilt Draft: 2006/1 (11) Born: 29-Apr-1983 Age: 34 Risk: N/A

Year	Team	G/GS	Snaps	Att	Comp	C%	Yds	TD	INT/Adj	FUM	ASR	NY/P	Rk	DVOA	Rk	DYAR	Rk	YAR	Runs	Yds	TD	DVOA	DYAR	QBR
2014	CHI	15/15	969	561	370	66.0%	3812	28	18/22	12	6.3%	6.0	26	-0.7%	21	398	16	351	39	191	2	38.3%	65	54.0
2015	CHI	15/15	992	483	311	64.4%	3659	21	11/14	8	5.2%	6.9	8	8.6%	9	659	10	556	38	201	1	43.7%	84	60.7
2016	CHI	5/5	275	137	81	59.1%	1059	4	5/8	6	10.8%	6.2	--	-18.5%	--	-69	--	-218	5	24	0	-0.1%	3	33.2

| 2015: | 50% Short | 30% Mid | 11% Deep | 9% Bomb | YAC: 5.6 (13) | ALEX: 3.1 | 2016: | 49% Short | 27% Mid | 14% Deep | 10% Bomb | YAC: 5.1 (--) | ALEX: 0.7 |

Jay Cutler's career will always be remembered as a long, drawn-out question mark. Until his final year in the league he could still make any throw from any platform. His arm talent was as impressive as anyone's. An inability to read defenses and a lack of poise in the pocket limited Cutler's value. As with Tony Romo, but to a lesser degree, Cutler was still talented enough to fill a role in the NFL when he retired. His age and recent durability issues mean that he would have probably had to play on a league-minimum salary while winning a roster spot in training camp.

Andy Dalton

Height: 6-2 Weight: 215 College: TCU Draft: 2011/2 (35) Born: 29-Oct-1987 Age: 30 Risk: Yellow

Year	Team	G/GS	Snaps	Att	Comp	C%	Yds	TD	INT/Adj	FUM	ASR	NY/P	Rk	DVOA	Rk	DYAR	Rk	YAR	Runs	Yds	TD	DVOA	DYAR	QBR
2014	CIN	16/16	1031	481	309	64.2%	3398	19	17/21	3	4.3%	6.5	19	-3.7%	24	237	21	238	60	169	4	-2.9%	26	55.2
2015	CIN	13/13	798	386	255	66.1%	3250	25	7/9	5	5.1%	7.7	3	31.7%	2	1135	4	1059	57	142	3	-8.1%	9	73.1
2016	CIN	16/16	1085	563	364	64.7%	4206	18	8/16	9	7.3%	6.6	15	7.6%	12	738	10	667	46	184	4	20.6%	60	58.3
2017	CIN			554	354	64.0%	4231	25	12	7		6.8		6.3%					56	189	2	10.7%		

| 2015: | 49% Short | 28% Mid | 14% Deep | 9% Bomb | YAC: 5.9 (8) | ALEX: 1.9 | 2016: | 48% Short | 34% Mid | 12% Deep | 6% Bomb | YAC: 5.1 (16) | ALEX: 0.8 |

Andy Dalton was born 30 years too late. Even though there are legitimate examples of quarterbacks who have won Super Bowls without being great (Joe Flacco, Trent Dilfer, Brad Johnson, Zombie Peyton Manning), Dalton was born into the sabermetric era and is thus constantly criticized. In a world of success cycles and competitive windows, the decent quarterback is never enough for the media. Dalton is somewhere between the 13th and 20th best quarterback in the NFL, and on a good team, that's enough. It just might not look like it this year if the offensive line in front of him can't block.

Chase Daniel

Chase Daniel   Height: 6-0   Weight: 225   College: Missouri   Draft: 2009/FA   Born: 7-Oct-1986   Age: 31   Risk: Yellow

Year	Team	G/GS	Snaps	Att	Comp	C%	Yds	TD	INT/Adj	FUM	ASR	NY/P	Rk	DVOA	Rk	DYAR	Rk	YAR	Runs	Yds	TD	DVOA	DYAR	QBR
2014	KC	3/1	67	28	16	57.1%	157	0	0/0	0	13.2%	4.4	--	-24.4%	--	-28	--	-18	4	15	0	84.8%	9	46.4
2015	KC	2/0	13	2	2	100.0%	4	0	0/0	0	-1.7%	2.0	--	-32.7%	--	-3	--	-1	2	-2	0	--	--	98.5
2016	PHI	1/0	6	1	1	100.0%	16	0	0/0	0	0.0%	11.0	--	360.8%	--	16	--	13	0	0	0	--	--	99.5
2017	NO			606	374	61.6%	4359	28	15	11		5.9		-3.6%					39	105	1	-3.0%		

2015: 100% Short   0% Mid   0% Deep   0% Bomb   YAC: 2.0 (–)   ALEX: -1.0   2016: 100% Short   0% Mid   0% Deep   0% Bomb   YAC: 11.0 (–)   ALEX: 0.0

If Jon Gruden had a nickname for Chase Daniel, it would have to be the Golden Clipboard. By the end of his current one-year deal, Daniel will have earned approximately $24 million in his nine years as a pro. He has thrown 78 passes. That works out to approximately $300,000 per pass attempt, $425,000 per completion, $50,000 per yard, or a price per touchdown of ... $24 million. Yes, he has thrown one touchdown (and one interception) in his entire $24 million career. Despite a reasonably high completion percentage, Daniel's career yards per attempt is a full yard below last season's league average of 7.2. Though he doesn't throw many interceptions, he takes a sack every 12 dropbacks. If that cautious mediocrity is the reason he keeps getting backup gigs, it's also the reason why he's never become more than a backup.

Austin Davis

Austin Davis   Height: 6-2   Weight: 221   College: Southern Mississippi   Draft: 2012/FA   Born: 2-Jun-1989   Age: 28   Risk: Yellow

Year	Team	G/GS	Snaps	Att	Comp	C%	Yds	TD	INT/Adj	FUM	ASR	NY/P	Rk	DVOA	Rk	DYAR	Rk	YAR	Runs	Yds	TD	DVOA	DYAR	QBR
2014	STL	10/8	548	284	180	63.4%	2001	12	9/12	5	9.5%	5.9	32	-8.8%	29	47	29	-2	16	36	0	4.6%	5	37.6
2015	CLE	3/2	159	94	56	59.6%	547	1	3/5	2	11.5%	4.0	--	-52.9%	--	-269	--	-287	7	33	0	-24.5%	-5	22.1
2017	SEA			530	334	63.1%	3738	19	14	12		5.8		-11.9%					42	101	1	-7.7%		

2015: 47% Short   39% Mid   8% Deep   6% Bomb   YAC: 3.8 (–)   ALEX: 0.9

Davis spent his 2016 season as the third-stringer for the Broncos behind Trevor Siemian and Paxton Lynch, and his only starting experience has come as an injury replacement in both St. Louis and Cleveland. His most notable accomplishments to this point in his career have probably been beating out Johnny Manziel for the right to start a game with the Browns, and completing 85 percent of his passes when he led the Rams to a home upset win over Seattle in 2014. People will more likely know Davis today as the guy Seattle signed instead of Colin Kaepernick for a backup role. If Davis sees meaningful action for Seattle this season, then something will have gone horribly, horribly wrong, but it would be Davis' chance to finally prove Brett Favre right after Favre claimed that he could be the next Tom Brady or Kurt Warner just a few short years ago.

Ryan Fitzpatrick

Ryan Fitzpatrick   Height: 6-2   Weight: 221   College: Harvard   Draft: 2005/7 (250)   Born: 24-Nov-1982   Age: 35   Risk: Red

Year	Team	G/GS	Snaps	Att	Comp	C%	Yds	TD	INT/Adj	FUM	ASR	NY/P	Rk	DVOA	Rk	DYAR	Rk	YAR	Runs	Yds	TD	DVOA	DYAR	QBR
2014	HOU	12/12	727	312	197	63.1%	2483	17	8/13	5	5.8%	7.2	6	6.7%	12	383	17	485	50	184	2	2.8%	32	55.3
2015	NYJ	16/16	1046	562	335	59.6%	3905	31	15/23	5	3.9%	6.6	14	3.5%	14	542	13	670	60	270	2	18.0%	73	63.6
2016	NYJ	14/11	765	403	228	56.6%	2710	12	17/20	10	4.8%	6.2	23	-22.6%	32	-319	32	-329	33	130	0	-19.5%	-11	45.4
2017	TB			553	309	55.8%	3994	23	18	7		6.1		-9.0%					37	127	1	1.0%		

2015: 42% Short   33% Mid   17% Deep   9% Bomb   YAC: 5.4 (19)   ALEX: 3.1   2016: 42% Short   32% Mid   19% Deep   7% Bomb   YAC: 4.9 (23)   ALEX: 1.7

A proposition: The "R" in DYAR should no longer stand for "replacement." It should stand for "Ryan Fitzpatrick" instead, and an individual quarterback's performance should be measured by how much better or worse he is than the Harvard product. This will raise the baseline performance a teeny bit—Fitzpatrick's career DVOA is -8.5%, a little higher than our current replacement level of -11.0%—but it makes logical sense. After all, who has replaced more quarterbacks, or been replaced more himself, than Fitzpatrick? He can never hang on to a job, but he is never out of work either. Fitzpatrick has played for six NFL teams, and passed for at least 700 yards in a season with each one of them. The only other quarterbacks who have done that are Gus Frerotte, Chris Chandler, and Steve Beuerlein. (Vinny Testaverde also makes the list if you count the old Cleveland Browns and the Baltimore Ravens as separate franchises.) Now Fitzpatrick is on the Buccaneers, his fifth team in the past six seasons, and he can be the first player to throw for 700 yards with seven teams if Jameis Winston is sidelined for just two or three games. Should that happen, it would not necessarily torpedo the Bucs' ship. Fitzpatrick has spent most of his career straddling the fine line between good backup and bad starter, and he has the deep ball (no starting quarterback had a higher share of his passes in the deep or bomb range last season) to give Tampa Bay's prolific weapons chances to make plays downfield.

Joe Flacco

						Height: 6-6		Weight: 236		College: Delaware			Draft: 2008/1 (18)		Born: 16-Jan-1985		Age: 32			Risk: Yellow

Year	Team	G/GS	Snaps	Att	Comp	C%	Yds	TD	INT/Adj	FUM	ASR	NY/P	Rk	DVOA	Rk	DYAR	Rk	YAR	Runs	Yds	TD	DVOA	DYAR	QBR
2014	BAL	16/16	1070	554	344	62.1%	3986	27	12/16	5	4.5%	6.7	13	15.5%	7	987	8	962	39	70	2	-12.9%	-1	67.3
2015	BAL	10/10	717	413	266	64.4%	2791	14	12/14	5	4.2%	6.3	21	-10.5%	26	17	27	55	13	23	3	6.8%	15	40.9
2016	BAL	16/16	1111	672	436	64.9%	4317	20	15/19	5	5.4%	5.8	28	-14.6%	29	-155	30	-44	21	58	2	15.8%	21	58.4
2017	BAL			629	401	63.7%	4265	24	14	7		5.8		-5.6%					19	40	1	2.7%		

2015:	59% Short	23% Mid	12% Deep	7% Bomb	YAC: 5.6 (14)	ALEX: 1.9	2016:	56% Short	29% Mid	9% Deep	6% Bomb	YAC: 4.8 (27)	ALEX: 0.8

Per Cian Fahey's work in the *Pre-Snap Reads Quarterback Catalogue*, Flacco finished 27th in accuracy percentage last year on passes 20 or more yards downfield. That was a number bettered by, among others, Alex Smith, Brian Hoyer, and Ryan Fitz-patrick. We went over a lot of damning statistics about Flacco in the Ravens chapter, but even the things that Flacco is supposed to do well, he did at a replacement level last season. And considering he threw fewer balls (roughly 15 percent of his attempts) between 11 and 20 yards, this is really all the Ravens had for a vertical passing game. The ball looks really pretty though, guys. Like, you wouldn't believe how pretty the deep ball is as it hits the ground harmlessly.

Nick Foles

						Height: 6-5		Weight: 243		College: Arizona			Draft: 2012/3 (88)		Born: 20-Jan-1989		Age: 28			Risk: Red

Year	Team	G/GS	Snaps	Att	Comp	C%	Yds	TD	INT/Adj	FUM	ASR	NY/P	Rk	DVOA	Rk	DYAR	Rk	YAR	Runs	Yds	TD	DVOA	DYAR	QBR
2014	PHI	8/8	545	311	186	59.8%	2163	13	10/12	4	2.7%	6.5	18	1.8%	19	264	19	280	16	68	0	9.5%	15	62.2
2015	STL	11/11	656	337	190	56.4%	2052	7	10/12	4	3.8%	5.6	34	-27.9%	37	-353	37	-428	17	20	1	32.0%	21	30.0
2016	KC	3/1	106	55	36	65.5%	410	3	0/1	0	7.1%	6.4	--	-9.9%	--	5	--	26	4	-4	0	--	--	35.3
2017	PHI			574	358	62.4%	4053	25	17	8		5.9		-11.9%					32	98	0	-3.3%		

2015:	51% Short	30% Mid	12% Deep	8% Bomb	YAC: 6.1 (3)	ALEX: 0.6	2016:	56% Short	27% Mid	7% Deep	9% Bomb	YAC: 5.5 (--)	ALEX: -1.0

Foles has officially downshifted into the "capable veteran backup and spot starter" role that always suited his talents. Now that the madness of his brief 2013 stardom and his disastrous 2015 brush with Jeff Fisher are both fading memories, Foles can bounce from team to team coached by Andy Reid disciples until he turns 40. Foles' two solid efforts last year came against the Colts and Jaguars, so don't grow too enamored with his 2016 totals. But he'll get the Eagles through a game or two if called upon.

Blaine Gabbert

						Height: 6-4		Weight: 234		College: Missouri			Draft: 2011/1 (10)		Born: 15-Oct-1989		Age: 28			Risk: Yellow

Year	Team	G/GS	Snaps	Att	Comp	C%	Yds	TD	INT/Adj	FUM	ASR	NY/P	Rk	DVOA	Rk	DYAR	Rk	YAR	Runs	Yds	TD	DVOA	DYAR	QBR
2014	SF	1/0	9	7	3	42.9%	38	1	0/0	0	0.3%	5.4	--	37.7%	--	22	--	18	1	5	0	-34.2%	-1	91.4
2015	SF	8/8	511	282	178	63.1%	2031	10	7/6	4	8.0%	6.1	27	-15.6%	31	-85	31	-118	32	185	1	16.2%	34	42.6
2016	SF	6/5	344	160	91	56.9%	925	5	6/8	0	5.5%	5.1	--	-25.4%	--	-158	--	-205	40	173	2	13.3%	52	60.3
2017	ARI			581	344	59.2%	3856	22	18	7		5.5		-18.9%					40	155	1	2.7%		

2015:	56% Short	28% Mid	12% Deep	4% Bomb	YAC: 6.1 (4)	ALEX: -2.4	2016:	48% Short	35% Mid	14% Deep	4% Bomb	YAC: 4.0 (--)	ALEX: -1.2

Gabbert opened the season as the 49ers' starter by default, due to injuries to his competition. He ended up demoted to third string by the end of the year. Gabbert has now started 40 games in the NFL. He has a career record of 9-31. He has never had a season with positive passing DVOA or DYAR. His career average of 6.0 yards per pass ranks dead last among the 47 active quarterbacks with at least 750 career pass attempts, and he is in the bottom five for completion rate, touchdown rate, and NFL passer rating as well. The athleticism that made Gabbert the 10th overall pick in 2011 is still there, and there's talk that Bruce Arians could groom him as a potential replacement for Carson Palmer, enticing a third fan base to ponder what could be if Gab-bert could ever put it all together on the field. But Gabbert's not a young prospect anymore, and there's little past precedent for someone playing *so* poorly in such a large sample size ever becoming a competent NFL starter. The best case for Gabbert is a Josh McCown-esque journeyman career; expecting anything more at this point is folly.

Jimmy Garoppolo

Height: 6-2   Weight: 226   College: Eastern Illinois   Draft: 2014/2 (62)   Born: 11-Feb-1991   Age: 26   Risk: Red

Year	Team	G/GS	Snaps	Att	Comp	C%	Yds	TD	INT/Adj	FUM	ASR	NY/P	Rk	DVOA	Rk	DYAR	Rk	YAR	Runs	Yds	TD	DVOA	DYAR	QBR
2014	NE	6/0	69	27	19	70.4%	182	1	0/0	0	14.0%	4.6	--	-13.8%	--	-5	--	-28	10	9	0	-14.3%	-1	19.2
2015	NE	5/0	13	4	1	25.0%	6	0	0/0	0	1.2%	1.5	--	-98.6%	--	-25	--	-21	5	-5	0	--	--	2.4
2016	NE	6/2	144	63	43	68.3%	502	4	0/0	2	3.6%	7.3	--	44.4%	--	225	--	182	10	6	0	-4.3%	1	89.9
2017	NE			563	376	66.8%	4325	30	14	9		6.9		11.5%					44	99	1	-1.8%		

2015:	75% Short	25% Mid	0% Deep	0% Bomb	YAC: 1.0 (–)	ALEX: 0.0	2016:	48% Short	37% Mid	10% Deep	6% Bomb	YAC: 5.8 (–)	ALEX: 1.8

With all the "will-they-or-won't-they" trade speculation this offseason, Garoppolo feels more like a theoretical projection of value than an actual player. In reality, the 25-year-old (he turns 26 in November) is now a highly regarded prospect thanks to six strong quarters which saw him ranked first in QBR and DVOA after two weeks. That's just enough of a tease to get everyone in a tizzy while also telling us very little at all. Garoppolo has 94 career passes through three seasons; the track record of quarterbacks drafted in the first two rounds to throw under 100 passes in their first three years is neither long nor illustrious. Garoppolo is the 20th quarterback to fit this criteria since the merger. Of the other 19, there's one resounding success in Aaron Rodgers and a lot of Pat White- and Jim Druckenmiller-level flotsam. It's an important reminder of how wide the spectrum of future outcomes is for Garoppolo, who will likely sit through another redshirt season, assuming Tom Brady keeps doing Tom Brady-ish things. Handsome Jimmy G may be a lock for the Dashing Clipboard Holders Hall of Fame, but little else about his career is assured.

Mike Glennon

Height: 6-6   Weight: 218   College: North Carolina State   Draft: 2013/3 (73)   Born: 12-Dec-1989   Age: 28   Risk: Yellow

Year	Team	G/GS	Snaps	Att	Comp	C%	Yds	TD	INT/Adj	FUM	ASR	NY/P	Rk	DVOA	Rk	DYAR	Rk	YAR	Runs	Yds	TD	DVOA	DYAR	QBR
2014	TB	6/5	363	203	117	57.6%	1417	10	6/8	2	7.7%	6.1	24	-3.1%	23	107	26	161	10	49	0	2.2%	6	56.0
2016	TB	2/0	15	11	10	90.9%	75	1	0/0	0	1.7%	6.8	--	65.8%	--	65	--	64	0	0	0	--	--	96.9
2017	CHI			527	321	61.0%	3738	22	16	8		6.1		-5.9%					28	53	1	-10.0%		

2016:	82% Short	18% Mid	0% Deep	0% Bomb	YAC: 3.7 (–)	ALEX: -2.0

Even if it's just lip service, the Bears are talking about Mike Glennon as their starting quarterback. Glennon will give the Bears an improvement over last season's flotsam, but that isn't saying much. Glennon is a different type of player from Matt Barkley or Jay Cutler. He will play to his skill set more consistently than either of those players did, but the important thing is that the Bears also play to his skill set. He's an athletic quarterback who can execute elongated play fakes and throw while on the move outside of the pocket. Glennon's best chance of succeeding will come from pushing the ball downfield off of play-action.

The Bears will offer Glennon solid pass protection, but the limited ability of his receivers will likely hamper his production. Kevin White has to stay healthy or Glennon will be throwing to a group of receivers who will struggle to consistently get open on vertical routes. White himself is largely unproven too, so even his health may not give the quarterback the type of receiver on which he likes to rely.

Jared Goff

Height: 6-4   Weight: 215   College: California   Draft: 2016/1 (1)   Born: 14-Oct-1994   Age: 23   Risk: Blue

Year	Team	G/GS	Snaps	Att	Comp	C%	Yds	TD	INT/Adj	FUM	ASR	NY/P	Rk	DVOA	Rk	DYAR	Rk	YAR	Runs	Yds	TD	DVOA	DYAR	QBR
2016	LARM	7/7	393	205	112	54.6%	1089	5	7/8	5	11.1%	3.8	34	-74.8%	34	-881	34	-819	8	16	1	-22.8%	-3	22.2
2017	LARM			543	325	59.9%	3324	14	14	11		5.1		-21.3%					37	78	2	-7.3%		

2016:	54% Short	33% Mid	8% Deep	5% Bomb	YAC: 5.1 (14)	ALEX: -2.5

There are only so many different ways to describe Goff's 2016 performance, but based on historical precedent, 2017 couldn't be any worse, right? 2015's worst quarterback, Nick Foles of the then-St. Louis Rams, finished with less than half the negative DYAR of Goff on 145 more pass attempts, meaning that Goff packed an incredible amount of suck into each of his 205 attempts. As strange as this is to say for a No. 1 overall pick entering his second season in the league, 2017 looks like a make-or-break season for Goff. If he continues to struggle, the Rams will likely be searching for a new answer at quarterback (possibly Sean McVay's old quarterback in Washington). Should Goff continue on his path to bust-dom, he will join the growing list of unsuccessful NFL quarterbacks who posted big numbers running an Air Raid offensive system in college.

Robert Griffin

Height: 6-2   Weight: 223   College: Baylor   Draft: 2012/1 (2)   Born: 12-Feb-1990   Age: 27   Risk: N/A

Year	Team	G/GS	Snaps	Att	Comp	C%	Yds	TD	INT/Adj	FUM	ASR	NY/P	Rk	DVOA	Rk	DYAR	Rk	YAR	Runs	Yds	TD	DVOA	DYAR	QBR
2014	WAS	9/7	457	214	147	68.7%	1694	4	6/6	9	13.7%	5.9	29	-34.2%	35	-374	35	-372	38	176	1	-25.5%	-23	30.8
2016	CLE	5/5	302	147	87	59.2%	886	2	3/5	4	12.9%	4.4	--	-36.0%	--	-270	--	-331	31	190	2	17.0%	39	45.0

2016: 54% Short   31% Mid   5% Deep   10% Bomb   YAC: 5.0 (--)   ALEX: -2.0

Shortly after Cleveland released him, Griffin publicly announced that his girlfriend was pregnant, and the couple was now engaged. That kind of happy news will make anyone optimistic. So Griffin can be forgiven for also announcing that he was continuing his training and not giving up on his NFL career. When the same team that trades for Brock Osweiler and retains Kevin Hogan doesn't want you back, it's time to find a new line of work. Even as bottom-of-the-barrel passers such as Blaine Gabbert and Austin Davis were signing with the Cardinals and Seahawks, Griffin couldn't even get a visit. It has been a spectacular collapse for Griffin, who now looks like one of the great one-year wonders of all time. Specifically, whatever pocket presence he ever had has vanished—his sack rate has been higher than 13 percent in each of the last two seasons he has played, much higher than that of any other quarterback in Washington in 2014 or in Cleveland last year.

Christian Hackenberg

Height: 6-4   Weight: 223   College: Penn State   Draft: 2016/2 (51)   Born: 14-Feb-1995   Age: 22   Risk: Yellow

Year	Team	G/GS	Snaps	Att	Comp	C%	Yds	TD	INT/Adj	FUM	ASR	NY/P	Rk	DVOA	Rk	DYAR	Rk	YAR	Runs	Yds	TD	DVOA	DYAR	QBR
2017	NYJ		522	297	56.9%	3519	15		19	9		5.7		-21.8%					39	59	1	-19.0%		

Hackenberg entered the NFL with a dismal QBASE projection that gave him an over 80 percent chance of being a bust, and so far has done little to prove that projection wrong. In two preseason games last year, Hackenberg went 17-of-47 for 159 yards (36 percent completion rate, 3.4 yards per pass) with one touchdown, two interceptions, one sack, and one fumble. As Ryan Fitzpatrick, Geno Smith, and Bryce Petty all struggled with poor play and injuries, never once was there any suggestion that Hackenberg would see the field, a damning indictment of his capabilities of running an NFL offense. In offseason practices this year, Hackenberg showed a penchant for drilling reporters with errant passes. The significance of that was overblown—incomplete sideline routes have to land somewhere, after all—but it's certainly not a good sign. Latest reports had Hackenberg narrowly ahead of Petty and behind Josh McCown in the Jets' wretched quarterback derby, but before the year is done he is likely to get a chance to show what he can do, for better or worse.

Chad Henne

Height: 6-2   Weight: 230   College: Michigan   Draft: 2008/2 (57)   Born: 2-Jul-1985   Age: 32   Risk: Green

Year	Team	G/GS	Snaps	Att	Comp	C%	Yds	TD	INT/Adj	FUM	ASR	NY/P	Rk	DVOA	Rk	DYAR	Rk	YAR	Runs	Yds	TD	DVOA	DYAR	QBR
2014	JAC	3/3	141	78	42	53.8%	492	3	1/2	1	16.2%	4.2	--	-54.3%	--	-249	--	-210	4	25	0	38.3%	10	16.1
2016	JAC	1/0	1	0	0	0.0%	0	0	0/0	--	--	--	--	--	--	--	--	--	1	-2	0	--	--	--
2017	JAC			561	323	57.7%	3457	19		17	6		5.0		-21.1%					33	114	0	-2.2%		

San Diego once parlayed four years of not letting Charlie Whitehurst throw a pass into acquiring a third-round pick and a 20-spot upgrade for their second-round pick. Alas, the Jaguars are two more seasons of not letting Henne play away from that point, plus Henne has actual NFL tape in the past and the Whitehurst situation could only happen with a young player and special late CBA rules, so we've seen through your clever move Dave Caldwell! If the Jaguars bench Bortles at the end of a lost season, it would likely be the much younger third-stringer Brandon Allen rather than Henne who gets the work.

Kevin Hogan

Height: 6-3   Weight: 218   College: Stanford   Draft: 2016/5 (162)   Born: 20-Oct-1992   Age: 25   Risk: Green

Year	Team	G/GS	Snaps	Att	Comp	C%	Yds	TD	INT/Adj	FUM	ASR	NY/P	Rk	DVOA	Rk	DYAR	Rk	YAR	Runs	Yds	TD	DVOA	DYAR	QBR
2016	CLE	4/0	50	26	14	53.8%	104	0	2/2	0	7.8%	3.4	--	-86.2%	--	-131	--	-133	8	105	1	108.2%	45	70.3
2017	CLE			500	272	54.5%	3046	16		21	10		5.1		-32.3%					91	440	5	15.3%		

2016: 62% Short   33% Mid   5% Deep   0% Bomb   YAC: 3.8 (--)   ALEX: 2.5

Only two players managed five runs of 15 yards or more in a single game last season: Carlos Hyde in Week 14 against the Jets, and Hogan, who pulled it off in Week 7 against Cincinnati, in a game where he didn't start and he played fewer than 70 percent of Cleveland's offensive snaps. Part of that outburst was due to Hogan's own athleticism—he had two scrambles for 35 yards, including a 28-yard touchdown—but mostly it looked like the Bengals were caught totally off guard that a Caucasian quarterback would ever keep the ball on an option play. On passing plays, Hogan showed why the Chiefs (who originally drafted him) had waived him before the season, and he played only six offensive snaps the rest of the year. Given the sorry state of Cleveland's offense, it's a little surprising Hogan and the option never appeared again. But he remains on the Browns roster, so there's always hope for 2017.

Brian Hoyer | Height: 6-2 | Weight: 215 | College: Michigan State | Draft: 2009/FA | Born: 13-Oct-1985 | Age: 32 | Risk: Red

Year	Team	G/GS	Snaps	Att	Comp	C%	Yds	TD	INT/Adj	FUM	ASR	NY/P	Rk	DVOA	Rk	DYAR	Rk	YAR	Runs	Yds	TD	DVOA	DYAR	QBR
2014	CLE	14/13	911	438	242	55.3%	3326	12	13/20	4	5.4%	6.8	10	-5.3%	25	166	24	255	24	39	0	-64.8%	-59	43.1
2015	HOU	11/9	674	369	224	60.7%	2606	19	7/6	6	7.5%	6.1	26	-3.0%	20	201	20	372	15	44	0	57.9%	26	59.6
2016	CHI	6/5	314	200	134	67.0%	1445	6	0/0	3	2.5%	7.1	6	19.4%	7	404	18	506	7	-2	0	-47.9%	-3	61.1
2017	SF			547	348	63.6%	3739	20	14	9		5.7		-14.8%					29	59	1	-10.4%		

| 2015: | 44% Short | 37% Mid | 11% Deep | 7% Bomb | YAC: 4.2 (36) | ALEX: 2.5 | 2016: | 51% Short | 30% Mid | 15% Deep | 5% Bomb | YAC: 5.2 (11) | ALEX: 1.3 |

Not only did Hoyer have zero interceptions in 200 attempts but Cian Fahey's *Pre-Snap Reads QB Catalogue* charting only charged him with four interceptable passes all season, none of which were dropped or otherwise misplayed by the defense. That is *not* sustainable, although it's notable that Hoyer's adjusted interception rate was second-best in the league in 2015 (1.6 percent) before he threw four interceptions in the playoff loss to the Chiefs. His interception rate was much higher—and his completion rate much lower—in his one previous season with Kyle Shanahan in Cleveland in 2014. This is in part because Shanahan asks his quarterbacks to throw much deeper than Hoyer did in Houston or Chicago. Hoyer averaged 10.4 air yards with Shanahan in Cleveland, third-highest in the league. He averaged just 8.0 air yards in 2016. The problem there is that Hoyer doesn't have the physical tools to be a deep-ball quarterback; he tends to float passes or miss his intended targets completely. Again, from the *PSR QB Catalogue*, Hoyer was one of the league's 10 most accurate quarterbacks when throwing short, but dropped to the bottom 10 when throwing deep passes or bombs.

Brett Hundley | Height: 6-3 | Weight: 226 | College: UCLA | Draft: 2015/5 (147) | Born: 15-Jun-1993 | Age: 24 | Risk: Yellow

Year	Team	G/GS	Snaps	Att	Comp	C%	Yds	TD	INT/Adj	FUM	ASR	NY/P	Rk	DVOA	Rk	DYAR	Rk	YAR	Runs	Yds	TD	DVOA	DYAR	QBR
2016	GB	4/0	22	10	2	20.0%	17	0	1/0	1	0.0%	1.7	--	-109.2%	--	-80	--	-75	3	-2	0	--	--	6.3
2017	GB			540	330	61.2%	3876	24	17	9		6.3		-2.7%					74	286	2	8.9%		

| | | | | | | | | | | | 2016: | 30% Short | 50% Mid | 10% Deep | 10% Bomb | YAC: 6.5 (--) | ALEX: 5.7 |

Brett Hundley will be just 24 years old entering his third season as the Green Bay Packers backup quarterback, and he is largely unchallenged for his position. Typically such a young player isn't guaranteed his spot the way the Packers have guaranteed Hundley his. That is a reflection on how high the franchise is on him. Hundley obviously won't take over the starting spot in Green Bay. He will only play if Rodgers is injured or, like last year, if the Packers need someone to take snaps in garbage time. But once he hits free agency, he will likely be given an opportunity to compete somewhere.

Cardale Jones | Height: 6-5 | Weight: 253 | College: Ohio State | Draft: 2016/4 (139) | Born: 29-Sep-1992 | Age: 25 | Risk: Yellow

Year	Team	G/GS	Snaps	Att	Comp	C%	Yds	TD	INT/Adj	FUM	ASR	NY/P	Rk	DVOA	Rk	DYAR	Rk	YAR	Runs	Yds	TD	DVOA	DYAR	QBR
2016	BUF	1/0	19	11	6	54.5%	96	0	1/1	0	9.9%	7.8	--	-84.6%	--	-62	--	-46	1	-1	0	-94.8%	-5	18.5
2017	BUF			483	290	60.0%	3181	22	17	11		5.6		-18.7%					86	472	4	20.9%		

| | | | | | | | | | | | 2016: | 27% Short | 64% Mid | 0% Deep | 9% Bomb | YAC: 4.2 (--) | ALEX: 5.0 |

Once seen as a potential No. 1 overall pick, the linebacker-sized Jones is facing an uphill climb simply to sustain employment. The buzz over the summer suggests that the 2016 fourth-rounder may have a difficult time making Buffalo's 53-man roster. With Tyrod Taylor and rookie Nathan Peterman likely locks, Jones will have to beat out veteran T.J. Yates, who already has familiarity with new offensive coordinator Rick Dennison's system after playing under Dennison from 2011 to 2013 in Houston. Given the new regime's ambivalence towards Taylor despite his relatively productive stretch as a starter, a mid-round Rex Ryan selection likely won't get much benefit of the doubt this preseason. Hopefully Jones played some school in addition to football at Ohio State.

Landry Jones

Height: 6-4   Weight: 218   College: Oklahoma   Draft: 2013/4 (115)   Born: 4-Apr-1989   Age: 28   Risk: Green

Year	Team	G/GS	Snaps	Att	Comp	C%	Yds	TD	INT/Adj	FUM	ASR	NY/P	Rk	DVOA	Rk	DYAR	Rk	YAR	Runs	Yds	TD	DVOA	DYAR	QBR
2015	PIT	7/2	109	55	32	58.2%	513	3	4/4	1	3.1%	8.7	--	-1.5%	--	37	--	-12	5	-5	0	--	--	35.9
2016	PIT	8/2	161	86	53	61.6%	558	4	2/3	0	4.9%	5.9	--	-13.7%	--	-14	--	46	6	-4	0	--	--	46.6
2017	PIT			553	337	61.0%	3883	25	19	8		6.7		4.9%					44	23	1	-25.0%		

2015:	45% Short	25% Mid	19% Deep	11% Bomb	YAC: 8.8 (--)	ALEX: -3.4	2016:	47% Short	29% Mid	14% Deep	9% Bomb	YAC: 4.6 (--)	ALEX: 1.9

Jones re-signed with the Steelers in March, but then Pittsburgh drafted Joshua Dobbs in the fourth round, which means Jones' job as Ben Roethlisberger's backup (an important job, given Roethlisberger's injury history) is far from guaranteed. Jones has had troubles with consistency and ball security, but he has also been explosive—a career average of 7.6 yards per pass is nothing to sneeze at, even in a tiny sample size of 141 passes.

Colin Kaepernick

Height: 6-5   Weight: 233   College: Nevada   Draft: 2011/2 (36)   Born: 3-Nov-1987   Age: 30   Risk: N/A

Year	Team	G/GS	Snaps	Att	Comp	C%	Yds	TD	INT/Adj	FUM	ASR	NY/P	Rk	DVOA	Rk	DYAR	Rk	YAR	Runs	Yds	TD	DVOA	DYAR	QBR
2014	SF	16/16	1049	478	289	60.5%	3369	19	10/12	8	9.9%	5.7	34	-8.4%	28	91	27	176	104	639	1	7.5%	88	55.9
2015	SF	9/8	504	244	144	59.0%	1615	6	5/8	5	10.3%	5.3	36	-21.5%	34	-182	35	-249	45	256	1	22.7%	63	47.1
2016	SF	12/11	690	331	196	59.2%	2241	16	4/7	9	9.7%	5.6	32	-17.5%	30	-145	29	-99	69	468	2	31.9%	134	55.2

2015:	59% Short	23% Mid	8% Deep	10% Bomb	YAC: 5.8 (9)	ALEX: 0.6	2016:	46% Short	37% Mid	14% Deep	4% Bomb	YAC: 5.7 (5)	ALEX: 0.4

In 2016, Kaepernick had the NFL's highest passing DVOA in the red zone (78.8%). He led all quarterbacks in rushing value, despite only playing in 12 games. He made significant strides as a pocket passer. He did all this with his three leading wide receivers each finishing in the bottom five of DYAR. He was given the Len Eshmont Award for inspirational and courageous play, San Francisco's most prestigious annual honor, voted on by his teammates. None of that means Kaepernick is an above-average quarterback, or that he should be handed a starting job somewhere. But when Josh McCown is a starting quarterback, and Trevone Boykin, Sean Mannion, and Jake Rudock are No. 2s, it is exceedingly difficult to come up with a justifiable reason why Kaepernick remains unsigned.

There are 144 quarterbacks in NFL history who threw at least 200 passes at age 29. If Kaepernick remains a free agent through the rest of the season, he will become only the second quarterback in that group to not appear on an NFL roster in his age-30 season. And the other was a very different case: Bobby Hebert, who sat out 1990 in a contract holdout and returned as the New Orleans starter in 1991.

Case Keenum

Height: 6-2   Weight: 209   College: Houston   Draft: 2012/FA   Born: 17-Feb-1988   Age: 29   Risk: Yellow

Year	Team	G/GS	Snaps	Att	Comp	C%	Yds	TD	INT/Adj	FUM	ASR	NY/P	Rk	DVOA	Rk	DYAR	Rk	YAR	Runs	Yds	TD	DVOA	DYAR	QBR
2014	2TM	2/2	165	77	45	58.4%	435	2	2/2	1	2.8%	5.3	--	-20.8%	--	-50	--	-43	10	35	0	4.3%	9	43.7
2015	STL	6/5	297	125	76	60.8%	828	4	1/4	3	3.1%	6.2	--	-1.1%	--	83	--	144	12	5	0	-70.7%	-17	47.7
2016	LARM	10/9	596	322	196	60.9%	2201	9	11/10	5	6.3%	6.0	26	-19.5%	31	-183	31	-174	20	51	1	22.2%	25	43.4
2017	MIN			565	341	60.4%	3792	22	19	7		5.9		-9.9%					56	149	0	-17.0%		

2015:	50% Short	31% Mid	7% Deep	11% Bomb	YAC: 5.3 (--)	ALEX: 0.2	2016:	53% Short	29% Mid	10% Deep	7% Bomb	YAC: 5.3 (8)	ALEX: 0.7

Case Keenum can feel somewhat aggrieved about last season. He was always going to be replaced by Jared Goff, but the assumption was that Goff would play well enough to take the job from him. In truth, Goff was given the job and was worse than Keenum had been. Keenum isn't worthy of a starting spot in the NFL, but his play has been more than good enough to justify a roster spot. Limited arm strength means Keenum would need an elite ability to diagnose coverages to be a starter. He doesn't have that, but he is smart enough to avoid completely shutting down the passing game when he plays.

Cody Kessler

Height: 6-1   Weight: 220   College: USC   Draft: 2016/3 (93)   Born: 11-Apr-1993   Age: 24   Risk: Red

Year	Team	G/GS	Snaps	Att	Comp	C%	Yds	TD	INT/Adj	FUM	ASR	NY/P	Rk	DVOA	Rk	DYAR	Rk	YAR	Runs	Yds	TD	DVOA	DYAR	QBR
2016	CLE	9/8	349	195	128	65.6%	1380	6	2/3	4	9.7%	5.8	29	-7.6%	22	50	24	80	11	18	0	-37.1%	-9	49.6
2017	CLE			557	364	65.3%	3975	20	13	10		6.0		-4.7%					34	88	1	-5.5%		

				2016:	47% Short	36% Mid	12% Deep	6% Bomb	YAC: 5.0 (21)	ALEX: -0.8

You can forgive Browns fans for being overly excited about Kessler's rookie campaign. By DVOA, it was the best season a Browns quarterback has had since Colt McCoy's rookie year in 2010, and among the top five seasons in Cleveland since the franchise returned in to the city in 1999. So be nice. Let them enjoy Kessler's decision-making and ability to exploit defensive mistakes (8.8 yards per play on play-action, nearly a full yard better than average), and don't point out how badly he struggled in obvious passing situations (5.2 net yards per pass without play-action, a full yard worse than average). Kessler enters training camp as a slight favorite in Cleveland's quarterback battle royale, but the ceiling looks pretty low here. Don't be surprised if a passer with more upside is taking snaps by the end of the year.

DeShone Kizer

| | | Height: 6-4 | | | Weight: 233 | | | College: Notre Dame | | | Draft: 2017/2 (52) | | Born: 3-Jan-1996 | | Age: 22 | | | Risk: Yellow |

Year	Team	G/GS	Snaps	Att	Comp	C%	Yds	TD	INT/Adj	FUM	ASR	NY/P	Rk	DVOA	Rk	DYAR	Rk	YAR	Runs	Yds	TD	DVOA	DYAR	QBR
2017	CLE		513	309		60.3%	3575	18	17	9		6.2		-12.5%					90	321	4	-0.6%		

Kizer is one of the more difficult quarterbacks to forecast in this year's draft class. He's big, with a strong arm, and plenty of college production. In two years at Notre Dame, he threw for 47 touchdowns and ran for 18 more. But he declined as a junior, completing less than 60 percent of his passes, and his overall numbers were inflated by a weak set of opposing defenses. He was also benched sporadically for Malik Zaire, though he never lost his starting job. Kizer is a year younger than either Patrick Mahomes or Deshaun Watson, and two years younger than Mitchell Trubisky, and has a lot of room for growth. But he may well be the best quarterback on Cleveland's roster right now, and Hue Jackson won't hesitate to play him if that's the case

Andrew Luck

| | | Height: 6-4 | | | Weight: 234 | | | College: Stanford | | | Draft: 2012/1 (1) | | Born: 12-Mar-1989 | | Age: 28 | | | Risk: Yellow |

Year	Team	G/GS	Snaps	Att	Comp	C%	Yds	TD	INT/Adj	FUM	ASR	NY/P	Rk	DVOA	Rk	DYAR	Rk	YAR	Runs	Yds	TD	DVOA	DYAR	QBR
2014	IND	16/16	1072	616	380	61.7%	4761	40	16/21	13	4.8%	7.1	7	9.2%	10	879	10	829	64	273	3	4.4%	40	63.8
2015	IND	7/7	508	293	162	55.3%	1881	15	12/16	3	5.4%	5.8	30	-17.5%	32	-126	33	-189	33	196	0	31.2%	59	47.6
2016	IND	15/15	1013	545	346	63.5%	4240	31	13/13	6	7.6%	6.8	10	7.3%	13	719	11	671	64	341	2	26.2%	93	71.2
2017	IND		592	380		64.1%	4540	34	14	5		6.7		9.6%					51	256	1	24.7%		
2015:	41% Short		34% Mid		16% Deep			9% Bomb		YAC: 4.3 (35)		ALEX: 2.5		2016:	47% Short		32% Mid		14% Deep		7% Bomb	YAC: 4.9 (22)	ALEX: 1.5

Coming up with negatives about Andrew Luck is like trying to name the most irredeemable character on *Game of Thrones*, but here are a couple. 1) He throws quite a few interceptable passes. Way more than Peyton Manning in his prime did, though certainly not an unacceptable amount. 2) He throws his body around a bit too much. He almost cost the Colts a game against Tennessee in Week 10 with a 3-for-12 second-half performance where he threw for 76 yards and was picked once and sacked twice. After the game he immediately went into concussion protocol, and given how great he is when he's on, it sure seems likely he was not his full self in those last two quarters. As long as Luck is cleared from offseason labrum surgery, it should be another stellar year of covering Ryan Grigson, Chuck Pagano, and Jim Irsay like a cat in a litter box.

Paxton Lynch

| | | Height: 6-7 | | | Weight: 244 | | | College: Memphis | | | Draft: 2016/1 (26) | | Born: 12-Feb-1994 | | Age: 23 | | | Risk: Red |

Year	Team	G/GS	Snaps	Att	Comp	C%	Yds	TD	INT/Adj	FUM	ASR	NY/P	Rk	DVOA	Rk	DYAR	Rk	YAR	Runs	Yds	TD	DVOA	DYAR	QBR
2016	DEN	3/2	176	83	49	59.0%	497	2	1/2	2	10.2%	5.0	--	-18.8%	--	-46	--	-57	11	25	0	-43.0%	-12	28.8
2017	DEN		554	321		57.9%	3755	19	15	11		5.8		-17.8%					61	270	1	-4.7%		
														2016:	38% Short		37% Mid		12% Deep		12% Bomb	YAC: 3.2 (--)	ALEX: 3.0

We covered a lot of Lynch's statistics, which are from a small sample size in 2016, in the Denver chapter. One area we did not touch on was YAC, or the adjusted figures we come up with for YAC+. An area of concern in Lynch's college scouting report was that his inaccuracy with ball placement would limit YAC for his receivers, an issue which did crop up during his three rookie year appearances. Denver's offense already had YAC issues in 2015, but with Trevor Siemian last year, the Broncos ranked 12th in YAC+ (plus-0.1). With Lynch, Denver's YAC+ was minus-1.3, which is the worst average for any quarterback with at least 50 passes last season. YAC is still mostly a receiver skill, and it hurts the numbers if Demaryius Thomas doesn't have one of his bubble screens go 80 yards for a touchdown, but this is something to keep an eye on if Lynch ends up starting for the Broncos in 2017.

Patrick Mahomes Height: 6-2   Weight: 225   College: Texas Tech   Draft: 2017/1 (10)   Born: 17-Sep-1995   Age: 22   Risk: Red

Year	Team	G/GS	Snaps	Att	Comp	C%	Yds	TD	INT/Adj	FUM	ASR	NY/P	Rk	DVOA	Rk	DYAR	Rk	YAR	Runs	Yds	TD	DVOA	DYAR	QBR
2017	KC			524	322	61.4%	3759	22	15	8		6.5		-3.5%					69	205	2	-0.6%		

The Anti-Alex should be an interesting quarterback to watch when he gets his chance. In using air yards data from ESPN Stats & Info, we found that Mahomes' 2016 ALEX on third down was plus-4.2, the type of number that would lead the NFL in most seasons. He's an aggressive playmaker, but still avoided interceptions fairly well despite the number of shootouts in which he was involved at Texas Tech. Mahomes had only one game in college with more than two interceptions.

Even if most high draft picks had good win-loss records in the NCAA, the knock on Mahomes' 13-16 record as a college starter is misguided. According to ESPN, Mahomes' QBR in wins (80.8) was barely higher than it was in losses (79.0). Texas Tech allowed an FBS-worst 43.5 points per game in 2016, and things weren't any better in 2015 when the Red Raiders allowed 43.6 points per game (ranked 125th out of 128 teams). In Mahomes' 29 starts, he led Texas Tech to an average of 42.5 points, but the team allowed 42.9 points per game. In the 16 losses, Mahomes led a scoring average of 35.6 points per game, but the team allowed 52.8 points per game. Mahomes was 0-10 when Tech allowed more than 45 points, but how absurd is that anyway? The Chiefs have allowed more than 45 points six times in franchise history. The kid will have a real defense in the NFL, perhaps one of the best in the league by the time he takes over.

Ryan Mallett Height: 6-7   Weight: 253   College: Arkansas   Draft: 2011/3 (74)   Born: 5-Jun-1988   Age: 29   Risk: Yellow

Year	Team	G/GS	Snaps	Att	Comp	C%	Yds	TD	INT/Adj	FUM	ASR	NY/P	Rk	DVOA	Rk	DYAR	Rk	YAR	Runs	Yds	TD	DVOA	DYAR	QBR
2014	HOU	3/2	157	75	41	54.7%	400	2	2/5	0	3.6%	5.3	--	14.5%	--	120	--	37	6	-2	0	31.6%	6	48.2
2015	2TM	8/6	421	244	136	55.7%	1336	5	6/10	0	3.0%	5.2	37	-12.3%	28	-19	28	-113	5	15	1	17.2%	8	55.1
2016	BAL	4/0	23	6	3	50.0%	26	0	1/1	0	0.7%	4.3	--	-84.9%	--	-29	--	-34	5	-6	0	--	--	4.7
2017	BAL			621	351	56.5%	3703	20	18	7		5.2		-21.7%					35	20	0	-25.0%		

| 2015: | 41% Short | 42% Mid | 12% Deep | 5% Bomb | YAC: 3.5 (37) | ALEX: -0.1 | 2016: | 67% Short | 0% Mid | 17% Deep | 17% Bomb | YAC: 6.3 (--) | ALEX: -4.5 |

Mallett has an arm to dream on and a head that's too busy sleeping in to use it. Luckily for him, he has not made any political statements that run counter to the general NFL sentiment, so he can continue to languish on the bench behind Joe Flacco. In a situation where a savvy team might have brought in competition for Flacco, the Ravens have instead given him such a low bar to clear that it's almost impossible for him to fail.

Eli Manning Height: 6-4   Weight: 218   College: Mississippi   Draft: 2004/1 (1)   Born: 3-Jan-1981   Age: 37   Risk: Red

Year	Team	G/GS	Snaps	Att	Comp	C%	Yds	TD	INT/Adj	FUM	ASR	NY/P	Rk	DVOA	Rk	DYAR	Rk	YAR	Runs	Yds	TD	DVOA	DYAR	QBR
2014	NYG	16/16	1109	601	379	63.1%	4410	30	14/20	7	4.7%	6.7	14	4.6%	15	642	11	735	12	31	1	41.3%	18	70.9
2015	NYG	16/16	1106	618	387	62.6%	4432	35	14/15	11	5.2%	6.6	13	-1.9%	19	404	18	535	20	61	0	-0.4%	5	60.5
2016	NYG	16/16	1061	598	377	63.0%	4027	26	16/26	7	3.8%	6.3	20	-6.5%	20	188	20	192	21	-9	0	-12.5%	0	51.8
2017	NYG			602	379	63.0%	4218	29	15	8		6.4		0.4%					21	21	0	-20.2%		

| 2015: | 50% Short | 34% Mid | 9% Deep | 7% Bomb | YAC: 5.4 (18) | ALEX: 1.1 | 2016: | 52% Short | 31% Mid | 9% Deep | 8% Bomb | YAC: 5.3 (9) | ALEX: 2.9 |

Manning produced six multi-interception games last season, and now has 23 of them in the last five years. A film review of Manning's 2016 interceptions reveals lots of examples of inexperienced receivers or terrible tight ends falling down, not fighting for contested passes, or just getting slants ripped from their hands by defenders. But there are also plenty of forced throws and short passes undercut by defenders Manning should have seen. And of course every quarterback suffers a few interceptions that were not his fault.

Manning's career 3.2 percent interception rate is much higher than those of his peers. Big Brother checked in at 2.7 percent even after his final-season debacle. Ben Roethlisberger is also at 2.7 percent; Philip Rivers, 2.6 percent; Joe Flacco and Drew Brees at 2.5 percent; and Tom Brady and Aaron Rodgers in rarified air at 1.8 percent and 1.5 percent. Contemporaries in Eli's neighborhood include Chad Henne (3.2 percent), Jay Cutler (3.3 percent), Josh McCown (3.3 percent), and Ryan Fitzpatrick (3.4 percent). Brett Favre also checks in at 3.2 percent, but interception rates have gradually declined since Favre's prime years.

Manning always occupied his own space: not good enough to be counted among Big Brother and his pals, but far too good to slum around with the Fitzpatricks of the world. The question now is whether he will age like an all-time great or succumb to the turnovers that derive from athletic decline like a mortal quarterback. The Giants have built their receiving corps to support the former, but a line and backfield which could hasten the latter.

Sean Mannion

Height: 6-6 | Weight: 229 | College: Oregon State | Draft: 2015/3 (89) | Born: 23-Apr-1992 | Age: 25 | Risk: Red

Year	Team	G/GS	Snaps	Att	Comp	C%	Yds	TD	INT/Adj	FUM	ASR	NY/P	Rk	DVOA	Rk	DYAR	Rk	YAR	Runs	Yds	TD	DVOA	DYAR	QBR
2015	STL	1/0	7	7	6	85.7%	31	0	0/0	0	-0.6%	4.4	--	4.3%	--	7	--	4	0	0	0	--	--	92.4
2016	LARM	1/0	16	6	3	50.0%	19	0	1/1	1	0.0%	3.2	--	-108.8%	--	-45	--	-53	1	-1	0	-373.2%	-20	0.4
2017	LARM			501	302	60.2%	3352	14	16	9		5.5		-17.5%					22	47	1	-7.3%		

| 2015: | 71% Short | 29% Mid | 0% Deep | 0% Bomb | YAC: 1.8 (--) | ALEX: -5.0 | 2016: | 86% Short | 0% Mid | 14% Deep | 0% Bomb | YAC: 4.7 (--) | ALEX: -6.0 |

In two seasons with the Rams, Mannion has played in one game per season and attempted a total of 13 passes. If the Rams were not so invested in Jared Goff's success, Mannion likely would have had a chance to win the starting job in an open competition at some point. But with Los Angeles betting it all on Goff, Mannion's only opportunity to play last year came in a Week 17 blowout loss to the Cardinals. He's a very prototypical quarterback from an earlier generation: big body, big arm, no mobility whatsoever. Mannion enters 2017 as Goff's primary backup, but he could get a chance to prove himself if Goff continues to perform at a historically bad level.

EJ Manuel

Height: 6-5 | Weight: 240 | College: Florida State | Draft: 2013/1 (16) | Born: 19-Mar-1990 | Age: 27 | Risk: Green

Year	Team	G/GS	Snaps	Att	Comp	C%	Yds	TD	INT/Adj	FUM	ASR	NY/P	Rk	DVOA	Rk	DYAR	Rk	YAR	Runs	Yds	TD	DVOA	DYAR	QBR
2014	BUF	5/4	259	131	76	58.0%	838	5	3/3	1	5.5%	5.8	--	-17.1%	--	-53	--	-36	16	52	1	-26.3%	-10	19.8
2015	BUF	7/2	155	84	52	61.9%	561	3	3/5	2	8.1%	5.7	--	-16.0%	--	-26	--	-12	17	64	1	20.8%	34	37.0
2016	BUF	6/1	78	26	11	42.3%	131	0	0/1	2	10.8%	3.9	--	-47.2%	--	-58	--	-22	8	22	0	-55.2%	-17	29.3
2017	OAK			567	345	60.8%	3767	20	13	12		5.7		-10.4%					54	175	2	0.3%		

| 2015: | 38% Short | 38% Mid | 14% Deep | 9% Bomb | YAC: 3.2 (--) | ALEX: 0.2 | 2016: | 26% Short | 48% Mid | 19% Deep | 7% Bomb | YAC: 2.5 (--) | ALEX: 4.5 |

After last season's disastrous ending, the Raiders needed some extra veteran insurance at quarterback. Manuel comes over after four years of failure in Buffalo. There's nothing he does particularly well, but he would have a much better collection of talent around him should he have to start any games for the Raiders. Based on the last four years, let's hope it does not come to that.

Marcus Mariota

Height: 6-4 | Weight: 222 | College: Oregon | Draft: 2015/1 (2) | Born: 30-Oct-1993 | Age: 24 | Risk: Red

Year	Team	G/GS	Snaps	Att	Comp	C%	Yds	TD	INT/Adj	FUM	ASR	NY/P	Rk	DVOA	Rk	DYAR	Rk	YAR	Runs	Yds	TD	DVOA	DYAR	QBR
2015	TEN	12/12	736	370	230	62.2%	2818	19	10/14	10	10.1%	6.3	17	-13.2%	29	-53	30	123	34	252	2	-0.6%	20	61.0
2016	TEN	15/15	963	451	276	61.2%	3426	26	9/11	8	5.4%	7.0	9	11.1%	10	681	13	719	60	349	2	9.5%	52	64.9
2017	TEN			502	314	62.5%	3897	27	11	10		7.0		8.0%					69	380	3	28.2%		

| 2015: | 38% Short | 40% Mid | 17% Deep | 5% Bomb | YAC: 5.1 (25) | ALEX: 1.3 | 2016: | 37% Short | 38% Mid | 16% Deep | 9% Bomb | YAC: 4.6 (29) | ALEX: 2.4 |

Onward and upward is the expected course of development for second-year NFL players after promising rookie seasons, and onward and upward indeed was the course Mariota took. He showed clear improvement from his rookie season in multiple areas. One area that stood out was showing off the ability to manipulate defenders with his eyes, freezing them to create passing lanes for receivers. His deep ball was improved, though room for further improvement remains. The mediocre YAC numbers are much more a reflection of the offense and the receivers than Mariota's accuracy. The upgrades in the receiving corps should help those numbers some, and Corey Davis quickly becoming a ball-winning perimeter receiver would give Mariota an option he badly needed in some situations last year. The broken leg that ended his season late in Week 16 kept him out of most off-season work, but he participated in OTAs and minicamp and should be a full go by training camp. As a fast rather than elusive runner, even the ankle ligament damage should not have too much of an effect on his game barring a significant setback. Unless the Titans run game or defense dramatically worsens, though, do not expect much increase in his volume stats.

AJ McCarron

Height: 6-3 | Weight: 220 | College: Alabama | Draft: 2014/5 (164) | Born: 13-Sep-1990 | Age: 27 | Risk: Red

Year	Team	G/GS	Snaps	Att	Comp	C%	Yds	TD	INT/Adj	FUM	ASR	NY/P	Rk	DVOA	Rk	DYAR	Rk	YAR	Runs	Yds	TD	DVOA	DYAR	QBR
2015	CIN	7/3	257	119	79	66.4%	854	6	2/2	1	8.5%	6.0	--	6.9%	--	151	--	138	14	31	0	-8.2%	2	64.4
2016	CIN	1/0	2	0	0	0.0%	0	0	0/0	--	--	--	--	--	--	--	--	--	0	0	0	--	--	--
2017	CIN			544	335	61.7%	3718	23	16	8		5.8		-12.7%					52	161	1	-6.1%		

| 2015: | 50% Short | 25% Mid | 17% Deep | 8% Bomb | YAC: 4.0 (--) | ALEX: 3.3 |

The Bengals played footsie with trading McCarron this offseason, but never found anyone willing to pay the reported second-round price. It's just as well, because what McCarron showed most in his 2015 playing time is that the Bengals had a lot of good skill position players around him. Still, he's got the right size and pedigree to be some team's Mike Glennon. His free agency status is somewhat up for grabs, as the Bengals believe he didn't accrue a year of service during a 2014 season when he spent all but three weeks on the NFI list. "That's for the lawyers," McCarron said via NFL.com.

Josh McCown

Height: 6-4   Weight: 215   College: Sam Houston State   Draft: 2002/3 (81)   Born: 4-Jul-1979   Age: 38   Risk: Red

Year	Team	G/GS	Snaps	Att	Comp	C%	Yds	TD	INT/Adj	FUM	ASR	NY/P	Rk	DVOA	Rk	DYAR	Rk	YAR	Runs	Yds	TD	DVOA	DYAR	QBR
2014	TB	11/11	630	327	184	56.3%	2206	11	14/13	10	10.4%	5.5	35	-41.9%	37	-665	36	-576	25	127	3	35.9%	47	35.7
2015	CLE	8/8	509	292	186	63.7%	2109	12	4/5	9	7.1%	6.2	23	-5.8%	23	110	23	81	20	98	1	0.7%	12	53.9
2016	CLE	5/3	262	165	90	54.5%	1100	6	6/10	7	10.5%	5.3	--	-34.4%	--	-269	--	-276	7	21	0	-37.8%	-6	35.1
2017	NYJ			544	316	58.1%	3562	15	17	15		5.3		-24.1%					39	113	0	-11.7%		

2015: 51% Short 33% Mid 11% Deep 5% Bomb YAC: 5.5 (17) ALEX: 2.7   2016: 43% Short 36% Mid 9% Deep 13% Bomb YAC: 5.2 (--) ALEX: 2.8

"Quarterback wins" are not exactly a popular statistic in the Football Outsiders universe. Writers and readers alike realize that they don't account for each quarterback's situation, and can be wildly inaccurate in the short term. Drew Brees, for example, has won just seven games in each of the past three years. That sounds like the record of a mediocre quarterback, not a passer who is still one of the best in the game. In the long term, though, both luck and defense tend to even out, and quarterback wins become a much more reliable measurement. Since he was drafted in 2001, Brees has won 131 games, more than anyone except Tom Brady and Peyton Manning. That's a very reasonable description of Brees' place in this era of the NFL.

Which brings us to Josh McCown. McCown was drafted in 2002, one year after Brees. In the 15 NFL seasons since, McCown has started and won a total of 18 regular-season games. That's at least ten fewer wins in the same time frame than either Jake Plummer, Drew Bledsoe, or Aaron Brooks, none of whom has played since 2006. It's four fewer than Derek Carr, who was drafted in 2014. And it's not even half as many as former Jets Mark Sanchez and Ryan Fitzpatrick. Neither of those quarterbacks will be remembered fondly in New York, but in all likelihood, McCown will fail to meet even those low standards for success.

McCown enters the season with minus-1,331 career passing DYAR, third-worst since 1989 behind Ryan Leaf (minus-1,388) and Blaine Gabbert (minus-1,928). McCown needs about minus-600 DYAR to pass Gabbert as the Worst Quarterback of the DVOA Era, and as you can see in the table, he has done that before. It would also help if Gabbert had a big year in Arizona, but that would be an even bigger miracle than McCown playing well in New York. Frankly, it's a mystery why either of these men is still in the league.

Colt McCoy

Height: 6-1   Weight: 216   College: Texas   Draft: 2010/3 (85)   Born: 5-Sep-1986   Age: 31   Risk: Yellow

Year	Team	G/GS	Snaps	Att	Comp	C%	Yds	TD	INT/Adj	FUM	ASR	NY/P	Rk	DVOA	Rk	DYAR	Rk	YAR	Runs	Yds	TD	DVOA	DYAR	QBR
2014	WAS	5/4	240	128	91	71.1%	1057	4	3/4	6	11.8%	6.5	--	-15.9%	--	-43	--	-9	16	66	1	-33.0%	-13	46.1
2015	WAS	2/0	44	11	7	63.6%	128	1	0/0	1	7.9%	9.5	--	20.9%	--	22	--	14	3	-3	0	--	--	36.8
2017	WAS			557	375	67.4%	3905	24	15	14		5.9		-9.0%					43	130	2	-2.8%		

2015: 55% Short 27% Mid 0% Deep 18% Bomb YAC: 11.6 (--) ALEX: 1.8

Albert Breer reported for MMQB.com in March that the Redskins believed they could win with Colt McCoy as their starting quarterback. This is how the team prepares for Kirk Cousins' departure: not by acquiring real potential replacements, but by spreading gossip about how much they love the 31-year-old backup who has never enjoyed anything close to legitimate NFL success. That kind of spin doctoring will only hasten Cousins' departure by poisoning the relationship between player and team. Maybe the team should be renamed the Washington Self-Fulfilled Prophecies.

Matt McGloin

Height: 6-1   Weight: 210   College: Penn State   Draft: 2013/FA   Born: 2-Dec-1989   Age: 28   Risk: Green

Year	Team	G/GS	Snaps	Att	Comp	C%	Yds	TD	INT/Adj	FUM	ASR	NY/P	Rk	DVOA	Rk	DYAR	Rk	YAR	Runs	Yds	TD	DVOA	DYAR	QBR
2014	OAK	1/0	24	19	12	63.2%	129	1	2/1	0	4.7%	6.1	--	-54.4%	--	-58	--	-63	2	3	0	8.1%	2	10.3
2015	OAK	2/0	42	32	23	71.9%	142	2	1/1	1	6.1%	3.6	--	-21.5%	--	-26	--	-46	0	0	0	--	--	18.8
2016	OAK	3/1	39	15	8	53.3%	50	0	0/0	0	0.0%	3.3	--	-4.0%	--	6	--	-18	3	-3	0	--	--	14.5
2017	PHI			572	358	62.5%	3804	23	20	12		5.6		-20.6%					30	59	0	-19.2%		

2015: 66% Short 25% Mid 6% Deep 3% Bomb YAC: 2.8 (--) ALEX: -0.5   2016: 50% Short 25% Mid 17% Deep 8% Bomb YAC: 1.1 (--) ALEX: 0.9

McGloin managed just 15 ineffectual passes in relief of Derek Carr in Week 17 before getting knocked out of the game with a shoulder injury. McGloin was a semi-healthy scratch in the playoffs while Connor Cook bumbled through the loss to the Texans, a sign that Jack Del Rio may have been ready for a youth movement behind Carr anyway. McGloin reunites with quarterback coach John DeFilippo in Philly and has third-string job security because the Eagles have no developmental quarterback on the roster other than the one who starts every week. McGloin may be the definition of a replacement-level quarterback, but at least he has found a niche.

Kellen Moore — Height: 6-0 — Weight: 197 — College: Boise State — Draft: 2012/FA — Born: 12-Jul-1989 — Age: 28 — Risk: Green

Year	Team	G/GS	Snaps	Att	Comp	C%	Yds	TD	INT/Adj	FUM	ASR	NY/P	Rk	DVOA	Rk	DYAR	Rk	YAR	Runs	Yds	TD	DVOA	DYAR	QBR
2015	DAL	3/2	167	104	61	58.7%	779	4	6/4	1	5.4%	6.9	--	-9.7%	--	10	--	16	2	-1	0	--	--	19.0
2017	DAL		488	304		62.4%	3563	24	16	7		6.5		-4.0%					26	17	1	-23.6%		

| 2015: | 40% Short | 39% Mid | 18% Deep | 3% Bomb | YAC: 5.8 (–) | ALEX: -0.1 |

Better to remain silent and be thought a fool than open your mouth and remove all doubt. Also, better to break your leg in August and be thought a plucky journeyman backup worth keeping around than start for several months and prove you belong in a Mountain West Conference broadcast booth. Moore is nearly reaching the age when career backups get the next contract because there must have been some reason they were kept around during the last contract. It's great work if you can get it. And the Cowboys are screwed if Moore has to play in any real games.

Matt Moore — Height: 6-3 — Weight: 202 — College: Oregon State — Draft: 2007/FA — Born: 9-Aug-1984 — Age: 33 — Risk: Red

Year	Team	G/GS	Snaps	Att	Comp	C%	Yds	TD	INT/Adj	FUM	ASR	NY/P	Rk	DVOA	Rk	DYAR	Rk	YAR	Runs	Yds	TD	DVOA	DYAR	QBR
2014	MIA	2/0	30	4	2	50.0%	21	0	0/0	0	0.0%	5.3	--	28.4%	--	8	--	13	2	-2	0	--	--	72.4
2015	MIA	1/0	7	1	1	100.0%	14	0	0/0	0	-1.2%	14.0	--	340.2%	--	12	--	11	3	-2	0	--	--	98.1
2016	MIA	4/3	190	87	55	63.2%	721	8	3/5	1	2.0%	8.5	--	34.7%	--	259	--	285	1	-1	0	--	--	82.9
2017	MIA		495	307		62.1%	3611	25	16	9		6.5		-4.6%					13	25	0	-12.6%		

| 2015: | 100% Short | 0% Mid | 0% Deep | 0% Bomb | YAC: 9.0 (–) | ALEX: – | 2016: | 58% Short | 22% Mid | 11% Deep | 9% Bomb | YAC: 6.6 (–) | ALEX: 3.3 |

He only started three games, but Moore's 34.7% DVOA would have only trailed MVP Matt Ryan (39.1%). He's not actually that good. After all, Moore entered 2016 with 129 career DYAR to his name. Still, the Dolphins have one of the best backups in the league. The drop-off from starter to backup at quarterback is smaller in Miami than it is for most teams.

Cam Newton — Height: 6-5 — Weight: 248 — College: Auburn — Draft: 2011/1 (1) — Born: 11-May-1989 — Age: 28 — Risk: Yellow

Year	Team	G/GS	Snaps	Att	Comp	C%	Yds	TD	INT/Adj	FUM	ASR	NY/P	Rk	DVOA	Rk	DYAR	Rk	YAR	Runs	Yds	TD	DVOA	DYAR	QBR
2014	CAR	14/14	927	448	262	58.5%	3127	18	12/14	9	8.4%	5.9	30	-14.5%	32	-105	32	-46	103	539	5	16.3%	146	56.9
2015	CAR	16/16	1077	495	296	59.8%	3837	35	10/14	5	6.9%	6.8	11	7.6%	12	630	11	855	132	636	10	8.1%	142	66.0
2016	CAR	15/14	1023	510	270	52.9%	3509	19	14/22	3	6.8%	6.0	25	-13.0%	28	-64	28	-64	90	359	5	-12.5%	-2	53.1
2017	CAR		513	310		60.4%	3680	25	12	5		6.5		2.4%					81	410	4	25.9%		

| 2015: | 34% Short | 42% Mid | 12% Deep | 11% Bomb | YAC: 5.0 (27) | ALEX: 3.0 | 2016: | 31% Short | 47% Mid | 12% Deep | 10% Bomb | YAC: 4.9 (24) | ALEX: 3.5 |

One number among many in a horrific season stands out. After posting a sterling 45.7% passing DVOA in the red zone in 2015, Newton plummeted to -25.4% last year. Those are passing numbers only, but Newton's unwillingness to run certainly factored into that number. Regardless, it must improve for Carolina to swing the pendulum back toward a winning record. Newton also struggled mightily on second down, with a -28.6% DVOA. He averaged 8.8 yards to go, high but hardly unprecedented—Andy Dalton had the same average distance on second down, and he put up a 13.5% DVOA.

KUBIAK expects Newton to bounce back—not to the levels of his MVP season in 2015, naturally, but enough to erase the bitter taste of 2016. The addition of short-game targets like Christian McCaffrey should bump Newton's completion rate back toward the 60 percent barrier, though the soft toss is hardly Newton's long suit. Aiming smaller may also cut down on his interceptable passes—Cian Fahey counted 27 in 510 attempts last year, the fifth-worst rate in the league. His projection also sees a further diminishment in Newton's rushing production. That hurt the Panthers offense last season, but is a necessary tweak if Newton is to survive another decade in the NFL.

Brock Osweiler

Height: 6-7   Weight: 242   College: Arizona State   Draft: 2012/2 (57)   Born: 22-Nov-1990   Age: 27   Risk: Red

Year	Team	G/GS	Snaps	Att	Comp	C%	Yds	TD	INT/Adj	FUM	ASR	NY/P	Rk	DVOA	Rk	DYAR	Rk	YAR	Runs	Yds	TD	DVOA	DYAR	QBR
2014	DEN	4/0	37	10	4	40.0%	52	1	0/0	0	11.3%	4.2	--	-19.7%	--	-5	--	1	8	0	0	-85.5%	-6	10.2
2015	DEN	8/7	515	275	170	61.8%	1967	10	6/10	4	7.2%	6.1	25	-3.2%	21	153	22	140	21	61	1	-6.1%	6	48.8
2016	HOU	15/14	977	510	301	59.0%	2957	15	16/21	5	5.4%	5.2	33	-26.8%	33	-558	33	-502	30	131	2	35.5%	54	55.3
2017	CLE			563	324	57.4%	3681	20	15	9		5.3		-20.2%					26	105	1	9.2%		

2015:	43% Short	38% Mid	11% Deep	8% Bomb	YAC: 5.2 (20)	ALEX: 1.7	2016:	47% Short	35% Mid	11% Deep	7% Bomb	YAC: 3.9 (33)	ALEX: 0.6

Osweiler produced so many high-attempt, low-production games in Houston last season that we had to start naming them after him. We awarded a quarterback with an "Osweiler" whenever he threw 40 or more passes but gained fewer than 200 yards. Including the playoffs, Osweiler had four Osweilers last season. No other quarterback since 1950 has had more than two in a year. Those Osweilers also tie Osweiler with Sam Bradford for second place in the career leaderboard behind Bernie Kosar, who had five. Kosar started 115 games in his career, while Bradford has started 78. Osweiler has only started 21.

And yet, he might still start more. The 2015 version of Osweiler, one that was benched for a haggard old man with no arm, would still have been better than almost any NuBrowns quarterback outside of 2007 Derek Anderson. It wouldn't be the most shocking thing if he ended up starting for the Browns this year. If not, though, Cleveland won't hesitate to cut him, absorb his massive cap hit, and happily go on with the 2018 second-round pick they acquired when they agreed to take his massive salary.

Carson Palmer

Height: 6-5   Weight: 230   College: USC   Draft: 2003/1 (1)   Born: 27-Dec-1979   Age: 38   Risk: Yellow

Year	Team	G/GS	Snaps	Att	Comp	C%	Yds	TD	INT/Adj	FUM	ASR	NY/P	Rk	DVOA	Rk	DYAR	Rk	YAR	Runs	Yds	TD	DVOA	DYAR	QBR
2014	ARI	6/6	410	224	141	62.9%	1626	11	3/5	3	4.1%	6.7	15	8.5%	11	285	18	400	8	25	0	-94.8%	-20	64.8
2015	ARI	16/16	1039	537	342	63.7%	4671	35	11/18	6	4.9%	8.1	1	34.4%	1	1698	1	1755	25	24	1	-31.7%	-10	82.2
2016	ARI	15/15	1045	597	364	61.0%	4233	26	14/21	14	6.7%	6.2	22	-7.8%	23	137	21	283	14	38	0	59.0%	19	58.9
2017	ARI			585	368	62.9%	4319	26	14	10		6.3		3.1%					18	43	0	-4.0%		

2015:	36% Short	37% Mid	16% Deep	11% Bomb	YAC: 5.1 (22)	ALEX: 4.3	2016:	41% Short	38% Mid	14% Deep	6% Bomb	YAC: 4.6 (30)	ALEX: -0.1

Palmer's stats dropped essentially across the board in 2016, but most notably in ALEX. In 2015, Palmer's plus-4.3 ALEX ranked second in the league, but he plummeted to sixth from the bottom last year at minus-0.2. A significant chunk of that can be attributed to the rise of David Johnson, who went from 57 targets in 2015 to 120 in 2016, but that doesn't explain all of it. Bruce Arians' offense generally loves the deep ball, but only 20 percent of Palmer's throws in 2016 were "deep" or "bombs," his lowest percentage since joining Arians in the desert. Mind you, Palmer still ranked sixth in the league with 9.54 air yards per pass, so it's not like he is transforming into Alex Smith or anything. It is possible, however, that age is beginning to take away Palmer's considerable arm strength. That might actually *increase* his air yards in 2017, however—a somewhat diminished Palmer could lead to Arizona running the ball more, setting up big pass plays as the defense creeps extra guys into the box.

Bryce Petty

Height: 6-3   Weight: 230   College: Baylor   Draft: 2015/4 (103)   Born: 31-May-1991   Age: 26   Risk: Green

Year	Team	G/GS	Snaps	Att	Comp	C%	Yds	TD	INT/Adj	FUM	ASR	NY/P	Rk	DVOA	Rk	DYAR	Rk	YAR	Runs	Yds	TD	DVOA	DYAR	QBR
2016	NYJ	6/4	245	133	75	56.4%	809	3	7/8	1	9.2%	5.0	--	-57.5%	--	-414	--	-342	5	19	0	-11.8%	0	19.4
2017	NYJ			543	319	58.6%	3333	15	19	8		5.1		-30.4%					43	117	1	-12.1%		

							2016:	54% Short	23% Mid	11% Deep	13% Bomb	YAC: 5.1 (--)	ALEX: 1.3

Petty showed enough in the 2015-16 preseasons (101 passes, 58 percent completion rate, 7.3 yards per pass) to indicate some level of competence. Then the Jets put him into action last November after injuries to Ryan Fitzpatrick and Geno Smith, and Petty fell on his face. The Jets scored a total of 52 points in the four games in which Petty threw 20 or more passes (including a relief appearance against Indianapolis in Week 13). His season came to an end in Week 16 when he tore the labrum in his non-throwing shoulder while trying to make a tackle against the Patriots. In that game, he became the first quarterback to give up at least one interception and two sacks without completing a pass since Troy Aikman in Week 1 of the 2000 season. Petty had surgery in January, but should be 100 percent going into OTAs. He is considered a distant third in the Jets' quarterback competition, which is the NFL equivalent of being a longshot in a wiener dog race.

Dak Prescott

Height: 6-2 | Weight: 226 | College: Mississippi State | Draft: 2016/4 (135) | Born: 29-Jul-1993 | Age: 24 | Risk: Green

Year	Team	G/GS	Snaps	Att	Comp	C%	Yds	TD	INT/Adj	FUM	ASR	NY/P	Rk	DVOA	Rk	DYAR	Rk	YAR	Runs	Yds	TD	DVOA	DYAR	QBR
2016	DAL	16/16	1013	459	311	67.8%	3667	23	4/7	9	5.3%	7.3	4	31.6%	3	1302	4	1220	57	282	6	43.6%	121	81.5
2017	DAL			491	330	67.2%	3721	24	10	9		6.9		9.7%					60	281	3	26.1%		

2016: 41% Short — 41% Mid — 13% Deep — 5% Bomb — YAC: 5.0 (20) — ALEX: 1.1

Including the postseason, Dak Prescott threw just 33 passes when trailing by 9 to 16 points last year (18-33-268, 3 TD, 1 INT). He attempted just 67 passes on 3rd-and-7 or longer (43-67-491, 3 TD, 2 INT), and attempted just 14 passes when trailing with less than four minutes to play, completing six for 73 yards and one touchdown.

For the sake of contrast, Carson Wentz threw 112 passes when trailing by 9 to 16 points; 89 in third-and-long situations; and 51 when trailing late.

Wentz threw over 100 more passes than Prescott as well, but that is precisely the point. Prescott was in a unique situation for a rookie quarterback: playing with constant leads, for an offense that was usually "on schedule" from a down-and-distance standpoint. Playing with a lead and avoiding third downs and late-game rally situations suppresses a quarterback's attempt totals to a degree, but it also improves his rate stats, because sack and interception percentages increase sharply when a quarterback is trailing or facing constant third-and-long situations.

For a quarterback like Tom Brady, a causality loop takes effect within the statistics. Brady's awesomeness puts him in awesome position for increased awesomeness. For an unheralded rookie playing behind the greatest offensive line in at least a generation, it's safe to assume that Prescott was benefiting more from the situation his teammates put him in than vice versa. As such, there is going to be volatility in his statistics. If the Cowboys dip from last year's 13-win level of play—and central tendency suggests they will—it will show up in Prescott's interception rate and other stats, even if he takes a step forward as a passer or on-field leader.

None of this is a knock against Prescott's long-term credentials as a franchise quarterback. It's just a reminder that a 23:4 touchdown-interception ratio is not really sustainable, and that expecting across-the-board improvements from Prescott is unrealistic, because he was already operating under near-ideal conditions.

Philip Rivers

Height: 6-5 | Weight: 228 | College: North Carolina State | Draft: 2004/1 (4) | Born: 8-Dec-1981 | Age: 36 | Risk: Yellow

Year	Team	G/GS	Snaps	Att	Comp	C%	Yds	TD	INT/Adj	FUM	ASR	NY/P	Rk	DVOA	Rk	DYAR	Rk	YAR	Runs	Yds	TD	DVOA	DYAR	QBR
2014	SD	16/16	1052	570	379	66.5%	4286	31	18/18	8	6.0%	6.8	12	12.6%	9	918	9	803	37	102	0	-10.0%	3	66.8
2015	SD	16/16	1153	661	437	66.1%	4792	29	13/16	4	5.5%	6.4	15	7.8%	11	847	8	780	17	28	0	-9.8%	1	59.4
2016	SD	16/16	1061	578	349	60.4%	4386	33	21/19	9	6.6%	6.8	11	1.4%	18	498	17	435	14	35	0	-9.3%	1	64.5
2017	LACH			588	367	62.3%	4312	28	13	6		6.3		3.5%					23	38	0	-10.0%		

2015: 56% Short — 29% Mid — 9% Deep — 6% Bomb — YAC: 6.0 (7) — ALEX: 0.6 | 2016: 49% Short — 32% Mid — 14% Deep — 6% Bomb — YAC: 5.8 (3) — ALEX: 1.3

If Rivers hands the ball off to Melvin Gordon more often this season to satisfy Anthony Lynn's offensive vision, then perhaps the Chargers can increase the amount of play-action passing. Rivers has always been quite effective while using play-action. The Chargers have ranked first or second in play-action DVOA in three of the last four years, including a league-best 83.9% DVOA last season. Unfortunately, Mike McCoy's Chargers were dead last in how often they used play-action passing from 2013 to 2015, and still in the bottom 10 last year at roughly 17 percent.

A change there under Lynn could help Rivers have a more effective season as he turns 36 this December. That sounds a bit old, but the prolific quarterbacks of this pass-crazed era have continued to thrive at that age. Kurt Warner (2007), Peyton Manning (2012), Tom Brady (2013), Drew Brees (2015), and Carson Palmer (2015) all threw at least 25 touchdown passes in their age-36 season, and all but Warner had at least 4,300 yards passing too.

Aaron Rodgers

Height: 6-2 | Weight: 223 | College: California | Draft: 2005/1 (24) | Born: 2-Dec-1983 | Age: 34 | Risk: Yellow

Year	Team	G/GS	Snaps	Att	Comp	C%	Yds	TD	INT/Adj	FUM	ASR	NY/P	Rk	DVOA	Rk	DYAR	Rk	YAR	Runs	Yds	TD	DVOA	DYAR	QBR
2014	GB	16/16	983	520	341	65.6%	4381	38	5/7	10	5.3%	7.6	2	32.2%	1	1564	2	1581	43	269	2	54.4%	104	82.6
2015	GB	16/16	1138	572	347	60.7%	3821	31	8/11	8	7.3%	5.7	32	-1.0%	17	406	17	258	58	344	1	37.1%	107	64.9
2016	GB	16/16	1066	610	401	65.7%	4428	40	7/11	8	5.6%	6.5	18	18.7%	8	1279	6	1299	67	369	4	22.4%	89	76.9
2017	GB			584	389	66.5%	4523	39	8	9		7.1		21.4%					59	260	2	20.6%		

2015: 50% Short — 30% Mid — 11% Deep — 8% Bomb — YAC: 5.6 (11) — ALEX: 3.5 | 2016: 46% Short — 32% Mid — 13% Deep — 8% Bomb — YAC: 5.1 (17) — ALEX: 3.8

Inconsistent weekly results over the first half of last season resulted in Rodgers becoming somewhat of a piñata. Rodgers didn't play well, but he also wasn't to blame for the offense's sluggish start to the season. The offense's biggest problem was the inconsistency of its receivers. Rodgers was just as accurate over the first half of the regular season as he was over the second, but his receivers were continually ruining big plays. Our charting marked Rodgers with 471 yards lost to receiver drops last year, even assuming 0 YAC on each pass. No other quarterback was over 400 yards. (The numbers are in the Statistical Appendix, page 454.) Cian Fahey's charting for *Pre-Snap Reads QB Catalogue 2017* ranked Rodgers in the top seven of accuracy to every level of the field, and he was the only quarterback to rank in the top 10 for every distance.

Ben Roethlisberger Height: 6-5   Weight: 240   College: Miami (Ohio)   Draft: 2004/1 (11)   Born: 2-Mar-1982   Age: 35   Risk: Yellow

Year	Team	G/GS	Snaps	Att	Comp	C%	Yds	TD	INT/Adj	FUM	ASR	NY/P	Rk	DVOA	Rk	DYAR	Rk	YAR	Runs	Yds	TD	DVOA	DYAR	QBR
2014	PIT	16/16	1104	608	408	67.1%	4952	32	9/14	8	5.8%	7.6	3	26.8%	3	1572	1	1505	33	27	0	-50.8%	-34	72.5
2015	PIT	12/11	794	469	319	68.0%	3938	21	16/18	1	4.3%	7.8	2	22.1%	4	1114	5	1056	15	29	0	-0.2%	4	76.9
2016	PIT	14/14	921	509	328	64.4%	3819	29	13/25	8	4.0%	7.0	8	12.1%	9	807	8	790	16	14	1	14.8%	7	66.3
2017	PIT			568	371	65.3%	4507	33	14	4		7.4		23.1%					26	29	0	-8.2%		

| 2015: | 44% Short | 31% Mid | 12% Deep | 13% Bomb | YAC: 4.6 (33) | ALEX: 7.1 | 2016: | 51% Short | 25% Mid | 14% Deep | 10% Bomb | YAC: 5.2 (10) | ALEX: 4.2 |

Remember how irritating it was when Brett Favre teased retirement every year in Green Bay for eons? We could be in for more of the same with Roethlisberger, who told everyone who would listen in January that he might retire. He finally committed to one more season, but refused to say that he would be back after that. Roethlisberger's lengthy injury list literally starts at his head and goes to his feet, with at least a half-dozen other maladies in various spots in between. Given that beating, retirement must sound tempting.

Then again, the chase for a third Super Bowl ring must sound tempting too, especially now that Roethlisberger is surrounded by what should be the best offensive talent he has ever enjoyed. To that end, Roethlisberger has made drastic changes to his playing style, getting the ball out quicker than ever before. Early in his career, about 30 to 35 percent of Roethlisberger's passes were "short" throws to receivers within 5 yards of the line of scrimmage. That rate has risen steadily ever since, peaking at 51 percent last year. Those short throws are replacing the "mid"-range routes of 6 to 15 yards, which once made up nearly half of Roethlisberger's passes but are now much less frequent. Meanwhile, the total rates of Roethlisberger's "deep" and "bomb" throws are as high as they have ever been. This change has been going on for more than a decade now, so it's not just an effect of Todd Haley's scheme or Le'Veon Bell's presence on the roster. An older, wiser Roethlisberger is relying more on the jab to keep things in control, then picking and choosing his spots for haymakers and knockouts. It's a sound plan to keep Roethlisberger out of the trainer's room—he has broken his personal record for lowest sack rate in each of the last three seasons—without totally sacrificing the offense's explosiveness. However, he must take better care of the football. Roethlisberger was second in adjusted interceptions behind Eli Manning last year, and was in the top 10 in 2015 too.

Jake Rudock Height: 6-3   Weight: 208   College: Michigan   Draft: 2016/6 (191)   Born: 23-Jan-1993   Age: 24   Risk: Yellow

Year	Team	G/GS	Snaps	Att	Comp	C%	Yds	TD	INT/Adj	FUM	ASR	NY/P	Rk	DVOA	Rk	DYAR	Rk	YAR	Runs	Yds	TD	DVOA	DYAR	QBR
2017	DET			548	341	62.3%	3653	20	17	10		5.7		-11.6%					57	138	1	-9.6%		

Rudock was a game manager at Iowa and Michigan before the Lions drafted him in the sixth round in 2016. With Dan Orlovsky gone as Matthew Stafford's backup, Rudock will have a chance to move up to No. 2, though he may battle with 2017 rookie Brad Kaaya, who put up bigger college numbers at Miami. Rudock lacks the arm strength to be a reliable starter in the NFL, so the Lions will have to hope that Stafford continues his ironman streak.

Matt Ryan Height: 6-4   Weight: 228   College: Boston College   Draft: 2008/1 (3)   Born: 17-May-1985   Age: 32   Risk: Green

Year	Team	G/GS	Snaps	Att	Comp	C%	Yds	TD	INT/Adj	FUM	ASR	NY/P	Rk	DVOA	Rk	DYAR	Rk	YAR	Runs	Yds	TD	DVOA	DYAR	QBR
2014	ATL	16/16	1064	628	415	66.1%	4694	28	14/18	5	5.1%	6.9	9	14.9%	8	1101	7	1072	29	145	0	4.8%	23	67.0
2015	ATL	16/16	1116	614	407	66.3%	4591	21	16/20	13	5.2%	6.8	10	-1.9%	18	389	19	669	36	63	0	-9.6%	3	61.8
2016	ATL	16/16	1021	534	373	69.9%	4944	38	7/10	4	6.6%	8.2	1	39.1%	1	1885	1	1765	35	117	0	12.7%	32	83.3
2017	ATL			552	363	65.8%	4383	32	14	5		7.0		16.5%					34	100	0	6.2%		

| 2015: | 47% Short | 39% Mid | 10% Deep | 4% Bomb | YAC: 4.5 (34) | ALEX: 0.6 | 2016: | 48% Short | 32% Mid | 12% Deep | 7% Bomb | YAC: 6.1 (1) | ALEX: -0.2 |

Ryan just missed becoming the 15th member of the 40.0% DVOA club. As is, he still finished with one of the 15 best seasons on record.

Top 15 Passing Seasons, 1989-2016

Name	Year	Team	DVOA
Peyton Manning	2004	IND	58.9%
Tom Brady	2007	NE	54.1%
Peyton Manning	2006	IND	51.3%
Tom Brady	2010	NE	46.7%
Aaron Rodgers	2011	GB	46.6%
Steve Young	1992	SF	45.1%
Randall Cunningham	1998	MIN	45.1%
Peyton Manning	2013	DEN	43.2%
Vinny Testaverde	1998	NYJ	42.2%
Mark Rypien	1991	WAS	41.9%
Philip Rivers	2009	SD	41.7%
Peyton Manning	2005	IND	41.7%
Chad Pennington	2002	NYJ	40.6%
Tom Brady	2009	NE	40.4%
Matt Ryan	2016	ATL	39.1%

Minimum 200 passes

Ryan's astounding 40.9% improvement from 2015 might not quite rank with Randall Cunningham's Lazarus Tale from 1998 (he was the Vikings backup in '97, and out of football entirely in '96), or Testaverde's 43.8% improvement as a 35-year-old from that same year (in retrospect, 1998 was quite an insane season). But it was amazing in that unlike most of the other names on this exclusive list, Ryan had never previously suggested he was capable of reaching such heights. He was very good, mind you, just not… don't say it, don't say it… *elite*. He did post a 30.9% DVOA in his rookie season, mainly by drafting behind a powerful rushing attack, but since then had settled into the mid-teens as his true value, making both 2015 and 2016 aberrations.

There are two countervailing trends at work here—the historic one that works against aging quarterbacks (Ryan will be 32), and the recent one that has seen great quarterbacks remain great well past the sell-by dates of most mortal athletes. Even during last season's wonderama, Ryan had plenty of moments where his iffy arm strength deserted him. While Ryan is highly unlikely to have another stinkeroo like 2015, he isn't likely to make a repeat appearance at the top of our stats tables either. Dropping back to his 2010-to-2014 level may cost the Falcons a couple of wins, and suggests he won't quite have the seemingly limitless brilliance of Manning or Brady as they pushed 40, but should serve the team just fine in the near term.

Mark Sanchez Height: 6-2 Weight: 227 College: USC Draft: 2009/1 (5) Born: 11-Nov-1986 Age: 31 Risk: Yellow

Year	Team	G/GS	Snaps	Att	Comp	C%	Yds	TD	INT/Adj	FUM	ASR	NY/P	Rk	DVOA	Rk	DYAR	Rk	YAR	Runs	Yds	TD	DVOA	DYAR	QBR
2014	PHI	9/8	625	309	198	64.1%	2418	14	11/11	7	7.2%	6.8	11	-1.4%	22	210	23	255	34	87	1	-25.9%	-15	58.2
2015	PHI	4/2	169	91	59	64.8%	616	4	4/4	1	8.5%	5.6	--	-46.9%	--	-227	--	-154	6	22	0	20.9%	7	38.9
2016	DAL	2/0	39	18	10	55.6%	93	0	2/2	0	14.5%	3.2	--	-96.5%	--	-119	--	-139	4	-2	0	-75.2%	-1	5.3
2017	CHI			514	308	59.8%	3467	19	19	11		5.8		-16.8%					36	83	1	-14.6%		

2015:	54% Short	33% Mid	12% Deep	1% Bomb	YAC: 5.4 (--)	ALEX: -2.0	2016:	65% Short	18% Mid	12% Deep	6% Bomb	YAC: 5.4 (--)	ALEX: 2.0

Mark Sanchez was signed to be a veteran backup who would not cause controversy for a first-year starter. Who knew at the time that he'd be not causing controversy for two quarterbacks instead of one? Sanchez shouldn't play in 2017, but he's almost assured of a roster spot because of his experience. The Bears aren't going to only carry two quarterbacks, not when one is a rookie who may not be ready to enter mid-game.

Tom Savage

| | | Height: 6-4 | | Weight: 228 | | College: Pittsburgh | | | Draft: 2014/4 (135) | | Born: 26-Apr-1990 | | Age: 27 | | | Risk: | Red |

Year	Team	G/GS	Snaps	Att	Comp	C%	Yds	TD	INT/Adj	FUM	ASR	NY/P	Rk	DVOA	Rk	DYAR	Rk	YAR	Runs	Yds	TD	DVOA	DYAR	QBR
2014	HOU	2/0	60	19	10	52.6%	127	0	1/0	2	4.2%	6.1	--	-24.2%	--	-20	--	-33	6	-6	0	-183.1%	-31	12.7
2016	HOU	3/2	146	73	46	63.0%	461	0	0/1	1	6.9%	5.5	--	-5.4%	--	31	--	21	6	12	0	32.0%	8	63.1
2017	HOU			544	344	63.3%	3578	19	16	10		5.7		-14.1%					47	159	1	-5.9%		

| | | | | | | | 2016: | 41% Short | | 47% Mid | | 7% Deep | | 5% Bomb | | YAC: 3.7 (--) | | ALEX: 0.0 |

All dialogue that circles around Savage starting and how he can hold off Deshaun Watson misses the forest for the trees for a few reasons. 1) It considers Savage as a good bet to improve when, despite some progression, he's still a gear too slow to run an effective NFL offense. 2) Even if he wasn't slow, he's practically never healthy long enough to show much. Savage has arm strength and can spin it, which are two big points in his favor given how the league currently scouts quarterbacks. This is probably still the high point of his NFL career. We don't mean this coming year—we mean the part where he's getting enough sunshine up his butt in OTAs to pretend like he's worth starting.

Matt Schaub

| | | Height: 6-5 | | Weight: 235 | | College: Virginia | | | Draft: 2004/3 (90) | | Born: 25-Jun-1981 | | Age: 36 | | | Risk: | Red |

Year	Team	G/GS	Snaps	Att	Comp	C%	Yds	TD	INT/Adj	FUM	ASR	NY/P	Rk	DVOA	Rk	DYAR	Rk	YAR	Runs	Yds	TD	DVOA	DYAR	QBR
2014	OAK	11/0	19	10	5	50.0%	57	0	2/3	2	22.9%	2.2	--	-220.7%	--	-158	--	-158	0	0	0	--	--	0.1
2015	BAL	2/2	137	80	52	65.0%	540	3	4/4	0	4.8%	6.2	--	-38.4%	--	-146	--	-71	4	10	0	-76.1%	-17	34.3
2016	ATL	4/0	21	3	1	33.3%	16	0	0/0	0	0.0%	5.3	--	-15.0%	--	-1	--	3	2	-2	0	--	--	18.4
2017	ATL			554	355	64.2%	3913	25	19	6		6.2		-1.1%					40	92	0	-9.0%		

| 2015: | 46% Short | | 33% Mid | | 14% Deep | | 7% Bomb | | YAC: 4.1 (--) | | ALEX: -0.1 | | 2016: | 33% Short | | 67% Mid | | 0% Deep | | 0% Bomb | | YAC: 5.0 (--) | | ALEX: -0.7 |

Since his 2013 meltdown in Houston, Schaub has thrown 93 passes in three seasons while backing up Derek Carr, Joe Flacco, and Matt Ryan. In that period he has collected north of $10 million, and just re-signed with the Falcons for at least $5 million more. He is the epitome of the "good guy, no waves" backup, the poster boy for what the NFL prizes in the role—as opposed to Colin Kaepernick. Schaub will ride the gravy train behind Ryan for at least another season, though so long as he cracks jokes in the meeting room and stands for the national anthem, there's no telling how long he'll last.

Trevor Siemian

| | | Height: 6-3 | | Weight: 220 | | College: Northwestern | | | Draft: 2015/7 (250) | | Born: 26-Dec-1991 | | Age: 26 | | | Risk: | Red |

Year	Team	G/GS	Snaps	Att	Comp	C%	Yds	TD	INT/Adj	FUM	ASR	NY/P	Rk	DVOA	Rk	DYAR	Rk	YAR	Runs	Yds	TD	DVOA	DYAR	QBR
2015	DEN	1/0	1	0	0	0.0%	0	0	0/0	--	--	--	--	--	--	--	--	--	1	-1	0	--	--	--
2016	DEN	14/14	904	486	289	59.5%	3401	18	10/13	4	7.0%	6.2	21	-7.1%	21	137	22	214	28	57	0	-17.0%	-4	55.8
2017	DEN			580	357	61.6%	3940	24	15	8		5.8		-10.8%					32	68	1	-12.5%		

| | | | | | | | 2016: | 41% Short | | 41% Mid | | 10% Deep | | 8% Bomb | | YAC: 4.9 (25) | | ALEX: 1.5 |

Even if Siemian winds up as Denver's backup this season, he will have already had one of the best careers for a quarterback drafted in the seventh round. The bar surely is low, but since the NFL moved to a seven-round draft in 1994, Siemian's 486 pass attempts rank sixth for all seventh-round picks. With an 8-6 record as a starter, he had more success than Tyler Thigpen (1-11) and Tim Rattay (5-13), the next two quarterbacks ahead of Siemian on the attempts list. That leaves just three names that we can say have been more successful than Siemian so far: Matt Cassel (2,624 attempts), Gus Frerotte (3,106 attempts), and Ryan Fitzpatrick (3,876 attempts). It's a pretty solid return on a seventh-round pick for John Elway and the Broncos.

Alex Smith

| | | Height: 6-4 | | Weight: 212 | | College: Utah | | | Draft: 2005/1 (1) | | Born: 7-May-1984 | | Age: 33 | | | Risk: | Yellow |

Year	Team	G/GS	Snaps	Att	Comp	C%	Yds	TD	INT/Adj	FUM	ASR	NY/P	Rk	DVOA	Rk	DYAR	Rk	YAR	Runs	Yds	TD	DVOA	DYAR	QBR
2014	KC	15/15	940	464	303	65.3%	3265	18	6/6	4	9.1%	5.9	28	4.1%	18	493	14	527	49	254	1	8.5%	38	49.4
2015	KC	16/16	989	470	307	65.3%	3486	20	7/11	4	8.6%	6.3	19	3.0%	15	468	15	359	84	498	2	11.5%	86	66.5
2016	KC	15/15	917	489	328	67.1%	3502	15	8/11	7	5.5%	6.5	17	9.4%	11	688	12	538	48	134	5	4.8%	26	66.1
2017	KC			531	351	66.1%	3716	20	9	7		6.2		0.5%					51	195	2	11.5%		

| 2015: | 49% Short | | 36% Mid | | 9% Deep | | 6% Bomb | | YAC: 6.3 (1) | | ALEX: -3.4 | | 2016: | 54% Short | | 32% Mid | | 9% Deep | | 5% Bomb | | YAC: 5.5 (6) | | ALEX: 0.5 |

How do you get Alex Smith to throw for 4,000 yards? Tell him it's third down with 4,500 yards to go.

In all seriousness, Smith passed for a career-high 3,502 yards last season. Since Smith was drafted in 2005, quarterbacks have passed for more yards than he did last year 164 times. By this point, we know exactly what type of quarterback Smith is. The same can likely be said for the Chiefs, hence the aggressive trade to get Patrick Mahomes in Kansas City.

Geno Smith   Height: 6-3   Weight: 208   College: West Virginia   Draft: 2013/2 (39)   Born: 10-Oct-1990   Age: 27   Risk: Red

Year	Team	G/GS	Snaps	Att	Comp	C%	Yds	TD	INT/Adj	FUM	ASR	NY/P	Rk	DVOA	Rk	DYAR	Rk	YAR	Runs	Yds	TD	DVOA	DYAR	QBR
2014	NYJ	14/13	816	367	219	59.7%	2525	13	13/15	8	7.5%	6.0	27	-12.5%	30	-33	30	-21	59	238	1	-34.3%	-65	35.4
2015	NYJ	1/0	65	42	27	64.3%	265	2	1/1	0	7.5%	5.5	--	11.0%	--	72	--	83	2	34	0	168.6%	14	66.2
2016	NYJ	2/1	33	14	8	57.1%	126	1	1/1	1	17.3%	6.2	--	-70.8%	--	-68	--	-83	2	9	0	39.6%	5	30.9
2017	NYG			596	376	63.2%	3999	20	21	11		5.4		-19.2%					36	130	1	5.4%		

2015: 37% Short   47% Mid   7% Deep   9% Bomb   YAC: 3.3 (–)   ALEX: 3.7   2016: 50% Short   43% Mid   7% Deep   0% Bomb   YAC: 10.4 (–)   ALEX: 1.5

Smith needed a miracle to keep his job with the Jets, and found disaster instead. He tore his ACL just 24 snaps into his first start of the season, which turned out to be his last in a Jets uniform. His limited playing time in 2017 was even worse than his numbers suggest—more than half his passing yardage (and 45 DYAR) came on one 69-yard touchdown pass against Baltimore, and 63 of those yards came after the catch. Still in New York but now wearing blue, Smith claimed to be 100 percent in OTAs. He is unlikely to see much action this year, considering Eli Manning has never missed a start since taking over as the Giants quarterback midway through the 2004 season. Smith is still young, and if he can spend a year on the bench rehabbing his body and his image, it wouldn't be the craziest thing if he got a chance to compete for a starting job somewhere else in 2018.

Matthew Stafford   Height: 6-2   Weight: 225   College: Georgia   Draft: 2009/1 (1)   Born: 7-Feb-1988   Age: 29   Risk: Yellow

Year	Team	G/GS	Snaps	Att	Comp	C%	Yds	TD	INT/Adj	FUM	ASR	NY/P	Rk	DVOA	Rk	DYAR	Rk	YAR	Runs	Yds	TD	DVOA	DYAR	QBR
2014	DET	16/16	1093	602	363	60.3%	4257	22	12/15	8	7.0%	6.2	22	-0.7%	20	423	15	544	43	93	2	-15.4%	-4	55.1
2015	DET	16/16	1033	592	398	67.2%	4262	32	13/14	4	7.3%	6.3	20	8.0%	10	804	9	637	44	159	1	11.4%	35	62.6
2016	DET	16/16	1037	594	388	65.3%	4327	24	10/16	3	6.1%	6.5	16	7.2%	14	761	9	768	37	207	2	29.3%	64	70.5
2017	DET			598	389	65.0%	4331	27	13	4		6.2		5.8%					43	149	1	10.3%		

2015: 56% Short   30% Mid   10% Deep   5% Bomb   YAC: 6.1 (5)   ALEX: -0.4   2016: 52% Short   31% Mid   10% Deep   7% Bomb   YAC: 5.8 (4)   ALEX: 1.7

Stafford is set to become a free agent in 2018, but expect the Lions to lock him up to a contract that should surpass the $25 million per season that Derek Carr signed on for in Oakland this summer. If 80 percent of success is showing up, then one of Stafford's best attributes is that he hasn't missed a start in any of the last six seasons. Despite 19 missed games in his first two seasons, Stafford has been an ironman ever since, active each week with a heavy workload that has to keep the Lions competitive.

He's not Aaron Rodgers or Tom Brady. He's not even Philip Rivers or Tony Romo when they were at their best, but Stafford is Detroit's franchise quarterback for the foreseeable future. That sure beats years of dealing with Joey Harrington, Charlie Batch, Scott Mitchell, and Andre Ware.

Drew Stanton   Height: 6-3   Weight: 230   College: Michigan State   Draft: 2007/2 (43)   Born: 7-May-1984   Age: 33   Risk: Green

Year	Team	G/GS	Snaps	Att	Comp	C%	Yds	TD	INT/Adj	FUM	ASR	NY/P	Rk	DVOA	Rk	DYAR	Rk	YAR	Runs	Yds	TD	DVOA	DYAR	QBR
2014	ARI	9/8	469	240	132	55.0%	1711	7	5/13	1	4.3%	6.5	20	4.2%	16	238	20	185	25	63	0	36.2%	27	58.0
2015	ARI	7/0	65	25	11	44.0%	104	0	2/2	0	7.2%	3.6	--	-57.4%	--	-82	--	-99	13	-13	0	--	--	12.3
2016	ARI	5/1	106	48	19	39.6%	192	2	3/2	0	1.9%	3.8	--	-50.9%	--	-119	--	-84	3	-3	0	--	--	26.9
2017	ARI			583	323	55.3%	3766	20	16	8		5.1		-17.8%					34	70	0	-15.0%		

2015: 32% Short   48% Mid   4% Deep   16% Bomb   YAC: 2.4 (–)   ALEX: 6.2   2016: 36% Short   40% Mid   11% Deep   13% Bomb   YAC: 4.1 (–)   ALEX: 5.4

Stanton started one game in 2016, and it was ugly. He completed fewer than 40 percent of his throws against a San Francisco defense that ranked 28th against the pass, which is less than ideal. He had a DVOA of 81.6% when targeting Larry Fitzgerald, and -50.9% when targeting anyone else. Stanton will battle Blaine Gabbert for the backup role in Arizona. Considering Stanton has been in the system since 2014 *and* was apparently told he was the starter-in-waiting if Carson Palmer retired, you'd hope he'd win that battle. At age 33, though, calling Stanton the "quarterback of the future" would be a massive stretch, unless he suddenly shapeshifts into a 24-year-old prospect overnight.

Ryan Tannehill

Height: 6-4 | Weight: 221 | College: Texas A&M | Draft: 2012/1 (8) | Born: 27-Jul-1988 | Age: 29 | Risk: Yellow

Year	Team	G/GS	Snaps	Att	Comp	C%	Yds	TD	INT/Adj	FUM	ASR	NY/P	Rk	DVOA	Rk	DYAR	Rk	YAR	Runs	Yds	TD	DVOA	DYAR	QBR
2014	MIA	16/16	1065	590	392	66.4%	4045	27	12/15	8	7.0%	5.8	33	4.1%	17	630	12	566	56	311	1	11.4%	51	59.1
2015	MIA	16/16	1026	586	363	61.9%	4208	24	12/15	10	7.6%	6.1	28	-10.6%	27	20	26	67	32	141	1	36.5%	49	43.2
2016	MIA	13/13	758	389	261	67.1%	2995	19	12/16	9	7.2%	6.7	14	-10.8%	25	10	25	92	39	164	1	-7.0%	8	54.6
2017	MIA			509	333	65.4%	3812	25	14	6		6.4		0.0%					36	150	1	16.5%		

2015: 45% Short | 34% Mid | 12% Deep | 9% Bomb | YAC: 5.1 (24) | ALEX: 1.6 | 2016: 53% Short | 30% Mid | 8% Deep | 9% Bomb | YAC: 5.5 (7) | ALEX: 1.2

The buzz this summer out of Miami is that this is the best offense Ryan Tannehill has ever been involved with. Or was it 2014, when Bullygate was laid to rest, and Lamar Miller was going to have his breakout year? Or was it 2015, when Jarvis Landry was no longer a rookie, DeVante Parker and Kenny Stills were going to stretch the field, and Jordan Cameron was the tight end Tannehill's been looking for? Or was it 2016, when Adam Gase was going to fix everything, and the team got a steal in Laremy Tunsil?

No, it really should be 2017, because center Mike Pouncey is healthy, Tunsil is now at left tackle, Jay Ajayi is the workhorse back, Julius Thomas is the latest tight end dream, and the top three receivers are all entering their second season of experience with the same offense. So yes, this has to be the year in which Tannehill puts it all together. "My goal is to go out and play at the level I know I can play consistently throughout the season, get better as the season goes on and play our best football in January," said Tannehill to the *Miami Herald* in July. "If I do that, the results will speak for itself." However, if the results are still "meh," then six years of Tannehill's career will also speak for him.

Tyrod Taylor

Height: 6-1 | Weight: 216 | College: Virginia Tech | Draft: 2011/6 (180) | Born: 3-Aug-1989 | Age: 28 | Risk: Green

Year	Team	G/GS	Snaps	Att	Comp	C%	Yds	TD	INT/Adj	FUM	ASR	NY/P	Rk	DVOA	Rk	DYAR	Rk	YAR	Runs	Yds	TD	DVOA	DYAR	QBR
2014	BAL	1/0	6	0	0	0.0%	0	0	0/0	--	--	--	--	--	--	--	--	--	4	-3	0	--	--	--
2015	BUF	14/14	923	380	242	63.7%	3035	20	6/11	8	8.5%	6.8	12	9.8%	8	536	14	486	104	568	4	19.8%	133	67.8
2016	BUF	15/15	969	436	269	61.7%	3023	17	6/6	4	9.2%	5.9	27	-2.1%	19	275	19	347	95	580	6	2.1%	65	68.2
2017	BUF			480	290	60.5%	3429	22	10	8		6.2		-6.1%					95	544	5	27.9%		

2015: 45% Short | 29% Mid | 10% Deep | 15% Bomb | YAC: 4.7 (32) | ALEX: 4.0 | 2016: 43% Short | 36% Mid | 13% Deep | 9% Bomb | YAC: 4.2 (31) | ALEX: 2.6

Taylor will be working with his third offensive coordinator in three seasons—not exactly ideal conditions as the new regime determines his fate as Buffalo's long-term starter. Under Greg Roman and Anthony Lynn, Taylor was the rare downfield passer who also took care of the ball. Last year, Taylor finished seventh in ALEX but also ranked fourth in adjusted interception rate. Among qualifying quarterbacks in each of the last two years, only Tom Brady, Aaron Rodgers, and Brian Hoyer posted better interception rates than Taylor. Even given his limitations as a progression reader, it's hard to argue with the results Taylor has delivered over his first two seasons as a starter.

Under Rick Dennison, Taylor's biggest adjustment will likely come from playing under center more. While the Bills have ranked third in shotgun usage each of the past two seasons, Dennison's Broncos ranked 14th in 2015 and 31st in 2016. In fact, along with the Falcons and Cardinals, the Broncos were one of three teams to deploy the shotgun on less than half their snaps. One possible upshoot of Dennison's system? Taylor should find himself passing from inside the pocket more frequently. No quarterback threw a higher percentage of his passes from outside the pocket in 2016, yet the Bills' offensive DVOA with Taylor rolling out or scrambling (-8.5%) was significantly worse than when he remained inside the pocket (35.6%). Ideally, these schematic changes will accentuate Taylor's strengths as a downfield passer, while also maintaining his viability as a weapon in the running game. Taylor was easily the most dynamic rushing quarterback in the league last season. He led all quarterbacks in total broken tackles (33), broken tackles to avoid sacks (14), and broken tackles beyond the line of scrimmage (19). Nobody else came close—the runners-up in those three categories were Jameis Winston (16), Winston and Russell Wilson (nine each), and Colin Kaepernick (12). There's no reason Taylor can't post another efficient season, which should have Bills fans wondering why ownership is so ready to move on.

Scott Tolzien

Height: 6-3 | Weight: 205 | College: Wisconsin | Draft: 2011/FA | Born: 9-Jan-1987 | Age: 30 | Risk: Green

Year	Team	G/GS	Snaps	Att	Comp	C%	Yds	TD	INT/Adj	FUM	ASR	NY/P	Rk	DVOA	Rk	DYAR	Rk	YAR	Runs	Yds	TD	DVOA	DYAR	QBR
2015	GB	3/0	10	1	1	100.0%	4	0	0/0	1	48.3%	-2.0	--	-321.5%	--	-14	--	-17	3	-3	0	-224.2%	-16	0.2
2016	IND	3/1	83	37	23	62.2%	216	1	2/4	1	7.7%	4.9	--	-33.6%	--	-59	--	-63	6	3	0	-103.5%	-25	31.8
2017	IND			567	356	62.8%	3762	22	17	9		5.4		-14.5%					41	89	1	-8.3%		

2015: 100% Short | 0% Mid | 0% Deep | 0% Bomb | YAC: 0.0 (--) | ALEX: -- | 2016: 38% Short | 27% Mid | 24% Deep | 11% Bomb | YAC: 3.5 (--) | ALEX: -1.6

With Brett Hundley taking over as Green Bay's backup, Tolzien was left to wander to Indianapolis. He did a halfway credible job in his one start last year, against the Steelers on Thanksgiving after their defense had turned the corner. The Colts have too many other issues to deal with to worry about upgrading on Tolzien, which is fine, as he's a passable second-stringer.

Mitchell Trubisky

Height: 6-2 Weight: 222 College: North Carolina Draft: 2017/1 (2) Born: 20-Aug-1994 Age: 23 Risk: Yellow

Year	Team	G/GS	Snaps	Att	Comp	C%	Yds	TD	INT/Adj	FUM	ASR	NY/P	Rk	DVOA	Rk	DYAR	Rk	YAR	Runs	Yds	TD	DVOA	DYAR	QBR
2017	CHI		504	287	56.9%		3575	19	20	8		6.2		-10.2%					54	197	3	11.8%		

If the Bears want to get the best from Mitchell Trubisky, they will play him. He won't be good as a rookie. Defenses will constantly bait him into mistakes and he would be a favorite to lead the league in turnovers if he survived 16 games. That's OK though. 2017 would be a development year for a quarterback who hasn't played a huge amount of football since leaving high school. What makes Trubisky worth playing is his potential for positive plays. He showed off poise, balance, footwork, and good eye level in college. Those traits mean he won't collapse if he faces pressure on a regular basis.

Trubisky's accuracy isn't particularly special. He's not Andrew Luck or Marcus Mariota as a prospect, but he is accurate enough to push the ball downfield regularly. Whether it's Trubisky or Mike Glennon at quarterback, the Bears offense would be at its best relying on a play-action heavy approach that swaps out efficiency for big chunks.

Deshaun Watson

Height: 6-2 Weight: 221 College: Clemson Draft: 2017/1 (12) Born: 14-Sep-1995 Age: 22 Risk: Yellow

Year	Team	G/GS	Snaps	Att	Comp	C%	Yds	TD	INT/Adj	FUM	ASR	NY/P	Rk	DVOA	Rk	DYAR	Rk	YAR	Runs	Yds	TD	DVOA	DYAR	QBR
2017	HOU		496	279	56.3%		3498	20	18	9		6.1		-15.4%					93	512	4	12.7%		

The learning curve for Watson will be steep. He can get happy feet in the pocket, especially when the first read is covered. His selection was one of traits rather than of established skill sets. Watson has the arm talent, if not the consistent accuracy. The leadership and intangibles, if not the body scouts want. As far as being brought along slowly, "being behind Tom Savage" is pretty counter-productive. So, here's the first swing Houston was willing to take on a first-round quarterback since David Carr. Odds are, it will be as uneven as Carr's first year was—though without the bloodbath the 2002 Texans offensive line created.

Brandon Weeden

Height: 6-4 Weight: 221 College: Oklahoma State Draft: 2012/1 (22) Born: 14-Oct-1983 Age: 34 Risk: Red

Year	Team	G/GS	Snaps	Att	Comp	C%	Yds	TD	INT/Adj	FUM	ASR	NY/P	Rk	DVOA	Rk	DYAR	Rk	YAR	Runs	Yds	TD	DVOA	DYAR	QBR
2014	DAL	5/1	89	41	24	58.5%	303	3	2/2	1	3.2%	7.0	--	-3.5%	--	21	--	25	6	-1	0	-158.1%	-26	15.4
2015	2TM	6/4	313	140	97	69.3%	1043	5	2/4	2	7.0%	6.5	--	3.8%	--	139	--	209	16	47	1	49.8%	27	66.2
2017	HOU		532	334	62.8%		3262	16	17	9		5.0		-25.1%					40	124	1	-4.7%		
2015:	50% Short			34% Mid		13% Deep		3% Bomb		YAC: 5.0 (--)		ALEX: -1.1												

There's an actual cottage industry of takes in Houston that go like this: Tom Savage isn't good, Deshaun Watson isn't ready, so Brandon Weeden is the best win-now quarterback on the roster. There are far, far, too many sports radio shows in this city. Here's a real take: Brandon Weeden looks like Alan Tudyk and plays like Alan Tudyk would if he were a quarterback.

Carson Wentz

Height: 6-5 Weight: 237 College: North Dakota State Draft: 2016/1 (2) Born: 30-Dec-1992 Age: 25 Risk: Green

Year	Team	G/GS	Snaps	Att	Comp	C%	Yds	TD	INT/Adj	FUM	ASR	NY/P	Rk	DVOA	Rk	DYAR	Rk	YAR	Runs	Yds	TD	DVOA	DYAR	QBR
2016	PHI	16/16	1127	607	379	62.4%	3782	16	14/19	14	5.4%	5.6	31	-12.0%	27	-36	27	12	46	150	2	-3.6%	16	52.8
2017	PHI		591	374	63.3%		4009	25	13	12		6.0		-6.2%					47	176	2	5.4%		
													2016:	51% Short		32% Mid		11% Deep		5% Bomb	YAC: 4.7 (28)	ALEX: 0.2	

Wentz visited quarterback guru Tom House (who by this point should have his name legally changed to "Quarterback Guru Tom House") for about 10 days in the early offseason. Depending on whom you speak to, Wentz's mechanical adjustments were: a) sweeping and career-altering; b) catastrophic and career-threatening; c) "subtle" (Doug Pederson's term); d) a source of controversy and scandal within Eagles headquarters; e) not all that necessary (quarterback coach John DeFilippo's opinion); or f) unlikely to stick or have an impact, anyway.

And those are just the opinions you get from polling the Football Outsiders staff.

DeFilippo said during minicamp that the changes were indeed minor and emphasized that better situational decision-making was more important to Wentz's development than the nuts and bolts of his delivery. From our perspective, throwing the ball downfield more often would help too.

The other major offseason Wentz storyline was about how desperately Wentz needed time off after his whirlwind rookie season. While lots of quarterbacks (Dak Prescott, for instance) go from the Senior Bowl to the combine to pre-draft workouts to the draft and rookie camp, Wentz had lots of other extraneous factors to contend with, including his rise from FCS obscurity and the Sam Bradford drama. In fact, Pederson and other coaches sounded more excited about Wentz's globe-trotting safaris than his practice sessions with House.

The moral of the story: quarterback evaluation is tough, quarterback development is tougher, and sometimes the best thing for all of us is to step away from football for a while to regain our perspective.

Russell Wilson

Height: 5-11   Weight: 204   College: Wisconsin   Draft: 2012/3 (75)   Born: 29-Nov-1988   Age: 29   Risk: Yellow

Year	Team	G/GS	Snaps	Att	Comp	C%	Yds	TD	INT/Adj	FUM	ASR	NY/P	Rk	DVOA	Rk	DYAR	Rk	YAR	Runs	Yds	TD	DVOA	DYAR	QBR
2014	SEA	16/16	1054	452	285	63.1%	3475	20	7/12	11	8.8%	6.6	17	5.5%	13	503	13	488	118	849	6	43.7%	269	62.5
2015	SEA	16/16	1050	483	329	68.1%	4024	34	8/11	7	9.0%	7.1	4	24.3%	3	1190	3	1159	103	553	1	17.4%	123	74.9
2016	SEA	16/16	1008	546	353	64.7%	4219	21	11/15	7	7.0%	6.7	13	4.0%	15	569	14	599	72	259	1	-12.3%	-1	63.2
2017	SEA			533	351	65.9%	4162	27	11	8		7.0		10.8%					88	471	3	16.5%		

2015:	48% Short	33% Mid	11% Deep	8% Bomb	YAC: 5.6 (16)	ALEX: 2.2	2016:	49% Short	31% Mid	12% Deep	9% Bomb	YAC: 5.0 (19)	ALEX: 0.9

All the pressure, the hits, and the scrambling for his life behind a shaky offensive line finally caught up to Wilson in 2016 as he suffered serious injuries to his ankle and knee in Weeks 1 and 3, respectively. Wilson admirably played through the injuries without missing a game, but the injuries prevented him from posing the same threat running the ball, with Wilson posting a negative rushing DVOA and DYAR for the first time in his career. The Seahawks hope that an offseason's worth of recovery will allow Wilson to regain his late-2015 form, when he was arguably the best quarterback in the league. If Seattle is going to make it to Minneapolis for Super Bowl LII, they will need Wilson firing on all cylinders to beat out the other NFC behemoths.

Jameis Winston

Height: 6-4   Weight: 230   College: Florida State   Draft: 2015/1 (1)   Born: 6-Jan-1994   Age: 24   Risk: Yellow

Year	Team	G/GS	Snaps	Att	Comp	C%	Yds	TD	INT/Adj	FUM	ASR	NY/P	Rk	DVOA	Rk	DYAR	Rk	YAR	Runs	Yds	TD	DVOA	DYAR	QBR
2015	TB	16/16	1093	535	312	58.3%	4042	22	15/22	6	5.8%	6.8	9	2.1%	16	467	16	495	54	213	6	7.6%	42	58.6
2016	TB	16/16	1123	567	345	60.8%	4090	28	18/20	10	5.9%	6.4	19	3.6%	16	556	15	539	53	165	1	-23.8%	-19	64.7
2017	TB			576	338	58.6%	4394	29	15	8		6.8		6.4%					58	201	2	2.2%		

2015:	36% Short	39% Mid	17% Deep	8% Bomb	YAC: 4.8 (31)	ALEX: 1.2	2016:	33% Short	42% Mid	17% Deep	8% Bomb	YAC: 3.9 (34)	ALEX: 3.3

Jameis Winston has *FN FAL* versatility: he can make every type of throw from just about any platform, whether that means rifling strikes between defenders, dropping touch passes into buckets, making sidearm throws on the run, or plopping simple screens over onrushing linemen. Alas, he also has Hollywood villain accuracy: Cian Fahey's *Pre-Snap Reads Quarterback Catalogue* charted Winston's accuracy as the third-lowest of any primary starter last year, while Sports Info Solutions charting data ranked him tied for first in off-target rate (passes marked overthrown or underthrown) at 18 percent. Overthrows were a particular issue: a league-leading 14 percent of his passes were charted as overthrown, head and shoulders above the average of 10 percent. That may partly account for the fact that the Buccaneers threw deep passes more often than all but two other teams, yet ranked 15th in success rate and 19th in DVOA. Remember young Eli Manning, with his reputation for perfect throws to a spot six feet over his receiver's head? Winston is displaying a similar tendency, which could be better news for the 6-foot-1 Chris Godwin than it is for the 5-foot-10 DeSean Jackson. Manning learned to compensate for his own recoil, and for a few years mid-career was one of the league's most efficient passers. Winston will need to do likewise to make the most of his wide array of targets.

Going Deep

Brandon Allen, JAC: Should the Jaguars be willing to move on from Blake Bortles during the season, it would make more sense to give this 2016 sixth-round pick a tryout than to give more time to veteran backup Chad Henne. Allen's play-action and dropback work at Arkansas fits with the new regime's offense, and let's be honest, Henne isn't taking you anywhere you want to be. Better to find out now if Allen is, like every sixth rounder, the next Tom Brady, or maybe Marc Bulger. Or even Bruce Gradkowski.

C.J. Beathard, SF: Beathard's 2016 season caused his draft prospects to plummet; a 57 percent completion rate and only 5.2 net yards per pass (including sacks) will do that for you. Slow mechanics, inconsistent touch, and lack of pocket presence made his third-round selection a surprise. Kyle Shanahan compares him to Kirk Cousins, citing how well both process the game, but Cousins was more accurate and had more success in college. On the other hand, Beathard's pro set experience and confidence when rolling out of the pocket mesh well with Shanahan's system.

Joshua Dobbs, PIT: The Steelers drafted Dobbs in the fourth round to compete with Landry Jones for the backup job. He led the SEC in passing efficiency as a senior, and would have ranked third in our QBASE projections (Patrick Mahomes and Mitchell Trubisky) had he been chosen in the top 100 picks. Dobbs is also known for his brainpower, since he graduated from Tennessee in May with a degree in aerospace engineering. Yes, he's a legit rocket scientist. NASA fans anxiously await the day when Matt Patricia has to design a defense to stop Dobbs.

Brandon Doughty, MIA: A seventh-rounder out of Western Kentucky, Doughty made Miami's initial 53-man roster but was relegated to the practice squad after Week 1. Ryan Tannehill had never missed a game until late last season, but the Dolphins went with veteran T.J. Yates instead of Doughty to back up Matt Moore. Doughty will battle with David Fales to be Miami's No. 3 quarterback, though most teams still prefer to only carry two quarterbacks.

Jeff Driskel, CIN: A sixth-round 2016 draft selection, Driskel is a tall, strong-armed quarterback who transferred to Louisana Tech after a dismal junior year at Florida. He was drafted by the 49ers, but the Bengals caught San Francisco trying to sneak him to the practice squad and claimed him on waivers. A classic All-Pro in shorts, Driskel will serve out the year as Cincy's third quarterback behind AJ McCarron.

David Fales, MIA: Fales once completed 72.5 percent of his passes for San Jose State in 2012, but hasn't seen much action in the NFL the last three years. He had one standout preseason performance, but he's now on his third pro team. Fales will hope to hang on as Miami's third quarterback behind Ryan Tannehill and Matt Moore.

Garrett Grayson, NO: Two years into his NFL career, Grayson still hasn't taken a single regular-season snap. If that changes this year, it probably means something has gone horribly wrong. The former third-round pick should be concerned for his job after the return of Chase Daniel to New Orleans.

Ryan Griffin, TB: What odds would you have gotten in summer 2013 that this R. Griffin would be the only one still employed as a quarterback in the NFL in four years' time? An undrafted free agent that year, Griffin has spent four years bouncing between the Saints and Bucs without throwing a regular-season pass for either team. Ryan Fitzpatrick's arrival leaves Griffin the third quarterback in Tampa Bay, setting up most of next year's comment to be an easy cut-and-paste of this year's comment.

Brad Kaaya, DET: Kaaya was a three-year starter at Miami, and was named ACC Rookie of the Year in 2014. However, he skipped his final season of eligibility and fell to the sixth round after some concerns with his accuracy and ability to get the ball down the field. Detroit is one of the best spots for him with its small-ball passing game, and the fact that Matthew Stafford's only other backup is 2016 sixth-round pick Jake Rudock.

Chad Kelly, DEN: There has probably never been a more relevant "Mr. Irrelevant" than Ole Miss quarterback Chad Kelly. His uncle is Jim Kelly, who was drafted the same year as John Elway. Before the draft, Buffalo's Hall of Famer assured Denver's that Chad is a good kid. Sure, not many kids allegedly get kicked out of school for yelling at coaches, or get barred from the combine for telling a club bouncer that he was going to get his AK-47 and "spray this place." On the field, Kelly tossed 50 touchdowns to 21 picks in two seasons at Ole Miss. He put up big numbers in a win over Alabama in 2015, and passed for 421 yards in a 48-43 loss against Nick Saban's defense last year. A torn ACL ended his season, but Kelly will have a chance to stick around in Denver given the lack of stability from Paxton Lynch and Trevor Siemian to this point.

Nathan Peterman, BUF: We're pessimistic about Peterman's prospects due to his age (23) and the fact that he played the easiest schedule of the quarterbacks drafted in 2017. Still, the fifth-round rookie might represent Buffalo's future if the new regime prefers a more traditional pocket passer than Tyrod Taylor.

Nate Sudfeld, WAS: Sudfeld impressed the Redskins enough in 2016 preseason and scout team drills to prevent them from signing a veteran free agent or drafting another developmental quarterback. He's essentially the quarterback of the future right now. Remember when Mike Shanahan set fire to the Donovan McNabb bridge, then entered the next offseason with Rex Grossman and John Beck as his quarterbacks? Next year, Colt McCoy will be Grossman and Sudfeld will be Beck.

Davis Webb, NYG: Webb possesses the Joe Flacco toolkit: a strong arm for throwing lovely deep balls, a no-nonsense demeanor, tall heightitude. The usual height-and-arm fetishists in the draftnik community touted Webb as a first-round talent, but NFL teams are finally wary of strapping dudes who look phenomenal in a clean pocket and an Air Raid offense. As a third-round pick, Webb should get at least a year to learn what an NFL huddle sounds like and how many steps are in a five-step drop. If forced to start this year, Webb won't be a Jared Goff-level disaster (the offense is too good), but it won't be pretty, either.

T.J. Yates, BUF: A future quarterbacks coach, but Yates was out of the league last year until Miami signed him after Ryan Tannehill's knee injury. The last time he played, for Houston in 2015, he couldn't complete half his passes. There's no reason for a team at Buffalo's position in the development cycle to keep Yates over Cardale Jones or Nathan Peterman.

Running Backs

In the following section we provide the last three years of statistics, as well as a 2017 KUBIAK projection, for every running back who either played a significant role in 2016 or is expected to do so in 2017.

The first line contains biographical data—each player's name, height, weight, college, draft position, birth date, and age. Height and weight are the best data we could find; weight, of course, can fluctuate during the offseason. **Age** is very simple, the number of years between the player's birth year and 2017, but birthdate is provided if you want to figure out exact age.

Draft position gives draft year and round, with the overall pick number with which the player was taken in parentheses. In the sample table, it says that David Johnson was chosen in the 2015 NFL draft in the third round with the 86th overall pick. Undrafted free agents are listed as "FA" with the year they came into the league, even if they were only in training camp or on a practice squad.

To the far right of the first line is the player's Risk for fantasy football in 2017. As explained in the quarterback section, the standard is for players to be marked Green. Players with higher than normal risk are marked Yellow, and players with the highest risk are marked Red. Players who are most likely to match or surpass our forecast—primarily second-stringers with low projections—are marked Blue. Risk is not only based on age and injury probability, but how a player's projection compares to his recent performance as well as our confidence (or lack thereof) in his offensive teammates.

Next we give the last three years of player stats. First come games played and games started (**G/GS**). Games played is the official NFL total and may include games in which a player appeared on special teams, but did not carry the ball or catch a pass. We also have a total of offensive **Snaps** for each season. The next four columns are familiar: **Runs**, rushing yards (**Yds**), yards per rush (**Yd/R**) and rushing touchdowns (**TD**).

The entry for fumbles (**FUM**) includes all fumbles by this running back, no matter whether they were recovered by the offense or defense. Holding onto the ball is an identifiable skill; fumbling it so that your own offense can recover it is not. (For more on this issue, see the essay "Pregame Show" in the front of the book.) This entry combines fumbles on both carries and receptions.

The next five columns give our advanced metrics for rushing: **DVOA** (Defense-Adjusted Value Over Average), **DYAR** (Defense-Adjusted Yards Above Replacement), and **YAR** (Yards Above Replacement), along with the player's rank (**Rk**) in both **DVOA** and **DYAR**. These metrics compare every carry by the running back to a league-average baseline based on the game situations in which that running back carried the ball. DVOA and DYAR are also adjusted based on the opposing defense. The methods used to compute these numbers are described in detail in the "Statistical Toolbox" introduction in the front of the book. The important distinctions between them are:

- DVOA is a rate statistic, while DYAR is a cumulative statistic. Thus, a higher DVOA means more value per play, while a higher DYAR means more aggregate value over the entire season.
- Because DYAR is defense-adjusted and YAR is not, a player whose DYAR is higher than his YAR faced a harder-than-average schedule. A player whose DYAR is lower than his YAR faced an easier-than-average schedule.

To qualify for ranking in rushing DVOA and DYAR, a running back must have had 100 carries in that season. Last year, 42 running backs qualified to be ranked in these stats, compared to 44 backs in 2015 and 43 backs in 2014.

Success Rate (**Suc%**), listed along with rank, represents running back consistency as measured by successful running plays divided by total running plays. (The definition for success is explained in the "Statistical Toolbox" introduction in the front of the book.) A player with high DVOA and a low Success Rate mixes long runs with plays on which he was stuffed at or behind the line of scrimmage. A player with low DVOA and a high Success Rate generally gets the yards needed, but rarely gets more. The league-average Success Rate in 2016 was 48 percent. Success Rate is not adjusted for the defenses a player faced.

We also give a total of broken tackles (**BTkl**) according to charting from Sports Info Solutions. This total includes broken tackles on both runs and receptions. Please note that last year SIS marked broken tackles roughly 15 more often than in 2015, and roughly 40 percent more often than in 2014 (when our broken tackle numbers still came from the old Football Outsiders game charting project). So most running backs with consistent playing time will be listed with more broken tackles in 2016; it doesn't necessarily mean they suddenly became more powerful or elusive.

The shaded columns to the right of broken tackles give data for each running back as a pass receiver. Receptions (**Rec**) counts passes caught, while Passes (**Pass**) counts total passes

David Johnson			Height: 6-1		Weight: 224		College: Northern Iowa			Draft: 2015/3 (86)		Born: 16-Dec-1991		Age: 26			Risk: Yellow	
Year	Team	G/GS	Snaps	Runs	Yds	Yd/R	TD	FUM	DVOA	Rk	DYAR	Rk	YAR	Suc%	Rk	BTkl	Rec	Pass	Yds	C%	Yd/C	TD	YAC	DVOA	Rk	DYAR	Rk
2015	ARI	16/5	412	125	581	4.6	8	3	15.7%	4	133	8	149	56%	3	27	36	57	457	63%	12.7	4	9.6	22.1%	12	120	6
2016	ARI	16/16	964	293	1239	4.2	16	5	5.1%	17	177	9	139	50%	13	80	80	121	879	67%	11.0	4	8.0	27.7%	4	274	1
2017	ARI			302	1368	4.5	11	5	2.5%								77	115	771	67%	10.0	2		5.5%			

thrown to this player, complete or incomplete. The next four columns list receiving yards (**Yds**), catch rate (**C%**), yards per catch (**Yd/C**), receiving touchdowns (**TD**), and average yards after the catch (**YAC**).

Our research has shown that receivers bear some responsibility for incomplete passes, even though only their catches are tracked in official statistics. Catch rate represents receptions divided by all intended passes for this running back. The average NFL running back caught 74 percent of passes in 2016. Unfortunately, we don't have room to post the best and worst running backs in receiving plus-minus, but you'll find the top 10 and bottom 10 running backs in this metric listed in the statistical appendix.

Finally we have receiving DVOA and DYAR, which are entirely separate from rushing DVOA and DYAR. To qualify for ranking in receiving DVOA and DYAR, a running back must have 25 passes thrown to him in that season. There are 53 running backs ranked for 2016, 58 backs for 2015, and 57 backs for 2014. Numbers without opponent adjustment (YAR, and VOA) can be found on our website, FootballOutsiders.com.

The italicized row of statistics for the 2017 season is our 2017 KUBIAK projection based on a complicated regression analysis that takes into account numerous variables including projected role, performance over the past two years, projected team offense and defense, historical comparables, height, age, experience of the offensive line, and strength of schedule.

It is difficult to accurately project statistics for a 162-game baseball season, but it is exponentially more difficult to accurately project statistics for a 16-game football season. Consider the listed projections not as a prediction of exact numbers,

Top 20 RB by Rushing DYAR (Total Value), 2016

Rank	Player	Team	DYAR
1	Ezekiel Elliott	DAL	339
2	LeSean McCoy	BUF	338
3	Le'Veon Bell	PIT	277
4	Mike Gillislee	BUF	256
5	Jordan Howard	CHI	219
6	Carlos Hyde	SF	204
7	Jay Ajayi	MIA	185
8	Bilal Powell	NYJ	182
9	David Johnson	ARI	177
10	Mark Ingram	NO	175
11	Isaiah Crowell	CLE	169
12	Rex Burkhead	CIN	163
13	Frank Gore	IND	159
14	Devonta Freeman	ATL	148
15	LeGarrette Blount	NE	131
16	Derrick Henry	TEN	131
17	Tim Hightower	NO	121
18	Chris Thompson	WAS	111
19	Rob Kelley	WAS	102
20	Darren Sproles	PHI	99

Top 20 RB by Rushing DVOA (Value per Rush), 2016

Rank	Player	Team	DVOA
1	Mike Gillislee	BUF	44.9%
2	LeSean McCoy	BUF	28.3%
3	Bilal Powell	NYJ	23.1%
4	Derrick Henry	TEN	19.6%
5	Le'Veon Bell	PIT	17.3%
6	Ezekiel Elliott	DAL	15.9%
7	Carlos Hyde	SF	15.3%
8	Isaiah Crowell	CLE	13.4%
9	Jordan Howard	CHI	12.3%
10	Tim Hightower	NO	11.9%
11	Mark Ingram	NO	11.3%
12	Tevin Coleman	ATL	9.7%
13	Jay Ajayi	MIA	9.3%
14	Devonta Freeman	ATL	6.4%
15	Rob Kelley	WAS	5.8%
16	Frank Gore	IND	5.6%
17	David Johnson	ARI	5.1%
18	LeGarrette Blount	NE	1.5%
19	Jacquizz Rodgers	TB	0.2%
20	Ryan Mathews	PHI	0.0%

Minimum 100 carries.

Top 10 RB by Receiving DYAR (Total Value), 2016

Rank	Player	Team	DYAR
1	David Johnson	ARI	274
2	Le'Veon Bell	PIT	165
3	James White	NE	163
4	Devonta Freeman	ATL	141
5	Tevin Coleman	ATL	136
6	Duke Johnson	CLE	134
7	LeSean McCoy	BUF	117
8	Spencer Ware	KC	115
9	Melvin Gordon	SD	105
10	Giovani Bernard	CIN	101

Top 10 RB by Receiving DVOA (Value per Pass), 2016

Rank	Player	Team	DVOA
1	Tevin Coleman	ATL	48.8%
2	Spencer Ware	KC	32.7%
3	Tim Hightower	NO	32.1%
4	David Johnson	ARI	27.7%
5	Ezekiel Elliott	DAL	26.9%
6	Devonta Freeman	ATL	24.9%
7	Giovani Bernard	CIN	22.4%
8	LeSean McCoy	BUF	21.2%
9	Melvin Gordon	SD	21.0%
10	James White	NE	20.1%

Minimum 25 passes.

but the mean of a range of possible performances. What's important is less the exact number of yards we project, and more which players are projected to improve or decline. Actual performance will vary from our projection less for veteran starters and more for rookies and third-stringers, for whom we must base our projections on much smaller career statistical samples. Touchdown numbers will vary more than yardage numbers.

For many rookie running backs, we'll also include a metric from our college football arsenal: **Highlight Yards**. Highlight Yards are those yards not included in adjusted line yards. So,

for example, if a runner gains 12 yards on a given carry, and we attribute 7.0 of those yards to the line (the ALY formula gives the offensive line 100 percent credit for all yards gained between zero and four yards and 50 percent credit between five and 10), then the player's highlight yardage on the play is 5.0 yards. Highlight Yards are shown as an average per opportunity, which means Highlight Yards divided by the total number of carries that went over four yards.

Finally, in a section we call "Going Deep," we briefly discuss lower-round rookies, free-agent veterans, and practice-squad players who may play a role during the 2017 season or beyond.

Ameer Abdullah   Height: 5-9   Weight: 205   College: Nebraska   Draft: 2015/2 (54)   Born: 13-Jun-1993   Age: 24   Risk: Green

Year	Team	G/GS	Snaps	Runs	Yds	Yd/R	TD	FUM	DVOA	Rk	DYAR	Rk	YAR	Suc%	Rk	BTkl	Rec	Pass	Yds	C%	Yd/C	TD	YAC	DVOA	Rk	DYAR	Rk
2015	DET	16/9	355	143	597	4.2	2	4	-8.9%	37	-2	37	21	51%	7	16	25	38	183	66%	7.3	1	7.7	-11.3%	40	6	40
2016	DET	2/2	57	18	101	5.6	0	0	16.5%	--	18	--	32	61%	--	7	5	5	57	100%	11.4	1	10.8	87.2%	--	33	--
2017	DET			163	671	4.1	3	2	-3.2%								26	38	185	68%	7.1	0		-11.4%			

Injuries have been a concern in Abdullah's young career. When healthy, he is the best all-around back on Detroit's roster, but he only lasted 23 (mostly good) touches last season before a Lisfranc tear ended his possible breakout year. He has that potential again this season, but it's wise to be skeptical of the fantasy numbers when a back with a shoddy injury history plays for an offense that loves to throw the ball, in particular to a back named Theo Riddick.

Jay Ajayi   Height: 6-0   Weight: 221   College: Boise State   Draft: 2015/5 (149)   Born: 15-Jun-1993   Age: 24   Risk: Red

Year	Team	G/GS	Snaps	Runs	Yds	Yd/R	TD	FUM	DVOA	Rk	DYAR	Rk	YAR	Suc%	Rk	BTkl	Rec	Pass	Yds	C%	Yd/C	TD	YAC	DVOA	Rk	DYAR	Rk
2015	MIA	9/0	158	49	187	3.8	1	0	-17.7%	--	-17	--	-3	39%	--	17	7	11	90	64%	12.9	0	11.1	38.1%	--	28	--
2016	MIA	15/12	582	260	1272	4.9	8	4	9.3%	13	185	7	126	43%	32	59	27	35	151	77%	5.6	0	4.9	-20.7%	47	-14	46
2017	MIA			289	1299	4.5	7	4	1.1%								36	50	279	72%	7.8	1		-1.1%			

The three 200-yard rushing games highlighted Ajayi's season, but his running style was defined by his ability to break tackles and create his own yardage. Ajayi averaged a league-best 3.5 yards after contact per rush. That stat is not always consistent from year to year, but we have seen some backs (Adrian Peterson, Marshawn Lynch, and LeGarrette Blount, to name a few) consistently produce yardage after contacting defenders. Ajayi looks to be in that mold, but for him to really develop into an every-down back, he'll have to get better as a receiver.

Ajayi had 55 broken tackles on runs last year, tied with Devonta Freeman for second-most, but only four broken tackles on receptions. He lost too many third-down snaps to a lesser player, Damien Williams. With Adam Gase looking to ride Ajayi this season, the former Boise State star is worth a high fantasy pick, but his lack of receiving versatility still keeps him behind the likes of Le'Veon Bell, Ezekiel Elliott, LeSean McCoy, and David Johnson.

Buck Allen   Height: 6-0   Weight: 221   College: USC   Draft: 2015/4 (125)   Born: 27-Aug-1991   Age: 26   Risk: Red

Year	Team	G/GS	Snaps	Runs	Yds	Yd/R	TD	FUM	DVOA	Rk	DYAR	Rk	YAR	Suc%	Rk	BTkl	Rec	Pass	Yds	C%	Yd/C	TD	YAC	DVOA	Rk	DYAR	Rk
2015	BAL	16/6	393	137	514	3.8	1	2	-3.2%	29	31	30	0	47%	19	23	45	62	353	73%	7.8	2	6.7	-6.2%	33	27	29
2016	BAL	8/0	41	9	34	3.8	0	0	-18.0%	--	-3	--	2	56%	--	3	3	4	15	75%	5.0	0	7.3	-12.1%	--	0	--
2017	BAL			25	107	4.3	0	1	-2.3%								15	19	100	79%	6.6	0		0.5%			

Made extraneous by the unearthing of Terrance West, Allen is a gamer who goes hard and can't quite compensate for his lack of burst or change of direction to find a path to starting. His conceptual understanding of the game is strong and he should be able to hack it for a few more years at least. But he's no better than the fourth-string back on the Baltimore roster, and could benefit from a change of scenery.

C.J. Anderson
Height: 5-8   Weight: 224   College: California   Draft: 2013/FA   Born: 2-Feb-1991   Age: 26   Risk: Red

Year	Team	G/GS	Snaps	Runs	Yds	Yd/R	TD	FUM	DVOA	Rk	DYAR	Rk	YAR	Suc%	Rk	BTkl	Rec	Pass	Yds	C%	Yd/C	TD	YAC	DVOA	Rk	DYAR	Rk
2014	DEN	15/7	495	179	849	4.7	8	1	17.5%	4	196	7	215	51%	10	46	34	44	324	77%	9.5	2	8.3	13.0%	14	65	13
2015	DEN	15/6	500	152	720	4.7	5	2	-3.2%	27	34	28	70	41%	41	31	25	36	183	69%	7.3	0	6.0	-27.8%	53	-23	51
2016	DEN	7/7	314	110	437	4.0	4	0	-13.5%	36	-23	35	9	39%	41	17	16	24	128	67%	8.0	1	6.8	-15.4%	--	-2	--
2017	DEN			195	848	4.4	9	2	0.6%								32	44	256	73%	8.0	0		-0.3%			

Anderson tends to look the part of a good featured back when the Broncos are in the national spotlight. He looked fantastic on opening night last season, when he gained 139 yards from scrimmage and scored two touchdowns against the Panthers. The last we saw of him, he had his only 100-yard rushing game of 2016 against the Texans on a Monday night. But in between those performances, Anderson was largely a non-factor, averaging 3.2 yards per carry in five games. He also missed the final nine games with a torn meniscus. New head coach Vance Joseph has said that Denver will employ a running back by committee approach, so look for Anderson to share touches with Jamaal Charles and Devontae Booker this year as that elusive first 1,000-yard rushing season evades him again.

Cameron Artis-Payne
Height: 5-10   Weight: 212   College: Auburn   Draft: 2015/5 (174)   Born: 23-Jun-1992   Age: 25   Risk: Blue

Year	Team	G/GS	Snaps	Runs	Yds	Yd/R	TD	FUM	DVOA	Rk	DYAR	Rk	YAR	Suc%	Rk	BTkl	Rec	Pass	Yds	C%	Yd/C	TD	YAC	DVOA	Rk	DYAR	Rk
2015	CAR	7/0	113	45	183	4.1	1	0	-9.2%	--	-1	--	-10	38%	--	7	5	5	58	100%	11.6	0	12.2	90.1%	--	31	--
2016	CAR	3/3	84	36	144	4.0	2	0	-4.5%	--	6	--	21	50%	--	8	1	1	11	100%	11.0	0	15.0	128.6%	--	8	--
2017	CAR			22	96	4.5	0	1	5.8%								4	5	25	80%	6.3	0		-1.1%			

Artis-Payne was a first-down wonder, with a 60 percent success rate and a 40.2% DVOA on 20 carries. His other 16 attempts were horrible, with a 36 percent success rate and minus-35.4% DVOA. With Christian McCaffrey around, CAP's snaps will be capped.

Matt Asiata
Height: 5-11   Weight: 220   College: Utah   Draft: 2011/FA   Born: 24-Jul-1987   Age: 30   Risk: Red

Year	Team	G/GS	Snaps	Runs	Yds	Yd/R	TD	FUM	DVOA	Rk	DYAR	Rk	YAR	Suc%	Rk	BTkl	Rec	Pass	Yds	C%	Yd/C	TD	YAC	DVOA	Rk	DYAR	Rk
2014	MIN	15/9	524	164	570	3.5	9	1	1.0%	17	69	20	75	52%	6	10	44	63	312	70%	7.1	1	7.7	-23.9%	48	-33	48
2015	MIN	16/0	199	29	112	3.9	0	0	-11.8%	--	-3	--	-1	38%	--	7	19	22	132	86%	6.9	0	10.5	-19.5%	--	-6	--
2016	MIN	16/6	407	121	402	3.3	6	1	-10.8%	33	-13	32	-15	50%	14	22	32	38	263	84%	8.2	0	8.2	11.5%	15	54	18
2017	DET			26	90	3.4	1	1	2.3%								15	18	105	83%	7.0	1		6.2%			

The arrival of Latavius Murray in Minnesota made Asiata redundant. Murray will take over the short-yardage role in the Vikings offense, tasked with running into the wall of bodies that never moves anywhere. Asiata has never been a great physical talent or a nuanced runner, but his well-rounded skill set means he is more than capable of filling a role within a variety of offenses. Asiata's pass-blocking and receiving ability make him a potential backup to Theo Riddick in his new home.

Peyton Barber
Height: 5-10   Weight: 228   College: Auburn   Draft: 2016/FA   Born: 27-Jun-1994   Age: 23   Risk: Green

Year	Team	G/GS	Snaps	Runs	Yds	Yd/R	TD	FUM	DVOA	Rk	DYAR	Rk	YAR	Suc%	Rk	BTkl	Rec	Pass	Yds	C%	Yd/C	TD	YAC	DVOA	Rk	DYAR	Rk
2016	TB	15/1	136	55	223	4.1	1	0	-17.2%	--	-19	--	11	47%	--	8	5	6	28	83%	5.6	0	2.8	-10.2%	--	1	--
2017	TB			35	132	3.7	0	1	-10.4%								7	8	51	88%	7.3	0		11.2%			

Though his name suggests a sordid backstory involving relatives of Eli and Tiki, Peyton is actually a cousin of former Cowboys running back Marion Barber. Injuries forced him onto the field last year, where he was basically the definition of replacement-level. This year, his special teams contributions might be enough for him to stick on the roster, but his playing time on offense will probably take a haircut. He doesn't have a return job with which to impress, and is not a viable third-down back. A downhill plodder with quick feet and good vision but limited agility, he may get occasional work in short-yardage situations. It's difficult to find any task at which at least two of his teammates aren't better—except, perhaps, staying healthy.

Le'Veon Bell

Height: 6-1   Weight: 230   College: Michigan State   Draft: 2013/2 (48)   Born: 18-Feb-1992 Age: 25   Risk: Red

Year	Team	G/GS	Snaps	Runs	Yds	Yd/R	TD	FUM	DVOA	Rk	DYAR	Rk	YAR	Suc%	Rk	BTkl	Rec	Pass	Yds	C%	Yd/C	TD	YAC	DVOA	Rk	DYAR	Rk
2014	PIT	16/16	927	290	1361	4.7	8	0	8.6%	9	205	5	283	51%	9	59	83	105	854	79%	10.3	3	9.8	38.4%	3	316	1
2015	PIT	6/6	301	113	556	4.9	3	0	28.1%	1	162	5	127	50%	10	19	24	26	136	92%	5.7	0	5.8	-21.3%	49	-10	48
2016	PIT	12/12	781	261	1268	4.9	7	4	17.3%	5	277	3	271	56%	3	61	75	94	616	80%	8.2	2	8.9	16.2%	12	165	2
2017	PIT			298	1520	5.1	8	3	17.6%								79	100	704	79%	8.9	1		22.5%			

At this point in his career, Bell's offensive production is unmatched in NFL history. Of the 135 players with at least 4,000 yards from scrimmage in their first four seasons, none can top Bell's average of 128.7 yards per game. Bell and Marcus Allen are the only players to average 80 yards a game rushing and 40 more receiving in their first four years. It was a no-brainer for Pittsburgh to use the franchise tag to stop Bell from leaving in free agency. That means Bell will make $12 million in 2017—about $4 million more than the next-highest paid running back, LeSean McCoy—but the two sides were unable to come to a long-term deal. In an interview with ESPN, Bell said he should get the money of a top running back, plus the money of a No. 2 receiver. That's overstating things a bit—more than three-quarters of Bell's targets came out of the backfield—but there's no question that Bell's receiving value is a big part of the package he offers as a player. Bell has not signed his franchise tender and could "hold out" from training camp in protest, but he's not likely to see much action until the games start anyway, as he recovers from groin surgery in March.

Giovani Bernard

Height: 5-8   Weight: 202   College: North Carolina   Draft: 2013/2 (37)   Born: 22-Nov-1991 Age: 26   Risk: Red

Year	Team	G/GS	Snaps	Runs	Yds	Yd/R	TD	FUM	DVOA	Rk	DYAR	Rk	YAR	Suc%	Rk	BTkl	Rec	Pass	Yds	C%	Yd/C	TD	YAC	DVOA	Rk	DYAR	Rk
2014	CIN	13/9	509	168	680	4.0	5	0	-8.1%	32	3	32	8	39%	38	19	43	59	349	73%	8.1	2	8.4	0.8%	22	48	21
2015	CIN	16/1	580	154	730	4.7	2	1	11.8%	8	131	10	130	49%	13	37	49	66	472	74%	9.6	0	9.3	14.6%	16	97	12
2016	CIN	10/2	394	91	337	3.7	2	1	-2.1%	--	24	--	22	49%	--	17	39	51	336	76%	8.6	1	6.4	22.4%	7	101	10
2017	CIN			86	372	4.3	1	1	3.6%								46	58	375	79%	8.2	1		10.8%			

If you're a subscriber to the theory that teams tell you how they view a player by how they use him, then the Bengals clearly think Bernard is a third-down back. He has only been used situationally since Jeremy Hill was drafted, and now he's behind Joe Mixon too. Coming off a late-season torn ACL, Bernard may not be cleared for September. In the final year of his rookie deal, it's pretty important that he shows something when he gets back on the field. He's the kind of guy the Patriots find and turn into a 1,000-yard rusher, but he must stay healthy to fulfil that promise. At his worst, last year's Bernard was a good third-down back. The potential for more is there if his body can take the pounding.

LeGarrette Blount

Height: 6-0   Weight: 247   College: Oregon   Draft: 2010/FA   Born: 5-Dec-1986 Age: 31   Risk: Green

Year	Team	G/GS	Snaps	Runs	Yds	Yd/R	TD	FUM	DVOA	Rk	DYAR	Rk	YAR	Suc%	Rk	BTkl	Rec	Pass	Yds	C%	Yd/C	TD	YAC	DVOA	Rk	DYAR	Rk
2014	2TM	16/1	231	125	547	4.4	5	1	1.6%	15	56	22	54	46%	19	14	10	12	54	83%	5.4	0	6.1	-15.3%	--	-1	--
2015	NE	12/6	308	165	703	4.3	6	1	0.2%	20	64	21	91	52%	6	23	6	7	43	86%	7.2	1	5.2	39.5%	--	21	--
2016	NE	16/8	527	299	1161	3.9	18	2	1.5%	18	131	14	84	44%	28	48	7	8	38	88%	5.4	0	6.1	-31.0%	--	-7	--
2017	PHI			176	684	3.9	9	2	-2.6%								7	9	45	78%	6.5	1		3.8%			

Blount averaged 25 carries and 99.3 yards in three September games last year (when Tom Brady was unavailable, of course), but averaged 18.3 carries for 60.3 yards in December and 11.7 for 36.3 in the playoffs. The Patriots didn't need much more than goal-line and fourth-quarter battering ram duties after Brady's return, which Blount handled well enough, so it is hard to tell if Blount was worn down late in the year by age/early-season use or just trapped in cog-in-the-machine mode.

Blount arrived at Eagles camp in great shape and spirits, looking and sounding like he was ready for some more 25-carry afternoons, but his near-uselessness as a receiver will limit his opportunities with the Eagles almost as much as it did with the Patriots. And, of course, the Eagles won't get to the 5-yard line as often as the Patriots did, so Blount's touchdown total will suffer.

Alfred Blue

Height: 6-2   Weight: 223   College: Louisiana St.   Draft: 2014/6 (181)   Born: 27-Apr-1991   Age: 26   Risk: Green

Year	Team	G/GS	Snaps	Runs	Yds	Yd/R	TD	FUM	DVOA	Rk	DYAR	Rk	YAR	Suc%	Rk	BTkl	Rec	Pass	Yds	C%	Yd/C	TD	YAC	DVOA	Rk	DYAR	Rk
2014	HOU	16/3	336	169	528	3.1	2	0	-21.3%	43	-88	43	-60	39%	36	6	15	18	113	83%	7.5	1	5.0	25.4%	--	41	--
2015	HOU	16/9	368	183	698	3.8	2	2	-0.2%	22	61	22	10	45%	29	20	15	16	109	94%	7.3	1	4.5	26.1%	--	31	--
2016	HOU	14/2	238	100	420	4.2	1	1	-7.2%	27	6	27	29	45%	24	10	12	16	40	75%	3.3	0	2.3	-59.7%	--	-42	--
2017	HOU			41	159	3.9	0	2	-8.5%								9	12	65	75%	7.3	1		0.5%			

A hilarious SB Nation draft packet preview of "bold predictions" theorized that the Texans should trade up with the Jets to try to acquire Mitchell Trubisky. The price? You guessed it: Alfred Blue. Alfred Blue's parents, named as Jets co-GMs, wouldn't make that trade. Blue is a run-right-at-the-tackles guy with little else to recommend. With D'Onta Foreman in town to play that sledgehammer role, Blue will likely see a large reduction in workload

Devontae Booker

Height: 5-11   Weight: 219   College: Utah   Draft: 2016/4 (136)   Born: 27-May-1992   Age: 25   Risk: Green

Year	Team	G/GS	Snaps	Runs	Yds	Yd/R	TD	FUM	DVOA	Rk	DYAR	Rk	YAR	Suc%	Rk	BTkl	Rec	Pass	Yds	C%	Yd/C	TD	YAC	DVOA	Rk	DYAR	Rk
2016	DEN	16/6	497	174	612	3.5	4	4	-21.1%	39	-95	41	-62	45%	27	24	31	45	265	69%	8.5	1	8.3	-31.4%	51	-41	50
2017	DEN			78	306	3.9	2	2	-5.6%								20	26	142	77%	7.1	0		0.1%			

Booker ranked next-to-last in rushing DYAR last season. He was dead last in receiving DYAR, which makes him a weird choice to be Denver's third-leading receiver in 2016, but he was. When healthy, C.J. Anderson is a better back than Booker. When healthy, which is a rarity these days, Jamaal Charles is a better back than Booker too. Last season, there was a six-game stretch following Anderson's season-ending knee injury last season when Booker was the Broncos' featured back, and he averaged 58 rushing yards per game and just 3.12 yards per carry. Booker is the only player since 2015 to have zero 20-yard runs on at least 150 carries.

The Broncos only used a fourth-round pick on Booker in 2016, so it's not a Paxton Lynch situation where they are motivated to get him on the field. While a better offensive line could help Booker out this year, he just hasn't shown anything impressive yet to warrant more touches. If anything, he deserves fewer opportunities.

Malcolm Brown

Height: 5-11   Weight: 224   College: Texas   Draft: 2015/FA   Born: 15-May-1993   Age: 24   Risk: Blue

Year	Team	G/GS	Snaps	Runs	Yds	Yd/R	TD	FUM	DVOA	Rk	DYAR	Rk	YAR	Suc%	Rk	BTkl	Rec	Pass	Yds	C%	Yd/C	TD	YAC	DVOA	Rk	DYAR	Rk
2015	STL	1/0	9	4	17	4.3	0	0	-5.9%	--	0	--	2	50%	--	1	1	1	-2	100%	-2.0	0	3.0	-184.6%	--	-9	--
2016	LARM	16/0	65	18	39	2.2	0	1	-67.0%	--	-44	--	-43	22%	--	4	3	3	46	100%	15.3	0	14.0	166.9%	--	25	--
2017	LARM			21	66	3.2	0	1	-18.1%								6	8	25	75%	4.1	0		-18.2%			

Starting running back Todd Gurley struggled in his second year with the Rams, so you can imagine how his backup fared behind one of the worst offensive lines in the league. Brown couldn't get anything going on his 18 carries, but at least he had a few nice catches out of the backfield. (How about that receiving DVOA!) Alas, the majority of Brown's touches occurred after it became clear that Los Angeles' season was ending in Week 17. If the Rams do mount a charge to the playoffs this season, Brown will likely not play a huge part in it. But hey, somebody has to start if Gurley gets injured; thus, the Risk of Blue.

Rex Burkhead

Height: 5-10   Weight: 214   College: Nebraska   Draft: 2013/6 (190)   Born: 2-Jul-1990   Age: 27   Risk: Yellow

Year	Team	G/GS	Snaps	Runs	Yds	Yd/R	TD	FUM	DVOA	Rk	DYAR	Rk	YAR	Suc%	Rk	BTkl	Rec	Pass	Yds	C%	Yd/C	TD	YAC	DVOA	Rk	DYAR	Rk
2014	CIN	9/0	33	9	27	3.0	1	0	-34.9%	--	-7	--	-2	22%	--	1	7	10	49	70%	7.0	0	5.6	-7.7%	--	3	--
2015	CIN	16/0	73	4	4	1.0	0	1	-222.9%	--	-30	--	-31	0%	--	0	10	15	94	67%	9.4	1	2.5	0.9%	--	13	--
2016	CIN	16/1	238	74	344	4.6	2	1	42.0%	--	163	--	126	62%	--	24	17	20	145	85%	8.5	0	8.4	7.3%	--	22	--
2017	NE			98	441	4.5	2	3	6.2%								26	32	235	81%	9.0	1		17.8%			

A career special-teamer with 13 carries over his first three seasons, Burkhead exploded down the stretch of a lost season for Cincinnati. Over the Bengals' final six games, Burkhead averaged 4.5 yards per carry. He did not get enough carries to qualify on the primary running back leaderboard, but his 163 rushing DYAR would have ranked 12th overall last season. Burkhead received a surprisingly pricey one-year, $3.15 million pact from the Patriots this offseason, though it's unclear if he'll receive the opportunity to reprise his late-season productivity. Fellow offseason arrival Mike Gillislee is the favorite to lead the team in carries, and receiving backs James White and Dion Lewis also loom on the depth chart. Bill Belichick invests heavily in special teams, so it's entirely possible he simply wanted the player who led Cincy with 12 special teams tackles in 2016. If Burkhead does get a chance in 2017, though, cue up all the lazy Danny Woodhead comps.

Travaris Cadet Height: 6-1 Weight: 210 College: Appalachian State Draft: 2012/FA Born: 1-Feb-1989 Age: 28 Risk: Red

Year	Team	G/GS	Snaps	Runs	Yds	Yd/R	TD	FUM	DVOA	Rk	DYAR	Rk	YAR	Suc%	Rk	BTkl	Rec	Pass	Yds	C%	Yd/C	TD	YAC	DVOA	Rk	DYAR	Rk
2014	NO	15/1	205	10	32	3.2	0	2	-55.8%	--	-18	--	-16	50%	--	0	38	51	296	75%	7.8	1	6.4	5.4%	18	57	15
2015	3TM	7/1	117	11	28	2.5	0	1	-69.0%	--	-26	--	-19	27%	--	2	17	22	214	77%	12.6	1	9.0	51.6%	--	78	--
2016	NO	15/1	247	4	19	4.8	0	0	5.8%	--	3	--	1	50%	--	6	40	54	281	74%	7.0	4	5.2	-1.2%	26	44	22
2017	NO			8	31	3.8	0	0	1.9%								35	41	291	85%	8.3	1		15.0%			

Ostensibly the passing-down back for the Saints, Cadet was outplayed by Mark Ingram and/or Tim Hightower in every phase of the game last year. A below-average receiver on first and second down, he became more effective on later downs—but his DVOA of 38.9% on third and fourth down was blown away by Hightower's 76.0%, never mind Ingram's 144.3%. Cadet played almost a quarter of his offensive snaps last year as a slot receiver or flanker, contributing one receiving touchdown from each of those positions. He only has 26 rushing attempts in 63 NFL games, so the passing game is his only chance to make an impact on offense. Even that potential is capped now, with rookie Alvin Kamara impinging on the veteran's territory. Kamara's ascension could leave Cadet with only kick return duty, where he has also underwhelmed: his 14.4-yard return average was the lowest on the team, and ranked 69th of the 74 players with at least four returns.

Ka'Deem Carey Height: 5-9 Weight: 207 College: Arizona Draft: 2014/4 (117) Born: 30-Oct-1992 Age: 25 Risk: Green

Year	Team	G/GS	Snaps	Runs	Yds	Yd/R	TD	FUM	DVOA	Rk	DYAR	Rk	YAR	Suc%	Rk	BTkl	Rec	Pass	Yds	C%	Yd/C	TD	YAC	DVOA	Rk	DYAR	Rk
2014	CHI	14/0	98	36	158	4.4	0	0	21.2%	--	47	--	48	53%	--	8	5	6	57	83%	11.4	0	8.6	43.5%	--	17	--
2015	CHI	11/1	77	43	159	3.7	2	1	21.2%	--	56	--	34	58%	--	4	3	3	19	100%	6.3	1	2.7	53.6%	--	18	--
2016	CHI	12/0	98	32	126	3.9	0	0	-6.4%	--	3	--	-6	38%	--	7	5	7	55	71%	11.0	0	12.0	41.5%	--	24	--
2017	CHI			13	51	3.9	0	1	-1.1%								5	6	32	83%	6.3	0		1.1%			

Largely a goal-line vulture over his first three seasons, Carey will now be reduced to competing with Tarik Cohen and Jeremy Langford for the scraps left over by Jordan Howard and Benny Cunningham. Carey is in a fortunate position because he has advantages over both of the backs he will be competing with. Cohen obviously has less experience at this level and less time with the coaching staff, while Langford has been an inefficient volume runner when given the opportunity. Langford may have been the starter ahead of Carey and Jordan Howard entering last season, but his lack of versatility becomes more important when competing for backup roles.

Jamaal Charles Height: 5-11 Weight: 200 College: Texas Draft: 2008/3 (73) Born: 27-Dec-1986 Age: 31 Risk: Yellow

Year	Team	G/GS	Snaps	Runs	Yds	Yd/R	TD	FUM	DVOA	Rk	DYAR	Rk	YAR	Suc%	Rk	BTkl	Rec	Pass	Yds	C%	Yd/C	TD	YAC	DVOA	Rk	DYAR	Rk
2014	KC	15/15	650	206	1033	5.0	9	5	19.9%	2	249	3	212	54%	2	30	40	60	291	68%	7.3	5	7.7	-13.5%	39	1	39
2015	KC	5/5	264	71	364	5.1	4	3	24.8%	--	96	--	90	48%	--	16	21	30	177	70%	8.4	1	9.8	-12.1%	42	3	42
2016	KC	3/0	27	12	40	3.3	1	0	2.6%	--	6	--	8	42%	--	0	2	3	14	67%	7.0	0	8.5	-64.0%	--	-11	--
2017	DEN			88	388	4.4	2	1	4.7%								27	39	213	69%	7.9	1		-5.5%			

Last season was the first time that Charles, regardless of carry total, failed to average 5.0 yards per carry. He comes to Denver, about to turn 31, with a different role in mind. Charles can serve as the team's best receiving back, only needing to spell C.J. Anderson and Devontae Booker when necessary. If that helps to keep him fresh, then the Broncos have a low-risk investment ($2.5 million for one year) in a player who was once special before injuries caught up to him.

Tevin Coleman

Height: 5-11   Weight: 206   College: Indiana   Draft: 2015/3 (73)   Born: 16-Apr-1993   Age: 24   Risk: Green

Year	Team	G/GS	Snaps	Runs	Yds	Yd/R	TD	FUM	DVOA	Rk	DYAR	Rk	YAR	Suc%	Rk	BTkl	Rec	Pass	Yds	C%	Yd/C	TD	YAC	DVOA	Rk	DYAR	Rk
2015	ATL	12/3	226	87	392	4.5	1	3	-11.9%	--	-12	--	13	49%	--	3	2	11	14	18%	7.0	0	5.5	-99.5%	--	-46	--
2016	ATL	13/0	353	118	520	4.4	8	1	9.7%	12	86	18	90	45%	25	24	31	40	421	78%	13.6	3	12.1	48.8%	1	136	5
2017	ATL			141	623	4.4	5	4	3.9%								39	49	403	80%	10.3	2		22.4%			

Coleman was flawed as a rookie but lived up to his vast potential in 2016, especially in the passing game, where he led all running backs in receiving DVOA. Coleman and fellow back Davonte Freeman upended the classic "Thunder and Lightning" combo that to date was the preferred paradigm. The two backs were mostly interchangeable, equally capable of slashing for tough yards, breaking a long gainer, or catching passes out of the backfield. The similarity gave Atlanta a decided strategic advantage, as defenses couldn't adjust when one back subbed in for the other. It will be interesting to see how Coleman's role changes with Kyle Shanahan gone. Steve Sarkisian tended to favor a more downhill power game while in college, as opposed to Shanny's beloved perimeter zone scheme. It's hard to imagine Sark upsetting the apple cart, but even subtle changes could allow defenses to hone in on tendencies when Coleman is in the game. Coleman is talented enough to thrive in any scheme, however.

Alex Collins

Height: 5-10   Weight: 217   College: Arkansas   Draft: 2016/5 (171)   Born: 26-Aug-1994   Age: 23   Risk: Green

Year	Team	G/GS	Snaps	Runs	Yds	Yd/R	TD	FUM	DVOA	Rk	DYAR	Rk	YAR	Suc%	Rk	BTkl	Rec	Pass	Yds	C%	Yd/C	TD	YAC	DVOA	Rk	DYAR	Rk
2016	SEA	11/0	141	31	125	4.0	1	2	-13.0%	--	-6	--	-8	35%	--	7	11	11	84	100%	7.6	0	7.4	35.7%	--	37	--
2017	SEA			22	82	3.6	1	0	-5.4%								9	11	52	82%	5.8	0		-2.5%			

A 2016 fifth-round pick out of Arkansas, Collins spent much of 2016 waiting his turn behind Christine Michael, Thomas Rawls, and C.J. Prosise, among others. While Michael has since departed, Eddie Lacy is now in town to compete for starter's carries. Collins will likely be relegated to waiting for one of the three backs ahead of him to get hurt. All three did in 2016, but even then Collins will need to prove that his two fumbles on 31 carries from 2016 were just a small-sample fluke for the Seattle coaching staff to trust him with a larger share of the workload.

James Conner

Height: 6-1   Weight: 233   College: Pittsburgh   Draft: 2017/3 (105)   Born: 5-May-1995   Age: 22   Risk: Green

Year	Team	G/GS	Snaps	Runs	Yds	Yd/R	TD	FUM	DVOA	Rk	DYAR	Rk	YAR	Suc%	Rk	BTkl	Rec	Pass	Yds	C%	Yd/C	TD	YAC	DVOA	Rk	DYAR	Rk
2017	PIT			53	255	4.9	1	1	12.1%								10	11	70	91%	7.0	0		3.3%			

As a sophomore in 2014, Conner was named ACC Player of the Year, leading the conference and finishing in the top ten in the country with 1,765 rushing yards and 26 touchdowns. Then came a torn MCL in the 2015 opener, excessive fatigue as he tried to rehab that injury, and finally a diagnosis of Hodgkin's lymphoma in December. Conner spent the first half of 2016 training for a return for football and going through a dozen rounds of chemotherapy. With a cancer-free declaration, Conner was again Pittsburgh's bell-cow back last year. His total numbers (1,092 rushing yards, 16 touchdowns) were down significantly from his 2014 campaign, but he finished on a high note, topping 100 yards four times in five games in October and November. Conner's Speed Score (99.7) and BackCAST projection (+9.1%) are decidedly mediocre, but given his unique medical history there is reason to believe he is being underrated by these metrics.

Dalvin Cook

Height: 5-10   Weight: 210   College: Florida State   Draft: 2017/2 (41)   Born: 10-Aug-1995   Age: 22   Risk: Yellow

Year	Team	G/GS	Snaps	Runs	Yds	Yd/R	TD	FUM	DVOA	Rk	DYAR	Rk	YAR	Suc%	Rk	BTkl	Rec	Pass	Yds	C%	Yd/C	TD	YAC	DVOA	Rk	DYAR	Rk
2017	MIN			184	816	4.4	5	5	3.1%								52	63	346	83%	6.7	1		-5.1%			

Dalvin Cook proved to be one of the more peculiar draft prospects from recent years. His tape was excellent. He consistently makes defenders miss, reads what the defense is doing in front of him, and races downfield for big plays. Yet when he went to the combine his testing proved to be disastrous, causing him to fall out of the first round. The Vikings are hoping that his ability as a running back matters more than his physical limitations in the NFL. It's not like the Florida State back was playing against a lower level of competition in college. Expecting Cook to put up huge numbers as a rookie would be irrational. Even if he proves to be a great player, the Vikings rotated their running backs last season and added Latavius Murray in free agency this year. Cook is the better receiver of the two, but Murray is likely to get the majority of goal-line carries.

Isaiah Crowell

Height: 5-11 Weight: 225 College: Alabama State Draft: 2014/FA Born: 8-Jan-1993 Age: 24 Risk: Yellow

Year	Team	G/GS	Snaps	Runs	Yds	Yd/R	TD	FUM	DVOA	Rk	DYAR	Rk	YAR	Suc%	Rk	BTkl	Rec	Pass	Yds	C%	Yd/C	TD	YAC	DVOA	Rk	DYAR	Rk
2014	CLE	16/4	382	148	607	4.1	8	3	-3.6%	25	30	25	43	44%	28	6	9	14	87	64%	9.7	0	7.6	-3.6%	--	8	--
2015	CLE	16/9	476	185	706	3.8	4	0	-4.0%	30	36	27	-21	41%	40	25	19	22	182	86%	9.6	1	11.9	17.9%	--	37	--
2016	CLE	16/16	568	198	952	4.8	7	2	13.4%	8	169	11	94	39%	40	37	40	53	319	75%	8.0	0	8.4	-2.4%	28	33	28
2017	CLE			227	973	4.3	7	3	-0.4%								39	52	326	75%	8.4	1		11.4%			

Though he was a full-time starter for the first time in 2016, Crowell's rushing numbers didn't change much from what he had done in prior seasons. He remained a boom-or-bust runner, who just happened to get a little more boom than he had before. More than 20 percent of his yardage total came on three runs: a 42-yard gain against Cincinnati, a 67-yarder against Pittsburgh, and an 85-yard touchdown against Baltimore. Take those three plays away, and Crowell's rushing average drops to 3.9 yards per carry—exactly what he did in his first two seasons. What was new for Crowell was his role in the passing game, which blossomed in Hue Jackson's offense. That seemed to drop off by the end of the year, though. In the first ten games of the season, he averaged 23.4 receiving yards per game, 11.1 yards per catch. After that, those averages fell to 14.2 and 4.5. Jackson said after the season he wanted to get Crowell more carries in 2017, but it's important to make sure he can contribute as a receiver as well.

Crowell was a restricted free agent this year, and didn't sign his one-year tender until May, hoping the Browns or someone else would break the bank to get him. That didn't happen, but if Crowell continues to grow, he will leave Cleveland with a very tough decision to make after the season.

Benny Cunningham

Height: 5-10 Weight: 217 College: Middle Tennessee State Draft: 2013/FA Born: 7-Jul-1990 Age: 27 Risk: Green

Year	Team	G/GS	Snaps	Runs	Yds	Yd/R	TD	FUM	DVOA	Rk	DYAR	Rk	YAR	Suc%	Rk	BTkl	Rec	Pass	Yds	C%	Yd/C	TD	YAC	DVOA	Rk	DYAR	Rk
2014	STL	16/2	396	66	246	3.7	3	1	1.7%	--	26	--	7	38%	--	12	45	53	352	85%	7.8	1	7.0	25.7%	8	109	6
2015	STL	16/1	282	37	140	3.8	0	1	-14.9%	--	-10	--	-29	38%	--	21	26	36	250	72%	9.6	0	9.2	28.3%	8	67	20
2016	LARM	11/0	179	21	101	4.8	0	1	-11.4%	--	-2	--	-14	48%	--	9	16	21	91	76%	5.7	0	5.0	-24.0%	--	-12	--
2017	CHI			23	100	4.3	0	1	2.6%								20	25	145	80%	7.3	0		5.3%			

The Rams downgraded when they let Benny Cunningham leave and replaced him with Lance Dunbar. Nothing against Dunbar—a good player, a good receiving back. But Cunningham can comfortably execute as a pass blocker, consistently picking up his assignments while showing off the strength to repel defenders. He is also capable of running routes out of the backfield before making defenders miss in space. Where he is most improved over Dunbar is as a runner. He can be trusted to make the right reads and run hard between the tackles.

Had he stayed in Los Angeles, Cunningham would have been the perfect complement to Todd Gurley. Now that he is in Chicago, he is a perfect complement to Jordan Howard. He should open the season as the team's third-down back.

Kenneth Dixon

Height: 5-10 Weight: 215 College: Louisiana Tech Draft: 2016/4 (134) Born: 21-Jan-1994 Age: 23 Risk: Green

Year	Team	G/GS	Snaps	Runs	Yds	Yd/R	TD	FUM	DVOA	Rk	DYAR	Rk	YAR	Suc%	Rk	BTkl	Rec	Pass	Yds	C%	Yd/C	TD	YAC	DVOA	Rk	DYAR	Rk
2016	BAL	12/0	258	88	382	4.3	2	1	5.1%	--	54	--	54	55%	--	34	30	41	162	73%	5.4	1	6.2	-20.6%	46	-14	47
2017	BAL			70	287	4.1	1	2	-3.2%								29	34	202	84%	7.1	1		10.3%			

If you believe in the talent, have some patience. Dixon was well-regarded for a small school prospect coming out last year, when an injury kept him from seeing the field until Week 5. He came back before he was fully ready to, and only demonstrated his skill from Week 9 on, in a situation that did nothing to help him. He was easily the best back Baltimore had last year, and despite getting saddled with a four-game suspension for violating the NFL's substance abuse policy, that remains true today. Remember his name in October. It might bail you out of some fantasy football conundrums.

Kenyan Drake

Height: 6-1 Weight: 210 College: Alabama Draft: 2016/3 (73) Born: 26-Jan-1994 Age: 23 Risk: Blue

Year	Team	G/GS	Snaps	Runs	Yds	Yd/R	TD	FUM	DVOA	Rk	DYAR	Rk	YAR	Suc%	Rk	BTkl	Rec	Pass	Yds	C%	Yd/C	TD	YAC	DVOA	Rk	DYAR	Rk
2016	MIA	16/1	109	33	179	5.4	2	0	38.1%	--	60	--	57	42%	--	3	9	10	46	90%	5.1	0	7.1	0.6%	--	8	--
2017	MIA			55	231	4.2	1	2	-2.6%								21	26	119	81%	5.7	1		-4.9%			

Drake returned a kickoff for a touchdown to help Alabama win a national championship in his final college game. His biggest splash as an NFL rookie was also a kick return for a touchdown, going 96 yards for the win against the Jets last year. Drake has that big-play ability in the open field and could be a nice complement to Jay Ajayi's power style.

Shaun Draughn Height: 6-0   Weight: 205   College: North Carolina   Draft: 2011/FA   Born: 7-Dec-1987   Age: 30   Risk: Green

Year	Team	G/GS	Snaps	Runs	Yds	Yd/R	TD	FUM	DVOA	Rk	DYAR	Rk	YAR	Suc%	Rk	BTkl	Rec	Pass	Yds	C%	Yd/C	TD	YAC	DVOA	Rk	DYAR	Rk
2014	3TM	10/0	20	10	19	1.9	0	0	-62.7%	--	-20	--	-22	40%	--	0	0	0	0	--	0.0	0	--	--	--	--	--
2015	2TM	11/6	263	78	273	3.5	1	1	-16.8%	--	-24	--	-27	40%	--	13	27	35	176	77%	6.5	0	6.5	-27.3%	52	-25	52
2016	SF	16/1	314	74	196	2.6	4	1	-0.7%	--	24	--	-26	32%	--	17	29	39	263	74%	9.1	2	6.4	14.2%	13	60	17
2017	NYG			28	104	3.7	0	1	-8.9%								16	23	117	70%	7.3	0		-5.8%			

Six teams have employed Draughn in the past five years, and none of the six thought he was worth keeping around. The Giants will be the seventh squad to kick the tires, but even there he seems redundant. Draughn's best asset is his receiving ability, but will he find a role on a team that already has Shane Vereen returning to health? Or will Draughn end up searching for Team No. 8?

Lance Dunbar Height: 5-8   Weight: 191   College: North Texas   Draft: 2012/FA   Born: 25-Jan-1990   Age: 27   Risk: Red

Year	Team	G/GS	Snaps	Runs	Yds	Yd/R	TD	FUM	DVOA	Rk	DYAR	Rk	YAR	Suc%	Rk	BTkl	Rec	Pass	Yds	C%	Yd/C	TD	YAC	DVOA	Rk	DYAR	Rk
2014	DAL	16/0	138	29	99	3.4	0	0	-16.9%	--	-10	--	-13	45%	--	7	18	22	217	82%	12.1	0	10.8	60.7%	--	88	--
2015	DAL	4/0	92	5	67	13.4	0	0	107.9%	--	13	--	16	40%	--	2	21	23	215	91%	10.2	0	7.2	23.1%	--	45	--
2016	DAL	13/0	139	9	31	3.4	1	1	39.8%	--	19	--	23	56%	--	1	16	24	122	67%	7.6	0	5.2	-17.5%	--	-5	--
2017	LARM			46	173	3.8	0	1	-9.5%								34	49	234	69%	6.9	0		-8.3%			

After five seasons as a backup in Dallas, Dunbar joins the Rams to serve as a backup to Todd Gurley in Los Angeles. Dunbar has never had more than 30 carries in a season and has generally been more impactful as a receiving threat out of the backfield than as a runner in his career. With Ezekiel Elliott commanding the vast majority of running back touches in Dallas in 2016, Dunbar did not have much of a chance to make an impact last season, but he caught 21 passes in just four games in 2015 before tearing multiple ligaments in his knee on a kickoff return that ended his season. If Dunbar can return to something resembling his small-sample 2015 form, he could be a very useful outlet for Jared Goff in the passing game.

Andre Ellington Height: 5-9   Weight: 199   College: Clemson   Draft: 2013/6 (187)   Born: 3-Feb-1989   Age: 28   Risk: Green

Year	Team	G/GS	Snaps	Runs	Yds	Yd/R	TD	FUM	DVOA	Rk	DYAR	Rk	YAR	Suc%	Rk	BTkl	Rec	Pass	Yds	C%	Yd/C	TD	YAC	DVOA	Rk	DYAR	Rk
2014	ARI	12/12	528	201	660	3.3	3	2	-12.3%	35	-29	36	-87	39%	37	13	46	65	395	72%	8.6	2	7.7	-2.6%	27	44	23
2015	ARI	10/2	213	45	289	6.4	3	1	24.4%	--	64	--	63	58%	--	7	15	24	148	63%	9.9	0	5.3	3.7%	--	27	--
2016	ARI	16/0	150	34	96	2.8	0	0	-26.8%	--	-25	--	-33	35%	--	5	12	19	85	63%	7.1	0	6.0	-4.3%	--	8	--
2017	ARI			45	197	4.4	0	1	-1.7%								24	37	230	65%	9.6	1		6.5%			

Ellington has shuttled back and forth between positions this offseason, spending an entire 71 days listed as a wide receiver before returning to the running backs room. Ellington has spent about a fifth of his snaps lined up as a wideout anyway, and there's no reason to expect that would change going forward. Ellington's biggest issue as a running back is a lack of physicality; he broke only five tackles last season and averaged just 2.0 yards after contact. He needs to be used in space to be effective—hence the idea of moving him to receiver. With David Johnson eating up snaps at running back and the healthy returns of John Brown and Jaron Brown, Ellington might find it difficult to see meaningful snaps.

Ezekiel Elliott Height: 6-0   Weight: 225   College: Ohio State   Draft: 2016/1 (4)   Born: 22-Jul-1995   Age: 22   Risk: Green

Year	Team	G/GS	Snaps	Runs	Yds	Yd/R	TD	FUM	DVOA	Rk	DYAR	Rk	YAR	Suc%	Rk	BTkl	Rec	Pass	Yds	C%	Yd/C	TD	YAC	DVOA	Rk	DYAR	Rk
2016	DAL	15/15	716	322	1631	5.1	15	5	15.9%	6	339	1	354	57%	2	69	32	40	363	80%	11.3	1	12.2	26.9%	5	82	11
2017	DAL			319	1545	4.8	14	4	11.4%								34	43	283	79%	8.3	1		14.5%			

The coaching staff that force-fed DeMarco Murray 392 regular-season carries two years ago wasn't going to fret about a small matter like overusing a rookie MVP candidate. Elliott touched the ball 377 times, counting the playoffs. The Cowboys did step back from the abyss late in the season, giving Elliott just 12 carries in the final two games. Curse of 370 fears should be allayed by the fact that Elliott wasn't quite pushed into the danger zone, and the Cowboys line practically spots even ordinary running backs the first 900 yards or so.

Elliott rushed 204 times for 1,120 yards on first downs alone, both the highest figures in the league last season by a wide margin. Murray assembled a jaw-dropping 261 carries for 1,289 yards on first downs just two years ago. Murray also tied Marshawn Lynch and LeSean McCoy for the league lead with 58 red zone carries for the Cowboys in 2014. Elliott rushed just 39 times in the red zone last year, but he gained 144 yards (third in the league) with a whopping 65 percent success rate. One way to prevent overuse is to make the most of your carries so you don't get used like a battering ram.

Kenneth Farrow
Height: 5-9 Weight: 219 College: Houston Draft: 2016/FA Born: 7-Mar-1993 Age: 24 Risk: Red

Year	Team	G/GS	Snaps	Runs	Yds	Yd/R	TD	FUM	DVOA	Rk	DYAR	Rk	YAR	Suc%	Rk	BTkl	Rec	Pass	Yds	C%	Yd/C	TD	YAC	DVOA	Rk	DYAR	Rk
2016	SD	13/2	189	60	192	3.2	0	2	-21.1%	--	-33	--	-27	52%	--	4	13	16	70	81%	5.4	0	6.8	-54.5%	--	-35	--
2017	LACH			37	128	3.5	1	1	-11.8%								9	11	72	82%	8.0	1		12.4%			

In 2016, Farrow had the lowest rate of broken tackles (5.5 percent) and lowest rushing average after contact (1.52 yards) for any running back with at least 50 touches. He will have to battle with Kenjon Barner and Andre Williams just to make the Chargers roster.

Josh Ferguson
Height: 5-10 Weight: 200 College: Illinois Draft: 2016/FA Born: 23-May-1993 Age: 24 Risk: Red

Year	Team	G/GS	Snaps	Runs	Yds	Yd/R	TD	FUM	DVOA	Rk	DYAR	Rk	YAR	Suc%	Rk	BTkl	Rec	Pass	Yds	C%	Yd/C	TD	YAC	DVOA	Rk	DYAR	Rk
2016	IND	16/0	133	15	20	1.3	0	0	-77.0%	--	-38	--	-46	13%	--	6	20	25	136	80%	6.8	0	8.1	-3.7%	31	14	34
2017	IND			13	30	2.3	0	1	-27.0%								10	12	83	83%	8.3	0		11.9%			

The modern NFL has created an interesting running back trend: nobody wants old backs, everyone has draft picks, and fantasy football owners are always looking for the next thing. In that spirit a lot of running backs are drafted on opportunity rather than talent. Matt Waldman's detailed tape work yielded a grade of 29th out of 35 backs for Ferguson. But suddenly he was the only young back on the Colts roster! And he was talked about during OTAs! And... yeah. You can put the shares of Ferguson right in the trash bin next to Jeremy Langford and Matt Jones. He was bad last year, the Colts drafted Marlon Mack, and the general manager who drafted Ferguson is now a special assistant for the Browns.

D'Onta Foreman
Height: 6-0 Weight: 233 College: Texas Draft: 2017/3 (89) Born: 24-Apr-1996 Age: 21 Risk: Green

Year	Team	G/GS	Snaps	Runs	Yds	Yd/R	TD	FUM	DVOA	Rk	DYAR	Rk	YAR	Suc%	Rk	BTkl	Rec	Pass	Yds	C%	Yd/C	TD	YAC	DVOA	Rk	DYAR	Rk
2017	HOU			85	336	4.0	1	2	-7.2%								19	30	131	63%	6.9	1		-20.4%			

230 pounds of run-you-over condensed into a football player. Foreman was the entire Texas offense last season, and has enough power to even bully some smaller NFL linebackers and safeties. However, as a whole, he struggles when he is asked to be more nimble and move east-to-west rather than north-to south. There's star potential here if Foreman learns to stay away from being cutesy and stops fumbling. And if not, Ron Dayne lasted a long time in the NFL too.

Justin Forsett
Height: 5-8 Weight: 194 College: California Draft: 2008/7 (233) Born: 14-Oct-1985 Age: 32 Risk: N/A

Year	Team	G/GS	Snaps	Runs	Yds	Yd/R	TD	FUM	DVOA	Rk	DYAR	Rk	YAR	Suc%	Rk	BTkl	Rec	Pass	Yds	C%	Yd/C	TD	YAC	DVOA	Rk	DYAR	Rk
2014	BAL	16/14	707	235	1266	5.4	8	1	6.7%	12	149	11	207	44%	29	25	44	60	263	75%	6.0	0	7.4	-33.5%	51	-64	55
2015	BAL	10/10	477	151	641	4.2	2	0	9.1%	10	117	13	101	46%	22	12	31	41	153	76%	4.9	0	4.5	-42.6%	57	-64	57
2016	3TM	9/6	265	87	291	3.3	1	2	-37.2%	--	-103	--	-103	34%	--	14	20	28	85	75%	4.3	0	4.8	-40.1%	52	-42	51

Forsett retired this offseason after playing for nearly a quarter of the league in his nine-year career. He peaked in 2014 when he rushed for 1,266 yards with the Ravens in his only Pro Bowl season. Forsett had one touchdown catch on his 210 career receptions, which pairs him with Gerald Riggs (zero scores on 201 catches) as the only players in NFL history to have 200 catches without multiple touchdowns. Forsett was consistently one of the least effective receiving backs in the game, but still averaged 4.7 yards per carry on the ground for his career.

Matt Forte

Height: 6-2 Weight: 218 College: Tulane Draft: 2008/2 (44) Born: 10-Dec-1985 Age: 32 Risk: Yellow

Year	Team	G/GS	Snaps	Runs	Yds	Yd/R	TD	FUM	DVOA	Rk	DYAR	Rk	YAR	Suc%	Rk	BTkl	Rec	Pass	Yds	C%	Yd/C	TD	YAC	DVOA	Rk	DYAR	Rk
2014	CHI	16/16	975	266	1038	3.9	6	2	0.9%	18	113	12	112	50%	12	30	102	131	808	79%	7.9	4	7.7	5.0%	19	127	3
2015	CHI	13/13	600	218	898	4.1	4	2	12.0%	7	192	2	147	48%	17	37	44	58	389	76%	8.8	3	8.0	23.5%	11	112	7
2016	NYJ	14/13	488	218	813	3.7	7	1	-8.8%	30	-2	30	-5	41%	37	38	30	43	263	70%	8.8	1	9.2	-5.6%	33	21	32
2017	NYJ			158	655	4.1	4	1	1.5%								32	45	231	71%	7.2	1		-6.4%			

Forte is one of nine players ever with at least 9,000 yards rushing and 4,000 receiving in his career. He needs 585 yards on the ground and 621 in the air to join Marshall Faulk, Tiki Barber, and Marcus Allen in the 10,000/5,000 club. It's not impossible that he'll get there this year, but it's highly improbable, especially as he loses more and more playing time to Bilal Powell. Forte's home-run speed is all but gone, but he still has a lot of value when it comes to short-yardage (65 conversions with 1 or 2 yards to go since 2014, third-most in the NFL), ball security (one fumble every 176 touches in the last three years, fourth-best among players with at least 500 touches), and catching passes out of the backfield (fifth in the league last year with 157 yards on running back screens—his receiving DVOA was killed by a trio of incomplete passes on third-and-1).

Leonard Fournette

Height: 6-0 Weight: 240 College: Louisiana St. Draft: 2017/1 (4) Born: 18-Jan-1995 Age: 22 Risk: Green

Year	Team	G/GS	Snaps	Runs	Yds	Yd/R	TD	FUM	DVOA	Rk	DYAR	Rk	YAR	Suc%	Rk	BTkl	Rec	Pass	Yds	C%	Yd/C	TD	YAC	DVOA	Rk	DYAR	Rk
2017	JAC			258	1117	4.3	7	3	4.5%								31	39	196	79%	6.3	1		-10.1%			

Add BackCAST to the list of people and things proclaiming Fournette's potential to be a special talent. His +142.2% score is the fourth-highest in the system's 20 years of data, adding support to the YouTube clips dating back to high school and GIFs of him treating SEC defenders like overmatched children. The realistic rookie season expectation for Fournette starts well short of what Ezekiel Elliott did last year, and where his season ends up depends on a couple key factors. First, what kind of run blocking can the Jaguars offensive line provide? It struggled mightily last season en route to finishing 27th in adjusted line yards, but might be improved this year. Second, how is his health? Fournette sparkled in 2015 but only flashed in 2016 thanks to a nagging left ankle injury. Third, how much can he do in the passing game? LSU's offense asked little of him here. Jacksonville will probably ask at least somewhat more, even as a rookie. Fourth, just how athletic is he? He is clearly big and fast, but how is his lateral movement? He did not do agility drills at the combine or his pro day. One thing that made Adrian Peterson so great was his ability to jump-cut across multiple gaps. If Fournette can do the same, he could become the same type of player. Either way, he will be counted on to provide a big upgrade and be a sustaining force for the Jaguars offense in 2017.

Devonta Freeman

Height: 5-8 Weight: 206 College: Florida St. Draft: 2014/4 (103) Born: 15-Mar-1992 Age: 25 Risk: Green

Year	Team	G/GS	Snaps	Runs	Yds	Yd/R	TD	FUM	DVOA	Rk	DYAR	Rk	YAR	Suc%	Rk	BTkl	Rec	Pass	Yds	C%	Yd/C	TD	YAC	DVOA	Rk	DYAR	Rk
2014	ATL	16/0	234	65	248	3.8	1	1	-22.9%	--	-38	--	-47	31%	--	15	30	37	225	81%	7.5	1	5.7	4.1%	20	33	26
2015	ATL	15/13	768	265	1056	4.0	11	3	-0.5%	24	90	15	122	46%	23	54	73	97	578	75%	7.9	3	6.0	-1.2%	28	68	19
2016	ATL	16/16	604	227	1079	4.8	11	1	6.4%	14	148	13	179	50%	12	63	54	65	462	83%	8.6	2	7.7	24.9%	6	141	4
2017	ATL			197	865	4.4	9	2	6.0%								51	67	457	76%	9.0	2		19.4%			

The best thing to happen to Freeman was the emergence of backfield mate Tevin Coleman and the other weapons in Atlanta. With much less usage, especially in the passing game (memories of repeated frantic checkdowns from Matt Ryan in 2015 still linger), his efficiency skyrocketed. Freeman's freshness was particularly evident through his violent engagement of defenders—only three players (David Johnson, Ezekiel Elliott, LeSean McCoy) broke more tackles than Freeman. But his red zone and goal-line success rates were lower than average. That may be why Atlanta drafted a banger, Brian Hill from Wyoming, to ease Freeman's burden—and possibly replace him if the club decides to let him go in free agency.

A fourth-round choice, Freeman is one of the best draft picks of the Thomas Dimitroff era, but the general manager may not re-sign the dynamic Freeman. The team will essentially have to decide whether to give Freeman big bucks or say goodbye to Tevin Coleman after 2018. Freeman's agent, Luther Campbell (yes, the former rapper of 2 Live Crew fame), is demanding a new deal that factors in Freeman's 27 touchdowns over the last two seasons. To his credit, Freeman hasn't made similar waves, taking part in team activities and being the good guy and teammate he has been throughout his career to date. Other teams, like Kyle Shanahan's 49ers, are watching contract developments in Atlanta closely.

Wayne Gallman   Height: 6-0   Weight: 215   College: Clemson   Draft: 2017/4 (140)   Born: 1-Oct-1994   Age: 23   Risk: Green

Year	Team	G/GS	Snaps	Runs	Yds	Yd/R	TD	FUM	DVOA	Rk	DYAR	Rk	YAR	Suc%	Rk	BTkl	Rec	Pass	Yds	C%	Yd/C	TD	YAC	DVOA	Rk	DYAR	Rk
2017	NYG			87	388	4.4	2	3	0.3%								14	20	106	70%	7.6	1		-12.1%			

Gallman was the third or fourth wheel in the Clemson offense in 2016, after Deshaun Watson, Mike Williams, and whoever else was having a big day (Artavis Scott, Jordan Leggett, Charone Peake in 2015). He's a tough, downhill runner with some power and moves in the open field. Gallman will bounce too many runs outside and doesn't have elite big-play capability, but he's a decent receiver who can work in a committee system because he's used to waiting his turn for touches. Gallman could well supplant Shane Vereen as the Giants' third-down back, though like Paul Perkins, he will have to prove he can handle the intricacies of an NFL passing attack.

Mike Gillislee   Height: 5-11   Weight: 208   College: Florida   Draft: 2013/5 (164)   Born: 1-Nov-1990   Age: 27   Risk: Green

Year	Team	G/GS	Snaps	Runs	Yds	Yd/R	TD	FUM	DVOA	Rk	DYAR	Rk	YAR	Suc%	Rk	BTkl	Rec	Pass	Yds	C%	Yd/C	TD	YAC	DVOA	Rk	DYAR	Rk
2015	BUF	5/1	112	47	267	5.7	3	1	20.9%	--	54	--	20	36%	--	4	6	7	29	86%	4.8	0	5.2	-4.0%	--	4	--
2016	BUF	15/1	284	101	577	5.7	8	0	44.9%	1	256	4	236	66%	1	19	9	11	50	82%	5.6	1	5.1	-48.0%	--	-18	--
2017	NE			188	879	4.7	8	4	8.9%								21	27	168	78%	8.0	2		13.6%			

It's not surprising that a running back from Buffalo led the NFL in yards per carry last year, but not many would have pegged Gillislee for that distinction over LeSean McCoy. Wildly productive on a per-play basis the past two seasons, Gillislee became the latest member of the Orchard Park-to-Foxborough pipeline and seems like the early favorite to assume the early-down role vacated by LeGarrette Blount. Playing in New England will likely cap Gillislee's volume, and the Patriots' RBBC is as flummoxing week-to-week as any in the league. Still, faced with the prospect of leading the backfield for the first time in his career, Gillislee enters 2016 as one of the more intriguing unheralded backs.

Melvin Gordon   Height: 6-1   Weight: 215   College: Wisconsin   Draft: 2015/1 (15)   Born: 13-Apr-1993   Age: 24   Risk: Yellow

Year	Team	G/GS	Snaps	Runs	Yds	Yd/R	TD	FUM	DVOA	Rk	DYAR	Rk	YAR	Suc%	Rk	BTkl	Rec	Pass	Yds	C%	Yd/C	TD	YAC	DVOA	Rk	DYAR	Rk
2015	SD	14/12	395	184	641	3.5	0	6	-17.4%	43	-68	43	-94	43%	32	38	33	37	192	89%	5.8	0	7.8	-16.1%	46	-5	45
2016	SD	13/11	659	254	997	3.9	10	2	-8.4%	29	2	29	83	45%	26	52	41	57	419	72%	10.2	2	10.1	21.0%	9	105	9
2017	LACH			304	1266	4.2	7	5	-3.9%								48	64	406	75%	8.5	2		10.3%			

Gordon was one of six running backs in 2016 with at least 40 broken tackles on runs (42) and at least 10 broken tackles on receptions (10). He's not a typical receiving back in the mold of LaDainian Tomlinson, Darren Sproles, or Danny Woodhead, but Gordon is still useful in the passing game. Still, we expect to see an uptick in his rushing production after Gordon just missed out on his first 1,000-yard season a year ago. Look for Anthony Lynn's Chargers to pound the rock with Gordon more than Mike McCoy ever did, and a career-best season should be the result of that.

Frank Gore   Height: 5-9   Weight: 215   College: Miami   Draft: 2005/3 (65)   Born: 14-May-1983   Age: 34   Risk: Yellow

Year	Team	G/GS	Snaps	Runs	Yds	Yd/R	TD	FUM	DVOA	Rk	DYAR	Rk	YAR	Suc%	Rk	BTkl	Rec	Pass	Yds	C%	Yd/C	TD	YAC	DVOA	Rk	DYAR	Rk
2014	SF	16/16	647	255	1106	4.3	4	2	6.3%	13	154	10	118	50%	11	19	11	19	111	58%	10.1	1	9.3	-14.4%	--	-1	--
2015	IND	16/16	690	260	967	3.7	6	4	-8.6%	36	0	36	-65	40%	42	41	34	58	267	59%	7.9	1	8.0	-32.1%	56	-60	56
2016	IND	16/16	650	263	1025	3.9	4	2	5.6%	16	159	12	88	49%	19	32	38	48	277	81%	7.3	4	7.6	0.7%	25	40	23
2017	IND			197	794	4.0	6	1	1.4%								29	40	192	73%	6.6	1		-5.3%			

Since 2012, there have been two running backs to carry the ball in an NFL season as a 34-year-old: Fred Jackson (2015) and John Kuhn (2016). There have been a grand total of two seasons since 1997 in which a running back 34 or older carried the ball 100 or more times: Emmitt Smith's farewell season in 2005, and Ricky Williams' change-of-pace role with the Ravens in 2011. This is the history Gore runs up against as Father Time continues to grab a cleat-hold of his burst. Gore is a conceptual mastermind of his position and should be able to take the workload if the Colts need it. It would probably be best for all parties involved if he didn't, because that would mean the Colts found a future at the position.

Todd Gurley Height: 6-1   Weight: 222   College: Georgia   Draft: 2015/1 (10)   Born: 3-Aug-1994   Age: 23   Risk: Green

Year	Team	G/GS	Snaps	Runs	Yds	Yd/R	TD	FUM	DVOA	Rk	DYAR	Rk	YAR	Suc%	Rk	BTkl	Rec	Pass	Yds	C%	Yd/C	TD	YAC	DVOA	Rk	DYAR	Rk
2015	STL	13/12	456	229	1106	4.8	10	3	10.0%	9	170	4	124	43%	36	46	21	26	188	81%	9.0	0	9.6	2.1%	25	25	31
2016	LARM	16/16	742	278	885	3.2	6	2	-14.4%	37	-66	37	-75	41%	36	56	43	58	327	74%	7.6	0	8.2	-9.9%	39	13	35
2017	LARM			266	1027	3.9	8	3	-6.7%								42	60	320	70%	7.6	0		-9.2%			

For fantasy players and regular Rams fans alike, Gurley was a major disappointment in 2016 after an electrifying rookie season that saw him take home Offensive Rookie of the Year honors. It certainly wasn't for a lack of opportunities, as Gurley saw a combined 321 touches between carries and receptions. However, with the Rams' quarterback situation a total mess, opposing teams were free to focus on stopping Gurley, daring Case Keenum or Jared Goff to beat them from behind a porous offensive line. The Rams' 2017 passing game doesn't even need to be average for Gurley to succeed, as the 2015 team ranked 31st at minus-13.5% passing DVOA. Compared to 2016's dead-last minus-38.4%, that team looks like the Greatest Show on Turf.

DuJuan Harris Height: 5-7   Weight: 197   College: Troy   Draft: 2011/FA   Born: 3-Sep-1988   Age: 29   Risk: N/A

Year	Team	G/GS	Snaps	Runs	Yds	Yd/R	TD	FUM	DVOA	Rk	DYAR	Rk	YAR	Suc%	Rk	BTkl	Rec	Pass	Yds	C%	Yd/C	TD	YAC	DVOA	Rk	DYAR	Rk
2014	GB	15/0	51	16	64	4.0	0	0	11.0%	--	14	--	13	56%	--	3	1	2	11	50%	11.0	0	10.0	23.1%	--	4	--
2015	2TM	4/1	98	48	189	3.9	0	1	-12.4%	--	-7	--	-31	38%	--	10	9	14	97	64%	10.8	0	10.9	12.1%	--	21	--
2016	SF	10/1	129	38	138	3.6	0	2	-28.1%	--	-31	--	-32	39%	--	11	8	9	115	89%	14.4	1	15.1	59.6%	--	36	--

Harris had an odd trek up and down the 49ers' depth chart in 2016. He started a clear fourth, behind not only starter Carlos Hyde but sophomore Mike Davis and journeyman Shaun Draughn as well. He received no offensive snaps at all in the first six weeks of the season, but then Hyde hurt his shoulder, and suddenly, Harris was back in the mix. Harris led the team with 113 snaps in San Francisco's next four games, first as Hyde's replacement, then as his primary backup—and then he was off the radar again, receiving just 16 snaps the rest of the way. Why Harris rose to prominence, and Draughn fell into the doghouse, remains a mystery, though the answer is probably *#LOL49ers*. Currently unsigned.

Derrick Henry Height: 6-3   Weight: 247   College: Alabama   Draft: 2016/2 (45)   Born: 17-Jul-1994   Age: 23   Risk: Blue

Year	Team	G/GS	Snaps	Runs	Yds	Yd/R	TD	FUM	DVOA	Rk	DYAR	Rk	YAR	Suc%	Rk	BTkl	Rec	Pass	Yds	C%	Yd/C	TD	YAC	DVOA	Rk	DYAR	Rk
2016	TEN	15/1	270	110	490	4.5	5	0	19.6%	4	131	15	139	55%	6	27	13	15	137	87%	10.5	0	9.5	46.9%	--	45	--
2017	TEN			120	531	4.4	5	2	7.7%								14	18	120	78%	8.5	0		9.4%			

Henry had a fine rookie season, with his physical running style translating well behind the Titans surprisingly effective offensive line. He performed well in the shotgun and from under center, did good work in the red zone, and was effective on all three downs. After not being asked to do much in the air at Alabama, he was effective when called upon and drew further praise this offseason for his improved hands. Just do not expect more than eight to ten carries per game as long as DeMarco Murray is available.

Tim Hightower Height: 6-0   Weight: 226   College: Richmond   Draft: 2008/5 (149)   Born: 23-May-1986   Age: 31   Risk: Green

Year	Team	G/GS	Snaps	Runs	Yds	Yd/R	TD	FUM	DVOA	Rk	DYAR	Rk	YAR	Suc%	Rk	BTkl	Rec	Pass	Yds	C%	Yd/C	TD	YAC	DVOA	Rk	DYAR	Rk
2015	NO	8/3	192	96	375	3.9	4	0	16.5%	--	110	--	95	56%	--	10	12	13	129	92%	10.8	0	11.2	56.5%	--	51	--
2016	NO	16/1	286	133	548	4.1	4	0	11.9%	10	121	16	99	52%	9	12	22	26	200	85%	9.1	1	9.5	32.1%	3	73	14
2017	SF			43	176	4.1	2	1	0.0%								8	10	61	80%	7.6	0		5.6%			

Hightower ranked ninth in the league in success rate. At first glance, that would indicate he is a prime short-yardage back. Keep in mind, though, that the Saints had the best run-blocking offensive line in football last season, and that Mark Ingram's success rate was even better than Hightower's. When Hightower is tackled, he is *tackled*—he only broke a tackle on 7.8 percent of his touches, second-worst in the NFL among qualified running backs. With San Francisco's more porous offensive line, Hightower may not be able to keep up his short-yardage success from 2016. Instead, his value to the 49ers is in the receiving game; his 87 percent catch rate since rejoining the league in 2015 is higher than any other back the 49ers currently employ. Running backs accounted for 25 percent of Shanahan's receptions in 2016, so there's volume to be had here if he gets the snaps.

Brian Hill   Height: 6-1   Weight: 219   College: Wyoming   Draft: 2017/5 (156)   Born: 9-Nov-1995   Age: 22   Risk: Green

Year	Team	G/GS	Snaps	Runs	Yds	Yd/R	TD	FUM	DVOA	Rk	DYAR	Rk	YAR	Suc%	Rk	BTkl	Rec	Pass	Yds	C%	Yd/C	TD	YAC	DVOA	Rk	DYAR	Rk
2017	ATL			35	172	4.9	1	1	8.8%								5	7	38	71%	7.5	0		-10.2%			

Hill fell in the draft in part due to a fractured wrist suffered late in the college season. A heavy-footed power back without much receiving talent (just 67 yards as a senior), he doesn't match the profile of Atlanta's current backs, meaning Wyoming's all-time leading rusher could carve out a role as a goal-line snowplow and late-game closer. Hill will find more expansive duty if the Falcons let Devonta Freeman leave after 2017.

Jeremy Hill   Height: 6-1   Weight: 233   College: Louisiana St.   Draft: 2014/2 (55)   Born: 10/20/1992   Age: 25   Risk: Yellow

Year	Team	G/GS	Snaps	Runs	Yds	Yd/R	TD	FUM	DVOA	Rk	DYAR	Rk	YAR	Suc%	Rk	BTkl	Rec	Pass	Yds	C%	Yd/C	TD	YAC	DVOA	Rk	DYAR	Rk
2014	CIN	16/8	501	222	1124	5.1	9	5	12.6%	6	204	6	231	54%	4	26	27	32	215	84%	8.0	0	8.3	-3.7%	30	17	31
2015	CIN	16/15	458	223	794	3.6	11	3	0.1%	21	85	16	64	49%	12	23	15	19	79	79%	5.3	1	5.8	-13.4%	--	0	--
2016	CIN	15/13	443	222	839	3.8	9	0	-5.0%	24	34	25	36	44%	29	32	21	27	174	78%	8.3	0	7.8	3.1%	23	27	30
2017	CIN			135	524	3.9	6	2	-1.0%								15	20	109	75%	7.3	0		-0.9%			

After an incredible first season, the Hill we were left with the last two years was the one most scouts saw from the beginning: an inconsistent runner who kicks people around when he's on, but runs too high and is too reliant on his offensive line when he's not. He was drastically out-produced by Rex Burkhead last year. The Bengals, apparently, came to the same conclusion, and they pounced on Joe Mixon in the second round. Hill is not exactly *persona non grata* in Cincinnati, but if he were to be benched, it would be earned.

Jordan Howard   Height: 6-0   Weight: 230   College: Indiana   Draft: 2016/5 (150)   Born: 2-Nov-1994   Age: 23   Risk: Yellow

Year	Team	G/GS	Snaps	Runs	Yds	Yd/R	TD	FUM	DVOA	Rk	DYAR	Rk	YAR	Suc%	Rk	BTkl	Rec	Pass	Yds	C%	Yd/C	TD	YAC	DVOA	Rk	DYAR	Rk
2016	CHI	15/13	654	252	1313	5.2	6	2	12.3%	9	219	5	246	49%	17	51	29	50	298	58%	10.3	1	10.3	-7.5%	36	17	33
2017	CHI			281	1425	5.1	8	3	14.9%								30	44	224	68%	7.5	1		-4.4%			

Jordan Howard is an emerging star who has the potential to be one of the best running backs in the NFL. In a similar vein to how Arizona's David Johnson excelled during his rookie season, Howard demonstrated great physicality and explosiveness when he was trusted with the ball last season. He is primarily a one-cut runner who can accelerate away from defenders or generate power with his short-area quickness. His physical prowess shouldn't overshadow his ability to make good decisions and anticipate his blocking before it develops in front of him. Although he didn't have a huge receiving role as a rookie, Howard showed off some ability in that area. Chances are the Bears won't rely on him to catch the ball much because of the offseason arrivals of Benny Cunningham and Tarik Cohen.

Kareem Hunt   Height: 5-10   Weight: 216   College: Toledo   Draft: 2017/3 (86)   Born: 6-Aug-1995   Age: 22   Risk: Green

Year	Team	G/GS	Snaps	Runs	Yds	Yd/R	TD	FUM	DVOA	Rk	DYAR	Rk	YAR	Suc%	Rk	BTkl	Rec	Pass	Yds	C%	Yd/C	TD	YAC	DVOA	Rk	DYAR	Rk
2017	KC			84	366	4.4	3	3	2.2%								21	25	151	84%	7.2	1		-0.6%			

Hunt is a big back who can catch the screens and checkdowns that he is guaranteed to see in a Kansas City offense. One plus that could lead to early playing time is Hunt's ball security, as he didn't fumble at all in 2016 over 303 total touches. Back-CAST didn't love him, as his projection ranked just 12th in this year's class, but Hunt should contribute as Spencer Ware's main backup this season.

Carlos Hyde   Height: 6-0   Weight: 230   College: Ohio St.   Draft: 2014/2 (57)   Born: 9/20/1991   Age: 26   Risk: Red

Year	Team	G/GS	Snaps	Runs	Yds	Yd/R	TD	FUM	DVOA	Rk	DYAR	Rk	YAR	Suc%	Rk	BTkl	Rec	Pass	Yds	C%	Yd/C	TD	YAC	DVOA	Rk	DYAR	Rk
2014	SF	14/0	292	83	333	4.0	4	1	3.0%	--	38	--	25	46%	--	21	12	16	68	75%	5.7	0	5.4	-38.5%	--	-21	--
2015	SF	7/7	295	115	470	4.1	3	1	3.9%	14	60	23	27	49%	14	24	11	15	53	73%	4.8	0	5.5	-33.9%	--	-18	--
2016	SF	13/13	535	217	988	4.6	6	5	15.3%	7	204	6	98	48%	21	51	27	34	163	82%	6.0	3	5.4	6.2%	19	38	25
2017	SF			234	1071	4.6	8	4	0.3%								38	49	277	78%	7.3	1		5.2%			

San Francisco has had the league's worst run-blocking offensive line for two years in a row, which is why it's a good thing they've had Hyde to bail them out—at least, when he has managed to stay healthy. Last season, Hyde averaged 3.0 yards after contact, fifth-best in the league. He broke a tackle on 20.9 percent of his touches, with the fourth-most broken tackles on running plays in the league (48). Averaging 4.6 yards per carry behind San Francisco's line was a minor miracle, considering the rest of their running backs averaged less than three. There are legitimate concerns as to how Hyde's power running style will fit in Shanahan's outside-zone run scheme, but it's not *that* different than the system Chip Kelly put into place last season. The rumors of him being traded or otherwise losing his starting job in 2017 seem greatly exaggerated, though they are the reason we're listing him with Risk of Red.

Mark Ingram   Height: 5-11   Weight: 215   College: Alabama   Draft: 2011/1 (28)   Born: 21-Dec-1989   Age: 28   Risk: Green

Year	Team	G/GS	Snaps	Runs	Yds	Yd/R	TD	FUM	DVOA	Rk	DYAR	Rk	YAR	Suc%	Rk	BTkl	Rec	Pass	Yds	C%	Yd/C	TD	YAC	DVOA	Rk	DYAR	Rk
2014	NO	13/9	470	226	964	4.3	9	3	2.7%	14	108	14	129	50%	13	30	29	36	145	81%	5.0	0	5.0	-40.9%	56	-54	54
2015	NO	12/10	534	166	769	4.6	6	2	6.6%	12	108	14	120	45%	30	34	50	60	405	83%	8.1	0	9.2	4.0%	21	59	21
2016	NO	16/14	530	205	1043	5.1	6	2	11.3%	11	175	10	223	56%	5	46	46	58	319	79%	6.9	4	7.1	10.6%	16	81	12
2017	NO			189	887	4.7	6	3	6.9%								43	55	313	78%	7.3	2		12.7%			

A 60-40 timeshare with Tim Hightower in 2016 produced the most effective season of Mark Ingram's career, whether by DVOA and DYAR or more traditional statistics such as yards from scrimmage and yards per carry. Ingram has never been a double-digit touchdown runner, but he finally added receiving touchdowns to his stat sheet last year, and that was enough to take him into double figures for the season. He also had 1,000 yards rushing for the first time, and has more than tripled his career receiving total in just the past two campaigns. If Ingram can continue to be this effective splitting carries with Adrian Peterson, that benefit alone might be enough to justify the latter's place on the roster.

Chris Ivory   Height: 6-0   Weight: 222   College: Tiffin   Draft: 2010/FA   Born: 22-Mar-1988   Age: 29   Risk: Yellow

Year	Team	G/GS	Snaps	Runs	Yds	Yd/R	TD	FUM	DVOA	Rk	DYAR	Rk	YAR	Suc%	Rk	BTkl	Rec	Pass	Yds	C%	Yd/C	TD	YAC	DVOA	Rk	DYAR	Rk
2014	NYJ	16/10	446	198	821	4.1	6	2	-0.6%	20	69	21	60	44%	25	33	18	27	123	67%	6.8	1	6.7	-15.4%	41	-2	41
2015	NYJ	15/14	537	247	1070	4.3	7	4	-11.5%	39	-31	40	23	43%	35	45	30	37	217	81%	7.2	1	9.2	-4.3%	32	21	32
2016	JAC	11/1	311	117	439	3.8	3	5	-34.3%	42	-125	42	-93	45%	22	22	20	28	186	71%	9.3	0	9.5	-12.0%	42	3	42
2017	JAC			25	101	4.0	1	1	1.1%								10	13	72	77%	7.2	0		1.3%			

Last year's "big physical back who is supposed to save the offense and make Blake Bortles' job easier" has become this year's... well, what is he? Certainly not that again, after finishing last in rushing DYAR and with Leonard Fournette the new leading man. "More expensive to cut than to keep" is a better answer, with last offseason's "five-year, $32 million deal" turning from treasure to trash quicker than expected. An illness cost him time early in the season, while a hamstring injury hampered him late. In between, he struggled behind a porous offensive line to find the running room where his bruising style is more effective. Pencil him in for third-string and a cap casualty next February or March.

Rashad Jennings

Height: 6-1   Weight: 231   College: Liberty   Draft: 2009/7 (250)   Born: 26-Mar-1985   Age: 32   Risk: N/A

Year	Team	G/GS	Snaps	Runs	Yds	Yd/R	TD	FUM	DVOA	Rk	DYAR	Rk	YAR	Suc%	Rk	BTkl	Rec	Pass	Yds	C%	Yd/C	TD	YAC	DVOA	Rk	DYAR	Rk
2014	NYG	11/9	418	167	639	3.8	4	1	7.0%	11	112	13	75	47%	16	26	30	41	226	73%	7.5	0	10.4	-29.3%	50	-35	49
2015	NYG	16/16	425	195	863	4.4	3	2	5.6%	13	117	12	161	56%	4	25	29	40	296	73%	10.2	1	10.7	-0.9%	27	29	27
2016	NYG	13/12	443	181	593	3.3	3	1	-20.5%	38	-86	40	-72	39%	39	16	35	43	201	84%	5.7	1	7.7	-25.6%	48	-28	49

One of the smartest, most socially-conscious players in the league, Jennings is currently a free agent after an impressive performance on *Dancing with the Stars*. Once a dangerous all-purpose committee back, Jennings became a plodding rusher and receiver with minimal burst last year. He still has potential value as a locker-room leader and backfield stabilizer, but the market was flooded with veteran rushers this offseason, so Jennings may have reached the end of the line.

Chris Johnson

Height: 5-11   Weight: 197   College: East Carolina   Draft: 2008/1 (24)   Born: 23-Sep-1985   Age: 32   Risk: Blue

Year	Team	G/GS	Snaps	Runs	Yds	Yd/R	TD	FUM	DVOA	Rk	DYAR	Rk	YAR	Suc%	Rk	BTkl	Rec	Pass	Yds	C%	Yd/C	TD	YAC	DVOA	Rk	DYAR	Rk
2014	NYJ	16/6	398	155	663	4.3	1	1	-6.0%	30	16	30	31	45%	24	10	24	34	151	71%	6.3	1	6.1	-13.8%	40	0	40
2015	ARI	11/9	366	196	814	4.2	3	2	-5.4%	31	26	32	24	47%	18	25	6	13	58	46%	9.7	0	10.5	-47.0%	--	-23	--
2016	ARI	4/0	42	25	95	3.8	1	0	-2.0%	--	7	--	19	48%	--	2	0	1	0	0%	0.0	0	0.0	-98.6%	--	-4	--
2017	*ARI*			*35*	*141*	*4.0*	*1*	*1*	*-4.6%*								*6*	*9*	*53*	*67%*	*8.8*	*0*		*1.3%*			

Johnson's two seasons in Arizona have both been cut short due to injury, leaving him just 463 yards short of becoming the 30th player with 10,000 career rushing yards. He has expressed a desire to come back to Arizona, but with fifth-round pick T.J. Logan joining David Johnson and Andre Ellington in the backfield, there may not be enough room for a 32-year-old coming off of sports hernia surgery. Johnson was still moderately effective in 2015, but that was two major injuries ago. (Late note: We guess there was room, because Johnson re-signed with Arizona right before we released the book. He's still probably not going to be very effective, but if he makes it through final cuts, he's probably the proper handcuff for David Johnson.)

David Johnson

Height: 6-1   Weight: 224   College: Northern Iowa   Draft: 2015/3 (86)   Born: 16-Dec-1991   Age: 26   Risk: Yellow

Year	Team	G/GS	Snaps	Runs	Yds	Yd/R	TD	FUM	DVOA	Rk	DYAR	Rk	YAR	Suc%	Rk	BTkl	Rec	Pass	Yds	C%	Yd/C	TD	YAC	DVOA	Rk	DYAR	Rk
2015	ARI	16/5	412	125	581	4.6	8	3	15.7%	4	133	8	149	56%	3	27	36	57	457	63%	12.7	4	9.6	22.1%	12	120	6
2016	ARI	16/16	964	293	1239	4.2	16	5	5.1%	17	177	9	139	50%	13	80	80	121	879	67%	11.0	4	8.0	27.7%	4	274	1
2017	*ARI*			*302*	*1368*	*4.5*	*11*	*5*	*2.5%*								*77*	*115*	*771*	*67%*	*10.0*	*2*		*5.5%*			

Bruce Arians says he wants Johnson to get "30 touches a game" in 2017. That has only happened once in NFL history (James Wilder in 1984), so take the under on that. Even if you take it as a statement of intent and not a strict goal, there are questions as to just how much more workload the Cardinals can put on him. Johnson was responsible for 34.4 percent of Arizona's yards from scrimmage last season, making him the most heavily used player in the league. Part of that was because he was such a weapon in the passing game. Johnson's 80 receptions weren't all screens and dumpoffs. His average target came 4.6 yards downfield, leading all running backs. Johnson also led all running backs with 28 targets in the slot and 18 targets split out wide, and had positive receiving DVOA no matter where he lined up. So, I guess what we're trying to say is David Johnson is *pretty good at football, you guys.*

Duke Johnson

Height: 5-9   Weight: 207   College: Miami   Draft: 2015/3 (77)   Born: 23-Sep-1993   Age: 24   Risk: Green

Year	Team	G/GS	Snaps	Runs	Yds	Yd/R	TD	FUM	DVOA	Rk	DYAR	Rk	YAR	Suc%	Rk	BTkl	Rec	Pass	Yds	C%	Yd/C	TD	YAC	DVOA	Rk	DYAR	Rk
2015	CLE	16/7	561	104	379	3.6	0	1	-1.4%	25	30	31	9	45%	26	47	61	74	534	82%	8.8	2	8.0	2.3%	23	68	18
2016	CLE	16/1	457	73	358	4.9	1	2	11.2%	--	54	--	45	45%	--	35	53	74	514	72%	9.7	0	8.0	19.2%	11	134	6
2017	*CLE*			*87*	*388*	*4.5*	*1*	*1*	*3.1%*								*60*	*78*	*533*	*77%*	*8.9*	*1*		*14.1%*			

The Browns clearly don't trust Johnson in scoring range. In his career, he has rushed or caught the ball on just 10 percent of Cleveland's plays inside the 10-yard line, less than half as often as he has been used over the rest of the field. On a related note, Johnson's total of three offensive touchdowns is tied with Darren McFadden for the lowest among the 77 players with at least 1,500 yards from scrimmage in the past two years. Johnson has been especially useless as a receiver inside the 10, with just one catch on six targets—and that one catch lost 5 yards. Even as the second runner on the depth chart in Cleveland, Johnson is fourth among running backs in receptions in the last two years, so he will have some sleeper value in PPR fantasy leagues. Just don't count on him for more than that as long as Isaiah Crowell is healthy.

Aaron Jones   Height: 5-9   Weight: 208   College: Texas-El Paso   Draft: 2017/5 (182)   Born: 2-Dec-1994   Age: 23   Risk: Green

Year	Team	G/GS	Snaps	Runs	Yds	Yd/R	TD	FUM	DVOA	Rk	DYAR	Rk	YAR	Suc%	Rk	BTkl	Rec	Pass	Yds	C%	Yd/C	TD	YAC	DVOA	Rk	DYAR	Rk
2017	GB		55	268	4.9	1	1	11.3%									10	13	70	77%	7.0	0		-7.5%			

Although he didn't run fast at the combine, Aaron Jones was one of the standout athletes from this year's class. He ranked high in both jumps, both shuttle drills, and the 3-cone. The Packers will be hoping that Jones' explosiveness translates from the college level, where he had a run over 40 yards in eight different games during his final season. The biggest challenge facing Jones is making that transition because he played at lowly Texas-El Paso in Conference USA.

Matt Jones   Height: 6-2   Weight: 231   College: Florida   Draft: 2015/3 (95)   Born: 7-Mar-1993   Age: 24   Risk: Red

Year	Team	G/GS	Snaps	Runs	Yds	Yd/R	TD	FUM	DVOA	Rk	DYAR	Rk	YAR	Suc%	Rk	BTkl	Rec	Pass	Yds	C%	Yd/C	TD	YAC	DVOA	Rk	DYAR	Rk
2015	WAS	13/0	340	144	490	3.4	3	5	-23.4%	44	-92	44	-54	46%	23	19	19	25	304	76%	16.0	1	14.0	38.9%	3	75	16
2016	WAS	7/7	221	99	460	4.6	3	3	10.2%	--	83	--	50	54%	--	19	8	8	73	100%	9.1	0	7.1	76.6%	--	45	--
2017	WAS			23	90	3.9	1	1	-4.5%								10	14	72	71%	7.2	0		-3.6%			

Jones was perma-benched after a disastrous game in Week 7 against the Lions last year, fumbling a potential touchdown into the end zone and botching a pair of exchanges with Kirk Cousins. Fumbles have plagued Jones throughout his two seasons, and the Redskins tried to shop him during the draft, but to no avail. Jones is a long shot to make the Washington roster this season. He is likely to join the Christine Michael/Knile Davis caravan of running backs who are too talented to ignore but too unreliable to actually use.

Kyle Juszczyk   Height: 6-1   Weight: 248   College: Harvard   Draft: 2013/4 (130)   Born: 23-Apr-1991   Age: 26   Risk: Green

Year	Team	G/GS	Snaps	Runs	Yds	Yd/R	TD	FUM	DVOA	Rk	DYAR	Rk	YAR	Suc%	Rk	BTkl	Rec	Pass	Yds	C%	Yd/C	TD	YAC	DVOA	Rk	DYAR	Rk
2014	BAL	16/14	454	0	0	--	0	2	--	--	--	--	--	--	--	2	19	27	182	70%	9.6	1	8.9	-6.7%	34	11	34
2015	BAL	16/11	383	2	3	1.5	0	0	-20.3%	--	-1	--	-4	0%	--	10	41	56	321	73%	7.8	4	6.6	7.0%	18	72	17
2016	BAL	16/7	463	5	22	4.4	1	0	72.5%	--	19	--	19	60%	--	7	37	49	266	76%	7.2	0	5.9	-11.9%	41	6	41
2017	SF			13	37	2.9	0	1	-10.9%								46	61	345	75%	7.5	1		3.1%			

The world's highest-paid fullback (and a deadly Scrabble word to boot) is considered an "offensive weapon" in Kyle Shanahan's offense. Juszczyk ranked ninth among running backs in receiving plus-minus in 2016 (plus-1.8), and his 1.3 air yards per target was above average for backs as well. Juszczyk was most valuable as a safety valve for Joe Flacco on third downs; he had a 9.5% DVOA and averaged 8.5 yards after the catch on third and fourth down. Juszcyzk was also a core special teams player for Baltimore, playing on 70 percent of their kicking snaps. Whether all of that is worth $5.25 million a year remains to be seen.

Alvin Kamara   Height: 5-10   Weight: 214   College: Tennessee   Draft: 2017/3 (67)   Born: 25-Jul-1995   Age: 22   Risk: Yellow

Year	Team	G/GS	Snaps	Runs	Yds	Yd/R	TD	FUM	DVOA	Rk	DYAR	Rk	YAR	Suc%	Rk	BTkl	Rec	Pass	Yds	C%	Yd/C	TD	YAC	DVOA	Rk	DYAR	Rk
2017	NO		38	174	4.6	1	2	8.8%									45	63	321	71%	7.1	2		-10.8%			

A highly-touted third-round pick, Kamara amassed over 1,000 receiving yards in his three years at the University of Tennessee and will compete directly with Travaris Cadet to be the Saints' main receiver out of the backfield. Though he will not carry the ball regularly—Cadet had only four carries in that role all of last season—Kamara will also see snaps as a true wide receiver from the slot and flanker positions. Though Reggie Bush was mediocre as the prototype for this role in Sean Payton's offense, it made Darren Sproles a top-five running back in receiving DYAR for three straight years, amassing almost 2,000 yards on 232 receptions. Cadet has been a disappointment, so Kamara has a terrific opportunity to take the lion's share of those targets. A word of caution though: our BackCAST projections flagged Kamara as a potential bust, suggesting that neither his athleticism nor his production merited taking him with a high-round pick. The NFL comparable mentioned in that article was ... Travaris Cadet.

Rob Kelley				Height: 6-0		Weight: 228		College: Tulane				Draft: 2016/FA			Born: 3-Oct-1992		Age: 25		Risk: Green		
Year	Team	G/GS	Snaps	Runs	Yds	Yd/R	TD	FUM	DVOA	Rk	DYAR	Rk	YAR	Suc%	Rk	BTkl	Rec	Pass	Yds	C%	Yd/C	TD	YAC	DVOA	Rk	DYAR	Rk
2016	WAS	15/9	343	168	704	4.2	6	0	5.8%	15	102	17	62	48%	20	43	12	18	82	67%	6.8	1	6.5	-4.8%	--	10	--
2017	WAS			133	534	4.0	4	1	-3.8%								13	19	95	68%	7.3	1		-3.4%			

Kelley impressed the Redskins with a great preseason as a rookie UDFA, took over for Matt Jones after Jones' fumbling spree against the Lions, hammered out a 67-321-4 rushing line over a three-week span, then settled into a 15-carry committee role with Chris Thompson. Kelley had knee surgery after last season but is healthy for training camp and penciled in as the starter. He offers zero receiving value, so both Thompson and rookie Samaje Perine are likely to siphon off significant touches. Our projection is based on the expectation that Perine will take the starting job around midseason.

Eddie Lacy				Height: 5-11		Weight: 240		College: Alabama				Draft: 2013/2 (61)			Born: 1-Jan-1990		Age: 28		Risk: Green		
Year	Team	G/GS	Snaps	Runs	Yds	Yd/R	TD	FUM	DVOA	Rk	DYAR	Rk	YAR	Suc%	Rk	BTkl	Rec	Pass	Yds	C%	Yd/C	TD	YAC	DVOA	Rk	DYAR	Rk
2014	GB	16/16	687	246	1139	4.6	9	3	9.8%	8	189	8	159	48%	15	51	42	55	427	76%	10.2	4	10.3	23.0%	9	112	4
2015	GB	15/12	471	187	758	4.1	3	4	-8.3%	35	3	35	42	49%	15	29	20	28	188	71%	9.4	2	10.7	-0.6%	26	20	33
2016	GB	5/5	166	71	360	5.1	0	0	20.4%	--	84	--	61	49%	--	26	4	7	28	57%	7.0	0	10.0	-45.4%	--	-12	--
2017	SEA			166	726	4.4	7	1	8.1%								19	26	160	73%	8.4	0		0.6%			

Lacy suffered an ankle injury in Week 5 that eventually landed him on injured reserve, ending not only his 2016 season but his time in Green Bay as well. After signing an incentive-laden one-year contract in Seattle, Lacy will have a chance to prove that his five games last season were not a mirage and cash in again on the free agent market at season's end. Lacy will have Thomas Rawls nipping at his heels should he falter early on, but sharing the repetitions at running back could also help both players to stay healthier in 2017. He may not have a guaranteed starter's workload, but if the P90X pays off for Lacy, he could make a major impact for the Seattle offense.

Jeremy Langford				Height: 6-0		Weight: 208		College: Michigan State				Draft: 2015/4 (106)			Born: 6-Dec-1991		Age: 26		Risk: Green		
Year	Team	G/GS	Snaps	Runs	Yds	Yd/R	TD	FUM	DVOA	Rk	DYAR	Rk	YAR	Suc%	Rk	BTkl	Rec	Pass	Yds	C%	Yd/C	TD	YAC	DVOA	Rk	DYAR	Rk
2015	CHI	16/2	391	148	537	3.6	6	0	12.7%	5	123	11	111	47%	20	13	22	42	279	52%	12.7	1	10.4	-6.6%	34	16	34
2016	CHI	12/3	248	62	200	3.2	4	2	-9.3%	--	-2	--	-9	56%	--	7	19	27	142	70%	7.5	0	6.8	-7.1%	35	9	40
2017	CHI			61	234	3.8	2	2	-2.1%								20	27	141	74%	7.0	0		-4.3%			

There is a very real chance that Jeremy Langford goes from starting running back one season to off the roster the next. Langford's lack of versatility becomes a greater issue when he's not the starter. He doesn't offer special teams value, he's not going to be the goal-line back, and there are at least two players on the roster who are better suited to play on third downs. Langford's projection for the Bears is solely that of a backup runner to Jordan Howard. Then again, if he were a good enough runner to justify a roster spot without fitting a role, he never would have lost his starting spot in the first place.

Dion Lewis				Height: 5-7		Weight: 195		College: Pittsburgh				Draft: 2011/5 (149)			Born: 27-Sep-1990		Age: 27		Risk: Green		
Year	Team	G/GS	Snaps	Runs	Yds	Yd/R	TD	FUM	DVOA	Rk	DYAR	Rk	YAR	Suc%	Rk	BTkl	Rec	Pass	Yds	C%	Yd/C	TD	YAC	DVOA	Rk	DYAR	Rk
2015	NE	7/6	298	49	234	4.8	2	2	28.1%	--	77	--	83	55%	--	25	36	50	388	72%	10.8	2	9.6	14.7%	15	78	14
2016	NE	7/5	163	64	283	4.4	0	1	21.0%	--	74	--	52	59%	--	20	17	24	94	71%	5.5	0	4.9	-31.9%	--	-25	--
2017	NE			59	303	5.2	1	2	16.4%								23	30	208	77%	9.1	1		14.9%			

Most would view Lewis' encore season in New England as a letdown, which seems unfair given that he was behind the eight-ball all season after starting the year on the PUP list. No, Lewis was not as spectacular as he had been in 2015, when he terrorized defenders in the open field with a 29.4 percent broken tackle rate (second among running backs). However, his 24.7

percent broken tackle rate in 2016 was quietly sixth among running backs with at least 80 touches. Some have speculated about Lewis' job security headed into training camp, but with an affordable $1.5 million cap hit and value on all three downs, that speculation doesn't really add up. Lewis' per-game touches may drop with the arrivals of Mike Gillislee and Rex Burkhead, as well as the ascent of James White as the passing back. That's not necessarily a bad thing given Lewis' injury history, though, and having the most versatile skill set in the Patriots' backfield should help him retain some value.

T.J. Logan   Height: 5-9   Weight: 196   College: North Carolina   Draft: 2017/5 (179)   Born: 3-Sep-1994   Age: 23   Risk: Yellow

Year	Team	G/GS	Snaps	Runs	Yds	Yd/R	TD	FUM	DVOA	Rk	DYAR	Rk	YAR	Suc%	Rk	BTkl	Rec	Pass	Yds	C%	Yd/C	TD	YAC	DVOA	Rk	DYAR	Rk
2017	ARI			28	137	4.9	0	1	7.3%								13	17	96	76%	7.4	1		-6.5%			

What Logan lacks in size he makes up for in explosive potential; he not only led all backs with a 4.37-second 40 at the combine, but his Speed Score of 107.5 was the third-best in the 2017 draft class. Logan's immediate impact is more likely to be as a kick returner; he averaged 27.2 yards per return at North Carolina and brought five back to the house. His ceiling is replacing Andre Ellington as the primary change-of-pace and home-run potential back. Logan dropped just one pass at North Carolina, so he could theoretically be used in that same passing-down situational role as Ellington, but his slim frame means that he'll likely never hold up as an every-down player.

Marshawn Lynch   Height: 5-11   Weight: 215   College: California   Draft: 2007/1 (12)   Born: 22-Apr-1986   Age: 31   Risk: Red

Year	Team	G/GS	Snaps	Runs	Yds	Yd/R	TD	FUM	DVOA	Rk	DYAR	Rk	YAR	Suc%	Rk	BTkl	Rec	Pass	Yds	C%	Yd/C	TD	YAC	DVOA	Rk	DYAR	Rk
2014	SEA	16/14	704	280	1306	4.7	13	3	23.1%	1	359	2	307	53%	5	88	37	48	367	77%	9.9	4	10.9	21.8%	11	93	9
2015	SEA	7/6	310	111	417	3.8	3	0	1.2%	19	47	25	54	50%	11	24	13	21	80	62%	6.2	0	6.7	-34.6%	--	-24	--
2017	OAK			226	927	4.1	10	2	4.3%								29	42	207	69%	7.1	1		-9.3%			

Lynch did not come out of retirement to be a marginal contributor. He saw an opportunity to play for his hometown team, a Super Bowl contender, in an offense that lost its leading rusher in Latavius Murray. When you have Lynch, you're going to feed him the ball… unless it's at the 1-yard line in Super Bowl XLIX. But quarterback Derek Carr has already promised that he will make that handoff should such a moment arise.

The question is what can the Raiders really expect from Lynch after a year off. In 2015, Lynch was mostly injured and ineffective for Seattle. He retired for 2016 and now returns as a 31-year-old running back with a good bit of mileage on his body. In NFL history, there have been 12 1,000-yard rushing seasons by a 31-year-old back. The kicker is that 10 of those players also had 1,000-plus yards as a 30-year-old runner. Lynch was rambling about the world, enjoying his retirement. While that could be a positive in terms of health, the fact is the NFL is an unkind game to older backs. A total of 93 players rushed for 500-plus yards at age 30, but that number drops to 52 at age 31. Only 12 running backs in league history have gained more rushing yards at age 31 than they did at age 30.

Running Backs: Largest Gain in Rushing Yards from Age 30 to Age 31 in NFL History

Rk	Player	Age-30 Yr	Team	Runs	Yards	YPC	Age-31 Yr	Team	Runs	Yards	YPC	Gain
1	Ricky Williams	2007	MIA	6	15	2.50	2008	MIA	160	659	4.12	644
2	Stephen Davis	2004	CAR	24	92	3.83	2005	CAR	180	549	3.05	457
3	Lenny Moore	1963	CLT	27	136	5.04	1964	CLT	157	584	3.72	448
4	Harvey Williams	1997	OAK	18	70	3.89	1998	OAK	128	496	3.88	426
5	Pete Banaszak	1974	OAK	80	272	3.40	1975	OAK	187	672	3.59	400
6	Curtis Martin	2003	NYJ	323	1308	4.05	2004	NYJ	371	1697	4.57	389
7	John Henry Johnson	1959	DET	82	270	3.29	1960	PIT	118	621	5.26	351
8	Sammy Morris	2007	NE	85	384	4.52	2008	NE	156	727	4.66	343
9	James Stewart	2001	DET	143	685	4.79	2002	DET	231	1021	4.42	336
10	**Ward Cuff**	**1942**	**NYG**	**38**	**189**	**4.97**	**1943**	**NYG**	**80**	**523**	**6.54**	**334**
11	James Brooks	1988	CIN	182	931	5.12	1989	CIN	221	1239	5.61	308
12	Joe Perry	1957	SF	97	454	4.68	1958	SF	125	758	6.06	304

Ricky Williams could be the closest parallel to Lynch, since he too retired at a young age (27) before returning to rush for 743 yards. He then missed another full season (suspension for substance abuse), then only rushed for 15 yards in one game in 2007 before suffering an injury. At age 31 in 2008, Williams rushed for 659 yards as part of the Wildcat offense, an increase of 644 yards over his age-30 season. Obviously, any positive yardage gained by Lynch this year is a boost over last year, but it is hard to expect him to return in full "Beast Mode" right away. Even if we use his 2015 numbers as a starting point, a 500-yard gain over that would put him just over 900 yards. Throw in some big touchdown numbers and clock-killing carries in the fourth quarter behind a strong offensive line, and the Raiders should be content with that action, boss.

Marlon Mack

Height: 5-11 Weight: 213 College: South Florida Draft: 2017/4 (143) Born: 7-Mar-1996 Age: 21 Risk: Blue

Year	Team	G/GS	Snaps	Runs	Yds	Yd/R	TD	FUM	DVOA	Rk	DYAR	Rk	YAR	Suc%	Rk	BTkl	Rec	Pass	Yds	C%	Yd/C	TD	YAC	DVOA	Rk	DYAR	Rk
2017	IND			83	391	4.7	2	2	8.5%								24	33	159	73%	6.6	1		-13.8%			

Mack is heading into a great situation insomuch as Frank Gore is the back he needs to learn from. As a college runner, Mack was a little too eager to head to the corner store and didn't earn many extra yards after contact. He's here for a reason: he was productive and has plenty of speed and skill. (That speed contributed to Mack having 9.3 highlight yards per opportunity last year, highest of any drafted running back.) But it's the refined technique of the position that someone like a Gore could teach him that will make the difference between a star and a committee partner. The footwork is there for Mack to be great. Whether he gets there is all about how well he does as a student of the game.

Doug Martin

Height: 5-9 Weight: 210 College: Boise State Draft: 2012/1 (31) Born: 13-Jan-1989 Age: 28 Risk: Yellow

Year	Team	G/GS	Snaps	Runs	Yds	Yd/R	TD	FUM	DVOA	Rk	DYAR	Rk	YAR	Suc%	Rk	BTkl	Rec	Pass	Yds	C%	Yd/C	TD	YAC	DVOA	Rk	DYAR	Rk
2014	TB	11/11	345	134	494	3.7	2	0	-12.9%	36	-21	34	5	36%	43	7	13	20	64	65%	4.9	0	4.8	-47.2%	--	-35	--
2015	TB	16/16	622	288	1402	4.9	6	5	-1.6%	26	81	18	150	48%	16	63	33	44	271	75%	8.2	1	7.0	-8.9%	38	11	36
2016	TB	8/8	322	144	421	2.9	3	1	-22.0%	40	-82	39	-76	42%	34	33	14	16	134	88%	9.6	0	7.6	24.7%	--	30	--
2017	TB			148	600	4.1	5	1	-0.6%								22	29	197	75%	9.0	0		17.3%			

Doug Martin has now missed at least five games in three of his five seasons as a pro, and begins his next with a three-game suspension. Though he has received public praise for his offseason work, there is more than a sneaking suspicion that it could be a ploy to entice potential trade partners. Jason Licht is on record stating that the team will not be saving him a seat if the running game is effective in his absence. None of his 2017 salary is guaranteed and the team owes him no more money until October, so it's likely that nothing will be decided one way or the other until he returns from his suspension in late September.

Ryan Mathews

Height: 6-0 Weight: 218 College: Fresno State Draft: 2010/1 (12) Born: 1-May-1987 Age: 30 Risk: Red

Year	Team	G/GS	Snaps	Runs	Yds	Yd/R	TD	FUM	DVOA	Rk	DYAR	Rk	YAR	Suc%	Rk	BTkl	Rec	Pass	Yds	C%	Yd/C	TD	YAC	DVOA	Rk	DYAR	Rk
2014	SD	6/6	165	74	330	4.5	3	1	11.3%	--	62	--	37	47%	--	8	9	10	69	90%	7.7	0	7.0	37.6%	--	32	--
2015	PHI	13/6	245	106	539	5.1	6	3	20.4%	3	133	9	106	53%	5	16	20	28	146	71%	7.3	1	7.6	-22.2%	50	-11	49
2016	PHI	13/8	287	155	661	4.3	8	3	0.0%	20	58	19	67	52%	8	21	13	14	115	93%	8.8	1	8.7	19.6%	--	33	--
2017	PHI			18	73	4.1	0	1	-1.3%								7	11	47	64%	6.8	0		-11.8%			

Mathews was a forgotten man around Eagles headquarters long before the team decided they would release him. He was absent from OTAs, as the team has been planning to release Mathews the moment he can pass a physical in the wake of the neck injury suffered last season.

When healthy, Mathews is a capable all-purpose runner with mediocre receiving chops and a habit of fumbling in the fourth quarter that followed him from coast to coast. Mathews is at the stage in his career where he is the back a team picks up after multiple injuries, then drops when they realize that the undrafted rookie is just as effective, but much cheaper and somehow less fumble prone.

Christian McCaffrey Height: 5-11   Weight: 202   College: Stanford   Draft: 2017/1 (8)   Born: 7-Jun-1996   Age: 21   Risk: Yellow

Year	Team	G/GS	Snaps	Runs	Yds	Yd/R	TD	FUM	DVOA	Rk	DYAR	Rk	YAR	Suc%	Rk	BTkl	Rec	Pass	Yds	C%	Yd/C	TD	YAC	DVOA	Rk	DYAR	Rk
2017	CAR			147	648	4.4	5	2	8.1%								62	85	594	73%	9.6	2		4.3%			

McCaffrey shot up draft boards despite a statistical decline from his sensational sophomore campaign, when he probably should have won the Heisman Trophy. His quickness in confined space, abrupt change of direction, and superb hands make McCaffrey the prime exemplar of a modern NFL back; one could argue he should have gone before Leonard Fournette due to his versatility and value on all three downs.

Scheme fit remains the large X-factor, along with how well a back ideally suited to a Bradyesque scalpel meshes with a Newtonian sledgehammer. Overuse is another quandary—counting returns, McCaffrey had nearly 700 touches over the last two seasons in Palo Alto. The Panthers would do well to resist the temptation to get McCaffrey the ball at every opportunity, at least as a rookie. But given his talent and the draft capital spent on him, that will be difficult.

LeSean McCoy Height: 5-11   Weight: 198   College: Pittsburgh   Draft: 2009/2 (53)   Born: 12-Jul-1988   Age: 29   Risk: Yellow

Year	Team	G/GS	Snaps	Runs	Yds	Yd/R	TD	FUM	DVOA	Rk	DYAR	Rk	YAR	Suc%	Rk	BTkl	Rec	Pass	Yds	C%	Yd/C	TD	YAC	DVOA	Rk	DYAR	Rk
2014	PHI	16/16	775	312	1319	4.2	5	4	-1.6%	24	87	15	93	45%	22	40	28	39	155	77%	5.5	0	6.6	-18.2%	43	-9	44
2015	BUF	12/12	598	203	895	4.4	3	2	8.8%	11	139	7	110	47%	21	39	32	50	292	64%	9.1	2	9.0	-2.0%	29	30	26
2016	BUF	15/15	645	234	1267	5.4	13	3	28.3%	2	338	2	244	51%	10	65	50	58	356	88%	7.1	1	7.6	21.2%	8	117	7
2017	BUF			250	1234	4.9	9	3	14.4%								48	64	399	75%	8.3	1		6.6%			

Adrian Peterson's release left McCoy as the standard-bearer for running back contracts, a fitting title for one of the few backs left who still serves as his team's offensive foundation. McCoy finished in the top five in rushing DVOA for the fourth time in the past six seasons, while also setting career-bests in both rushing DVOA and DYAR. The 29-year-old has had his share of nagging injuries the past two seasons, but that has yet to sap any of his trademark agility. Indeed, McCoy's 23 percent broken tackle rate ranked fourth among running backs with at least 150 touches.

Now that Rick Dennison is aboard as Buffalo's new offensive coordinator, the hope is that he won't mess with a good thing by overhauling the shotgun-heavy gap-rushing scheme in which McCoy has thrived. Of course, Dennison's Denver background suggests a lot more zone runs from under center. McCoy has thrived in a zone scheme before, having led the league in rushing DYAR and rushing yards in 2013 under Chip Kelly, but it's questionable whether the Bills have the athletes on the offensive line to run a similar scheme. McCoy isn't a sure thing given these circumstances and his injury history, but as long as he's on the field, he should remain one of the higher volume three-down backs in the game.

Darren McFadden Height: 6-1   Weight: 211   College: Arkansas   Draft: 2008/1 (4)   Born: 27-Aug-1987   Age: 30   Risk: Green

Year	Team	G/GS	Snaps	Runs	Yds	Yd/R	TD	FUM	DVOA	Rk	DYAR	Rk	YAR	Suc%	Rk	BTkl	Rec	Pass	Yds	C%	Yd/C	TD	YAC	DVOA	Rk	DYAR	Rk
2014	OAK	16/12	513	155	534	3.4	2	1	-13.9%	37	-33	37	-40	40%	35	14	36	56	212	64%	5.9	0	7.3	-37.5%	53	-75	56
2015	DAL	16/10	614	239	1089	4.6	3	3	-0.4%	23	83	17	103	50%	8	22	40	53	328	75%	8.2	0	7.9	6.9%	19	56	22
2016	DAL	3/1	48	24	87	3.6	0	0	-15.7%	--	-7	--	-3	46%	--	4	3	5	17	60%	5.7	0	8.3	-11.2%	--	1	--
2017	DAL			70	334	4.8	1	1	9.4%								19	27	157	70%	8.3	0		1.8%			

McFadden missed most of last season with an elbow injury he suffered at home in June. He returned in Week 16 to replace Alfred Morris as the back who mops up blowouts for Ezekiel Elliott. McFadden is just two years removed from a 1,000-yard season and has enough screen-and-go capability to play a third-down role. Signed to a one-year deal in the offseason, he has the inside track to supplant Morris as Elliott's long reliever and perhaps inherit some of Lance Dunbar's scant touches.

Jerick McKinnon Height: 5-9   Weight: 209   College: Georgia Southern   Draft: 2014/3 (96)   Born: 5-Mar-1992   Age: 25   Risk: Blue

Year	Team	G/GS	Snaps	Runs	Yds	Yd/R	TD	FUM	DVOA	Rk	DYAR	Rk	YAR	Suc%	Rk	BTkl	Rec	Pass	Yds	C%	Yd/C	TD	YAC	DVOA	Rk	DYAR	Rk
2014	MIN	11/6	331	113	538	4.8	0	0	11.5%	7	82	16	72	42%	34	12	27	41	135	66%	5.0	0	6.4	-53.1%	57	-83	57
2015	MIN	16/0	160	52	271	5.2	2	0	15.3%	--	50	--	61	50%	--	17	21	29	173	72%	8.2	1	8.4	2.4%	22	27	28
2016	MIN	15/7	510	159	539	3.4	2	0	-11.0%	34	-15	33	-56	42%	35	32	43	53	255	81%	5.9	2	6.3	-10.7%	40	10	36
2017	MIN			59	221	3.7	1	1	-8.3%								25	33	186	76%	7.4	0		2.4%			

The Vikings needed to figure out how much they believed in Jerick McKinnon this offseason. The departure of Adrian Peterson created an opening for McKinnon to move into a starting role. Adding Latavius Murray and Dalvin Cook to the backfield suggests that they don't trust McKinnon to be that guy. At this point it looks like McKinnon will be the Vikings' third-down back. For all of his athleticism and explosiveness, McKinnon is still trying to prove his ability as both a runner and a receiver. His limited development since entering the NFL is the reason why the Vikings weren't comfortable handing him a starting role this offseason.

Jeremy McNichols Height: 5-9 Weight: 214 College: Boise State Draft: 2017/5 (162) Born: 26-Dec-1995 Age: 22 Risk: Red

Year	Team	G/GS	Snaps	Runs	Yds	Yd/R	TD	FUM	DVOA	Rk	DYAR	Rk	YAR	Suc%	Rk	BTkl	Rec	Pass	Yds	C%	Yd/C	TD	YAC	DVOA	Rk	DYAR	Rk
2017	TB			126	532	4.2	5	2	3.9%								21	29	164	72%	7.8	1		-7.3%			

A lot of what happens in the Buccaneers backfield will be decided in September: Doug Martin's suspension moves everybody else up a slot on the depth chart, where there's a good chance Jeremy McNichols will be in the mix for touches on passing downs and as a backup to Jacquizz Rodgers. When (if?) Martin returns, McNichols is currently competing to be the backup to a backup, a much less enticing prospect unless he can excel in those September opportunities. In the long term, McNichols is widely considered a fifth-round steal: a versatile three-down back who could have a productive starting career as Martin's eventual replacement. He might become that guy as early as this coming season, but he has a bit of a logjam to negotiate first.

Christine Michael Height: 5-10 Weight: 220 College: Texas A&M Draft: 2013/2 (62) Born: 9-Nov-1990 Age: 27 Risk: N/A

Year	Team	G/GS	Snaps	Runs	Yds	Yd/R	TD	FUM	DVOA	Rk	DYAR	Rk	YAR	Suc%	Rk	BTkl	Rec	Pass	Yds	C%	Yd/C	TD	YAC	DVOA	Rk	DYAR	Rk
2014	SEA	10/0	73	34	175	5.1	0	1	10.0%	--	25	--	19	50%	--	8	1	2	12	50%	12.0	0	18.0	23.8%	--	3	--
2015	2TM	8/2	100	54	243	4.5	0	0	13.2%	--	51	--	29	48%	--	11	3	6	16	50%	5.3	0	6.0	-70.0%	--	-14	--
2016	2TM	15/7	398	148	583	3.9	7	2	-0.6%	21	52	21	48	49%	15	29	22	29	107	76%	4.9	1	5.6	-42.2%	53	-44	52

An explosive if not necessarily reliable running back originally drafted by the Seahawks, Michael did not live up to the hope that he would be the true successor to Marshawn Lynch in Seattle. Michael finished 2016 as the Seahawks' leading rusher despite being cut after nine games, which says more about the state of the Seattle running attack last year than it does about him. Michael signed a small free agent deal with Green Bay but was cut after the draft and subsequently picked up by the Colts in their effort to acquire every non-Lynch former Seattle running back available. Alas, Michael went down with an undisclosed injury in mid-June, landing on injured reserve with no timetable for a return. Undaunted by this, the Colts continued their search for former Seahawks running backs by signing Troymaine Pope to take his place on the active roster.

Lamar Miller Height: 5-11 Weight: 212 College: Miami Draft: 2012/4 (97) Born: 25-Apr-1991 Age: 26 Risk: Green

Year	Team	G/GS	Snaps	Runs	Yds	Yd/R	TD	FUM	DVOA	Rk	DYAR	Rk	YAR	Suc%	Rk	BTkl	Rec	Pass	Yds	C%	Yd/C	TD	YAC	DVOA	Rk	DYAR	Rk
2014	MIA	16/16	642	216	1099	5.1	8	2	17.8%	3	246	4	239	57%	1	24	38	52	275	73%	7.2	1	6.1	-10.7%	37	9	37
2015	MIA	16/16	631	194	872	4.5	8	1	1.7%	18	81	19	105	43%	34	26	47	57	397	82%	8.4	2	9.0	-3.6%	31	32	25
2016	HOU	14/14	623	268	1073	4.0	5	2	-10.5%	32	-21	34	29	45%	23	37	31	39	188	79%	6.1	1	6.0	-14.4%	44	-1	44
2017	HOU			276	1205	4.4	5	3	-0.3%								35	43	260	81%	7.4	3		19.6%			

Finally, we got to see what Lamar Miller could do with a steady workload. Oh… that's it? There were obviously some mitigating factors: the Houston quarterback situation brought down the offense, and they tried to pound Miller up the middle a bit much. Miller has the speed to attack a defense outside of the tackle box, but the Texans ran up the middle on 64 percent of their carries and were below average there while telegraphing most of them. Miller should remain the lead back this year, but nothing is guaranteed after that if he has another lackluster season.

Joe Mixon Height: 6-1 Weight: 228 College: Oklahoma Draft: 2017/2 (48) Born: 24-Jul-1996 Age: 21 Risk: Yellow

Year	Team	G/GS	Snaps	Runs	Yds	Yd/R	TD	FUM	DVOA	Rk	DYAR	Rk	YAR	Suc%	Rk	BTkl	Rec	Pass	Yds	C%	Yd/C	TD	YAC	DVOA	Rk	DYAR	Rk
2017	CIN			170	693	4.1	7	3	2.8%								26	36	184	72%	7.1	1		-12.7%			

There was a lot of debate about who was the top back in the extremely gifted running back class of 2017. Offseason issues knocked Mixon down to the second round, but he might be the most talented of them all. Mixon has prototype back size with no glaring deficiencies, and is a patient runner who plays the game at a level beyond his years. While we as a staff have taken more of a wait-and-see approach on his playing time, there are a lot of ways to get snaps in a backfield that's suddenly very empty outside of the underperforming Jeremy Hill. Mixon's status as someone you may not want to root for notwithstanding, he could be a fantasy football league winner à la Ezekiel Elliott last year.

Ty Montgomery
Height: 6-0 · Weight: 216 · College: Stanford · Draft: 2015/3 (94) · Born: 22-Jan-1993 · Age: 24 · Risk: Green

Year	Team	G/GS	Snaps	Runs	Yds	Yd/R	TD	FUM	DVOA	Rk	DYAR	Rk	YAR	Suc%	Rk	BTkl	Rec	Pass	Yds	C%	Yd/C	TD	YAC	DVOA	Rk	DYAR	Rk
2015	GB	6/3	242	3	14	4.7	0	0	-28.6%	--	2	--	4	--	--	4	15	19	136	79%	9.1	2	6.1	32.3%	--	74	--
2016	GB	15/6	392	77	457	5.9	3	2	17.6%	--	86	--	105	55%	--	25	44	56	348	79%	7.9	0	7.3	-4.2%	32	33	27
2017	GB			156	797	5.1	5	3	11.3%								50	66	433	76%	8.7	2		18.3%			

It's unclear how good Ty Montgomery can be as a running back. He needs to continue to improve as a pass blocker, both in terms of picking up his assignments and holding up against the physically superior beings that play in defensive fronts. Unsurprisingly, given his playing style at Stanford, Montgomery is a natural runner who anticipates his blocking and can work his way through holes in the defense to create big plays. He obviously has the athleticism to take advantage of the space he finds too. From a talent perspective, Montgomery has the physical ability and has shown flashes of the mental ability required to be a full-time back.

His size isn't a big concern either. Sure, he'll struggle with linebackers and defensive ends in pass protection, but most running backs do. Six-foot, 216 pounds is a fine frame for a running back.

The question is about Montgomery's snap-to-snap consistency. He only carried the ball 102 times in 19 games last year. How will his decision-making, ball security, and athleticism hold up if he is asked to carry the ball 20 times in consecutive games? He had 11 carries in back-to-back games during the playoffs, but his high for the season was 16. The optimist will point to his 162 yards on those 16 carries, but the realist will know that we need to be wary of Montgomery's workload until he forces us not to be.

Alfred Morris
Height: 5-10 · Weight: 219 · College: Florida Atlantic · Draft: 2012/6 (173) · Born: 12-Dec-1988 · Age: 29 · Risk: Red

Year	Team	G/GS	Snaps	Runs	Yds	Yd/R	TD	FUM	DVOA	Rk	DYAR	Rk	YAR	Suc%	Rk	BTkl	Rec	Pass	Yds	C%	Yd/C	TD	YAC	DVOA	Rk	DYAR	Rk
2014	WAS	16/16	595	265	1074	4.1	8	2	-1.4%	23	77	17	77	46%	18	28	17	26	155	65%	9.1	0	9.1	-8.7%	36	7	38
2015	WAS	16/16	385	202	751	3.7	1	0	-15.0%	41	-52	42	9	39%	44	12	10	13	55	77%	5.5	0	3.8	-27.6%	--	-10	--
2016	DAL	14/0	130	69	243	3.5	2	0	-7.7%	--	3	--	11	52%	--	13	3	6	11	50%	3.7	0	3.7	-53.4%	--	-13	--
2017	DAL			25	93	3.7	0	0	-6.3%								3	4	18	75%	6.0	0		-4.6%			

Morris had 56 yards on 17 carries mopping up the fourth quarter of a 35-10 rout of the Browns in Week 9, then saw his role in the offense nearly disappear as the Cowboys faced tougher opponents in the playoff chase. He returned for 15 yards on nine touches in the meaningless Week 17 game, production which revealed just how little tread is left on Morris' tires. He will battle Darren McFadden for the right to caddie for Ezekiel Elliott in camp. Watch the camp battle and injury log and grab the handcuff back if you like, but don't expect a scrap of production as long as Zeke is healthy.

DeMarco Murray
Height: 6-0 · Weight: 213 · College: Oklahoma · Draft: 2011/3 (71) · Born: 12-Feb-1988 · Age: 29 · Risk: Red

Year	Team	G/GS	Snaps	Runs	Yds	Yd/R	TD	FUM	DVOA	Rk	DYAR	Rk	YAR	Suc%	Rk	BTkl	Rec	Pass	Yds	C%	Yd/C	TD	YAC	DVOA	Rk	DYAR	Rk
2014	DAL	16/16	782	392	1845	4.7	13	5	14.8%	5	382	1	369	54%	3	51	57	64	416	89%	7.3	0	8.8	3.0%	21	58	14
2015	PHI	15/8	482	193	702	3.6	6	2	-12.1%	40	-29	39	19	45%	31	33	44	55	322	80%	7.3	1	8.7	-9.3%	39	13	35
2016	TEN	16/16	861	293	1287	4.4	9	4	-5.3%	25	42	24	140	50%	11	49	53	67	377	79%	7.1	3	6.5	-3.2%	30	40	24
2017	TEN			279	1247	4.5	9	3	7.3%								48	62	381	77%	7.9	1		11.0%			

Murray drew plenty of plaudits for rebounding from his Chip Kelly experience to lead the AFC in rushing yards. While still acknowledging him as a big upgrade to what Tennessee had before, our numbers were less effusive. For one thing, strength of schedule mattered **a lot**. Murray had 98 more YAR than DYAR, the third-biggest downward adjustment in rush value in the past 30 years. For another, he fell off dramatically as the season went on. Heavy workloads—he had at least 21 carries from Week 4 to Week 8—and a foot injury held him back. From Week 10 on, he had a rushing DVOA of minus-16.3%, and in four of seven games averaged less than 4.0 yards per carry. Mike Mularkey loves to pile carries on a single back, and Murray is in line for that job again this year. With a capable backup on hand in Derrick Henry, though, Mularkey should look to establish a more balanced workload so Murray is fresher come December and maybe even January rather than again emulating the Cowboys' apparent "run him into the ground by midseason" strategy from 2014.

Latavius Murray Height: 6-2   Weight: 223   College: UCF   Draft: 2013/6 (181)   Born: 21-Feb-1991   Age: 26   Risk: Green

Year	Team	G/GS	Snaps	Runs	Yds	Yd/R	TD	FUM	DVOA	Rk	DYAR	Rk	YAR	Suc%	Rk	BTkl	Rec	Pass	Yds	C%	Yd/C	TD	YAC	DVOA	Rk	DYAR	Rk
2014	OAK	15/3	275	82	424	5.2	2	1	1.7%	--	35	--	26	44%	--	3	17	23	143	74%	8.4	0	9.0	-6.6%	--	8	--
2015	OAK	16/16	680	266	1066	4.0	6	4	-5.6%	32	32	29	27	39%	43	39	41	53	232	77%	5.7	0	6.0	-30.6%	55	-47	54
2016	OAK	14/12	525	195	788	4.0	12	2	-3.4%	23	46	23	100	49%	16	36	33	43	264	77%	8.0	0	8.5	-9.4%	38	10	37
2017	MIN			130	526	4.1	6	2	1.1%								17	21	136	81%	8.0	0		10.5%			

Playing behind the Oakland Raiders offensive line is nothing like playing behind the Minnesota Vikings offensive line. Latavius Murray is about to find this out. The Raiders offensive line gave Murray time to read the defense after he got the ball and, more importantly, space to accelerate before crossing the line of scrimmage. That time and space will likely disappear in Minnesota.

Murray played consistently well in Oakland. He's a better runner than given credit for and can create both through contact and in space. He was never trusted to stay on the field in a full-time role because of his limited skill set. Murray is more diverse than Adrian Peterson, but he's still not a versatile receiving option. He is a better pass blocker and less likely to fumble the ball, which is why the Vikings were happy to pick him up in the offseason.

Jamize Olawale Height: 6-1   Weight: 240   College: North Texas   Draft: 2012/FA   Born: 17-Apr-1989   Age: 28   Risk: Green

Year	Team	G/GS	Snaps	Runs	Yds	Yd/R	TD	FUM	DVOA	Rk	DYAR	Rk	YAR	Suc%	Rk	BTkl	Rec	Pass	Yds	C%	Yd/C	TD	YAC	DVOA	Rk	DYAR	Rk
2014	OAK	16/0	112	2	0	0.0	0	0	-106.9%	--	-14	--	-13	0%	--	0	5	6	18	83%	3.6	2	1.4	58.5%	--	28	--
2015	OAK	14/3	156	24	110	4.6	1	0	33.5%	--	44	--	44	58%	--	5	9	11	84	82%	9.3	0	7.4	28.5%	--	28	--
2016	OAK	16/7	263	17	47	2.8	2	0	-9.4%	--	-1	--	-3	35%	--	8	12	14	227	86%	18.9	1	14.4	84.8%	--	71	--
2017	OAK			16	56	3.4	1	1	0.9%								12	15	119	80%	9.9	0		19.2%			

The two longest pass completions for the 2016 Raiders both went to Olawale. Maybe he lulled defenses to sleep with four years of nothingness, but he was as wide open as it gets on a 68-yard catch against Tampa Bay and a 75-yard touchdown against Houston. The latter required one cut at midfield, and over the final 50 yards Olawale showed some of that vintage fullback speed to the end zone. Don't expect him to come close to matching those career highlights in 2017.

Branden Oliver Height: 5-8   Weight: 203   College: Buffalo   Draft: 2014/FA   Born: 7-May-1991   Age: 26   Risk: Green

Year	Team	G/GS	Snaps	Runs	Yds	Yd/R	TD	FUM	DVOA	Rk	DYAR	Rk	YAR	Suc%	Rk	BTkl	Rec	Pass	Yds	C%	Yd/C	TD	YAC	DVOA	Rk	DYAR	Rk
2014	SD	14/7	373	160	582	3.6	3	0	-5.5%	28	20	29	24	44%	26	29	36	45	271	80%	7.5	1	9.4	15.3%	12	68	12
2015	SD	8/1	90	31	108	3.5	0	0	10.1%	--	27	--	23	48%	--	5	13	15	112	87%	8.6	0	10.4	37.4%	--	39	--
2017	LACH			29	105	3.7	1	1	-5.7%								26	31	225	84%	8.6	1		17.0%			

Oliver flashed some big-play potential back in 2014, but injuries have robbed him of the last season and a half. He could still be the best back behind Melvin Gordon on the Chargers roster, and Anthony Lynn loved using Mike Gillislee to back up LeSean McCoy in Buffalo last season. Still, expectations should be super low for a player who has 31 carries since 2015.

Samaje Perine Height: 5-11   Weight: 233   College: Oklahoma   Draft: 2017/4 (114)   Born: 16-Sep-1995   Age: 22   Risk: Blue

Year	Team	G/GS	Snaps	Runs	Yds	Yd/R	TD	FUM	DVOA	Rk	DYAR	Rk	YAR	Suc%	Rk	BTkl	Rec	Pass	Yds	C%	Yd/C	TD	YAC	DVOA	Rk	DYAR	Rk
2017	WAS			151	608	4.0	6	3	-3.1%								13	16	86	81%	6.6	0		-9.0%			

Run "Samaje Perine" through your Scot McCloughan decoder ring and it translates as "Frank Gore." Perine rushed for 1,713 yards and 21 touchdowns as a freshman for Oklahoma in 2014, and 1,349 yards with 16 touchdowns in 2015. He then gave way to Joe Mixon, but still gained 1,060 yards and scored 12 touchdowns in a reduced role. Mixon's elevation to the starting job was a disguised blessing for Perine, because: a) it lowered his workload; b) it forced him into a complementary role that emphasized his blocking and receiving abilities; and c) it made Perine's outstanding character stand out in stark relief. Perine is well-suited to a committee role, but he is so multi-talented that it's hard to believe that he will be unable to push Rob Kelley for the starting job.

Paul Perkins

Height: 5-10   Weight: 208   College: UCLA   Draft: 2016/5 (149)   Born: 16-Nov-1994   Age: 23   Risk: Green

Year	Team	G/GS	Snaps	Runs	Yds	Yd/R	TD	FUM	DVOA	Rk	DYAR	Rk	YAR	Suc%	Rk	BTkl	Rec	Pass	Yds	C%	Yd/C	TD	YAC	DVOA	Rk	DYAR	Rk
2016	NYG	14/1	289	112	456	4.1	0	1	-6.1%	26	11	26	22	44%	30	18	15	24	162	63%	10.8	0	11.3	-14.4%	--	-1	--
2017	NYG			176	788	4.5	4	3	1.2%								23	35	167	66%	7.2	0		-13.3%			

Ben McAdoo officially named Perkins the starting running back in May. Perkins' role increased steadily last season, from two to five touches early in the year, to a 50-50 split of carries with Rashad Jennings, to a featured role in the season finale and playoff loss. Perkins wasn't outstanding, but he was more effective than Jennings, and his value as both a receiver and pass protector remained limited even as his workload increased. McAdoo is sold on Perkins, but remember that McAdoo came from an offense that was sold on Ryan Grant and James Starks as a championship-caliber backfield tandem for several years.

Adrian Peterson

Height: 6-2   Weight: 217   College: Oklahoma   Draft: 2007/1 (7)   Born: 21-Mar-1985   Age: 32   Risk: Red

Year	Team	G/GS	Snaps	Runs	Yds	Yd/R	TD	FUM	DVOA	Rk	DYAR	Rk	YAR	Suc%	Rk	BTkl	Rec	Pass	Yds	C%	Yd/C	TD	YAC	DVOA	Rk	DYAR	Rk
2014	MIN	1/1	43	21	75	3.6	0	0	-1.8%	--	5	--	-4	43%	--	1	2	3	18	67%	9.0	0	10.0	53.4%	--	10	--
2015	MIN	16/16	665	327	1485	4.5	11	7	2.2%	17	143	6	133	45%	25	51	30	36	222	83%	7.4	0	8.6	-16.3%	47	-5	47
2016	MIN	3/3	84	37	72	1.9	0	1	-49.1%	--	-57	--	-63	38%	--	2	3	6	8	50%	2.7	0	3.7	-109.4%	--	-30	--
2017	NO			147	617	4.2	5	3	2.5%								23	28	191	82%	8.3	1		11.0%			

It is difficult to overstate how bad Adrian Peterson's numbers were during his brief sojourn out of the treatment room last year. None of his splits do him any favors. On first-down carries, Peterson accrued an unspeakable minus-70.8% DVOA. On second down, he "improved" to minus-39.5%. On runs from the shotgun, his DVOA was minus-60.4%. On pass targets… oh, you get the picture. Overall, Peterson's DVOA, both rushing and receiving, was the worst of any back with at least 20 carries. Maybe that was purely a combination of his injuries and the state of the Vikings offensive line. Maybe a healthy Peterson behind much better blockers will get back to his Hall-of-Fame level. Or maybe he's a 32-year-old running back with a growing injury history, and the best he can hope for is a few years of second fiddle to pad out his resume for Canton. Whatever the case, his signing for the Saints this offseason makes for an intriguing subplot to their season.

Bilal Powell

Height: 5-10   Weight: 205   College: Louisville   Draft: 2011/4 (126)   Born: 27-Oct-1988   Age: 29   Risk: Green

Year	Team	G/GS	Snaps	Runs	Yds	Yd/R	TD	FUM	DVOA	Rk	DYAR	Rk	YAR	Suc%	Rk	BTkl	Rec	Pass	Yds	C%	Yd/C	TD	YAC	DVOA	Rk	DYAR	Rk
2014	NYJ	15/1	237	33	141	4.3	1	0	7.6%	--	22	--	24	45%	--	3	11	15	92	73%	8.4	0	8.7	2.2%	--	14	--
2015	NYJ	11/2	367	70	313	4.5	1	2	1.0%	--	25	--	48	46%	--	20	47	63	388	75%	8.3	2	8.9	-3.3%	30	36	24
2016	NYJ	16/4	531	131	722	5.5	3	1	23.1%	3	182	8	197	56%	4	49	58	75	388	79%	6.7	2	7.2	-1.9%	27	49	20
2017	NYJ			164	790	4.8	4	2	8.8%								54	82	389	66%	7.2	1		-15.2%			

In the last four games of the year, Powell had 411 yards rushing and 552 yards from scrimmage, ranking third and second in the NFL in those respective categories. Powell's success was keyed by an ability to make defenders miss—he averaged one broken tackle every 2.7 carries, the best rate of any qualifying running back last year. It gave Jets fans a glimmer of hope, one source of optimism in what was otherwise a wasted season. Now, here's your reality check: Powell is entering his age-29 season and has just 2,331 career rushing yards. He has only three 100-yard rushing games in his career, and two of them came in that four-game stretch at the end of last year. And his value as a receiver is built on volume rather than efficiency; only once has he had a positive receiving DVOA in a season, and in that year he only had 15 targets. Powell will probably end up the feature back in New York ahead of a 32-year-old Matt Forte, but he's starting to get old himself. His ceiling doesn't look that high, and his time as the Jets' top running back should be short.

C.J. Prosise   Height: 6-0   Weight: 220   College: Notre Dame   Draft: 2016/3 (90)   Born: 20-May-1994   Age: 23   Risk: Green

Year	Team	G/GS	Snaps	Runs	Yds	Yd/R	TD	FUM	DVOA	Rk	DYAR	Rk	YAR	Suc%	Rk	BTkl	Rec	Pass	Yds	C%	Yd/C	TD	YAC	DVOA	Rk	DYAR	Rk
2016	SEA	6/2	147	30	172	5.7	1	0	19.6%	--	38	--	18	52%	--	6	17	19	208	89%	12.2	0	6.9	55.2%	--	62	--
2017	SEA			81	364	4.5	2	1	7.4%								50	64	437	78%	8.7	2		10.5%			

Prosise enters 2017 in line for an expanded role in both the running and passing games as Seattle's third-down back. A former wide receiver at Notre Dame, Prosise was a matchup nightmare in passing packages and his 62 receiving DYAR would have ranked 17th in the league among running backs had he met the minimum threshold for inclusion in the rankings. It's safe to say that Prosise will be seeing more than 19 targets this season if he is able to escape the injury bug and suit up for more than six games. Prosise played a huge role in Seattle's prime-time road win against the Patriots, accounting for 153 total yards on 24 touches; if he can stay on the field, it will definitely help the Seahawks' chances of returning to their past heights.

Donnel Pumphrey   Height: 5-8   Weight: 176   College: San Diego State   Draft: 2017/4 (132)   Born: 6-Dec-1994   Age: 23   Risk: Green

Year	Team	G/GS	Snaps	Runs	Yds	Yd/R	TD	FUM	DVOA	Rk	DYAR	Rk	YAR	Suc%	Rk	BTkl	Rec	Pass	Yds	C%	Yd/C	TD	YAC	DVOA	Rk	DYAR	Rk
2017	PHI			36	176	4.9	1	1	6.6%								19	27	141	70%	7.4	1		-12.4%			

There are small running backs, there are tiny running backs, and there are backs who could step onto a junior high basketball court and not even look like the star of the team. Pumphrey falls into that third category. His San Diego State game film is tasty, but his calves and wrists are twig-like.

The Eagles clearly plan to ease Pumphrey into Darren Sproles' role as change-up back, designated matchup headache out of the backfield, and punt returner. But Pumphrey has little experience as a return man, and Sproles is about 20 pounds heavier and far beefier.

Pumphrey is the little guy everyone will be rooting for, including us, but don't go overboard. Yes, Warrick Dunn succeeded with similar measurements, but there are lots of tiny, talented running backs in the world, while there was only one Warrick Dunn.

Thomas Rawls   Height: 5-9   Weight: 215   College: Central Michigan   Draft: 2015/FA   Born: 8-Aug-1993   Age: 24   Risk: Yellow

Year	Team	G/GS	Snaps	Runs	Yds	Yd/R	TD	FUM	DVOA	Rk	DYAR	Rk	YAR	Suc%	Rk	BTkl	Rec	Pass	Yds	C%	Yd/C	TD	YAC	DVOA	Rk	DYAR	Rk
2015	SEA	13/7	289	147	830	5.6	4	1	26.4%	2	216	1	224	62%	1	27	9	11	76	82%	8.4	1	8.4	5.8%	--	13	--
2016	SEA	9/7	303	109	349	3.2	3	0	-9.0%	31	-2	31	-26	41%	38	20	13	17	96	76%	7.4	0	6.3	10.9%	--	22	--
2017	SEA			130	555	4.3	4	2	2.8%								14	19	108	74%	7.7	0		2.5%			

Rawls burst onto the scene in his rookie year after Marshawn Lynch went down with an injury, but a broken ankle suffered against the Ravens prematurely ended his 2015 season. Unfortunately for Seattle, his sophomore season featured more time on the shelf than impact on the field. Rawls still broke a tackle on nearly one out of every five carries, without a doubt a useful skill behind the Seattle offensive line, but his production nosedived after leading the league in DYAR as a rookie. Rawls now faces competition from the newly signed Eddie Lacy for early-down carries, and C.J. Prosise is poised to take on a larger role in the passing game if he can stay healthy. Rawls could definitely bounce back from an efficiency standpoint, but given the wealth of options at Seattle's disposal, he will have a hard time living up to the potential he showed as a rookie.

Jalen Richard   Height: 5-8   Weight: 207   College: Southern Mississippi   Draft: 2016/FA   Born: 15-Oct-1993   Age: 24   Risk: Blue

Year	Team	G/GS	Snaps	Runs	Yds	Yd/R	TD	FUM	DVOA	Rk	DYAR	Rk	YAR	Suc%	Rk	BTkl	Rec	Pass	Yds	C%	Yd/C	TD	YAC	DVOA	Rk	DYAR	Rk
2016	OAK	16/0	237	83	491	5.9	1	0	16.7%	--	76	--	97	49%	--	23	29	39	194	74%	6.7	2	4.9	-8.8%	37	9	39
2017	OAK			58	260	4.5	1	2	1.4%								26	33	192	79%	7.4	1		5.9%			

Richard ranked fifth in yards after contact per rush (3.11) among players with at least 75 carries last year. His 75-yard touchdown run in New Orleans in his NFL debut really helped that comeback effort for the Raiders, but Richard never earned much more playing time in a crowded backfield. Even though leading rusher Latavius Murray has departed, the addition of Marshawn Lynch should keep Richard as just an occasional ballcarrier in this offense.

Theo Riddick

Height: 5-10   Weight: 201   College: Notre Dame   Draft: 2013/6 (199)   Born: 4-May-1991   Age: 26   Risk: Green

Year	Team	G/GS	Snaps	Runs	Yds	Yd/R	TD	FUM	DVOA	Rk	DYAR	Rk	YAR	Suc%	Rk	BTkl	Rec	Pass	Yds	C%	Yd/C	TD	YAC	DVOA	Rk	DYAR	Rk
2014	DET	14/2	172	20	51	2.6	0	0	-34.4%	--	-22	--	-17	40%	--	4	34	50	316	68%	9.3	4	9.0	14.7%	13	76	11
2015	DET	16/1	470	43	133	3.1	0	1	-24.5%	--	-29	--	-19	42%	--	40	80	99	697	81%	8.7	3	8.2	24.6%	10	201	2
2016	DET	10/8	423	92	357	3.9	1	0	-9.8%	--	-5	--	-1	42%	--	33	53	67	371	79%	7.0	5	7.3	3.9%	21	67	15
2017	DET			54	187	3.5	1	1	-12.2%								60	75	514	80%	8.6	1		13.6%			

Matthew Stafford and Jim Bob Cooter love themselves some Theo Riddick. Riddick was on pace for another 80-catch season before injury cost him his final six games. The only reason Riddick had 20 more carries last season (92) than his first three seasons combined was the early injury to Ameer Abdullah. Riddick has only rushed for 50 yards twice in his 54-game career, as he has always been more comfortable as a receiver. With Abdullah back, look for Riddick to remain the top receiving back in this offense.

Jacquizz Rodgers

Height: 5-6   Weight: 196   College: Oregon State   Draft: 2011/5 (145)   Born: 6-Feb-1990   Age: 27   Risk: Green

Year	Team	G/GS	Snaps	Runs	Yds	Yd/R	TD	FUM	DVOA	Rk	DYAR	Rk	YAR	Suc%	Rk	BTkl	Rec	Pass	Yds	C%	Yd/C	TD	YAC	DVOA	Rk	DYAR	Rk
2014	ATL	16/1	350	58	217	3.7	1	1	-11.4%	--	-7	--	7	40%	--	12	29	40	173	73%	6.0	1	6.4	-5.8%	33	18	30
2015	CHI	5/0	41	14	41	2.9	0	0	2.1%	--	7	--	-1	36%	--	2	1	3	10	33%	10.0	0	14.0	-85.8%	--	-13	--
2016	TB	10/5	341	129	560	4.3	2	0	0.2%	19	47	22	64	49%	18	22	13	16	98	81%	7.5	0	6.9	9.3%	--	19	--
2017	TB			87	361	4.1	1	2	-1.7%								17	22	167	77%	9.8	0		18.0%			

Until the injury bug struck the Buccaneers depth chart last year, six-year veteran Jacquizz Rodgers had never carried the ball more than 100 times in a single season, or eclipsed 4.0 yards per carry. He achieved both last time out, and was the only Buccaneers back to post a (marginally) positive rushing DVOA. Pocket Herculizz now looks set to be an opening-day starter for the first time in his career, but between Doug Martin's impending return and ripples of offseason excitement around fifth-round pick Jeremy McNichols, he will have to do more than scrape replacement level to retain that job beyond the end of September.

Charles Sims

Height: 6-0   Weight: 214   College: West Virginia   Draft: 2014/3 (69)   Born: 9/19/1990   Age: 27   Risk: Red

Year	Team	G/GS	Snaps	Runs	Yds	Yd/R	TD	FUM	DVOA	Rk	DYAR	Rk	YAR	Suc%	Rk	BTkl	Rec	Pass	Yds	C%	Yd/C	TD	YAC	DVOA	Rk	DYAR	Rk
2014	TB	8/0	231	66	185	2.8	1	2	-42.1%	--	-84	--	-77	35%	--	9	19	27	190	70%	10.0	0	10.4	-4.4%	31	12	33
2015	TB	16/0	457	107	529	4.9	0	2	2.6%	16	50	24	71	57%	2	36	51	70	561	73%	11.0	4	9.5	29.2%	7	150	3
2016	TB	7/2	238	51	149	2.9	1	1	-33.6%	--	-52	--	-56	39%	--	17	24	32	190	75%	7.9	1	7.3	3.5%	22	32	29
2017	TB			13	51	3.9	0	1	-2.5%								13	17	110	76%	8.5	0		7.6%			

With Doug Martin suspended for the first three games of the season, Sims was expected to get the first crack at the starting job for the Buccaneers. Instead, he may end up the odd man out by the time Martin's roster exemption expires. Injuries limited Sims to only seven ineffective appearances last season, the second time already in his young career that he's missed half the season and fallen below 3.0 yards per carry. Like most Buccaneers backs, he was much more effective in the passing game, but for Sims that still meant barely above replacement level. Jacquizz Rodgers and Peyton Barber proved themselves adequate if unspectacular replacements during Martin's most recent absence, and rookie Jeremy McNichols is already turning heads during the offseason. That spells trouble for Sims, as he is also the only backup halfback in Tampa Bay who does not have a special teams role to help secure his roster spot.

Wendell Smallwood

Height: 5-10   Weight: 208   College: West Virginia   Draft: 2016/5 (153)   Born: 29-Jan-1994   Age: 23   Risk: Red

Year	Team	G/GS	Snaps	Runs	Yds	Yd/R	TD	FUM	DVOA	Rk	DYAR	Rk	YAR	Suc%	Rk	BTkl	Rec	Pass	Yds	C%	Yd/C	TD	YAC	DVOA	Rk	DYAR	Rk
2016	PHI	13/3	164	77	312	4.1	1	1	-3.4%	--	17	--	9	49%	--	12	6	13	55	46%	9.2	0	8.3	-27.6%	--	-9	--
2017	PHI			118	508	4.3	2	2	-2.2%								20	26	165	77%	8.3	0		6.8%			

Smallwood had some fine games in 2016, including 13 carries for 70 yards in the Falcons win and 79 yards of mop-up duty in the blowout victory over the Steelers. He also carried once for a 5-yard loss and a fourth-quarter fumble against the Cowboys. Smallwood then spent December on the IR with an MCL injury. It was like a miniaturized version of a Ryan Mathews season, but the Eagles saw enough that they liked to bring Smallwood back this year. With LeGarrette Blount on hand and Darren Sproles and Donnell Pumphrey expected to share third-down duties, Smallwood now looks like the "other guy" in the rotation, which is what he was last year. An "other guy" cannot afford another year of injuries and fourth-quarter fumbles.

Darren Sproles   Height: 5-6   Weight: 181   College: Kansas State   Draft: 2005/4 (130)   Born: 20-Jun-1983   Age: 34   Risk: Green

Year	Team	G/GS	Snaps	Runs	Yds	Yd/R	TD	FUM	DVOA	Rk	DYAR	Rk	YAR	Suc%	Rk	BTkl	Rec	Pass	Yds	C%	Yd/C	TD	YAC	DVOA	Rk	DYAR	Rk
2014	PHI	15/0	337	57	329	5.8	6	2	30.4%	--	86	--	87	41%	--	18	40	63	387	65%	9.7	0	10.1	-3.1%	28	37	24
2015	PHI	16/4	393	83	317	3.8	3	1	14.8%	--	80	--	64	49%	--	14	55	83	388	66%	7.1	1	6.5	-24.9%	51	-50	55
2016	PHI	15/5	511	94	438	4.7	2	0	17.6%	--	99	--	83	52%	--	36	52	71	427	73%	8.2	2	7.9	3.0%	24	65	16
2017	PHI			80	364	4.5	1	1	4.8%								50	71	379	70%	7.6	1		-2.1%			

Sproles posted his career high in carries at age 33 last year, which is not how it is supposed to work for any running back, let alone a 5-foot-6 scatback. The Eagles recognized that Sproles' 2016 success was unsustainable, hence the signing of LeGarrette Blount to absorb carries and the draft selection of obvious replacement Donnell Pumphrey.

Look for Sproles' offensive role to be curtailed this season, though he should still get a fair share of touches between punt returns, third-down duties, and the many two-back looks the Eagles rolled out during OTAs. Sproles has had a remarkable career as an all-purpose contributor across three teams. The end is coming soon, but it's not quite here yet.

James Starks   Height: 6-2   Weight: 218   College: Buffalo   Draft: 2010/6 (193)   Born: 25-Feb-1986   Age: 31   Risk: N/A

Year	Team	G/GS	Snaps	Runs	Yds	Yd/R	TD	FUM	DVOA	Rk	DYAR	Rk	YAR	Suc%	Rk	BTkl	Rec	Pass	Yds	C%	Yd/C	TD	YAC	DVOA	Rk	DYAR	Rk
2014	GB	16/0	260	85	333	3.9	2	1	-8.6%	--	0	--	-8	40%	--	14	18	29	140	62%	7.8	0	6.7	-27.1%	49	-20	46
2015	GB	16/4	528	148	601	4.1	2	5	-15.8%	42	-46	41	-49	43%	37	18	43	53	392	81%	9.1	3	11.4	17.3%	14	97	10
2016	GB	9/4	265	63	145	2.3	0	1	-29.6%	--	-54	--	-75	32%	--	7	19	26	134	77%	7.1	2	8.3	-28.1%	50	-20	48

It didn't look like age had caught up to James Starks last season. Starks averaged a pitiful 2.3 yards per attempt, but his physical burst and strength could still be seen. The challenge for Starks has always been his consistency making decisions and his limited overall skill set. He lacks subtlety in his footwork and can't run different routes or line up in different spots of the field as a receiver. 31-year-old running backs don't often thrive in the NFL, and Starks' career is likely over.

Jonathan Stewart   Height: 5-10   Weight: 235   College: Oregon   Draft: 2008/1 (13)   Born: 21-Mar-1987   Age: 30   Risk: Green

Year	Team	G/GS	Snaps	Runs	Yds	Yd/R	TD	FUM	DVOA	Rk	DYAR	Rk	YAR	Suc%	Rk	BTkl	Rec	Pass	Yds	C%	Yd/C	TD	YAC	DVOA	Rk	DYAR	Rk
2014	CAR	13/8	546	175	809	4.6	3	2	1.3%	16	72	18	71	51%	7	32	25	31	181	81%	7.2	1	8.6	7.8%	16	35	25
2015	CAR	13/13	607	242	989	4.1	6	3	-6.2%	34	23	33	78	43%	33	49	16	21	99	76%	6.2	1	7.3	-5.4%	--	10	--
2016	CAR	13/13	565	218	824	3.8	9	3	-11.8%	35	-29	36	9	44%	31	46	8	21	60	38%	7.5	0	9.3	-70.1%	--	-67	--
2017	CAR			177	744	4.2	8	2	3.3%								15	19	109	79%	7.3	0		6.4%			

Goal-line stats tend to regress to the mean from year to year, but Stewart has steadily improved the last couple of seasons. Only three backs (Ezekiel Elliott, David Johnson, and Mike Gillislee) had a better touchdown percentage from in close with a minimum of ten carries. Stewart scored 9 touchdowns on 16 carries, 1.7 touchdowns over expectation. Most likely those numbers fall a bit in 2017. Stewart also excelled on third and fourth down (64 percent success rate, 16.8% DVOA) despite Cam Newton's obvious hesitation to run on the money downs in 2016.

In most other areas, however, Stewart is on the decline. Stewart's catch rate fell off a cliff in 2016, usually a foreshadowing of bad days ahead. Carolina drafted Christian McCaffrey to become the feature back as soon as possible, and to haul in those Cam cannonballs thrown from close range. Stewart may well soon find himself as a quality backup, not dissimilar from the role his old backfield mate, DeAngelo Williams, occupied in Pittsburgh. Whether that is with the Panthers or not remains to be seen.

Chris Thompson   Height: 5-8   Weight: 187   College: Florida State   Draft: 2013/5 (154)   Born: 20-Oct-1990   Age: 27   Risk: Green

Year	Team	G/GS	Snaps	Runs	Yds	Yd/R	TD	FUM	DVOA	Rk	DYAR	Rk	YAR	Suc%	Rk	BTkl	Rec	Pass	Yds	C%	Yd/C	TD	YAC	DVOA	Rk	DYAR	Rk
2014	WAS	2/0	30	3	12	4.0	0	0	18.5%	--	3	--	3	67%	--	0	6	7	27	86%	4.5	1	6.0	-12.4%	--	1	--
2015	WAS	13/0	274	35	216	6.2	0	2	8.0%	--	22	--	25	43%	--	8	35	48	240	73%	6.9	2	4.7	-15.6%	45	-5	46
2016	WAS	16/0	489	68	356	5.2	3	2	33.9%	--	111	--	99	53%	--	30	49	62	349	79%	7.1	2	5.1	10.6%	17	77	13
2017	WAS			64	316	4.9	1	2	6.8%								53	74	361	72%	6.8	1		-6.9%			

Jay Gruden and erstwhile offensive coordinator Sean McVay were creative about getting the most from the diminutive Thompson. They used Thompson as a traditional third-down back, of course, but they also packaged him in plays that let him get to the edge on toss-crack type runs. Eighteen of Thompson's 68 rushes netted 8 yards or more; 14 of those rushes were listed in the play-by-play as going around left or right end. It will be interesting to see if Thompson's role is as dynamic with McVay gone, or if Lance Dunbar gets all the successful sweeps in Los Angeles while Thompson waits for third down.

Mike Tolbert Height: 5-9 Weight: 243 College: Coastal Carolina Draft: 2008/FA Born: 23-Nov-1985 Age: 32 Risk: Green

Year	Team	G/GS	Snaps	Runs	Yds	Yd/R	TD	FUM	DVOA	Rk	DYAR	Rk	YAR	Suc%	Rk	BTkl	Rec	Pass	Yds	C%	Yd/C	TD	YAC	DVOA	Rk	DYAR	Rk
2014	CAR	8/6	220	37	78	2.1	0	0	-53.2%	--	-72	--	-68	27%	--	2	12	17	93	71%	7.8	0	8.3	-39.4%	--	-21	--
2015	CAR	16/3	422	62	256	4.1	1	0	9.8%	--	54	--	53	56%	--	12	18	23	154	78%	8.6	3	7.6	25.3%	--	56	--
2016	CAR	16/2	324	35	114	3.3	0	0	-18.6%	--	-14	--	-7	37%	--	11	10	15	72	67%	7.2	1	8.7	0.2%	--	11	--
2017	BUF			41	166	4.1	1	2	6.0%								15	21	113	71%	7.5	0		1.6%			

Orchard Park is one of the league's few remaining fullback sanctuaries. The Bills, who used two-back sets on a league-high 57 percent of their running plays last season, inked Tolbert and Patrick DiMarco this offseason to pave lanes for LeSean Mc-Coy. Tolbert is the slightly more viable option to actually have the ball in his hands, as he's had at least 40 touches every year since his rookie season in 2008. Moreover, during his time in Carolina, he had nearly as many carries within 5 yards of the goal line (34) as Jonathan Stewart (38). So while Tolbert's primary value is as a blocker, expect a few short-yardage totes, especially if one of the Bills' top two backs goes down.

Robert Turbin Height: 5-10 Weight: 222 College: Utah State Draft: 2012/4 (106) Born: 2-Dec-1989 Age: 28 Risk: Green

Year	Team	G/GS	Snaps	Runs	Yds	Yd/R	TD	FUM	DVOA	Rk	DYAR	Rk	YAR	Suc%	Rk	BTkl	Rec	Pass	Yds	C%	Yd/C	TD	YAC	DVOA	Rk	DYAR	Rk
2014	SEA	16/3	260	74	310	4.2	0	1	9.5%	--	57	--	41	61%	--	5	16	20	186	80%	11.6	2	10.5	83.3%	--	104	--
2015	2TM	10/0	150	50	199	4.0	1	0	13.5%	--	45	--	32	48%	--	9	7	10	23	70%	3.3	0	3.7	-89.2%	--	-31	--
2016	IND	15/0	300	47	164	3.5	7	0	32.2%	--	96	--	83	61%	--	17	26	35	179	74%	6.9	1	8.4	-14.2%	43	-1	43
2017	IND			45	156	3.4	2	2	-5.8%								17	23	113	74%	6.7	1		-2.1%			

The prototype late-2000s third-down back, before David Johnson changed the position. Turbin doesn't have great long speed but he brings good blocking and reliable pass-catching to the table. On any other roster, a 2012 draftee with zero 100-touch seasons would probably be in danger of losing his roster spot. In Indianapolis? Turbin might be the safest back they've got.

Shane Vereen Height: 5-10 Weight: 205 College: California Draft: 2011/2 (56) Born: 2-Mar-1989 Age: 28 Risk: Yellow

Year	Team	G/GS	Snaps	Runs	Yds	Yd/R	TD	FUM	DVOA	Rk	DYAR	Rk	YAR	Suc%	Rk	BTkl	Rec	Pass	Yds	C%	Yd/C	TD	YAC	DVOA	Rk	DYAR	Rk
2014	NE	16/6	595	96	391	4.1	2	0	-7.4%	--	4	--	-2	41%	--	15	52	77	447	68%	8.6	3	7.3	-3.1%	29	49	20
2015	NYG	16/0	431	61	260	4.3	0	1	-4.8%	--	9	--	20	41%	--	15	59	81	494	73%	8.4	4	7.2	8.4%	17	103	9
2016	NYG	5/1	117	33	158	4.8	1	2	-7.8%	--	1	--	14	45%	--	13	11	19	94	58%	8.5	0	8.0	-33.6%	--	-19	--
2017	NYG			82	379	4.6	3	2	7.9%								56	85	454	66%	8.1	1		-5.4%			

Vereen tore his triceps twice last season and also suffered a concussion. He took a pay cut in the offseason to remain with the Giants. The team needs him healthy as their third-down back, because starter Paul Perkins is a work-in-progress as an all-purpose player.

Terron Ward Height: 5-7 Weight: 201 College: Oregon State Draft: 2015/FA Born: 15-Feb-1992 Age: 25 Risk: Red

Year	Team	G/GS	Snaps	Runs	Yds	Yd/R	TD	FUM	DVOA	Rk	DYAR	Rk	YAR	Suc%	Rk	BTkl	Rec	Pass	Yds	C%	Yd/C	TD	YAC	DVOA	Rk	DYAR	Rk
2015	ATL	13/0	114	29	95	3.3	1	0	-12.3%	--	-4	--	-6	38%	--	2	9	13	73	69%	8.1	0	6.6	-33.4%	--	-11	--
2016	ATL	5/0	66	31	151	4.9	0	0	-2.8%	--	7	--	14	48%	--	4	1	2	11	50%	11.0	0	9.0	28.3%	--	4	--
2017	ATL			17	73	4.2	1	1	3.9%								7	9	62	78%	8.9	1		14.1%			

Atlanta's Super Bowl collapse left Ward's older brother, Broncos safety T.J. Ward, as the only member of the family with a ring. Knowing sibling rivalry, it's possible T.J. was rooting for the Patriots. Terron will likely spend even more time watching from the bench than he did in 2016, with rookie Brian Hill expected to snatch away the third-string role.

Spencer Ware Height: 5-10 Weight: 228 College: Louisiana St. Draft: 2013/6 (194) Born: 23-Nov-1991 Age: 26 Risk: Green

Year	Team	G/GS	Snaps	Runs	Yds	Yd/R	TD	FUM	DVOA	Rk	DYAR	Rk	YAR	Suc%	Rk	BTkl	Rec	Pass	Yds	C%	Yd/C	TD	YAC	DVOA	Rk	DYAR	Rk
2015	KC	11/2	159	72	403	5.6	6	0	25.8%	--	106	--	144	58%	--	12	6	6	5	100%	0.8	0	2.0	-167.8%	--	-42	--
2016	KC	14/14	546	214	921	4.3	3	4	-2.7%	22	54	20	72	53%	7	55	33	42	447	79%	13.5	2	11.4	32.7%	2	115	8
2017	KC			198	945	4.8	7	2	10.0%								28	35	235	80%	8.4	1		19.3%			

He's no Jamaal Charles, but Ware has been a good reclamation project for the Chiefs. Ware was second in the NFL with an average of 4.76 receiving yards after first contact. He even had 129 receiving yards in Week 1 against San Diego, but we can probably chalk that up as an outlier—he has never had more than 54 receiving yards in any other game. Now that Charles is in Denver, Ware can enter the season without looking over his shoulder at the other backs. Then again, the Chiefs parted ways with their WR1 and general manager in June. You can never be too comfortable in this business.

DeAndre Washington Height: 5-8 Weight: 204 College: Texas Tech Draft: 2016/5 (143) Born: 22-Feb-1993 Age: 24 Risk: Green

Year	Team	G/GS	Snaps	Runs	Yds	Yd/R	TD	FUM	DVOA	Rk	DYAR	Rk	YAR	Suc%	Rk	BTkl	Rec	Pass	Yds	C%	Yd/C	TD	YAC	DVOA	Rk	DYAR	Rk
2016	OAK	14/2	241	87	467	5.4	2	1	7.0%	--	55	--	78	47%	--	14	17	23	115	74%	6.8	0	6.8	-12.9%	--	1	--
2017	OAK			89	400	4.5	2	2	4.6%								22	28	158	79%	7.2	1		4.4%			

Washington flashed at times last year, but the Raiders still made the splash signing of coaxing Marshawn Lynch out of retirement. Washington is the player most likely to reap the benefits should Lynch falter in his return, but he will most likely be part of a committee approach again.

Dwayne Washington Height: 6-2 Weight: 226 College: Washington Draft: 2016/7 (236) Born: 24-Apr-1994 Age: 23 Risk: Red

Year	Team	G/GS	Snaps	Runs	Yds	Yd/R	TD	FUM	DVOA	Rk	DYAR	Rk	YAR	Suc%	Rk	BTkl	Rec	Pass	Yds	C%	Yd/C	TD	YAC	DVOA	Rk	DYAR	Rk
2016	DET	12/2	230	90	265	2.9	1	0	-19.3%	--	-39	--	-58	36%	--	15	10	15	62	67%	6.2	0	7.6	-20.1%	--	-5	--
2017	DET			75	287	3.8	2	2	-6.5%								12	14	93	86%	7.8	1		11.5%			

Washington dipped under the running back Mendoza line last season: he averaged 2.9 yards per carry. Rookie or not, few backs ever return to prominence after falling under 3.0 yards per carry. Some of the recent names to sink that low include Andre Williams (2015), Tre Mason (2015), Donald Brown (2014), Trent Richardson (2013), Bernard Pierce (2013), and Willis McGahee (2013). We'd show you how little those backs did after that season, but we have already written too much about a RB4 on a team that rarely runs the ball anyway. Either Washington or Zach Zenner will likely be cut before the season starts.

Charcandrick West Height: 5-10 Weight: 205 College: Abilene Christian Draft: 2014/FA Born: 2-Jun-1991 Age: 26 Risk: Blue

Year	Team	G/GS	Snaps	Runs	Yds	Yd/R	TD	FUM	DVOA	Rk	DYAR	Rk	YAR	Suc%	Rk	BTkl	Rec	Pass	Yds	C%	Yd/C	TD	YAC	DVOA	Rk	DYAR	Rk
2014	KC	6/0	4	0	0	--	0	0	--	--	--	--	--	--	--	0	0	1	0	0%	--	0	0.0	-135.3%	--	-7	--
2015	KC	15/9	497	160	634	4.0	4	1	2.8%	15	77	20	74	45%	27	29	20	34	214	59%	10.7	1	11.9	-20.4%	48	-13	50
2016	KC	15/2	358	88	293	3.3	1	0	-25.5%	--	-60	--	-56	36%	--	19	28	34	188	82%	6.7	2	6.5	-3.0%	29	21	31
2017	KC			32	131	4.0	0	1	-4.7%								13	17	86	76%	6.6	0		-2.9%			

West is clearly behind Spencer Ware on the Chiefs' depth chart, and he'll have to hold off rookie Kareem Hunt to remain relevant this year. It was only in Week 17 when West put in his best game of the season at San Diego with 116 yards from scrimmage and two touchdowns. Naturally, Ware was inactive that day to allow West that opportunity. If the Chiefs felt more confident in West's abilities, they wouldn't have needed to draft Hunt in the third round.

Terrance West   Height: 5-9   Weight: 225   College: Towson   Draft: 2014/3 (94)   Born: 1/28/1991   Age: 26   Risk: Yellow

Year	Team	G/GS	Snaps	Runs	Yds	Yd/R	TD	FUM	DVOA	Rk	DYAR	Rk	YAR	Suc%	Rk	BTkl	Rec	Pass	Yds	C%	Yd/C	TD	YAC	DVOA	Rk	DYAR	Rk
2014	CLE	14/6	401	171	673	3.9	4	1	-5.7%	29	21	28	39	47%	17	21	11	13	64	85%	5.8	1	4.8	17.5%	--	20	--
2015	2TM	8/0	125	62	231	3.7	0	2	-17.2%	--	-22	--	-35	42%	--	8	4	5	21	80%	5.3	0	4.5	-40.7%	--	-7	--
2016	BAL	16/13	443	193	774	4.0	5	2	-8.2%	28	3	28	-10	42%	33	49	34	45	236	76%	6.9	1	7.0	4.9%	20	50	19
2017	BAL			184	799	4.3	7	3	4.7%								24	34	169	71%	7.0	0		-6.2%			

Per charting from Bleacher Report's Marcus Mosher, West excelled on runs with six in the box last year, averaging 4.9 yards per carry on 59 attempts. On runs with seven or more in the box, not so much. West blossomed into a pretty useful player after the Browns gave up on him in 2014. He has improved since then, to the point where he can be the lead bruising back of a committee à la LeGarrette Blount. But if he wants to maintain his hold on his job and keep Kenneth Dixon from taking his snaps, he'll have to do better against base personnel. It would be nice if his offensive line gave him a hand in the process.

James White   Height: 5-9   Weight: 204   College: Wisconsin   Draft: 2014/4 (130)   Born: 3-Feb-1992   Age: 25   Risk: Green

Year	Team	G/GS	Snaps	Runs	Yds	Yd/R	TD	FUM	DVOA	Rk	DYAR	Rk	YAR	Suc%	Rk	BTkl	Rec	Pass	Yds	C%	Yd/C	TD	YAC	DVOA	Rk	DYAR	Rk
2014	NE	3/0	31	9	38	4.2	0	0	-7.1%	--	0	--	4	56%	--	0	5	5	23	100%	4.6	0	4.8	4.0%	--	5	--
2015	NE	14/1	290	22	56	2.5	2	0	-22.1%	--	-12	--	-13	32%	--	9	40	54	410	74%	10.3	4	8.7	33.3%	5	140	4
2016	NE	16/4	426	39	166	4.3	0	0	7.8%	--	24	--	24	51%	--	16	60	86	551	70%	9.2	5	8.8	20.1%	10	163	3
2017	NE			61	248	4.1	1	1	-1.2%								63	84	600	75%	9.5	2		15.6%			

The Super Bowl LI hero received a three-year, $12 million extension this offseason that secures his place as the heir to the all-important third-down back role in New England. The Patriots have had a running back catch at least 40 passes in five straight seasons, and White's 60 catches in 2016 were a Brady-Belichick era record for a running back. As the team's highest paid running back by average annual value, White is a logical candidate to maintain an expanded role in the passing game. The efficiency is certainly there, as White is the only running back to finish in the top 10 of receiving DVOA and DYAR each of the past two seasons. Still, with the Patriots restocking their backfield and receiving corps over the offseason, volume figures to remain an issue. The Super Bowl was only White's fourth career game with double-digit touches, and he has never had more than seven carries in a game. Thus, White's workload figures to vacillate week-to-week, despite New England's trust in his long-term outlook.

Fozzy Whittaker   Height: 5-10   Weight: 202   College: Texas   Draft: 2012/FA   Born: 2-Feb-1989   Age: 28   Risk: Green

Year	Team	G/GS	Snaps	Runs	Yds	Yd/R	TD	FUM	DVOA	Rk	DYAR	Rk	YAR	Suc%	Rk	BTkl	Rec	Pass	Yds	C%	Yd/C	TD	YAC	DVOA	Rk	DYAR	Rk
2014	CAR	10/1	84	32	145	4.5	1	0	22.7%	--	33	--	37	41%	--	2	5	6	60	83%	12.0	1	15.6	53.6%	--	24	--
2015	CAR	15/1	155	25	108	4.3	1	0	2.0%	--	11	--	20	44%	--	6	12	15	64	80%	5.3	0	9.3	-42.5%	--	-21	--
2016	CAR	16/0	308	57	265	4.6	0	1	-24.1%	--	-34	--	-7	37%	--	16	25	33	226	76%	9.0	0	9.5	6.2%	18	37	26
2017	CAR			41	195	4.7	0	1	8.8%								16	20	131	80%	8.2	0		9.9%			

Foswhitt apparently means "zombie," as Whitaker keeps plowing forward. He even had his first 100-yard game of his career in September, though the extra carries reduced his efficiency. Whitaker has always possessed very good hands, and he caught more than half of the completed passes to Carolina running backs in 2016. The Panthers clearly value him, as they re-signed him to a two-year deal in the offseason, though it seems likely Christian McCaffrey takes most of his targets.

Damien Williams   Height: 5-11   Weight: 221   College: Oklahoma   Draft: 2014/FA   Born: 3-Apr-1992   Age: 25   Risk: Green

Year	Team	G/GS	Snaps	Runs	Yds	Yd/R	TD	FUM	DVOA	Rk	DYAR	Rk	YAR	Suc%	Rk	BTkl	Rec	Pass	Yds	C%	Yd/C	TD	YAC	DVOA	Rk	DYAR	Rk
2014	MIA	16/0	158	36	122	3.4	0	0	-9.7%	--	-2	--	-6	47%	--	12	21	27	187	78%	8.9	1	7.2	40.1%	2	90	10
2015	MIA	16/0	159	16	59	3.7	0	1	-49.1%	--	-28	--	-27	31%	--	7	21	28	142	75%	6.8	1	4.2	-7.4%	35	10	37
2016	MIA	15/0	160	35	115	3.3	3	1	6.3%	--	22	--	9	37%	--	14	23	31	249	74%	10.8	3	9.0	12.5%	14	45	21
2017	MIA			34	132	3.9	1	1	-3.4%								17	22	119	77%	7.0	0		0.2%			

Williams has been borderline useless as a runner (3.4 yards per carry since 2014), but he is the best receiving back on the Dolphins roster. Williams actually ranked 54th in YAC+ at his position in 2015, but moved up to fourth with his best season yet in 2016. He's not fantasy relevant and may do even less this year if Jay Ajayi can contribute more on third down.

DeAngelo Williams Height: 5-8   Weight: 210   College: Memphis   Draft: 2006/1 (27)   Born: 25-Apr-1983   Age: 34   Risk: N/A

Year	Team	G/GS	Snaps	Runs	Yds	Yd/R	TD	FUM	DVOA	Rk	DYAR	Rk	YAR	Suc%	Rk	BTkl	Rec	Pass	Yds	C%	Yd/C	TD	YAC	DVOA	Rk	DYAR	Rk
2014	CAR	6/6	135	62	219	3.5	0	1	-15.2%	--	-17	--	-22	45%	--	7	5	6	44	83%	8.8	0	11.4	-3.3%	--	4	--
2015	PIT	16/10	701	200	907	4.5	11	3	12.1%	6	184	3	162	50%	9	31	40	47	367	85%	9.2	0	9.2	30.5%	6	109	8
2016	PIT	9/4	271	98	343	3.5	4	0	-12.8%	--	-17	--	25	46%	--	20	18	27	118	67%	6.6	2	7.1	-15.7%	45	-3	45

The Steelers made little effort to re-sign Williams in free agency, and the market seems pretty grim, as you would expect for a 34-year-old running back. Someone could bring him in as a goal-line back—he has a dozen rushing touchdowns inside the 5-yard line in the last two years, putting him in the top ten in that category—but otherwise, this looks like the end of the line. If so, Williams finishes as one of just 11 runners in NFL history to gain at least 8,000 yards and average at least 4.5 yards per carry. With no football to keep him busy, Williams appeared at a July pay-per-view event for Impact Wrestling, teaming with Quinn "Moose" Ojinnaka, who played seven years in the NFL himself. You can think of Impact Wrestling as pro wrestling's equivalent of the USFL, only instead of shutting down after three seasons they have somehow managed to hemorrhage money for 15 years. NFL stars Frank Wycheck and Adam Jones have also worked with the group. They currently have a show on Thursday nights on something called Pop TV between re-runs of *The Young and the Restless* and *Taxi*. Billy Corgan of Smashing Pumpkins fame tried to buy them in 2016 and ended up suing them instead. This is all true, and there's a lot more, but those stories belong in a different book.

Jamaal Williams Height: 6-0   Weight: 212   College: BYU   Draft: 2017/4 (134)   Born: 3-Apr-1995   Age: 22   Risk: Green

Year	Team	G/GS	Snaps	Runs	Yds	Yd/R	TD	FUM	DVOA	Rk	DYAR	Rk	YAR	Suc%	Rk	BTkl	Rec	Pass	Yds	C%	Yd/C	TD	YAC	DVOA	Rk	DYAR	Rk
2017	GB			95	390	4.1	4	2	3.9%								19	23	131	83%	6.9	0		-6.9%			

Daniel Jeremiah of NFL Network compared Jamaal Williams to James Starks. The rest of this should really write itself. Starks was a tall back who showed off explosiveness but was a more linear athlete than the Packers would have preferred. Williams has a similar athletic profile and has the same limitations as a receiver. He won't elevate his run blocking with subtle movements or great anticipation in his vision. Williams is the definition of a point-and-go runner. He picks his spot, hits it hard, and hopes to break through any defenders in his way. Without Eddie Lacy or Starks on the roster, Williams should be the favorite for short-yardage carries, assuming the Packers don't continue to rely on fullback Aaron Ripkowski in those situations.

Joe Williams Height: 5-11   Weight: 210   College: Utah   Draft: 2017/4 (121)   Born: 4-Sep-1993   Age: 24   Risk: Blue

Year	Team	G/GS	Snaps	Runs	Yds	Yd/R	TD	FUM	DVOA	Rk	DYAR	Rk	YAR	Suc%	Rk	BTkl	Rec	Pass	Yds	C%	Yd/C	TD	YAC	DVOA	Rk	DYAR	Rk
2017	SF			78	357	4.6	2	2	2.0%								14	18	71	78%	5.1	0		-21.7%			

Williams had the second-highest Speed Score at the combine, running a 4.41 40 at 210 pounds. He also was reportedly a favorite of both coach Kyle Shanahan and running backs coach Bobby Turner, who fell in love with him despite questions over his dismissal from UConn and his month-long retirement at Utah. There are worse situations for a rookie to be in than having two coaches firmly in your corner. His success at Utah jumps out on film and on the stat sheet—with 7.1 highlight yards per opportunity, Williams produced more than his fair share of explosive plays in 2016. Is all that enough to unseat Carlos Hyde as San Francisco's starter, as has been rumored? Probably not as a rookie, but keep in mind that a) Tevin Coleman got 34 percent of Atlanta's offensive snaps last season despite being the second running back; b) Hyde's rookie contract expires at the end of 2017; and c) Hyde's a Trent Baalke player, not a Lynchahan selection. The situation seems ripe for Williams to have an opportunity to earn the feature back role come 2018 if he is able to perform as a rookie.

Jonathan Williams Height: 5-11   Weight: 220   College: Arkansas   Draft: 2016/5 (156)   Born: 2-Feb-1994   Age: 23   Risk: Red

Year	Team	G/GS	Snaps	Runs	Yds	Yd/R	TD	FUM	DVOA	Rk	DYAR	Rk	YAR	Suc%	Rk	BTkl	Rec	Pass	Yds	C%	Yd/C	TD	YAC	DVOA	Rk	DYAR	Rk
2016	BUF	11/0	92	27	94	3.5	1	2	-32.9%	--	-31	--	-40	41%	--	5	1	2	0	50%	0.0	0	2.0	-74.0%	--	-6	--
2017	BUF			96	419	4.4	4	4	1.8%								10	13	82	77%	8.2	0		5.8%			

Following Mike Gillislee's offseason departure, Williams will move into the vacated role of LeSean McCoy's squire. McCoy has missed five games the past two seasons while picking up a variety of dings and dents along the way, meaning that Williams will likely start at least a game or two in 2017. For Williams, the real key to unlocking carries will be improving his goal-line performance. In a tiny seven-carry sample size last year, Williams compiled a minus-20.1% rushing DVOA in the red zone. Buffalo showed a willingness to give Gillislee touches in part because of his prowess near the end zone, a skill Williams needs to pick up if he's going to be anything more than a McCoy handcuff.

Kerwynn Williams Height: 5-8   Weight: 195   College: Utah State   Draft: 2013/7 (230)   Born: 9-Jun-1991   Age: 26   Risk: Green

Year	Team	G/GS	Snaps	Runs	Yds	Yd/R	TD	FUM	DVOA	Rk	DYAR	Rk	YAR	Suc%	Rk	BTkl	Rec	Pass	Yds	C%	Yd/C	TD	YAC	DVOA	Rk	DYAR	Rk
2014	ARI	5/0	89	53	246	4.6	0	1	2.6%	--	23	--	31	58%	--	5	2	6	11	33%	5.5	0	6.5	-56.6%	--	-12	--
2015	ARI	6/0	51	27	142	5.3	1	1	-27.1%	--	-19	--	-9	37%	--	3	2	2	16	100%	8.0	0	3.5	60.8%	--	8	--
2016	ARI	10/0	51	18	157	8.7	2	0	78.7%	--	69	--	62	56%	--	4	1	2	6	50%	6.0	0	7.0	-6.6%	--	1	--
2017	ARI			13	59	4.5	0	1	6.4%								6	9	47	67%	7.9	0		-1.4%			

Williams was cut by the Cardinals twice in 2016, first in training camp and then in October. He did end up with 18 rushing attempts in the last month of the season after injuries forced Arizona to dig deep into their depth. Williams now finds himself in an out-and-out fight to be the primary backup to David Johnson. He is competing with Andre Ellington, who was briefly moved to receiver during the offseason, re-signed veteran Chris Johnson, and fifth-round rookie T.J. Logan. When given an opportunity, Williams *has* averaged 5.6 yards per attempt, so he has shown some sparks. Williams is a fighter; he has been cut eight times in his four-year career, yet keeps bouncing back. Maybe he has finally found a situation he can stick with. Either way, a healthy Johnson is getting 75 percent (or more) of Arizona's running back snaps, so his backup will be more of an emergency player.

Danny Woodhead Height: 5-9   Weight: 200   College: Chadron State   Draft: 2008/FA   Born: 25-Jan-1985   Age: 32   Risk: Yellow

Year	Team	G/GS	Snaps	Runs	Yds	Yd/R	TD	FUM	DVOA	Rk	DYAR	Rk	YAR	Suc%	Rk	BTkl	Rec	Pass	Yds	C%	Yd/C	TD	YAC	DVOA	Rk	DYAR	Rk
2014	SD	3/0	68	15	38	2.5	0	0	-30.3%	--	-14	--	-21	33%	--	2	5	6	34	83%	6.8	0	6.6	46.4%	--	24	--
2015	SD	16/2	594	98	336	3.4	3	0	-5.5%	--	13	--	14	45%	--	21	80	108	755	76%	9.4	6	8.9	25.8%	9	235	1
2016	SD	2/1	55	19	116	6.1	0	0	33.7%	--	30	--	38	63%	--	0	6	8	35	75%	5.8	1	5.2	26.0%	--	18	--
2017	BAL			67	280	4.2	0	2	-1.0%								63	88	502	72%	8.0	2		2.1%			

Another consummate third-down back. Woodhead has little power and his whole game is about speed and burst, which is a problem after two lost seasons in three years, the last of which was due to a torn ACL. In an uncertain backfield, Woodhead could surprise and have a bigger share of the targets than expected. He could also fall behind Kenneth Dixon upon Dixon's return and never be heard from again. Isn't the life of an NFL running back exciting?

T.J. Yeldon Height: 6-1   Weight: 226   College: Alabama   Draft: 2015/2 (36)   Born: 2-Oct-1993   Age: 24   Risk: Blue

Year	Team	G/GS	Snaps	Runs	Yds	Yd/R	TD	FUM	DVOA	Rk	DYAR	Rk	YAR	Suc%	Rk	BTkl	Rec	Pass	Yds	C%	Yd/C	TD	YAC	DVOA	Rk	DYAR	Rk
2015	JAC	12/12	620	182	740	4.1	2	0	-3.2%	28	39	26	31	42%	38	38	36	46	279	78%	7.8	1	8.3	5.7%	20	52	23
2016	JAC	15/13	576	130	465	3.6	1	2	-24.8%	41	-81	38	-57	38%	42	42	50	68	312	74%	6.2	1	7.1	-27.9%	49	-52	53
2017	JAC			75	301	4.0	1	1	-4.8%								28	37	217	76%	7.7	0		3.1%			

Might T.J. Yeldon be a good NFL player in a good situation? The idea seems plausible, but Jacksonville is certainly not a good situation, and Yeldon certainly has not transcended it. His inconsistent workloads continued, with just four games with double-digit carries. Of course, opening the season with 21 carries for 39 yards in Chris Ivory's absence did not help his case to be the lead back. The best hope is that the arrival of Leonard Fournette will do what Ivory could not: turn Yeldon into more of a situational player who can be effective on eight carries a game. He ran better from shotgun than he did from under center and is a better bet to take passing game reps than either Fournette or Ivory. It might work out, and certainly cannot hurt.

Zach Zenner			Height: 5-11		Weight: 222		College: South Dakota State			Draft: 2015/FA			Born: 13-Sep-1991 Age: 26			Risk: Yellow		
Year	Team	G/GS	Snaps	Runs	Yds	Yd/R	TD	FUM	DVOA	Rk	DYAR	Rk	YAR	Suc%	Rk	BTkl	Rec	Pass	Yds	C%	Yd/C	TD	YAC	DVOA	Rk	DYAR	Rk
2015	DET	6/1	46	17	60	3.5	0	0	-0.4%	--	6	--	-1	53%	--	0	2	3	11	67%	5.5	0	6.0	-23.4%	--	-1	--
2016	DET	14/4	293	88	334	3.8	4	1	-3.1%	--	21	--	9	48%	--	15	18	23	196	78%	10.9	0	11.4	51.4%	--	80	--
2017	DET			73	293	4.0	2	2	2.5%								14	18	120	78%	8.6	1		11.3%			

With the league's most injury-riddled backfield, the Lions relied on Zenner late in the year. He didn't mind when his peers, namely Seattle's Michael Bennett, referred to him as "the best white running back in the league." It's not a competition many enter these days. Carolina rookie Christian McCaffrey will likely take that title now, and Zenner will likely remain a backup now that the Lions have Ameer Abdullah and Theo Riddick healthy again.

Going Deep

Kenjon Barner, LACH: Barner has bounced around with the Panthers and Eagles, two of the teams more committed to the running back position in recent years. A long-time Chip Kelly favorite, Barner scored his first two NFL rushing touchdowns in Doug Pederson's offense last year, but now he's a deep-roster back who will have to compete with Melvin Gordon, Branden Oliver, and Kenneth Farrow just to make the Chargers roster.

Kapri Bibbs, SF: It looked like Bibbs would get his first significant NFL role last season after C.J. Anderson went down with a torn meniscus, but Bibbs managed just 29 carries before suffering a high ankle sprain that ended his season. Bibbs does have experience in the zone-blocking scheme the 49ers are switching to, but his spot on the 53-man roster is tenuous at best. He'll have to show special teams value to beat out UDFA Matt Breida (Georgia Southern) for the fourth running back slot.

Mack Brown, WAS: Brown was activated for the London game in Week 8 as part of the "Anyone but Matt Jones Initiative" in the Redskins backfield. He played special teams until Week 16, when he ripped off a 61-yard run in garbage time against the Bears. Even with Jones on the way out, Brown will be hard-pressed to make a depth chart led by Rob Kelley, Chris Thompson, and Samije Perine. Brown does have a good chance of landing on another roster if Washington releases him.

Tarik Cohen, CHI: Tarik Cohen was compared to Darren Sproles coming out of FCS school North Carolina A&T. Nothing new there. Cohen is actually worthy of that comparison when it comes to style of play. He could spend as much time lining up out wide or playing on passing downs as he does lining up in the backfield to run the ball. Cohen's elusiveness and explosiveness in the open field is what will determine how much he can play early in his career. The Bears will look to him for big plays rather than consistency, giving him a role somewhat similar to Jalen Richard's in Oakland.

Orleans Darkwa, NYG: The bad penny of the Giants roster. Darkwa picked up a few early-season starts when Rashad Jennings was hurt but accomplished nothing. He's the ultimate replacement-level running back. The Giants signed him to a one-year deal in March, because they often find themselves in need of replacement-level backs, and Darkwa already has a parking space.

Knile Davis, PIT: Davis had the highest Speed Score among 2013 running back prospects, but aside from a pair of touchdowns on kickoff returns, he hasn't had much luck translating his physical gifts into on-field success. After spending 2016 with the Jets, Packers, and Chiefs (twice), he signed to compete with James Conner and Fitzgerald Toussaint for the backup spot behind Le'Veon Bell.

Mike Davis, SEA: Davis averaged just 2.0 yards per carry in two years in San Francisco. The 49ers offensive line was bad, but not that bad. Davis is insurance in case injuries strike Thomas Rawls, Eddie Lacy, C.J. Prosise, Alex Collins, Shaun Alexander, Chris Warren, John L. Williams, Felix Hernandez, Pete Carroll, Macklemore, and Sir Mix-a-Lot. If all go down in training camp, Davis has a chance to make the 53-man roster.

Matthew Dayes, CLE: Dayes ran for 1,166 yards in 2016, the first thousand-yard rusher at North Carolina State in 14 years, but dropped to the seventh round thanks in part to a 4.66-second 40-yard dash at his pro day. He'll be the third running back in Cleveland this fall.

Tyler Ervin, HOU: Billed as a speedy third-down back with return ability—basically, compared to Darren Sproles by over-zealous scouts—Ervin received zero carries for the Texans last year. He handled 14 kick returns and 27 punt returns, muffing four of them (plus two more in the playoffs) because he had to live up to the true calling of Texans Special Teamer. As a punt returner on a pure statistical level, he wasn't half-bad last year. But Ervin looked as lost and confused as anyone on the perennially last-place special teams unit.

Corey Grant, JAC: The latest in the long line of whodats to rush for 100 yards in Week 17, Grant is a screens-and-draws type perimeter runner who put up 18 carries for 122 yards against a Colts defense that was bad even at full strength. Depending on just how embryonic Leonard Fournette's passing-game skills are, Grant could potentially seize a situational role. Just don't expect more, and that would be true regardless of depth chart.

Jonathan Grimes, FA: Grimes had a nice 2015 season for the Texans (56 carries for 282 yards, 20.0% DVOA), but was confined to spot duty last year after Lamar Miller came over in free agency. Entering his age-27 season without much of a resume besides "do-it-all backup," and no rumored market for his services as we go to press, it's likely the end of the line for ol' Grimey.

De'Angelo Henderson, DEN: He's not on the talent level of DeAngelo Williams or (assuming here) "How Does It Feel" D'Angelo, but De'Angelo Henderson was a productive rusher for Coastal Carolina with three straight 1,150-yard seasons. He is a smaller back, but there is an opportunity here to make the team behind C.J. Anderson (consistently inconsistent), Jamaal Charles (consistently injured), and Devontae Booker (unproven).

Ronnie Hillman, FA: The selection of Devontae Booker in 2016's draft led to Denver's release of Hillman. The Vikings scooped him up after Adrian Peterson went down, but Hillman was of no use (2.8 yards per carry) behind a bad offensive line. Similar things can be said about his short stay in San Diego, and the Chargers released him in March. He'll only be 26 in September, but there aren't many suitors for a back who generally struggles to crack 3.0 yards per carry.

Akeem Hunt, HOU: Easily the fastest back the Texans have in terms of hitting the hole, Hunt had eight carries for 52 yards against the Jaguars in Week 10, prompting fantasy football speculation due to Lamar Miller's injuries. He gained 57 yards over the next seven games. Hunt does return kicks and has some explosiveness, so he's a fine end-of-roster back and could find himself active often if Alfred Blue loses the backup spot to D'Onta Foreman.

Daniel Lasco, NO: In a crowded Saints backfield, 2016 seventh-rounder Lasco will probably be the fifth of five running backs on the final 53-man roster. Last year, he managed only 13 touches in seven games. Assuming he does retain his roster spot in September, it will be almost exclusively for special teams.

Keith Marshall, WAS: At the 2016 combine, Marshall ran a 4.31-second 40-yard dash at 219 pounds, good for a Speed Score of 126.9, the highest such number on record. He has had terrible luck with injuries, including a torn ACL in 2013 that more or less killed his production in college, and a sprained elbow that cost him his entire rookie season. Marshall may get lost in the shuffle in Washington's crowded backfield this year, but his upside is high enough that a practice-squad spot somewhere seems assured.

Devante Mays, GB: A physically gifted back, Mays fell to the seventh round because of an ankle injury that hampered his final season at Utah State. He's not a nuanced runner or deceptive in space, but he has the right combination of size and explosiveness to run through holes and over defenders.

Elijah McGuire, NYJ: McGuire went over 1,200 yards from scrimmage in all four seasons at Louisiana-Lafayette despite playing through a foot injury in his senior year. The Jets grabbed him in the sixth round despite questions about his physicality, both as a runner and a blocker.

Bobby Rainey, FA: Last seen stepping out of bounds at the 3-yard line after fielding a kickoff return against the Packers in the playoffs. Presumed to be seeking employment in another industry.

Denard Robinson, FA: Robinson had a better rushing DVOA than either Chris Ivory or T.J. Yeldon, but it was still just minus-24.4%. His only significant action came in Weeks 11 and 12, and 30 carries for 92 yards against a pair of bottom-12 run defenses has not earned him a contract anywhere this offseason.

C.J. Spiller, KC: About the only difference between C.J. Spiller and Christine Michael at this point is that Spiller at least used to be good. Spiller is on his fifth team since 2014, and he only had 68 yards from scrimmage with the Jets and Seahawks last year. There's a bit of a void in Kansas City with Jamaal Charles moving on, but rookie Kareem Hunt could make it hard for Spiller to catch on even as a dump-pass option for Alex Smith.

Fitzgerald Toussaint, PIT: Toussaint has only gained 172 yards from scrimmage in three NFL seasons, but he may have found a home in the kicking game. He was third on the Steelers with 248 special teams snaps last year after playing only 76 special teams snaps in his first two NFL seasons.

Brandon Wilds, NYJ: An undrafted rookie out of South Carolina, Wilds was called from the Jets' practice squad to the main roster when the depth chart fell to pieces in December. He played like you'd expect a late-season practice squad call-up to play and is a long shot to make the Jets' roster this year.

Andre Williams, LACH: Williams was a power back lacking in power with the Giants. He spent most of 2016 on the practice squad in San Diego, but did rush for 87 yards in the Week 17 finale, albeit with the Chiefs not having the strongest run defense in the league. Williams has caught an abysmal 19 of his 42 career targets, which won't be appreciated by Philip Rivers. He has a lot of competition in the backfield and would be a fourth back at best in Los Angeles.

Wide Receivers

In the following two sections we provide the last three years of statistics, as well as a 2017 KUBIAK projection, for every wide receiver and tight end who either played a significant role in 2016 or is expected to do so in 2017.

The first line contains biographical data—each player's name, height, weight, college, draft position, birth date, and age. Height and weight are the best data we could find; weight, of course, can fluctuate during the off-season. **Age** is very simple, the number of years between the player's birth year and 2017, but birth date is provided if you want to figure out exact age.

Draft position gives draft year and round, with the overall pick number with which the player was taken in parentheses. In the sample table, it says that Brandin Cooks was chosen in the 2014 NFL draft with the 20th overall pick in the first round. Undrafted free agents are listed as "FA" with the year they came into the league, even if they were only in training camp or on a practice squad.

To the far right of the first line is the player's Risk for fantasy football in 2017. As explained in the quarterback section, the standard is for players to be marked Green. Players with higher than normal risk are marked Yellow, and players with the highest risk are marked Red. Players who are most likely to match or surpass our forecast—primarily second-stringers with low projections—are marked Blue. Risk is not only based on age and injury probability, but how a player's projection compares to his recent performance as well as our confidence (or lack thereof) in his offensive teammates.

Next we give the last three years of player stats. Note that rushing stats are not included for receivers, but that any receiver with at least five carries last year will have his 2016 rushing stats appear in his team's chapter.

Next we give the last three years of player stats. First come games played and games started (**G/GS**). Games played represents the official NFL total and may include games in which a player appeared on special teams, but did not play wide receiver or tight end. We also have a total of offensive **Snaps** for each season. Receptions (**Rec**) counts passes caught, while Passes (**Pass**) counts passes thrown to this player, complete or incomplete. Receiving yards (**Yds**) is the official NFL total for each player.

Catch rate (**C%**) includes all passes listed in the official play-by-play with the given player as the intended receiver, even if those passes were listed by our game charters as "Thrown Away," "Tipped at Line," or "Quarterback Hit in

Motion." The average NFL wide receiver has caught between 58 and 60 percent of passes over the last three seasons; tight ends caught between 64 and 65 percent of passes over the last three seasons.

Plus/minus (+/-) is a metric that we introduced in *Football Outsiders Almanac 2010*. It estimates how many passes a receiver caught compared to what an average receiver would have caught, given the location of those passes. Unlike simple catch rate, plus/minus does not consider passes listed as "Thrown Away," "Tipped at Line," or "Quarterback Hit in Motion." Player performance is compared to a historical baseline of how often a pass is caught based on the pass distance, the distance required for a first down, and whether it is on the left, middle, or right side of the field. Note that plus/minus is not scaled to a player's target total.

Yards per catch (**Yd/C**) and receiving touchdowns (**TD**) are standard stats. Drops (**Drop**) list the number of dropped passes according to charting from Sports Info Solutions. Our totals may differ from the drop totals kept by other organizations.

Next we list yards after catch (**YAC**), rank (**Rk**) in yards after catch, and **YAC+.** YAC+ is similar to plus-minus; it estimates how much YAC a receiver gained compared to what we would have expected from an average receiver catching passes of similar length in similar down-and-distance situations. This is imperfect—we don't specifically mark what route a player runs, and obviously a go route will have more YAC than a comeback—but it does a fairly good job of telling you if this receiver gets more or less YAC than other receivers with similar usage patterns. We also give a total of broken tackles (**BTkl**) according to Sports Info Solutions charting.

The next five columns include our main advanced metrics for receiving: **DVOA** (Defense-Adjusted Value Over Average), **DYAR** (Defense-Adjusted Yards Above Replacement), and **YAR** (Yards Above Replacement), along with the player's rank in both DVOA and DYAR. These metrics compare every pass intended for a receiver and the results of that pass to a league-average baseline based on the game situations in which passes were thrown to that receiver. DVOA and DYAR are also adjusted based on the opposing defense and include Defensive Pass Interference yards on passes intended for that receiver. The methods used to compute these numbers are described in detail in the "Statistical Toolbox" introduction in the front of the book. The important distinctions between them are:

Brandin Cooks					Height: 5-10		Weight: 189		College: Oregon St.			Draft: 2014/1 (20)		Born: 25-Sep-1993		Age: 24		Risk: Green	
Year	Team	G/GS	Snaps	Rec	Pass	Yds	C%	+/-	Yd/C	TD	Drop	YAC	Rk	YAC+	BTkl	DVOA	Rk	DYAR	Rk	YAR	Short	Mid	Deep	Bomb
2014	NO	10/7	534	53	69	550	77%	+9.7	10.4	3	1	3.2	75	-2.3	1	9.7%	26	124	34	125	51%	29%	9%	11%
2015	NO	16/12	959	84	130	1138	65%	+5.8	13.5	9	3	4.6	41	-0.8	4	7.1%	40	192	21	186	44%	20%	19%	17%
2016	NO	16/12	880	78	118	1173	67%	+8.7	15.0	8	6	4.9	31	+0.1	4	11.6%	20	226	16	212	32%	38%	9%	20%
2017	NE			72	109	1087	66%	--	15.1	8						20.0%								

- DVOA is a rate statistic, while DYAR is a cumulative statistic. Thus, a higher DVOA means more value per pass play, while a higher DYAR means more aggregate value over the entire season.

- Because DYAR is defense-adjusted and YAR is not, a player whose DYAR is higher than his YAR faced a harder-than-average schedule. A player whose DYAR is lower than his YAR faced an easier-than-average schedule.

To qualify for ranking in YAC, receiving DVOA, or receiving DYAR, a wide receiver must have had 50 passes thrown to him in that season. We ranked 93 wideouts in 2016, 87 wideouts in 2015, and 87 in 2014. Tight ends qualify with 25 targets in a given season; we ranked 46 tight ends in 2016, 51 tight ends in 2015, and 50 in 2014.

The final four columns break down pass length based on charting from Sports Info Solutions. The categories are **Short** (5 yards or less), **Mid** (6-15 yards), **Deep** (16-25 yards), and **Bomb** (26 or more yards). These numbers are based on distance in the air only and include both complete and incomplete passes.

The italicized row of statistics for the 2017 season is our 2017 KUBIAK projection based on a complicated regression analysis that takes into account numerous variables including projected role, performance over the past two years, projected team offense and defense, projected quarterback statistics, historical comparables, height, age, and strength of schedule.

It is difficult to accurately project statistics for a 162-game baseball season, but it is exponentially more difficult to accurately project statistics for a 16-game football season. Consider the listed projections not as a prediction of exact numbers, but as the mean of a range of possible performances. What's important is less the exact number of yards we project, and more which players are projected to improve or decline. Actual performance will vary from our projection less for veteran starters and more for rookies and third-stringers, for whom we must base our projections on much smaller career statistical samples. Touchdown numbers will vary more than yardage numbers. Players facing suspension or recovering from injury have those missed games taken into account.

Note that the receiving totals for each team will add up to higher numbers than the projection for that team's starting quarterback, because we have done KUBIAK projections for more receivers than will actually make the final roster.

A few low-round rookies, guys listed at seventh on the depth chart, and players who are listed as wide receivers but really only play special teams are briefly discussed at the end of the chapter in a section we call "Going Deep."

Two notes regarding our advanced metrics: We cannot yet fully separate the performance of a receiver from the performance of his quarterback. Be aware that one will affect the other. In addition, these statistics measure only passes thrown to a receiver, not performance on plays when he is not thrown the ball, such as blocking and drawing double teams.

Top 20 WR by DYAR (Total Value), 2016

Rank	Player	Team	DYAR
1	Julio Jones	ATL	458
2	Michael Thomas	NO	431
3	Jordy Nelson	GB	382
4	T.Y. Hilton	IND	360
5	Cole Beasley	DAL	341
6	Mike Evans	TB	309
7	Antonio Brown	PIT	295
8	Adam Thielen	MIN	270
9	Doug Baldwin	SEA	263
10	Pierre Garcon	WAS	262
11	A.J. Green	CIN	250
12	DeSean Jackson	WAS	241
13	Amari Cooper	OAK	231
14	Davante Adams	GB	230
15	Rishard Matthews	TEN	229
16	Brandin Cooks	NO	226
17	Terrance Williams	DAL	214
18	Michael Crabtree	OAK	212
19	Marqise Lee	JAC	211
20	Willie Snead	NO	206

Top 20 WR by DVOA (Value per Play), 2016

Rank	Player	Team	DVOA
1	Taylor Gabriel	ATL	33.7%
2	Julio Jones	ATL	31.7%
3	Michael Thomas	NO	31.6%
4	Terrance Williams	DAL	31.1%
5	Cole Beasley	DAL	31.0%
6	Adam Thielen	MIN	26.2%
7	Malcolm Mitchell	NE	19.6%
8	Jordy Nelson	GB	19.2%
9	A.J. Green	CIN	19.1%
10	Eli Rogers	PIT	18.3%
11	Chris Hogan	NE	18.0%
12	T.Y. Hilton	IND	17.3%
13	DeSean Jackson	WAS	16.4%
14	Pierre Garcon	WAS	16.3%
15	Rishard Matthews	TEN	14.4%
16	Doug Baldwin	SEA	13.0%
17	Willie Snead	NO	12.5%
18	Marqise Lee	JAC	12.2%
19	Travis Benjamin	SD	12.1%
20	Brandin Cooks	NO	11.6%

Minimum 50 targets

Davante Adams

Height: 6-1 **Weight:** 212 **College:** Fresno St. **Draft:** 2014/2 (53) **Born:** 12/24/1992 **Age:** 25 **Risk:** Green

Year	Team	G/GS	Snaps	Rec	Pass	Yds	C%	+/-	Yd/C	TD	Drop	YAC	Rk	YAC+	BTkl	DVOA	Rk	DYAR	Rk	YAR	Short	Mid	Deep	Bomb
2014	GB	16/11	738	38	66	446	58%	+1.0	11.7	3	4	4.6	44	+0.2	2	-9.0%	59	19	63	28	32%	50%	11%	6%
2015	GB	13/12	763	50	94	483	53%	-7.1	9.7	1	6	3.0	78	-1.7	6	-27.8%	84	-109	86	-131	39%	38%	16%	8%
2016	GB	16/15	915	75	121	997	62%	+1.8	13.3	12	9	5.2	23	+0.6	14	11.3%	21	230	14	216	39%	27%	21%	13%
2017	GB			68	108	892	63%	--	13.1	9						10.4%								

Davante Adams is a great example of how a great quarterback can elevate a middling receiver. Adams doesn't excel at anything in particular. He's not a good route-runner, doesn't possess great size or ball skills, and isn't a field-stretching athlete. Adams also comes with major inconsistency catching the ball. He missed at least six touchdowns last year that he should have caught. That doesn't become the focus because Aaron Rodgers is able to consistently create opportunities for him to be productive. Adams can still put up numbers with the best receivers in the league even while not sharing any of the traits of the best receivers in the league.

Now that he is 24 years of age, this would be the time for Adams to take a step forward. His adjustment period from college should be long over. If he can become more consistent catching the ball and show off the strong footwork he occasionally showed last season—against Seattle, for example—he can be a reliable starter with any quarterback rather than someone who hinges on Rodgers being exceptional.

Nelson Agholor

Height: 6-0 **Weight:** 198 **College:** USC **Draft:** 2015/1 (20) **Born:** 24-May-1993 **Age:** 24 **Risk:** Green

Year	Team	G/GS	Snaps	Rec	Pass	Yds	C%	+/-	Yd/C	TD	Drop	YAC	Rk	YAC+	BTkl	DVOA	Rk	DYAR	Rk	YAR	Short	Mid	Deep	Bomb
2015	PHI	13/12	670	23	44	283	52%	-3.0	12.3	1	2	4.0	--	-0.9	4	-21.3%	--	-31	--	-16	44%	31%	13%	11%
2016	PHI	15/14	883	36	70	365	53%	-4.9	10.1	2	6	3.3	73	-1.6	7	-23.3%	86	-60	88	-60	39%	37%	12%	12%
2017	PHI			16	29	147	55%	--	9.2	0						-32.0%								

When Agholor caught a 40-yard touchdown from Carson Wentz in Week 16 against the Giants, a palpable wave of shock rippled across the Philadelphia area. After nearly two seasons of misery and a midseason benching, Agholor looked like a lost cause. Indeed, take away that sweet reception, and he was 7-61-0 (8.7 yards per catch) on 17 targets in December.

Agholor looked genuinely revived during OTAs. Chalk it up to increased competition from Alshon Jeffery/Torrey Smith/ rookies, the peppy new drills instituted by position coach Mike Groh, and extreme professional jeopardy. Chip Kelly's developmental techniques did not suit Agholor. They turned a Jeremy Maclin-like prospect into a robotic route-runner with no faith in his own hands. Agholor is up against the clock to unlearn all of his bad habits before September cuts.

Kamar Aiken

Height: 6-2 **Weight:** 219 **College:** UCF **Draft:** 2011/FA **Born:** 30-May-1989 **Age:** 28 **Risk:** Green

Year	Team	G/GS	Snaps	Rec	Pass	Yds	C%	+/-	Yd/C	TD	Drop	YAC	Rk	YAC+	BTkl	DVOA	Rk	DYAR	Rk	YAR	Short	Mid	Deep	Bomb
2014	BAL	16/0	273	24	32	267	75%	+3.5	11.1	3	1	2.5	--	-1.4	0	29.7%	--	106	--	100	22%	56%	13%	9%
2015	BAL	16/14	937	75	127	944	59%	-0.1	12.6	5	2	2.8	80	-1.4	10	-2.7%	57	101	46	118	28%	42%	17%	13%
2016	BAL	16/6	595	29	50	328	58%	-1.0	11.3	1	2	3.4	66	-1.5	3	-15.5%	78	-11	77	-12	46%	26%	22%	7%
2017	IND			24	39	312	62%	--	13.0	3						1.9%								

After a year as a high-volume sponge with a surprisingly decent DVOA for a bad offense in 2015, the Ravens phased Aiken out of their passing attack to focus on Mike Wallace and Dennis Pitta. Promised a fair shake at a starting job by new Colts general manager Chris Ballard, Aiken definitely has the talent to beat out Phillip Dorsett in three-wide sets. At worst he's Indy's new Darrius Heyward-Bey, picking up the blocking slack. At best, he has already proven he can gobble up targets from Joe Flacco. How will he do with a better quarterback?

Keenan Allen

Height: 6-2 **Weight:** 206 **College:** California **Draft:** 2013/3 (76) **Born:** 27-Apr-1992 **Age:** 25 **Risk:** Red

Year	Team	G/GS	Snaps	Rec	Pass	Yds	C%	+/-	Yd/C	TD	Drop	YAC	Rk	YAC+	BTkl	DVOA	Rk	DYAR	Rk	YAR	Short	Mid	Deep	Bomb
2014	SD	14/14	837	77	122	783	63%	+1.4	10.2	4	1	3.9	57	-0.8	6	-8.0%	57	43	55	29	46%	38%	11%	4%
2015	SD	8/8	540	67	89	725	75%	+8.0	10.8	4	2	3.5	67	-0.8	6	11.9%	22	173	24	181	47%	41%	8%	5%
2016	SD	1/1	27	6	7	63	86%	+1.4	10.5	0	0	3.0	--	-0.5	0	36.8%	--	33	--	29	38%	63%	0%	0%
2017	LACH			86	119	1025	72%	--	11.9	6						10.8%								

Sometimes a player gets hit with an "injury prone" label and it turns out to be true. Allen had durability concerns out of college, which is why he slipped to the third round. After a stellar rookie season in 2013, he has played in fewer games each season even though his role clearly wants to grow in this offense. Allen was averaging 8.4 catches per game in 2015 before a kidney injury ended his season, then he was off to a fast start in last season's opener (six catches for 63 yards) when he tore his ACL on a non-contact play right before halftime. He will likely return to being Philip Rivers' most targeted receiver, but there is obviously some risk in counting on him for your fantasy team.

Geronimo Allison			Height: 6-3			Weight: 202			College: Illinois				Draft: 2016/FA			Born: 18-Jan-1994			Age: 23		Risk: Yellow
Year	Team	G/GS	Snaps	Rec	Pass	Yds	C%	+/-	Yd/C	TD	Drop	YAC	Rk	YAC+	BTkl	DVOA	Rk	DYAR	Rk	YAR	Short	Mid	Deep	Bomb
2016	GB	10/2	185	12	22	202	55%	-0.1	16.8	2	3	4.2	--	+0.3	1	15.2%	--	47	--	51	24%	43%	19%	14%
2017	GB			13	23	195	57%	--	15.0	2						3.2%								

Unless the Packers make an unforeseen move with one of their top three receivers, Geronimo Allison doesn't have any room to grow. Allison will likely be the Packers' fourth receiver, but he will spend training camp fending off competition for that spot rather than trying to move up. He can feel somewhat aggrieved by that. Allison played well when given opportunities last year. His long frame and natural ball skills allowed him to consistently pluck the ball from the air away from his body. Allison isn't necessarily a noted route-runner or athlete, but he was effective enough in both areas to take advantage of his length.

Danny Amendola			Height: 5-11			Weight: 186			College: Texas Tech				Draft: 2008/FA			Born: 2-Nov-1985			Age: 32		Risk: Green
Year	Team	G/GS	Snaps	Rec	Pass	Yds	C%	+/-	Yd/C	TD	Drop	YAC	Rk	YAC+	BTkl	DVOA	Rk	DYAR	Rk	YAR	Short	Mid	Deep	Bomb
2014	NE	16/4	456	27	42	200	64%	-1.3	7.4	1	2	2.7	--	-2.6	0	-17.7%	--	-16	--	-14	49%	30%	12%	9%
2015	NE	14/7	576	65	87	648	75%	+8.2	10.0	3	2	4.1	54	-0.8	12	8.6%	33	139	30	132	53%	36%	9%	2%
2016	NE	12/4	267	23	29	243	79%	+4.2	10.6	4	0	3.2	--	-1.8	0	27.0%	--	85	--	96	38%	48%	7%	7%
2017	NE			10	15	110	67%	--	11.0	0						2.3%								

Amendola has had enough postseason moments for two championship teams that Patriots fans have essentially pardoned him for being a free-agent bust who has taken a pay cut three straight offseasons. Though injuries seem to push him into the rotation every January, 2016 was the second time in three seasons that Amendola had fewer than 30 catches and 250 yards. With Brandin Cooks' arrival and Malcolm Mitchell's promising rookie year, Amendola is a depth option who has the trust of the coaching staff, but little more.

Robby Anderson			Height: 6-3			Weight: 190			College: Temple				Draft: 2016/FA			Born: 9-May-1993			Age: 24		Risk: Yellow
Year	Team	G/GS	Snaps	Rec	Pass	Yds	C%	+/-	Yd/C	TD	Drop	YAC	Rk	YAC+	BTkl	DVOA	Rk	DYAR	Rk	YAR	Short	Mid	Deep	Bomb
2016	NYJ	16/8	717	42	78	587	54%	+0.6	14.0	2	6	2.8	84	-1.6	2	-17.9%	81	-31	80	-24	24%	32%	14%	30%
2017	NYJ			50	94	699	53%	--	14.0	3						-11.1%								

Anderson never gained a thousand yards in a season in college and wasn't invited to the combine, but wowed scouts with a 4.36-second 40-yard dash at Temple's pro day. The Jets took a flyer on him as a prospect, and he ended up starting eight games after Eric Decker's injury. Playing in an offense that often found itself in desperate situations, he became a constant target on bomb passes—30 percent of his targets traveled more than 25 yards downfield. No other wideout ran bomb routes on more than 25 percent of his targets. That's how you get statlines like "4-of-12 for 61 yards" and "6 of 11 for 99 yards." Anderson was Bryce Petty's favorite receiver—he gained 312 yards on passes from Petty, when no other wideout topped even 100 yards—so his projection might go up should Petty win the Jets' quarterback battle this summer.

Anderson was arrested in May and charged with obstructing police (a misdemeanor) and resisting arrest with violence (a felony) following an altercation with a police officer at a Florida music festival. His trial is scheduled to begin on September 11, one day after the Jets' season opener, and the league is unlikely to punish him until the legal issue is resolved.

Tavon Austin Height: 5-8 Weight: 174 College: West Virginia Draft: 2013/1 (8) Born: 15-Mar-1991 Age: 26 Risk: Yellow

Year	Team	G/GS	Snaps	Rec	Pass	Yds	C%	+/-	Yd/C	TD	Drop	YAC	Rk	YAC+	BTkl	DVOA	Rk	DYAR	Rk	YAR	Short	Mid	Deep	Bomb
2014	STL	15/8	534	31	44	242	70%	-1.8	7.8	0	2	5.5	--	-0.9	8	-5.8%	--	24	--	13	67%	20%	7%	7%
2015	STL	16/15	742	52	88	473	60%	-6.1	9.1	5	2	6.8	3	-0.6	34	-30.6%	86	-122	87	-122	57%	24%	8%	11%
2016	LARM	15/15	732	58	106	509	55%	-12.5	8.8	3	10	4.7	37	-1.6	20	-39.1%	94	-219	94	-199	57%	24%	14%	5%
2017	LARM			67	114	660	59%	--	9.9	3							-21.9%							

It would be easy to copy and paste much of Austin's comment from last year because many of the same issues remain true, but instead of playing the 2016 season on a rookie contract, Austin inked an extension potentially worth $42 million last August. His 46 rushing DYAR, while still positive, was a far cry from his record-setting 253 rushing DYAR as a wide receiver in 2015. Normally, this wouldn't be a huge problem for a wide receiver, but Austin derives most of his value from carrying the ball as opposed to catching it. (Austin carried the ball 28 times for 159 yards and a touchdown last season.) While the dynamic quarterback duo of Case Keenum and Jared Goff did not set the world on fire, Austin failed to help his quarterbacks out, dropping 9.4 percent of the passes thrown his direction on the way to finishing dead last in receiving DYAR for the second year in a row. Catching the ball tends to be an important part of the job description for a player getting paid like a No. 1 wide receiver. If Austin wants to keep his spot on the team heading into 2018, when the team can reasonably get out from under his contract, he will need to be a factor in the passing game. His KUBIAK projection includes another 28 carries for 161 yards and a touchdown.

Doug Baldwin Height: 5-11 Weight: 189 College: Stanford Draft: 2011/FA Born: 21-Sep-1988 Age: 29 Risk: Green

Year	Team	G/GS	Snaps	Rec	Pass	Yds	C%	+/-	Yd/C	TD	Drop	YAC	Rk	YAC+	BTkl	DVOA	Rk	DYAR	Rk	YAR	Short	Mid	Deep	Bomb
2014	SEA	16/16	879	66	99	825	68%	+6.1	12.5	3	3	5.2	24	-0.2	8	5.5%	34	137	32	140	38%	38%	18%	6%
2015	SEA	16/16	798	78	103	1069	76%	+13.3	13.7	14	1	5.6	14	+1.0	15	39.6%	1	414	2	391	40%	38%	14%	7%
2016	SEA	16/15	896	94	128	1128	76%	+12.9	12.0	7	5	4.9	30	-0.4	12	13.0%	16	263	9	287	52%	28%	12%	9%
2017	SEA			92	131	1146	70%	--	12.5	7							13.8%							

After exploding into the national consciousness in 2015, Baldwin followed up with another strong season in 2016. While he did not come close to matching his DYAR, DVOA, and touchdown totals from 2015 (when he finished second, first, and first, respectively), Baldwin was still among the league leaders at his position despite the major drop-off in performance for Seattle's offense as a whole. The former undrafted free agent from Stanford did earn his first Pro Bowl appearance as an injury replacement for Larry Fitzgerald, even though his 2015 season was much more deserving of the nod. Due in part to Seattle's struggles running the ball, Baldwin set career highs in targets, receptions, and receiving yards. Even with tight end Jimmy Graham returning to form after the knee injury that ended his 2015 season, Baldwin remains the clear No. 1 receiver in an offense that could improve significantly if Seattle gets that whole offensive line thing sorted out.

Cole Beasley Height: 5-8 Weight: 177 College: Southern Methodist Draft: 2012/FA Born: 26-Apr-1989 Age: 28 Risk: Green

Year	Team	G/GS	Snaps	Rec	Pass	Yds	C%	+/-	Yd/C	TD	Drop	YAC	Rk	YAC+	BTkl	DVOA	Rk	DYAR	Rk	YAR	Short	Mid	Deep	Bomb
2014	DAL	16/2	434	37	49	420	76%	+4.0	11.4	4	0	6.6	6	+2.1	4	16.7%	13	117	36	134	47%	45%	4%	4%
2015	DAL	16/3	563	52	75	536	69%	+1.2	10.3	5	4	6.2	7	+1.4	7	-1.9%	53	64	58	73	68%	30%	1%	1%
2016	DAL	16/6	604	75	99	833	77%	+9.5	11.1	5	4	5.3	19	+0.7	11	31.0%	5	341	5	342	45%	49%	3%	2%
2017	DAL			68	96	726	71%	--	10.7	3							12.0%							

Beasley was absolutely deadly on short passes: 73 catches on 95 targets (76.8 percent), 769 yards, five touchdowns, and an average of 5.9 YAC. He was also a machine on third-and-medium, with 19 conversions (including touchdowns) out of 21 targets on third-and-7 or less. Ryan Switzer looks poised to take away some of Beasley's opportunities, but that's only because we assume all short, white receivers are interchangeable and only the Patriots have room for more than one of them on a roster. The more likely threat to Beasley's production is a healthy Dez Bryant: Beasley's biggest games (like 6-58-2 against the Packers) came when Dez was unavailable or limited.

Odell Beckham   Height: 5-11   Weight: 198   College: Louisiana St.   Draft: 2014/1 (12)   Born: 5-Nov-1992   Age: 25   Risk: Green

Year	Team	G/GS	Snaps	Rec	Pass	Yds	C%	+/-	Yd/C	TD	Drop	YAC	Rk	YAC+	BTkl	DVOA	Rk	DYAR	Rk	YAR	Short	Mid	Deep	Bomb
2014	NYG	12/11	771	91	130	1305	70%	+11.1	14.3	12	2	5.3	20	+0.2	14	25.8%	9	396	6	429	33%	40%	14%	12%
2015	NYG	15/15	998	96	158	1450	61%	+4.6	15.1	13	4	6.2	8	+2.0	12	10.3%	27	304	10	345	25%	50%	9%	16%
2016	NYG	16/16	1002	101	169	1367	60%	+0.3	13.5	10	10	5.2	24	+0.8	32	-1.1%	52	161	29	177	38%	38%	15%	10%
2017	NYG			97	158	1307	61%	--	13.5	11						9.8%								

Beckham's numbers on passes more than 25 yards downfield are unspectacular: 4-of-17, 193 yards, one touchdown, one interception. No team in its right mind would let Beckham beat them deep, so Ben McAdoo had to be creative with his deployment. Beckham lined up inside in 3-by-1 packages to find mismatches and ran lots and lots of shallow crosses to get the ball in space. There were also some option-y wrinkles that are best left un-talked about.

Brandon Marshall and the Giants' other new weapons should make it impossible for opponents to assign their best cornerback and a deep safety to Beckham every time he splits wide. That should increase Beckham's deep effectiveness without taking away the catch-and-run business underneath. All of the new personalities could also create a not-enough-balls scenario and off-field melodrama, but there's no formula for predicting how all of these personalities will react above the Bunsen burner of the Big Apple media.

Josh Bellamy   Height: 6-0   Weight: 206   College: Louisville   Draft: 2012/FA   Born: 18-May-1989   Age: 28   Risk: Blue

Year	Team	G/GS	Snaps	Rec	Pass	Yds	C%	+/-	Yd/C	TD	Drop	YAC	Rk	YAC+	BTkl	DVOA	Rk	DYAR	Rk	YAR	Short	Mid	Deep	Bomb
2014	CHI	4/0	11	0	1	0	0%	-0.3	0.0	0	0	0.0	--	+0.0	0	-90.7%	--	-6	--	-7	0%	0%	0%	100%
2015	CHI	16/3	437	19	34	224	56%	-2.1	11.8	2	2	3.6	--	-1.9	2	-16.8%	--	-11	--	-12	48%	24%	12%	15%
2016	CHI	16/2	304	19	38	282	50%	-2.9	14.8	1	5	2.7	--	-1.1	4	-11.2%	--	4	--	14	16%	47%	21%	16%
2017	CHI			4	8	43	50%	--	10.9	0						-24.2%								

Josh Bellamy is never going to get a better opportunity to establish himself than the one he got last year. While playing more than 300 snaps on offense, Bellamy failed to make a positive impression. He wasn't reliable at the catch point and didn't show off a diverse route tree or enough explosiveness to justify opportunities on screens or end-arounds. His role for the Bears is likely to remain on special teams rather than in the offense now that Markus Wheaton and Kendall Wright are on the roster.

Kelvin Benjamin   Height: 6-5   Weight: 240   College: Florida St.   Draft: 2014/1 (28)   Born: 5-Feb-1991   Age: 26   Risk: Yellow

Year	Team	G/GS	Snaps	Rec	Pass	Yds	C%	+/-	Yd/C	TD	Drop	YAC	Rk	YAC+	BTkl	DVOA	Rk	DYAR	Rk	YAR	Short	Mid	Deep	Bomb
2014	CAR	16/15	925	73	145	1008	50%	-7.8	13.8	9	7	2.3	86	-2.0	3	-11.8%	67	9	67	33	18%	49%	15%	18%
2016	CAR	16/13	801	63	118	941	53%	-5.1	14.9	7	8	3.7	64	+0.1	14	3.0%	46	145	33	128	11%	63%	18%	7%
2017	CAR			67	125	991	54%	--	14.8	8						2.1%								

Benjamin opened eyes at summer OTAs, and not in a good way—people had to spread their peepers wide in order to take in the fullness of Benjamin's newly blubbery "physique." The apparent weight gain wasn't a good sign for a player looking to keep his role as option No. 1 in the passing game. Overrated as a rookie in 2014 despite a 1,000-yard season and nine touchdowns (which primarily came from being force-fed the ball to the tune of 145 targets), Benjamin then blew out his knee and missed Carolina's Super Bowl season in 2015. His numbers last year were certainly better than they were in 2014, but inconsistency remains Benjamin's weakness.

Benjamin's big body is incapable of creating much downfield separation (true even before the knee injury), and he hasn't been the point-of-contact ball winner Carolina expected. The girth did help him box out defenders in the red zone, where, alone among Panthers receivers, he was effective (41.2% DVOA). While he struggled when lined up on the perimeter (-2.8% DVOA, 49 percent catch rate on 75 targets), Benjamin was much more efficient from the slot (13.1% DVOA, 61 percent catch rate on 44 targets). The hope is that newcomers Russell Shepard and Curtis Samuel can use their speed to loosen up the middle for Benjamin and fellow wide, wide receiver Devin Funchess—their lack of movement beyond straight-line route running stagnated the offense last season.

Travis Benjamin   Height: 5-10   Weight: 172   College: Miami   Draft: 2012/4 (100)   Born: 29-Dec-1989   Age: 28   Risk: Blue

Year	Team	G/GS	Snaps	Rec	Pass	Yds	C%	+/-	Yd/C	TD	Drop	YAC	Rk	YAC+	BTkl	DVOA	Rk	DYAR	Rk	YAR	Short	Mid	Deep	Bomb
2014	CLE	16/0	383	18	46	314	39%	-6.5	17.4	3	3	2.4	--	-2.6	2	-10.2%	--	9	--	5	20%	35%	15%	30%
2015	CLE	16/15	851	68	125	966	54%	-4.1	14.2	5	4	4.8	34	-0.4	8	-8.7%	69	38	65	37	37%	31%	18%	13%
2016	SD	14/8	548	47	75	677	63%	+3.3	14.4	4	6	5.2	21	+0.6	4	12.1%	19	144	35	110	43%	28%	9%	19%
2017	LACH			20	34	299	59%	--	14.9	2							2.4%								

Benjamin was hoping to fill the retired Malcom Floyd's shoes as a deep threat, but peaked early in his first season with the Chargers, putting up 115 yards and two touchdowns in Week 2. He was eventually surpassed in production by Tyrell Williams and Dontrelle Inman despite playing 14 games, and that's even with Keenan Allen missing nearly the entire season. Add in first-round pick Mike Williams, and it's not looking good for Benjamin to be more than a role player this year. Benjamin was also more effective out of the slot (32.0% DVOA) than he was lined up out wide (-15.2% DVOA).

Anquan Boldin   Height: 6-1   Weight: 218   College: Florida State   Draft: 2003/2 (54)   Born: 3-Oct-1980   Age: 37   Risk: N/A

Year	Team	G/GS	Snaps	Rec	Pass	Yds	C%	+/-	Yd/C	TD	Drop	YAC	Rk	YAC+	BTkl	DVOA	Rk	DYAR	Rk	YAR	Short	Mid	Deep	Bomb
2014	SF	16/16	952	83	131	1062	63%	+3.6	12.8	5	7	4.8	34	+0.6	12	9.3%	28	222	19	240	33%	48%	14%	5%
2015	SF	14/13	762	69	111	789	62%	-4.0	11.4	4	3	4.1	53	-0.9	11	-7.9%	65	41	64	13	52%	34%	9%	5%
2016	DET	16/16	830	67	95	584	71%	+4.1	8.7	8	5	3.4	67	-0.4	9	5.2%	41	140	38	152	59%	35%	4%	1%

Boldin, who turns 37 in October, has plans to play a 15th season in the NFL. He has been linked to the Chiefs or a return to the Ravens, but remains a free agent as we prepare to publish. He led the Lions with eight touchdown catches last season, still providing toughness and a reliable pair of hands, but his yards per catch dropped to 8.7. The veteran ranks 14th all-time in receiving yards (13,779), and he only needs 567 yards to move into 10th place. He may have to wait for someone to get injured before a team brings him in this year.

Tyler Boyd   Height: 6-1   Weight: 197   College: Pittsburgh   Draft: 2016/2 (55)   Born: 15-Nov-1994   Age: 23   Risk: Green

Year	Team	G/GS	Snaps	Rec	Pass	Yds	C%	+/-	Yd/C	TD	Drop	YAC	Rk	YAC+	BTkl	DVOA	Rk	DYAR	Rk	YAR	Short	Mid	Deep	Bomb
2016	CIN	16/2	739	54	81	603	67%	+3.4	11.2	1	2	3.7	60	-0.9	3	2.4%	47	96	53	85	39%	38%	19%	4%
2017	CIN			44	68	520	65%	--	11.8	3							1.5%								

Boyd's rookie year was about the sum of the skeptical view of him coming out of Pittsburgh: he's a good intermediate receiver who shows a little wiggle in tight areas, but other than that doesn't really offer a game-breaking trait. As a No. 2 receiver, a player like this is stretched, which is why Brandon LaFell wound up with 100 targets last year. But should John Ross stay healthy, Boyd is a much better fit as a jack-of-all-trades slot man, where his skills will play up a little. As long as you don't expect Boyd to leave any scorch marks on the backs of his defenders, you won't be disappointed.

Kenny Britt   Height: 6-3   Weight: 218   College: Rutgers   Draft: 2009/1 (30)   Born: 19-Sep-1988   Age: 29   Risk: Green

Year	Team	G/GS	Snaps	Rec	Pass	Yds	C%	+/-	Yd/C	TD	Drop	YAC	Rk	YAC+	BTkl	DVOA	Rk	DYAR	Rk	YAR	Short	Mid	Deep	Bomb
2014	STL	16/13	783	48	84	748	57%	+2.9	15.6	3	2	3.5	67	-1.2	2	12.4%	18	163	28	161	35%	22%	13%	30%
2015	STL	16/14	650	36	72	681	50%	-1.4	18.9	3	3	3.3	73	-1.4	5	11.0%	26	139	31	141	16%	47%	15%	22%
2016	LARM	15/15	789	68	111	1002	61%	+3.1	14.7	5	5	4.4	43	+0.3	13	6.4%	37	166	28	177	32%	44%	13%	12%
2017	CLE			66	118	832	56%	--	12.6	5							-4.2%								

Britt did the impossible last season: he was a productive wide receiver for the Rams, becoming the first player on the team to gain even 800 receiving yards in a season since Torry Holt in 2007. So of course, they opted not to re-sign him in free agency. That wasn't the only questionable decision the Rams have made in the past year. Through ten weeks of the 2016 season (which included the Rams' bye week), Britt was 11th among qualifying wide receivers in receiving yards and fifth in DYAR, with a DVOA of 28.3%. Then the Rams benched Case Keenum for Jared Goff, and over the last seven weeks of the year Britt was 44th in yardage and 12th from the bottom in DYAR, with a DVOA of -22.3%. This is really the story of Britt's entire career, where he has played with one horrible quarterback after another from Nashville to St. Louis to Los Angeles—and now, in all likelihood, Cleveland.

Kenny Britt's Primary Quarterbacks

Year	Age	Tm	QB	C%	Rk	Y/A	Rk	DVOA	Rk
2009	21	TEN	V.Young	58.7%	22	7.3	13	13.9%	14
2010	22	TEN	K.Collins	57.6%	30	6.6	27	-3.2%	26
2011	23	TEN	M.Hasselbeck	61.6%	10	6.9	20	0.5%	17
2012	24	TEN	J.Locker	56.4%	31	6.9	21	-23.6%	32
2013	25	TEN	R.Fitzpatrick	62.0%	14	7.0	19	-3.6%	20
2014	26	STL	A.Davis	63.4%	17	7.0	24	-8.8%	30
2015	27	STL	N.Foles	56.4%	35	6.1	36	-27.9%	37
2016	28	LARM	C.Keenum	60.9%	23	6.8	25	-19.6%	31

Yuck. None of those passers were especially good, and Vince Young in 2009 was the last one who could take regular advantage of Britt's deep speed. This makes it even more amazing that Britt has averaged 15.8 yards per catch in his career, fifth-best among active players with at least 200 catches. Britt's tenure with the Titans included torn knee ligaments and multiple arrests, but those were all five years ago. Britt is coming off his best season, and at age 29 might even last long enough to play in Cleveland's next playoff game.

Antonio Brown

Height: 5-10 | Weight: 186 | College: Central Mighican | Draft: 2010/6 (195) | Born: 10-Jul-1988 | Age: 29 | Risk: Green

Year	Team	G/GS	Snaps	Rec	Pass	Yds	C%	+/-	Yd/C	TD	Drop	YAC	Rk	YAC+	BTkl	DVOA	Rk	DYAR	Rk	YAR	Short	Mid	Deep	Bomb
2014	PIT	16/16	1061	129	181	1698	71%	+16.5	13.2	13	5	4.6	39	-0.2	18	25.7%	10	554	1	525	36%	39%	15%	10%
2015	PIT	16/16	1029	136	193	1834	70%	+18.2	13.5	10	4	4.4	45	-0.5	18	19.7%	9	517	1	490	38%	29%	21%	12%
2016	PIT	15/15	975	106	154	1284	69%	+8.1	12.1	12	4	3.8	56	-1.0	13	11.1%	22	295	7	306	41%	27%	22%	9%
2017	PIT			105	152	1357	69%	--	12.9	11						18.9%								

In February, the Steelers signed Brown to a four-year extension worth up to $68 million, with $19 million guaranteed. By the time that contract is through, Brown should own all the Steelers' receiving records (he needs 368 catches, 3,706 yards, and 35 touchdowns to catch Hines Ward in all three categories). Cementing the future of the best wideout in franchise history, and one of the best in this era of the NFL, was a wise move. The next wise move should be to use that wideout to the best of his ability. This year, thanks to Sports Info Solutions, we have data on specific pass routes for the first time. Brown's most frequent route, the wide receiver screen, was also his worst—he had minus-31.1% DVOA and averaged just 4.6 yards on those plays. After the screen, Brown's next-most common routes were the drag (-4.6% DVOA/5.7 yards per target), the curl (7.6%/6.9), the go/fly (46.2%/14.9), the slant (10.7%/7.9), and the fade (50.2%/12.3). There is certainly some selection bias in these numbers. Ben Roethlisberger, like any quarterback, is more likely to throw deeper passes when receivers are wide open on those plays. Still, wide receiver screens only happen by design, never by accident, and Brown's results on screens are worse than almost any other play the Steelers could call, running or passing. This is true for most wide receivers, by the way, but a lot of teams are desperate for options and have no choice but to force the ball to their best players. The Steelers are not one of those teams.

Corey Brown

Height: 5-11 | Weight: 180 | College: Ohio State | Draft: 2014/FA | Born: 16-Dec-1991 | Age: 26 | Risk: Green

Year	Team	G/GS	Snaps	Rec	Pass	Yds	C%	+/-	Yd/C	TD	Drop	YAC	Rk	YAC+	BTkl	DVOA	Rk	DYAR	Rk	YAR	Short	Mid	Deep	Bomb
2014	CAR	13/3	307	21	36	296	58%	-0.2	14.1	2	1	2.5	--	-2.4	2	7.7%	--	59	--	67	24%	42%	16%	18%
2015	CAR	14/11	753	31	54	447	57%	+3.8	14.4	4	2	2.6	83	-1.1	3	8.8%	32	89	50	101	14%	41%	27%	18%
2016	CAR	16/8	587	27	53	276	51%	-2.1	10.2	1	3	4.2	49	-0.4	3	-25.8%	89	-55	85	-63	40%	42%	7%	11%
2017	BUF			14	26	182	54%	--	13.0	1						-10.9%								

Like most of the Panthers offense, the artist formerly known as Philly saw a significant dip in efficiency last season. Only five qualifying wide receivers posted a worse DVOA in 2016, three of whom resided in the wasteland of the 49ers' offense. Moving to Buffalo may give Brown an opportunity to receive more reps in a thin receiving corps, though he will probably just settle into the same No. 4 receiver role he occupied in Carolina. Brown needs a good preseason just to secure a roster spot given his extremely modest one-year deal.

John Brown

| | | Height: 5-10 | | Weight: 179 | | | College: Pittsburg St. (KS) | | | Draft: 2014/3 (91) | | | Born: 4-Mar-1990 | | | Age: 27 | | Risk: Yellow |

Year	Team	G/GS	Snaps	Rec	Pass	Yds	C%	+/-	Yd/C	TD	Drop	YAC	Rk	YAC+	BTkl	DVOA	Rk	DYAR	Rk	YAR	Short	Mid	Deep	Bomb
2014	ARI	16/5	633	48	103	696	47%	-7.3	14.5	5	2	3.8	62	-1.7	0	-12.5%	69	1	69	-5	21%	43%	22%	15%
2015	ARI	15/11	826	65	101	1003	64%	+6.6	15.4	7	5	4.8	32	+0.0	7	29.9%	4	352	5	345	27%	37%	14%	22%
2016	ARI	15/6	595	39	73	517	53%	-0.6	13.3	2	1	2.7	88	-1.5	1	-1.9%	57	61	61	69	17%	51%	20%	13%
2017	ARI			63	104	880	61%	--	14.0	5							0.8%							

For the past three offseasons, Brown has lived with Carson Palmer, in an attempt to help build chemistry between the two. It's not chemistry that Brown has to worry about, however, but biology—much of the explosiveness and big-play ability he showed in 2015 were sapped by sickle-cell issues and a cyst in his spine. Playing through pain for most of the year, it's not a surprise that Brown wasn't nearly as effective. Reports out of camp say that the issues are under control, which is great news both for Brown and for Arizona fans. Remember, Brown ranked 14th in receiving plus-minus two years ago and was just 11 DYAR behind Larry Fitzgerald. Fans of exciting football should hope Brown has made a full recovery.

Dez Bryant

| | | Height: 6-2 | | Weight: 225 | | | College: Oklahoma State | | | Draft: 2010/1 (24) | | | Born: 4-Nov-1988 | | | Age: 29 | | Risk: Yellow |

Year	Team	G/GS	Snaps	Rec	Pass	Yds	C%	+/-	Yd/C	TD	Drop	YAC	Rk	YAC+	BTkl	DVOA	Rk	DYAR	Rk	YAR	Short	Mid	Deep	Bomb
2014	DAL	16/16	896	88	137	1320	64%	+6.7	15.0	16	4	4.6	41	+0.1	18	27.0%	5	430	5	456	31%	39%	17%	13%
2015	DAL	9/9	444	31	72	401	43%	-8.5	12.9	3	6	4.2	49	+0.1	6	-26.8%	83	-86	85	-88	24%	44%	17%	15%
2016	DAL	13/13	688	50	96	796	52%	-2.0	15.9	8	4	2.9	82	-0.9	6	7.5%	32	153	31	154	13%	48%	26%	13%
2017	DAL			67	120	975	56%	--	14.6	10							3.7%							

Bryant missed three early-season games with a knee injury, battled a back injury through the latter half of the season, lost his father the day before the Steelers game, went toe-to-toe with several of the NFL's top cornerbacks in his own division, and played with a rookie quarterback (albeit a magnificent one) in the league's most run-heavy offense. Under the circumstances, a 50-796-8 stat line is pretty remarkable. Bryant wasn't really healthy enough to battle the likes of Janoris Jenkins or Josh Norman, but his 9-132-2 playoff performance against the Packers demonstrated what he is still capable of against lesser cornerbacks. Bryant won't be targeted for a dozen passes per game very often if the Cowboys stick to their run-heavy plan. But if healthy, he'll do a lot more damage with the targets he gets.

Martavis Bryant

| | | Height: 6-4 | | Weight: 221 | | | College: Clemson | | | Draft: 2014/4 (118) | | | Born: 20-Dec-1991 | | | Age: 26 | | Risk: Red |

Year	Team	G/GS	Snaps	Rec	Pass	Yds	C%	+/-	Yd/C	TD	Drop	YAC	Rk	YAC+	BTkl	DVOA	Rk	DYAR	Rk	YAR	Short	Mid	Deep	Bomb
2014	PIT	10/3	295	26	49	549	53%	-0.8	21.1	8	3	7.3	--	+1.7	2	22.9%	--	137	--	129	31%	22%	14%	33%
2015	PIT	11/5	511	50	92	765	54%	-3.7	15.3	6	6	7.0	2	+1.7	14	-2.4%	54	75	56	47	30%	34%	10%	26%
2017	PIT			59	103	980	57%	--	16.6	7							12.8%							

Everyone was saying the right things about Bryant's return this spring. Bryant himself showed up 10 pounds bigger, which demonstrated that he had put his year in purgatory to good use. He also claimed the birth of his son had changed him, and he realized he needed to change the company he kept to succeed in life. Steelers wide receiver coach Richard Mann says Bryant was more humble and mature. "Obviously, he has a long way to go," said offensive coordinator Todd Haley, "but he's off to a good start." It all sounds promising, but it's hard not to be skeptical of a player with Bryant's track record.

But then you scan his game logs, and what he has done in limited time, as a No. 2 receiver, and the numbers jump out at you. Only eight wide receivers had more total touchdowns in 2014 and 2015, and keep in mind Bryant missed 11 games in those two years. Since Bryant was drafted, the only player with at least 50 catches and a better average per catch is DeSean Jackson. Bryant has also averaged 11.6 yards on 12 career runs, including gains of 40 and 44 yards in the 2015 playoffs. Bryant is a big-play specialist with few peers in the modern NFL, and a perfect complement for a team with a pair of YAC machines like Antonio Brown and Le'Veon Bell.

Brice Butler   Height: 6-3   Weight: 205   College: San Diego State   Draft: 2013/7 (209)   Born: 29-Jan-1990   Age: 27   Risk: Green

Year	Team	G/GS	Snaps	Rec	Pass	Yds	C%	+/-	Yd/C	TD	Drop	YAC	Rk	YAC+	BTkl	DVOA	Rk	DYAR	Rk	YAR	Short	Mid	Deep	Bomb
2014	OAK	15/0	271	21	36	280	58%	-0.1	13.3	2	1	4.0	--	-0.4	2	1.9%	--	42	--	24	26%	57%	9%	9%
2015	DAL	7/2	261	12	26	258	46%	-0.9	21.5	0	2	8.0	--	+3.5	2	0.3%	--	28	--	30	17%	50%	25%	8%
2016	DAL	16/3	429	16	32	219	50%	-2.4	13.7	3	2	1.2	--	-2.0	1	-10.4%	--	6	--	21	25%	38%	19%	19%
2017	DAL			17	31	286	55%	--	16.8	2						-6.6%								

Butler caught five balls for 41 yards as a starter when Dez Bryant was out against the 49ers, then spent most of the season catching occasional 21-yard passes when opponents were too scattered by the other Cowboys weapons to cover a No. 4 receiver. The Cowboys re-signed Butler to a one-year contract in the offseason, but his role as the designated blocker in spread formations who sometimes sneaks deep just screams "Noah Brown," so don't assume anything.

Michael Campanaro   Height: 5-9   Weight: 192   College: Wake Forest   Draft: 2014/7 (218)   Born: 25-Jan-1991   Age: 26   Risk: Green

Year	Team	G/GS	Snaps	Rec	Pass	Yds	C%	+/-	Yd/C	TD	Drop	YAC	Rk	YAC+	BTkl	DVOA	Rk	DYAR	Rk	YAR	Short	Mid	Deep	Bomb
2014	BAL	4/0	65	7	9	102	78%	+1.1	14.6	1	0	5.0	--	+1.0	0	60.5%	--	50	--	47	33%	44%	22%	0%
2015	BAL	4/0	54	5	6	35	83%	+0.4	7.0	0	0	5.4	--	+0.0	1	-10.9%	--	1	--	-1	67%	33%	0%	0%
2016	BAL	3/0	17	0	1	0	0%	-0.9	0.0	0	1	0.0	--	--	0	-112.1%	--	-8	--	-7	100%	0%	0%	0%
2017	BAL			11	17	134	65%	--	12.2	0						2.2%								

Campanaro's NFL career to date has been a reminder of the things that all of us need to remember when it comes to dubbing players The Next Wes Welker. Wes Welker, himself, was not particularly more talented than several other players who played his role for various colleges. A little faster, sure. A little more sure-handed, yes. But the main differentiator is that players who play at Welker's size get punished by NFL physicality. Campanaro could easily be a store-brand Welker if he could stay healthy. He has been on IR twice in the last two years, between a 2015 herniated disc and an injury settlement in training camp last year. In 2014, he missed a big chunk of midseason with hamstring issues. If he could take a hit half as well as Welker, Campanaro would be a pretty valuable NFL player. So far, that's a pretty big if.

Sammie Coates   Height: 6-1   Weight: 212   College: Auburn   Draft: 2015/3 (87)   Born: 31-Mar-1993   Age: 24   Risk: Green

Year	Team	G/GS	Snaps	Rec	Pass	Yds	C%	+/-	Yd/C	TD	Drop	YAC	Rk	YAC+	BTkl	DVOA	Rk	DYAR	Rk	YAR	Short	Mid	Deep	Bomb
2015	PIT	6/0	34	1	2	11	50%	-0.3	11.0	0	0	4.0	--	+0.3	0	-26.8%	--	-2	--	-2	0%	100%	0%	0%
2016	PIT	14/5	313	21	49	435	43%	-4.0	20.7	2	6	5.4	--	-0.1	3	-12.7%	--	0	--	2	24%	24%	10%	41%
2017	PIT			12	23	202	52%	--	16.8	2						3.7%								

Talk about a season that turned south in a hurry. Coates peaked in Week 5, with six catches for 139 yards and two touchdowns against the Jets. At that point, he was 15th in DYAR, with a 28.0% DVOA and a 61 percent catch rate. He was targeted 18 times the rest of the season, catching only two passes for 14 yards. That's an 11 percent catch rate and minus-89.9% DVOA. He didn't even finish with enough targets to qualify for our wide receiver leaderboards. If he had, he would have edged out Torrey Smith for the highest drop rate in the league—and considering he had more catches and more drops than Smith, you could argue that Coates had the worst hands in the league last year. He had the worst left hand for sure, suffering two broken fingers on that side. That, and the hamstring woes he suffered late in the season, no doubt played a big part in his struggles. There were conflicting reports that Coates had hand surgery after the season, though a sports hernia injury was confirmed. Even with better health this year, the return of Martavis Bryant could push Coates out of the starting lineup, or even off the team entirely.

Randall Cobb   Height: 5-11   Weight: 190   College: Kentucky   Draft: 2011/2 (64)   Born: 22-Aug-1990   Age: 27   Risk: Green

Year	Team	G/GS	Snaps	Rec	Pass	Yds	C%	+/-	Yd/C	TD	Drop	YAC	Rk	YAC+	BTkl	DVOA	Rk	DYAR	Rk	YAR	Short	Mid	Deep	Bomb
2014	GB	16/16	922	91	127	1287	72%	+8.4	14.1	12	2	6.4	7	+1.9	10	35.7%	1	479	4	501	46%	32%	21%	2%
2015	GB	16/15	1050	79	129	829	61%	-2.3	10.5	6	6	5.5	18	+0.2	16	-5.1%	60	77	53	54	46%	37%	14%	2%
2016	GB	13/10	681	60	84	610	71%	+3.4	10.2	4	1	6.0	10	+0.6	15	6.6%	35	133	39	131	56%	31%	10%	4%
2017	GB			52	78	545	67%	--	10.5	4						-0.9%								

Randall Cobb's career was meant to be much better than this. The 27-year-old has managed just one 1,000-yard season, and that was three years ago. Since then he has dealt with health issues while accumulating less than 900 yards in each season. Cobb's inability to consistently get open in Mike McCarthy's scheme is his biggest issue. His quickness through his routes isn't what it was early in his career, meaning he is more reliant on having option routes or being schemed open. That's not something McCarthy emphasizes. Despite his limited effectiveness, the Packers don't appear to be actively trying to replace him. He will still play a significant number of snaps when healthy and is more likely to move into the backfield on passing downs than to come off the field to give Geronimo Allison an opportunity.

Brandon Coleman   Height: 6-6   Weight: 220   College: Rutgers   Draft: 2014/FA   Born: 22-Jun-1992   Age: 25   Risk: Green

Year	Team	G/GS	Snaps	Rec	Pass	Yds	C%	+/-	Yd/C	TD	Drop	YAC	Rk	YAC+	BTkl	DVOA	Rk	DYAR	Rk	YAR	Short	Mid	Deep	Bomb
2015	NO	16/4	430	30	49	454	61%	+2.3	15.1	2	1	4.0	--	-0.5	2	17.9%	--	113	--	104	25%	33%	29%	13%
2016	NO	16/4	365	26	38	281	68%	+2.2	10.8	3	2	2.8	--	-1.2	0	12.2%	--	77	--	80	26%	47%	16%	11%
2017	NO			28	45	323	62%	--	11.6	2						2.2%								

A big-bodied but slow receiver, Brandon Coleman remains on the Saints roster as an auxiliary target for passing downs and red zone use. All three of his touchdowns came from inside the 10-yard line. As the old saying goes, if the shoe fits...

Corey Coleman   Height: 5-11   Weight: 194   College: Baylor   Draft: 2016/1 (15)   Born: 6-Jul-1994   Age: 23   Risk: Yellow

Year	Team	G/GS	Snaps	Rec	Pass	Yds	C%	+/-	Yd/C	TD	Drop	YAC	Rk	YAC+	BTkl	DVOA	Rk	DYAR	Rk	YAR	Short	Mid	Deep	Bomb
2016	CLE	10/10	533	33	73	413	45%	-3.6	12.5	3	4	2.9	81	-1.6	10	-22.9%	85	-57	87	-84	32%	34%	15%	19%
2017	CLE			65	120	889	54%	--	13.7	5						-9.1%								

Coleman was a hit early in his rookie campaign, with seven catches for 173 yards and two scores in his first two games. Then he broke his hand in practice, and didn't play again until Week 9. By that point, the Browns were playing a hellish game of musical chairs with their quarterbacks, none of whom were able to make a deep connection with Coleman. He averaged fewer than 10 yards per catch the rest of the way and failed to gain even 50 yards in a single game. Hue Jackson dubbed Coleman "the guy" after the departure of Terrelle Pryor—and, more notably, after the signing of Kenny Britt. Coleman had a monstrous Playmaker Score projection coming out of college, and he has absolute Pro Bowl potential if the Browns can ever find anyone to get him the ball.

Chris Conley   Height: 6-2   Weight: 213   College: Georgia   Draft: 2015/3 (76)   Born: 25-Oct-1992   Age: 25   Risk: Yellow

Year	Team	G/GS	Snaps	Rec	Pass	Yds	C%	+/-	Yd/C	TD	Drop	YAC	Rk	YAC+	BTkl	DVOA	Rk	DYAR	Rk	YAR	Short	Mid	Deep	Bomb
2015	KC	16/5	369	17	31	199	55%	-1.1	11.7	1	3	4.1	--	-0.1	3	2.7%	--	39	--	39	23%	45%	16%	16%
2016	KC	16/11	818	44	69	530	64%	+1.6	12.0	0	3	3.4	69	-0.4	3	1.1%	49	74	56	57	30%	50%	12%	8%
2017	KC			53	85	621	62%	--	11.7	3						-6.2%								

There will be a pattern with comments on Kansas City's wide receivers. First, they all need to step up now that Jeremy Maclin is gone. Second, they all fared worse in DVOA when lined up in the slot compared to being out wide, which is odd when you consider that Alex Smith would be expected to do better with throws where the receiver is closer to him. Conley had the biggest difference of them all as he had minus-34.2% DVOA in the slot compared to 15.3% DVOA out wide. Despite averaging 18.3 yards per catch as a senior at Georgia, Conley hasn't been a big playmaker in his first two seasons. He is more of a possession receiver in Andy Reid's offense, but he improved last year, and he'll have to improve even more now that Jeremy Maclin is gone. (Is there an echo in here?)

Brandin Cooks   Height: 5-10   Weight: 189   College: Oregon St.   Draft: 2014/1 (20)   Born: 25-Sep-1993   Age: 24   Risk: Green

Year	Team	G/GS	Snaps	Rec	Pass	Yds	C%	+/-	Yd/C	TD	Drop	YAC	Rk	YAC+	BTkl	DVOA	Rk	DYAR	Rk	YAR	Short	Mid	Deep	Bomb
2014	NO	10/7	534	53	69	550	77%	+9.7	10.4	3	1	3.2	75	-2.3	1	9.7%	26	124	34	125	51%	29%	9%	11%
2015	NO	16/12	959	84	130	1138	65%	+5.8	13.5	9	3	4.6	41	-0.8	4	7.1%	40	192	21	186	44%	20%	19%	17%
2016	NO	16/12	880	78	118	1173	67%	+8.7	15.0	8	6	4.9	31	+0.1	4	11.6%	20	226	16	212	32%	38%	9%	20%
2017	NE			72	109	1087	66%	--	15.1	8						20.0%								

Cooks' arrival is one of the primary forces driving the Patriots hype machine this offseason, a fire Robert Kraft stoked further by comparing Cooks to Randy Moss and not so subtly evoking 2007 comparisons. Realistically, Cooks is less of a pure burner and more a versatile threat to line up all over the formation and serve as both a capable possession weapon and occasional deep threat. After seeing an average of 123 targets the past two seasons, Cooks is likely to see a decline in volume this year, especially if Edelman and Rob Gronkowski remain relatively healthy. Still, being a talented versatile chess piece in a Patriots offense is never a bad thing, and Cooks should retain the efficiency he enjoyed with Drew Brees his first three seasons.

Amari Cooper Height: 6-1   Weight: 211   College: Alabama   Draft: 2015/1 (4)   Born: 18-Jun-1994   Age: 23   Risk: Green

Year	Team	G/GS	Snaps	Rec	Pass	Yds	C%	+/-	Yd/C	TD	Drop	YAC	Rk	YAC+	BTkl	DVOA	Rk	DYAR	Rk	YAR	Short	Mid	Deep	Bomb
2015	OAK	16/15	900	72	130	1070	55%	-6.6	14.9	6	10	5.2	23	+0.0	11	-1.0%	50	122	37	130	33%	43%	13%	10%
2016	OAK	16/14	997	83	132	1153	63%	+0.8	13.9	5	4	5.3	18	+0.0	12	8.8%	28	231	13	185	43%	35%	12%	10%
2017	OAK			89	144	1244	62%	--	14.0	9						5.8%								

Make no mistake about it: Cooper has had a fine start to his career, with back-to-back 1,000-yard seasons. It's just that in this era of Julio Jones, A.J. Green, Antonio Brown, and Odell Beckham Jr. (to name a few), it's harder for Cooper to really stand out. He cut down his drops from his rookie season, but there are still rough patches in his game, like all the times he would catch a pass just out of bounds in the end zone. Cooper's DVOA in the red zone was just minus-44.3% largely for that reason. Cooper also cost himself a long touchdown against the Chargers after stepping out of bounds before coming back in to catch the pass. KUBIAK sees his touchdown production finally matching his yardage totals in 2017.

Pharoh Cooper Height: 5-11   Weight: 203   College: South Carolina   Draft: 2016/4 (117)   Born: 7-Mar-1995   Age: 22   Risk: Green

Year	Team	G/GS	Snaps	Rec	Pass	Yds	C%	+/-	Yd/C	TD	Drop	YAC	Rk	YAC+	BTkl	DVOA	Rk	DYAR	Rk	YAR	Short	Mid	Deep	Bomb
2016	LARM	10/3	211	14	20	106	70%	-0.8	7.6	0	0	5.1	--	-1.2	2	-36.0%	--	-30	--	-27	63%	37%	0%	0%
2017	LARM			14	21	127	67%	--	9.1	0						-13.4%								

Cooper had a small role in his rookie season in large part because Tavon Austin ate up touches that might otherwise have gone to the youngster out of South Carolina. In addition to the returning Austin, he now has to fight with another Cooper (third-round rookie Cooper Kupp) and free agent Robert Woods to carve out a larger stake in the Los Angeles offense. With several different mouths to feed in the receiving corps, and a small spoon to feed them with, it will be difficult for Jared Goff to get Cooper the ball frequently enough for him to be a difference-maker in 2017.

Michael Crabtree Height: 6-2   Weight: 215   College: Texas Tech   Draft: 2009/1 (10)   Born: 14-Sep-1987   Age: 30   Risk: Green

Year	Team	G/GS	Snaps	Rec	Pass	Yds	C%	+/-	Yd/C	TD	Drop	YAC	Rk	YAC+	BTkl	DVOA	Rk	DYAR	Rk	YAR	Short	Mid	Deep	Bomb
2014	SF	16/16	722	68	108	698	64%	-0.8	10.3	4	5	3.9	58	-1.2	9	-9.9%	63	24	59	50	47%	30%	17%	6%
2015	OAK	16/15	809	85	146	922	58%	-6.7	10.8	9	6	3.1	75	-1.4	14	-13.0%	76	-4	77	3	41%	37%	13%	8%
2016	OAK	16/16	835	89	145	1003	61%	+0.1	11.3	8	11	2.8	83	-1.4	12	5.3%	40	212	18	171	36%	43%	10%	10%
2017	OAK			85	132	963	64%	--	11.3	8						1.4%								

Crabtree was drafted to be a No. 1 receiver/savior for the 49ers in 2009, but never really earned that reputation. In Oakland, he's better suited as the No. 2 guy behind Amari Cooper. Crabtree's raw numbers in 2016 were almost identical to what he did in 2015, right down to having three 100-yard games in both seasons. The difference in his much better advanced metrics is largely due to situational football. On third/fourth down, Crabtree's DVOA went from minus-29.0% (his worst down in 2015) to 13.4% (his best down in 2016). In the red zone, where he was the team's best option, Crabtree's DVOA went from minus-49.9% to 16.1%.

Jamison Crowder

Height: 5-8   Weight: 185   College: Duke   Draft: 2015/4 (105)   Born: 17-Jun-1993   Age: 24   Risk: Green

Year	Team	G/GS	Snaps	Rec	Pass	Yds	C%	+/-	Yd/C	TD	Drop	YAC	Rk	YAC+	BTkl	DVOA	Rk	DYAR	Rk	YAR	Short	Mid	Deep	Bomb
2015	WAS	16/6	734	59	78	604	76%	+5.1	10.2	2	2	5.7	12	+0.1	4	-4.4%	59	52	62	49	69%	17%	12%	3%
2016	WAS	16/9	784	67	99	847	68%	+2.8	12.6	7	3	5.6	13	+0.8	11	4.6%	44	129	42	127	59%	21%	15%	5%
2017	WAS			65	94	789	69%	--	12.1	5							3.0%								

Crowder went 31-462-3 over one five-game stretch in which DeSean Jackson and Jordan Reed were unavailable and/or limited, then settled into a more reasonable five-target role as a slot specialist. Crowder is nifty off the line, will make defenders miss, and can slip past the secondary on deep routes at times. Jay Gruden said during OTAs that Crowder could have a 1,000-yard season this year and that he plans to get the receiver on the field as much as possible. That's great news for Crowder and a less-than-ringing endorsement of Terrelle Pryor and Brian Quick.

Victor Cruz

Height: 6-1   Weight: 200   College: Massachusetts   Draft: 2010/FA   Born: 11-Nov-1986   Age: 31   Risk: Red

Year	Team	G/GS	Snaps	Rec	Pass	Yds	C%	+/-	Yd/C	TD	Drop	YAC	Rk	YAC+	BTkl	DVOA	Rk	DYAR	Rk	YAR	Short	Mid	Deep	Bomb
2014	NYG	6/6	372	23	41	337	56%	-1.4	14.7	1	6	7.7	--	+2.5	7	-9.0%	--	13	--	21	29%	37%	22%	12%
2016	NYG	15/12	766	39	72	586	54%	-1.5	15.0	1	5	4.8	33	+0.5	6	-11.7%	73	6	74	23	29%	47%	10%	13%
2017	CHI			19	33	218	58%	--	11.5	1							-9.5%								

Cruz was a delight to watch and cover for several years: a local-hero feel-good camp story who became a salsa-dancing Super Bowl sensation before disappearing into an injury fog. Now the injuries have taken away all of his lateral burst; he went on a brief offseason free agent tour, but no one wanted a fading slot receiver with no special teams value. We never really got to see the Cruz-Odell Beckham tandem we were once promised, at least not at full capacity. But we'll always have 2011.

Corey Davis

Height: 6-3   Weight: 209   College: Western Michigan   Draft: 2017/1 (5)   Born: 11-Jan-1995   Age: 22   Risk: Yellow

Year	Team	G/GS	Snaps	Rec	Pass	Yds	C%	+/-	Yd/C	TD	Drop	YAC	Rk	YAC+	BTkl	DVOA	Rk	DYAR	Rk	YAR	Short	Mid	Deep	Bomb
2017	TEN			53	92	815	58%	--	15.4	4							2.0%								

Davis was phenomenally productive for the Western Michigan Broncos, setting the FBS record for career receiving yards. He had more than 1,400 yards and at least 12 receiving touchdowns in each of his past three seasons, finishing his career with 1,500 yards on a 70 percent catch rate in 2016, with a showcase Cotton Bowl performance against Wisconsin. As the fifth overall pick in the draft, he should get an opportunity to play significant snaps early. His role will likely be a limited one, replacing Tajae Sharpe as the designated receiver who lines up outside. Reports after his return from the ankle injury that kept him out of the pre-draft process and the early offseason were suitably effusive, praising the size, speed, and physicality that led the Titans to draft him so early. The Titans did not have a receiver last year who could win one-on-one matchups the way Davis potentially can.

Eric Decker

Height: 6-3   Weight: 217   College: Minnesota   Draft: 2010/3 (87)   Born: 15-Mar-1987   Age: 30   Risk: Green

Year	Team	G/GS	Snaps	Rec	Pass	Yds	C%	+/-	Yd/C	TD	Drop	YAC	Rk	YAC+	BTkl	DVOA	Rk	DYAR	Rk	YAR	Short	Mid	Deep	Bomb
2014	NYJ	15/15	812	74	115	962	64%	+5.4	13.0	5	5	4.4	47	-0.2	1	9.4%	27	199	24	176	33%	44%	15%	9%
2015	NYJ	15/13	906	80	132	1027	61%	+4.2	12.8	12	5	2.7	82	-1.1	1	13.6%	17	278	12	290	23%	48%	22%	7%
2016	NYJ	3/3	211	9	21	194	43%	-2.2	21.6	2	0	3.3	--	-0.5	0	17.3%	--	48	--	43	15%	45%	25%	15%
2017	TEN			43	76	564	57%	--	13.1	7							-1.6%								

The hip and shoulder issues that ruined Decker last season are now in the past. Fully recovered, he made a wise decision signing with Tennessee, where he will get to play a supporting role behind Corey Davis as the headliner. Decker has led two teams in receiving yardage—the 2011 Broncos and 2014 Jets—and in those two years he finished 71st and 24th in DYAR. When he has had a Demaryius Thomas or Brandon Marshall across the field, though, he has finished fourth, fourth, and 12th. Part of this is that the quarterbacks who made him a leading receiver were Tim Tebow and Geno Smith, but Decker is still best suited to a secondary role at this point in his career. Decker breaks tackles about as often as you do, and he's of little use as a deep threat, but his big body and fine hands make him very effective on mid-range routes.

Stefon Diggs

Height: 6-0   Weight: 195   College: Maryland   Draft: 2015/5 (146)   Born: 29-Nov-1993   Age: 24   Risk: Yellow

Year	Team	G/GS	Snaps	Rec	Pass	Yds	C%	+/-	Yd/C	TD	Drop	YAC	Rk	YAC+	BTkl	DVOA	Rk	DYAR	Rk	YAR	Short	Mid	Deep	Bomb
2015	MIN	13/9	654	52	84	720	62%	+4.0	13.8	4	2	5.6	15	+0.8	14	3.8%	43	108	44	85	35%	39%	15%	10%
2016	MIN	13/11	693	84	111	903	76%	+11.3	10.8	3	5	3.8	57	-0.8	9	8.2%	29	186	24	218	55%	28%	10%	7%
2017	MIN			85	122	983	70%	--	11.6	6							10.9%							

At 23 years of age, Stefon Diggs is about to conclude his development. The Vikings receiver is still waiting for his first 1,000-yard season, but would have had one last year if he had stayed healthy. Diggs missed three games, but more importantly, he played at less than 100 percent in many more. He showed off explosiveness through his routes early in the year before fading from the offense as the season wore on. After a 164-yard output in Week 10, Diggs didn't eclipse 60 yards in a game over the remainder of the season. He had fewer than 30 yards in each of his final two games before missing the Week 17 victory over the Bears.

Diggs was overshadowed by Adam Thielen in 2016 because Thielen stayed healthy and was able to get open more consistently downfield. When healthy, Diggs offers his quarterback a diverse skill set, and there's a good chance he posts his first 1,000-yard season in 2017.

Josh Doctson

Height: 6-2   Weight: 202   College: TCU   Draft: 2016/1 (22)   Born: 3-Dec-1992   Age: 25   Risk: Red

Year	Team	G/GS	Snaps	Rec	Pass	Yds	C%	+/-	Yd/C	TD	Drop	YAC	Rk	YAC+	BTkl	DVOA	Rk	DYAR	Rk	YAR	Short	Mid	Deep	Bomb
2016	WAS	2/0	31	2	6	66	33%	-0.8	33.0	0	0	7.5	--	+1.5	0	-9.3%	--	2	--	-3	20%	60%	0%	20%
2017	WAS			34	58	532	59%	--	15.7	3							7.4%							

Doctson is an injured Achilles tendon with a human attached to it. He injured the foot during May minicamp last year. Since then, his timetable for recovery has increased quadratically. First he was a week or two away, then about four weeks away, then on the PUP list, then (after two brief early-season appearances) on injured reserve. The Redskins were reportedly taking things extra slowly with Doctson during this year's OTAs, which presumably means he will be on the field before his 40th birthday. Doctson was a draftnik favorite long before he got Scot McCloughan's seal of approval, but when an injury that was never considered serious sidelines a player for more than a year, it's a sign that he may not be built to last long in the NFL.

Phillip Dorsett

Height: 5-10   Weight: 185   College: Miami   Draft: 2015/1 (29)   Born: 5-Jan-1993   Age: 25   Risk: Green

Year	Team	G/GS	Snaps	Rec	Pass	Yds	C%	+/-	Yd/C	TD	Drop	YAC	Rk	YAC+	BTkl	DVOA	Rk	DYAR	Rk	YAR	Short	Mid	Deep	Bomb
2015	IND	11/0	212	18	39	225	46%	-2.8	12.5	1	0	3.3	--	-1.5	0	-32.4%	--	-59	--	-49	32%	27%	19%	22%
2016	IND	15/7	795	33	59	528	56%	-1.7	16.0	2	5	4.5	39	-0.1	2	10.2%	25	107	50	86	38%	23%	13%	25%
2017	IND			38	68	549	56%	--	14.4	4							-2.4%							

Dorsett is doing exactly what he was drafted to do. Last season, he had 140 DYAR on 23 deep targets, which put him in the top 20 of all receivers on deep-ball DYAR. Now, perhaps you're saying, "isn't having a one-dimensional speedster with a small frame and no chance of winning contested deep balls a bad use of a first-round draft pick? Wasn't he kind of an odd pick considering all the other holes the Colts had in 2015?" Well, yes, but Ryan Grigson thought Dorsett was special. Now Grigson is in Cleveland, and Dorsett might be a free agent soon! Pep up, Browns fans!

Julian Edelman

Height: 6-0   Weight: 198   College: Kent State   Draft: 2009/7 (232)   Born: 22-May-1986   Age: 31   Risk: Green

Year	Team	G/GS	Snaps	Rec	Pass	Yds	C%	+/-	Yd/C	TD	Drop	YAC	Rk	YAC+	BTkl	DVOA	Rk	DYAR	Rk	YAR	Short	Mid	Deep	Bomb
2014	NE	14/13	805	92	133	972	69%	+7.1	10.6	4	10	4.6	40	-0.1	8	0.2%	42	137	31	102	53%	34%	9%	4%
2015	NE	9/9	525	61	88	692	69%	+2.6	11.3	7	6	5.1	25	+0.5	15	8.1%	35	144	28	159	51%	36%	6%	7%
2016	NE	16/13	875	98	159	1106	62%	-4.0	11.3	3	10	5.0	29	+0.2	12	-9.2%	68	43	65	38	46%	33%	12%	8%
2017	NE			85	123	968	69%	--	11.4	5							7.1%							

The Patriots showed faith in Edelman's twilight years this offseason, inking the 31-year-old to an extension that will keep him in New England through 2019. Of course, the organization also protected itself with a team-friendly deal, which may come in handy. Edelman exhibited some early signs of erosion last season, posting a negative DVOA for the first time since he became a starter and seeing his catch rate dip below the 70 percent range he had occupied every year since 2013. Still, Tom

Brady's most trusted target will always have some value to the offense so long as he's healthy. Last year was only the second time in his eight-year career that Edelman played 16 games, but in both instances he received more than 150 targets. Something to watch moving forward will be how carefully the Patriots manage Edelman during the regular season. Edelman only played 78 percent of the offensive snaps last year despite being available for every game; in contrast, he played 85 percent of the snaps during his last fully healthy season in 2013. Even if he does remain healthy, Edelman should naturally see a target decrease with the arrival of Brandin Cooks and a potentially healthier season from Rob Gronkowski. Regardless, his rapport with Brady is deep enough that he should have a fairly high floor whenever he's on the field.

Quincy Enunwa   Height: 6-2   Weight: 225   College: Nebraska   Draft: 2014/6 (209)   Born: 31-May-1992   Age: 25   Risk: Red

Year	Team	G/GS	Snaps	Rec	Pass	Yds	C%	+/-	Yd/C	TD	Drop	YAC	Rk	YAC+	BTkl	DVOA	Rk	DYAR	Rk	YAR	Short	Mid	Deep	Bomb
2015	NYJ	12/6	522	22	46	315	48%	-6.9	14.3	0	5	6.7	--	+1.9	7	-27.0%	--	-48	--	-40	42%	28%	23%	7%
2016	NYJ	16/13	873	58	105	857	55%	-9.0	14.8	4	7	6.1	7	+1.1	13	-4.5%	63	69	58	72	42%	37%	16%	5%
2017	NYJ			75	133	1031	56%	--	13.7	6							-9.8%							

In a passing attack that often seemed limited to running back screens and desperate long bombs, Enunwa was effective as a tackle-breaking YAC producer. Witness his 69-yard touchdown against the Ravens, where he took a simple curl over the middle, spun away from a pair of defenders, and zipped down the field for a score. If Enunwa's going to have success in 2017, he'll need more plays like that where he does all the work himself, because the New York offense seems ill-suited to helping him out in any way. Enunwa goes into this year with 80 career receptions, the most of any Jets wideout or tight end, and with Eric Decker and Brandon Marshall gone he is clearly the team's top wide receiver. That's why his KUBIAK projection is higher than you were probably expecting. Yes, the Jets will be terrible, but terrible teams tend to pass a lot, and somebody has to catch those passes once in a while.

Mike Evans   Height: 6-5   Weight: 231   College: Texas A&M   Draft: 2014/1 (7)   Born: 21-Aug-1993   Age: 24   Risk: Green

Year	Team	G/GS	Snaps	Rec	Pass	Yds	C%	+/-	Yd/C	TD	Drop	YAC	Rk	YAC+	BTkl	DVOA	Rk	DYAR	Rk	YAR	Short	Mid	Deep	Bomb
2014	TB	15/15	768	68	123	1051	55%	+3.8	15.5	12	4	2.5	82	-2.3	4	11.4%	21	222	17	234	21%	38%	22%	19%
2015	TB	15/14	857	74	148	1206	50%	-6.2	16.3	3	10	3.3	74	-0.9	4	2.8%	44	187	22	153	14%	46%	23%	16%
2016	TB	16/16	950	96	173	1321	55%	+2.3	13.8	12	8	1.8	94	-1.9	2	10.0%	26	309	6	312	13%	54%	21%	13%
2017	TB			88	162	1305	54%	--	14.8	11							3.1%							

In just his fourth season as a professional, Mike Evans already has an outside chance to become Tampa Bay's leading receiver of all time. That says plenty about the Buccaneers' history, but it also gives an idea of just how consistent Evans' usage has been since he was drafted seventh overall in 2014. He recovered from a relative down year in 2015 to rank sixth in DYAR last season, and has accumulated 3,700 yards and 27 touchdowns across his first three years. Another 1,000-yard season looks inevitable, no matter how shiny the allure of Jameis Winston's new toys.

Larry Fitzgerald   Height: 6-3   Weight: 225   College: Pittsburgh   Draft: 2004/1 (3)   Born: 31-Aug-1983   Age: 34   Risk: Yellow

Year	Team	G/GS	Snaps	Rec	Pass	Yds	C%	+/-	Yd/C	TD	Drop	YAC	Rk	YAC+	BTkl	DVOA	Rk	DYAR	Rk	YAR	Short	Mid	Deep	Bomb
2014	ARI	14/13	857	63	104	784	61%	-1.2	12.4	2	1	5.3	22	+0.4	8	-5.8%	55	54	54	58	37%	37%	20%	6%
2015	ARI	16/16	984	109	146	1215	75%	+14.7	11.1	9	2	4.2	48	-0.6	8	18.9%	10	363	4	356	42%	40%	14%	3%
2016	ARI	16/16	1052	107	152	1023	72%	+7.3	9.6	6	4	3.4	68	-1.1	16	-6.8%	65	71	57	119	53%	35%	11%	1%
2017	ARI			101	151	1040	67%	--	10.3	8							1.2%							

Does Fitzgerald just... not age? He led the league in receptions last year at age 33, a feat that has only been done two other times. One name you know: Jerry Rice in 1996. The other is familiar to you if you're an old-school Cardinals fan: MacArthur Lane back in 1976. Fitzgerald was also the youngest player to ever lead the league in receptions back in 2005, so he basically spits on expected age curves. Fitzgerald has aged gracefully in part because Bruce Arians has transitioned him into a slot receiver. In 2016, Fitzgerald had minus-0.1% DVOA in the slot, but fell to minus-30.7% when lined up wide. Managing to successfully transition inside has added years to Fitzgerald's career.

Michael Floyd   Height: 6-3   Weight: 220   College: Notre Dame   Draft: 2012/1 (13)   Born: 27-Nov-1989   Age: 28   Risk: Yellow

Year	Team	G/GS	Snaps	Rec	Pass	Yds	C%	+/-	Yd/C	TD	Drop	YAC	Rk	YAC+	BTkl	DVOA	Rk	DYAR	Rk	YAR	Short	Mid	Deep	Bomb
2014	ARI	16/14	944	47	100	841	48%	-5.2	17.9	6	3	2.5	83	-2.4	2	-1.9%	47	81	44	81	15%	41%	16%	29%
2015	ARI	15/6	652	52	89	849	58%	+2.8	16.3	6	3	4.1	52	+0.0	4	24.0%	8	256	14	227	12%	46%	26%	17%
2016	2TM	15/8	746	37	76	488	49%	-4.0	13.2	5	5	1.9	92	-1.7	2	-5.6%	64	43	67	58	15%	50%	20%	15%
2017	MIN			20	39	262	51%	--	13.1	2						-12.9%								

Floyd's disastrous 2016 season has left his career in flux. Being on his third team in two seasons is the least of his problems, as Floyd was also suspended for the first four games of the year after serving jail time for an extreme DUI charge this offseason. On the field, the former first-rounder set career-lows in catches and yards, while his receiving DVOA and DYAR figures were his worst since his rookie season. Now in Minnesota, Floyd will battle Laquon Treadwell for No. 3 receiver reps in a fairly low-volume offense, assuming he can overcome his personal demons first.

Will Fuller   Height: 6-0   Weight: 186   College: Notre Dame   Draft: 2016/1 (21)   Born: 16-Apr-1994   Age: 23   Risk: Green

Year	Team	G/GS	Snaps	Rec	Pass	Yds	C%	+/-	Yd/C	TD	Drop	YAC	Rk	YAC+	BTkl	DVOA	Rk	DYAR	Rk	YAR	Short	Mid	Deep	Bomb
2016	HOU	14/13	829	47	92	635	51%	-2.4	13.5	2	6	4.7	35	-0.2	7	-14.8%	77	-15	78	-15	25%	29%	22%	24%
2017	HOU			48	90	724	53%	--	15.1	4						-5.4%								

Will Ginn Junior did exactly what was expected of him in his rookie season. He provided some field-stretching ability to an offense that couldn't do anything with it, he returned a punt to the house, and he dropped a lot of balls on concentration errors that bordered on the amateur. He'll continue to be a field-stretching target in his second year. Perhaps by the end of his rookie contract, the Texans will have a quarterback who can take advantage of that. Stranger things have happened.

Devin Funchess   Height: 6-4   Weight: 232   College: Michigan   Draft: 2015/2 (41)   Born: 21-May-1994   Age: 23   Risk: Yellow

Year	Team	G/GS	Snaps	Rec	Pass	Yds	C%	+/-	Yd/C	TD	Drop	YAC	Rk	YAC+	BTkl	DVOA	Rk	DYAR	Rk	YAR	Short	Mid	Deep	Bomb
2015	CAR	16/5	493	31	63	473	49%	-5.1	15.3	5	3	3.6	63	-0.4	3	-10.7%	73	9	73	32	15%	63%	12%	10%
2016	CAR	15/7	494	23	58	371	40%	-8.9	16.1	4	5	4.5	42	+1.0	2	-7.4%	66	26	68	28	15%	56%	15%	14%
2017	CAR			27	59	412	46%	--	15.3	4						-9.1%								

Funchess was a risky player for Carolina to trade up and select in the second round of the 2015 draft, a converted tight end without dominant traits. Nevertheless, after a blah rookie season, Funchess seemed to be on the verge of justifying the move after a strong 2016 training camp. Then he was simply awful during the regular season. Funchess had the lowest catch rate of any wideout with 50 or more targets. Also worrying was the lack of separation and regular miscommunication with Cam Newton.

For the Panthers attack to open up, Funchess needs to improve, but the prognosis for that isn't great. He's unlikely to suddenly be able to open space on defenders who squatted on his routes and pushed him around, despite size disadvantages. Funchess is at a crossroads. The Panthers are clearly attempting to move their offense away from the style they imagined Funchess would benefit from, but that's a tough transition to accomplish overnight, and strong play could prevent the loss of targets to the newcomers in Carolina. Otherwise, he's a dead contract walking.

Taylor Gabriel   Height: 5-8   Weight: 167   College: Abilene Christian   Draft: 2014/FA   Born: 17-Feb-1991   Age: 26   Risk: Green

Year	Team	G/GS	Snaps	Rec	Pass	Yds	C%	+/-	Yd/C	TD	Drop	YAC	Rk	YAC+	BTkl	DVOA	Rk	DYAR	Rk	YAR	Short	Mid	Deep	Bomb
2014	CLE	16/2	610	36	74	621	51%	-5.4	17.3	1	2	7.3	3	+1.2	4	-9.0%	60	21	61	19	32%	33%	17%	18%
2015	CLE	13/4	401	28	48	241	58%	-4.4	8.6	0	4	3.9	--	-2.3	2	-31.8%	--	-74	--	-95	51%	30%	13%	6%
2016	ATL	13/3	349	35	51	579	71%	+4.4	16.5	6	0	7.7	1	+1.9	7	33.7%	1	181	25	185	37%	39%	8%	16%
2017	ATL			48	74	619	65%	--	12.9	5						9.0%								

On September 3, Gabriel was released by the Browns. The next day, he was signed by the Falcons. Five months later, he was in the Super Bowl. Timing truly is everything in life.

Gabriel actually played fewer snaps than he had in Cleveland during the first two years of his career, but he made them count, leading the league in receiving DVOA thanks to his proficiency at taking wide receiver screens and skittering like a bug across a pond all the way to paydirt. (He also got help from finishing just one target over the qualifying minimum.) One sour note: in a sea of great efficiency numbers among Falcons receivers, Gabriel's third down inefficiency (-22.7% DVOA) stood out. It's hard to imagine Gabriel repeating his once-in-a-lifetime season, but so long as he keeps that speed and elusiveness Gabriel will have a role in Atlanta's high-octane attack.

Pierre Garcon

Height: 6-0   Weight: 210   College: Mount Union   Draft: 2008/6 (205)   Born: 8-Aug-1986   Age: 31   Risk: Yellow

Year	Team	G/GS	Snaps	Rec	Pass	Yds	C%	+/-	Yd/C	TD	Drop	YAC	Rk	YAC+	BTkl	DVOA	Rk	DYAR	Rk	YAR	Short	Mid	Deep	Bomb
2014	WAS	16/14	872	68	105	752	65%	+0.1	11.1	3	0	5.0	29	-0.1	6	-14.6%	75	-15	76	0	49%	33%	9%	9%
2015	WAS	16/16	811	72	111	777	65%	+3.9	10.8	6	2	2.3	86	-2.1	3	2.4%	45	128	33	129	39%	33%	20%	8%
2016	WAS	16/16	808	79	114	1041	69%	+8.8	13.2	3	2	4.3	45	-0.1	13	16.3%	14	262	10	256	38%	41%	15%	6%
2017	SF			80	128	973	63%	--	12.2	6							-2.7%							

Fantasy football players take note: the last time Garcon played in a Kyle Shanahan offense, he received 181 targets, one of the 20 highest seasons since targets started being recorded in the '90s. He wasn't very *effective* on said targets (-5.2% DVOA), but Washington was terrible in 2013. Apart from Garcon, Washington's receiving corps that year featured the corpse of Santana Moss, a rookie Jordan Reed, and mediocre-at-best players like Leonard Hankerson, Logan Paulsen, Aldrick Robinson, and Josh Morgan. That left Shanahan with very few other options than to throw everything at Garcon and hope something stuck.

Now, take a look at San Francisco's receiving corps. It's not exactly the days of Jerry Rice and John Taylor out there. Garcon could be in line for major work once again.

Ted Ginn

Height: 5-11   Weight: 178   College: Ohio State   Draft: 2007/1 (9)   Born: 12-Apr-1985   Age: 32   Risk: Red

Year	Team	G/GS	Snaps	Rec	Pass	Yds	C%	+/-	Yd/C	TD	Drop	YAC	Rk	YAC+	BTkl	DVOA	Rk	DYAR	Rk	YAR	Short	Mid	Deep	Bomb
2014	ARI	16/0	151	14	26	190	54%	-0.7	13.6	0	2	3.3	--	-1.9	1	-15.5%	--	-6	--	-4	35%	27%	19%	19%
2015	CAR	15/13	670	44	96	739	46%	-6.4	16.8	10	7	5.5	19	+1.4	2	-2.5%	55	77	52	106	14%	50%	12%	24%
2016	CAR	16/8	687	54	95	752	57%	-2.9	13.9	4	6	3.4	70	-1.6	5	-10.8%	72	13	72	15	31%	46%	7%	16%
2017	NO			47	81	754	58%	--	16.0	5							3.9%							

In theory, Ted Ginn was signed as a free agent to replace the outgoing Brandin Cooks. In practice, Ginn will be the Saints' No. 3 receiver, a pure deep threat in a role not unlike Devery Henderson's or Robert Meachem's in days of yore. Ginn still has, shall we say, inconsistent hands, but his speed has never been questioned. He should also see action as an occasional punt returner and, potentially, kickoff returner—two positions where the Saints are in dire need of an upgrade from last season.

Chris Godwin

Height: 6-1   Weight: 209   College: Penn State   Draft: 2017/3 (84)   Born: 27-Feb-1996   Age: 21   Risk: Yellow

Year	Team	G/GS	Snaps	Rec	Pass	Yds	C%	+/-	Yd/C	TD	Drop	YAC	Rk	YAC+	BTkl	DVOA	Rk	DYAR	Rk	YAR	Short	Mid	Deep	Bomb
2017	TB			18	34	259	53%	--	14.4	2							-5.9%							

A big-bodied outside receiver with the speed to test defenses deep, Godwin's scouting reports suggest an ideal fit for both Tampa Bay's offense and their quarterback. In particular, his ability to adjust to the ball in flight, extend to catch the ball away from his body, and consistently bring in contested receptions should pay dividends quickly. His one obvious roadblock will be playing time, as he has very little experience in the slot and will be competing with DeSean Jackson for snaps on the outside.

Kenny Golladay

Height: 6-4   Weight: 218   College: Northern Illinois   Draft: 2017/3 (96)   Born: 1-Jan-1994   Age: 24   Risk: Red

Year	Team	G/GS	Snaps	Rec	Pass	Yds	C%	+/-	Yd/C	TD	Drop	YAC	Rk	YAC+	BTkl	DVOA	Rk	DYAR	Rk	YAR	Short	Mid	Deep	Bomb
2017	DET			43	62	538	69%	--	12.5	4							7.1%							

Golladay is the tallest wideout on Detroit's roster, and he has a good shot to be the No. 3 after Golden Tate and Marvin Jones. Golladay's size would make him a natural fit on the outside, while Tate can play in the slot. Detroit needed this type of draft pick after letting Anquan Boldin go in the offseason. Golladay won't make fans forget about Calvin Johnson, but we could have said the same thing about the Marvin Jones signing last year.

Marquise Goodwin Height: 5-9   Weight: 183   College: Texas   Draft: 2013/3 (78)   Born: 19-Nov-1990   Age: 27   Risk: Red

Year	Team	G/GS	Snaps	Rec	Pass	Yds	C%	+/-	Yd/C	TD	Drop	YAC	Rk	YAC+	BTkl	DVOA	Rk	DYAR	Rk	YAR	Short	Mid	Deep	Bomb
2014	BUF	10/0	89	1	9	42	11%	-3.0	42.0	0	0	6.0	--	-1.4	0	-95.0%	--	-58	--	-62	22%	22%	22%	33%
2015	BUF	2/0	28	2	2	24	100%	+0.7	12.0	0	0	1.0	--	-2.2	0	69.3%	--	13	--	15	0%	100%	0%	0%
2016	BUF	15/9	638	29	68	431	43%	-7.1	14.9	3	3	2.8	86	-0.9	1	-23.8%	87	-56	86	-50	16%	55%	14%	16%
2017	SF			40	79	604	51%	--	15.1	4						-10.5%								

Goodwin has been a major tease so far. There's no questioning his athletic prowess—He competed at the 2012 Olympics! He ran a 4.27-second 40 at the combine!—but he hasn't put it all together on the field. He has missed 24 games with injuries in his first four seasons, and when he has been on the field, he has been inconsistent. It's possible, however, Buffalo wasn't using him properly. Kyle Shanahan used the similarly diminutive yet quick Taylor Gabriel to great effect in Atlanta last year, getting him the ball in space and letting him turn on the afterburners, and he led the league with 7.7 yards after catch. Expect more screens and deep posts and fewer comebacks and fly routes for Goodwin in 2016 as the 49ers try to get him the ball and let that speed loose.

A.J. Green Height: 6-4   Weight: 207   College: Georgia   Draft: 2011/1 (4)   Born: 31-Jul-1988   Age: 29   Risk: Yellow

Year	Team	G/GS	Snaps	Rec	Pass	Yds	C%	+/-	Yd/C	TD	Drop	YAC	Rk	YAC+	BTkl	DVOA	Rk	DYAR	Rk	YAR	Short	Mid	Deep	Bomb
2014	CIN	13/13	648	69	116	1041	59%	+4.2	15.1	6	2	4.5	46	+0.3	9	4.1%	38	158	29	161	23%	45%	20%	12%
2015	CIN	16/16	932	86	132	1297	65%	+13.2	15.1	10	3	3.9	57	-0.3	6	26.5%	7	414	3	403	26%	38%	22%	13%
2016	CIN	10/10	554	66	100	964	66%	+6.8	14.6	4	3	3.9	54	-1.1	9	19.1%	9	250	11	232	30%	42%	12%	15%
2017	CIN			94	148	1349	64%	--	14.4	8						11.0%								

The hamstring injury that effectively ended Green's season was a mixed blessing for the Bengals. It came at a time where they were already effectively out of the playoff race, and it won't be serious enough to hamper Green in the future. We're not sure there's much analysis needed with Green himself: he was on his way to a career year before getting hurt, and since he was drafted in 2011 he has been a bona fide No. 1 receiver on a Hall of Fame path. Our only complaint is that the Bengals used Green a bit too much on go routes last year when he's much more effective using his route-running skills in the middle of the field. Hopefully John Ross will provide some amount of attention for opposing safeties next year.

Dorial Green-Beckham Height: 6-5   Weight: 237   College: Oklahoma   Draft: 2015/2 (40)   Born: 12-Apr-1993   Age: 24   Risk: N/A

Year	Team	G/GS	Snaps	Rec	Pass	Yds	C%	+/-	Yd/C	TD	Drop	YAC	Rk	YAC+	BTkl	DVOA	Rk	DYAR	Rk	YAR	Short	Mid	Deep	Bomb
2015	TEN	16/5	580	32	67	549	48%	-2.5	17.2	4	3	4.5	42	+0.8	4	1.8%	47	77	54	90	23%	35%	36%	6%
2016	PHI	15/7	642	36	74	392	49%	-8.6	10.9	2	7	4.2	51	-0.0	4	-18.6%	82	-34	81	-31	28%	54%	16%	3%

Green-Beckham looks like Randy Moss' older brother until the moment arrives to do something football-related,. Then he becomes a big, fast dude who got by on raw talent since the moment he strapped on a helmet and lacks the focus and gumption to do anything more than run fast in a straight line and get out-jumped or out-muscled for the ball. DGB will get several more NFL opportunities after the Eagles cut him, based solely on measurables. He will disappoint at every stop.

Cobi Hamilton Height: 6-2   Weight: 212   College: Arkansas   Draft: 2013/6 (197)   Born: 13-Nov-1990   Age: 27   Risk: Blue

Year	Team	G/GS	Snaps	Rec	Pass	Yds	C%	+/-	Yd/C	TD	Drop	YAC	Rk	YAC+	BTkl	DVOA	Rk	DYAR	Rk	YAR	Short	Mid	Deep	Bomb
2016	PIT	11/8	385	17	28	234	61%	+0.7	13.8	2	1	1.3	--	-3.3	0	14.9%	--	64	--	62	31%	31%	17%	21%
2017	PIT			4	7	54	57%	--	13.4	0						-2.3%								

The Bengals drafted Hamilton in 2013, and he spent the next three years on practice squads in Cincinnati, Philadelphia, Miami, and Carolina. Pittsburgh joined that list in 2016, then promoted Hamilton to the active roster a day before the Week 6 game against Miami. He rewarded them with a 23-yard touchdown catch against the Dolphins. Hamilton bounced in and out of the starting lineup through the rest of the regular season and playoffs but was rarely a significant factor—his biggest game came in a meaningless Week 17 contest against Cleveland, when he caught three passes for 54 yards and a game-winning touchdown in overtime. It was a nice story, and the Steelers signed Hamilton to a one-year, $540,000 deal for 2017. None of that money is guaranteed, though, and Hamilton will have to fight to keep his spot on Pittsburgh's deep roster.

Justin Hardy   Height: 5-10   Weight: 192   College: East Carolina   Draft: 2015/4 (107)   Born: 18-Dec-1991   Age: 26   Risk: Green

Year	Team	G/GS	Snaps	Rec	Pass	Yds	C%	+/-	Yd/C	TD	Drop	YAC	Rk	YAC+	BTkl	DVOA	Rk	DYAR	Rk	YAR	Short	Mid	Deep	Bomb
2015	ATL	9/1	337	21	36	194	58%	-1.6	9.2	0	2	3.1	--	-1.0	0	-24.8%	--	-32	--	-20	42%	48%	3%	6%
2016	ATL	16/3	290	21	31	203	68%	+2.2	9.7	4	0	2.3	--	-1.5	1	14.8%	--	70	--	73	41%	48%	3%	7%
2017	ATL			20	31	208	65%	--	10.4	2							-3.3%								

Hardy's value is versatility—he can play either wideout spot or the slot competently enough at the pro level. Unfortunately, he isn't as good at any of the roles as the current Falcons starters, so unless injury hits, Hardy watches more than he gets a chance to prove himself. He went from walk-on to become the all-time leading receiver at East Carolina (Zay Jones surpassed him last year), so Hardy isn't the quitting type. He has been spotted with an inordinate number of Julio Jones voodoo dolls, however.

Andrew Hawkins   Height: 5-7   Weight: 175   College: Toledo   Draft: 2008/FA   Born: 10-Mar-1986   Age: 31   Risk: Red

Year	Team	G/GS	Snaps	Rec	Pass	Yds	C%	+/-	Yd/C	TD	Drop	YAC	Rk	YAC+	BTkl	DVOA	Rk	DYAR	Rk	YAR	Short	Mid	Deep	Bomb
2014	CLE	15/15	647	63	113	824	57%	-5.2	13.1	2	3	6.4	9	+1.1	9	-11.4%	66	11	65	29	40%	41%	15%	4%
2015	CLE	8/8	415	27	43	276	63%	-1.4	10.2	0	0	4.7	--	-0.5	1	-26.0%	--	-42	--	-44	54%	37%	7%	2%
2016	CLE	16/5	647	33	54	324	61%	-1.1	9.8	3	3	3.9	55	-0.5	8	-12.5%	75	1	75	3	52%	30%	14%	4%
2017	NE			12	19	123	63%	--	10.2	0							-7.4%								

Hawkins signed with New England in free agency, which didn't make much sense for either side. It's a mystery why a stacked team like New England would bother with a low-upside veteran like Hawkins, but at least they can just cut him if it doesn't work out. It's also a mystery why Hawkins chose the Patriots over a team with greater need at receiver, but apparently the allure of a championship ring won out over job security.

Carlos Henderson   Height: 5-11   Weight: 199   College: Louisiana Tech   Draft: 2017/3 (82)   Born: 19-Dec-1994   Age: 23   Risk: Yellow

Year	Team	G/GS	Snaps	Rec	Pass	Yds	C%	+/-	Yd/C	TD	Drop	YAC	Rk	YAC+	BTkl	DVOA	Rk	DYAR	Rk	YAR	Short	Mid	Deep	Bomb
2017	DEN			19	32	273	59%	--	14.4	2							1.5%								

Henderson is a speedster who was named Conference USA's Offensive and Special Teams Player of the Year. His flaw is that he relies too heavily on speed at times instead of technique on his route running. Let's just say that special teams, namely kick returns, will be more of his bag in 2017, but the Broncos do have a real need for a No. 3 receiver. With players such as Cody Latimer and Bennie Fowler not exactly stepping up, Henderson could impress with a good summer performance.

Rashard Higgins   Height: 6-1   Weight: 196   College: Colorado State   Draft: 2016/5 (172)   Born: 7-Oct-1994   Age: 23   Risk: Green

Year	Team	G/GS	Snaps	Rec	Pass	Yds	C%	+/-	Yd/C	TD	Drop	YAC	Rk	YAC+	BTkl	DVOA	Rk	DYAR	Rk	YAR	Short	Mid	Deep	Bomb
2016	CLE	16/0	183	6	12	77	50%	-0.9	12.8	0	1	5.2	--	+1.4	1	-26.4%	--	-14	--	-11	33%	50%	0%	17%
2017	CLE			18	36	233	50%	--	13.0	1							-17.5%								

Higgins barely ever saw the field in his first season and never caught more than two passes in a game. He put up some big numbers in college, but has limited athleticism and upside. He'll need to make major strides in his second season if he's going to last long, because players like this rarely get many chances to show what they can do.

Tyreek Hill   Height: 5-9   Weight: 185   College: West Alabama   Draft: 2016/5 (165)   Born: 1-Mar-1994   Age: 23   Risk: Yellow

Year	Team	G/GS	Snaps	Rec	Pass	Yds	C%	+/-	Yd/C	TD	Drop	YAC	Rk	YAC+	BTkl	DVOA	Rk	DYAR	Rk	YAR	Short	Mid	Deep	Bomb
2016	KC	16/1	418	61	83	593	73%	+3.9	9.7	6	6	4.5	41	-1.1	26	0.8%	50	87	55	67	60%	21%	6%	12%
2017	KC			73	101	774	72%	--	10.6	5							5.2%								

This is one of the toughest comments to write, and it's not just because Hill is Good At Football, Bad At Life. How good is his game? We know that his work as a first-team All-Pro return specialist is impressive, and he should be a threat on that front in 2017. The Chiefs have been consistently great on special teams, which is hard to do. The expectations are super high for Hill, who was ranked 36th on the Top 100 Players of 2017 by NFL Network. But can Hill can be a legitimate No. 1 wide receiver now that Jeremy Maclin is gone?

We only have one season of data to go on, but that doesn't seem likely. Hill is more of a deluxe gadget player. What if Percy Harvin were healthy? What if Tavon Austin wasn't terrible?

Hill can line up in the backfield and follow blocks for touchdown runs of 68 and 70 yards (against the Titans and Broncos, respectively). He can go deep, as he caught 3-of-8 targets on go/fly routes. But the Chiefs have to prove that Hill can run more of a varied route tree if we are to believe that he will be a 1,000-yard receiving threat.Last season, half of Hill's targeted routes were curls (22) and wide receiver screens (23). You would think he would be a good screen option, but his minus-58 DYAR on those plays was the third-worst total in the league. Alex Smith had 72 DYAR on his 28 other screens to wideouts, so that wasn't the problem. On third and fourth down, Hill's DVOA dropped to -34.2%. We'll see if Hill can still balance his return duties with a bigger role on offense, but caution should be exercised in projecting his production this season.

Hill had 24 carries for 267 yards and 3 touchdowns last year, leading all wide receviers with 119 rushing DYAR. This year's KUBIAK projection includes 28 carries for 263 yards and a touchdown.

T.Y. Hilton Height: 5-10 Weight: 183 College: Florida International Draft: 2012/3 (92) Born: 14-Nov-1989 Age: 28 Risk: Green

Year	Team	G/GS	Snaps	Rec	Pass	Yds	C%	+/-	Yd/C	TD	Drop	YAC	Rk	YAC+	BTkl	DVOA	Rk	DYAR	Rk	YAR	Short	Mid	Deep	Bomb
2014	IND	15/15	831	82	131	1345	63%	+11.9	16.4	7	5	4.5	45	-0.1	5	16.5%	14	303	11	283	22%	45%	14%	19%
2015	IND	16/15	925	69	134	1124	51%	-7.8	16.3	5	1	5.5	17	+0.9	8	-7.7%	64	52	61	77	24%	44%	17%	15%
2016	IND	16/16	947	91	155	1448	59%	+6.3	15.9	6	10	3.8	58	-0.4	6	17.3%	12	360	4	333	22%	45%	22%	11%
2017	IND			90	152	1445	59%	--	16.1	8						6.8%								

Hilton makes his bread with his speed, but per Matt Harmon's Reception Perception charting, Hilton only ran go routes on 10.4 percent of his targets in 2016. In other words: diminish the rest of his game all you want, but the speed allows everything else to work, because nobody wants to get caught flat-footed against him. Hilton had an extremely successful year on contested catches as well. In short: he is a No. 1 receiver, not a No. 1 receiver just because he plays with Andrew Luck in a high-volume pass offense.

Chris Hogan Height: 6-1 Weight: 220 College: Monmouth Draft: 2012/FA Born: 24-Oct-1988 Age: 29 Risk: Green

Year	Team	G/GS	Snaps	Rec	Pass	Yds	C%	+/-	Yd/C	TD	Drop	YAC	Rk	YAC+	BTkl	DVOA	Rk	DYAR	Rk	YAR	Short	Mid	Deep	Bomb
2014	BUF	16/2	461	41	61	426	67%	+1.0	10.4	4	2	4.6	43	-0.6	5	-8.1%	58	21	60	10	51%	32%	14%	3%
2015	BUF	16/4	612	36	59	450	61%	+1.3	12.5	2	5	2.8	81	-1.8	5	-12.4%	75	1	75	15	38%	28%	12%	22%
2016	NE	15/14	830	38	58	680	66%	+5.3	17.9	4	4	6.3	6	+1.4	2	18.0%	11	145	34	158	41%	23%	16%	20%
2017	NE			22	35	360	63%	--	16.3	2						17.9%								

This was your 2016 league leader in yards per catch. We can assure you this is really Chris Hogan's player comment, and that we did not mean to print "Julio Jones" or "DeSean Jackson" above. Hogan somehow emerged as a dangerous deep threat in his first Patriots season, blowing away his previous career average of 11.0 yards per catch. The cherry on top was his 180-yard, two-score romp in the AFC Championship Game, which set a Patriots franchise record for receiving yards in a playoff game. Hogan was likely going to see strong regression even before the arrival of Brandin Cooks, but now he'll have to battle Malcolm Mitchell simply to stay in three-receiver sets. Aiding Hogan will be his versatility, as he actually received more targets last year from the slot than in a wide alignment. He'll almost certainly see his numbers tilt back towards more of a possession receiver profile this season, but Hogan's productivity in 2016 should at least keep him in the receiver rotation.

Andre Holmes Height: 6-5 Weight: 206 College: Hillsdale Draft: 2011/FA Born: 16-Jun-1988 Age: 29 Risk: Red

Year	Team	G/GS	Snaps	Rec	Pass	Yds	C%	+/-	Yd/C	TD	Drop	YAC	Rk	YAC+	BTkl	DVOA	Rk	DYAR	Rk	YAR	Short	Mid	Deep	Bomb
2014	OAK	16/13	714	47	98	693	48%	-4.6	14.7	4	4	4.1	52	-0.4	1	-7.2%	56	42	56	22	25%	36%	22%	18%
2015	OAK	16/1	346	14	33	201	42%	-2.7	14.4	4	2	3.1	--	-0.3	1	-15.9%	--	-8	--	-7	30%	30%	17%	23%
2016	OAK	16/2	261	14	25	126	56%	-1.0	9.0	3	1	1.9	--	-1.8	2	-9.9%	--	6	--	0	46%	38%	13%	4%
2017	BUF			22	42	299	52%	--	13.6	3						-8.0%								

Holmes fell out of favor in Oakland just as the Raiders turned things around, leading him to move to the Bills on a modest three-year deal this offseason. The good news is that Holmes has the inside track to the No. 3 WR spot. The bad news is that Buffalo used 11 personnel on just 46 percent of its snaps last season, 30th in the league. Rick Dennison's arrival as offensive coordinator may not change that much, as the Broncos ranked only 26th in 11 personnel usage last season. At 6-foot-5, Holmes is the biggest body on an already large receiving corps, which may give an opportunity to earn some split end reps when the Bills do go to three-receiver sets.

DeAndre Hopkins   Height: 6-1   Weight: 214   College: Clemson   Draft: 2013/1 (27)   Born: 6-Jun-1992   Age: 25   Risk: Green

Year	Team	G/GS	Snaps	Rec	Pass	Yds	C%	+/-	Yd/C	TD	Drop	YAC	Rk	YAC+	BTkl	DVOA	Rk	DYAR	Rk	YAR	Short	Mid	Deep	Bomb
2014	HOU	16/16	1053	76	127	1210	60%	+4.4	15.9	6	2	4.9	32	+0.3	7	10.3%	23	237	15	223	22%	43%	23%	13%
2015	HOU	16/16	1150	111	192	1521	58%	+4.5	13.7	11	3	2.0	87	-1.7	5	4.8%	41	268	13	307	15%	54%	20%	11%
2016	HOU	16/16	1086	78	151	954	52%	-6.1	12.2	4	4	3.3	74	-0.6	6	-9.3%	70	43	66	27	23%	55%	13%	9%
2017	HOU			81	153	1096	53%	--	13.5	9						-8.0%								

Was it a down year for the offense, or a down year for Hopkins? The answer is really just "yes." Hopkins struggled at times to get off man coverage, particularly later in the season when Jalen Ramsey ate his lunch. At the same time, the Texans didn't really take advantage of Hopkins' skills, providing him a quarterback who couldn't even put it in the correct vicinity. The Texans picked up his fifth-year option, but this might be a buy-low opportunity they miss out on if they don't talk extension now.

Adam Humphries   Height: 5-11   Weight: 195   College: Clemson   Draft: 2015/FA   Born: 24-Jun-1993   Age: 24   Risk: Green

Year	Team	G/GS	Snaps	Rec	Pass	Yds	C%	+/-	Yd/C	TD	Drop	YAC	Rk	YAC+	BTkl	DVOA	Rk	DYAR	Rk	YAR	Short	Mid	Deep	Bomb
2015	TB	13/0	437	27	40	260	68%	-0.8	9.6	1	2	4.6	--	-0.7	4	-4.1%	--	26	--	24	53%	33%	15%	0%
2016	TB	15/4	650	55	83	622	66%	-0.1	11.3	2	4	6.9	2	+1.6	4	-1.9%	56	68	59	77	55%	32%	10%	3%
2017	TB			39	64	459	61%	--	11.8	2						-4.5%								

Humphries is the least likely incumbent receiver to be affected by Tampa Bay's offseason acquisitions. While DeSean Jackson, Mike Evans, and Chris Godwin will all battle for playing time on the outside of the formation, Humphries is the clear favorite to man the slot as the regular third receiver. When Vincent Jackson went down for the season last October, Humphries became Tampa Bay's most effective wide receiver on third and fourth down: his 14.7% DVOA and 8.8 yards per target eclipsed even Mike Evans, though tight end Cameron Brate was still the most reliable option overall. Humphries also had by far the best yards after catch figure of any Buccaneers wideout, a testament to his role in the offense. Though he is unlikely to see a high target share, Humphries should fulfill a similar role to similar effect this year.

Allen Hurns   Height: 6-3   Weight: 195   College: Miami   Draft: 2014/FA   Born: 12-Nov-1991   Age: 26   Risk: Red

Year	Team	G/GS	Snaps	Rec	Pass	Yds	C%	+/-	Yd/C	TD	Drop	YAC	Rk	YAC+	BTkl	DVOA	Rk	DYAR	Rk	YAR	Short	Mid	Deep	Bomb
2014	JAC	16/8	788	51	97	677	53%	-6.8	13.3	6	5	4.2	51	-0.7	5	-14.4%	74	-13	75	-16	38%	37%	13%	11%
2015	JAC	15/15	865	64	105	1031	61%	+5.2	16.1	10	1	5.4	20	+1.2	5	16.1%	12	236	16	243	29%	36%	30%	6%
2016	JAC	11/11	635	35	76	477	46%	-7.8	13.6	3	6	6.0	9	+1.1	4	-24.0%	88	-71	89	-63	42%	26%	26%	6%
2017	JAC			64	116	875	55%	--	13.7	6						-5.4%								

Receiving plus-minus tells the story of Hurns' season as simply as possible. His fantastic work in 2015 hauling in vaguely accurate Blake Bortles passes earned him a big-money extension last offseason. 2016? No such luck. Cian Fahey's *Pre-Snap Reads Quarterback Catalogue 2017* lists Hurns with eight failed receptions and no created ones. A shoulder injury probably did not help. The hamstring injury that ended his season certainly did not, and led him to add bulk this offseason. Marqise Lee played well in Hurns' role in his absence, and Hurns needs to rebound to his 2015 form to stave off the threat.

Dontrelle Inman   Height: 6-3   Weight: 205   College: Virginia   Draft: 2011/FA   Born: 31-Jan-1989   Age: 28   Risk: Green

Year	Team	G/GS	Snaps	Rec	Pass	Yds	C%	+/-	Yd/C	TD	Drop	YAC	Rk	YAC+	BTkl	DVOA	Rk	DYAR	Rk	YAR	Short	Mid	Deep	Bomb
2014	SD	7/0	120	12	17	158	71%	+2.5	13.2	0	1	1.2	--	-2.7	1	24.0%	--	49	--	42	12%	47%	35%	6%
2015	SD	14/7	691	35	63	486	56%	-0.5	13.9	3	3	5.1	26	+1.0	4	-6.2%	61	32	67	35	32%	38%	24%	6%
2016	SD	16/16	958	58	97	810	60%	+2.2	14.0	4	6	3.7	62	-0.7	5	5.5%	38	140	37	134	24%	51%	20%	5%
2017	LACH			12	21	156	57%	--	13.0	1						-7.3%								

Inman has improved each season, but he'll be greatly affected by Tyrell Williams' emergence, the drafting of Mike Williams, and the return of Keenan Allen. Given that Travis Benjamin has the fifth-highest cap number on the team this year ($6.5 million compared to $2.75 million for Inman), Inman can stake his claim as the best No. 4 or No. 5 wide receiver in the league right now. That's not a bad title to hold when you play for the Chargers and injuries are almost to be expected by this point.

DeSean Jackson   Height: 5-9   Weight: 169   College: California   Draft: 2008/2 (49)   Born: 1-Dec-1986   Age: 31   Risk: Yellow

Year	Team	G/GS	Snaps	Rec	Pass	Yds	C%	+/-	Yd/C	TD	Drop	YAC	Rk	YAC+	BTkl	DVOA	Rk	DYAR	Rk	YAR	Short	Mid	Deep	Bomb
2014	WAS	15/13	755	56	95	1169	60%	+0.8	20.9	6	1	8.5	1	+2.5	3	27.0%	6	306	10	300	36%	33%	6%	24%
2015	WAS	9/9	359	30	49	528	61%	+5.3	17.6	4	0	5.3	22	-0.6	4	12.7%	20	97	47	99	27%	29%	18%	27%
2016	WAS	15/15	707	56	100	1005	56%	+4.3	17.9	4	6	5.1	28	+0.3	4	16.4%	13	241	12	233	26%	34%	15%	25%
2017	TB			53	100	943	53%	--	17.8	5						6.8%								

Tampa Bay's most exciting new attraction since Busch Gardens, DeSean Jackson is a veteran of multiple 1,000-yard seasons catching passes from such luminaries as Michael Vick, Nick Foles, and the three-headed monster of Robert Griffin, Kirk Cousins, and Colt McCoy. As such, he should have no trouble settling in with Jameis Winston as the speedy counterpunch to Mike Evans. A word of caution though: most of Jackson's DYAR last year came on corner, post, and fly routes—the same deep balls on which Jameis Winston is most likely to miss. Why should Busch Gardens get all the good rollercoasters?

Vincent Jackson   Height: 6-5   Weight: 241   College: Northern Colorado   Draft: 2005/2 (61)   Born: 14-Jan-1983   Age: 34   Risk: N/A

Year	Team	G/GS	Snaps	Rec	Pass	Yds	C%	+/-	Yd/C	TD	Drop	YAC	Rk	YAC+	BTkl	DVOA	Rk	DYAR	Rk	YAR	Short	Mid	Deep	Bomb
2014	TB	16/16	903	70	142	1002	49%	-7.8	14.3	2	1	2.1	87	-1.8	5	-12.3%	68	4	68	30	11%	56%	19%	15%
2015	TB	10/9	533	33	62	543	53%	-1.2	16.5	3	1	3.1	76	-0.9	2	11.2%	25	111	42	104	11%	56%	31%	2%
2016	TB	5/5	313	15	32	173	47%	-2.6	11.5	0	3	1.1	--	-2.9	0	-20.0%	--	-18	--	-19	9%	58%	30%	3%

Jackson has the third-most receiving yards in Buccaneers history, only 700 yards short of the franchise record, but the NFL has scant sentiment for 34-year-old receivers who missed at least six games in each of their previous two seasons. Though he has expressed his desire to play this season, it seems unlikely unless some team is hit very hard by injuries. Assuming he retires instead, he does so ranked 56th all-time in career receiving yards.

Alshon Jeffery   Height: 6-3   Weight: 216   College: South Carolina   Draft: 2012/2 (45)   Born: 14-Feb-1990   Age: 27   Risk: Red

Year	Team	G/GS	Snaps	Rec	Pass	Yds	C%	+/-	Yd/C	TD	Drop	YAC	Rk	YAC+	BTkl	DVOA	Rk	DYAR	Rk	YAR	Short	Mid	Deep	Bomb
2014	CHI	16/16	956	85	145	1133	59%	+0.1	13.3	10	5	5.5	19	+0.1	7	11.1%	22	278	13	266	38%	31%	12%	18%
2015	CHI	9/8	506	54	94	807	57%	+1.8	14.9	4	1	3.3	71	-1.1	3	4.1%	42	126	35	134	20%	44%	17%	18%
2016	CHI	12/12	692	52	94	821	55%	+2.3	15.8	2	5	3.7	63	-0.7	6	5.0%	42	132	40	140	19%	48%	21%	12%
2017	PHI			70	124	1006	56%	--	14.4	8						3.9%								

Jeffery suffered through a contract-year bad-luck trifecta in 2016: nagging injuries, a four-game suspension, and revolving-door quarterback play. Hamstring and knee injuries plagued him early in the year. By the time he got healthy, Brian Hoyer was the Bears quarterback. By the time he gelled with Hoyer, the league slapped a substance-abuse policy suspension on him. And by the time Jeffery returned, Matt Barkley was at quarterback and the team was going through the motions.

Jeffery is now two full seasons removed from his 1,000-yard seasons, but he just turned 27 in February, so he is certainly young enough to bounce back now that he's with an organization and quarterback with a bit more forward momentum. Jeffery was the best receiver on the field by far in Eagles OTAs, though that isn't much of a feat. If healthy, Jeffery will become Carson Wentz's go-to receiver, and his catch radius and 50-50 ball retrieval skills will be major assets.

Charles Johnson Height: 6-2   Weight: 215   College: Grand Valley State   Draft: 2013/7 (216)   Born: 27-Feb-1989   Age: 28   Risk: Blue

Year	Team	G/GS	Snaps	Rec	Pass	Yds	C%	+/-	Yd/C	TD	Drop	YAC	Rk	YAC+	BTkl	DVOA	Rk	DYAR	Rk	YAR	Short	Mid	Deep	Bomb
2014	MIN	12/6	440	31	59	475	53%	-3.1	15.3	2	2	5.6	18	+1.2	1	-16.2%	78	-16	77	2	26%	41%	16%	17%
2015	MIN	11/4	218	9	13	127	69%	+1.1	14.1	0	0	3.1	--	-1.4	1	19.5%	--	37	--	40	43%	7%	36%	14%
2016	MIN	16/7	405	20	37	232	54%	-1.3	11.6	0	0	3.5	--	-1.4	2	-17.0%	--	-13	--	-9	32%	29%	21%	18%
2017	CAR			4	7	46	57%	--	11.5	0						-8.7%								

When Carolina agreed to re-sign Charles Johnson the defensive end, was it part of the deal that they would also sign Charles Johnson the former Vikings wideout as well, thus confusing fans should either fail to perform up to snuff? More likely, the Panthers signed C.J. the receiver as part of their commitment to getting faster. Forty percent of his fifty targets in the last two seasons have been charted as either Deep or Bomb, and that number could rise with Cam Newton delivering the passes. Or, more likely, Johnson won't even make it past final cuts.

Julio Jones Height: 6-3   Weight: 220   College: Alabama   Draft: 2011/1 (6)   Born: 3-Feb-1989   Age: 28   Risk: Green

Year	Team	G/GS	Snaps	Rec	Pass	Yds	C%	+/-	Yd/C	TD	Drop	YAC	Rk	YAC+	BTkl	DVOA	Rk	DYAR	Rk	YAR	Short	Mid	Deep	Bomb
2014	ATL	15/15	868	104	163	1593	64%	+7.2	15.3	6	4	5.2	25	+0.4	14	16.2%	15	356	7	353	34%	26%	30%	10%
2015	ATL	16/16	970	136	203	1871	67%	+10.6	13.8	8	7	4.7	38	-0.1	21	8.5%	34	343	6	409	37%	41%	15%	7%
2016	ATL	14/14	705	83	129	1409	64%	+7.9	17.0	6	5	4.7	36	+0.2	9	31.7%	2	458	1	469	32%	30%	24%	14%
2017	ATL			97	156	1451	62%	--	15.0	8							11.2%								

About the only concerns with Quintorris Lopez "Julio" Jones are nagging injuries (he has played a full 16-game season just twice in his six-year career), and an odd dip in his broken tackle numbers, which could actually be a positive—J.J. may have realized that fighting for extra yards may lead to those missed games. He also put up a surprisingly poor red zone DVOA of minus-20.0%. While Jones is thought of mainly as a flanker, he actually lined up in the slot almost as often as he lined up out wide (68 targets outside, 67 inside), and his numbers were noticeably better from the slot.

Julio Jones, Slot vs. Split Wide, 2016

Lined Up	Targets	DVOA	Yards	YPC	YAC
Slot	67	37.2%	883	16.5	5.2
Wide	68	26.5%	658	12.4	4.2

In a more perfect world, Jones would have followed up his otherworldly grab late in the Super Bowl with the game-clinching touchdown. Such a sequence would not only have brought forth a deserved Super Bowl ring (and perhaps the MVP trophy), but would have taken his fame and status to new heights.

Marvin Jones Height: 6-2   Weight: 199   College: California   Draft: 2012/5 (166)   Born: 12-Mar-1990   Age: 27   Risk: Yellow

Year	Team	G/GS	Snaps	Rec	Pass	Yds	C%	+/-	Yd/C	TD	Drop	YAC	Rk	YAC+	BTkl	DVOA	Rk	DYAR	Rk	YAR	Short	Mid	Deep	Bomb
2015	CIN	16/13	901	65	104	816	63%	+5.3	12.6	4	3	4.6	40	-0.6	11	7.6%	37	171	25	149	42%	23%	13%	23%
2016	DET	15/15	879	55	103	930	53%	-3.5	16.9	4	9	4.3	47	+0.0	7	10.9%	23	202	21	200	26%	37%	24%	14%
2017	DET			65	112	921	58%	--	14.2	5							-0.2%								

Signed to replace Calvin Johnson, Jones looked like a home run for Detroit early in the year. He had 205 yards and two touchdowns in Green Bay in Week 3, but never had another 100-yard game the rest of the season. He didn't score a touchdown after Week 6. While he only missed one full game, health was a concern, as Jones was listed on the injury report for his hamstring, foot, thigh, and quadriceps. Jones had four games where he was held to 16 receiving yards or less last season. Megatron only had eight such games in his 137-game career. With Anquan Boldin gone, Jones will have to become a more consistent threat for Matthew Stafford this season.

T.J. Jones | Height: 5-11 | Weight: 188 | College: Notre Dame | Draft: 2014/6 (189) | Born: 19-Jul-1992 | Age: 25 | Risk: Red

Year	Team	G/GS	Snaps	Rec	Pass	Yds	C%	+/-	Yd/C	TD	Drop	YAC	Rk	YAC+	BTkl	DVOA	Rk	DYAR	Rk	YAR	Short	Mid	Deep	Bomb
2015	DET	10/0	159	10	18	132	56%	-1.8	13.2	1	1	4.1	--	-0.9	1	-7.8%	--	7	--	-5	39%	33%	22%	6%
2016	DET	3/0	52	5	14	93	36%	-3.2	18.6	0	1	6.0	--	-1.3	1	-33.6%	--	-20	--	-18	46%	8%	23%	23%
2017	DET			22	39	283	56%	--	12.9	2						-6.2%								

Jones has hung around Detroit for three years now, but has yet to make an impact. His only catches last season were in the final few weeks, and he has just 15 career catches. The Lions could use some receiver help after Golden Tate and Marvin Jones, but Jones will have to fight off rookie Kenny Golladay for that role.

Zay Jones | Height: 6-2 | Weight: 201 | College: East Carolina | Draft: 2017/2 (37) | Born: 30-Mar-1995 | Age: 22 | Risk: Red

Year	Team	G/GS	Snaps	Rec	Pass	Yds	C%	+/-	Yd/C	TD	Drop	YAC	Rk	YAC+	BTkl	DVOA	Rk	DYAR	Rk	YAR	Short	Mid	Deep	Bomb
2017	BUF			60	97	766	62%	--	12.8	5						-3.9%								

The all-time FBS receptions leader should get an opportunity to contribute right away in the next chapter of his career. With Robert Woods' departure and the dearth of quality receiving options behind Sammy Watkins, Jones effectively inherits the No. 2 receiver role from the outset. Aiding his adjustment will be the presence of receivers coach Phil McGeoghan, who served as his position coach at East Carolina. But while the volume and system familiarity should be helpful, Jones still profiles as a prospect facing a difficult NFL transition. Playmaker Score is very pessimistic on Jones' outlook in part because of his possession receiver skill set. Explosive plays and touchdowns tend to correlate well with NFL success; Jones averaged only 10.7 yards per catch for his NCAA career (11.1 ypc his senior season) and scored eight times in an offense that threw 554 passes. None of this is to say that Jones is preordained to fail, especially since the Bills appear ready to feature him with Watkins approaching free agency after the season. However, given Tyrod Taylor's strengths as a deep passer, it would behoove Jones to expand his skill set if he's to fulfill the No. 1 receiver ambitions Buffalo surely has planned for him.

Jermaine Kearse | Height: 6-1 | Weight: 209 | College: Washington | Draft: 2012/FA | Born: 6-Feb-1990 | Age: 27 | Risk: Red

Year	Team	G/GS	Snaps	Rec	Pass	Yds	C%	+/-	Yd/C	TD	Drop	YAC	Rk	YAC+	BTkl	DVOA	Rk	DYAR	Rk	YAR	Short	Mid	Deep	Bomb
2014	SEA	15/14	792	38	69	537	55%	-1.0	14.1	1	3	5.9	11	+0.4	4	-9.1%	61	19	62	22	31%	33%	23%	13%
2015	SEA	16/16	771	49	68	685	72%	+7.5	14.0	5	3	4.8	37	+0.4	6	29.8%	5	227	19	217	28%	43%	21%	9%
2016	SEA	16/15	828	41	89	510	46%	-5.3	12.4	1	3	3.4	71	-1.4	7	-28.7%	91	-114	92	-90	29%	41%	17%	13%
2017	SEA			35	63	459	56%	--	13.1	2							-10.6%								

In 2015, Kearse set career highs in receptions, receiving yards, and catch rate. He parlayed that performance into a three-year free-agent deal with Seattle, and his level of play immediately plummeted. If finishing near the bottom in both DVOA and DYAR in 2016 wasn't enough, Kearse also led the league in offensive pass interference penalties, taking an already rough season from bad to worse. His true ability almost certainly lies somewhere in the middle of those two campaigns, and he will likely have one last opportunity this season to preserve his roster spot, with rookie third-round pick Amara Darboh breathing down his neck as a cheaper potential replacement. Kearse has made some crucial catches in postseasons past, but he will need to deliver a performance closer to 2015's if he wants to hang onto his job as one of Russell Wilson's secondary weapons moving forward.

Jeremy Kerley | Height: 5-9 | Weight: 188 | College: TCU | Draft: 2011/5 (153) | Born: 8-Nov-1988 | Age: 29 | Risk: Yellow

Year	Team	G/GS	Snaps	Rec	Pass	Yds	C%	+/-	Yd/C	TD	Drop	YAC	Rk	YAC+	BTkl	DVOA	Rk	DYAR	Rk	YAR	Short	Mid	Deep	Bomb
2014	NYJ	16/7	734	38	75	409	51%	-4.3	10.8	1	3	3.9	55	-0.7	2	-21.2%	83	-51	82	-67	29%	52%	15%	3%
2015	NYJ	16/1	223	16	26	152	62%	-2.2	9.5	2	1	5.9	--	+1.0	3	-5.3%	--	14	--	10	50%	46%	4%	0%
2016	SF	16/13	790	64	115	667	56%	-9.0	10.4	3	3	3.3	72	-1.4	4	-26.4%	90	-124	93	-94	42%	38%	19%	1%
2017	SF			47	75	489	63%	--	10.4	2							-14.3%								

Kerley's DVOA and catch-rate splits by down were something to see in 2016. On first and second down, Kerley hovered around minus-15.0% DVOA and a 68 percent catch rate—not great numbers, but better than any other 49ers receiver could manage. On third downs, however, he plummeted to minus-45.4% DVOA and a 36 percent catch rate. It's not an issue of sample size or harder-to-catch passes. Nor is it a one-year phenomenon—he dropped off on third downs in 2015, as well. The fact that Kerley was the 49ers' leading receiver in 2016 and had the fifth-lowest receiving plus-minus in the league tells you just about all you need to know about San Francisco's passing attack.

Cooper Kupp			Height: 6-2		Weight: 204		College: Eastern Washington			Draft: 2017/3 (69)		Born: 15-Jun-1993		Age: 24		Risk: Red		
Year	Team	G/GS	Snaps	Rec	Pass	Yds	C%	+/-	Yd/C	TD	Drop	YAC	Rk	YAC+	BTkl	DVOA	Rk	DYAR	Rk	YAR	Short	Mid	Deep	Bomb
2017	LARM			37	62	493	60%	--	13.3	3						0.4%								

The third-round rookie from FCS Eastern Washington would have made a risky blackjack player as a senior—he was hitting on 17 quite often, posting 117 receptions, 1,700 receiving yards, and 17 touchdowns. Kupp started off the season hot in an upset of interstate foe Washington State with 12 catches for 206 yards and three touchdowns, and helped lead the Eagles to the FCS Final Four before they lost to Youngstown State. Kupp projects as the Rams' third receiver, but he also went 5-of-7 as a passer with 19.3 yards per attempt as a senior. The Rams already have Tavon Austin for gadget plays; why not double down with Kupp?

Brandon LaFell			Height: 6-3		Weight: 211		College: Louisiana St.			Draft: 2010/3 (78)		Born: 4-Nov-1986		Age: 31		Risk: Green		
Year	Team	G/GS	Snaps	Rec	Pass	Yds	C%	+/-	Yd/C	TD	Drop	YAC	Rk	YAC+	BTkl	DVOA	Rk	DYAR	Rk	YAR	Short	Mid	Deep	Bomb
2014	NE	16/13	913	74	119	953	62%	-0.2	12.9	7	3	5.0	31	+0.3	8	5.7%	33	174	27	158	34%	43%	16%	7%
2015	NE	11/7	659	37	74	515	50%	-8.9	13.9	0	6	6.1	9	-0.2	1	-20.1%	82	-43	82	-52	39%	32%	11%	18%
2016	CIN	16/14	1010	64	107	862	60%	-2.0	13.5	6	3	5.5	15	+0.6	5	10.8%	24	202	22	180	38%	40%	16%	6%
2017	CIN			20	37	262	54%	--	13.1	2						-8.3%								

At this point in his career, LaFell is a known quantity. Need someone to soak up targets for you in the face of injuries? LaFell can do it. Need someone to be at all dynamic or coverage-busting? Draft someone to play ahead of LaFell. That's what the Bengals did with John Ross, slotting LaFell into his ideal position: backup plan.

Jarvis Landry			Height: 5-11		Weight: 205		College: Louisiana St.			Draft: 2014/2 (63)		Born: 11/28/1992		Age: 25		Risk: Green		
Year	Team	G/GS	Snaps	Rec	Pass	Yds	C%	+/-	Yd/C	TD	Drop	YAC	Rk	YAC+	BTkl	DVOA	Rk	DYAR	Rk	YAR	Short	Mid	Deep	Bomb
2014	MIA	16/11	683	84	112	758	75%	+8.7	9.0	5	3	5.1	26	-0.3	10	-0.8%	45	102	39	86	58%	36%	4%	2%
2015	MIA	16/14	868	110	167	1157	66%	+2.3	10.5	4	6	4.8	33	-1.1	33	-7.1%	63	72	57	55	48%	36%	9%	6%
2016	MIA	16/16	892	94	131	1136	72%	+6.2	12.1	4	5	6.6	4	+1.2	30	4.8%	43	174	26	190	55%	33%	10%	2%
2017	MIA			96	137	1080	70%	--	11.3	5						6.7%								

Landry's minus-64 DYAR on wide receiver screens was the second-worst total in the league in 2016, ahead of only Tavon Austin (minus-74 DYAR). Landry did some of his best work on slants (72 DYAR), corners (68 DYAR), and dig routes (64 DYAR), but the Dolphins still insist on using him more on short curls (minus-13 DYAR), out routes (minus-13 DYAR), and those unproductive screens. Landry's DVOA in the slot (3.5%) was also less than that of his teammates DeVante Parker (63.1%) and Kenny Stills (10.4%), though Miami still threw 104 passes to Landry in the slot compared to 59 combined for his two teammates.

Marqise Lee			Height: 6-0		Weight: 192		College: USC			Draft: 2014/2 (39)		Born: 11/25/1991		Age: 26		Risk: Green		
Year	Team	G/GS	Snaps	Rec	Pass	Yds	C%	+/-	Yd/C	TD	Drop	YAC	Rk	YAC+	BTkl	DVOA	Rk	DYAR	Rk	YAR	Short	Mid	Deep	Bomb
2014	JAC	13/8	492	37	68	422	54%	-5.7	11.4	1	4	4.8	36	-0.4	7	-20.3%	82	-41	81	-37	48%	38%	6%	8%
2015	JAC	10/1	240	15	32	191	47%	-3.4	12.7	1	2	6.1	--	+0.9	5	-13.4%	--	-2	--	9	43%	27%	10%	20%
2016	JAC	16/6	817	63	105	851	60%	-0.7	13.5	3	5	5.5	14	+1.0	10	12.2%	18	211	19	192	29%	43%	15%	12%
2017	JAC			67	115	871	58%	--	13.0	5						-4.8%								

A season ago, Lee looked like the likely odd man out among the Jaguars' trio of receivers who had debuted with Blake Bortles. Now, each of the three has had a season in the top 20 in DVOA and DYAR, and Jacksonville has some difficult decisions to make. Lee's biggest on-field improvement was better work at the catch point. We didn't see this in Lee's drop rate, but rather in setting up for Bortles. He also was one of the main drivers/recipients of Bortles' garbage-time production. Lee had a

DVOA of 53.5% when the Jaguars were down by more than a touchdown, compared to minus-9.0% otherwise. Even so, more good play could lead to more playing time should Allen Hurns' struggles continue.

Tyler Lockett

Height: 5-10   Weight: 182   College: Kansas State   Draft: 2015/3 (69)   Born: 28-Sep-1992   Age: 25   Risk: Green

Year	Team	G/GS	Snaps	Rec	Pass	Yds	C%	+/-	Yd/C	TD	Drop	YAC	Rk	YAC+	BTkl	DVOA	Rk	DYAR	Rk	YAR	Short	Mid	Deep	Bomb
2015	SEA	16/8	664	51	69	664	74%	+8.1	13.0	6	2	5.0	28	-0.4	7	35.1%	3	249	15	242	38%	29%	10%	22%
2016	SEA	15/9	558	41	68	597	63%	-0.1	14.6	1	2	5.7	12	-0.2	3	5.5%	39	99	52	105	52%	19%	12%	16%
2017	SEA			48	75	666	64%	--	13.9	4						8.6%								

The speed demon from Kansas State had a relatively disappointing sophomore season after bursting onto the scene as an all-purpose threat in his rookie year. After dealing with some nagging leg injuries early in the season, Lockett landed on injured reserve with a broken fibula suffered while diving for a catch near the end zone in Week 16 against the Cardinals. Before the injury, Lockett had won the No. 2 wide receiver job from Jermaine Kearse late in the year, so if Lockett can be back to full speed when Week 1 in Green Bay rolls around, he should again be in line to contribute as a receiver, a runner (he carried the ball 6 times for 114 yards and a touchdown), and a returner this season.

Ricardo Louis

Height: 6-2   Weight: 215   College: Auburn   Draft: 2016/4 (114)   Born: 23-Mar-1994   Age: 23   Risk: Red

Year	Team	G/GS	Snaps	Rec	Pass	Yds	C%	+/-	Yd/C	TD	Drop	YAC	Rk	YAC+	BTkl	DVOA	Rk	DYAR	Rk	YAR	Short	Mid	Deep	Bomb
2016	CLE	16/3	316	18	36	205	50%	-2.5	11.4	0	4	5.1	--	+0.1	4	-42.6%	--	-82	--	-73	48%	32%	10%	10%
2017	CLE			37	67	464	55%	--	12.5	2						-12.1%								

Save for two plays in Week 17, all of Louis' targets, catches, and yardage came from Week 3 to Week 8, when Corey Coleman was out with a broken hand. He showed nothing in those six weeks to indicate he deserved more playing time, but many players struggle as rookies before improving in Year 2. Louis had better be one of them, for Cleveland's sake—the Browns are paper-thin at wideout behind Coleman and Kenny Britt.

Jeremy Maclin

Height: 6-0   Weight: 198   College: Missouri   Draft: 2009/1 (19)   Born: 11-May-1988   Age: 29   Risk: Yellow

Year	Team	G/GS	Snaps	Rec	Pass	Yds	C%	+/-	Yd/C	TD	Drop	YAC	Rk	YAC+	BTkl	DVOA	Rk	DYAR	Rk	YAR	Short	Mid	Deep	Bomb
2014	PHI	16/16	1022	85	143	1318	59%	-1.5	15.5	10	2	5.8	12	+0.8	4	7.4%	30	222	18	245	31%	39%	16%	14%
2015	KC	15/15	828	87	124	1088	70%	+9.6	12.5	8	3	3.8	59	-0.7	3	11.3%	24	234	18	217	28%	50%	11%	11%
2016	KC	12/12	629	44	76	536	58%	-2.1	12.2	2	4	3.1	77	-1.5	4	-4.3%	62	50	62	29	26%	52%	15%	7%
2017	BAL			63	106	762	59%	--	12.1	6						-3.8%								

Few June cuts are as surprising as the Chiefs' decision to dump Maclin, their assumed No. 1 wide receiver heading into 2017. Maclin did struggle to stay healthy in Kansas City, and he was coming off a career-low 536 receiving yards. Still, this was not expected. Baltimore was a good spot for Maclin to land now that Steve Smith is no longer there. While Mike Wallace and Breshad Perriman are a bit similar in style, Maclin does have the ability to play in the slot. He just may not excel there, evident by his minus-27.4% DVOA in the slot compared to 18.6% DVOA out wide last year.

Brandon Marshall

Height: 6-4   Weight: 229   College: UCF   Draft: 2006/4 (119)   Born: 23-Mar-1984   Age: 33   Risk: Yellow

Year	Team	G/GS	Snaps	Rec	Pass	Yds	C%	+/-	Yd/C	TD	Drop	YAC	Rk	YAC+	BTkl	DVOA	Rk	DYAR	Rk	YAR	Short	Mid	Deep	Bomb
2014	CHI	13/13	753	61	106	721	58%	-2.1	11.8	8	4	3.8	60	-0.8	7	-3.3%	48	78	46	82	31%	49%	8%	13%
2015	NYJ	16/16	1059	109	173	1502	63%	+7.0	13.8	14	8	4.0	56	+0.0	15	9.3%	31	303	11	343	26%	46%	17%	11%
2016	NYJ	15/15	901	59	127	788	46%	-14.0	13.4	3	10	3.0	80	-1.0	6	-16.1%	79	-35	82	-29	18%	44%	30%	8%
2017	NYG			54	96	694	56%	--	12.9	7						-3.7%								

Marshall likely could have found more targets and more money elsewhere, but at this point in his career he was wise to sign a $12 million, two-year contract with the Giants. Marshall's days as an effective No. 1 are probably done—he was last in the league in plus-minus last year, and only Michael Crabtree dropped more passes. But with Odell Beckham (and perhaps Sterling

Shepard as well) drawing more attention from opposing defenses, Marshall could feast on third cornerbacks and hole-in-zone coverage. Marshall is an odd oxymoron: a very public personality who's also a very quiet superstar. Since he was drafted, only Larry Fitzgerald has more catches or more yardage, and only Fitz, Antonio Gates, and Calvin Johnson have more receiving touchdowns. But he can also be a bit of a headache, and for all that production, there's a reason Marshall has been traded three times and released once in the past eight years. Between that and his age, he's not likely to be with the Giants long, but he could make a big impact in a short tenure. That's what he has done everywhere else, after all.

Jordan Matthews Height: 6-3 Weight: 212 College: Vanderbilt Draft: 2014/2 (42) Born: 7/16/1992 Age: 25 Risk: Green

Year	Team	G/GS	Snaps	Rec	Pass	Yds	C%	+/-	Yd/C	TD	Drop	YAC	Rk	YAC+	BTkl	DVOA	Rk	DYAR	Rk	YAR	Short	Mid	Deep	Bomb
2014	PHI	16/10	764	67	103	872	65%	+0.1	13.0	8	3	5.8	15	+0.8	6	11.6%	20	194	25	214	47%	37%	13%	4%
2015	PHI	16/12	919	85	128	997	66%	+2.2	11.7	8	5	4.9	31	+0.4	10	-1.8%	52	112	41	120	48%	34%	14%	4%
2016	PHI	14/13	844	73	117	804	62%	+0.8	11.0	3	10	3.2	75	-1.8	5	-13.2%	76	-4	76	2	41%	31%	20%	8%
2017	PHI			69	108	738	64%	--	10.7	5						-6.0%								

Matthews was the Eagles' empty-calorie king when it came to binging on micro passes. On throws 5 or fewer yards down-field, Matthews was 38-of-52 for 184 yards (3.53 yards per pass), one touchdown, and just eight first downs. Screens, flats, extremely quick outs: you name it, Matthews caught it for zero to 6 yards.

A very minor-sounding injury kept Matthews out of OTAs and minicamps for weeks. If Matthews cannot stick as the Eagles slot receiver, he may fall off the back of the roster: Nelson Agholor practiced like his helmet was on fire throughout the offseason, rookie Mack Hollins is a potential special teams ace, and fellow rookie Shelton Gibson is a likely redshirt. Matthews may have been angling for a trade during his absence. A change of scenery could do him some good.

Rishard Matthews Height: 6-0 Weight: 217 College: Nevada Draft: 2012/7 (227) Born: 12-Oct-1989 Age: 28 Risk: Yellow

Year	Team	G/GS	Snaps	Rec	Pass	Yds	C%	+/-	Yd/C	TD	Drop	YAC	Rk	YAC+	BTkl	DVOA	Rk	DYAR	Rk	YAR	Short	Mid	Deep	Bomb
2014	MIA	14/0	210	12	23	135	57%	-0.3	11.3	2	1	3.5	--	-1.0	2	-14.5%	--	-3	--	-15	35%	35%	26%	4%
2015	MIA	11/11	520	43	61	662	70%	+6.3	15.4	4	4	5.7	13	+1.4	2	36.4%	2	235	17	237	28%	47%	17%	8%
2016	TEN	16/10	782	65	108	945	60%	+3.2	14.5	9	3	3.1	76	-0.5	6	14.4%	15	229	15	218	21%	49%	16%	15%
2017	TEN			60	98	830	61%	--	13.8	7						6.5%								

Matthews spent the first half of the season in a timeshare with Andre Johnson, which was even weirder to watch than to write about. After seven weeks, the Titans decided they should play the guy with the 21.8% DVOA and not the one with the minus-25.1% DVOA, and Matthews rightfully ascended to playing a lot. He did particularly well in the red zone, finishing fourth in the league with 102 DYAR. The additions the Titans made to the receiving corps this offseason will likely not have too big an effect on his production.

Cameron Meredith Height: 6-3 Weight: 207 College: Illinois State Draft: 2015/FA Born: 21-Sep-1992 Age: 25 Risk: Yellow

Year	Team	G/GS	Snaps	Rec	Pass	Yds	C%	+/-	Yd/C	TD	Drop	YAC	Rk	YAC+	BTkl	DVOA	Rk	DYAR	Rk	YAR	Short	Mid	Deep	Bomb
2015	CHI	11/0	136	11	16	120	69%	+0.6	10.9	0	0	3.4	--	-2.1	2	-6.3%	--	7	--	4	31%	38%	25%	6%
2016	CHI	14/10	703	66	98	888	68%	+2.8	13.5	4	7	4.5	40	-0.3	14	4.1%	45	128	43	158	40%	37%	18%	4%
2017	CHI			66	116	880	57%	--	13.3	5						-3.9%								

Injuries at wide receiver gave Cameron Meredith a chance to show the Bears what he could do last year. Meredith showed off his inconsistency, dropping too many passes and looking uncertain in his routes at times. He also showed off an ability to get open downfield and make plays on the ball in the air. Meredith finished the season strong with at least 60 yards in each of his final five games. At 24 years of age entering his third season, Meredith is still developing and could very easily take a step forward with more playing time. Adding Kendall Wright and Markus Wheaton to the roster creates more competition for him, but Meredith's size means he will play outside more than either of those players.

Braxton Miller   Height: 6-1   Weight: 201   College: Ohio State   Draft: 2016/3 (85)   Born: 30-Nov-1992   Age: 25   Risk: Red

Year	Team	G/GS	Snaps	Rec	Pass	Yds	C%	+/-	Yd/C	TD	Drop	YAC	Rk	YAC+	BTkl	DVOA	Rk	DYAR	Rk	YAR	Short	Mid	Deep	Bomb
2016	HOU	10/6	379	15	28	99	54%	-3.0	6.6	1	5	3.5	--	-1.9	3	-48.3%	--	-79	--	-74	56%	41%	4%	0%
2017	HOU			35	65	373	54%	--	10.6	1						-23.9%								

A Senior Bowl superstar, Miller's transition from college quarterback/wideout/weapon to NFL wide receiver happened on exactly the wrong team. Miller's lack of readiness forced the Texans into a lot of two tight-end sets. If Miller uses last year as a learning experience, he has all the physical talent you could ask of a wide receiver and needs only the technique that accompanies it. To his credit, he seems to be a hard worker with a good head on his shoulders. And, to the credit of his detractors, those are pretty much the words you would use to describe someone who has shown no aptitude at the NFL level yet.

Malcolm Mitchell   Height: 6-0   Weight: 198   College: Georgia   Draft: 2016/4 (112)   Born: 20-Jul-1993   Age: 24   Risk: Green

Year	Team	G/GS	Snaps	Rec	Pass	Yds	C%	+/-	Yd/C	TD	Drop	YAC	Rk	YAC+	BTkl	DVOA	Rk	DYAR	Rk	YAR	Short	Mid	Deep	Bomb
2016	NE	14/6	538	32	48	401	67%	+2.4	12.5	4	4	5.2	22	+1.2	6	19.6%	7	132	41	143	35%	35%	21%	8%
2017	NE			17	27	229	63%	--	13.5	2						7.5%								

Mitchell had a nice rookie season in an offense notoriously difficult on inexperienced receivers. Despite missing the majority of the preseason with an elbow injury, Mitchell actually had the best DVOA of any Patriots wide receiver, earning enough trust to play in three-receiver sets during the postseason. All this is very promising for Mitchell's future... except for the fact that he's almost certain to see a downturn in production this season, through no fault of his own. Brandin Cooks' arrival leaves Mitchell fighting for No. 3 receiver scraps with Chris Hogan, and that's before accounting for the return of Rob Gronkowski, who was healthy for only six games last season. With Cooks, Hogan, and Julian Edelman all under contract for at least the next two seasons, Mitchell will need to take a big leap forward at some point to reassume a regular role.

Donte Moncrief   Height: 6-2   Weight: 221   College: Mississippi   Draft: 2014/3 (90)   Born: 8-Jun-1993   Age: 24   Risk: Green

Year	Team	G/GS	Snaps	Rec	Pass	Yds	C%	+/-	Yd/C	TD	Drop	YAC	Rk	YAC+	BTkl	DVOA	Rk	DYAR	Rk	YAR	Short	Mid	Deep	Bomb
2014	IND	16/2	411	32	49	444	65%	+3.1	13.9	3	2	6.5	--	+1.2	9	-0.2%	--	47	--	61	48%	20%	11%	22%
2015	IND	16/10	836	64	105	733	61%	-0.3	11.5	6	2	4.2	51	-0.3	7	1.1%	49	110	43	121	35%	43%	17%	6%
2016	IND	9/7	468	30	56	307	54%	-2.9	10.2	7	3	2.6	89	-1.1	4	-1.9%	58	50	63	49	35%	39%	17%	9%
2017	IND			66	109	781	61%	--	11.8	6						-4.3%								

A touchdown machine in 2016, Moncrief continued his 2015 pattern of looking like a terrific talent when he was on the field, then struggling with nagging injuries for weeks at a time. Last season those injuries kept him off the field, whereas in previous years they had just kept him from starting and playing at 100 percent. The Colts have a keeper on pure talent, but, as with Dwayne Allen, the injuries could make them lean towards pushing him out the door as we enter the last year of his rookie contract. There's nothing that Moncrief can't do on the field—he just has to stay there.

Chris Moore   Height: 6-1   Weight: 206   College: Cincinnati   Draft: 2016/4 (107)   Born: 16-Jun-1993   Age: 24   Risk: Green

Year	Team	G/GS	Snaps	Rec	Pass	Yds	C%	+/-	Yd/C	TD	Drop	YAC	Rk	YAC+	BTkl	DVOA	Rk	DYAR	Rk	YAR	Short	Mid	Deep	Bomb
2016	BAL	15/0	162	7	16	46	44%	-3.8	6.6	0	3	2.7	--	-2.1	0	-66.1%	--	-68	--	-63	69%	13%	13%	6%
2017	BAL			11	21	126	52%	--	11.4	0						-20.1%								

Moore's game at Cincinnati was "run downfield, look for ball, repeat." So filling the Jacoby Jones Memorial role in Baltimore's offense was a natural fit for his skill set. Now if he could learn to return kicks like Jones, he might have a more-defined future in the NFL. As it stands, he needs some growth somewhere to be good enough to get a guaranteed roster spot.

J.J. Nelson

Height: 5-10   Weight: 156   College: Alabama-Birmingham   Draft: 2015/5 (159)   Born: 24-Apr-1992   Age: 25   Risk: Yellow

Year	Team	G/GS	Snaps	Rec	Pass	Yds	C%	+/-	Yd/C	TD	Drop	YAC	Rk	YAC+	BTkl	DVOA	Rk	DYAR	Rk	YAR	Short	Mid	Deep	Bomb
2015	ARI	11/2	148	11	27	299	41%	+0.0	27.2	2	0	5.1	--	+0.4	2	25.7%	--	84	--	82	7%	24%	34%	34%
2016	ARI	15/6	471	34	74	568	46%	-5.5	16.7	6	7	5.1	27	+1.2	5	-2.3%	59	62	60	70	12%	45%	22%	22%
2017	ARI			46	95	780	48%	--	17.0	6							-3.0%								

Nelson was forced into a larger role in 2016 thanks to injuries to John Brown and Jaron Brown, and it's hard to argue he wasn't exciting. His 19.3 yards per reception over the past two years tops anyone with at least 25 catches. By that metric, he has been the league's best home run hitter. He ranked sixth in the league in YAC+ (plus-1.2) and was targeted an average of 17.0 yards downfield. That's all great when he was catching the ball, but that was far from a guarantee; Nelson was only 75th in receiving plus-minus (minus-5.5), meaning that even after adjusting for the deep shots he was given, he wasn't hauling in enough passes. In baseball terms, that makes him more Joey Gallo than Aaron Judge; you have to put up with a lot of strikeouts to get to the good stuff.

Jordy Nelson

Height: 6-2   Weight: 217   College: Kansas State   Draft: 2008/2 (36)   Born: 31-May-1985   Age: 32   Risk: Yellow

Year	Team	G/GS	Snaps	Rec	Pass	Yds	C%	+/-	Yd/C	TD	Drop	YAC	Rk	YAC+	BTkl	DVOA	Rk	DYAR	Rk	YAR	Short	Mid	Deep	Bomb
2014	GB	16/16	959	98	151	1519	65%	+11.6	15.5	13	3	5.1	27	+0.6	11	26.8%	8	482	2	487	27%	45%	16%	12%
2016	GB	16/16	1015	97	152	1257	64%	+7.6	13.0	14	9	3.7	61	+0.1	3	19.2%	8	382	3	366	26%	43%	19%	12%
2017	GB			90	139	1286	65%	--	14.3	12							19.9%								

Jordy Nelson's importance to the Packers was emphasized more by his absence in 2015 than it ever could have been by his presence. When he returned in 2016 he put up impressive numbers, but had a tougher time getting open on vertical routes. Nelson averaged at least 15.0 yards per reception in each of the four seasons that preceded his injury. He only averaged 13.0 yards per reception in 2016. He still put up big total numbers, but it was obvious that he wasn't at the same peak that he had been previously.

Putting another 12 months between him and his surgery will only help Nelson reclaim that lost athleticism. The positive signs for the Packers are that Nelson looked more explosive towards the end of last season than he did at the beginning. The concerning issue is that Nelson is now going to be a 32-year-old playing a young man's position. The benefit that comes from time after surgery will need to fend off the decline that comes with age.

DeVante Parker

Height: 6-3   Weight: 209   College: Louisville   Draft: 2015/1 (14)   Born: 20-Jan-1993   Age: 24   Risk: Yellow

Year	Team	G/GS	Snaps	Rec	Pass	Yds	C%	+/-	Yd/C	TD	Drop	YAC	Rk	YAC+	BTkl	DVOA	Rk	DYAR	Rk	YAR	Short	Mid	Deep	Bomb
2015	MIA	14/4	468	26	50	494	52%	+1.3	19.0	3	3	3.8	61	-0.7	6	11.4%	23	93	48	90	13%	57%	13%	17%
2016	MIA	15/8	736	56	88	744	64%	+4.6	13.3	4	3	4.2	50	-0.2	6	7.8%	31	141	36	141	33%	39%	9%	19%
2017	MIA			64	109	905	59%	--	14.1	7							3.2%								

Each year you will find numerous stories that talk of a player showing up in "the best shape of his life" for offseason work. Parker has been that player for Miami this summer. He has apparently figured out that staying healthy is key to having success in this league, so he's getting "the best sleep" of his life. His practice habits are much better. He's going "hard all the time now," and according to the *Miami Herald*'s Armando Salguero, "it is game-speed hard." *Oh, so hard.* That all sounds great, but we'll see if it translates in September when the games matter.

So far, Parker has shown he has first-round talent, but the consistency has not been there. He really is the most talented wideout on Miami's roster, but the offense has continued to feed Jarvis Landry more even though Parker is capable of bigger plays. A third-year breakout would not be unusual for a receiver of Parker's caliber. Roddy White (2007 Falcons) and Demaryius Thomas (2012 Broncos) have both done that as first-round picks in the last decade. Even Braylon Edwards (2007 Browns) once exploded for 1,289 yards and 16 touchdowns in his third season after two lesser years. Parker is a good fit for Adam Gase's offense, but we'll just have to see if he has earned more trust from Ryan Tannehill.

Cordarrelle Patterson Height: 6-2   Weight: 216   College: Tennessee   Draft: 2013/1 (29)   Born: 17-Mar-1991   Age: 26   Risk: Yellow

Year	Team	G/GS	Snaps	Rec	Pass	Yds	C%	+/-	Yd/C	TD	Drop	YAC	Rk	YAC+	BTkl	DVOA	Rk	DYAR	Rk	YAR	Short	Mid	Deep	Bomb
2014	MIN	16/7	566	33	67	384	49%	-4.8	11.6	1	1	4.8	35	+0.1	7	-25.0%	85	-64	85	-46	39%	37%	12%	12%
2015	MIN	16/1	58	2	2	10	100%	+0.4	5.0	0	0	2.0	--	-4.9	1	13.1%	--	3	--	2	50%	50%	0%	0%
2016	MIN	16/8	531	52	70	453	74%	+3.5	8.7	2	2	6.4	5	+0.4	19	-9.5%	71	17	71	28	70%	18%	9%	3%
2017	OAK			30	45	319	67%	--	10.6	2							-2.8%								

It is hard to believe that Patterson was a first-round selection by the Vikings in 2013, but after reflecting on that draft's first round, it may not be that crazy. Even Tavon Austin went No. 8, and Patterson at least hasn't cost a team that much money or draft capital. Patterson is quite arguably the best kickoff returner in the league, but he leaves a lot to be desired as a wideout. Last season, Patterson split his time evenly out wide and in the slot on his 70 targets, and he did have 19 screen passes. He's a little more than just a bubble-screen receiver, but not by much. Patterson caught 1-of-8 passes thrown more than 15 yards beyond the line of scrimmage, and had two drops. On the plus side, he did have 2016's second-highest broken-tackle rate (32.2 percent) for anyone with at least 50 touches.

Quinton Patton Height: 6-0   Weight: 204   College: Louisiana Tech   Draft: 2013/4 (128)   Born: 9-Aug-1990   Age: 27   Risk: N/A

Year	Team	G/GS	Snaps	Rec	Pass	Yds	C%	+/-	Yd/C	TD	Drop	YAC	Rk	YAC+	BTkl	DVOA	Rk	DYAR	Rk	YAR	Short	Mid	Deep	Bomb
2014	SF	4/0	86	3	8	44	38%	-1.4	14.7	0	0	0.0	--	-5.4	0	-37.2%	--	-18	--	-18	38%	50%	0%	13%
2015	SF	16/4	424	30	57	394	53%	-5.6	13.1	1	3	7.1	6	+1.6	6	-14.7%	79	-9	78	-23	48%	33%	12%	8%
2016	SF	14/14	701	37	63	408	59%	-2.8	11.0	0	3	5.4	16	-0.1	4	-29.5%	92	-84	91	-64	43%	36%	16%	5%

You know your team is desperate at wide receiver when they add a guy who couldn't even stick in San Francisco. That's just what the Jets did in May when they added Patton. Then a few weeks later they put him on IR for undisclosed reasons, then released him with an injury settlement. Patton might get another chance somewhere if he gets healthy, but even then he'll be a 27-year-old wide receiver with just one touchdown catch in his career and severely limited upside.

Charone Peake Height: 6-2   Weight: 209   College: Clemson   Draft: 2016/7 (241)   Born: 16-Oct-1992   Age: 25   Risk: Yellow

Year	Team	G/GS	Snaps	Rec	Pass	Yds	C%	+/-	Yd/C	TD	Drop	YAC	Rk	YAC+	BTkl	DVOA	Rk	DYAR	Rk	YAR	Short	Mid	Deep	Bomb
2016	NYJ	15/1	323	19	35	186	54%	-3.0	9.8	0	2	3.7	--	-0.8	2	-32.6%	--	-51	--	-44	53%	25%	22%	0%
2017	NYJ			15	27	164	56%	--	10.9	0							-19.3%								

Peake's rookie season was very weird. He saw as many as ten targets in a single game as a reserve player, but he wasn't targeted even one time in his only start. He never caught a touchdown pass, but he did score a 40-yard touchdown against Seattle when he scooped up a Ryan Fitzpatrick fumble that the Seahawks thought was an incomplete pass. By default, Peake enters camp as the Jets' third receiver, but he is in severe danger of losing that job to rookies ArDarius Stewart and Chad Hansen.

Breshad Perriman Height: 6-2   Weight: 212   College: UCF   Draft: 2015/1 (26)   Born: 10-Sep-1993   Age: 24   Risk: Yellow

Year	Team	G/GS	Snaps	Rec	Pass	Yds	C%	+/-	Yd/C	TD	Drop	YAC	Rk	YAC+	BTkl	DVOA	Rk	DYAR	Rk	YAR	Short	Mid	Deep	Bomb
2016	BAL	16/1	484	33	66	499	50%	-5.9	15.1	3	5	5.2	25	+0.6	2	-8.7%	67	21	70	20	28%	40%	13%	19%
2017	BAL			52	97	798	54%	--	15.3	6							-0.8%								

Noted *Boondocks* philosopher Gin Rummy offered the following quote: "What I'm saying is that there are known knowns and that there are known unknowns. But there are also unknown unknowns; things we don't know that we don't know." In that spirit, we present Breshad Perriman's NFL career: a physical dream of an NFL talent who played zero NFL snaps in 2015 and was arguably not fully healthy at all last year either. He led Baltimore in failed receptions in 2016, but what does that really tell us? This is the kind of player who makes projections feel pointless. Either he's going to turn around and play up to his draft status, or he's going to get a two-sentence blurb in *FOA 2018* and be out of the book the year after that.

Terrelle Pryor

Height: 6-6   Weight: 233   College: Ohio State   Draft: 2011/3 (SUP)   Born: 20-Jun-1989   Age: 28   Risk: Red

Year	Team	G/GS	Snaps	Rec	Pass	Yds	C%	+/-	Yd/C	TD	Drop	YAC	Rk	YAC+	BTkl	DVOA	Rk	DYAR	Rk	YAR	Short	Mid	Deep	Bomb
2015	CLE	3/2	91	1	8	42	13%	-2.8	42.0	0	1	5.0	--	-2.3	1	-67.7%	--	-34	--	-32	0%	71%	14%	14%
2016	CLE	16/15	899	77	140	1007	55%	-1.8	13.1	4	7	2.8	85	-1.4	6	-2.5%	60	112	49	115	20%	52%	12%	16%
2017	WAS			71	125	1106	57%	--	15.6	7						3.9%								

Pryor is already one of the more unusual players in NFL history. He is one of six players all-time (and the first since Marlin Briscoe in the 1970s) to gain 1,000 yards passing and 1,000 yards receiving in his career, and if he repeats his 2016 output this season, he'll be the only member of the 2,000/2,000 club. While he has maxed out his quarterback ceiling as an option threat and gadget passer, his limits as a receiver remain unknown. His performance in Cleveland is difficult to evaluate. His DVOA was much higher than the Browns' other wideouts, and he was no doubt held back by the pile of rejects who were throwing him passes. But some of that damage was also self-inflicted. His YAC+ was worse than average, as were his rates of drops and broken tackles. He was maddeningly inconsistent even late in the year. He had five catches for 97 yards in Week 11 against Pittsburgh and then six for 131 a week later against the Giants, but followed that with eight catches for 58 yards over his next three games. Pryor apparently overestimated the demand for his services in free agency, signing with Washington late in the process for one year and just $6 million. If he continues to develop this season—and remember, he's only 28—he could get a major payday in 2018.

Brian Quick

Height: 6-4   Weight: 220   College: Appalachian State   Draft: 2012/2 (33)   Born: 5-Jun-1989   Age: 28   Risk: Red

Year	Team	G/GS	Snaps	Rec	Pass	Yds	C%	+/-	Yd/C	TD	Drop	YAC	Rk	YAC+	BTkl	DVOA	Rk	DYAR	Rk	YAR	Short	Mid	Deep	Bomb
2014	STL	7/7	339	25	39	375	64%	+4.1	15.0	3	1	2.9	--	-1.0	1	24.5%	--	115	--	119	16%	42%	21%	21%
2015	STL	13/2	351	10	32	102	31%	-7.6	10.2	0	1	3.9	--	-0.7	0	-56.7%	--	-110	--	-118	22%	41%	19%	19%
2016	LARM	16/8	691	41	77	564	53%	-3.7	13.8	3	4	4.3	46	+0.2	6	-17.1%	80	-28	79	-15	34%	41%	11%	15%
2017	WAS			10	20	141	50%	--	14.1	2						-12.8%								

You expect big results out of second-round draft picks, and Quick paid off for the Rams with 105 catches, 1,499 yards, and 10 touchdowns. Except that was not in 2016—that was his entire five-year tenure with the team. Quick couldn't even nail down a starting role on one of the NFL's worst wideout squads. He joins a Washington team that is loaded with unproven receivers, but his spot on the roster is not guaranteed. ESPN's John Keim reported that Quick was behind not only Terrelle Pryor, Jamison Crowder, and Josh Doctson in OTAs, but also 2014 fifth-rounder Ryan Grant, 2016 UDFA Maurice Harris, and rookie sixth-rounder Robert Davis.

Paul Richardson

Height: 6-0   Weight: 175   College: Colorado   Draft: 2014/2 (45)   Born: 4/13/1992   Age: 25   Risk: Green

Year	Team	G/GS	Snaps	Rec	Pass	Yds	C%	+/-	Yd/C	TD	Drop	YAC	Rk	YAC+	BTkl	DVOA	Rk	DYAR	Rk	YAR	Short	Mid	Deep	Bomb
2014	SEA	15/6	497	29	44	271	66%	+4.1	9.3	1	1	2.2	--	-2.6	2	-15.2%	--	-8	--	-1	35%	43%	8%	15%
2015	SEA	1/0	6	1	1	40	100%	+0.7	40.0	0	0	12.0	--	+3.4	0	253.5%	--	21	--	21	0%	0%	0%	100%
2016	SEA	15/0	338	21	36	288	58%	+2.9	13.7	1	0	4.6	--	+0.3	1	7.9%	--	56	--	61	25%	44%	16%	16%
2017	SEA			19	33	262	58%	--	13.8	1						-2.6%								

After Tyler Lockett went down with a gruesome leg injury against the Cardinals in Week 16, Richardson filled the void in a major way by making three spectacular catches against the Lions in the wild-card round of the playoffs (even if one of them technically should not have counted). The story with Richardson has always been that of a talented player who just could not stay healthy after the Seahawks selected him in the second round in 2014. With Doug Baldwin and Jimmy Graham entrenched as the top two targets for Seattle in 2017, and Tyler Lockett perhaps regaining his rookie level of performance after he returns to the field, Richardson may not see many balls thrown his way. But on the occasions when Russell Wilson does look his way? Get your popcorn ready.

Seth Roberts

Height: 6-2 | Weight: 195 | College: West Alabama | Draft: 2014/FA | Born: 22-Feb-1991 | Age: 26 | Risk: Yellow

Year	Team	G/GS	Snaps	Rec	Pass	Yds	C%	+/-	Yd/C	TD	Drop	YAC	Rk	YAC+	BTkl	DVOA	Rk	DYAR	Rk	YAR	Short	Mid	Deep	Bomb
2015	OAK	16/5	565	32	55	480	58%	-0.8	15.0	5	4	4.2	50	-0.2	2	13.3%	19	114	38	127	39%	43%	11%	7%
2016	OAK	16/6	749	38	77	397	49%	-12.3	10.4	5	9	5.3	20	+0.4	14	-18.6%	83	-37	84	-54	47%	38%	10%	5%
2017	OAK			35	66	463	53%	--	13.2	4						-10.9%								

Roberts was one of the league's worst No. 3 receiving options in 2016. In fact, he gained more yards on one play (a tackle-breaking 41-yard game-winning overtime touchdown in Tampa Bay) than he did in 14 of his regular-season games played. Derek Carr was a minus-13.1 in passing plus-minus while targeting Roberts, and plus-5.6 to everyone else in Oakland. Tight end Jared Cook could be a more attractive option in the slot than Roberts this season.

Aldrick Robinson

Height: 5-10 | Weight: 182 | College: Southern Methodist | Draft: 2011/6 (178) | Born: 11-Apr-1988 | Age: 29 | Risk: Green

Year	Team	G/GS	Snaps	Rec	Pass	Yds	C%	+/-	Yd/C	TD	Drop	YAC	Rk	YAC+	BTkl	DVOA	Rk	DYAR	Rk	YAR	Short	Mid	Deep	Bomb
2014	WAS	5/0	25	1	3	6	33%	-0.7	6.0	0	0	8.0	--	+0.1	0	-71.5%	--	-14	--	-11	33%	33%	0%	33%
2016	ATL	16/1	315	20	32	323	63%	+1.5	16.2	2	1	3.8	--	+0.3	1	24.5%	--	91	--	90	19%	52%	26%	3%
2017	SF			11	19	178	58%	--	16.2	1						3.8%								

Kyle Shanahan has brought in a lot of His Guys to help install his system, and Robinson might be the one with the least non-Shanahan upside. Robinson spent 2012, 2013, and 2016 with Shanahan in Washington and Atlanta, putting up about 16 catches and 300 yards per season; typical fourth-receiver material. His non-Shanahan years saw him waived in 2014 and out of the league in 2015. He is a deep threat, but no more than a streak-runner. 49ers fans may overrate him, however, because he exploded for 111 yards against their team in Week 15 last season. That one game accounts for 12 percent of Robinson's *career* yardage.

Allen Robinson

Height: 6-2 | Weight: 220 | College: Penn St. | Draft: 2014/2 (61) | Born: 8/24/1993 | Age: 24 | Risk: Green

Year	Team	G/GS	Snaps	Rec	Pass	Yds	C%	+/-	Yd/C	TD	Drop	YAC	Rk	YAC+	BTkl	DVOA	Rk	DYAR	Rk	YAR	Short	Mid	Deep	Bomb
2014	JAC	10/8	516	48	81	548	59%	-0.2	11.4	2	1	3.3	71	-1.0	3	-11.1%	64	10	66	9	27%	53%	9%	11%
2015	JAC	16/16	983	80	151	1400	53%	+1.4	17.5	14	5	4.5	43	+0.2	8	14.0%	16	318	8	343	22%	30%	30%	17%
2016	JAC	16/16	1047	73	151	883	48%	-10.4	12.1	6	10	2.8	87	-1.2	5	-12.0%	74	8	73	-16	24%	41%	24%	11%
2017	JAC			73	127	979	57%	--	13.4	9						0.4%								

Robinson led the NFL in touchdown catches in 2015, drawing praise that went well beyond Matt Harmon. But as was the case with Allen Hurns opposite him, 2016 was a season to forget for Robinson. His frustration, sometimes with his teammates and sometimes with himself, was visible at times. Four games under 20 yards and just two over 100 was not what anybody expected from him in 2016. The increased focus on the run offense might limit his volume in 2017 unless the defense struggles, but it will make his work on downfield passes maybe even more important.

Chester Rogers

Height: 6-1 | Weight: 180 | College: Grambling State | Draft: 2016/FA | Born: 12-Jan-1994 | Age: 23 | Risk: Green

Year	Team	G/GS	Snaps	Rec	Pass	Yds	C%	+/-	Yd/C	TD	Drop	YAC	Rk	YAC+	BTkl	DVOA	Rk	DYAR	Rk	YAR	Short	Mid	Deep	Bomb
2016	IND	14/2	434	19	34	273	56%	-0.6	14.4	0	3	2.8	--	-0.8	2	5.4%	--	51	--	41	41%	15%	38%	6%
2017	IND			11	18	174	61%	--	15.8	2						11.0%								

Rogers drew exuberant praise at OTAs this year, being called "outstanding" by general manager Chris Ballard and "a guy that you love" by offensive coordinator Rob Chudzinski. A UDFA from Grambling, Rogers seems likely to offer some combination of injury-driven targets and punt returns in 2017. But between the lack of pedigree and the "hard worker" praise, we might be looking at a Seth Roberts ceiling rather than an actual game-changer.

Eli Rogers   Height: 5-10   Weight: 180   College: Louisville   Draft: 2015/FA   Born: 23-Dec-1992   Age: 25   Risk: Yellow

Year	Team	G/GS	Snaps	Rec	Pass	Yds	C%	+/-	Yd/C	TD	Drop	YAC	Rk	YAC+	BTkl	DVOA	Rk	DYAR	Rk	YAR	Short	Mid	Deep	Bomb
2016	PIT	13/8	550	48	66	594	73%	+4.3	12.4	3	2	4.3	48	-0.6	4	18.3%	10	150	32	150	45%	31%	15%	9%
2017	PIT			37	55	466	67%	--	12.6	2							9.0%								

Rogers was a nice surprise in his first healthy NFL season, lining up primarily in the slot and giving Ben Roethlisberger a reliable target on curl, slant, and drag routes. He finished as Pittsburgh's second-leading wideout despite missing two games with a toe injury and a third for unspecified disciplinary reasons, allegedly for showing up late for a walkthrough. To some degree, he's redundant on a team that has Antonio Brown, but then that just gives them quality depth behind one of their best players. Rogers is expected to stay in the slot this year, with Brown, Martavis Bryant, and second-round rookie JuJu Smith-Schuster handling duties outside.

John Ross   Height: 5-11   Weight: 188   College: Washington   Draft: 2017/1 (9)   Born: 27-Nov-1994   Age: 23   Risk: Red

Year	Team	G/GS	Snaps	Rec	Pass	Yds	C%	+/-	Yd/C	TD	Drop	YAC	Rk	YAC+	BTkl	DVOA	Rk	DYAR	Rk	YAR	Short	Mid	Deep	Bomb
2017	CIN			51	84	772	61%	--	15.1	4							7.1%								

The fastest 40-yard-dash in combine history. The No. 1 wide receiver prospect by our Playmaker Score metrics. And somehow, it still seems like he's not a sure thing. Concerns about Ross' size should be mollified by his performance in the red zone at Washington, but he also has a lengthy injury history and is going to have to survive NFL punishment. Cincinnati will at least get field-stretching ability out of him this year, but Ross' health will determine just how smart this pick looks in three years.

Eddie Royal   Height: 5-9   Weight: 184   College: Virginia Tech   Draft: 2008/2 (42)   Born: 21-May-1986   Age: 31   Risk: N/A

Year	Team	G/GS	Snaps	Rec	Pass	Yds	C%	+/-	Yd/C	TD	Drop	YAC	Rk	YAC+	BTkl	DVOA	Rk	DYAR	Rk	YAR	Short	Mid	Deep	Bomb
2014	SD	16/11	760	62	91	778	68%	+7.0	12.5	7	3	5.8	13	-0.1	6	12.8%	17	183	26	159	51%	22%	16%	11%
2015	CHI	9/9	477	37	50	238	74%	-1.0	6.4	1	3	4.8	35	-1.8	8	-34.0%	87	-81	84	-83	71%	24%	2%	4%
2016	CHI	9/1	311	33	43	369	77%	+1.8	11.2	2	0	5.9	--	+0.7	4	0.6%	--	41	--	38	58%	33%	9%	0%

There's no question that Eddie Royal can still be a quality NFL receiver. Royal's game should age well as a slot receiver who runs precise routes. So long as he has his quickness, he will be able to get open. The problem for Royal is his health. He played nine games in each of his two seasons with the Bears before being released. But Royal should be able to play three or four more seasons for somebody if he can stay healthy.

Curtis Samuel   Height: 5-11   Weight: 196   College: Ohio State   Draft: 2017/2 (40)   Born: 11-Aug-1996   Age: 21   Risk: Red

Year	Team	G/GS	Snaps	Rec	Pass	Yds	C%	+/-	Yd/C	TD	Drop	YAC	Rk	YAC+	BTkl	DVOA	Rk	DYAR	Rk	YAR	Short	Mid	Deep	Bomb
2017	CAR			45	77	467	58%	--	10.4	3							-12.5%								

Samuel put up more than 1,500 total yards as a combo running back/wideout in Columbus, with a sturdy 76 percent catch rate. But there is reason to question his ability to become a pro wide receiver. Only 51 percent of his receptions were successful plays by our baselines. Samuel seldom ran pro-style routes at Ohio State, instead usually lining up as an H-back and taking advantage of linebackers. His hands are only middling, and pre-draft scouting reports noted his tendency to body-catch far too often. Due to his small size, he could struggle against press man coverage, and he didn't do much blocking for his fellow Buckeyes.

Samuel's sky-high Playmaker Score (97.4 percent) is artificially boosted by his heavy rushing numbers. In that regard, he resembles Dexter McCluster, and the best-case analogue is probably Tavon Austin. The Panthers would probably take that—Austin has been disappointing for a top-ten pick, but his production is viable for a second-rounder. On the other hand, Samuel could turn into fellow Buckeyes alum Jalin Marshall, a tweener without a true NFL position. That would be a real waste for Carolina.

Emmanuel Sanders Height: 5-11   Weight: 186   College: Southern Methodist   Draft: 2010/3 (82)   Born: 17-Mar-1987   Age: 30   Risk: Green

Year	Team	G/GS	Snaps	Rec	Pass	Yds	C%	+/-	Yd/C	TD	Drop	YAC	Rk	YAC+	BTkl	DVOA	Rk	DYAR	Rk	YAR	Short	Mid	Deep	Bomb
2014	DEN	16/16	1000	101	141	1404	72%	+16.3	13.9	9	0	3.5	65	-1.4	6	29.6%	4	481	3	457	40%	27%	15%	19%
2015	DEN	15/15	859	76	137	1135	55%	-0.7	14.9	6	6	4.8	36	+0.0	5	-4.1%	58	90	49	110	24%	38%	19%	20%
2016	DEN	16/16	869	79	137	1032	58%	+2.4	13.1	5	3	3.0	79	-0.9	12	-3.3%	61	103	51	82	29%	42%	14%	16%
2017	DEN			77	132	1012	58%	--	13.1	7						-2.0%								

Sanders signed a contract extension last September for about $11 million per season, or $3 million less than teammate Demaryius Thomas. It wouldn't be hard to argue that Sanders has outplayed Thomas in each of the last three seasons, with fewer drops and an ability to make tough grabs down the field that he rarely ever showed in Pittsburgh. Last season, Thomas did better in advanced metrics, though that's largely because Sanders did not fare well with rookie Paxton Lynch. He had a 0.0% DVOA on passes from Trevor Siemian, but minus-15.3% DVOA on passes from Lynch. Sanders had 71 DYAR on 13 dig routes (only Julio Jones had more among wide receivers), but only 32 DYAR on his other 125 targets.

Mohamed Sanu Height: 6-2   Weight: 211   College: Rutgers   Draft: 2012/3 (83)   Born: 22-Aug-1989   Age: 28   Risk: Green

Year	Team	G/GS	Snaps	Rec	Pass	Yds	C%	+/-	Yd/C	TD	Drop	YAC	Rk	YAC+	BTkl	DVOA	Rk	DYAR	Rk	YAR	Short	Mid	Deep	Bomb
2014	CIN	16/13	986	56	98	790	57%	-6.7	14.1	5	6	5.8	16	+0.7	6	0.1%	43	99	40	91	35%	40%	12%	12%
2015	CIN	16/4	643	33	49	394	67%	-0.2	11.9	0	0	6.2	--	+1.0	7	-8.3%	--	16	--	14	57%	23%	15%	4%
2016	ATL	15/15	744	59	81	653	73%	+5.7	11.1	4	2	4.9	32	+0.2	10	6.5%	36	123	44	135	41%	44%	11%	4%
2017	ATL			58	84	678	69%	--	11.7	5						10.3%								

Sanu left Cincinnati for Arthur Blank's big dollars, and to be a consistent No. 2 option. In many cases, this results in heartbreak, but not only did Mo get to escape playoff purgatory for a Super Bowl start, he boosted his efficiency even as his targets significantly rose. The No. 2 extends to his preferred down, as in second—the lion's share of Sanu's good work took place there (27.5% DVOA, vs. 0.9% on first down and minus-3.8% on third/fourth). He lined up in the slot on 70 of his 80 targets; those ten out wide were forgettable indeed (-26.9% DVOA). Sanu's play tended to wax and wane in Cincy, and that could well happen in 2017, though Matt Ryan is more dependable on that front than Andy Dalton. Sanu's aggressive blocking will make him valuable even if his receiving numbers drop.

Tajae Sharpe Height: 6-2   Weight: 194   College: Massachusetts   Draft: 2016/5 (140)   Born: 23-Dec-1994   Age: 23   Risk: Blue

Year	Team	G/GS	Snaps	Rec	Pass	Yds	C%	+/-	Yd/C	TD	Drop	YAC	Rk	YAC+	BTkl	DVOA	Rk	DYAR	Rk	YAR	Short	Mid	Deep	Bomb
2016	TEN	16/10	786	41	83	522	49%	-5.9	12.7	2	2	2.1	91	-1.8	3	-9.2%	69	23	69	8	20%	43%	28%	8%
2017	TEN			5	9	68	56%	--	13.6	1						-6.8%								

Last June, Sharpe was a revelation, the fifth-round rookie who kept drawing praise from coaches and quickly surpassed older and more pedigreed players. Ultimately, his seven catches and 76 yards in the season opener proved to be his high marks for the season. His precision and ability to follow directions proved less important than his inability to separate or win in contested situations. He averaged just 28 receiving yards per game after Week 3, lost his starting role by season's end, missed minicamp and OTAs with a foot injury that should be healed by training camp, and allegedly beat up a bar patron after the Titans drafted Corey Davis (as of late June, no criminal charges had been filed). Sharpe is no lock to make the team after Tennessee's offseason additions, and seems unlikely to earn regular snaps barring injury even if he does.

Russell Shepard Height: 6-1   Weight: 195   College: Louisiana St.   Draft: 2013/FA   Born: 17-Sep-1990   Age: 27   Risk: Green

Year	Team	G/GS	Snaps	Rec	Pass	Yds	C%	+/-	Yd/C	TD	Drop	YAC	Rk	YAC+	BTkl	DVOA	Rk	DYAR	Rk	YAR	Short	Mid	Deep	Bomb
2014	TB	16/0	154	4	8	63	50%	-0.3	15.8	0	0	5.5	--	+2.2	1	-11.7%	--	1	--	4	13%	50%	13%	25%
2015	TB	13/2	209	3	9	28	33%	-1.9	9.3	1	1	0.3	--	-2.4	0	-29.2%	--	-12	--	-12	22%	22%	33%	22%
2016	TB	14/4	434	23	40	341	58%	+1.0	14.8	2	0	3.3	--	-0.2	2	15.7%	--	89	--	98	13%	46%	31%	10%
2017	CAR			8	15	107	53%	--	13.4	0						-7.4%								

Nice pickup by the Panthers. The fiery Shepard was a special teams demon (and captain) in Tampa Bay, but jumped NFC South clubs to play on the third unit and go deep for passes from Cam Newton. Carolina's interest probably runs back to a Week 5 game against the Bucs, when Shepard clobbered Ted Ginn on a punt return, forcing a key fumble. Shepard's gunner numbers fell off last season as he was forced to play more wideout than usual due to a rash of injuries; as such, he recorded career receiving highs across the board. The Panthers will reportedly give Shepard every chance to play regularly and take targets from the likes of Devin Funchess.

Sterling Shepard   Height: 5-10   Weight: 194   College: Oklahoma   Draft: 2016/2 (40)   Born: 10-Feb-1994   Age: 23   Risk: Green

Year	Team	G/GS	Snaps	Rec	Pass	Yds	C%	+/-	Yd/C	TD	Drop	YAC	Rk	YAC+	BTkl	DVOA	Rk	DYAR	Rk	YAR	Short	Mid	Deep	Bomb
2016	NYG	16/16	1005	65	105	683	62%	-3.3	10.5	8	5	4.0	53	-0.6	9	-1.8%	55	91	54	101	35%	48%	11%	6%
2017	NYG			55	91	685	60%	--	12.5	6						-1.7%								

Shepard on passes marked as "short middle" in the play-by-play last year: 25-of-32, 297 yards, two touchdowns, 18 first downs, and 9.3 yards per target. Shepard should be effective in the same ways this season, but how many targets will be left once Odell Beckham and Brandon Marshall get fed? Shepard had a zero-target afternoon against the Browns last season because the Giants were trying to force-feed Beckham and Victor Cruz. Eli Manning actually apologized to Shepard after the game. This season, Eli may have to graduate to greeting cards.

JuJu Smith-Schuster   Height: 6-1   Weight: 215   College: USC   Draft: 2017/2 (62)   Born: 22-Nov-1996   Age: 21   Risk: Green

Year	Team	G/GS	Snaps	Rec	Pass	Yds	C%	+/-	Yd/C	TD	Drop	YAC	Rk	YAC+	BTkl	DVOA	Rk	DYAR	Rk	YAR	Short	Mid	Deep	Bomb
2017	PIT			18	27	199	67%	--	11.1	2						3.0%								

Smith-Schuster drew comparisons to Anquan Boldin before the draft as a player who can make up for a lack of blazing speed with good size and an ability to catch balls in traffic over the middle. Early reports on Pittsburgh OTAs had him working in the slot, where he would theoretically compete with Eli Rogers for playing time, but it's just as easy to see both on the field at the same time, along with Martavis Bryant and Antonio Brown split wide. That would be quite a formidable group if the Steelers wanted to spread the field with four wide receivers, something they did only seven times in 2016.

Steve Smith   Height: 5-9   Weight: 185   College: Utah   Draft: 2001/3 (74)   Born: 12-May-1979   Age: 38   Risk: N/A

Year	Team	G/GS	Snaps	Rec	Pass	Yds	C%	+/-	Yd/C	TD	Drop	YAC	Rk	YAC+	BTkl	DVOA	Rk	DYAR	Rk	YAR	Short	Mid	Deep	Bomb
2014	BAL	16/16	822	79	134	1065	59%	-3.7	13.5	6	5	4.7	37	+0.3	13	-5.4%	53	79	45	57	33%	44%	12%	11%
2015	BAL	7/7	348	46	73	670	63%	+2.3	14.6	3	1	5.6	16	+0.3	6	9.4%	30	125	36	113	36%	38%	20%	6%
2016	BAL	14/14	721	70	101	799	69%	+3.3	11.4	5	4	4.0	52	-0.4	16	7.2%	33	158	30	149	47%	40%	6%	6%

Smith leaves behind a legacy of big talk from a man who always acted taller than his stature. Securing an NFL Network gig for the next few years should only boost his Hall of Fame odds further, as he continues to create viral content by opening his mouth and being Steve Smith. The Baltimore years weren't always things of beauty, but the chip on Smith's shoulder fit right in with the persona of the team. Smith finishes with 2,146 receiving DYAR over his 16-year career, a number that is far short of the greats but also influenced by playing on a run-first team as the lone star-caliber target for most of his career. Well, that and 16 games of Matt Moore and Jimmy Clausen in 2010 that resulted in minus-150 DYAR.

Torrey Smith   Height: 6-1   Weight: 204   College: Maryland   Draft: 2011/2 (58)   Born: 26-Jan-1989   Age: 28   Risk: Green

Year	Team	G/GS	Snaps	Rec	Pass	Yds	C%	+/-	Yd/C	TD	Drop	YAC	Rk	YAC+	BTkl	DVOA	Rk	DYAR	Rk	YAR	Short	Mid	Deep	Bomb
2014	BAL	16/16	788	49	92	767	53%	-3.0	15.7	11	5	3.4	69	-1.0	6	26.8%	7	310	9	304	16%	46%	17%	22%
2015	SF	16/12	775	33	62	663	53%	+0.3	20.1	4	4	6.6	5	+1.1	1	14.3%	14	134	32	112	20%	42%	20%	17%
2016	SF	12/12	643	20	49	267	41%	-7.4	13.4	3	5	3.1	78	-1.2	2	-33.0%	93	-78	90	-69	31%	35%	15%	19%
2017	PHI			35	70	516	50%	--	14.7	4						-10.9%								

Smith was trapped for two seasons on a 49ers team both unwilling and unable to give him the kind of deep opportunities he regularly enjoyed with the Ravens. It was a weird case of a one-dimensional player getting stuck on a team with no use for his dimension, like Yngwie Malmsteen joining a reggae band. His 2016 numbers were especially bad—Smith was 5-for-17 last year on targets listed as "deep" (more than 15 yards downfield) on the play-by-play, for 139 yards, two touchdowns, two interceptions, and one play longer than 30 yards (a 53-yard completion from Colin Kaepernick). Now with the franchise that made "Air Yards" a storyline last year, Smith must prove he can still get separation along the boundary and provide a useful mix of catches and defensive pass interference penalties. Smith looked good and sounded eager to assume a leadership role during OTAs, but competition in Philly is surprisingly stiff, so nothing is guaranteed.

Willie Snead

Height: 5-11 **Weight:** 195 **College:** Ball State **Draft:** 2014/FA **Born:** 17-Oct-1992 **Age:** 25 **Risk:** Green

Year	Team	G/GS	Snaps	Rec	Pass	Yds	C%	+/-	Yd/C	TD	Drop	YAC	Rk	YAC+	BTkl	DVOA	Rk	DYAR	Rk	YAR	Short	Mid	Deep	Bomb
2015	NO	15/8	780	69	101	984	68%	+8.8	14.3	3	2	5.0	28	+0.5	9	10.1%	28	175	23	198	35%	42%	14%	9%
2016	NO	15/4	740	72	104	895	69%	+2.5	12.4	4	4	5.4	17	+0.8	12	12.5%	17	206	20	195	53%	32%	13%	2%
2017	NO			71	104	939	68%	--	13.2	7						14.6%								

The league-mandated Scrappy Undrafted Slot Guy (TM), Snead spent last season quietly hauling in a handful of receptions in almost every game, a consistent tally of between 35 and 80 yards, and the occasional touchdown. His one big game was a massive 9-for-9, 172-yard, one-touchdown performance against Oakland on opening day; he managed 723 total yards the rest of the year. The departure of Brandin Cooks makes Snead the team's No. 2 receiver behind Michael Thomas, a role he filled productively in 2015, and gives him a reasonable chance to post the first 1,000-yard season of his young career.

ArDarius Stewart

Height: 5-11 **Weight:** 204 **College:** Alabama **Draft:** 2017/3 (79) **Born:** 1-Jan-1993 **Age:** 25 **Risk:** Red

Year	Team	G/GS	Snaps	Rec	Pass	Yds	C%	+/-	Yd/C	TD	Drop	YAC	Rk	YAC+	BTkl	DVOA	Rk	DYAR	Rk	YAR	Short	Mid	Deep	Bomb
2017	NYJ			32	53	413	60%	--	12.9	2						-2.5%								

The Jets drafted Stewart hoping he could make an impact right away, but then he underwent separate surgeries on his thumb and groin, knocking him out of OTAs and minicamp and threatening to limit him in training camp. At Alabama, Stewart was somewhat lost in Calvin Ridley's shadow, but his Playmaker Rating of 73.4 percent suggests cautious optimism. The Crimson Tide made fine use of Stewart's versatility, using him on screens out of the backfield, fly sweeps, reverses, and kickoff returns. Stewart was also noted for his blocking and went 2-of-2 for 36 yards as a passer. Given the alternatives, the Jets might want to play him at quarterback.

Kenny Stills

Height: 6-0 **Weight:** 194 **College:** Oklahoma **Draft:** 2013/5 (144) **Born:** 22-Apr-1992 **Age:** 25 **Risk:** Yellow

Year	Team	G/GS	Snaps	Rec	Pass	Yds	C%	+/-	Yd/C	TD	Drop	YAC	Rk	YAC+	BTkl	DVOA	Rk	DYAR	Rk	YAR	Short	Mid	Deep	Bomb
2014	NO	15/7	617	63	84	931	75%	+15.5	14.8	3	3	3.0	80	-1.6	2	30.3%	3	285	12	301	32%	35%	19%	15%
2015	MIA	16/8	594	27	63	440	43%	-5.9	16.3	3	4	3.8	60	-1.3	0	-17.2%	80	-22	80	-26	16%	34%	26%	23%
2016	MIA	16/16	795	42	81	726	52%	-2.7	17.3	9	3	4.6	38	+0.5	4	6.8%	34	121	45	144	24%	40%	17%	19%
2017	MIA			43	82	707	52%	--	16.5	6						3.5%								

When Stills dropped a completely wide-open touchdown bomb in Week 1 in Seattle, fans may have thought it was going to be another long year for him in Miami. His 2015 debut went poorly, and he finished that Seattle game with one grab on five targets for 16 yards. However, Stills did improve, and he became effective enough to the point where he scored in nine different games last year, including four straight to end the regular season. Stills should remain the third wideout in Miami's passing game, offering more of a deep threat than DeVante Parker and Jarvis Landry. Stills also remains a case study for the impact of good quarterback play on a receiver's stats. In New Orleans with Drew Brees, Stills had a receiving plus-minus of plus-21.9. In Miami, he has been below average with both Ryan Tannehill (minus-7.5) and Matt Moore (minus-1.1). In 2016, Stills was actually not at his best on go/fly routes (32 DYAR), but instead did most of his damage (95 DYAR) on post/corner routes.

Jaelen Strong

Height: 6-2   Weight: 217   College: Arizona State   Draft: 2015/3 (70)   Born: 25-Jan-1994   Age: 23   Risk: Green

Year	Team	G/GS	Snaps	Rec	Pass	Yds	C%	+/-	Yd/C	TD	Drop	YAC	Rk	YAC+	BTkl	DVOA	Rk	DYAR	Rk	YAR	Short	Mid	Deep	Bomb
2015	HOU	10/1	282	14	24	161	58%	-0.8	11.5	3	1	4.5	--	+0.3	1	7.1%	--	35	--	45	50%	27%	14%	9%
2016	HOU	8/2	300	14	24	131	58%	-2.0	9.4	0	1	2.3	--	-2.5	0	-29.5%	--	-32	--	-44	57%	35%	4%	4%
2017	HOU			14	24	149	58%	--	10.6	0						-16.5%								

A big-bodied possession threat, Strong is rapidly running out of chances to show that he belongs in the NFL. Strong's a non-factor on special teams, and despite the third-round pedigree and a nice Playmaker Score coming out of Arizona State, has thus far been unable to play ahead of Keith Mumphery. With only Braxton Miller clearly in his path to playing time, this is Strong's last real chance.

Ryan Switzer

Height: 5-8   Weight: 181   College: North Carolina   Draft: 2017/4 (133)   Born: 4-Nov-1994   Age: 23   Risk: Red

Year	Team	G/GS	Snaps	Rec	Pass	Yds	C%	+/-	Yd/C	TD	Drop	YAC	Rk	YAC+	BTkl	DVOA	Rk	DYAR	Rk	YAR	Short	Mid	Deep	Bomb
2017	DAL			15	22	161	68%	--	10.7	1						-0.5%								

The SB Nation Cowboys site "Blogging the Boys" ran a Switzer article in early May with the headline "Why 'Fearless' Ryan Switzer Will Quickly Become a Fan Favorite in Dallas." Hey, we love the SB Nation Network, and we know how important it is to generate clickability in a headline, but … can we try a tiny bit harder than slapping the "fan favorite" label on, and praising the courage of, the latest little white guy? What is this, Barstool?

Switzer is, in fact, short, muscular, quick and Caucasian, but those are no reasons to get problematic with the dog whistling. Come to think of it, this player comment may be problematic as well, since it reinforces a stereotype while ostensibly trying to combat a stereotype. As long as we don't mention Cole Beasley … rats, we just did. When did everything become so fraught with semiotic peril? Switzer should replace Lucky Whitehead as the Cowboys' return man and as a package screens-and-reverses player, OK? And you are allowed to like him for any reason you wish. Don't @ us, please.

Golden Tate

Height: 5-10   Weight: 199   College: Notre Dame   Draft: 2010/2 (60)   Born: 2-Aug-1988   Age: 29   Risk: Green

Year	Team	G/GS	Snaps	Rec	Pass	Yds	C%	+/-	Yd/C	TD	Drop	YAC	Rk	YAC+	BTkl	DVOA	Rk	DYAR	Rk	YAR	Short	Mid	Deep	Bomb
2014	DET	16/16	924	99	144	1331	69%	+4.9	13.4	4	2	7.0	4	+1.5	18	6.7%	31	214	22	244	49%	33%	13%	4%
2015	DET	16/16	926	90	128	813	70%	+1.7	9.0	6	5	5.9	10	+0.1	27	-1.7%	51	113	39	74	58%	32%	7%	3%
2016	DET	16/16	866	91	135	1077	67%	+3.0	11.8	4	9	6.8	3	+0.9	27	-1.8%	54	114	48	111	50%	34%	6%	9%
2017	DET			92	132	1001	70%	--	10.9	5						4.7%								

Tate has had an interesting career. He was a pseudo-No. 1 receiver in Seattle, where he was effective on both deep passes and after the catch. He looked the part of a budding star in 2014 when the Lions needed him to step up while Calvin Johnson was injured. He was relegated to more of a dink-and-dunk approach under Jim Bob Cooter's offense in 2015. Then last year, with Johnson gone entirely, Tate fell somewhere between his first two Detroit seasons, but still logged more than 90 receptions for the third straight year. Still, it's a wonder whether the Lions are utilizing him best by not going to him downfield more. Tate's 29 wide receiver screens led the league. Tate's YAC+ was plus-0.8 in Seattle and is plus-0.9 in Detroit, but his average depth of target has fallen from 11.1 yards in the Emerald City to 7.2 yards in Motown.

Jordan Taylor

Height: 6-5   Weight: 210   College: Rice   Draft: 2015/FA   Born: 18-Feb-1992   Age: 25   Risk: Green

Year	Team	G/GS	Snaps	Rec	Pass	Yds	C%	+/-	Yd/C	TD	Drop	YAC	Rk	YAC+	BTkl	DVOA	Rk	DYAR	Rk	YAR	Short	Mid	Deep	Bomb
2016	DEN	16/0	277	16	25	209	64%	+1.5	13.1	2	0	5.3	--	+1.5	2	2.7%	--	32	--	29	29%	50%	21%	0%
2017	DEN			19	31	222	61%	--	11.7	1						-6.3%								

Taylor is best known for helping Peyton Manning rehab when he was an undrafted rookie on the practice squad in 2015. He got into the real games last season and caught his first two NFL touchdowns, but the Broncos still seem disinterested in getting a third receiver to step up in this offense. Taylor will have to battle with Cody Latimer, Bennie Fowler, and rookie Carlos Henderson for playing time.

Taywan Taylor   Height: 5-11   Weight: 203   College: Western Kentucky   Draft: 2017/3 (72)   Born: 2-Mar-1995   Age: 22   Risk: Yellow

Year	Team	G/GS	Snaps	Rec	Pass	Yds	C%	+/-	Yd/C	TD	Drop	YAC	Rk	YAC+	BTkl	DVOA	Rk	DYAR	Rk	YAR	Short	Mid	Deep	Bomb
2017	TEN			17	28	231	61%	--	13.6	1						0.8%								

Taylor was assigned jersey No. 13, and spent a lot of time at minicamp getting compared to the man whose role he inherits, Kendall Wright. Like Wright, he projects at least initially as a slot receiver, with sufficient but not notable size; good run-after-catch ability; maybe not the fastest top gear; and, crucially for the Titans, outstanding collegiate production. Taylor had 1,730 receiving yards to lead S&P+'s No. 4 passing offense. He's unlikely to average 17.7 yards per catch against NFL defenses, and the June arrival of Eric Decker further reduces his already modest volume expectation. But Tennessee needed the dimension Wright brought, and Taylor has shown no sign of bringing the inconsistency-related headaches that made Wright's career so frustrating.

Adam Thielen   Height: 6-2   Weight: 195   College: Minnesota State   Draft: 2013/FA   Born: 22-Aug-1990   Age: 27   Risk: Yellow

Year	Team	G/GS	Snaps	Rec	Pass	Yds	C%	+/-	Yd/C	TD	Drop	YAC	Rk	YAC+	BTkl	DVOA	Rk	DYAR	Rk	YAR	Short	Mid	Deep	Bomb
2014	MIN	16/2	152	8	13	137	62%	+0.3	17.1	1	0	4.3	--	+0.2	0	31.3%	--	43	--	44	8%	62%	15%	15%
2015	MIN	16/2	218	12	18	144	67%	+1.4	12.0	0	0	3.9	--	+0.0	3	-8.4%	--	6	--	-5	29%	53%	12%	6%
2016	MIN	16/10	786	69	92	967	75%	+12.2	14.0	5	2	4.3	44	-0.3	9	26.2%	6	270	8	299	40%	29%	19%	12%
2017	MIN			69	96	890	72%	--	12.9	5						17.0%								

Adam Thielen was one of the revelations of the 2016 season. Partially because of injury to teammate Stefon Diggs, Thielen was the surprise leading receiver for the Vikings last year. He has secured himself a starting role moving into 2017, and if he replicates his performances from 2016 he will remain in that spot for a long time. Thielen immediately built a rapport with Sam Bradford, whose ability to throw with anticipation highlight's Thielen's athleticism and ability to create space downfield. With Laquon Treadwell remaining an unknown, Thielen, Diggs, Bradford, and Dalvin Cook figure to make up the foundation of the Vikings offense moving forward.

Demaryius Thomas   Height: 6-3   Weight: 224   College: Georgia Tech   Draft: 2010/1 (22)   Born: 25-Dec-1987   Age: 30   Risk: Yellow

Year	Team	G/GS	Snaps	Rec	Pass	Yds	C%	+/-	Yd/C	TD	Drop	YAC	Rk	YAC+	BTkl	DVOA	Rk	DYAR	Rk	YAR	Short	Mid	Deep	Bomb
2014	DEN	16/16	1021	111	184	1619	60%	-3.8	14.6	11	8	5.8	14	+1.2	7	9.2%	29	317	8	282	43%	32%	19%	6%
2015	DEN	16/16	937	105	177	1304	59%	-3.3	12.4	6	9	4.7	39	+0.0	15	-8.7%	70	56	60	80	38%	38%	16%	9%
2016	DEN	16/16	890	90	144	1083	63%	+1.6	12.0	5	10	3.6	65	-0.6	11	2.1%	48	172	27	149	31%	49%	10%	10%
2017	DEN			96	154	1185	62%	--	12.3	7						-0.5%								

Over the last two seasons, Thomas has played with four different quarterbacks. Here are his receiving plus-minus figures with each passer: Peyton Manning, plus-2.2; Trevor Siemian, plus-1.0; Paxton Lynch, plus-0.5; and Brock Osweiler minus-5.4.

At least Osweiler is long out of the picture, but Thomas had his lowest yardage total in the last five years in 2016. Thomas was one of seven wide receivers to get credit for a Pro Bowl selection in the AFC last year, but he wasn't as effective as the Broncos would like given his big contract. Without stellar quarterback play the last two seasons, Thomas has only caught 11 touchdowns combined after having 11 scores in 2014 alone. It's not just about the quarterbacks: his 55-yard touchdown against the Bengals last season was his only score longer than 11 yards, so he hasn't been turning the short throw into a long gain as well as he used to.

Michael Thomas   Height: 6-3   Weight: 212   College: Ohio State   Draft: 2016/2 (47)   Born: 3-Mar-1994   Age: 23   Risk: Yellow

Year	Team	G/GS	Snaps	Rec	Pass	Yds	C%	+/-	Yd/C	TD	Drop	YAC	Rk	YAC+	BTkl	DVOA	Rk	DYAR	Rk	YAR	Short	Mid	Deep	Bomb
2016	NO	15/12	865	92	121	1137	76%	+11.4	12.4	9	4	5.1	26	+1.1	17	31.6%	3	431	2	408	48%	36%	13%	3%
2017	NO			95	142	1279	67%	--	13.5	10						15.1%								

Last year, Michael Thomas ascended to become the third member of DYAR's rookie receiver trinity: Thomas, Randy Moss, and Odell Beckham have the three best rookie seasons on record. Thomas was remarkably consistent in his effectiveness. He was the team's most productive receiver whether on first, second, or third down; inside the red zone or out; in his own half of the field or the opponent's. He led the team in DYAR in 11 of 16 games, as well as for the season as a whole. Moss and Beckham saw their DYAR drop slightly following their outstanding rookie years, but both also eclipsed 1,400 yards and 10 touchdowns in their sophomore seasons. With Brandin Cooks now in New England and Willie Snead no threat for the No. 1 spot, there's little reason to think that Thomas won't approach those numbers.

Laquon Treadwell Height: 6-2   Weight: 221   College: Mississippi   Draft: 2016/1 (23)   Born: 14-Jun-1995   Age: 22   Risk: Yellow

Year	Team	G/GS	Snaps	Rec	Pass	Yds	C%	+/-	Yd/C	TD	Drop	YAC	Rk	YAC+	BTkl	DVOA	Rk	DYAR	Rk	YAR	Short	Mid	Deep	Bomb
2016	MIN	9/1	80	1	3	15	33%	+0.2	15.0	0	0	0.0	--	-4.6	0	-38.8%	--	-8	--	-5	0%	75%	0%	25%
2017	MIN			37	59	452	63%	--	12.2	3						0.7%								

Although he's only entering his second season, the pressure is on Laquon Treadwell. The Vikings have two young, established starters who are inarguably ahead of Treadwell for the foreseeable future. They also have former first-round pick Michael Floyd, who is trying to redeem himself after falling out of favor in Arizona. Floyd is young enough to stay on the roster for years if he wins the No. 3 receiver job over Treadwell this season.

The big concern for Treadwell is that his skill set doesn't have one standout trait on which he can rely. He's not fast—in fact, he's closer to slow than he is to average for an NFL receiver. He's tall, but he's not a physically-imposing specimen who can expect to bully NFL athletes at the catch point. Treadwell doesn't run great routes and he wasn't a consistent catcher of the ball in college. And he doesn't have a clear role that he can fill—such as deep threat or a goal-line fade receiver—until he becomes a viable starter.

Mike Wallace Height: 6-0   Weight: 199   College: Mississippi   Draft: 2009/3 (84)   Born: 1-Aug-1986   Age: 31   Risk: Green

Year	Team	G/GS	Snaps	Rec	Pass	Yds	C%	+/-	Yd/C	TD	Drop	YAC	Rk	YAC+	BTkl	DVOA	Rk	DYAR	Rk	YAR	Short	Mid	Deep	Bomb
2014	MIA	16/16	819	67	115	862	58%	+3.2	12.9	10	4	3.5	63	-1.0	10	11.8%	19	221	20	216	27%	39%	19%	15%
2015	MIN	16/12	751	39	72	473	54%	-2.7	12.1	2	4	4.3	47	-0.5	4	-6.4%	62	36	66	16	35%	37%	20%	8%
2016	BAL	16/16	872	72	116	1017	62%	+3.8	14.1	4	8	5.8	11	+1.3	14	0.0%	51	114	47	122	28%	44%	15%	13%
2017	BAL			67	112	856	60%	--	12.8	5						-1.9%								

There are very few NFL players who are more predictable than Mike Wallace. Wallace is here to do three things: win on 9 routes, get you sold enough on 9 routes to have success on the comeback and corner, and make you wonder how on Earth someone with this much natural talent could be so bad at every other aspect of playing wide receiver. The volume will be there without Steve Smith, but the fantasy results will be more impressive than their real world implications.

Bryan Walters Height: 6-0   Weight: 190   College: Cornell   Draft: 2010/FA   Born: 4-Nov-1987   Age: 30   Risk: N/A

Year	Team	G/GS	Snaps	Rec	Pass	Yds	C%	+/-	Yd/C	TD	Drop	YAC	Rk	YAC+	BTkl	DVOA	Rk	DYAR	Rk	YAR	Short	Mid	Deep	Bomb
2014	SEA	13/0	106	6	11	57	55%	-0.8	9.5	0	0	6.5	--	-0.6	0	-27.2%	--	-12	--	-19	60%	20%	20%	0%
2015	JAC	11/1	313	32	45	368	71%	+4.1	11.5	1	1	3.8	--	-1.1	0	11.4%	--	87	--	86	45%	36%	19%	0%
2016	JAC	10/3	321	24	35	231	71%	+2.2	9.6	2	0	4.3	--	-0.1	3	12.5%	--	70	--	56	64%	33%	3%	0%

Walters had another surprisingly useful season catching a bunch of 5-yard passes from the slot, value he mostly offset by doing little on punt returns even when he did not fumble. If healthy (the Jaguars cut him with an injury settlement in May), he could easily do the same for some other team.

Sammy Watkins Height: 6-1   Weight: 211   College: Clemson   Draft: 2014/1 (4)   Born: 14-Jun-1993   Age: 24   Risk: Red

Year	Team	G/GS	Snaps	Rec	Pass	Yds	C%	+/-	Yd/C	TD	Drop	YAC	Rk	YAC+	BTkl	DVOA	Rk	DYAR	Rk	YAR	Short	Mid	Deep	Bomb
2014	BUF	16/16	1027	65	128	982	51%	-8.5	15.1	6	2	5.3	21	+0.9	9	-5.7%	54	71	48	48	30%	33%	23%	14%
2015	BUF	13/13	714	60	96	1047	63%	+9.6	17.5	9	2	3.0	77	-1.2	2	28.9%	6	312	9	312	28%	29%	13%	30%
2016	BUF	8/8	382	28	52	430	54%	+0.6	15.4	2	3	1.9	93	-1.8	2	-1.3%	53	48	64	56	18%	50%	16%	16%
2017	BUF			69	129	1076	53%	--	15.6	9						2.8%								

Fresh off the first 1,000-yard season by a Bills receiver since 2012, Watkins plummeted as far as any young receiver in the league last year. A badly mismanaged left foot injury forced Watkins to undergo multiple surgeries, leaving him with a significant medical red flag on his file. Thus, after seemingly living up to his promise as a No. 1 receiver, Watkins isn't even guaranteed a spot on the roster beyond 2017 after Buffalo declined his fifth-year option. Judging Watkins by his numbers from last season isn't really fair, given that he played hobbled after repeatedly reaggravating his injury. However, it's also a large leap of faith to assume he's the same player who finished seventh in receiving plus-minus and sixth in yards per catch in 2015 . If he is indeed healthy, Watkins should receive plenty of volume given his connection with Tyrod Taylor. When Watkins has been on the field, he has received 37.2 percent of Buffalo's targets, the second-highest target share in that span behind only Julio Jones. With only a second-round rookie and a few veteran retreads added to the roster, Watkins should remain the clear top target this season whenever he plays. Beyond that, the outlook is surprisingly murky for someone who was one of the game's brightest young receivers at this time last year.

Dede Westbrook Height: 6-0 Weight: 178 College: Oklahoma Draft: 2017/4 (110) Born: 21-Nov-1993 Age: 24 Risk: Yellow

Year	Team	G/GS	Snaps	Rec	Pass	Yds	C%	+/-	Yd/C	TD	Drop	YAC	Rk	YAC+	BTkl	DVOA	Rk	DYAR	Rk	YAR	Short	Mid	Deep	Bomb
2017	JAC			16	28	248	57%	--	15.5	1						2.9%								

The 2016 Heisman Trophy finalist and fourth-round pick drew pre-draft comparisons to Titus Young for his rare combination of athletic explosiveness, thin frame (6-foot-0 and just 178 pounds), and massive character red flags (some nasty domestic violence allegations, and unfavorable comparisons to fellow Sooner Joe Mixon). He is also overage, turning 24 in November. Playmaker Score sees only performance and athleticism, and a 77 percent catch rate for 19.1 yards per grab is impressive even against Big 12 defenses. Jacksonville's depth at wide receiver will likely limit Westbrook's role as a rookie to special teams and the occasional go route.

Markus Wheaton Height: 5-11 Weight: 189 College: Oregon Draft: 2013/3 (79) Born: 7-Feb-1991 Age: 26 Risk: Green

Year	Team	G/GS	Snaps	Rec	Pass	Yds	C%	+/-	Yd/C	TD	Drop	YAC	Rk	YAC+	BTkl	DVOA	Rk	DYAR	Rk	YAR	Short	Mid	Deep	Bomb
2014	PIT	16/11	745	53	86	644	62%	+4.7	12.2	2	1	3.2	76	-1.2	8	-0.2%	44	84	43	69	20%	52%	17%	11%
2015	PIT	16/8	699	44	79	749	56%	+0.0	17.0	5	3	3.6	66	-0.7	4	12.4%	21	159	27	140	22%	47%	15%	16%
2016	PIT	3/2	97	4	9	51	44%	-0.9	12.8	1	1	2.0	--	-0.4	0	-25.8%	--	-9	--	-7	22%	22%	33%	22%
2017	CHI			34	62	494	55%	--	14.5	3						-2.3%								

It was somewhat surprising that the Pittsburgh Steelers let Markus Wheaton leave in free agency. Wheaton hadn't lived up to expectations and played some of his worst football for the team that drafted him during his final year there, but he is a better player than Cobi Hamilton. Wheaton can play inside or outside while showing off the athleticism to get open on vertical routes or shorter horizontal routes. Wheaton's ball skills need to get better and he's not a physically strong receiver, but should prove to be a valuable complementary piece in Chicago.

Kevin White Height: 6-3 Weight: 215 College: West Virginia Draft: 2015/1 (7) Born: 25-Jun-1992 Age: 25 Risk: Yellow

Year	Team	G/GS	Snaps	Rec	Pass	Yds	C%	+/-	Yd/C	TD	Drop	YAC	Rk	YAC+	BTkl	DVOA	Rk	DYAR	Rk	YAR	Short	Mid	Deep	Bomb
2016	CHI	4/4	191	19	36	187	53%	-2.0	9.8	0	2	2.8	--	-2.1	3	-35.6%	--	-64	--	-70	32%	32%	24%	12%
2017	CHI			52	101	731	51%	--	14.1	5						-7.6%								

Kevin White continues to keep the Bears waiting. There weren't many flashes of brilliance from White during the four games he managed to play in 2016, but at 25 years of age it's still too early to write him off. White has the size and athleticism to bully NFL defensive backs. His route-running will need to be refined—and he can't do that without being healthy so that's a major concern—but his ball skills should remain unblemished.

The Bears spent a top-10 pick on White because he could stretch defenses and give his quarterback a greater margin for error with his accuracy. Without Alshon Jeffery, he will be the Bears' best big-play threat and their No. 1 receiver by default. That's a lot of pressure for the NFL's version of Joel Embiid.

Mike Williams
Height: 6-4   Weight: 218   College: Clemson   Draft: 2017/1 (7)   Born: 4-Oct-1994   Age: 23   Risk: Red

Year	Team	G/GS	Snaps	Rec	Pass	Yds	C%	+/-	Yd/C	TD	Drop	YAC	Rk	YAC+	BTkl	DVOA	Rk	DYAR	Rk	YAR	Short	Mid	Deep	Bomb
2017	LACH			43	79	602	54%	--	14.0	4						-8.5%								

Do you know who Eric Bishop is? That is the legal name of the actor best known as Jamie Foxx. Many celebrities use a fake name to stand out, or to comply with standards for accreditation. This is why Michael B. Jordan, star of *Creed* and *Fruitvale Station*, is not simply called Michael Jordan, star of *Space Jam* and the greatest player in NBA history.

The NFL should really think of adopting a similar rule, or at least a special case that bans any other player from calling himself "Mike Williams." Pro Football Reference only returns eight results for Mike Williams, but it sure feels like there have been more, and it doesn't help that most of them are wide receivers. This particular Mike Williams hopes not be a bust like the big target from USC who went to Detroit in 2005, and hopes to stick around longer than the one who went to Tampa Bay in 2010. By his height, Williams is expected to be a good catch radius receiver and red zone target. However, his career-high touchdown mark of 11 at Clemson last season isn't that impressive, nor is his 15.4 yards per reception in his college career. He's the type of big receiver that Philip Rivers developed with in this league (think Vincent Jackson, who also ran near 4.5 in the 40-yard dash), but don't count on rookie stardom with the other pieces the Chargers have in place.

Terrance Williams
Height: 6-2   Weight: 208   College: Baylor   Draft: 2013/3 (74)   Born: 18-Sep-1989   Age: 28   Risk: Green

Year	Team	G/GS	Snaps	Rec	Pass	Yds	C%	+/-	Yd/C	TD	Drop	YAC	Rk	YAC+	BTkl	DVOA	Rk	DYAR	Rk	YAR	Short	Mid	Deep	Bomb
2014	DAL	16/16	811	37	65	621	57%	+3.4	16.8	8	2	3.0	78	-1.4	2	30.6%	2	220	21	239	17%	39%	19%	25%
2015	DAL	16/13	789	52	93	840	56%	-0.7	16.2	3	4	5.3	21	+0.8	5	7.4%	38	140	29	147	17%	45%	27%	11%
2016	DAL	16/15	745	44	61	594	72%	+6.8	13.5	4	2	3.8	59	-0.3	6	31.1%	4	214	17	218	19%	51%	22%	8%
2017	DAL			42	69	549	61%	--	13.1	4						10.1%								

Williams was 17-277-1 during the four early-season games when Dez Bryant was injured or limited. He then embarked on a long stretch of one- or two-catch games, ending the season with four receptions (but one devastating drop) against the Packers in the playoffs. Williams signed a new four-year contract with the Cowboys in March, to the surprise of many who thought that Williams would seek increased targets elsewhere while the Cowboys would economize at a low-priority position in the offense. Williams' primary role will be to burn No. 2 cornerbacks deep while both safeties are busy with Bryant, the running game, and everything else the Cowboys can throw at a defense. He needs to do that more often to justify his new contract.

Tyrell Williams
Height: 6-3   Weight: 204   College: Western Oregon   Draft: 2015/FA   Born: 12-Feb-1992   Age: 25   Risk: Green

Year	Team	G/GS	Snaps	Rec	Pass	Yds	C%	+/-	Yd/C	TD	Drop	YAC	Rk	YAC+	BTkl	DVOA	Rk	DYAR	Rk	YAR	Short	Mid	Deep	Bomb
2015	SD	7/0	30	2	6	90	33%	-0.7	45.0	1	0	25.5	--	+18.8	0	21.9%	--	15	--	10	17%	0%	33%	50%
2016	SD	16/12	891	69	118	1059	58%	+0.4	15.3	7	9	6.0	8	+1.7	8	9.0%	27	201	23	174	41%	26%	22%	11%
2017	LACH			53	93	780	57%	--	14.7	5						-1.7%								

As a rookie in 2015, Williams caught an 80-yard touchdown in Denver in Week 17. He wasn't on anyone's radar heading into last season, but injuries to Keenan Allen and Stevie Johnson opened up a lot of opportunities for him, and he delivered by leading the Chargers in targets, receptions, and receiving yards. It was one of the more surprising 1,000-yard receiving seasons in NFL history. Allen Hurns (2015 Jaguars) and Victor Cruz (2011 Giants) are the only other undrafted players since 1990 to gain 1,000 yards receiving in their second seasons. Williams also led all wideouts in YAC+, and was the top receiver on drag routes with a league-high 29 of them for 103 DYAR. Stefon Diggs (22) was the only other player with at least 20 drag routes last season. However, with Allen's return, the drafting of Mike Williams at No. 7 overall, and Anthony Lynn's ground-and-pound philosophy, it is unlikely that Williams will exceed last season's numbers.

Albert Wilson Height: 5-9 Weight: 200 College: Georgia State Draft: 2014/FA Born: 12-Jul-1992 Age: 25 Risk: Yellow

Year	Team	G/GS	Snaps	Rec	Pass	Yds	C%	+/-	Yd/C	TD	Drop	YAC	Rk	YAC+	BTkl	DVOA	Rk	DYAR	Rk	YAR	Short	Mid	Deep	Bomb
2014	KC	12/2	215	16	28	260	57%	-0.9	16.3	0	1	7.4	--	+2.7	6	14.8%	--	57	--	56	38%	38%	12%	12%
2015	KC	14/12	654	35	57	451	61%	-1.0	12.9	2	2	6.3	6	+1.0	10	1.5%	48	61	59	59	38%	36%	16%	11%
2016	KC	16/5	466	31	51	279	61%	-4.4	9.0	2	5	4.8	34	-0.8	7	-22.1%	84	-37	83	-48	58%	26%	12%	4%
2017	KC			35	58	397	60%	--	11.3	1						-11.4%								

Wilson's biggest contribution in 2016 was a 55-yard touchdown run in Atlanta on a fake punt. He simply took the quick snap and ran right down the middle of the field, only needing to beat one Atlanta player. Wilson also had his second-most productive receiving game of the season that day (48 yards on four grabs). Otherwise, he never gained more than 52 yards from scrimmage in any of his other 16 games, including the playoffs where he caught a 5-yard touchdown against Pittsburgh. Wilson's average yards per catch have fallen sharply over the past two years, and he is at best the fourth receiving option in Kansas City.

Robert Woods Height: 6-0 Weight: 201 College: USC Draft: 2013/2 (41) Born: 10-Apr-1992 Age: 25 Risk: Red

Year	Team	G/GS	Snaps	Rec	Pass	Yds	C%	+/-	Yd/C	TD	Drop	YAC	Rk	YAC+	BTkl	DVOA	Rk	DYAR	Rk	YAR	Short	Mid	Deep	Bomb
2014	BUF	16/15	899	65	104	699	63%	-0.3	10.8	5	5	3.1	77	-1.9	2	-11.4%	65	11	64	12	43%	32%	19%	7%
2015	BUF	14/9	774	47	80	552	59%	-2.8	11.7	3	2	3.3	72	-0.7	3	-14.6%	78	-12	79	-3	26%	55%	12%	8%
2016	BUF	13/10	633	51	75	613	67%	+7.2	12.0	1	2	2.5	90	-1.6	3	7.9%	30	117	46	123	31%	46%	13%	10%
2017	LARM			69	120	859	58%	--	12.5	3						-10.7%								

After four years in Buffalo, Woods returns home to Southern California as a free agent on a five-year contract. Known for his blocking, Woods had a solid but unspectacular season for Buffalo and set a career high in catch rate. If he can replicate that performance in Los Angeles, it would give Jared Goff a reliable target in a receiver group that leaves much to be desired. While Woods is a useful player and will have a chance to shine in an expanded role, you generally don't pay $7 million per year for a blocking receiver who has never eclipsed 700 yards in a single season. The cost of living in Los Angeles is high… but not that high.

Kendall Wright Height: 5-10 Weight: 196 College: Baylor Draft: 2012/1 (20) Born: 12-Nov-1989 Age: 28 Risk: Green

Year	Team	G/GS	Snaps	Rec	Pass	Yds	C%	+/-	Yd/C	TD	Drop	YAC	Rk	YAC+	BTkl	DVOA	Rk	DYAR	Rk	YAR	Short	Mid	Deep	Bomb
2014	TEN	14/11	662	57	93	715	61%	-1.2	12.5	6	1	6.4	8	+0.8	14	-3.3%	49	67	50	48	46%	26%	18%	9%
2015	TEN	10/9	412	36	60	408	60%	+0.3	11.3	3	3	4.0	55	-0.9	8	-8.1%	66	21	70	17	29%	46%	12%	14%
2016	TEN	11/4	309	29	43	416	67%	+2.9	14.3	3	1	4.3	--	+0.2	3	21.9%	--	119	--	115	36%	45%	10%	10%
2017	CHI			22	36	247	61%	--	11.2	1						-6.3%								

The Bears got a bargain in Kendall Wright. The former Titans receiver signed a one-year prove-it deal with the Bears in the offseason. Wright is a lightning-quick receiver who can create separation against press coverage or find the soft spots in zones consistently. He was primarily used as a possession receiver in Tennessee but can get open vertically too because of his electric athleticism. He is a smaller receiver who has dealt with durability issues throughout his career, including last season, while also drawing the ire of different coaching staffs for freelancing his routes.

If the reality check that comes with being an afterthought in free agency makes Wright a more disciplined player, he could easily develop into the Bears' best receiver. Talent has never been a problem for Wright. While the Bears' quarterbacks are obviously a downgrade from Marcus Mariota, Wright only played with Mariota for a short period. Most of his career was spent playing with passers who are inferior to Mike Glennon and, most likely, Mitchell Trubisky. Some were even worse than Mark Sanchez.

Going Deep

Rodney Adams, MIN: Drops and a lack of size are big concerns for the fifth-round pick out of South Florida. Adams should immediately compete for special teams time as a returner, but early in his career, his value to the offense will only be as a deep threat on shot plays. With Michael Floyd and Laquon Treadwell as the Vikings' primary backups, it's unlikely Adams sees the field on offense much this season.

DeMarcus Ayers, PIT: Ayers spent most of his first NFL season on the practice squad after the Steelers drafted him in the seventh round out of Houston. He was called up in mid-December, and Pittsburgh gave him a dozen targets in a rest-the-starters game against Cleveland in Week 17. The Steelers are loaded at wide receiver and Ayers is no lock to make the team.

Jace Billingsley, DET: Billingsley has earned the nickname "White Thunder" from teammate Golden Tate. He's part wide receiver, part running back, and can also be a return specialist. He was productive last preseason with 12 catches (including two touchdowns), but had to settle for a spot on the practice squad. A similar fate could await him this fall.

Jaron Brown, ARI: Brown has been an incredibly consistent receiver for the Cardinals, which usually is a compliment. In this case, though, we mean that in his four NFL seasons, Brown has caught 11 passes three times and doubled it to 22 once. Brown signed an extension after tearing his ACL in October, indicating that he is still in Arizona's plans. Our advanced statistical analysis and deeply-rooted mathematical insights would suggest that perhaps he'll catch 33 passes some year. Numerology is advanced stats, right?

Noah Brown, DAL: A seventh-round pick from Ohio State, Brown was the best blocking receiver in this draft class, a Jermaine Kearse-level brawler in the open field whose work jumped out when draftniks were scouting teammates like Curtis Samuel and opponents like Jabrill Peppers. Brown also had a four-touchdown game against Oklahoma and possesses the measurables of a starting wide receiver. A fractured leg in 2015 limited his role in the Buckeyes offense and hampered his draft stock. Brown's skill set is almost perfectly tailored to at least Brice Butler's role, if not Terrance Williams'. The Cowboys could use a block-first receiver who doesn't expect the ball much, but can cause trouble when he gets it.

Aaron Burbridge, SF: Burbridge had a Playmaker Score of just 24.4% at Michigan State. He's a plodding, big-bodied receiver with inconsistent hands and no playmaking skills after he catches the pass. Burbridge is a solid route-runner and the second-largest receiver on the 49ers' roster, and he did escape the first culling of the new regime, so he still has a chance to stick around. But he seems a long shot to surpass his seven receptions from last season.

K.D. Cannon, NYJ: After gaining more than 3,000 yards receiving in three seasons, Cannon skipped his senior season at Baylor to enter the NFL draft. He had tantalizing gifts, as shown by his 86.4% Playmaker Score. He went undrafted, but the 49ers guaranteed him $45,000 as a free agent—and then cut him after two days of running in shorts. The Jets scooped him up, in hopes he can develop into a downfield threat.

Leonte Carroo, MIA: It's not that Miami has already given up on the 2016 third-round pick, but the truth is most teams don't get much out of their No. 4 wide receiver. Carroo is clearly that, at best, behind Jarvis Landry, DeVante Parker, and Kenny Stills. He wasn't able to carve out a role for himself in Adam Gase's offense last year, and ended up with just three catches. Now he may be battling 2016 sixth-round pick Jakeem Grant and 2016 UDFA Rashawn Scott for his roster spot.

Jehu Chesson, KC: By releasing Jeremy Maclin, the Chiefs showed they are either confident in Chesson, or convinced they can thrive without throwing to their wide receivers. Chesson showed big-play ability for Michigan in 2015, but a knee injury at the end of that season slowed him for much of 2016, when he struggled to separate. A fourth-round pick with post-injury health concerns doesn't sound like a match made in Alex Smith's heaven, but there should be opportunities for Chesson to see the field this season.

Stacy Coley, MIN: This receiver from the University of Miami is more intriguing than most seventh-round picks. He has found a nice fit with the Vikings as a potential vertical complement to the primary starters. He needs to develop technically and there are character concerns, but his raw talent gives him a legitimate chance at making the back end of the Vikings roster.

Cody Core, CIN: A good special-teamer who somehow out-produced college teammate Laquon Treadwell in their rookie seasons, Core is ticketed for the "in case of massive injury problems" emergency case in 2017. He's got NFL-caliber size and speed, but the hands and the consistency come and go.

Amara Darboh, SEA: After serving as Michigan's No. 1 receiver this past season, Darboh will be fighting for snaps and targets in 2017 because of the depth already present at the Seattle skill positions. Darboh profiles as a potential replacement for Jermaine Kearse down the road, but the third-round selection enters camp fighting for the fourth or fifth receiver job on a team that also employs star tight end Jimmy Graham and running back C.J. Prosise, a converted wide receiver. Darboh's journey to the NFL is nothing short of inspiring given the hardships he faced growing up as a refugee from Sierra Leone, but with so many players ahead of him on the depth chart, it will be tough for Darboh to stand out on offense as a rookie.

Robert Davis, WAS: A sixth-round pick from Georgia State, Davis is the next Niles Paul. He's a big receiver who works the middle of the field well, with a man-among-boys style in the Sun Belt conference that roughly translates into a possession-receiving-and-special-teaming role in the NFL. Paul was a college receiver who has stuck for years in Washington as a tiny tight end. Davis could go the same route.

Harry Douglas, TEN: As a marginal player, your best bet is to find a good situation; be versatile; earn your coaches' trust; and never, ever, ever get comfortable. Douglas fits the profile to a "T." He has spent most of his career with both Mike Mularkey and offensive coordinator Terry Robiskie, who speak of his reliability. He can play inside and outside and fill in on punt returns. And he knows he is guaranteed nothing. He filled in for Kendall Wright and Tajae Sharpe in the slot and outside last year, but the offseason arrival of three receivers likely to be ahead of him on the depth chart make his roster spot as precarious as it has ever been.

Malachi Dupre, GB: LSU has produced some high-quality NFL receivers—including Odell Beckham and Jarvis Landry—but Dupre didn't show off that kind of quality. His size (6-feet-2, 196 pounds) is likely the only reason he is getting a shot in the NFL. A strong training camp could land him a practice-squad spot.

Bruce Ellington, SF: In the time it took to write this sentence, Ellington was injured again. In his first three NFL seasons, Ellington has more weeks on the injured list (27) than career receptions (19). He missed the start of OTAs this year with yet another soft tissue injury. When healthy, Ellington is an explosive athlete, but a healthy Ellington sighting ranks right up there with Sasquatch in the Bay Area's cryptozoology handbook.

Isaiah Ford, MIA: A seventh-round pick from Virginia Tech, Ford could serve as a poor man's Kenny Stills-style deep threat, but he'll need to bulk up to handle the more physical nature of NFL cornerbacks. It doesn't help that Miami already has a fairly crowded wide receiver depth chart.

Devin Fuller, ATL: The Falcons' seventh-round pick in 2016, Fuller lost his rookie season to shoulder surgery. He possesses great speed, but rarely played to that at UCLA. He doesn't figure to get many opportunities to do so in Atlanta, unless it is on special teams.

Shelton Gibson, PHI: Gibson is a pure boundary receiver who went 84-1,898-17 in just over two seasons as a regular at West Virginia, an average of 22.6 yards per reception. He's dangerous on the fly route, the comeback route that looks like a fly route until he stops, and the screen. College boundary receivers are most likely to translate to the NFL if: a) they are crafty enough in their first steps off the line of scrimmage to beat jams and create initial separation, and b) they can block enough to stay on the field and do more than clear safeties out. Gibson has both of those traits, making him a promising lid-lifter. That said, he looked raw in OTAs and is stuck behind Torrey Smith as the Eagles' designated deep threat, so this may be a redshirt year for the Philadelphia fifth-round pick.

Jakeem Grant, MIA: Grant steadily improved as a receiver each year at Texas Tech, but the Dolphins really only used him on special teams last season. He returned a punt 74 yards for a touchdown, but also struggled with four fumbles. Grant dropped the only pass target he had all season, so he'll have to show more this August to earn offensive snaps in 2017.

Ryan Grant, WAS: Grant's semi-regular role as the blocking receiver and decoy in trips formations was gradually usurped by Maurice Harris last season. It's not a role to get excited about in the first place.

Rashad Greene, JAC: Imprecise quarterbacks and shifty slot receivers rarely go well together, and so it has been with Greene and Blake Bortles. 2016 was a season to forget for Greene, who struggled to stay in the lineup, coughed up the ball on too many punt returns, and ended the season on injured reserve with an Achilles injury. The arrival of Dede Westbrook in the draft, who can do similar things, further reduces his chances of making the team and playing a role in 2017.

Chad Hansen, NYJ: Hansen spent one year at Idaho State and two years at Cal. He led the Pac-12 with 92 catches and 1,249 yards as a junior, then skipped his senior season to enter the draft. The Jets drafted him in the fourth round, and injuries to ArDarius Stewart might open up playing time for him as a rookie.

Darrius Heyward-Bey, PIT: Heyward-Bey was the seventh overall pick of the 2009 draft, so you would have to call him a bust—but for a bust, he sure has lasted for a long time. He had only six catches in 2016 and might not stick on the league's deepest receiver corps in Pittsburgh, but he should still catch on with some team looking for a home-run hitter who also blocks and plays special teams.

Mack Hollins, PHI: This fourth-rounder is a toolsy prospect who got lost among the crowded North Carolina receiving corps after some early-career injuries set him back. Getting stuck behind Ryan Switzer, Austin Proehl, and others became a disguised blessing for Hollins, who emerged as North Carolina's special teams captain, drastically increasing his chances of sticking in the NFL as a fourth or fifth wideout. Look for Hollins to become part of the Eagles' always-excellent coverage teams. As for an offensive role, Hollins will again be waiting at the end of a long line.

Josh Huff, TB: Though his prospects at receiver are less than enticing, Josh Huff has a great chance to make the Buccaneers roster in September as a kick returner. Tampa Bay's recent history is utterly devoid of return talent: Huff has more kick return touchdowns in his three-year career (two) than the franchise has in its past six seasons (one).

Justin Hunter, PIT: Hunter was a second-round pick in 2013, but has never been more than a third wideout in four seasons with the Titans, Bills, and Dolphins. He signed with the Steelers, but Martavis Bryant's return from suspension means that Hunter may never have a chance to show the big-play ability that made him a star for the Tennessee Volunteers.

Jeff Janis, GB: Janis has shown flashes of his vertical ability and athleticism in the NFL, but he hasn't proven that he can run routes or consistently catch the ball. 2017 is a make-or-break season for him.

Cody Latimer, DEN: Even if Latimer makes the team, why should we expect him to do anything in the regular season? He has 16 catches in three years in Denver and could never even get comfortable with Peyton Manning at quarterback. The Broncos have badly needed a third receiver to step up since 2015, but Latimer, a former second-round pick, has been a bust to this point.

Roger Lewis, NYG: Lewis made the Giants as an undrafted rookie last year, generated a few big plays early, earned a start in place of Victor Cruz, and had a miserable game against the Bengals: one catch, one drop, one interception when he fell down instead of contesting the ball when it arrived. Lewis then suffered a Week 11 concussion and disappeared from the team's picture. He could still make the Giants roster as a fourth receiver, which would make him about the 11th option in the Giants offense.

Josh Malone, CIN: A height-weight-speed dream, Malone is 6-foot-3 and 208 pounds, with a 4.4 40-yard dash at the combine, and he broke Robert Meachem's yards-per-reception record at Tennessee by more than a yard. A.J. Green has already compared him to a young Marvin Jones. The downside is that Malone still needs a lot of technical work. The Bengals drafted him near the end of the fourth round, but he shouldn't be pressed into service this year given how much talent the Bengals have ahead of him on the depth chart.

Jalin Marshall, NYJ: Marshall was New York's primary punt returner and fifth wide receiver last year. In March he was issued a four-game suspension for PEDs, and then the Jets added five rookie wideouts to the roster, likely signaling an end to his time with Gang Green.

Vince Mayle, BAL: One of the overlooked disasters of the mid-teens Cleveland drafts, Mayle was selected in the fourth round in 2015 and waived before training camp ended. He was nicknamed—we're not making this up—"Little LeBron" for his basketball prowess in grade school. Anyone could float to a third receiver role on Baltimore's receiver depth chart, but Mayle might be better off giving basketball another shot.

Tanner McEvoy, SEA: McEvoy played quarterback, tight end, and wide receiver at Wisconsin before settling in as an undrafted rookie wideout for the Seahawks. That versatility came in handy during his rookie season, as he blocked a punt, caught nine passes (two for touchdowns) on 11 targets, and completed a 43-yard pass on a trick play. He will compete in training camp to be the fifth or sixth wide receiver and have a role on special teams for the Seahawks.

Isaiah McKenzie, DEN: McKenzie returned five punts for touchdowns at Georgia, so special teams is likely his best hope of making an impact as a rookie. There will be comparisons to Kansas City's Tyreek Hill, but the overall skill set is not that good. McKenzie is also just 5-foot-7, which usually means a gadget player who will see a few bubble screens in the NFL if he's lucky. Return specialist or bust for this fifth-round pick.

David Moore, SEA: A seventh-round pick in 2017, Moore attended East Central University (Division II) in Oklahoma. Moore had 1,079 receiving yards and a school-record 13 receiving touchdowns as a junior, then 878 yards and ten touchdowns in his senior season. Moore faces an uphill battle to make the 53-man roster out of training camp and may be destined for the practice squad.

Keith Mumphery, FA: Two years into the Keith Mumphery Era, the Texans were still trying to figure out what it is he's actually good at. It isn't special teams—he got pulled off returns in 2016 in favor of Tyler Ervin. It isn't receiving—he caught 43.8 percent of his targets in 2015 and had just 69 yards on 10 receptions last season. Mr. Mumphery, what is it, you would say, you do here? (It turns out nothing, because the Texans cut him in June.)

Jordan Norwood, FA: Norwood has been around since 2009, but has never been more than a deep-bench wideout, good for a 200-yard season here and there. He started six games for Denver last year, but the Broncos need more out of a starter than the production they were getting from Norwood. Currently unsigned.

Walter Powell, BUF: The sometimes kick returner had his first career reception in 2016, his third season in the league. Powell does hold some special teams value and should get an opportunity to compete for a roster spot amid the morass that is the Bills wide receiver depth chart. However, barring more injuries at the position in 2017, don't expect Powell to hold an offensive role again this season.

Josh Reynolds, LARM: A fourth-round rookie from Texas A&M, Reynolds posted 1,039 receiving yards as the No. 2 target for the Aggies in 2016 behind former top recruit Christian Kirk. Reynolds was a big-play threat for Texas A&M, averaging 17.0 yards per catch and 10.9 yards per target for an explosive Aggies offense that ranked 28th in IsoPPP+ in 2016. At 6-foot-3, Reynolds could serve as a red zone target for Jared Goff as well, giving him a good chance at carving out a somewhat productive role from Day 1.

Andre Roberts, ATL: Roberts never played for Chip Kelly, but the erstwhile Eagles and Niners coach still cost him heavily. Roberts was signed after four seasons in Arizona to be the No. 2 man in Washington, only to see Kelly shockingly cut DeSean Jackson. The 'Skins snapped Jackson up, relegating Roberts down the food chain, and he never blossomed into a featured receiver. Now on his fourth team, Roberts replaces the departed Aldrick Robinson as the No. 4 wideout, and will handle returns. Only three players had more value on punt returns in 2016.

Demarcus Robinson, KC: The release of Jeremy Maclin helps to keep open a spot for a player like Robinson, a 2016 fourth-round pick. Robinson drew Mike Wallace comparisons as a deep threat at Florida. He only played six offensive snaps (zero targets) for Kansas City in 2016. Unproven vertical threats don't exactly hit things off in this type of passing game, but Robinson provides something different than Albert Wilson, Tyreek Hill, and De'Anthony Thomas. He's nowhere near Maclin of course, but he is at least a warm body with a 6-foot-1 frame and the ability to play outside the numbers.

Travis Rudolph, NYG: Remember the story of the Florida State player who ate lunch with an autistic child sitting all alone in the cafeteria during a team visit to a local elementary school? Rudolph was that player. The Giants love guys like Rudolph; they probably had to outbid Tom Coughlin for his rookie free-agent services. Rudolph's 4.65 combine 40 kept him out of the draft pool. He flashes good route running and toughness on tape to go with his high character. He's a practice squad/special teams stash. If rumors that he is faster than his 40 time prove true, he's a potential steal.

Devin Smith, NYJ: A second-round pick out of Ohio State in 2014, Smith has been limited by injuries to just ten catches in 14 games in his first two seasons, and now will miss the 2017 season with his second torn ACL. A sad case of a talented player and what might have been.

Rod Streater, BUF: Streater was last spotted as an effective receiver in Oakland in 2013, catching 60 passes and topping 900 yards from scrimmage. Since then, he has been an afterthought, bouncing from the Raiders to the Chiefs to the 49ers in an exchange of conditional 2019 seventh-round picks—a sure sign of a high-valued player, there. Buffalo is in need of depth at wideout, and Streater is as good of a camp body as anyone else.

Damore'ea Stringfellow, MIA: Back in 2014, Stringfellow was charged with three misdemeanors for altercations he got into with Seahawks fans after Super Bowl XLVIII. He transferred from the University of Washington to Ole Miss and had his best season in 2016. While he was expected to be a late-round pick, he went undrafted and signed with the Dolphins. Stringfellow is a big "catch radius" receiver, but his lack of production and special teams flexibility could make it difficult for him to crack Miami's roster this year.

Trent Taylor, SF: Taylor is absolutely tiny—just 5-foot-8 and 181 pounds. Only ten or so guys in NFL history have made a living as a receiver at that size or smaller, but Kyle Shanahan is very familiar with one of them: Taylor Gabriel, who worked with the 49ers' new head coach in both Cleveland and Atlanta. San Francisco drafted Taylor in the fifth round. There's no doubting Taylor's college production, as he put up an insane 327 receptions and 4,179 yards at Louisiana Tech. He'll need to show some punt returning skills to have a major impact in 2017.

De'Anthony Thomas, KC: With Tyreek Hill in town, the Chiefs no longer have much use for Thomas outside of depth. Thomas had 11 touches on offense last season, lost his punt returner job to Hill, and wasn't nearly as successful on kick returns as his new teammate, who is really what the Chiefs thought they were getting in Thomas when they selected him in the fourth round in 2014.

Mike Thomas, LARM: Not to be confused with Saints receiver Michael Thomas, who was the far superior player as a rookie, Mike Thomas from Southern Miss had a disappointing first season in which he was only targeted nine times. However, with Tavon Austin missing offseason practices recovering from an injury, Thomas impressed both Sean McVay and Jared Goff with his effort and speed on the outside. Now, this is fairly typical for the offseason, when players are almost always "in the best shape of their life," but maybe this will be the time when the OTA praise results in making regular-season plays. But after the NFL handed him a four-game suspension for PED use, that seems unlikely.

Deonte Thompson, CHI: Thompson is 28 years old and has journeyed around the league. He has always played well in pre-season games and when given opportunities in the regular season, but will never be a regular contributor because his skill set lacks any one great trait. He's useful on kickoff returns, though.

Derel Walker, TB: Walker went undrafted the same year Mike Evans, his teammate at Texas A&M, was picked seventh overall. He spent the past two years starring in the CFL to the tune of 2,699 yards and 16 touchdowns for the Edmonton Eskimos. Another big outside target at 6-foot-2, he has a chance to stick as further depth after impressing during OTAs.

Lucky Whitehead, DAL: The Cowboys' primary return man for two seasons, Whitehead was inactivated for missing team meetings last season and did not do much with the returns and limited offensive touches he was given. Rookie Ryan Switzer is a near-lock to replace him.

Chad Williams, ARI: Arizona's third-round pick dominated against FCS competition at Grambling State, which is pretty much the bare minimum of what you're required to do if you're going to be an NFL prospect. His hands have been compared to Anquan Boldin's, which is setting the bar way too high. Williams will open up his career as Arizona's No. 5 receiver, giving him time to adjust to NFL playbooks, defenses, and route-running requirements. Good hands, a physical presence, and a strong running style are good building blocks for a prospect; just don't expect too much out of Williams too soon.

Jarius Wright, MIN: The Vikings rushed to extend Jarius Wright back in 2015, meaning that the receiver has three years left on his current deal. He initially got $7 million in guaranteed money, so what remains of that is the strongest argument for giving him a roster spot. Wright's production fell from 34 receptions for 442 yards in 2015 to 11 receptions for a mere 67 yards in 2016.

DeAngelo Yancey, GB: Chosen near the end of the fifth round, Yancey played on a bad team at Purdue and didn't show off a diverse route tree. He has size and enough athleticism to win vertically, so he could carve out a role on special teams while working his way into contention for playing time on offense.

Tight Ends

Top 20 TE by DYAR (Total Value), 2016

Rank	Player	Team	DYAR
1	Travis Kelce	KC	261
2	Jimmy Graham	SEA	204
3	Martellus Bennett	NE	197
4	Cameron Brate	TB	149
5	Eric Ebron	DET	149
6	Hunter Henry	SD	148
7	Rob Gronkowski	NE	136
8	Greg Olsen	CAR	134
9	Jack Doyle	IND	131
10	Dwayne Allen	IND	108
11	Austin Hooper	ATL	106
12	Delanie Walker	TEN	102
13	Jordan Reed	WAS	102
14	Vernon Davis	WAS	96
15	Gary Barnidge	CLE	89
16	Erik Swoope	IND	85
16	Zach Miller	CHI	85
16	Levine Toilolo	ATL	85
19	Zach Ertz	PHI	75
20	Tyler Eifert	CIN	57

Top 20 TE by DVOA (Value per Play), 2016

Rank	Player	Team	DVOA
1	Austin Hooper	ATL	46.8%
2	Rob Gronkowski	NE	44.5%
3	Hunter Henry	SD	33.4%
4	Martellus Bennett	NE	33.4%
5	Travis Kelce	KC	26.0%
6	Jimmy Graham	SEA	25.1%
7	Dwayne Allen	IND	21.8%
8	Cameron Brate	TB	20.4%
9	Eric Ebron	DET	20.1%
10	Jack Doyle	IND	18.7%
11	Vernon Davis	WAS	16.8%
12	Zach Miller	CHI	12.5%
13	Gary Barnidge	CLE	10.0%
14	Jordan Reed	WAS	9.9%
15	Tyler Eifert	CIN	9.6%
16	Delanie Walker	TEN	8.4%
17	Greg Olsen	CAR	8.3%
18	Vance McDonald	SF	6.7%
19	Mychal Rivera	OAK	6.4%
20	Dion Sims	MIA	6.3%

Minimum 25 targets

Dwayne Allen
Height: 6-3 Weight: 255 College: Clemson Draft: 2012/3 (64) Born: 24-Feb-1990 Age: 27 Risk: Green

Year	Team	G/GS	Snaps	Rec	Pass	Yds	C%	+/-	Yd/C	TD	Drop	YAC	Rk	YAC+	BTkl	DVOA	Rk	DYAR	Rk	YAR	Short	Mid	Deep	Bomb
2014	IND	13/13	619	29	50	395	58%	-2.7	13.6	8	4	5.6	13	+1.2	3	22.7%	6	104	12	91	34%	46%	16%	4%
2015	IND	13/12	509	16	29	109	55%	-1.7	6.8	1	0	3.1	46	-1.5	0	-31.4%	49	-48	45	-59	56%	37%	7%	0%
2016	IND	14/14	611	35	52	406	67%	+2.8	11.6	6	2	3.4	41	-0.5	0	21.8%	7	108	10	96	28%	60%	10%	2%
2017	NE			23	35	261	66%	--	11.3	4						11.3%								

Allen became the Patriots' latest veteran tight end import this offseason, leaving Indianapolis after five seasons in a rare trade between the two franchises. The Colts utilized him as mostly a blocker and red zone threat, though he showed a bit of versatility last season with nearly half his targets coming from the slot. The problem with the "red zone threat" label is that Allen has been largely average in that part of the field the last two seasons since an eye-popping 55.3% red zone DVOA in 2014. And apart from a memorable Monday night three-touchdown game against the sad-sack Jets, Allen has otherwise caught just four touchdowns the past two seasons combined. New England has traditionally been a two-tight end base offense with a healthy Rob Gronkowski; in 2015, 12 personnel was their most frequently used grouping (43 percent) despite Scott Chandler and Asante Cleveland serving as the Gronk sidekicks. Allen should receive a healthy number of reps for a second tight end, vulturing the occasional touchdown whenever defenses get lost scrambling to cover the Patriots' more heralded weapons.

Gary Barnidge
Height: 6-6 Weight: 243 College: Louisville Draft: 2008/5 (141) Born: 22-Sep-1985 Age: 32 Risk: N/A

Year	Team	G/GS	Snaps	Rec	Pass	Yds	C%	+/-	Yd/C	TD	Drop	YAC	Rk	YAC+	BTkl	DVOA	Rk	DYAR	Rk	YAR	Short	Mid	Deep	Bomb
2014	CLE	13/2	358	13	25	156	52%	-2.8	12.0	0	0	3.2	43	-1.4	2	-0.3%	27	10	29	-5	46%	29%	21%	4%
2015	CLE	16/13	942	79	125	1043	63%	+1.5	13.2	9	4	4.6	24	+0.3	8	19.7%	9	218	3	188	35%	51%	13%	1%
2016	CLE	16/16	968	55	81	612	68%	+3.0	11.1	2	4	3.7	30	-0.9	3	10.0%	13	89	15	81	44%	46%	8%	3%

Barnidge's role in the passing game shrunk a bit after his Cinderella 2015 season, and his age combined with the drafting of David Njoku made him expendable, but it's surprising he remained unsigned as of early July. Target for target, he was still the most reliable receiver Cleveland had last year. He was best with a hand in the dirt (22.3% DVOA), not in the slot (7.6%), so the rise of spread formations across the league may be working against him. Last word had him in talks with the Broncos, Bills, and Jaguars. None of those teams had a ranking tight end with a positive DVOA last year, so any would seem like a good fit for Barnidge.

Martellus Bennett
Height: 6-6   Weight: 259   College: Texas A&M   Draft: 2008/2 (61)   Born: 10-Mar-1987   Age: 30   Risk: Yellow

Year	Team	G/GS	Snaps	Rec	Pass	Yds	C%	+/-	Yd/C	TD	Drop	YAC	Rk	YAC+	BTkl	DVOA	Rk	DYAR	Rk	YAR	Short	Mid	Deep	Bomb
2014	CHI	16/15	954	90	128	916	70%	+1.6	10.2	6	8	5.0	17	-0.1	19	3.0%	20	88	14	51	57%	31%	12%	1%
2015	CHI	11/11	728	53	80	439	66%	-0.9	8.3	3	3	4.3	31	-1.0	9	-10.7%	35	-18	38	-30	55%	29%	13%	4%
2016	NE	16/12	868	55	73	701	75%	+3.9	12.7	7	3	7.6	3	+2.3	14	33.4%	4	197	3	164	65%	27%	7%	1%
2017	GB			59	85	717	69%	--	12.2	6							13.5%								

Retaining Jared Cook to help stretch the defense might have made sense for the Packers if he had shown more consistency last season. Instead the Packers have swapped him out for a tight end who has a style that is less ideal for the personnel they have, but is a significantly better player. Bennett's value as a blocker and receiver is so far above what Cook offered that he has to improve the offense. He will immediately be the best possession receiver the Packers have over the middle of the field while Jordy Nelson and Davante Adams focus on working outside.

Because of the Patriots' depth and variety on offense, Bennett was often on the periphery of the game plan. He won't be a focal point in Green Bay either, but he should play a bigger role than he did last year. The Packers will benefit massively from his ability to make defenders miss after the catch with his athleticism.

Cameron Brate
Height: 6-5   Weight: 235   College: Harvard   Draft: 2014/FA   Born: 13-Jul-1991   Age: 26   Risk: Green

Year	Team	G/GS	Snaps	Rec	Pass	Yds	C%	+/-	Yd/C	TD	Drop	YAC	Rk	YAC+	BTkl	DVOA	Rk	DYAR	Rk	YAR	Short	Mid	Deep	Bomb
2014	TB	5/1	44	1	1	17	100%	+0.3	17.0	0	0	4.0	--	-0.3	0	114.4%	--	9	--	8	0%	100%	0%	0%
2015	TB	14/4	341	23	30	288	77%	+3.8	12.5	3	0	2.2	51	-2.0	1	33.6%	4	81	15	85	23%	50%	20%	7%
2016	TB	15/10	709	57	81	660	70%	+6.9	11.6	8	4	2.4	45	-1.4	3	20.4%	8	149	4	146	30%	53%	15%	1%
2017	TB			41	62	503	66%	--	12.3	5							10.8%								

Brate had a breakout season in 2016, scoring more than a quarter of the Buccaneers' receiving touchdowns while ranking second in both yards and catches. He was Tampa Bay's most efficient receiver on third down, and only Jordy Nelson had more touchdown catches in the red zone. The team showed their appreciation by picking O.J. Howard in the first round of April's draft. Brate remains the official starter for now, but the same was true for Austin Seferian-Jenkins this time last year. At the very least, Brate will see Howard eat into his playing time and targets. In all likelihood, those roles will be reversed by the end of the year.

Trey Burton
Height: 6-3   Weight: 235   College: Florida   Draft: 2014/FA   Born: 29-Oct-1991   Age: 26   Risk: Green

Year	Team	G/GS	Snaps	Rec	Pass	Yds	C%	+/-	Yd/C	TD	Drop	YAC	Rk	YAC+	BTkl	DVOA	Rk	DYAR	Rk	YAR	Short	Mid	Deep	Bomb
2014	PHI	15/0	6	0	0	0	--	--	--	0	--	--	--	--	--	--	--	--	--	--	--	--	--	--
2015	PHI	16/0	63	3	4	54	75%	+0.0	18.0	0	0	10.3	--	+6.2	1	40.2%	--	12	--	15	50%	50%	0%	0%
2016	PHI	15/4	331	37	60	327	62%	-2.2	8.8	1	5	3.6	33	-1.3	3	-27.9%	44	-83	44	-70	47%	38%	12%	3%
2017	PHI			24	36	217	67%	--	9.1	1							-10.6%								

Burton is officially a tight end this season after spending the last three years as a nominal H-back/fullback. He was a frequent recipient of the overcomplicated screen passes the Eagles ran last year when nothing else in their offense worked. Burton could replace Brent Celek as the Eagles' second tight end, but should not earn 60 targets this season unless starter Zach Ertz is hurt or the whole Eagles offense collapses into a screen-pass white dwarf star.

Garrett Celek | Height: 6-5 | Weight: 252 | College: Michigan State | Draft: 2012/FA | Born: 29-May-1988 | Age: 29 | Risk: Red

Year	Team	G/GS	Snaps	Rec	Pass	Yds	C%	+/-	Yd/C	TD	Drop	YAC	Rk	YAC+	BTkl	DVOA	Rk	DYAR	Rk	YAR	Short	Mid	Deep	Bomb
2014	SF	3/1	35	2	2	53	100%	+1.2	26.5	0	0	3.5	--	-2.8	0	169.2%	--	24	--	23	0%	0%	50%	50%
2015	SF	11/8	399	19	28	186	68%	+1.1	9.8	3	0	5.2	17	+0.5	1	5.4%	21	25	29	29	62%	27%	12%	0%
2016	SF	16/6	605	29	50	350	58%	-1.5	12.1	3	6	4.2	21	+0.3	2	-9.0%	30	-6	31	-23	28%	60%	13%	0%
2017	SF			31	47	329	66%	--	10.6	2						-3.1%								

Celek could see a significant increase in his usage in 2017. Kyle Shanahan has made a point out of talking him up this off-season, and the 49ers attempted (and failed) to trade Vance McDonald during the draft. Is Celek actually a better player than McDonald? Celek has put up better red zone DVOA in each of the past two seasons, but that's a relatively small sample size as San Francisco was rarely *in* the red zone. Celek also managed to somehow drop more passes than McDonald did in 2016, which feels like it belongs on *Ripley's Believe It or Not*. Shanahan used multi-tight end sets more than a quarter of the time in Atlanta, so there's definitely room for Celek to have a big role, but the rumors having him well ahead of McDonald seem out of place for now—more smoke than fire.

Charles Clay | Height: 6-3 | Weight: 239 | College: Tulsa | Draft: 2011/6 (174) | Born: 13-Feb-1989 | Age: 28 | Risk: Green

Year	Team	G/GS	Snaps	Rec	Pass	Yds	C%	+/-	Yd/C	TD	Drop	YAC	Rk	YAC+	BTkl	DVOA	Rk	DYAR	Rk	YAR	Short	Mid	Deep	Bomb
2014	MIA	14/14	745	58	84	605	69%	+3.6	10.4	3	1	4.4	22	-1.0	6	-6.9%	31	2	31	8	52%	34%	14%	0%
2015	BUF	13/13	764	51	77	528	66%	-1.5	10.4	3	5	4.6	22	-0.9	11	-6.0%	32	6	32	-2	54%	25%	18%	3%
2016	BUF	15/15	871	57	87	552	66%	-2.3	9.7	4	7	3.4	37	-1.2	10	-6.5%	27	4	27	6	41%	40%	16%	2%
2017	BUF			57	90	571	63%	--	10.0	3						-6.7%								

It's not a good sign when a player's contract structure provides more job security than his actual performance, but that's where Clay sits after a disappointing 2016. Thanks to a $10 million roster bonus converted to a signing bonus in February 2016, Clay's cap hit will be $9 million each of the next three years, with at least $4.5 million in potential dead money every season. Worst of all, the ailing knee injury Clay managed all of last season has lingered into 2017, leading the Bills to announce that they'll need to manage his practice reps this season. None of this bodes well for a player who averaged a career-low 9.7 yards per catch in 2016. A healthier season from Sammy Watkins and quick development from Zay Jones could lessen Clay's burden in the passing game, but he'll still receive a healthy snap and target count simply due to the Bills' lack of options at the position. Thus, after posting nearly identical stat lines his first two seasons in Buffalo, expect similar results in Year 3 so long as Clay can manage his knee problems.

Jared Cook | Height: 6-6 | Weight: 246 | College: South Carolina | Draft: 2009/3 (89) | Born: 7-Apr-1987 | Age: 30 | Risk: Yellow

Year	Team	G/GS	Snaps	Rec	Pass	Yds	C%	+/-	Yd/C	TD	Drop	YAC	Rk	YAC+	BTkl	DVOA	Rk	DYAR	Rk	YAR	Short	Mid	Deep	Bomb
2014	STL	16/6	682	52	99	634	53%	-8.1	12.2	3	3	5.1	16	+0.6	6	-13.4%	37	-39	41	-47	40%	43%	13%	3%
2015	STL	16/12	673	39	75	481	52%	-6.6	12.3	0	3	5.1	18	-0.1	3	-23.5%	44	-76	51	-71	41%	39%	13%	7%
2016	GB	10/5	329	30	51	377	59%	-1.7	12.6	1	2	4.9	13	+0.2	3	-11.5%	33	-15	32	-7	35%	39%	18%	8%
2017	OAK			51	80	591	64%	--	11.6	3						-4.4%								

Cook did not light things up with Aaron Rodgers last year, but he made perhaps the catch of the season for the Packers to set up a game-winning field goal in Dallas in the playoffs. Cook had 229 yards and two touchdowns in three playoff games, the first time in his career he reached the postseason. While Rodgers wanted him back in Green Bay, Derek Carr will get to try out Cook now, and Cook should be an upgrade over Clive Walford. Just don't expect him to block well or reliably produce catches the way he did in January.

Vernon Davis

Height: 6-3		Weight: 250		College: Maryland			Draft: 2006/1 (6)		Born: 31-Jan-1984		Age: 33		Risk: Green											

Year	Team	G/GS	Snaps	Rec	Pass	Yds	C%	+/-	Yd/C	TD	Drop	YAC	Rk	YAC+	BTkl	DVOA	Rk	DYAR	Rk	YAR	Short	Mid	Deep	Bomb
2014	SF	14/14	830	26	51	245	51%	-3.5	9.4	2	4	1.9	49	-2.2	3	-28.4%	46	-66	45	-71	29%	44%	17%	10%
2015	2TM	15/9	621	38	58	395	66%	+2.5	10.4	0	3	3.8	39	-0.9	4	-8.8%	34	-6	34	1	41%	37%	15%	7%
2016	WAS	16/14	673	44	59	583	75%	+4.7	13.3	2	4	5.4	8	+0.7	11	16.8%	11	96	14	100	48%	33%	12%	7%
2017	WAS			37	58	410	64%	--	11.1	2						-3.1%								

Davis unexpectedly pulled his career out of free fall by signing on as Jordan Reed's backup and proving to be both a valuable insurance policy and a useful matchup headache as a No. 2 tight end. Washington rewarded Davis with a three-year, $15 million contract in the offseason. That's a lot of money for a 33-year-old role player who still doesn't block worth a lick. If Washington's other offseason investments on offense work out, there won't be enough footballs to go around for Davis to earn his money.

A.J. Derby

Height: 6-4		Weight: 255		College: Arkansas			Draft: 2015/6 (202)		Born: 20-Sep-1991		Age: 26		Risk: Green											

Year	Team	G/GS	Snaps	Rec	Pass	Yds	C%	+/-	Yd/C	TD	Drop	YAC	Rk	YAC+	BTkl	DVOA	Rk	DYAR	Rk	YAR	Short	Mid	Deep	Bomb
2016	2TM	10/3	226	16	20	160	80%	+2.6	10.0	0	1	3.2	--	-1.3	1	-6.7%	--	1	--	1	37%	58%	5%	0%
2017	DEN			28	42	291	67%	--	10.4	2						-3.4%								

Remember when Shredder became Super Shredder in the first Teenage Mutant Ninja Turtles sequel? That's kind of what we have here with Wes Welker turning into A.J. Derby, and it's not just because they both wear No. 83 and joined Denver via New England. Unfortunately, Derby goes down about as easily as Super Shredder did, and he's not nearly the consistent threat of a Welker. However, he has a chance to stick around just because of what little proven production the Broncos have at that position.

Seth DeValve

Height: 6-4		Weight: 244		College: Princeton			Draft: 2016/4 (138)		Born: 29-Jan-1993		Age: 24		Risk: Green											

Year	Team	G/GS	Snaps	Rec	Pass	Yds	C%	+/-	Yd/C	TD	Drop	YAC	Rk	YAC+	BTkl	DVOA	Rk	DYAR	Rk	YAR	Short	Mid	Deep	Bomb
2016	CLE	12/2	94	10	12	127	83%	+1.9	12.7	2	0	4.4	--	+1.0	4	57.5%	--	52	--	55	42%	42%	17%	0%
2017	CLE			22	30	255	73%	--	11.6	2						7.9%								

DeValve got off to a slow start as a rookie, with only 24 snaps (11 on offense) in the first seven games of the year. That's partly because he was slowed by a hamstring injury during training camp, and then a knee injury knocked him out for four games. Those snapcounts climbed to 165 and 82 from that point onward, and DeValve had at least one catch in each of his last eight games. Cleveland coaches and beat writers alike were praising DeValve's physical and mental improvement in OTAs. The Browns were just 23rd in usage of two-tight end sets last year, but that should go up if DeValve can carry this performance into the regular season.

Jack Doyle

Height: 6-6		Weight: 258		College: Western Kentucky			Draft: 2013/FA		Born: 5-May-1990		Age: 27		Risk: Yellow											

Year	Team	G/GS	Snaps	Rec	Pass	Yds	C%	+/-	Yd/C	TD	Drop	YAC	Rk	YAC+	BTkl	DVOA	Rk	DYAR	Rk	YAR	Short	Mid	Deep	Bomb
2014	IND	16/1	399	18	22	118	82%	+0.9	6.6	2	0	6.0	--	+0.0	4	-4.6%	--	4	--	-2	82%	14%	5%	0%
2015	IND	16/2	332	12	14	72	86%	+1.1	6.0	1	0	4.7	--	-1.0	2	-7.9%	--	-1	--	-1	93%	7%	0%	0%
2016	IND	16/14	750	59	75	584	79%	+6.2	9.9	5	4	4.2	23	-0.2	7	18.7%	10	131	9	96	56%	35%	9%	0%
2017	IND			59	76	583	78%	--	9.9	4						6.1%								

Typecast as a blocking tight end for the first few years of his career, Doyle blossomed in 2016 after Coby Fleener fled to New Orleans and Dwayne Allen got hurt yet again. Doyle is not going to burn his opponents on pure speed or physicality, but he's a reliable possession receiver with a big frame and a willingness to fight for balls in traffic.

Eric Ebron

| | | Height: 6-4 | | Weight: 250 | | College: North Carolina | | | Draft: 2014/1 (10) | | Born: 10-Apr-1993 | | Age: 24 | | Risk: Green | |

Year	Team	G/GS	Snaps	Rec	Pass	Yds	C%	+/-	Yd/C	TD	Drop	YAC	Rk	YAC+	BTkl	DVOA	Rk	DYAR	Rk	YAR	Short	Mid	Deep	Bomb
2014	DET	13/7	445	25	47	248	53%	-4.0	9.9	1	4	5.0	18	+0.3	1	-28.6%	47	-65	44	-49	50%	26%	11%	13%
2015	DET	14/8	613	47	70	537	67%	-2.4	11.4	5	7	6.2	8	+1.3	3	6.5%	18	64	18	81	57%	35%	7%	0%
2016	DET	13/13	708	61	85	711	72%	+3.1	11.7	1	7	4.6	14	+0.3	3	20.1%	9	149	5	141	40%	49%	10%	1%
2017	DET			58	84	704	69%	--	12.1	5						9.1%								

Some of the vitriol directed at Ebron is probably from fantasy fans who are angry that he had one touchdown catch in 2014 and 2016. The rest is probably from Detroit fans wondering why the team drafted Ebron 10th overall when Odell Beckham Jr. was still on the board. Can you imagine two years of Calvin Johnson and Beckham together? However, Ebron is Detroit's guy, and he has improved each season. He hasn't justified his draft status yet, but things could be worse.

Ebron's lack of red zone success is a problem. Matthew Stafford only targeted him eight times there in 2016, compared to far more opportunities for Anquan Boldin (23), Golden Tate (18), Theo Riddick (15), and Marvin Jones (15). The fact that Ebron's DVOA (33.9%) was higher than all but Riddick's from that group might suggest that he deserves more of those scoring chances. There was a similar trend in 2015 when Ebron only had eight red zone targets, but still had the best red zone DVOA (71.2%) on the team.

Tyler Eifert

| | | Height: 6-6 | | Weight: 251 | | College: Notre Dame | | | Draft: 2013/1 (21) | | Born: 8-Sep-1990 | | Age: 27 | | Risk: Red | |

Year	Team	G/GS	Snaps	Rec	Pass	Yds	C%	+/-	Yd/C	TD	Drop	YAC	Rk	YAC+	BTkl	DVOA	Rk	DYAR	Rk	YAR	Short	Mid	Deep	Bomb
2014	CIN	1/1	8	3	3	37	100%	+1.1	12.3	0	0	2.7	--	-1.6	0	47.1%	--	11	--	13	33%	33%	33%	0%
2015	CIN	13/12	751	52	74	615	70%	+7.2	11.8	13	5	4.5	28	+0.4	5	42.0%	1	247	1	230	40%	44%	16%	0%
2016	CIN	8/2	428	29	47	394	62%	+3.5	13.6	5	1	5.0	10	+1.0	0	9.6%	15	57	18	79	33%	53%	13%	3%
2017	CIN			61	92	770	66%	--	12.6	8						15.0%								

For consideration: touchdown-catching tight end, never healthy. Eifert has caught 18 touchdowns in 14 starts over the last two years, with a hulking frame matched with uncommon size, speed, and route-running ability. He has also played just 22 games over the last three years, and his health is in question again as the Bengals head to training camp. Coming off back surgery, Eifert was non-committal on being full-go at the start of camp in April. Sadly, health is a skill.

Evan Engram

| | | Height: 6-3 | | Weight: 234 | | College: Ole Miss | | | Draft: 2017/2 (23) | | Born: 2-Sep-1994 | | Age: 23 | | Risk: Red | |

Year	Team	G/GS	Snaps	Rec	Pass	Yds	C%	+/-	Yd/C	TD	Drop	YAC	Rk	YAC+	BTkl	DVOA	Rk	DYAR	Rk	YAR	Short	Mid	Deep	Bomb
2017	NYG			44	67	586	66%	--	13.3	4						10.6%								

The Giants finally have a quality tight end for the first time since Jeremy Shockey left. Engram outperformed O.J. Howard during Senior Bowl week; Howard was the better blocker, but Engram looked incredibly skilled and polished as a receiver, and he didn't crumple into a ball during blocking drills. Engram is a "move" tight end who should be deadly when sliding all over the formation and drawing coverage from whichever linebacker is left after Odell Beckham, Brandon Marshall, and Sterling Shepard divvy up the secondary. Pass protection? Shmass protection. That's what Rhett Ellison and Will Tye are for.

Zach Ertz

| | | Height: 6-5 | | Weight: 249 | | College: Stanford | | | Draft: 2013/2 (35) | | Born: 10-Nov-1990 | | Age: 27 | | Risk: Yellow | |

Year	Team	G/GS	Snaps	Rec	Pass	Yds	C%	+/-	Yd/C	TD	Drop	YAC	Rk	YAC+	BTkl	DVOA	Rk	DYAR	Rk	YAR	Short	Mid	Deep	Bomb
2014	PHI	16/5	587	58	89	702	65%	+3.5	12.1	3	2	3.9	31	-0.5	3	13.3%	12	127	8	130	34%	37%	23%	6%
2015	PHI	15/7	788	75	112	853	67%	+4.9	11.4	2	4	4.0	36	-0.5	4	0.2%	27	56	19	55	45%	36%	19%	0%
2016	PHI	14/12	851	78	106	816	74%	+11.4	10.5	4	3	3.4	39	-1.1	2	3.4%	22	75	17	106	51%	36%	10%	3%
2017	PHI			72	102	749	71%	--	10.4	4						-1.1%								

Ertz led the Eagles in receptions, receiving yards, and touchdowns by default last year because all of the wide receivers stunk. A 13-139-2 performance in the meaningless season finale juiced Ertz's numbers considerably in what was otherwise a very ordinary year. The same thing happened in 2015, when Ertz finished the season with 22-274-0 in a pair of meaningless games. A cynic might point out that Ertz has a knack for stat-padding in meaningless situations. A shrewd fantasy gamer would set that question aside, point to Ertz's long early-season stretches of mediocre productivity, note that the Eagles now have many other weapons, and suggest that you draft a tight end more likely to help you in September.

Gerald Everett

| | | Height: 6-3 | | | Weight: 239 | | College: South Alabama | | | | Draft: 2017/2 (44) | | | Born: 25-Jun-1994 | | Age: 23 | | Risk: Yellow |

Year	Team	G/GS	Snaps	Rec	Pass	Yds	C%	+/-	Yd/C	TD	Drop	YAC	Rk	YAC+	BTkl	DVOA	Rk	DYAR	Rk	YAR	Short	Mid	Deep	Bomb
2017	LARM			24	41	297	59%	--	12.4	2						3.9%								

It's been a winding road for Gerald Everett: two years at community college, one season at Alabama-Birmingham before they shut down their football program, then two years at South Alabama, and finally the second round of the 2017 draft. He was one of the best athletes at tight end in a rookie class chock-full of them, and should have plenty of opportunities alongside second-year player Tyler Higbee. Departed veteran Lance Kendricks had a catch rate of 57 percent in 2016 to go with eight dropped passes, so Los Angeles will be hoping for a more reliable set of hands from their new tight end prospect.

C.J. Fiedorowicz

| | | Height: 6-5 | | | Weight: 265 | | College: Iowa | | | | Draft: 2014/3 (65) | | | Born: 10/22/1991 | | Age: 26 | | Risk: Yellow |

Year	Team	G/GS	Snaps	Rec	Pass	Yds	C%	+/-	Yd/C	TD	Drop	YAC	Rk	YAC+	BTkl	DVOA	Rk	DYAR	Rk	YAR	Short	Mid	Deep	Bomb
2014	HOU	15/8	471	4	7	28	57%	-0.9	7.0	1	0	2.5	--	-1.5	0	-19.1%	--	-5	--	-4	71%	14%	14%	0%
2015	HOU	16/14	650	17	24	167	71%	+0.0	9.8	1	1	4.5	--	-0.1	0	-19.6%	--	-19	--	-9	78%	22%	0%	0%
2016	HOU	15/15	678	54	89	559	61%	-2.8	10.4	4	7	3.9	26	+0.0	6	-18.8%	39	-67	40	-31	46%	50%	4%	0%
2017	HOU			52	83	585	63%	--	11.3	3						-4.2%								

Fiedorowicz casually tripled his career reception total last year, although that wasn't saying much. In many ways, he was a beneficiary of the circumstances. The Texans refused to give their receivers anything easy, making it difficult for Brock Osweiler to connect with DeAndre Hopkins. And so, when Osweiler tightened up and stopped throwing 50/50 balls, the way forward for this offense was over the middle through the arms of Fiedoriwicz. Fiedorowicz has decent hands, but he's no better than a fourth option on a good offense because he offers very little after the catch. If the Texans run a better offense this year, Fiedorowicz's role will stagnate. If they don't, 100 empty targets are in play.

Coby Fleener

| | | Height: 6-6 | | | Weight: 247 | | College: Stanford | | | | Draft: 2012/2 (34) | | | Born: 20-Sep-1988 | | Age: 29 | | Risk: Green |

Year	Team	G/GS	Snaps	Rec	Pass	Yds	C%	+/-	Yd/C	TD	Drop	YAC	Rk	YAC+	BTkl	DVOA	Rk	DYAR	Rk	YAR	Short	Mid	Deep	Bomb
2014	IND	16/12	787	51	92	774	55%	-3.6	15.2	8	5	5.8	11	+1.3	3	10.1%	15	112	10	115	35%	38%	19%	8%
2015	IND	16/11	732	54	84	491	64%	-0.3	9.1	3	3	3.3	42	-1.4	2	-15.9%	40	-49	46	-38	49%	31%	17%	4%
2016	NO	16/8	663	50	82	631	61%	-1.9	12.6	3	4	4.2	22	+0.0	0	-4.5%	25	16	24	18	49%	24%	23%	4%
2017	NO			49	79	622	62%	--	12.7	4						5.3%								

Fleener underwhelmed in his first year with the Saints, failing to match either the raw or advanced statistics posted one year prior by then-35-year-old Benjamin Watson. Fleener tallied just three touchdowns, fumbled twice, and averaged under 40 yards per game. He lost playing time to Josh Hill in midseason; then over the last four games, with Hill back on injured reserve, Fleener scraped together a *total* of 84 yards. The only time he topped even 60 yards after Week 6 came against the rock-bottom Lions pass defense in his team's worst offensive performance of the season. Regardless of how Fleener performs, his position on the roster is secure: he was signed to a backloaded five-year, $36 million contract last offseason, because the Saints can't go a full offseason without throwing wads of cash at somebody. Releasing him would cost $12.2 million in dead money to save a mere $5.8 million in salary, so for now his $9 million cap hit isn't going anywhere.

Antonio Gates

| | | Height: 6-4 | | | Weight: 260 | | College: Kent State | | | | Draft: 2003/FA | | | Born: 18-Jun-1980 | | Age: 37 | | Risk: Yellow |

Year	Team	G/GS	Snaps	Rec	Pass	Yds	C%	+/-	Yd/C	TD	Drop	YAC	Rk	YAC+	BTkl	DVOA	Rk	DYAR	Rk	YAR	Short	Mid	Deep	Bomb
2014	SD	16/14	770	69	98	821	70%	+7.8	11.9	12	1	3.7	34	-0.5	1	24.1%	4	204	2	224	45%	39%	8%	8%
2015	SD	11/4	496	56	85	630	66%	+3.2	11.3	5	3	4.3	32	+0.0	4	13.1%	11	113	7	91	46%	43%	10%	1%
2016	SD	14/9	585	53	93	548	57%	-5.2	10.3	7	8	3.5	35	-0.2	4	-6.6%	28	4	28	6	42%	45%	11%	2%
2017	LACH			39	63	395	62%	--	10.1	6						0.8%								

Gates is 37 years old and averaged a career-low 10.3 yards per reception last season. He still caught seven touchdowns and has a great connection with Philip Rivers, but time is obviously drawing to a close on his career. Gates only needs one touchdown to surpass Tony Gonzalez (111) for the most in NFL history by a tight end. That will almost certainly happen early in the season, but by the end of the year, Gates will have fully passed the torch to Hunter Henry as the new featured tight end for the Chargers.

Jimmy Graham Height: 6-6   Weight: 260   College: Miami   Draft: 2010/3 (95)   Born: 24-Nov-1986   Age: 31   Risk: Yellow

Year	Team	G/GS	Snaps	Rec	Pass	Yds	C%	+/-	Yd/C	TD	Drop	YAC	Rk	YAC+	BTkl	DVOA	Rk	DYAR	Rk	YAR	Short	Mid	Deep	Bomb
2014	NO	16/13	775	85	124	889	69%	+3.7	10.5	10	5	3.5	40	-0.7	7	6.8%	17	124	9	113	41%	46%	10%	2%
2015	SEA	11/11	571	48	74	605	65%	+2.3	12.6	2	2	4.6	27	-0.3	4	14.8%	10	110	8	72	37%	49%	11%	3%
2016	SEA	16/15	790	65	96	923	69%	+3.7	14.2	6	5	5.0	12	+0.3	9	25.1%	6	204	2	194	34%	45%	17%	4%
2017	SEA			66	102	822	65%	--	12.4	8							12.0%								

Graham gave the Seahawks more than they could have possibly expected in his first season back after tearing his patellar tendon in 2015. Graham set single-season franchise records in catches and receiving yards for a tight end and finished second at the position in DYAR, which is what the Seahawks were hoping for when they traded away center Max Unger and a first-round pick in exchange for Graham and a fourth-rounder in 2015. However, Seattle struggled in the red zone in 2016, finishing 28th in touchdowns per red zone appearance, which is not what the team had in mind when they acquired Graham. A common refrain among Seahawks fans is that Graham isn't seeing enough red zone targets compared to someone like receiver Jermaine Kearse, but when the opponent is well aware of the threat of Graham, they will try to force another player to beat them. An improved running game would likely open up more opportunities for Graham to score more touchdowns in 2016.

Ladarius Green Height: 6-6   Weight: 237   College: Louisiana-Lafayette   Draft: 2012/4 (110)   Born: 27-Jan-1991   Age: 26   Risk: N/A

Year	Team	G/GS	Snaps	Rec	Pass	Yds	C%	+/-	Yd/C	TD	Drop	YAC	Rk	YAC+	BTkl	DVOA	Rk	DYAR	Rk	YAR	Short	Mid	Deep	Bomb
2014	SD	14/4	289	19	25	226	76%	+2.8	11.9	0	1	6.0	8	+0.5	1	15.9%	9	41	18	32	60%	20%	20%	0%
2015	SD	13/11	662	37	63	429	59%	+0.7	11.6	4	4	6.0	11	+1.3	3	11.8%	13	78	16	42	50%	32%	14%	4%
2016	PIT	6/2	140	18	34	304	53%	-2.1	16.9	1	2	5.4	6	+0.6	3	-0.4%	24	14	25	33	28%	34%	34%	3%

Green was supposed to break out after finally escaping Antonio Gates' shadow, but instead he suffered by far his worst season as a pro. That's largely due to injuries, as he spent most of the season on the sidelines with ankle and concussion issues, but he was also a bad fit in Pittsburgh's scheme. The Steelers used Green more on deep routes than the Chargers ever did, but that's not where Green's strengths lie. The Steelers released him after he failed a physical in May. Green says he is hoping to play again, but he remains in the NFL's concussion protocol, and there's a good chance the head injuries will have ended his career.

Virgil Green Height: 6-5   Weight: 240   College: Nevada   Draft: 2011/7 (204)   Born: 3-Aug-1988   Age: 29   Risk: Green

Year	Team	G/GS	Snaps	Rec	Pass	Yds	C%	+/-	Yd/C	TD	Drop	YAC	Rk	YAC+	BTkl	DVOA	Rk	DYAR	Rk	YAR	Short	Mid	Deep	Bomb
2014	DEN	13/9	394	6	6	74	100%	+1.7	12.3	1	0	7.7	--	+2.8	0	71.5%	--	35	--	41	83%	0%	17%	0%
2015	DEN	16/5	383	12	15	173	80%	+1.8	14.4	1	0	10.1	--	+5.9	3	51.3%	--	66	--	62	79%	21%	0%	0%
2016	DEN	12/11	494	22	37	237	59%	-2.0	10.8	1	3	4.6	16	-0.4	4	-14.8%	37	-19	35	-11	35%	53%	9%	3%
2017	DEN			30	47	271	64%	--	9.0	2							-9.4%								

Green is entering his seventh season with the Broncos, but has just 57 catches in his career. He notched a career-high 22 receptions last season, but saw A.J. Derby eat up some of his receiving duties. Green is athletic, but still suited to be more of a blocker while the team continues exploring other options for a receiving tight end.

Jermaine Gresham Height: 6-5   Weight: 261   College: Oklahoma   Draft: 2010/1 (21)   Born: 16-Jun-1988   Age: 29   Risk: Yellow

Year	Team	G/GS	Snaps	Rec	Pass	Yds	C%	+/-	Yd/C	TD	Drop	YAC	Rk	YAC+	BTkl	DVOA	Rk	DYAR	Rk	YAR	Short	Mid	Deep	Bomb
2014	CIN	15/15	875	62	79	460	78%	+5.2	7.4	5	2	4.2	25	-1.3	12	-21.9%	44	-73	48	-76	71%	25%	3%	1%
2015	ARI	15/12	596	18	32	223	56%	-0.1	12.4	1	1	4.1	33	-0.8	0	-14.0%	38	-16	36	-11	43%	43%	10%	3%
2016	ARI	16/14	835	37	61	391	61%	-1.3	10.6	2	7	3.7	29	-0.7	9	-18.7%	38	-48	38	-40	46%	46%	9%	0%
2017	ARI			35	56	400	63%	--	11.4	4							2.7%							

Gresham got a big new deal in the offseason, making a cool $7 million per year to stick as Arizona's top tight end. Now, maybe the Cardinals will consider actually using tight ends to justify the expenditure. Despite playing on 73 percent of Arizona's offensive snaps, Gresham was only sixth on the team in targets behind four separate wide receivers and a running back. While some of his value comes from his excellent run blocking, you would hope a tight end to whom you're paying that much money would have a more significant role in the offense going forward.

Ryan Griffin Height: 6-6   Weight: 247   College: Connecticut   Draft: 2013/6 (201)   Born: 11-Jan-1990   Age: 27   Risk: Green

Year	Team	G/GS	Snaps	Rec	Pass	Yds	C%	+/-	Yd/C	TD	Drop	YAC	Rk	YAC+	BTkl	DVOA	Rk	DYAR	Rk	YAR	Short	Mid	Deep	Bomb
2014	HOU	16/2	334	10	16	91	63%	-1.1	9.1	1	2	3.6	--	-1.0	0	-2.7%	--	5	--	7	56%	19%	19%	6%
2015	HOU	9/4	351	20	34	251	59%	-2.2	12.6	2	2	5.0	19	+0.1	2	11.5%	14	42	22	39	44%	41%	9%	6%
2016	HOU	16/5	507	50	74	442	68%	+0.1	8.8	2	6	3.4	42	-1.1	4	-22.9%	43	-77	43	-62	53%	33%	13%	1%
2017	HOU			34	55	364	62%	--	10.7	1							-7.8%							

Texans prime-time games harmed a lot of innocent bystanders last year, and one casual side product of that was an overintense dose of Ryan Griffin. Nothing says hopeless like two end-of-half drives where you go to your second-string tight end seven times. Griffin is a competent catch-first second tight end—a hype-less Mychal Rivera.

Xavier Grimble Height: 6-4   Weight: 257   College: USC   Draft: 2014/FA   Born: 22-Sep-1992   Age: 25   Risk: Green

Year	Team	G/GS	Snaps	Rec	Pass	Yds	C%	+/-	Yd/C	TD	Drop	YAC	Rk	YAC+	BTkl	DVOA	Rk	DYAR	Rk	YAR	Short	Mid	Deep	Bomb
2016	PIT	13/2	197	11	21	118	52%	-2.8	10.7	2	2	3.5	--	-0.8	1	-8.5%	--	-2	--	-13	55%	30%	15%	0%
2017	PIT			21	32	237	66%	--	11.3	3							3.0%							

From the moment he signed his first contract, Grimble has been a first-stringer on the NFL's All-Name team (along with his cousin, Barkevious Mingo). Now he could be a first-stringer in real life. Grimble spent two years bouncing around with the Giants, 49ers, and Patriots before seeing his first NFL action in Pittsburgh last year. He looks to be a more dangerous receiver than Jesse James, and could take over as the starter this season if he can play more consistently.

Rob Gronkowski Height: 6-6   Weight: 264   College: Arizona   Draft: 2010/2 (42)   Born: 14-May-1989   Age: 28   Risk: Red

Year	Team	G/GS	Snaps	Rec	Pass	Yds	C%	+/-	Yd/C	TD	Drop	YAC	Rk	YAC+	BTkl	DVOA	Rk	DYAR	Rk	YAR	Short	Mid	Deep	Bomb
2014	NE	15/10	825	82	131	1124	63%	+2.3	13.7	12	5	5.6	14	+1.3	24	19.7%	7	237	1	253	34%	45%	17%	4%
2015	NE	15/15	939	72	120	1176	60%	-0.1	16.3	11	1	7.7	2	+3.3	14	21.0%	7	235	2	211	35%	40%	19%	6%
2016	NE	8/6	354	25	38	540	66%	+4.5	21.6	3	1	9.1	1	+5.0	7	44.5%	2	136	7	142	22%	38%	27%	14%
2017	NE			73	109	1064	67%	--	14.6	11							22.9%							

Gronk was well on his way to a career year before a troublesome back injury ended his season after just eight games. On one hand, it was the fifth consecutive season he failed to make it through 16 games, and the third surgery for a back that appears increasingly likely to prematurely end his career at some point. On the other hand, Gronkowski was as spectacular as ever during his six-week stretch of health, a reminder of his status as the game-changer who lifts a great Patriots offense to even higher levels. Gronk's 21.6 yards per reception were not only a career-high, but the best single-season mark of any tight end with at least 25 catches since the merger. His plus-5.0 YAC+ was the best of his career, and the fourth time in his seven-year career he has led the league in that category. His broken tackle rate of 28 percent was best among all tight ends last year. As always, a healthy Gronk is in the discussion for the most dangerous non-quarterback in the game. Besides his health, the most intriguing part of Gronk's 2017 season will be whether or not he sustains last year's deep-ball usage, as he saw significant spikes in "deep" and "bomb" target rates from his previous career norms. His per-game volume may also decrease with the offensive skill -position cupboard so well-stocked, giving the Patriots other options as they dance around the annual problem of protecting their fragile tight end for the long haul. Still, at age 28, Gronk remains firmly at the peak of his powers, bad news for defenders so long as he's still standing.

Hunter Henry   Height: 6-5   Weight: 250   College: Arkansas   Draft: 2016/2 (35)   Born: 7-Dec-1994   Age: 23   Risk: Yellow

Year	Team	G/GS	Snaps	Rec	Pass	Yds	C%	+/-	Yd/C	TD	Drop	YAC	Rk	YAC+	BTkl	DVOA	Rk	DYAR	Rk	YAR	Short	Mid	Deep	Bomb
2016	SD	15/10	573	36	53	478	68%	+3.6	13.3	8	2	5.4	6	+2.2	5	33.4%	3	148	6	140	43%	37%	18%	2%
2017	LACH			54	84	702	64%	--	13.0	7						11.2%								

Tight ends are known for slow development as rookies. Since the NFL went to a 16-game season in 1978, only Keith Jackson (1988) and Jeremy Shockey (2002) had more than 700 receiving yards as rookies. While Hunter Henry did not produce that much, he did have to share snaps with a future Hall of Famer in Antonio Gates. If 2016 is any indication, he'll be just fine as a successor. The Chargers are hard to project with Keenan Allen returning from injury and the addition of Mike Williams, but Henry should be one of the team's most reliable targets this year.

Tyler Higbee   Height: 6-6   Weight: 249   College: Western Kentucky   Draft: 2016/4 (110)   Born: 1-Jan-1993   Age: 25   Risk: Red

Year	Team	G/GS	Snaps	Rec	Pass	Yds	C%	+/-	Yd/C	TD	Drop	YAC	Rk	YAC+	BTkl	DVOA	Rk	DYAR	Rk	YAR	Short	Mid	Deep	Bomb
2016	LARM	16/6	405	11	29	85	38%	-7.2	7.7	1	4	2.4	46	-2.5	1	-68.5%	46	-109	46	-111	56%	33%	7%	4%
2017	LARM			35	60	354	58%	--	10.1	3						-10.2%								

Perhaps Higbee thought he might be getting a chance to shine when the Rams cut tight end Lance Kendricks, but then Los Angeles went and drafted Gerald Everett in the second round to play a big role as a rookie. Sean McVay made use of multiple tight ends during his time with Washington, and the Rams are hoping that Everett and Higbee can form a duo somewhat close to what McVay had in the nation's capital with Jordan Reed and Vernon Davis. Theis pair will likely be a thrift-store version of that combination, at least in Year 1, but if Higbee can fix his issues with dropped passes, he could prove to be a useful cog in the Rams' new offense.

Josh Hill   Height: 6-5   Weight: 229   College: Idaho State   Draft: 2013/FA   Born: 21-May-1990   Age: 27   Risk: Yellow

Year	Team	G/GS	Snaps	Rec	Pass	Yds	C%	+/-	Yd/C	TD	Drop	YAC	Rk	YAC+	BTkl	DVOA	Rk	DYAR	Rk	YAR	Short	Mid	Deep	Bomb
2014	NO	16/3	288	14	20	176	70%	+0.9	12.6	5	1	7.1	--	+2.2	0	32.0%	--	57	--	58	68%	11%	16%	5%
2015	NO	16/7	424	16	30	120	53%	-6.0	7.5	2	0	4.8	21	-0.3	2	-27.9%	48	-44	43	-42	73%	17%	10%	0%
2016	NO	9/8	362	15	22	149	68%	+1.7	9.9	1	2	5.1	--	+0.3	0	-20.4%	--	-20	--	-17	63%	21%	16%	0%
2017	NO			28	42	286	67%	--	10.2	2						-1.0%								

When healthy, Josh Hill's playing time has increased every season since he joined the Saints as an undrafted free agent. Last year, after missing three games with a sprained ankle leading into the Week 5 bye, he played 65% of the team's offensive snaps from Week 6 to Week 12—more than supposed No.1 tight end Coby Fleener. Despite the increase in usage, Hill only had three games all year with more than a single catch. He finished the season on injured reserve with a fractured fibula.

Austin Hooper   Height: 6-4   Weight: 254   College: Stanford   Draft: 2016/3 (81)   Born: 4-Nov-1994   Age: 23   Risk: Green

Year	Team	G/GS	Snaps	Rec	Pass	Yds	C%	+/-	Yd/C	TD	Drop	YAC	Rk	YAC+	BTkl	DVOA	Rk	DYAR	Rk	YAR	Short	Mid	Deep	Bomb
2016	ATL	14/3	405	19	27	271	70%	+2.8	14.3	3	2	3.8	27	-0.4	1	46.8%	1	106	11	95	48%	33%	7%	11%
2017	ATL			40	64	517	63%	--	12.9	6						10.5%								

Meet the top tight end in DVOA, and this year's presumptive first-stringer in Atlanta. Sure, it was a small sample, but Hooper, who wasn't slated to play much until Jacob Tamme went down, showed very good athleticism and physicality as a rookie. It comes honestly—Hooper was a defensive lineman at fabled De La Salle High School in California, and switched positions when recruited by Tight End U, a.k.a. Stanford. Sixteen of his 19 catches moved the chains, and he looks like a solid red zone target with a quick first step to go with his size. Hooper benefited mightily from defenses bewildered by the many other Falcons playmakers, and he is unlikely to maintain anything like his 2016 efficiency, but he could develop into an above-average starter.

O.J. Howard Height: 6-6   Weight: 251   College: Alabama   Draft: 2017/1 (19)   Born: 19-Nov-1994   Age: 23   Risk: Red

Year	Team	G/GS	Snaps	Rec	Pass	Yds	C%	+/-	Yd/C	TD	Drop	YAC	Rk	YAC+	BTkl	DVOA	Rk	DYAR	Rk	YAR	Short	Mid	Deep	Bomb
2017	TB	36	59	485	61%	--	13.5	4	9.6%	8	4	5.6	13	+1.2	3	22.7%	6	104	12	91	34%	46%	16%	4%

Much has been written about the potential for O.J. Howard to shine in the Buccaneers offense, but he will first have to dislodge Cameron Brate as the starter. If Dirk Koetter was willing to change his base offense to accommodate two tight ends, he would have done so last year with Brate and Luke Stocker when his No. 2 receiver was a pair of crutches tied together with a discarded baseball glove. Howard is noted for his ability as a blocker in addition to his receiving prowess—he was used more as a blocker than a receiver at Alabama, but still had almost 600 yards receiving in 2016. That versatility should ensure that he sees plenty of on-field action, but there are many mouths to feed in the Buccaneer Palace canteen.

Jesse James Height: 6-7   Weight: 261   College: Penn State   Draft: 2015/5 (160)   Born: 4-Jun-1994   Age: 23   Risk: Green

Year	Team	G/GS	Snaps	Rec	Pass	Yds	C%	+/-	Yd/C	TD	Drop	YAC	Rk	YAC+	BTkl	DVOA	Rk	DYAR	Rk	YAR	Short	Mid	Deep	Bomb
2015	PIT	8/2	181	8	11	56	73%	+1.1	7.0	1	0	2.5	--	-1.6	0	-13.3%	--	-5	--	0	70%	10%	20%	0%
2016	PIT	16/13	855	39	60	338	65%	-3.9	8.7	3	5	3.2	43	-0.9	1	-13.7%	34	-26	37	-21	49%	42%	7%	2%
2017	PIT			33	46	346	72%	--	10.5	4							8.4%								

James' big postseason performance (12 catches in 16 targets for 159 yards in three games) raised eyebrows of fantasy owners around the world, wondering if the youngster was starting to blossom into a sleeper candidate. The Steelers have too many weapons to expect James to top 50 yards very often, but the folks in Pittsburgh must have been excited to see the youngster play so well after not doing much in his career up to that point. James is still very young—he was born the same year as first-round draft pick O.J. Howard—and should have plenty of time to develop. On the other hand, there is plenty of room for improvement here. James had four more drops than he had broken tackles, tied for the highest such margin among tight ends.

Travis Kelce Height: 6-5   Weight: 255   College: Cincinnati   Draft: 2013/3 (63)   Born: 5-Oct-1989   Age: 28   Risk: Yellow

Year	Team	G/GS	Snaps	Rec	Pass	Yds	C%	+/-	Yd/C	TD	Drop	YAC	Rk	YAC+	BTkl	DVOA	Rk	DYAR	Rk	YAR	Short	Mid	Deep	Bomb
2014	KC	16/11	668	67	87	862	77%	+9.9	12.9	5	4	7.2	4	+2.2	12	23.0%	5	174	4	196	53%	35%	12%	0%
2015	KC	16/16	923	72	103	875	70%	+0.2	12.2	5	5	7.3	4	+1.8	14	9.3%	16	110	9	108	57%	35%	8%	0%
2016	KC	16/15	888	85	117	1125	73%	+4.8	13.2	4	8	7.4	4	+2.5	12	26.0%	5	261	1	222	55%	33%	8%	4%
2017	KC			88	123	1081	72%	--	12.3	5							11.9%								

Rob Gronkowski is one of a kind, but Kelce would be considered a good outcome for an attempt at human cloning. He's a big, lovable goofball, and would fit right in on the cast of *Peaky Blinders*. Kelce had his first 1,000-yard season in 2016, and took advantage of Gronk's troubled health to earn his first All-Pro selection. He only had four touchdowns, but that says a lot about playing with Alex Smith as his quarterback.

Kelce's 2016 was dominated by drags and slants. No tight end was targeted more on either route, and he easily led the NFL with 88 DYAR on 14 slants and 82 DYAR on 19 drag routes. The other unique thing the Chiefs do with Kelce is line him up wide for a screen pass. He had 49 DYAR on eight of those last season, while all other NFL tight ends combined for 34 such screens withr minus-95 DYAR. For all the talk about what Tyreek Hill might do without Jeremy Maclin around, the Chiefs should look to unleash Kelce to even greater highs this season.

Lance Kendricks

Height: 6-3 Weight: 243 College: Wisconsin Draft: 2011/2 (47) Born: 30-Jan-1988 Age: 29 Risk: Red

Year	Team	G/GS	Snaps	Rec	Pass	Yds	C%	+/-	Yd/C	TD	Drop	YAC	Rk	YAC+	BTkl	DVOA	Rk	DYAR	Rk	YAR	Short	Mid	Deep	Bomb
2014	STL	16/14	594	27	38	259	71%	+1.4	9.6	5	2	3.9	32	-1.0	0	11.8%	13	51	15	52	64%	25%	11%	0%
2015	STL	15/12	570	25	40	245	63%	-1.5	9.8	2	1	5.2	16	-0.3	2	-13.6%	37	-17	37	-7	62%	27%	3%	8%
2016	LARM	16/16	826	50	87	499	57%	-6.4	10.0	2	8	5.5	5	+0.5	6	-19.7%	40	-70	42	-89	65%	24%	10%	1%
2017	GB			26	38	263	68%	--	10.1	2						0.1%								

It would have made sense for the Packers to add some speed to the tight end position to complement Martellus Bennett and offset the departure of Jared Cook. Instead they added Lance Kendricks, who is primarily a blocking tight end. The positive spin on Kendricks is that he has played with bad quarterbacks over the course of his career in offenses that didn't excel at scheming receivers open or deceiving the defense. Aaron Rodgers should be able to make him an effective player in a limited role and he should be an improvement over Richard Rodgers, but Kendricks isn't a difference-maker by any definition.

George Kittle

Height: 6-4 Weight: 247 College: Iowa Draft: 2017/5 (146) Born: 9-Oct-1993 Age: 24 Risk: Red

Year	Team	G/GS	Snaps	Rec	Pass	Yds	C%	+/-	Yd/C	TD	Drop	YAC	Rk	YAC+	BTkl	DVOA	Rk	DYAR	Rk	YAR	Short	Mid	Deep	Bomb
2017	SF			20	31	228	65%	--	11.4	2						-4.3%								

Kittle was, at best, C.J. Beathard's fourth target at Iowa, with just 48 receptions in his college career. What kept him in the starting lineup was his blocking ability—arguably the best in the class, making him a perfect choice for filling the H-back hole San Francisco has struggled with since Delanie Walker left town. Kittle only had one drop in his 48 receptions as well, so he's capable enough when targeted. Reports from San Francisco say it's unlikely both Vance McDonald and Garrett Celek make the final roster, so Kittle will likely play a significant role as a rookie.

Vance McDonald

Height: 6-4 Weight: 267 College: Rice Draft: 2013/2 (55) Born: 13-Jun-1990 Age: 27 Risk: Red

Year	Team	G/GS	Snaps	Rec	Pass	Yds	C%	+/-	Yd/C	TD	Drop	YAC	Rk	YAC+	BTkl	DVOA	Rk	DYAR	Rk	YAR	Short	Mid	Deep	Bomb
2014	SF	8/4	214	2	7	30	29%	-1.3	15.0	0	0	13.0	--	+8.0	0	-99.1%	--	-46	--	-46	60%	20%	0%	20%
2015	SF	14/11	473	30	46	326	65%	-0.5	10.9	3	5	6.1	9	+1.2	4	-19.2%	43	-34	40	-29	52%	28%	13%	7%
2016	SF	11/11	442	24	45	391	53%	-4.6	16.3	4	3	8.6	2	+4.3	2	6.7%	18	41	19	22	41%	36%	16%	7%
2017	SF			33	53	370	62%	--	11.2	3						-4.7%								

When the first thing your new coach and general manager try to do is try to trade you away, that's probably a sign. When no one else in the league is willing to pony up anything to acquire you in a trade, that's also probably a sign. Don't write McDonald off entirely just yet, though. He ranked higher in DVOA than most 49ers players at any position have in recent years, and he finished second among tight ends in YAC+, due in large part to two 60-plus-yard touchdowns. He can do very good things with the ball in his hands; the trouble is getting the ball in his hands to begin with. Jerry Rice may have dunked his hands in stickum in the '80s, but McDonald apparently has chosen molten lead. McDonald's receiving plus-minus was fourth-worst among tight ends, and his battle with the drops has been an ongoing subplot to his career.

Zach Miller

Height: 6-4 Weight: 233 College: Nebraska-Omaha Draft: 2009/6 (180) Born: 4-Oct-1984 Age: 33 Risk: Red

Year	Team	G/GS	Snaps	Rec	Pass	Yds	C%	+/-	Yd/C	TD	Drop	YAC	Rk	YAC+	BTkl	DVOA	Rk	DYAR	Rk	YAR	Short	Mid	Deep	Bomb
2015	CHI	15/14	579	34	46	439	74%	+5.0	12.9	5	0	6.5	6	+2.4	12	25.6%	5	104	11	105	57%	26%	14%	2%
2016	CHI	10/8	511	47	64	486	73%	+3.1	10.3	4	1	4.6	15	+0.3	9	12.5%	12	85	16	87	58%	29%	11%	2%
2017	CHI			46	68	511	68%	--	11.1	4						6.7%								

Zach Miller has been shockingly productive considering his circumstances over the past two seasons. But he also turns 33 in October, has a terrible history of injuries, and doesn't possess a particularly impressive skill set. Miller can stretch the defense, but he's not a noted vertical tight end. He can make receptions in different areas of the field, but he's not a possession receiver. He is an assignment blocker rather than an impact blocker. Miller probably will have another reasonable season and be a useful spot start when your fantasy tight end has a bye week. With Adam Shaheen arriving as a second-round pick and Dion Sims signed to a large free-agent contract, some Bears reporters think he'll be elsewhere by Week 1.

David Njoku

Height: 6-4 | Weight: 246 | College: Miami | Draft: 2017/1 (29) | Born: 10-Jul-1996 | Age: 21 | Risk: Yellow

Year	Team	G/GS	Snaps	Rec	Pass	Yds	C%	+/-	Yd/C	TD	Drop	YAC	Rk	YAC+	BTkl	DVOA	Rk	DYAR	Rk	YAR	Short	Mid	Deep	Bomb
2017	CLE			50	76	556	66%	--	11.1	3						-1.7%								

Technically, Njoku will replace Gary Barnidge in the Browns' starting lineup, but he will also replace Terrelle Pryor as the big target with freaky athleticism in the passing game. Njoku is two inches shorter than Pryor and a few pounds heavier, but he split time between wide receiver and tight end with the Hurricanes and figures to see plenty of action in the slot or out wide this fall. He was Miami's No.3 target last year, and used mostly as a deep threat, averaging 16.2 yards per catch. He had eight touchdowns in just 43 catches, and those touchdowns averaged 24.0 yards apiece. His best highlights came against Duke, when he showed an ability get open deep on a 76-yard touchdown, and also tackle-breaking agility and open-field speed, taking a shallow cross to the house for a 58-yard score. However, he also scored five red zone touchdowns, so he can be effective close to the goal line too. Njoku was a national champion high-jumper in high school and blew up at the combine, finishing third or better among tight ends in the vertical jump, broad jump, and 3-cone drill. He struggled with drops at times and needs to add some mass if he's going to be an effective blocker, but the ceiling here is sky-high and it's quite reasonable to expect Njoku to play in a Pro Bowl soon.

Greg Olsen

Height: 6-6 | Weight: 254 | College: Miami | Draft: 2007/1 (31) | Born: 11-Mar-1985 | Age: 32 | Risk: Green

Year	Team	G/GS	Snaps	Rec	Pass	Yds	C%	+/-	Yd/C	TD	Drop	YAC	Rk	YAC+	BTkl	DVOA	Rk	DYAR	Rk	YAR	Short	Mid	Deep	Bomb
2014	CAR	16/16	1067	84	123	1008	68%	+5.1	12.0	6	1	4.0	29	-0.3	1	14.7%	10	178	3	183	37%	49%	12%	3%
2015	CAR	16/16	1057	77	124	1104	62%	+3.3	14.3	7	2	4.5	29	+0.3	1	8.9%	17	132	6	184	28%	48%	15%	9%
2016	CAR	16/16	1033	80	129	1073	62%	+2.5	13.4	3	3	4.4	17	+0.2	2	8.3%	17	134	8	123	22%	52%	18%	8%
2017	CAR			79	130	1024	61%	--	13.0	6						5.9%								

Olsen keeps chugging on as one of the most consistent players in football, even as he's passed age 30. For five straight seasons he has played in every game and finished with a positive DVOA. He was also in the top ten in DYAR four times in those five seasons (he was 14th in 2013). For three straight years he has gone over 1,000 yards. Speed and slipperiness are all the rage in Charlotte these days, but Olsen is the consistent glue that is center of gravity in the offense. Look for more of the same from him this season.

Dennis Pitta

Height: 6-5 | Weight: 245 | College: BYU | Draft: 2010/4 (114) | Born: 29-Jun-1985 | Age: 32 | Risk: N/A

Year	Team	G/GS	Snaps	Rec	Pass	Yds	C%	+/-	Yd/C	TD	Drop	YAC	Rk	YAC+	BTkl	DVOA	Rk	DYAR	Rk	YAR	Short	Mid	Deep	Bomb
2014	BAL	3/3	166	16	21	125	76%	+1.1	7.8	0	1	3.4	--	-1.8	2	-3.5%	--	5	--	0	55%	40%	5%	0%
2016	BAL	16/12	811	86	121	729	71%	+2.7	8.5	2	8	3.4	38	-1.4	7	-19.7%	41	-96	45	-65	57%	35%	7%	2%

Just when you thought it was safe for the Ravens to have a victory at the tight end position. Pitta was presumed to be a re-tirement candidate after what amounts to three lost years with a degenerative hip condition. It was a remarkable story when he came out of nowhere to lead the Ravens in targets last year, regardless of how productive he was. Then, in this year's OTAs, the voodoo curse that was put on the Ravens tight end position had its revenge, and he got knocked the wrong way on his hip again. The Ravens released him, and he is likely looking at the end of the line. There are *Walking Dead* episodes with a lower attrition rate than the Ravens' tight end depth chart.

Jordan Reed

Height: 6-2 | Weight: 236 | College: Florida | Draft: 2013/3 (85) | Born: 3-Jul-1990 | Age: 27 | Risk: Red

Year	Team	G/GS	Snaps	Rec	Pass	Yds	C%	+/-	Yd/C	TD	Drop	YAC	Rk	YAC+	BTkl	DVOA	Rk	DYAR	Rk	YAR	Short	Mid	Deep	Bomb
2014	WAS	11/2	364	50	65	465	77%	+1.9	9.3	0	0	5.7	12	+0.5	10	-10.8%	35	-15	35	-8	66%	28%	6%	0%
2015	WAS	14/8	704	87	114	952	76%	+9.6	10.9	11	2	5.4	15	+0.9	19	20.1%	8	206	4	213	64%	25%	11%	1%
2016	WAS	12/8	568	66	89	686	74%	+6.9	10.4	6	1	4.0	25	-0.2	12	9.9%	14	102	13	130	49%	37%	12%	2%
2017	WAS			86	122	931	70%	--	10.8	8						7.6%								

Reed missed two early-season games with a concussion. He missed two late-season games and was ineffective in two others due to a shoulder injury he suffered on Thanksgiving against the Cowboys. When healthy, Reed remains outstanding. But injuries may be slowly turning an Antonio Gates-level talent into a possession receiver with only a fraction of his original big-play capability.

Mychal Rivera   Height: 6-3   Weight: 242   College: Tennessee   Draft: 2013/6 (184)   Born: 8-Sep-1990   Age: 27   Risk: Green

Year	Team	G/GS	Snaps	Rec	Pass	Yds	C%	+/-	Yd/C	TD	Drop	YAC	Rk	YAC+	BTkl	DVOA	Rk	DYAR	Rk	YAR	Short	Mid	Deep	Bomb
2014	OAK	16/10	818	58	99	534	59%	-2.7	9.2	4	7	3.0	44	-1.8	1	-22.6%	45	-97	49	-112	51%	31%	14%	4%
2015	OAK	16/0	401	32	46	280	70%	+1.4	8.8	1	1	3.9	38	-1.6	2	-25.7%	45	-51	48	-56	55%	20%	18%	7%
2016	OAK	13/2	313	18	25	192	72%	+2.0	10.7	1	3	3.4	36	-1.1	0	6.4%	19	23	22	17	46%	29%	21%	4%
2017	JAC			30	49	331	61%	--	11.0	2						-4.6%								

The case in favor of Mychal Rivera having a role in Jacksonville is that 1) he's a tight end; 2) most teams throw the ball to one at least occasionally, unless they are Chan Gailey's Jets; 3) Jacksonville signed him; and 4) Marcedes Lewis, Ben Koyack, and Neal Sterling are not likely to be the guy. As long as they aren't expecting Rivera to do more than catch the ball reasonably well and maybe fall forward for an extra yard, and do not ask him to be more than a situational blocker, the Jaguars should be satisfied with what they get.

Richard Rodgers   Height: 6-4   Weight: 257   College: California   Draft: 2014/3 (98)   Born: 1/22/1992   Age: 25   Risk: Yellow

Year	Team	G/GS	Snaps	Rec	Pass	Yds	C%	+/-	Yd/C	TD	Drop	YAC	Rk	YAC+	BTkl	DVOA	Rk	DYAR	Rk	YAR	Short	Mid	Deep	Bomb
2014	GB	16/5	478	20	30	225	67%	-0.1	11.3	2	1	2.4	47	-2.5	1	-10.9%	36	-8	34	-7	59%	24%	10%	7%
2015	GB	16/12	799	58	85	510	68%	+2.4	8.8	8	2	4.0	35	-0.9	4	-3.7%	30	21	30	30	55%	36%	5%	4%
2016	GB	16/6	604	30	47	271	64%	+0.5	9.0	2	4	3.5	34	-1.1	2	-9.1%	32	-6	30	-1	39%	45%	11%	5%
2017	GB			17	27	176	63%	--	10.3	2						-3.2%								

Richard Rodgers wasn't even close to becoming the Packers starting tight end after Jared Cook's departure. Rodgers has proven to be inconsistent in the NFL but more importantly he has been inconsistent while showing off a limited skill set. He's not a great athlete or nuanced route-runner, and his blocking skills are replacement-level at best. If Rodgers is going to play any role in the Packers offense, he will need to outperform Lance Kendricks through training camp.

Kyle Rudolph   Height: 6-6   Weight: 265   College: Notre Dame   Draft: 2011/2 (43)   Born: 9-Nov-1989   Age: 28   Risk: Yellow

Year	Team	G/GS	Snaps	Rec	Pass	Yds	C%	+/-	Yd/C	TD	Drop	YAC	Rk	YAC+	BTkl	DVOA	Rk	DYAR	Rk	YAR	Short	Mid	Deep	Bomb
2014	MIN	9/8	434	24	34	231	71%	+1.8	9.6	2	3	4.8	20	+0.3	1	0.0%	25	17	25	11	65%	26%	6%	3%
2015	MIN	16/16	847	49	73	495	67%	+6.0	10.1	5	3	3.9	37	-0.4	7	-6.3%	33	5	33	12	63%	20%	14%	3%
2016	MIN	16/16	969	83	132	840	63%	-1.9	10.1	7	7	4.3	19	-0.2	5	-9.1%	31	-17	34	3	50%	40%	10%	1%
2017	MIN			78	112	750	70%	--	9.6	5						0.3%								

Kyle Rudolph has never lived up to expectations. He remains the Vikings' starting tight end and a focal point of the passing game, but not because of consistently great performances. Rudolph has never faced real competition for his starting spot, and the Vikings have always been trying to address greater issues around him with their equity in the offseason. Rudolph has the physical ability to get open, but doesn't run great routes. He has the size to beat defenders at the catch point, but doesn't consistently catch passes that he should. The lack of consistency in his play is unlikely to disappear at this point of his career. He may look like Rob Gronkowski, but that's where the comparisons end.

Austin Seferian-Jenkins   Height: 6-5   Weight: 262   College: Washington   Draft: 2014/2 (38)   Born: 9/29/1992   Age: 25   Risk: Red

Year	Team	G/GS	Snaps	Rec	Pass	Yds	C%	+/-	Yd/C	TD	Drop	YAC	Rk	YAC+	BTkl	DVOA	Rk	DYAR	Rk	YAR	Short	Mid	Deep	Bomb
2014	TB	9/9	447	21	38	221	55%	-0.0	10.5	2	2	2.0	48	-1.8	1	-18.7%	40	-29	38	-30	30%	55%	15%	0%
2015	TB	7/3	218	21	39	338	54%	-2.9	16.1	4	1	4.6	26	+1.2	3	5.0%	23	33	25	62	26%	50%	21%	3%
2016	2TM	9/2	190	13	20	154	65%	-0.5	11.8	1	3	2.2	--	-1.2	1	15.4%	--	32	--	37	29%	57%	5%	10%
2017	NYJ			39	64	466	60%	--	12.1	3						-1.6%								

Seferian-Jenkins' second-round draft status in 2014 gives him the highest pedigree among the Jets' tight ends and receivers this year, and his seven career receiving touchdowns (second on the team behind Matt Forte) make him arguably the most accomplished among them as well. He claims to have been sober since January, kicking a drinking problem that has followed him since college, and continues to go to rehab in hopes of preventing a relapse. He has also lost 20 pounds, and was reportedly the star of New York's OTAs. He'll be suspended for two games following a DUI arrest last September, but otherwise all signs point to a rebirth for the winner of the 2013 John Mackey Award as college football's top tight end. The Jets have ignored the position recently—as a group, Jets tight ends have only 26 catches since head coach Todd Bowles arrived in 2015, less than half as many as any other team. However, with a barren depth chart at wide receiver and a new offensive coordinator in John Morton who has a track record with head coaches who like tight ends (Jim Harbaugh, Jon Gruden, Sean Payton), Seferian-Jenkins has a good chance to make a splash this year.

Adam Shaheen   Height: 6-6   Weight: 278   College: Ashland   Draft: 2017/2 (45)   Born: 1-Jan-1994   Age: 24   Risk: Green

Year	Team	G/GS	Snaps	Rec	Pass	Yds	C%	+/-	Yd/C	TD	Drop	YAC	Rk	YAC+	BTkl	DVOA	Rk	DYAR	Rk	YAR	Short	Mid	Deep	Bomb
2017	CHI			16	24	209	67%	--	13.0	1						11.3%								

Adam Shaheen is huge. The 6-foot-6, 278-pound tight end ran a 4.79-second 40-yard dash at the combine and looked even faster on the field in college. Part of that was playing against a lower level of competition. In the NFL, Sheehan will be an average athlete for a tight end, but maybe an above- average one when you consider the size advantage he will have down the field. So long as he can hold up against the physicality of linebackers and defensive backs, Sheehan should always have the advantage when trying to play the ball in the air. Shaheen probably won't play a huge amount as a rookie, but if the Bears are smart they will design specific plays to incorporate him while going in search of big yards.

Dion Sims   Height: 6-5   Weight: 262   College: Michigan State   Draft: 2013/4 (106)   Born: 18-Feb-1991   Age: 26   Risk: Green

Year	Team	G/GS	Snaps	Rec	Pass	Yds	C%	+/-	Yd/C	TD	Drop	YAC	Rk	YAC+	BTkl	DVOA	Rk	DYAR	Rk	YAR	Short	Mid	Deep	Bomb
2014	MIA	14/2	507	24	36	284	67%	+2.1	11.8	2	1	4.6	21	-0.3	1	11.1%	14	42	17	56	55%	24%	18%	3%
2015	MIA	13/4	457	18	25	127	72%	+0.8	7.1	1	1	4.9	20	-0.4	0	-27.7%	47	-35	42	-36	60%	20%	16%	4%
2016	MIA	14/11	701	26	35	256	74%	+2.7	9.8	4	0	5.0	11	+0.6	3	6.3%	20	34	20	36	64%	27%	3%	6%
2017	CHI			22	34	231	65%	--	10.5	2						-1.4%								

Dion Sims had a real chance to be a long-term starter in Miami, but never took the opportunities he was given. Sims was a better blocker than Jordan Cameron but couldn't perform well enough as a receiver to hold the starting job. Talent isn't a question for Sims. He can adjust to the ball in the air against tight coverage, is athletic enough to get open, and will make impact blocks at the point of attack on running plays. Getting him to do it for four quarters each week is the challenge.

Jonnu Smith   Height: 6-3   Weight: 248   College: Florida International   Draft: 2017/3 (100)   Born: 22-Aug-1995   Age: 22   Risk: Green

Year	Team	G/GS	Snaps	Rec	Pass	Yds	C%	+/-	Yd/C	TD	Drop	YAC	Rk	YAC+	BTkl	DVOA	Rk	DYAR	Rk	YAR	Short	Mid	Deep	Bomb
2017	TEN			18	27	231	67%	--	12.8	2						9.0%								

For Smith's NFL.com draft profile, Lance Zierlein compared Smith to Delanie Walker. Fitting, then, that his likely NFL future is to supplant Walker come 2018 or 2019. Like Walker, lack of height and bulk means he is unlikely to be a base option as an in-line blocker, notwithstanding the Titans talking him up in June. The Tennessee team chapter notes the rarity of successful mid-major tight ends, although Smith was reasonably successful as the Golden Panthers' No. 2 target, averaging more than 12 yards per catch. Unless he can function well as an in-line blocker or Walker gets injured, though, Smith's rookie impact is likely to be quite modest both on the field and from a fantasy perspective.

Erik Swoope | Height: 6-5 | Weight: 246 | College: Miami | Draft: 2014/FA | Born: 8-May-1992 | Age: 25 | Risk: Blue

Year	Team	G/GS	Snaps	Rec	Pass	Yds	C%	+/-	Yd/C	TD	Drop	YAC	Rk	YAC+	BTkl	DVOA	Rk	DYAR	Rk	YAR	Short	Mid	Deep	Bomb
2015	IND	1/0	6	0	0	0	--	--	--	0	--	--	--	--	--	--	--	--	--	--	--	--	--	--
2016	IND	16/4	245	15	22	297	68%	+1.0	19.8	1	2	8.9	--	+5.0	0	46.7%	--	85	--	81	36%	32%	32%	0%
2017	IND			31	47	399	66%	--	12.9	4						10.4%								

Slated for an expanded role this year, there's a lot to be excited about with Swoope. It wasn't many targets, but he was often a deep threat and worked his way into the correct spots. Swoope faced a steep learning curve since he was purely a basketball player at Miami, but he was able to train with Jimmy Graham and make his way up the Colts roster from the practice squad. Still just 25, with a lot of positive indicators and not much competition from the Colts receiving corps, he might play a bigger fantasy role than you'd think in 2017.

Julius Thomas | Height: 6-5 | Weight: 251 | College: Portland State | Draft: 2011/4 (129) | Born: 27-Jun-1988 | Age: 29 | Risk: Red

Year	Team	G/GS	Snaps	Rec	Pass	Yds	C%	+/-	Yd/C	TD	Drop	YAC	Rk	YAC+	BTkl	DVOA	Rk	DYAR	Rk	YAR	Short	Mid	Deep	Bomb
2014	DEN	13/10	691	43	62	489	69%	+4.3	11.4	12	1	3.8	33	-0.5	3	24.7%	2	140	6	142	58%	31%	8%	3%
2015	JAC	12/10	541	46	80	455	58%	-4.3	9.9	5	5	3.2	44	-0.8	3	-17.7%	41	-57	49	-42	50%	34%	14%	1%
2016	JAC	9/6	449	30	51	281	59%	-3.5	9.4	4	1	3.4	40	-0.8	0	-13.8%	35	-23	36	-39	51%	41%	6%	2%
2017	MIA			54	88	571	61%	--	10.6	5						-1.6%								

Thomas ranked fourth and second in DVOA when Peyton Manning was delivering his passes in Denver, but finished 41st and 35th when Blake Bortles became his delivery man. He signed a modest contract (two years, $12.2 million) to play for the Dolphins, but simply reuniting with Adam Gase's offense is not a magic cure-all for Thomas' recent struggles. On the bright side, it is hard to imagine that he could do any worse for the Dolphins than free agent Jordan Cameron did at this position.

Will Tye | Height: 6-2 | Weight: 262 | College: Stony Brook | Draft: 2015/FA | Born: 4-Nov-1991 | Age: 26 | Risk: Green

Year	Team	G/GS	Snaps	Rec	Pass	Yds	C%	+/-	Yd/C	TD	Drop	YAC	Rk	YAC+	BTkl	DVOA	Rk	DYAR	Rk	YAR	Short	Mid	Deep	Bomb
2015	NYG	13/7	543	42	62	464	68%	-0.5	11.0	3	4	4.6	23	+0.2	11	5.1%	22	51	20	44	64%	25%	10%	0%
2016	NYG	16/10	680	48	70	395	69%	-1.5	8.2	1	4	3.8	28	-0.8	11	-22.2%	42	-68	41	-64	68%	24%	6%	3%
2017	NYG			25	36	235	69%	--	9.4	2						-5.3%								

Tye was never anything more than a pedestrian short receiver with a running style reminiscent of Mr. Potato Head in the *Toy Story* movies. He made up for it, however, by being a below-average blocker. The Giants have finally figured out what real tight ends look like and how to acquire them, so Tye's best chance at staying on the team is the Giants' penchant for keeping role players around forever.

Clive Walford | Height: 6-4 | Weight: 251 | College: Miami | Draft: 2015/3 (68) | Born: 21-Oct-1991 | Age: 26 | Risk: Green

Year	Team	G/GS	Snaps	Rec	Pass	Yds	C%	+/-	Yd/C	TD	Drop	YAC	Rk	YAC+	BTkl	DVOA	Rk	DYAR	Rk	YAR	Short	Mid	Deep	Bomb
2015	OAK	16/2	439	28	50	329	56%	-2.1	11.8	3	1	4.4	30	-0.8	5	-4.1%	31	10	31	-6	38%	32%	26%	4%
2016	OAK	15/8	702	33	52	359	63%	-0.1	10.9	3	5	3.7	31	-0.9	3	-4.7%	26	9	26	-17	39%	53%	6%	2%
2017	OAK			23	35	257	66%	--	11.2	3						2.4%								

Walford is a useful pass protector, but the young tight end failed to take any steps forward as a receiver in his second season. Thus, the Raiders brought in Jared Cook to spruce up the receiving power of this unit.

Delanie Walker   Height: 6-1   Weight: 241   College: Central Missouri   Draft: 2006/6 (175)   Born: 12-Aug-1984   Age: 33   Risk: Green

Year	Team	G/GS	Snaps	Rec	Pass	Yds	C%	+/-	Yd/C	TD	Drop	YAC	Rk	YAC+	BTkl	DVOA	Rk	DYAR	Rk	YAR	Short	Mid	Deep	Bomb
2014	TEN	15/14	769	63	106	890	59%	-1.2	14.1	4	3	6.0	10	+1.4	14	-5.6%	30	12	28	9	40%	40%	14%	6%
2015	TEN	15/10	688	94	133	1088	71%	+9.9	11.6	6	5	4.1	34	-0.3	11	13.0%	12	174	5	164	42%	42%	12%	4%
2016	TEN	15/10	707	65	103	800	64%	+3.2	12.3	7	6	4.3	20	-0.4	11	8.4%	16	102	12	102	32%	44%	15%	8%
2017	TEN			62	92	777	67%	--	12.5	5						9.3%								

Walker and Vernon Davis became just the sixth and seventh tight ends in NFL history to average at least 12.0 yards per catch after their 32nd birthday. Walker did his best work on third downs, posting a 40.4% DVOA and leading all tight ends with 101 DYAR. He was also, once again, a big part of Marcus Mariota's success in the red zone. He tied for the team lead with 18 red zone targets and finished third among tight ends with 69 red zone DYAR.

Walker's likely 2017 role will resemble his 2016 one, playing largely from the slot in base personnel and in-line in 11. He is unlikely to see 2015-like volume barring a *King Ralph*-style accident in the wide receiver room and a defensive collapse, but that just makes him less valuable to your fantasy team. It does not affect the Titans.

Benjamin Watson   Height: 6-3   Weight: 255   College: Duke   Draft: 2004/1 (32)   Born: 18-Dec-1980   Age: 37   Risk: Red

Year	Team	G/GS	Snaps	Rec	Pass	Yds	C%	+/-	Yd/C	TD	Drop	YAC	Rk	YAC+	BTkl	DVOA	Rk	DYAR	Rk	YAR	Short	Mid	Deep	Bomb
2014	NO	16/8	571	20	31	136	65%	+0.5	6.8	2	2	3.9	30	-1.5	1	-21.3%	43	-29	39	-29	68%	21%	11%	0%
2015	NO	16/16	984	74	110	825	67%	+5.1	11.1	6	5	3.3	43	-1.0	3	4.9%	24	87	13	102	48%	33%	14%	6%
2017	BAL			47	60	496	78%	--	10.5	4						12.4%								

Most 36-year-old tight ends coming off torn ACLs are heading for retirement, but as the last man standing after this offseason's derailment of the Baltimore tight end position, Watson might be the healthiest target they have in camp. And given Baltimore's need to have someone to catch passes this year, Watson could benefit. The words "36-year-old tight end" don't exactly fill us with promise, but volume is volume.

Maxx Williams   Height: 6-4   Weight: 249   College: Minnesota   Draft: 2015/2 (55)   Born: 12-Apr-1994   Age: 23   Risk: Red

Year	Team	G/GS	Snaps	Rec	Pass	Yds	C%	+/-	Yd/C	TD	Drop	YAC	Rk	YAC+	BTkl	DVOA	Rk	DYAR	Rk	YAR	Short	Mid	Deep	Bomb
2015	BAL	14/7	477	32	48	268	67%	+0.0	8.4	1	2	4.6	25	-1.0	1	-14.6%	39	-23	39	-40	57%	30%	11%	2%
2017	BAL			30	46	296	65%	--	9.9	1	-7.5%	1	0	3.1	46	-1.5	0	-31.4%	49	-48	45	-59	56%	37%	7%	0%
2017	NE			23	35	261	66%	--	11.3	4						11.3%								

Because John Harbaugh is one of those "we can't disclose actual surgeries" guys, here's what we know about Maxx Williams. 1) He went under the knife in April for what Harbaugh would say was a knee surgery "no other player has had." 2) He currently has no timetable to return. 3) He is a candidate to open the season on the PUP list. 4) He is a Ravens tight end and likely spends his rehab time trying to catch the Road Runner with Wile E. Coyote. He was a talent coming out of Minnesota and may still become the Kyle Rudolph-esque player he was thought to be. But obviously, all short-term expectations should be muted.

Jason Witten   Height: 6-6   Weight: 265   College: Tennessee   Draft: 2003/3 (69)   Born: 6-May-1982   Age: 35   Risk: Yellow

Year	Team	G/GS	Snaps	Rec	Pass	Yds	C%	+/-	Yd/C	TD	Drop	YAC	Rk	YAC+	BTkl	DVOA	Rk	DYAR	Rk	YAR	Short	Mid	Deep	Bomb
2014	DAL	16/16	1047	64	90	703	71%	+6.0	11.0	5	2	3.6	37	-0.7	3	17.9%	8	146	5	171	31%	53%	12%	3%
2015	DAL	16/16	1019	77	104	713	74%	+7.9	9.3	3	0	3.0	48	-1.3	3	-1.9%	28	36	24	37	45%	46%	7%	2%
2016	DAL	16/16	1018	69	95	673	73%	+4.7	9.8	3	3	3.7	32	-0.6	10	-7.2%	29	0	29	25	46%	45%	9%	0%
2017	DAL			62	82	587	76%	--	9.5	4						3.2%								

Witten was 17-of-21 for 204 yards with 10 first-down conversions on play-action passes last season. Many of those play-action passes came on first downs; overall, Witten caught 24-281-1 with 12 first downs on 32 first-down targets.

If you are going to extend the career of a 35-year-old tight end who still blocks well, creating a run-heavy offense that lets him exploit early-down play-action is one way to do it. That said, Witten posted his lowest yardage total since his rookie season and has now dipped below 10 yards per catch for two consecutive years. The Cowboys chose not to draft a tight end from the deepest class in history, so there is no heir apparent on the roster for their future Hall of Famer except mega-project Rico Gathers. Fortunately, the current Cowboys offense does not require all that much from Witten besides leadership, blocking, and occasional first-down mismatch exploitation.

Going Deep

Jerell Adams, NYG: An athletic, productive player at South Carolina, Adams inherited the No. 2 tight end role for the Giants last year when Larry Donnell fell out of favor. Adams is basically an off-brand Evan Engram, so he might have trouble staying on the roster now that the Giants have invested in the real thing.

Daniel Brown, CHI: The Bears' tight end depth chart became crowded this offseason. Adam Shaheen was a high pick in this year's draft. Dion Sims is an established player and capable backup. Brown won't be pushing for playing time on the Bears, but quality play in the preseason could land him an opportunity on another team's practice squad.

Jake Butt, DEN: We're not talking out of our ass when we say this could be a real steal for Denver, which has struggled to find a receiving tight end since Julius Thomas left. Butt won the John Mackey Award for best college tight end, but slipped to the fifth round after he tore his ACL in the Orange Bowl. Butt may not be able to contribute much in his rookie season, but he could be a reliable target, and the source of many puns, for the Broncos in the near future.

Brent Celek, PHI: Celek's 75-971-8 season occurred so long ago that Donovan McNabb was his quarterback and Brian Westbrook was still on the Eagles roster. Celek is still occasionally useful in a system that deploys lots of multi-tight end sets. But if everything the Eagles tried to do this offseason comes to fruition, there should be few targets left for a 31-year-old tight end.

Larry Donnell, FA: Donnell was chugging along in his traditional role as the Giants' ineffective tight end before a concussion sidelined him early in the season. He returned to fumble away a reception in Week 7 against the Rams, and the Giants realized they could get roughly the same level of ineffectiveness from Will Tye. Donnell was still a free agent at press time, because if you can't make it as a tight end for one of the New York teams, you can't make it anywhere.

Gavin Escobar, KC: Escobar never developed into the Jason Witten padawan the Cowboys were expecting, and rugged-blocking Geoff Swaim claimed the No. 2 tight end role from him before getting hurt in the middle of last season. Escobar is now in Kansas City, where they collect backup tight ends like old tin beer signs and use them in creative ways that rarely involve more than four or five targets per month.

Anthony Fasano, MIA: Can you believe that Fasano was a second-round pick in Bill Parcells' last season as a head coach in 2006? He never quite lived up to the second-round status, but he can be a useful run blocker and occasional pass receiver for the Dolphins. Fasano played for Miami in 2008-2012, then went to Tennessee, and has now returned.

Rico Gathers, DAL: A 6-foot-6, 280-pound former Baylor basketball player who spent the 2016 season on the practice squad, Gathers is a throwback to the days when teams drafted basketball players to play tight end instead of drafting the quality tight ends coming out of Alabama, Ole Miss, etc. When Gathers somehow emerges with a 70-catch season, Jerry Jones will get to explain how he pioneered the idea of scouting power forwards as tight ends.

Crockett Gillmore, BAL: Dealing with what he called a "broken back," Gillmore managed to find himself just eight receptions in 2016. He has managed through injuries to his shoulders, hamstring, and thighs over the past two years. Right now a healthy Gillmore would be the third tight end on the Baltimore roster behind Benjamin Watson and Maxx Williams, but these are Baltimore tight ends. When we wrote the rough draft of these comments, it said "fourth tight end" and mentioned Dennis Pitta. By the start of the season, Gillmore might be the only tight end available to play.

Demetrius Harris, KC: It's not uncommon to see a team with a star receiving tight end have more of an in-line blocker as the No. 2 guy on the depth chart. That's the role Harris served for the Chiefs, and he had the fifth-worst receiving plus-minus (minus-4.0) in 2016 among tight ends. He was arrested in March for possession of marijuana, and the team brought in Gavin Escobar for more competition at the positon.

Temarrick Hemingway, LARM: Hemingway was buried on the depth chart as a rookie, appearing in eight games without logging a single catch. With second-round rookie Gerald Everett paired with 2016 draftee Tyler Higbee atop the depth chart, Hemingway is unlikely to have much of a role outside of special teams and heavy packages near the goal line.

Jeff Heuerman, DEN: We might never know for sure what the Broncos had in Heuerman, a third-round pick who tore his ACL in 2015. He only has nine catches in 12 career games, and John Elway is already talking about his roster spot not being a sure thing after the team drafted Jake Butt in the fifth round this year. Heuerman had also been playing behind Virgil Green and A.J. Derby.

Cole Hikutani, SF: Few coaches used three tight ends as often as Kyle Shanahan did in Atlanta. None used it as effectively, as shown by Atlanta's 54.9% DVOA. That gives hope to Hikutini, who played in college at Sacramento State and then Louisville. A non-factor as a blocker, he was targeted as a priority UDFA because of his size, athleticism, and ball skills. With the tight end position one large question mark in San Francisco, and Shanahan's love of his big formations, Hikutini could play the role of Austin Hooper in 2017 and haul in 20 receptions as the third tight end.

Ben Koyack, JAC: The realistic upside for Koyack is that he becomes a reliable second tight end as a blocker and receiver this season, behind either Marcedes Lewis or Mychal Rivera. The downside is that the 2015 seventh-rounder fails to crack even Jacksonville's limited depth chart.

Tyler Kroft, CIN: Kroft, a 2015 third-rounder, has the ability to be more than he's shown on the field. He's a good blocker who has flashed possession-receiver skills in a limited sample. The Bengals preferred C.J. Uzomah as a receiver last season, and with the addition of John Ross should again have no reason to give Kroft more than the standard 20 targets this year.

Jordan Leggett, NYJ: Leggett caught a team-high 15 total touchdowns the last two seasons at Clemson, even though he had 14 fewer receptions than Mike Williams and 83 fewer than Artavis Scott in those two years. At 6-foot-5, you'd expect him to offer a tempting target in the red zone, but he has described himself as lazy in the past, so you can't help but question what kind of blocker he'll be. With Austin Seferian-Jenkins suspended for two games, Leggett will get a quick audition to show he deserves playing time. Otherwise, this fifth-round rookie will probably be playing second fiddle the rest of the year.

Marcedes Lewis, JAC: Back before the 2014 offseason, Lewis was coming off a down season and was glossed over at an offseason event where the marquee showing was Gus Bradley's fire. Now, three years later, Bradley is gone but Lewis may be in line for a bigger role. After a second consecutive down season, Lewis may be approaching the mini-tackle stage of his career, but that will be a useful role for Jacksonville, if not your fantasy team.

Troy Niklas, ARI: So far in his NFL career, Niklas has eight receptions and seven starts. He also has six surgeries, as doctors have had to work on his ankles, hand, wrist, and groin. When he has been on the field, he has drawn praise from Bruce Arians, but "when" is doing a lot of heavy lifting in that sentence. If he's healthy, he'll get regular work in two tight-end sets. If.

Niles Paul, WAS: Paul, a nominal tight end who is really a special-teamer and package wide receiver, missed half of last season with a shoulder injury. He posted an Instagram photo of himself backflipping off a boat in Thailand in February, so he should be able to compete for a job this summer in the crowded Washington backfield. The bad news is that Josh Doctson re-injured his Achilles while watching Paul's video.

Michael Roberts, DET: Roberts had one of 2016's most interesting college stat lines at Toledo: 45 catches for 533 yards and 16 touchdowns. Yes, 16 touchdowns on just 45 grabs. Those scores were largely of the short, red zone variety, so the "Bubba Franks 2.0" comparison may be spot on for the fourth-round pick. Detroit doesn't have a lot of competition after Eric Ebron, and after losing Anquan Boldin, Roberts could be the player to step up in 2017 for those Matthew Stafford bullet passes in the end zone.

Jeremy Sprinkle, WAS: Sprinkle is best known for getting suspended from the Belk Bowl for shoplifting from Belk. It's almost like a team of comedy writers spent all night brainstorming the dumbest thing that could happen to a college football player, gave up from exhaustion, scribbled something about "Belk" on a legal pad, and lo, Jeremy Sprinkle was born unto an unsuspecting world. When not bilking Belk, Sprinkle is a punishing run blocker and capable short receiver, the kind the NCAA rarely produces these days and a worthy designated blocker off the bench for Jordan Reed and Vernon Davis. The shoplifting incident, which involved a complementary swag bag Sprinkle tried to overstuff, is probably not a sign of serious character flaws. Fifth-rounder Sprinkle will be a useful role player, if not a fantasy superstar.

Phillip Supernaw, TEN: The departure of blocking tight end Anthony Fasano creates an opportunity for Supernaw to move from H-back and second tight end to primary in-line blocker, with Delanie Walker the move tight end and third-round pick Jonnu Smith more likely Walker's heir. It's a big transition, but Mike Mularkey was optimistic about it this offseason.

Jacob Tamme, FA: Nine years in the NFL: seven with Peyton Manning, two with Matt Ryan, four of which were MVP campaigns for his quarterbacks. Tamme had shoulder surgery in mid-2016, and remains unsigned. If this is it for him, he leaves after a pretty charmed career, even if his individual stats never goggled the eyes.

Levine Toilolo, ATL: Best known for playing the ukulele on *Hard Knocks* a couple years back, Devine Levine did just enough in the unstoppable Falcons offense to earn another contract with the team. On the other hand, he had ten blown blocks, third-most among tight ends, so clearly Atlanta doesn't care much about the physical part of Toilolo's game.

C.J. Uzomah, CIN: Cincy's regular move tight end while Tyler Eifert was injured, Uzomah gave the Bengals roughly league-average production but was in no way a target sponge or a matchup weapon. As long as he's behind Eifert, Uzomah has a clear path to the field because of Eifert's inability to stay healthy. But Uzomah is more of a good second tight end than a fantasy football breakout waiting to happen.

Nick Vannett, SEA: A third-round selection out of Ohio State, Vannett served as Seattle's third-string tight end in his rookie season. He suffered an ankle injury in the preseason before catching three passes for 32 yards in nine games in a limited role behind Jimmy Graham and Luke Willson. The coaching staff is high on Vannett, and Graham and Willson are both set to be free agents after 2017, meaning Vannett could have a chance to expand his role both in 2017 and beyond.

Luke Willson, SEA: The 2016 season was the first of Willson's career where he did not receive enough targets to be ranked in the tight end DYAR table, finishing 24th, 24th, and 27th in 2013, 2014, and 2015, respectively. Seattle brought Willson back on a one-year contract this offseason, and with 2016 third-rounder Nick Vannett waiting in the wings, Willson does not appear to be in the team's plans after 2017. In the short term, however, Willson would probably get the first crack at replacing Jimmy Graham in the event of an injury.

2017 Kicker Projections

L isted below are the 2017 KUBIAK projections for kickers. Due to the inconsistency of field goal percentage from year to year, kickers are projected almost entirely based on team forecasts, although a handful of individual factors do come into play:

• More experience leads to a slightly higher field goal percentage in general, with the biggest jump between a kicker's rookie and sophomore seasons.

• Kickers with a better career field goal percentage tend to get more attempts, although they are not necessarily more accurate.

• Field goal percentage on kicks over 40 yards tends to regress to the mean.

Kickers are listed with their total fantasy points based on two different scoring systems. For **Pts1**, all field goals are worth three points. For **Pts2**, all field goals up to 39 yards are worth three points, field goals of 40-49 yards are worth four points, and field goals over 50 yards are worth five points. Kickers are also listed with a Risk of Green, Yellow, or Red, as explained in the introduction to the section on quarterbacks.

Note that field goal totals below are rounded, but "fantasy points" are based on the actual projections, so the total may not exactly equal (FG * 3 + XP).

Fantasy Kicker Projections, 2017

Kicker	Team	FG	Pct	XP	Pts1	Pts2	Risk	Kicker	Team	FG	Pct	XP	Pts1	Pts2	Risk
Stephen Gostkowski	NE	31-36	86%	49	142	157	Green	Jason Myers	JAC	25-32	78%	34	110	125	Red
Graham Gano	CAR	30-37	81%	45	135	149	Yellow	Dustin Hopkins	WAS	25-32	78%	35	110	122	Green
Adam Vinatieri	IND	31-35	89%	41	134	150	Yellow	Steven Hauschka	BUF	23-30	77%	38	108	120	Yellow
Dan Bailey	DAL	31-37	84%	40	132	148	Green	Greg Zuerlein	LARM	26-31	84%	29	108	124	Red
Matt Prater	DET	32-36	89%	36	131	151	Yellow	Cairo Santos	KC	25-30	83%	33	108	121	Green
Mason Crosby	GB	28-31	90%	47	130	143	Green	Wil Lutz	NO	22-26	85%	41	108	120	Red
Matt Bryant	ATL	30-34	88%	41	130	146	Green	Chandler Catanzaro	NYJ	27-35	77%	25	107	120	Yellow
Phil Dawson	ARI	29-35	83%	37	124	139	Yellow	Roberto Aguayo	TB	21-26	81%	41	104	115	Red
Sebastian Janikowski	OAK	28-33	85%	40	124	138	Green	Zane Gonzalez	CLE	25-30	83%	30	104	115	Red
Ryan Succop	TEN	27-31	87%	42	122	135	Green	Kai Forbath	MIN	23-27	85%	35	103	114	Red
Caleb Sturgis	PHI	29-33	88%	35	122	136	Yellow	Aldrick Rosas	NYG	23-28	82%	34	102	113	Red
Chris Boswell	PIT	27-31	87%	41	121	134	Green	Robbie Gould	SF	23-28	82%	31	100	111	Green
Justin Tucker	BAL	30-35	86%	30	120	141	Yellow								
Jake Elliott	CIN	25-33	76%	42	118	129	Red								
Blair Walsh	SEA	26-32	81%	40	117	130	Green								

Kicker	Team	FG	Pct	XP	Pts1	Pts2	Risk
Josh Lambo	LACH	27-33	82%	36	117	130	Yellow
Nick Novak	HOU	29-35	83%	29	116	130	Yellow
Connor Barth	CHI	27-33	82%	33	113	127	Yellow
Brandon McManus	DEN	27-32	84%	31	113	128	Yellow
Andrew Franks	MIA	26-31	84%	35	112	125	Yellow

Other kickers who may win jobs:							
Kicker	Team	FG	Pct	XP	Pts1	Pts2	Risk
Harrison Butker	CAR	26-33	79%	43	121	133	Red
Randy Bullock	CIN	27-34	79%	41	123	137	Yellow
Cody Parkey	CLE	26-32	81%	29	106	119	Red
Nick Folk	TB	23-27	85%	39	109	121	Red

2017 Fantasy Defense Projections

Listed below are the 2017 KUBIAK projections for fantasy team defense. The projection method is discussed in an essay in *Pro Football Prospectus 2006*, the key conclusions of which were:

• Schedule strength is very important for projecting fantasy defense.
• Categories used for scoring in fantasy defense have no consistency from year-to-year whatsoever, with the exception of sacks and interceptions.

Fumble recoveries and defensive touchdowns are forecast solely based on the projected sacks and interceptions, rather than the team's totals in these categories from a year ago. This is why the 2017 projections may look very different from the fantasy defense values from the 2016 season. Safeties and shutouts are not common enough to have a significant effect on the projections. Team defenses are also projected with Risk factor of Green, Yellow, or Red; this is based on the team's projection compared to performance in recent seasons.

In addition to projection of separate categories, we also give an overall total based on our generic fantasy scoring formula: one point for a sack, two points for a fumble recovery or interception, and six points for a touchdown. Remember that certain teams (in particular, the Seahawks) will score better if your league also gives points for limiting opponents' scoring or yardage. Special-teams touchdowns are listed separately and are not included in the fantasy scoring total listed.

Fantasy Team Defense Projections, 2017

Team	Fant Pts	Sack	Int	Fum Rec	Def TD	Risk	ST TD	Team	Fant Pts	Sack	Int	Fum Rec	Def TD	Risk	ST TD
CAR	110	42.7	13.9	10.1	3.2	Green	0.6	TB	95	37.0	13.1	9.1	2.3	Green	0.7
SEA	109	42.6	14.0	10.3	2.9	Red	0.6	TEN	95	38.3	13.8	9.1	1.8	Yellow	0.5
LARM	108	44.9	14.9	9.0	2.6	Yellow	0.5	GB	93	33.1	15.0	7.8	2.4	Yellow	0.7
NYG	106	37.4	14.3	10.7	3.1	Yellow	0.5	DAL	93	37.5	11.5	10.2	1.9	Red	0.6
KC	106	38.9	16.6	8.4	2.9	Green	1.4	BAL	92	37.5	14.9	8.2	1.5	Yellow	0.6
NE	105	39.7	16.1	9.1	2.5	Red	0.4	ATL	91	34.2	12.3	9.1	2.3	Yellow	0.8
PIT	103	40.0	16.6	8.6	2.2	Yellow	0.5	CIN	91	36.2	12.8	7.5	2.3	Yellow	0.6
ARI	102	41.1	14.8	9.0	2.2	Green	0.7	DET	89	32.0	12.3	9.7	2.2	Red	0.9
OAK	98	35.5	13.8	9.8	2.6	Yellow	0.8	WAS	86	31.0	13.4	6.9	2.4	Yellow	0.7
DEN	98	38.6	14.5	8.5	2.2	Green	0.5	MIA	85	32.7	10.9	9.3	2.0	Yellow	0.7
PHI	97	35.9	13.0	9.0	2.9	Green	1.3	BUF	85	34.0	11.2	9.3	1.6	Green	0.7
JAC	97	37.0	14.4	9.0	2.2	Red	0.5	NO	84	33.5	10.7	7.9	2.3	Green	0.6
MIN	97	32.0	14.3	9.9	2.7	Green	0.9	NYJ	84	31.0	11.3	8.0	2.5	Green	0.4
LACH	97	38.2	13.0	9.2	2.3	Yellow	0.8	SF	84	30.0	11.7	8.2	2.3	Green	0.6
IND	95	34.5	14.8	9.3	2.1	Yellow	0.7	CHI	83	31.1	13.0	7.5	1.9	Green	0.8
HOU	95	39.3	13.2	9.1	1.9	Yellow	0.4	CLE	78	30.6	10.8	6.9	1.9	Green	0.6

Projected Defensive Leaders, 2017

Solo Tackles			Total Tackles			Sacks			Interceptions		
Player	Team	Tkl	Player	Team	Tkl	Player	Team	Sacks	Player	Team	Int
K.Alexander	TB	98	L.Kuechly	CAR	143	J.J.Watt	HOU	14.1	M.Peters	KC	4.0
T.Smith	JAC	98	B.Wagner	SEA	142	K.Mack	OAK	13.8	T.Mathieu	ARI	3.4
A.Ogletree	LARM	98	C.Kirksey	CLE	141	V.Beasley	ATL	12.8	X.Howard	MIA	3.4
N.Bowman	SF	94	K.Alexander	TB	138	V.Miller	DEN	12.4	H.Clinton-Dix	GB	3.3
L.Kuechly	CAR	92	A.Ogletree	LARM	136	J.Bosa	LACH	11.9	K.Coleman	CAR	3.2
L.Collins	NYG	91	S.Lee	DAL	136	J.Houston	KC	11.6	R.Nelson	OAK	3.0
C.Kirksey	CLE	89	N.Bowman	SF	134	C.Jones	ARI	11.3	L.Collins	NYG	2.9
J.Cyprien	TEN	88	R.Jones	MIA	126	D.Hunter	MIN	11.2	B.Grimes	TB	2.9
R.Jones	MIA	88	L.David	TB	125	E.Ansah	DET	11.1	R.Jones	MIA	2.9
S.Lee	DAL	87	T.Smith	JAC	124	C.Dunlap	CIN	10.6	E.Thomas	SEA	2.7
B.Wagner	SEA	86	K.J.Wright	SEA	123	C.Avril	SEA	10.1	A.J.Bouye	JAC	2.7
M.Jack	JAC	86	B.McKinney	HOU	121	J.Clowney	HOU	9.9	D.Slay	DET	2.7

College Football Introduction and Statistical Toolbox

The last four college football seasons have produced four different national champions. That may not be a particularly noteworthy fact in the context of college football history, but it is significant to call out as we embark on yet another season in which the Alabama Crimson Tide find themselves atop our preseason projections.

Alabama has spent the better part of the last decade at the top of the college football landscape, of course, hauling in more talented players than any other program and deploying them with ruthless efficiency to consistently compete for and win conference and national championships. The Crimson Tide are the only program to have made the College Football Playoff field in each of its first three iterations, and they're more likely than any other program to make another playoff run this fall.

Nevertheless, and it bears repeating, Alabama will not necessarily win the national championship. The ultimate fate of the season is not pre-ordained.

The other three programs that have claimed a national championship since 2013 are ranked right behind Alabama in our preseason forecast. The Ohio State Buckeyes, Florida State Seminoles, and Clemson Tigers also have talent advantages relative to the majority of the competition they'll face, and each program has enjoyed very consistent year-over-year success as well. All four programs at the top of our projections have each lost fewer than ten total games over the last five seasons. No other program in college football has fewer than 14 losses in the same span.

And not only are Alabama, Ohio State, Florida State, and Clemson all well-positioned for future championship success, they're also led by the only four active FBS head coaches who have reached the pinnacle of the sport. Nick Saban, Urban Meyer, Jimbo Fisher, and Dabo Swinney are the only coaches heading into the season who have previously won championships as head coaches. For comparison, ten years ago we entered the 2007 season with three times as many teams (12 total) led by head coaches who were previous national championship winners.

Of course, unpredictability is a frequent refrain in this sport and in our annual forecasts, and that 2007 season ten years ago remains one of our favorite reference points. It's still stunning to recall Appalachian State's upset of Michigan to kick off the year; Stanford upending USC as a 41-point underdog; Pittsburgh defeating top-ranked West Virginia in an epic Backyard Brawl to conclude the regular season; and two-loss LSU improbably leaping into position to play for and win the national championship.

We may never see anything quite like that season play out again, but there is certainly potential for programs outside our projected top four to make a championship run of their own

in 2017. The Oklahoma Sooners rank No. 5 in our ratings, but have the third-best opportunity to reach the College Football Playoff. The USC Trojans, No. 6 in our projections, are the most likely power conference champion, and they'll be right in the mix for the playoff as well. Among teams ranked outside our projected top ten, the Wisconsin Badgers have the best potential to contend for a playoff berth deep into the year, and may find themselves in a de facto playoff qualifier in the Big Ten Championship game at season's end.

Perhaps one or more of the preseason heavyweights will fall flat on their faces, and perhaps a truly unexpected contender will emerge to take their place. We're not alone in projecting Alabama and other power programs to have the best opportunity for success in 2017, but we're also not alone in looking forward to finding out which teams will defy expectations this fall.

Welcome to the college football section of Football Outsiders Almanac and our deep dive into the numbers that will shape the 2017 season. Since 2003, Brian Fremeau has been developing and enhancing the drive-based Fremeau Efficiency Index (FEI) and its companion statistics; for the last ten years, Bill Connelly has explored play-by-play and drive data to refine his system, the S&P+ ratings. Both systems are opponent-adjusted and effective in evaluating team strengths and weaknesses.

The College Statistical Toolbox section that follows this introduction explains the methodology of FEI, S&P+, F/+, and other stats you will encounter in the college chapters of this book. There are similarities to Football Outsiders' NFL-based DVOA ratings in the combined approach, but college football presents a unique set of challenges different from the NFL. All football stats must be adjusted according to context, but how? If Team A and Team B do not play one another and don't share any common opponents, how can their stats be effectively compared? Should a team from the SEC or Big 12 be measured against that of an average team in its own conference, or an average team across all conferences?

Our mission is to continue to drill deeper into the statistical measures that fuel success on the field for each and every FBS team, though this book is particularly focused on the playoff and conference contenders for the year ahead. Each of the 50 team capsules provides a snapshot of that team's projection for 2017 and the statistical factors that went into the projection. The capsules also included a game-by-game graphic highlighting our projected win likelihoods for the year ahead. Supplementing the stat work, college football staff writers Chad Peltier and Ian Boyd explore player and coaching personnel changes, offensive and defensive advantages and deficiencies, and schedule highlights and pitfalls in a thorough summary of each team's keys to the upcoming season.

For each of the 130 FBS teams, we project the likelihood of every possible regular-season record, conference and non-conference alike. We have included division, overall conference, and College Football Playoff projections for every team as well.

By taking two different statistical approaches to reach one exciting series of answers to college football's most important questions, we're confident we have the tools to answer key questions and spark new insights to the game we love. Enjoy the college football section of *Football Outsiders Almanac 2017*, and join us at www.FootballOutsiders.com/college throughout the season.

College Statistics Toolbox

Regular readers of FootballOutsiders.com may be familiar with the FEI and S&P+ stats published throughout the year. Others may be learning about our advanced approach to college football stats analysis for the first time by reading this book. In either case, this College Statistics Toolbox section is highly recommended reading before getting into the conference chapters. The stats that form the building blocks for F/+, FEI, and S&P+ are constantly being updated and refined.

Each team profile begins with a statistical snapshot. The projected overall and conference records—rounded from the team's projected Mean Wins—are listed alongside the team name in the header. Other stats and rankings provided in the team snapshot and highlighted in the team capsules are explained below.

DRIVE-BY-DRIVE DATA

Fremeau Efficiency Index: The Fremeau Efficiency Index (FEI) is based on opponent-adjusted drive efficiency. Approximately 20,000 possessions are contested annual in FBS vs. FBS games. First-half clock-kills and end-of-game garbage drives are filtered out. Unadjusted game efficiency is a measure of net success on non-garbage possessions, the success of the offensive, defensive, and special teams units in terms of maximizing the team's own scoring opportunities and minimizing those of its opponent. FEI opponent adjustments are calculated with an emphasis placed on quality performances against good teams, win or lose.

Offensive and Defensive FEI: Maximizing success on offensive possessions and minimizing success on opponent possessions begins with an understanding of the value of field position. An average offense facing an average defense may expect to score 2.1 points on average at the conclusion of the drive. If that drive begins at the offense's own 15-yard line, the average scoring value is only 1.5 points. If it begins at the opponent's 15-yard line, the average scoring value is 4.9 points. Offensive and defensive efficiency are in part a function of the variable value of starting field position.

Likewise, drive-ending field position is an important component as well. Touchdowns represent the ultimate goal of an offensive possession, but drives that fall short of the end zone can add scoring value as well. National field goal success rates correlate strongly with proximity to the end zone, and an offense that drives deep into opponent territory to set up a chip-shot field goal generates more scoring value than one that ends a drive at the edge of or outside field goal range.

The basic value generated by an offense on a given possession is the difference between the drive-ending value and the value of field position at the start of the drive. Offensive efficiency is the average per-possession value generated or lost by the offense. Defensive efficiency is the average per-possession value generated or lost by the defense. Offensive FEI and Defensive FEI are the opponent-adjusted per-possession values generated or lost by these units.

PLAY-BY-PLAY DATA

Success Rates: More than one million plays over the last ten years in college football have been collected and evaluated to determine baselines for success for every situational down in a game. Similar to DVOA, basic success rates are determined

No. 1 Alabama Crimson Tide (11-1, 7-1)

2017 Projections

F/+	48.4 (1)
FEI	.325 (1)
S&P+	34.0 (1)
Total Wins	10.5
Conf Wins	6.9
SOS	.056 (12)
Conf SOS	.109 (14)
Div Champ	73%
Conf Champ	44%
CFP Berth	47%

Projection Factors

2016 F/+	81.0 (1)
2016 FEI	.350 (1)
2016 S&P+	34.0 (1)
5-Year F/+	68.9 (1)
5-Year FEI	.328 (1)
5-Year S&P+	27.5 (1)
2-Yr/5-Yr Recruiting	1/1
Ret. Offense	64% (61)
Ret. Defense	59% (84)
Ret. Total	62% (73)

Projected Win Likelihood by Game

Date	Opponent (Proj Rank)	PWL	Projected Loss	Projected Win
Sep 2	vs Florida St. (3)	70%		
Sep 9	vs Fresno St. (111)	99%		
Sep 16	vs Colorado St. (44)	97%		
Sep 23	at Vanderbilt (50)	94%		
Sep 30	vs Ole Miss (26)	92%		
Oct 7	at Texas A&M (20)	78%		
Oct 14	vs Arkansas (37)	96%		
Oct 21	vs Tennessee (24)	91%		
Nov 4	vs LSU (7)	79%		
Nov 11	at Mississippi St. (34)	88%		
Nov 18	vs Mercer (FCS)	100%		
Nov 25	at Auburn (10)	69%		

by national standards. The distinction for college football is in defining the standards of success. We use the following determination of a "successful" play:

• First-down success = 50 percent of necessary yardage.
• Second-down success = 70 percent of necessary yardage.
• Third-/Fourth-down success = 100 percent of necessary yardage.

On a per-play basis, these form the standards of efficiency for every offense in college football. Defensive success rates are based on preventing the same standards of achievement.

Equivalent Points and Points per Play: All yards are not created equal. A 10-yard gain from a team's own 15-yard line does not have the same value as a 10-yard gain that goes from the opponent's 10-yard line into the end zone. Based on expected scoring rates by field position, we calculate a point value for each play in a drive. Equivalent Points (EqPts) are calculated by subtracting the value of the resulting yard line from the initial yard line of a given play. This assigns credit to the yards that are most associated with scoring points, the end goal in any possession.

With EqPts, the game can be broken down and built back up again in a number of ways. With the addition of penalties, turnovers, and special teams play, EqPts provides an accurate assessment of how a game was played on a play-by-play basis. Average EqPts per play (PPP) measures consistency, while IsoPPP measures EqPts per play on successful plays only as a way to isolate of explosiveness.

S&P: Like OPS (on-base percentage plus slugging average) in baseball, we created a measure that combines consistency with power. S&P represents a combination of efficiency (Success Rates) and explosiveness (Points per Play) to most accurately represent the effectiveness of a team or individual player.

A boom-or-bust running back may have an excellent per-carry average and PPP, but his low Success Rate will lower his S&P. A consistent running back who gains between 4 and 6 yards every play, on the other hand, will have a strong Success Rate but possibly low PPP. The best offenses in the country can maximize both efficiency and explosiveness on a down-by-down basis. Reciprocally, the best defenses can limit both.

S&P+: As with the FEI stats discussed above, context matters in college football. Adjustments are made to the S&P unadjusted data with a formula that takes into account a team's production, the quality of the opponent, and the quality of the opponent's opponent. To eliminate the noise of less-informative blowout stats, we filtered the play-by-play data to include only those that took place when the game was "close." This excludes plays where the score margin is larger than 28 points in the first quarter, 24 points in the second quarter, 21 points in the third quarter, or 16 points in the fourth quarter.

Beginning in 2013, we also factored in a drive efficiency measure that is calculated in a similar fashion to PPP, by comparing the expected value of a given drive (based on starting field position) to the actual value a team produces and adjusting it for the opponent at hand. The ability to finish drives is a singular skill that isn't perfectly encapsulated in a measure that only looks at play-by-play data.

The combination of the play-by-play and drive data gives us S&P+, a comprehensive measure that represents a team's efficiency and explosiveness as compared to all other teams in college football. S&P+ values are calibrated around an average rating of 100. An above-average team, offensively or defensively, will have an S&P+ rating greater than 100. A below-average team will have an S&P+ rating lower than 100. The "+" adjustment can be used for other components, as well, such as Success Rate+ and PPP+.

Five Factors: In January 2014, Bill Connelly introduced a new set of concepts for analysis and debate within the realm of college football stats. At Football Study Hall, a college football stats site within the SB Nation network, he wrote the following: "Over time, I've come to realize that the sport comes down to five basic things, four of which you can mostly control. You make more big plays than your opponent, you stay on schedule, you tilt the field, you finish drives, and you fall on the ball. Explosiveness, efficiency, field position, finishing drives, and turnovers are the five factors to winning football games."

Unlike the Four Factors used by ESPN's Dean Oliver for discussion of basketball, these factors are heavily related to each other, and at press time, work to unpack each one is still ongoing. But for team tables in this section, we are including the following measures, which represent each of the five factors as currently constituted: Success Rate+ (the opponent-adjusted version of Success Rate), IsoPPP+ (an opponent-adjusted look at the average PPP gained only in successful plays), FPA (Brian Fremeau's Field Position Advantage measure), Red Zone S&P+, and Adjusted Turnover Margin (a comparison of a team's actual turnover margin to what would have been expected with neutral luck).

Highlight Yards: Highlight yards represent the yards gained by a runner outside of those credited to the offensive line through Adjusted Line Yards. The ALY formula, much like the same stat in the NFL, gives 100 percent credit to all yards gained between 0 and 4 yards and 50 percent strength to yards between 5 and 10. If a runner gains 12 yards in a given carry, and we attribute 7.0 of those yards to the line, and the player's highlight yardage on the play is 5.0 yards. Beginning in 2013, we began calculating highlight yardage averages in a slightly different manner: Instead of dividing total highlight yardage by a player's overall number of carries, we divide it only by the number of carries that gain more than 4 yards; if a line is given all credit for gains smaller than that, then it makes sense to look at highlight averages only for the carries on which a runner got a chance to create a highlight.

Opportunity Rate: Opportunity Rate represents the percentage of a runner's carries that gained at least 5 yards. This gives us a look at a runner's (and his line's) consistency and efficiency to go along with the explosiveness measured by Highlight Yards.

Adjusted Score/Adjusted Points: Taking a team's single-game S&P+ for both offense and defense, and applying it to a normal distribution of points scored in a given season, can give us an interesting, descriptive look at a team's performance in a given game and season. Adjusting for pace and opponent, Adjusted Score asks the same question of every team in every game: if Team A had played a perfectly average opponent in a given game, how would they have fared? Adjusted Score allows us to look at in-season trends as well, since the week-to-week baseline is opponent-independent.

COMBINATION DATA

F/+: Introduced in *Football Outsiders Almanac 2009*, the F/+ measure combines FEI and S&P+. There is a clear distinction between the two individual approaches, and merging the two diminishes certain outliers caused by the quirks of each method. The resulting metric is both powerfully predictive and sensibly evaluative.

Program F/+: Relative to the pros, college football teams are much more consistent in year-to-year performance. Breakout seasons and catastrophic collapses certainly occur, but generally speaking, teams can be expected to play within a reasonable range of their baseline program expectations. The idea of a Football Outsiders program rating began with the introduction of Program FEI in *Pro Football Prospectus 2008* as a way to represent those individual baseline expectations.

As the strength of the F/+ system has been fortified with more seasons of full drive-by-drive and play-by-play data, the Program F/+ measure has emerged. Program F/+ is calculated from five years of FEI and S&P+ data. The result not only represents the status of each team's program power, but provides the first step in projecting future success. For each team statistical profile, we provide each team's five-year ratings profile and other projection factors that are included in the formula for the Projected FEI, Projected S&P+, and Projected F/+ ratings.

Recruiting success rates are based on a blend of Rivals.com and 247Sports.com recruiting ratings. The ranking for each team's two-year recruiting success and five-year recruiting success reflect the potential impact for both recent star-studded classes and the depth of talent for each team. Our returning experience data represents the percentage of production that returns to the roster this fall rather than a simple count of players labeled as starters. Program F/+ ratings are a function of program ratings and these recruiting and returning production transition factors.

Strength of Schedule: Unlike other rating systems, our Strength of Schedule (SOS) calculation is not a simple average of the Projected F/+ data of each team's opponents. Instead, it represents the likelihood that an elite team (a typical top-five team) would win every game on the given schedule. The distinction is valid. For any elite team, playing No. 1 Alabama and No. 130 UAB in a two-game stretch is certainly more difficult than playing No. 65 Syracuse and No. 66 Temple. An average rating might judge these schedules to be equal.

The likelihood of an undefeated season is calculated as the product of individual game projected win likelihoods. Generally speaking, an elite team may have a 75 percent chance of defeating a team ranked No. 10, an 85 percent chance of defeating a team ranked No. 20, and a 95 percent chance of defeating a team ranked No. 40. Combined, the elite team has a 61 percent likelihood of defeating all three ($0.75 \times 0.85 \times 0.95 = 0.606$).

A lower SOS rating represents a lower likelihood of an elite team running the table, and thus a stronger schedule. For our calculations of FBS versus FCS games, with all due apologies to North Dakota State, et al., the likelihood of victory is 100 percent in the formula.

Mean Wins and Win Probabilities: To project records for each team, we use Projected F/+ and win likelihood formulas to estimate the likelihood of victory for a given team in its individual games. The probabilities for winning each game are added together to represent the average number of wins the team is expected to tally over the course of its scheduled games. Potential conference championship games and bowl games are not included.

The projected records listed next to each team name in the conference chapters are rounded from the mean wins data listed in the team capsule. Mean Wins are not intended to represent projected outcomes of specific matchups; rather, they are our most accurate forecast for the team's season as a whole. The correlation of mean projected wins to actual wins is 0.69 for all games, 0.61 for conference games.

Win likelihoods are also used to produce the likelihood of each team winning a division or championship. Our College Football Playoff appearance likelihoods are a function of each team's likelihood to go undefeated or finish the season with one loss, as well as the strength of the team's conference and overall schedule, factors that the CFP selection committee considers in their process.

The Win Probability tables that appear in each conference chapter are also based on the game-by-game win likelihood data for each team. The likelihood for each record is rounded to the nearest whole percent.

Brian Fremeau and Bill Connelly

NCAA Top 50 Teams

No. 1 Alabama Crimson Tide (11-1, 7-1)

2017 Projections

F/+	48.4 (1)
FEI	.325 (1)
S&P+	34.0 (1)
Total Wins	10.5
Conf Wins	6.9
SOS	.056 (12)
Conf SOS	.109 (14)
Div Champ	73%
Conf Champ	44%
CFP Berth	47%

Projection Factors

2016 F/+	81.0 (1)
2016 FEI	.350 (1)
2016 S&P+	34.0 (1)
5-Year F/+	68.9 (1)
5-Year FEI	.328 (1)
5-Year S&P+	27.5 (1)
2-Yr/5-Yr Recruiting	1/1
Ret. Offense	64% (61)
Ret. Defense	59% (84)
Ret. Total	62% (73)

Projected Win Likelihood by Game

Date	Opponent (Proj Rank)	PWL
Sep 2	vs Florida St. (3)	70%
Sep 9	vs Fresno St. (111)	99%
Sep 16	vs Colorado St. (44)	97%
Sep 23	at Vanderbilt (50)	94%
Sep 30	vs Ole Miss (26)	92%
Oct 7	at Texas A&M (20)	78%
Oct 14	vs Arkansas (37)	96%
Oct 21	vs Tennessee (24)	91%
Nov 4	vs LSU (7)	79%
Nov 11	at Mississippi St. (34)	88%
Nov 18	vs Mercer (FCS)	100%
Nov 25	at Auburn (10)	69%

The Crimson Tide lost the national championship last season but were nevertheless the most dominant team throughout the course of the season, managing 12 games with a 96 percent or higher S&P+ performance and 13 games with an S&P+ win expectancy of 98 percent or higher—and that was with a true freshman quarterback and evolved offensive scheme. Despite a few notable NFL departures, Alabama returns the most talented roster in college football. There are really only four questions marks for Alabama this season: 1. Jalen Hurts' development with new offensive coordinator (his third in three games!) Brian Daboll. 2. Replacing stars on both lines in Cam Robinson and Jonathan Allen. 3. Replacing three-quarters of the linebackers, including Reuben Foster, Tim Williams, and Ryan Anderson. 4. The potential weakness at cornerback after losing Marlon Humphrey.

The only offenses that have had any success against the Crimson Tide defense over the last few years have featured mobile quarterbacks who are comfortable throwing low-percentage deep passes (i.e., Chad Kelly, Deshaun Watson). Because Alabama often asks its corners to play on islands, any inadequacies in man coverage or slowed pass rush can result in explosive plays. Alabama ranked second in passing S&P+ and 13th in passing IsoPPP. The Crimson Tide didn't face many top-end passing offenses last season (USC was still starting Max Browne for their opening matchup), but nevertheless allowed more than 400 passing yards in three games—against Ole Miss, Arkansas, and Clemson. While Alabama's safety duo of Minkah Fitzpatrick and Ronnie Harrison is clearly elite, the departure of Humphrey puts Alabama cornerbacks in a precarious position. Senior Tony Brown has likely secured one of the top spots after taking over the STAR spot when Eddie Jackson went down last season, but there's a battle for the other position.

The linebacker corps is the unit most impacted by departures to the NFL, losing Foster, Williams, and Anderson. There's both talent and (non-starting) experience waiting in the wings, though. Shaun Dion Hamilton and Rashaan Evans had the second- and fourth-most tackles among linebackers last year, so they—along with players like Keith Holcombe, Anfernee Jennings, and Christian Miller—should be keep the Alabama front seven every bit as elite as we're accustomed to. True freshman elite athlete Dylan Moses could also make a push for playing time as well.

Alabama had few weaknesses last year aside from a consistent intermediate and deep passing game (75th in passing success rate) and occasionally struggling to finish drives (averaging 4.6 points per trip inside the 40, 54th). Jalen Hurts had an extremely successful freshman season, but nevertheless averaged just 6.6 yards per attempt. The good news for the passing game is that freshman Jerry Jeudy looks ready to contribute immediately, leading the spring game receivers with five catches for 134 yards. Jeudy and veteran Calvin Ridley should form a dangerous duo for Hurts.

Finally, Alabama long benefited from two stars on both lines in Cam Robinson and Jonathan Allen, who have now finally gone off to the NFL. Alabama has plenty of former blue chippers on the roster, but these two were a cut above even their typically elite line talent. On the defensive side, the most obvious replacement is Da'shawn Hand, the former top defensive end recruit.

For a repeat national championship appearance, Alabama's two biggest hurdles will be the passing game's consistency and the cornerbacks' development. The toughest game is likely the season opener against Florida State—which is convenient because that's also the game they can most afford to lose.

No. 2 Ohio State Buckeyes (10-2, 8-1)

2017 Projections

F/+	47.4 (2)
FEI	.269 (2)
S&P+	26.0 (2)
Total Wins	10.2
Conf Wins	7.7
SOS	.155 (53)
Conf SOS	.243 (58)
Div Champ	51%
Conf Champ	33%
CFP Berth	29%

Projection Factors

2016 F/+	61.3 (3)
2016 FEI	.277 (3)
2016 S&P+	24.6 (5)
5-Year F/+	53.4 (2)
5-Year FEI	.262 (3)
5-Year S&P+	20.7 (2)
2-Yr/5-Yr Recruiting	2/2
Ret. Offense	68% (50)
Ret. Defense	57% (92)
Ret. Total	63% (72)

Projected Win Likelihood by Game

Date	Opponent (Proj Rank)	PWL
Aug 31	at Indiana (43)	84%
Sep 9	vs Oklahoma (5)	61%
Sep 16	vs Army (96)	99%
Sep 23	vs UNLV (117)	99%
Sep 30	at Rutgers (93)	99%
Oct 7	vs Maryland (79)	99%
Oct 14	at Nebraska (45)	85%
Oct 28	vs Penn St. (8)	65%
Nov 4	at Iowa (58)	87%
Nov 11	vs Michigan St. (46)	93%
Nov 18	vs Illinois (95)	99%
Nov 25	at Michigan (13)	54%

31-0 stings. The Buckeyes got embarrassed by Clemson in the College Football Playoff semifinals, showing the country what many fans had seen all season—the offense needed drastic changes. And Urban Meyer made those changes by pulling in Kevin Wilson, former Indiana head coach, to take over for his two offensive coordinators. Joining Wilson is former Chip Kelly assistant Ryan Day.

Wilson will work broadly within Urban Meyer's system, and some of his biggest changes may seem subtle from the outside. For instance, in the Ohio State spring game, we already saw evidence of not only an increased willingness to throw deep—something that was nearly nonexistent last year, when the Buckeyes ranked 105th in passing IsoPPP—but also frequent crossing routes that targeted the middle of the field. These are high(er) percentage throws that the Buckeyes desperately needed, since they were also 95th in passing success rate and 64th in passing S&P+ overall. Just replace Ohio State's co-offensive coordinators with Kevin Wilson and re-run the Buckeyes' 2016 season and they would likely be in great shape. But then you remember how young Ohio State was overall last season—they were the youngest Power-5 team in the country after their monster 2015 NFL draft class—and you start to see the potential for the Buckeyes in 2017.

Ohio State has clearly the second-most talented roster behind Alabama. Their 2017 signing day just furthered that, with the second-rated class overall and 19 blue chip prospects. Ohio State added players like five-star defensive end Chase Young to go along with last year's five-star end signees Nick Bosa and Jonathan Cooper, and it's likely that none of the three will be full-time starters to open the season due to players like Tyquan Lewis, Sam Hubbard, and Dre'Mont Jones. That's how talented the Buckeyes have gotten under Urban Meyer.

But nevertheless, the Buckeyes have problems that could hold them back from another run at a championship. The biggest three are efficient quarterback play, explosive receivers (obviously these first two are connected), and replacing three-quarters of the secondary.

J.T. Barrett returns for his senior season after throwing for 2,555 yards on a low 5.9 yards per attempt. Barrett was 95th in passing success rate and completed just 61.5 percent of his throws. One of the major problems was that the Buckeyes really only used one receiver: H-back Curtis Samuel. Samuel was arguably more explosive and valuable than Percy Harvin was at Florida, with 771 yards rushing and a 60.8 percent opportunity rate, and 865 yards receiving with a 76.3 percent catch rate. Unfortunately, Samuel, second-leading receiver Noah Brown, and fourth-leading receiver Dontre Wilson are all gone. The leading returning receivers are sophomore K.J. Hill and tight end Marcus Baugh. Hill had a promising freshman season with a 75 percent catch rate and 14.6 yards per catch, but the receivers as a whole still vastly underperformed relative to their talent level. It was never a question of talent, but scheme (route combinations, coaching) and whether Barrett was comfortable enough to throw the deep ball and accurate enough to put the ball in tight windows. There's no real competition—after all, Barrett's career production has been insane—but Joe Burrow and redshirt freshman Dwayne Haskins are exciting options down the line. The general expectation is that Kevin Wilson should help immediately, while receivers like Binjimen Victor, Austin Mack, Demario McCall, and Parris Campbell should help.

So maybe the real concern is in the secondary that lost Gareon Conley, Marcus Lattimore, and Malik Hooker to the NFL, all in the first round of the draft. Those three led the eighth-best passing S&P+ defense and helped fuel the third-best turnover margin at plus-15. So the departure of three top-flight defensive backs, along with the idea that replacing members of the secondary has the greatest impact on future defensive S&P+, gives some cause for concern. But those fears are somewhat alleviated by the insane talent that Ohio State has ready to fill those needs. Junior Denzel Ward wasn't a full-time starter but rotated with Marcus Lattimore last season. Shaun Wade and Jeffrey Okudah are two true freshman early enrollees, along with JUCO transfer (and former Alabama blue chip player) Kendall Sheffield. Ohio State is replacing blue chip talent with arguably more recruited players—it's just a matter of how long before they get up to speed on defense.

Passing-related issues are the big concerns on both sides of the ball. But there are reasons to think that the Buckeyes have put the pieces together to solve all of those problems in what should be another playoff-challenging season at least.

No. 3 Florida State Seminoles (9-3, 7-1)

2017 Projections

F/+	46.8 (3)
FEI	.230 (3)
S&P+	25.7 (3)
Total Wins	9.4
Conf Wins	6.5
SOS	.042 (7)
Conf SOS	.215 (54)
Div Champ	43%
Conf Champ	29%
CFP Berth	20%

Projection Factors

2016 F/+	47.0 (7)
2016 FEI	.190 (9)
2016 S&P+	21.7 (6)
5-Year F/+	43.6 (4)
5-Year FEI	.196 (4)
5-Year S&P+	18.8 (3)
2-Yr/5-Yr Recruiting	3/5
Ret. Offense	60% (79)
Ret. Defense	80% (13)
Ret. Total	70% (39)

Projected Win Likelihood by Game

Date	Opponent (Proj Rank)	PWL
Sep 2	vs Alabama (1)	30%
Sep 9	vs UL-Monroe (121)	99%
Sep 16	vs Miami-FL (23)	78%
Sep 23	vs NC State (31)	86%
Sep 30	at Wake Forest (62)	91%
Oct 14	at Duke (59)	90%
Oct 21	vs Louisville (16)	69%
Oct 27	at Boston College (78)	99%
Nov 4	vs Syracuse (65)	97%
Nov 11	at Clemson (4)	44%
Nov 18	vs Delaware St. (FCS)	100%
Nov 25	at Florida (14)	53%

With Clemson losing Deshaun Watson, Florida State has a chance to retake the ACC, coming in at one spot higher than the Tigers in our F/+ projections. The Seminoles, after closing out last season with a bowl win over Michigan, have a significant amount of experienced talent returning, led by the return of safety Derwin James.

The Seminoles went 10-3 last season, and apart from an early-season no-show performance against Lamar Jackson and Louisville, lost their other two games by a combined five points.

The Seminoles had two big problems last season. First, after Derwin James' injury, the defense had a tendency to allow big plays (103rd in defensive IsoPPP, 80th in opponent 20-plus-yard plays). It was kind of all-or-nothing for the Seminoles, as they excelled in pressuring opposing quarterbacks (20th in overall havoc rate and sixth in defensive line havoc), but were liable to give up a big play if the initial pass rush didn't connect.

Second, the defense struggled to stop the run against dual-threat quarterbacks. The Seminoles were 31st in rushing defensive S&P+, 47th in adjusted line yards, and 44th in opportunity rate, but that's despite holding opposing offenses to less than 100 rushing yards in six of their last eight games. The big two problem games were against Louisville and South Florida, teams that both have excellent rushing quarterbacks (both of those quarterbacks had opportunity rates of 56 percent and highlight yards per opportunity of more than 7.8 yards). The pass rush has been a real strength (second overall adjusted sack rate) and should continue to be in 2017 despite losing Demarcus Walker and his 16 sacks from last season—junior

Josh Sweat and sophomore Brian Burns should break 20 sacks between them.

Third, despite consistently opening holes for Dalvin Cook, Florida State's offensive line has been mediocre in pass protection, ranking 63rd in adjusted sack rate. Deondre Francois had a solid freshman season, but it's difficult to average better than a 58.8 percent completion rate and 7.1 yards per attempt when you're constantly trying to escape the opposing pass rush. Francois will also have to contend with losing his top four targets—Travis Rudolph, Jesus Wilson, Kermit Whitfield, and Dalvin Cook. But juniors Nyqwan Murray and Auden Tate should be ready to step up as the next in line. Tate in particular is an exciting target at 6-foot-5.

Finally, Florida State must replace the always-underrated Dalvin Cook at running back. Jacques Patrick, a junior, is next in line. Despite being a fellow five-star recruit coming out of high school, he was a step down from Cook statistically, averaging 1.2 highlight yards per opportunity and 2.7 percent opportunity rate lower than Cook (giving him a still-respectable 5.7 highlight yards per opportunity and 39.3 percent opportunity rate). Most around the program are more excited to see what incoming five-star running back Cam Akers can do, however. Akers was the top running back and second overall player in last year's 247 Sports composite rankings.

Florida State is in a strong position to compete for the playoff this year. If Deondre Francois and his offensive line can be more consistent, the run defense can improve, and the Jacques Patrick/Cam Akers duo can fill in for Cook, then the Seminoles will likely have all the pieces they need to challenge Clemson and Alabama.

No. 4 Clemson Tigers (10-2, 6-2)

2017 Projections

F/+	45.6 (4)
FEI	.214 (4)
S&P+	22.3 (6)
Total Wins	9.5
Conf Wins	6.2
SOS	.089 (24)
Conf SOS	.164 (37)
Div Champ	31%
Conf Champ	21%
CFP Berth	16%

Projection Factors

2016 F/+	68.9 (2)
2016 FEI	.320 (2)
2016 S&P+	26.9 (2)
5-Year F/+	44.8 (3)
5-Year FEI	.270 (2)
5-Year S&P+	18.6 (4)
2-Yr/5-Yr Recruiting	13/12
Ret. Offense	32% (120)
Ret. Defense	62% (73)
Ret. Total	47% (116)

Projected Win Likelihood by Game

Date	Opponent (Proj Rank)	PWL
Sep 2	vs Kent St. (120)	99%
Sep 9	vs Auburn (10)	64%
Sep 16	at Louisville (16)	53%
Sep 23	vs Boston College (78)	99%
Sep 30	at Virginia Tech (25)	67%
Oct 7	vs Wake Forest (62)	96%
Oct 13	at Syracuse (65)	92%
Oct 28	vs Georgia Tech (27)	83%
Nov 4	at NC State (31)	73%
Nov 11	vs Florida St. (3)	56%
Nov 18	vs Citadel (FCS)	100%
Nov 25	at South Carolina (32)	74%

The defending national champion Tigers are one of the most interesting teams for 2017, having to replace all-time great quarterback Deshaun Watson; running back Wayne Gallman; leading receiver Mike Williams; two of the other top three receiving targets; team leader in sacks Carlos Watkins; and leading cornerback Cordrea Tankersley. The Tigers have been a top-25 caliber team throughout head coach Dabo Swinney's tenure at Clemson, but the Deshaun Watson era saw the Tigers rise from top 25 to top two and win a national title. Clemson went from 24th, 23rd, and 16th in FEI rating from 2012 to 2014 to second in each of the last two seasons. That puts the Tigers at second behind only Alabama in the overall weighted five-year program FEI ratings. The question now is whether the Tigers will fall back to the 20s or stay among the top ten teams in the post-Watson era.

The 2016 Tigers did a lot right. They had a fierce pass rush (seventh in adjusted sack rate, third in overall havoc rate). They were one of the most efficient passing teams in the country (third overall in passing S&P+, fourth in passing success rate). They protected Watson extremely well (fourth in adjusted sack rate allowed), and controlled passing downs on defense (fourth in passing downs S&P+). They weren't overwhelmingly explosive on offense or defense (104th and 85th in unadjusted offensive and defensive IsoPPP) and Watson had a tendency for risk-taking and throwing interceptions, particularly when the run game was slowed (71st in turnover margin), but they managed only a single loss despite eight games decided by a touchdown or less.

That final stat is where Watson's departure may hurt the most: close games. If the Tigers find themselves in eight games that are decided by a touchdown or less in 2017, then they can't take it for granted that either junior Kelly Bryant, freshman Hunter Johnson, or sophomores Zerrick Cooper or Tucker Israel will have the same success. The quarterback room is talented but diverse. Bryant has the most time in the system, but has a limited ceiling as a pure passer. He is much more effective as a runner. Cooper and Johnson are similar in that they are both highly effective passers, but the choice is somewhat between experience (Cooper) and ceiling (Johnson). Johnson is an early enrollee five-star recruit that was the second-rated pro-style quarterback.

Whoever wins the battle will at least have one of the best wide receiver groups to throw to. Despite losing Williams and Artavis Scott, the trio of Deon Cain as an explosive threat and Ray Ray McCloud and Hunter Renfrow as more high-percentage receivers should be formidable. No one is as physically gifted as Williams, but McCloud might be an upgrade over Scott. A big part of Clemson's success last season was that the wide receiver rotation was so deep—six players had at least 60 targets and 470 receiving yards. Clemson will need younger players like Diondre Overton and Cornell Powell to step up. The new starting quarterback will also inherit maybe the best offensive line in the ACC, headlined by left tackle Mitch Hyatt. The line was fourth in adjusted sack rate and in adjusted line yards (but 63rd in opportunity rate, which shows how many efficient runs Wayne Gallman had that still failed to gain 5 yards!).

The defense should be one of the best in the country and will anchor the Tigers until they work out the quarterback and running back situations. The defensive line is particularly explosive despite losing Carlos Watkins. The Tigers have seemed to lose their top pass-rusher in each of the last three drafts, but have nevertheless had someone new emerge. This year's line will be anchored by Dexter Lawrence, Christian Wilkins, and Clelin Farrell.

No. 5 Oklahoma Sooners (10-2, 7-2)

2017 Projections

F/+	45.4 (5)
FEI	.203 (5)
S&P+	22.8 (5)
Total Wins	9.7
Conf Wins	7.3
SOS	.091 (26)
Conf SOS	.200 (49)
Div Champ	-
Conf Champ	46%
CFP Berth	32%

Projection Factors

2016 F/+	46.4 (8)
2016 FEI	.206 (7)
2016 S&P+	19.1 (10)
5-Year F/+	40.6 (6)
5-Year FEI	.192 (5)
5-Year S&P+	16.9 (6)
2-Yr/5-Yr Recruiting	11/14
Ret. Offense	60% (77)
Ret. Defense	73% (40)
Ret. Total	67% (54)

Projected Win Likelihood by Game

Date	Opponent (Proj Rank)	PWL	Projected Loss / Projected Win
Sep 2	vs UTEP (127)	99%	
Sep 9	at Ohio St. (2)	39%	
Sep 16	vs Tulane (89)	99%	
Sep 23	at Baylor (30)	72%	
Oct 7	vs Iowa St. (63)	96%	
Oct 14	vs Texas (19)	66%	
Oct 21	at Kansas St. (28)	71%	
Oct 28	vs Texas Tech (64)	96%	
Nov 4	at Oklahoma St. (21)	60%	
Nov 11	vs TCU (18)	72%	
Nov 18	at Kansas (114)	99%	
Nov 25	vs West Virginia (69)	97%	

Baker Mayfield is back for one more chance at the College Football Playoff with the Sooners even though we now know that head coach Bob Stoops won't be. Mayfield was one of four key offensive stars that had the Sooners as the top S&P+ offense last season. The problem for 2017 is that the other three are all off to the NFL. That includes running backs Samaje Perine and Joe Mixon as well as electric receiver Dede Westbrook. The Sooners have two major questions for 2017. First, can the defense improve enough from last year's 55th-ranked S&P+ unit to compensate for potential offensive regression? Second, how will the team fare with new head coach and former offensive coordinator Lincoln Riley running the show in Norman?

Outside of early losses to Houston and Ohio State, the Oklahoma offense was nearly unstoppable. They were the top-rated S&P+ passing offense, 14th in rushing S&P+, third in finishing drives (with an average of 5.44 points per trip inside the 40), and ninth in explosiveness. But out of the 3,078 rushing yards the Sooners gained last season, 2,334 have moved on to the NFL. Out of Baker Mayfield's nearly 4,000 passing yards and 358 attempts, Dede Westbrook accounted for 1,524 receiving yards and 28.3 percent of his targets. All in all, those three players accounted for 3,858 yards last season. In addition to Westbrook's departure, Mayfield also lost two of his top three other receiving targets in Joe Mixon and Geno Lewis. That's a lot of firepower to replace.

The two most likely candidates to replace Westbrook's production at wide receiver are Jeff Mead and Mark Andrews. Andrews is the leading returning receiver and was second-most targeted last season, but averaged 3 yards per catch less than Westbrook and had a 12 percent lower catch rate. Mead was the seventh-leading receiver last season and had just a 55 percent catch rate, but has drawn rave reviews throughout the spring. Both targets are 6-foot-5, presenting significant challenges for cornerbacks in man coverage. There is also hype surrounding JUCO transfer Marquise Brown, who is similar to Westbrook in terms of breakaway speed, even if he is shorter.

It will be much more difficult to replace Mixon and Perine's production on the ground. That combination was lethal because of Mixon's explosiveness, speed, and impact in the receiving game, and Perine's size and between-the-tackles ability. The duo could handle a high number of carries, and even though Mixon was both more explosive and efficient than Perine, the drop-off between them wasn't significant enough that the offense had to worry or shift its strategy. It's not clear whether the Sooners have the personnel to approximate that combination in 2017. The next-leading back is Abdul Adams, who had similar numbers to Perine, if slightly more explosive and less efficient (6.6 highlight yards per opportunity and a 35.8 percent opportunity rate). The wildcard is JUCO transfer Marcelias Sutton, a smaller, versatile back who was recruited as an athlete.

The defense dragged the Sooners down last season but has the potential to be a little better in 2017. Oklahoma suffered from a lack of havoc (91st in overall havoc rate), pass rush (99th in adjusted sack rate), and depth, going from an average of 28th in first-quarter defensive S&P+ to 116th in the fourth quarter. Leading tackler Jordan Evans has gone, but sack leader Ogbonnia Okoronkwo should be the team's defensive leader this season, and Caleb Kelly is another player to watch in the linebacker group. The Sooners particularly struggled on passing downs (62nd in passing downs S&P+), but the cornerback duo of Parnell Motley and All-Big 12 cornerback Jordan Thomas should be solid.

The key for Oklahoma will be giving Baker Mayfield reliable receiving options, having a running back emerge to give the offense balance, and developing a pass rush to take the burden off of the two cornerbacks. Games against Ohio State, Texas, and Oklahoma State are the keys to another playoff challenge in 2017.

No. 6 USC Trojans (10-2, 8-1)

2017 Projections

F/+	44.8 (6)
FEI	.192 (6)
S&P+	22.0 (7)
Total Wins	10.0
Conf Wins	7.7
SOS	.167 (57)
Conf SOS	.342 (63)
Div Champ	94%
Conf Champ	47%
CFP Berth	36%

Projection Factors

2016 F/+	43.1 (11)
2016 FEI	.178 (12)
2016 S&P+	19.3 (9)
5-Year F/+	34.5 (8)
5-Year FEI	.165 (10)
5-Year S&P+	15.1 (8)
2-Yr/5-Yr Recruiting	7/4
Ret. Offense	58% (82)
Ret. Defense	67% (61)
Ret. Total	63% (71)

Projected Win Likelihood by Game

Date	Opponent (Proj Rank)	PWL
Sep 2	vs W. Michigan (70)	98%
Sep 9	vs Stanford (9)	61%
Sep 16	vs Texas (19)	73%
Sep 23	at California (68)	93%
Sep 29	at Washington St. (36)	76%
Oct 7	vs Oregon St. (61)	95%
Oct 14	vs Utah (41)	90%
Oct 21	at Notre Dame (17)	56%
Oct 28	at Arizona St. (49)	84%
Nov 4	vs Arizona (67)	97%
Nov 11	at Colorado (60)	89%
Nov 18	vs UCLA (35)	86%

After a 1-3 start, it appeared as though the 2016 Trojans were going to be one of the most disappointing teams yet in a rough decade for the USC program. Then their third loss featured redshirt freshman quarterback Sam Darnold taking over and only narrowly losing to the Utah Utes in what ended up being USC's last loss of the season. With Darnold established at the helm, the Trojans went on a tear across the Pac-12, winning their nine remaining games by an average margin of 17.3 points. That stretch included a 21-17 win over the Colorado Buffaloes, a 26-13 road win over the Washington Huskies, and a 52-49 shootout victory over the Penn State Nittany Lions in the Rose Bowl. Once Darnold was settled in at quarterback, it could be easily argued that the Trojans were the best team in the Pac-12 and perhaps even the entire nation.

Darnold now returns at quarterback, suggesting that the 2017 Trojans could be just as great, if not better. The first challenge in living up to that expectation is replacing both starting offensive tackles; three of the top four receiving targets; and star cornerback/kick returner Adoree' Jackson (five interceptions, four special teams touchdowns). Besides the major impact that Jackson's playmaking regularly had in big, tightly contested games, the concern is now whether the Trojans can build another precise, pro-style passing attack with so many crucial components no longer on campus.

Those concerns aside, it was Darnold's tremendous talent that allowed all of the Trojans' excellent offensive linemen and receivers to finally showcase their own abilities in the first place. Head coach Clay Helton should find it relatively straightforward to reload around Darnold for this coming fall. He has some important pieces to work with such as rising junior tackle Chuma Edoga; tight ends Daniel Imatorbhebhe and Taylor McNamara (five combined touchdowns); and receiver Deontay Burnett (164 receiving yards and three touchdowns in the Rose

Bowl). The Trojans also welcome back Ronald Jones after his 1,082-yard year in his first season as the starting running back.

The Trojans played good defense in 2016, and they have played good defense this decade when directed by current defensive coordinator Clancy Pendergast. The defensive coach has had two strong seasons in Los Angeles in 2013 and then again last year when brought back to replace Justin Wilcox. The Trojans were very aggressive last year and played a lot of press-man coverage, which helped them rank highly by S&P+ in every regard in 2016 except IsoPPP. This indicated that when they got beat, they were often beat badly with explosive plays.

There's a lot to work with in the cast of returning starters, with junior defensive end Porter Gustin and junior linebacker Cameron Smith coming back to lead the defensive front after combining for 20 tackles for loss and 6.5 sacks a year ago. The Trojans also enjoy the return of junior defensive tackle Rasheem Green, who had another six sacks in 2016. With all of that talent stepping into their upperclassmen seasons, the Trojans should be a force up front.

The secondary will try to mitigate the loss of Jackson with an up-and-coming secondary that returns starting safeties junior Marvell Tell and redshirt senior Chris Hawkins while plugging in Jack Jones, a former five-star recruit, into Jackson's spot. Nickelback Ajene Harris may be an underrated component as well. He intercepted two passes and broke up four in his first season at defensive back after moving from wide receiver.

The Trojans will have to replace a few star players across both sides of the ball next season, but they are reloading with recruiting classes that have been ranked in the top 10 for the last four consecutive seasons, and perhaps the nation's best player in Darnold.

No. 7 LSU Tigers (9-3, 5-3)

2017 Projections

F/+	44.6 (7)	2016 F/+	50.4 (6)
FEI	.178 (7)	2016 FEI	.198 (8)
S&P+	23.3 (4)	2016 S&P+	24.6 (4)
Total Wins	8.8	5-Year F/+	39.8 (7)
Conf Wins	5.0	5-Year FEI	.186 (7)
SOS	.028 (3)	5-Year S&P+	17.3 (5)
Conf SOS	.033 (1)	2-Yr/5-Yr Recruiting	5/3
Div Champ	9%	Ret. Offense	59% (80)
Conf Champ	6%	Ret. Defense	40% (118)
CFP Berth	4%	Ret. Total	50% (111)

**Projection Factors**

Projected Win Likelihood by Game

Date	Opponent (Proj Rank)	PWL	Projected Loss / Projected Win
Sep 2	vs BYU (40)	84%	
Sep 9	vs Chattanooga (FCS)	100%	
Sep 16	at Mississippi St. (34)	74%	
Sep 23	vs Syracuse (65)	96%	
Sep 30	vs Troy (74)	98%	
Oct 7	at Florida (14)	49%	
Oct 14	vs Auburn (10)	62%	
Oct 21	at Ole Miss (26)	66%	
Nov 4	at Alabama (1)	21%	
Nov 11	vs Arkansas (37)	87%	
Nov 18	at Tennessee (24)	64%	
Nov 25	vs Texas A&M (20)	73%	

The drama-rich final years of the Les Miles era have finally come to a close in Baton Rouge. The head coach nearly lost his job in 2015, but hung on thanks to an outpouring of fan support combined with a victory over Texas A&M in the season's final game. Then when the Tigers struggled out of the gate in 2016 and went down to Auburn 18-13 in a final display of offensive ineptitude, Miles was pushed out and replaced by Ed Orgeron on an interim basis. The Tigers finished 6-2 down the stretch with narrow losses to SEC West champion Alabama and SEC East champion Florida, and Orgeron was named permanent head coach.

His first priority was retaining star defensive coordinator Dave Aranda, who had coached up the already strong LSU defense into the nation's third best unit per S&P+. Then the Tigers brought in rising star offensive coordinator Matt Canada from Pittsburgh. Canada had a brilliant 2016 season highlighted by a 43-42 shootout victory over the eventual national champion Clemson Tigers.

Aranda's job in Year 2 may be more difficult due to the heavy losses LSU is taking from graduation and early departure to the NFL. The Tigers' top four tacklers are all gone, and six total starters have to be replaced. The front was hit hardest, with starting linebackers Duke Riley and Kendell Beckwith moving on along with strongside end Lewis Neal and defensive end/tackle Davon Godchaux. Star safety Jamal Adams is also off to the NFL, so the main characters in LSU's game plans from 2016 are almost all gone.

They do return junior pass-rushing star Arden Key, who had 12 sacks a year ago, and still have some experience in the secondary in returning defensive backs John Battle, Kevin Tolliver II, and Donte Jackson. Everywhere else, Aranda will be looking

to demonstrate his bona fides once more by coaching up a new class of talented LSU recruits to play high-level defense.

Canada is inheriting an offense that was solid in 2016 but has some dominant components that might finally be fashioned into an elite unit under his more creative direction. Running back Derrius Guice returns after running for 1,387 yards at 7.6 yards per carry with 15 touchdowns while splitting time with the NFL-bound Leonard Fournette. Starting quarterback Danny Etling is also back, but leading receivers Travin Dural and Malachi Dupre have gone pro.

Canada likes to build his offense around inside runs, with jet sweeps, outside pass options, and play-action liberally sprinkled in with specific designs to punish defenses for how they try to defend the runs. Meanwhile the offensive line returns starting guards Maea Teuhema and William Clapp and fullback J.D. Moore to help plow the road for Guice and create a lot of stress for opponents trying to handle those inside runs without conceding too much elsewhere.

It's just too easy to see ways for Canada to successfully leverage the Tigers' inside run game with its star components into easy opportunities for their passing game, which will include some premium athletes at the receiver positions that stand to benefit.

The challenge for this team is a nasty schedule that includes a neutral site opener against the scrappy BYU Cougars; road trips to Florida and Tennessee from the SEC East; and then road games against SEC West foes Ole Miss, Mississippi State, and Alabama. To only play six home games makes for a tough slate, and for none of those six to include their bouts with the other SEC conference frontrunners paints a bleak picture for this young team in Year 1 with the new regime.

No. 8 Penn State Nittany Lions (10-2, 7-2)

2017 Projections

F/+	43.0 (8)
FEI	.159 (11)
S&P+	21.4 (8)
Total Wins	10.0
Conf Wins	7.1
SOS	.161 (55)
Conf SOS	.179 (44)
Div Champ	28%
Conf Champ	18%
CFP Berth	15%

Projection Factors

2016 F/+	43.5 (10)
2016 FEI	.180 (11)
2016 S&P+	19.4 (8)
5-Year F/+	19.1 (31)
5-Year FEI	.125 (16)
5-Year S&P+	9.7 (26)
2-Yr/5-Yr Recruiting	18/21
Ret. Offense	79% (26)
Ret. Defense	68% (55)
Ret. Total	74% (27)

Projected Win Likelihood by Game

Date	Opponent (Proj Rank)	PWL	Projected Loss	Projected Win
Sep 2	vs Akron (119)	99%		
Sep 9	vs Pittsburgh (38)	88%		
Sep 16	vs Georgia St. (115)	99%		
Sep 23	at Iowa (58)	84%		
Sep 30	vs Indiana (43)	90%		
Oct 7	at Northwestern (33)	72%		
Oct 21	vs Michigan (13)	62%		
Oct 28	at Ohio St. (2)	35%		
Nov 4	at Michigan St. (46)	81%		
Nov 11	vs Rutgers (93)	99%		
Nov 18	vs Nebraska (45)	91%		
Nov 25	at Maryland (79)	98%		

The 2016 season was a major breakthrough for the Penn State program and third-year head coach James Franklin. The unmistakable key to this successful season was the hiring of Fordham head coach Joe Moorhead as offensive coordinator to bring the up-tempo spread offense to State College. What followed was sophomore quarterback Trace McSorley accounting for 3,979 total yards and 36 touchdowns while leading the Nittany Lions to an 11-3 season and a Big 10 championship.

In 2017 the Lions will have to replace leading receiver Chris Godwin (982 yards and 11 touchdowns), but the rest of their skill players are back. The leader of this group is running back Saquon Barkley, who thrived in the new spread offense running for 1,496 yards and 18 touchdowns. Saeed Blacknall might be the heir to Godwin as the primary deep threat after averaging 12.9 yards per target. Tight end Mike Gesicki is arguably one of the more underrated players in the Big 10 and nearly left early for the NFL draft. The senior had 678 receiving yards and five touchdowns in 2016 while also serving as a run blocker for Barkley and a pass protector for McSorley.

Perhaps even more significant than returning all of these breakthrough performers will be the improvements coming along the Penn State offensive line, which has been the weakest part of the team for several years now as they recover from NCAA sanctions. The line played much better in 2016, ranking 26th in adjusted sack rate, but still struggled in the run game, finishing 120th in adjusted line yards. They are poised to make another leap of improvement with potentially four starters returning and young players like redshirt sophomore Ryan Bates and sophomore Connor McGovern coming into greater prominence after gaining valuable experience.

The defense is losing some valuable players in starting defensive ends Garrett Sickels and Evan Schwan (12 combined sacks), and they lost starting cornerback John Reid in spring. However, they return star safety Marcus Allen and middle linebacker Jason Cabinda, who leads an emerging linebacker corps that should be a team strength in 2017. Both defensive tackles are returning starters, and if the Lions can plug in new impact players outside at end this could prove to be as strong a defensive unit as they had a year ago, when they ranked 14th in S&P+.

Perhaps the biggest factor for Penn State is how well the rest of the league adjusts to handle their spread offense, which brought an aggressiveness and explosiveness that really threatened the league's practice of slower tempo. Because of their willingness to throw it deep early and often, the Nittany Lions are never out of a game and can put a lot of pressure on opponents to embrace their up-tempo style or risk being left behind in a shootout. You can hold Penn State down for a few quarters, but you'd better be padding a sizable lead for when your own pass rush starts to wear down and McSorley starts finding time to hit targets downfield.

Now that they're in Year 2 in this offense with their quarterback returning and their line improving, the Nittany Lions' ability to run the ball and aggressively attack teams down the field figures to improve. If the top-20 recruiting classes that Franklin has been bringing in over the last few years are ready to step into the spotlight, then Penn State could be back in contention for another Big 10 title, and perhaps this time a playoff spot as well.

No. 9 Stanford Cardinal (9-3, 7-2)

2017 Projections

F/+	42.9 (9)
FEI	.180 (8)
S&P+	18.6 (12)
Total Wins	9.3
Conf Wins	6.8
SOS	.100 (30)
Conf SOS	.151 (33)
Div Champ	34%
Conf Champ	17%
CFP Berth	13%

Projection Factors

2016 F/+	24.3 (25)
2016 FEI	.102 (30)
2016 S&P+	11.1 (23)
5-Year F/+	40.8 (5)
5-Year FEI	.149 (11)
5-Year S&P+	16.4 (7)
2-Yr/5-Yr Recruiting	16/16
Ret. Offense	76% (38)
Ret. Defense	74% (36)
Ret. Total	75% (22)

Projected Win Likelihood by Game

Date	Opponent (Proj Rank)	PWL	Projected Loss / Projected Win
Aug 26	vs Rice (118)	99%	
Sep 9	at USC (6)	39%	
Sep 16	at San Diego St. (48)	81%	
Sep 23	vs UCLA (35)	84%	
Sep 30	vs Arizona St. (49)	91%	
Oct 7	at Utah (41)	78%	
Oct 14	vs Oregon (22)	72%	
Oct 26	at Oregon St. (61)	87%	
Nov 4	at Washington St. (36)	74%	
Nov 10	vs Washington (11)	60%	
Nov 18	vs California (68)	97%	
Nov 25	vs Notre Dame (17)	68%	

On paper the Cardinal wouldn't necessarily seem to be poised for a top-10 season. They just went 10-3, after all, while being led by the third and eighth overall picks in the 2017 NFL draft in defensive lineman Solomon Thomas and running back Christian McCaffrey. On top of that, the Cardinal found their quarterback of the future down the stretch in 2016 when redshirt junior-to-be Keller Chryst took over—only to lose him for six months when he suffered a knee injury in the Sun Bowl.

Thomas amazingly led the Cardinal in tackles despite playing in the trenches, and it was a weekly struggle for Stanford head coach David Shaw not to just give McCaffrey the ball on every play. Yet despite all those losses and Chryst's uncertain timetable for return, Stanford has some momentum building up that could make them a contender in a deep Pac-12.

One of their strongest points is that the running game is likely to remain just as potent, if not better, after successfully sorting out their offensive line depth chart. David Bright moved out to left tackle and has locked that position down, while massive sophomore guard Nick Herbig (6-foot-4 and 346 pounds) has taken over at the left guard spot after a promising freshman year. Fullback Daniel Marx also returns for his senior year, and running back Bryce Love ran for 783 yards at 7 yards per carry while splitting time with McCaffrey in 2016.

If either Chryst returns to his prior form or senior Ryan Burns is improved, than the passing game should be better, with a solidified offensive line and the return of targets like wide receiver Trenton Irwin and tight end Dalton Schultz. The Cardinal are usually keyed by the play of their offensive line, and stand to improve considerably from having the advantage in the trenches once more in the Pac-12.

The defensive plan for replacing Thomas will be to feature returning nose tackle Harrison Phillips (six sacks) and versatile linebacker Joey Alfieri (five sacks), who will both move around and disrupt opponents up front. The Cardinal like to play a lot of nickel and dime sub-packages while leaning on secondary coach Duane Akina to produce defensive backs who can play man coverage and free up the big Stanford linebackers to focus on dominating the box. Stanford is losing safeties Dallas Lloyd and Zach Hoffpauir, but returns Justin Reid at that position and is loaded at cornerback with Quenton Meeks (eight passes defended), Alijah Holder (eight) and Alameen Murphy (seven) all returning. Add in a deep and versatile stable of linebackers and Stanford should be able to create chaos up front with shifting fronts and blitzes while matching up to the league's better passing games with its own talented secondary.

Shaw has been bringing in some strong recruiting classes for the last four years, building out Stanford into a national brand with their academics, pro-style schemes, and cutting edge strength and conditioning program. Their prospective starting lineup in 2017 will feature both an offense and a defense that are filled with blue chip recruits and players who have been in their program for three years or more. With the line established and the defense loaded with the right components to piece together another top-20 or better unit, this team could be poised for a big season if quarterback sorts out.

No. 10 Auburn Tigers (8-4, 5-3)

2017 Projections

F/+	42.3 (10)
FEI	.157 (13)
S&P+	20.0 (9)
Total Wins	8.4
Conf Wins	5.0
SOS	.028 (2)
Conf SOS	.057 (7)
Div Champ	12%
Conf Champ	7%
CFP Berth	5%

Projection Factors

2016 F/+	37.9 (13)
2016 FEI	.152 (14)
2016 S&P+	17.6 (13)
5-Year F/+	26.9 (19)
5-Year FEI	.127 (14)
5-Year S&P+	13.9 (14)
2-Yr/5-Yr Recruiting	9/7
Ret. Offense	72% (43)
Ret. Defense	60% (79)
Ret. Total	66% (56)

Projected Win Likelihood by Game

Date	Opponent (Proj Rank)	PWL
Sep 2	vs Ga. Southern (94)	99%
Sep 9	at Clemson (4)	37%
Sep 16	vs Mercer (FCS)	100%
Sep 23	at Missouri (52)	82%
Sep 30	vs Mississippi St. (34)	84%
Oct 7	vs Ole Miss (26)	77%
Oct 14	at LSU (7)	38%
Oct 21	at Arkansas (37)	74%
Nov 4	at Texas A&M (20)	55%
Nov 11	vs Georgia (15)	62%
Nov 18	vs UL-Monroe (121)	99%
Nov 25	vs Alabama (1)	31%

The 2016 season played out pretty strangely for head coach Gus Malzahn's Auburn Tigers. They struggled some on offense early and were held under 20 points in early contests with Clemson, LSU, and Texas A&M. Surprisingly it was their defense that kept them in games while Malzahn's offense faced uncharacteristic troubles. The Tigers later went on a tear, winning six straight before fizzling again late when facing Georgia, Alabama, and Oklahoma. It was one of the tougher schedules in college football and the Auburn offense lacked enough firepower to get through it.

Malzahn made two major moves before 2016. The first was replacing defensive coordinator Will Muschamp, who left for the head coaching job at South Carolina. Malzahn hired another Nick Saban disciple in Kevin Steele and the Tigers thrived under the continuity, leaping from 29th in S&P+ on defense to ninth. The other was welcoming junior college quarterback transfer John Franklin III, an explosive running quarterback who played a role in the Netflix documentary series on East Mississippi Community College, "Last Chance U." Franklin ran for 430 yards and two touchdowns, but couldn't win the quarterback job and rescue the Tigers from lackluster play at that position.

This offseason Malzahn made two more similar moves to try to achieve a breakthrough for his team, which has gone just 11-13 in SEC play since it went to the national title game in 2013. The first was hiring a rising coaching star who started in the Alabama high school system, Chip Lindsey from Arizona State. Lindsey will bring a more updated version of the run-centric offense that Malzahn prefers, with a greater focus on giving the quarterback passing options outside on running plays to punish teams that load the box.

Opponents will likely need to load the box as Auburn re-turns running backs Kamryn Pettway (1,224 rushing yards) and Kerryon Johnson (895 rushing yards) along with their escort, fullback Chandler Cox. The Tigers also return three starters along the offensive line and welcome in a pair of transfers in FCS center Casey Dunn from Jacksonville State and Florida State guard Wilson Bell, who started 18 games blocking for star running back Dalvin Cook.

The other major move Malzahn made was welcoming in another transfer quarterback, Jarrett Stidham, who played at Baylor in 2015 as a true freshman. Stidham was possibly the most talented quarterback Baylor had seen yet, but he transferred to a community college for the 2016 season after head coach Art Briles was fired, making him eligible to transfer and play immediately in the 2017 season. Stidham had a strong command of a similar offense at Baylor and could be an enormous boost to the Auburn offense. Franklin is moving to wide receiver to help provide Stidham with more targets outside.

On defense the Tigers are replacing star players such as nickel Jonathan Ford, defensive end Carl Lawson, and defensive tackle Montravius Adams. Their defensive line was getting pushed around in the spring game against the Auburn offensive line and they'll need to find some impact players to match last year's results. The two starting inside linebackers both return, as do all of the starters in the secondary save for the nickel or "star" defensive back, so the Tigers could take another step forward if they can find some strong replacements.

True sophomore Daniel Thomas played very well in place of Ford when he was injured late in the year, and Auburn's underclassmen ranks are filled with big blue chip recruits along the defensive line. Malzahn's last five recruiting classes were all ranked in the top 10 by 247's composite rankings, so there's a lot to work with in Auburn.

No. 11 Washington Huskies (10-2, 7-2)

2017 Projections

F/+	41.7 (11)
FEI	.162 (10)
S&P+	18.1 (13)
Total Wins	10.1
Conf Wins	7.2
SOS	.234 (65)
Conf SOS	.238 (57)
Div Champ	47%
Conf Champ	23%
CFP Berth	20%

Projection Factors

2016 F/+	50.8 (5)
2016 FEI	.229 (5)
2016 S&P+	20.6 (7)
5-Year F/+	25.4 (21)
5-Year FEI	.178 (8)
5-Year S&P+	11.3 (22)
2-Yr/5-Yr Recruiting	28/27
Ret. Offense	75% (40)
Ret. Defense	50% (110)
Ret. Total	63% (70)

Projected Win Likelihood by Game

Date	Opponent (Proj Rank)	PWL
Sep 1	at Rutgers (93)	99%
Sep 9	vs Montana (FCS)	100%
Sep 16	vs Fresno St. (111)	99%
Sep 23	at Colorado (60)	86%
Sep 30	at Oregon St. (61)	86%
Oct 7	vs California (68)	96%
Oct 14	at Arizona St. (49)	81%
Oct 28	vs UCLA (35)	83%
Nov 4	vs Oregon (22)	70%
Nov 10	at Stanford (9)	40%
Nov 18	vs Utah (41)	88%
Nov 25	vs Washington St. (36)	84%

The Huskies have two big-picture questions for 2017: can they win the Pac-12 and make a repeat trip to the College Football Playoff even though USC appears to be surging? And did the Huskies hit their ceiling in last year's loss in the semi-finals, or can Washington get even better?

The Huskies were the 24th-most talented team last season in 247 Sports' College Team Talent Composite last season, which measures the entire team's composite recruiting rankings. They averaged an 85.62 recruiting ranking. For comparison, the other playoff members averaged 92.69 (Alabama), 91.43 (Ohio State), and 89.00 (Clemson). It looks like the Huskies definitely punched above their weight when it comes to talent and performance—as is typical for a Chris Peterson-coached team.

And Washington seems primed for a showdown with USC in the Pac-12 Championship Game based on the talent returning. Essentially the entire 15th-ranked S&P+ offense returns, while most of the big pieces of the front seven on defense do as well. There are only a few big departures. First, and most critical for the Huskies next season, is that wide receiver John Ross went off to the NFL in the first round of the draft. He set the record for the fastest 40 at the modern NFL combine with a 4.22 time. Junior quarterback Jake Browning is definitely going to miss that breakaway speed, especially when Ross received 33.1 percent of his passing targets last season.

The cupboard isn't bare, though, with Dante Pettis (15.5 yards per catch, 1.3 higher than Ross, and 72.6 percent catch rate, again better than Ross) and Chico McClatcher (18.5 yards per catch) ready to assume leading roles. And the offense is stabilized by not only those second- and third-leading receivers and Browning returning, but also the two leading rushers in Myles Gaskin and Lavon Coleman. Those two quietly ran for 2,228 yards last season, and Coleman averaged 7.2 highlight yards per opportunity, with over a 50 percent efficiency rate.

The only other major concern for Huskies fans hoping for a repeat is whether the secondary can survive the losses of Budda Baker, Kevin King, and Sidney Jones. There's talent on the roster, including blue chip young guys like Austin Joyner, Byron Murphy, and Isaiah Gilchrist. It's just a matter of whether that young talent is ready to go. Last year's Huskies defense was tenth in rushing S&P+ and fifth in passing S&P+, so it's fair to expect the passing numbers to fall this season. But the run defense should be just as solid.

The schedule is extremely manageable as well. Besides a matchup against Colorado in their fourth game, the Huskies likely won't be seriously challenged until a critical two-game stretch against Oregon and Stanford in November. Those two games will likely determine the Pac-12 North winner. Current S&P+ projections favor Stanford by about a field goal, but the Huskies are favored by more than a touchdown in all other games.

No. 12 Wisconsin Badgers (10-2, 8-1)

2017 Projections

F/+	41.6 (12)
FEI	.157 (12)
S&P+	18.6 (11)
Total Wins	10.4
Conf Wins	7.7
SOS	.327 (70)
Conf SOS	.398 (64)
Div Champ	79%
Conf Champ	28%
CFP Berth	25%

Projection Factors

2016 F/+	45.5 (9)
2016 FEI	.210 (6)
2016 S&P+	18.2 (11)
5-Year F/+	33.0 (10)
5-Year FEI	.175 (9)
5-Year S&P+	14.0 (13)
2-Yr/5-Yr Recruiting	36/34
Ret. Offense	66% (58)
Ret. Defense	68% (56)
Ret. Total	67% (52)

Projected Win Likelihood by Game

Date	Opponent (Proj Rank)	PWL	Projected Loss / Projected Win
Sep 1	vs Utah St. (75)	98%	
Sep 9	vs Fla. Atlantic (92)	99%	
Sep 16	at BYU (40)	76%	
Sep 30	vs Northwestern (33)	83%	
Oct 7	at Nebraska (45)	80%	
Oct 14	vs Purdue (97)	99%	
Oct 21	vs Maryland (79)	83%	
Oct 28	at Illinois (95)	99%	
Nov 4	at Indiana (43)	79%	
Nov 11	vs Iowa (58)	92%	
Nov 18	vs Michigan (13)	60%	
Nov 25	at Minnesota (57)	82%	

Wisconsin had one of the most surprising runs of 2016. Preseason projections weren't optimistic for the Badgers, who were ranked 36th in last year's projections. They had LSU, Michigan State, Iowa, Michigan, and Ohio State all on the schedule (and with the latter four all in a row starting in late September!), so it was understandable why nearly everyone was down on a team that managed ten wins in 2015. But we were proven wrong, as the Badgers managed another double-digit-win season, including victories over three of those five dangerous opponents. The Badgers also only lost by a touchdown in each of their three losses (to Michigan, Ohio State, and Penn State). To get yet another 10-plus-win season in 2017, the Badgers will likely play with the same script: decent, decidedly unflashy offense, and elite defense.

The offense has a few notable departures from last season, including part-time starting quarterback Bart Houston. Houston and 2017 starter Alex Hornibrook split passing attempts nearly down the middle last season, but Houston averaged 1.8 yards per attempt more than the then-freshman Hornibrook. Houston reclaimed the job from Hornibrook for the last four games, with efficient performances in each. Hornibrook loses third-leading receiver Robert Wheelwright, but the top two targets, Jazz Peavy and potential All-American tight end Troy Fumagalli, should keep the receiving game near where it was last season. Peavy showed some big-play ability, averaging nearly 15 yards per catch, while Fumagalli is a huge (6-foot-6) target with reliable hands (71.2 percent catch rate). Wisconsin teams are never huge passing teams—Joel Stave nearly got to 3,000 passing yards in 2015, but their combined 2,507 yards last season was on par with Badgers teams going back to 2012, after Russell Wilson's lone year in Madison.

The offense will instead be centered on the running game, which lost key pieces in a unit that was disappointingly just 48th in rushing S&P+ and 108th in opportunity rate. Those departed players include first round pick offensive tackle Ryan Ramczyk, stalwart rusher Corey Clement, and senior Dare Ogunbowale. Though Clement had nearly 1,400 yards last season, he and the run game overall were inefficient, averaging just a 30.7 percent opportunity rate. The hope is that there will be some addition by subtraction. Sophomore Bradrick Shaw likely takes the top spot, and he was at least consistent in his more limited time last season (43.2 percent opportunity rate). The run game will also get a boost from Pitt transfer Chris James. James was originally a high-three star recruit and should be a solid option on third downs.

While the offense looks to be maybe slightly improved from last season, the defense takes a few hits from the losses of T.J. Watt and Vince Biegel at linebacker, Sojourn Shelton at corner, and Leo Musso at safety. That's a lot of lost playmaking ability. The Badgers defense was 13th overall in havoc rate, and those four players led the team in sacks (11.5 for Watt, four for Biegel), tackles for loss (15.5 for Watt), interceptions (five for Musso and four for Shelton), and pass breakups (12 for Shelton). The 2016 Badgers defense was incredibly experienced, made a lot of big plays, limited explosive plays (11th) and control the red zone (3.6 points per trip inside the 40, tenth). There's still plenty of talent on the roster, but it's hard not to imagine some step back in playmaking ability on defense.

No. 13 Michigan Wolverines (9-3, 7-2)

2017 Projections

F/+	40.4 (13)
FEI	.133 (16)
S&P+	19.8 (10)
Total Wins	9.2
Conf Wins	6.8
SOS	.090 (25)
Conf SOS	.141 (28)
Div Champ	20%
Conf Champ	13%
CFP Berth	9%

Projection Factors

2016 F/+	58.9 (4)
2016 FEI	.242 (4)
2016 S&P+	26.8 (3)
5-Year F/+	29.7 (18)
5-Year FEI	.190 (6)
5-Year S&P+	14.3 (10)
2-Yr/5-Yr Recruiting	4/19
Ret. Offense	46% (98)
Ret. Defense	22% (127)
Ret. Total	34% (126)

Projected Win Likelihood by Game

Date	Opponent (Proj Rank)	PWL	Projected Loss / Projected Win
Sep 2	vs Florida (14)	50%	
Sep 9	vs Cincinnati (77)	98%	
Sep 16	vs Air Force (104)	99%	
Sep 23	at Purdue (97)	99%	
Oct 7	vs Michigan St. (46)	89%	
Oct 14	at Indiana (43)	78%	
Oct 21	at Penn St. (8)	38%	
Oct 28	vs Rutgers (93)	99%	
Nov 4	vs Minnesota (57)	91%	
Nov 11	at Maryland (79)	97%	
Nov 18	at Wisconsin (12)	40%	
Nov 25	vs Ohio St. (2)	46%	

Last year was supposed to be the year for the Wolverines. And until a fluky 14-13 loss to Iowa in November, it was. Michigan was loaded with upperclassmen who would go on to be drafted. A year after archrivals Ohio State dominated the NFL draft, Michigan would send the most players through the draft in 2017 with 11. That was a school record and a testament to Brady Hoke's recruiting prowess. But after the Wolverines lost again to Ohio State in The Game, Jim Harbaugh's second season back in Ann Arbor felt like a missed opportunity.

For 2017, 11 of Michigan's top 13 players in total tackles are now gone, including Jabrill Peppers; top defensive ends Taco Charlton and Chris Wormley; both safeties; and both cornerbacks, including star Jourdan Lewis. On offense, Michigan loses starting running back De'Veon Smith and the top three receiving targets, including star tight end Jake Butt. Michigan is last in the country in overall returning starters according to Phil Steele's charts, and third-to-last in Bill Connelly's returning production rankings. So how can Michigan avoid the dreaded rebuilding year as Big Ten East rivals Ohio State and Penn State carry contrasting high expectations into 2017? Well, through high accumulated talent and a darn good coaching staff.

Jim Harbaugh turned Wilton Speight into a solid quarterback last season. Speight averaged just 6.8 yards per attempt and completed only 61.6 percent of his passes, but managed to keep the passing game at a top-30 level nonetheless. The offense overall was 41st, due a lack of explosive production and just average efficiency. In fact, the Wolverines offense overall seemed to lack star power. That's not due to recruiting—for instance, the Wolverines have had three five-star running backs on their rosters over the last three years (Derrick Green, Ty Issac, and Kareem Walker, who redshirted last season and will likely fight for third string this season). But it has been much more of a committee approach to produce steady, but not eye-popping results. The Wolverines were 49th in rushing S&P+

and 28th in passing S&P+. But despite the experience advantage that Speight, a senior, brings to the passing game, the run game might be in better shape with sophomore Chris Evans taking on the leading role. As a freshman last year and easily the less-heralded running back recruit, Evans was the best running back on the team despite receiving just half of De'Veon Smith's carries—6.9 yards per carry and a 47.2 percent opportunity rate. The passing game will have to rely heavily on underclassmen after losing its three top targets. But there's no shortage of young talent coming in, including five-star top 2017 receiver Donovan Peoples-Jones and four-star Tarik Black.

The defense was the backbone of Michigan's 2016 title aspirations. It was the second overall S&P+ unit, first in overall S&P+ efficiency, eighth in defensive FEI, and first in finishing drives, holding opponents to just 3.09 points per trip inside the 40. And while we've already discussed all of the new starters that Michigan has to break in, especially on the line and in the secondary, the defensive line should surprisingly be one of the top in the country just a year after leading the country in adjusted sack rate and ranking seventh in defensive line havoc rate. That's because Michigan returns Maurice Hurst, Bryan Mone, Chase Winovich, and last year's top overall recruit Rashaan Gary. That's not to mention their 2017 recruiting class, which includes five-star second-ranked defensive tackle Aubrey Solomon.

Michigan has a ton of talent on its roster and some decent defensive experience that just wasn't starting last year. There are really just two challenges. First, with all of that talent, the big concerns are the losses in the secondary and at wide receiver, where returning productions seems to have the highest correlation year-to-year with next year's offensive and defensive S&P+. Second, there still aren't stars on offense, unless Evans can break out at running back or if Peoples-Jones can emerge as a true freshman at wide receiver.

No. 14 Florida Gators (9-3, 6-2)

2017 Projections

F/+	40.4 (14)
FEI	.146 (14)
S&P+	17.8 (15)
Total Wins	8.6
Conf Wins	5.6
SOS	.069 (15)
Conf SOS	.169 (39)
Div Champ	44%
Conf Champ	18%
CFP Berth	11%

Projection Factors

2016 F/+	30.8 (16)
2016 FEI	.126 (21)
2016 S&P+	14.1 (15)
5-Year F/+	29.8 (17)
5-Year FEI	.121 (18)
5-Year S&P+	13.8 (15)
2-Yr/5-Yr Recruiting	8/10
Ret. Offense	81% (21)
Ret. Defense	53% (103)
Ret. Total	67% (50)

Projected Win Likelihood by Game

Date	Opponent (Proj Rank)	PWL
Sep 2	vs Michigan (13)	50%
Sep 9	vs No. Colorado (FCS)	100%
Sep 16	vs Tennessee (24)	73%
Sep 23	at Kentucky (55)	81%
Sep 30	vs Vanderbilt (50)	90%
Oct 7	vs LSU (7)	51%
Oct 14	vs Texas A&M (20)	68%
Oct 28	vs Georgia (15)	51%
Nov 4	at Missouri (52)	80%
Nov 11	at South Carolina (32)	68%
Nov 18	vs UAB (130)	99%
Nov 25	vs Florida St. (3)	47%

Florida's 2016 felt all too familiar for Gators fans: nearly double-digit wins, a trip to the SEC Championship Game, but no quarterback production and a resulting middling offense. A top-5 S&P+ defense was wasted by the offense's inability to move the ball (or score if it did get in the red zone, since the offense ranked 112th in points per trip inside the 40).

Florida is the Wisconsin of the SEC: elite defense and poor offense where two quarterbacks—one a senior and the other an underclassman—split passing yards nearly equally. Austin Appleby and the returning Luke Del Rio were nearly identical. Both averaged around 6 yards per attempt, under a 61 percent completion rate, and had nearly a 1:1 ratio of touchdowns to interceptions. But even though Del Rio returns for his junior season, odds are that he won't be the starting quarterback. After the spring, where Del Rio sat out due to shoulder surgery, redshirt freshman Feleipe Franks looks to have the lead over classmate Kyle Trask. Franks came to Gainesville as a high-ceiling (.9721 in the 247 Sports composite), but raw recruit whom analysts expected would need two or three years of development before assuming the starting job.

But Franks will have some more competition from recently announced Notre Dame graduate transfer Malik Zaire. Zaire's reputation was built on three games—the 2014 season bowl win over LSU, and then the first two games of the 2015 season when he started over his eventual replacement (and this year's NFL draft pick) DeShone Kizer before getting injured. Zaire was part of a quarterback rotation at Notre Dame last season before eventually ceding the job to Kizer. Zaire will likely be the most athletic quarterback on the roster and add a running dimension to the Florida offense. If Franks isn't ready for the starting job yet, Zaire certainly has sufficient experience to lead the Gators in 2017. The only problem is that even with Zaire or Franks, the Gators still don't have a developed passing threat to lead the offense.

Zaire, Franks, and Florida fans can at least expect to see the greatest concentration of offensive skill talent since the Urban Meyer days. Jordan Scarlett is the first in the running back committee, and the offensive line is deeper than it has been in recent seasons. It will need to be, because last year's offensive line offered decent pass protection but extremely poor run blocking, ranking 99th in adjusted line yards and 110th in opportunity rate. Antonio Callaway, now a junior, led the Gators with 721 yards last season, but former blue chip sophomore Tyrie Cleveland flashed big-play potential (averaging 21.3 yards per catch) despite extremely limited action due to hamstring injuries.

The defense has been consistently among the best in the country for years, but might take a step back this season due to personnel losses, including corners Teez Tabor and Quincy Wilson, lineman Caleb Brantley, and linebacker Jarrad Davis. But sophomore Jabari Zuniga led the team in sacks as a freshman, defensive lineman Cece Jefferson was a five-star recruit, and Chauncey Gardner was a high four-star recruit with three interceptions as a freshman last season, so the talent is likely there to get back up to elite level.

The Gators have early tough matchups with Michigan and Tennessee, but neither of those teams should give the defense much of a challenge while new starters work their way in. Look for plenty of low-scoring games early in Florida's 2017 season as well.

No. 15 Georgia Bulldogs (9-3, 6-2)

2017 Projections		Projection Factors	
F/+	39.6 (15)	2016 F/+	3.4 (59)
FEI	.189 (7)	2016 FEI	.046 (54)
S&P+	13.4 (20)	2016 S&P+	-.2 (68)
Total Wins	8.6	5-Year F/+	32.7 (12)
Conf Wins	5.6	5-Year FEI	.108 (24)
SOS	.073 (16)	5-Year S&P+	12.5 (18)
Conf SOS	.161 (36)	2-Yr/5-Yr Recruiting	6/6
Div Champ	43%	Ret. Offense	77% (35)
Conf Champ	17%	Ret. Defense	85% (5)
CFP Berth	11%	Ret. Total	81% (9)

Projected Win Likelihood by Game

Date	Opponent (Proj Rank)	PWL	Projected Loss	Projected Win
Sep 2	vs Appalachian St. (54)	90%		
Sep 9	at Notre Dame (17)	47%		
Sep 16	vs Samford (FCS)	100%		
Sep 23	vs Mississippi St. (34)	81%		
Sep 30	at Tennessee (24)	57%		
Oct 7	at Vanderbilt (50)	79%		
Oct 14	vs Missouri (52)	89%		
Oct 28	vs Florida (14)	49%		
Nov 4	vs South Carolina (32)	80%		
Nov 11	at Auburn (10)	38%		
Nov 18	vs Kentucky (55)	90%		
Nov 25	at Georgia Tech (27)	63%		

Georgia went from firing Mark Richt after a double-digit-win season to a disappointing 8-5 last year under new head coach Kirby Smart. After Smart's first season, the primary concern is that Georgia is headed towards a future like Will Muschamp-era Florida: a team coached by a former elite defensive coordinator with a strong defense and no offense to speak of. It's too early to tell if that's true or not as Georgia fans expect the typical second-year bump.

Last year was always going to be a transition year as Georgia quickly changed quarterbacks, going from Virginia grad transfer Grayson Lambert to true freshman elite recruit Jacob Eason. Eason, with prototypical size and excellent throwing mechanics, nevertheless was faced with depleted offensive line and wide receiver talent and a large and complicated playbook from first-year offensive coordinator Jim Chaney. Last year's offense only had a single S&P+ offense performance better than 65 percent—and that was a 76 percent performance against North Carolina in the season opener.

With Eason and yet another five-star freshman quarterback recruit in Jake Fromm, the Bulldogs are set at quarterback for the immediate future, and the backfield is loaded, with Sony Michel and Nick Chubb returning for their final seasons. But wide receiver, offensive line, and play calling remain difficult questions for the Bulldogs. Last year's offensive line was 101st in adjusted line yards, 94th in stuff rate, and 58th in adjusted sack rate. JUCO transfer D'Marcus Hayes, five-star freshman Isaiah Wilson, high-four star freshman Andrew Thomas, and four-star Netori Johnson might all challenge for playing time this season. Wilson has the highest ceiling, but Hayes and Thomas might challenge if veterans Ben Cleveland or Dyshon Sims can't lock down spots. Just as critical to the line's poor performance was the shift away from a zone-blocking scheme, and Georgia just might not have had the talent or size to handle the increase in one-on-one matchups.

Similarly, Jacob Eason was thrown into the starting role running a pro-style offense under center after operating out of the shotgun throughout his record-setting high school career. It was a difficult situation, especially because the run game was so hot-and-cold, but Eason also showed a tendency to overthrow at times. He also lacked help at wide receiver. Isaiah McKenzie emerged as a capable primary target and freshman Isaac Nauta showed potential at tight end, but the Bulldogs expected more from Terry Godwin and freshman Riley Ridley, who have both shown potential in the past. Sophomores Charlie Woerner and Tyler Simmons, along with veteran Javon Wims, should all challenge for playing time as well. They will get help from Mark Webb and early enrollee Jeremiah Holloman, who should help upgrade the wide receiver room's talent base. But offensive line and wide receiver still remain the big questions for Georgia this offseason.

Georgia's defense got a decent amount of praise, especially in comparison to the offense, but they had their problems too at just 35th in S&P+ and 36th in FEI. The main problems were finishing drives (which was even worse for the offense); allowing 4.8 points per trip inside the 40 (95th); getting tackles for loss (101st in stuff rate) and general run defense (41st in adjusted line yards); and getting pressure from its defensive line (116th in defensive line havoc rate, 34th in adjusted sack rate). But the Bulldogs lost Alabama graduate transfer Maurice Smith and Quincy Mauger in the defensive backfield, and the baseline talent there is a little lower than ideal for SEC play. They have Richard LeCounte III, the second-rated safety, coming in, and veteran Dominick Sanders is around for another year, but the secondary might be a problem spot this season. Additionally, even though the front seven is loaded with former elite recruits like Lorenzo Carter and Trent Thompson, the front seven has arguably underperformed up to this point, which will make things tougher on the thin secondary. Georgia is almost assuredly the most talented team in the SEC East, but there are definitely enough question marks for the East race to be close again in 2017.

No. 16 Louisville Cardinals (10-2, 6-2)

2017 Projections

F/+	39.4 (16)
FEI	.131 (17)
S&P+	18.0 (14)
Total Wins	9.7
Conf Wins	5.9
SOS	.155 (52)
Conf SOS	.178 (43)
Div Champ	23%
Conf Champ	15%
CFP Berth	12%

Projection Factors

2016 F/+	36.7 (14)
2016 FEI	.140 (17)
2016 S&P+	18.1 (12)
5-Year F/+	25.9 (20)
5-Year FEI	.131 (12)
5-Year S&P+	11.6 (20)
2-Yr/5-Yr Recruiting	34/33
Ret. Offense	58% (84)
Ret. Defense	80% (15)
Ret. Total	69% (45)

Projected Win Likelihood by Game

Date	Opponent (Proj Rank)	PWL
Sep 2	vs Purdue (97)	99%
Sep 9	at North Carolina (39)	74%
Sep 16	vs Clemson (4)	47%
Sep 23	vs Kent St. (120)	99%
Sep 30	vs Murray St. (FCS)	100%
Oct 5	at NC State (31)	66%
Oct 14	vs Boston College (78)	98%
Oct 21	at Florida St. (3)	31%
Oct 28	at Wake Forest (62)	85%
Nov 11	vs Virginia (72)	97%
Nov 18	vs Syracuse (65)	94%
Nov 25	at Kentucky (55)	80%

The Cardinals may have gone 9-4 and produced a Heisman winner in quarterback Lamar Jackson, but you'd hardly know it based on their end-of-season tailspin and the resulting backlash. After starting 9-1, with their only loss to the eventual national champions by less than a touchdown, opposing teams began to figure the Cardinals offense out—specifically, that they could dominate the Louisville offensive line. Louisville finished with the tenth-best S&P+ offense in the country, but that was after losses to Houston, arch-rival Kentucky, and LSU in their bowl game. Against Houston and LSU, the Cardinals managed ten points or less and their offensive percentile performances were 24 and 2 percent.

On the surface, the Cardinals offense didn't have any problems. They were first in rushing S&P+ and opportunity rate, 21st in passing S&P+, 19th in finishing drives, seventh in IsoPPP, and eighth in success rate. But the Cardinals unraveled at the seams. They fumbled frequently—and had bad fumble luck—and gave up an absurd number of sacks. The Cardinals ended up with a minus-7 overall turnover margin, but Jackson only threw nine interceptions. Instead, the Cardinals finished dead last in fumbles lost with 22. For comparison, Texas was tied for 101st in fumbles lost, but had half the number of fumbles as Louisville! Jackson, as both the team's leading rusher (with 214 carries, Jackson had the 14th-most carries of any player in the country—only Navy quarterback Will Worth had more as a quarterback) and sack victim, had eight fumbles, five of which were lost. But the next three run-

ning backs all lost every fumble they had, which is obviously terrible luck. Jackson was also sacked 46 times—or 10.1 percent of the time he dropped back to pass.

So those things are obviously bad, but do they mean anything for 2017? After all, fumble luck is largely inconsistent year-to-year, right? Well, yes and no. First of all, the fumble luck may be better, but that doesn't mean the offensive line will improve. Three veterans return, they signed five freshmen in February, and Mike Summers returns to coach the offensive line, but improvement is far from a sure thing. It's also tough when a lot of the skill talent around Jackson is gone, including top running back Brandon Radcliff and the top three receiving targets, James Quick, Jamari Staples, and Cole Hikutini. Jaylen Smith is likely the top guy at wide receiver and four other players had at least 150 yards last year, but the Cardinals will need more targets out wide.

Bobby Petrino lost defensive coordinator Todd Grantham in the offseason to Mississippi State, and while the defense didn't have as noticeable an end of year decline as the offense, it was still volatile week-to-week. The defense still finished 19th in S&P+ and FEI and primarily had problems with field position (which could be related to offensive turnovers) and in allowing big plays, ranking 94th in IsoPPP. The Cardinals defense returns seven players and 80 percent of its production from last season (15th). That stability on one side of the ball might be necessary as the Cardinals try to bring their offense back to early 2016 standards.

No. 17 Notre Dame Fighting Irish (9-3)

2017 Projections			Projection Factors		
F/+	36.5 (17)		2016 F/+	21.6 (29)	
FEI	.124 (19)		2016 FEI	.085 (42)	
S&P+	14.7 (17)		2016 S&P+	10.5 (26)	
Total Wins	8.7		5-Year F/+	31.9 (13)	
Conf Wins	.		5-Year FEI	.119 (20)	
SOS	.105 (33)		5-Year S&P+	14.3 (9)	
Conf SOS	.		2-Yr/5-Yr Recruiting	10/8	
Div Champ	.		Ret. Offense	58% (83)	
Conf Champ	.		Ret. Defense	56% (96)	
CFP Berth	2%		Ret. Total	57% (86)	

Projected Win Likelihood by Game

Date	Opponent (Proj Rank)	PWL	Projected Loss	Projected Win
Sep 2	vs Temple (66)	93%		
Sep 9	vs Georgia (15)	53%		
Sep 16	at Boston College (78)	94%		
Sep 23	at Michigan St. (46)	75%		
Sep 30	vs Miami-OH (86)	99%		
Oct 7	at North Carolina (39)	71%		
Oct 21	vs USC (6)	44%		
Oct 28	vs NC State (31)	76%		
Nov 4	vs Wake Forest (62)	92%		
Nov 11	at Miami-FL (23)	49%		
Nov 18	vs Navy (71)	96%		
Nov 25	at Stanford (9)	32%		

All of college football joked incessantly about Notre Dame's dismal 4-8 season, but they finished a respectable 29th in the F/+. So what happened to the Fighting Irish to get such a poor record from such a decent season, at least statistically? Seven of their eight losses came by eight points or less. Four of those losses were by a field goal or less. That's either some terrible luck or performance in close games, depending on how you look at it. Just some regression to the mean in performance in close games should indicate that the Irish will have a better 2017 than 2016, right?

That's probably right, but there are still some reasons for caution. First, Notre Dame had the 2015 Ohio State two-quarterback problem: rotating Malik Zaire and DeShone Kizer ended up being a bad thing for everybody, but now both are gone—one to the NFL and one to Florida. Brandon Wimbush, the former third-ranked dual-threat quarterback in the 247 Sports composite, might be better than either one of them, but he's still a brand new starter.

Speaking of new starters, Notre Dame is going to have a lot of them in 2017. The Irish return just 58 percent (83rd) of offensive production and 56 percent (96th) of defensive production. In addition to Zaire and Kizer, notable losses include running back Tarean Folston, wide receiver Torii Hunter Jr., defensive lineman Issac Rochell, cornerback Cole Luke, and linebacker James Onwualu.

Another problem: last year's pass defense was terrible by Notre Dame standards. At 86th in passing S&P+, the defense couldn't pressure opposing quarterbacks, ranking just 115th in adjusted sack rate and 102nd in overall havoc rate. Without pressure, quarterbacks could pick the Irish apart. Only departed senior Cole Luke had more than one interception (and he only had two), while only linebacker Nyles Morgan had more than three sacks (with four). There simply weren't a lot of big plays coming from the defensive personnel. Notre Dame had fallen down the 247 Sports composite overall team talent rankings to ninth, but they still averaged a 90.03 (four-star) rating, so the talent is far from bare.

So between the pass defense, the new quarterback, and the high overall turnover, you'd think that there wouldn't be too many reasons for optimism next year. But while those could be challenges, there are also plenty of reasons to be optimistic, too. First, Brian Kelly sourced some new coordinators. On defense, Kelly hired Wake Forest's Mike Elko, who managed to turn Wake Forest's poor recruiting into the 31st-best FEI defense last season. Offensively, Kelly took a step back and hired Memphis' Chip Long, who had the 27th-best FEI offense last season. Long's use of run-pass options should fit well with Brandon Wimbush's skill set. Second, there's a lot to like about Notre Dame's wide receiver corps. Equanimeous St. Brown is 6-foot-5 and led the team with 961 yards, 16.6 yards per catch, and a 66 percent catch rate, but Kevin Stepherson showed a lot of promise as a freshman, and C.J. Sanders should round out a solid starting group.

No. 18 TCU Horned Frogs (9-3, 6-3)

2017 Projections

F/+	35.8 (18)
FEI	.134 (15)
S&P+	12.9 (21)
Total Wins	8.9
Conf Wins	6.2
SOS	.119 (39)
Conf SOS	.147 (31)
Div Champ	-
Conf Champ	14%
CFP Berth	9%

Projection Factors

2016 F/+	9.8 (51)
2016 FEI	.040 (56)
2016 S&P+	5.2 (47)
5-Year F/+	23.1 (25)
5-Year FEI	.082 (35)
5-Year S&P+	10.1 (24)
2-Yr/5-Yr Recruiting	27/35
Ret. Offense	92% (5)
Ret. Defense	77% (23)
Ret. Total	85% (2)

Projected Win Likelihood by Game

Date	Opponent (Proj Rank)	PWL
Sep 2	vs Jackson St. (FCS)	100%
Sep 9	at Arkansas (37)	67%
Sep 16	vs SMU (84)	98%
Sep 23	at Oklahoma St. (21)	45%
Oct 7	vs West Virginia (69)	94%
Oct 14	at Kansas St. (28)	58%
Oct 21	vs Kansas (114)	99%
Oct 28	at Iowa St. (63)	83%
Nov 4	vs Texas (19)	59%
Nov 11	at Oklahoma (5)	28%
Nov 18	at Texas Tech (64)	84%
Nov 24	vs Baylor (30)	74%

It's hard to find a signature win on TCU's schedule from last season. They embarrassed Baylor 62-22 and had a 31-9 win over Texas, but lost to Kansas State and Georgia in their last two games of the season. The defense couldn't stop anyone on the ground (63rd in rushing S&P+ and 83rd in adjusted line yards), while the passing game was plagued by both inefficiency and a lack of explosive plays despite Texas A&M transfer Kenny Hill taking over. It was easy to expect some regression after Treyvone Boykin's departure, but TCU lacked a go-to receiver and Hill struggled with accuracy at times. Leading receiver Taj Williams had just a 51.9 percent catch rate.

The good news is that nearly everyone returns for 2017. In fact, with 92 percent of offensive production returning, the Horned Frogs are fifth in returning offensive production and second overall in total team returning production. Every receiver with more than 20 targets is expected to return. KaVontae Turpin, who made a splash as a freshman in 2015, returns after ranking fifth on the team last season in receiving yards and sitting out spring practice. Also on offense, running back Kyle Hicks had a solid 1,000-yard season and returns, along with sophomore Darius Anderson. Anderson made the most of his 27 carries last year, averaging a 66.7 percent opportunity rate and 6.2 highlight yards per opportunity—more than either Hicks or Hill.

Hill will be a senior and should certainly benefit from a largely veteran receiving corps, but that group of receivers didn't do him many favors last season.

On defense, TCU was solid in pass defense largely due to an excellent pass rush (tenth in adjusted sack rate) but struggled to stop the run or get tackles behind the line (108th in stuff rate). While a large percentage of the defense returns for 2017, leading pass-rusher Josh Carraway is among the departures. The defensive line was hit the hardest, with Aaron Curry and James McFarland also gone. That's not to mention the loss of safety Denzel Johnson, who tied for the team lead in tackles for loss. With turnover on the line it's hard to expect the run defense to get too much better—until you look at the surprising amount of blue chip redshirt freshman and true freshman linemen who can make an impact. Assuming Mat Boesen and Chris Bradley can lead the pass rush and approximate last year's production, then the returning secondary should keep the pass defense stable overall. Look for ULM transfer Ben Banogu to make a difference in havoc creation.

No. 19 Texas Longhorns (8-4, 6-3)

2017 Projections

F/+	35.0 (19)
FEI	.109 (22)
S&P+	14.8 (16)
Total Wins	8.5
Conf Wins	6.2
SOS	.085 (22)
Conf SOS	.171 (40)
Div Champ	-
Conf Champ	17%
CFP Berth	10%

Projection Factors

2016 F/+	10.7 (49)
2016 FEI	.025 (57)
2016 S&P+	7.3 (36)
5-Year F/+	11.9 (44)
5-Year FEI	.032 (54)
5-Year S&P+	7.5 (37)
2-Yr/5-Yr Recruiting	19/15
Ret. Offense	84% (15)
Ret. Defense	80% (12)
Ret. Total	82% (6)

Projected Win Likelihood by Game

Date	Opponent (Proj Rank)	PWL
Sep 2	vs Maryland (79)	97%
Sep 9	vs San Jose St. (108)	99%
Sep 16	at USC (6)	28%
Sep 28	at Iowa St. (63)	82%
Oct 7	vs Kansas St. (28)	71%
Oct 14	vs Oklahoma (5)	34%
Oct 21	vs Oklahoma St. (21)	60%
Oct 28	at Baylor (30)	59%
Nov 4	at TCU (18)	41%
Nov 11	vs Kansas (114)	99%
Nov 18	at West Virginia (69)	87%
Nov 24	vs Texas Tech (64)	92%

Tom Herman's debut season at Texas comes with a surprising level of expectations for a program that hasn't had sustained success since Colt McCoy left Austin. Herman's eventual ascension to the Texas job seemed preordained since about the midway point of his first season at Houston, but some LSU flirtations and just the right amount of Charlie Strong uncertainty kept things interesting in the Herman sweepstakes. Herman came into a good situation at Houston, with experienced players and just the right amount of talent to make something happen (ironically, Strong appears to have that at South Florida, too). Texas looks like it has a decent enough baseline despite depleted talent relative to the Vince Young/Colt McCoy years—after all, their 247 Sports team talent composite ranking was 11th last season, just one spot behind the national champion Clemson Tigers.

Herman inherits sophomore Shane Buechele, who threw for nearly 3,000 yards even if the passing offense ranked just 67th in passing S&P+. Buechele faded somewhat in the last four games, averaging 6.2 yards per attempt compared to 8.5 during his first eight games. His interception rate also increased from 2.5 percent to 3.3 percent. And it's not just from quality of competition—Texas faced Texas Tech and Kansas in that last period. Part of the problem was undoubtedly the offensive line, which forced Buechele into a 7.3 percent sack rate, 110th in the country. It also struggled with run blocking, ranking 59th in adjusted line yards and 38th in opportunity rate. Buechele will likely win the job under Herman even if he's not a prototypical dual-threat quarterback. But his lack of fit with Herman's system may be somewhat overstated—removing all of the sacks he took last season, Buechele rushed for 4.3 yards per carry with a 45.6 percent opportunity rate. Those numbers won't blow you away and Buechele won't offer breakaway capabilities, but potentially enough to keep defenses honest with the threat of quarterback keep or run-pass options. And if Herman ultimately decides to move on at quarterback, he recruited blue chip dual-threat prospect Sam Ehlinger, who offers superior athletic ability right off the bat. Texas has had quarterback competitions for years, but this is by far the highest talent level to compete.

Outside of quarterback, the Texas offense has two other notable questions. First, Herman hired former Ohio State co-offensive coordinator and quarterback coach Tim Beck. Beck wasn't exactly Buckeyes fans' favorite, so his hire was seen by many as an interesting choice. Second, D'Onta Foreman will be sorely missed in burnt orange. Seeing what the 2,000-yard rusher could have done in Herman's system would have been excellent. Foreman was run into the ground with the third-most carries in the country, but he had excellent production despite the reliance the offense had on him. His replacement is Chris Warren III, a junior who had similar numbers but a slight drop-off in explosiveness. (Warren and Foreman could pass for middle linebackers at 250 pounds each.) Sophomore Kyle Porter was a blue chip freshman with limited action but less efficiency than either Foreman or Warren last season. Herman also brought in Toneil Carter, who enrolled early for spring practice, as another challenger.

While the offense slowed down some after initially looking like it could win shootouts, the 45th-ranked FEI defense also had problems stopping the run (50th in opportunity rate) and allowing efficient passing (75th in unadjusted success rate). But the good news is that almost everyone returns—80 percent of production (12th). In fact, overall, Texas returns the sixth most production and the third-most total starters. Most of the starters were sophomores last year—it was a young defense. Herman's defensive coordinator Todd Orlando transformed Houston's defense into the 15th-ranked FEI unit last season, so there's reason to feel positive about what he can do with a more experienced and talented Texas team. Overall, things should look bright for Texas fans. They've got the coach, they've got at least one quarterback, and they have a team with a strong amount of returning starters. That's a heck of a foundation to build a program with.

No. 20 Texas A&M Aggies (8-4, 4-4)

2017 Projections

F/+	34.4 (20)
FEI	.113 (21)
S&P+	13.4 (19)
Total Wins	7.6
Conf Wins	4.0
SOS	.034 (4)
Conf SOS	.043 (4)
Div Champ	3%
Conf Champ	2%
CFP Berth	1%

Projection Factors

2016 F/+	23.7 (26)
2016 FEI	.100 (31)
2016 S&P+	10.8 (24)
5-Year F/+	30.8 (15)
5-Year FEI	.120 (19)
5-Year S&P+	14.1 (11)
2-Yr/5-Yr Recruiting	12/9
Ret. Offense	39% (108)
Ret. Defense	64% (67)
Ret. Total	52% (107)

Projected Win Likelihood by Game

Date	Opponent (Proj Rank)	PWL
Sep 3	at UCLA (35)	62%
Sep 9	vs Nicholls St. (FCS)	100%
Sep 16	vs UL-Lafayette (109)	99%
Sep 23	vs Arkansas (37)	71%
Sep 30	vs South Carolina (32)	74%
Oct 7	vs Alabama (1)	22%
Oct 14	at Florida (14)	33%
Oct 28	vs Mississippi St. (34)	75%
Nov 4	vs Auburn (10)	45%
Nov 11	vs New Mexico (112)	99%
Nov 18	at Ole Miss (26)	52%
Nov 25	at LSU (7)	27%

The Aggies are in a weird place, coming off of an 8-5 season and losing their final two games to LSU and Kansas State.

The Kevin Sumlin Aggies regularly seem to run out of juice in October, and last year it all started to go downhill beginning with the Alabama game. After the Tide's 33-14 win, the Aggies would lose four of their next six games, only beating New Mexico State and UTSA, which were both ranked in the hundreds in S&P+. Quarterback Trevor Knight's sole season with the Aggies was fine, but he led just the 43rd-ranked passing S&P+ offense and completed only 53.3 percent of his passes on 6.3 yards per attempt. Along with Knight's departure, nearly every receiver not named Christian Kirk left as well. In a string of shifting offensive strategies and personnel in the post-Johnny Manziel era at Texas A&M, nearly the entire passing offense will be different in 2017. That's not to mention the new faces we'll see on defense—top overall pick in the NFL draft, Myles Garrett, joins Shaan Washington and Justin Evans, the two top tacklers, as defensive departures.

The Aggies offense will be undoubtedly built around three players in 2017: wide receiver Christian Kirk and running backs Trayveon Williams and Keith Ford. Offensive linemen Avery Gennesy and Jermaine Eluemunor are both gone, which is a big hit after last year's line managed to be 14th in adjusted line yards, but stability at offensive coordinator under Noel Mazzone should help. And there's a big need for some stability after what we saw from the quarterbacks in the

Aggies' spring game. There is a three-way race between Jake Hubenak, Nick Starkel, and true freshman blue chip Kellen Mond. Hubenak is the steady, experienced, but low-ceiling pick; Starkel is a more prototypical pro-style option; and Mond is the least developed passer, by far the best runner, and likely has the highest ceiling. The problem with the Aggies offense is that besides breaking in a new quarterback and receivers behind Kirk, the established offensive stars won't be able to do much without a quality offensive line—and that's a big question mark right now.

On the defensive side of the ball, the biggest questions are on the defensive line. Myles Garrett leaving is bad enough, considering he was the top overall NFL draft pick for a reason—his replacement is unlikely to totally equal either his production or the amount opposing coordinators had to game-plan around him. But the Aggies lose Daeshon Hall too (not to mention Claude George and Shaan Washington behind them). Zaycoven Henderson has had solid production, but the line is nevertheless a critical concern. That's intensified by the fact that even with Garrett and Hall, the defense was 53rd in opportunity rate, 37th in adjusted sack rate, and 60th in passing S&P+.

No. 21 Oklahoma State Cowboys (9-3, 6-3)

2017 Projections

F/+	34.2 (21)
FEI	.117 (20)
S&P+	12.7 (22)
Total Wins	8.9
Conf Wins	6.3
SOS	.173 (58)
Conf SOS	.211 (51)
Div Champ	-
Conf Champ	15%
CFP Berth	10%

Projection Factors

2016 F/+	29.2 (17)
2016 FEI	.147 (15)
2016 S&P+	11.1 (22)
5-Year F/+	23.6 (24)
5-Year FEI	.123 (17)
5-Year S&P+	9.9 (25)
2-Yr/5-Yr Recruiting	40/36
Ret. Offense	78% (30)
Ret. Defense	56% (97)
Ret. Total	67% (49)

Projected Win Likelihood by Game

Date	Opponent (Proj Rank)	PWL
Aug 31	vs Tulsa (76)	96%
Sep 8	at South Alabama (106)	99%
Sep 16	at Pittsburgh (38)	67%
Sep 23	vs TCU (18)	55%
Sep 30	at Texas Tech (64)	82%
Oct 14	vs Baylor (30)	72%
Oct 21	at Texas (19)	41%
Oct 28	at West Virginia (69)	86%
Nov 4	vs Oklahoma (5)	40%
Nov 11	at Iowa St. (63)	81%
Nov 18	vs Kansas St. (28)	70%
Nov 25	vs Kansas (114)	99%

The 2017 season has a chance to be one of the more special years in Oklahoma State history under current head coach Mike Gundy. They were explosive last year on offense with a 4,000-yard passer in quarterback Mason Rudolph, a 1,000-yard rusher in freshman running back Justice Hill, a 1,000-yard receiver in James Washington, and an 800-yard receiver in Jalen McCleskey. All of these players now return in 2017, and Gundy supplemented the rest of the roster by taking a couple of grad transfers in former starting Cal left tackle Aaron Cochran and Clemson cornerback Adrian Baker.

The Cowboys are also welcoming back receiver Marcell Ateman, who had 766 receiving yards and five touchdowns in 2015 before injury cost him 2016, and welcoming in former five-star recruit Tyron Johnson, who sat out 2016 after transferring from LSU.

This is the strongest collection of offensive skill players that

Oklahoma State has been able to field since 2011, when they returned a similar assortment of skill players and proceeded to go 11-1 and win their only Big 12 title of the Gundy era. Their offensive line is also poised for a good year with three returning starters from a breakthrough 2016 unit.

The only hangup is at tight end, where the Cowboys say farewell to key blocker Zac Veatch and versatile hybrid Blake Jarwin. While they are a spread offense, the Oklahoma State system is at its best when utilizing a blocking tight end to help its run game. With the run game established, the spread-out receivers are even better positioned to burn opponents on screens and play-action passes down the field. The Cowboys have an assistant dedicated to developing players at this position, and if he can get a walk-on like Britton Abbott (a 6-foot-2, 255 pound redshirt junior) up to speed on all of the necessary blocks, then this system should really hum in 2017.

Oklahoma State is generally very solid on defense, but they have struggled over the last few years since losing cornerback Justin Gilbert to the NFL after three phenomenal seasons in Stillwater. The addition of Clemson transfer Adrian Baker could be huge here, and the Cowboys already moved their top corner Ramon Richards to safety in anticipation of locking down the position with new blood.

If they can find a lockdown corner on their roster, the Cowboys are generally well drilled and capable of working in concert to outnumber opponents elsewhere on the field. The trick is having the talent somewhere to win one-on-one battles so that help can be shifted elsewhere, and most often that talent needs to be at cornerback. Defensive coordinator Glenn Spencer has a few schemes to help his players outnumber opponents but he has lacked an elite corner since Gilbert graduated. Up front, OSU is saying goodbye to a very effective pair of defensive tackles in Motekiaia Maile and Vincent Taylor, the latter of whom was just drafted, but they return a trio of young defensive ends who might be ready to grow into effective pass-rushers in 2017.

Oklahoma State has a lot of things going right for them. If they can find enough depth on their roster from years of mid-level Big 12 recruiting to surround their established stars, this team could be as good a bet as their rivals in Norman to win the conference.

No. 22 Oregon Ducks (9-3, 6-3)

2017 Projections

F/+	33.8 (22)
FEI	.124 (18)
S&P+	11.7 (23)
Total Wins	9.0
Conf Wins	6.2
SOS	.154 (51)
Conf SOS	.165 (38)
Div Champ	17%
Conf Champ	9%
CFP Berth	6%

Projection Factors

2016 F/+	-10.0 (78)
2016 FEI	-.064 (83)
2016 S&P+	-1.2 (74)
5-Year F/+	34.5 (9)
5-Year FEI	.056 (46)
5-Year S&P+	13.2 (17)
2-Yr/5-Yr Recruiting	23/22
Ret. Offense	76% (37)
Ret. Defense	91% (3)
Ret. Total	84% (3)

Projected Win Likelihood by Game

Date	Opponent (Proj Rank)	PWL	Projected Loss	Projected Win
Sep 2	vs Southern Utah (FCS)	100%		
Sep 9	vs Nebraska (45)	84%		
Sep 16	at Wyoming (80)	95%		
Sep 23	at Arizona St. (49)	73%		
Sep 30	vs California (68)	93%		
Oct 7	vs Washington St. (36)	76%		
Oct 14	at Stanford (9)	28%		
Oct 21	at UCLA (35)	61%		
Oct 28	vs Utah (41)	81%		
Nov 4	at Washington (11)	30%		
Nov 18	vs Arizona (67)	92%		
Nov 25	vs Oregon St. (61)	90%		

The Mark Helfrich era of Oregon football dissipated very quickly, leaving him to catch all the heat for issues that may have been similarly challenging for Chip Kelly had he remained in Eugene rather than heading to the NFL. The major issue was the retirement of longtime defensive coordinator Nick Aliotti, who ran the show on that side of the ball long before Kelly arrived and then retired after spending one year with Helfrich in an attempt to ease the transition from Kelly.

Oregon's defensive S&P+ rank slipped from 25th to 39th in 2014 in Year 1 post-Aliotti, but that was still strong enough to help the Ducks win the Pac-12, beat the Florida State Seminoles in the playoffs, and reach the national championship game. Then they collapsed in 2015, falling to 94th, leading Helfrich to make a change and bring in former Michigan Wolverines head coach Brady Hoke to fix the defense. Hoke's defense was even worse, slipping now all the way down to 119th in S&P+.

The Ducks never lost their edge on offense in this time and continued to churn out great units, but replaced Helfrich this past offseason to try and stem their decline in recruiting going up against rival Pac-12 north schools Stanford and Washington while reinvigorating the program. They opted for South Florida's Willie Taggart, fresh off a 10-2 season with the Bulls that came largely as a result of embracing a spread-option offense similar to what Kelly made popular at Oregon. South Florida didn't play particularly good defense in 2015—in fact they were pretty poor—but the next step at Oregon was to secure the services of another former USF head coach, Colorado's immensely successful defensive coordinator Jim Leavitt.

Now Taggart will be aiming to maintain the course on offense at Oregon with returning quarterback Justin Herbert and their talented ensemble. Leading receivers Charles Nelson and Darren Carrington return, along with star running back Royce Freeman and all five starters along the offensive line. So long as the Ducks don't overhaul too much of their offense and move away from what was working well, they should be poised to put forth a very strong unit in 2017.

On defense Leavitt is inheriting a pretty talented roster for a 4-8 team, with multiple returning starters across the defensive line and the secondary. In particular, it looks like they'll build around sophomore safety Brenden Schooler, who was a lonely bright spot in their 2016 defense, and rising nickelback junior Fotu Leiato, an Internet star for his violent high school highlight reel.

With multiple returning starters on the defensive line and these two run-stopping defensive backs returning under Leavitt's guidance, it's reasonable to expect that Oregon will finally play sound and solid run defense once more. If paired with another typically explosive Ducks offense, that could make them competitive in the Pac-12 again.

No. 23 Miami Hurricanes (9-3, 5-3)

2017 Projections		Projection Factors	
F/+	32.8 (23)	2016 F/+	40.6 (12)
FEI	.098 (24)	2016 FEI	.188 (10)
S&P+	13.5 (18)	2016 S&P+	16.3 (14)
Total Wins	8.8	5-Year F/+	17.4 (33)
Conf Wins	5.5	5-Year FEI	.127 (13)
SOS	.156 (54)	5-Year S&P+	9.6 (28)
Conf SOS	.215 (53)	2-Yr/5-Yr Recruiting	17/17
Div Champ	38%	Ret. Offense	37% (113)
Conf Champ	12%	Ret. Defense	55% (101)
CFP Berth	8%	Ret. Total	46% (119)

Projected Win Likelihood by Game

Date	Opponent (Proj Rank)	PWL
Sep 2	vs Bethune-Cook (FCS)	100%
Sep 9	at Arkansas St. (81)	95%
Sep 16	at Florida St. (3)	23%
Sep 23	vs Toledo (56)	85%
Sep 29	at Duke (59)	79%
Oct 12	vs Georgia Tech (27)	67%
Oct 21	vs Syracuse (65)	91%
Oct 28	at North Carolina (39)	66%
Nov 4	vs Virginia Tech (25)	63%
Nov 11	vs Notre Dame (17)	51%
Nov 18	vs Virginia (72)	94%
Nov 24	at Pittsburgh (38)	65%

Year 1 for the Mark Richt era in Miami went pretty well with a 9-4 record and then the No. 13 recruiting class per 247 the following February. Year 2 will have to include an overhaul on offense, where starting quarterback Brad Kaaya is moving on to the NFL, but it could include some exciting defense.

The Hurricanes' defense was very stout in Year 1 while plugging in a trio of true freshman linebackers in Shaquille Quarterman, Michael Pinckney, and Zach McCloud. The three of them combined for 21 tackles for loss and 8.5 sacks while learning how to play at the ACC level against opponents like Florida State, North Carolina, Notre Dame, Virginia Tech, Pittsburgh, and West Virginia.

They were also playing behind a young defensive line that now returns all four starters, including budding star defensive end Joe Jackson, who had 7.5 sacks last year as yet another true freshman starter. With all of these young athletes, the potential for this defensive front in Year 2 in this new defensive scheme is pretty tremendous, and could catapult the Hurricanes to the top of the Coastal Division standings.

The secondary is a bigger question after losing a couple of starters, but it does return safety Jaquan Johnson and cornerback Malek Young. The Hurricanes were excellent at stopping big plays in 2016, finishing sixth nationally in IsoPPP, and have vigorously embraced the modern "rugby" style tackling to ensure that they regularly get opposing ballcarriers on the ground.

The offense is losing Kaaya but brings back four starters along the offensive line as well as running back Mark Walton, who had 1,357 yards and 15 touchdowns in 2016. Their second-most targeted and most explosive wide receiver, Ahmmon Richards, is also back to ease the transition for the new starting quarterback. The Hurricanes also welcome back backup tight end Christopher Herndon IV, who caught 28 balls and got a lot of action a year ago in their double-tight end sets. The quarterback job is still an unsettled battle between redshirt junior Mark Rosier and true sophomore Evan Shireffs.

Mark Richt coaches a pro-style passing attack that is central to his offense. These two quarterbacks are in Year 2 under his tutelage, and their ability to master his system is probably what will set this team's ceiling. If they can get their passing game up to Richt's standards with one of these first-year quarterbacks working with this supporting cast, the team's ceiling could really surprise people across the country.

No. 24 Tennessee Volunteers (8-4, 4-4)

2017 Projections		Projection Factors	
F/+	30.5 (24)	2016 F/+	25.4 (23)
FEI	.098 (25)	2016 FEI	.130 (20)
S&P+	11.2 (24)	2016 S&P+	9.6 (28)
Total Wins	7.6	5-Year F/+	19.1 (32)
Conf Wins	4.1	5-Year FEI	.103 (26)
SOS	.040 (6)	5-Year S&P+	9.3 (30)
Conf SOS	.051 (6)	2-Yr/5-Yr Recruiting	14/13
Div Champ	7%	Ret. Offense	42% (105)
Conf Champ	3%	Ret. Defense	61% (78)
CFP Berth	2%	Ret. Total	51% (109)

Projected Win Likelihood by Game

Date	Opponent (Proj Rank)	PWL
Sep 4	vs Georgia Tech (27)	56%
Sep 9	vs Indiana St. (FCS)	100%
Sep 16	at Florida (14)	27%
Sep 23	vs Massachusetts (110)	99%
Sep 30	vs Georgia (15)	43%
Oct 14	vs South Carolina (32)	69%
Oct 21	at Alabama (1)	9%
Oct 28	at Kentucky (55)	70%
Nov 4	vs Southern Miss (88)	98%
Nov 11	at Missouri (52)	70%
Nov 18	vs LSU (7)	36%
Nov 25	vs Vanderbilt (50)	82%

The Tennessee Volunteers and head coach Butch Jones are facing tough expectations for their 2017 season. Despite boasting what was probably the best team in the SEC East, the Volunteers fell short of winning the division in 2016 due to a variety of factors that included injuries, a tough scheduling draw, and some disastrous losses to Vanderbilt and South Carolina that wasted head-to-head victories over Georgia and Florida.

Now Jones is under some pressure to produce more wins than their 4-4 finish in SEC play a year ago, but he must do so in a year with tougher competition and without starting quarterback Joshua Dobbs, who was drafted by the Pittsburgh Steelers. The competition within the SEC East will be increased with Florida entering Year 3 in the Jim McElwain era while plugging in grad transfer quarterback Malik Zaire. The Kirby Smart Georgia Bulldogs will be in Year 2 of their new regime and return their starting quarterback along with their star running backs. The bigger window of opportunity for Tennessee to break through and win the SEC East was last year, but the pressure will now be on to win it this season.

The Tennessee offense that Jones has built in Knoxville is geared around a "smashmouth spread" approach to running the football that quarterback Dobbs greatly aided with his own abilities as a runner. Both of his potential replacements, junior Quinten Dormady and redshirt freshman Jarrett Guarantano, are pocket passers who don't offer the same kind of running ability. The Vols are returning four starters from a very strong offensive line that should help ease that transition, and running back John Kelly returns after running for 681 yards as a backup in 2016.

The Volunteers defense can only stand to improve after a year in which both star linebackers went down with injury, as did one of their top backups. Middle linebacker Darrin Kirkland Jr., was poised to break out in 2016, but spent half the season on the bench. He's now back, along with a much more seasoned supporting cast around him at defensive tackle, outside linebacker, and safety.

If Tennessee can find another pass-rusher to replace Derek Barnett, who had 13 sacks last year and was drafted by the Philadelphia Eagles, there are a lot of players returning for second-year defensive coordinator Bob Shoop who should be ready to make a leap playing in this system.

No. 25 Virginia Tech Hokies (9-3, 5-3)

2017 Projections

F/+	29.6 (25)
FEI	.092 (27)
S&P+	11.0 (25)
Total Wins	9.1
Conf Wins	5.3
SOS	.254 (68)
Conf SOS	.266 (60)
Div Champ	30%
Conf Champ	10%
CFP Berth	7%

Projection Factors

2016 F/+	29.2 (18)
2016 FEI	.135 (18)
2016 S&P+	12.0 (17)
5-Year F/+	19.9 (29)
5-Year FEI	.109 (23)
5-Year S&P+	8.4 (34)
2-Yr/5-Yr Recruiting	37/28
Ret. Offense	34% (118)
Ret. Defense	79% (17)
Ret. Total	56% (92)

Projected Win Likelihood by Game

Date	Opponent (Proj Rank)	PWL
Sep 3	vs West Virginia (69)	87%
Sep 9	vs Delaware (FCS)	100%
Sep 16	at East Carolina (103)	99%
Sep 23	vs Old Dominion (98)	99%
Sep 30	vs Clemson (4)	33%
Oct 7	at Boston College (78)	90%
Oct 21	vs North Carolina (39)	76%
Oct 28	vs Duke (59)	86%
Nov 4	at Miami-FL (23)	37%
Nov 11	at Georgia Tech (27)	47%
Nov 18	vs Pittsburgh (38)	75%
Nov 24	at Virginia (72)	85%

Just like Miami and Tennessee, the Virginia Tech Hokies' greatest challenge is replacing a starting quarterback—in their case, Jerod Evans. The JUCO transfer was the perfect fit for new head coach Justin Fuente's spread offense as a dual-threat player with a strong arm who was coming along very well under Fuente's tutelage. Then Evans left early for the NFL, leaving redshirt freshman Josh Jackson to begin his run as the new starting quarterback a year earlier than ideal.

Jackson is also a good fit for Fuente's system, which has made pros of past quarterbacks such as Andy Dalton (while Fuente was at TCU) and Paxton Lynch (while Fuente was at Memphis). There's often a learning curve in Year 1, particularly for freshman starters, so Virginia Tech may take a step back while initiating a new leader on offense. Jackson is a solid runner who ran spread-option quarterback runs at high school in Michigan, so the Hokies could lean on that dimension while he learns the ropes in the Virginia Tech passing game.

Their defense is basically a self-propelled unit at this point under defensive coordinator Bud Foster, who has been on the defensive staff at Virginia Tech since 1987, and the defensive coordinator since 1995. Star linebackers Tremaine Edmunds and Andrew Motuapuaka are back, along with four out of their five starting defensive backs and another two starters on the defensive line.

Cornerback Brandon Facyson has flashed great potential ever since his fantastic freshman season in 2013 and "whip" or "nickel" defensive back Mook Reynolds was a breakout performer in 2016 with two interceptions and two sacks.

Their defense could be elite this season and if Fuente can coach up his young offense—which does return starting running back Travon McMillian (676 rushing yards, seven touchdowns) and wide receiver Cam Phillips (983 receiving yards, five touchdowns) along with three starters on the offensive line—then they might go on a run in conference play.

No. 26 Ole Miss Rebels (8-4, 4-4)

2017 Projections

F/+	28.8 (26)
FEI	.087 (28)
S&P+	10.8 (26)
Total Wins	7.6
Conf Wins	3.9
SOS	.045 (9)
Conf SOS	.048 (5)
Div Champ	2%
Conf Champ	1%
CFP Berth	1%

Projection Factors

2016 F/+	18.8 (35)
2016 FEI	.069 (47)
2016 S&P+	9.7 (27)
5-Year F/+	31.5 (14)
5-Year FEI	.106 (25)
5-Year S&P+	14.0 (12)
2-Yr/5-Yr Recruiting	20/18
Ret. Offense	37% (114)
Ret. Defense	63% (71)
Ret. Total	50% (110)

Projected Win Likelihood by Game

Date	Opponent (Proj Rank)	PWL
Sep 2	vs South Alabama (106)	99%
Sep 9	vs Tenn-Martin (FCS)	100%
Sep 16	at California (68)	81%
Sep 30	at Alabama (1)	8%
Oct 7	at Auburn (10)	23%
Oct 14	vs Vanderbilt (50)	80%
Oct 21	vs LSU (7)	34%
Oct 28	vs Arkansas (37)	71%
Nov 4	at Kentucky (55)	68%
Nov 11	vs UL-Lafayette (109)	99%
Nov 18	vs Texas A&M (20)	48%
Nov 23	at Mississippi St. (34)	53%

Ole Miss should have been poised for a big 2017 season, but is now dealing with self-imposed sanctions of scholarship reductions, the possibility of more sanctions from the NCAA, and a good deal of uncertainty around the program. And just weeks before the season, head coach Hugh Freeze abruptly resigned due to the revelation of escort-service calls in his phone records.

It will be a year of new beginnings for the Rebels in many ways. On offense the Rebels brought in Sam Houston State offensive coordinator Phil Longo, an up-and-comer in the style of Air Raid spread offense that Ole Miss has used under Freeze to stand apart in the rough-and-tumble SEC West.

Longo will be working with sophomore quarterback Shea Patterson, whom Ole Miss intended to redshirt a year ago but had to press into service when starter Chad Kelly went down with injury. Patterson was highly recruited and might be the most talented quarterback in Oxford since Eli Manning. Patterson showed a lot of athleticism and skill when taking down Texas A&M on the road in his first collegiate start, mixing in some scrambling ability and the passing acumen that made him a highly rated prospect. He'll also be working behind a young but talented offensive line featuring fellow sophomore former five-star Greg Little at left tackle.

Former Ole Miss secondary coach Wesley McGriff steps in to lead the defense, after stints in the NFL and at Auburn, where he helped Kevin Steele revitalize the Tigers defense last season. He's bringing some NFL techniques and more man coverage to the Rebels defense and an overall simplicity designed to improve the execution of the unit, particularly up front.

The Rebels are also plugging in a sophomore, former five-star recruit at defensive tackle in Benito Jones, and they have a pretty young secondary that's looking to absorb McGriff's instruction. With all of the youth across the roster and uncertainty regarding the program's fate, expectations won't be quite as high for this team, but they have a very talented young roster that'll be starting to come of age in Oxford this season.

No. 27 Georgia Tech Yellow Jackets (8-4, 5-3)

2017 Projections

F/+	26.8 (27)
FEI	.093 (26)
S&P+	8.6 (31)
Total Wins	7.5
Conf Wins	4.9
SOS	.118 (38)
Conf SOS	.212 (52)
Div Champ	19%
Conf Champ	6%
CFP Berth	3%

Projection Factors

2016 F/+	14.3 (43)
2016 FEI	.074 (46)
2016 S&P+	5.8 (45)
5-Year F/+	19.3 (30)
5-Year FEI	.085 (32)
5-Year S&P+	8.6 (33)
2-Yr/5-Yr Recruiting	54/51
Ret. Offense	62% (70)
Ret. Defense	82% (10)
Ret. Total	72% (29)

Projected Win Likelihood by Game

Date	Opponent (Proj Rank)	PWL
Sep 4	vs Tennessee (24)	44%
Sep 9	vs Jacksonville St. (FCS)	100%
Sep 16	at Central Florida (73)	83%
Sep 23	vs Pittsburgh (38)	71%
Sep 30	vs North Carolina (39)	72%
Oct 12	at Miami-FL (23)	33%
Oct 21	vs Wake Forest (62)	85%
Oct 28	at Clemson (4)	18%
Nov 4	at Virginia (72)	83%
Nov 11	vs Virginia Tech (25)	53%
Nov 18	at Duke (59)	72%
Nov 25	vs Georgia (15)	38%

The Yellow Jackets are coming off a nice three-year stretch in which they had quarterback Justin Thomas at the helm. He was an ideal operator for head coach Paul Johnson's triple-option "flexbone" offense and ran for over 1,000 yards in Year 1 while leading the team to an 11-3 record and top-ten ranking. The program did take a significant step back in Year 2 of the Thomas era, finishing 3-9 and 1-7 in the ACC, but rebounded in 2016 with a 9-4 season.

Now Thomas is gone and the Yellow Jackets need to find a way to replace the explosive running ability the quarterback brought to their system. The Georgia Tech defense has been fairly consistent over the last three years, ranking 66th in defensive S&P+ in 2014, 55th in 2015, and then 57th in 2016. The big difference from their big 2014 season and every other year under Johnson was how wildly effective Thomas was running the football.

In 2017 Johnson will be choosing between junior Taquon Marshall or perhaps junior Matthew Jordan if he returns from an injury he incurred in spring practice. At their B-back and A-back positions, which are the running backs in the flexbone

offense, Georgia Tech has a lot of talent coming back. Sophomore Dedrick Mills was the breakout star of 2016, running for 771 yards and 12 touchdowns at 5.1 yards per carry, and all of the leading rushers save for Thomas are back. However, the two strongest seasons Johnson has had at Georgia Tech (2009 and 2014) both featured quarterbacks who ran for over 1,000 yards. If the Yellow Jackets don't get a major impact from that dimension of their offense, they seem to be a pretty consistently 7-6 kind of football program.

On defense, Georgia Tech has four of the top six tacklers back, but has to replace defensive lineman Patrick Gamble, who had 10.5 tackles for loss and 7.5 sacks last season. Georgia Tech hasn't been able to consistently develop defensive linemen who can rush the passer and could be in for a step backwards unless senior Antonio Simmons or junior Anree Saint-Amour is ready to break out at defensive end.

No. 28 Kansas State Wildcats (8-4, 5-4)

2017 Projections		Projection Factors	
F/+	26.2 (28)	2016 F/+	19.4 (34)
FEI	.101 (23)	2016 FEI	.098 (33)
S&P+	7.5 (35)	2016 S&P+	7.7 (31)
Total Wins	8.0	5-Year F/+	22.7 (26)
Conf Wins	5.4	5-Year FEI	.111 (22)
SOS	.149 (50)	5-Year S&P+	9.1 (31)
Conf SOS	.171 (41)	2-Yr/5-Yr Recruiting	68/60
Div Champ	-	Ret. Offense	79% (24)
Conf Champ	6%	Ret. Defense	61% (77)
CFP Berth	3%	Ret. Total	70% (36)

Projected Win Likelihood by Game

Date	Opponent (Proj Rank)	PWL
Sep 2	vs C. Arkansas (FCS)	100%
Sep 9	vs Charlotte	99%
Sep 16	at Vanderbilt (50)	64%
Sep 30	vs Baylor (30)	60%
Oct 7	at Texas (19)	29%
Oct 14	vs TCU (18)	42%
Oct 21	vs Oklahoma (5)	29%
Oct 28	at Kansas (114)	99%
Nov 4	at Texas Tech (64)	75%
Nov 11	vs West Virginia (69)	89%
Nov 18	at Oklahoma St. (21)	30%
Nov 25	vs Iowa St. (63)	85%

The Wildcats are a very intriguing team coming off their 9-4 2016 season and entering Bill Snyder's 26th year as the head coach of the team. They rarely look exemplary on paper due to mediocre recruiting rankings, yet they regularly field well-coached teams that win a lot of games within the Big 12 conference.

Snyder's record when returning his starting quarterback is generally very good. When Jake Waters returned in 2014 and the Wildcats went 9-4, it was the first time that a returning starting quarterback had failed to win 11 games for Snyder. The 2017 Wildcats return starting quarterback Jesse Ertz fresh off a season in which he ran for 1,012 yards and 12 touchdowns while passing for another 1,755 yards and nine touchdowns.

Eight other starters from the 2016 Wildcats offense also return, including the starting center and offensive tackles and a pair of guards who split time at the same position and now each own their own starting role. Kansas State has to replace wide receiver Deantre Burton after a 404-yard season but is plugging in former blue chip recruit and Cal transfer Carlos

Strickland to replace him. This offense really hit its stride down the stretch of 2016, going 6-1 with the sole loss a narrow 43-37 defeat at the hands of Oklahoma State. They may now prove to be one of the best, if not the best, offense in a league filled with exceptional offenses.

The defense is facing a much stiffer challenge in having to replace NFL-bound defensive end Jordan Willis after a season with 11.5 sacks, along with both starting linebackers and two starting safeties. They do return their cornerback tandem of Duke Shelley and D.J. Reed, who combined to intercept six passes and break up 20 more, along with up-and-coming safety Kendall Adams, who added two more picks.

Assuming the Wildcat offense is as potent as it would seem is likely, the ceiling for the K-State season will likely be set by how well they replace Willis up front. They return Reggie Walker fresh off a redshirt season in which he had 6.5 sacks playing across from Willis, and are now counting on him to key their pass-rush. With development from Walker and the other young players up front, Kansas State could put together a Big 12 championship season.

No. 29 Boise State Broncos (10-2, 7-1)

2017 Projections

F/+	25.2 (29)
FEI	.079 (31)
S&P+	8.8 (29)
Total Wins	9.8
Conf Wins	7.0
SOS	.471 (93)
Conf SOS	.713 (72)
Div Champ	53%
Conf Champ	32%
CFP Berth	2%

Projection Factors

2016 F/+	28.3 (19)
2016 FEI	.132 (19)
2016 S&P+	11.6 (19)
5-Year F/+	23.6 (23)
5-Year FEI	.127 (15)
5-Year S&P+	9.6 (27)
2-Yr/5-Yr Recruiting	64/64
Ret. Offense	60% (74)
Ret. Defense	50% (112)
Ret. Total	55% (95)

Projected Win Likelihood by Game

Date	Opponent (Proj Rank)	PWL
Sep 2	vs Troy (74)	92%
Sep 9	at Washington St. (36)	49%
Sep 14	vs New Mexico (112)	99%
Sep 22	vs Virginia (72)	91%
Oct 6	at BYU (40)	55%
Oct 14	at San Diego St. (48)	61%
Oct 21	vs Wyoming (80)	95%
Oct 28	at Utah St. (75)	83%
Nov 4	vs Nevada (105)	99%
Nov 11	at Colorado St. (44)	60%
Nov 18	vs Air Force (104)	99%
Nov 25	at Fresno St. (111)	99%

Boise State has continued to chug along under head coach Bryan Harsin. The halcyon days of winning 12 or 13 games every season and trying to earn a spot in a BCS bowl or even the National Championship appear to be over, but the 2017 Broncos may surprise. The big challenge confronting the Broncos is a more difficult schedule that has resulted from playing in the Mountain West Conference rather than the Western Athletic Conference, which they dominated in the 2000s.

To confront that schedule, Boise State has a veteran passer, Brett Rypien, who is entering his third season as the starting quarterback in this offense after a strong 2016 performance. Building out a passing game in college requires chemistry between the quarterback and his targets and an offensive line with at least one truly talented tackle surrounded by other starters who work well in concert. Boise State returns starting left tackle Archie Lewis and Rypien's second-favorite target in 2016, Cedrick Wilson, who averaged 11.9 yards per target while racking up 1,129 receiving yards and 11 touchdowns. In the run game Boise State must replace explosive running back Jeremy McNichols, but they have three returning tight ends who have played a lot to help pave the way for the new starter.

The Broncos defense is losing six of the top seven tacklers, but the two most disruptive members of the defensive line return in tackle David Moa and defensive end Jabril Frazier, who combined for 12.5 sacks in 2016. Thanks to the rise of 298-pound sophomore Sonatane Lui, Moa will now be transitioning from nose tackle, which he had to play due to the Broncos' lack of size, to a 3-technique position. From his new position, Moa should be freed up to avoid double-teams more easily and be even more disruptive.

That would help a defensive backfield which will be experiencing a youth movement. Redshirt junior linebacker Leighton Vander Esch leads an interior that will be reloading with underclassmen and first-time starters. Junior cornerback Tyler Horton is back after a solid sophomore season to try and anchor the secondary.

If the rankings on Harsin's recruiting classes are to be believed, this could be the best Boise State team we've seen since the Chris Petersen-coached squads that put this program on the map at the turn of the decade.

No. 30 Baylor Bears (8-4, 5-4)

2017 Projections

F/+	24.8 (30)
FEI	.074 (33)
S&P+	9.1 (28)
Total Wins	7.8
Conf Wins	5.1
SOS	.137 (46)
Conf SOS	.150 (32)
Div Champ	-
Conf Champ	3%
CFP Berth	2%

Projection Factors

2016 F/+	9.7 (52)
2016 FEI	.046 (53)
2016 S&P+	4.6 (50)
5-Year F/+	33.0 (11)
5-Year FEI	.097 (28)
5-Year S&P+	13.5 (16)
2-Yr/5-Yr Recruiting	24/32
Ret. Offense	45% (103)
Ret. Defense	67% (62)
Ret. Total	56% (93)

Projected Win Likelihood by Game

Date	Opponent (Proj Rank)	PWL
Sep 2	vs Liberty (FCS)	100%
Sep 9	vs UTSA (83)	96%
Sep 16	at Duke (59)	70%
Sep 23	vs Oklahoma (5)	28%
Sep 30	at Kansas St. (28)	40%
Oct 14	at Oklahoma St. (21)	28%
Oct 21	vs West Virginia (69)	88%
Oct 28	vs Texas (19)	41%
Nov 4	at Kansas (114)	99%
Nov 11	vs Texas Tech (64)	79%
Nov 18	vs Iowa St. (63)	83%
Nov 24	at TCU (18)	26%

Projecting the 2017 Baylor Bears football season is very difficult due to the utter turmoil the program has endured for the last year and the total transformation that has occurred as a result. Much of the talent that recruiting rankings suggest should be in Waco for new head coach Matt Rhule (hired from Temple) has transferred out of the program or been removed from the team.

Statistical projections of what the Baylor Bears are capable of based off what they have done the last several years under deposed head coach Art Briles and his staff are likely to be very different now that the legendary coach has been removed in disgrace. Briles brought a revolutionary spread offense that Rhule will now seek to replace with a modern, pro-style offense. The Baylor offensive line has been grievously depleted by injuries and attrition and even lost starting center Tanner Thrift after the spring due to a knee injury. The adjustment to the new offensive system could take time before the Bears are able to get anywhere close to matching the results that became normal under Briles.

On defense, which is Rhule's area of particular expertise, Baylor is moving away from a simple, anti-spread zone defense designed by Phil Bennett (now the defensive coordinator at Arizona State) to a system with more man coverage and more overall variety. The new system will depend heavily on the defensive line, where Baylor was thin in 2016 but could potentially be much stronger in 2017. Starting defensive end K.J. Smith is back after a 2016 season with 11 tackles for loss and seven sacks. Longtime utility man Byron Bonds is back after being injured for the 2016 season, and redshirt junior nose tackle Ira Lewis is back after a promising first season as a starter.

Rhule also has something to work with at linebacker in redshirt senior Taylor Young, who had nine tackles for loss and 4.5 sacks a year ago. Defensive back Travon Blanchard could be another key piece for the Bears on defense if reinstituted this fall.

Rhule has a depleted roster to work with, but there's still some talent on hand. If Baylor can adjust sooner rather than later on offense, they may be able to avoid a lost season while rebuilding the program.

No. 31 North Carolina State Wolfpack (7-5, 4-4)

2017 Projections

F/+	24.3 (31)
FEI	.066 (35)
S&P+	9.5 (27)
Total Wins	7.1
Conf Wins	4.4
SOS	.083 (20)
Conf SOS	.158 (35)
Div Champ	3%
Conf Champ	2%
CFP Berth	1%

Projection Factors

2016 F/+	21.7 (28)
2016 FEI	.085 (43)
2016 S&P+	10.6 (25)
5-Year F/+	3.4 (55)
5-Year FEI	.048 (48)
5-Year S&P+	3.8 (50)
2-Yr/5-Yr Recruiting	46/40
Ret. Offense	83% (17)
Ret. Defense	58% (90)
Ret. Total	71% (34)

Projected Win Likelihood by Game

Date	Opponent (Proj Rank)	PWL
Sep 2	vs South Carolina (32)	52%
Sep 9	vs Marshall (100)	98%
Sep 16	vs Furman (FCS)	100%
Sep 23	at Florida St. (3)	14%
Sep 30	vs Syracuse (65)	85%
Oct 5	vs Louisville (16)	35%
Oct 14	at Pittsburgh (38)	53%
Oct 28	at Notre Dame (17)	25%
Nov 4	vs Clemson (4)	27%
Nov 11	at Boston College (78)	86%
Nov 18	at Wake Forest (62)	70%
Nov 25	vs North Carolina (39)	69%

The Wolfpack, seemingly out of nowhere, had an incredible defense in 2016, and defensive line in particular. The good news is that most of the standout players are returning for 2017. The offense wasn't nearly as efficient, ranking 55th in the S&P+, but can build on quarterback Ryan Finley.

The defense ranked 11th in the S&P+ and was just as good defending the run (12th) as the pass (15th). It was incredibly efficient and buoyed by playmakers in the front seven. Ranking 21st overall in havoc rate, Airius Moore, Bradley Chubb, Kentavius Street, and Darian Roseboro all had 9.5 tackles for loss or more. Chubb and Roseboro also had seven or more sacks. This was a disruptive front, and all of those guys return. Safety Josh Jones left for the NFL early, and defensive backs Dravious Wright and Niles Clark were seniors, so the secondary may be a little shaky as it looks for new faces. But if the front seven can control the run (11th in adjusted line yards) and get to the quarterback (44th in adjusted sack rate) like they did last season, then the defense can make up for inexperience in the back end.

The offense will be led by Finley, the Boise State transfer. Finley had a solid debut season with the Wolfpack, but what was maybe most remarkable was how effectively he distributed the ball around the field. Five players had target rates of ten percent or more, and four of those players return for 2017. Stephen Louis showed signs of big-play ability with an average of nearly 20 yards per catch but a 50 percent catch rate, while running back Nyheim Hines and tight end Jaylen Samuels were more reliable targets. None of Finley's top receivers had success rates over 60 percent, suggesting poor catch rates and/or short passes. But since Finley and his top receivers all return, there's good reason to think the passing game will be even better than in 2016. However, leading running back Matthew Dayes is off to the NFL, so either Reggie Gallaspy II or Dakwa Nichols is likely to take over. N.C. State had five running backs with ten or more carries last season and they were all more or less interchangeable—though Dayes was more efficient than Gallaspy, while Gallaspy is more explosive than the other two. The two top backs were both injured for parts of spring practice.

No. 32 South Carolina Gamecocks (6-6, 4-4)

2017 Projections

F/+	23.2 (32)
FEI	.084 (30)
S&P+	6.8 (36)
Total Wins	6.5
Conf Wins	3.8
SOS	.077 (18)
Conf SOS	.145 (30)
Div Champ	5%
Conf Champ	2%
CFP Berth	1%

Projection Factors

2016 F/+	-14.0 (84)
2016 FEI	-.071 (88)
2016 S&P+	-3.6 (79)
5-Year F/+	16.2 (37)
5-Year FEI	.012 (62)
5-Year S&P+	6.7 (42)
2-Yr/5-Yr Recruiting	21/20
Ret. Offense	91% (7)
Ret. Defense	72% (44)
Ret. Total	81% (8)

Projected Win Likelihood by Game

Date	Opponent (Proj Rank)	PWL
Sep 2	vs NC State (31)	48%
Sep 9	at Missouri (52)	60%
Sep 16	vs Kentucky (55)	75%
Sep 23	vs Louisiana Tech (82)	95%
Sep 30	at Texas A&M (20)	26%
Oct 7	vs Arkansas (37)	63%
Oct 14	at Tennessee (24)	31%
Oct 28	vs Vanderbilt (50)	74%
Nov 4	at Georgia (15)	20%
Nov 11	vs Florida (14)	32%
Nov 18	vs Wofford (FCS)	100%
Nov 25	vs Clemson (4)	26%

Will Muschamp's rookie season with South Carolina went better than most people expected. At 6-7 the Gamecocks weren't exactly lighting the world on fire, but wins over Vanderbilt, Tennessee, and Missouri highlighted a season that could have been much worse.

The biggest revelation was the emergence of an offense from quarterback Jake Bentley, a freshman who took over halfway through the season, and running back Rico Dowdle. Bentley had four games of over 200 passing yards, including a stellar 390-yard performance against South Florida in the bowl game. Bentley was a four-star quarterback and likely got just enough time to develop before grabbing the starting job from the Perry Orth/Brandon McIlwain rotation. Even though Bentley showed promise, the early-season quarterback rotation issues had South Carolina at 94th in passing S&P+. And before freshman Dowdle seized control of the top running back spot around the same time, the running game was in a similar state (109th). Dowdle was by far the best option that South Carolina had, averaging 5.7 yards per carry, 41.8 percent opportunity rate, and 5.5 highlight yards per opportunity. That's over a yard better per carry than any of the other backs

and about a six percent better opportunity rate. And that's despite an offensive line that ranked 111th in adjusted line yards and 116th in adjusted sack rate. At this point, now that playmakers have been identified, the biggest thing holding the Gamecocks back is the line, which added five new signees with this year's recruiting class.

Another reason for optimism besides Bentley and Dowdle: the young and deep collection of receivers. Deebo Samuel and Bryan Edwards were the top targets, but two sophomore tight ends impressed as well, especially Hayden Hurst. Hurst, Samuel, and Edwards should be the core receiving group. In fact, every receiver with ten or more targets last season was a freshman or sophomore. Considering how young the talent was overall, it's a little amazing that the offense was even as good as it was.

The defense wasn't exactly up to Muschamp standards yet, which is unfortunate because a lot of the top contributors were juniors or seniors last year. The biggest loss is probably Darius English, with his 13 tackles for loss and nine sacks. The Gamecocks did add four-star defensive back Jamyest Williams and three four-star defensive ends, so they should be worked in as soon as they pick up the defensive scheme.

No. 33 Northwestern Wildcats (9-3, 6-3)

2017 Projections

F/+	22.9 (33)
FEI	.084 (29)
S&P+	6.6 (37)
Total Wins	8.7
Conf Wins	6.0
SOS	.251 (66)
Conf SOS	.278 (61)
Div Champ	15%
Conf Champ	5%
CFP Berth	3%

Projection Factors

2016 F/+	13.8 (45)
2016 FEI	.085 (40)
2016 S&P+	4.6 (49)
5-Year F/+	7.7 (49)
5-Year FEI	.074 (38)
5-Year S&P+	3.2 (52)
2-Yr/5-Yr Recruiting	48/48
Ret. Offense	67% (55)
Ret. Defense	77% (22)
Ret. Total	72% (30)

Projected Win Likelihood by Game

Date	Opponent (Proj Rank)	PWL
Sep 2	vs Nevada (105)	98%
Sep 9	at Duke (59)	67%
Sep 16	vs Bowling Green (90)	97%
Sep 30	at Wisconsin (12)	18%
Oct 7	vs Penn St. (8)	28%
Oct 14	at Maryland (79)	85%
Oct 21	vs Iowa (58)	75%
Oct 28	vs Michigan St. (46)	72%
Nov 4	at Nebraska (45)	57%
Nov 11	vs Purdue (97)	98%
Nov 18	vs Minnesota (57)	75%
Nov 25	at Illinois (95)	95%

Northwestern was a frustrating, but ultimately disappointing team in 2016. The Wildcats lost their first two games of the season, to Western Michigan and Illinois State, by a combined three points. Pat Fitzgerald deserves some credit for getting the team out of that tailspin and managing seven wins, including quality victories over Duke, Iowa, and the bowl conquest over Pitt. Northwestern has lately struggled with efficiency on offense, but has managed to field top-end defenses in prototypical Big Ten West style.

Two of Northwestern's top three offensive playmakers return in 2017, including quarterback Clayton Thorson and running back Justin Jackson. As a rising senior, Jackson has more career carries (855) than any returning FBS player after being top-20 in carries per game as a freshman then top-10 in each of the last two seasons. Jackson has always been reliable for over 20 carries a game. The problem has been that he's not the most efficient back (32.2 percent opportunity rate). The bigger freshman John Moten IV was steadier last season with a 50.7 percent opportunity rate, but Jackson improved dramatically in his explosiveness from the previous season, getting 13 more 10-plus-yard runs and averaging 7.0 highlight yards per opportunity. Similar to Jackson, Clayton Thorson was inefficient and high-volume, but he was also not very explosive,

completing just 58.6 percent of his passes and averaging only 5.8 yards per attempt. But worse, his top target Austin Carr (who devastated Ohio State with eight catches for 158 yards, his season high) is gone. Flynn Nagel looks like his most likely replacement, but he had an 11 percent lower success rate. Carr's absence will likely hurt some.

The Northwestern defense has a weird mix. They ranked 39th in defensive FEI and 32nd in S&P+ (which is great for the talent they typically bring in), 37th in rushing S&P+ and 49th in passing S&P+. But they were also 70th in standard downs S&P+ and 16th in passing downs S&P+. Combine that with two other stats—eighth in finishing drives with 3.56 points allowed per opponent trip inside the 40 and a plus-9 turnover margin (14th)—and you get a picture of Northwestern as a bend-don't-break defense that excelled at the margins. The Wildcats didn't get stops until the red zone and were decimated on standard downs, but were one of the country's best defenses on later downs. It's a unique mix, but it was effective overall. Best of all, the Wildcats return almost everyone except pass-rusher Ifeadi Odenigbo, who had ten sacks last season. He had more sacks than the next two best defenders, so the Wildcats will need a pass-rusher to emerge and replace his production.

No. 34 Mississippi State Bulldogs (6-6, 3-5)

2017 Projections

F/+	22.2 (34)	
FEI	.059 (37)	
S&P+	8.6 (30)	
Total Wins	6.2	
Conf Wins	2.6	
SOS	.036 (5)	
Conf SOS	.039 (3)	
Div Champ	0%	
Conf Champ	0%	
CFP Berth	0%	

Projection Factors

2016 F/+	0.9 (63)
2016 FEI	-.019 (69)
2016 S&P+	3.5 (56)
5-Year F/+	22.0 (27)
5-Year FEI	.031 (56)
5-Year S&P+	11.4 (21)
2-Yr/5-Yr Recruiting	31/25
Ret. Offense	72% (44)
Ret. Defense	59% (85)
Ret. Total	65% (63)

Projected Win Likelihood by Game

Date	Opponent (Proj Rank)	PWL	Projected Loss / Projected Win
Sep 2	vs Charleston So. (FCS)	100%	
Sep 9	at Louisiana Tech (82)	88%	
Sep 16	vs LSU (7)	26%	
Sep 23	at Georgia (15)	19%	
Sep 30	at Auburn (10)	16%	
Oct 14	vs BYU (40)	66%	
Oct 21	vs Kentucky (55)	74%	
Oct 28	at Texas A&M (20)	25%	
Nov 4	vs Massachusetts (110)	99%	
Nov 11	vs Alabama (1)	12%	
Nov 18	at Arkansas (37)	46%	
Nov 23	vs Ole Miss (26)	47%	

Mississippi State had a rough 2016, including a loss to South Alabama to start the year. But the Bulldogs showed high potential with several upsets as well, including a huge 55-20 Egg Bowl win over Ole Miss and a win over Texas A&M. Nick Fitzgerald quickly won the job to be Dak Prescott's replacement at quarterback, and he managed to be a surprisingly electric runner as the Bulldogs figured out their post-Prescott offensive identity. As Fitzgerald settled into the role, the pass defense became the more pressing issue.

The Bulldogs offense under Fitzgerald is interesting. He's got prototypical pro-style size at 6-foot-5 and 230 pounds, but ran for 1,454 yards, had nearly a 50 percent opportunity rate, and averaged 8.7 highlight yards per opportunity. And he came out of high school as a three-star recruit, 40th among dual-threat quarterbacks. As Dan Mullen joked late last season, they only

had to beat out UT-Chattanooga to land Fitzgerald. But he wasn't much of a passer against Power-5 teams, leading the No. 58 passing S&P+ offense. The passing offense is a little more diminished with the graduation of Fred Ross as well. But Malik Dear and Keith Mixon should complement Donald Gray again this season, so Fitzgerald should have enough targets even in a run-first offense. Aeris Williams should again be an effective, if less explosive, running back as well (45.3 percent opportunity rate, 3.3 highlight yards per opportunity).

But the major problem with last year's team, and likely for this season as well, was the pass defense, which ranked 104th in S&P+. That's an even bigger requirement since Mississippi State is likely to see better passing games in-conference with an older Jalen Hurts, a Matt Canada-led LSU, and Austin Allen at Arkansas. The Bulldogs struggled to get any pressure on opposing quarterbacks, ranking 103rd in adjusted sack rate. But now the Bulldogs have lost leading tackler Richie Brown and the top two havoc-generators, Jonathan Calvin and A.J. Jefferson, who combined for 22 tackles for loss and 11 sacks.

There weren't any other standout defenders last season. JUCO transfer (and former Georgia Bulldog) Chauncey Rivers can provide some immediate pass rush help, but there's still a big gap left from that missing production.

No. 35 UCLA Bruins (6-6, 4-5)

2017 Projections

F/+	22.2 (35)
FEI	.069 (34)
S&P+	7.5 (34)
Total Wins	6.4
Conf Wins	4.5
SOS	.061 (14)
Conf SOS	.089 (12)
Div Champ	3%
Conf Champ	2%
CFP Berth	1%

Projection Factors

2016 F/+	3.6 (58)
2016 FEI	.012 (60)
2016 S&P+	2.8 (58)
5-Year F/+	25.2 (22)
5-Year FEI	.063 (42)
5-Year S&P+	11.1 (23)
2-Yr/5-Yr Recruiting	15/11
Ret. Offense	68% (49)
Ret. Defense	40% (119)
Ret. Total	54% (99)

Projected Win Likelihood by Game

Date	Opponent (Proj Rank)	PWL	Projected Loss / Projected Win
Sep 3	vs Texas A&M (20)	38%	
Sep 9	vs Hawaii (116)	99%	
Sep 16	at Memphis (47)	57%	
Sep 23	at Stanford (9)	16%	
Sep 30	vs Colorado (60)	80%	
Oct 14	at Arizona (67)	73%	
Oct 21	vs Oregon (22)	39%	
Oct 28	at Washington (11)	17%	
Nov 3	at Utah (41)	52%	
Nov 11	vs Arizona St. (49)	72%	
Nov 18	at USC (6)	14%	
Nov 24	vs California (68)	86%	

Things were rough for UCLA after Josh Rosen went down halfway through the season. To that point Rosen was on track for nearly a 4,000-yard passing season, but senior replacement Mike Fafaul led just the No. 75 passing S&P+ offense in his place. Jim Mora, who is always rumored to be looking around for a new job, brought in Jedd Fisch as the new offensive coordinator in January. Most recently Fisch was Michigan's passing game coordinator, making Wilton Speight into a decent quarterback last season. He'll have an easier time with Rosen, but the bigger question is whether the run game will be anything better than abysmal despite decent talent on the roster.

Besides growing hot seat talk surrounding Mora, the big storylines for UCLA's season will likely be Rosen's return and whether Fisch can get anything out of the running game. The run game, and standard downs by extension, were abysmal, ranking 126th and 115th respectively. Both Nate Starks and Soso Jamabo were blue chip runners in high school (Jamabo was even a five-star and the second-rated back in the country), but the offense was dead last in allowing tackles for loss and

124th in both adjusted line yards and opportunity rate. That imbalance, especially in a supposedly pro-style (i.e., non-Air Raid) offense, really hurts. Both Starks and Jamabo return (Jamabo was more efficient, with a 34.1 percent opportunity rate to Starks' 23.5 percent, though they received equal carries—maybe that's a place to start!), but it really all starts with the offensive line. The line was fine in pass protection (30th in adjusted sack rate), and the passing game should be fine with last year's top two targets returning, but that poor of a running game is inexcusable and holds the entire team back.

The good news is that the defense was pretty solid and should be solid again in 2017. Finishing 26th overall, the Bruins benefited from now-Atlanta Falcon Takkarist McKinley and his havoc generation. That's not to mention linebacker Jaylon Brown, who also departed after leading the team in tackles while racking up tackles for loss, sacks, and interceptions. But UCLA benefits from some excellent recruiting on defense, including top overall 247 Sports recruit defensive end Jaelan Phillips, five-star cornerback Darnay Holmes, and four-star defensive tackle Greg Rogers.

No. 36 Washington State Cougars (7-5, 4-5)

2017 Projections			Projection Factors	
F/+	21.6 (36)		2016 F/+	19.8 (32)
FEI	.074 (32)		2016 FEI	.123 (22)
S&P+	6.2 (40)		2016 S&P+	6.2 (41)
Total Wins	6.9		5-Year F/+	-1.4 (65)
Conf Wins	4.4		5-Year FEI	.068 (41)
SOS	.107 (34)		5-Year S&P+	0.0 (66)
Conf SOS	.124 (21)		2-Yr/5-Yr Recruiting	51/54
Div Champ	2%		Ret. Offense	67% (54)
Conf Champ	1%		Ret. Defense	72% (41)
CFP Berth	1%		Ret. Total	69% (43)

Projected Win Likelihood by Game

Date	Opponent (Proj Rank)	PWL
Sep 2	vs Montana St. (FCS)	100%
Sep 9	vs Boise St. (29)	51%
Sep 16	vs Oregon St. (61)	79%
Sep 23	vs Nevada (105)	98%
Sep 29	vs USC (6)	24%
Oct 7	at Oregon (22)	24%
Oct 13	at California (68)	73%
Oct 21	vs Colorado (60)	78%
Oct 28	at Arizona (67)	71%
Nov 4	vs Stanford (9)	26%
Nov 11	at Utah (41)	50%
Nov 25	at Washington (11)	16%

The Cougars appear to have settled into a Mike Leach route. Despite ending the season with three straight losses, Washington State finished with eight wins and was only slowed down on offense by Minnesota in the Holiday Bowl and Washington in the Apple Cup. With Luke Falk returning for his senior year and another 600-plus pass attempts, if the Cougars can avoid a third-straight season-opening FCS loss, then another seven or eight wins are on the table again for 2017.

Washington State was exactly what you'd expect them to be. Despite ranking 64th in the 247 Sports Team Talent Composite last season, the offense passed more than anyone in the country on standard downs; was fairly efficient doing so (33rd in passing S&P+, 21st in passing success rate); was effective running the ball despite only running on barely a third of standard downs; and was average on defense (63rd). Washington State is, ironically, what the best version of Kliff Kingsbury's Texas Tech would be—high-efficiency, pass-first offense and middle-of-the-road defense (if only the Red Raiders could field even an adequate defense!).

That team mostly returns for 2017. Falk, of course, is back, along with the top three running backs and seven players return who each had at least 35 receiving targets last season. The

Leach system allows a lot of skill players to cycle through the offense, so those ten players (plus some fresh faces) should get a lot of activity again in 2017.

The Cougars defense was more effective against the run than the pass (44th to 103rd in defensive S&P+) and interestingly was far more effective getting run stops behind the line than getting sacks (seventh in stuff rate, 110th in adjusted sack rate). The big difference maker was Hercules Mata'afa, who had 13.5 tackles for loss and five sacks as a sophomore. Unfortunately, the biggest playmaker in the secondary, Shalom Luani (with his four interceptions) is gone for 2017. Washington State lived and died on defense by stopping the run fairly effectively and then forcing turnovers, going plus-6 on the season. As Luani was responsible for four of those, Leach will need to find a replacement playmaker in the secondary.

In 2017, Washington State thankfully draws an easier season opener against Montana State. Boise State, Oregon, and USC are the difficult first-half matchups, but there's also a difficult final three games, much like last season, against Stanford, Utah and the Huskies. The win/loss total might be a little worse in 2017, but it should be a similar-quality team overall.

No. 37 Arkansas Razorbacks (6-6, 3-5)

2017 Projections			Projection Factors	
F/+	20.0 (37)		2016 F/+	7.9 (56)
FEI	.045 (45)		2016 FEI	.023 (58)
S&P+	8.6 (32)		2016 S&P+	5.2 (48)
Total Wins	5.9		5-Year F/+	17.0 (35)
Conf Wins	2.6		5-Year FEI	.040 (52)
SOS	.026 (1)		5-Year S&P+	9.0 (32)
Conf SOS	.035 (2)		2-Yr/5-Yr Recruiting	26/31
Div Champ	0%		Ret. Offense	55% (90)
Conf Champ	0%		Ret. Defense	58% (89)
CFP Berth	0%		Ret. Total	57% (90)

Projected Win Likelihood by Game

Date	Opponent (Proj Rank)	PWL
Aug 31	vs Florida A&M (FCS)	100%
Sep 9	vs TCU (18)	34%
Sep 23	vs Texas A&M (20)	29%
Sep 30	vs New Mexico St. (125)	99%
Oct 7	at South Carolina (32)	37%
Oct 14	at Alabama (1)	4%
Oct 21	vs Auburn (10)	26%
Oct 28	at Ole Miss (26)	29%
Nov 4	vs Coastal Carolina (124)	99%
Nov 11	at LSU (7)	13%
Nov 18	vs Mississippi St. (34)	54%
Nov 24	vs Missouri (52)	70%

How many years can Arkansas go either 7-6 or 8-5 under Bret Bielema before fans start wanting something more? Bobby Petrino managed to get double-digit-win seasons out of the Razorbacks before his sudden departure. Last year's team finished with a 7-6 record, including late losses to Missouri and Virginia Tech, and the Razorbacks lose a lot, including leading rusher Rawleigh Williams III, five of the top six receiving targets, team sack leader Jeremiah Ledbetter, and tackle leader Brooke Ellis. But quarterback Austin Allen (who threw for 3,430 yards on 7.3 yards per attempt), four starting offensive linemen, and second-leading rusher Devwah Whaley return, forming the core of the Razorbacks' team.

Arkansas has benefited immeasurably from the Allen brothers. Austin Allen and his brother Brandon have been steady in Bielema's offense even though the coach is known for running a ground-first attack going back to his Wisconsin days. But Austin Allen's first year as a starter produced the 22nd-ranked passing S&P+ attack despite the line performing poorly (107th in adjusted line yards and 92nd in adjusted sack rate). Four of last year's starters return, so you would imagine a more experi-

enced line would help. The major issue is that it's unclear who Allen will throw to now that leading targets Drew Morgan and Keon Hatcher are gone. Jared Cornelius is the top target, and running back Devwah Whaley was solid as a pass catcher, but behind them it's all unproven receivers. Assuming the offensive line grows (dead last in power success rate and 109th in stuff rate!), Devwah Whaley could have a breakout year. He was a high four-star recruit and had nearly identical production to Rawleigh Williams as a freshman last season.

The Arkansas defense had plenty of issues last season, ranking 79th in passing S&P+ and 112th against the run. It's never good to be in the 100s in defensive rushing S&P+, but it's nearly fatal when you're in the same division as Leonard Fournette and now Derius Guice, Bo Scarbrough, and Damien Harris. Paul Rhodes comes in as the new defensive coordinator, and he's also responsible for installing a 3-4 despite running a 4-3 for most of his career. With so much changing on defense—personnel, coordinator, and scheme—it's hard to be anything but optimistic considering where they started from in 2016.

No. 38 Pittsburgh Panthers (7-5, 4-4)

2017 Projections

F/+	18.0 (38)
FEI	.039 (48)
S&P+	7.8 (33)
Total Wins	6.5
Conf Wins	4.1
SOS	.130 (43)
Conf SOS	.306 (62)
Div Champ	9%
Conf Champ	3%
CFP Berth	1%

Projection Factors

2016 F/+	26.4 (21)
2016 FEI	.120 (23)
2016 S&P+	11.2 (20)
5-Year F/+	15.5 (39)
5-Year FEI	.084 (33)
5-Year S&P+	7.8 (35)
2-Yr/5-Yr Recruiting	33/41
Ret. Offense	44% (104)
Ret. Defense	44% (115)
Ret. Total	44% (122)

Projected Win Likelihood by Game

Date	Opponent (Proj Rank)	PWL
Sep 2	vs Youngstown St. (FCS)	100%
Sep 9	at Penn St. (8)	12%
Sep 16	vs Oklahoma St. (21)	33%
Sep 23	at Georgia Tech (27)	29%
Sep 30	vs Rice (118)	99%
Oct 7	at Syracuse (65)	66%
Oct 14	vs NC State (31)	47%
Oct 21	at Duke (59)	61%
Oct 28	vs Virginia (72)	85%
Nov 9	vs North Carolina (39)	59%
Nov 18	at Virginia Tech (25)	25%
Nov 24	vs Miami-FL (23)	35%

Pitt may have finished only 8-5 with a bowl loss to Northwestern, but it did manage wins over both Penn State and Clemson, signaling a high ceiling and a low floor. At 20th in S&P+ last season, Pitt's losses to Oklahoma State, North Carolina, Virginia Tech, and Miami are all defensible because those teams were all similarly ranked in the advanced stats, but the downfall against Northwestern was surprising. Pitt also surprised with Nathan Peterman's play (2,855 passing yards, 8.8 yards per attempt), which led to Peterman getting drafted and offensive coordinator Matt Canada heading to LSU. Pitt's offense should look much different next year after losing Canada and Peterman, and also running back James Conner and tight end Scott Orndoff.

The two biggest names in the quarterback competition to replace Peterman are likely last year's backup, redshirt sophomore Ben DiNucci (who completed three of his nine pass attempts with two interceptions), and USC transfer Max Browne. Browne is the favorite to win the job and has an extremely high ceiling—he was a five-star prospect out of high school who

just couldn't put it all together in Los Angeles. Whoever wins the job will have a few quality receivers, including big-play threat Jester Weah (24.2 yards per catch), Quadree Henderson, and promising sophomore Tre Tipton. To replace Conner, the Panthers have the versatile Henderson, sophomore Chawntez Moss, and a pair of four-star freshmen in A.J. Davis and Todd Sibley. Sibley, a former Ohio State commit, provides a downhill, between-the-tackles running threat.

The Pitt defense struggled with explosive runs (80th in rushing IsoPPP despite ranking 14th in opportunity rate) and struggled with the pass overall despite frequently getting to the quarterback (53rd in passing S&P+ and 100th in passing success rate despite being 23rd in adjusted sack rate). The bad news is that the Pitt defense was senior-heavy—they are 115th in returning defensive production, with notable holes from edge rusher Ejuan Price and Shakir Soto. Jordan Whitehead is the returning leader of the secondary, but the Panthers will need to replace major contributors at all three levels of the defense.

No. 39 North Carolina Tar Heels (6-6, 3-5)

2017 Projections			Projection Factors		
F/+	17.4 (39)		2016 F/+	26.3 (22)	
FEI	.046 (44)		2016 FEI	.119 (24)	
S&P+	6.5 (38)		2016 S&P+	11.1 (21)	
Total Wins	6.5		5-Year F/+	14.5 (41)	
Conf Wins	3.4		5-Year FEI	.094 (31)	
SOS	.148 (49)		5-Year S&P+	6.9 (41)	
Conf SOS	.199 (48)		2-Yr/5-Yr Recruiting	29/24	
Div Champ	4%		Ret. Offense	19% (127)	
Conf Champ	1%		Ret. Defense	64% (69)	
CFP Berth	1%		Ret. Total	41% (125)	

Projected Win Likelihood by Game

Date	Opponent (Proj Rank)	PWL	Projected Loss / Projected Win
Sep 2	vs California (68)	81%	
Sep 9	vs Louisville (16)	26%	
Sep 16	at Old Dominion (98)	93%	
Sep 23	vs Duke (59)	74%	
Sep 30	at Georgia Tech (27)	28%	
Oct 7	vs Notre Dame (17)	29%	
Oct 14	vs Virginia (72)	85%	
Oct 21	at Virginia Tech (25)	25%	
Oct 28	vs Miami-FL (23)	34%	
Nov 9	at Pittsburgh (38)	41%	
Nov 18	vs W. Carolina (FCS)	100%	
Nov 25	at NC State (31)	31%	

North Carolina is coming off of an 8-5 season that produced the NFL draft's top quarterback, Mitchell Trubisky. Trubisky's departure means that the Tar Heels will have their third starting quarterback in three seasons. There are three contenders for that starting job: Nathan Elliott, a three-star sophomore quarterback who was efficient on nine garbage-time pass attempts behind Trubisky last season; Chazz Surratt, a four-star redshirt freshman who is more athletic than Elliott (some recruiting services had him as an athlete rather than quarterback) but needs time to develop as a passer; and LSU transfer Brandon Harris. Harris is the most interesting option here and has the highest ceiling despite not putting up big numbers in Les Miles' LSU offense. But while Harris has the highest ceiling and the most experience, he's not assured the starting job, particularly because that would mean 2018 would see yet another new starting quarterback for head coach Larry Fedora. But whomever wins the job will also have a new set of skill players around him—both running backs, Elijah Hood and T.J. Logan, are gone, as are four of Trubisky's top five receiving targets. That's how the Tar Heels earned the very last spot in the returning offensive production rankings.

Senior receiver Austin Proehl is the leading returner (49.3 percent success rate last season), but some new faces will need to emerge. The defense was actually the main problem with last year's Tar Heels, ranking 76th in defensive FEI. But most of the main playmakers from last year's defense return, including pass-rusher Malik Carney.

No. 40 BYU Cougars (9-4)

2017 Projections			Projection Factors		
F/+	17.3 (40)		2016 F/+	19.8 (31)	
FEI	.062 (36)		2016 FEI	.109 (28)	
S&P+	4.8 (46)		2016 S&P+	7.2 (37)	
Total Wins	9.3		5-Year F/+	21.7 (28)	
Conf Wins	-		5-Year FEI	.115 (21)	
SOS	.252 (67)		5-Year S&P+	9.4 (29)	
Conf SOS	-		2-Yr/5-Yr Recruiting	55/67	
Div Champ	-		Ret. Offense	34% (117)	
Conf Champ	-		Ret. Defense	70% (47)	
CFP Berth	0%		Ret. Total	52% (106)	

Projected Win Likelihood by Game

Date	Opponent (Proj Rank)	PWL	Projected Loss / Projected Win
Aug 26	vs Portland St. (FCS)	100%	
Sep 2	vs LSU (7)	16%	
Sep 9	vs Utah (41)	59%	
Sep 16	vs Wisconsin (12)	24%	
Sep 29	at Utah St. (75)	76%	
Oct 6	vs Boise St. (29)	45%	
Oct 14	at Mississippi St. (34)	34%	
Oct 21	at East Carolina (103)	93%	
Oct 28	vs San Jose St. (108)	98%	
Nov 4	at Fresno St. (111)	96%	
Nov 10	at UNLV (117)	98%	
Nov 18	vs Massachusetts (110)	98%	
Nov 25	at Hawaii (116)	97%	

BYU is coming off of a solid 9-4 debut season for head coach Kalani Sitake. Long-time quarterback Taysom Hill has finally exhausted his eligibility, leaving former four-star quarterback Tanner Mangum to take over. Mangum proved his worth in 2015 when he took over for the injured Hill and threw for 3,377 yards at 7.6 yards per attempt. But while Mangum is an excellent talent, he's a much different quarterback than Hill. While last year's offense could count on Hill's legs (with a crazy 57.8 percent opportunity rate), Hill didn't lead much of a passing game despite a senior-heavy receiving corps—the Cougars were 90th in passing S&P+ and dead last in passing IsoPPP.

Mangum is the nearly the opposite quarterback. He's an efficient passer and promising NFL prospect, but he's not a runner—in 2015 he averaged 3 yards per carry and a 27.3 percent opportunity rate. And with leading rusher Jamaal Williams gone (1,375 yards, 41 percent opportunity rate), that's a huge blow to the run game. Compounding the rebuilt offense is the departure of Hill's top three receiving targets, who combined for 48 percent of total receiving targets. On the whole, just 34 percent of offensive production returns next year, which is 118th in the country. Moroni Laulu-Pututau returns and should be one of the top targets next year—but it's unclear how the offense is going to produce explosive plays without someone young emerging. At least the Cougars can count on a mostly experienced defense, which finished 29th in S&P+ last season and returns 70 percent of its production (42nd). BYU could count on an excellent run defense, and that shouldn't change for Sitake's second year.

No. 41 Utah Utes (6-6, 4-5)

2017 Projections

F/+	16.7 (41)
FEI	.056 (40)
S&P+	5.0 (45)
Total Wins	6.0
Conf Wins	3.7
SOS	.077 (19)
Conf SOS	.093 (13)
Div Champ	1%
Conf Champ	1%
CFP Berth	0%

Projection Factors

2016 F/+	15.8 (39)
2016 FEI	.085 (41)
2016 S&P+	6.0 (43)
5-Year F/+	17.0 (34)
5-Year FEI	.096 (29)
5-Year S&P+	7.0 (39)
2-Yr/5-Yr Recruiting	35/42
Ret. Offense	59% (81)
Ret. Defense	37% (123)
Ret. Total	48% (115)

Projected Win Likelihood by Game

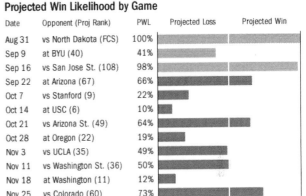

Date	Opponent (Proj Rank)	PWL	Projected Loss	Projected Win
Aug 31	vs North Dakota (FCS)	100%		
Sep 9	at BYU (40)	41%		
Sep 16	vs San Jose St. (108)	98%		
Sep 22	at Arizona (67)	66%		
Oct 7	vs Stanford (9)	22%		
Oct 14	at USC (6)	10%		
Oct 21	vs Arizona St. (49)	64%		
Oct 28	at Oregon (22)	19%		
Nov 3	vs UCLA (35)	49%		
Nov 11	vs Washington St. (36)	50%		
Nov 18	at Washington (11)	12%		
Nov 25	vs Colorado (60)	73%		

Head coach Kyle Whittingham is facing a very tough rebuild in 2017 with his Utah football program. The Utes went 9-4 in 2016 and finished three games back of Colorado for the Pac-12 South crown. Now they have to go back up against the Buffaloes and the Trojans after losing star running back Joe Williams, star safety Marcus Williams, and four starters along the offensive line.

To address those losses and Utah's perennial mid-level performance on that side of the ball, Whittingham hired rising star coach Troy Taylor to take over the offense. Taylor had been a star high school coach in Folsom, California, and then took over play calling at Eastern Washington for the 2016 season. What followed was Eastern Washington's former walk-on quarterback throwing for over 5,000 yards, including 418 against Washington State in a huge upset, and Whittingham snatching Taylor up to update the Utes' passing game.

The Utes return starting quarterback Troy Williams but they could also turn to former Alabama quarterback Cooper Bateman, who walked on this spring. Blazing fast sophomore running back Devonta'e Henry-Cole is looking to step in for Joe Williams at running back after a breakout spring. If Taylor can work with a rebuilt offensive line and install the kind of passing game they had at Eastern Washington, this could be a game-changer for the Utah program.

On defense, things proceed as normal, with several starters back across their typically fierce defensive line along with both starting linebackers. The secondary is getting hit hard by graduation and Marcus Williams leaving early for the NFL after picking off five passes last year. They do return leading tackler and strong safety Chase Hansen, a big, hard-hitting enforcer in the middle of the field. The Utes normally play pretty stout defense, and with defensive tackles Filipo Mokofisi and Lowel Lotulelei back after combining for 16.5 tackles for loss in 2016, they could be in for another strong year.

No. 42 Houston Cougars (9-3, 6-2)

2017 Projections		Projection Factors	
F/+	14.8 (42)	2016 F/+	20.4 (30)
FEI	.051 (41)	2016 FEI	.118 (26)
S&P+	4.3 (49)	2016 S&P+	7.0 (39)
Total Wins	9.2	5-Year F/+	8.0 (48)
Conf Wins	6.0	5-Year FEI	.094 (30)
SOS	.673 (117)	5-Year S&P+	2.3 (57)
Conf SOS	.741 (76)	2-Yr/5-Yr Recruiting	56/70
Div Champ	39%	Ret. Offense	51% (92)
Conf Champ	21%	Ret. Defense	58% (91)
CFP Berth	1%	Ret. Total	55% (96)

Projected Win Likelihood by Game

Date	Opponent (Proj Rank)	PWL	Projected Loss	Projected Win
Sep 2	at UTSA (83)	83%		
Sep 9	at Arizona (67)	63%		
Sep 16	vs Rice (118)	98%		
Sep 23	vs Texas Tech (64)	74%		
Sep 30	at Temple (66)	62%		
Oct 7	vs SMU (84)	92%		
Oct 14	at Tulsa (76)	75%		
Oct 19	vs Memphis (47)	60%		
Oct 28	vs East Carolina (103)	97%		
Nov 4	at South Florida (51)	46%		
Nov 18	at Tulane (89)	87%		
Nov 24	vs Navy (71)	82%		

It's Year 1 for the Cougars in the post-Tom Herman era, and his offensive coordinator Major Applewhite is now taking over for the budding program. The last two years made for a magical run for the Cougars that included three wins over top-10 opponents in Florida State, Oklahoma, and Louisville, and an AAC title in 2015. Now Herman is out the door, defensive coordinator Todd Orlando followed him to Austin to coach Texas, and quarterback Greg Ward Jr., is gone after going 27-7 in three years as the starter.

The plan at quarterback would seem to be to replace Ward with Texas A&M transfer Kyle Allen, but it's also possible they'll turn to sophomore D'Eriq King, a lightning-quick, 5-foot-10, 170-pounder who might as well be called Greg Ward III.

The offensive line returns multiple players who shuffled in and out of the starting lineup over the last two years as the Cougars dealt with injuries, and might now finally be a team strength. They'll be looking to pave the way for returning running back Duke Catalon, who ran for 528 yards last year and added another 324 receiving yards catching the ball out of the backfield. Catalon is a versatile, talented player who could thrive if the offensive line becomes a position of strength. If he continues to have injuries, they can turn to former walk-on Dillon Birden, who ran for 4.7 yards per carry and six touchdowns last year.

Continuity is the overall plan at Houston, and Applewhite hired former Miami defensive coordinator Mark D'Onofrio to maintain the same 3-4 scheme that had the Cougars playing at a top-25 level on defense last year. The Cougars have to replace some really good players in rush linebacker Tyus Bowser, rover Steven Taylor, and cornerback Howard Wilson. However, they return defensive tackle Ed Oliver, who started as a true freshman last year and had 22.5 tackles for loss, five sacks, and nine pass break-ups. It's possible that Oliver will be the best defensive player in the entire country in his sophomore campaign. The Cougars also return safety Garrett Davis and middle linebacker Matthew Adams to stabilize things in 2017.

No. 43 Indiana Hoosiers (7-5, 5-4)

2017 Projections		Projection Factors	
F/+	14.7 (43)	2016 F/+	3.1 (60)
FEI	.030 (55)	2016 FEI	-.010 (64)
S&P+	6.5 (39)	2016 S&P+	4.3 (53)
Total Wins	7.3	5-Year F/+	-1.2 (64)
Conf Wins	4.7	5-Year FEI	-.012 (71)
SOS	.138 (47)	5-Year S&P+	2.6 (54)
Conf SOS	.143 (29)	2-Yr/5-Yr Recruiting	61/53
Div Champ	1%	Ret. Offense	63% (67)
Conf Champ	0%	Ret. Defense	96% (1)
CFP Berth	0%	Ret. Total	79% (13)

Projected Win Likelihood by Game

Date	Opponent (Proj Rank)	PWL	Projected Loss	Projected Win
Aug 31	vs Ohio St. (2)	16%		
Sep 9	at Virginia (72)	70%		
Sep 16	vs Florida Int'l (107)	97%		
Sep 23	vs Ga. Southern (94)	96%		
Sep 30	at Penn St. (8)	10%		
Oct 14	vs Michigan (13)	22%		
Oct 21	at Michigan St. (46)	44%		
Oct 28	at Maryland (79)	78%		
Nov 4	vs Wisconsin (12)	21%		
Nov 11	at Illinois (95)	90%		
Nov 18	vs Rutgers (93)	96%		
Nov 25	at Purdue (97)	90%		

The Hoosiers 2016 season was decidedly mixed in results. They went 6-7 and endured some scandal over player discipline philosophy that led to the ouster of head coach Kevin Wilson and his replacement with first-year defensive coordinator Tom Allen. Indiana was having great initial success in finally building a strong defense to match Wilson's perpetually explosive offenses, and they finished ranked 31st in S&P+ even as the offense struggled and slipped to 67th.

Rebuilding the offense without Wilson around could be tricky with top two receivers Mitchell Paige and Ricky Jones leaving along with star running back Devine Redding. The Hoosiers do bring back starting quarterback Richard Lagow and 2016 freshman All-American left tackle Coy Cronk, along with two other starting linemen. Allen hired Mike DeBord from Tennessee to bring the Volunteers' potent style of run game to Indiana and be more physical overall on offense. When a defensive coordinator pushes out a successful offensive approach in order to empha-

size the run game that's often a warning sign, but DeBord has a strong resume coaching offensive lines to run the ball efficiently.

There are no doubts, however, about Allen's defense, which was very strong in 2016 and now returns all of its leading tacklers. Weakside linebacker Tegray Scales is the headliner after a season where he led the team with 109 tackles, 23.5 tackles for loss, and seven sacks. Cornerback Rashard Fant is also back despite having another brilliant season. The senior defensive back has broken up 39 passes in two years.

The rest of the secondary returns all of their starters and is supported up front by nickel linebacker Marcelino Ball, who had two interceptions and eight pass break-ups last year as a true freshman. The Hoosiers are hoping to get more pressure from their defensive line so they can rely slightly less on their brutally effective blitz package, but even if they don't these linebackers and defensive backs are very effective in Allen's aggressive and pressure-oriented schemes.

No. 44 Colorado State Rams (9-3, 7-1)

2017 Projections

F/+	14.0 (44)
FEI	.037 (51)
S&P+	5.2 (43)
Total Wins	9.1
Conf Wins	6.7
SOS	.203 (63)
Conf SOS	.815 (85)
Div Champ	39%
Conf Champ	23%
CFP Berth	1%

Projection Factors

2016 F/+	13.8 (46)
2016 FEI	.054 (51)
2016 S&P+	7.1 (38)
5-Year F/+	-6.5 (76)
5-Year FEI	.019 (59)
5-Year S&P+	-1.5 (74)
2-Yr/5-Yr Recruiting	69/79
Ret. Offense	84% (16)
Ret. Defense	74% (34)
Ret. Total	79% (14)

Projected Win Likelihood by Game

Date	Opponent (Proj Rank)	PWL
Aug 26	vs Oregon St. (61)	70%
Sep 1	vs Colorado (60)	62%
Sep 9	vs Abil Christian (FCS)	100%
Sep 16	at Alabama (1)	3%
Sep 30	at Hawaii (116)	96%
Oct 7	at Utah St. (75)	72%
Oct 14	vs Nevada (105)	97%
Oct 20	at New Mexico (112)	95%
Oct 28	vs Air Force (104)	97%
Nov 4	at Wyoming (80)	80%
Nov 11	vs Boise St. (29)	40%
Nov 18	vs San Jose St. (108)	97%

The Rams have slipped over the last two years since Jim McElwain left to take over Florida and Mike Bobo, former offensive coordinator for Mark Richt and the Georgia Bulldogs, took over. They've gone 14-12 in those two seasons, 10-6 against the rest of the Mountain West.

They'll have a tough time achieving breakthrough in 2017 while playing in the same division as the Boise State Broncos and Wyoming Cowboys, both of whom return big-time quarterbacks and talented teams. Air Force and New Mexico also lurk after finishing above the Rams in 2016.

That said, there's a lot going positively for Colorado State in 2017, with quarterback Nick Stevens back for his senior year and surrounded by playmakers who had strong 2016 seasons. Running backs Dalyn Dawkins and Izzy Matthews ran for 919 yards and 734 yards respectively, with Dawkins bringing some pop between the 20-yard lines and Matthews finishing drives (13 touchdowns). Wide receiver Michael Gallup was the focus of the passing game, catching 76 balls for 1,285 yards and 14

touchdowns. They're all back for another go in 2017.

The defense is a bit worse off, losing linebacker Kevin Davis, who led the team in tackles and tackles for loss. The other top linebackers are back, as well as three of the top four defensive backs. Rising sophomore Toby McBride was the most productive defensive lineman a year ago despite serving as a back-up. He now returns with a chance to become a featured component. The Rams are rather small overall up front after losing all of their lineman who were 280 pounds or heavier and will be counting on bulking up returning starters like Jakob Buys, who was 6-foot-4 and 264 pounds a year ago.

The plan will be to rely on movement up front in the form of stunts and twists by the defensive line and linebackers to utilize their team speed and cause problems for opponents. It's a style that has been known to work, but it's hard to beat top offensive lines like those Wyoming and Boise State will be bringing into Mountain West play without really explosive playmaking of the sort Colorado State didn't get in 2016.

No. 45 Nebraska Cornhuskers (7-5, 5-4)

2017 Projections			Projection Factors		
F/+	13.9 (45)		2016 F/+	8.1 (55)	
FEI	.033 (54)		2016 FEI	.021 (59)	
S&P+	5.6 (42)		2016 S&P+	5.5 (46)	
Total Wins	6.7		5-Year F/+	16.9 (36)	
Conf Wins	4.7		5-Year FEI	.056 (47)	
SOS	.114 (37)		5-Year S&P+	7.5 (36)	
Conf SOS	.174 (42)		2-Yr/5-Yr Recruiting	22/26	
Div Champ	3%		Ret. Offense	26% (126)	
Conf Champ	1%		Ret. Defense	65% (65)	
CFP Berth	1%		Ret. Total	46% (121)	

Projected Win Likelihood by Game

Date	Opponent (Proj Rank)	PWL	Projected Loss / Projected Win
Sep 2	vs Arkansas St. (81)	90%	
Sep 9	at Oregon (22)	17%	
Sep 16	vs Northern Illinois (85)	92%	
Sep 23	vs Rutgers (93)	95%	
Sep 29	at Illinois (95)	90%	
Oct 7	vs Wisconsin (12)	20%	
Oct 14	vs Ohio St. (2)	15%	
Oct 28	at Purdue (97)	90%	
Nov 4	vs Northwestern (33)	43%	
Nov 11	at Minnesota (57)	47%	
Nov 18	at Penn St. (8)	10%	
Nov 24	vs Iowa (58)	63%	

The Mike Riley era in Nebraska is now entering Year 3 after a solid Year 2, with a 9-4 record and second-place finish in the Big 10 West. For the last two years Riley has been forcing a bit of a square peg into a round hole using dual-threat quarterback Tommy Armstrong Jr., in his pro-style offense. They ended up adjusting the scheme to utilize Armstrong in their running game, but now he's moving on and the Cornhuskers can move closer to the pro-style offense that Riley prefers to run.

Another issue confronting Riley in implementing his new system was the offensive line, which had been stockpiled with shorter, scrappy blockers recruited and developed to execute outside zone blocking. Riley prefers bigger players up front to plow the road straight ahead on inside zone. The Cornhuskers are bigger up front now and returning all five starters from a year ago.

Changes on offense could be painful, though. The quarterback, running back, and three of the top four wide receivers will be new starters. However, the Cornhuskers do return De'Mornay Pierson-El, an explosive slot receiver, and leading receiver Stanley Morgan Jr. There's enough here to work with if the Cornhuskers can finally get Riley's downhill run game working this season.

On defense, Riley made a big move this offseason firing longtime defensive coordinator Mark Banker, whom he'd worked with for 20 years. Riley replaced Banker with Bob Diaco, who had been a successful defensive coordinator at Notre Dame before becoming head coach at Connecticut and then getting fired himself. Diaco will bring a 3-4 defense to Lincoln, and the Cornhuskers already have the size up front to execute that vision.

The defensive backfield is losing its top two linebackers and top run-support safety Nathan Gerry. However, they do return their other top two safeties from their nickel defense and some up-and-coming linebackers such as Dedrick Young and Alex Davis. All in all, Nebraska is moving closer to realizing Riley's vision for the program, but they may take a step back this season while integrating new players and a new defense.

No. 46 Michigan State Spartans (6-6, 4-5)

2017 Projections			Projection Factors		
F/+	13.7 (46)		2016 F/+	1.0 (62)	
FEI	.036 (52)		2016 FEI	-.018 (67)	
S&P+	5.1 (44)		2016 S&P+	3.4 (57)	
Total Wins	6.1		5-Year F/+	30.0 (16)	
Conf Wins	4.1		5-Year FEI	.069 (39)	
SOS	.086 (23)		5-Year S&P+	12.2 (19)	
Conf SOS	.115 (17)		2-Yr/5-Yr Recruiting	25/23	
Div Champ	0%		Ret. Offense	35% (115)	
Conf Champ	0%		Ret. Defense	52% (107)	
CFP Berth	0%		Ret. Total	44% (123)	

Projected Win Likelihood by Game

Date	Opponent (Proj Rank)	PWL	Projected Loss / Projected Win
Sep 2	vs Bowling Green (90)	95%	
Sep 9	vs W. Michigan (70)	80%	
Sep 23	vs Notre Dame (17)	25%	
Sep 30	vs Iowa (58)	63%	
Oct 7	at Michigan (13)	11%	
Oct 14	at Minnesota (57)	47%	
Oct 21	vs Indiana (43)	56%	
Oct 28	at Northwestern (33)	28%	
Nov 4	vs Penn St. (8)	19%	
Nov 11	at Ohio St. (2)	7%	
Nov 18	vs Michigan St. (79)	88%	
Nov 25	at Rutgers (93)	89%	

The Spartans had about as bad a year as you can imagine in 2016. The program was rocked after multiple players were charged with sexual assault and there were reports of team turmoil in the wake of their first losing season (3-9) since 2009, by far the worst season since Mark Dantonio took over the program in 2007.

The 2017 team will be breaking in new starters at 17 of the 22 starting positions on offense and defense. Prospective quarterback Brian Lewerke could bring a valuable new dimension to their offense with his running abilities—he averaged 9.4 yards per carry a year ago. He'll be working with an offensive line returning center Brian Allen but starting over with underclassmen and first-year starters at the other four positions.

Lead running back L.J. Scott returns after running for 994 yards a year ago at 5.4 yards per carry. Junior wide receiver Felton Davis III is the only target with any significant production to his name at this point.

The Spartans defense, which has been the backbone of the program during the Dantonio era, is also starting over. They do return defensive tackles Mike Panusiuk and Raequan Williams, who showed promise after being forced into action early last year by injuries. They also bring back their leading tackler in linebacker Chris Frey. With some stability up front and a new generation established, the Spartans run defense stands to improve and approach their old standards.

The secondary, once famous as a "no fly zone," is facing the hardest rebuild. Vayante Copeland, long regarded as the next great cornerback at Michigan State, was removed from the team, and the Spartans will likely start a true sophomore in Justin Layne and a true freshman in Josiah Scott. They'll also be starting over at safety and choosing between four different players each in their third year in the program.

With Penn State, Michigan, and Ohio State all fielding top teams this coming year, there's a good chance that Michigan State will have to claw its way back to the top of the Big 10 East over multiple seasons.

No. 47 Memphis Tigers (10-2, 6-2)

2017 Projections

F/+	13.5 (47)
FEI	.056 (38)
S&P+	3.0 (61)
Total Wins	9.8
Conf Wins	6.4
SOS	.698 (118)
Conf SOS	.794 (80)
Div Champ	54%
Conf Champ	30%
CFP Berth	2%

Projection Factors

2016 F/+	15.7 (40)
2016 FEI	.085 (39)
2016 S&P+	5.9 (44)
5-Year F/+	3.4 (54)
5-Year FEI	.058 (45)
5-Year S&P+	2.2 (58)
2-Yr/5-Yr Recruiting	65/75
Ret. Offense	87% (11)
Ret. Defense	51% (109)
Ret. Total	69% (44)

Projected Win Likelihood by Game

Date	Opponent (Proj Rank)	PWL
Aug 31	vs UL-Monroe (121)	98%
Sep 9	at Central Florida (73)	70%
Sep 16	vs UCLA (35)	44%
Sep 23	vs S. Illinois (FCS)	100%
Sep 30	at Georgia St. (115)	95%
Oct 6	at Connecticut (122)	97%
Oct 14	vs Navy (71)	81%
Oct 19	at Houston (42)	40%
Oct 27	vs Tulane (89)	94%
Nov 3	at Tulsa (76)	73%
Nov 18	vs SMU (84)	91%
Nov 25	vs East Carolina (103)	96%

The Tigers had to replace NFL quarterback Paxton Lynch and head coach Justin Fuente in 2016, but they maintained their positive course with a solid 8-5 season and now seem poised to challenge for the AAC West title and a shot in the AAC Championship Game.

New head coach Mike Norvell rolled out a new variety of spread offense that included more pass options on their run plays and more double-tight end and double-running back sets to create a physical run game. Running back Doroland Dorceus ran for 810 yards at 6.1 yards per carry and now returns for his senior year. Junior college transfer quarterback Riley Ferguson was brilliant in Year 1 in this system, throwing for 3,698 yards with 32 touchdowns and 10 interceptions.

Top receivers Anthony Miller (1,434 yards, 14 touchdowns) and Phil Mayhue (677 yards, four touchdowns) are also back, along with three starters on the offensive line to help re-form what might now be the best offense in the division.

The defense has a tougher task, with both starting cornerbacks moving on after holding the unit together in 2016. However, the Tigers are plugging in former Oklahoma Sooners cornerbacks Tito Windham and Marcus Green to take on that task, along with another transfer at safety in former Missouri Tiger Shaun Rupert. The linebacker corps could be ready for a big step up with starters Curtis Akins and Genard Avery returning. Avery and returning safety Jonathan Cook led the team in tackles in 2016. Avery also led the team in tackles for loss with 11 and sacks with five.

The Tigers need to maintain their offensive surge down the stretch in 2016 and improve on defense to win the AAC, but they have the pieces to make each happen.

No. 48 San Diego State Aztecs (10-2, 7-1)

2017 Projections		Projection Factors	
F/+	13.3 (48)	2016 F/+	15.3 (41)
FEI	.044 (47)	2016 FEI	.063 (49)
S&P+	4.0 (52)	2016 S&P+	7.5 (33)
Total Wins	9.6	5-Year F/+	5.0 (53)
Conf Wins	7.1	5-Year FEI	.059 (44)
SOS	.489 (96)	5-Year S&P+	2.5 (56)
Conf SOS	.816 (86)	2-Yr/5-Yr Recruiting	74/73
Div Champ	98%	Ret. Offense	79% (27)
Conf Champ	39%	Ret. Defense	53% (104)
CFP Berth	2%	Ret. Total	66% (55)

Projected Win Likelihood by Game

Date	Opponent (Proj Rank)	PWL	Projected Loss	Projected Win
Sep 2	vs UC Davis (FCS)	100%		
Sep 9	at Arizona St. (49)	43%		
Sep 16	vs Stanford (9)	19%		
Sep 23	at Air Force (104)	92%		
Sep 30	vs Northern Illinois (85)	92%		
Oct 7	at UNLV (117)	95%		
Oct 14	vs Boise St. (29)	39%		
Oct 21	vs Fresno St. (111)	97%		
Oct 28	at Hawaii (116)	95%		
Nov 4	at San Jose St. (108)	94%		
Nov 18	vs Nevada (105)	97%		
Nov 24	vs New Mexico (112)	98%		

The 2016 San Diego State Aztecs carved out an impressive achievement as the Mountain West champions in a year in which both Wyoming and Boise State were playing great football in the opposing East division. The Aztecs lost a narrow game to Wyoming earlier in the year before avenging themselves in the title game. Then they went into the Las Vegas Bowl and capped a brilliant season with a 34-10 beating of the Houston Cougars. All of these wins were achieved with a physical, pounding run game that put Donnel Pumphrey over 2,000 rushing yards and Rashaad Penny over 1,000. While Pumphrey moved on, Penny returns for 2017. Quarterback Christian Chapman is also back after managing games for the Aztecs run game and defense a year ago.

The Aztecs' supporting cast is getting gutted, with Pumphrey and four starters on the offensive line now moving on from San Diego. But fullback Nick Bawden returns as an es-

cort for Penny and the other running backs. If the coaches feel Chapman is up for shouldering a greater load for the offense, his top receiver Mikah Holder is back for his senior season.

The defense was a major strength for San Diego State in 2016, perhaps even moreso than the running game. They return six starters but lose a potent combination up front in defensive linemen Alex Barrett and Kyle Kelly, who combined for 20.5 tackles for loss and 13.5 sacks. Noble Hall and Sergio Phillips return to anchor the front and try to keep their defensive backfield clear.

The secondary has a mixed report. They return three starters from a year ago, including safety Kameron Kelly (who had five picks in 2016), but lose cornerback Damonte Kazee, who had seven interceptions. The Aztecs have been playing top-25 defense per S&P+ for two years now and hope their program's culture can fill in the losses with new stars.

No. 49 Arizona State Sun Devils (5-6, 3-6)

2017 Projections		Projection Factors	
F/+	12.7 (49)	2016 F/+	-15.9 (87)
FEI	.047 (43)	2016 FEI	-.078 (90)
S&P+	3.3 (58)	2016 S&P+	-4.5 (83)
Total Wins	5.4	5-Year F/+	15.7 (38)
Conf Wins	3.3	5-Year FEI	.004 (64)
SOS	.104 (32)	5-Year S&P+	7.2 (38)
Conf SOS	.119 (18)	2-Yr/5-Yr Recruiting	38/30
Div Champ	1%	Ret. Offense	72% (45)
Conf Champ	1%	Ret. Defense	70% (48)
CFP Berth	0%	Ret. Total	71% (35)

Projected Win Likelihood by Game

Date	Opponent (Proj Rank)	PWL	Projected Loss	Projected Win
Aug 31	vs New Mexico St. (125)	98%		
Sep 9	vs San Diego St. (48)	57%		
Sep 16	at Texas Tech (64)	57%		
Sep 23	vs Oregon (22)	27%		
Sep 30	at Stanford (9)	9%		
Oct 14	vs Washington (11)	19%		
Oct 21	at Utah (41)	36%		
Oct 28	vs USC (6)	16%		
Nov 4	vs Colorado (60)	68%		
Nov 11	at UCLA (35)	28%		
Nov 18	at Oregon St. (61)	53%		
Nov 25	vs Arizona (67)	74%		

The Sun Devils' 10-win seasons in 2013 and 2014 are fading into history now for head coach Todd Graham, who finds himself on the hot seat after consecutive losing seasons. Their former star offensive coach, Mike Norvell, is now the head coach at Memphis, and last year's offensive coordinator Chip

Lindsey is now the offensive coordinator at Auburn.

On defense, the Sun Devils brought in former Baylor defensive coordinator Phil Bennett, who runs a similar defense to the aggressive 4-2-5 quarters scheme favored by Graham himself. The defense has been poor for a few years now, dropping in the S&P+ defensive rankings from 26th in 2013 to 41st in 2014, then 81st in 2015, then 114th in 2016.

Bennett will try to blend a little more conservatism into their approach in order to protect a unit that was regularly mauled in 2016. He'll have a fair amount to work with, starting with "devil" linebacker Koron Crump, who had nine sacks last year, and then continuing with fellow linebacker and leading tackler D.J. Calhoun, who had 4.5 sacks. Bennett's main task will be to shore up the secondary so they can survive the occasions when pressures featuring Crump and Calhoun don't get to the quarterback quickly.

On offense, the Sun Devils return quarterback Manny Wilkins, who ran for 471 yards but only threw for 2,329 yards at 6.1 yards per attempt. They're adding Alabama transfer Blake Barnett, who has already found himself sharing the top spot on the depth chart with Wilkins after spring practice. Both main running backs Demario Richards and wildcat-operator Kalen Ballage are back, as well as three of the top four receivers (a list which includes Ballage).

Ballage is the main feature of the offense. New offensive coordinator Billy Napier, who was coaching the receivers at Alabama last year, will want to employ every trick he learned from Lane Kiffin to get the senior as many touches as possible this coming season. At 6-foot-2 and 227 pounds, Ballage brings a rare combination of quickness, skill, and sheer power. If the Sun Devils can clean up their defense and get him even more touches next season (he averaged 14 per game in 2016), they should be able to make major strides from a year ago, even if they can't quite hurdle USC or other Pac-12 South opponents.

No. 50 Vanderbilt Commodores (5-7, 2-6)

2017 Projections

F/+	12.6 (50)
FEI	.056 (39)
S&P+	2.4 (63)
Total Wins	5.0
Conf Wins	2.2
SOS	.053 (10)
Conf SOS	.065 (8)
Div Champ	0%
Conf Champ	0%
CFP Berth	0%

Projection Factors

2016 F/+	2.3 (61)
2016 FEI	.040 (55)
2016 S&P+	-0.5 (71)
5-Year F/+	-6.2 (75)
5-Year FEI	.015 (61)
5-Year S&P+	-2.1 (80)
2-Yr/5-Yr Recruiting	59/47
Ret. Offense	94% (3)
Ret. Defense	68% (59)
Ret. Total	81% (10)

Projected Win Likelihood by Game

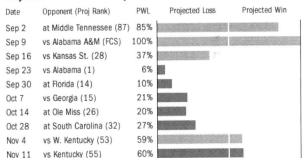

Date	Opponent (Proj Rank)	PWL
Sep 2	at Middle Tennessee (87)	85%
Sep 9	vs Alabama A&M (FCS)	100%
Sep 16	vs Kansas St. (28)	37%
Sep 23	vs Alabama (1)	6%
Sep 30	at Florida (14)	10%
Oct 7	vs Georgia (15)	21%
Oct 14	at Ole Miss (26)	20%
Oct 28	at South Carolina (32)	27%
Nov 4	vs W. Kentucky (53)	59%
Nov 11	vs Kentucky (55)	60%
Nov 18	vs Missouri (52)	59%
Nov 25	at Tennessee (24)	18%

Three years into the Derek Mason era at Vanderbilt and the Commodores are starting to look like the team many expected Mason to build. They have been strong on defense, even ranking 12th in defensive S&P+ in 2015 before slipping to a respectable 40th in 2016. However, they have struggled on offense, mostly due to an inefficient passing game that has struggled to work off a solid running game.

The offense has ranked 113th and 123rd in passing downs per S&P+ over the last two years, largely due to an inability to protect their quarterbacks. In a few starts in 2015 quarterback Kyle Shurmur had a sack rate of 8.0 percent, which only decreased to 7.9 percent in 2016 when he took over the starting role. Probably in part due to that poor protection, Shurmur has thrown only 14 touchdowns but 13 interceptions thus far in his career with the Commodores.

The 2017 offensive line will be without left tackle Will Holden, now with the Arizona Cardinals, but should be a year deeper into the development of some of Mason's recruits over the last few years. The Commodores also return their top two tight ends to help boost both the run game and their protection sets. Shurmur returns all of his top receivers from a year ago, headlined by senior C.J. Duncan, who had 494 yards in 2016. Overall, Vanderbilt needs to do a great deal more damage with their play-action passing game.

The defense brings back most of the rank-and-file, but has to replace second-round draft pick linebacker Zach Cunningham, who had 16.5 tackles for loss a year ago. Mason's sure-tackling secondary returns largely intact, including safeties LaDarius Wiley and Ryan White, who finished second and third on the team in tackles last season. Vanderbilt is hoping that linebacker Oren Burks can build on a solid 2016 and replace Cunningham, while a defensive line loaded with seniors helps set up their linebackers to run free to the ball and wreak havoc on the blitz.

Vanderbilt's schedule includes an early test against Big 12 contender Kansas State prior to a murderer's row of Alabama, Florida, Georgia, and Ole Miss. If the Commodores can survive that run, things get easier as they face the rest of the SEC East.

NCAA Win Projections

Projected Win Probabilities For ACC Teams

ACC Atlantic	Overall Wins													Conference Wins								
	12-0	11-1	10-2	9-3	8-4	7-5	6-6	5-7	4-8	3-9	2-10	1-11	0-12	8-0	7-1	6-2	5-3	4-4	3-5	2-6	1-7	0-8
Boston College	-	-	-	-	-	1	5	14	32	27	17	3	1	-	-	-	-	1	9	24	41	25
Clemson	3	19	29	25	15	7	2	-	-	-	-	-	-	8	31	35	20	5	1	-	-	-
Florida State	2	13	30	29	15	7	3	1	-	-	-	-	-	14	38	34	12	2	-	-	-	-
Louisville	5	20	31	27	13	3	1	-	-	-	-	-	-	4	25	37	25	7	2	-	-	-
NC State	-	1	4	14	23	27	20	9	2	-	-	-	-	-	3	14	28	31	18	5	1	-
Syracuse	-	-	-	-	1	7	21	34	26	9	2	-	-	-	-	-	1	6	26	38	25	4
Wake Forest	-	-	-	-	-	2	7	17	26	26	16	5	1	-	-	1	2	15	31	32	17	2
ACC Coastal	12-0	11-1	10-2	9-3	8-4	7-5	6-6	5-7	4-8	3-9	2-10	1-11	0-12	8-0	7-1	6-2	5-3	4-4	3-5	2-6	1-7	0-8
Duke	-	-	-	2	3	10	19	26	22	13	4	1	-	-	-	1	5	14	28	29	19	4
Georgia Tech	-	2	6	14	27	28	14	6	2	1	-	-	-	-	7	23	30	28	9	3	-	-
Miami-FL	2	9	22	27	23	11	4	2	-	-	-	-	-	2	17	33	27	15	6	-	-	-
North Carolina	-	-	1	6	14	23	27	18	9	2	-	-	-	-	1	4	13	28	30	18	5	1
Pittsburgh	-	-	2	6	16	25	27	15	7	2	-	-	-	-	3	11	25	28	22	9	2	-
Virginia	-	-	-	-	1	4	10	23	31	24	6	1	-	-	-	-	-	4	18	38	31	9
Virginia Tech	2	11	26	31	19	8	3	-	-	-	-	-	-	2	13	28	32	18	6	1	-	-

Projected Win Probabilities For American Teams

American East	Overall Wins													Conference Wins								
	12-0	11-1	10-2	9-3	8-4	7-5	6-6	5-7	4-8	3-9	2-10	1-11	0-12	8-0	7-1	6-2	5-3	4-4	3-5	2-6	1-7	0-8
Central Florida	-	1	4	8	20	27	23	11	5	1	-	-	-	1	3	12	24	31	22	6	1	-
Cincinnati	-	-	2	8	19	29	21	12	5	3	1	-	-	-	3	11	28	31	19	7	1	-
Connecticut	-	-	-	-	-	-	1	3	9	24	35	28	-	-	-	-	-	1	4	20	44	31
East Carolina	-	-	-	-	-	1	3	9	23	32	23	9	-	-	-	-	1	6	18	37	29	9
South Florida	11	28	33	18	7	2	1	-	-	-	-	-	-	13	33	33	15	5	1	-	-	-
Temple	-	3	8	22	28	22	12	4	1	-	-	-	-	2	11	25	31	18	10	3	-	-
American West	12-0	11-1	10-2	9-3	8-4	7-5	6-6	5-7	4-8	3-9	2-10	1-11	0-12	8-0	7-1	6-2	5-3	4-4	3-5	2-6	1-7	0-8
Houston	3	13	25	26	19	9	3	2	-	-	-	-	-	8	26	34	23	7	2	-	-	-
Memphis	6	22	33	24	10	3	2	-	-	-	-	-	-	13	37	33	15	2	-	-	-	-
Navy	-	-	1	7	17	27	23	15	8	2	-	-	-	-	2	11	25	32	20	8	2	-
SMU	-	-	-	1	6	14	26	26	18	7	2	-	-	-	-	2	10	23	31	26	8	-
Tulane	-	-	-	-	2	6	13	24	28	18	7	2	-	-	-	-	1	10	24	34	24	7
Tulsa	-	-	-	2	7	15	25	26	16	7	2	-	-	-	2	6	18	26	29	16	3	-

Projected Win Probabilities For Big 12 Teams

Big 12	Overall Wins													Conference Wins									
	12-0	11-1	10-2	9-3	8-4	7-5	6-6	5-7	4-8	3-9	2-10	1-11	0-12	9-0	8-1	7-2	6-3	5-4	4-5	3-6	2-7	1-8	0-9
Baylor	1	3	8	20	28	25	10	4	1	-	-	-	-	-	2	10	23	33	24	7	1	-	-
Iowa State	-	-	-	-	-	3	12	23	31	21	8	2	-	-	-	-	1	7	19	33	30	10	-
Kansas	-	-	-	-	-	-	-	-	2	7	25	41	25	-	-	-	-	-	-	-	4	27	69
Kansas State	-	3	10	20	30	22	9	4	2	-	-	-	-	1	4	15	26	31	17	5	1	-	-
Oklahoma	6	18	33	27	12	3	1	-	-	-	-	-	-	13	34	31	16	5	1	-	-	-	-
Oklahoma State	2	11	24	25	22	10	4	2	-	-	-	-	-	3	13	28	31	18	6	1	-	-	-
TCU	2	7	24	30	22	11	3	1	-	-	-	-	-	3	12	28	31	19	6	1	-	-	-
Texas	1	6	15	29	27	16	5	1	-	-	-	-	-	2	14	27	31	18	7	1	-	-	-
Texas Tech	-	-	-	-	2	5	14	29	27	17	5	1	-	-	-	-	1	8	18	33	30	9	1
West Virginia	-	-	-	-	-	1	5	13	24	34	18	4	1	-	-	-	1	2	11	32	36	17	1

Projected Win Probabilities For Big 10 Teams

Big Ten East	Overall Wins													Conference Wins									
	12-0	11-1	10-2	9-3	8-4	7-5	6-6	5-7	4-8	3-9	2-10	1-11	0-12	9-0	8-1	7-2	6-3	5-4	4-5	3-6	2-7	1-8	0-9
Indiana	-	1	3	14	26	29	18	7	2	-	-	-	-	-	1	3	16	36	31	11	2	-	-
Maryland	-	-	-	-	-	-	2	5	21	37	26	9	-	-	-	-	-	-	2	11	30	45	12
Michigan	2	11	28	29	22	6	2	-	-	-	-	-	-	5	19	39	27	8	2	-	-	-	-
Michigan State	-	-	1	4	10	22	29	21	10	3	-	-	-	-	-	2	10	24	35	22	6	1	-
Ohio State	13	30	32	18	5	2	-	-	-	-	-	-	-	20	38	30	10	2	-	-	-	-	-
Penn State	6	26	34	21	9	3	1	-	-	-	-	-	-	6	29	35	22	6	2	-	-	-	-
Rutgers	-	-	-	-	-	-	2	12	24	36	20	6	-	-	-	-	-	-	2	13	32	40	13
Big Ten West	12-0	11-1	10-2	9-3	8-4	7-5	6-6	5-7	4-8	3-9	2-10	1-11	0-12	9-0	8-1	7-2	6-3	5-4	4-5	3-6	2-7	1-8	0-9
Illinois	-	-	-	-	-	-	-	3	9	23	35	24	6	-	-	-	-	-	2	10	32	40	16
Iowa	-	-	2	4	12	25	30	18	8	1	-	-	-	-	-	1	6	20	33	29	10	1	-
Minnesota	-	1	4	12	22	27	23	8	3	-	-	-	-	-	1	5	18	33	27	13	3	-	-
Nebraska	-	-	3	6	19	30	25	12	4	1	-	-	-	-	1	6	18	33	28	12	2	-	-
Northwestern	1	6	19	31	25	12	4	2	-	-	-	-	-	1	10	27	30	24	7	1	-	-	-
Purdue	-	-	-	-	-	-	1	3	8	21	36	25	6	-	-	-	-	-	1	10	30	43	16
Wisconsin	15	34	30	14	5	2	-	-	-	-	-	-	-	22	40	27	9	2	-	-	-	-	-

Projected Win Probabilities For Conference USA Teams

Conf USA East	Overall Wins													Conference Wins								
	12-0	11-1	10-2	9-3	8-4	7-5	6-6	5-7	4-8	3-9	2-10	1-11	0-12	8-0	7-1	6-2	5-3	4-4	3-5	2-6	1-7	0-8
Charlotte	-	-	-	-	1	3	9	19	26	26	13	3	-	-	-	-	2	10	23	34	24	7
Florida Atlantic	-	-	1	4	11	20	26	22	10	4	2	-	-	-	2	10	25	28	23	10	2	-
Florida International	-	-	-	-	2	8	19	25	21	17	7	1	-	-	-	2	11	24	32	22	8	1
Marshall	-	-	-	1	4	10	19	24	21	14	5	2	-	-	1	5	15	26	29	17	6	1
Middle Tennessee	-	-	1	4	10	21	28	22	10	4	-	-	-	1	10	28	30	20	10	1	-	-
Old Dominion	-	-	-	3	6	17	28	25	13	6	2	-	-	-	2	9	23	30	24	10	2	-
Western Kentucky	19	41	26	9	3	2	-	-	-	-	-	-	-	54	36	9	1	-	-	-	-	-
Conf USA West	12-0	11-1	10-2	9-3	8-4	7-5	6-6	5-7	4-8	3-9	2-10	1-11	0-12	8-0	7-1	6-2	5-3	4-4	3-5	2-6	1-7	0-8
Louisiana Tech	-	1	3	14	27	26	19	7	3	-	-	-	-	2	14	30	30	17	6	1	-	-
North Texas	-	-	-	1	5	10	20	27	21	12	3	1	-	-	-	4	15	29	31	15	5	1
Rice	-	-	-	-	1	3	8	18	24	24	14	6	2	-	-	3	11	22	32	22	9	1
Southern Miss	-	-	3	11	23	28	20	10	4	1	-	-	-	1	11	28	31	20	8	1	-	-
UAB	-	-	-	-	1	3	8	19	25	28	12	4	-	-	-	-	3	11	23	33	23	7
UTEP	-	-	-	-	-	1	3	8	18	26	28	13	3	-	-	1	2	9	24	34	24	6
UTSA	-	2	9	19	27	23	12	6	2	-	-	-	-	5	18	32	31	10	3	1	-	-

Projected Win Probabilities For Independent Teams

Independents	Overall Wins												
	12-0	11-1	10-2	9-3	8-4	7-5	6-6	5-7	4-8	3-9	2-10	1-11	0-12
Army	-	-	1	3	6	18	28	25	13	5	1	-	-
BYU*	3	15	28	31	17	4	2	-	-	-	-	-	-
Massachusetts	-	-	-	-	-	1	6	20	33	26	11	3	-
Notre Dame	1	8	18	27	24	14	6	2	-	-	-	-	-

*BYU will play 13 regular season games; for projected overall records, 12-0 means 13-0, 11-1 means 12-1, etc.

Projected Win Probabilities For MAC Teams

MAC East	Overall Wins													Conference Wins								
	12-0	11-1	10-2	9-3	8-4	7-5	6-6	5-7	4-8	3-9	2-10	1-11	0-12	8-0	7-1	6-2	5-3	4-4	3-5	2-6	1-7	0-8
Akron	-	-	-	-	-	2	7	18	31	27	13	2	-	-	-	-	4	14	30	32	17	3
Bowling Green	-	-	-	1	3	9	17	26	23	14	6	1	-	-	5	14	28	29	18	5	1	-
Buffalo	-	-	-	-	1	3	7	15	26	27	16	5	-	-	-	-	2	8	20	34	26	10
Kent State	-	-	-	-	-	3	10	21	28	25	11	2	-	-	-	1	5	18	30	27	17	2
Miami-OH	-	1	5	14	20	28	16	10	4	2	-	-	-	2	13	26	28	20	9	2	-	-
Ohio	-	1	3	7	19	26	20	15	7	2	-	-	-	-	3	10	21	30	23	10	2	1
MAC West	12-0	11-1	10-2	9-3	8-4	7-5	6-6	5-7	4-8	3-9	2-10	1-11	0-12	8-0	7-1	6-2	5-3	4-4	3-5	2-6	1-7	0-8
Ball State	-	-	1	4	13	23	28	17	9	4	1	-	-	-	1	8	19	30	27	12	3	-
Central Michigan	-	-	-	-	1	3	9	18	26	24	14	4	1	-	-	3	10	25	27	24	10	1
Eastern Michigan	-	-	-	2	3	6	13	23	24	17	8	3	1	-	-	2	7	20	31	26	12	2
Northern Illinois	-	-	1	4	13	22	29	19	9	3	-	-	-	-	3	17	30	31	14	4	1	-
Toledo	4	29	36	19	7	4	1	-	-	-	-	-	-	37	37	20	6	-	-	-	-	-
Western Michigan	-	-	2	12	31	33	15	5	2	-	-	-	-	7	30	39	17	6	1	-	-	-

Projected Win Probabilities For MWC Teams

MWC Mountain	Overall Wins													Conference Wins								
	12-0	11-1	10-2	9-3	8-4	7-5	6-6	5-7	4-8	3-9	2-10	1-11	0-12	8-0	7-1	6-2	5-3	4-4	3-5	2-6	1-7	0-8
Air Force	-	-	-	-	1	3	11	21	29	22	10	3	-	-	-	-	2	11	29	32	22	4
Boise State	6	24	31	23	11	4	1	-	-	-	-	-	-	29	44	23	4	-	-	-	-	-
Colorado State	-	7	27	32	21	10	3	-	-	-	-	-	-	19	45	28	7	1	-	-	-	-
New Mexico	-	-	-	-	-	2	7	23	29	24	13	2	-	-	-	-	2	5	22	38	27	6
Utah State	-	-	2	6	19	29	24	13	5	2	-	-	-	1	10	29	33	20	6	1	-	-
Wyoming	-	-	1	5	15	28	30	15	5	1	-	-	-	-	3	15	34	30	16	2	-	-
MWC West	12-0	11-1	10-2	9-3	8-4	7-5	6-6	5-7	4-8	3-9	2-10	1-11	0-12	8-0	7-1	6-2	5-3	4-4	3-5	2-6	1-7	0-8
Fresno State	-	-	-	-	-	-	2	8	22	31	26	9	2	-	-	1	7	19	34	28	10	1
Hawaii	-	-	-	-	-	2	8	15	30	27	14	4	-	-	-	-	1	12	25	32	25	5
Nevada	-	-	-	-	-	2	10	25	28	23	10	2	-	-	-	-	7	23	34	27	8	1
San Diego State	2	15	37	33	11	2	-	-	-	-	-	-	-	26	55	17	2	-	-	-	-	-
San Jose State*	-	-	-	-	1	3	7	15	29	27	14	4	-	-	-	1	5	18	29	29	16	2
UNLV	-	-	-	1	3	5	14	22	27	18	9	1	-	-	-	2	8	20	28	26	13	3

*San Jose State will play 13 regular season games; for projected overall records, 12-0 means 13-0, 11-1 means 12-1, etc.

Projected Win Probabilities For Pac-12 Teams

Pac 12 North	Overall Wins													Conference Wins									
	12-0	11-1	10-2	9-3	8-4	7-5	6-6	5-7	4-8	3-9	2-10	1-11	0-12	9-0	8-1	7-2	6-3	5-4	4-5	3-6	2-7	1-8	0-9
California	-	-	-	-	-	2	4	12	25	31	20	6	-	-	-	-	-	1	7	23	31	29	9
Oregon	-	2	10	25	30	18	8	5	2	-	-	-	-	1	11	30	33	19	5	1	-	-	-
Oregon State	-	-	-	-	2	7	17	24	26	17	5	2	-	-	-	-	1	6	17	31	29	13	3
Stanford	3	16	26	27	17	8	2	1	-	-	-	-	-	5	22	33	26	10	3	1	-	-	-
Washington	8	29	34	17	9	2	1	-	-	-	-	-	-	11	31	31	20	6	1	-	-	-	-
Washington State	-	-	3	10	20	29	21	11	4	2	-	-	-	-	1	5	15	26	28	18	6	1	-
Pac 12 South	12-0	11-1	10-2	9-3	8-4	7-5	6-6	5-7	4-8	3-9	2-10	1-11	0-12	9-0	8-1	7-2	6-3	5-4	4-5	3-6	2-7	1-8	0-9
Arizona	-	-	-	1	4	9	18	27	23	13	4	1	-	-	-	-	2	6	15	28	30	15	4
Arizona State	-	-	-	2	8	15	23	27	15	8	2	-	-	-	-	1	5	14	23	33	18	5	1
Colorado	-	-	-	-	1	4	15	24	27	18	8	3	-	-	-	1	2	9	22	34	20	10	2
UCLA	-	-	2	5	16	27	25	15	7	3	-	-	-	-	-	4	14	27	31	17	6	1	-
USC	8	26	27	23	11	4	1	-	-	-	-	-	-	25	36	26	10	2	1	-	-	-	-
Utah	-	-	2	5	10	21	27	23	9	3	-	-	-	-	-	1	6	19	31	27	13	3	-

Projected Win Probabilities For SEC Teams

SEC East	Overall Wins													Conference Wins								
	12-0	11-1	10-2	9-3	8-4	7-5	6-6	5-7	4-8	3-9	2-10	1-11	0-12	8-0	7-1	6-2	5-3	4-4	3-5	2-6	1-7	0-8
Florida	-	2	10	17	24	25	13	5	3	1	-	-	-	6	20	30	28	11	4	1	-	-
Georgia	-	2	9	17	27	24	13	4	3	1	-	-	-	4	19	32	28	13	4	-	-	-
Kentucky	-	-	-	-	2	7	14	25	27	17	7	1	-	-	-	1	5	13	26	32	18	5
Missouri	-	-	1	4	11	22	28	22	10	2	-	-	-	-	-	1	4	14	24	31	20	6
South Carolina	-	-	2	6	16	25	23	18	8	2	-	-	-	-	1	7	19	31	25	14	3	-
Tennessee	-	-	2	6	17	28	24	15	6	2	-	-	-	-	1	9	25	35	20	9	1	-
Vanderbilt	-	-	-	-	1	4	11	20	27	24	10	3	-	-	-	-	2	10	26	34	22	6
SEC West	12-0	11-1	10-2	9-3	8-4	7-5	6-6	5-7	4-8	3-9	2-10	1-11	0-12	8-0	7-1	6-2	5-3	4-4	3-5	2-6	1-7	0-8
Alabama	20	35	26	14	4	1	-	-	-	-	-	-	-	28	42	23	6	1	-	-	-	-
Arkansas	-	-	1	3	8	21	31	22	11	3	-	-	-	-	-	1	4	15	31	30	15	4
Auburn	-	1	6	15	27	25	16	6	3	1	-	-	-	2	9	25	32	21	9	2	-	-
LSU	-	2	7	20	28	24	13	4	2	-	-	-	-	1	10	20	33	24	10	2	-	-
Mississippi State	-	-	1	3	12	24	27	20	11	2	-	-	-	-	-	1	5	16	31	30	14	3
Ole Miss	-	2	6	18	28	26	13	5	2	-	-	-	-	-	1	8	23	32	25	9	2	-
Texas A&M	-	2	9	19	26	23	14	6	1	-	-	-	-	-	2	10	24	28	25	9	2	-

Projected Win Probabilities For Sun Belt Teams

Sun Belt	Overall Wins													Conference Wins								
	12-0	11-1	10-2	9-3	8-4	7-5	6-6	5-7	4-8	3-9	2-10	1-11	0-12	8-0	7-1	6-2	5-3	4-4	3-5	2-6	1-7	0-8
Appalachian State	7	46	35	10	2	-	-	-	-	-	-	-	-	78	20	2	-	-	-	-	-	-
Arkansas State	-	-	1	5	17	29	25	14	5	3	1	-	-	7	22	33	25	9	3	1	-	-
Coastal Carolina	-	-	-	1	3	8	16	26	26	12	7	1	-	-	-	2	5	16	30	29	15	3
Georgia Southern	-	-	-	2	7	19	27	27	13	4	1	-	-	-	1	10	21	35	21	10	2	-
Georgia State	-	-	-	-	2	10	19	28	23	12	4	2	-	-	1	3	11	26	31	19	8	1
Idaho	-	-	-	-	2	6	13	23	30	19	6	1	-	-	-	1	9	20	29	28	12	1
New Mexico State	-	-	-	-	-	2	4	12	22	29	20	10	1	-	-	1	3	14	25	31	20	6
South Alabama	-	-	-	1	4	10	22	28	22	10	3	-	-	-	2	7	20	30	23	15	3	-
Texas State	-	-	-	-	-	2	5	17	27	28	16	5	-	-	-	-	2	12	28	31	22	5
Troy	-	-	3	22	35	26	10	3	1	-	-	-	-	20	41	27	10	2	-	-	-	-
UL-Lafayette	-	-	-	-	2	9	24	25	25	11	3	1	-	-	1	7	20	31	27	12	2	-
UL-Monroe	-	-	-	-	-	1	5	13	24	28	18	9	2	-	-	2	9	22	30	23	12	2

NCAA F/+ Projections

NCAA Teams, No. 1 to No. 130

Rk	Team	Rec	Conf	F/+	MW	CW	SOS	Rk	CSOS	Rk	Div	Conf	CFP
1	Alabama	11-1	7-1	48.4%	10.5	6.9	0.056	12	0.109	14	73.4%	44.1%	46.6%
2	Ohio State	10-2	8-1	47.4%	10.2	7.7	0.155	53	0.243	58	51.3%	33.3%	29.1%
3	Florida State	9-3	7-1	46.8%	9.4	6.5	0.042	7	0.215	54	43.2%	29.3%	19.5%
4	Clemson	10-2	6-2	45.6%	9.5	6.2	0.089	24	0.164	37	31.0%	21.1%	16.3%
5	Oklahoma	10-2	7-2	45.4%	9.7	7.3	0.091	26	0.200	49	-	45.7%	31.9%
6	USC	10-2	8-1	44.8%	10.0	7.7	0.167	57	0.342	63	93.5%	46.7%	35.7%
7	LSU	9-3	5-3	44.6%	8.8	5.0	0.028	3	0.033	1	9.4%	5.6%	4.1%
8	Penn State	10-2	7-2	43.0%	10.0	7.1	0.161	55	0.179	44	27.9%	18.1%	15.2%
9	Stanford	9-3	7-2	42.9%	9.3	6.8	0.100	30	0.151	33	34.1%	17.0%	12.5%
10	Auburn	8-4	5-3	42.3%	8.4	5.0	0.028	2	0.057	7	12.1%	7.3%	4.6%
11	Washington	10-2	7-2	41.7%	10.1	7.2	0.234	65	0.238	57	46.7%	23.4%	19.7%
12	Wisconsin	10-2	8-1	41.6%	10.4	7.7	0.327	70	0.398	64	79.0%	27.7%	25.2%
13	Michigan	9-3	7-2	40.4%	9.2	6.8	0.090	25	0.141	28	19.9%	12.9%	9.0%
14	Florida	9-3	6-2	40.4%	8.6	5.6	0.069	15	0.169	39	44.0%	17.6%	10.9%
15	Georgia	9-3	6-2	39.6%	8.6	5.6	0.073	16	0.161	36	42.7%	17.1%	10.6%
16	Louisville	10-2	6-2	39.4%	9.7	5.9	0.155	52	0.178	43	22.6%	15.4%	11.7%
17	Notre Dame	9-3	-	36.5%	8.7	0.0	0.105	33	-	-	-	-	1.6%
18	TCU	9-3	6-3	35.8%	8.9	6.2	0.119	39	0.147	31	-	14.1%	9.0%
19	Texas	8-4	6-3	35.0%	8.5	6.2	0.085	22	0.171	40	-	16.5%	9.5%
20	Texas A&M	8-4	4-4	34.4%	7.6	4.0	0.034	4	0.043	4	2.8%	1.7%	1.0%
21	Oklahoma State	9-3	6-3	34.2%	8.9	6.3	0.173	58	0.211	51	-	14.8%	9.5%
22	Oregon	9-3	6-3	33.8%	9.0	6.2	0.154	51	0.165	38	17.0%	8.5%	5.8%
23	Miami-FL	9-3	5-3	32.8%	8.8	5.5	0.156	54	0.215	53	37.9%	12.1%	7.6%
24	Tennessee	8-4	4-4	30.5%	7.6	4.1	0.040	6	0.051	6	6.6%	2.6%	1.5%
25	Virginia Tech	9-3	5-3	29.6%	9.1	5.3	0.254	68	0.266	60	30.0%	9.6%	6.5%
26	Ole Miss	8-4	4-4	28.8%	7.6	3.9	0.045	9	0.048	5	2.1%	1.2%	0.7%
27	Georgia Tech	8-4	5-3	26.8%	7.5	4.9	0.118	38	0.212	52	18.8%	6.0%	3.2%
28	Kansas State	8-4	5-4	26.2%	8.0	5.4	0.149	50	0.171	41	-	5.6%	3.2%
29	Boise State	10-2	7-1	25.2%	9.8	7.0	0.471	93	0.713	72	53.0%	31.8%	1.6%
30	Baylor	8-4	5-4	24.8%	7.8	5.1	0.137	46	0.150	32	-	3.3%	1.9%
31	NC State	7-5	4-4	24.3%	7.1	4.4	0.083	20	0.158	35	3.1%	2.1%	1.1%
32	South Carolina	6-6	4-4	23.2%	6.5	3.8	0.077	18	0.145	30	5.1%	2.0%	1.0%
33	Northwestern	9-3	6-3	22.9%	8.7	6.0	0.251	66	0.278	61	15.1%	5.3%	3.3%
34	Mississippi State	6-6	3-5	22.2%	6.2	2.6	0.036	5	0.039	3	0.2%	0.1%	0.1%
35	UCLA	6-6	4-5	22.2%	6.4	4.5	0.061	14	0.089	12	3.1%	1.6%	0.8%
36	Washington State	7-5	4-5	21.1%	6.9	4.4	0.107	34	0.124	21	2.2%	1.1%	0.6%
37	Arkansas	6-6	3-5	20.0%	5.9	2.6	0.026	1	0.035	2	0.1%	0.0%	0.0%
38	Pittsburgh	7-5	4-4	18.0%	6.5	4.1	0.130	43	0.306	62	8.8%	2.8%	1.4%
39	North Carolina	6-6	3-5	17.4%	6.5	3.4	0.148	49	0.199	48	3.7%	1.2%	0.6%
40	BYU	9-4	-	17.3%	9.3	0.0	0.252	67	-	-	-	-	0.0%
41	Utah	6-6	4-5	16.7%	6.0	3.7	0.077	19	0.093	13	1.4%	0.7%	0.4%
42	Houston	9-3	6-2	14.8%	9.2	6.0	0.673	117	0.741	76	38.6%	21.2%	1.0%
43	Indiana	7-5	5-4	14.7%	7.3	4.7	0.138	47	0.143	29	0.6%	0.4%	0.2%
44	Colorado State	9-3	7-1	14.0%	9.1	6.7	0.203	63	0.815	85	38.5%	23.1%	1.1%
45	Nebraska	7-5	5-4	13.9%	6.7	4.7	0.114	37	0.174	42	3.1%	1.1%	0.5%
46	Michigan State	6-6	4-5	13.7%	6.1	4.1	0.086	23	0.115	17	0.4%	0.2%	0.1%
47	Memphis	10-2	6-2	13.5%	9.8	6.4	0.698	118	0.794	80	54.0%	29.7%	1.5%
48	San Diego State	10-2	7-1	13.3%	9.6	7.1	0.489	96	0.816	86	98.4%	39.4%	1.9%
49	Arizona State	5-7	3-6	12.7%	5.4	3.3	0.104	32	0.119	18	1.1%	0.6%	0.3%
50	Vanderbilt	5-7	2-6	12.6%	5.0	2.2	0.053	10	0.065	8	0.3%	0.1%	0.1%

Rk	Team	Rec	Conf	F/+	MW	CW	SOS	Rk	CSOS	Rk	Div	Conf	CFP
51	South Florida	10-2	6-2	12.4%	10.2	6.4	0.831	129	0.857	99	64.1%	28.9%	1.5%
52	Missouri	6-6	2-6	12.2%	6.2	2.3	0.136	44	0.140	27	0.8%	0.3%	0.2%
53	Western Kentucky	11-1	7-1	12.1%	10.7	7.4	0.794	124	0.923	125	91.8%	68.9%	3.8%
54	Appalachian State	10-2	8-0	11.8%	10.5	7.7	0.523	99	0.923	121	-	76.4%	3.8%
55	Kentucky	5-7	2-6	11.6%	5.4	2.4	0.113	36	0.157	34	0.5%	0.2%	0.1%
56	Toledo	10-2	7-1	11.1%	10.0	7.1	0.612	108	0.916	114	69.8%	38.4%	1.9%
57	Minnesota	7-5	5-4	11.0%	7.1	4.7	0.224	64	0.248	59	2.3%	0.8%	0.4%
58	Iowa	6-6	4-5	10.9%	6.2	3.8	0.122	42	0.134	25	0.5%	0.2%	0.1%
59	Duke	5-7	2-6	6.3%	4.9	2.4	0.174	59	0.224	55	0.6%	0.2%	0.1%
60	Colorado	5-7	3-6	6.3%	5.4	3.0	0.177	60	0.198	47	0.6%	0.3%	0.2%
61	Oregon State	5-7	3-6	6.2%	4.5	2.7	0.093	29	0.112	16	0.0%	0.0%	0.0%
62	Wake Forest	5-7	2-6	5.4%	4.6	2.4	0.077	17	0.138	26	0.2%	0.1%	0.1%
63	Iowa State	5-7	3-6	5.1%	5.2	2.8	0.120	40	0.127	22	-	0.0%	0.0%
64	Texas Tech	5-7	3-6	3.6%	4.5	2.9	0.109	35	0.134	24	-	0.0%	0.0%
65	Syracuse	5-7	2-6	2.7%	4.9	2.0	0.043	8	0.086	11	0.0%	0.0%	0.0%
66	Temple	8-4	5-3	2.6%	7.8	5.0	0.477	94	0.768	77	20.9%	9.4%	0.4%
67	Arizona	5-7	3-6	1.4%	4.8	2.6	0.180	61	0.193	45	0.3%	0.1%	0.1%
68	California	3-9	2-7	-0.3%	3.3	2.0	0.060	13	0.084	10	0.0%	0.0%	0.0%
69	West Virginia	4-8	2-7	-0.9%	4.4	2.4	0.085	21	0.110	15	-	0.0%	0.0%
70	Western Michigan	8-4	6-2	-2.5%	8.3	6.1	0.364	77	0.829	97	24.7%	13.6%	0.6%
71	Navy	7-5	4-4	-3.7%	6.5	4.1	0.413	85	0.672	69	4.1%	2.3%	0.1%
72	Virginia	4-8	2-6	-3.9%	4.1	1.8	0.141	48	0.197	46	0.2%	0.0%	0.0%
73	Central Florida	7-5	4-4	-4.9%	6.8	4.2	0.672	116	0.794	81	8.0%	3.6%	0.2%
74	Troy	9-3	7-1	-6.1%	8.7	6.7	0.361	76	0.923	118	-	16.4%	0.8%
75	Utah State	7-5	5-3	-6.4%	6.7	5.2	0.373	78	0.776	79	6.6%	3.9%	0.1%
76	Tulsa	6-6	4-4	-8.1%	5.6	3.6	0.420	86	0.724	74	2.4%	1.3%	0.1%
77	Cincinnati	7-5	4-4	-9.9%	6.7	4.2	0.450	92	0.795	82	6.8%	3.1%	0.1%
78	Boston College	3-9	1-7	-10.1%	3.5	1.2	0.092	27	0.124	20	0.0%	0.0%	0.0%
79	Maryland	3-9	1-8	-11.1%	2.9	1.4	0.054	11	0.083	9	0.0%	0.0%	0.0%
80	Wyoming	7-5	4-4	-14.0%	6.5	4.4	0.479	95	0.680	70	2.0%	1.2%	0.1%
81	Arkansas State	7-5	6-2	-14.7%	7.5	5.9	0.641	111	0.921	116	-	6.3%	0.3%
82	Louisiana Tech	7-5	5-3	-15.7%	7.2	5.3	0.575	102	0.822	88	29.7%	7.4%	0.3%
83	UTSA	8-4	6-2	-16.9%	7.6	5.6	0.661	114	0.923	124	39.8%	9.9%	0.5%
84	SMU	5-7	3-5	-17.1%	5.4	3.0	0.439	89	0.696	71	0.8%	0.5%	0.0%
85	Northern Illinois	6-6	5-3	-17.4%	6.2	4.6	0.618	110	0.823	94	3.5%	1.9%	0.1%
86	Miami-OH	7-5	5-3	-20.4%	7.2	5.2	0.573	101	0.923	122	49.4%	22.2%	1.0%
87	Middle Tennessee	6-6	5-3	-20.5%	6.1	5.1	0.648	112	0.822	90	5.3%	4.0%	0.2%
88	Southern Miss	7-5	5-3	-21.8%	7.0	5.2	0.616	109	0.923	123	24.6%	6.2%	0.3%
89	Tulane	4-8	2-6	-21.9%	4.4	2.1	0.357	74	0.728	75	0.1%	0.0%	0.0%
90	Bowling Green	6-6	4-4	-23.3%	5.7	4.3	0.605	105	0.888	111	25.7%	11.6%	0.5%
91	Ball State	6-6	4-4	-23.4%	6.2	3.8	0.755	123	0.873	100	1.1%	0.6%	0.0%
92	Florida Atlantic	6-6	4-4	-25.2%	5.9	4.0	0.448	91	0.822	87	0.8%	0.6%	0.0%
93	Rutgers	3-9	2-7	-25.3%	3.2	1.5	0.093	28	0.133	23	0.0%	0.0%	0.0%
94	Georgia Southern	6-6	4-4	-25.4%	5.6	4.0	0.387	80	0.823	93	-	0.4%	0.0%
95	Illinois	2-10	1-8	-25.7%	2.1	1.4	0.167	56	0.202	50	0.0%	0.0%	0.0%
96	Army	6-6	-	-26.2%	5.8	0.0	0.402	83	-	-	-	-	0.0%
97	Purdue	2-10	1-8	-26.3%	2.0	1.4	0.136	45	0.235	56	0.0%	0.0%	0.0%
98	Old Dominion	6-6	4-4	-26.9%	5.6	4.0	0.583	104	0.884	107	1.2%	0.9%	0.0%
99	Ohio	7-5	4-4	-27.1%	6.6	3.9	0.861	130	0.888	112	17.7%	8.0%	0.4%
100	Marshall	5-7	3-5	-27.6%	4.8	3.4	0.666	115	0.884	108	0.8%	0.6%	0.0%
101	Central Michigan	5-7	3-5	-27.8%	4.8	3.0	0.807	128	0.873	101	0.6%	0.3%	0.0%
102	Eastern Michigan	4-8	3-5	-28.0%	4.4	2.8	0.707	119	0.823	95	0.3%	0.1%	0.0%
103	East Carolina	3-9	2-6	-28.1%	3.1	1.9	0.497	97	0.664	68	0.2%	0.1%	0.0%
104	Air Force	4-8	2-6	-30.8%	3.9	2.2	0.335	71	0.598	66	0.0%	0.0%	0.0%
105	Nevada	4-8	3-5	-31.9%	4.1	2.9	0.337	72	0.554	65	0.2%	0.1%	0.0%
106	South Alabama	5-7	4-4	-32.0%	5.0	3.8	0.529	100	0.921	117	-	0.1%	0.0%

Rk	Team	Rec	Conf	F/+	MW	CW	SOS	Rk	CSOS	Rk	Div	Conf	CFP
107	Florida International	5-7	3-5	-32.1%	4.6	3.1	0.743	121	0.884	109	0.1%	0.1%	0.0%
108	San Jose State	4-9	3-5	-32.6%	3.7	2.5	0.340	73	0.770	78	0.1%	0.1%	0.0%
109	UL-Lafayette	5-7	4-4	-32.7%	4.9	3.7	0.394	82	0.824	96	-	0.1%	0.0%
110	Massachusetts	4-8	-	-33.0%	3.8	0.0	0.357	75	-	-	-	-	0.0%
111	Fresno State	4-8	3-5	-33.2%	3.9	2.8	0.101	31	0.720	73	0.4%	0.1%	0.0%
112	New Mexico	4-8	2-6	-33.7%	3.8	2.0	0.389	81	0.600	67	0.0%	0.0%	0.0%
113	North Texas	5-7	3-5	-33.8%	5.1	3.5	0.806	127	0.923	126	2.8%	0.7%	0.0%
114	Kansas	2-10	0-9	-34.3%	2.2	0.4	0.121	41	0.124	19	-	0.0%	0.0%
115	Georgia State	5-7	3-5	-35.1%	4.9	3.3	0.445	90	0.884	104	-	0.2%	0.0%
116	Hawaii	4-8	2-6	-35.3%	3.6	2.2	0.611	107	0.835	98	0.1%	0.0%	0.0%
117	UNLV	4-8	3-5	-35.7%	4.3	2.8	0.376	79	0.879	102	0.8%	0.3%	0.0%
118	Rice	4-8	3-5	-37.3%	3.6	3.1	0.405	84	0.923	119	2.3%	0.6%	0.0%
119	Akron	4-8	2-6	-37.7%	3.7	2.5	0.422	87	0.815	84	2.2%	1.0%	0.0%
120	Kent State	4-8	3-5	-37.8%	3.9	2.6	0.265	69	0.907	113	3.9%	1.7%	0.1%
121	UL-Monroe	3-9	3-5	-38.9%	3.3	3.0	0.201	62	0.885	110	-	0.0%	0.0%
122	Connecticut	2-10	1-7	-39.3%	2.2	1.0	0.735	120	0.799	83	0.0%	0.0%	0.0%
123	Idaho	4-8	3-5	-39.6%	4.4	2.8	0.750	122	0.884	103	-	0.2%	0.0%
124	Coastal Carolina	5-7	3-5	-40.1%	4.6	2.6	0.660	113	0.823	92	-	0.0%	0.0%
125	New Mexico State	3-9	2-6	-40.9%	3.3	2.3	0.579	103	0.823	91	-	0.0%	0.0%
126	Buffalo	4-8	2-6	-42.1%	3.6	2.0	0.799	126	0.916	115	1.2%	0.5%	0.0%
127	UTEP	3-9	2-6	-42.1%	2.8	2.1	0.423	88	0.884	106	0.5%	0.1%	0.0%
128	Charlotte	4-8	2-6	-43.0%	3.9	2.2	0.611	106	0.822	89	0.0%	0.0%	0.0%
129	Texas State	4-8	2-6	-43.7%	3.6	2.2	0.799	125	0.884	105	-	0.0%	0.0%
130	UAB	4-8	2-6	-46.8%	3.7	2.1	0.523	98	0.923	120	0.3%	0.1%	0.0%

BackCAST 2017

Last year, Football Outsiders introduced BackCAST, a metric that projects the likelihood of success for running back prospects available in the NFL draft. BackCAST follows Speed Score, which evaluates running backs based on 40-yard dash time and weight. Like Speed Score, BackCAST uses 40-yard dash time and weight in its projections, but it also includes college statistics from each prospect that correlate to NFL success. BackCAST also projects whether each running back is likely to be heavily involved in the receiving game, or is more of a "ground-and-pound" back.

As we stated last year, BackCAST was (and is) a work in progress, and there was a good chance that we would be able to improve the model in the future. We have used the last 12 months to reconfigure BackCAST in a way that we believe will make it more effective going forward.

Let's start with what stays the same. BackCAST still uses 40-yard dash time and weight, the two holdovers from Speed Score. BackCAST also uses each prospect's receiving yards per game. However, BackCAST is removing the metrics Yards Over Expected Per Game (YOE/G) and Peak Attempts in exchange for two new metrics: Adjusted Yards Per Attempt and Attempts Over Expected Per Season (AOEPS).

YOE/G created a baseline for the strength of each prospect's college team's running game and compared the performance of the prospect against that baseline. More specifically, YOE/G compared the player's yards per attempt during his entire college career to the yards per attempt of all other teammates to record rushing attempts during the player's career, as well as the year before the player started at the college. The idea behind this metric was to control for situations where the running back's system or supporting cast inflated (or deflated) his numbers.

Indeed, when we first started building BackCAST, one of our goals was to create a metric that would address the "Wisconsin running back problem," where running backs from certain schools with consistently strong offensive lines tended to be overdrafted. When that metric seemed to correlate with success, it was easy to rationalize including it in the model. It even had some good anecdotes to support it; for example, the baseline led to a low projection for super-bust Trent Richardson.

Having had more time to work on the model, we subjected the "baseline" theory to more scrutiny, and it did not hold up. When isolated, the baseline was just noise that was mixed with other factors that correlate with success. Specifically, what YOE/G was really doing was measuring efficiency and volume, sort of like an extremely primitive DYAR for college running backs. Put more simply, it's one thing to average 6.5 yards per carry after 30 carries, but it's quite another to average 6.5 yards over 550 carries. Similarly, most players with high YOE/G had a high yards per attempt average and a lot of carries.

The new BackCAST removes the "baseline" noise in the prior version and measures yards per carry directly with an adjustment for running backs with low attempt numbers. If the running back prospect has at least an "average" number of total carries for a drafted running back (518), BackCAST assumes that his yards per attempt is reliable and uses it for the metric. However, if the running back has less than 518 carries (for example, 450), BackCAST recalculates the yards per attempt by adding the difference between the average number of carries for a drafted running back and the prospect's running back's carries (in the example, 518 - 450 = 68) and assumes those extra carries each gained 5.36 yards (the average yards per carry of a drafted running back). These adjustments prevent a running back with good efficiency numbers but few carries from skewing the results.

After we removed YOE/G and added adjusted yards per attempt, we were able to take a much closer look at the best way to measure the relationship between total rushing attempts and NFL success. The metric that ended up working best to predict NFL success together with adjusted yards per attempt is one we're calling Attempts Over Expected Per Season (AOEPS). AOEPS gives the running back credit for soaking up a high volume of his team's attempts early in his career. Typically, the most special prospects become significant factors in the running game early in their college careers and increasingly dominate as they gain more experience. An average drafted running back has 19.4 percent of his team's carries as a freshman, 29.2 percent as a sophomore, 36.5 percent as a junior, and 42.4 percent as a senior. Thus, a running back who soaked up 29.4 percent, 39.2 percent, 46.5 percent, and 52.4 percent of his team's rushing attempts during a four-year career would have an AOEPS of 10 percent, because he averaged 10 percent more of his team's rushing attempts than would be expected for a drafted running back.

Although these changes to the model may seem dramatic, they don't significantly change the projections for 90 percent of individual prospects. BackCAST still likes big, fast, efficient running backs who dominated in their backfields in college. However, the differences do cause big shifts for some running back prospects whom BackCAST significantly downgraded or upgraded due to a team baseline or unusual usage patterns in college. One of those running backs happens to be last year's standout rookie Ezekiel Elliott. Originally, BackCAST graded Elliott as a good prospect but probably overrated as a top-ten pick. The baseline hurt Elliott's projection significantly, and he also had an unusual usage pattern in college—he was used extensively as a freshman, but did not earn an unusually large share of Ohio State's carries over the latter years of his college career. The new BackCAST (correctly, it seems) grades Elliott as an elite prospect.

The list of the top 20 projected running backs according to BackCAST is a good list, but not a perfect one (Table 1). Ricky Williams is the No. 1 prospect with LaDainian Tomlinson at No. 4, but the players between them (T.J. Duckett and Ron Dayne) will not be going to the Hall of Fame. However, where BackCAST really shines is in its list of the first- and second-round picks with the lowest BackCAST projections

(Table 2). That list identifies such second-round busts as Kenny Irons, Brandon Jackson, and Monterio Hardesty.

One other change that we have not made this year, but expect to make in the near future, is to switch the independent variables being projected from each running back's total rushing and receiving yards for his first five years in the NFL to each running back's total rushing and receiving DYAR for his first five years in the NFL. However, we do not expect the switch to result in dramatic changes to the model.

In sum, BackCAST (as revised) includes the following factors:

• The prospect's weight at the NFL combine;
• The prospect's forty-yard dash at the NFL combine. If he did not run at the combine, BackCAST uses his pro day time;
• The prospect's yards per attempt, with an adjustment for running backs who had fewer career carries than an average drafted running back;
• The prospect's "AOEPS," which measures how much, on average, the prospect's team used him in the running game during his career relative to the usage of an average drafted running back during the same year of eligibility; and
• The prospect's receiving yards per game in his college career.

BackCAST is expressed in terms of the percentage that the running back is projected to over-perform or under-perform the average running back prospect. For example, a player who has a +50.0% BackCAST score is expected to be 1.5 times as productive as the average drafted running back. Conversely, a player with a BackCAST score of -50.0% is expected to be only half as productive as the average drafted running back.

BackCAST also includes "RecIndex," which measures whether the player is likely to be a ground-and-pound two-down back, a player who catches passes out of the backfield more often than he takes handoffs, or something in between. In short, RecIndex measures the likelihood that the player records a disproportionately high or low number of receiving yards versus his rushing yards. The two factors that are significant in predicting RecIndex are receiving yards per game in college and weight, as smaller players are more likely to be receiving backs.

Our new and improved BackCAST suggests that we had an amazing class of running backs in the 2017 NFL draft. This class was so good that I had to double-check things after the first time I ran the numbers, as I was sure that some sort of error in my spreadsheets caused BackCAST to rate this class too highly. Indeed, if you compare the prospects below to the top-20 historical BackCAST projections above, you will notice that not one, not two, but *three* of this season's rookies would make the list of the top-ten prospects in BackCAST's database.

Leonard Fournette, LSU
Drafted by Jacksonville (Round 1, Pick 4)
BackCAST Score: +142.2%
RecIndex: -0.01

Leonard Fournette has an amazing size/speed combination. The average drafted running back is 216 pounds and runs a 4.55 40-yard dash. Fournette, by contrast, is faster than the average running back at 4.51 seconds and nearly a full standard deviation heavier at 240 pounds. Fournette dropped to 228 pounds at his pro day, but unfortunately for football analytics

Table 1. Top BackCAST projections, 1998-2016

Name	Year	Rnd	Pick	School	BackCAST
Ricky Williams	1999	1	5	Texas	+185.7%
T.J. Duckett	2002	1	18	Michigan St.	+160.6%
Ron Dayne	2000	1	11	Wisconsin	+150.8%
LaDainian Tomlinson	2001	1	5	TCU	+134.2%
Darren McFadden	2008	1	4	Arkansas	+130.3%
Ronnie Hillman	2012	3	67	San Diego St.	+126.3%
DeAngelo Williams	2006	1	27	Memphis	+115.7%
Todd Gurley	2015	1	10	Georgia	+115.2%
Ezekiel Elliott	2016	1	4	Ohio St.	+114.7%
Rudi Johnson	2001	4	100	Auburn	+113.1%
Luke Staley	2002	7	214	BYU	+112.8%
Willis McGahee	2003	1	23	Miami	+111.5%
Edgerrin James	1999	1	4	Miami	+111.2%
Steven Jackson	2004	1	24	Oregon St.	+109.8%
Curtis Enis	1998	1	5	Penn St.	+109.5%
Reggie Bush	2006	1	2	USC	+108.6%
LenDale White	2006	2	45	USC	+105.7%
Kevin Jones	2004	1	30	Virginia Tech	+105.6%
Derrick Henry	2016	2	45	Alabama	+99.6%
Knowshon Moreno	2009	1	12	Georgia	+97.9%
Michael Turner	2004	5	154	N. Illinois	+97.6%

Table 2. Lowest BackCAST projections for Players Chosen in Rounds 1-2, 1998-2016

Name	Year	Rnd	Pick	School	BackCAST
Joe Montgomery	1999	2	49	Ohio St.	-77.8%
Brandon Jackson	2007	2	63	Nebraska	-59.0%
Kenny Irons	2007	2	49	Auburn	-56.2%
John Avery	1998	1	29	Mississippi	-38.4%
Chris Henry	2007	2	50	Arizona	-37.0%
Travis Henry	2001	2	58	Tennessee	-34.5%
Julius Jones	2004	2	43	Notre Dame	-30.5%
Christine Michael	2013	2	62	Texas A&M	-24.2%
Montario Hardesty	2010	2	59	Tennessee	-23.6%
Ameer Abdullah	2015	2	54	Nebraska	-22.2%
Mike Cloud	1999	2	54	Boston College	-12.8%
Carlos Hyde	2014	2	57	Ohio St.	-11.3%
Montee Ball	2013	2	58	Wisconsin	-9.3%
DeShaun Foster	2002	2	34	UCLA	-6.7%
Joseph Addai	2006	1	30	LSU	-5.5%
Chris Perry	2004	1	26	Michigan	-5.2%
David Wilson	2012	1	32	Virginia Tech	-4.7%
Robert Edwards	1998	1	18	Georgia	+2.1%
Isaiah Pead	2012	2	50	Cincinnati	+4.5%
J.J. Johnson	1999	2	39	Mississippi St.	+7.7%

enthusiasts, he did not run the 40-yard dash again.

Fournette was also no slouch when it came to production. Fournette had an AOEPS of +11.76%, even after missing a good third of his junior season to injury (and also, perhaps, due to a desire to preserve his health for the NFL draft). Fournette also averaged more than 6.2 yards per attempt during his career. Fournette does not absolutely blow you away in the receiving game, but his RecIndex is greater than the typical running back. (The median running back has a negative RecIndex, which is balanced by a smaller group of third-down specialist backs.)

Despite Fournette's obvious talent and optimistic projection, the Jaguars' decision to use the fourth overall pick on a running back is nonetheless curious. NFL running backs, even the good ones, typically have only short windows of success—often followed by a period of being a "veteran presence" and not much else. With Blake Bortles' development flat-lining, it is hard to imagine a scenario in which Fournette meaningfully contributes to a Super Bowl run.

Dalvin Cook, Florida State
Drafted by Minnesota (Round 2, Pick 41)
BackCAST Score: +136.0%
RecIndex: +0.61

For the analytically-minded, it is hard to argue against the Vikings passing on re-signing the aging Adrian Peterson in exchange for spending a second-round pick on one of BackCAST's best projected running backs of all-time.

Dalvin's Cook's projection is so high because he sports an unusual combination of usage and efficiency. When a college running back is the focal point of his team's offense, his opponents will scheme against him. Although the running back can still be efficient, it would take a unique talent to post peak efficiency numbers while carrying an unusually large load.

There have been plenty of running backs who have been used as heavily as Cook or have been as efficient as Cook, but only one running back ever who has been used as heavily and been as efficient as Cook. Ricky Williams is the only other running back prospect to ever score an AOEPS above 20 percent and to average more than 6.0 yards per attempt.

You could make a case for drafting Cook over top-ranked prospect Fournette. Although Fournette has an awesome projection, his particular profile somewhat matches other running backs who boasted great projections but ultimately disappointed. BackCAST was also high on Ron Dayne and T.J. Duckett, for example, who scored highly in large part due to unusual size/speed combinations. It is a bit harder to find a bust whose high projection, like Cook's, had more to do with college production. Also, Cook has an excellent RecIndex, which means that even if he does not succeed as a traditional running back, he likely has some value as a Reggie Bush-type back who can catch passes out of the backfield.

As much as the numbers like Cook, however, BackCAST does not, and cannot, take into account a player's likelihood of running into the personal conduct policy. Cook has had a number of run-ins with the law, and a high-profile case could derail what could otherwise be an extremely promising career.

Joe Mixon, Oklahoma
Drafted by Cincinnati (Round 2, Pick 48)
BackCAST Score: +115.7%
RecIndex: +0.90

The Cincinnati Bengals have a history of gambling on talented prospects with checkered pasts, and pasts do not come much more checkered than Joe Mixon's.

As humans, we condemn the off-the-field actions of Joe Mixon in the strongest terms. BackCAST, however, is a mathematical construct that does not make any moral judgments and has no way to factor in the effect of a prospect's off-the-field actions. If nothing else, BackCAST's positive outlook on Mixon's talent is a testament to the potential that Mixon has squandered.

Mixon was not quite as heavily used as Fournette or Cook, but he was more efficient, averaging more than 6.7 yards per carry—the highest of any running back in this year's class. Mixon was also a prolific receiver, and he therefore also has the second-highest RecIndex of any running back in this class.

Brian Hill, Wyoming
Drafted by Atlanta (Round 5, Pick 156)
BackCAST Score: +84.6%
RecIndex: -0.07

The defending NFC champions grabbed some great insurance in case either Devonta Freeman or Tevin Coleman suffers from injury or ineffectiveness next year. Brian Hill is a major BackCAST sleeper who the Falcons stole in the fifth round. Indeed, Hill's strong BackCAST projection would theoretically put him on top of a weaker draft class. Hill's 4.54-second 40-yard dash is "average" for a drafted running back, but Hill is a big back at 219 pounds, which gives him a good size/speed combination. The Cowboys used Hill heavily, and his +20.6% AOEPS is better than any other running back in this class save for Dalvin Cook. Hill's biggest drawback is his lower average of 5.53 yards per attempt, although that is not unusually low for a running back with a workload as heavy as Hill's.

Marlon Mack, South Florida
Drafted by Indianapolis (Round 4, Pick 143)
BackCAST Score: +80.8%
RecIndex: +0.10

With Frank Gore already long in the tooth, the Colts were prudent to look to the mid-rounds for a near-to medium-term replacement. Although not quite the sleeper that Hill is, Mack could be a pleasant surprise for a team that spends a mid-round pick on him. Due to a strong freshman season, Mack posts a +11.5% AOEPS. It is hard to say whether AOEPS under- or overrates him. As his career progressed, Mack ceded carries to running quarterback Quinton Flowers, but he also lost carries to fellow running back D'Ernest Johnson. Mack also posted a strong 6.2 yards per carry, which, combined with his good AOEPS, makes him a sort of discounted Dalvin Cook.

Christian McCaffrey, Stanford
Drafted by Carolina (Round 1, Pick 8)
BackCAST Score: +76.2%
RecIndex: +0.99

Typically, when a first-round running back prospect comes in sixth on BackCAST's list, it would be time for an explanation about why the prospect is overrated. McCaffrey, however, is simply a victim of being a fairly "average" first-round prospect in a draft full of historically great prospects and strong sleepers. McCaffrey's projection suffers a bit because he had few carries as a freshman and lost carries to Bryce Love as a junior. Overall, McCaffrey is a strikingly similar prospect to Marlon Mack. McCaffrey has much better receiving numbers, but Mack edges him slightly in AOEPS and size/speed combination.

The Carolina Panthers used a lot of draft capital to nab McCaffrey with the eighth pick in the first round. The Panthers obviously hope McCaffrey will jump start a running game that ranked 20th in the NFL in yards per attempt, despite sporting one of the best rushing quarterbacks in the NFL. McCaffrey also has great receiving potential, with the highest RecIndex in this class.

Rookie NFL running backs develop more quickly than any position, and the Panthers are only a year removed from a Super Bowl appearance, so filling an immediate need with a solid player does make a certain kind of sense, even given the analytics research that suggests that a first-round running back is usually a bad investment.

Samaje Perine, Oklahoma
Drafted by Washington (Round 4, Pick 114)
BackCAST Score: +72.9%
RecIndex: -0.27

Samaje Perine is rather slow with a 4.65-second 40-yard dash, but he is an absolute load at 233 pounds. Perine somehow managed to post a nice AOEPS despite the fact that he had to share the backfield with Joe Mixon during his sophomore and junior seasons. That freshman season, however, was particularly impressive: Perine ran the ball 263 times for 1,713 yards, working out to an average of 6.51 yards per attempt. One could only imagine what Perine's college numbers may have looked like if he had not had to share the load with Mixon.

Perine obviously fills the Alfred Morris role as a running back who can gain yards on the ground but will frustrate fantasy owners in points per reception leagues. Perine was not particularly explosive in the passing game. He never had more than 108 yards receiving in any single season, hence the low RecIndex.

POTENTIAL BUST ALERT

Alvin Kamara, Tennessee
Drafted by New Orleans (Round 3, Pick 67)
BackCAST Score: -30.4%
RecIndex: +0.71

Alvin Kamara had trouble getting carries for the Tennessee Volunteers, posting a -14.2% AOEPS. It would be one thing if Kamara had been stuck behind a particularly talented teammate, but the available evidence does not suggest that Kamara was permanently locked in some sort of Thurman Thomas/Barry Sanders situation (both played for Oklahoma State at the same time). Kamara was the clear second running back behind Jalen Hurd as a sophomore (though, in all fairness, Hurd was considered a possible future high-round draft pick at the time). During Kamara's junior year, Hurd battled injuries and his production cratered, resulting in an abrupt decision to transfer from Tennessee. Even with Hurd out of the picture, Kamara barely edged out sophomore running back and former three-star recruit John Kelly for carries. It certainly could be the case that Tennessee's coaches failed to realize what they had in Kamara and that his NFL career will prove them wrong for failing to give him the rock enough times to shine. However, Kelly was actually more productive than Kamara on a per-carry basis, so Tennessee's coaches were not clearly wrong to platoon their backs.

Other signs that Kamara could be a transcendent talent stuck in a bad situation are just not there. Kamara ran a 4.56-second 40-yard dash at 214 pounds—those are firmly average numbers. Kamara averaged more than 6 yards per carry, which is good, but not unusual for a back with relatively low attempts, nor is it a number that makes Kamara stand out amongst the running back prospects in this class.

Despite his poor projection on the ground, Kamara may have landed in the best situation possible. The New Orleans Saints also have Adrian Peterson and Mark Ingram, who will likely constitute most of the Saints' ground game. The Saints are probably expecting Kamara to catch passes out of the backfield and little else. Despite his poor BackCAST, Kamara has a high RecIndex, so he certainly has the potential to flourish in this role. On our website, before Kamara was drafted by the Saints, we suggested that Kamara's upside might be Travaris Cadet, a running back with only four rushing attempts but 40 receptions in 2016. Now Kamara could quite literally take over Cadet's role.

Table 3 provides the BackCAST and RecIndex numbers for all of the Division I FBS halfback prospects selected in this year's NFL draft.

Nathan Forster

Table 3. BackCAST Projections for Drafted Running Backs, 2017

Name	School	Rnd	Pick	Team	40	Weight	AEOPS	Adj Y/A	RecYd/G	BackCAST	RecIndex
Leonard Fournette	LSU	1	4	JAC	240	4.51	11.8%	6.22	16.4	142.2%	-0.01
Dalvin Cook	Florida St.	2	41	MIN	210	4.49	20.7%	6.50	24.6	136.0%	0.61
Joe Mixon	Oklahoma	2	48	CIN	228	4.45	1.9%	6.16	35.8	115.7%	0.90
Brian Hill	Wyoming	5	156	ATL	219	4.54	20.6%	5.53	10.9	84.6%	-0.07
Marlon Mack	South Florida	4	143	IND	213	4.50	11.5%	6.16	13.8	80.8%	0.10
Christian McCaffrey	Stanford	1	8	CAR	202	4.48	9.1%	6.21	32.8	76.2%	0.99
Samaje Perine	Oklahoma	4	114	WAS	233	4.65	11.9%	6.02	8.9	72.9%	-0.27
Jeremy McNichols	Boise St.	5	162	TAM	214	4.49	8.3%	5.61	32.0	69.5%	0.86
Elijah McGuire	La-Lafayette	6	188	NYJ	214	4.53	1.9%	6.06	27.3	50.3%	0.66
D'Onta Foreman	Texas	3	89	HOU	233	4.58	-3.4%	6.26	5.4	43.9%	-0.42
Elijah Hood	North Carolina	7	242	OAK	232	4.59	2.0%	5.89	6.4	43.5%	-0.37
Kareem Hunt	Toledo	3	86	KC	216	4.62	6.0%	6.32	12.6	40.6%	0.03
Aaron Jones	UTEP	5	182	GB	208	4.56	1.7%	6.25	18.5	27.8%	0.34
Donnel Pumphrey	San Diego St.	4	132	PHI	176	4.48	12.8%	6.05	19.2	12.0%	0.63
James Conner	Pittsburgh	3	105	PIT	233	4.65	-1.2%	5.59	10.6	9.1%	-0.20
Wayne Gallman	Clemson	4	140	NYG	215	4.60	8.5%	5.06	11.6	-3.1%	-0.01
Matt Dayes	N.C. State	7	252	CLE	205	4.47	-5.2%	5.19	20.7	-22.6%	0.46
Jamaal Williams	BYU	4	134	GB	210	4.59	0.1%	5.37	13.2	-26.0%	0.10
Alvin Kamara	Tennessee	3	67	NO	214	4.56	-14.2%	5.69	28.5	-30.4%	0.71
T.J. Logan	North Carolina	5	179	ARI	196	4.37	-10.5%	5.42	13.5	-31.6%	0.23
Joe Williams	Utah	4	121	SF	190	4.41	-11.9%	5.75	10.1	-49.8%	0.13
Christopher Carson	Oklahoma St.	7	249	SEA	218	4.58	-16.9%	5.23	14.2	-71.5%	0.08
Khalfani Muhammad	California	7	241	TEN	170	4.38	-10.8%	5.65	13.0	-81.9%	0.42

FO Rookie Projections

Over the years, Football Outsiders has developed a number of methods for forecasting the NFL success of highly-drafted players at various positions. You've now read about BackCAST; here is a rundown of the other methods and what they say about players drafted in 2017.

Quarterbacks: QBASE

The QBASE (Quarterback Adjusted Stats and Experience) system analyzes the last 20 years of rookie quarterbacks chosen among the top 100 picks of the NFL draft, and uses regression analysis to determine which factors helped predict their total passing DYAR in Years 3-5 of their careers. (We use these years to account for the fact that many highly-drafted quarterbacks may not play regularly until their second or even third seasons.)

The primary factor in QBASE is the quarterback's college performance, analyzed with three metrics: completion rate, yards per attempt adjusted based on touchdowns and interceptions, and team passing S&P+ from Football Outsiders' college stats. We then adjust based on strength of schedule and strength of teammates. The latter element gives credit based on the draft-pick value of offensive linemen and receivers drafted in the quarterback's draft year as well as the projected draft position of younger teammates in 2017.

The measurement of past performance is then combined with two other factors: college experience and draft position. The latter factor accounts for what scouts will see but a statistical projection system will not, including personality, leadership, and projection of physical attributes to the next level.

QBASE also looks at the past performance of quarterbacks compared to their projection and using 50,000 simulations, produces a range of potential outcomes for each prospect: Elite quarterback (over 2500 DYAR in Years 3-5), Upper Tier quarterback (1500-2500 DYAR), Adequate Starter (500-1500 DYAR), or Bust (less than 500 DYAR in Years 3-5).

Here are QBASE projections for quarterbacks chosen in the top 100 picks of the 2016 NFL draft:

Player	College	Tm	Rd	Pick	QBASE	Elite	Upper Tier	Adequate	Bust
M.Trubisky	UNC	CHI	1	2	456	4.4%	15.6%	30.8%	49.3%
P.Mahomes	T.TECH	KC	1	10	793	9.7%	17.9%	26.7%	45.7%
D.Watson	CLEM	HOU	1	12	282	3.5%	11.8%	28.3%	56.5%
D.Kizer	ND	CLE	2	52	-181	3.0%	9.8%	21.8%	65.5%
D.Webb	CAL	NYG	3	87	238	4.4%	13.6%	25.2%	56.9%

Edge Rushers: SackSEER

SackSEER is a method that projects sacks for edge rushers, including both 3-4 outside linebackers and 4-3 defensive ends, using the following criteria:

• An "explosion index" that measures the prospect's scores in the forty-yard dash, the vertical jump, and the broad jump in pre-draft workouts.
• Sacks per game, adjusted for factors such as early entry in the NFL Draft and position switches during college.
• Passes defensed per game.
• Missed games of NCAA eligibility due to academic problems, injuries, benchings, suspensions, or attendance at junior college.

SackSEER outputs two numbers. The first, SackSEER Rating, solely measures how high the prospect scores compared to players of the past. The second, SackSEER Projection, represents a forecast of sacks for the player's first five years in the NFL. It synthesizes metrics with conventional wisdom by adjusting based on the player's expected draft position (interestingly, not his actual draft position) based on pre-draft analysis at the site NFLDraftScout.com.

Here are the SackSEER numbers for edge rushers drafted in the first three rounds of the 2017 draft, along with two later-round picks that had a high SackSEER Rating.

Name	College	Team	Rnd	Pick	SackSEER Projection	SackSEER Rating
M.Garrett	TXAM	CLE	1	1	31.9	98.7%
S.Thomas	STAN	SF	1	3	24.2	78.7%
D.Barnett	TEN	PHI	1	14	25.5	81.7%
C.Harris	MIZZ	MIA	1	22	14.8	17.5%
T.McKinley	UCLA	ATL	1	26	22.7	78.7%
T.Charlton	MICH	DAL	1	28	20.8	47.3%
T.Watt	WIS	PIT	1	30	26.5	91.3%
T.Bowser	HOU	BAL	2	47	26.5	92.0%
R.Anderson	BAMA	WAS	2	49	6.3	3.3%
D.Smoot	ILL	JAC	3	68	7.3	33.4%
J.Willis	KSST	CIN	3	73	23.6	93.3%
D.Hall	TXAM	CAR	3	77	13.4	59.6%
T.Williams	BAMA	BAL	3	78	14.3	35.5%
T.Basham	OHIO	IND	3	80	16.6	64.5%
D.Rivers	YSU	NE	3	83	17.6	33.4%
T.Hendrickson	FAU	NO	3	103	15.7	90.0%
D.Wise	ARK	NE	4	131	12.4	63.0%
I.Odenigbo	NW	MIN	7	220	4.8	62.7%

SackSEER was created by Nathan Forster.

Wide Receivers: Playmaker Score

Playmaker Score projects success for NFL wide receivers using the following criteria:

- The wide receiver's peak season for receiving yards per team attempt and receiving touchdowns per team attempt.
- Differences between this prospect's peak season and most recent season, to adjust for players who declined in their final college year.
- College career yards per reception.
- Rushing attempts per game.
- Vertical jump from pre-draft workouts.
- A binary variable that rewards players who enter the draft as underclassmen.

Like SackSEER, Playmaker Score outputs two numbers. The first, Playmaker Rating, solely measures how high the prospect scores compared to players of the past. The second, Playmaker Projection, represents a forecast of average receiving yards per year in the player's first five seasons, synthesizing metrics with conventional wisdom by adjusting based on the player's expected draft position.

Here are the Playmaker Score numbers for players drafted in the first three rounds of the 2017 draft, along with later-round picks (and one UDFA) with a high Playmaker Rating. Cooper Kupp (Rams) and Chad Williams (Cardinals) do not have Playmaker Scores because they played at the FCS level:

Name	College	Team	Rnd	Pick	Playmaker Projection	Playmaker Rating
C.Davis	WMU	TEN	1	5	669	90.6%
M.Williams	CLEM	LACH	1	7	514	70.9%
J.Ross	WASH	CIN	1	9	694	96.9%
Z.Jones	ECU	BUF	2	37	286	37.6%
C.Samuel	OHST	CAR	2	40	565	97.4%
J.Smith-Schuster	USC	PIT	2	62	425	80.3%
T.Taylor	WKU	TEN	3	72	407	79.1%
A.Stewart	BAMA	NYJ	3	79	377	73.4%
C.Henderson	LTECH	DEN	3	82	541	97.4%
C.Godwin	PSU	TB	3	84	487	87.0%
K.Golladay	NILL	DET	3	96	286	71.3%
A.Darboh	MICH	SEA	3	106	233	29.9%
D.Westbrook	OKLA	JAC	4	110	440	93.7%
J.Reynolds	TXAM	LARM	4	117	303	83.9%
S.Gibson	WVU	PHI	5	166	293	81.7%
I.Ford	VTECH	MIA	7	237	275	85.0%
M.Dupre	LSU	GB	7	247	353	80.5%
K.Cannon	BAY	NYJ	UDFA	--	292	86.4%

Playmaker Score was originally created by Vincent Verhei and then further developed by Nathan Forster.

Top 25 Prospects

Every year, Football Outsiders takes it upon ourselves to put together a list of the NFL's best and brightest that have barely played. Eighty percent of the draft-day discussion is about first-round picks, and 10 percent is about the players that should have been first-round picks, but instead went in the second round.

This list is about the others. Everybody knows that Marcus Mariota and Myles Garrett are good. There's a cottage industry around the idea of hyping every draft's No. 1 quarterback as a potential superstar. This is a list of players that have a strong chance to make an impact in the NFL despite their lack of draft stock and the fact that they weren't immediate NFL starters. Previous instances of the list have hyped players such as Geno Atkins, Elvis Dumervil, Malcolm Butler, and Jamaal Charles before they blew up. Rotoworld has referred to this list as "an all-star team of waiver pickups" after we hit on players such as Arian Foster and Miles Austin. Last year's list included David Johnson, Danielle Hunter, and Super Bowl star Grady Jarrett.

This is the 11th anniversary of the list. We're still relying on the same things we always do: scouting, statistics, measurables, context, expected role, and what we hear from other sources. The goal is to bring your attention to players who are still developing in their second and third seasons, even after the draftniks have forgotten them.

Here's our full criteria:

• Drafted in the third round or later, or signed as an undrafted free agent
• Entered the NFL between 2014 and 2016
• Fewer than 500 career offensive or defensive snaps
• Have not signed a contract extension (players who have bounced around the league looking for the right spot, however, still qualify for the list)
• Age 26 or younger in 2017

This year, there weren't any prospects head-and-shoulders above the rest of the crew, like we've seen in past instances. Last year, David Johnson was an easy top prospect, for example. We actually had to have a bit of a debate to settle on the top of the list. And the No. 1 prospect is a bit polarizing because of this.

1 Tyreek Hill, WR, Kansas City
418 offensive snaps | fifth-round pick, 2016, age 23

Most famous for being another of the NFL's myriad domestic violence cases, Hill was drafted in the fifth round by the Chiefs because he's simply too fast to ignore. Oklahoma State dismissed him from the team after he was arrested for reportedly assaulting his pregnant girlfriend, and he ended up at Division II West Alabama. Hill reportedly ran a 4.24 40-yard dash at his pro day, which is no surprise for a high school track All-American.

At first, Hill was just a special teams maven, but with injuries to Jamaal Charles and Jeremy Maclin sapping their speed, the Chiefs began to turn to him more in their horizontal passing game. With Maclin now cut, Hill enters 2017 as their No. 1 option in the passing game. The doubters will point to a small sample size of snaps where he actually played wide receiver, but he impressed in the ones where he did, breaking press coverage repeatedly. Maybe he's only a speedy gadget receiver. Or, maybe he's Antonio Brown.

2 Austin Hooper, TE, Atlanta
405 offensive snaps | third-round pick, 2016, age 22

Hooper came out of Stanford with a pedigree as a great blocking tight end, but he wasn't utilized much in the passing game by the Cardinal, with only 34 targets his junior season. However, outside evaluators such as Matt Waldman of the *Rookie Scouting Portfolio* loved what they saw of Hooper. He tested well and also looked the part on the field.

Hooper had a 47.1% receiving DVOA in his rookie year for the Falcons. Granted, some of that came because Kyle Shanahan's second tight ends often get a lot of leeway to make big plays. But with no ball-dominant second option in the Atlanta passing game, and Jacob Tamme gone, Hooper could make the leap this year and become a true TE1 for fantasy football purposes.

3 Javon Hargrave, DT, Pittsburgh
492 defensive snaps | third-round pick, 2016, age 24

Hargrave combines impressive burst inside with advanced hand technique, and the only reason he was still around this late in the draft was that he played at South Carolina State. He ranked third in sacks at the FCS level, with 16, while playing at defensive tackle.

For the Steelers, who are usually pretty conservative bringing rookies along, Hargrave earned a lion's share of the snaps at nose tackle last season. Much as Grady Jarrett has been for Atlanta, we expect Hargrave to eventually be a run-down dominator with a chance to play a little on passing downs as well. Although Pittsburgh's run defense was a bit up-and-down in 2016, that was more about injuries to Ryan Shazier and Cameron Heyward than Hargrave's play.

4 Brett Hundley, QB, Green Bay
22 offensive snaps | fifth-round pick, 2015, age 24

The story on Hundley hasn't changed much from last year. He's still an incredibly athletic quarterback who was ruined at UCLA by a bad offensive system and a lack of supporting weapons. Hundley saw limited playing time last preseason because of an ankle injury, and limited playing time last season because he is behind Aaron Rodgers.

We've started to see some talk about Hundley's trade value, though the Packers aren't typically a team that leaks a ton to the media. With two years left on his rookie deal, the time to strike probably would've been this offseason. If only he were as tall and dreamy as Mike Glennon, then maybe someone would've spent actual draft-pick value to get him.

5 Elandon Roberts, LB, New England
270 defensive snaps | sixth-round pick, 2016, age 23

A big part of the reason Jamie Collins was traded to the Browns was the quick development of Roberts, who started sliding into Bill Belichick's defensive packages much sooner than anticipated. Roberts didn't time or test well in the pre-draft process, but he was highly regarded at Houston as both a leader and a playmaker after he helped lead the Cougars back to national prominence. He reeled off 19 tackles for loss and six sacks, along with five passes defensed in 14 games.

With the Patriots, Roberts' average gain on his run tackles was just 2.7 yards, which is a very low number for an off-ball linebacker. He's a downhill player who is at his best when being aggressive right off the snap. Although his timed speed (4.60 40-yard dash) wasn't very impressive for a player his size, he plays faster than that. Roberts lost playing time to Kyle Van Noy down the stretch, but still profiles to develop into a three-down linebacker.

6 Kenneth Dixon, RB, Baltimore
258 offensive snaps | fifth-round pick, 2016, age 23

Dixon missed the first four weeks of last season and came back without much burst as he tried to recover from a pre-season MCL tear. Dixon will also miss the first four weeks of next season after getting popped for a substance-abuse violation in the offseason. It's those last six weeks of last season that give him some promise: he's absolutely Baltimore's most talented running back, whether they believe it or not.

It's hard to understand how Dixon made it to the fifth round. Wildly productive, he held the career FBS touchdown record for a few days at the end of his senior season, before Keenan Reynolds snagged it back. He was first-team All-Conference —as a freshman at Louisiana Tech. He's a great receiver out of the backfield. He doesn't go down on first contact, and he gets the most out of every run. Perhaps the Ravens think he is untrustworthy at this point, but on talent alone, he should be the lynchpin of their offense next season. Well, for 12 games of next season.

7 C.J. Prosise, RB, Seattle
147 offensive snaps | third-round pick, 2016, age 23

How could you watch last year's New England-Seattle Sunday Night Football game and not think that Prosise has a chance to be a star? He dominated out of the backfield as a receiver in ways few current non-David Johnson backs do. And this makes perfect sense, as Prosise was a converted receiver playing running back at Notre Dame.

The only question at this point is how good he can be as a traditional running back. Prosise has some skill to read blocks, but he often tried to press the hole a bit too early for the Fighting Irish. In theory, all the talent is here for Prosise to be a three-down back. Seattle has covered him up with Eddie Lacy and Thomas Rawls, so there's not much fantasy value to be had. But even becoming the next Shane Vereen in an NFL world where Theo Riddick is becoming a household name is a big feat.

8 Michael Pierce, DE, Baltimore
375 defensive snaps | undrafted, 2016, age 24

Coming out of Samford, here's how well-known Pierce was: He has no NFL.com draft profile, and ESPN's page of his traits returns only "N/As." At his pro day, Pierce ran a 4.98 40-yard-dash. That might not sound like much, but there aren't many 320-plus-pounders with that kind of speed. His production was weak in college (3.5 sacks in 47 games), but there was definitely something to work with. The Ravens quickly swooped in on him after the draft.

As a rookie, Pierce picked up two sacks and nine hurries in limited time, while also destroying running games to the tune of a 94 percent stop rate on 33 runs. There's some concern over whether he's an actual pass-rusher or not, but he definitely showed enough for Baltimore to take a longer look at him in their passing-down fronts. It's not very often a player with these traits slips through the draft cracks. Baltimore is reaping the rewards for finding him.

9 Andrew Billings, DT, Cincinnati
0 defensive snaps | fourth-round pick, 2016, age 21

After missing 2016 with a knee injury, Billings heads into training camp as the presumed starting nose tackle for the Bengals. He was a hell of a prospect, with elite strength and nimble feet at Baylor, where he was the co-Big 12 Defensive Player of the Year at 20 years old. He racked up 26.5 tackles for loss in his last two years of college.

The question with Billings is: Is he a nose tackle, or is he more? Nose tackles don't have a ton of value in today's NFL, and the reason he slipped to the fourth round is because scouts looked at his body and saw a two-down player. The upside for Billings' skill set is to become Star Lotulelei, with the speed and power to win in any gap and be a factor on pass-rushing downs.

10 Nick Vigil, LB, Cincinnati
111 defensive snaps | third-round pick, 2016, age 24

Another of the Bengal Babies who are getting their first real chance this year, Vigil tested out very highly at the combine as a line of scrimmage defender. Vigil's short shuttle and 3-cone drill times were both in the top 10 percent of all inside linebackers over the last 18 years. His NFL.com draft profile includes this in weaknesses: "Instincts make him seem more athletic and fast than he might actually be." Sign us up for that weakness.

The question with Vigil will be the muscle he's able to add and what it does to his speed. He was merely 230 pounds at the combine. A best-case athletic scenario might be something like Kiko Alonso with the Bills before the injuries wrecked his career. After a successful cup of coffee in 2016, Vigil was dubbed "much better" by defensive coordinator Paul Guenther in OTAs and should be in line for a big role in 2017.

11 Owamagbe Odighizuwa, EDGE, New York Giants
396 defensive snaps | third-round pick, 2015, age 25

It was widely reported that Odighizuwa was considering quitting football this offseason, taking some time away from the Giants before showing up to OTAs. It's hard to really find a way to quantify that into a list. Either you believe in the talent, or you don't. The truth of the matter is that Odighizuwa has been hosed by the Giants, who went out and signed Olivier Vernon and Damon Harrison to keep him from really seeing the field.

But that takes nothing away from Odighizuwa's talent; he has shined every time he has been on the field. Our pre-draft metrics would have loved him, provided UCLA hadn't hidden him at end in a 3-4 defense. All Odighizuwa needs is a chance to play. If you believe in the college tape, it's insulting that he hasn't been given the chance yet. If you look at the reality of the situation, where the Giants brought in Devin Taylor this offseason, Odighizuwa might not get the chance with the Giants.

12 Jonathan Bullard, DT, Chicago
297 defensive snaps | third-round pick, 2016, age 23

Tabbed for this list the instant the draft ended in 2016, the Bears have instead done everything they could to make it appear that Bullard's value is down. Bullard tested like a star tackle, and some thought he should be playing end. SackSEER believed the former, calling for a more modest 12.1 sacks over the first five years of his career as projected at end. But even if you liked Bullard as a Geno Atkins-esque 3-technique, he was still perceived as a very hot commodity in the 2016 draft.

So naturally, he received fewer snaps than known mediocrities Mitch Unrein and Cornelius Washington last year, and notched just one sack and four hurries in his small sample size. Defensive coordinator Vic Fangio told the *Chicago Sun-Times* "I don't think he was quite ready for that last year, both physically or mentally." That's a pretty damning quote. The opportunity is here. The talent should be here. But whereas we might have slotted him in the top 10 if he were eligible for our list before last season, we're less sure about him now.

13 Terrance Mitchell, CB, Kansas City
239 defensive snaps | undrafted, 2014, age 25

Mitchell had a huge half-year as the Chiefs stopped the bleeding next to Marcus Peters down the stretch. Targeted in an obscene 30 percent of his snaps after joining the starting lineup, Mitchell had a 57 percent success rate and allowed an average of just 4.9 adjusted yards per attempt. He added eight defensed passes.

As a prospect, Mitchell has been on the radar for a bit, but never had a real opportunity. He spent time on the Bears active roster in 2014, but has also served two stints with the Cowboys, and one with the Texans last offseason before getting claimed by the Chiefs at final cuts. Mitchell had horrendous tested deep speed, with a 4.63 40-yard-dash that put him in the 11th percentile of all drafted cornerbacks since 1999. He was regarded as a mid-round prospect coming out of Oregon by most draftniks, but went undrafted in part due to a torn pec-

toral muscle. We at FO have seen a lot of small sample-size success seasons by cornerbacks in our day, so we're wary that Mitchell is suddenly a star. But on paper, it all seems to make sense that he could become a solid No. 2 corner.

14 Paul Perkins, RB, New York Giants
289 offensive snaps | fifth-round pick, 2016, age 22

Perkins has a couple of major gifts on his side. He has the Marshawn Lynch-esque ability to stop-and-start while evading defenders. He has the elusiveness to be a consistent between-the-tackles runner despite a lack of true burn-you speed down the field. In a lot of ways, his strengths set him up to be the next Devonta Freeman, another successful graduate from this list.

Perkins, however, did not test anything like Freeman at the combine. In fact, his combine was pretty disappointing as he managed a pedestrian 4.54 40-yard dash at 208 pounds. His pedestrian pass protection coming out of UCLA also helped him fall to the fifth round. He also has to overcome the inherent inertia of the New York Giants running back depth chart. Wayne Gallman is a higher-round pick than Perkins, while a healthy Shane Vereen offers more in the passing game and Orleans Darkwa seems to get 50 carries a year no matter what else happens. Perkins is a compelling talent, but there are reasons to doubt that he's a three-down back at this point.

15 Parker Ehinger, G, Kansas City
229 offensive snaps | fourth-round pick, 2016, age 24

Ehinger likely would have played his way right off this list had he not torn his ACL soon after ascending to the starting job. Considered a bit of a tweener at tackle after playing there at Cincinnati, the Chiefs immediately moved Ehinger to guard, where we have him with just five blown blocks in his small sample last year.

Ehinger is not expected to be full-go at training camp, but as soon as he is ready to go, the Chiefs should find themselves with a functional-to-good guard with near-tackle agility. If Ehinger can find just a little more power, he could be a star.

16 D.J. Reader, DT, Houston
404 defensive snaps | fifth-round pick, 2016, age 23

Unlike the other nose tackles on the list, there's not much doubt that Reader isn't a three-down lineman. He's a pure run-plugger, but he did that job very well in his first season as Vince Wilfork's understudy. Now with Wilfork retired and the Texans without much else at the position, Reader should be a starter this year. His 90 percent stop rate on 20 runs last year shows promise.

In putting this list together though, we have an obvious bias towards passing-game players. We think Reader is a terrific prospect at a nose tackle, and might have even put him above some of the players ahead of him if we were ranking players just on their floors. But there's only so much value a run-only player can have in a pass-first league.

17 P.J. Williams, CB, New Orleans
82 defensive snaps | third-round pick, 2015, age 24

Williams has the size and talent to be a strong boundary corner. Williams is a physical freak, with video of a 60-inch box jump that went viral as he was coming out of the draft. The only thing that has held back Williams' ascension is his early-career injury history. A torn hamstring ended his 2015 season before it began, and a severe concussion cut his 2016 season after just a handful of snaps.

Williams still has a huge opportunity for playing time, even with Marshon Lattimore on the team, but this is probably his last real chance to impress the Saints. Another year on the sideline would make it extremely hard for an NFL team to count on him. And while his upside is higher than some players ahead of him on the list, we have to measure that against the chance that he never plays another NFL snap.

18 A.J. Derby, TE, Denver
191 offensive snaps | fifth-round pick, 2015, age 25

Derby had the size, speed, and skill to be star college tight end, but resisted the change for many years, even transferring from Iowa to Arkansas to try to stay at quarterback. Without much statistical track record, and coming out of college with an injury that caused him to miss his bowl game and most of the combine, it was a surprise that he was actually drafted. But under the watchful eye of Bill Belichick, Derby blossomed to the point that the Patriots were able to deal him to Denver and recoup their initial investment.

Given the lack of a real established tight end in Denver, Derby doesn't have much to beat out to see playing time. He's certainly the best receiving option the Broncos have at the position. New offensive coordinator Mike McCoy's tenure with the Chargers heavily emphasized tight ends, and while Derby is no Antonio Gates, he should see a little more involvement than he did last year.

19 Justin Simmons, S, Denver
296 defensive snaps | third-round pick, 2016, age 23

Simmons got some experience last year while T.J. Ward was out, and is probably the free safety of the future in Denver. Simmons showed off his range at the combine by posting 97th percentile scores in the 20-yard shuttle and 60-yard shuttle. His lanky frame makes him somewhat awkward as an NFL tackler, and scouts also dinged his single-high safety instincts coming out of Boston College.

However, that range will play anywhere. The question is just where he'll be most effective in Denver, with Ward and Darian Stewart both coming up on the end of their useful shelf life. He probably fits best as a single-high safety from a pure athletic standpoint. It's the development of his instincts and reads that will ultimately determine the right spot for him.

20 Miles Killebrew, S, Detroit
149 defensive snaps | fourth-round pick, 2016, age 24

A rangy, hard-hitting safety in the Deone Bucannon "safety who is really a linebacker" mold, Killebrew projects to see plenty of time in Detroit's secondary going forward. Glover Quin is getting closer to 30, and under Teryl Austin the Lions have been very open to dime defenses, going with them 18 percent of the time in 2016.

Killebrew's 40-yard dash at the combine was brutal, with a 4.65-second time that put him in the bottom 20 percent of all safeties since 1999. However, his jumps were explosive and once he got up to top speed he managed pretty well at Southern Utah. It's all projection this deep on the list, but Killebrew has the tools to be an NFL moneybacker.

21 B.J. Finney, G/C, Pittsburgh
300 offensive snaps | undrafted, 2015, age 25

Finney was a reserve lineman for the Steelers in 2016, after spending most of 2015 on the practice squad. The Kansas State lineman was heavily decorated for Bill Snyder's Wildcats, a Remington Trophy Finalist in 2014 and a first-team All-Big 12 center. He has the wrestling background that has come to define inside maulers such as former Patriot Stephen Neal. Scouts were worried about his quickness in college, and his short arms didn't do him any favors with front offices.

But when put on the spot in relief of Ramon Foster, Finney quietly did an excellent job last year. He helped key the Steelers in their dominant win over the Chiefs and wasn't anywhere near as overmatched against the Eagles as the right side of the offensive line. Maybe he isn't the next Andrew Norwell—the Panthers guard who went from UDFA to star—but he has all the tools to be a good NFL drive blocker.

22 Cody Kessler, QB, Cleveland
349 offensive snaps | third-round pick, 2016, age 24

Kessler was never drafted with the expectation that he could be a star quarterback, but he has a lot of the traits that can keep a quarterback in the league for a long time. He's fairly accurate underneath, he makes good decisions with the ball, and he's got the bulk to take the NFL beating. His major downsides are a) that he's 6-foot-1 and b) that he lacks NFL arm strength.

Still, Matt Flynn has that same package and was in the league for how many years? With a -7.5% DVOA last year, Kessler was essentially a league-average passer in a bad offense. He was benched for a reason, and there's no reason to hold a banquet in his honor for not being the worst player on the Browns. But Kessler could absolutely be a solid backup quarterback or Brian Hoyer-type. This league literally has someone start Josh McCown every year, that's how low the bar is.

23 Tyler Higbee, TE, Los Angeles Rams
405 offensive snaps | fourth-round pick, 2016, age 24

Higbee's first year with the Rams was spent doing his best Bo Scaife impersonation for Jeff Fisher's dying offense. He finished with the worst DYAR of any qualifying tight end in the league, generating minus-109 on just 29 passes while Jared Goff sailed them all over his head. That number, in that sample size, is essentially meaningless. But it does show you how lost the Rams were.

Higbee arrived at Western Kentucky as a 190-pound wideout and built himself into a 250-pound tight end. He maintained a lot of the wideout agility, too, which showed at the college level. New head coach Sean McVay has gotten terrific seasons out of Niles Paul and Jordan Reed, and Higbee certainly has the talent to hang with Paul's best seasons. Whether McVay lets that happen rather than turning rookie Gerald Everett into the focal point at the position is an open question.

24 Rashard Higgins, WR, Cleveland
183 offensive snaps | fifth-round pick, 2016, age 22

The death blow for an outside player's draft stock is a 4.64 40-yard dash at the combine. Higgins had a very high rating in our Playmaker Score metric, at 89.5%. He had a similar projection to what Antonio Brown would have had ... and what Dez White would have had. You can see the hit-or-miss nature of small-school wideout projection.

The 40 time belies the real problem with Higgins: he's a technically-skilled, smart receiver. But he also lacks a high ceiling because there's no physical upside here. Higgins is never going to post up against a press-outside corner like Dez Bryant can. There's not a lot in front of him on the depth chart in Cleveland, where Kenny Britt and Corey Coleman are joined by a deluge of younger receivers. But Higgins may need to take another step to be more than a solid underneath threat.

25 A.J. McCarron, QB, Cincinnati
259 offensive snaps | fourth-round pick, 2014, age 26

McCarron didn't exactly set the world on fire in his small sample with the Bengals, but adequate quarterbacking is worth something. McCarron's statistics, including a 6.9% DVOA on 132 dropbacks, were heavily influenced by a great supporting cast. Whenever McCarron gets his chance, you can expect some adequate game-manager type play. Nothing inspiring or worthy of a thinkpiece, but every era needs its Jon Kitna.

McCarron is in a bit of an interesting dispute with the Bengals, who don't want his 2014 season to count as an accrued year for the purposes of free agency. Assuming this is just wishful thinking, McCarron very well may find himself as the next winner of the Brock Osweiler/Mike Glennon Memorial Enormous Contract. The only real problem with that idea is that those guys had big arms, and McCarron has never had that.

Honorable Mention

QB Vernon Adams, Montreal Alouettes
EDGE Ronald Blair, San Francisco
CB Kendall Fuller, Washington
WR Roger Lewis, New York Giants
QB Cardale Jones, Buffalo
RB Robert Kelley, Washington
EDGE Dean Lowry, Green Bay
RB Jalen Richard, Oakland
RB Dwayne Washington, Detroit
G Christian Westerman, Cincinnati

Rivers McCown

Fantasy Projections

Here are the top 275 players according to the KUBIAK projection system, ranked by projected fantasy value (FANT) in 2017. We've used the following generic scoring system:

- 1 point for each 10 yards rushing, 10 yards receiving, or 20 yards passing
- 6 points for each rushing or receiving TD, 4 points for each passing TD
- -2 points for each interception or fumble lost
- Kickers: 1 point for each extra point, 3 points for each field goal
- Team defense: 2 points for a fumble recovery, interception, or safety, 1 point for a sack, and 6 points for a touchdown.

These totals are then adjusted based on each player's listed Risk for 2017:

- Green: Standard risk, no change
- Yellow: Higher than normal risk, value dropped by five percent
- Red: Highest risk, value dropped by 10 percent
- Blue: Significantly lower than normal risk, value increased by five percent

Note that fantasy totals may not exactly equal these calculations, because each touchdown projection is not necessarily a round number. (For example, a quarterback listed with 2 rushing touchdowns may actually be projected with 2.4 rushing touchdowns, which will add 14 fantasy points to the player's total rather than 12.) Fantasy value does not include adjustments for week-to-week consistency,

Players are ranked in order based on marginal value of each player, the idea that you draft based on how many more points a player will score compared to the worst starting player at that position, not how many points a player scores overall. We've ranked players in five league configurations:

- Flex Rk: 12 teams, starts 1 QB, 2 RB, 2 WR, 1 FLEX (RB/WR), 1 TE, 1 K, and 1 D.
- 3WR Rk: 12 teams, starts 1 QB, 2 RB, 3 WR, 1 TE, 1 K, and 1 D.
- PPR Rk: 12 teams, starts 1 QB, 2 RB, 2 WR, 1 FLEX (RB/WR), 1 TE, 1 K, and 1 D. Also adds one point per reception to scoring.
- 10-3WR Rk: same as 3WR, but with only 10 teams.
- 10-PPR Rk: same as PPR, but with only 10 teams.

The rankings also include half value for the first running back on the bench, and reduce the value of kickers and defenses to reflect the general drafting habits of fantasy football players. We urge you to draft using common sense, not a strict reading of these rankings.

A customizable spreadsheet featuring these projections is also available at FootballOutsiders.com for a $20 fee. This spreadsheet is updated based on injuries and changing forecasts of playing time during the preseason, and also has a version which includes individual defensive players.

The projection for Doug Martin incorporates three weeks of "replacement-level" value, accounting for the fact that a fantasy team that drafts Martin will still get points from a bench player during the weeks he is suspended.

Player	Team	Bye	Pos	Age	PaYd	PaTD	INT	Ru	RuYd	RuTD	Rec	RcYd	RcTD	FL	Fant	Risk	Flex Rk	3WR Rk	PPR Rk	10-3WR Rk	10-PPR Rk
David Johnson	ARI	8	RB	26	0	0	0	302	1368	11	77	771	2	2	269	Yellow	1	1	1	1	1
Ezekiel Elliott	DAL	6	RB	22	0	0	0	319	1545	14	34	283	1	2	257	Yellow	2	2	6	2	6
Le'Veon Bell	PIT	9	RB	25	0	0	0	298	1520	8	79	704	1	1	244	Red	3	3	2	3	2
LeSean McCoy	BUF	6	RB	29	0	0	0	250	1234	9	48	399	1	1	208	Yellow	4	4	14	4	14
Melvin Gordon	LACH	9	RB	24	0	0	0	304	1266	7	48	406	2	2	204	Yellow	5	6	16	6	16
Antonio Brown	PIT	9	WR	29	0	0	0	4	28	0	105	1357	11	0	201	Green	6	5	3	5	3
Jordan Howard	CHI	9	RB	23	0	0	0	281	1425	8	30	224	1	1	201	Yellow	7	9	25	7	29
Aaron Rodgers	GB	8	QB	34	4523	39	8	59	260	2	0	0	0	4	377	Yellow	8	11	13	9	12
DeMarco Murray	TEN	8	RB	29	0	0	0	279	1247	9	48	381	1	1	199	Red	9	12	19	11	20
Mike Evans	TB	11	WR	24	0	0	0	0	0	0	88	1305	11	0	196	Green	10	7	7	8	7
Julio Jones	ATL	5	WR	28	0	0	0	0	0	0	97	1451	8	0	195	Green	11	8	4	10	4
Odell Beckham	NYG	8	WR	25	0	0	0	0	0	0	97	1307	11	0	193	Green	12	10	5	12	5
Devonta Freeman	ATL	5	RB	25	0	0	0	197	865	9	51	457	2	1	193	Green	13	15	18	15	18
T.Y. Hilton	IND	11	WR	28	0	0	0	0	0	0	90	1445	8	0	191	Green	14	13	8	13	8
Jordy Nelson	GB	8	WR	32	0	0	0	0	0	0	90	1286	12	0	191	Yellow	15	14	9	14	9
Lamar Miller	HOU	7	RB	26	0	0	0	276	1205	5	35	260	3	2	186	Green	16	16	34	16	37
Todd Gurley	LARM	8	RB	23	0	0	0	266	1027	8	42	320	0	2	182	Green	17	19	29	18	33
Tom Brady	NE	9	QB	40	4813	36	8	39	65	1	0	0	0	3	357	Yellow	18	20	23	20	19
Michael Thomas	NO	5	WR	23	0	0	0	2	10	0	95	1279	10	0	179	Yellow	19	17	10	17	10

Player	Team	Bye	Pos	Age	PaYd	PaTD	INT	Ru	RuYd	RuTD	Rec	RcYd	RcTD	FL	Fant	Risk	Flex Rk	3WR Rk	PPR Rk	10-3WR Rk	10-PPR Rk
Amari Cooper	OAK	10	WR	24	0	0	0	2	10	0	89	1244	9	0	176	Green	20	18	11	19	11
Jay Ajayi	MIA	11	RB	24	0	0	0	289	1299	7	36	279	1	2	176	Red	21	22	42	21	44
Leonard Fournette	JAC	8	RB	22	0	0	0	258	1117	7	31	196	1	1	174	Green	22	24	51	23	51
Rob Gronkowski	NE	9	TE	28	0	0	0	0	0	0	73	1064	11	0	153	Red	23	23	28	24	24
A.J. Green	CIN	6	WR	29	0	0	0	0	0	0	94	1349	8	0	171	Yellow	24	21	12	22	13
Andrew Luck	IND	11	QB	28	4540	34	14	51	256	1	0	0	0	3	345	Yellow	25	25	32	25	27
Mark Ingram	NO	5	RB	28	0	0	0	189	887	6	43	313	2	2	165	Green	26	28	43	26	45
Isaiah Crowell	CLE	9	RB	24	0	0	0	227	973	7	39	326	1	1	164	Yellow	27	30	55	29	57
Drew Brees	NO	5	QB	38	4833	35	12	25	25	1	0	0	0	3	341	Yellow	28	31	36	28	32
Carlos Hyde	SF	11	RB	26	0	0	0	234	1071	8	38	277	1	2	163	Red	29	32	58	31	61
Spencer Ware	KC	10	RB	26	0	0	0	198	945	7	28	235	1	1	161	Green	30	33	65	33	70
DeAndre Hopkins	HOU	7	WR	25	0	0	0	0	0	0	81	1096	9	0	160	Green	31	26	20	27	21
Brandin Cooks	NE	9	WR	24	0	0	0	6	31	0	72	1087	8	0	159	Green	32	27	24	30	28
Doug Baldwin	SEA	6	WR	29	0	0	0	2	13	0	92	1146	7	0	158	Green	33	29	15	32	15
Marshawn Lynch	OAK	10	RB	31	0	0	0	226	927	10	29	207	1	1	158	Red	34	35	71	34	77
Ty Montgomery	GB	8	RB	24	0	0	0	156	797	5	50	433	2	1	157	Green	35	37	46	35	47
Mike Gillislee	NE	9	RB	27	0	0	0	188	879	8	21	168	2	2	156	Green	36	38	79	38	88
Christian McCaffrey	CAR	11	RB	21	0	0	0	147	648	5	62	594	2	1	155	Yellow	37	40	38	39	41
Greg Olsen	CAR	11	TE	32	0	0	0	0	0	0	79	1024	6	0	136	Green	38	36	31	37	25
Russell Wilson	SEA	6	QB	29	4162	27	11	88	471	3	0	0	0	4	331	Yellow	39	42	44	40	38
Matt Ryan	ATL	5	QB	32	4383	32	13	34	100	0	0	0	0	2	330	Green	40	44	47	42	39
Demaryius Thomas	DEN	5	WR	30	0	0	0	0	0	0	96	1185	7	0	152	Yellow	41	34	17	36	17
Travis Kelce	KC	10	TE	28	0	0	0	0	0	0	88	1081	5	0	131	Yellow	42	43	35	44	26
Allen Robinson	JAC	8	WR	24	0	0	0	0	0	0	73	979	9	0	149	Green	43	39	30	41	34
Dez Bryant	DAL	6	WR	29	0	0	0	0	0	0	67	975	10	0	148	Yellow	44	41	39	43	42
C.J. Anderson	DEN	5	RB	26	0	0	0	195	848	9	32	256	1	1	146	Red	45	54	86	62	95
Sammy Watkins	BUF	6	WR	24	0	0	0	0	0	0	69	1076	9	0	145	Red	46	45	45	45	46
Bilal Powell	NYJ	11	RB	29	0	0	0	164	790	4	54	389	1	1	145	Green	47	55	57	64	60
Jordan Reed	WAS	5	TE	27	0	0	0	0	0	0	86	931	8	0	126	Red	48	52	41	50	35
Emmanuel Sanders	DEN	5	WR	30	0	0	0	2	9	0	77	1012	7	0	144	Green	49	46	33	46	36
Larry Fitzgerald	ARI	8	WR	34	0	0	0	0	0	0	101	1040	8	0	143	Yellow	50	47	21	47	22
Michael Crabtree	OAK	10	WR	30	0	0	0	0	0	0	85	963	8	0	143	Green	51	48	26	48	30
Dalvin Cook	MIN	9	RB	22	0	0	0	184	816	5	52	346	1	2	143	Yellow	52	56	62	66	67
Davante Adams	GB	8	WR	25	0	0	0	0	0	0	68	892	9	0	142	Green	53	49	40	49	43
Jarvis Landry	MIA	11	WR	25	0	0	0	4	32	0	96	1080	5	0	141	Green	54	50	22	51	23
Terrelle Pryor	WAS	5	WR	28	0	0	0	8	31	0	71	1106	7	0	141	Red	55	51	49	52	49
Kelvin Benjamin	CAR	11	WR	26	0	0	0	0	0	0	67	991	8	0	140	Yellow	56	53	52	53	52
Tevin Coleman	ATL	5	RB	24	0	0	0	141	623	5	39	403	2	2	140	Green	57	60	78	69	86
Jimmy Graham	SEA	6	TE	31	0	0	0	0	0	0	66	822	8	0	121	Yellow	58	58	63	54	55
Tyrod Taylor	BUF	6	QB	28	3429	22	10	95	544	5	0	0	0	4	317	Green	59	62	61	56	54
Golden Tate	DET	7	WR	29	0	0	0	8	38	0	92	1001	5	0	136	Green	60	57	27	55	31
Derek Carr	OAK	10	QB	26	4171	29	11	38	93	1	0	0	0	3	313	Green	61	65	64	60	58
Willie Snead	NO	5	WR	25	0	0	0	2	10	0	71	939	7	0	135	Green	62	59	48	57	48
Alshon Jeffery	PHI	10	WR	27	0	0	0	0	0	0	70	1006	8	0	133	Red	63	61	59	58	63
Ben Roethlisberger	PIT	9	QB	35	4507	33	14	26	29	0	0	0	0	2	310	Yellow	64	69	66	65	62
Tyreek Hill	KC	10	WR	23	0	0	0	28	261	1	73	774	5	0	132	Yellow	65	63	54	59	56
Eddie Lacy	SEA	6	RB	27	0	0	0	166	726	7	19	160	0	0	132	Green	66	73	134	74	148
Jameis Winston	TB	11	QB	23	4394	29	15	58	201	2	0	0	0	4	309	Yellow	67	70	67	68	64
Julian Edelman	NE	9	WR	31	0	0	0	8	52	0	85	968	5	0	131	Green	68	64	37	61	40
Frank Gore	IND	11	RB	34	0	0	0	197	794	6	29	192	1	1	130	Yellow	69	76	120	78	134
Terrance West	BAL	10	RB	26	0	0	0	184	799	7	24	169	0	1	129	Yellow	70	79	131	79	145
Jonathan Stewart	CAR	11	RB	30	0	0	0	177	744	8	15	109	0	1	129	Green	71	80	156	80	158
Pierre Garcon	SF	11	WR	31	0	0	0	0	0	0	80	973	6	0	128	Yellow	72	66	53	67	53
Quincy Enunwa	NYJ	11	WR	25	0	0	0	3	13	0	75	1031	6	0	127	Red	73	67	60	70	65
Tyler Eifert	CIN	6	TE	27	0	0	0	0	0	0	61	770	8	0	108	Red	74	75	95	73	80
Cam Newton	CAR	11	QB	28	3680	25	12	81	410	4	0	0	0	3	304	Yellow	75	82	73	77	68
Martavis Bryant	PIT	9	WR	26	0	0	0	3	17	0	59	980	7	0	126	Red	76	68	74	71	82
Delanie Walker	TEN	8	TE	33	0	0	0	0	0	0	62	777	5	0	107	Green	77	78	83	76	71
Dak Prescott	DAL	6	QB	24	3721	24	10	60	281	3	0	0	0	5	303	Green	78	86	76	83	69
Joe Mixon	CIN	6	RB	21	0	0	0	170	693	7	26	184	1	1	125	Yellow	79	83	139	85	151
LeGarrette Blount	PHI	10	RB	31	0	0	0	176	684	9	7	45	0	1	125	Green	80	84	175	86	177
Hunter Henry	LACH	9	TE	23	0	0	0	0	0	0	54	702	7	0	106	Yellow	81	81	103	82	92
Stephen Gostkowski	NE	9	K	33	--	--	--	--	--	--	--	--	--	0	155	Green	82	72	88	63	79
Stefon Diggs	MIN	9	WR	25	0	0	0	2	9	0	85	983	6	0	124	Yellow	83	71	50	72	50
DeVante Parker	MIA	11	WR	25	0	0	0	2	14	0	64	905	7	0	123	Yellow	84	74	70	75	76

Player	Team	Bye	Pos	Age	PaYd	PaTD	INT	Ru	RuYd	RuTD	Rec	RcYd	RcTD	FL	Fant	Risk	Flex Rk	3WR Rk	PPR Rk	10-3WR Rk	10-PPR Rk
Keenan Allen	LACH	9	WR	25	0	0	0	0	0	0	86	1025	6	0	122	Red	85	77	56	81	59
Martellus Bennett	GB	8	TE	30	0	0	0	0	0	0	59	717	6	0	103	Yellow	86	90	100	89	87
Matthew Stafford	DET	7	QB	29	4331	27	13	43	149	1	0	0	0	2	299	Yellow	87	94	84	93	72
Doug Martin	TB	11	RB	28	0	0	0	171	698	5	29	256	1	1	121	Yellow	88	87	146	90	153
Andy Dalton	CIN	6	QB	30	4231	25	12	56	189	2	0	0	0	4	298	Yellow	89	100	87	96	75
Kyle Rudolph	MIN	9	TE	28	0	0	0	0	0	0	78	750	5	0	101	Yellow	90	93	72	95	66
Kirk Cousins	WAS	5	QB	29	4316	26	15	25	84	2	0	0	0	5	297	Green	91	101	89	99	78
Rishard Matthews	TEN	8	WR	28	0	0	0	2	13	0	60	830	7	0	119	Yellow	92	85	80	87	89
Marqise Lee	JAC	8	WR	26	0	0	0	5	28	0	67	871	5	0	118	Green	93	88	68	91	73
Mike Wallace	BAL	10	WR	31	0	0	0	2	11	0	67	856	5	0	118	Green	94	89	69	92	74
Paul Perkins	NYG	8	RB	23	0	0	0	176	788	4	23	167	0	1	118	Green	95	91	162	97	165
Eric Ebron	DET	7	TE	24	0	0	0	0	0	0	58	704	5	0	99	Green	96	99	104	103	93
Marcus Mariota	TEN	8	QB	24	3897	27	11	69	380	3	0	0	0	5	295	Red	97	108	92	108	81
DeSean Jackson	TB	11	WR	31	0	0	0	0	0	0	53	943	5	0	116	Yellow	98	92	97	98	109
Dan Bailey	DAL	6	K	29	--	--	--	--	--	--	--	--	--	0	146	Green	99	95	102	84	96
Donte Moncrief	IND	11	WR	24	0	0	0	2	10	0	66	781	6	0	114	Green	100	96	75	104	83
Adam Thielen	MIN	9	WR	27	0	0	0	2	10	0	69	890	5	0	114	Yellow	101	97	77	105	85
Marvin Jones	DET	7	WR	27	0	0	0	2	12	0	65	921	5	0	114	Yellow	102	98	81	106	90
Chiefs D	KC	10	D	--	--	--	--	--	--	--	--	--	--	0	116	Green	103	102	105	88	99
Matt Bryant	ATL	5	K	42	--	--	--	--	--	--	--	--	--	0	143	Green	104	105	106	94	103
Corey Coleman	CLE	9	WR	23	0	0	0	3	13	0	65	889	5	0	112	Yellow	105	103	90	111	97
John Brown	ARI	8	WR	27	0	0	0	2	12	0	63	880	5	0	112	Yellow	106	104	93	112	102
Zach Ertz	PHI	10	TE	27	0	0	0	0	0	0	72	749	4	0	93	Yellow	107	121	96	125	84
Cameron Meredith	CHI	9	WR	26	0	0	0	2	11	0	66	880	5	0	111	Yellow	108	106	91	113	98
Matt Prater	DET	7	K	33	--	--	--	--	--	--	--	--	--	0	141	Yellow	109	114	112	100	105
Mason Crosby	GB	8	K	33	--	--	--	--	--	--	--	--	--	0	141	Green	110	115	113	101	106
Adam Vinatieri	IND	11	K	45	--	--	--	--	--	--	--	--	--	0	141	Yellow	111	116	114	102	107
Jamison Crowder	WAS	5	WR	25	0	0	0	4	27	0	65	789	5	0	110	Green	112	109	85	117	94
Kenny Britt	CLE	9	WR	29	0	0	0	0	0	0	66	832	5	0	110	Green	113	110	82	116	91
J.J. Nelson	ARI	8	WR	25	0	0	0	5	22	0	46	780	6	0	110	Yellow	114	111	124	118	140
Allen Hurns	JAC	8	WR	26	0	0	0	0	0	0	64	875	6	0	109	Red	115	117	98	121	110
Graham Gano	CAR	11	K	30	--	--	--	--	--	--	--	--	--	0	139	Yellow	116	122	117	109	111
Seahawks D	SEA	6	D	--	--	--	--	--	--	--	--	--	--	0	111	Yellow	117	123	118	107	108
Breshad Perriman	BAL	10	WR	25	0	0	0	2	11	0	52	798	6	0	108	Yellow	118	119	119	126	133
Matt Forte	NYJ	11	RB	32	0	0	0	158	655	4	32	231	1	1	108	Yellow	119	107	170	114	173
Philip Rivers	LACH	9	QB	36	4312	28	13	23	38	0	0	0	0	3	285	Yellow	120	144	107	145	100
Carson Wentz	PHI	10	QB	25	3959	25	13	47	176	2	0	0	0	6	285	Green	121	145	108	146	101
Justin Tucker	BAL	10	K	28	--	--	--	--	--	--	--	--	--	0	138	Green	122	125	121	110	113
Coby Fleener	NO	5	TE	29	0	0	0	0	0	0	49	622	4	0	88	Green	123	136	158	144	136
Tyrell Williams	LACH	9	WR	26	0	0	0	2	13	0	53	780	5	0	106	Green	124	126	115	132	130
Duke Johnson	CLE	9	RB	24	0	0	0	87	388	1	60	533	1	0	106	Green	125	112	99	119	112
Samaje Perine	WAS	5	RB	22	0	0	0	151	608	6	13	86	0	2	106	Blue	126	113	187	120	192
Sebastian Janikowski	OAK	10	K	39	--	--	--	--	--	--	--	--	--	0	136	Green	127	131	123	115	115
Jeremy Maclin	BAL	10	WR	29	0	0	0	2	12	0	63	762	6	0	105	Yellow	128	130	101	140	114
Brandon Marshall	NYG	8	WR	33	0	0	0	0	0	0	54	694	7	0	104	Yellow	129	132	122	141	137
Ameer Abdullah	DET	7	RB	24	0	0	0	163	671	3	26	185	0	1	104	Green	130	118	179	124	179
Austin Hooper	ATL	5	TE	23	0	0	0	0	0	0	40	517	6	0	85	Green	131	150	176	152	160
Giants D	NYG	8	D	--	--	--	--	--	--	--	--	--	--	0	106	Yellow	132	137	126	122	116
Eagles D	PHI	10	D	--	--	--	--	--	--	--	--	--	--	0	106	Green	133	138	127	123	117
Sterling Shepard	NYG	8	WR	23	0	0	0	3	14	0	55	685	6	0	103	Green	134	135	116	147	132
Patriots D	NE	9	D	--	--	--	--	--	--	--	--	--	--	0	105	Yellow	135	141	133	127	119
Corey Davis	TEN	8	WR	22	0	0	0	3	18	0	53	815	4	0	102	Yellow	136	139	129	148	143
C.J. Prosise	SEA	6	RB	23	0	0	0	81	364	2	50	437	2	0	102	Green	137	120	132	128	146
Ryan Succop	TEN	8	K	31	--	--	--	--	--	--	--	--	--	0	132	Green	138	146	136	131	124
Vikings D	MIN	9	D	--	--	--	--	--	--	--	--	--	--	0	104	Green	139	147	137	129	121
Jordan Matthews	PHI	10	WR	25	0	0	0	0	0	0	69	738	5	0	101	Green	140	142	94	150	104
Chris Boswell	PIT	9	K	26	--	--	--	--	--	--	--	--	--	0	131	Green	141	151	140	208	187
Raiders D	OAK	10	D	--	--	--	--	--	--	--	--	--	--	0	103	Green	142	152	141	133	125
Panthers D	CAR	11	D	--	--	--	--	--	--	--	--	--	--	0	103	Red	143	153	142	134	126
Cardinals D	ARI	8	D	--	--	--	--	--	--	--	--	--	--	0	103	Yellow	144	154	143	135	127
Rams D	LARM	8	D	--	--	--	--	--	--	--	--	--	--	0	103	Red	145	155	144	136	128
Kenny Stills	MIA	11	WR	25	0	0	0	0	0	0	43	707	6	0	100	Yellow	146	148	161	153	164
Steelers D	PIT	9	D	--	--	--	--	--	--	--	--	--	--	0	102	Yellow	147	158	147	209	188
Ted Ginn	NO	5	WR	32	0	0	0	9	61	0	47	754	5	0	99	Red	148	156	159	155	162
Latavius Murray	MIN	9	RB	27	0	0	0	130	526	6	17	136	0	1	99	Green	149	124	192	130	200

Player	Team	Bye	Pos	Age	PaYd	PaTD	INT	Ru	RuYd	RuTD	Rec	RcYd	RcTD	FL	Fant	Risk	Flex Rk	3WR Rk	PPR Rk	10-3WR Rk	10-PPR Rk
Cameron Brate	TB	11	TE	26	0	0	0	0	0	0	41	503	5	0	80	Green	150	172	181	165	169
Eli Manning	NYG	8	QB	36	4218	29	15	21	21	0	0	0	0	4	276	Yellow	151	183	128	169	118
Phil Dawson	ARI	8	K	42	--	--	--	--	--	--	--	--	--	0	129	Yellow	152	162	150	219	191
Chargers D	LACH	9	D	--	--	--	--	--	--	--	--	--	--	0	101	Green	153	163	151	214	190
Kevin White	CHI	9	WR	26	0	0	0	2	8	0	52	731	5	0	98	Yellow	154	159	149	157	154
Tavon Austin	LARM	8	WR	26	0	0	0	28	161	1	67	660	3	0	97	Yellow	155	164	109	160	120
Will Fuller	HOU	7	WR	23	0	0	0	3	17	0	48	724	4	0	97	Green	156	165	153	161	155
Tyler Lockett	SEA	6	WR	26	0	0	0	8	63	0	48	666	4	0	97	Green	157	166	154	162	156
James White	NE	9	RB	25	0	0	0	61	248	1	63	600	2	1	97	Green	158	127	111	137	123
Shane Vereen	NYG	8	RB	28	0	0	0	82	379	3	56	454	1	1	97	Yellow	159	128	135	138	149
Adrian Peterson	NO	5	RB	32	0	0	0	147	617	5	23	191	1	1	97	Red	160	129	189	139	196
Julius Thomas	MIA	11	TE	29	0	0	0	0	0	0	54	571	5	0	78	Red	161	177	173	174	157
Zay Jones	BUF	6	WR	22	0	0	0	3	15	0	60	766	5	0	96	Red	162	168	138	164	150
Charles Clay	BUF	6	TE	28	0	0	0	0	0	0	57	571	3	0	77	Green	163	182	164	175	142
Carson Palmer	ARI	8	QB	38	4319	26	14	18	43	0	0	0	0	5	273	Yellow	164	189	145	182	129
Eric Decker	TEN	8	WR	30	0	0	0	0	0	0	43	564	7	0	95	Green	165	169	168	166	171
Jason Witten	DAL	6	TE	35	0	0	0	0	0	0	62	587	4	0	76	Yellow	166	186	160	180	139
Jack Doyle	IND	11	TE	27	0	0	0	0	0	0	59	583	4	0	76	Yellow	167	187	166	181	147
Joe Flacco	BAL	10	QB	32	4265	24	14	19	40	1	0	0	0	3	272	Yellow	168	193	148	185	131
Mohamed Sanu	ATL	5	WR	28	0	0	0	0	0	0	58	678	5	0	94	Green	169	173	130	170	144
Derrick Henry	TEN	8	RB	23	0	0	0	120	531	5	14	120	0	1	94	Blue	170	133	208	142	214
Jeremy Hill	CIN	6	RB	25	0	0	0	135	524	6	15	109	0	1	93	Yellow	171	134	211	143	220
Blake Bortles	JAC	8	QB	25	3892	25	16	56	297	3	0	0	0	5	270	Red	172	202	152	189	135
Cole Beasley	DAL	6	WR	28	0	0	0	2	10	0	68	726	3	0	92	Green	173	178	110	176	122
Taylor Gabriel	ATL	5	WR	26	0	0	0	5	33	0	48	619	5	0	92	Green	174	179	165	177	168
John Ross	CIN	6	WR	23	0	0	0	3	19	0	51	772	4	0	92	Red	175	180	169	178	172
Jared Cook	OAK	10	TE	30	0	0	0	0	0	0	51	591	3	0	73	Yellow	176	191	182	188	170
C.J. Fiedorowicz	HOU	7	TE	26	0	0	0	0	0	0	52	585	3	0	73	Yellow	177	192	180	187	167
Deshaun Watson	HOU	7	QB	22	3498	20	18	93	512	4	0	0	0	4	268	Yellow	178	208	155	194	138
Robert Woods	LARM	8	WR	25	0	0	0	2	9	0	69	859	3	0	90	Red	179	188	125	186	141
Jeremy McNichols	TB	11	RB	22	0	0	0	126	532	5	21	164	1	1	90	Red	180	140	209	149	217
Evan Engram	NYG	8	TE	23	0	0	0	0	0	0	44	586	3	0	70	Red	181	205	193	200	180
Rob Kelley	WAS	5	RB	25	0	0	0	133	534	4	13	95	1	0	88	Green	182	143	221	151	226
David Njoku	CLE	9	TE	21	0	0	0	0	0	0	50	556	3	0	69	Yellow	183	207	185	203	175
Zach Miller	CHI	9	TE	33	0	0	0	0	0	0	46	511	4	0	68	Red	184	210	194	205	181
Antonio Gates	LACH	9	TE	37	0	0	0	0	0	0	39	395	6	0	68	Yellow	185	211	201	206	186
Erik Swoope	IND	11	TE	25	0	0	0	0	0	0	31	399	4	0	68	Blue	186	212	212	207	194
Ryan Tannehill	MIA	11	QB	29	3812	25	14	36	150	1	0	0	0	3	263	Yellow	187	223	167	213	152
Darren Sproles	PHI	10	RB	34	0	0	0	80	364	1	50	379	1	1	85	Green	188	149	171	154	174
Danny Woodhead	BAL	10	RB	32	0	0	0	67	280	0	63	502	2	1	84	Yellow	189	157	157	156	159
Robby Anderson	NYJ	11	WR	24	0	0	0	3	14	0	50	699	3	0	82	Yellow	190	213	178	211	178
Benjamin Watson	BAL	10	TE	37	0	0	0	0	0	0	47	496	4	0	63	Red	191	224	199	225	184
O.J. Howard	TB	11	TE	23	0	0	0	0	0	0	36	485	4	0	63	Red	192	225	219	226	206
Theo Riddick	DET	7	RB	26	0	0	0	54	187	1	60	514	1	1	81	Green	193	160	163	158	166
Thomas Rawls	SEA	6	RB	24	0	0	0	130	555	4	14	108	0	1	81	Yellow	194	161	238	159	240
Jermaine Gresham	ARI	8	TE	29	0	0	0	0	0	0	35	400	4	0	62	Yellow	195	229	220	227	207
Randall Cobb	GB	8	WR	27	0	0	0	9	40	0	52	545	4	0	80	Green	196	216	174	216	176
Sam Bradford	MIN	9	QB	30	4109	23	12	26	30	1	0	0	0	4	257	Yellow	197	237	172	234	161
Terrance Williams	DAL	6	WR	28	0	0	0	0	0	0	42	549	4	0	79	Green	198	219	186	221	189
Phillip Dorsett	IND	11	WR	25	0	0	0	2	10	0	38	549	4	0	79	Green	199	220	188	222	195
Rex Burkhead	NE	9	RB	27	0	0	0	98	441	2	26	235	1	1	79	Yellow	200	167	217	163	223
Jesse James	PIT	9	TE	23	0	0	0	0	0	0	33	346	4	0	59	Green	201	236	226	240	212
Alex Smith	KC	10	QB	33	3716	20	9	51	195	2	0	0	0	4	255	Yellow	202	241	177	243	163
Marquise Goodwin	SF	11	WR	27	0	0	0	2	14	0	40	604	4	0	76	Red	203	230	200	231	210
Torrey Smith	PHI	10	WR	28	0	0	0	0	0	0	35	516	4	0	76	Green	204	231	203	232	211
Giovani Bernard	CIN	6	RB	26	0	0	0	86	372	1	46	375	1	1	76	Red	205	170	190	167	197
Jamaal Williams	GB	8	RB	22	0	0	0	95	390	4	19	131	0	1	76	Green	206	171	239	168	241
Austin Seferian-Jenkins	NYJ	11	TE	25	0	0	0	0	0	0	39	466	3	0	57	Red	207	240	231	245	213
Chris Conley	KC	10	WR	26	0	0	0	0	0	0	53	621	3	0	74	Yellow	208	234	184	241	185
Mike Williams	LACH	9	WR	23	0	0	0	3	22	0	43	602	4	0	74	Red	209	235	198	242	209
Chris Thompson	WAS	5	RB	27	0	0	0	64	316	1	53	361	1	1	74	Green	210	174	183	171	182
Marlon Mack	IND	11	RB	21	0	0	0	83	391	2	24	159	1	1	73	Blue	211	175	230	172	236
Kareem Hunt	KC	10	RB	22	0	0	0	84	366	3	21	151	1	1	73	Green	212	176	242	173	245
Tyler Boyd	CIN	6	WR	23	0	0	0	4	20	0	44	520	3	0	72	Green	213	239	191	246	199
Vernon Davis	WAS	5	TE	33	0	0	0	0	0	0	37	410	2	0	52	Green	214	248	236	250	218

Player	Team	Bye	Pos	Age	PaYd	PaTD	INT	Ru	RuYd	RuTD	Rec	RcYd	RcTD	FL	Fant	Risk	Flex Rk	3WR Rk	PPR Rk	10-3WR Rk	10-PPR Rk
Titans D	TEN	8	D	--	--	--	--	--	--	--	--	--	--	0	100	Green	215	233	196	220	193
Jamaal Charles	DEN	5	RB	31	0	0	0	88	388	2	27	213	1	1	69	Yellow	216	181	240	179	242
Kenny Golladay	DET	7	WR	24	0	0	0	4	26	0	43	538	4	0	68	Red	217	247	210	249	219
Wendell Smallwood	PHI	10	RB	23	0	0	0	118	508	2	20	165	0	1	68	Red	218	184	251	183	254
Blair Walsh	SEA	6	K	27	--	--	--	--	--	--	--	--	--	0	127	Green	219	238	197	235	201
DeAndre Washington	OAK	10	RB	24	0	0	0	89	400	2	22	158	1	1	67	Green	220	185	248	184	251
Dwayne Allen	NE	9	TE	27	0	0	0	0	0	0	23	261	4	0	48	Green	221	253	258	254	249
Seth Roberts	OAK	10	WR	26	0	0	0	0	0	0	35	463	4	0	66	Yellow	222	249	225	252	232
Vance McDonald	SF	11	TE	27	0	0	0	0	0	0	33	370	3	0	47	Red	223	256	253	255	239
Caleb Sturgis	PHI	10	K	28	--	--	--	--	--	--	--	--	--	0	126	Yellow	224	242	202	244	208
Cowboys D	DAL	6	D	--	--	--	--	--	--	--	--	--	--	0	98	Green	225	243	204	236	202
Bucs D	TB	11	D	--	--	--	--	--	--	--	--	--	--	0	98	Green	226	244	205	237	203
Broncos D	DEN	5	D	--	--	--	--	--	--	--	--	--	--	0	98	Yellow	227	245	206	238	204
Jaguars D	JAC	8	D	--	--	--	--	--	--	--	--	--	--	0	98	Yellow	228	246	207	239	205
Markus Wheaton	CHI	9	WR	26	0	0	0	0	0	0	34	494	3	0	64	Green	229	252	227	253	233
Tyler Higbee	LARM	8	TE	24	0	0	0	0	0	0	35	354	3	0	45	Red	230	260	255	262	243
Clive Walford	OAK	10	TE	26	0	0	0	0	0	0	23	257	3	0	44	Green	231	262	262	265	255
Devin Funchess	CAR	11	WR	24	0	0	0	0	0	0	27	412	4	0	62	Yellow	232	255	249	256	252
Alvin Kamara	NO	5	RB	22	0	0	0	38	174	1	45	321	2	1	62	Yellow	233	190	214	190	222
Trevor Siemian	DEN	5	QB	26	3940	24	15	32	68	1	0	0	0	4	239	Red	234	270	195	270	183
Josh Doctson	WAS	5	WR	25	0	0	0	0	0	0	34	532	3	0	61	Red	235	257	245	261	247
Curtis Samuel	CAR	11	WR	21	0	0	0	6	30	0	45	467	3	0	60	Red	236	258	222	263	229
Cooper Kupp	LARM	8	WR	24	0	0	0	0	0	0	37	493	3	0	60	Red	237	259	243	264	246
Dion Lewis	NE	9	RB	27	0	0	0	59	303	1	23	208	1	1	60	Green	238	194	254	191	257
Jonathan Williams	BUF	6	RB	23	0	0	0	96	419	4	10	82	0	2	60	Red	239	195	268	192	268
Colts D	IND	11	D	--	--	--	--	--	--	--	--	--	--	0	95	Yellow	240	250	215	247	215
Texans D	HOU	7	D	--	--	--	--	--	--	--	--	--	--	0	95	Yellow	241	251	216	248	216
Adam Humphries	TB	11	WR	25	0	0	0	4	25	0	39	459	2	0	59	Green	242	261	228	268	234
Wayne Gallman	NYG	8	RB	23	0	0	0	87	388	2	14	106	1	1	59	Green	243	196	263	193	263
Laquon Treadwell	MIN	9	WR	22	0	0	0	4	22	0	37	452	3	0	58	Yellow	244	265	241	269	244
Darren McFadden	DAL	6	RB	30	0	0	0	70	334	1	19	157	0	1	58	Blue	245	197	257	195	259
Jacquizz Rodgers	TB	11	RB	27	0	0	0	87	361	1	17	167	0	1	58	Green	246	198	260	196	261
Falcons D	ATL	5	D	--	--	--	--	--	--	--	--	--	--	0	94	Green	247	254	218	251	221
T.J. Yeldon	JAC	8	RB	24	0	0	0	75	301	1	28	217	0	1	57	Blue	248	199	250	197	253
Kenneth Dixon	BAL	10	RB	23	0	0	0	70	287	1	29	202	1	1	57	Green	249	200	252	198	256
Devontae Booker	DEN	5	RB	25	0	0	0	78	306	2	20	142	1	1	57	Green	250	201	259	199	260
Joe Williams	SF	11	RB	24	0	0	0	78	357	2	14	71	0	1	56	Blue	251	203	265	201	265
D'Onta Foreman	HOU	7	RB	21	0	0	0	85	336	1	19	131	1	1	55	Green	252	204	261	202	262
Jeremy Kerley	SF	11	WR	29	0	0	0	0	0	0	47	489	2	0	54	Yellow	253	272	229	273	235
Eli Rogers	PIT	9	WR	25	0	0	0	0	0	0	37	466	2	0	54	Yellow	254	273	247	274	250
Josh Lambo	LACH	9	K	27	--	--	--	--	--	--	--	--	--	0	120	Yellow	255	263	223	257	224
Nick Novak	HOU	7	K	36	--	--	--	--	--	--	--	--	--	0	120	Yellow	256	264	224	258	225
Jalen Richard	OAK	10	RB	24	0	0	0	58	260	1	26	192	1	1	53	Blue	257	206	256	204	258
Mike Glennon	CHI	9	QB	28	3738	22	16	28	53	1	0	0	0	4	230	Yellow	258	275	213	275	198
Brandon McManus	DEN	5	K	26	--	--	--	--	--	--	--	--	--	0	119	Yellow	259	266	232	266	230
Cairo Santos	KC	10	K	26	--	--	--	--	--	--	--	--	--	0	119	Green	260	267	233	267	231
Redskins D	WAS	5	D	--	--	--	--	--	--	--	--	--	--	0	91	Green	261	268	234	259	227
Bengals D	CIN	6	D	--	--	--	--	--	--	--	--	--	--	0	91	Yellow	262	269	235	260	228
Jeremy Langford	CHI	9	RB	26	0	0	0	61	234	2	20	141	0	1	51	Green	263	209	266	210	266
Zach Zenner	DET	7	RB	26	0	0	0	73	293	2	14	120	1	1	50	Yellow	264	214	271	212	271
Dustin Hopkins	WAS	5	K	27	--	--	--	--	--	--	--	--	--	0	118	Green	265	271	237	271	237
Ravens D	BAL	10	D	--	--	--	--	--	--	--	--	--	--	0	89	Red	266	274	244	272	238
Jerick McKinnon	MIN	9	RB	25	0	0	0	59	221	1	25	186	0	1	47	Blue	267	215	264	215	264
Robert Turbin	IND	11	RB	28	0	0	0	45	156	2	17	113	1	1	45	Green	268	217	272	217	272
Dwayne Washington	DET	7	RB	23	0	0	0	75	287	2	12	93	1	1	45	Red	269	218	274	218	274
Kyle Juszczyk	SF	11	RB	26	0	0	0	13	37	0	46	345	1	0	44	Green	270	221	246	223	248
Kenyan Drake	MIA	11	RB	23	0	0	0	55	231	1	21	119	1	1	43	Blue	271	222	270	224	270
Branden Oliver	LACH	9	RB	26	0	0	0	29	105	1	26	225	1	1	40	Green	272	226	269	228	269
Lance Dunbar	LARM	8	RB	27	0	0	0	46	173	0	34	234	0	0	39	Red	273	227	267	229	267
Aaron Jones	GB	8	RB	23	0	0	0	55	268	1	10	70	0	1	39	Green	274	228	275	230	275
Donnel Pumphrey	PHI	10	RB	23	0	0	0	36	176	1	19	141	1	1	37	Green	275	232	273	233	273

Statistical Appendix

Broken Tackles by Team, Offense

Rk	Team	Plays	Plays w/ BTkl	Pct	Total BTkl
1	WAS	969	124	12.8%	149
2	DET	933	115	12.3%	128
3	KC	937	111	11.8%	133
4	BAL	1027	121	11.8%	145
5	MIA	873	102	11.7%	130
6	ATL	945	107	11.3%	127
7	CLE	913	103	11.3%	117
8	BUF	955	106	11.1%	131
9	OAK	1008	111	11.0%	129
10	LARM	900	99	11.0%	120
11	NE	1012	111	11.0%	131
12	DAL	963	103	10.7%	128
13	ARI	1035	110	10.6%	130
14	SF	942	97	10.3%	110
15	NYG	977	99	10.1%	117
16	CHI	930	94	10.1%	111
17	PIT	986	98	9.9%	113
18	NYJ	962	95	9.9%	123
19	PHI	1034	102	9.9%	113
20	GB	974	96	9.9%	121
21	TEN	963	94	9.8%	108
22	MIN	953	91	9.5%	102
23	CAR	1008	95	9.4%	118
24	SEA	953	84	8.8%	93
25	JAC	1011	88	8.7%	106
26	CIN	996	85	8.5%	102
27	DEN	963	82	8.5%	96
28	TB	1015	84	8.3%	107
29	NO	1058	87	8.2%	98
30	SD	970	76	7.8%	90
31	IND	971	74	7.6%	84
32	HOU	1023	77	7.5%	90

Play total includes Defensive Pass Interference.

Broken Tackles by Team, Defense

Rk	Team	Plays	Plays w/ BTkl	Pct	Total BTkl
1	DEN	1018	75	7.4%	83
2	JAC	974	72	7.4%	79
3	GB	936	71	7.6%	79
4	MIN	944	72	7.6%	86
5	OAK	950	74	7.8%	83
6	SD	972	76	7.8%	93
7	DAL	966	76	7.9%	82
8	TEN	977	78	8.0%	94
9	HOU	911	74	8.1%	88
10	NO	959	81	8.4%	98
11	WAS	1003	89	8.9%	105
12	BAL	946	84	8.9%	97
13	NYJ	947	86	9.1%	92
14	IND	978	89	9.1%	105
15	NYG	1013	95	9.4%	114
16	KC	1022	96	9.4%	112
17	CAR	973	92	9.5%	104
18	SEA	967	94	9.7%	108
19	ARI	960	95	9.9%	103
20	CLE	1027	102	9.9%	120
21	TB	964	97	10.1%	124
22	ATL	1009	102	10.1%	125
23	MIA	1036	106	10.2%	115
24	NE	959	99	10.3%	120
25	PIT	953	101	10.6%	116
26	CHI	954	102	10.7%	116
27	SF	1048	113	10.8%	132
28	LARM	990	107	10.8%	125
29	BUF	961	110	11.4%	124
30	DET	923	106	11.5%	116
31	PHI	927	117	12.6%	131
32	CIN	990	126	12.7%	142

Play total includes Defensive Pass Interference.

Most Broken Tackles, Defenders

Rk	Player	Team	BTkl	Rk	Player	Team	BTkl	Rk	Player	Team	BTkl
1	R.Shazier	PIT	20	8	A.Ogletree	LARM	16	18	L.David	TB	14
2	K.Alexander	TB	19	8	M.Smith	OAK	16	18	J.Hughes	BUF	14
3	R.McLeod	PHI	18	12	M.Barron	LARM	15	18	D.Jackson	IND	14
3	T.Smith	JAC	18	12	A.Bethea	SF	15	18	M.Jenkins	PHI	14
3	V.Burfict	CIN	18	12	W.Compton	WAS	15	18	K.Minter	ARI	14
6	D.Bucannon	ARI	17	12	S.Davis	PIT	15	18	Z.Orr	BAL	14
6	J.Collins	CLE	17	12	C.Graham	BUF	15	18	T.Porter	CHI	14
8	V.Hargreaves	TB	16	12	D.Kirkpatrick	CIN	15	18	P.Posluszny	JAC	14
8	D.Johnson	KC	16	18	K.Alonso	MIA	14				

Top 20 Defenders, Broken Tackle Rate

Rk	Player	Team	BTkl	Tkl	Rate
1	K.Joseph	OAK	0	44	0.0%
2	J.McCourty	TEN	2	55	3.5%
3	V.Bell	NO	2	50	3.8%
4	B.Grimes	TB	2	46	4.2%
4	L.Kuechly	CAR	3	68	4.2%
6	P.Amukamara	JAC	2	45	4.3%
7	A.Williamson	TEN	3	65	4.4%
8	X.Rhodes	MIN	2	40	4.8%
9	T.Davis	DEN	3	59	4.8%
10	M.Foster	WAS	5	80	5.9%
11	D.Sorensen	KC	3	43	6.5%
12	L.Ryan	NE	5	70	6.7%
13	H.Clinton-Dix	GB	4	55	6.8%
13	V.Miller	DEN	4	55	6.8%
15	J.Taylor	CLE	3	40	7.0%
16	A.J.Bouye	HOU	4	49	7.5%
16	C.Harris	DEN	4	49	7.5%
18	J.Freeman	CHI	6	73	7.6%
19	R.Wilson	KC	5	57	8.1%
20	J.Ryan	GB	4	45	8.2%

Broken Tackles divided by Broken Tackles + Solo Tackles.
Special teams not included; min. 40 Solo Tackles

Bottom 20 Defenders, Broken Tackle Rate

Rk	Player	Team	BTkl	Tkl	Rate
1	R.Shazier	PIT	20	47	29.9%
2	S.Davis	PIT	15	45	25.0%
3	J.Casillas	NYG	13	40	24.5%
3	C.Pryor	NYJ	13	40	24.5%
5	T.Porter	CHI	14	45	23.7%
6	M.Jenkins	PHI	14	48	22.6%
7	D.Bucannon	ARI	17	59	22.4%
8	R.McLeod	PHI	18	63	22.2%
9	C.Graham	BUF	15	53	22.1%
10	V.Burfict	CIN	18	64	22.0%
11	W.Compton	WAS	15	54	21.7%
12	D.Revis	NYJ	11	40	21.6%
12	T.Young	BAL	11	40	21.6%
14	N.Bellore	SF	12	44	21.4%
15	D.Ihenacho	WAS	13	48	21.3%
16	L.Joyner	LARM	12	45	21.1%
17	C.Conte	TB	13	49	21.0%
18	D.Jackson	IND	14	53	20.9%
19	V.Hargreaves	TB	16	63	20.3%
20	D.Johnson	KC	16	64	20.0%

Broken Tackles divided by Broken Tackles + Solo Tackles.
Special teams not included; min. 40 Solo Tackles

Most Broken Tackles, Running Backs

Rk	Player	Team	BTkl
1	D.Johnson	ARI	80
2	E.Elliott	DAL	69
3	L.McCoy	BUF	65
4	D.Freeman	ATL	63
5	L.Bell	PIT	61
6	J.Ajayi	MIA	59
7	T.Gurley	LARM	56
8	S.Ware	KC	55
9	M.Gordon	SD	52
10	J.Howard	CHI	51
10	C.Hyde	SF	51
12	D.Murray	TEN	49
12	B.Powell	NYJ	49
12	T.West	BAL	49
15	L.Blount	NE	48
16	M.Ingram	NO	46
16	J.Stewart	CAR	46
18	R.Kelley	WAS	43
19	T.J.Yeldon	JAC	42
20	M.Forte	NYJ	38

Most Broken Tackles, WR/TE

Rk	Player	Team	BTkl
1	O.Beckham	NYG	32
2	J.Landry	MIA	30
3	G.Tate	DET	27
4	T.Hill	KC	26
5	T.Austin	LARM	20
6	C.Patterson	MIN	19
7	M.Thomas	NO	17
8	L.Fitzgerald	ARI	16
8	S.Smith	BAL	16
10	R.Cobb	GB	15
11	D.Adams	GB	14
11	K.Benjamin	CAR	14
11	M.Bennett	NE	14
11	C.Meredith	CHI	14
11	S.Roberts	OAK	14
11	M.Wallace	BAL	14
17	K.Britt	LARM	13
17	A.Brown	PIT	13
17	Q.Enunwa	NYJ	13
17	P.Garcon	WAS	13

Most Broken Tackles, Quarterbacks

Rk	Player	Team	Behind LOS	Beyond LOS	BTkl	Rk	Player	Team	Behind LOS	Beyond LOS	BTkl
1	T.Taylor	BUF	14	19	33	5	R.Wilson	SEA	9	3	12
2	J.Winston	TB	9	7	16	7	A.Luck	IND	6	4	10
3	C.Newton	CAR	7	8	15	7	C.Wentz	PHI	2	8	10
4	C.Kaepernick	SF	2	12	14	9	B.Bortles	JAC	2	7	9
5	M.Stafford	DET	5	7	12	9	B.Osweiler	HOU	3	6	9

Best Broken Tackle Rate, Offensive Players (min. 80 touches)

Rk	Player	Team	BTkl	Touch	Rate	Rk	Player	Team	BTkl	Touch	Rate
1	O.Beckham	NYG	32	102	31.4%	11	D.Sproles	PHI	36	146	24.7%
2	T.Hill	KC	26	85	30.6%	12	R.Kelley	WAS	43	180	23.9%
3	J.Landry	MIA	30	99	30.3%	13	T.J.Yeldon	JAC	42	180	23.3%
4	K.Dixon	BAL	34	118	28.8%	14	T.Austin	LARM	20	86	23.3%
5	D.Johnson	CLE	35	126	27.8%	15	L.McCoy	BUF	65	283	23.0%
6	G.Tate	DET	27	101	26.7%	16	T.Riddick	DET	33	145	22.8%
7	R.Burkhead	CIN	24	91	26.4%	17	D.Freeman	ATL	63	281	22.4%
8	B.Powell	NYJ	49	189	25.9%	18	S.Ware	KC	55	247	22.3%
9	C.Thompson	WAS	30	117	25.6%	19	D.Henry	TEN	27	123	22.0%
10	D.Lewis	NE	20	81	24.7%	20	T.West	BAL	49	227	21.6%

Top 20 Defenders, Passes Defensed

Rk	Player	Team	PD
1	B.Grimes	TB	24
2	A.J.Bouye	NYG	21
3	R.Alford	ATL	19
3	C.Hayward	SD	19
3	J.Norman	WAS	19
6	J.Jenkins	NYG	18
6	M.Peters	KC	18
8	D.Amerson	OAK	17
8	M.Butler	NE	17
10	A.J.Bouye	HOU	16
10	L.McKelvin	PHI	16
12	B.Maxwell	MIA	15
12	R.Sherman	SEA	15
14	T.Brock	SF	14
14	R.Cockrell	PIT	14
14	S.Nelson	KC	14
14	J.Ramsey	JAC	14
14	D.Shead	SEA	14
19	7 tied with		13

Top 20 Defenders, Defeats

Rk	Player	Team	Dfts
1	P.Brown	BUF	31
2	L.David	TB	29
2	K.Mack	OAK	29
2	V.Miller	DEN	29
5	K.Alexander	TB	28
5	L.Alexander	BUF	28
5	S.Lee	DAL	28
8	Z.Brown	BUF	27
8	M.Golden	ARI	27
8	T.Smith	JAC	27
8	K.Wright	SEA	27
12	Z.Orr	BAL	26
12	P.Posluszny	JAC	26
14	N.Bradham	PHI	25
14	C.Jordan	NO	25
14	E.Kendricks	MIN	25
14	N.Perry	GB	25
18	9 tied with		24

Note: Based on the definition given in the Statistical Toolbox, not NFL totals.

Top 20 Defenders, Run Tackles for Loss

Rk	Player	Team	TFL
1	J.Clowney	HOU	14
2	C.Jordan	NO	13
3	P.Brown	BUF	12
3	Z.Brown	BUF	12
3	B.Graham	PHI	12
3	T.Smith	JAC	12
7	A.Donald	LARM	11
7	S.Lee	DAL	11
7	S.Richardson	NYJ	11
10	M.Bennett	SEA	10
10	K.Dansby	CIN	10
10	T.Jefferson	ARI	10
10	K.Mack	OAK	10
10	W.Mercilus	HOU	10
10	K.Short	CAR	10
16	N.Bradham	PHI	9
16	L.David	TB	9
16	C.Kirksey	CLE	9
16	P.Posluszny	JAC	9
16	J.Ryan	GB	9
16	L.Williams	NYJ	9
16	K.Wright	SEA	9

Top 20 Defenders, Quarterback Hits

Rk	Player	Team	Hits
1	A.Donald	LARM	24
1	T.Johnson	MIN	24
3	B.Irvin	OAK	22
4	B.Graham	PHI	20
4	K.Mack	OAK	20
8	E.Griffen	MIN	18
6	C.Jordan	NO	19
6	O.Vernon	NYG	19
9	G.Atkins	CIN	17
9	C.Dunlap	CIN	17
9	M.Golden	ARI	17
9	T.Murphy	WAS	17
13	J.Casey	TEN	16
13	N.Fairley	NO	16
15	E.Ansah	DET	14
15	C.Avril	SEA	14
15	M.Bennett	SEA	14
15	D.Buckner	SF	14
15	W.Mercilus	HOU	14
15	B.Wagner	SEA	14
15	C.Wake	MIA	14
15	L.Williams	NYJ	14

Top 20 Defenders, QB Knockdowns (Sacks + Hits)

Rk	Defender	Team	KD
1	A.Donald	LARM	33
2	C.Wake	MIA	31
3	B.Irvin	OAK	30
3	K.Mack	OAK	30
5	M.Golden	ARI	30
6	O.Vernon	NYG	29
7	E.Griffen	MIN	28
8	G.Atkins	CIN	27
8	C.Jordan	NO	27
10	C.Avril	SEA	26
10	T.Johnson	MIN	26
10	V.Miller	DEN	26
10	T.Murphy	WAS	26
14	L.Alexander	BUF	25
14	C.Dunlap	CIN	25
16	N.Fairley	NO	24
16	B.Graham	PHI	24
16	C.Jones	ARI	24
19	C.Campbell	ARI	23
19	W.Mercilus	HOU	23
19	L.Williams	NYJ	23

Full credit for whole and half sacks; includes sacks cancelled by penalty. Does not include strip sacks.

Top 20 Defenders, Hurries

Rk	Defender	Team	Hur
1	O.Vernon	NYG	66
2	B.Graham	PHI	52
3	C.Jordan	NO	50
3	K.Mack	OAK	50
5	C.Dunlap	CIN	48
6	A.Donald	LARM	44
7	E.Griffen	MIN	42
7	M.Ingram	SD	42
9	R.Kerrigan	WAS	40
10	C.Avril	SEA	39
11	V.Beasley	ATL	38
11	B.Irvin	OAK	38
11	V.Miller	DEN	38
14	G.Atkins	CIN	37
15	C.Wake	MIA	36
16	N.Suh	MIA	35
17	J.Clowney	HOU	33
17	J.Hughes	BUF	33
17	D.Morgan	TEN	33
20	C.Campbell	ARI	31
20	D.Fowler	JAC	31
20	W.Mercilus	HOU	31

Top 20 Quarterbacks, QB Hits

Rk	Player	Team	Hits
1	C.Palmer	ARI	87
1	J.Winston	TB	87
3	A.Luck	IND	85
4	R.Wilson	SEA	75
5	M.Ryan	ATL	74
6	C.Wentz	PHI	71
7	S.Bradford	MIN	68
7	K.Cousins	WAS	68
9	P.Rivers	SD	67
10	C.Newton	CAR	62
11	B.Osweiler	HOU	59
12	B.Bortles	JAC	57
12	T.Siemian	DEN	57
14	R.Tannehill	MIA	56
15	J.Flacco	BAL	51
16	M.Stafford	DET	49
17	D.Brees	NO	48
17	R.Fitzpatrick	NYJ	48
19	E.Manning	NYG	47
20	A.Rodgers	GB	45

Top 20 Quarterbacks, QB Knockdowns (Sacks + Hits)

Rk	Player	Team	KD
1	C.Palmer	ARI	127
2	A.Luck	IND	126
3	J.Winston	TB	120
4	R.Wilson	SEA	117
5	M.Ryan	ATL	114
6	S.Bradford	MIN	102
7	P.Rivers	SD	101
7	C.Wentz	PHI	101
9	C.Newton	CAR	99
10	K.Cousins	WAS	90
11	B.Bortles	JAC	89
11	T.Siemian	DEN	89
13	B.Osweiler	HOU	87
14	M.Stafford	DET	86
15	J.Flacco	BAL	84
16	R.Tannehill	MIA	83
16	T.Taylor	BUF	83
18	A.Rodgers	GB	81
19	D.Brees	NO	79
20	A.Dalton	CIN	75

Includes sacks cancelled by penalties
Does not include strip sacks or "self sacks" with no defender listed.

Top 10 Quarterbacks, Knockdowns per Pass

Rk	Player	Team	KD	Pct
1	C.Kessler	CLE	54	23.6%
2	J.Goff	LARM	53	21.4%
3	A.Luck	IND	126	20.1%
4	R.Tannehill	MIA	83	18.9%
5	M.Ryan	ATL	114	18.9%
6	R.Wilson	SEA	117	18.6%
7	J.Winston	TB	120	18.5%
8	C.Palmer	ARI	127	18.4%
9	C.Newton	CAR	99	17.2%
10	S.Bradford	MIN	102	16.5%

Min. 200 passes; includes passes cancelled by penalty

Bottom 10 Quarterbacks in Knockdowns per Pass

Rk	Player	Team	KD	Pct
1	D.Carr	OAK	39	6.3%
2	M.Barkley	CHI	19	7.9%
3	M.Mariota	TEN	46	9.0%
4	B.Roethlisberger	PIT	51	9.2%
5	B.Hoyer	CHI	20	9.3%
6	E.Manning	NYG	69	10.6%
7	D.Brees	NO	79	10.9%
8	J.Flacco	BAL	84	11.4%
9	A.Smith	KC	63	11.7%
10	A.Dalton	CIN	75	11.8%

Min. 200 passes; includes passes cancelled by penalty

Top 10 Most Passes Tipped at Line, Quarterbacks

Rk	Player	Team	Total
1	B.Bortles	JAC	21
2	A.Luck	IND	16
2	T.Siemian	DEN	16
2	C.Wentz	PHI	16
5	J.Winston	TB	15
6	S.Bradford	MIN	14
6	A.Dalton	CIN	14
8	D.Brees	NO	13
8	R.Tannehill	MIA	13
10	R.Fitzpatrick	NYJ	12
10	E.Manning	NYG	12
10	B.Osweiler	HOU	12

Top 10 Tipped at the Line, Defenders

Rk	Player	Team	Total
1	C.Dunlap	CIN	15
2	J.Pierre-Paul	NYG	7
2	A.Robinson	DET	7
4	J.Crick	DEN	6
4	A.Ogletree	LARM	6
4	N.Suh	MIA	6
7	C.Campbell	ARI	5
7	J.Casey	TEN	5
7	A.Donald	LARM	5
7	D.Irving	DAL	5
7	C.Jordan	NO	5

2016 Quarterbacks with and without Pass Pressure

Rank	Player	Team	Plays	Pct Pressure	DVOA with Pressure	Yds with Pressure	DVOA w/o Pressure	Yds w/o Pressure	DVOA Dif	Rank
1	B.Hoyer	CHI	206	18.0%	-34.1%	4.0	42.0%	7.8	-76.0%	6
2	B.Roethlisberger	PIT	534	18.5%	-38.5%	3.8	51.7%	7.9	-90.3%	9
3	D.Carr	OAK	610	18.7%	-45.7%	4.1	55.4%	7.6	-101.1%	15
4	D.Brees	NO	702	19.2%	-55.5%	3.5	50.3%	8.1	-105.8%	19
5	M.Mariota	TEN	506	21.1%	-72.4%	2.1	61.3%	8.5	-133.7%	29
6	C.Keenum	LARM	358	21.2%	-116.6%	1.4	19.5%	7.4	-136.1%	30
7	E.Manning	NYG	632	22.2%	-76.7%	3.2	28.8%	7.2	-105.5%	17
8	A.Smith	KC	541	23.1%	-46.9%	2.8	46.1%	7.6	-93.0%	10
9	B.Bortles	JAC	716	23.5%	-60.6%	3.2	27.2%	6.9	-87.9%	8
10	A.Dalton	CIN	634	23.8%	-77.7%	3.2	54.8%	7.8	-132.6%	28
11	S.Bradford	MIN	601	24.5%	-72.2%	3.4	36.7%	7.1	-108.9%	21
12	M.Barkley	CHI	227	24.7%	-99.1%	4.5	37.2%	8.3	-136.3%	31
13	K.Cousins	WAS	642	24.9%	-54.5%	4.7	65.5%	8.9	-120.0%	25
14	T.Siemian	DEN	540	25.7%	-71.7%	3.3	29.6%	7.3	-101.3%	16
15	T.Brady	NE	461	25.8%	-31.6%	4.9	81.1%	8.8	-112.6%	23
16	C.Wentz	PHI	665	26.3%	-71.0%	3.0	29.1%	6.7	-100.0%	13
17	R.Fitzpatrick	NYJ	449	26.7%	-95.9%	3.1	17.1%	7.5	-113.0%	24
18	R.Tannehill	MIA	434	26.7%	-108.8%	2.6	54.8%	8.2	-163.7%	34
19	J.Flacco	BAL	714	27.5%	-79.8%	3.1	32.6%	7.0	-112.4%	22
20	A.Rodgers	GB	694	28.1%	-3.3%	5.5	54.1%	7.5	-57.3%	1
21	M.Stafford	DET	667	28.5%	-34.1%	4.7	38.6%	7.5	-72.6%	4
22	P.Rivers	SD	629	29.1%	-85.8%	3.6	54.2%	8.1	-140.0%	33
23	C.Newton	CAR	560	29.1%	-94.8%	2.1	42.6%	7.6	-137.4%	32
24	D.Prescott	DAL	513	29.4%	-30.5%	4.2	77.4%	8.8	-107.9%	20
25	B.Osweiler	HOU	558	29.9%	-100.6%	2.1	21.0%	6.8	-121.5%	26
26	M.Ryan	ATL	598	30.3%	-32.9%	4.5	90.5%	10.0	-123.3%	27
27	C.Palmer	ARI	653	30.8%	-72.8%	3.5	32.9%	7.5	-105.7%	18
28	J.Winston	TB	641	31.7%	-24.9%	4.0	45.3%	7.7	-70.2%	3
29	C.Kaepernick	SF	403	34.5%	-57.2%	3.7	38.4%	7.1	-95.6%	12
30	C.Kessler	CLE	223	34.5%	-47.2%	3.3	46.7%	7.2	-93.8%	11
31	A.Luck	IND	635	34.6%	-27.4%	4.9	48.6%	8.2	-76.0%	5
32	R.Wilson	SEA	634	34.9%	-51.6%	4.1	49.1%	8.3	-100.7%	14
33	T.Taylor	BUF	533	35.3%	-21.3%	4.9	46.4%	7.0	-67.7%	2
34	J.Goff	LARM	235	40.4%	-126.5%	2.2	-45.2%	5.0	-81.3%	7

Includes scrambles and Defensive Pass Interference. Does not include aborted snaps.
Minimum: 200 passes.

WR: Highest Slot/Wide Ratio of Targets

Player	Team	Slot	Wide	Slot%
J.Crowder	WAS	94	3	97%
J.Kerley	SF	110	5	96%
W.Snead	NO	92	6	94%
E.Rogers	PIT	59	6	91%
R.Cobb	GB	67	8	89%
A.Hawkins	CLE	47	6	89%
S.Shepard	NYG	94	12	89%
C.Beasley	DAL	86	11	89%
M.Sanu	ATL	70	10	88%
D.Baldwin	SEA	111	16	87%
T.Boyd	CIN	70	11	86%
A.Hurns	JAC	67	11	86%
A.Boldin	DET	81	14	85%
S.Roberts	OAK	63	11	85%
Q.Enunwa	NYJ	80	17	82%
J.Edelman	NE	128	31	81%
J.Landry	MIA	104	27	79%
L.Fitzgerald	ARI	121	32	79%
T.Austin	LARM	77	22	78%
C.Brown	CAR	41	12	77%

Min. 50 passes

WR: Highest Wide/Slot Ratio of Targets

Player	Team	Slot	Wide	Wide%
M.Jones	DET	10	100	91%
V.Cruz	NYG	8	65	89%
Beckham	PHI	10	65	87%
D.Parker	MIA	13	75	85%
R.Anderson	NYJ	14	63	82%
M.Mitchell	NE	11	39	78%
T.Pryor	CLE	33	111	77%
C.Coleman	CLE	17	54	76%
A.J.Green	CIN	25	77	75%
B.Perriman	BAL	17	52	75%
B.Marshall	NYJ	33	97	75%
C.Conley	KC	18	50	74%
M.Goodwin	BUF	18	50	74%
A.Brown	PIT	42	115	73%
P.Garcon	WAS	31	84	73%
A.Jeffery	CHI	26	70	73%
O.Beckham	NYG	48	125	72%
M.Wallace	BAL	33	83	72%
D.Thomas	DEN	43	107	71%
J.J.Nelson	ARI	22	53	71%

Min. 50 passes

Top 10 WR Better Lined Up Wide

Player	Team	Slot	Wide	Slot	Wide	Dif
J.Kearse	SEA	40	50	-56.0%	-8.4%	47.6%
J.Maclin	KC	35	40	-27.4%	18.6%	46.0%
T.Hill	KC	44	35	-17.6%	26.9%	44.4%
D.Adams	GB	33	80	-14.0%	29.5%	43.5%
D.Bryant	DAL	29	69	-19.5%	18.7%	38.2%
N.Agholor	PHI	35	38	-42.0%	-7.7%	34.4%
B.Cooks	NO	79	39	-0.7%	32.1%	32.8%
G.Tate	DET	58	78	-18.1%	11.5%	29.6%
C.Meredith	CHI	67	32	-3.6%	19.9%	23.6%
J.J.Nelson	ARI	22	53	-18.0%	4.5%	22.5%

Min. 20 targets from each position

Top 10 WR Better Lined Up in Slot

Player	Team	Slot	Wide	Slot	Wide	Dif
T.Ginn	CAR	35	59	24.4%	-33.2%	57.6%
P.Garcon	WAS	31	84	54.1%	3.0%	51.1%
T.Benjamin	SD	45	30	32.0%	-15.2%	47.2%
T.Williams	DAL	24	36	59.7%	15.0%	44.7%
R.Matthews	TEN	63	45	31.8%	-11.5%	43.3%
A.Robinson	JAC	51	108	10.9%	-24.8%	35.7%
T.Y.Hilton	IND	119	37	25.5%	-8.5%	34.0%
K.Britt	LARM	38	76	28.7%	-4.9%	33.6%
S.Watkins	BUF	22	30	19.4%	-11.6%	30.9%
L.Fitzgerald	ARI	121	32	-0.1%	-30.7%	30.5%

Min. 20 targets from each position

Top 10 TE Highest Rate of Targets from WR Positions (Slot/Wide)

Player	Team	Tight	Slot	Wide	Back	WR%
J.Cook	GB	10	32	9	1	79%
A.Gates	SD	21	68	6	0	78%
G.Olsen	CAR	27	94	5	5	76%
D.Walker	TEN	27	70	6	1	73%
T.Kelce	KC	32	69	16	0	73%
C.Brate	TB	23	53	6	0	72%
J.Reed	WAS	27	48	13	1	69%
T.Burton	PHI	19	36	4	1	67%
Z.Ertz	PHI	37	66	4	0	65%
E.Ebron	DET	31	46	10	0	64%

Min. 25 passes

Top 10 TE Lowest Rate of Targets from WR Positions (Slot/Wide)

Player	Team	Tight	Slot	Wide	Back	WR%
D.Sims	MIA	32	2	1	0	9%
V.Green	DEN	33	4	0	0	11%
V.McDonald	SF	39	6	0	0	13%
W.Tye	NYG	57	11	0	2	16%
J.Gresham	ARI	52	10	0	0	16%
G.Celek	SF	41	8	1	0	18%
M.Lewis	JAC	24	5	1	0	20%
T.Higbee	LARM	23	4	2	0	21%
C.J.Fiedorowicz	HOU	67	20	1	1	24%
A.Hooper	ATL	20	7	1	0	29%

Min. 25 passes

Top 10 RB Highest Rate of Targets from WR Positions (Slot/Wide)

Player	Team	Back	Slot	Wide	Tight	WR%
T.Cadet	NO	30	18	6	0	44%
D.Johnson	ARI	76	28	18	0	38%
J.Richard	OAK	26	8	6	0	35%
C.Sims	TB	21	3	8	0	34%
T.Coleman	ATL	29	7	4	0	28%
D.Freeman	ATL	50	9	7	0	24%
C.Michael	2TM	22	0	7	0	24%
J.White	NE	63	9	11	2	24%
M.Forte	NYJ	33	8	2	0	23%
T.Montgomery	GB	44	11	1	0	21%

Min. 25 passes

Top 10 Teams, Pct Passes Dropped

Rk	Team	Passes	Drops	Pct
1	ATL	511	16	3.1%
2	CIN	510	18	3.5%
3	TEN	464	20	4.3%
4	MIN	556	24	4.3%
5	MIA	442	20	4.5%
6	DAL	460	21	4.6%
7	WAS	562	26	4.6%
8	TB	544	26	4.8%
9	DEN	516	25	4.8%
10	NO	633	31	4.9%

Bottom 10 Teams, Pct Passes Dropped

Rk	Team	Passes	Drops	Pct
23	OAK	566	40	7.1%
24	SD	530	38	7.2%
25	IND	543	39	7.2%
26	CAR	517	38	7.4%
27	CLE	514	38	7.4%
28	PHI	564	42	7.4%
29	KC	519	39	7.5%
30	LARM	500	38	7.6%
31	SF	461	36	7.8%
32	NYJ	518	43	8.3%

Top 20 Players, Passes Dropped

Rk	Player	Team	Total
1	M.Crabtree	OAK	11
2	T.Austin	LARM	10
2	O.Beckham	NYG	10
2	J.Edelman	NE	10
2	T.Y.Hilton	IND	10
2	B.Marshall	NYJ	10
2	J.Matthews	PHI	10
2	A.Robinson	JAC	10
2	D.Thomas	DEN	10
10	D.Adams	GB	9
10	M.Jones	DET	9
10	J.Nelson	GB	9
10	S.Roberts	OAK	9
10	G.Tate	DET	9
10	T.Williams	SD	9
16	L.Bell	PIT	8
16	K.Benjamin	CAR	8
16	Q.Enunwa	NYJ	8
16	M.Evans	TB	8
16	A.Gates	SD	8
16	J.Howard	CHI	8
16	T.Kelce	KC	8
16	L.Kendricks	LARM	8
16	D.Pitta	BAL	8
16	M.Wallace	BAL	8

Top 20 Players, Pct. Passes Dropped

Rk	Player	Team	Drops	Passes	Pct
1	C.Spiller	2TM	5	13	38.5%
2	R.Kelley	WAS	5	18	27.8%
3	D.Harris	KC	6	31	19.4%
4	J.Stewart	CAR	4	21	19.0%
5	B.Miller	HOU	5	28	17.9%
6	C.Anderson	DEN	4	24	16.7%
7	J.Howard	CHI	8	50	16.0%
8	T.Higbee	LARM	4	29	13.8%
9	J.Bellamy	CHI	5	38	13.2%
10	J.Richard	OAK	5	39	12.8%
11	S.Coates	PIT	6	49	12.2%
12	F.Whittaker	CAR	4	33	12.1%
13	G.Celek	SF	6	50	12.0%
14	S.Roberts	OAK	9	77	11.7%
15	J.Gresham	ARI	7	61	11.5%
16	R.Turbin	IND	4	35	11.4%
17	I.Crowell	CLE	6	53	11.3%
18	R.Louis	CLE	4	36	11.1%
19	S.Draughn	SF	4	39	10.3%
20	T.Smith	SF	5	49	10.2%

Min. four drops

Top 20 Yards Lost to Drops by Quarterbacks

Rk	Player	Team	Drops	Yds
1	A.Rodgers	GB	34	471
2	C.Newton	CAR	36	389
3	D.Carr	OAK	39	370
4	J.Flacco	BAL	41	349
5	B.Osweiler	HOU	32	340
6	M.Stafford	DET	39	325
7	R.Fitzpatrick	NYJ	29	318
8	C.Palmer	ARI	30	311
9	P.Rivers	SD	38	308
10	E.Manning	NYG	40	306
11	J.Winston	TB	25	284
12	B.Bortles	JAC	34	279
13	C.Wentz	PHI	42	276
14	T.Siemian	DEN	23	235
15	A.Luck	IND	36	231
16	D.Brees	NO	31	229
17	M.Barkley	CHI	17	210
18	A.Smith	KC	37	206
19	D.Prescott	DAL	20	197
20	R.Tannehill	MIA	19	196

Based on yardage in the air, no possible YAC included.

Top 20 Intended Receivers on Interceptions

Rk	Player	Team	Total
1	D.Hopkins	HOU	9
1	T.Williams	SD	9
3	M.Evans	TB	8
3	B.Marshall	NYJ	8
5	A.Jeffery	CHI	7
5	A.Robinson	JAC	7
7	R.Anderson	NYJ	6
7	K.Stills	MIA	6
9	T.Austin	LARM	5
9	T.Ginn	CAR	5
9	T.Y.Hilton	IND	5
9	M.Lee	JAC	5
9	D.Parker	MIA	5
9	T.Pryor	CLE	5
9	E.Sanders	DEN	5
9	S.Shepard	NYG	5
17	17 tied with		4

Top 10 Plus/Minus for Running Backs

Rk	Player	Team	Pass	+/-
1	L.McCoy	BUF	58	+4.9
2	D.Freeman	ATL	65	+4.6
3	T.Montgomery	GB	56	+4.1
4	M.Ingram	NO	58	+3.9
5	T.Hightower	NO	26	+3.4
6	D.Murray	TEN	67	+2.6
7	T.Cadet	NO	54	+2.5
8	D.Williams	MIA	31	+2.2
9	C.Thompson	WAS	62	+2.1
10	K.Juszczyk	BAL	49	+1.8

Min. 25 passes; plus/minus adjusted for passes tipped/thrown away.

Bottom 10 Plus/Minus for Running Backs

Rk	Player	Team	Pass	+/-
1	J.Howard	CHI	50	-8.9
2	J.White	NE	86	-4.8
3	D.Williams	PIT	27	-4.4
4	K.Dixon	BAL	41	-3.3
5	M.Gordon	SD	57	-2.5
6	T.Gurley	LARM	58	-2.3
7	R.Turbin	IND	35	-1.4
8	J.Langford	CHI	27	-1.3
9	J.Starks	GB	26	-1.2
10	R.Jennings	NYG	43	-1.1

Min. 25 passes; plus/minus adjusted for passes tipped/thrown away.

Top 10 Plus/Minus for Wide Receivers

Rk	Player	Team	Pass	+/-
1	D.Baldwin	SEA	128	+12.9
2	A.Thielen	MIN	92	+12.2
3	M.Thomas	NO	121	+11.4
4	S.Diggs	MIN	111	+11.3
5	C.Beasley	DAL	99	+9.5
6	P.Garcon	WAS	114	+8.8
7	B.Cooks	NO	118	+8.7
8	A.Brown	PIT	154	+8.1
9	J.Jones	ATL	129	+7.9
10	J.Nelson	GB	152	+7.6

Min. 50 passes; plus/minus adjusted for passes tipped/thrown away.

Bottom 10 Plus/Minus for Wide Receivers

Rk	Player	Team	Pass	+/-
1	B.Marshall	NYJ	127	-14.0
2	T.Austin	LARM	106	-12.5
3	S.Roberts	OAK	77	-12.3
4	A.Robinson	JAC	151	-10.4
5	J.Kerley	SF	115	-9.0
6	Q.Enunwa	NYJ	105	-9.0
7	D.Funchess	CAR	58	-8.9
8	D.Green-Beckham	PHI	74	-8.6
9	A.Hurns	JAC	76	-7.8
10	T.Smith	SF	49	-7.4

Min. 50 passes; plus/minus adjusted for passes tipped/thrown away.

Top 10 Plus/Minus for Tight Ends

Rk	Player	Team	Pass	+/-
1	Z.Ertz	PHI	106	+11.4
2	J.Reed	WAS	89	+6.9
3	C.Brate	TB	81	+6.9
4	J.Doyle	IND	75	+6.2
5	T.Kelce	KC	117	+4.8
6	J.Witten	DAL	95	+4.7
7	V.Davis	WAS	59	+4.7
8	R.Gronkowski	NE	38	+4.5
9	M.Bennett	NE	73	+3.9
10	J.Graham	SEA	96	+3.7

Min. 25 passes; plus/minus adjusted for passes tipped/thrown away.

Bottom 10 Plus/Minus for Tight Ends

Rk	Player	Team	Pass	+/-
1	T.Higbee	LARM	29	-7.2
2	L.Kendricks	LARM	87	-6.4
3	A.Gates	SD	93	-5.2
4	V.McDonald	SF	45	-4.6
5	D.Harris	KC	31	-4.0
6	J.James	PIT	60	-3.9
7	J.Thomas	JAC	51	-3.5
8	C.J.Fiedorowicz	HOU	89	-2.8
9	C.Clay	BUF	87	-2.3
10	T.Burton	PHI	60	-2.2

Min. 25 passes; plus/minus adjusted for passes tipped/thrown away.

Top 10 Quarterbacks, Yards Gained on Defensive Pass Interference

Rk	Player	Team	Pen	Yds
1	B.Bortles	JAC	18	313
2	D.Carr	OAK	19	287
3	A.Rodgers	GB	7	239
4	A.Luck	IND	10	230
5	K.Cousins	WAS	7	215
6	M.Ryan	ATL	10	171
7	R.Wilson	SEA	8	170
8	M.Stafford	DET	13	162
9	J.Winston	TB	11	155
10	M.Mariota	TEN	11	154

Top 10 Receivers, Yards Gained on Defensive Pass Interference

Rk	Player	Team	Pen	Yds
1	D.Jackson	WAS	5	169
2	A.Robinson	JAC	9	166
3	J.Jones	ATL	6	132
4	M.Crabtree	OAK	6	124
5	M.Jones	DET	7	111
6	M.Lee	JAC	4	104
7	D.Thomas	DEN	7	101
8	P.Dorsett	IND	3	100
9	A.Cooper	OAK	7	99
10	D.Hopkins	HOU	8	87

Top 10 Defenders, Yards Allowed on Defensive Pass Interference

Rk	Player	Team	Pen	Yds
1	N.Lawson	DET	4	124
2	J.McCourty	TEN	3	105
3	T.Young	BAL	5	104
4	K.Jackson	HOU	4	101
5	N.Carroll	PHI	7	91
6	R.Alford	ATL	6	85
7	D.J.Hayden	OAK	6	82
8	R.Cockrell	PIT	4	81
9	S.Moore	NO	5	80
10	X.Rhodes	MIN	3	78

Top 20 First Downs/Touchdowns Allowed, Coverage

Rk	Player	Team	Yards	Rk	Player	Team	Yards
1	V.Hargreaves	TB	43	11	N.Carroll	PHI	33
2	B.Carr	DAL	39	11	M.Cooper	ARI	33
3	R.Alford	ATL	36	11	J.Mills	PHI	33
3	D.Shead	SEA	36	11	Q.Rollins	GB	33
5	C.Hayward	SD	35	11	L.Ryan	NE	33
5	J.McCourty	TEN	35	16	P.Amukamara	JAC	32
5	S.Nelson	KC	35	17	T.Brock	SF	31
8	P.Cox	TEN	34	17	L.McKelvin	PHI	31
8	J.Norman	WAS	34	17	S.Moore	NO	31
8	T.Porter	CHI	34	17	J.Ramsey	JAC	31

Includes Defensive Pass Interference.

Top 20 Passing Yards Allowed, Coverage

Rk	Player	Team	Yards	Rk	Player	Team	Yards
1	V.Hargreaves	TB	892	11	M.Cooper	ARI	637
2	L.McKelvin	PHI	802	12	M.Butler	NE	636
3	J.McCourty	TEN	765	13	N.Carroll	PHI	624
4	B.Carr	DAL	703	14	R.Darby	BUF	623
5	T.Porter	CHI	698	15	S.Smith	OAK	612
6	D.Amerson	OAK	692	16	P.Cox	TEN	611
7	D.Shead	SEA	688	17	S.Nelson	KC	608
8	A.Burns	PIT	654	18	Q.Rollins	GB	606
9	R.Sherman	SEA	650	19	P.Gaines	KC	602
10	R.Alford	ATL	638	20	J.Mills	PHI	600

Includes Defensive Pass Interference.

Fewest Yards After Catch Allowed, Coverage by Cornerbacks

Rk	Player	Team	YAC
1	T.Newman	MIN	0.7
2	B.Callahan	CHI	1.6
3	N.Lawson	DET	1.8
4	J.Bradberry	CAR	1.8
5	P.Amukamara	JAC	1.8
6	W.Gay	PIT	2.1
7	C.Harris	DEN	2.1
8	T.Brock	SF	2.2
9	B.Skrine	NYJ	2.2
10	J.Mills	PHI	2.3
11	D.Trufant	ATL	2.4
12	L.Ryan	NE	2.4
13	R.Cockrell	PIT	2.4
14	A.Jones	CIN	2.5
15	T.Waynes	MIN	2.5
16	D.Rodgers-Cromartie	NYG	2.6
17	C.LeBlanc	CHI	2.7
18	R.Alford	ATL	2.7
19	J.Smith	BAL	2.8
20	J.Ramsey	JAC	2.8

Min. 50 passes or 8 games started.

Most Yards After Catch Allowed, Coverage by Cornerbacks

Rk	Player	Team	YAC
1	R.Sherman	SEA	6.4
2	P.Gaines	KC	6.2
3	S.Smith	OAK	6.1
4	L.McKelvin	PHI	6.1
5	A.Burns	PIT	5.5
6	V.Hargreaves	TB	5.0
7	J.Haden	CLE	5.0
8	J.Shaw	CIN	4.9
9	A.J.Bouye	HOU	4.7
10	T.Porter	CHI	4.6
11	J.Ward	SF	4.6
12	R.Melvin	IND	4.5
13	B.Poole	ATL	4.4
14	P.Cox	TEN	4.3
15	P.Peterson	ARI	4.3
16	T.Young	BAL	4.3
17	R.Darby	BUF	4.0
17	B.McCain	TEN	4.0
19	M.Cooper	ARI	3.9
20	Q.Rollins	GB	3.9

Min. 50 passes or 8 games started.

Most Dropped Interceptions, 2014-2016

Rk	Player	Team	2016	2015	2014	Total
1	M.Jenkins	PHI	1	2	3	6
2	P.Cox	SF/TEN	0	1	4	5
3	K.Alexander	TB	1	3	0	4
3	A.Hal	HOU	1	2	1	4
3	J.Jenkins	STL/NYG	3	0	1	4
3	D.Kirkpatrick	CIN	1	2	1	4
3	K.Lewis	HOU/BAL	0	1	3	4
3	J.Norman	CAR/WAS	3	1	0	4
3	R.Parker	KC	2	0	2	4
3	D.Rodgers-Cromartie	NYG	0	4	0	4
3	J.Smith	BAL	1	2	1	4
3	E.Weddle	SD/BAL	3	1	0	4
3	K.Wright	SEA	0	2	2	4

Fewest Avg Yards on Run Tackle, Defensive Line or Edge Rusher

Rk	Player	Team	Tkl	Avg
1	M.Bennett	SEA	28	0.5
2	A.Donald	LARM	36	0.7
3	C.Jordan	NO	46	0.8
4	B.Graham	PHI	49	0.8
5	K.Short	CAR	45	0.9
6	B.Allen	PHI	25	1.0
7	J.Bosa	SD	28	1.1
8	J.Mauro	ARI	28	1.1
9	J.Clowney	HOU	41	1.1
10	M.Pierce	BAL	33	1.3
11	S.Tuitt	PIT	29	1.3
12	L.Williams	NYJ	57	1.4
13	W.Hayes	LARM	34	1.4
14	A.Jones	JAC	27	1.4
15	M.Daniels	GB	26	1.4
16	F.Cox	PHI	33	1.5
17	L.Guion	GB	28	1.6
18	P.Sims	CIN	34	1.6
19	C.Liuget	SD	31	1.6
20	D.Peko	CIN	34	1.7

Min. 25 run tackles

Fewest Avg Yards on Run Tackle, LB

Rk	Player	Team	Tkl	Avg
1	D.Lee	NYJ	33	2.3
2	N.Bowman	SF	26	2.4
3	S.Thompson	CAR	28	2.4
4	L.David	TB	41	2.5
5	D.Smith	TB	25	2.6
6	N.Bellore	SF	55	2.6
7	N.Bradham	PHI	52	2.6
8	D.Kennard	NYG	42	2.6
9	W.Woodyard	TEN	35	2.7
10	C.Greenway	MIN	28	2.7
10	E.Roberts	NE	28	2.7
10	R.Shazier	PIT	42	2.7
13	K.Toomer	SD	48	2.8
14	L.Kuechly	CAR	54	2.9
15	D.Hightower	NE	35	2.9
16	S.Moore	ARI	40	3.0
17	D.Campbell	ATL	27	3.0
18	N.Kwiatkoski	CHI	29	3.0
19	J.Ryan	GB	59	3.0
20	K.Van Noy	NE	34	3.0

Min. 25 run tackles

Fewest Avg Yards on Run Tackle, DB

Rk	Player	Team	Tkl	Avg
1	K.Vaccaro	NO	28	3.6
2	K.Chancellor	SEA	48	3.7
3	T.Jefferson	ARI	54	4.1
4	L.Collins	NYG	59	4.3
5	J.Cyprien	JAC	72	4.3
6	K.Byard	TEN	25	4.4
7	L.Ryan	NE	24	4.4
8	T.Wilson	DET	42	4.5
9	M.Jenkins	PHI	31	4.7
10	C.Pryor	NYJ	31	4.7
11	D.Swearinger	ARI	32	4.9
12	K.Neal	ATL	35	5.0
13	L.Joyner	LARM	25	5.1
14	H.Smith	MIN	50	5.1
15	C.Geathers	IND	28	5.2
16	J.Addae	SD	27	5.3
17	M.Burnett	GB	36	5.5
18	M.Griffin	CAR	23	5.6
19	E.Berry	KC	37	5.8
20	D.Worley	CAR	25	5.8

Min. 20 run tackles

Top 20 Offensive Tackles, Blown Blocks

Rk	Player	Pos	Team	Sacks	All Pass	All Run	Total
1	T.Clemmings	LT	MIN	9.5	20	12	32
2	M.Schwartz	RT	KC	8.0	23	7	30
3	D.Stephenson	RT	DEN	3.0	20	8	28
4	C.Clark	RT	HOU	5.5	22	5	27
4	M.Remmers	LT/RT	CAR	8.5	20	7	27
6	B.Bulaga	RT	GB	1.5	16	10	26
6	G.Fant	LT	SEA	6.0	19	7	26
6	J.James	RT	MIA	5.3	18	8	26
6	D.Smith	LT	TB	3.0	15	11	26
10	D.Free	RT	DAL	5.5	14	11	25
10	R.Schraeder	RT	ATL	5.0	18	7	25
12	T.Brown	RT	SF	4.5	12	12	24
12	R.Havenstein	RT	LARM	5.8	20	4	24
12	J.Matthews	LT	ATL	5.5	17	7	24
15	E.Flowers	LT	NYG	4.0	19	4	23
15	A.Howard	RT	OAK	5.5	18	5	23
17	T.Decker	LT	DET	7.5	14	8	22
17	A.Pasztor	RT	CLE	8.0	16	6	22
17	J.Peters	LT	PHI	4.0	15	7	22
20	J.Barksdale	RT	SD	7.0	14	7	21
20	K.Beachum	LT	JAC	6.0	14	7	21
20	M.Cannon	RT	NE	2.5	14	7	21
20	C.Ogbuehi	RT	CIN	4.5	14	7	21

Top 20 Offensive Tackles in Snaps per Blown Block

Rk	Player	Pos	Team	Sacks	All Pass	All Run	Total	Snaps	Snaps per BB
1	J.Conklin	RT	TEN	1.0	3	4	7	1060	151.4
2	Z.Strief	RT	NO	2.5	8	0	8	1124	140.5
3	C.Glenn	LT	BUF	2.0	5	0	5	656	131.2
4	T.Williams	LT	WAS	1.0	2	5	7	796	113.7
5	A.Whitworth	LT	CIN	2.5	6	4	10	1065	106.5
6	M.Gilbert	RT	PIT	3.0	3	5	8	847	105.9
7	L.Johnson	RT	PHI	0.5	3	1	4	407	101.8
8	M.Newhouse	RT	NYG	2.0	3	2	5	461	92.2
9	J.Thomas	LT	CLE	3.0	9	3	12	1030	85.8
10	A.Villanueva	LT	PIT	4.0	10	3	13	1083	83.3
11	J.Veldheer	LT	ARI	1.0	5	2	7	577	82.4
12	D.Bakhtiari	LT	GB	4.8	9	4	13	1057	81.3
13	D.Penn	LT	OAK	2.5	7	8	15	1111	74.1
14	T.Lewan	LT	TEN	2.3	7	7	14	989	70.6
15	T.Smith	LT	DAL	4.5	8	4	12	837	69.8
16	R.Wagner	RT	BAL	3.5	10	4	14	924	66.0
17	D.Brown	LT	HOU	0.0	6	6	12	778	64.8
18	M.Moses	RT	WAS	4.5	14	2	16	1020	63.8
19	J.Haeg	RT	IND	4.5	14	1	15	953	63.5
20	J.Reitz	RT	IND	3.0	7	0	7	423	60.4

Minimum: 400 snaps

Top 20 Interior Linemen, Blown Blocks

Rk	Player	Pos	Team	Sacks	All Pass	All Run	Total
1	R.Saffold	LG	LARM	2.5	14	10	24
2	C.Chester	RG	ATL	6.0	14	9	23
2	B.Fusco	RG	MIN	3.5	13	10	23
2	G.Ifedi	RG	SEA	4.5	18	5	23
2	K.Pamphile	LG	TB	4.0	15	8	23
2	J.Thuney	LG	NE	3.0	15	8	23
7	J.Garnett	RG	SF	5.0	15	7	22
7	M.Glowinski	LG	SEA	2.0	12	10	22
9	Z.Beadles	C/LG	SF	1.5	14	7	21
9	C.Boling	LG	CIN	4.5	8	13	21
9	G.Glasgow	C/LG	DET	2.0	14	7	21
9	A.Marpet	RG	TB	2.0	10	11	21
9	S.Mason	RG	NE	4.5	15	6	21
14	M.Iupati	LG	ARI	2.5	12	8	20
15	T.Barnes	C	LARM	5.3	11	8	19
15	T.Turner	RG	CAR	2.5	14	5	19
17	J.Allen	RG	HOU	4.0	10	8	18
17	O.Franklin	LG	SD	2.5	13	5	18
17	M.Garcia	LG	DEN	4.0	9	9	18
17	J.Hawley	C	TB	2.5	9	9	18
17	J.Kelce	C	PHI	0.0	6	12	18
17	A.Levitre	LG	ATL	3.0	10	8	18
17	A.Norwell	LG	CAR	4.0	13	5	18

Top 20 Interior Linemen in Snaps per Blown Block

Rk	Player	Pos	Team	Sacks	All Pass	All Run	Total	Snaps	Snaps per BB
1	Z.Martin	RG	DAL	1.5	2	0	2	1060	530.0
2	R.Groy	C	BUF	0.0	1	1	2	541	270.5
3	T.Frederick	C	DAL	0.0	1	5	6	1060	176.7
4	R.Kalil	C	CAR	1.0	2	1	3	506	168.7
5	L.Tunsil	LG	MIA	0.5	3	2	5	802	160.4
6	S.Wisniewski	C/G	PHI	0.0	2	2	4	607	151.8
7	B.Jones	C	TEN	1.8	5	2	7	1060	151.4
8	J.Miller	RG	BUF	2.0	5	2	7	1047	149.6
9	N.Mangold	C	NYJ	0.0	1	2	3	433	144.3
10	J.Evans	RG	NO	2.5	4	4	8	1137	142.1
11	R.Hudson	C	OAK	0.0	3	5	8	1119	139.9
12	G.Jackson	RG	OAK	0.5	5	3	8	1118	139.8
13	M.Unger	C	NO	1.0	5	3	8	1090	136.3
14	M.Paradis	C	DEN	1.0	2	6	8	1080	135.0
15	M.Yanda	RG	BAL	0.5	4	3	7	898	128.3
16	T.Swanson	C	DET	0.0	2	4	6	766	127.7
17	A.Shipley	C	ARI	0.5	5	4	9	1148	127.6
18	R.Kelly	C	IND	1.5	7	1	8	1020	127.5
19	Tardif	RG	KC	0.0	3	4	7	892	127.4
20	B.Brooks	RG	PHI	1.0	6	2	8	991	123.9

Minimum: 400 snaps

Top 20 Non-Offensive Linemen, Blown Blocks

Rk	Player	Pos	Team	Sacks	All Pass	All Run	Total
1	L.Kendricks	TE	LARM	2.0	6	10	16
2	L.Stocker	TE	TB	1.0	4	7	11
3	L.Toilolo	TE	ATL	1.5	3	7	10
4	V.Davis	TE	WAS	1.0	1	8	9
4	R.Rodgers	TE	GB	0.0	1	8	9
4	J.Witten	TE	DAL	1.0	4	5	9
7	G.Celek	TE	SF	1.0	2	6	8
8	B.Celek	TE	PHI	0.0	2	5	7
8	C.Clay	TE	BUF	0.5	2	5	7
8	E.Dickson	TE	CAR	0.5	5	2	7
8	J.Doyle	TE	IND	1.5	3	4	7
8	J.Graham	TE	SEA	0.0	0	7	7
8	D.Sims	TE	MIA	0.5	3	4	7
8	C.Walford	TE	OAK	0.0	0	7	7
15	D.Allen	TE	IND	2.5	5	1	6
15	G.Barnidge	TE	CLE	1.5	3	3	6
15	Z.Ertz	TE	PHI	0.0	0	6	6
15	J.Felton	FB	BUF	0.0	1	5	6
15	C.J.Fiedorowicz	TE	HOU	0.0	1	5	6
15	W.Tye	TE	NYG	0.0	0	6	6
15	M.Mulligan	TE	DET	0.0	1	5	4

Most Penalties, Offense

Rk	Player	Team	Pen	Yds
1	G.Robinson	LARM	15	90
1	M.Remmers	CAR	15	85
3	T.Lewan	TEN	14	123
3	C.Clark	HOU	14	50
5	E.Flowers	NYG	13	97
5	D.DeCastro	PIT	13	77
5	J.Peters	PHI	13	55
8	D.Smith	TB	12	100
8	D.Dotson	TB	12	95
8	J.Parnell	JAC	12	85
11	J.James	MIA	11	81
11	T.Brown	SF	11	80
11	R.Okung	DEN	11	62
14	V.Alexander	OAK	10	83
14	D.Brees	NO	10	78
14	J.Thuney	NE	10	75
14	K.Beachum	JAC	10	75
14	T.Clemmings	MIN	10	75
14	D.Penn	OAK	10	72
14	A.Marpet	TB	10	62
14	T.Turner	CAR	10	60
14	R.Schraeder	ATL	10	60
14	E.Fisher	KC	10	52

Includes declined and offsetting, but not special teams or penalties on turnover returns.

Most False Starts, Offense

Rk	Player	Team	Pen
1	D.Free	DAL	8
2	L.Johnson	PHI	7
2	M.Remmers	CAR	7
4	J.Barksdale	SD	6
5	D.Ferguson	NYJ	5
5	C.Hairston	SD	5
5	B.Jones	HOU	5
5	B.Marshall	NYJ	5
5	J.Peters	PHI	5
5	A.Smith	CIN	5
5	L.Smith	OAK	5
5	Z.Strief	NO	5
5	J.Thomas	CLE	5
5	J.Witten	DAL	5
15	15 tied with		4

Most Penalties, Defense

Rk	Player	Team	Pen	Yds	Rk	Player	Team	Pen	Yds
1	J.Norman	WAS	15	79	8	N.Carroll	PHI	9	93
2	R.Alford	ATL	12	130	8	A.J.Bouye	HOU	9	92
3	X.Rhodes	MIN	11	113	8	B.Skrine	NYJ	9	86
4	D.J.Hayden	OAK	10	102	8	D.Kirkpatrick	CIN	9	82
4	B.Maxwell	MIA	10	99	8	J.Hughes	BUF	9	80
4	M.Smith	OAK	10	77	8	V.Davis	IND	9	69
4	W.Young	CHI	10	58	8	J.Phillips	MIA	9	50
8	A.Burns	PIT	9	107	8	J.Clowney	HOU	9	20
8	A.Donald	LARM	9	97	18	15 tied with		8	

Includes declined and offsetting, but not special teams or penalties on turnover returns.

Top 10 Kickers, Gross Kickoff Value over Average

Rk	Player	Team	Kick Pts+	Net Pts+	Kicks
1	S.Hauschka	SEA	+3.2	+5.6	84
2	D.Hopkins	WAS	+3.2	-1.5	89
3	M.Crosby	GB	+3.0	-8.7	86
4	C.Sturgis	PHI	+2.8	+14.3	81
5	J.Tucker	BAL	+2.7	+6.8	79
6	A.Franks	MIA	+2.5	+6.0	74
7	C.Boswell	PIT	+2.2	-1.4	77
8	J.Myers	JAC	+2.0	+0.1	70
9	R.Gould	NYG	+2.0	-1.5	42
10	G.Gano	CAR	+1.7	+4.7	84

Min. 20 kickoffs; squibs and onside not included

Bottom 10 Kickers, Gross Kickoff Value over Average

Rk	Player	Team	Kick Pts+	Net Pts+	Kicks
1	N.Novak	HOU	-5.9	-13.1	68
2	B.McManus	DEN	-4.9	-1.7	75
3	W.Lutz	NO	-4.7	-5.1	88
4	P.Dawson	SF	-4.1	-2.9	38
5	M.Bosher	ATL	-3.8	-2.9	105
5	C.Catanzaro	ARI	-2.9	-4.9	80
7	P.McAfee	IND	-2.8	+1.2	83
8	S.Martin	DET	-2.6	-2.4	73
8	B.Walsh	MIN	-2.4	-8.8	40
10	S.Janikowski	OAK	-1.0	+5.3	86

Min. 20 kickoffs; squibs and onside not included

Top 10 Punters, Gross Punt Value over Average

Rk	Player	Team	Punt Pts+	Net Pts+	Punts
1	J.Hekker	LARM	+18.8	+29.2	98
2	M.King	OAK	+8.2	-5.5	81
3	S.Martin	DET	+7.6	+10.7	62
4	B.Wing	NYG	+7.4	+10.6	93
5	B.Anger	TB	+6.1	+13.6	70
6	S.Koch	BAL	+5.8	-1.0	80
7	M.Bosher	ATL	+4.7	+2.5	44
8	T.Morstead	NO	+3.7	+0.8	57
9	P.O'Donnell	CHI	+2.7	-1.4	68
10	S.Lechler	HOU	+2.4	-13.0	72

Min. 20 punts

Bottom 10 Punters, Gross Punt Value over Average

Rk	Player	Team	Punt Pts+	Net Pts+	Punts
1	L.Edwards	NYJ	-12.6	-21.1	77
2	C.Schmidt	BUF	-9.2	-2.9	75
3	R.Quigley	ARI	-8.1	-2.5	35
4	J.Ryan	SEA	-6.7	-5.6	72
5	D.Butler	ARI	-6.3	-8.9	32
6	M.Darr	MIA	-5.2	-3.5	91
7	B.Pinion	SF	-2.7	+5.1	100
8	J.Schum	GB	-2.6	+0.1	56
9	J.Locke	MIN	-2.2	+5.9	74
10	R.Dixon	DEN	-1.9	+3.3	89

Min. 20 punts

Top 10 Kick Returners, Value over Average

Rk	Player	Team	Pts+	Returns
1	C.Patterson	MIN	+10.4	25
2	M.Lee	JAC	+10.3	18
3	A.Erickson	CIN	+10.2	29
4	J.Todman	IND	+9.2	16
5	K.Drake	MIA	+8.0	13
6	T.Hill	KC	+6.1	14
6	W.Smallwood	PHI	+5.8	9
8	B.Cunningham	LARM	+4.8	22
8	K.Barner	PHI	+4.3	9
10	J.Huff	2TM	+3.2	13

Min. eight returns

Bottom 10 Kick Returners, Value over Average

Rk	Player	Team	Pts+	Returns
1	T.Ervin	HOU	-4.4	13
2	T.Cadet	NO	-3.5	10
3	J.Marshall	NYJ	-3.4	13
4	R.Smith	TB	-3.4	10
5	A.Ellington	ARI	-3.2	10
6	G.Atkinson	CLE	-2.9	8
7	T.Jones	OAK	-2.8	8
8	M.Murphy	NO	-2.4	7
9	K.Davis	2TM	-2.4	10
10	R.Louis	CLE	-2.3	9

Min. eight returns

Top 10 Punt Returners, Value over Average

Rk	Player	Team	Pts+	Returns
1	T.Hill	KC	+20.6	39
2	M.Sherels	MIN	+12.3	20
3	J.Crowder	WAS	+10.3	27
4	A.Roberts	DET	+8.5	20
5	B.Tate	BUF	+7.7	26
6	D.Sproles	PHI	+4.6	17
7	W.Fuller	HOU	+4.4	11
8	E.Weems	ATL	+3.8	24
9	J.Richard	OAK	+3.4	34
10	T.Ervin	HOU	+3.2	27

Min. eight returns

Bottom 10 Punt Returners, Value over Average

Rk	Player	Team	Pts+	Returns
1	C.Jones	NE	-6.5	11
2	R.Greene	JAC	-6.4	21
3	D.Harris	NYG	-6.3	29
4	J.Norwood	DEN	-6.1	25
5	D.Hester	BAL	-5.0	25
6	A.Jones	CIN	-4.4	10
7	A.Erickson	CIN	-4.4	28
7	T.Ginn	CAR	-4.3	29
9	J.Marshall	NYJ	-4.2	18
10	B.Walters	JAC	-4.0	17

Min. eight returns

Top 20 Special Teams Plays

Rk	Player	Team	Plays	Rk	Player	Team	Plays
1	N.Ebner	NE	19	7	S.McManis	CHI	12
2	M.Hull	MIA	18	7	J.Schobert	CLE	12
2	M.Thomas	MIA	18	7	J.Tartt	SF	12
4	B.Trawick	OAK	15	16	D.Alexander	KC	11
4	E.Weems	ATL	15	16	J.Holton	OAK	11
6	J.Martin	NYJ	14	16	D.Mayo	CAR	11
7	L.Alexander	BUF	12	16	J.Meeks	BUF	11
7	J.Bethel	ARI	12	16	R.Nelson	HOU	11
7	A.Burbridge	SF	12	16	P.Onwuasor	BAL	11
7	R.Burkhead	CIN	12	16	C.Reynolds	LARM	11
7	D.Jones	MUL	12	16	D.Watson	DEN	11
7	T.Matakevich	PIT	12	20	7 tied with		11

Plays = tackles + assists; does not include onside or end-half squib kicks.

Top 10 Offenses, 3-and-out per drive

Rk	Team	Pct
1	ATL	14.5%
2	WAS	15.2%
3	NO	15.8%
4	CAR	17.0%
5	SEA	18.4%
6	SD	18.6%
7	BAL	19.0%
8	DAL	19.2%
9	TB	19.4%
10	KC	19.9%

Top 10 Defenses, 3-and-out per drive

Rk	Team	Pct
1	HOU	29.0%
2	JAC	27.5%
3	LARM	26.8%
4	DEN	26.7%
5	CAR	25.8%
6	CHI	25.8%
7	NE	24.9%
8	NYG	24.7%
9	ARI	24.6%
10	BUF	24.6%

Top 10 Offenses, Yards per drive

Rk	Team	Yds/Dr
1	ATL	40.53
2	WAS	39.81
3	NO	38.27
4	GB	36.73
5	DET	35.70
6	DAL	35.63
7	NE	35.48
8	IND	35.11
9	CIN	33.97
10	PIT	33.80

Top 10 Defenses, Yards per drive

Rk	Team	Yds/Dr
1	ARI	25.25
2	HOU	26.72
3	DEN	27.00
4	BAL	27.62
5	NYG	27.85
6	SEA	28.58
7	MIN	28.71
8	NE	28.82
9	JAC	29.05
10	SD	30.08

Bottom 10 Offenses, 3-and-out per drive

Rk	Team	Pct
23	TEN	22.2%
24	JAC	22.3%
25	DET	22.4%
26	CLE	23.5%
27	NE	24.9%
28	MIA	29.2%
29	SF	30.6%
30	DEN	30.7%
31	NYG	31.0%
32	LARM	31.6%

Bottom 10 Defenses, 3-and-out per drive

Rk	Team	Pct
23	MIA	19.8%
24	PIT	19.7%
25	TB	19.0%
26	WAS	18.9%
27	DET	18.7%
28	SF	18.4%
29	IND	17.8%
30	GB	17.4%
31	KC	15.5%
32	NO	12.0%

Bottom 10 Offenses, Yards per drive

Rk	Team	Yds/Dr
23	NYJ	29.43
24	BAL	29.00
25	CAR	28.83
26	HOU	28.77
27	NYG	28.27
28	MIA	28.15
29	CLE	27.94
30	DEN	27.48
31	SF	25.02
32	LARM	22.36

Bottom 10 Defenses, Yards per drive

Rk	Team	Yds/Dr
23	DAL	33.04
24	KC	33.67
25	CHI	33.96
26	ATL	34.51
27	CLE	34.83
28	GB	35.10
29	IND	35.84
30	DET	36.05
31	WAS	36.38
32	NO	36.71

Top 10 Offenses, avg LOS to start drive

Rk	Team	LOS
1	OAK	31.4
2	NE	30.7
3	CAR	30.4
4	MIN	30.4
5	KC	30.4
6	PHI	30.3
7	ARI	30.0
8	GB	29.5
9	MIA	28.9
10	SEA	28.9

Top 10 Defenses, avg LOS to start drive

Rk	Team	LOS
1	NE	24.9
2	OAK	25.1
3	ATL	26.1
4	KC	26.3
5	TEN	26.6
6	IND	26.6
7	DET	26.6
8	MIN	26.8
9	LARM	26.9
9	CAR	27.0

Top 10 Offenses, Points per drive

Rk	Team	Pts/Dr
1	ATL	3.06
2	NO	2.65
3	GB	2.60
4	DAL	2.54
5	NE	2.53
6	WAS	2.40
7	IND	2.30
8	PIT	2.26
9	BUF	2.18
10	TEN	2.16

Top 10 Defenses, Points per drive

Rk	Team	Pts/Dr
1	NE	1.42
2	NYG	1.43
3	DEN	1.51
4	SEA	1.60
4	HOU	1.67
6	BAL	1.71
7	MIN	1.73
8	KC	1.76
9	ARI	1.79
10	CIN	1.85

Bottom 10 Offenses, avg LOS to start drive

Rk	Team	LOS
23	NYJ	27.2
24	NO	27.2
25	WAS	27.2
26	LARM	27.0
27	PIT	26.9
28	CIN	26.5
29	JAC	26.4
30	DET	25.2
31	CHI	24.8
32	CLE	23.4

Bottom 10 Defenses, avg LOS to start drive

Rk	Team	LOS
23	BUF	29.1
24	NYJ	29.2
24	NO	29.2
26	CHI	29.4
27	ARI	29.5
28	HOU	29.6
29	CLE	29.9
30	JAC	30.8
31	SF	31.3
32	SD	31.4

Bottom 10 Offenses, Points per drive

Rk	Team	Pts/Dr
23	BAL	1.71
24	JAC	1.66
25	DEN	1.61
26	SF	1.59
27	NYG	1.56
28	CHI	1.54
29	HOU	1.50
30	NYJ	1.49
31	CLE	1.45
32	LARM	1.17

Bottom 10 Defenses, Points per drive

Rk	Team	Pts/Dr
23	SD	2.12
24	WAS	2.19
24	IND	2.22
26	DET	2.28
27	ATL	2.29
27	GB	2.29
29	CHI	2.33
30	SF	2.41
31	CLE	2.47
32	NO	2.50

Top 10 Offenses, Better DVOA with Shotgun

Rk	Team	% Plays Shotgun	DVOA Shot	DVOA Not	Yd/Play Shot	Yd/Play Not	DVOA Dif
1	NE	53%	44.3%	-1.0%	7.0	4.9	45.3%
2	DET	84%	6.9%	-32.8%	6.0	4.0	39.7%
3	PIT	66%	26.5%	-10.7%	6.4	5.3	37.2%
4	TEN	56%	27.6%	-6.9%	6.7	4.8	34.5%
5	CIN	64%	19.5%	-9.5%	6.1	4.6	29.0%
6	DAL	51%	31.2%	10.3%	6.6	5.7	20.9%
7	JAC	75%	-5.9%	-25.7%	5.6	4.4	19.8%
8	HOU	67%	-14.0%	-33.6%	5.4	3.8	19.6%
9	BUF	80%	14.3%	-2.1%	5.9	5.1	16.4%
10	CAR	78%	-4.3%	-19.8%	5.7	4.3	15.4%

Top 10 Offenses, Better DVOA with Play-Action

Rk	Team	% PA	DVOA PA	DVOA No PA	Yd/Play PA	Yd/Play No PA	DVOA Dif
1	SD	17%	83.9%	-1.5%	9.6	6.5	85.5%
2	LARM	16%	15.6%	-48.9%	8.3	5.1	64.5%
3	TB	22%	67.0%	7.2%	8.1	6.3	59.8%
4	PHI	19%	46.1%	-7.6%	8.3	5.4	53.7%
5	MIN	19%	50.1%	-1.0%	9.2	6.0	51.0%
6	ARI	15%	35.1%	-11.6%	8.6	6.0	46.7%
7	KC	17%	58.5%	15.0%	9.2	6.2	43.5%
8	NYJ	16%	6.9%	-30.5%	8.0	5.8	37.4%
9	NYG	15%	33.0%	0.4%	7.6	6.2	32.5%
10	SEA	20%	40.6%	8.3%	8.7	6.7	32.3%

Bottom 10 Offenses, Better DVOA with Shotgun

Rk	Team	% Plays Shotgun	DVOA Shot	DVOA Not	Yd/Play Shot	Yd/Play Not	DVOA Dif
23	NO	55%	17.1%	13.7%	6.6	5.8	3.4%
24	IND	60%	4.8%	2.3%	6.2	5.4	2.5%
25	ATL	40%	25.7%	24.0%	6.7	6.9	1.7%
26	DEN	43%	-12.9%	-11.8%	5.6	4.9	-1.1%
27	SEA	70%	-4.4%	0.8%	5.9	5.9	-5.2%
28	NYJ	68%	-25.2%	-16.2%	5.4	5.1	-9.0%
29	PHI	67%	-10.7%	3.2%	5.1	5.3	-13.9%
30	ARI	49%	-15.2%	1.4%	5.5	5.5	-16.6%
31	SF	99%	-7.4%	16.0%	5.0	5.3	-23.4%
32	LARM	59%	-49.8%	-23.5%	4.5	4.6	-26.3%

Bottom 10 Offenses, Better DVOA with Play-Action

Rk	Team	% PA	DVOA PA	DVOA No PA	Yd/Play PA	Yd/Play No PA	DVOA Dif
23	DAL	24%	45.3%	40.7%	8.8	7.0	4.6%
24	CHI	20%	10.3%	7.2%	7.7	6.8	3.2%
25	ATL	27%	53.3%	50.5%	10.3	7.8	2.8%
26	TEN	18%	20.6%	31.1%	8.3	6.6	-10.4%
27	DET	16%	9.4%	20.5%	6.7	6.8	-11.1%
28	CAR	18%	-9.0%	5.0%	6.0	6.6	-14.0%
29	PIT	14%	12.7%	33.7%	8.3	6.9	-21.0%
30	GB	15%	11.8%	41.2%	6.4	6.9	-29.5%
31	HOU	17%	-40.2%	-10.2%	6.3	5.4	-29.9%
32	BAL	18%	-26.8%	7.3%	5.7	6.2	-34.1%

Top 10 Defenses, Better DVOA vs. Shotgun

Rk	Team	% Plays Shotgun	DVOA Shot	DVOA Not	Yd/Play Shot	Yd/Play Not	DVOA Dif
1	CAR	60%	-12.1%	3.3%	5.5	5.8	-15.4%
2	KC	67%	-7.7%	5.9%	5.7	5.6	-13.6%
3	GB	66%	-2.1%	10.1%	6.0	6.0	-12.2%
4	DEN	59%	-23.4%	-12.1%	5.1	4.5	-11.3%
5	SEA	64%	-14.8%	-4.3%	5.0	5.3	-10.5%
6	ARI	70%	-14.9%	-11.2%	5.1	4.6	-3.7%
7	TB	56%	-4.2%	-1.5%	6.3	5.5	-2.8%
8	MIA	65%	1.1%	2.5%	5.7	5.8	-1.4%
9	PHI	66%	-12.9%	-11.6%	5.7	6.0	-1.3%
10	CIN	66%	0.4%	1.6%	5.6	5.4	-1.3%

Top 10 Defenses, Better DVOA vs. Play-Action

Rk	Team	% PA	DVOA PA	DVOA No PA	Yd/Play PA	Yd/Play No PA	DVOA Dif
1	HOU	15%	-31.5%	2.8%	5.7	6.1	-34.3%
2	DAL	15%	-3.4%	14.6%	7.7	6.3	-18.1%
3	PHI	17%	-22.0%	-6.7%	7.8	6.6	-15.3%
4	BUF	20%	4.2%	18.2%	7.5	6.9	-14.1%
5	JAC	23%	-1.6%	11.9%	6.1	6.2	-13.5%
6	WAS	21%	6.2%	18.7%	6.9	7.0	-12.5%
7	TB	21%	-10.5%	0.7%	7.4	7.1	-11.2%
8	PIT	17%	-5.0%	2.7%	7.2	6.4	-7.7%
9	SD	17%	-3.4%	0.3%	7.4	6.7	-3.8%
10	SF	25%	24.2%	21.7%	8.3	6.8	2.6%

Bottom 10 Defenses, Better DVOA vs. Shotgun

Rk	Team	% Plays Shotgun	DVOA Shot	DVOA Not	Yd/Play Shot	Yd/Play Not	DVOA Dif
23	LARM	71%	2.9%	-12.0%	5.5	4.9	14.9%
24	CHI	71%	9.8%	-5.2%	6.2	4.5	15.0%
25	WAS	65%	12.9%	-2.6%	6.2	5.2	15.5%
26	BUF	63%	14.1%	-1.5%	6.2	5.1	15.6%
27	DET	62%	25.6%	8.7%	6.4	5.6	16.8%
28	NO	61%	22.1%	4.8%	6.6	5.7	17.2%
29	NE	73%	3.4%	-13.9%	5.5	4.7	17.3%
30	SF	51%	24.5%	1.3%	6.7	5.5	23.1%
31	DAL	73%	8.3%	-15.6%	5.8	4.7	24.0%
32	NYJ	67%	14.9%	-15.9%	6.4	4.7	30.8%

Bottom 10 Defenses, Better DVOA vs. Play-Action

Rk	Team	% PA	DVOA PA	DVOA No PA	Yd/Play PA	Yd/Play No PA	DVOA Dif
23	IND	18%	42.8%	13.7%	8.9	6.6	29.2%
24	CLE	21%	50.7%	20.2%	9.3	6.8	30.5%
25	DET	21%	60.8%	28.7%	9.2	6.5	32.1%
26	BAL	18%	26.9%	-5.9%	7.6	6.2	32.8%
27	LARM	18%	40.7%	6.5%	8.1	5.9	34.1%
28	SEA	21%	30.8%	-5.1%	8.5	6.2	35.8%
29	OAK	19%	48.7%	6.5%	9.7	6.8	42.2%
30	DEN	13%	16.2%	-33.3%	7.7	5.2	49.4%
31	NYG	21%	33.1%	-17.4%	9.3	5.7	50.5%
32	GB	17%	58.0%	4.3%	9.3	7.0	53.7%

2016 Defenses with and without Pass Pressure

Rank	Team	Plays	Pct Pressure	DVOA with Pressure	Yds with Pressure	DVOA w/o Pressure	Yds w/o Pressure	DVOA Dif	Rank
1	DEN	625	32.2%	-63.7%	3.4	-8.8%	6.3	-54.8%	1
2	ARI	630	32.1%	-92.1%	2.8	29.9%	7.3	-122.0%	31
3	PHI	617	31.6%	-63.8%	4.5	13.7%	7.7	-77.4%	9
4	MIA	662	31.4%	-40.6%	4.7	29.9%	7.3	-70.5%	4
5	MIN	615	31.2%	-77.2%	2.9	35.3%	7.3	-112.5%	27
6	CIN	652	30.8%	-58.7%	3.2	34.5%	7.5	-93.2%	15
7	CAR	682	30.2%	-77.4%	3.6	36.0%	7.7	-113.4%	28
8	NYG	678	29.2%	-80.8%	3.3	23.3%	7.5	-104.1%	24
9	BUF	579	29.0%	-49.9%	3.1	40.9%	8.2	-90.8%	14
10	SEA	597	28.6%	-47.7%	3.8	23.5%	7.3	-71.2%	5
11	LARM	647	28.4%	-56.1%	3.4	40.6%	7.3	-96.7%	20
12	WAS	645	28.4%	-61.1%	3.4	45.1%	8.0	-106.2%	25
13	CHI	602	28.1%	-29.8%	5.1	26.0%	7.2	-55.8%	2
14	NO	644	27.3%	-30.3%	4.5	49.8%	8.5	-80.1%	11
15	JAC	614	27.2%	-61.2%	3.9	34.4%	7.1	-95.6%	18
16	GB	638	27.0%	-80.3%	2.5	48.0%	8.8	-128.4%	33
17	OAK	595	26.9%	-61.7%	3.5	41.6%	8.8	-103.3%	23
18	SD	646	26.8%	-56.3%	4.0	20.3%	7.5	-76.6%	7
19	BAL	630	26.7%	-72.1%	3.3	26.1%	7.3	-98.2%	21
20	ATL	720	26.4%	-53.6%	3.8	32.5%	7.2	-86.1%	12
21	NYJ	598	26.3%	-39.2%	4.3	51.4%	8.0	-90.7%	13
22	HOU	588	26.2%	-54.5%	3.8	15.2%	7.1	-69.7%	3
23	TEN	704	24.9%	-53.8%	3.0	45.4%	7.8	-99.2%	22
24	PIT	651	24.7%	-56.8%	3.7	20.3%	7.2	-77.1%	8
25	TB	619	24.7%	-89.2%	3.5	24.2%	8.1	-113.4%	29
26	NE	657	24.7%	-69.7%	2.9	39.3%	7.2	-109.0%	26
27	KC	659	24.4%	-89.0%	3.8	25.1%	7.4	-114.1%	30
28	CLE	590	23.7%	-69.0%	3.3	57.1%	8.2	-126.1%	32
29	DAL	687	23.1%	-61.7%	3.4	33.5%	7.2	-95.2%	17
30	DET	603	23.1%	-24.9%	4.5	54.9%	7.9	-79.8%	10
31	SF	579	22.6%	-35.1%	3.8	39.3%	8.0	-74.4%	6
32	IND	651	19.0%	-59.4%	3.1	37.1%	7.9	-96.5%	19
NFL AVERAGE		635	27.1%	-60.3%	3.6	33.5%	7.6	-93.8%	

Includes scrambles and Defensive Pass Interference. Does not include aborted snaps.

Author Bios

Editor-in-Chief and NFL Statistician

Aaron Schatz is the creator of FootballOutsiders.com and the proprietary NFL statistics within *Football Outsiders Almanac*, including DVOA, DYAR, adjusted line yards, and the KUBIAK fantasy football projections. He writes regularly for ESPN Insider and *ESPN The Magazine*, and he has done custom research for a number of NFL teams. *The New York Times Magazine* referred to him as "the Bill James of football." Readers should feel free to blame everything in this book on the fact that he went to high school six miles from Gillette Stadium before detouring through Brown University and eventually landing in Sashi Brown's hometown of Framingham, Massachusetts. He promises that someday Bill Belichick will retire, the Patriots will be awful, and he will write very mean and nasty things about them.

Layout and Design

Vincent Verhei has been a writer and editor for Football Outsiders since 2007. In addition to writing for *Football Outsiders Almanac 2017*, he did all layout and design on the book. During the season, he writes the "Quick Reads" column covering the best and worst players of each week according to Football Outsiders metrics. His writings have also appeared in *ESPN The Magazine* and in Maple Street Press publications, and he has done layout on a number of other books for Football Outsiders and Prospectus Entertainment Ventures. His other night job is as a writer and podcast host for pro wrestling/MMA website Figurefouronline.com. He is a graduate of Western Washington University.

College Football Statisticians

Bill Connelly has contributed college football play-by-play stats to Football Outsiders for nearly a decade. He's also the College Sports Editor and Analytics Director for SB Nation, where he runs the college football blog Football Study Hall. His most recent book, *The 50 Best* College Football Teams of All-Time*, was released in March. He grew up a numbers and sports nerd in western Oklahoma, but now lives in Missouri with his wife, pets, and young daughter.

Brian Fremeau has been analyzing college football drive stats for Football Outsiders since 2006. A lifelong Fighting Irish fan, Brian can be found every home football Saturday in Notre Dame Stadium. He can be found there every day, in fact, due to his campus facility operations responsibilities. He lives in South Bend, Indiana with his wife and two daughters.

Contributors

Greg A. Bedard is the columnist, editor and owner of BostonSportsJournal.com, recently launched after a 20-year award-winning career in traditional media. He was formerly a senior NFL writer for *Sports Illustrated* and TheMMQB.com. He's also covered the NFL for *The Boston Globe*, the *Milwaukee Journal-Sentinel*, and *The Palm Beach Post*. Greg's film work has earned the respect of several coaches and front office executives, including Bill Belichick, Mike McCarthy and Bill O'Brien. He's a Massachusetts native and resident, and graduated from Rutgers University. When he's not studying football, he's coaching softball and baseball, and helping his wife shuttle their children to various sporting events in the Greater Boston area.

Ian Boyd is a history major graduate from the University of Texas, now based in southeast Michigan, who loves studying the trends and stories of college football. You can also find his work at the websites Inside Texas and Football Study Hall.

It was a single moment that brought **Cian Fahey** to the NFL when he was 12 years old. Like many fans, it came at the behest of a family member. Unlike most fans, it came at 1am on Christmas Eve in Ireland. His uncle Dex had implored him to watch on as Brett Favre threw one of his many game-winning touchdown passes. The excitement of that moment began a journey that would stretch over the next decade and more. When not writing for Football Outsiders, Cian has published his own annual books of quarterback analysis, most recently *Pre-Snap Reads QB Catalogue 2017*.

Nathan Forster played wide receiver for his freshman football team, but unfortunately graduated before Matt Millen left the broadcast booth. He graduated with a B.A. in English from the University of Michigan and a J.D. from Boston College Law School, which naturally lead him to develop regression models that project the success of NFL Draft prospects. Nathan and his love-hate relationship with the Detroit Lions currently reside in the greater Boston area with his wife, Sarah, and daughter, Lily.

Tom Gower joined the FO writing staff in 2009. He has degrees from Georgetown University and the University of Chicago, whose football programs have combined for an Orange Bowl appearance and seven Big Ten Titles but are still trying to find success after Pearl Harbor. His work has also appeared at NBCSports.com, NBC Sports World, ESPN.com, and in *ESPN The Magazine*. He roots for the Tennessee Titans from the Chicago suburbs.

Scott Kacsmar has covered the NFL as a full-time analyst since 2011. He joined Football Outsiders as an Assistant Editor in 2013. Some of his unique contributions include the first standardized database of fourth-quarter comebacks and game-winning drives, quantifying catch radius and ALEX. He will not stop writing about the value of drive stats, the dominance of the quarterback sneak, and he continues to help the NFL fix the most mundane of statistical errors, such as Tony Graziani's 1998 rushing totals. His work has appeared on SI.com, Bleacher Report, ESPN Insider and NFL Network. Scott lives near Pittsburgh and has an Industrial Engineering degree from the University of Pittsburgh.

Bryan Knowles grew up watching Joe Montana and Steve Young ply their trade at quarterback, so he has somewhat overly-inflated expectations of how quarterbacks should perform. This has certainly done him no favors over the past decade or so of watching the San Francisco 49ers. A graduate of UC Davis and San Jose State University, he has opted to eschew all the useful advice those august institutions have supplied him with and become a sportswriter instead. He's also written for Bleacher Report and Fansided, and currently lives in Chicago with a wife who for some reason puts up with him.

Rivers McCown has written for ESPN.com, Bleacher Report, *USA Today*, and Deadspin, among other places. He's edited for Football Outsiders, *Rookie Scouting Portfolio*, and *Pre-Snap Reads Quarterback Catalogue*. He lives in Houston, Texas. He wants more jobs.

Chad Peltier was raised to be an Ohio State fan, but four years of "Run the damn ball, Bobo!" at the University of Georgia and living in Athens have made him a Bulldawg fan as well. In addition to writing two columns on college football at Football Outsiders, Chad also contributes to the SB Nation blogs Land Grant Holy Land and Football Study Hall. He currently lives in New Haven, Connecticut, working in aerospace and defense, but misses SEC country.

Anglo-Scot (so, Briton) **Andrew Potter** blames Mega Drive classics John Madden Football and Joe Montana Sports Talk Football for his Transatlantic love of the gridiron game. He joined Football Outsiders in 2013 to help with the infamous Twitter Audibles experiment, and still compiles Audibles at the Line to this day. He also authors the weekly Injury Aftermath report and co-authors Scramble for the Ball with Bryan Knowles. Though outwardly a fan of the New Orleans Saints, inwardly the Inverness resident still yearns for his first gridiron love: NFL Europe's Scottish Claymores.

This is **Mike Tanier**'s 13th *Football Outsiders Almanac* or *Almanac*-like publication. He has been with FO since the days of individual kicker comments and publisher-mandated May deadlines, since before NFL Game Rewind made verifying plays or scouting an unknown player a breeze, since before social networking as we now know it, and since before any of us could ever get a press credential, let alone sometimes chew the ear of an actual player/coach/GM. Mike has gone from *The New York Times* to Sports on Earth to NFL lead writer at Bleacher Report, another thing that didn't exist when we starting writing annuals. He no longer teaches high-school math in Joe Flacco's hometown, but still lives with his wife and two sons just one minute from the base of the Walt Whitman Bridge in South Jersey.

Robert Weintraub is the author of the *New York Times* bestseller *No Better Friend: One Man, One Dog, and their Extraordinary Story of Courage and Survival in WWII,* as well as *The Victory Season* and *The House That Ruth Built.* He has also been a regular contributor to Sports on Earth, Slate, Grantland, *Columbia Journalism Review*, and *The New York Times.*

Carl Yedor was born and raised in Seattle, Washington, and his first vivid football memory was "We want the ball, and we're going to score." As an undergrad at Georgetown University, he worked with the varsity football team to implement football research into their strategy and game planning, drawing on his coursework in statistics and his high school experience as an undersized offensive guard and inside linebacker. He lives in Arlington, Virginia and works as a consultant at IBM in addition to writing for Football Outsiders

Acknowledgements

We want to thank all the Football Outsiders readers, all the people in the media who have helped to spread the word about our website and books, and all the people in the NFL who have shown interest in our work. This is our 13th annual book as part of the *Pro Football Prospectus* or *Football Outsiders Almanac* series. Bill James only wrote a dozen editions of the *Bill James Baseball Abstract*, so we now officially have him beat. Then again, we couldn't do this if we were just one guy, or without the help and/or support from all these people:

• FO outgoing techmaster Steven Steinman and incoming techmaster Dave Bernreuther.

• Jason Beattie for the Philip Rivers caricature in the Los Angeles Chargers chapter.

• Mike Harris for help with the season simulation.

• Premium programmer Sean McCall, Excel macro master John Argentiero, and drive stats guru Jim Armstrong.

• Our offensive line guru Ben Muth.

• Jason McKinley, creator of Offensive Line Continuity Score.

• Jeremy Snyder, our incredibly prolific transcriber of old play-by-play gamebooks.

• Roland Beech of the Sacramento Kings, formerly of Two-MinuteWarning.com, who came up with the original ideas behind our individual defensive stats.

• Our editors at ESPN.com and *ESPN The Magazine*, including Daniel Kaufman, Scott Miller, and Chris Sprow.

• Our friends at Sports Info Solutions who have really expanded what we can do with game charting, including Dan Foehrenbach, Matt Manocherian, Scott Spratt, Greg Thomas, and Ben Jedlovic.

• Bill Simmons, for constantly promoting us on his podcast, and Peter King, for lots of promotion on The MMQB.

• Michael Katzenoff at the NFL, for responding to our endless questions about specific items in the official play-by-play.

• All the friends we've made on coaching staffs and in front offices across the National Football League, who generally don't want to be mentioned by name. You know who you are.

• Our comrades in the revolution: Doug Drinen (creator of the indispensable Pro Football Reference), Bill Barnwell (our long lost brother), Brian Burke and the guys from ESPN Stats & Information, Neil Paine, Robert Mays, Danny Kelly, Kevin Clark, and K.C. Joyner, plus the kids at Numberfire, the football guys from footballguys.com, and our friends at Prospectus Entertainment Ventures.

• Also, our scouting buddies, including Andy Benoit, Chris Brown, Greg Cosell, Doug Farrar, and Russ Lande.

• Joe Alread, Justin Patel, and William Schautz, who handle the special Football Outsiders cards in Madden Ultimate Team, and the other folks at EA Sports who make FO a part of the Madden universe.

• Interns who helped prepare data over the past year or for this book specifically, including Keegan Abdoo, James Burnett, Dave Cavallaro, Rob Eves, Andrew Fisher, Thomas Ribaudo, Matthew Russo, Brent Schwartz, and Michael Valverede.

• All those who volunteered their time and effort for the Football Outsiders game charting project in past seasons. We would like to specifically thank charters who also pitched in this year to help us check our charting from multiple sources: Mike Bonner, Jason Dooley, Michael Dunn, Dave DuPlantis, and Matthew Weston.

And as always, thanks to our family and friends for putting up with this nonsense.

Aaron Schatz

Follow Football Outsiders on Twitter

Follow the official account announcing new Football Outsiders articles at **@fboutsiders**. You can follow other FO and *FOA 20186* writers at these Twitter addresses:

Greg A. Bedard: **@GregABedard**
Ian Boyd: **@Ian_A_Boyd**
Bill Connelly: **@SBN_BillC**
Cian Fahey: **@cianaf**
Brian Fremeau: **@bcfremeau**
Tom Gower: **@ThomasGower**
Scott Kacsmar: **@FO_ScottKacsmar**
Bryan Knowles: **@BryKno**
Rivers McCown: **@RiversMcCown**
Ben Muth: **@FO_WordofMuth**
Chad Peltier: **@cgpeltier**
Andrew Potter: **@bighairyandy**
Aaron Schatz: **@FO_ASchatz**
Mike Tanier: **@MikeTanier**
Vince Verhei: **@FO_VVerhei**
Robert Weintraub: **@robwein**
Carl Yedor: **@CarlYedor61**

Follow Football Outsiders on Facebook

https://www.facebook.com/footballoutsiders

About Sports Info Solutions

The mission of Sports Info Solutions (SIS) is to provide the most accurate, in-depth, timely professional sports data, including cutting-edge research and analysis, striving to educate professional teams and the public about sports analytics. SIS is thrilled to work with nearly every Major League Baseball team and a growing number of National Football League teams in service of that goal.

SIS opened its doors back in 2002 and has been on the leading edge of the advanced statistical study of sports ever since. The early years were dedicated to pioneering the analytical landscape in baseball, where SIS successfully played a large role in the growth of trends such as defensive shifting. More recently, SIS recognized the growing need for football analytics and launched a new operation to mirror its industry-leading baseball data collection operation.

That operation began with a partnership with Football Outsiders in 2015, one that continues to propel the industry forward by linking the most comprehensive, objective data provider with the most reputable source for football analysis.

SIS has built its success thanks to its staff of expert scouts and an army of highly trained video scouts who chart thousands of NFL, FBS, MLB, and MiLB games annually. SIS collects valuable data that cannot be found any place else, and each game is reviewed multiple times to ensure that the data is as accurate as possible. The company records everything from basic box score data to advanced defensive coverages and route information. The company's analysts and programmers dissect the data, producing a variety of predictive studies and analytics that are used by high-profile clients throughout the sports industry.

Sports Info Solutions was founded by John Dewan, who has been a leader in baseball analytics for more than 25 years. From his first partnership with Bill James as the Executive Director of Project Scoresheet to co-founding STATS, Inc. and his 15-year tenure as CEO, companies under John's leadership have continually broken new ground in sports data and analytics.

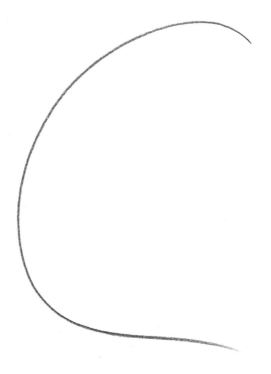

Made in the USA
Middletown, DE
30 August 2017